Quick Reference Handbook Set

BASIC KNOWLEDGE and MODERN TECHNOLOGY

Contributors

Titles given below are as of the time of the author's contributions to the book.

Elvin Abeles
Former Associate Editor
Collier's Encyclopedia

Frank Alweis
Director, Honor School
James Monroe High School

Roy O. Billett
Professor of Education, Emeritus
Boston University

Lawrence D. Brennan
Professor, Business Writing and Speaking
New York University

Oscar Cargill
Head, Department of English
Graduate School of Arts and Science
New York University

Bradford Chambers
Author; Editor, *Home Library Press*

Allan Danzig
Assistant Professor,
Department of English
Lafayette College

Mary F. Doherty
Librarian
The Metropolitan Museum of Art

John R. Dugan
Professor of Law
New York Law School

David Ebner
Author, *Elementary Algebra*

Willard Hutcheon
Lecturer, Philosophy
The City University of New York

William Jaber
Geographer

Steele M. Kennedy
Former Education Editor and
Director of Information Services
New Jersey State
Department of Education

Jerome E. Leavitt
Professor of Education
Portland State College

Paul B. Panes
Director, The Reading Institute
New York University

Thomas N. Pappas
Dean of Academic Administration
Warner Pacific College

Ernest D. Partridge, Jr.
Assistant Professor of Philosophy
and Education
Paterson State College

Mario Pei
Professor, Romance Languages,
Emeritus
Columbia University

Louis M. Pell
Chairman, Department of English
Columbia Grammar School

Gary Ruse
Vice-President, First National Bank
Gordon, Nebraska

Robert M. Segal
Editor
Stravon Educational Press

Clem Stein, Jr.
Merchandising Supervisor
Sears, Roebuck and Co.

Mitchell Weiner
Director
College Entrance Tutoring Service

Consulting Editors

Calvin D. Linton, Ph.D.
Dean, Columbian College
The George Washington University

Edward H. Litchfield, Ph.D.
Chancellor
University of Pittsburgh

Coordinating Editor

Stephen W. Hines

Associate Editor

Mary Bray Wheeler

Editorial Assistant

Genon Hickerson Neblett

Updating Editors

Alice C. Ewing
John A. Fribley
Steve Pemberton
Susan Kirby

THE VARSITY COMPANY
NASHVILLE, TENNESSEE 37214

Published in Nashville, Tennessee, by Thomas Nelson, Inc., Publishers and distributed in Canada by Lawson Falle, Ltd., Cambridge, Ontario.

The *Quick Reference Handbook Set—Basic Knowledge and Modern Technology,* replaces *The Complete Reference Handbook,* copyright © 1964 by Stravon Publishers; the *Quick Reference Encyclopedia,* copyright © 1976 by Thomas Nelson, Inc., Publishers; and *The Quick Reference Handbook of Basic Knowledge,* copyright © 1979, revised 1982, 1984 by Thomas Nelson, Inc., Publishers.

ACKNOWLEDGMENTS

Library of Congress Cataloging-in-Publication Data

Quick reference handbook set—basic knowledge and modern technology.

Includes index.
1. Handbooks, vade-mecums, etc. I. Abeles, Elvin, 1909- . II. Title: Basic knowledge and modern technology. III. Title: Basic knowledge.
AG106.Q53 1987 031 .02 87-10581
ISBN 0-8407-3005-5

Manufactured in the United States of America

1 2 3 4 5 6 7 8 9 10 11 12 13 14 15 — 88 87

PICTURE ACKNOWLEDGMENTS

Air France, 350; Alaska Travel Division, 299; Alinari–Art Reference Bureau, 125 (b); American Airlines, 300 (t), 301, 308, 313 (t), 321, 324, 334; Anderson–Art Reference Bureau, 125 (t); Arab Information Center, 369, 391, 424; Argosy Gallery, 705, 718, 726; Austrian News and Information Bureau, 352; Bahamas News Bureau, 353; The Bettmann Archive, Inc., 131; BOAC, 88, 89, 90, 372, 373, 379, 389, 393, 394, 401, 418, 420; Brazilian Government Trade Bureau, 356; British European Airways, 95, 376, 384, 423; Canadian Consulate General, 359 (b), 360; Chamber of Commerce of Metropolitan St. Louis, 318; Cincinnati Chamber of Commerce, 327; Civic Promotion Division of Commerce of South Bend, 309; Colorado Department of Public Relations, 302; Connecticut Development Committee, 303; Consul General of Chile, 363; Delaware State Development Department, 304; Ewing Galloway, 126 (m), 126 (b), 127 (t), 127 (m), 128 (t), 128 (b), 130, 132 (m), 133 (l), 133 (r), 135 (l), 135 (r), 136 (b), 138 (m.r.), 138 (b.r.), 139 (l), 139 (r), 140 (t.l.), 140 (b.l.), 141 (t), 142 (t.l.), 142 (m), 142 (t.r.), 142 (b.r.), 143, 144 (t.l.), 144 (b.l.), 144 (b.r.), 145, 146 (l), 146 (b), 147 (t.l.), 148 (l), 148 (t.r.), 149 (t.l.), 149 (t.r.), 150 (t.r.), 150 (b.r.); Irish Tourist Office, 93; Italian Tourist Office, 89; Japan Air Lines, 97; Japan Tourist Association, 386; Library of Congress, 210, 212, 756; The Metropolitan Museum of Art, 132 (b), 136 (t); Miami Bureau, 305; Montana Highway Commission, 319 (t); NASA, 270 (t), 271, 272, 793; National Park Service, 300 (b), 306 (t), 306 (b), 307, 311, 313 (b), 315, 317, 326, 328, 333, 337; Nebraska Game Commission, 319 (b); Netherlands Information Service, 397; New York–Historical Society, 206, 207 (t), 207 (b), 694; North Carolina Department of Conservation and Development, 325; Northwest Orient Airlines, 331 (r); Ontario Department Travel and Publicity, 359 (t); Oregon State Highway Department, 329; Philippine Tourist and Travel Association, 402; Rhode Island Development Council, 331 (l); Scandinavian Travel Commission, 368; "Sni-Yan," 403; Spanish Ministry of Tourism, 95; Standard Oil Company, (N.J.), 312; TWA Airlines, 314, 320, 323; Union Pacific Railroad, 340; United Nations, 370, 381, 390, 438 (t), 438 (b), 440, 441, 442, 443, 445; United Press International, 270 (b.l.), 270 (b.r.), 275, 364, 425, 426, 427, 695, 697, 703, 704, 707, 715, 717, 719, 720, 732, 734, 739, 745, 748; U.S. Army, 258, 259 (t), 259 (b), 260, 261, 263, 264, 265, 267, 268, 269, 274 (t), 274 (b); U.S. Navy, 205, 216 (b), 216 (t), 262; Utah Tourist and Publicity Council, 335 (t); Vermont Development Department, 335 (b); Venezuela Ministry of Tourism, 421; Vilko Zuber, 91; Virginia Department of Conservation and Economic Development, 336; West Virginia Department of Commerce, 338; White House, The, 255, 256; White House Historical Association, 217, 219, 220, 221, 222, 223, 224, 225, 226, 227, 228, 229, 230, 231, 232, 233, 234, 235, 236, 237, 238, 239, 240, 241, 242, 243, 244, 245, 246, 247, 248, 249, 250, 251, 252, 253, 254, 255; World Wide Photos, 134, 138 (l), 140 (b.r.), 147 (b.r.); Wisconsin Conservation Department, 339

The letters in the parentheses next to the page numbers stand for the following: t = top of page; m = middle of page; b = bottom of page; r = right side of page; l = left side of page; b.l. = bottom left of page; b.r. = bottom right of page; m.r. = middle right of page; t.l. = top left of page; t.r. = top right of page.

CONTENTS

PREFACE

The reference book is the indispensable tool of students, writers, and researchers. Without it they would be lost in a maze of books in their effort to find even the simplest information. The function of the reference book is to save its user this time-consuming labor and to permit him to spend his time on the more creative aspects of his work.

Today, thousands of reference books are available. Some are so comprehensive that they defeat their own purpose. Even after considerable time has been spent searching through oversized pages printed in the smallest type, the reader may still not find the information he requires. Of course, there can be no one perfect reference book, and the publisher of this *Quick Reference Handbook—Basic Knowledge and Modern Technology* does not claim to have published it. But he did aim to produce a book that contains the kind of information that high school and college students and the assistants to business executives generally need.

In evaluating the primary use of this handbook, the publisher and his staff held that the principal reference need would involve the writing aspects of the student's or assistant's duties. Thus, a decision was made to include the chapter "Communication Through Language." Thorough material on basic tools and using the tools fully explains the use of punctuation marks, grammar, spelling, vocabulary, writing effective sentences and paragraphs, and the principles of applied writing. In each instance the goal was to supply a source where the student, the writer, or the researcher could readily look up the required information. Thus, for example: If a student had had a paper returned by his English instructor marked "faulty parallelism," he could find an example of such faulty parallelism in this book and also the correct form.

Other situations the student may be involved in, such as the writing of letters of application and employment resumés, are fully discussed in the chapter "Special Compositions." Rather than present theory alone, the editorial staff polled dozens of outstanding employers on their views as to what they regard as effective letters and employment resumés. Some of these views are reproduced in the book and provide an authentic picture of how employers evaluate the letters and resumés of those who apply to them for jobs.

A time-consuming phase of most students' activities is the technical preparation of reports and manuscripts. Many students literally waste hours in the formal preparation of such reports. They have no idea how their reports should be typed: the spacing, the capitalization, the indentation, the subdivision, the arrangement of footnotes, the bibliography, the tables, the appearance of the typed pages of the manuscript, etc.

Probably the greatest handicap the student has in using reference books is the lack of facility for comprehension and speed in reading. The best reference material will not serve its purposes if the user is not able to read reasonably fast and, of course, to understand clearly what he is reading. Therefore, a section has been included which outlines methods that students may follow to improve both their reading comprehension and their reading speed.

Every book may be said to have some research value, and every good author contributes to this great reference pool. Throughout history, outstanding writers have made major contributions to man's understanding. There are a number of contributors to whom man constantly has recourse, both to sustain himself and to discover his origins and his development—cultural, intellectual, and even physical. Some of these people and their works are described in the section of the reference book entitled "Authors and Their Works."

This edition contains more detailed sections on mathematics and science to enhance the handbook's usefulness and bring it closer to the goal of being a comprehensive study aid. The material in Chapters Eight–Sixteen was originally published by Doubleday and Company and is used by special permission.

Fundamental reference material, which all students and business executives have occasion to use, occupies over one-half of the book. Such information includes detailed descriptions of the governmental structure of the United States, the fifty individual states of the United States, and its outlying areas. The history of each country in the world is presented. A concise explanation of the functions and agencies of the United Nations is also given.

In an effort to provide the most up-to-date information that would be useful to students and those in business alike, this volume contains a complete chapter on "Computer Science." This material is an introduction/overview and, along with the glossary of computer terms, will serve to broaden the reader's understanding of this vital area.

The background on the development of computers helps to explain how this science has become so important in the world of today.

The reader will find biographical sketches of four hundred well-known people from American history in Chapter Eighteen, which was written especially for the new edition by Dr. Thomas N. Pappas of Warner Pacific College. The biographical sketches of famous American authors will be found in Chapter Four, while American presidents are described in Chapter Six.

The sections on the business world and accounting are designed to be of value to those readers whose interest is not primarily in research but rather in opportunities in the business world. Included in these sections is practical, useful information that business personnel may need in the competent performance of their duties, including material on secretarial functions, banking, investments, insurance, and real estate.

Since it is anticipated that some of the users of the *Quick Reference Handbook—Basic Knowledge and Modern Technology* will be high-school seniors, extensive information on the College Entrance Examination Board, its tests and questionnaires, is given, including sample test questions and answers. A complete list of accredited two-year and four-year colleges is also supplied.

Much other useful material is provided in the form of charts, tables, and lists, such as metric conversions, two thousand commonly misspelled words, and two thousand foreign words and phrases commonly in use in the English language. The complete Constitution of the United States, mathematical and scientific information, space terms, music terms, cookery and nutrition, and a sixteen-page atlas, especially prepared for this book and containing the most up-to-the-minute political and geographic developments and changes in the world, are also included.

HOW TO USE THIS BOOK

In referring to material in this book on punctuation, grammar, rules of spelling, capitalization, and abbreviations, the reader should bear in mind that not all authorities are in agreement with the rules and examples cited. For example: Several authoritative reference books exist, such as *A Manual of Style* published by the University of Chicago, *Words into Print,* published by Meredith Publishing Company, the *New York Times Style Book,* and the *United States Government Printing Office Style Manual.* These books frequently differ as to which words are to be capitalized, hyphenated, italicized, and abbreviated. They may not, for example, agree as to which numerals are to be spelled out and which are to be left as numerals. For example, in the use of abbreviations: *A Manual of Style* abbreviates North Dakota as N.D. The *Style Manual* of the United States Government prefers N.Dak. *A Manual of Style* abbreviates New Mexico as N.M. The *Style Manual* of the United States Government prefers N.Mex. *A Manual of Style* abbreviates Oregon as Ore. The *Style Manual* of the United States Government prefers Oreg.

The final authority for a student should be the particular school he attends. If a school has a particular preference, this should be ascertained by the student and he should use the preferred style. Ultimately, the only time the style needs to be changed is when the material is considered for publication.

Quick Reference Handbook Set

BASIC KNOWLEDGE and MODERN TECHNOLOGY

CHAPTER ONE

COMMUNICATION THROUGH LANGUAGE

BASIC TOOLS

Punctuation Marks

Many of us look on marks of punctuation as annoying inventions of English teachers to make the hard job of writing even harder. Consequently, we ignore punctuation whenever we can, which is most of the time, and turn over the job of inserting the proper marks to instructors, copy editors, or to anyone else likely to get a mysterious pleasure from the process.

Actually, punctuation is almost as essential to clear writing as words themselves are. It is the function of words to identify meanings, and it is the function of punctuation to package the meanings in usable clumps, like phrases, clauses, and sentences. Imagine trying to read this page if all the letters were run together (for spacing is punctuation, too) from top to bottom, with no capital letters, no breaks, no clumping of word groups. Punctuation really *says* things, just as words do, but it says them more economically. A period, for example, says "Pause here. A complete thought has been expressed." And so with all the other marks.

Punctuation also serves another vital function, that of stylistic effectiveness. When you speak, of course, you use physical means to achieve clarity and vigor. You raise and lower your voice; you emphasize a point with a gesture of your finger; you speak rapidly and then slowly to provide contrast; you say particular words with unusual stress. None of this could be passed on to your reader, however, if you did not use punctuation marks. The reader of a well-punctuated page almost feels as if he were listening to you speak.

So do not underestimate the importance of punctuation. No writing is good if it is not clear, and no writing is clear if it is not well punctuated.

TERMINAL MARKS

Marks of punctuation that have the power to end a sentence are called "terminal marks." A sentence may be brought to an end without necessarily being complete; that is, it does not have to possess a full subject and predicate. The terminal mark may be used with a phrase, or even a single word. The following are examples of how terminal marks may be used:

Questions and Answers

What are you doing? Not much.

Imperatives

Do it now. Go. Don't.

Exclamations

What luck! Bah! Humbug!

We generally think that the period, question mark, and exclamation mark are the only terminal marks. This is not so. Two other marks have the power to end a sentence. The dash can interrupt or summarily end a sentence before it is completed; and the colon–essentially a mark of introduction–can terminate an introductory statement when what follows it begins with a capital letter.

Dash as a Terminal Mark

"I swear I never again will drive a—" The mad honking of automobiles cut him short.

Colon as a Terminal Mark

In conclusion, I make this promise: If elected, I shall serve you to the best of my ability.

These are only incidental uses of the dash and colon, however. The three chief terminal marks are still the period, question mark, and exclamation mark.

Note: To avoid confusion with examples and quoted material, we will use block paragraphs in the following sections on punctuation and grammar.

Period

The period (.) is the most common terminal mark of punctuation. It presents few problems to students. The only difficulties ordinarily encountered are in distinguishing between abbreviations that take periods and abbreviations that are accepted as the shortened forms of proper names and do not take periods. The other difficulty with the period is its use in relation to other marks of punctuation. The rules for use of the period are given below.

A period is used at the end of a declarative sentence.

We have nothing to fear but fear itself.
–*Franklin D. Roosevelt*

A period is used at the end of an imperative sentence.

Go at once.
She said, "Help me."

Do not use a period when an imperative sentence is so strong that it becomes an exclamation. Such a sentence is followed by an exclamation mark. Whether an imperative sentence is ended by a period or an exclamation mark depends entirely on the degree of emphasis desired.

"Go at once!" he shouted.
"Help!" she cried.

A period is used at the end of a sentence that is interrogative in form but to which an answer is not required.

Children, will you stop that noise at once.

A period is used to represent a decimal point.

17.4°   75.2% $1.75

A period is used after figures and letters to represent principal divisions of lists.

IV. Gross income
  A. Expenses
    1. Net income
      a. Net earnings per share

Do not use a period when the figures or letters are in parentheses.

(IV) Gross income
  (A) Expenses
    (1) Net income
      (a) Net earnings per share

A period is used with most abbreviations.

A.M.   P.M.   Mrs.   Ave.   etc.
Mon.   Jan.   treas.   i.e.   M.D.
F.D.R.   John F. Kennedy   L.B.J.

Do not use a period after a person's nickname, or after the shortened form of a person's name.

Sue   Hank   Doug   Bob

Do not use a period after letters of the alphabet used in place of a person's name.

Mr. A told Mr. B   X said to Y

Do not use a period after the call letters of radio and TV stations.

WPIX   KLOB   ABCTV

Do not use a period after familiar shortened forms of common words.

tab   ad   el   lab   electro

Do not use a period with abbreviations that are accepted as the shortened forms of proper names.

OWI   Pan Am   MiG
TWA   FBI   SAC

Do not use a period after Roman numerals except to represent principal divisions of lists.

Henry V   Act III   Vol. II
Ecclesiastes II   Matthew V

Do not use a period after ordinal endings of numbers.

3rd   6th   21st   92nd

Do not use a period with mathematical equations, trigonometrical terms, or chemical symbols.

$y \times 4 = y^2$ log   sin H_2O

Do not use a period with the abbreviated form of the words *manuscript* and *manuscripts*.

MS MSS

Do not use periods with the following miscellaneous abbreviations (notice the proper spacings):

S O S (radio distress call)
I O U (I owe you)
A B C's (Know your A B C's)

Do not use a period after the initials of the writer and the secretary in business letters (which appear in the bottom left-hand corner).

JRS:BS HTB:fn rmm:ns tdc/al

In Relation to Other Marks of Punctuation

The period is not used in addition to a question mark or an exclamation mark at the end of a sentence. It is always placed inside closing quotation marks.

The period is placed outside the closing parenthesis when the parenthesis encloses the last word of a sentence. The period is placed inside the closing parenthesis only when what is enclosed in parentheses is a complete sentence and the first letter is capitalized.

This is called the law of natural selection (Darwinism).

This is called the law of natural selection. (This law cannot be too highly stressed in the study of biology.)

When a sentence ends with an abbreviation that requires a period of its own, no second period is added.

For your first day in school, you must remember to take paper, pencils, erasers, etc.

Question Mark

The question mark (?) follows an interrogative word, phrase, clause, or sentence. It has the power to end a sentence, yet it may also punctuate a quotation within a sentence without ending the sentence. This mark is always used to indicate a question.

A question mark should follow every direct question.

Have you done your homework?

"What time is it?" he asked.

Do not use a question mark after an indirect question.

I was asked if I had finished my homework.

He asked what time it was.

Do not use a question mark at the end of an interrogative sentence to which no answer is required.

Will you please enter my name on your mailing list.

Do not use a question mark after a question that is actually an exclamation.

How could you! How dare you!

A declarative expression may be transformed into a question by the mere addition of a question mark.

The train was late. The train was late?

Really. Really?

A question mark is enclosed in parentheses after a fact that is doubtful.

America was first visited by a white man in A.D. 1000 (?).

The crowd numbered 650 (?) cheering students.

A question mark in parentheses should not be used to indicate irony.

Poor This is a great (?) book.

Better This is hardly a great book.

When more than one question is asked in a sentence, a question mark may or may not be used depending upon the degree of emphasis desired. For emphasis, each separate question begins with a capital letter and terminates with its own question mark. A single question mark is used at the end of a sentence when the questions within the sentence are related and form a unified thought.

The teacher asked, "How large is Berlin? What is its population? and In what country is it located?"

How am I expected to know the size, population, and location of a city when I don't have an atlas?

More than one question mark placed for special emphasis does not conform to accepted usage. A period or a comma is never used in addition to the question mark.

Wrong Did you really like that play?.

Right Did you really like that play?

Wrong "Will you come with us?," she asked.

Right "Will you come with us?" she asked.

The question mark should be placed inside quotation marks if it belongs to the quotation (as shown in the example immediately above). It should be placed outside quotation marks if it does not belong to the quotation.

Who first said, "Haste makes waste"?

Exclamation Mark

The exclamation mark (!) adds forceful emphasis to a declarative word, expression, or sentence. The exclamation mark is used after a strong command or exhortation.

"Get out!" she screamed.

"Don't shoot!" he pleaded.

The exclamation mark is used after an expression of strong emotion.

What a stroke of luck!

How the mighty are fallen!

An interjection is a word that expresses emotion. It may be strong enough on its own merit not to require an exclamation mark. The exclamation mark merely helps to strengthen it.

Oh, what a beautiful day.

Wow! What a blizzard.

The exclamation mark is placed either immediately after an interjection that begins a sentence, or at the end of the sentence introduced by an interjection.

Whew! That was a close call.

Oh, what a beautiful day!

COMMA

The comma is a comparatively weak but subtle mark of punctuation. It is used–and misused–more frequently than any other punctuation mark. This is because the comma has such varied functions. Chiefly, it introduces, separates, and encloses. In addition, it indicates omission. None of these functions is performed by the comma with the authority or finality of such marks as the colon, semicolon, or dash. All the comma indicates is a mild pause, hence its subtle, elusive nature. In the rules for comma usage that follow, the term "to separate" means that the comma separates a word, phrase, or clause from the rest of the sentence. A single comma is used to separate. The term "to enclose" means that an expression appearing within a sentence is enclosed in commas. Two commas are used to enclose: one comma is placed immediately preceding, and the other following, the expression. When an expression to be enclosed ends the sentence, a period is used instead of the second enclosing comma.

Quoted References

A comma is used to introduce a short quotation, maxim, or proverb.

Helen said, "It's a lovely day."

The saying is, "Time waits for no man."

Do not use a comma to introduce a formal quotation or a quotation that consists of two or more sentences. A colon is used instead of the comma (see page 9). Do not use a comma to introduce a quoted word or phrase that is the subject or object of a sentence.

"Fourscore and seven years ago" is the most famous opening passage of any address ever made.

The president spoke on "Our Relations with Latin America."

Obey the "Slow down" signs.

Must you always ask "Why?"

Can't you say "Thank you" occasionally?

Do not use a comma preceding a quotation introduced by the conjunction *that*.

Wrong The travel poster suggested that, "California is the land of sunshine."

Right The travel poster suggested that "California is the land of sunshine."

A comma is used after a quotation to separate such expressions as *he said* and *she replied*. Commas are used to enclose such expressions when they break into or interrupt a quotation.

"It's a grand day," Bill said.

"The weather is perfect," she said, "for the Winter Carnival."

Do not use a comma in addition to a question mark or mark of exclamation following a quotation.

Wrong "Do you think we can leave early?," she asked.

Right "Do you think we can leave early?" she asked.

Series Separation

Commas are used to separate words, phrases, and clauses in a series. (In journalistic writing the comma is frequently omitted before the final conjunction in a series. This practice is not sanctioned in formal writing.)

> Our American professors like their literature clear, cold, pure, and very dead. –*Sinclair Lewis*

> All the things I really like to do are either immoral, illegal, or fattening.–*Alexander Woollcott*

Do not use commas when the conjunction is repeated before each item in a series.

Wrong It rained, and thundered, and hailed.

Right It rained and thundered and hailed.

Do not use a comma after the last item in a series.

Wrong We planted roses, violets, and nasturtiums, in our garden.

Right We planted roses, violets, and nasturtiums in our garden.

Commas are used to separate two or more coordinate adjectives modifying the same noun. Adjectives may be considered coordinate when they are in a series and the coordinating conjunction *and* can be readily substituted for the comma.

> Caroline is a comely, tow-headed girl.

> John is a short, stocky, powerful wrestler.

Do not use the comma to separate adjectives that appear as part of a compound noun, that is, if *and* cannot be readily substituted for the comma.

Wrong She is a comely, little girl.

Right She is a comely little girl.

Do not use the comma to separate one adjective that modifies another.

Wrong He has a deep, tan sunburn.

Right He has a deep tan sunburn.

Separation in Compound Sentences

A comma is used to separate the main (independent) clauses of a sentence joined by coordinating conjunctions like *and, but, or, nor, for,* and *yet.*

> It's better to give than to lend, and it costs about the same.–*Philip Gibbs*

> My folks didn't come over on the *Mayflower,* but they were there to meet the boat.–*Will Rogers*

> We do not know what to do with this short life, yet we want another which will be eternal.–*Anatole France*

> Arguments are extremely vulgar, for everybody in good society holds exactly the same opinions.–*Oscar Wilde*

Do not use a comma to separate main clauses when the clauses already contain commas within them. A semicolon is used instead of the comma (see page 10).

Do not use a comma to separate main clauses when they are short and are closely connected in thought, provided that the omission of the comma will not lead to a misreading.

Wrong Grace picked up the photo that stood on the table and walked away. (The omission of the comma in this sentence could be misread as referring to picking up a photo that walked away.)

Right Grace picked up the photo that stood on the table, and walked away.

Do not use a comma to separate main clauses when the second clause has the same subject as the first clause and the subject is not repeated.

> She was a brunette by birth but a blonde by habit.–*Arthur Baer*

> Poverty is very good in poems but very bad in the house; very good in maxims and sermons but very bad in practical life.–*Henry Ward Beecher*

A comma is used to separate an introductory subordinate phrase or clause from a main clause. Such clauses often begin with subordinating conjunctions (*when, if, because, since, while, as,* etc.).

> Where all think alike, no one thinks very much.–*Walter Lippmann*

> When you get to the end of your rope, tie a knot and hang on.–*Franklin Delano Roosevelt*

> If you're there before it's over, you're on time.–*James J. Walker*

A comma is used to separate an introductory phrase containing a participle or an infinitive used as an adjective or an adverb.

> Drawing on my fine command of knowledge, I said nothing.–*Robert Benchley*

> To keep your friends, treat them kindly; to kill them, treat them often.–*George D. Prentice*

Do not use a comma to separate a gerund or an infinitive phrase that is the subject of the sentence.

Wrong Writing carelessly, causes bad grades.

Right Writing carelessly causes bad grades.

> To profit from good advice requires more wisdom than to give it.–*John Churton Collins*

Parenthetical Expressions, Appositives

Commas are used to enclose such parenthetical expressions as the following: *to tell the truth, in the main, generally speaking, you must admit, I should say, I know, I believe, we may understand, in short, for one thing, in the long run, for the most part, in fact,* and *it is true.*

Thomas Carlyle

> Opera in English is, in the main, just about as sensible as baseball in Italian.–*H. L. Mencken*

> The greatest of faults, I should say, is to be conscious of none.–*Thomas Carlyle*

Commas are used to enclose the parenthetical expressions *for example, for instance,* and *that is.*

> Take, for example, the poets we have been reading.

> Consider the books we have been reading, for instance.

> This is not an adequate map, that is, not from an artist's point of view.

Commas are used to enclose nonlimiting (also called "nonrestrictive") phrases and clauses within a sentence. Though it may add information and help clarify meaning, a nonlimiting phrase or clause is not necessary to identify the word or words it modifies. It can be omitted from the sentence without changing the meaning. A limiting (also called "restrictive") phrase or clause, however, is necessary to identify the word or words it modifies. An integral part of the sentence, a limiting phrase or clause is *not* enclosed in commas.

Nonlimiting: *The Spirit of St. Louis,* which Lindbergh flew across the Atlantic, was a single-engine airplane.

Limiting: The airplane that Lindbergh flew across the Atlantic was *The Spirit of St. Louis.*

Commas are used to enclose a parenthetical aside that interrupts the free flow, or thought, of a sentence and that can be omitted without changing the meaning of the sentence. An aside–like other parenthetical expressions–may add information, but the essential thought of the sentence is complete without it.

> That, like it or not, is the way to learn to write; whether I have profited or not, that is the way.–*Robert Louis Stevenson*

> Age carries all things, even the mind, away.–*Virgil*

Commas are used to enclose words in apposition. An appositive is a noun or a pronoun (or any group of words used as a noun or a pronoun) that is set beside another noun or pronoun having the same meaning. An appositive adds information, but it is not absolutely essential to the meaning or clarity of the sentence.

> Helen, my sister, is coming to the prom.

> Roger Martin Du Gard, the author, was a close friend of André Gide.

Do not use commas to enclose limiting or "restrictive" appositives. A limiting appositive is absolutely necessary to the meaning and clarity of the sentence, because it actually identifies a particular person or thing. A limiting appositive is frequently part of a name.

> My sister Helen is coming to the prom. (My sister Helen is coming, not my sister Barbara.)

> The author Roger Martin Du Gard was a close friend of André Gide.

Expressions Not in Normal Order

Commas are used to enclose an expression that does not appear in its normal order in the sentence.

Not normal order: A cynic is a man who, when he smells flowers, looks around for a coffin.–*H. L. Mencken*

Normal order: A cynic is a man who looks around for a coffin when he smells flowers.

Omissions

A comma is used to take the place of one or more omitted words. Usually the comma takes the place of a verb or verb phrase.

> To love and win is the best thing; to love and lose, the next best.–*William Makepeace Thackeray*

> To eat is human; to digest, divine.–*Mark Twain*

Direct Address

A comma is used to separate a word or words in direct address, either at the beginning or the end of a sentence. When an expression in direct address appears within the sentence, commas are used to enclose it.

> Sir, I wish to leave the room.

> I move, Mr. Chairman, that the motion be put to a vote.

Contrasts

A comma is used to separate letters, words, phrases, or clauses that are contrasted. Such contrasts are generally introduced by the word *not.*

> We live in deeds, not years; in thoughts, not breaths.–*Philip James Bailey*

> Genius is born, not paid.–*Oscar Wilde*

Direct Questions

A comma is used to separate a direct question from the rest of the sentence. The first word of the direct question may be capitalized or not, depending upon how much the writer wishes to emphasize the question.

> The question is, where do we go from here?

> Have you ever asked yourself the question, Why am I here?

> I wondered, what do I do next?

Interjections

A comma is used to separate mild interjections from the rest of the sentence. When the interjection appears within the sentence, commas are used to enclose it. (An interjection becomes an exclamation when it is followed by an exclamation mark [see page 4].)

> Well, let me see now.

> Oh, why, oh, why did I ever do that?

Do not use a comma when such words as *well* and *why* are used as adverbs.

> Well done, team.

> Why am I not good enough for you?

Do not use a comma immediately following the vocative *O* (that is, when *O* is used to emphasize the name of a person or persons being addressed).

> O ye Gods, grant us what is good, whether we pray for it or not, but keep evil from us, even though we pray for it.–*Plato*

However, you should use a comma after the interjection *O*.

> O, for a draught of vintage!–*John Keats*

Yes and No

A comma is used to separate the words *Yes* and *No* from the rest of the sentence.

> Yes, it was a wonderful book.

> No, you are not to leave.

> I have already given my answer and that is, no.

Do not use a comma when the word *Yes* or *No* is a direct object.

> Jane answered yes to the suggestion.

> I said to tell him no.

Emphasis

A comma may be used to separate a word or words strictly for emphasis, or to add an element of surprise. This is a subtle use of the comma. The dash is used more frequently for emphasis and surprise (see page 11).

> I spent a year in that town, one Sunday. –*Warwick Deeping*

> One would think that only a policeman would be safe in the subway, these days.

Ordinal Adverbs

Commas are used to separate ordinal adverbs (*first, second, third,* etc.) and ordinal adverb phrases such as *in the first place* and *in the second place.*

> First, I wish to announce that the library will be open during the Christmas recess; second, that all borrowed books must be returned on or before the first day of classes.

> In the first place, there isn't time; in the second, we don't have the facilities to do a proper job.

Figures

Commas are used to separate the digits in figures above 999. The comma is placed preceding every third digit, counting backward from the last digit. Note that in sums of money the digits denoting cents are not counted.

1,000 1,999 2,000 12,605
$99.00 $999,000 $1,000,000
$2,105,602,000.46

Do not use the comma in numbers denoting dates.

The Trojan War began in 1194 B.C.

George Orwell's *1984* is a remarkable book.

Do not use the comma in page numbers, telephone numbers, and street numbers. The comma is also not generally used in serial numbers.

You will find the reference on page 1201.

Please phone me at 212-8915.

Do not use the comma in decimals.

.1329 .89641

Do not use the comma in numbers denoting dimensions, weights, and measures.

6 ft. 3 in. 10 feet 11 inches

11 hr. 38 min. 11 hours 38 minutes

Commas are used to enclose the year when the year immediately follows the name of the month.

In December, 1964, John moved to Los Angeles.

May 8, 1945, was the day Germany formally surrendered, ending World War II in Europe.

A comma is used to separate unrelated figures that appear next to each other.

In 1960, 68,837,000 presidential votes were cast–an increase of 6,800,000 from the presidential election of 1956.

Addresses

Commas are used to enclose the name of a state when it immediately follows the name of a city or town.

John moved from Denver, Colorado, to Los Angeles, California.

Do not use the comma in addresses to separate digits in street numbers, nor to separate the street number from the street itself.

This is to notify you that I have moved my address from 1135 Biscayne Blvd., Miami, Florida, to 1060 Park Ave., New York, N.Y.

Titles and Degrees

Commas are used to enclose an abbreviation or phrase that denotes a person's title or degree, when it follows the person's name.

Lyndon B. Johnson, President of the United States, will address the United Nations.

Henry Nathan, M.D., and Lester Hawthorne, Ph.D., are the expert witnesses for the defense.

Initials

Commas are used to enclose a person's initials when the initials follow the person's name.

The authors are Johnson, L. M., and Scott, N. R.

Letters

A comma is used to separate the salutation of a friendly, informal letter from the body of the letter.

Dear Bill, Dear Susan, Dear Mother,

Do not use a comma after the salutation in a formal business letter. A colon is used instead.

Dear Mr. Marks: Dear Sir:

A comma is used to separate the complimentary close of both informal and business letters from the writer's signature.

Sincerely, Yours truly,

COLON

The colon (:) is a formal mark of punctuation. It has two functions only: to introduce and to separate. As a mark of introduction, the colon introduces formal quotations, restatements or clarifying examples, and lists or enumerations. As a mark of separation, the colon separates the salutation in a formal letter from the main body of the letter, titles from subtitles, scenes of plays from acts, etc. A colon is used to introduce a formal quotation.

Franklin D. Roosevelt said: "We have nothing to fear but fear itself."

The first line of Franz Kafka's *The Trial* reads: "Someone must have been telling lies about Joseph K., for without having done anything wrong he was arrested one fine morning."

Do not use a colon to introduce a maxim, a proverb, or a quotation of a single sentence in ordinary dialogue.

The saying is, "A stitch in time saves nine."

John said, "Let's go to the movies."

A colon is used to introduce all quotations longer than one sentence.

As John left the theatre he said: "I liked the play. I must recommend it to my friends."

The colon may take the place of such expressions as *in effect, in other words,* and *namely* to introduce new statements, restatements, and clarifying examples.

Readers are of two sorts: one who carefully goes through a book, and the other who as carefully lets the book go through him. –*Douglas Jerrold*

James Russell Lowell

Whatever you may be sure of, be sure of this: that you are dreadfully like other people.– *James Russell Lowell*

The colon is used to introduce formal lists and enumerations.

I have come to the following conclusions:

Kindly forward the items listed:

Mix the ingredients as follows:

The colon is used in reference to time to separate hours from minutes.

10:15 A.M. 6:50 P.M.

The colon is used to separate a subtitle from a main title.

Wheat: The Staff of Life

My Father: A Memoir of Mark Twain

The colon is used to separate a scene from an act in a play.

Act III: scene ii

The colon is used to separate verse from chapter in the Bible.

The Song of Solomon 2:1

Ezekiel 10:6

In reference matter, the colon is used to separate the home office from the name of a publishing firm.

Chapel Hill, N.C.: University of North Carolina Press

New York: Basic Books

The colon is used following the salutation in a formal business letter.

Dear Mr. Jones: Dear Sir: Gentlemen:

In Relations to Other Marks of Punctuation

The colon takes the place of the period after an abbreviation, such as *etc.*

The following synthetic materials contain dacron, nylon, aquilon, etc:

When the colon appears together with closing quotation marks, the colon always follows the quotation marks.

The teacher said, "Please answer the following questions":

The colon always follows a closing parenthesis.

The librarian recommended the following books (all by Maugham):

The colon commonly used to be joined with the dash. This is no longer accepted usage.

Wrong We must follow these rules:–

Right We must follow these rules:

SEMICOLON

The semicolon, consisting of a period atop a comma (;), is strictly a mark of separation. Unlike a colon, it does not introduce; unlike a comma, it does not enclose; and, unlike a period, it does not terminate. Its sole function is to separate parts of sentences that cannot be separated by the comma. It marks a greater break or a longer pause than the comma, yet it does not carry the full authority of the period and other terminal marks to end a sentence.

A semicolon separates main (independent) clauses of a sentence when those clauses are not already joined by coordinating conjunctions like *and, but or, neither, nor, for,* and *yet.*

Abraham Lincoln

With educated people, I suppose, punctuation is a matter of rule; with me it is a matter of feeling. But I must say I have a great respect for the semicolon; it's a useful little chap. –*Abraham Lincoln*

A semicolon separates the main (independent) clauses of a sentence when the clauses are joined by coordinating conjunctions but when one or more already contain commas.

> Don't ever prophesy; for if you prophesy wrong, nobody will forget it; and if you prophesy right, nobody will remember it. –*Josh Billings*

> If you have charm, you don't need to have anything else; and if you don't have it, it doesn't matter what else you have.–*James M. Barrie*

A semicolon separates main (independent) clauses of a sentence that are joined by conjunctive adverbs like *thus, however, consequently, therefore, accordingly, besides,* and *moreover.*

> I do best in subjects that relate to science; consequently, I plan to major in science next year.

> He is taking six courses this semester; however, he has given up his part-time job and will have more time to study.

A semicolon separates items in a series when parts of the items are already separated by commas. The reason is that without the semicolon, the main parts would be indistinguishable.

> The winners were: John, first; Bill, second; Tom, third.

> New York Central has railroad stations in Chicago, Illinois; Sante Fe, New Mexico; and Los Angeles, California.

In Relation to Other Marks of Punctuation

A semicolon is always placed outside quotation marks.

> Play the "Appassionata Sonata"; play it with feeling this time.

A semicolon appearing next to words in parentheses is always placed after the closing parenthesis.

> The advanced math course intrigues me (with the possible exception of geometry); basketball practice, however, intrigues me more.

DASH

The dash (—) is roughly twice the length of a hyphen. On the typewriter it is indicated by two successive hyphens. The dash is extraordinarily versatile. It can perform any one of the four major functions of punctuation: introduction, separation, enclosure, and termination. In addition, the dash can indicate interruption and omission (of words, letters, figures). The dash is often used indiscriminately, especially by beginning writers, precisely because it is so versatile. It is, after all, a conspicuous, highly obtrusive mark of punctuation. Properly used, the dash is an ideal method of injecting an element of irony or surprise into a sentence, but to accomplish this it must be used sparingly. Other marks of punctuation can usually take the place of the dash, and they should be substituted for it whenever one of the rules given below does not completely justify its use.

In the past, other marks of punctuation–the colon, in particular–were commonly used with the dash. Proper usage now requires the dash to stand alone. Do not confuse the dash with the shorter hyphen (see page 14).

The dash indicates a sudden break or change of thought.

> Where was I on the night of last July 10? I was in my home–no, let me think, maybe I was at the theater.

> Are you–do you feel all right?

The dash is used following a direct quotation to indicate an interruption in discourse.

> "Really, now you ask me," said Alice, very much confused, "I don't think—"

> "Then you shouldn't talk," said the Hatter.–*Lewis Carroll*

Dashes may be used to set off a parenthetical thought to give it strong emphasis. Recourse to this use of the dash should be sparing.

Yesterday, December 7, 1941–a date which will live in infamy–the United States of America was suddenly and deliberately attacked by naval and air forces of the Empire of Japan.–*Franklin D. Roosevelt*

Sometimes a parenthetical expression already contains punctuation within it and the expression cannot be enclosed in parentheses because it properly belongs to the sentence. Then dashes are used to set it off. This use of the dash frequently takes the place of commas that might otherwise be misread as series commas.

His clothes–dirty, shabby, torn–belied his circumstances.

The dash may be used as a substitute for the expressions *that is, in other words,* and *namely.*

He admits that there are two sides to every question–his own and the wrong side. –*Channing Pollock*

The dash may be used to set off a word or group of words to add an element of surprise, to show an unexpected turn of thought.

Josh Billings

There are two things in life for which we are never fully prepared, and that is–twins. –*Josh Billings*

A pun is the lowest form of humor–when you don't think of it first. –*Oscar Levant*

The dash is used before a summarizing expression such as *all such, these,* and *all these.*

Barrymore, Gielgud, Evans–these were great Hamlets in their time.

The dash may be used to indicate a word, or part of a word, that has been omitted.

That fellow is a d—— fool.

A dash is used to indicate inclusion in dates, to take the place of the words *to* or *through.*

Vacation will be June–September.

I was in the Army 1963–1965.

Do not use the dash to indicate inclusion when the words *from* or *between* precede the date.

Wrong Vacation will be from June–September.

Right Vacation will be from June to [*or* through] September.

In Relation to Other Marks of Punctuation

When the dash ends a sentence, all other terminal marks (period, question mark, exclamation mark) are omitted.

PARENTHESES

When an expression cannot be sufficiently set off by commas or dashes, parentheses are used to enclose it. Generally, in order for a statement to be enclosed in parentheses, it must have no grammatical relationship to the rest of the sentence. Whatever is said in the parentheses should not be referred to again in the sentence. Statements within parentheses are completely independent of the rest of the sentence. Parentheses are used to set off a comment that may be only remotely connected to the meaning of the sentence itself.

The astronomer reported (as the result of too much star-gazing, I suppose) that the mean distance between the moon and the earth was 238 miles.

Parentheses are used to enclose references and directions.

The book was hailed by at least one critic (see *The Saturday Review,* Nov. 30, 1963, page 43).

Parentheses may be used to enclose figures or letters marking the order of a series.

(1) .... (2) .... (3) ....
(a) .... (b) .... (c) ....

BRACKETS

Brackets ([]), like parentheses, enclose statements that are independent of the rest of the sentence. Unlike parentheses, brackets enclose parenthetical material inserted by someone other than the author of the sentence. Brackets are generally used by editors to supply missing material to make an author's meaning clearer, or to draw attention to an author's error of fact. Brackets are used to enclose an explanatory comment in quoted material.

She [Gertrude Stein] used to counsel Hemingway at great length.

Brackets are used to enclose a correction of a quoted statement of fact.

Douglas Fairbanks Junior [Senior] was married to Mary Pickford.

Brackets are used to enclose the word *sic,* which is Latin for "thus," to call attention to the fact that some remarkable or inaccurate expression, misspelling, or error is being quoted literally.

In his speech he suggested that Li'l Abner was the most literate [sic] cartoon in America.

Brackets may be used to take the place of parentheses within parentheses.

An interesting comment on the Witches Sabbath is contained in the author's previous book (see *Medieval Europe,* pp. 204-229 [2d ed.]).

QUOTATION MARKS

A chief function of quotation marks (" ") is to identify words spoken in direct discourse. Another chief function is to identify words said or written by one person and quoted or reproduced by another. In addition, quotation marks may be used to distinguish words from other words that surround them in a sentence. Used this way, they approach–but not quite–the distinguishing function of italics. Modern journalistic practice is to use quotation marks as an actual substitute for italics. Newspapers and magazines often use quotation marks, for example, to set off the titles of books and plays–a practice not countenanced in formal writing. Formal writing limits the distinguishing strength of quotation marks to subdivisions, such as the titles of chapters of books and the titles of stories and articles appearing in books or magazines. Quotation marks are used at the beginning and end of every direct quotation. A direct quotation consists of the exact words of a speaker and the exact words used in reproducing a quoted passage.

"Speak for yourself, John," suggested Priscilla.

"Even when laws have been written down," said Aristotle, "they ought not always to remain unaltered."

Quotation marks are not used with an indirect quotation.

Aristotle suggested that even when laws are written down, they ought not always to remain unaltered.

When a quotation consists of more than one paragraph, place the quotation marks at the beginning of each new paragraph and at the end of the last paragraph only.

Quotation marks may be used to set off slang terms in formal writing, not generally, however, in informal writing, and almost never in dialogue.

The policeman was annoyed by a group of young men who said they did not "dig" his actions.

He has the job "sewed up."

Quotation marks are used to set off quoted references to chapter headings of a book, titles of articles, stories, poems, etc., appearing in magazines and other periodicals.

Chapter II: "My Early Years"

Have you read "Backstairs at the White House" in last month's *Digest?*

Quotation marks are used to set off the title of a book series.

"Great Art of Western Civilization" series.

Quotation marks are used to set off quoted references to the title of a lecture, sermon, or speech unless it has been established as virtually public domain.

Dr. Jones will speak on "The Meaning of Christmas."

the Sermon on the Mount

the Gettysburg Address

Quotation marks are used to set off quoted reference to the titles of songs and short musical works.

"Say It with Music"

"Slaughter on Tenth Avenue"

Quotation marks are used to set off quoted reference to the titles of paintings and sculpture.

"Nude Descending a Staircase" by Duchamp

"Bird in Flight" by Brancusi

A single quotation mark is used to enclose a quotation within a quotation. Double quotation marks are used to enclose an additional quotation within the second.

> He said: "John told me that Mary said, 'You know that Henry hasn't heard "Alexander's Rag Time Band" yet.' "

In Relation to Other Marks of Punctuation

The period and comma are always placed inside the quotation marks.

> Henry Ford said, "History is the bunk."

> Although Anne said, "That was a fine play," she did not meant it.

A colon or semicolon after a quotation always appears outside the quotation marks.

> "Television is taking the place of movies": This suggestion grows in truth each day.

> Mary said, "Of course not"; and she meant it.

All other marks of punctuation are placed inside the quotation marks if they refer specifically to the quotation. They are placed outside if they refer, not to the quotation, but to the sentence as a whole.

> "Has it occurred to you that your parents have been waiting all day?" he asked.

> Did you remember to say "Thank you"?

> She exclaimed, "My gosh, I forgot!"

Quotation marks may be omitted when a single word is used.

> What can we do if they all say yes?

APOSTROPHE

The apostrophe mark (') is essentially a spelling device used to indicate the possessive case of nouns and the plural of letters and figures. As a mark of punctuation, it is used to denote the omission of one or more letters or figures. The apostrophe also denotes the omission of letters in words.

o'clock	shouldn't
haven't	don't

Do not use the apostrophe in words that are accepted shortened forms. Generally, such words would otherwise have an apostrophe preceding their first letter.

phone	cello
Frisco	plane
possum	copter

The apostrophe denotes the omission of figures.

> the Spirit of '76 the class of '63

POINTS OF ELLIPSIS

The points of ellipsis consist of three consecutive periods (. . .). They indicate an omission, a lapse of time, or a particularly long pause. When the points of ellipsis fall at the end of a sentence, a fourth–the terminal period–is added.

The points of ellipsis indicate the deliberate omission of one or more words from a quoted passage.

> The playbill quoted Wolcott Gibbs as saying "I couldn't leave the theatre . . ." when what he really said was "I couldn't leave the theatre soon enough."

A full line of points of ellipsis indicates the omission of one or more paragraphs from a quoted passage. It may also indicate the omission of one or more lines of poetry.

The points of ellipsis indicate passage of time.

> Three . . . two . . . one . . . zero.

The points of ellipsis may be used as a substitute for the expression *and so forth.*

> The glamor of motion pictures is usually represented by the *heroes,* Cary Grant, Troy Donohue, . . . , and the *heroines,* Audrey Hepburn, Tuesday Weld, ...

The points of ellipsis may be used to indicate that a statement is deliberately left unfinished.

> Even before the act was half over, I thought, "Well. . . ."

The points of ellipsis are often used in advertising writing between short groups of words for emphasis; but the practice is not acceptable in formal writing.

> Don't hesitate . . . send for your copy today.

The points of ellipsis are often used in textbooks, examinations, and commercial coupons to indicate words to be filled in.

> Four kinds of citrus fruit are . . . , . . . , . . . , ...

> Enclosed find $ . . . for . . . copies at . . . each.

> Name . . . .
> Address . . . .
> City . . . . .State . . . . . .Zip . . . .

In Relation to Other Marks of Punctuation

The points of ellipsis are always placed inside quotation marks, whether they fall at the beginning or end of the sentence.

> Jean said, ". . . and, furthermore, I wouldn't have gone even if. . . ."

HYPHEN

The hyphen is both a word connector and a word separator. As a connector, it joins compound words. As a word separator, it marks the division of an uncompleted word at the end of a line when there is no room for all of it, so that part of the word must be carried over to the next line. Such division of words is known as *syllabication*. Below are presented other, minor uses of the hyphen.

The hyphen is used to indicate inclusion of numbers in street addresses, social security numbers, account numbers, etc.

> 38-14 Sunset Blvd.
>
> 032-16-1379
>
> Library of Congress Catalogue Card Number 64-20010

The hyphen is used between inclusive page numbers.

> For a discussion of the causes of the war, see pp. 29-138.

ASTERISK AND SUPERIOR FIGURE

The asterisk (*), once the universal mark of omission, is now little more than a reference mark. Even in this capacity it is rapidly being superseded by the superior figure. The asterisk may be used as a footnote reference when only a few such references are planned.

> Allergy diseases are often caused by psychogenic factors.*
>
> *William Nesbitt, *Psychosomatic Medicine* (Philadelphia: Saunders, 1959), pp. 26-49.

The superior figure is used when many footnote references are planned.

> "It is proper for an escort to precede a lady through a revolving door."[4]
>
> [4]Sophie Hadida, *Manners for Millions* (New York: Permabooks, 1934), p. 38.

BAR (VIRGULE)

The bar is a diagonal line. It has two principal functions: to serve as a mark of separation and to indicate the omission of words. The bar also appears in such expressions as *and/or*. This use of the bar, however, is not acceptable in formal writing. When running together lines of quoted poetry, use the bar to indicate the correct ending of lines.

> A thing of beauty is a joy forever;/Its loveliness increases; it will never/Pass into nothingness; but still will keep/A bower quiet for us, and a sleep/Full of sweet dreams, and health, and quiet breathing./–*John Keats*

Use the bar, in addresses, to separate the letters *c* and *o* to form the symbol meaning *in care of.*

% Richard Watts Smith	% Miss Helen Jones

The bar is sometimes used in informal notes and memoranda in the contractions of dates.

January 8, 1964	1/8/64
June 29, 1970	6/29/70

The bar is occasionally used in business reports and in technical writing to indicate the omission of such words as *per* and *as*. Note that when the bar is used in abbreviations, the period that ordinarily follows the abbreviation is omitted.

barrels per day	barrels/day	bbls/day
bill of lading	B/L	

Use the bar on the typewriter in place of the caret.

> Into the street the Piper stept,
>
> a
>
> Smiling first/little smile. . . .
>
> –*Robert Browning*

CARET

The word *caret* is Latin and literally means "it is missing." The caret (^) is used to indicate where letters or words are to be inserted in a written line, or between lines. Use the caret freely on rough drafts, sparingly–if at all–on the finished composition. A single page with more than one insertion should be rewritten or retyped.

The keyboards of standard typewriters do not carry the caret, and the current practice is to use the bar as follows:

find
Look before, or you'll / youself behind.
–Poor Richard's Almanac

The caret itself has to be written in by hand. Write the caret as an inverted *v*. Since it is such a conspicuous mark, the caret should be made small and in light, not heavy, lines.

s
We visited the capitol in Boston, Ma‸achusetts.

upon
All experience is an arch, to build‸.–*Henry Brooks Adams*

DITTO MARKS

Ditto marks (″) are pairs of inverted commas, used where considerable repetition occurs, to take the place of words and groups of words. Ditto itself is derived from the Latin *dicere* (to say) and means "the aforementioned thing." The marks are restricted chiefly to lists and tabulations.

The ditto is another mark that does not appear on standard typewriter keyboards. Quotation marks are the acceptable substitute.

Grammar

Few words can be classified absolutely as one or another of the eight parts of speech traditionally distinguished in our language. Most of us would automatically say that *swim* is a verb; yet in the sentence *He went for a swim,* it is clearly a noun. An even more confusing example is *up:*

> The proposal was on the *up* and up. (noun)
>
> The auctioneer encouraged us to *up* our bid. (verb)
>
> His time was *up.* (adjective, modifying *time*)
>
> We flew *up* and over the clouds. (adverb, modifying *flew*)
>
> He went *up* the stairs. (preposition)

It is clear that we may assign a word to a grammatical class only by considering its use, or *function,* in its context. Grammar is a way of talking about the relationship of words.

NOUNS

A *noun* is a name. It indicates a person, place, or thing.

> The *fireman* climbed to the *top* of the *ladder.*

Not all "things" are concrete objects. A noun may also name a quality, an action, or a concept.

> The *brutality* of the *murder* underlined its *injustice.*

Nouns may be further classified according to five types:

1. A *common* noun names a class or group of persons, places, or things. A title is ordinarily treated as a common noun.

   My *father* is a *history professor.*

   But if it used as a specific name or as part of one it is considered a proper noun.

   I introduced *Father* to *Professor White* of the *Department of History.*

2. A *concrete* noun names a particular or specific member of a class or group that can be seen, heard, touched, smelled, or tasted–one that can be perceived by the senses.

   Naomi Swift, the famous contralto, sang a fourth *aria.* In her *hair* the *rose* glowed as red as *wine.*

3. An *abstract* noun names a quality or concept.

   Continued *apathy* will compromise the *freedom* we enjoy under *democracy.*

4. A *proper* noun names a specific person, place, or thing; it is capitalized.

   After *President Jefferson* returned from *Monticello* he addressed *Congress.*

5. A *collective* noun is a proper or common noun which names a group of persons or things.

   group crowd pack

Note: Nouns can belong to more than one type.

Concrete, common, and collective: He joined a *brotherhood* to meet friends.

Concrete, proper, and collective: He was a member of the *Brotherhood* of RR Engineers.

Abstract, common, and collective: He believed in the *brotherhood* of man.

A noun may be a single word:

The *attorney* is Adams;

or a compound word:

Richard Adams became *attorney general;*

or a phrase:

Hunting the elusive fox was strenuous sport;

or a clause:

That he could have been lying was out of the question.

Gender

The *gender* of a noun presents no problem in English. *Masculine nouns* refer to males (boy, father), *feminine* to females (woman, girl). All others are *neuter.* A number of nouns have masculine and feminine forms clearly marked by differences of pronunciation or of spelling (aviator, aviatrix; alumnus, alumna; fiancé, fiancée). Except in the case of the last example, the tendency seems to be toward using masculine forms in place of the feminine (aviator, etc.).

Number

The *number* of a noun is a way of indicating how many persons, places, and things it refers to. A noun is *singular* if it names one, and *plural* if it names two or more.

Case

The *case* of a noun is determined by what it does in a sentence. If it is *doing* something, it is in the nominative (or subjective) case, as in "The *teacher* graded my paper." If something is *being done to it,* the noun is usually in the objective (or accusative) case, as in "The teacher graded my *paper.*" If the noun is said to own something, it is in the possessive (or genitive) case, as in "the *dog's* tail."

Since the forms of nominative and objective nouns are identical, there is no problem in English of writing them correctly. Even the genitive case causes little difficulty in its grammatical relationships.

Use of Nouns

As *subject* (nominative case): The subject of a sentence is the person, place, or thing about which the statement is made or question asked.

The *girl* enjoyed dancing.

Didn't the *boy* know how to dance?

As *object* (objective, or accusative, case): The *direct object* of a sentence is the person, place, or thing directly affected by the action of a transitive verb.

The car crossed the *bridge.*

The college announced *that tuition would go up again.* (clause as object)

The *indirect object* is indirectly affected by the action of a transitive verb. It precedes the direct object, unless it is a prepositional phrase.

He sent *his mother* a birthday present.

He sent a birthday present *to his mother.*

As *subjective complement* (nominative case), also called the *predicate nominative.* The complement is a noun related directly to the subject, not the verb.

He is the heaviest *player* on the team.

Jenny seemed the last *person* you'd expect to get into trouble.

A linking verb (see page 21) connects subject and subjective complement.

As *objective complement* (objective case): Completes the sense of a transitive verb, related directly to the direct object, not the verb.

She called her best friend a green-eyed *monster.*

Linus considers Beethoven the only *composer.*

As *appositive:* An appositive is a noun that usually follows another noun with the same meaning. It takes the same case as the noun with which it is in apposition.

Our next-door neighbor, a *veteran* of World War II, refuses to join the American Legion. (*Veteran* is in apposition with *neighbor;* both are nominative.)

He finally joined the VFW, a livelier *organization.* (*Organization* is in apposition with *VFW,* both are objective.)

In *direct address:*

Darling, I agree.

Be good, my *dear,* and let who will be clever.

PRONOUNS

A *pronoun* refers to a person, place, or thing without naming it.

She bit *his* arm. Wash *it* with *this.*

Everyone who wants to come is welcome.

There are *four,* you say?

The noun (or pronoun) for which a pronoun substitutes is called its *antecedent.* Thus, in the first example above, *arm* is the antecedent of *it.* The antecedents of *she, his,* and *this* are implied; both speaker and hearer (or writer and reader) know who *she* and *he* are, and *this* refers to an object physically present. The antecedent of *who* in the second example, is *Everyone.* Pronouns may be classified according to seven types:

1. *Personal* pronouns substitute for the name of the person speaking, the person spoken to, or the person or object spoken of. Personal pronouns can be troublesome because, unlike nouns (which rarely change their forms except in the possessive case), most pronouns take a different form for each of the three cases: nominative, objective, and possessive.

	NOMINATIVE	OBJECTIVE	POSSESSIVE
1ST PERSON			
singular	I	me	my, mine
plural	we	us	our, ours
2ND PERSON			
singular	you	you	your, yours
plural	you	you	your, yours
3RD PERSON			
singular			
masculine	he	him	his
feminine	she	her	her, hers
neuter	it	it	its, of it
either gender	one	one	one's
plural	they	them	their, theirs

2. *Relative* pronouns link a subordinate clause with an independent one, referring to a noun or pronoun in the independent clause.

We smiled at the clerk *who* had been so pleasant.

The batter hit a line drive *which* sent two men home.

There is no difficulty of declension with most relative pronouns; only *who* and *whom* (and their related compound forms) present problems. The distinction between these has virtually disappeared in speech, but is still maintained in writing.

NOMINATIVE	OBJECTIVE	POSSESSIVE
who	whom	whose
whoever	whomever	whosever
which	which	of which
that	that	whose
what	what	——
as	as	——

Who and its related forms refer to people, *which* to other living creatures and to things; *that* may be used for either persons or things. *What* is the equivalent of *that which* when used as a relative pronoun. *As* appears in a dependent clause, when *such* or *the same* has appeared in the independent clause.

Ours is the same *as* yours.

Note: Except for the word *one's,* the possessive case of both personal and relative pronouns has no apostrophe.

3. *Interrogative* pronouns introduce questions. They include *who* (objective, *whom;* possessive, *whose*), *which,* and *what.*

Who saw him leave?
Whom do you mean?
Which are the best roads from here?
What is the direction you want to take?

Who (and its related forms) inquires about a person, *which* about a person or thing in a group, *what* about anything.

Note: Remember that the objective form *(whom):* is the object of a verb or a preposition.

Whom did Petrarch love?
Whom do you get them from?

Whose, which, and *what* also function as interrogative adjectives, when instead of substituting for a noun they modify it.

Which roads are best?
What direction are you taking?

4. *Demonstrative* pronouns point out specific persons or things. Principal ones are *this* (plural, *these*) and *that* (plural, *those*).

This is the least flattering of all the photos.
Have you seen *those?*

Note: Demonstrative pronouns may also function as demonstrative adjectives.

This photo is more flattering than *those others.*

5. *Indefinite* pronouns point out persons or things, but less specifically than demonstrative pronouns. A great number in this classification include the following:

SINGULAR INDEFINITE PRONOUNS

another	everything
anyone	somebody
each	such
either	

PLURAL INDEFINITE PRONOUNS

both	many
few	several

SINGULAR OR PLURAL INDEFINITE PRONOUNS

all	most
any	none
more	some

The only problem likely to arise with the use of the indefinite pronoun is that of number; see *Agreement,* page 19.

Note: Except for the words *none* and *plenty,* indefinite pronouns can function as adjectives as well.

6. *Reflexive* pronouns refer back to the subject. A reflexive pronoun is usually the direct object of a verb.

   We dressed *ourselves* hastily.

Reflexive pronouns may also be used for emphasis.

   Many feared the Senate *itself* was discredited.

In formal English the reflexive form is not used as a substitute for either subject or object; this is likely to be a practical problem only in the first person.

   Myrna and I (not: *myself*) made all the arrangements.

   They asked Myrna and *me* (not: *myself*) to chaperone the dance.

7. *Reciprocal* pronouns are compound indefinite pronouns which indicate some mutual relationship between two or more persons and things.

   The lovers lived only for *each other.*

   All members of the company saw *one another* every day.

Case of Pronouns

The case rules that apply to nouns apply also to pronouns. Unlike nouns, however, pronouns frequently change their form according to whether they are in the nominative, objective, or possessive case. For this reason the case rules for pronouns are given separately below. A pronoun used as the subject of a verb takes the nominative case.

Right John and *I* are invited, aren't *we*?

When a verb is omitted but understood, be sure to supply it mentally in order to determine whether the pronoun is used as its subject.

Wrong John knows more than *her.*

You are as good a player as *me.*

Right John knows more than *she* (does). (*She* is the subject of the omitted verb *does.*).

Right You are as good a player as *I* (am).

A pronoun used as a predicate nominative takes the nominative case. A predicate nominative is a noun or pronoun that follows *am, is, are, was, were, be, been,* and that refers back to the subject.

Wrong Knock. Knock. Who's there? It's *me.*

Could that be *her* already?

It might have been *him.*

Right Knock. Knock. Who's there? It's *I.* (*I* is the predicate nominative after the verb *is.*)

Could that be *she* already?

It might have been *he.*

Do not permit such interrupting expressions as *do you suppose, believe, think, say,* etc., to affect the case of *who* and *whom.*

Wrong *Whom* do you believe was the guilty person?

Right *Who* do you believe was the guilty person? (*Who* is the subject of *was,* not the object of *believe.*)

Be careful not to confuse the subject of a verb with the object of a preposition.

Wrong I will vote for *whomever* is the best candidate.

Right I will vote for *whoever* is the best candidate. (*Whoever* is the subject of *is.* The object of the preposition *for* is the whole clause *whoever is the best candidate.*)

A pronoun that is the subject of an infinitive takes the objective case. The infinitive is the form of the verb preceded by *to: to be, to dance,* etc.

Wrong Do you expect John and *I* to be ready?

Right Do you expect John and *me* to be ready? (*Me* is the subject together with *John* of the infinitive *to be.*)

A pronoun that follows the infinitive *to be* takes the objective case.

Wrong Mary took John to be *I*.

Right Mary took John to be *me*.

A pronoun used as the object of a verb, of an infinitive, or of a preposition, or as the indirect object, takes the objective case.

Wrong *Who* did you ask to the party?

Right *Whom* did you ask to the party? (*Whom* is the object of the verb *ask*.)

Wrong The time has come for *we* students to get to work.

Right The time has come for *us* students to get to work. (*Us* is the object of the preposition *for*.)

Wrong The coach gave John and *I* a briefing.

Right The coach gave John and *me* a briefing. (*John* and *me* are the indirect objects of the verb *gave*.)

A pronoun used in apposition with a noun takes the same case as the noun.

Wrong The instructor wants us all–Harry, Sam, and *I*–to stay after class.

Right The instructor wants us all–Harry, Sam, and *me*–to stay after class. (*Harry, Sam,* and *me* are in apposition with *us* and therefore take the same case.)

A pronoun used before a gerund takes the possessive case. A *gerund* is a verbal used as a noun. It has the same form as the verb's present or perfect participle.

Wrong I was sure of *him* winning the prize.

Right I was sure of *his* winning the prize. (*Winning* is the gerund. It is the object of the preposition *of*.)

The case form of the relative pronouns *who* and *whoever* depends upon how the pronoun is used in the clause it introduces.

Right I already know *who* will come to the party. (*Who* is the subject of the verb *come* and is therefore in the nominative case.)

The captain, *whom* I have never met, has asked to see me. (*Whom* is the direct object of the verb *met* and is therefore in the objective case.)

Agreement

Since pronouns are substitute words for other words, there must be agreement between them; otherwise the meaning of the substitute word will not be clear. The word for which a pronoun substitutes and to which it refers is its antecedent. A pronoun does not necessarily agree with its antecedent in case; but it must always agree with it in gender, number, and person.

The problem words are *each, either, neither, every, everyone, anybody, nobody, everybody, somebody.* In informal speech, we generally treat these words as collectives and we make the pronouns that refer to them singular or plural according to sound or whim. In formal writing, these words are treated as singular; therefore, a pronoun that has any one of these words as an antecedent should also be singular.

Informal Each of us knew what *we* were doing.

Formal Each of us knew what *he* was doing.

Informal Everybody should know what *they* want out of life.

Formal Everybody should know what *he* wants out of life.

Informal Will everyone please open *their* book to page 56.

Formal Will everyone please open *his* book to page 56.

Informal Every city and town had a large increase in *their* population.

Formal Every city and town had a large increase in *its* population.

When an antecedent includes mixed sexes and calls for a singular number, the use of *their* as an all-inclusive pronoun is wrong. The use of the double pronouns *he or she, his or her, him or her* is also undesirable. The pronoun that should be used for both sexes is *he, his, him.*

Wrong Every man, woman, and child should wear *their* life jacket.

Undesirable Every man, woman, and child should wear *his or her* life jacket.

Right Every man, woman, and child should wear *his* life jacket.

Use the pronoun *who* to refer to people, *which* to animals other than humans and to things, and *that* for either persons or things.

Wrong *Which* is that person?

Right *Who* is that person?

There are two exceptions to the above rule. *Which* may be used to refer to persons considered as a group. Also, when a reference to an animal results in the awkward *of which* construction, the acceptable alternative is *whose*.

Right Anthropologist believe that the race *which* gave America its first settlers was Mongoloid.

Awkward I claim that the cheetah, the speed *of which* has been timed at seventy miles an hour, is the world's fastest four-legged animal.

Right I claim that the cheetah, *whose* speed has been timed at seventy miles an hour, is the world's fastest four-legged animal.

When two antecedents are joined by *or* or *nor,* the pronoun should agree with the nearer antecedent.

Wrong Neither the President nor the members of the Cabinet could foresee *his* fate.

Right Neither the President nor the members of the Cabinet could foresee *their* fate.

Reference

A pronoun may be grammatically correct. It may agree in every way–in person, number, and gender–with its antecedent, and it may have just the right case form. Yet if the antecedent is not immediately clear, all the effort will be utterly wasted. The reader must be able to tell at a single glance exactly what your pronoun refers to. One of the worst writing sins you can commit is to force your reader to reread the sentence or refer back to a previous sentence to find your meaning. This sin is frequently caused by an ambiguous or misplaced pronoun. A pronoun should have a clearly defined antecedent and should be placed as near the antecedent as possible.

Indefinite I had a fascinating time in Mexico. *They* are a colorful people. (The antecedent of the pronoun *They* may be obvious to the writer, but not to the reader. Who are *They?*)

Definite I had a fascinating time on my trip to Mexico. Mexicans are a colorful people.

Definite I had a fascinating time on my trip to Mexico. It is a colorful country.

Shun the indefinite use of the pronoun *it.* In certain idiomatic phrases the indefinite use of *it* is acceptable. (*It is a fine day. It is a fact. It is necessary. It is likely. It is true.*) But when *it* is not part of an accepted idiom, avoid the indefinite use altogether.

Indefinite In the chapter on the second voyage, it reveals that Columbus sent five hundred Indian slaves as a gift to Queen Isabella.

Definite The chapter on the second voyage reveals that Columbus sent five hundred Indian slaves as a gift to Queen Isabella.

Avoid the use of the impersonal *it* and the pronoun *it* in the same sentence.

Indefinite The car is in rough shape, and it will probably cost more to repair it than the price of a new one.

Definite The car is in rough shape, and the cost of repairing it will probably be more than the price of a new one.

Shun the indefinite use of the pronouns *you* and *they.* The indefinite use of these pronouns is acceptable in informal speech, but not in formal writing. In formal writing use *one* and *everyone.*

Informal In this class *you* are not permitted to take notes.

Formal In this class *one* (or *a student*) is not permitted to take notes.

Informal *They* greet tourists warmly in Holland.

Formal *Everyone* greets tourists warmly in Holland.

VERBS

A *verb* is a word or group of words that indicates action, condition (being), or process.

> They *began* the boat race this morning; by six this evening they *will have sailed* halfway to the island.
>
> He *was* a good dog. The house *seems* empty without him.
>
> The rose *had become* an even deeper crimson.

Types of Verbs

Verbs may be classified according to four types:

1. A *transitive* verb requires a direct object to complete its meaning.

   Hilda *bathed* the *baby*. (The subject, *Hilda*, performs the action upon the direct object, *baby*.)

   Ulysses *plunged* the *stake* into the Cyclops' eye. (The verb *plunged* is transitive and the direct object is *stake*.)

2. An *intransitive* verb is complete within itself and does not require a direct object.

   Let us *pray*.
   We *felt* relieved.
   We *plunged* into the pool and *swam*. Then we *lay* in the sun.

Most verbs, like *plunge*, can be either transitive or intransitive. But *lie* is intransitive only. It is a troublesome verb because its past tense *lay* is frequently confused with the present tense of transitive *lay*.

	TRANSITIVE	INTRANSITIVE
PRESENT TENSE	lay (something down)	lie (on my bed)
PAST TENSE	laid (something down)	lay (on my bed)
PAST PARTICIPLE	have laid (something down)	have lain (on my bed)

3. A *linking* verb or *copula* joins the subject to its complement, which is a predicate noun or adjective. The more common ones are:

appear	look
be	seem
become	smell
feel	taste
grow	turn

Most of these verbs are not exclusively linking verbs.

USED AS LINKING VERBS	USED AS OTHER VERBS
It *grew* colder.	He *grew* a beard. (Transitive verb)
That *tasted* bad.	They *will taste* their soup. (Transitive verb)
He *turned* pirate.	She stopped and *turned*. (Intransitive verb)

4. An *auxiliary* verb helps the main verb of the sentence. It may be formed from *have, can, may, be, shall, will, might, must,* and *do,* and appears before the main verb in a verb phrase.

   We *can* go if we like.

   She *might have been* told earlier.

   I *am* finishing my letter.

Principal Parts

Verbs in English have three principal parts:

INFINITIVE OR BASIC FORM	to walk to sleep	to go to bite
PAST TENSE, USED IN THE SIMPLE PAST	walked slept	went bit
PAST PARTICIPLE, "USED TO" FORM COMPOUND TENSES	(has) walked (has) slept	(has) gone (has) bitten

Regular (or *weak*) verbs form their principal parts by adding *-ed, -d,* or *-t* to the infinitive.

wanted placed dealt

Irregular (or *strong*) verbs change or retain the vowel of the infinitive and do not add *-ed, -d,* or *-t*.

throw, threw, thrown

choose, chose, chosen

Intransitive sit, sat, sat

Transitive set, set, set

Sometimes a verb may have more than one form:

shine, shone (or shined), shone (or shined)

dream, dreamed (or dreamt), dreamed (or dreamt)

Consult a recent dictionary if there is any question of a form's being nonstandard:

see, saw (*not standard:* seen), have seen

Person and Number

Person and number present few problems in English verbs; the verb form usually changes only in the third person singular of the present tense, where an *s* is added (*I jump, he jumps; I cry, she cries*). A notable exception is the highly irregular verb *be*, but this is so frequently used it presents no practical difficulty.

Tense

The tense of a verb indicates the time of its action. There are six tenses in English:

1. The *present* tense uses three forms for positive statements.

SIMPLE PRESENT: We *know*, you *say*, he *rides*

PROGRESSIVE: I *am rushing*, you *are moving*, he *is standing* still

EMPHATIC: I *do move*, he *does ride*

In questions or in negative statements, the progressive or emphatic form is generally used.

PROGRESSIVE: *Are* you *coming?* She *is* not *coming*

EMPHATIC: *Does* he *swim?* They *do* not *swim*

2. The *past* tense indicates past time not continuing to the present. It uses three forms for positive statements.

SIMPLE PAST: I *took*, you *jumped*, she *sank*

PROGRESSIVE: He *was flying*, we *were laughing*

EMPHATIC: You *did believe*, they *did prove*

In questions or in negative statements, the progressive or emphatic form is generally used.

3. The *perfect* (or *present perfect*) tense indicates past time continuing to the present. It is formed by adding the past participle to *have* or *has*.

I *have shown* her the ring.

Have you *been* here long?

He *has filled* the tub.

4. The *past perfect* tense indicates past time occurring before a definite time in the past. It is formed by adding the past participle to *had*.

We *had been* in the new house for a week.

You *had come* to visit us.

Had she *set* the table yet?

Note: In the examples immediately above, any subsequent actions would still be in the past (She *set* the table when I arrived). But an action subsequent to those in the examples for the present perfect would naturally be in the present (He has filled the tub. He *is washing* now).

5. The *future* tense indicates future time continuing from the present. It has three forms.

We *will* not *leave*.

You *will be having* dinner.

Is he *going to tell* us?

The old distinction between *shall* (simple futurity) and *will* (future of determination) has virtually disappeared except in formal writing. It may also be used in the first person, to make clear an important difference in attitude.

I *shall* do it. (compliance)

I *will* do it. (desire)

6. The *future perfect* tense indicates future time occurring before a definite time in the future. It is formed by adding the past participle to the future tense of *have*.

He *shall have seen* them before you do.

Will they *have escaped* (before the house burns down)?

Note: The present tense may be used for future time (I *leave* for home tomorrow); past time, especially to add immediacy to a narrative (It *is* dark, this Christmas Eve, as Washington *approaches* Trenton); to make a statement that is presumably true at any time (Too many cooks *spoil* the broth); or to discuss a fictional past (When Huck *sneaks* ashore from the raft, we *see* intrepidity at its height).

Voice

A verb is in the *active voice* when its subject performs the action.

Tennyson published *In Memoriam* in 1850. (*Tennyson* is the subject and the verb *published* is in the active voice.)

A verb is in the *passive voice* when its subject is acted upon.

In Memoriam was published by Tennyson in 1850. (*In Memoriam* is the subject and the verb *published* is in the passive voice.)

Except for a reason of deliberate emphasis, choose the active voice in preference to the passive voice. It will make your writing more lively and vigorous. *Betty gave a party for all the children* is livelier than *A party was given by Betty for all the children*.

Mood

The *mood* of a verb refers to the manner in which a statement is expressed. There are three moods in English.

1. The *indicative* mood states a fact.

I *spent* the holiday in New York.

He *knew* you *had come*.

2. The *imperative* mood gives a command.

Stop!

Try and *make* me.

3. The *subjunctive* mood expresses a wish, a doubt, or a condition contrary to fact.

I wish he *were* somewhere else.

We wondered if we *were* going to get away with it.

Note: The past subjunctive of the verb *be*, which is *were* in all three persons and both numbers, is the only subjunctive of any real importance in English. In informal writing and in speech, the indicative *was* is an acceptable substitute. Other uses of the subjunctive are consciously formal (We request that this *be* omitted from the report; if this *prove* false I shall resign), or preserved in automatic phrases (*come* what may, whatever it *cost*). The subjunctive mood has largely disappeared.

Finite and Infinite Verbs (Verbals)

A *finite* verb is capable of making a complete and independent assertion.

She *finished* the book.

You *have done* a good job.

A finite verb is limited to a specific person, by a noun or a pronoun (the bear *roars;* he *climbs*). It is also limited in number, either singular or plural (she *laughs;* they *laugh*). And it is limited in time, by a tense form (we *sit;* we *sat*). A finite verb serves as a main verb in a sentence or clause.

She *had eaten* before we *began.*

An *infinite* verb, or *verbal,* is not thus limited. It cannot be used to make a sentence of the typical subject-verb pattern, but is characteristically used in subordinate constructions. (A clear understanding of the difference between a finite verb and a verbal will eliminate most careless sentence fragments from your writing.) There are three classes of verbals:

1. The *infinitive* is one of the present forms of a verb, with *to* either present or understood.

	ACTIVE	PASSIVE
PRESENT	(to push)	(to) be pushed
PERFECT	(to) have pushed	(to) have been pushed

Most versatile of the verbals, the infinitive may be used as a noun:

To ride is good sport. (subject)

She wanted *to play* with the puppies. (object of a verb)

They wanted nothing but *to be left* alone. (object of a preposition)

His intention was *to have kissed* her. (subjective complement)

as an adjective:

Ned Creeth is my choice *to represent* us. (modifies *choice*)

It was courageous *to volunteer.* (modifies *courageous*)

as an adverb:

I am sorry *to disappoint* you. (modifies *sorry*)

To find work, he moved to the city. (modifies *moved*)

with an auxiliary as part of a finite verb:

We must *find* a way. (*to* understood)

2. The *participle* is one of the present or past participle forms of a verb.

	ACTIVE	PASSIVE
PRESENT	trying	being tried
PAST	having tried	having been tried

It may be used as an adjective:

He shot the *leaping* deer.

The *broken* vase lay near the window.

Having paid our respects, we left.

as part of a finite verb:

We were *playing* leapfrog.

I have *had* enough for now.

in an absolute construction (a phrase grammatically independent of any other part of the sentence):

The city *having been taken,* Caesar moved on. (The entire phrase *The city having been taken* is the absolute construction.)

3. The *gerund* is one of the present participial forms of a verb, and is used as a noun.

Kissing is pleasant, but *being kissed* is a perfect joy. (subject, active and passive)

Many prefer *going* to the movies. (object of a verb)

Others waste their time in *bowling.* (object of a preposition)

Uncle Jack's favorite recreation is *sleeping.* (subjective complement)

Problems in Use

The following are some persistent problems in the use of verbs and verbals:

SHALL (SHOULD) and WILL (WOULD)
In questions, *will* is properly used in all persons. However, *shall* is often used to convey a sense of propriety or obligation. *Won't* is the regular negative form.

Shall I write to thank her?

What *shall* I do to avoid it?

What *won't* you do?

Do not overuse *shall.* It is neither more correct nor more elegant than *will.*
Should and *would* suggest doubt or uncertainty.

That *should* be all right. (contrast: That *will* be all right.)

In polite requests, *would* and *should* are used for the first person, *would* for the second.

I *would* (or *should*) be very grateful for your help.

Would you please pass the hominy grits?

CAN and MAY
Can and *may* are used to show ability and possibility, respectively.

You *can* do it if you try.

We *may* arrive in time.

Can is used increasingly to express permission.

Can I come in?

You *can* choose the one you want.

This use of *can* is still not considered formally correct. In writing, and even in speaking, it is preferable to use *may.*

May I come in?

You *may* choose the one you want.

LIE, SIT, RISE
Lie, sit, and *rise* are intransitive verbs. They should not be confused with their transitive counterparts *lay, set,* and *raise.* The best way to avoid difficulty with these troublesome pairs is simply to memorize their principal parts, and then to decide whether a construction calls for a transitive or intransitive verb.

	TRANSITIVE	INTRANSITIVE
PRESENT	lay, set, raise (something)	lie, sit, rise
PAST	laid, set, raised (something)	lay, sat, rose
PAST PARTICIPLE	(have) laid, set, raised (something)	(have) lain, sat, risen

Remember that a hen *sets* on her eggs, and the sun *sets* in the west.

GET
The past participle of the verb *get* is either *got* or *gotten.* The latter seems the more common. (The only past participle of *forget* is *forgotten.*) Avoid *have got* and *have got to* (meaning *must*) where *have* and *have to* are sufficient.

Wrong I have got some here.
I haven't got any more.
I have got to leave soon.

Right I have some here.
I haven't any more.
I have to leave soon.

AIN'T
Ain't is a contraction of *am not, are not,* and occasionally *have not;* despite its long history in English, it is a nonstandard form. Use the equally convenient contractions *I'm not, aren't,* and *haven't.* However, there is no completely satisfactory form for the first person singular negative interrogative: *am I not* is too formal for most speakers, and the clumsy *aren't I* is not everywhere accepted.

Misuse of Past Tense

One of the most common verb errors is to use the past tense instead of the past participle. Use the past participle whenever there is an auxiliary or helping verb.

Wrong It wasn't until I left the house that I noticed I had *forgot* my books.

Right It wasn't until I left the house that I noticed I had *forgotten* my books. (The auxiliary verb *had* demands the past participle.)

Sequence of Tenses

Avoid unnecessary shifts from one tense to another in the same sentence. Make a verb in a subordinate clause (or an infinitive or a participle) agree in time with the verb in the main clause.

Wrong Whenever he *said* yes, she *says* no. (The verb *said* in the subordinate clause does not agree in time with the verb *says* in the main clause.)

Right Whenever he *says* yes, she *says* no. (Both verbs agree.)

Whenever he *said* yes, she *said* no. (Both verbs agree.)

An exception to the above rule applies when one states a universal truth (a statement that is true regardless of time).

Sally *said* that it *is* better to be wise than virtuous. (Disagreement between verbs is acceptable because a universal truth requiring the present tense is stated.)

When two past actions are stated in the same sentence, use the past perfect tense for the earlier action.

Wrong Fred realized just in time that he already *drank* too much.

Right Fred realized just in time that he *had* already *drunk* too much. (The action of the second verb occurred before that of the first verb.)

After *if,* use the auxiliary verb *had* instead of *would have.*

Wrong If you would have used your head, you wouldn't be in this mess.

Right If you had used your head, you wouldn't be in this mess.

The past infinitive is often used to express action not yet completed at the time of the main or preceding verb. This is wrong. The present infinitive is demanded in such constructions.

Wrong We wanted *to have finished* the job by tonight.

Right We wanted *to finish* the job by tonight. (The present infinitive *to finish* is demanded because its action has not yet taken place at the time of the main verb *wanted.*)

Agreement of Subject and Verb

A verb must always agree with its subject in person and number. It is often difficult to tell which is the true subject, or whether a subject is considered singular or plural. The rules below govern the agreement of subject and verb.

The following pronouns, often taken to be plural, are singular and therefore require a singular verb: *each, everyone, everybody, either,* and *neither.*

Wrong Each of the candidates *are* competent.

Neither of us *are* ready.

Right Each of the candidates *is* competent.

Neither of us *is* ready.

The following nouns, plural in form, are considered singular in meaning and therefore require a singular verb: *news, economics, mathematics, politics, mumps,* and *measles. The United States* also takes a singular verb.

Wrong The economics of the plan *are* hazardous.

Right The economics of the plan *is* hazardous.

The United States *has* treated the American Indians abominably.

A collective noun generally takes a singular verb. However, when the individuals of the group are considered, the verb is plural.

Our team always *wins.*

The family *is* worried about my late hours. (Family regarded as a single unit–more usual.)

The family *have* gone about their chores. (Individuals of the family considered–less usual.)

The words *there* and *here* are not subjects. In constructions introduced by *there* and *here,* look for the true subject to ascertain the number of the verb.

Wrong *There's* several ways to skin a cat.

Right There *are* several ways to skin a cat.

Fractions take a singular verb when bulk or a total number or amount is considered, a plural verb when individuals are considered. This rule applies also to words such as *all, any, none, some, more,* and *most.*

Two-thirds of the student body *was* present.

Two-thirds of the students *were* present.

All the money *has* somehow vanished.

All the members of the team *are* on the honor list.

When the word *number* is preceded by the definite article *the,* it usually takes a singular verb. When it is preceded by the indefinite article *a,* it takes a plural verb.

The number on the team who can be counted on in a tight spot *is* small.

A number of the team *have* proved their worth.

When subjects are contrasted, the verb agrees with the affirmative subject.

Wrong She, not I, *am* responsible.

Right She, not I, *is* responsible.

When the subject is a relative pronoun, look for the pronoun's antecedent to determine whether the verb is singular or plural. Relative pronouns are *who, which,* and *that.*

Wrong Joe is one of the few students who *has* maintained an A average.

Right Joe is one of the few students who *have* maintained an A average. (The antecedent of the relative pronoun *who* is *students,* hence it takes a plural verb.)

Words joined to a subject by *as well as, in addition to, with, together with, including,* and *rather than* do not affect the verb.

Wrong The entire student body, as well as most of the members of the faculty, *have* denounced President Green's decision.

Right The entire student body, as well as most of the members of the faculty, *has* denounced President Green's decision.

A compound subject joined by *and* generally takes a plural verb.

Wrong Her arrival and departure *was* not even noticed.

Right Her arrival and departure *were* not even noticed.

Do not use a plural verb when the subject is a compound that is regarded as a single entity.

The long and short of the matter *is* that our front line is weak.

Spaghetti and meat balls *is* my favorite.

Bread and butter *is* all that we have for supper.

Singular subjects joined by *and* but preceded by *every* take a singular verb.

Wrong Every man, woman, and child *are* accounted for.

Right Every man, woman, and child *is* accounted for.

Singular subjects joined by *or, either . . . or, nor,* or *neither . . . nor,* take a singular verb.

Wrong Neither Adams nor Williams *are* present.

Right Neither Adams nor Williams *is* present.

When a verb has two or more subjects differing in person or number and connected by *or, either . . . or, nor,* or *neither . . . nor,* the verb agrees with the subject nearer it.

Wrong Either he or you *is* wrong.

Right Either he or you *are* wrong. (The verb agrees in person with the pronoun nearer it.)

Wrong Either new players or a new play *are* needed.

Right Either new players or a new play *is* needed. (The verb agrees in number with the noun nearer it.)

Irregular Verbs

To find the proper form of irregular verbs, consult a reliable dictionary. It is important to know how dictionaries enter the forms of irregular verbs. The main entry for all verbs is the infinitive (without the *to*) or present tense form. Following the verb's phonetic respelling comes, first, the past tense form, next, the past participial form, and finally, the present participial form. Acceptable variant forms are given. However, if any one form is the same as the one immediately preceding it, that form is not repeated. For verbs that are not irregular, the past tense and the past participle, when not given, are assumed to be formed in the usual way by adding *-d* or *-ed.*

ADJECTIVES AND ADVERBS

Adjectives and adverbs are *modifiers,* words which change the meaning of other words to make them clearer, more exact, weaker, or stronger.

An *adjective* modifies a noun or pronoun. It may answer the questions How many? What kind? Which one?

HOW MANY?

three brothers   *one* dollar   *many* men

WHAT KIND?

early bird   *whole* truth   *beautiful* girl

WHICH ONE?

this visit   *whose* jug?   *her* book

Note that *this, whose,* and *her*–often used as pronouns–here function as *pronominal adjectives.* A pronominal adjective always accompanies a noun.

Also note that the indefinite article *a* (*an*) identifies something as one of its kind (*a* boy, *an* apple), or serves as a substitute for *each* or *every* (once *a* week). The definite article *the* identifies one or more persons or objects by separating them from all others of their kind. Both articles are therefore adjectives.

An *adverb* modifies a verb, adjective, or other adverb. It may answer the questions How? When? Where? How much?

HOW?

Come *quickly.*   It moves *clockwise.*

WHEN?

They arrived *yesterday.*

WHERE?

They went *home*. *Here* it is.

HOW MUCH?

We are more active now, but *only partly* happy.

In addition, there are the conjunctive adverbs *(however, moreover, nevertheless, therefore),* and adverbs of assertion and concession (*yes, no, not, maybe, probably).*

Many adverbs may be distinguished from adjectives by their *-ly* ending *(happy, happily; hard, hardly; particular, particularly).* But some of the more common adverbs do not end in *-ly: now, quite, there, then, up, down, for.* The last four of these can also be adjectives; there is a long list of adjectives and adverbs with identical forms, including *better, early, fast, much, straight,* and *well.*

Some adverbs have two forms: *loud, loudly; slow, slowly; soft, softly; quick, quickly; wrong, wrongly.* Sometimes there is a clear difference of meaning between the two.

He tried *hard.*	He *hardly* tried.
She came *late.*	*Lately* she has been coming at dinner time.

With others, choice depends on sound or on level of usage. The *-ly* ending is more common in formal writing. It is almost invariably used when the adverb precedes the verb *(Tightly* he gripped the narrow ledge). The short form is used especially in commands (hold on *tight;* go *slow).* Do not drop the *-ly* from the adverbs *considerably, really, sincerely,* and the like. For any question of the standard form consult a dictionary.

Adjectives and adverbs in English do not change their forms to indicate person, number, or case. However, they do change their forms to indicate degrees of comparison. They are compared in three degrees, frequently by adding *-er* and *-est.*

	POSITIVE	COMPARATIVE	SUPERLATIVE
ADJECTIVE	long	longer	longest
ADVERB	far	farther	farthest

Some have irregular comparisons, but these rarely cause difficulty:

	POSITIVE	COMPARATIVE	SUPERLATIVE
ADJECTIVE	good	better	best
	bad	worse	worst
	many, much	more	most
ADVERB	well	better	best
	best	worse	worst

Words of two syllables may have comparisons in *-er* and *-est,* or may use *more (less)* and *most (least);* the choice is determined by rhythm and emphasis. Words of three or more syllables are compared only with *more (less)* and *most (least).*

	POSITIVE	COMPARATIVE	SUPERLATIVE
ADJECTIVE	lovely	lovelier; more (less) lovely	loveliest; most (least) lovely
	beautiful	more (less) beautiful	most (least) beautiful
ADVERB	beautifully	more (less) beautifully	most (least) beautifully

In informal speech, or for reasons of emphasis, the superlative is often used in place of the comparative. But the general rule in formal writing is to use the comparative in comparing two things, the superlative for three or more.

Informal Put your *best* foot forward.
May the *best* team win.

Formal The *better* team won decisively.
Rome is the *oldest* of European capitals.

Absolute adjectives cannot, strictly speaking, be compared; something is either *dead, possible, full, perfect, unique,* or it isn't. But in informal usage absolute adjectives are often modified by comparisons, either for emphasis ("*deader* than a doornail") or because some of them have virtually lost their absolute meaning ("this box is *emptier* than that"). In formal usage, "more nearly empty" would be preferable.

Things compared should be of the same kind.

Wrong Marlowe's plays are not so highly regarded as Shakespeare.

Right Marlowe's plays are not so highly regarded as those of Shakespeare (or *as Shakespeare's).*

Other is used only when the things compared are of the same class.

Wrong Helen is more intelligent than any *other* boy.

Right Helen is more intelligent than any boy.
She reads more widely than any *other* student.

Do not use *other* with superlative comparisons.

Wrong Helen was the most intelligent of all the *other* students.

Right Helen was the most intelligent of all the students.

An adjective may precede a noun (or pronoun), or follow one. Or an adjective may follow a linking verb (copula).

> The *tired* nations sought a peace, one *secure* and *permanent. (Tired* precedes and modifies the noun *nations. Secure* and *permanent* follow and modify the pronoun *one;* this word order is not common but completely acceptable.)

> They hoped it would not prove *illusory. (Illusory* follows the linking verb *prove* and modifies the pronoun *it.)*

Notice in the example immediately above that an adjective, like a noun, may serve as subjective complement. This is not true of adverbs:

Wrong It seems *truly.*
Right It seems *true.*

Through frequent use, *I feel badly* is now sometimes acceptable in informal speech; but to be formally correct, say:

> I feel *bad.*

> I feel *ill.*

> I feel *well.* (meaning: I do not feel ill.)

> I feel *good.* (meaning: I feel positively happy, *or* healthy.)

PREPOSITIONS

A *preposition* connects a noun or pronoun with another word in the sentence, and establishes the relationship between them.

> Peter walked *to* the store. (connecting *walked* and *store*)

> He returned *with* them. (connecting *returned* and *them*)

Since word relationships are more difficult concepts to handle than "plain facts," prepositions are probably the most difficult parts of speech to make satisfactory rules for. Many are used in expressions that are impossible to analyze logically, the meaning of which is usually clear to the native speaker of English: *compare with* and *compare to,* for instance, or *differ from* and *differ with.* Rules in such cases are cumbersome and possibly misleading. The best way to learn proper use of prepositions is by paying attention to the speech and writing of people who use English accurately. Some of the more common prepositions:

about	beneath	in
above	beside	of
along	between	on
among	by	over
at	during	to
before	except	with
behind	for	without
below	from	

The noun or pronoun introduced by the preposition is called *the object of the preposition* and must be in the objective case. This rule gives trouble only in the case of coordinated pronouns. Thus,

> The waiter brought some *for her and me.* (NOT: *she and I*)

A preposition with its object is called a *prepositional phrase* and is used as an adjective or an adverb.

> The boy *with the dog* is my brother. (adjective, modifying noun *boy)*

> They are all playing *with the dog.* (adverb, modifying verb *are playing)*

> He threw his hat *over the fence.* (adverb, modifying verb *threw)*

In informal conversation, prepositions are sometimes doubled, though this is not really necessary to the meaning of the sentence. Double prepositions are rarely used in writing.

Informal We left *at about* nine o'clock.

Formal We left *about* nine o'clock.

Never repeat the same preposition near the beginning and at the end of a sentence: She is the person *for* whom I took all that trouble *for.* This is a mark of carelessness. However, contrary to a frequent yet mistaken belief, a preposition may be used at the end of a sentence, whenever it sounds natural to the rhythm of the sentence.

> Where does she come *from?*

> Whom did she go *with?*

The first example below is obviously a much more natural (and effective) sentence, despite the two prepositions with which it ends, than the second example.

> That's the kind of stupidity I won't put *up with.*

> That's the kind of stupidity *up with which* I will not put.

One classic example ends with no fewer than five prepositions:

What did you put the book you were being read *to out of away for?*

This sentence, too clumsy for formal, written English, is perfectly clear (though not very elegant) as spoken language.

Problem Prepositions

As already stated, the major problem with most prepositions is their idiomatic use. The following prepositions often pose problems in general usage.

AMONG, BETWEEN
Among is used when more than two persons or things are considered. *Between* is used when only two are considered. This rule, which may be relaxed in informal conversation, must be rigidly followed in written English.

Divide the money *among* Frank, John, and Bill.

We must choose *between* Frank and John.

An exception to this rule occurs when a mutual or reciprocal relationship is indicated. In this event, *between* is used for more than two.

A treaty was concluded *between* the three nations.

Frank, John, and Bill agreed *between* them that they would divide the prize.

AT, IN
At and *in* may often be used interchangeably. However, certain rules govern their usage when they indicate place or locality.

In is used when the reference to the interior of a building is stressed; *at,* when the site itself is stressed.

Please meet me *in* the reception room of the dean's office.

Classes will be held *at* Judson Hall.

In is used before the names of countries; *at* before the names of business firms, office buildings, schools, universities, etc.

The International Conference will be held next year *in* Switzerland.

I was educated *at* Princeton.

In is used before the name of a city to give the impression of permanence; *at,* to indicate a temporary stay.

John goes to school *at* Trenton, but he lives *in* Philadelphia.

Following a brief stay *at* Mexico City, we spent a month *in* Oaxaca.

In is used before the name of a city in local addresses; *at,* before the street number.

Bill lives *in* Newark *at* 562 Kensington Avenue.

BELOW, BENEATH, UNDER, UNDERNEATH
These prepositions are generally used interchangeably, and in most cases one will be as grammatically correct as the other. Choice is usually determined by courtesy. Thus, the use of *beneath* may imply inferiority or contempt where *below* would be more courteous. The example below implies inferiority:

Mary is in the class *beneath* me.

To substitute the word *below* does not make the construction more grammatically correct; however, it does make it more courteous and more in accord with accepted usage.

Mary is in the class *below* me.

BESIDE, BESIDES
Beside is used to mean *next to. Besides* (ordinarily an adverb) is used to mean *in addition to* or *moreover.*

Please sit *beside* me.

Besides a dog, I have three cats. (*Besides* modifies the verb *have.*)

IN, INTO
In refers to position. *Into* denotes motion from without to within.

We ate a buffet supper *in* the living room.

We marched *into* the dining room.

ON, ONTO, ON TO
On refers to position upon something; *onto* denotes motion toward the upper surface of something; the two-word form *on to* is used when *on* belongs to the verb.

I rode *on* the horse.

I got *onto* the horse.

I hung *on to* the horse.

ITEMS IN A SERIES
Items in a series must always be parallel in form. This means that when a preposition is used to introduce a series, it should be either repeated before each ensuing item or dropped before each ensuing item.

Wrong I shall send invitations to John, Bill, and to Mary.

Right I shall send invitations to John, to Bill, and to Mary.

Right I shall send invitations to John, Bill, and Mary.

CONJUNCTIONS

A *conjunction* connects words, phrases, or clauses.

black *and* blue (words)

with the group *but* not part of it (phrases)

He agreed, *though* he had reservations. (clauses)

Conjunctions may be classified according to four types:

A *coordinating conjunction* connects equal words, phrases, or clauses. There are six coordinating conjunctions. These are: *and, but, for, nor, or, yet.*

We didn't walk, *nor* did we drive.

It rained, *yet* we enjoyed the farm.

A coordinating conjunction may occasionally introduce a sentence closely related in thought to the preceding one.

We managed to win the first game. *But* we never had a chance for the championship.

Correlative conjunctions are used in pairs to connect equal elements that are parallel in form. They replace a coordinating conjunction for greater emphasis.

We will go to Yellowstone Park *or* Yosemite. (coordinating conjunction)

We will go *either* to Yellowstone Park *or* Yosemite. (correlative conjunctions)

The most common correlative conjunctions are *both . . . and, neither . . . nor, either . . . or, whether . . . or,* and *not only . . . but (also).*

I didn't care *whether* we went *or* stayed home.

At the party we met *not only* the Jacksons *but* the Blairs.

Not only the husbands came *but also* the children.

A *conjunctive adverb* connects clauses in addition to modifying a verb (or clause). The most common are:

accordingly	however	nevertheless
also	indeed	still
besides	likewise	then
furthermore	meanwhile	therefore
hence	moreover	thus

A group of words may also serve as a conjunctive adverb:

in fact	for that reason
in the first place	on the contrary
in the meantime	on the other hand

The conjunctive adverb always has a semicolon before it when it is used between independent clauses.

I hadn't set the clock; *hence*, I was late.

The search may have ended; *indeed*, it's likely.

We tried the engine; but *in the meantime*, the tire had gone flat.

A *subordinating conjunction* introduces a dependent clause and subordinates it to an independent clause. It establishes the relation between the two clauses. This relation may be one of

CAUSE: *as, because, inasmuch as, since*

We went indoors, *as* it had grown quite dark.

Since he likes animals, they like him.

COMPARISON: *as . . . as, so . . . as, than*

Chaucer's language is not *so* difficult *as* you may think.

There was more smoke *than* (there was) fire.

CONCESSION: *although, though, while*

Although he works hard, he's not very efficient.

He doesn't write well, *though* he tries.

CONDITION: *if, provided that, unless*

She'll come *provided that* you do.

Unless you run you won't catch her.

MANNER: *as, as if, as though*

Do *as* you would be done by.

It seemed *as though* he would win.

PLACE: *where, wherever, whence, whither*

Where one is good, two are better.

"And *whence* they come and *whither* they shall go
The dew upon their feet shall manifest."

PURPOSE: *in order that, so that, that*

So *that* there will be enough for all, take no more than you need.

They died *that* we may live.

RESULT: *so that, so . . . that, such . . . that*

He studied hard, *so that* finally he was the recognized expert in the field.

Such was his optimism *that* we all were prepared for success.

TIME: *after, as, before, since, till, until, when, while*

Ruth arrived *as* they were leaving.

Until you spoke I didn't know you were there.

Troublesome Conjunctions

The following are troublesome conjunctions:

AND, ALSO

Also should not be used in place of *and* to connect items in a series.

Wrong I study English, French, Spanish, *also* Russian.

Right I study English, French, Spanish, and Russian.

AND, ETC.

The abbreviation *etc.* means "and so forth." It is incorrect to use *and* to connect the last item in a series when the last item is followed by *etc.*

Wrong We need eggs, bacon, and bread, etc.

Right We need eggs, bacon, bread, *etc.*

AND WHICH, AND WHO

These should not be used unless preceded in the same sentence by *which* or *who.*

Wrong I am looking for a course with four credits *and which* holds classes on Wednesday mornings.

Right I am looking for a course *which* offers four credits *and which* holds classes on Wednesday mornings.

AND, BUT

And is used to show addition; *but,* to show contrast.

Wrong Mary and I have been invited to a party, *and* I have to take care of my younger brother.

Right Mary and I have been invited to a party, *but* I have to take care of my younger brother.

AS, AS IF, LIKE

As and *as if* are respectably used as conjunctions to introduce clauses of various kinds and to connect comparisons. *Like,* which is gaining respectability as a conjunction in informal usage, is treated only as a preposition in formal writing. Grammarians shudder when they see *like* usurping the role of *as* and *as if.*

Informal You act *like* you're hurt.

Formal You act *as if* you were hurt.

AS, BECAUSE, SINCE

Any one of these may be used to introduce clauses of cause or reason, that is, to connect the stated cause with a fact already given.

I came *because* I was worried.

As you won't go, I will stay.

Since I can, I will.

However, *because* is limited to introducing clauses of cause or reason. *As* and *since* are also used to introduce clauses involving time. To introduce duration of time, use *as.* To introduce sequence of time, use *since.*

I worked less and less *as* each day passed. (time duration)

I haven't done any work *since* last you were here. (time sequence)

BECAUSE, FOR

Because is used when the reason it introduces is based upon fact. *For* is used when the reason it introduces is based upon opinion or speculation.

Come inside, *because* it is raining. (The reason given is an established fact.)

We are going to have a storm, *for* there is a ring around the moon. (The reason given is based on speculation.)

IF, WHETHER

If introduces clauses of supposition or condition involving uncertainty or doubt.

If I had known you were coming, I would have prepared a feast. (implies uncertainty)

If may also stand for *even though* or *whenever.*

If I am wrong, you are not right. (implies *even though*)

If I do not know, I try to find out. (implies *whenever*)

On the other hand, *whether* introduces clauses which involve an alternative. The alternative may be stated or understood. (*Whether* is the conjunction most likely to be used when followed by *or*.)

It will not make any difference *whether* I know or not. (alternative stated)

Please let me know *whether* I am right. (alternative implied)

WHEN, WHERE
When should not be used to introduce a definition unless the definition involves a time element; *where* should not be used unless the definition involves place or location.

Wrong A foul is *when* (or *where*) the ball leaves the court.

Right A foul is made *when* the ball leaves the court during the playing period. (time involved)

Right A foul is made at the place *where* the ball crosses the foul line. (place involved)

WHEN, WHILE
When refers to a fixed period of time; *while* to duration of time.

When you are willing to talk, I will listen. (fixed time: as soon as you are ready to talk)

While you talk, I will listen. (time duration: during the time that you talk)

WHILE, ALTHOUGH, BUT, WHEREAS
While is often used colloquially to mean *although, but,* and *whereas.*

Colloquial I like Mary, *while* I like Jeanne better.

Formal I like Mary, *but* I like Jeanne better.

Colloquial Mary is fat, *while* Jeanne is slim.

Formal Mary is fat, *whereas* Jeanne is slim.

INTERJECTIONS

An interjection is a word of exclamation which expresses emotion, but which has no grammatical relation to the rest of the sentence.

Oh! Hey! Whoa! Ouch! Ha, ha! Boo!

Many words that generally serve as other parts of speech may be used as interjections:

Well! Heavens! Nuts! Run! Good!

SENTENCES

The division of words into eight main parts of speech–a useful way to point out their individual characteristics–is technically termed *accidence.* But words are seldom used alone; how they are put together in sentences is termed *syntax.*

A *sentence* is a group of words expressing a complete thought. It may make a statement, ask a question, give a command, or express an exclamation.

Antarctica is the seventh continent.

Are Europe and Asia separate continents?

See America first!

So this is Africa!

However, a complete thought may be expressed by a single word: a man entering an elevator and saying, "Down"; the answers ("Are you going?") "No," ("Where is it?") "Here," or ("How do you feel?") "Happy." The concept of a *complete thought* is satisfied by such limited sentences as the telegraphic ARRIVING LAGUARDIA FRIDAY. HOME BEFORE SIX. LOVE STANLEY; or the journalistic headline LABOR UNIONS/HIT JOB LOSSES. But in addition, readers expect most sentences to be *grammatically complete.*

Grammatical Completion

The grammatically complete *simple sentence* consists of a subject and a predicate. The *subject* is a noun or a noun equivalent (pronoun in the nominative case, noun clause, gerund, infinitive) naming the person, place, or thing with which the sentence is chiefly concerned. The *predicate* is the verb or verb phrase asserting something about the subject.

Children (subject) *play* (predicate).

This simple sentence may be expanded and made more complicated (or significant) in various ways.

The subject may be modified:

Happy children play.

The predicate may be modified:

Children play *hard.*

Or the verb may be given a complement:

Children play *games.*

It becomes a *compound sentence* when two or more subjects attach to a single predicate:

Children and *adults* play.

or when two or more predicates follow from a single subject:

Children *play* and *sleep.*

or when two or more simple sentences closely related in thought are joined by commas, semicolons, or coordinating conjunctions:

Children play, men work, and women manage.

However complicated it may become, the sentence rests on the solid base of subject and predicate. This is true in the *declarative sentence* (above), the *interrogative sentence:*

Do children play?

the *exclamatory sentence:*

How happily the children play!

and the *imperative sentence:*

Play, children! (the subject, *you,* is understood)

The sentence may be made more flexible and expressive by the use of phrases and clauses.

Phrases

A *phrase* is a group of words used as a single part of speech (noun, adjective, adverb, or verb). It does not contain a subject and a predicate.

NOUN PHRASE:	It is impossible *not to pity him; trying to help* him is a problem.
ADVERBIAL PHRASE:	*By Monday* they were gone. I hung it *on the wall.*
ADJECTIVE PHRASE:	A man *of honor,* a name *to admire.*
VERB PHRASE:	He *has asked* for you; he *must have forgotten* already.

Phrases may also be classified by form:

A *prepositional phrase* consists of a preposition and its object, and any accompanying modifiers. It is used as an adjective or adverb.

At once they left *for the big town.* (prepositional phrases used as adverbs)

The man *with the hoe.* (used as adjective)

He felt lost *in the impersonal clamor* (used as adverb) *of the advertising industry.* (used as adjective)

An *infinitive phrase* consists of an infinitive (and its object, if present), and any accompanying modifiers. It is used as a noun, adjective, or adverb.

I want *to see* (infinitive) *the moon* (object). (infinitive phrase used as noun)

Professor Thomson is the man *to know.* (used as adjective)

A diplomat must be able *to make* (infinitive) *the most* (object) *of the existing situation.* (prepositional phrase, adjective modifying *the most,* used as adverb)

A *participial phrase* consists of a participle (and its object, if present), and any accompanying modifiers. It is used as an adjective.

Thinking quickly, he regained his poise.

The plane *carrying* (participle) *the serum* (object) arrived in time.

Shirley, *earnestly* (adverb modifying the next word, *talking*) *talking* (participle) *to the group* (prepositional phrase, adverb modifying *talking*), signaled Carrie to wait.

A *gerund phrase* consists of a gerund (and its object, if present), and any accompanying modifiers. It is used as a noun.

Daily *swimming* kept him in trim.

Flying (gerund) *a kite* (object) can be hard work.

His editor advised *writing* (gerund) *on a totally new subject.* (prepositional phrase, adjective modifying *writing*)

A *verb phrase* consists of a verb and its auxiliaries.

I *will have seen* him by then.

The Senate *could* hardly *have foreseen* the result of its action.

Clauses

A *clause* is a group of words containing a subject and a predicate. It may be independent or dependent. An *independent clause* is, essentially, a sentence; it differs only in its capitalization and/or punctuation. In the following example the independent clause can stand alone by capitalizing *he* and adding a period after *plotters*.

> Mindful of his honor, *he avoided every contact with the plotters* and refused to listen to their schemes.

A *dependent clause* cannot stand alone. It is connected to an independent clause by a relative pronoun, present or implied (*who, which, that*), or by a subordinating conjunction (*after, because, since, while,* etc.) and functions as a part of the sentence–as noun, adjective, or adverb.

> *That everyone was against him* was his constant complaint. (noun clause, subject)
>
> He estimated *which of the problems he could solve.* (noun clause, object of verb)
>
> In the afternoon we came to *what was evidently the main road.* (noun clause, object of preposition *to*)
>
> The man *who fails at everything he tries* may not be trying. (adjective clause, modifying *man*)
>
> He may succeed *if he tries a completely new approach.* (adverbial clause, modifying *succeed*)

A dependent clause need not be so complete as these examples. Often, especially in spoken language and informal writing, the connective between independent clause and dependent adjective clause is merely implied and not expressed.

> The man *he said was coming* never showed up. (*Who* or *that* is understood.)

Sometimes in informal speech or writing a dependent clause contains neither subject nor verb.

> *When crossing,* look both ways. (*When you are crossing* is understood.)
>
> His clothes were old *though clean.* (*Though they were clean* is understood.)

Constructions such as these are called *elliptical clauses.* When properly related to the main clause, an elliptical clause adds economy and punch to writing. The dependent clause used as an adjective (*adjective clause*) is called *restrictive* if it adds information necessary to identify the subject, or restricts it to a special case.

> The boy *you met last Friday* telephoned again.
>
> The man *who can plan ahead* is automatically at an advantage.
>
> Rebellions *that are successful* are recorded as revolutions.

If the subject requires no further identification after being named, the clause is *nonrestrictive,* and simply adds additional information.

> Jaspar, *who never gave up,* finally hit on a way to catch the chipmunk.

There is only one Jaspar being discussed, and the reader presumably knows who he is; the nonrestrictive clause is not essential to the meaning of the sentence, though it enriches it. Here are two more examples of nonrestrictive clauses.

> He sat on the table, *which could barely support him.*
>
> She was sure that the man, *whom she had not met,* must be her long-lost brother.

Who (whom) and *which* may introduce either restrictive or nonrestrictive clauses, but *that* introduces only restrictive clauses. Relative pronouns may be omitted only in restrictive clauses.

> The man *we hoped to see* has left. (Restrictive *who* is understood.)
>
> We all liked the pie *she baked.* (Restrictive *that* is understood.)

Nonrestrictive clauses are set off by commas, and often the various choices of punctuation can give the sentence radically different meanings.

RESTRICTIVE CLAUSE: Engineers who have little understanding of theory are rarely put in charge of a program.

NON-RESTRICTIVE CLAUSE: Engineers, who have little understanding of theory, are rarely put in charge of a program.

The first is a warning; the second is a sneer. (For the specific rules on punctuating restrictive and nonrestrictive clauses, see page 6.)

Sentence Diagraming

A sentence is a basic unit of language, a communication in words, having at least one independent finite verb with its subject. Sentences can be simple, compound and complex. A simple sentence contains one independent clause.

Dogs bark.

A compound sentence contains two or more independent clauses joined by a coordinating conjunction:

He tried hard, but he had no talent.

or by a conjunctive adverb preceded by a semicolon:

It had begun to rain; however, we had umbrellas.

or by a semicolon (or colon) alone:

Saturday is a day of activity; Sunday is a day of rest.

A complex sentence contains an independent clause with one or more dependent clauses. (You may wish to review the previous grammar section if you are unfamiliar with these terms.)

He whispered that he saw the suspect enter the bank when the clock struck eleven.

Sentence diagraming is a method used to identify the parts of a sentence and their relationship to each other. A diagram is a picture of this relationship. Diagraming sentences reveals the independent clause(s) and any adjectives, adverbs, phrases and dependent clauses. The following explanations and examples illustrate the use of this skill to build correct and effective usage. These basic building blocks are the foundation of good writing in school, business, and the home.

THE SIMPLE SENTENCE

A simple sentence consists of a subject, verb, and any modifiers. The basic form for diagraming is:

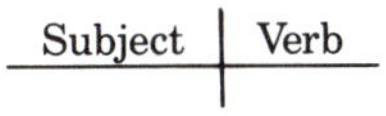

Dogs bark.

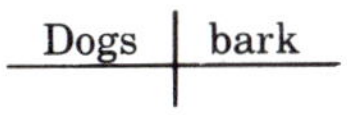

Notice that a single vertical line separates the subject from the verb and that the punctuation is not included in the diagram. The first step in diagraming a sentence is to find the verb. Then isolate the simple subject by asking who or what is doing the action.

The brown dog barks.

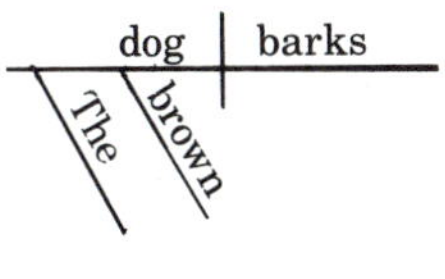

In this sentence the verb is *barks* and the simple subject is *dog*. Any adjectives are written on slanted lines under the word they describe. In this case, *the* and *brown* are written on slanted lines under *dog*.

In the same way, adverbs are written on slanted lines under the verb, adverb or adjective they describe.

The heavy chains rattle loudly.

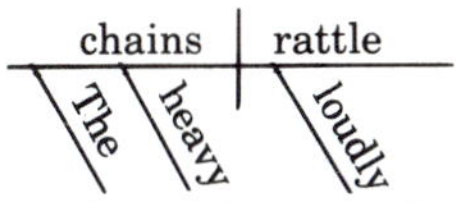

Loudly is the adverb modifying the verb *rattle*.

The heavy chains rattled very loudly.

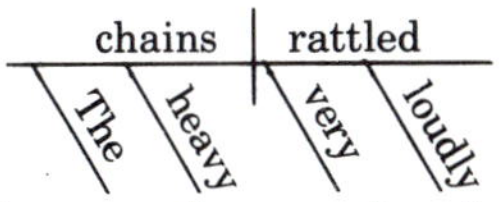

In this example, *very* is an adverb describing the adverb *loudly*.

The very heavy door shut.

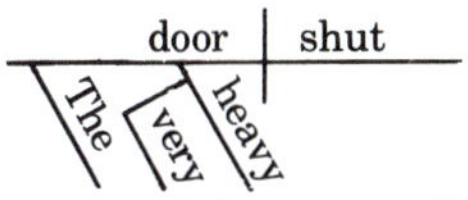

When the adverb modifies an adjective, it is written below the adjective. Sometimes there are several adjectives and adverbs, but each is diagramed beneath the word it modifies. The basic form is:

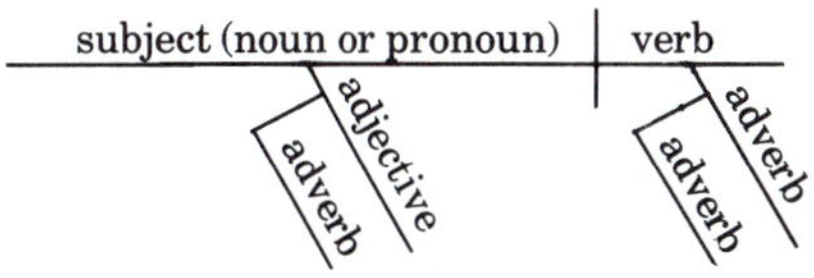

The willow's long leaves rustled very softly.

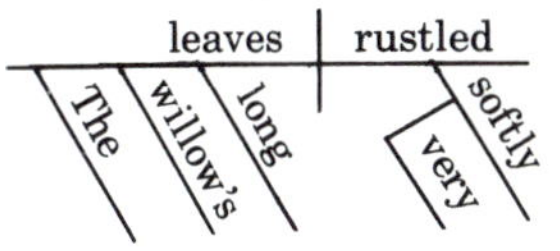

A rather deep stream flowed quite swiftly nearby.

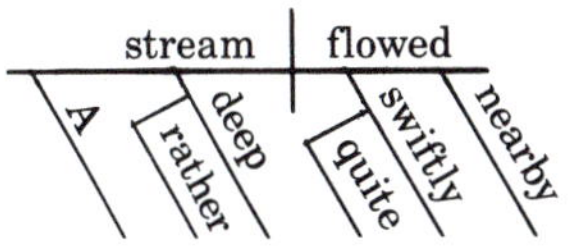

If there are two subjects or verbs, the form is:

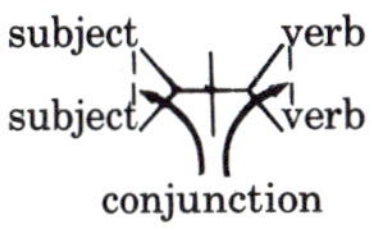

Notice that the conjunction is written on the dotted line between the two related words.

Dick and Katherine are coming but are late.

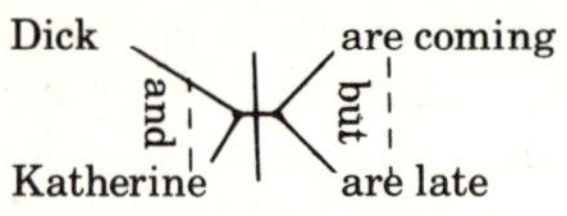

A small but valuable diamond was discovered.

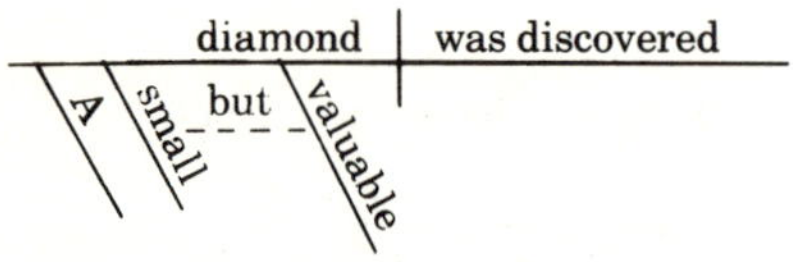

Jamie, Clay and I cheered and sang heartily.

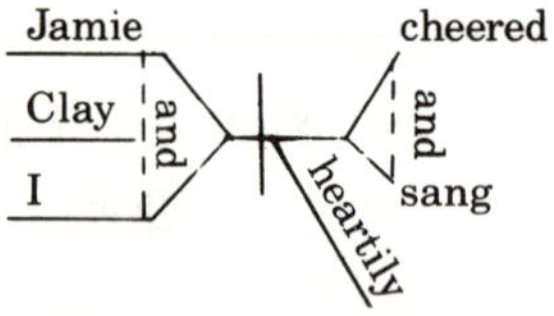

Prepositional phrases are groups of words added to the simple sentences as modifiers. The phrase consists of a preposition, the object of the preposition and any modifiers of the object. When diagraming, the phrase goes below the word(s) it modifies. The preposition is on a slanted line and the object of the preposition is on a horizontal line connected to the slanted line.

Seven states can be seen from Lookout Mountain in Tennessee.

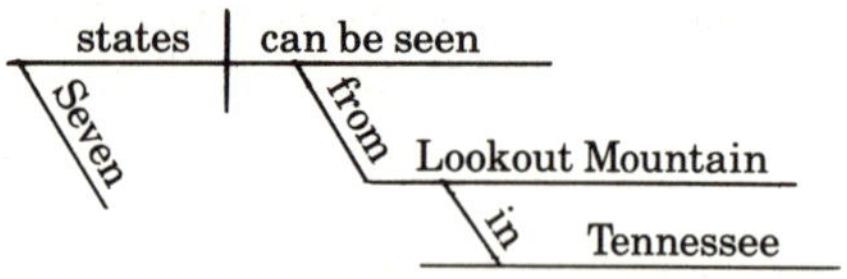

In this sentence, *from Lookout Mountain* is the prepositional phrase modifying the verb *can be seen*. The prepositional phrase *in Tennessee* modifies the object of the preposition, *Lookout Mountain*.

The mother of the children watched from the window.

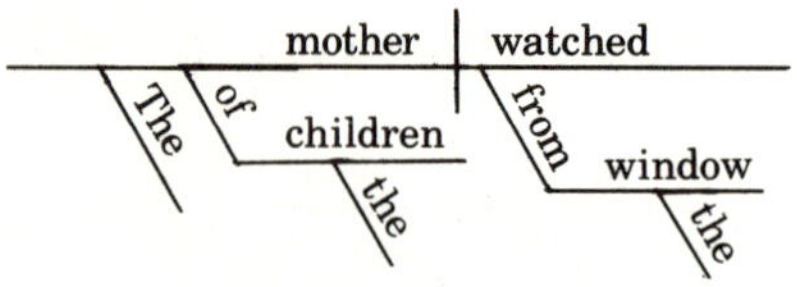

The present from Mom and Dad was delivered to Jamie and Clay.

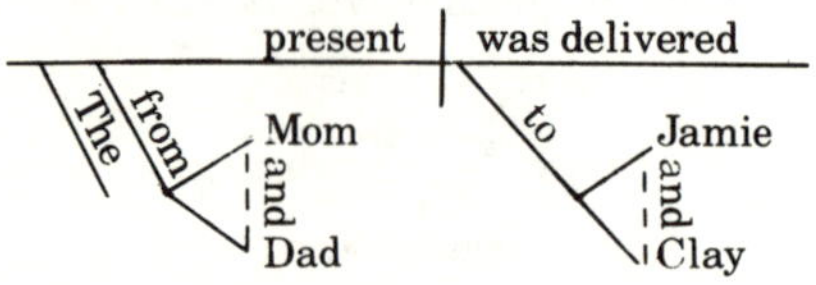

There are two prepositional phrases in these sentences; one is used as an adjective and the other as an adverb.

Across the street stood a car with a flat tire.

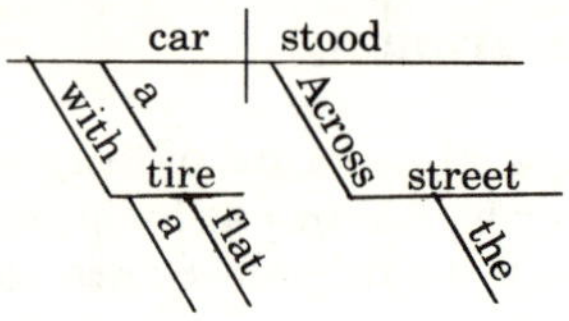

Notice that a phrase may appear at the beginning of the sentence. Don't be confused, but discover whether it is used as an adjective or an adverb.

The three most common complements are the direct object, the indirect object, and the subjective complement (predicate nominative or predicate adjective). The direct object tells what receives the action of the verb. When diagraming, the direct object appears on the main line following the verb and separated from it by a vertical line.

People own rabbits.

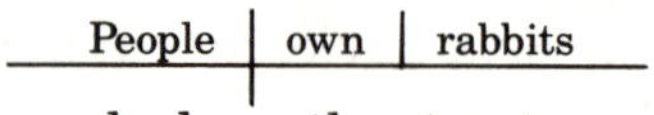

The new people down the street recently bought six grey rabbits from Mr. Smallwood.

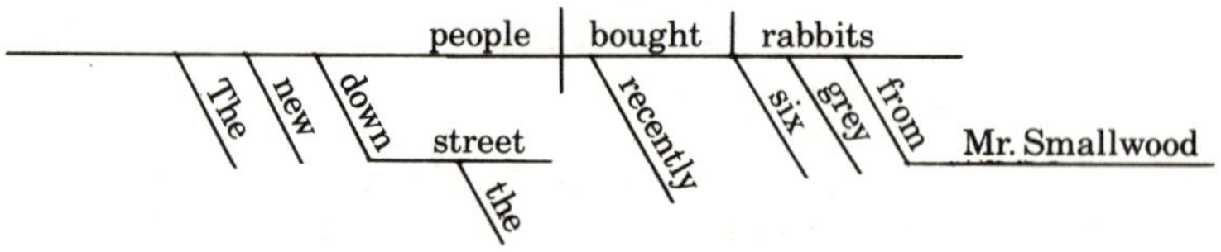

Two young rabbits were nibbling fresh dandelions and tasty clover in our yard.

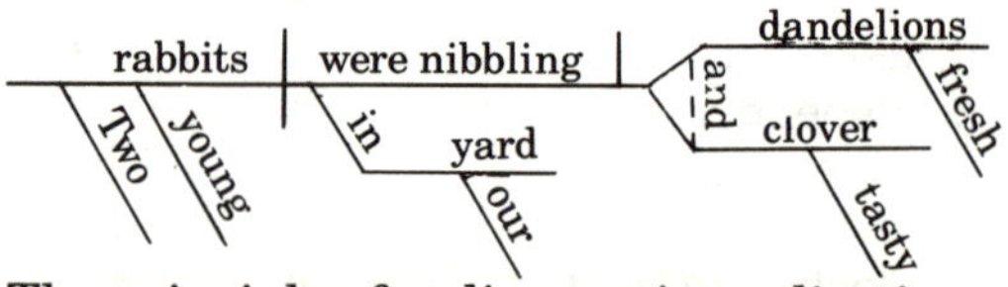

The principles for diagraming adjectives, phrases and two or more objects apply to diagraming direct objects.

The indirect object answers the question "To whom?" or "For whom?" It is diagramed like the object of a preposition and written under the verb.

Mrs. Hall baked us cookies.

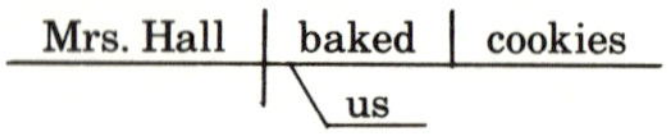

Brian showed the boys a new game.

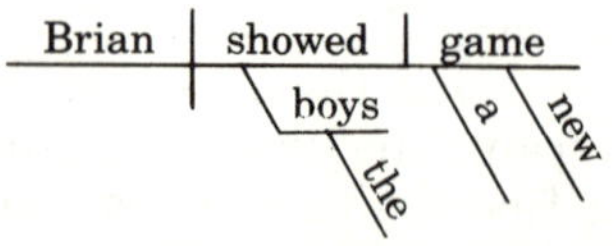

Douglas gave Susan and me his notebooks.

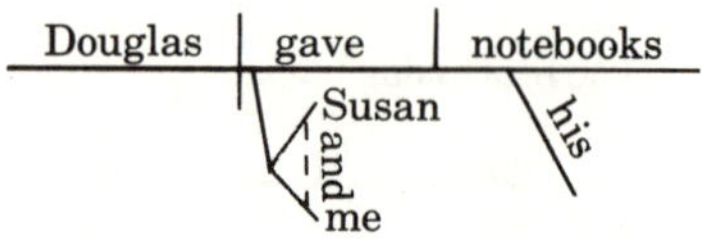

Any adjectives are written on slanted lines under the indirect object. Compound indirect objects follow the same rules for diagraming any compound form.

The subjective complement refers to the subject, describing or limiting it. When diagraming, the subjective complement follows the verb and is separated by a slanted line.

Doug is president.

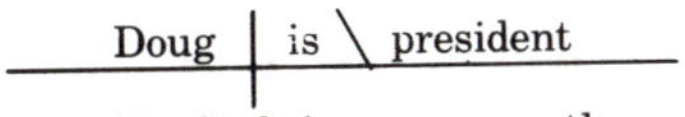

The little boys grew restless.

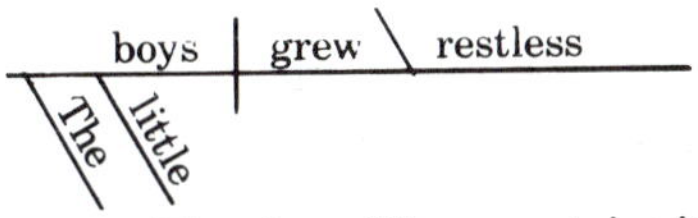

The view of the mountains is majestic and sweeping.

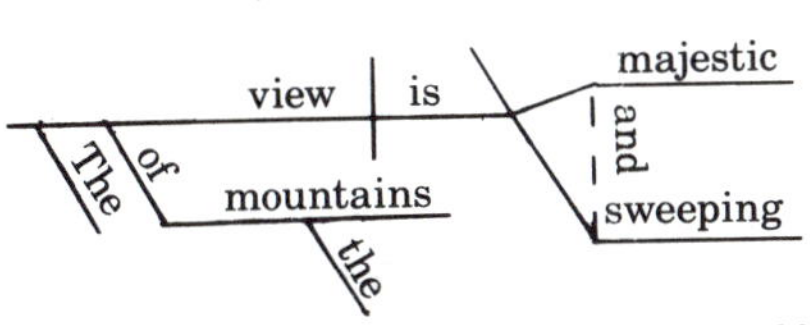

Diamonds are extremely hard but quite brittle.

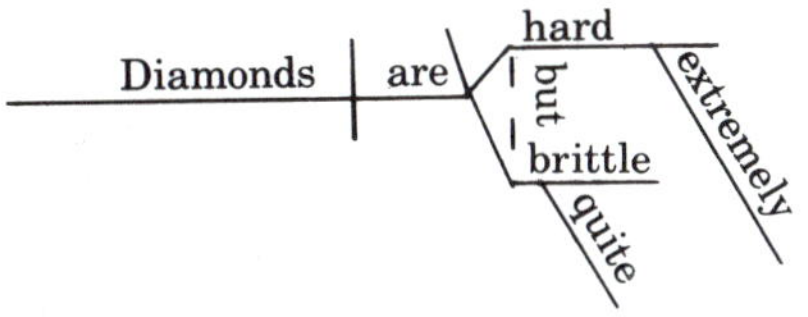

When a phrase is used as the subject or object, it is diagramed using this symbol:

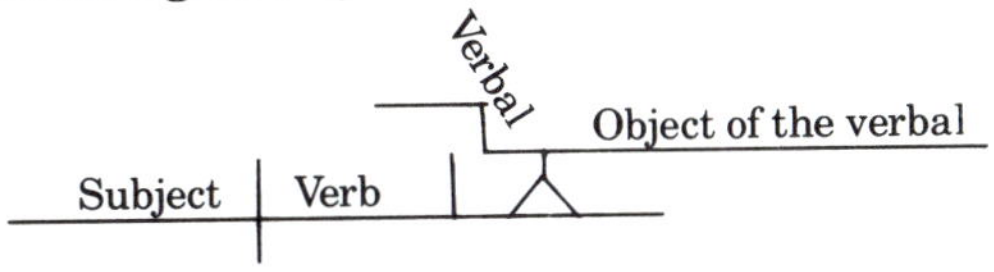

Gerund phrases serve as nouns and therefore function as subject, complement, or object of a preposition.

He enjoys watching television.

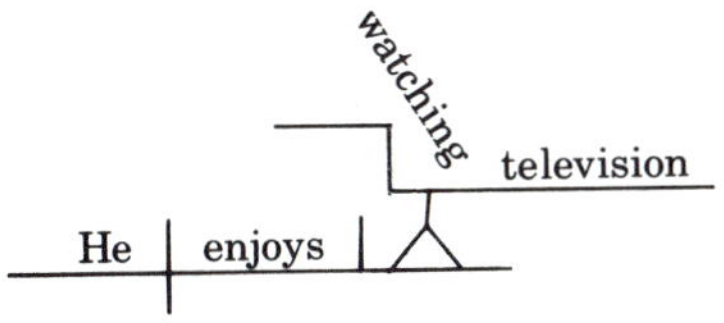

The gerund phrase, *watching television,* is the object of the verb, *enjoys.*

Susan's editor advised writing on a new subject.

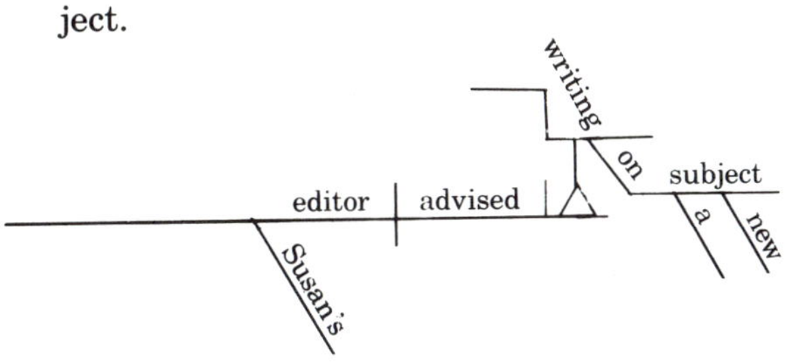

In this example, *on a new subject* is a prepositional phrase functioning as an adjective modifying the gerund, *writing*. The gerund functions as the object of the verb.

Telling lies creates trouble.

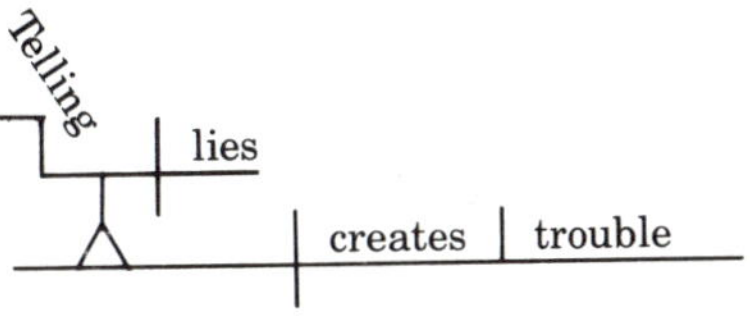

If a phrase functions as the subject, it is diagramed in the position of the subject.

THE COMPOUND SENTENCE

Diagraming a compound sentence is easy because the principles for diagraming any compound part (subject, verb, object and so on) apply.

I watched television and Susan read a book.

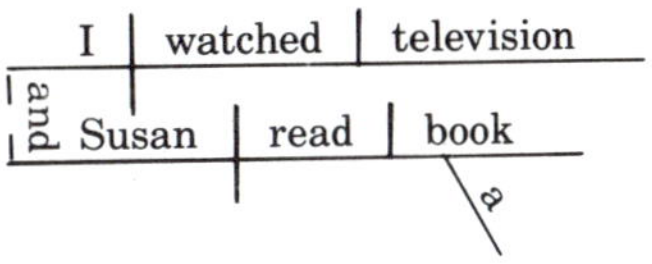

In the U.S., we celebrate religious and national holidays, but national holidays are more numerous.

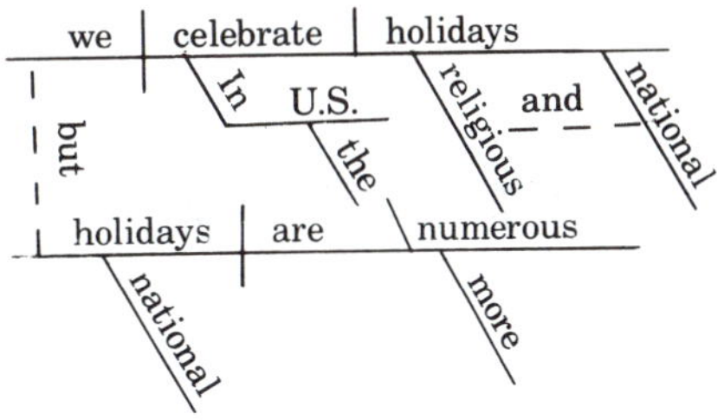

Notice that this compound sentence illustrates diagraming a prepositional phrase, compound adjectives and a subjective complement.

THE COMPLEX SENTENCE

The complex sentence contains at least one independent clause and one or several dependent clauses. Dependent clauses cannot stand alone and function as nouns, adjectives or adverbs.

The teacher said that the answer was correct.

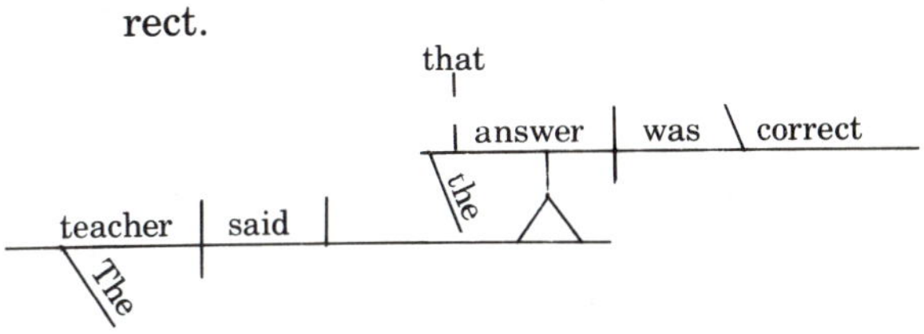

In this example, the independent clause is *The teacher said* and the dependent clause is *that the answer was correct*. The clause is the object of the verb, *said*. Within the clause is a subject, *answer,*

verb, *was,* and subjective complement, *correct.*

They arrived late because the weather was bad.

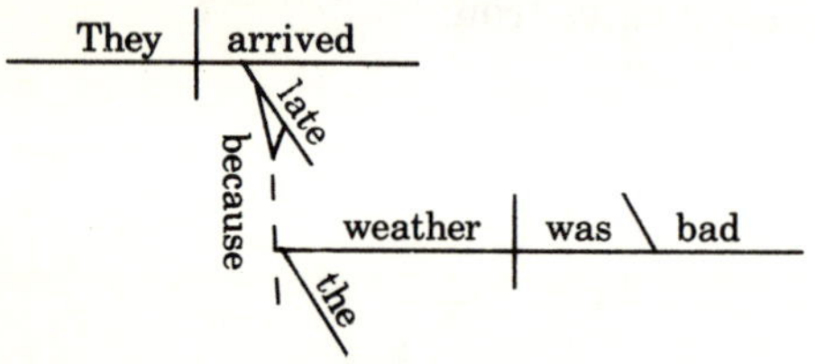

The dependent clause, *because the weather was bad,* functions as an adverb modifying the adverb, *late.* Notice that the subordinating conjunction (after, because, since, etc.) or the relative pronoun (who, which, that) appears on a dotted line in the diagram. The symbol, ⋏ , can appear above or below the main line and attached to a horizontal or slanted line, depending on its function.

He bought a typewriter which was guaranteed.

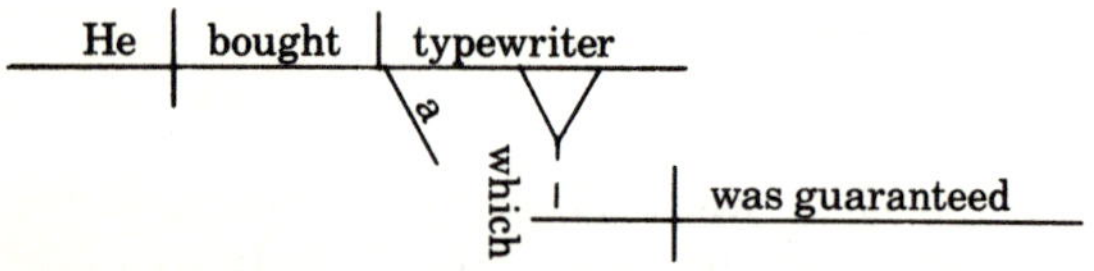

Which was guaranteed is a dependent clause modifying *typewriter.*

A compound-complex sentence has two independent clauses and one or more dependent clauses. Although this type of sentence may appear long and involved, the same rules for diagraming apply. First, identify the verbs. Second, isolate the subjects of the verbs. Third, identify the adjectives and adverbs. In this third step, separate the dependent clauses from the independent. For further discussion on the differences between dependent and independent clauses, see the preceding section on clauses.

Beth was tired, but she walked to the third floor because she wanted the exercise.

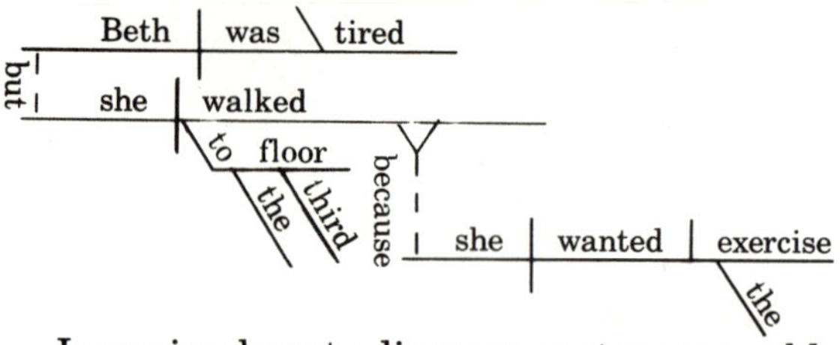

Learning how to diagram sentences enables the student to identify the parts of a sentence and to learn how the parts relate to each other. The simplest subject-verb sentence is the foundation for more precise sentences. Diagrams are visual aids which will help students to improve their grammatical skills.

Spelling and Vocabulary

Spelling is not the horrendous problem that many students think it is. By the time they have reached senior high school, and certainly by the time they finish college, most people have learned most of the words they will ever use, and they spell most of them correctly. The problem is caused by those few words which are misspelled over and over again. Another, but quite separate, problem is the rapid rate at which new words are added to our vocabularly, notably those emerging from enlarging technology and from areas of professional specialization.

For the average person afflicted with habits of bad spelling, corrective measures are not difficult to determine or apply. If you fall in this category, you probably spell most words quite correctly, and only fall down, with depressing recurrence, on certain kinds of words. To improve, you need not relearn how to spell, but only ferret out and concentrate on those specific areas where you have trouble. You will probably find that your problems are confined to certain special areas. Perhaps you are confused by words with *-able* or *-ible* endings, or by the question of whether to double final consonants or not. Once you have a list of such troublesome words–and the real job is running them down–you can take effective curative measures. Brief but regular periods devoted to memorizing the correct spellings will quickly produce results, particularly if the memorizing period is just before you go to bed.

BUILDING A VOCABULARY

We tend to avoid words we do not know how to spell, and in so doing we forget them by nonuse. With the spelling handicap reduced we can explore the various ways of acquiring a large and useful vocabulary.

In school the teacher advises, "Look up in the

dictionary every word you don't know and write it, with its definition, in a notebook. Then examine the meaning of its root, or roots, also possible suffix and/or prefix. Pronounce the word over to yourself, and finally use it in speaking and writing." This remains the surest technique, but it is slow, and demands more conscientious application than most people are prepared to bring to it.

The best way to build a vocabulary is to broaden one's intellectual horizons. An interest and a delight in words and the ideas they convey will bring about attentive listening and wide and thorough reading. It can give impetus to frequent use of the dictionary, memorization of selected vocabulary lists, and the study of the origin and development of words (etymology).

We all possess three basic vocabularies–a speaking, a writing, and a reading vocabulary. Of the three, the reading vocabularly contains by far the largest number of words. As we read extensively, all three vocabularies will expand, but at surprisingly different rates. The reading vocabulary increases the fastest. Only relatively few words will seep down into the speaking and writing vocabularies. We recognize any number of words when we see them in print, but they are neither on the tips of our tongues nor on the points of our pens–ready for us to use when they are applicable.

The main problem is to make the newly learned words accessible when we are speaking–but more especially when we are writing. The words we have learned must become familiar friends; not only should they be recognizable when we see and hear them again, but they should be instantly available.

A much surer way than the list method for making a new word your very own is to use the word in a sentence of your own construction. Don't attempt to do this with every new word you come upon. Be selective. Take the words that appeal to and interest you–words that you think you may want to use again in the future. When a word does appeal to you, go to the dictionary for help in defining it precisely. When you have the definition (or, rather, definitions, for most words have a number of meanings), don't simply accept the dictionary example of how it is used. Compose your own illustrative sentence to fix the new-found word in your mind. Let the sentence express something that is essentially *you*–some interest of yours. Perhaps the word can be used in relation to some hobby or to a friend.

A few words of caution: Don't be too quick to flaunt the new words in public. Don't insist on forcing them into your very next composition or report. You may have a fair idea of the meaning of a word; you may have a good sentence in mind. At the same time, you may not be using the word in precisely its right context. A good idea is to wait a bit before exposing the word to public hearing or view. For example, if the word has to do with biology, try the sentence out on a friend who is at home in this field, and make sure from him that you are using it correctly. This is the most creative way of fixing new words in your mind. It can be guaranteed to work, and even more important, the new words will be ready for recall and use when the occasion arises.

PRONUNCIATION

Just as important as the written word is the spoken or sounded word. The sounded word precedes the written word by thousands of years, and of course without the one there could not be the other. And just as there are correct ways to use words in writing, so are there correct ways to sound them in speaking.

English is supposedly a phonetic language. That is, the letters of our alphabet stand for sounds, and the way words are spoken or pronounced is supposed to correspond to the way they are spelled. In practice it doesn't always work out that way. In the early years, English was more or less phonetic, but time has brought drastic changes in pronunciation, while changes in spelling have not kept pace. (It is an interesting paradox that the language has been remarkably liberal in the matter of pronunciation yet remarkably conservative in the matter of spelling.) It is the gulf that has been created between pronunciation and spelling–widened during the last several centuries by the invention of the printing press–that has transformed English from a phonetic to a most unphonetic language.

To fill this gulf, our dictionaries respell countless thousands of words according to the way they are actually sounded in practice, and they construct elaborate phonetic alphabets that correspond to the true sounds (see page 38). The dictionaries don't always succeed, however, since there is considerable difference in the way people speak. Still, the dictionaries are our only guide, and if you follow the phonetic respellings of a reputable dictionary, you will be sure of pronouncing words correctly in most instances.

In the United States, there are three more or less distinct types of pronunciation–the northeastern, the southern, and the northwestern. Even when pronunciation differs from the norm or standard as given in dictionaries, it is nevertheless considered correct and proper as long as the pronunciation is used by the educated people of any one of these regions.

Common Errors

Do not sound the *t* in most words ending in *-sten* and *stle*.

fasten
wrestle
chasten

Do not sound the *t* in the following words:

often
soften

Beware of dropping the *g* in words that end in *-ing* and in *-ength*.

believing *not* believin'

thinking *not* thinkin'

Beware of dropping the letters *d, t,* and *l*. Even in the South, the practice of dropping these letters is regarded as vulgar by educated Southerners.

old *not* ol'

just *not* jus'

self *not* se'f

Beware of dropping the letter *r*. In New England and the South, correct pronunciation sanctions the substitution of the short *a* for the letter *r* in certain words. But to drop the *r* altogether in these words is regarded as vulgar (not *do'* for *door* or *fo'* for *for*). In these same regions, on the other hand, it is perfectly proper to drop the *r* in words such as *car* and *farther*.

Beware of the so-called intrusive *r*. Do not insert an *r* in a word where it does not belong, nor between two words when one word ends with a vowel and the following word begins with a vowel.

spoil *not* spurl

law and order *not* lawr and order

the idea (*not* idear) of it

USE OF THE DICTIONARY

Do you prize the dictionary as the most valuable tool in your possession to help you choose and use words properly? If you answer no, you are among a majority of students who feel the same way. If you answer yes, you are in a minority who understand what the dictionary is–and who also know how to use it. For the chief reason most people neglect the dictionary is that they just don't know what it's all about. The following pages show how to use the dictionary the way it should be used.

Meanings of Words

A word sometimes has as many as fifty or sixty different meanings or shades of meaning. This is not common, but the point to remember is that a word doesn't necessarily have just one meaning. Most words have several meanings, according to the ways they are used in a sentence. Moreover, the same word changes its form, usually its spelling, and often its pronunciation, according to the part of speech it takes. Therefore, never take the definition immediately following an entry as final. You must read–or at least scan–all its definitions. Different meanings are usually numbered.

Spelling

Occasionally an entry will have two or more different spellings of the same word. This means that all given spellings are in general use. All are acceptable, but the one given first is usually the preferred form. Irregular spellings of the plural form of a word are also given. Regular formations, however, are not given. Thus, when a plural spelling is omitted we can take it for granted that the word forms its plural in the regular way, by adding *s* to the singular and by adding *-es* to words ending in *s, x, z, ch,* and *sh*. Plurals of compound words are also generally omitted when they are formed in the same way as the plurals of the main word. British spelling variations are preceded by the abbreviation *Brit.* Such forms are acceptable in Great Britain, not in the United States.

Inflectional Forms

Often a word is spelled in various ways according to its use; we call these various spellings the *inflectional forms* of the word. For example, plurals of nouns are inflectional forms of the nouns, various tenses of verbs are inflectional forms of the verbs, while comparative and intensive forms of adjectives are their inflectional forms.

A good dictionary lists the inflectional forms that are irregular or that give trouble in spelling. When two inflected forms are listed for a verb, the first is the form for both the past tense and the past participle. When three forms are given, the first is the form for the past tense, the second the past participle, and the third the present participle.

Inflections formed in the regular way are seldom given, even in good dictionaries. In addition to the spelling of plurals, forms regarded as regular inflections include, for verbs, present tenses formed by adding *-s* or *-es,* past tenses and past participles formed by adding *-ed,* and present participles formed by adding *-ing.* Comparatives and superlatives formed in the regular way (by adding *-er* and *-est* to the positive form) are also omitted in most entries.

Usage Labels

Various labels signify a word's status in actual usage. These labels are extremely important. They indicate under what circumstances a word may properly be used. The conventional labels are: *colloquial* (used in conversation but not in formal writing), *slang* (restricted to rare occasions in informal conversation and informal writing), *obsolete* (no longer used), *archaic* (used only in special contexts, as in church ritual, but no longer in general use), *poetic* (restricted to poetry), *dialect* (restricted to special geographical areas), and *British* (characteristically British rather than American). Words that have more than one meaning are generally treated as follows: when the label follows the number introducing a definition, it applies to that definition only; when it precedes a number, it applies to all the definitions that follow.

Syllable Division

The division of all words into syllables is a universal practice of dictionaries. This is done partly as an aid to pronunciation and word derivation, and partly to show how a word is divided at the end of a line when there isn't enough space to write the full word on the same line. Syllable division is indicated by centered dots or small dashes. Some dictionaries divide the word's main entry into syllables, others indicate them in the phonetic respelling (see below) that immediately follows the entry. Many persons confuse the dot (·) or short dash (-) with the longer, heavier dash (–) that indicates a hyphen in compound words. The following is a sample compound word entry in Webster's *New World Dictionary* (note the difference between the syllable dot and the hyphen):

hel·ter–skel·ter

Accent Marks

Dictionary entries also carry accent marks (′) to indicate which particular syllable or part of the word should be stressed. Some dictionaries place the accent marks in the entry itself, others in the respelling that follows the entry. The important thing to remember is that the accent mark appears immediately *after* the syllable to be stressed. When two syllables in a word are to be accented, the syllable that receives the lighter stress is marked by a light accent mark (′). It should be pronounced with less stress than syllables marked with the dark accent mark, but with more stress than syllables that carry no accent mark at all. Words of one syllable have no accent marks. Instead of light and dark marks, some dictionaries use single and double accent marks. The single mark indicates heavy stress; double marks, light stress.

Phonetic "Respelling"

A wide gulf often exists between how words are spelled and how they are pronounced (see page 36). For this reason, all good dictionaries give the phonetic spelling of troublesome words, in addition to the way they are conventionally spelled. The phonetic spelling indicates how to sound out the various parts of a word in actual speech. It is termed the "respelling." Surprisingly few people know how to handle a respelling, but it is very simple.

A word respelling may consist of a simple rearrangement or substitution of vowels and consonants. It may also consist of symbols called "diacritical marks," which appear over the vowels. These marks indicate when a vowel is to be pronounced long, short, etc. It is not necessary to know the names of these marks, and it is not even necessary to memorize how to make the sounds of any particular mark. For they appear in a key at the bottom (or top) of each page (or alternate page) of all good dictionaries. And next to each mark is a short word that anyone can readily pronounce and that shows just what sound is called for. Sometimes the mark is contained in the short word instead of appearing separately. The marks appear in alphabetical order for ready reference. All you need to pronounce a word is to refer to this key listing. You find the vowel with the diacritical mark that corresponds to the mark in the respelling of the word given in the main entry. You pronounce it just as it is sounded in the short word given in the key.

Suppose that we want to be sure of the proper pronunciation of the name of the composer Wagner. The entry in Webster's *New World Dictionary* (Compact Desk Edition) gives the following respelling after the main entry:

väg′nẽr

Now we immediately know that the beginning letter *W* is pronounced as a *V*. But how about the *ä* and the *ẽ*? These are termed "two-dot *a*" and "tilde *e*" respectively, but we don't need to know this. At the bottom of the page is the following key list:

> **fat**, **āpe**, **bâre**, **cär**; **ten**, **ēven**, **ovẽr**; **is**, **bīte**; **lot**, **gō**, **hôrn**, **tōōl**, **look**; **oil**, **out**; **up**, **ūse**, **fũr**; ə for *a* in *ago*; ***th***in, ***th***en; **zh**, leisure; **n**, ring; **ë**, Fr. leur; **ö**, Fr. feu; Fr. mo***n***; **ü**, Fr. duc; **kh**, G. ich, doch. ‡ foreign; < derived from

We can see that the *a* with the two dots above it is in the short word *cär,* so we know that the *a* in *Wagner* is pronounced as the *a* in *car.* Similarly, the *e* is contained in the short word *ovẽr,* which is how the *e* in *Wagner* should be sounded.

If while you are reading you come upon an unfamiliar word, such as mores, you can not only learn its meaning but also its pronunciation. According to the dictionary, the phonetic respelling is:

môr′ēz,-āz

This word has two acceptable pronunciations as shown by the two possible endings, ēz and āz. The one shown first is the most common or preferred pronunciation. According to the key at the bottom of the dictionary page, the symbol ô sounds like the o in horn. The bar over the ē and the ā signals the long vowel sound, ē as in even and ā as in ape.

Sometimes the respelling shows the substitution of other consonants. For instance, the respelling of acetate is as′ə tāt and of plunge is plunj. In these examples, the dictionary tells you to pronounce the c as an s in acetate and the ge as a j in plunge. Other examples of this respelling include:

barge	barj
baroque	bərōk′
orange	ôr′inj
juice	jōōs

A comprehensive version of the phonetic key appears in the front pages of your dictionary. Ordinarily the simpler key on the pages with the entries is sufficient. Phonetic alphabets vary somewhat between dictionaries, but when you are acquainted with the markings of one, you will be able to interpret the others easily.

One mark that may give some trouble is the so-called *schwa,* or inverted *e* (ə). Not all dictionaries employ the schwa, but it is coming into increasing use, and you should know about it.

When the schwa (ə) appears in a respelling, it always takes the place of a vowel. It is a sign that the vowel is reduced in strength of stress. It has an enfeebled *uh* sound, as the *a* has in the words *ago* and *about.* The schwa can present difficulties, as you can't be sure just how to sound it in every case. You will soon get the knack of it, however, after you see it used a number of times in a dictionary. Its purpose, to repeat, is to reduce, almost to ignore, the vowel's stress. The schwa's importance will be apparent when you realize how dull and unpleasant English would sound if every vowel were clearly stressed and enunciated. To relieve the monotony of vowel enunciation, there are times when vowels should lose their force, and the schwa tells us just when to pass quickly over them.

For example, the phonetic respelling for fortitude is:

fôr′tətōōd′

The o with a housetop over it we have already discussed and know that it sounds like the o in horn. By looking in the key, we find that the long bar over the oo means that it sounds like tool. The schwa has the same sound as the a in ago. By using the phonetic pronunciation guide printed in the dictionary, you can easily string the sounds together and correctly pronounce any word.

Word Derivation

The chief languages upon which English is founded are Anglo-Saxon, Old Norse, Old French, Middle English, Latin, and Greek. The abbreviations used by dictionaries to specify the language (or languages) from which a word is derived are, in order of their appearance above: AS., ON., OF., ME., L., and Gk. Additional language abbreviations are listed in the front of the dictionary. The symbol > means "derived from." Generally, word derivation information appears in brackets, either at the beginning or at the end of the entry. A question mark following the derivation signifies that it is only a guess and at best is uncertain.

Frequently Misspelled Words

Words shown with an asterisk below also have an alternate correct spelling. See any good dictionary for the alternate spelling.

A
abominable
abridgment
absence
abundance
abundant
academic
academically
academy
accelerating
accentuation
acceptable
acceptance
accepting
accessible
accessory*
accidental
accidentally
acclaim
accommodate
accompanied
accompanies
accompaniment
accompanying
accomplish
accountant
accuracy
accurate
accurately
accuser
accuses
accusing
accustom
achievement
achieving
acknowledgment*
acquaintance
acquire
across
actuality
actually
acutely
adequately
adhering
admirable
admissible*
admission
admittance
adolescence
adolescent
advancement
advantageous
adversaries
advertisement*
advertiser*
advertising*
advice
advise
aerial
aesthetic
affect
affiliate
afraid
against
ageless
aging
aggravate
aggressive
alibis
allegedly
allergies
alleviate
allotment
allotted
allowed
allows
all right*
all together
already
altar
alter
alternate
alternative
altogether
amateur
amenable
amiable
amicably
among
amount
amplified
amusing
analogies
analysis
arriving
artfully
article
artificial
ascent
ascetic
asinine
asphalt
asphyxiation
aspiration
assassin
assemblies
assertiveness
assiduous
assignment
assimilate
assistance
associating
assortment
assuming
asthma
astonish
astronaut
astute
asylum
atheist
athlete
athletic
atrocious
atrocity
attachment
attack
attempts
attendance
attendant
attended
attirement
attitude
attractive
attribute
audacious
audacity
audience
augment
auspicious
authenticity
author
authoritarian
authoritative
authority
authorization
authorize
autumn
available
awareness
awesome
awfully

B
babbling
balancing
ballerina
balminess
bankruptcy
bare
barely
bargain
barrenness
barrier
barroom
bashfulness
basically
basis
battling
bawdiness
bazaar
bearable
beauteous
beautified
beautiful
beautifying
beauty
become
becoming
before
began
beggar
beginner
beginning
begrudging
beguile
behaving
behavior
belatedly
belief
believe
belittling
belligerence
beneath
benefactor
beneficent
beneficial
benefited*
benevolence
benign
biannual
bicycle
bicycling
bigamy
bigger
biggest
binoculars
biscuit
biting
bitten
blameless
bluing
blurred
blurry
boastfully
bohemian
boisterous
boloney
booby trap
boring
born
borne
bossiness
botanical
bottling
boulevard
bouncing
boundary
bounties
braggadocio
breath
breathe
breezier
brief
brilliance
brilliant
brimming
Britain
Britannica
brochure
bronchial
brutally
budget
bulging
bulletin
bumptious
buoy
buoyant
buried
bursar
bury
bushiness
business
busy

C
cabaret
cafeteria
caffeine
calamity
calculation
calendar
callous
callus
calves
camaraderie
canceled*
candescence
canniness
canning
canoeing
capably
capacity
capitalism
capital
capitol
capricious
captaincy
captivity
careen
career
careless
cargoes
caribou
caricature
caring
carnally
carousing
carpentry
carpeted
carried
carrier
carries
carrousel*
carrying
cascade
casserole
casually
cataclysmal
cataloged*
catalyst
catastrophe

category
caught
causally
causing
caustic
cautious
ceaseless
celibacy
celluloid
cemetery
centrifugal
centuries
ceramics
cerebellum
certainly
certificate
certified
cessation
chafe
chagrined
chalice
challenge
chancing
changeable
changing
chaotic
characteristic
characterized
charging
charlatan
chastise
chatty
chauffeur
chauvinism
cheerier
chief
children
chilliness
chiseling*
chivalry
choice
choose
choosing
chose
choreography*
Christianity
chronically
chronicle
cigarette
cinema
cipher
circling
circuit
circulating
circumstantial
cite
citizen
corporal
correlate
correspondent
corroborate
corruption
council
counsel
counselor*
countenance
countries
courtesy
cowardice
cozier
crazily
create
credibility
crescendo
crescent
crevice
criminally
cringing
criticism
criticize
crucially
crudely
cruelly
cruelty
crystal
cultivating
cultural
cunning
curing
curiosity
curious
curriculum
cycle
cynicism

D

dahlia
dallying
dauntless
dazedly
debatable*
deceased
deceitfully
deceive
decent
decided
decision
dedicating
deductible
defenseless
deferred
deficiency
define
definitely
definition
degeneracy
deliberating
delicately
delightfully
delinquency
demoralize
denied
denominational
denouncement
department
dependent*
deplorable
depreciate
depressant
depression
derangement
derisive
descend
describe
description
desert
deservedly
desirability
desire
desolately
despair
desperate
desperation
despising
despondency
desert
dessert
destitution
destruction
detach
deteriorate
determining
detriment
deuce
devastating
development*
deviation
device
devise
dexterity
diabolic
diagonally
dialogue
dictionary
difference
different
difficult
dilapidated
dolorous
dominant
dormitories
double
doubtfulness
drastically
dropped
drudgery
dually
during
duteous
dye
dyed
dyeing
dying

E

eager
easel
easily
eccentric
echelon
ecstasy*
eczema
edified
educating
eerily
effect
efficiency
efficient
effortlessly
egotistical
eighth
eightieth
either
elaborate
elapse
elegy
element
elementary
eligible
eliminate
emaciate
embarrass
embarrassment
embellish
embitter
emergencies
emerging
eminence
emperor
emphasize
employment
emptiness
emulate
enabling
excruciating
excusing
exercise
existence
existent
expelled
expense
experience
experiment
explanation
expulsion
extensively
extenuate
extremely

F

fabricator
facetious
facility
facing
facsimile
factually
fallacy
falsely
falsified
familiar
families
fanatical
fancied
fantasies
fantasy
farewell
fascinate
fashions
fastidious
fatally
fatigue
favorable
favorite
feasible
ferocity
fertility
fetish
fiancé
fiancée
fickleness
fictitious
fidelity
field
fierce
fifteenth
figuring
finally
financially
financier
finesse
fitfully
flamboyant
flammable
flatterer
flexible
flimsiness
flippancy
flourish
fluidity
fluorescent
forbearance
forbidding
foreigners
forfeit
forgotten
formally
formerly
formidable
fortieth
fortitude
fortunately
forty
forward
fourth
freer
frequency
friendliness
frightfully
frivolous
fulfill
fundamentally
furrier
further

G

gaiety
galvanizing
gamble
gambol
garish
garnishee
garrulous
gaseous
gauche
gauging
gazette
generally
generating
generic
geniality
genius
gentlest
gesticulating
ghastliest
gladden
glamorous
glamour*
glorified

gluttony
government
governor
gradually
grammar
grammatically
grandeur
grandiloquence
grandiose
graphically
gratefully
gratification
gratuitous
greasing
grieving
grimacing
group
grudgingly
gruesome
guaranteed
guidance
guiding
guileless
guillotine
gullible
gutturally
gypped

H

habitable
hackneyed
hallucination
halving
hamster
handicapped
handled
handsomely
happen
happened
happiness
harangue
harassment
harmfully
harmonizing
hear
height
heinous
hemorrhage
hereditary
heresy
heretofore
heroes
heroic
heroine
hesitancy
heterogeneity
heuristic
hibernate
hierarchy
hilarity
hindrance
hirable
hoarsely
holocaust
homage
homely
homilies
homogeneous
hopeful
hopeless
hoping
horizontally
horrendous
horrified
hospitality
hospitalization
huge
human
humane
humanistic
humidified
humiliating
humorist
humorous
hundred
hundredth
hunger
hungrily
hungry
hydrophobia
hygiene
hygienic
hyphenation
hypnotizing
hypocrisy
hypocrite
hypothesis
hysterical

I

icicle
ideally
ideologies
idiocy
idiomatic
idiosyncrasy
ignoramus
ignorance
ignorant
illegible
illiteracy
illuminate
illusory
imagery
imaginary
imagination
imagine
imbibing
imitating
immaculate
immanent
immediately
immense
immigrant
imminent
immobilized
impartially
impasse
impeccable
impeding
imperceptible
impersonally
impinging
implausible
imploring
impoliteness
importance
impresario
impressionistic
improbability
improvement
inadequacy
inappeasable
inattentively
incalculable
incessantly
incidentally
incomparable
incomprehensible
inconceivable
inconsequential
inconstancy
incorrigible
increase
indefinite
independence
independent
indeterminate
indexes*
indispensable
individually
industries
inebriation
inefficiency
inevitable
inexcusable
inferred
infinitely
inflame
irreverence
irreversible
irritable
irritating
irruptive
issuing
itinerary
its
it's

J

jauntily
jealousy
jeopardy
jettison
jocundity
jolliness
jovially
judgment*
judicially
juiciness
juvenile

K

kaleidoscope
keenness
khaki
kidnaped*
kindlier
kinescope
knowledge

L

laboratory
laborer
laboriously
labyrinth
laconic
laid
lamentable
languorous
largess*
laryngitis
lascivious
lassitude
lately
later
laureate
lazier
lead (v.)
lead (n.)
leafy
learnedly
legacy
legality
legibility
leisurely
lengthening
leniency
lenses
lesion
lethally
lethargy
letup
levying
libelous*
liberally
libidinous
license*
licentious
liege
likelihood
likely
likeness
limousine
linage
lineage
listener
literally
literary
literate
literature
litigation
liveliest
livelihood
liveliness
lives
lodging
loneliness
lonely
longitudinal
looniness
loose
lose
losing
loss
lugubrious
luminosity
lustfulness
luxury
lyricism

M

macabre*
macaroni
mademoiselle
magazine
magnanimity
magnificence
magnificent
maintenance
malefactor
malleable
manageability
management
minority
minuscule
minutes
miraculous
mirrored
misalliance
misanthrope
miscalculation
miscellaneous
mischief
mischievous
misconstruing
mismanagement
misshapen
misspell
mistakable
moderately
moisturize
mollification
momentarily
monetary
monitor
monopolies
monosyllable
monotonous
monstrosity
moodily
moral
morale
morally
morbidity
morosely
mortally
mortifying
mosaic
mosquitoes
motif
mottoes*
mousiness
movable*
mucilage
multiplicity
multitudinous
mundanely
munificent
musically
musing
mutuality
mysterious

N

naïve*
naïveté*
namely
narcissus
narrative
natively

naturalistic
naturally
naughtily
nauseate
nearly
necessary
needlessly
nefarious
negativism
negligence
negligible
Negroes
neighbor
neither
neurotic
nevertheless
nicety
niggardly
nihilism
nimbly
nineteen
ninetieth
ninety
ninth
noble
noisily
nominally
noncombustible
normally
nostalgia
noticeable
noticing
notifying
notoriety
nourishment
nudity
nuisance
nullify
numerous
nuptial

O

obedience
objectively
obliging
obliquely
obliterate
obsequious
observance
obsess
obsolescent
obstacle
obstinately
obtuseness
occasion
occupancy
occupying
occur
occurred
occurrence
occurring
o'clock
oculist
oddly
odoriferous
odyssey
Oedipus
off
offense
offensively
officially
officiating
officious
omission
omit
omitted
oncoming
opaque
operate
opinion
opponent
opportunely
opportunity
oppose
opposite
oppression
optimism
optionally
oracular
orating
orderliness
ordinarily
ordinary
organization
original
ornamental
ornateness
orthodoxy
oscillate
ostentatious
ostracism
outrageous
outweigh
overdevelopment
overrun

P

pacified
pageant
paid
painstaking
palatable
palladium
palpitating
pamphlets
pancreas
panicky
pantomime
papier-mâché*
parable
parading
paradoxically
parallel
paralleled
paralyzed
parental
parentheses
parenthesis
parliament
paroxysm
parsimonious
partaking
partiality
participating
participial
participle
particular
passable
passed
passionately
passivity
past
pasteurize
pastime
pastoral
pastorale
pastries
pathetically
pathologist
patriarch
patriotically
patrolling
patronize
paunchy
pausing
peace
pealing
peculiar
pecuniary
pedagogue
pedagogy
pedantic
pedestrian
peeve
peignoir
penetrate
penicillin
penitent
penniless
penology
penury
perambulating
perceive
perceptible
percipience
peremptorily
perfidious
performance
perfunctory
perilous
periodic
permanent
permit
perpetually
persevering
persistent
personal
personally
personnel
perspicacity
persuade
pertain
perversely
pessimism
pestilence
petticoat
petulancy
pharmaceutical
phase
phenomenon
philosophy
phlegmatic
phobia
phonetically
phosphoric
photogenic
phraseology
phrasing
physical
physician
physique
pianos
picayune
piccolo
picnicked*
pictorially
piece
piecing
piling
pinnacle
piquancy
pirouette
piteous
pitifulness
placating
placidity
prevalent
primitive
principal
principle
prisoners
privilege
probably
procedure
proceed
producible
profession
professor
proficient
prognosticating
progressively
prominent
promissory
pronounce
pronunciation
pronouncing
propaganda
propagate
prophecy*
prophesy*
psychoanalysis
psychology
psychopathic
psychosomatic
ptomaine
puerile
pugnacity
punctilious
purposeless
pursue

Q

quadruplicate
quantity
quarreled*
queasiness
querulous
questionnaire
queue
quiescent
quintessence
quipster
quixotic
quotable
quotient

R

rabies
raconteur
radiating
raising
ramification
rapidity
reproducible
repudiating
repulsion
reputable
requisite
rescind
resembling
resignedly
resources
respectful
response
responsible
restaurant
resurrect
resuscitate
retaliating
retrieve
revealed
revenging
reverence
revering
reversible
revising
revocable
revolutionize
rhapsodies
rhinoceros
rhyming
rhythm
ricochet
ridicule
ridiculous
rigidity
risqué
ritualistic
rogue
rollicking
romantically
roommate
rottenness
rudely

S

sabbatical
sacrifice
sadistically
safety
salacious
salutary
sanatorium*
sanitarium*
sapphire
sarsaparilla
satellite
satiety
satisfied
satisfy

saturating
sauerkraut
saxophone
scandalous
scared
scarred
scene
schedule
schemer
scintillating
scissors
sclerosis
scoundrelly
scrupulous
scurrilous
scurrying
secretive
secureness
sedentary
seducible*
seemingly
seize
self-abasement
self-conscious
semantics
senatorial
sensitivity
sensuality
sentence
sentience*
sentimentality
separable
separate
separation
sergeant*
serviceable
seventieth
sexually
Shakespearean*
shamefacedly
shellacked*
shepherd
shining
short circuit
short-lived
shredded
shrinkage
shrubbery
shyly
sibilance
sickliness
similar
simile
sincerely
situating
skied
skyscraper
slatternly
sleepily
sleigh
sleight of hand
sliest
slipperiness
slurred
smoky*
smuggest
snobbery
snowcapped
sobriety
sociability
socialistic
sociology
solemnity
solicitude
solidity
solitaire
solvable
somnambulist
soothe
sophomore
soporific
sorcery
sorely
sorrier
source
souvenir
spaghetti
sparing
sparsely
speaking
spectrum
speech
speedometer
spirituality
spitefulness
sponsor
spontaneity
spurious
squalid
squarely
squaring
stabilization
suspicious
sustenance
swimming
syllabication
syllable
symbol
sympathetic
symphonic
synonymous
synthesis
systematically

T

tableau
tabooed*
taciturn
tactically
talkativeness
tangible
tassel
tasteless
taught
taut
tawdriness
technique
tedious
telepathy
temperament
temporarily
tenacious
tendency
tentatively
tenuous
terminology
terrifically
terrifying
testicle
thankfully
thatched
themselves
theories
theory
therapeutic
therefore
thesaurus
theses
thesis
thieve
thinkable
thirstily
thirties
thorough
thought
thriving
through
ticklish
timidity
timing
tiresomely
titillate
to
tobaccos
together
tolerable
tomato
tomatoes
tomorrow
too
topography
tormentor
torpedoes
torrential
totally
tousled*
tragedy
tragically
tranquillity*
transcendental
transferred
translucence
transmitter
transparent
treachery
tremendous
trichinosis
tricycle
trivially
tropical
truculence
tubular
tumultuous
tuneful
turmeric*
turquoise
tying
typewriter
tyranny

U

ugliness
ukulele*
ultimately
umbrella
unaccountable
unanimous
unconcernedly
unctuous
undeniable
undoubtedly
unfortunately
uniformity
uniquely
unlikely
unnecessary
unoccupied
unprincipled
unruliness
unusually
urbanely
useful
useless
using
utterly

V

vacating
vacillate
vacuum
validity
valuable
vanquish
vaporous
variegated
varies
various
velocity
venerable
vengeance
ventriloquist
veracity
veritable
vernacular
versatility
vicarious
vicissitude
villain
vinegar
virtually
virulence
visibility
visitor
visualize
vitally
vivacity
vocalist
vociferous
voicing
voluminous
voluntarily
voluptuous
voracity
voucher
vulnerable

W

wakefully
wantonness
wariness
warrant
watery
weakened
wearisome
weather
weighty
weird
weren't
wheeze
where
whether
whistling
whole
wholly
whose
wieldy
wiliness
willfully*
winery
wintry
wireless
wishful
witticism
woeful
wonderfully
wondrous
workable
worrying
wrathfully
wrench
wretchedness
writhe
writhing
writing
wryly

Misuse of the Word

FAULTY DICTION

Aggravate, *to increase,* does not mean *to irritate.*

Ain't, a contraction of *am not,* should be avoided.

Alternative, *one of two things,* may not correctly be applied to more than two.

Among should be applied to more than two persons or things; *between* to two.

Any (every, no, some) place should not be used adverbially for *anywhere (everywhere, nowhere, somewhere).*

And which should be used only when preceded by *which.*

As should not take the place of *that* or *whether,* and preferably not of *because.*

As . . . as are correlatives to be used with positive; with negative use *so . . . as.*

As good as and **better than** are idioms. If they are used in the same sentence, neither *as* nor *than* may be omitted. The following sentence is, therefore, incorrect: *Brazil is as good, if not better, than Argentina in climate.*

As yet is redundant. Omit *as.*

Awful means *profoundly impressive.* It should not be used loosely to mean *very bad.*

Badly should not be used for *very much.*

Balance should not be used for *remainder* except in connection with a financial statement.

Barefoot is preferred to *barefooted.*

Because should not be used instead of *that* if preceded by *the reason why . . . is.* Nor should it be used instead of *the fact that.*

Blame it on him should not be used for *place the blame for it on him* or *blame him for it.*

Bring up or **rear** is preferable to *raise* in speaking of children.

Bursted, bust, and **busted** should not be used for *burst.*

But should not be used with a negative in expressions like *isn't but.*

But what is less desirable than *but that.*

Cannot but should not be confused with *can but.*

Certainly should not be overused.

Claim is a strong word. It should not be used for *maintain.*

Common, meaning *shared similarly,* should not be confused with *mutual,* meaning *reciprocal.* The expression *a friend in common* is naturally preferable to *a common friend.*

Comparison. Two standards should not be combined in one sentence. *Largest (tallest, best)* should be followed by a singular; if preceded by *one of,* by a plural. It is, therefore, incorrect to say, *The* Paul Revere *is New England's fastest, and one of America's best, planes.*

Considerable is overused. It may not be used as a noun.

Contact, used as a verb in business, should be avoided.

Could of is illiterate for *could have.*

Cute is used colloquially to mean *clever.* The word should be avoided.

Criticize, in literature, means *to judge.*

Date may not be used as a verb to mean *make an appointment,* or as a noun to mean *the one with whom an appointment has been made;* it is colloquial for *appointment.*

Different from is the preferred idiom.

Don't, a contraction of *do not,* may not be used in the third person singular.

Drownded is illiterate.

Each other should be used only with two persons or things; *one another* with more than two.

Either and **neither** should be used only with two persons or things. The elements of the correlatives *either . . . or* and *neither . . . nor* may not be interchanged.

Enthuse, a colloquialism, may not be used in formal writing.

Etc. is an overused and almost meaningless abbreviation. It should not be used, especially with *and.*

Every bit is colloquial.

Except, which is not a conjunction, should not be used for *unless.*

Expect should not be used for *think* or *suppose.*

Extra means *beyond that which is usual,* not *extraordinarily.*

Feel bad (not *badly*) is correct but confusing; *feel ill* is preferable. *Feel good* refers to a moral, not a physical, state.

Fellow is colloquial when it means *person* or *fiancé.*

Fewer is used with number; *less* with degree or quantity.

Fine means *finished, refined,* or *perfect.* It should not be used loosely.

Fix (up) is colloquial for *to arrange* or *to repair.*

Former may be used with only two persons or things; likewise *latter.*

Get to go is provincial for *to be able to go.*

Goings on is a vulgar expression.

Good may not be used as an adverb to mean *well.*

Got is an abused word: it is colloquial for *possess,* as is *have got* for *must.*

Gotten, except in a few crystallized expressions, has now been supplanted by *got.*

Grand means *magnificent* or *impressive.* It should be used with care.

Guess, when used to mean *believe* or *suppose,* although possessing a long history in that sense, should be used infrequently if at all.

Had ought is illiterate.

Hardly should not be used with a negative in expressions like *couldn't hardly.*

Have got is both colloquial and redundant. Omit *got.*

Heap(s) is colloquial when meaning *much* or *many.*

Hear to it is vulgar.

Honorable should be preceded by *the* and followed by the first name or *Mr.*

If is less desirable than *whether* after *ask, doubt,* and similar words.

Inside of for *within* is colloquial; in other cases, *of* should be omitted.

Kind and **sort** are singular: *this kind* or *these sorts.*

Kind of and **sort of** are colloquial when meaning *rather.* These phrases in sentences like *You plan to create a kind of game preserve?* should not be followed by the indefinite article, for the noun is used generically.

Lady is correctly applied to one of culture or social distinction; *woman* is, however, entirely correct and is preferred in compounds like *saleswoman.*

Learn means *to gain knowledge; teach* means *to give instruction.* These words must not be confused.

Let's, a contraction of *let us,* should not be followed by *we, don't,* or any other illogical words.

Like, never a conjunction, may not be followed by a clause, thus taking the place of *as* or *as if.*

Line is slang for *kind,* as in *line of work.*

Literally means *true to the fact.* It should not be used untruly for intensification.

Locate means *to place;* it is colloquial when it means *to take up residence.*

Lose out is redundant; omit *out.*

Lovely means *delicate* or *exquisite.* It should not be overused colloquially to mean *very pleasing.*

Mad means *insane* or *enraged,* not *angry.*

Mean, as an adjective, is a synonym for *humble* or *ignoble;* it is colloquial for *ill-tempered* or *selfish.*

Mighty means *powerful* or *wonderful. Mighty tired* is, therefore, incorrect.

Miss, Ms., Mr., Dr., Professor, and similar titles must be followed by the name.

More than means *in a greater number* or *amount;* it should not be confused with *over,* meaning *beyond.*

Mrs. should never be followed by the title or profession of the husband or a married woman: *Mrs. Judge Watson, Mrs. Lawyer Williams, Mrs. Major Wilkinson, Mrs. Director of Public Works Warren.*

Nice means *discriminating, pleasing, or scrupulous.* A more precise word is preferred.

No good is colloquial when used to modify a noun.

Notorious means *discreditably known; noted* means *celebrated.*

No use, except in informal speech, should be preceded by *of.*

Nowhere near is colloquial for *not nearly.*

Of is redundant when preceded by *outside (the house)* or *off;* it is illiterate when used for *have,* as in *could of.*

On account of is not a conjunction and may not be followed by a clause.

One repeated is stiff: *One may earn one's living if one tries.* The shift from *one* to *he* or *his* is sometimes awkward. *A person . . . his . . . he* is perhaps preferable to either.

One of, followed by a group into which it falls, does not govern the number of the verb which follows the group. Thus it is correct to say, *Black Beauty is one of the horses which run at Havre de Grace.*

Only should be placed properly in a sentence. Note the difference in meaning: *Only America won the war. American only won the war. America won the only war. America won the war only.*

Out loud, a colloquialism, should be replaced by *aloud.*

Outside of, meaning *besides* or *except for,* is objectionable.

Over with is redundant; omit *with.*

Overly is unknown to good usage.

Party means one person on one of two sides of a cause, or one entire group. It does not mean *any person.*

Per, coming from the Latin, should be used only with Latin words like *annum, capita, cent,* not with *acre, dozen,* and similar words.

Per cent should be used only after numbers; otherwise *percentage* should be used.

Perfectly is an abused and often unnecessary adjective, as in *perfectly darling* or *perfectly beautiful.*

Piano, voice, violin, vocal, and **instrumental** should not be used alone when speaking of instruction: *lessons* or *instruction* should follow.

Plan on is redundant; omit *on.*

Proven, except in the law, is archaic; *proved* is the modern past participle.

Quite means *completely;* when used to mean *to a great extent,* it is colloquial. It should not be used as by the English, excessively and often absurdly, as a meaningless ejaculation.

Quite a (bit, few, little, number) is colloquial.

Rarely ever and **seldom ever** should be avoided as confusions of *hardly ever* or *rarely (seldom) if ever.*

Real is an adjective or a noun; *really* is an adverb. *I was real happy* is, therefore, incorrect.

Render means *to give, to yield, to extract,* or *to inflict.* One may *render lard,* but one should not *render a vocal selection.*

Reverend should be preceded by *the* and followed by the first name or *Mr.*

Right, meaning *precisely (right here and now)* or *to a large degree (right nice girl)* is colloquial. *Right smart* is dialectal.

Right along (away, off) is colloquial.

Run, when meaning *to conduct* or *to manage,* is colloquial.

Said, when meaning *previously mentioned,* should be avoided except in the law. *Aforesaid* is permissible.

Same, except in the law, should not be used as a pronoun.

Says is the third person singular of *say;* it may not be used with *I. Says* should not be used when the past tense, *said,* is required.

See where is a misuse of *see that.*

Show is colloquial for *drama* or *concert.*

Show up is colloquial for *appear.*

So should not be used as a mere intensive in an incomplete construction: *I am so angry. Because* is preferable to the colloquial *so* in joining coordinate clauses: *He came; so we held a reception* should be rephrased: *Because he came, we held a reception. So* should not be used instead of *so that.* The correlative *as . . . as* are used positively; *so . . . as* are used negatively.

Some is colloquial for *somewhat.*

Stop means *to arrest progress.* A person *stays* at a hotel.

Such should not be used as a mere intensive in an incomplete construction: *I have heard such good things about you* is incomplete. A clause of result following *such* should be introduced by *that,* not *as: There was such a noise that I could not hear.* A relative clause following *such* should be introduced by *as: He will follow such directions as the governor may give.*

Superlatives should not be used for intensification in an incomplete construction, as in *I had the best time.*

Sure is slang when it means *certainly. Surely* should be used.

Suspicion may never be used as a verb.

Take or **take it** should not be used to introduce an example.

The should not take the place of *a: Bittersweet candy is fifty cents the pound* is incorrect because a specific pound is not intended.

That is used colloquially to mean *to such a degree: I am not that tired that I must rest. So* should be used.

There as an expletive should be avoided.

This here *(these here, that there, those there)* is a vulgarism.

These should not be used loosely without any feeling of the demonstrative: *He is one of these modern cowboys who broadcast.*

Those should be followed by a relative clause: *He is one of those militarists* should be completed by adding a clause like *who would involve us in war;* or *He is a militarist.*

Through should not be used before a gerund: *I am through working* should be changed to *I have finished my work.*

Try and should be replaced by *try to.*

Ugly means *hideous* or *offensive morally.* It is used colloquially to mean *unpleasant.*

Up is redundant when preceded by a verb. It may not be used as a verb to mean *to increase,* as in *He upped the price ten dollars.*

Used to could is illiterate.

Verse, when used with the indefinite article, means *a line of poetry.* It should not be confused with *stanza,* a group of verses.

Very much is preferred to *very* when followed by a past participle not yet recognized as an adjective.

Way must be preceded by a preposition if used adverbially: *He works in that way.*

Who is this? when spoken over the telephone is both illogical and impolite.

Which as a relative pronoun should be used if the antecedent is inanimate or an animal; *who* if the antecedent is a person.

Without may not be used as a conjunction.

WORDS COMMONLY CONFUSED

accept, to receive
except, to exclude

access, approach
excess, superfluity

affect, to influence
effect, to execute

aisle, passage
isle, island

alley, lane
ally, associate

all ready, entirely prepared
already, at this time

all together, grouped
altogether, completely

allusion, indirect reference
illusion, deceptive appearance

altar, table
alter, vary

anachorism, violation of geography
anachronism, violation of time

angel, spiritual being
angle, corner

barbarous, almost savage
barbaric, showy, lacking restraint

berth, sleeping compartment
birth, beginning

beside, by the side of
besides, in addition to

boarder, one who takes meals
border, margin

Calvary, site of Christ's crucifixion
cavalry, horsemen

canvas, cloth
canvass, to solicit

capital, principal
capitol, statehouse

censor, examine
censure, condemn

centrifugal, proceeding from center
centripetal, proceeding toward center

chord, combination of tones
cord, small rope

cite, summon, quote
site, position

clothes, garments
cloths, fabrics

coarse, common, harsh
course, route

complement, addition, to add
compliment, to praise

congenial, kindred in taste
genial, cheerful

conscience, moral faculty
conscious, cognizant

consul, commercial representative
council, assembly
counsel, advice, attorney

contemptible, despicable
contemptuous, insolent

continual, in close succession
continuous, uninterrupted

corps, unit of organized establishment
corpse, dead body

credible, trustworthy
creditable, deserving of praise
credulous, inclined to believe

currant, raisin
current, motion

dairy, place for milk and its products
diary, daily record

desert, arid region; v. t., to leave, to abandon
dessert, course at end of meal

disinterested, uninfluenced by personal advantage
uninterested, apathetic

dual, twofold
duel, combat

elegy, lament
eulogy, commendatory oration

emigrant, one who leaves
immigrant, one who enters

enormity, wickedness
enormousness, immensity

euphemism, softened statement
euphony, pleasant sound
euphuism, artificial statement

exceptional, uncommon
exceptionable, objectionable

factious, dissentient
factitious, artificial
fictitious, feigned
fractious, unruly

faint, swoon
feint, pretense

farther, applied to distance, space
further, applied to extent, degree

forceful, possessing power
forcible, violent

feat, deed
feet, terminals of legs

formally, conventionally
formerly, heretofore

forth, onward
fourth, ordinal of *four*

hanged, executed
hung, suspended

healthful, wholesome
healthy, well, vigorous

ingenious, clever
ingenuous, candid

indict, to charge
indite, to write

inhumane, lacking in human kindness
inhuman (also *unhuman*), savage

later, afterward
latter, the second of two

lay (also past of *lie*), to place
lie, to recline

liable, obliged
likely, probably

lightening, relieving
lightning, flashing of light

loose, unattached
lose, to miss

luxuriant, profuse
luxurious, costly, ornate

mantel, shelf
mantle, cloak

misogamist, marriage hater
misogynist, woman hater

noted, renowned
notorious, disgraceful

O, used in invocation
oh, exclamation

observance, act of custom
observation, attentive consideration

passed, crossed
past, bygone

persecute, to afflict
prosecute, to carry on

personal, private
personnel, group collectively employed

plain, level land
plane, level surface

practical, useful, skillful
practicable, feasible

precedence, priority
precedents, antecedents

principal, chief
principle, doctrine

prodigy, wonder
progeny, offspring

propose, to offer
purpose, to resolve

prophecy, prediction
prophesy, to predict

quiet, undisturbed
quite, wholly

raise, to erect (in good use, not a noun)
rise, to ascend

recipe, formula
receipt, written acknowledgment

respectful, deferential
respective, individual

sciolist, pretender
scholiast, commentator

sensual, fleshly
sensuous, pertaining to the senses

sentiment, feeling
sentimentality, excessive feeling

stationary, fixed
stationery, paper

statue, image
stature, height
statute, law

stimulant, alcoholic beverage
stimulus, incentive

specie, coin
species, variety

suit, apparel
suite, set

their, possessive of *they*
there, in that place

therefor, for that
therefore, hence

to, toward
too, also
two, the number

troop, a collection
troupe, company of actors

venal, mercenary
venial, excusable

waive, to relinquish
wave, to swing

weather, condition of atmosphere
whether, if

who's, contraction of *who is* or *who has*
whose, possessive of *who*

your, possessive of you
you're, contraction of *you are*

USING THE TOOLS

Effective Sentences

To write effective sentences, you must learn not only to avoid certain basic errors, but also how to employ the tools of good writing. Often the "tool" to be used is simply on the other side of the coin from the error to be avoided. For example, to correct a *wordy* sentence, you take all unnecessary words out of the sentence; however, you should try to avoid wordiness by writing concisely, by writing no unnecessary words in the first place. Below you will find some constructive suggestions on how to write effective sentences.

Note the word *effective*. It carries the implication that, in writing, we wish to *do* something to our reader, to have an "effect" on him. If we don't take the time and make the necessary effort to determine what this effect is to be, our sentences will be ineffective. On the other hand, if we do assign a purpose to everything we write, something specific that we want to say–a "point of view"–we will have found one pathway toward errorless and effective writing.

MAKING SENTENCES EFFECTIVE

Use Concrete Language

A good writer uses concrete and definite words frequently, and avoids vague or abstract words. Concrete language gives the reader a specific picture rather than a general statement. It builds images that the reader can readily grasp.

General The lovely sounds of nature woke me.

Specific The wind in the trees and a bird's chirping woke me.

Be Positive

Good writing makes direct, positive statements; it avoids indirect, non-committal language. Use the word "not" only when the negative idea is emphatic; otherwise express what you want to say in the positive form.

Indirect He did not like Mr. Harvey's approach to grammar.

Direct He disliked Mr. Harvey's approach to grammar.

Indirect I did not think the trip would be very interesting.

Direct I thought the trip would be a bore.

Indirect Mr. Alexander was perhaps our best committee chairman. He was not long-winded, he was never biased, and he never failed to get the business before us covered.

Direct Mr. Alexander was the best committee chairman we ever had. He was direct, unbiased, and efficient.

Use the Active Voice

A careless writer uses the passive voice when there is no specific reason for doing so, and thereby weakens his effectiveness. Use the passive voice only when the subject is unknown or when the fact that something was *done to* the subject is of primary importance. Otherwise use the active voice. (See *Verbs: Voice.*)

Vary Your Sentences

A good stylist avoids monotonous writing by keeping his sentences varied, in both structure and length. To achieve a varied style one must keep one's ear open to the *sound* of his writing. (See *Basic Sentence Errors: Monotony.*)

Use a Climactic Order

Gain emphasis by placing important words or ideas at the important positions in the sentence–at the beginning or at the end, especially at the end. Sentences which state supporting ideas first and which withhold the important idea until the end are known as "climactic" or "periodic" sentences. Sentences which state the important idea first and then add supporting ideas are called "loose" sentences. Either kind of sentence is effective, but a preponderance of one or the other is decidedly ineffective and artificial. Whatever kind of sentence you select to express an idea, be sure to tuck away illustrative details and parenthetical expressions in the middle of the sentence. As a rule, loose sentences are preferred in informal writing; periodic sentences are more common in formal writing.

Periodic The alternative we must avoid at all costs is armed conflict.

Loose Armed conflict is the alternative we must avoid at all costs. (Important idea expressed first and followed by explanatory comment)

Periodic Against the spangled backdrop of a dark night sky filled with unending stars shone the moon, white and fluorescent.

Loose A white, fluorescent moon shone against the spangled backdrop of a dark night sky filled with unending stars.

Euphony and Rhythm

Euphony is the smooth, pleasant flow of agreeable sounds. An experienced writer chooses and arranges his words so that they form patterns of sound that are rhythmical and euphonious when read aloud. The more experienced and skillful the writer, the more pleasant are the sounds he produces. The ability to produce these sound effects comes only from experience.

Do not repeat words that have the same sound. Do not alliterate. Do not confuse rhythm with rhyme. An alliteration is the repetition of an initial sound in two or more words in the same phrase or clause. It is an eye-catching device used by advertising copy writers, but it has no place in formal prose writing. Rhyme, the repetition of end sounds, is a device of verse, not of prose. The first example below illustrates how euphony can be destroyed by alliteration; the second, by rhyme.

Alliteration In a fury I flew into the fray.

Rhyme I yearn to learn who she is.

Figures of Speech

A prevalent belief among students is that figures of speech are old-fashioned and should be confined to rhetoric and poetry. This is a false belief. We all use figurative language every day, and more often than not, without realizing it. *Hungry as a bear, quick as lightning, time flies, drive a bargain*–these are common figurative expressions. A figure of speech is any deviation from the literal meaning or ordinary use of words designed to make a thought clearer or more forceful. Suppose we express how a girl sings by comparing her with a nightingale. *May sings like a nightingale.* We do not say literally how May sings. We suggest the image of the nightingale and leave it to the reader's imagination to know the quality of May's voice. This is communication in figurative language. The example of May's voice is a figure of speech known as a *simile*. The simile expresses a figurative resemblance or comparison between essentially different things. One thing is said to be like another, and the resemblance is usually introduced by *like* or *as*. *Hungry as a bear* and *quick as lightning* are also similes. Actually, the best similes compare things which are in most respects unlike, but which have at least one point of striking resemblance.

The "Intentional Fragment"

The grammatical structure of the sentence has been analyzed. We have already stated that a sentence need not necessarily contain a subject and a verb, although by far the majority of our written sentences do. Expressions such as "Why not?" or a conversational colloquialism such as "Me, too" are considered to be sentences. In writing, the sentence that intentionally lacks a subject or a verb is called an "intentional fragment." Professional writers use intentional fragments for stylistic effect. Beginning writers, however, are best advised not to use fragments of any kind.

Idioms

In every language, combinations of words have developed which appear completely proper to the natives of the country where the language is spoken, but which sound peculiar to a foreign visitor. Such expressions are known as *idioms*.

Sometimes idioms conform to grammatical rules, and at other times they may conflict with such rules, but idiomatic usage has established the expression as proper.

The prepositional idiom is a type of expression that gives even the native some difficulty. A seemingly well-written sentence will be ruined by a careless use of a prepositional idiom. The trouble arises in determining the correct preposition. For example: Is it *faced with* or *faced by*? Idiomatic usage has established *faced by* as the proper expression. To determine which preposition an idiom takes, see a good dictionary.

Synonyms

Synonyms are good words to become familiar with. They help give variety to sentences, and their proper use avoids repetitious phrases. A *synonym* actually is a word that means the same or nearly the same as another word. Practical students often resort to synonyms as a device to avoid using words they do not know how to spell. A student may want to use *lugubrious* on his essay examination but, unsure of the spelling, resorts to the word *dismal*. Careless substitution can change the subtle meaning of a sentence, even if it would appear that the two words are almost identical. To *plagiarize* and to *copy* often mean the same thing; there is, however, a distinct difference. To *plagiarize* definitely means to steal another person's literary effort and pass it off as one's own, whereas one may *copy* another person's work, with or without intent to steal it.

Antonyms

This is a word that means the opposite of another word. But even antonyms can be useful in giving sentences a greater variety if properly used. *Happy* and *sad* are antonyms. Seemingly, it would appear they are not interchangeable in a sentence, yet the writer may feel that the word *happy* is too strong, and he may decide, despite the admonition against the use of the negative, that *not sad* is just the right state he is trying to describe.

BASIC SENTENCE ERRORS

The Fragment

The *fragment* is a statement that fails to state a complete thought; it is an incomplete sentence. Generally, the error can be corrected by simply attaching the fragment to the sentence before or after it, as in each of the corrections below. Unintentional fragments used as complete sentences generally consist of phrases, appositives, or dependent clauses.

Fragment The soldiers stood stoically in the rain. *Cursing quietly over their wretched luck.* (verbal phrase incorrectly used as a complete sentence)

Complete The soldiers stood stoically in the rain, cursing quietly over their wretched luck.

Fragment He was an unbelievable person. *A man as well read and as outspoken as any I've ever met.* (an appositive incorrectly used as a complete sentence)

Complete He was an unbelievable person, a man as well read and as outspoken as any I've ever met.

Fragment The settlers were careful to place twenty-four-hour guards around the encampment. *So that they would not be caught off guard by an Indian attack at any time.* (dependent clause used incorrectly as a complete sentence)

Complete The settlers were careful to place twenty-four-hour guards around the encampment, so that they would not be caught off guard by an Indian attack at any time.

The Run-on Sentence

The *run-on sentence* occurs when the writer has failed to separate properly two sentences or independent clauses, with the result that the two "run into" each other. Two major types of run-on sentences occur. The first type contains no punctuation at all between the sentences. Such sentences are known as "fused sentences" or "stringiness." The second type of run-on sentence is one in which a comma has been improperly used. This is often called a "comma splice."

Run-on Let us be wary but let us not fall prey to fear. (fused: failure to use punctuation between independent clauses)

Improved Let us be wary, but let us not fall prey to fear.

Run-on A soft answer turns away wrath, grievious words stir up anger. (comma splice: comma incorrectly used to separate independent clauses)

Improved A soft answer turns away wrath; grievous words stir up anger.

To avoid writing run-on sentences, one must know the four possible ways of connecting independent clauses. (See also *Punctuation: The Comma.*) As a general rule, if the ideas are to receive equal emphasis, use the period and place the ideas in different sentences, or use the semicolon alone. If one idea is more important than the other, use the comma and a coordinating conjunction, or the semicolon and a conjunctive adverb.

Mixed Constructions

A *mixed construction* results when one part of a sentence does not agree grammatically with another part of the sentence. The two major types of mixed construction involve subject and verb disagreement, and pronoun and antecedent disagreement.

Wrong A series of lectures were given by Mr. Olsen. (Plural verb *were* does not agree with singular subject *series.*)

Right A series of lectures was given by Mr. Olsen. (Verb agrees with subject.)

Wrong Sometimes circumstantial evidence will convict a person of a crime they did not commit. (Plural pronoun *they* does not agree with singular antecedent *person.*)

Right Sometimes circumstantial evidence will convict a person of a crime he did not commit. (Pronoun agrees with antecedent.)

Dangling Modifiers

The *dangling modifier* is a verbal phrase that either has no word in the sentence to modify or is placed in such a way that it appears to modify unintended words in the same sentence.

Dangling Making a flying tackle, Sam's shoe came off. (The participial phrase is *Making a flying tackle,* but the subject of the clause that follows is *shoe. Making a flying tackle* cannot possibly refer to a shoe.)

Improved Making a flying tackle, Sam lost his shoe. (*Sam* is now the subject to which the participial phrase properly refers.)

Dangling To be sure of a good seat, your tickets must be bought far in advance. (The understood subject of the infinitive phrase *To be sure* is not the same as the subject of the clause that follows.)

Improved To be sure of a good seat, you must buy your tickets far in advance. (The infinitive phrase modifies *you,* the subject of the sentence.)

Dangling After waiting an hour, the train finally came. (The train waited an hour? Obviously not. *After waiting an hour* has no word in this sentence to modify.)

Improved After waiting an hour, we finally caught our train. (*After waiting an hour* refers to *we,* the subject of the sentence.)

Squinting Modifiers

A *squinting modifier* is one that is carelessly placed so that it appears to modify both the words preceding and the words following it. The reader has to stop reading to figure out what is being modified.

Squinting The man who shoved his way to the platform angrily addressed the crowd. (What does *angrily* modifiy? The way the man made his way to the platform? Or the way he addressed the crowd?)

Improved The man who angrily shoved his way to the platform addressed the crowd. *OR* The man who shoved his way to the platform addressed the crowd angrily.

There are two types of verbal phrase constructions that are independent of the rest of the sentence and that need not modify the subject of the clause that follows it. The first type is the *absolute phrase* consisting of a noun or pronoun followed by a participle.

The play having finished, the audience left.

The second type of verbal phrase that can be independent of the rest of the sentence is a phrase that states a general truth. A general truth does not refer to the action of a specific person or thing. Such expressions as *taking everything into consideration* and *to put it another way* are verbal phrases that can stand apart from the rest of the sentence.

Monotony

The most common form of this fault is the dull repetition of a subject-verb sentence pattern. Monotony also occurs when the writer fails to vary the length of his sentences. Monotony results, in fact, from any continued, dull repetition of sentence structure or length.

Not Varied He opened the car door. He stepped out. He walked towards the store. He tried to remember all the things his wife had told him to buy. He hated shopping!

Varied Opening the car door, he stepped out and walked towards the store, trying to remember all the things his wife had told him to buy. How he hated shopping!

Faulty Parallelism

A series of related ideas of equal importance can often be most effectively expressed by writing them in what is called "parallel form." Parallelism, which treats like ideas in like form, balances words, phrases, and clauses against one another. In a series, for example, words should be in the same class and in the same parts of speech. One may begin a series of parallel forms, then lose the parallelism, and thus commit the error known as "faulty parallelism."

Not Parallel Although very good-looking, Ted was modest, shy, and didn't talk much. (The parallel adjectives *modest* and *shy* demand a third adjective rather than a clause to follow them, in order that the sentence should read smoothly and clearly.)

Parallel Although very good-looking, Ted was modest, shy, and quiet.

Not Parallel The man at the desk ordered me to be silent, to sit down, and that I should wait until I was spoken to. (The two infinitives and the phrase beginning *and that* constitute unparallel form.)

Parallel The man at the desk ordered me to be silent, to sit down, and to wait until I was spoken to. (A third infinitive has been added to complete the parallelism begun by the first two.)

Correlative Conjunctions and Parallelism

The use of the correlative conjunctions can lead the writer to make mistakes in parallelism. These conjunctions–*either . . . or, neither . . . nor, not only . . . but also*–help tighten sentence structure and strength expression, but they must be used logically. That is, the same kinds of words and the same grammatical structure must appear on both sides of the correlatives, otherwise, parallelism and sense and effectiveness will be lost.

Not Parallel Al is both a marvelous athlete and he dresses very well. (A modifying phrase on one side and an independent clause on the other)

Parallel Al is both a marvelous athlete and a fine dresser. (Modifying phrase on either side)

Not Parallel Your grandmother has not only a sharp mind but also her humor is lively.

Parallel Your grandmother has not only a sharp mind but also a lively humor.

Mixed Metaphor

Combining two different comparisons or figures of speech that are inconsistent or incongruous with each other, produces the "mixed metaphor." The writer must be careful to maintain logic as he adds color with images and comparisons; he must make sure his comparisons "fit" one another. A "ship of state" cannot get "lost in the woods of diplomatic entanglements" (ships don't sail in the woods); "her eyes" could not be "glistening pebbles in the twilight sky" (pebbles do not glisten in the sky).

Mixed With determination Ellen dug into the sea of work before her.

Logical With determination Ellen dug into the pile of work before her. *OR* With determination Ellen plunged into the sea of work before her.

Mixed Now, friend, chew upon this branch of my thoughts: all good looks are a snare that no man should let himself be drowned in.

Logical Now, friend, chew upon this morsel of my thoughts: all good looks are a snare that no man should let himself be trapped in.

Inadequate Subordination

Immature minds seldom use subordination. It takes maturity to select one idea over another and to subordinate it to the important one. A child, for example, is likely to give new facts equal importance. Learning about Columbus, the child is likely to say: "Columbus was born in Portugal. He was given three ships by the Queen of Spain. He became famous as the discoverer of America. He died in poverty and neglect." A more mature version of these facts would be: "Columbus, who was born in Portugal, was given three ships by the Queen of Spain. He became famous as the discoverer of America; however, he died in poverty and neglect." Two simple words, the relative pronoun *who* and the conjunctive adverb *however,* place the facts about Columbus in truer perspective, by subordinating the less important facts to the more important ones.

Inadequate subordination is the sign not only of immaturity but of ineffective writing. It results in short, choppy sentences. The writer who combines ideas in sentences without proper subordination inevitably is guilty of an excessive number of *and* and *so* clauses. The rule to remember is: Put subordinate ideas in subordinate (dependent) clauses (or phrases), and main ideas in main (independent) clauses.

Inadequate Subordination Tom was tired of listening to the lecture, and no one could see him, and so he slipped quietly out of the room. (Three ideas are placed in independent clauses, thereby giving each idea equal importance and resulting in no subordination at all.)

Improved Tom was tired of listening to the lecture, and since no one could see him, he slipped quietly out of the room. (One idea has been made subordinate to the other two, by putting it in a dependent clause.) *OR* Since Tom was tired of listening to the lecture and as no one could see him, he slipped quietly out of the room. (two ideas made subordinate)

Faulty Subordination

When combining several ideas in one sentence, be sure not to make the mistake of subordinating the main idea. The less important of two ideas should always be in a dependent clause or phrase. Never introduce the main idea of a sentence with a conjunctive adverb.

Weak Although he easily won the club tennis championship, he showed some signs of fatigue. (The main idea of the sentence is weakly introduced by the subordinating conjunction *Although*. The subordinate idea is in an independent clause.)

Improved Although he showed some signs of fatigue, he easily won the club tennis championship. (The subordinate idea is properly placed in a subordinate clause, and the main idea is properly placed in the independent clause.)

"Fine" Writing

"Fine" writing is a ruse to cover up absence of knowledge. It is the use of big, pretentious words for simple, direct words. It is word exhibitionism at its worst. Students often resort to "fine" writing to impress, to make the reader think that they know what they are talking about. "Fine" writing is a puerile, sophomoric device, and it impresses nobody. Of course, writers often inject pretentious words into the speech of teenage delinquents, race track touts, and hoodlums of diverse sorts. This they do for comic irony, and the results can be hilarious. But it is pathetic to hear the same words uttered by high school and college students.

There is nothing wrong with big words, but they should normally be used only to express meanings and shades of meaning for which simpler words do not exist.

Split Infinitives

To split an infinitive is to insert an expression between the *to* and the verb. The inserted expression is usually an adverb (to *entirely* comprehend). The reason that split infinitives used to be condemned is that *to* is historically a preposition. Grammarians at one time insisted that a preposition should never be separated from its object by any other words. The rule now generally accepted sanctions the split infinitive when it results in a clearer meaning or a pleasanter sound. In the illustrations of acceptable split infinitives below, note how a transposition of the *to* would affect the meaning and the rhythm of the sentences.

> Do you want us to really enjoy ourselves?
>
> The judge refused to summarily dismiss the case.
>
> He failed to entirely comprehend the charge.

The Double Negative

Avoid the double negative. Use a single negative to express a negative idea.

Wrong I haven't no money left.

Right I have no money left.

The following are troublesome words. They are all negative, or negative by implication, so should not be accompanied by a second negative word.

barely	no one
hardly	none
neither	not
never	nothing
nobody	only

Unneeded Words

Beware of repeating ideas already expressed.

Repetitious	Repeat what you said again.
Concise	Repeat what you said.
Repetitious	The reason I didn't do my homework was on account of the fact that I forgot the assignment.
Better	The reason I didn't do my homework was that I forgot the assignment.
Concise	I didn't do my homework because I forgot the assignment.

Let us go one step further. We don't simply say that May has a voice *like* a nightingale, but we say that her voice *is* the voice of a nightingale. *May has the voice of a nightingale.* The two voices are equated. This is a *metaphor.* It is simply an expanded simile. A simile states that one thing is *like* another; a metaphor, that one thing *is* another.

Simile	He mouths a sentence as curs mouth a bone.
Metaphor	All the world's a stage, And all the men and women merely players.

Similes and metaphors are the most common figures of speech. Other common figures of speech are: *hyperbole* (extravagant but deliberate and fanciful exaggeration), *litotes* (deliberate understatement), *personification* (infusing life into inanimate things), and *metonymy* (naming one thing in terms of another which is part of it or associated with it).

Hyperbole	Thanks a million.
Litotes	Faulkner is not a bad writer (meaning he is a great writer).
Personification	Time flies.
Metonymy	She set a good table (meaning she prepared a good meal).

Weak Words

The weakest words in the English language are the intensives *very, little, rather,* and *pretty.* An *intensive* is a word that supposedly makes another word more forceful and emphatic. But the use of an adjective (as an adverb) to intensify another adjective often has the opposite effect. This is especially true of adjectives that have been used so often with so little regard for their true meanings that they have lost all the force they once had. Take the words *awful, dreadful, fearful,* and *horrible.* These are potent words when used to mean "to inspire awe" *(awful),* "to inspire dread" *(dreadful),* "to instill fear" *(fearful),* "to excite horror" *(horrible).* However, when these words are loosely used as intensives, they languish into impotence. They are especially absurd when they intensify words that contradict their own meanings. Expressions such as *awfully nice* and *horribly sorry* are not only feeble and placid but absurdly contradictory. The following is a list of words that should not be used as intensives. Unless you know the true meanings of these words, do not use them at all.

amazing	gorgeous	splendid
awful	grand	stunning
colossal	horrible	stupendous
devastating	huge	superb
dreadful	little	terrible
enormous	magnificent	terrific
fabulous	marvelous	tremendous
fearful	pretty	very
frightful	rather	wonderful

Slang

Slang is unacceptable in either ordinary conversation or formal writing. If it belongs anywhere, it is in light banter in an informal setting–but only if it is original and lively. Effective slang usually is a cleverly humorous or dramatically surprising play on words, achieved by taking words out of context, juxtaposing unexpected words, using very compressed metaphors, and the like. Unfortunately, slang ages quickly and becomes stale.

Why, then, is it so popular? Its chief attraction is that it makes a single word do so much. In an instant, a word of slang can communicate a reasonably exact meaning, suggest a humorous comparison, arouse emotion, and suggest personality. Think of how much more is said in the single word "Scram!" than in the sentence, "You may go now." In this very flexibility of slang lies one of its chief dangers: It may be used for so many things that it becomes a crutch for one's vocabulary. One may, for example, use the slang word "dig" in a variety of contexts: "I don't dig (understand) this equation"; "I dig (feel satisfied with) the mark I got in English"; "Baby, I dig (am attracted to) you." With so handy a word available the lazy or obtuse person will overuse it, quite failing to make distinct the various meanings he actually intends. Such dependence on slang prevents the development of a good vocabulary.

In sum, therefore, if you wish to inject slang into the dialogue of your fictional characters, by all means do so–with care and with a sparing hand. Incidentally, never enclose slang words within quotation marks, either single or double.

Solecisms

A *solecism* is the violation of correct grammatical structure. It is considered a blunder, not an illiteracy or a barbarism, and is usually the result of carelessness.

Colloquialisms

The chances are you have only a vague idea of what a colloquialism is. Most students confuse it with provincialisms or localisms and think it refers to sectional peculiarities of speech. Most students also attach some sort of stigma to the word and try to avoid using words or expressions that are labeled colloquial in the dictionary. A colloquialism really has nothing to do with sectional peculiarities, and there is nothing "bad" or improper about using it–under certain circumstances. The word simply labels expressions that are more acceptable in familiar or ordinary conversation than in formal speech and writing. For example, the president of a college, or the principal of a school, when talking with his colleagues, may quite properly use colloquialisms. However, when he dons cap and gown to deliver an address at the annual commencement exercises, he scrupulously avoids colloquialisms. The difference is in the setting.

It is perfectly all right to use colloquialisms when you are talking with members of your family, with friends, and when writing friendly letters and informal reports. An example of a colloquialism and its equivalent formal form is given below.

Colloquialism	What a close shave!
Formal	What a narrow escape!

Jargon

Dictionaries define *jargon* as language that is "unintelligible." This is an unfortunately broad definition. We usually associate the term with the "bureaucratic jargon" of officialdom, now widely referred to as *governmentese.* In this sense *jargon* has partly derisive, partly humorous connotations. In a stricter sense, *jargon* is the specialized vocabulary of persons who are engaged in the same trade or profession. The intelligibility of the specialized vocabularly naturally excludes the outsider, but for the insider it is loaded with meaning. A single expression can stand for a thought or idea that might otherwise take ten, twenty, or even a hundred words to express with a standard vocabulary. As long as the expression is kept within the specialized group, it is perfectly necessary and legitimate. It is only when the expression is employed outside the field in contexts where other vocabulary is available that it becomes jargon in the commonly accepted sense of the term. Thus, the expression "relate to" is a favorite in the vocabulary of psychologists. Employed by a psychologist outside his professional setting, or by the layman, this same expression loses its specialized meaning and becomes absurd jargon.

Trite Expressions and Clichés

A trite expression is an overused expression. It has been used so much that when the reader sees the first word or two, he can anticipate what follows. And when the reader can anticipate your words, you cannot hold his attention. "A good time was had by all" is a trite expression. A cliché is a figure of speech or turn of words that may have been original and clever once upon a time but that has become trite and stale through overuse. Like an oft-repeated joke, *it wears its welcome thin* (the expression in italics is a cliché). How do you tell when a cliché is a cliché? As happens with jokes, you hear one and you think it is original, or you think one up yourself. You hasten to tell it to your friends. But they have already heard it countless times. So it is with clichés. You must consciously be on the lookout for them in whatever you read or hear. Whenever you spot a cliché, make a mental note not to use it in your own writing.

Provincialisms and Localisms

A *provincialism* is a word, phrase, or idiom peculiar to a major geographical section or region. A *localism* is peculiar to a limited locality. When used in speech by persons who live in a particular section or locality, they are legitimate and proper. Since provincialisms and localisms are not in national usage, however, they do not appear in formal, expository writing. Obviously, both are essential to the speech of characters in fiction.

Barbarisms

Barbarism is the name grammarians give to the gross misuse of words. To use *eats* for *food,* as in "Pass me the eats," would be termed a barbarism. Another example of a barbarism is the use of *learn* for *teach,* as in "That will learn you a lesson."

Effective Paragraphs

Any reader is aware that an indented sentence means a new paragraph. In dialogue, such indentation shows merely that a new speaker is being quoted. But the indentation at the beginning of the paragraph always indicates some change of subject or approach–in the description, the narration, the argument–whatever the type of the writing may be.

The new paragraph, however, does more for us than indicate a change in thought. For the paragraph is the real building block of any prose writing. The casual letter-writer, the student, the professional journalist, the novelist–all use paragraphing in their letters, essays, articles, or novels. In order to function correctly, that is, to fit neatly among the other blocks as well as help to hold them up, the paragraph must, itself, be a carefully completed and finely shaped unit. Perhaps the best definition of a *paragraph* might be: *the carefully rounded development of a single impression or idea.*

The reader should bear in mind that no absolute criteria exist for determining a good paragraph. There is agreement that a paragraph should contain the stylistic elements which effectively convey the writer's idea, or purpose. Such a paragraph is effective–it is good.

Paragraphs may be purely descriptive, or narrative, or expository, or they may include any mixture of these major types of writing. The principles of good paragraph-writing discussed below can be applied to all types of paragraphs.

PRINCIPLES

The Topic Idea

A good writer knows exactly why he is starting a new paragraph and why he is ending it. Within that one paragraph he is trying to say essentially *one thing* as clearly and as completely as he possibly can. That one thing we call the "topic idea" of a paragraph. Often this topic idea is expressed in a *topic sentence* that generally comes at or near the beginning of the paragraph. The topic sentence, however, need not come at the beginning, nor does the paragraph have to have a topic sentence, so long as the single idea is clear.

Adequate Development

The topic idea can be conveyed only if the writer makes sufficient effort to "show what he means" to his reader. The different methods of "showing" are enumerated below, but it is important to remember that no matter how you construct your paragraph, it must give enough details, facts, examples, or reasons to hold and convince the reader.

Inadequate Everyone should play some sport from which he gets both enjoyment and physical toughening. Sports have always been considered important. They make you strong and you can have a lot of fun with them. Furthermore, friendships can be made through sports. Nobody can deny that for many reasons, sports are a "must."

In the above paragraph, note that most of the sentences are mere restatements of the topic sentence or of each other, and that they are extremely general. The way to construct your paragraphs well consists of your ability to give details, facts, specifics, in concise and *concrete* language.

Unity

The well-written paragraph sticks relentlessly to its topic idea and departs from that idea only to bring in closely related material. A careless writer, on the other hand, "wanders" from his topic, and thereby loses the concentrated focus, or "unity," that writing must have if it is to be effective. The best way to keep each paragraph unified is to make the subject of most of your sentences the same as the subject of your topic sentence; hold on to your subject, and you will hold on to your topic idea.

Transition

Transition is "going across" or–in writing–getting the reader smoothly from one thought to another, one image to another, one sentence to the next. You can achieve good transition by practicing these two important principles:

a) *Arrange the sentences of each paragraph in logical order so that each follows the one before it as naturally as possible.*

Failure to build the paragraph on such a predetermined order can result in confusion and lack of transition. Presenting images or events simply in their *order of occurrence in time* or in their "narrative order" is one of the most common methods of developing a paragraph logically.

You could also arrange the ideas or arguments in a predetermined "order of importance."

b) *Wherever necessary, use words and phrases that tie your ideas together as closely as possible.*

These words and phrases, sometimes called "transitional devices," can be categorized under three headings: pronouns, key (or "echo") words, and connectives.

1) Pronouns

Using pronouns whose antecedents are the subject of the paragraph makes transition stronger. The most useful of these for transitional purposes are the demonstratives: *this, that, these, those.*

> Nothing in the way of equipment was overlooked. It was because of *this* preparation that the expedition was so successful.

2) Key words

These are words that relate to or "echo" the topic idea, and their inclusion holds the paragraph–and the reader–to the subject.

> The men fought the *fire* mightily for three days. However, the *blaze* was too much for them; the *flames* would not be extinguished. Such *holocausts* cost Americans millions of acres in valuable forest every year.

3) Connective words and phrases

This group of transitional devices is extensive, and we use many of them quite naturally in our everyday speech. The group includes all conjunctions–subordinate, correlative, and coordinate–plus a large number of "connective" adverbs and adverb phrases.

The following paragraph has employed transitional words and phrases. Note that the "flow" is smooth and its thought easy to follow.

> My black, furry poodle, Totor, is a real problem to me. *Ever since* I bought him from a pet shop, he has caused me nothing but trouble. *However,* I do like him, *because* he has such a charming, lively personality. *But* this liveliness is also the source of my problem, *for* it leads him to do the most dreadful things. *For instance,* he hops up on the kitchen table and eats a whole ham. *Then* he chews the caps off the milk bottles and drinks all the cream. *And* he is always stealing shoes and chewing them apart. *Nevertheless,* he is worth it, *mostly because* I have learned how to outfox him–most of the time.

Necessary Design

The good paragraph is organically dependent upon its topic sentence or topic idea for its overall construction. It has a logical design that arises out of the purpose of the paragraph. Thus, if your purpose is to describe a room by putting the reader into the scene, your details would be arranged in an order in which he might see them, were he standing in the room. If, in another paragraph, your purpose is to convince your reader of a certain fact, you would list your points in such a way that they would have maximum effect on him (perhaps in an ascending or "climactic" order of importance).

DEVELOPING A PARAGRAPH

The way the writer develops his topic idea in any single paragraph must always be determined by the topic idea and the purpose that the writer has in mind for the paragraph. The six major ways in which a writer can develop a topic idea within any paragraph are described below:

Enumerate Examples or Illustrations

Sometimes we may be saying something that we cannot explain clearly, and our listener may suggest, "Well, suppose you give me an example." Examples, or illustrations, provide us with a way of putting something abstract and perhaps difficult to comprehend into images or pictures that are easy to understand. Examples are almost exactly the same as details, except that they are used for the specific purpose of making a general point. You give an example of something; you make an illustration of a point. Hence, this method of developing a paragraph is especially useful in *expository* and *argumentative* writing.

Use a Single Illustration

Often the easiest way to "say what you mean" is to tell a simple story that says it for you. Such a method of developing a topic idea can help you define a word, make a point clear, or explain an idea. Hence, the "single-illustration paragraph" is used most frequently in *expository* and *argumentative* writing.

Explain by Definition

In *expository* writing, we can sometimes more clearly discuss an idea or concept by *defining* the word that embodies the idea. The definition should expand the basic idea by presenting other ideas with which the reader is already familiar.

Explain by Analogy

An *analogy* is a single illustration that describes or explains one thing by describing something quite different, but at the same time similar, so that there is a clear parallel between the two. George Orwell's much-discussed novel *Animal Farm* is an analogy in the form of a novel. In this book, Orwell presents his attitude toward the aftermath of the Russian Revolution by telling a story of a group of very human animals on a farm. The analogy is often more dramatic than a simple illustration because of its suggestive powers. Thus, for example, Orwell's use of animals immediately suggests that the historical figures whom they represent were somewhat less than human in their behavior.

Illustrate by Comparison and/or Contrast

This method of developing a paragraph can take one of three forms, depending on the topic idea and the purpose of the writer:

a) showing comparisons or similarities
b) showing contrasts or dissimilarities
c) showing both comparisons and contrasts

As you can see, the third is a combination of the first two methods. This approach is especially useful when describing abstract ideas.

Give Reasons

The paragraph that uses reasons to develop its topic idea will be more effective if the reasons are listed in some logical or dramatic order, not haphazardly. The reasons are listed in increasing order of importance. Since the end of the paragraph–like the end of a sentence, or of an essay, or of a speech–is a high point of emphasis, this order is commonly used and is very effective. A "clincher" sentence is used at the end of the paragraph to restate the topic sentence for greater emphasis.

The Total Composition

Every composition has a clearly defined introduction, body, and conclusion, but these are not labeled as such or set apart when the paper is written.

The introduction should (1) arouse the reader's interest; (2) state the main idea of the composition; and (3) possibly preview the main topics. It contains your thesis statement (see "The Research Paper") and a number of other sentences designed to introduce your topic and let the reader know what the paper is about. This is your road map, guiding you through the rest of your paper until you reach your destination.

The body of the composition must develop, support, and explain the main ideas stated in your introduction, or thesis paragraph. It should include appropriate, specific examples and details to back up your thesis. An outline is essential for a well-constructed paper.

The conclusion of the paper should clinch the main points made in the body of the composition. It pulls together the details of the paper into a final statement, giving a feeling of completeness. It should not contain any new evidence. Depending on your objective, the conclusion may simply summarize your position, emphasize a main point, draw a conclusion, or even spur the reader to action.

However, the best ideas and the most detailed research are all to no avail if the end product, the written paper, is not *well* written, if it does not communicate effectively to the reader. Therefore, the mechanics of composition are of paramount importance to you. The three key words to consider in writing are *unity, coherence,* and *emphasis.*

The principle of unity applies to all components of the paper, to the paragraphs which are the building blocks of the paper like bricks in a wall, and to the paper as a whole. Each paragraph should contain only one thought, with the topic sentence controlling the idea of the whole paragraph. By the same token, each paragraph should develop, explain, or expand on the main point of the composition. Do not wander off on tangents; eliminate anything that does not fulfill your thesis statement.

Following the principle of coherence makes the paper understandable. It has to do with arranging your ideas in a clear order according to a definite plan, with the ideas linked together clearly and expressed in vivid, interesting language. Paragraphs should flow naturally from one to another with ideas arranged in logical order. Smooth transitions from one paragraph to the next are essential for the reader to understand the relationship between the ideas expressed in the individual paragraphs. Therefore transitions could be likened to the mortar holding together the separate building blocks of a wall.

Here are some linking expressions to bridge gaps between paragraphs.

To go from one point to another: finally, moreover, besides, in addition to, another, in the next place, also, furthermore, to sum up.

To indicate another time: next, soon, meanwhile, then, later, finally.

To indicate results: therefore, thus, consequently, as a result.

To show contrast: nevertheless, however, on the other hand, instead, in spite of.

To show relationships: accordingly, similarly, likewise.

To introduce examples: for instance, for example.

Style, the way words are put together, is extremely important in getting ideas across from your mind to your reader's mind. We all use our language in different ways. In everyday conversation we use contractions, slang, colloquialisms, even dialect. This is fine. In addition to our spoken language, we have our written language. When we write letters to friends, or even informal papers, we write in a chatty, informal style. This is fine too. Then there is formal written language. For serious papers informality is totally out of place, so do not use contractions, slang, or colloquial expressions. While avoiding being stodgy or flowery, do be formal or objective in expression, and refrain from using second person (you) or first person (I).

A writer must also be very careful not to be guilty of plagiarism, which is using another person's ideas, words, or even sentence structure as one's own without giving proper credit to the original author.

The third principle of writing concerns emphasis, meaning devoting more space to the more important points and explaining what needs to be explained fully. Put yourself in the reader's place and try to see if another person would have any unanswered questions after reading the paper. Would they really understand what you are trying to say?

It has been said that there is no such thing as good writing, only rewriting. All really great authors polish their works many times. After you have gotten your thoughts down on paper the first time, read it aloud to yourself and listen to what it has to say. Get another person to read it to see if it is understandable to an outsider. After you have reworked the paper for sense and style of writing, go over it again checking your grammar and punctuation. Make a third check just for spelling. After you have copied your paper in its final form, always go over it again proofreading for any copying errors.

Typed papers are always double spaced. If you write by hand, use blue or black ink on one side only of standard notebook paper.

Put the title in the center of the first line. Do not underline it or put it in quotes. Skip a line and begin the paper proper, indenting paragraphs one-half inch. Leave a margin on the left side to coincide with the red line of the notebook paper (about one and one-half inches). Leave a margin on the right side half the width of the left-hand margin. Do not skip lines between paragraphs and do not write on the last blue line at the bottom of the page. On all pages except the first, begin writing on the first blue line. Do not number the first page of the paper but number all other pages of the paper proper in the upper right-hand corner. Outline, end notes, and bibliography pages are not numbered. Never turn in a paper containing crossed-out words. For an example of a title page, see the model at the end of "The Research Paper."

CHAPTER TWO

SPECIAL COMPOSITIONS

Written communication falls into four kinds of writing: exposition, argument, description, and narration. Expository writing is to inform or explain. Argument is used to persuade by reason and/or emotion. Description paints a picture appealing to the five senses. Narration gives an account of action or events.

Probably more than 95 percent of contemporary writing is expository for it includes most scientific and technical books, textbooks, philosophical and political tracts (when not contentious), much of biography and history, the bulk of magazine writing, recipes and formulas, essays and editorials, and reviews and criticism, whether of art, music, or literature. Patches of exposition may be found also in argumentation, narration, and description. When a debater pauses to explain or clarify a situation, the temporary digression may serve to strengthen his case. He is then no longer contending for a point but is engaging in exposition. If the author of a detective story pauses to discuss the layout of the apartment in which the crime occurs he is similarly engaged in exposition. In a book like Rachel Carson's *The Sea Around Us,* the text is about evenly divided among narration, description, and exposition.

Since expository writing is so important, we will go into detail about some specific kinds: the research paper, the book report (or review), the précis, and the science project report.

THE RESEARCH PAPER

A research (or library or term) paper is a documented prose work resulting from an organized analysis of a subject. It presents the results of careful investigation of some chosen topic in an interesting, orderly, and clear manner. It is an original paper by a student who has searched with intelligence through varied sources, selecting facts that he recognizes as essential to his stated subject. The student takes a relevant idea from one author, a telling quotation from another and, having gathered together a body of such information, will then, by using his imagination and knowledge, create something new. It is written in his own words unless a direct quotation is attributed to its original author.

STEPS TO FOLLOW

1. CHOOSE, THEN LIMIT YOUR SUBJECT. You will do best with a subject that interests you, that you can understand, that has sufficient information available about it, that is limited in its scope so that it can be covered adequately in a paper of the assigned length.

2. SURVEY YOUR RESOURCES. Check the card catalog of the library for books dealing with

your proposed topic. Determining the key word to look under is a basic problem in library research. No matter what library tool you use—card catalog, *Readers' Guide,* indexes to books—you must ask yourself this question: "What key word will lead me to the information I seek?" The same key word does not always apply to every reference tool. For instance, the *Readers' Guide* may use "Impeachment," while the card catalog may use "Presidents—U.S.—Impeachment." Remember the topic may encompass many subject headings. For instance, the broad subject of "Crime and Criminals" would include these subject headings and many more: Crime prevention; Criminal law; Administration of justice; Juvenile delinquency; Murder; Organized crime; Police; Prisons; Punishment; Racketeering; Social ethics, etc.

Write down the call numbers for books you think you could use, then go to the shelves to find them. Look at books with similar call numbers. Scan tables of contents to see what the books are about. In the card catalog also note references to pamphlets and clippings in the library's Vertical File and to nonbook materials such as filmstrips and multimedia kits. Consider knowledgeable people in the field to interview. Systematically look at the various issues of the *Readers' Guide,* checking off each volume as you finish it.

3. MAKE A PRELIMINARY STATEMENT OF OBJECTIVE (THESIS STATEMENT). At some point during your survey of resources, you may find there is not enough information on your topic. Change topics immediately. If you find much information, you will need to narrow it very soon, but surveying your resources helps you see the different facets of the topic, to help with your narrowing decision. But very soon you must focus in on your chosen objective in order to find all you need to know about it and not to waste time on information not essential to it. Making a preliminary thesis statement helps keep you on track.

Possible topics:

The Supreme Court—No! Impossibly broad!

Recent Supreme Court Decisions—No! Still impossible!

Supreme Court Decisions Pertaining to School Desegregation—Still too big!

The Effect of Supreme Court Decisions on Nashville Schools—OK.

Thesis Statement: Dramatic changes in the structure of Nashville's school system occurred in the 1950s, in 1971, and in 1983 as a result of Supreme Court decisions.

4. MAKE A WORKING BIBLIOGRAPHY. Once you have settled on what you are looking for, it is time to begin gathering material in earnest. Set up a Working Bibliography on a sheet of notebook paper listing everything that might possibly be of use to you. Here you copy all magazine articles exactly as the information is given you in the *Readers' Guide.* Make notations of those unavailable in your school library so you can check the public library. Scratch off those that prove useless. Enter all books, pamphlets, nonbook materials, people. The Working Bibliography is a good place to list all the varied subject headings you need to check to find available material. This is a valuable tool, so preserve it carefully until you have finished your paper.

5. SCAN YOUR MATERIAL. As you find information, glance through it quickly to see if it contains information you want. You must understand the material and then translate it into an intelligible presentation of your own. Ask yourself, "What is the author trying to say?" "What are the main points he is trying to make?" If the answers to these questions have a bearing on your thesis, prepare to go over the material more thoroughly.

6. MAKE A BIBLIOGRAPHY CARD, separate, complete, and accurate, for each source of information you consult. Do this before you take any notes from that source and keep your master bibliography cards separate from your note cards.

For a book, get your information from the title page and, if no date is listed there, the copyright date from the back of the title page. Book information includes author (full name, last name first), title, place of publication, publisher, and date.

For a magazine you must have the author of the article (if any); name of magazine; its volume number in arabic numerals; its date; and the pages the article is found on, such as pp. 37–41.

7. TAKE GOOD NOTES. If they are prepared properly, writing the paper is relatively easy, and you should not have to consult your sources again. Follow this procedure:

(a) write on 3 x 5 or 4 x 6 cards;

(b) write on one side of the card only;

(c) put only one idea from one source to a card;

(d) include on each card four things—(1) a slug, identification of the specific subject treated on the card; (2) the source, shortened title or author's name so you can tell where the information came from; (3) your notes; (4) the exact page where the material appears.

Do not write down obvious, easily remembered,

well known, or general information. As you read, stop to think what the main idea is. Close your eyes and say it in your own words. Write the notation on the notecard. Check back to see that you have understood the idea correctly. Be careful to avoid misrepresentation by lifting material out of context or by twisting the interpretation to suit your own conclusion. Put the information in your own words, never using words in the book. However, if you think you would like to quote the material from your source, copy it exactly and enclose it in quotation marks.

Here are samples of a bibliography card and a note card made from it.

> Muir, Frank
> Christmas Customs & Traditions
> New York, Taplinger Publishing Company
> 1975

> Preparations - Cookery Muir
> Stir Up Sunday - Sun. before Advent
> last time to make Christmas
> pudding to be ready in time.
> p.22 Gets name from Church Collect for
> that day which begins "Stir up
> we beseech thee, O Lord, the wills of
> thy faithful people...."

8. During this reading process, MAKE A PRELIMINARY OUTLINE, so you can see exactly what information you need on various points and how much you will need. (See "Outlining.") Outline topics make good slugs for notecards.

9. CONTINUE READING AND NOTE TAKING. Remember the outline is like a skeleton which your paper will flesh out. The preliminary outline may show that your skeleton lacks an arm, or one arm is much smaller than the other. Your reading and note taking now can fill in what the outline revealed was needed.

10. MAKE UP AN INTERESTING TITLE.

11. WRITE YOUR THESIS STATEMENT IN ITS FINAL FORM. Remember the thesis tells exactly what your paper is about, what it is to cover; and the outline shows how you accomplish the objective of the thesis. In the preliminary stages you may need to adjust both the original thesis and the original outline. Now is the time to get your thesis in precise final form. Play with words, work to express your thesis so it will convey exactly the ideas you want it to in an interesting manner.

12. REVISE OUTLINE into its final form.

13. WRITE AN INTERESTING INTRODUCTION that (1) attracts the reader's attention; (2) states what the paper is about; and (3) previews the main topics. Incorporate your thesis in the introduction.

14. SORT YOUR NOTE CARDS to conform to your outline. Write the paper in your words using formal, objective style. Avoid the use of "you" and "I." The research paper is not an informal essay, although you need to make it interesting and may use imagination in making deductions and drawing conclusions.

Have your end note page beside you and make your end notes as you write. Be specific but do not worry about exact form at this time, as you can go back and set your end notes in precise form later. Just be sure your numbers coincide. End note[1] in your paper must refer to [1]on your end note page.

Even though you are writing in your own words, you have used information supplied by others. You will also want to use direct quotations (but only sparingly, to emphasize an important point or as proof of your conclusions). These must be acknowledged. Use a footnote or an end note to give credit for a direct quotation; to give credit for an original or unusually interesting opinion or interpretation which you have put in your own words; to give credit for all statistics, figures, definitions, illustrations. The question always arises, "Since I knew nothing about this subject before researching it, do I have to footnote every piece of information used?" Obviously that would be impractical. If the ideas seem to be general knowledge of authorities in the field, do not footnote unless you are quoting exactly. (See "Endnoting/Footnoting" for exact details.)

Direct quotations are handled in two different ways. For a short quotation (one that would be four typed lines or less) enclose it in quotation marks and "work it in smoothly as part of your own sentence."[1]

A long quotation (one that is five lines or more of type) should be handled this way:

Double-space (or skip a line of notebook paper) above and below the quotation. Single-space the quotation if you are typing. Indent the quoted material an extra half-inch on each side. Do not use quotation marks around it. Remember always at the end of a quotation, whether it is short or long, that you must put a number slightly above the line to refer to the same number in your footnotes.[2]

15. WRITE A GOOD CONCLUSION that rounds out your paper, sums it up, gives a feeling of completeness.

16. REVISE YOUR PAPER.

17. COPY YOUR PAPER, then proofread for copying errors. Doublecheck footnotes for accuracy and for form.

18. MAKE YOUR BIBLIOGRAPHY. Arrange your bibliography cards alphabetically according to the author's last name. If there is no author, alphabetize by the first word of the title (skipping "A," "An," and "The." If the reference is published by an organization with no author, use the organization as author. Make your bibliography according to the prescribed forms. Often teachers want you to include in your bibliography only the sources you actually used in writing the paper, not a complete listing of sources you may have consulted. (See "Bibliography.")

19. MAKE THE TITLE PAGE. (See form.)

20. ASSEMBLE THE PAPER. The usual order is: (1) title page; (2) outline, which substitutes for a table of contents in a school paper; (3) the paper itself; (4) end notes; (5) bibliography.

ABBREVIATIONS

Common abbreviations found in doing research are:

ca., c.	about (circa)
ch., chs.	chapter, chapters
cf.	compare, confer
et al.	and others (**et alii** or **alibi**)
ed.	edited, edition, editor
e.g.	for example (**exempli gratia**)
f., ff.	and the following page, pages
illus.	illustrated
ibid.	in the same place (**ibidem**) (obsolete)
id.	the same (**idem**)
l., ll.	line, lines
i.e.	that is (**id est**)
loc. cit.	in the place cited (**loco citato**) (obsolete)
lit.	literally
MS, MSS	Manuscript, Manuscripts
N.B.	note well (**nota bene**)
n.d.	no date given
no., nos.	number, numbers
op. cit.	in the work cited (**opere citato**) (obsolete)
p., pp.	page, pages
trans.	translator/translation
viz.	namely
vol., vols.	volume, volumes

OUTLINING

An outline is to a paper what a road map is to a journey. The thesis statement states your destination, and the outline shows you how to get there. Thesis: I am going to Yazoo City, Mississippi, from Nashville, Tennessee. Outline: Take I-40 to Memphis; then I-55 toward Jackson; at Exit 181 go west on Highway 16. . . . The purpose of outlining is to prevent wandering off the subject; to give a quick overall view of the essay; to insure proportionate space to each part; to aid in organizing and giving order to the essay; to enable you to spot missing or irrelevant matter. Some ways to organize are: by time, by space, by likenesses and differences, in order of importance, by cause and effect.

An outline includes only main ideas and important details. Flesh in the outline when you write the paper.

There must always be under any topic more than one subtopic. Subtopics are divisions of the topic above them, and you cannot divide anything into fewer than two parts. If you find yourself wanting to use a single subtopic, rewrite the topic above it so that this "sub idea" is included in the main topic.

Wrong: C. Hostesses
        1. Those who nag
Right: C. Nagging Hostesses

A subtopic must belong under the main topic beneath which it is placed. It must be closely related to the topic above it.

Wrong: A. Dull games
        1. Bingo
        2. Not enough refreshments

Terms such as "Introduction," "Body," and "Conclusion" should not be included in the outline. Of course, you should have them as definite parts of your paper (though never so designated) but these are not topics that you intend to discuss.

There are two kinds of outlines, the topic and the sentence. The topic is composed of words or phrases throughout all divisions. It is used for conciseness and brevity, and no end punctuation is needed. A sentence outline uses sentences throughout its divisions, so end punctuation is needed. It is fuller, clearer, and more exact than a topic outline.

How to Prepare an Outline

To outline a chapter in a book is easy because the information was outlined before it was written. The difficult part of outlining is taking a large body of information and organizing it into a logical, coherent form. Here are some tips to help you do this for your research paper. Notice it is in sentence outline form.

I. Select the subject of your paper.
  A. Decide on a general topic.
    1. Survey available resources.
    2. Note the various aspects of the subject.
  B. Limit your topic to a narrow aspect that can be adequately covered in a paper of your designated length.
  C. Write a thesis statement that exactly pinpoints your objective.

II. Make a rough draft of your outline.
  A. Jot down at random all the points about your paper that come to mind.
  B. Group similar ones together.
  C. Decide what pattern would be best to follow.
    1. It could be chronological.
    2. It could be spatial (geographical).
    3. It could be a study of contrasts or comparisons.
    4. It could be cause-and-effect.
    5. It could be a study of influences.
  D. Write a simple topic outline.
    1. Choose two to four most important points for the major divisions.
    2. Place remaining ideas as subtopics under them.
  E. Assess the result.
    1. Consider if you are fulfilling your thesis statement.
    2. Consider if you have covered the subject adequately.
    3. Check to see that each subtopic falls logically under its larger topic.
    4. Eliminate any material that does not fit.
      (a) This means irrelevant matter.
      (b) This means unnecessary (too detailed) matter for an outline.
    5. Determine if you need to look for additional information.
      (a) Should this information be for an added topic?
      (b) Should it be to expand on an existing topic?

III. Write the outline in final sentence form.
  A. Word the main topics to make them concise, clear, and parallel.*
  B. Fill in the subtopics by the same criteria.
  C. See that the outline is in correct outline form.

* Parallelism means using similar wording for various divisions of equal rank. Here is a topic outline illustrating this.

Wrong
How to Do the Laundry
I. Sorting by colors
II. To start the machine
III. Proper water temperature
IV. How to handle delicate fabrics

Right
How to Do the Laundry
I. Sorting by colors
II. Starting the machine
III. Choosing proper water temperature
IV. Handling delicate fabrics

Picture of an Outline

Title of Paper

Thesis Statement: . . . .
I. Major division
  A. Subdivision
    1. Sub-subdivision
      a.
        (1)
          (a)
          (b)
        (2)
      b.
    2.
  B.
II.

FOOTNOTING/ENDNOTING

The distinction has been made that footnotes are properly used in dissertations and end notes are to be used in research papers. The difference is that footnotes appear at the bottom of the page containing the cited material, while end notes are arranged on one or two pages at the end of the paper. It is much easier to do end notes because in footnotes the writing has to be spaced very carefully to allow sufficient room at the bottom of the page. Teachers vary in which they require. People generally speak of footnotes to mean both those at the foot of the page and those at the end of the paper.

These instructions are for end notes.

* Number them consecutively throughout the paper.

* In the body of your paper put a number slightly above the line *at the end* of the material to be acknowledged. No period follows an end note number.

* On your end note page put the same number as its corresponding number in the paper (again above the line and without a period). Indent the first line of each end note and start the second line even with the left margin.

* The author's *given name* should be written *first.*

When the same source is repeated, it is not necessary to give the full information about that source a second time. Use a shortened form to identify the reference. Formerly Latin terms such as "ibid.," "op. cit.," and "loc. cit." were used. These are now considered obsolete. When the same source is used a second or subsequent time, simply write the end note number, then the author's last name, and then the page number on which the material can be found.

If you have made your bibliography cards properly, you will have there all the information you will need for your end notes, except for the exact page on which that bit of material was found, which will be on your note card. Never end note for several pages in a source; the only time you would indicate two pages is when the sentence on the source page runs over onto a second page.

Examples of End Notes

(First use of book by one author)

[1]Robert W. Kirk, *First Aid for Pets* (New York: E. P. Dutton, 1978), p. 40.

(Second and subsequent uses of preceding book)

[2]Kirk, p. 41.

(First use of book by two authors)

[3]Mary Bray Wheeler and Genon Hickerson Neblett, *Hidden Glory: The Life and Times of Hampton Plantation, Legend of the South Santee* (Nashville: Rutledge Hill Press, 1983), pp. 21-22.

(For a book with no author)

[4]*Webster's Geographical Dictionary* (Springfield: G. & C. Merriam Co., 1981), p. 535.

(For an organization as author)

[5]U.S. Department of Commerce, Bureau of the Census, *Statistical Abstract of the United States 1982-83* (Washington, D.C.: Government Printing Office, 1982), p. 1065.

(For a book with an editor)

[6]Lois Decker O'Neill, ed., *The Women's Book of World Records and Achievements* (New York: Doubleday, 1979), p. 84.

(For a magazine article with an author; note the volume number before the date.)

[7]Michael M. Lombardo, "The Intolerable Boss," *Psychology Today,* 18 (Jan., 1984), p. 45.

(For the same article, second and subsequent quotings)

[8]Lombardo, p. 46.

(For a magazine article with no author)

[9]"The Muffin-Mix Scare," *Time,* 123 (Feb. 13, 1984), p. 20.

(For the same article, second and subsequent quotings)

[10]*Time,* p. 22.*

*If you are quoting from several *different* issues of *Time,* include the date in parentheses: *Time,* (Feb. 13, 1984), p. 22. This will indicate which issue you refer to.

(For a newspaper article with a by-line)

[11]Patricia McCormack, "Special Diet Urged to Thwart Cancer," *Nashville Tennessean* (Feb. 11, 1984), Sec. D, p. 2.

(For a newspaper article with no by-line)

[12]"Moslems Take West Beirut," *Nashville Banner* (Feb. 8, 1984), Sec. A., p. 1.

(For an encyclopedia article)

[13]"Jet Propulsion," *World Book Encyclopedia* (1979 ed.), vol. 11, p. 386.

(For an interview)

[14]Richard Fulton, Mayor of Nashville, interviewed by Mary Smith (Metropolitan Courthouse, Nashville, Tenn.), 10 A.M., Jan. 15, 1984.

(For a personal letter)

[15]Personal letter from Lamar Alexander, Governor of Tennessee, to Jason Jones, Feb. 16, 1984.

(For material from one source quoted in another)

[16]James Boswell, *The Life of Samuel Johnson,* quoted by Robert Byrne in *Cat Scan* (New York: Atheneum, 1983), p. 7.

If there are two or more works by the same author, or two or more authors with the same name, a shortened title of the cited work is used after the author's last name. Let us assume you are quoting from two books by Louise Davis, *Nashville Tales* and *Frontier Tales.*

(First citation)

[17]Louise Littleton Davis, *Nashville Tales* (Gretna, LA: Pelican Publishing Co., 1981), p. 35.

(Second citation)

[18]Davis, *Nashville,* p 4.

Notice the differences between the pattern of end notes and of a bibliography. In end notes the arrangement is strictly numerical in the order the material is cited from the work; the author's first name comes first; the first line is indented and the second line is flush with the left-hand margin. In a bibliography the arrangement is alphabetical by the author's last name and the first line is flush with the left-hand margin with the second line being indented. Here is a bibliography of the works cited in the example of footnotes.

BIBLIOGRAPHY

Alexander, Lamar, Governor of Tennessee, to Jason Jones, Feb. 16, 1984.

Byrne, Robert. *Cat Scan.* New York: Atheneum, 1983.

Davis, Louise Littleton. *Frontier Tales.* Gretna, LA: Pelican Publishing Co., 1980.

———, *Nashville Tales.* Gretna, LA: Pelican Publishing Co., 1981.

Fulton, Richard, Mayor of Nashville, interviewd by Mary Smith, Metropolitan Courthouse, Nashville, Tenn., 10 A.M., Jan. 15, 1984.

"Jet Propulsion." *World Book Encyclopedia,* 1979 ed., vol. 11, p. 386.

Kirk, Robert W. *First Aid for Pets.* New York: E. P. Dutton, 1978.

Lombardo, Michael M. "The Intolerable Boss." *Psychology Today,* 18 (Jan., 1984), pp. 45–48.

McCormack, Patricia. "Special Diet Urged to Thwart Cancer." *Nashville Tennessean* (Feb. 8, 1984), Sec. D. p. 2.

"Muffin-Mix Scare." *Time,* 123 (Feb. 13, 1984), pp. 20–21.

O'Neill, Lois Decker, ed. *The Women's Book of World Records and Achievements.* New York: Doubleday, 1979.

U.S. Department of Commerce, Bureau of the Census, *Statistical Abstract of the United States 1982–83.* Washington, D.C.: Government Printing Office, 1982.

Webster's Geographical Dictionary. Springfield: G. & C. Merriam Co., 1981.

Wheeler, Mary Bray, and Neblett, Genon Hickerson. *Hidden Glory: The Life and Times of Hampton Plantation, Legend of the South Santee.* Nashville: Rutledge Hill Press, 1983.

You will find slight variations, especially in punctuation, among the many handbooks available showing forms for footnotes and bibliographies. The important thing for you to do is to choose one source as your model and then be scrupulous in following it exactly so your paper is consistent throughout.

(Sample of Title Page)

RAIN OF DEATH: THE IMPACT OF ACID RAIN

ON NATURAL RESOURCES IN THE UNITED STATES

by

Nathan Elliott

American History, Fourth Period

February 21, 1984

Argumentative Writing

That category of writing which attempts to strengthen a view already held, to weaken or undermine such a view, or to persuade the reader to adopt another is called argumentation. The name, though well established, is unfortunate, for one immediately infers that it involves a contentious type of discussion. Persuasion would be a better name, for the aim is to incline another's will to one's own view rather than to controvert it or break it. The writer who conceives his task as persuasion must also assume (even though he may suspect the contrary to be true) that his reader has not taken a firm position, and, as a reasonable man, would be delighted to follow him into his stand. Therefore, from the very start, he tries to confine his attack, so far as he must attack, to issues rather than to persons. The attitude of the persuader must be understanding and generous. He writes, "It would appear . . . ," "It seems . . ." rather than "It is . . ." or "It must be. . . ."

Analysis of the Question

1. DEFINITION OF TERMS

Should a writer wish to contend that New York City is the true capital of America, he would have to define what he means by his terms. Does he mean "Greater New York," or does he mean the financial district? Does "true" have the same sense as "real"? Is "capital" used as "the governing political center" or the "dominant financial center"? By "America" does he mean the United States, North America, or the Western Hemisphere? It will be observed that until these terms are clarified the issue is confused. The process of clarification which must be undertaken by the writer at the outset is known as "defining the terms."

2. HISTORY OF THE QUESTION

Many issues are of long standing and have been discussed before. If the previous discussion has swayed public opinion in any discernible way, the writer may possibly profit by rehearsing previous discussions if their results favor him. Such a presentation is known as "giving the history of the question." If, on the other hand, he can show that his view has in the past received scant attention, has been rudely treated or suppressed, he may actually profit from rehearsing this history.

3. DETERMINING THE ISSUES

Whenever there is a difference of opinion, the holders of opposing views frequently find themselves separated on a multiplicity of issues, many of which may be extremely trivial. If one urges trivial issues, even successfully, when major issues are decisive, his power to persuade will fail. The best way to determine the major issues is to set up the chief issues for each side and to select the ones that collide most sharply; these are the major issues.

Planning Persuasive Measures

Once he has determined the issues, the writer plans the order in which he will present them. He will have to decide on one of two approaches, depending on whether he feels he can easily overcome opposition or will have to work hard to be persuasive. In the former situation he should choose and present his strongest point first, with the intent of putting his opposition to rout; in the latter, he should study the issues to see if there is not one that may be conceded to him without too great a struggle, and use that as an entering wedge. To persuade successfully one must consider every possible factor that can be turned to advantage, but yet must avoid seeming to do so. The tone of persuasion should be concessive, generous.

Briefing

If the issue involves grave consequences or the opposition is entrenched and well armed, it is wise to prepare a formal brief, covering the major issues and indicating the proof to be supplied. The practice of briefing, incidentally, provides an excellent discipline for the reasoning faculties. The form is well established and should be conscientiously adhered to:

The United States should support the U.N., *for*

I. It is the major instrument for world peace, *for*
   A. Balance of power is impossible, *for*
      1. Unilateral action can undermine the balance, *for*
         a. China does not accept Russian leadership in the East.
         b. France is uncooperative in the West.

B. Treaties are good only so long as the parties will honor them.
C. Neutral nations within the organization are a deterrent to immoral action.

II. It is a major instrument for social betterment, *for*
A. Its agencies combat disease and crime, etc.

Proof

1. TESTIMONIAL EVIDENCE

Once the writer has outlined his case, either in his own mind or in a formal brief, his next step is to muster the best proofs of his arguments that he can summon. Such proof is called evidence, and of evidence there are two kinds, testimonial and circumstantial. The first is the evidence of persons or witnesses; the second is that of the facts in the case.

Testimonial evidence is persuasive to the degree that the fairness and credibility of the witness may not be impugned. If the witness has something to gain from his testimony, its value is greatly reduced; in fact, it may be disproportionately reduced if the fact is discovered first by the opposition. The best witness is one who has no personal motivation in his testimony. In certain instances, in order to be judged reliable a witness should have no physical or mental handicaps. If a motorist has driven through a red light, and it can be shown that the only witness to his act is color blind, the case against him may be dismissed. Witnesses may be called upon to estimate the alleged speed of a traveling car, but if they cannot judge distances approximately in the courtroom their evidence may be impugned. The testimony of a witness may be impaired by showing that his morality is suspect because of some past dereliction, for while it is open to question whether a man who has stolen will lie, the world is all too ready to suspect that he will.

Whenever an issue involves special technical or scientific knowledge, it is customary to solicit the testimony of experts. In technical language, this is known as *the appeal to authority.* If responsibility in a boiler explosion is an issue, the testimony of an engineer is obviously worth more than that of a ribbon clerk, but if the quality of yardgoods is in question, the clerk, particularly if he is also a buyer for the store, is the better witness. The appeal to authority may also be invoked to summon the expert testimony of those dead and revered, as for example that of John Marshall (Chief Justice of the United States, 1801-1935) on constitutional questions. But so far as the expert testimony is concerned, it must be remembered that it is good only in the field of competency.

2. CIRCUMSTANTIAL EVIDENCE

Circumstantial evidence is evidence from the facts, but it is evidence from the facts as determined by human reasoning. One car, out of control, collides with another, catapulting its occupant into the street. An eyewitness may testify that the victim is a casualty of reckless driving, but it is disclosed that the victim, an elderly man and quite ill, was being driven to a hospital, and an autopsy reveals that he had been dead some time when the accident occurred. The facts of the autopsy, especially the blood clot closing the aorta, are interpreted as more convincing than the testimony of the eyewitness, though they are all circumstantial facts. (The illustration is a mixed one, for here the facts are presented by a physician and are reinforced by his authority; nevertheless, the court acts on his arrangement of them.) A man caught near the scene of a crime with a recently fired revolver of the same caliber as that of a bullet extracted from the body of the slain man has an impressive array of facts against him, despite a lack of any witness to the shooting. If we conclude he is guilty of the crime, our conclusion is based wholly on our reasoning from the facts. There may be others, however, that we have not taken into consideration. What if he was a friend of the victim who had picked up the murderer's gun and was searching for him? It must ever be kept in mind that in large areas of human experience circumstantical evidence at best produces only a "reasonable certainty."

3. TESTING CAUSAL RELATIONSHIPS

The initial presumptions that both the driver of the car out of control and the friend with the murderer's weapon in his hand were guilty are based upon one of the most fundamental tenets of all human thinking; namely, that nothing takes place without a cause. When the mind deals with an effect (natural death, in the first instance, and violent death, in the second) and searches for its cause, it is likely to commit certain well-known errors. The situation may be searched from the other direction, that is, from cause to effect. First, we may ask if the assumed cause was adequate to produce the effect. In both instances that we have hypothesized, it was; hence, the ready conclusion of guilt. Second, we may ask if the assumed cause is the only cause that could have operated. We have seen that, in each instance, it was not. When we are arguing that a certain cause will produce a "known" effect, we have these variants of the common errors to consider: Is the cause strong enough in this instance to produce the effect? May not some other cause intervene in the relationship?

The Argument from Analogy

Nothing is more enticing to a thinker bent on persuasion than the argument from analogy. It is based on the presumption that if two things have some elements in common, they have others also–a presumption which, of course, does not necessarily follow. Just as persons are always seeing family resemblances, they are quick to apprehend resemblances between things or situations.

There are two tests of real value with an analogy: (1) Are the resemblances really essential or vital resemblances? and (2) Despite the resemblances between the things compared, are there still more important differences between them? Dissenting from the relief measures that Franklin D. Roosevelt put into effect, William Allen White wrote, "If I was the underdog, I should bury my bones against the day of hunger." Mr. White believed that Roosevelt did not understand the "underdog" and, hence, would abandon him. Unfortunately for his analogy, many of the underdogs had no bones to bury, save those that Roosevelt's measures provided.

Generalizing Processes

1. INDUCTION

Every person who reasons inevitably generalizes. After discovering that a law operates in several examples of a kind, the mind finds it an enormous convenience to assume that it operates in all examples of that kind. When a scientist draws a conclusion from a reasonable number of cases, it is called an *induction*. We must remember, however, that there are few perfect inductions, that is, not *all* cases have been surveyed or could be surveyed.

There are four tests that an induction may be subjected to: Is the relative number of the instances observed, as compared with those unobserved, sufficiently large? Are the observed instances fair examples? Are there no invalidating exceptions? Is there an initial probability that the generalization is true?

2. DEDUCTION

It is a general assumption that all science is a product of the inductive method, but scientists frequently imply that the discovery or law was a "hunch" or generalization for which the proof had later to be found by laborious investigation. Be that as it may, there is an almost equal tendency to assume generalizations and to find the assumed law operating in the instance under discussion. This process is called deduction. It is possible to state all deductions in this form, known as a *syllogism:*

All iron objects are subject to oxidation.
A steel rail is an iron object.
Therefore, a steel rail is subject to oxidation.

In the above syllogism, the statement "All iron objects are subject to oxidation" is called *the major premise;* "A steel rail is an iron object," *the minor premise;* and "Therefore, a steel rail is subject to oxidation," *the conclusion.* Mere ability to put a deduction in syllogistic form, however, does not guarantee its validity. Thus, for example:

All men are liars *(major premise).*
Green is a man *(minor premise).*
Therefore, Green is a liar *(conclusion).*

This syllogism is completely correct *if* we accept the major premise. But the major premise is the result of a previous faulty induction.

The ancients discovered that the syllogistic statement could be readily tested for its validity. It must conform to these rules:

a. Every syllogism has three, and only three, terms.

b. Every syllogism contains three, and only three, propositions or statements.

c. The middle term must be distributed (that is, universally applied), once at least, and must not be ambiguous.

d. No term must be distributed in the conclusion which was not distributed in one of the premises.

e. From negative premises nothing can be inferred.

f. If one premise is negative, the conclusion must be negative; and vice versa, to prove a negative conclusion one of the premises must be negative.

g. From two particular premises no conclusion can be drawn.

h. If one premise be particular, the conclusion must be particular.

A *term* denotes an individual or group of individuals or an attribute or a group of attributes. Thus in the syllogism attempting to show Green a liar, the terms are men (man), liars (liar), and Green. The *middle term* is the term which does not appear in the conclusion. With the help of a book on logic, or without it by trial and error, one may discover the complete validity of these rules.

The Common Fallacies

Thus far we have examined errors which occur in logical processes of reasoning, but a person engaged in the process of persuasion may adopt one of two illogical processes of reasoning and be quite unaware that they are illogical processes. Indeed, in practice they may each prove quite effective until an opponent exposes them. They are the common fallacies of *ignoring the question* and of *begging the question.*

1. IGNORING THE QUESTION

A writer ignores the question by substituting an issue which appears to be the same as the one under discussion. Because every writer becomes identified with the cause for which he stands, one of the commonest exhibitions of this fallacy occurs whenever an opponent attacks the writer, rather than his cause or the real issue under discussion.

2. BEGGING THE QUESTION

Whenever a reasoner assumes as true the thing which he is trying to establish, he is said to beg the question. Two forms of this fallacy are common: first, using question-begging epithets, and second, arguing in a circle. The first of these errors is regularly indulged in by impassioned or dishonest propagandists. When one writes, "In the *decadent* South a Negro can expect *no* justice from the *brutal* police," he is really begging the question; purged of these epithets, the proposition should read: In Chicago, Detroit, New York, or the South, the Negro can expect little justice from the police.

Refutation

In formal debate, replying to an opponent is usually left to the rebuttal speeches, though in presenting his case the debater may anticipate counterarguments. In a persuasive article there is no opportunity for rebuttal; hence the anticipation must be complete. Experienced writers know, as a rule, what may be offered in opposition to their views. Yielding an unimportant issue creates an impression of a judicious, a reasonable mind. It is in refutation that the reasoner probably should be most conscious, not of his ability to contend, but of his ability to persuade. Even if there is no chance of this with a dogmatic opponent, the persuasive attitude may win over more undecided listeners and readers than the dogmatism of the opponent. The successful reasoner treats his opponent with respect.

Narrative Writing

That form of writing which presents an event or a sequence of events involving animate beings is called narrative writing. While usually the actors in such a narrative are human beings, narrative writing is not restricted to their participation. The range of actors may be from insects and animals to trolls and fairies, to mechanical creatures and visitors from other planets. One thinks of the fat spider which disturbed little Miss Muffet, the boll weevil, Br'er Rabbit, Donald Duck, the Three Bears, the Rat-Wife, the Snow Princess, Superman, Tommy Tractor, Frankenstein, and the Man from Mars, whose antics may, or may not, bear some resemblance to human behavior. They do, however, have the capacity to carry the reader through an event or series of episodes, a characteristic which represents the primary function of characters in narrative writing.

Simple Narrative

The simplest event that can occur presents an actor in a role that is to some slight degree worth remarking. The commonest form of this narrative is the anecdote; the more familiar the actor, the less the writer has to supply by way of characterization. In repeating the legend of Newton's discovery of the law of gravitation from the falling apple which struck him on the head, the writer can count on persons' generally knowing who Newton was. Elaboration turns an anecdote into a narrative allusion or after-dinner story. A narrative anecdote–it need not be true–that strikes at some foible in human behavior or belief is usually well received.

Fictional Narrative

Characters

To assure plausibility in a fictional narrative, start with the persons to be involved in the action. Ivan Turgenev, the Russian novelist, told the young Henry James that his fictions began "*always* with the vision of some person or persons, who hovered before him, soliciting him, as the active or passive figure, interesting him and appealing to him *just as they were and by what they were*" [italics ours]. That is, Turgenev started with a real person and transferred that person with his or her potentialities to his book. No procedure more surely guarantees plausibility than this one, for once the character is established he or she can do nothing "out of character"–both the artist and his reader would be instantly aware of the inconsistency. An axiomatic statement in fiction is, "Character governs action."

Plot

The persons in a work of fiction should determine the action; if they do not, it will not move. If three persons are placed together and two of them have traits that clash, the third is either bound to take sides or disintegrate, either through his effort to remain neutral or shift sides–and a "plot" is born. Imposing a plot on characters already assembled leads to distortion, unnaturalness, and eventually to implausibility. Increasing the number of characters usually multiplies the possibility of plot intricacy because of the alignment of loyalties. There are only two restrictions on the ramifications of plot: (1) The behavior of the characters must be wholly consistent with their natures, and (2) the high cost of typesetting limits the extent of any story. For the latter reason, three-volume novels and twenty-thousand-word short stories are not the fashion of the twentieth century, though they were common enough in the nineteenth.

All conflicts in life move toward either stalemate or some sort of resolution, but in fiction they must move toward resolution. The ultimate clash of forces we term the *climax* of the tale; the results or consequences of this collision we call the *dénouement*. It is the highest art to make this as brief as possible.

Setting

The leisurely novel of the nineteenth century took much pains to set the stage fully for the action of its story. Frequently these novels began with a descriptive passage on which the author expended much conscious art.

But few writers could afford it today. Forced to economize, they have done so by eliminating extended descriptions of their stages. Instead they give the details of their settings as they proceed with their narratives. Scattering graphic bits of description through the narrative seems the best way to impress upon the reader with the greatest economy of means the setting for modern narrative. In order to impart a real sense of the scene, the writer should prepare a good many notes on his setting in order to select from among them.

Point of View

After a writer has chosen his characters, determined the nature of the conflict among them (even perhaps imagined the course of his plot), and determined where the events of his narrative will take place, he still must ask himself an important question: From what point of view shall I tell this story? He must follow this in his mind by other questions: Should the narrator be outside the tale? Should he know everything that takes place?

Should he be a participant in the action? Should he be a major figure or a minor figure? Should he be a limited or prejudiced observer?

If the narrator is to be outside the tale, he may definitely be identified with the author. Both Fielding and Thackeray do this and are frankly partisan in the conflicts which they imagine. The advantage of this point of view is that converts are more readily made to the author's views; but the limitations are those of partisanship–the intruding voice, the sense of manipulated characters. Because of these intrusions the narrative is always fiction–it loses a degree of verisimilitude; it becomes something less than life, whereas, if art is selective, it should be something more than life. Another choice from outside the action is to adopt what is known as the "omniscient" point of view. Still another choice remains–to plant a spectator on the periphery of the tale to report what goes on.

The recent tendency of writers of fiction seems to be to locate the point of view "in" one of the participants in action in the tale, either a major or a minor character. The author may identify with the hero of the tale and become this "I" narrator of his own adventure. The merit of this is its immediacy; it has, however, the grave limitation of closing to the reader the emotions and thoughts (save as they are overt) of other characters in the tale. And what is more boring than one who talks all the time?

Dialogue

Just as character determines the action in a narrative, so also character determines the dialogue. Relations between characters define what they will express and what they will repress. The talk must advance the story, and it does this either by revealing hidden motives or by suggesting aims and devices. The author has to remember also that a character can divine more than is said from what is unskillfully repressed. To expose the play of mind on mind is one of the most exciting challenges of a writer's career. No talk in good narrative should be pointless.

Description

That form of writing which depicts objects, living things, and the static elements in fantasies is called *description.* It is the vehicle through which we become acquainted with the world, its animals and machines, and the furnishings of its dreams and visions.

Independent Description

Required to write a description of a given thing, the writer should ask himself for whom he is describing it. If he is a professional writer preparing material for a wholesale hardware magazine distributed to retailers, he may assume some knowledge of his object or device, but if he is the same writer describing the same device for the general catalog of a mail order house, he can assume very little; he also has the limitation of space since so many objects are presented through his medium. The amount of description will be further reduced if the catalog uses illustrations and formulas, but his familiarity must include these to compensate for what is not depicted or formularized. The householder without experience may write as good an advertisement of the home he wishes to sell as would the real estate agent (he should; he knows it better) but he does not know so well the purchaser or what will appeal to that purchaser.

Contributory Description

Skill in descriptive writing makes for interest in horticultural books, pleas for the preservation of wildlife, travel literature, and adventure stories, though these works may be chiefly narrative or persuasive. As with independent description, it is helpful to the reader to discover in an involved description a familiar image that will help him to see the scene with his mind's eye.

Long descriptive passages in fictional narrative are not so frequent today as they once were. The fiction writer manages to weave more of his descriptive detail into his narrative as it proceeds. The device is an old one; it is merely utilized more commonly now.

The Book Report/Review

Three conventional ways of writing about books are: (1) book reports, (2) book reviews, and (3) literary criticism. The book report is the traditional method whereby a teacher checks to see that an assignment has been completed and understood. It is the most elementary form. The third type, literary criticism, is an analysis, evaluation and judgment, presupposing critical knowledge on the part of the critic and the reader. You can work up to this.

The second type, the book review, is about halfway between the two, combining elements of both of the other types. Its purpose is (a) to inform the readership that a certain book is available; (b) to tell enough about the book to whet the appetite for someone to want to read it or to allow the reader to decide that he does not want to read it; (c) to make some judgment about its merit, although many reviewers are not acknowledged literary critics.

Students in elementary and middle schools need a lot of practice in doing book reports so when they reach high school they can move up into reviewing and make a good start toward real critiquing.

The way to approach writing a standard book report varies depending on the kind of book and the teacher's objective in making the assignment, so the teacher will often give specific guidelines to follow. However, there are many helpful hints the wise student will utilize which can make the difference between an "A" and a "C" report.

Many different kinds of short compositions can be used as book reports and are more interesting than a mere retelling of the story. Some suggestions include having the student write a sequel or a different ending to the story. The pupil can write an eyewitness report of a major event in the book, describing events from his point of view. Letter writing is an interesting approach where the student addresses one of the characters. Perhaps the student would like to transform the characters into animals and explain why he or she is similar to the animal selected. There are many new approaches to writing a book report that are limited only by the student's creativity and imagination.

In addition there are many ways to add appeal to a book report. A variety of projects serve to illustrate characters, plot, theme and so on. These visual aids are fun for the students, making reading more enjoyable. Here are some suggestions:

1. Make a poster including scenes from the story. Magazines and periodicals can provide material or the student can draw pictures of the setting, costumes or action of the story.

2. Construct a mobile showing various aspects of the story. Cut out the pieces from heavy paper or cardboard and color them.

3. Illustrate the sequence of events on a time line. This is especially adaptable for books about history. Time lines can be three-dimensional and set up on a table. The student's written report should carefully follow the sequence of events.

4. Show the setting of a book by making a travel brochure. A report on a history book should note points of interest, historical homes, good restaurants, taverns or inns, all mentioned in the story. This idea can be adapted for science books about exotic animals or unusual tribes by showing their origins.

5. The student may wish to provide original illustrations for the book. A series of pictures can be painted on heavy paper or butcher paper. A cartoon format is interesting and can be mounted on the classroom wall.

6. Stage sets can be made in boxes. Doll house furniture and pipe cleaner figures illustrate the setting and characters. Trees cut from sponges and paper mache hills make an outdoor scene. Students must read the book carefully in order to construct accurate representations of the setting.

Keep in mind always that a book report is a hybrid, part fact and part fancy. It gives hard information about the book, yet it is your own creation, giving your opinion and judgment of it. Any report should tell at the beginning the author's full name, the title, the publisher, and the date of publication. It also makes very clear exactly what kind of book is being reviewed (fiction, or biography, or factual book about science, current events, history, etc.). Each type is judged by different standards which will be discussed later.

But no matter what kind of book is read, good book reporters and good book reviewers always read with the review constantly in the back of their minds. They mark in the book (if it belongs to them) or they make notes as they read to help them remember important things they want to say about the book and to help them find pertinent passages to quote in the review.

And they read imaginatively which is a skill that

is necessary to complete the act of writing, for the greatest work ever written is only a piece of paper until a reader reacts to it. The reader actually helps create literature by responding to what the writer has to say. A thoughtful and imaginative reader considers both what the writer tries to say and how he says it. This gives him or her greater enjoyment in reading, and the critical skills develop with use, just as muscles do.

Usually when you finish a book you have a feeling. It may be of sorrow that the book has ended, or of satisfaction, or even of exhilaration. It may be a let-down feeling or plain indifference. Before you lose these emotions, before they fade away, jot down random notes capturing these reactions to the book. Then let your thoughts simmer on the back burner before actually writing the review.

The following is an example of a report written as a news story. The student chose a book about the Wright brothers, inventors of the airplane. There are guidelines to writing a news story. First, give all the facts, including exact names of people and places (traditionally this is done by answering the questions: who, what, when, where, why and how). Tell the events in the order of their importance, using direct quotations accurately. A short eye-catching headline is important.

← KITTY HAWK NEWS-HERALD →

WRIGHT BROTHERS TAKE TO THE SKY!

Kitty Hawk, N.C., Dec. 18, 1903. Yesterday, December 17, 1903, was a day of discovery at Kitty Hawk, North Carolina. Early in the morning as the mists rose from the hills, the Wright brothers made the first successful airplane flight. The brothers flew a glider with a wing span of 40 feet and a width of 6½ feet. They spent several days building a track for takeoff on Kill Devil Hill.

It was an exciting moment when Wilbur and Orville Wright tossed a coin to see who would make the first flight. Wilbur won the toss. Wilbur had bad luck and fell. His brother climbed into the awkward machine and took off down the hill. Mounting into the sky, he covered about 120 feet in 12 seconds. What a sensation, to fly like a bird! Later in the day, Wilbur tried again. This time he flew 825 feet in 59 seconds. However, he crashed, wrecking the glider. Before these brave and daring men returned to their bicycle shop in Dayton, Ohio, I asked them for their reactions to the day's events. Orville replied, "Although our airplane is a mass of splintered wood and twisted wires, we are both very happy. We feel that we are conquering the air at last."

For many years Wilbur and Orville Wright studied the soaring birds and had built larger box kites. These interests led to experiments with flying machines culminating in the glider with two wings, a rudder, and a small engine run on gasoline.

Where will these discoveries lead us and what does the future hold? Will we one day fly as naturally as the birds? Only time will tell.

REVIEWING FICTION

Most likely the majority of your class assignments for review will be in fiction, so you need to keep in mind these elements of literature as you read. First there is *characterization.* A writer may want to describe actions or ideas, but he must also describe the people who do the acting or have the ideas.

Then there is *motivation,* which means the reasons for the characters' actions. The writer should try to make his characters act like real people.

The *setting* is the place in which a character's story occurs. Literary characters, like the persons who read about them, do not exist in a vacuum. They act and react with one another, responding to the world in which they live.

The *plot* tells what happens to the characters in the story. It is built around a series of events that take place within a definite period of time. The leading character has a problem, he faces the problem, he overcomes it or is overcome by it.

Theme is what the author is trying to say, the basic idea behind writing the novel, the statement the author wants to make to the world. Seldom is it expressed in direct words; more often it is implied by the entire work. The mark of a sophisticated reader is being able to understand from the book what the author is trying to say above and beyond the simple story line of who did what to whom. The author may be saying that he thinks life is meaningless, that animals are superior to people, that love is the greatest power on earth, that all people need other people and cannot live alone, or whatever, *ad infinitum.*

Style is the way a writer uses words to create literature, to evoke emotions, to describe beauty or ugliness, to make characters come to life, to make events seem real.

As a mature reader you will understand these elements of literature and will assess them as you read, for they will color your evaluation.

You are now ready to plan your review. You have your notes made during the reading and your notes taken when you finished, and you have allowed your thoughts to take form. Ask yourself these questions:

* What was the author's real goal in writing the book? What was his theme? What was he trying to make me see, feel, or think? Did he accomplish his objective?

* Was the plot convincing? Did the incidents follow one another logically so I felt the story really could have happened?

* Did the characters seem human? Did I really care what happened to them? Did they act like real people or like puppets on a string? Did I learn anything about human nature after meeting these characters?

* Was the dialogue believable? Was it in keeping with the personalities of the characters? Did the dialogue move the story along or hinder it?

* Did the setting come to life? Could I actually see in my mind's eye the places described? Did the author fill in with vivid details?

* Was the style suitable to the plot and theme? Did it blend with the book or was I conscious of inept wording so it detracted from the story?

Make notes of your answers to these questions giving specific details to justify your reasons. Criticize where criticism is justified, but do not feel you must be critical to sound smart.

Summarize the plot briefly, never going into lengthy detail nor revealing an unexpected ending which would spoil the suspense if someone else were to read it. Never, never give a blow-by-blow account of the action; you are not rewriting the book but are judging the elements of the book and evaluating it as a whole. You may describe one particular scene in detail to try to capture the flavor of the book for your audience.

Take into consideration the exact nature of the book. If it is an historical novel, it is set in some specific place and period, so be sure to note the time, place, events, and historical persons involved. For instance, if you read the book *Tituba of Salem Village,* look up Tituba in an encyclopedia and point out that she was a real person and tell how the book followed (or did not follow) the actual events in her life. Read a little about the witchcraft trials in Salem, Massachusetts, so you can fix the book knowledgeably in its historical background.

Sometimes the title of the book needs explanation. If you read *The Magnificent Mutineers,* you should certainly include a paragraph about how mutineers, who are usually thought of as criminals, could be considered "magnificent."

Now ask yourself, What information do I want to get across to my readers about this book, what will *my* theme be? Take all your notes and form them into a logical outline that covers all that you want to say. Begin with the most factual parts and end with your own personal impressions.

Necessary for any good writing is a good introduction which entices the reader to read on and gives an overview of what is to come. Then the body of the work presents all the points the writer wishes to make. Equally critical is the conclusion that wraps up the writing, giving a feeling of completeness to the work.

The reviewer's own style of writing is important, with one word following another logically and interestingly, and with good paragraphs leading from one to the other smoothly. Use of transitional words or phrases between paragraphs helps the reader to follow the writer's meaning. All writing must be grammatically correct, with no misspelled words, and properly proofread.

Revise and polish your rough draft. Read the review over objectively. How do you think a reader of *your* work would evaluate it? Does it make a point? Does it give sufficient information for an outsider to form a valid opinion of the book? Is it dull? Is it a trustworthy evaluation? Be as thorough and critical of your own work as you were of the author's work!

REVIEWING A BIOGRAPHY

In reviewing a biography you must do much more than just tell the facts of the person's life which anyone can look up in an encyclopedia. Do summarize the person's life, telling when and where he lived and why he was worthy of having a book written about him.

A main factor to consider is what the author was trying to say about the person, what area of his life the author stressed. For instance, a biography about Thomas Jefferson might focus on Jefferson the president and what he did during his administration, such as enlarging the country through the Louisiana Purchase. Or the author might aim at showing how multitalented he was in the sciences and the arts. Or the concentration could be on his role in the Revolution as the author of the Declaration of Independence. Perhaps the main thrust was on the personality of Jefferson and his relationships with the people he loved.

Ask yourself these questions:

* Is the biographee presented as a real human being, with good traits and faults, or is he made into a stereotype, someone who is not quite real?

* Do the times and places come alive? Is the setting made real?

* Does the author explain what factors influenced the person? What conditions, or events, or people helped make the person what he became?

* Are the conversations as recorded believable?

* How does the author's style help or hinder the reading of the book?

* Would I have liked to have known the main character?

REVIEWING A SCIENCE BOOK

Here are some questions to ask yourself:

* Was the material easily understood? Did the author explain things clearly? Did I need more background to understand it or did the author write in too simple a manner?

* Were the facts accurate as far as I can tell?

* Were there enough illustrations, pictures, diagrams, and charts to help explain things?

* What are the author's qualifications? Is he a recognized authority in the field? How did he get his information, by actual experience or by research?

* What new sort of knowledge did I learn from reading the book? Is it just new to me or is it brand new scientific information? If it is new, does everyone agree with the author in his assessment of it? For instance, a book detailing how some scientists believe that birds are the direct descendants of dinosaurs would require relating this theory to older theories. Or a book about the discovery of "Lucy," a seven-million-year-old skeleton, would require fitting this information into opinions held by other scientists about how long man has been on this earth. But a book describing the life cycle of a butterfly might present nothing new or controversial although the information in it was new to you and helped enlarge your knowledge of the world about you.

REVIEWING HISTORY AND CURRENT EVENTS

* This type of book often deals with subjects from one point of view alone. What was the author's point of view? What was his purpose in writing it? Does he present only one side of a controversial question or did he look at it from many angles? For instance, a book about nuclear weapons can be slanted to the author's feeling or it can show different perspectives.

* Did my attitude change as I read the book?

* Was the book written in a clear manner so I could understand the various implications discussed?

* Did I feel the author distinguished fact from interpretation? Could I tell when hard facts were being given, those that can be checked elsewhere, and when the author was giving his assessment of the facts? Did he tell all the facts or did he distort or omit any? (This is a difficult thing to pinpoint, but reading a book with this possibility in mind helps open your eyes to the insidious nature of propaganda.)

* What are the author's qualifications for writing the book, his personal background?

A Précis

A précis is a concise summary of the essential points of a longer piece of writing in your own words, usually one-fourth to one-third as long as the original. Learning how to do this provides excellent training in reading for comprehension and in mastering the technique of clear, concise, and accurate writing. It is a useful skill, if mastered, and will be a valuable tool both for school work and later in the business world.

Fully recognize first of all that a précis is not a paraphrase, which is a restatement in different words of what the original said, often of the same length as or longer than the original. A précis, unlike a paraphrase, cuts wordage to the minimum, simplifying and getting to the essential meaning in very few words. It contains no details, examples, or illustrations, and it does not allow any comment or interpretation on your part. The French meaning of the word, "exact," "terse," describes it accurately.

Follow these steps:

* Read the selection quickly for a general overview.
* Reread it paragraph by paragraph several times very thoughtfully.
* In each paragraph look for the topic sentence and restate it, first to yourself, then write it down in your own words.
* Combine these ideas into a statement of the whole. Eliminate any that do not directly bear on the main idea of the paper.
* Revise your version checking to see that it is absolutely accurate in accordance with the author's version and that it follows the original in the same sequence of thoughts and facts.
* Go through your précis and cut it to one-fourth or one-third of the original length by tightening each sentence, cutting any extra words. Substitute a phrase for a clause or one word for a phrase.

Examples:

Wordy: If you do your studying right after school, you will be able to watch television at night.

Terse: Afternoon studying leaves night time free for TV watching.

Wordy: Miss Brown spoke to me in a pleasant manner.

Terse: Miss Brown spoke to me pleasantly.

Science Project Report

Writing a science project report involves a special format, although not all of the items listed below must be included for every project, as the nature of the investigation sometimes imposes limitations. However, knowing what can be required helps the student in planning and executing a successful project conducted according to approved scientific methods.

The writing must be clear and concise, using formal style, which means no colloquial expressions, no contractions, and in the third person (avoiding the words "you" and "I.") Define all terms that might need clarification.

1. *Title:* This should convey exactly what the report is about, being very specific and factual in wording. Cute or catchy titles are out of place. For example, "Sit, Lie Down, Play Dead" would not be a suitable title for a research report about how to train a dog. Instead, "Training a Dog to Follow Simple Commands," would be better.

2. *Abstract:* A one-paragraph summary of the report should introduce the paper telling the purpose of the project, general methods or procedures used, and the main results produced or conclusions reached. The reason for writing the abstract is to allow another busy scientist to decide if he/she wishes to study the entire report.

3. *Introduction:* This includes the importance of the area under investigation, why you chose it, something of the historical background, and an overview of what other people have done in the field. This literary support requires using the *Readers' Guide* or other indexes to find references to what has already been done on the subject. You will need to document (give credit to) the sources you consulted. Either use conventional footnotes or put in parentheses after a statement a shortened version of the source (Jones, *Science Reports,* 1984) to refer to the work in a bibliography which you will include following the paper itself.

4. *The Problem:* Clearly state what it is you planned to do. Tell if you were testing several hypotheses, were looking for a hypothesis, were suggesting a theory, or were reporting some observations made under certain specific, controlled conditions. If possible, include how your problem relates to other theories. A hypothesis is a tentative assumption made in order to draw out and test its logical consequences.

5. *Hypotheses:* State all hypotheses that you were testing and, if possible, what the results of your experiments will mean as to the acceptance or rejection of these hypotheses.

6. *Procedures:* Describe in detail exactly how you did your experiments so other people can do the same thing with the same results. List all

equipment you used, a step-by-step account of procedures followed, an exact description of the conditions influencing the results. Include all failures as well as successes so others will not waste time doing things that will not work. Diagrams and drawings can be used.

7. *Observations and Interpretations:* Record chronologically, perhaps in diary form, the facts you observed as you were conducting your experiments. Compile tables or graphs to present statistics, measurements, and other numerical data. Explain what your observations mean in connection with the hypothesis that was being tested.

8. *Conclusions:* Each hypothesis should be examined in light of your observations and interpretations so that the hypothesis may be rejected outright or accepted with reservations for more testing. Rarely does student work result in a fully accepted hypothesis.

9. *Generalizations:* Here you tell the implication or meaning of your research in relation to its larger field of science. Perhaps your study can suggest some new problems or further areas of study.

10. *Summary:* Write a brief summary of your investigation, listing the principal findings of the project.

Letters and Employment Resumes*

Whenever you write a letter–whether personal or business–those lines of writing become *you* in the mind of your reader. Your letters will, of course, vary in purpose and formality, as the occasion requires, yet each letter you write is, for your reader, like a face-to-face meeting with you. Let your letters be a credit to you in appearance, appropriateness, and good taste; make them also carry something of the naturalness and vitality your reader would experience in a person-to-person visit. Practically all letters can be included within three general classifications:

1. *The social "duty" letter,* a type of letter–formal or informal–demanded by good manners

2. *The personal letter,* a type of informal letter written to share the pleasures of life with friends and relatives

3. *The business letter,* a type of letter written in the conduct of commercial, professional, or administrative affairs

THE SOCIAL "DUTY" LETTER

Social "duty" letters are used as invitations, to acknowledge invitations, to thank friends for favors and gifts, to console relatives and friends in times of trouble. You will want to know how to write them.

Formal Social Letters

Very formal affairs–weddings, receptions, and formal dinners–still require a formal correspondence ritual. Guests are invited in a nonpersonal, formal manner, as is to be seen in the example below. The invitations are usually engraved or printed; they may be written in longhand. Guests responding to such invitations employ the same formal, nonpersonal language that they find in the invitation, but the responses are always handwritten.

INVITATION

Mr. and Mrs. Eugene Parsons
request the honor of your presence
at the marriage of their daughter

*The acute accent over the final *e* in resumé has been omitted in the text of this chapter as this seems to be the rule in most United States business correspondence. In formal writing, the acute accent should be included even if the mark has to be inserted by hand. The Merriam–Webster *Third New International Dictionary* also carries the accent over the first *e*.

Sue Ellen
to
Mr. Harvey Henderson
on Saturday, the first of June
at ten o'clock
Saint Mark's Church
New York

ACCEPTANCE
Thomas Olderbach
accepts with pleasure
the kind invitation of
Mr. and Mrs. Eugene Parsons
to the marriage of their daughter
Sue Ellen
to
Mr. Harvey Henderson
on Saturday, the first of June
at ten o'clock
Saint Mark's Church
New York

Informal Social Letters

Most social occasions that require letters are informal. When a hostess wants a few friends to attend a small dinner party, she does not send out engraved invitations. She writes a short personal note to each of them or she may even telephone. When a weekend guest returns home, he writes a so-called bread-and-butter thank-you note to his hostess.

Dear Mrs. Parsons,

That Saturday morning sunrise over the valley, those gay voices of the twins, and that stimulating table talk are still with me. Every moment of the weekend was perfect, but one–departure. How I hated to have it end!

I loved every moment at Oakridge Manor and I want to thank you very much for a wonderful time.

Sincerely,
Harvey Henderson

Gifts, favors, congratulations, and condolences–all are acknowledged in short notes which are set up like letters, rather than formal announcements. These social letters are written in natural, everyday language, with a friendliness of style appropriate to the relationship between writer and reader. Although a telephone call, greeting card, bouquet, or telegram may substitute for social letters on some occasions, letters are to be written:

Whenever you receive gifts, courtesies, favors, congratulations, or good wishes

Whenever you stay overnight as a guest in someone's home

Whenever you receive an invitation to a dinner or luncheon

Whenever you express or acknowledge condolence

In addition to such "duty" letters, there are innumerable kinds of social notes which it is always becoming to write. There are "cheer-up" notes which you send to the sick. There are "well-done," "best-wishes," "happy-journey," and "welcome-home" notes you can write on other occasions.

Stationery for the Social Letter

Formal social letters should be written on a good quality, white, side-folded letter sheet approximately 5½ inches x 7½ inches, in black or blue-black ink. Informal social letters may also be written on this type of stationery, on greeting cards, or on any of the personal stationery used in friendly correspondence. Less formal social letters may be typed, including the following, which at one time were handwritten only: letters of sympathy and replies to letters of sympathy, letters expressing and letters acknowledging good wishes, and letters acknowledging wedding gifts.

THE PERSONAL LETTER

Those letters which help us share with friends and relatives the joys of living are called *personal letters*. There is a single test for evaluating the personal letter: Does it provide the writer and the reader with shared satisfaction of friendship? The few principles of personal letterwriting that do exist are designed to help writer and reader enjoy to the full the pleasures of correspondence.

1. Note how Thackeray's daughter achieves the vividness of face-to-face contact in a letter:

I have been imagining you in my favorite corner of my favorite city. Have you opened your windows and looked out, does it smell–rumble–taste–Paris? I'm sure it does. Even the little tin water cans are unlike anything anywhere else.

2. Make your letters as cheerful and constructive as you can; nobody likes a complaining, gloomy, nagging letter.

3. Avoid any statement or hint that writing is a chore. It is impolite to tell a correspondent that you

just could not get around to writing, that there is nothing to say, or that you are hastily dashing off a few lines.

4. Avoid putting into a letter any statement that could prove unbecoming if the letter were to fall into the hands of another. Remember, letters are permanent records.

Stationery for the Personal Letter

Close friends may correspond on any kind of stationery available, the only restrictions rising from personal choice and consideration for the reader. Untidy, blotted, scratched-out, or soiled letters are unbecoming to the writer and a discourtesy to the reader. Legibility is only common politeness. Writing in pencil, writing around the edges of the sheet, or writing on lined paper may also be resented, even among friends.

THE BUSINESS LETTER

The importance of the letter as a tool in business, government, the professions, and other administrative activities has developed the type known as *the business letter*.

For all practical purposes, the great variety of business letters may be classified under four basic headings:

1. *Letters that handle routine business.* Most business letters have a simple, routine mission; they carry needed details and short statements of information from businessman to businessman. Letters that order goods, acknowledge orders, and handle remittances make up the bulk of mail interchanged by business organizations. The main qualities these routine letters must possess are brevity and clearness. They must be complete in supplying all details as to style, color, price, conditions, procedures, and the like.

2. *Letters that grant requests.* Many business letters are written to grant requests; they supply information sought by other businessmen and the public; they send out samples and booklets; they open charge accounts; they make adjustments. When a request is granted, it should be done graciously and with good will, usually in the opening sentence of the letter:

> We are pleased to send the samples of Kioba Fabric requested in your letter of January 23.

The middle of the letter can then supply the necessary detail. The ending is usually a further statement of good will.

3. *Letters that deny requests.* Many business letters have to deny requests. The best tactics for making a denial are (a) open with a statement that the reader will find agreeable–*we appreciate very much your detailed description of your recent experience with our Toast-Browner;* (b) give reasons for the denial; (c) make the denial; (d) seek the good will of the reader.

4. *Letters that persuade and sell.* Many business letters have a persuasive mission; they must move the minds and wills of their readers. Some of them must assist in selling goods and services; some of them must collect money; some of them must debate issues. All of them must employ techniques of persuasion.

The sales letter is usually constructed on a patterning of steps which lead to the sale–attention, desire, conviction, and action.

	DEAR MR. JONES:
Attention	Did you ever wish that your typewriter had an eraser key–one that could correct the original and all copies with a stroke of the finger? Well, here's your chance to get something even better–TYPERASO*–the magic insert and carbon pack that is self-erasing.
Desire	With TYPERASO an error can be corrected with the flick of a key. All you have to do is slip the TYPERASO mounting over the error, pull up the TYPERASO carbon, and strike any key. In an instant, the error is gone. What a saving to you in time, money, and nerves.
Conviction	TYPERASO has been approved by all leading banks, insurance companies, and typewriter manufacturers. We will give you double your money back if you are not delighted with your TYPERASO pack.
Action	Pick up a TYPERASO pack at any office supply store. There's a pack waiting for you right now.
	Sincerely,

*This is an imaginary product.

FORMATS OF THE LETTER

The general setup of a letter on a page is called its *format*. Formal invitations and replies, as already noted, are set up like announcements; their formats are different from the more usual letter formats.

Parts of the Letter

There are seven basic parts of a letter. Business and other "official" letters require all seven, and often several additional ones. Social and personal letters usually omit one or two of these parts, as explained below.

1. HEADING. The writer's address, engraved, printed, or written at the top of the sheet, constitutes the heading of the letter. As noted, personal stationery may have the writer's monogram, or name and address, or name alone, or address alone, imprinted upon the letter sheet. If the address does not appear on personal stationery, it must be written or typed at the top of the sheet. This same practice is followed in preparing a business letter when an individual (say, a job applicant) does not have printed letterhead stationery. Business firms and most other organizations have their names and addresses imprinted at the top of their letter sheets.

2. DATE LINE. All letters must be dated. The usual place for a letter date is to the top and right, on a lower line than the heading. Informal social letters, however, often carry their dates as a last element of the letter, at the left margin. The most usual form of date employed in letters is *January 23, 1965,* but social letters often omit the year; sometimes they are dated with a mere *Monday,* or *At home*. Never use such forms as January 23rd, 1965 or 1/23/65.

3. INSIDE ADDRESS. Business and other "official" letters always carry the name and address of the recipient of the letter. This *inside address* is generally placed four or five lines below the date line, beginning flush with the left margin.

4. SALUTATION. The greeting, *Dear Tom* or *Dear Sir,* so characteristic of the letter format, is called the *salutation*. In social and personal letters the salutation is followed by a comma and is generally informal–*Dear Tom, Tom dear,* etc. In business letters the salutation is followed by a colon and is generally formal, unless the writer and reader enjoy a close acquaintanceship–*Dear Mr. Smith:, Dear Sir:*. The formality of the salutation must always match the formality of the complimentary close. See table on Forms of Address, pp. 73-74.

5. BODY. The part of the letter which carries the message is called the *body*.

6. COMPLIMENTARY CLOSE. The closing, *Sincerely yours* or *Very truly yours,* is called the *complimentary close*. In social and personal letters the complimentary close may take such forms as *Affectionately* or *With love,* but in business letters more formal complimentary closes are employed–*Cordially, Sincerely, Yours very truly,* or (to superiors) *Respectfully, Respectfully yours.*

7. SIGNATURE. All letters, typed and handwritten, must be signed by the writer. In social and personal letters the signature may be very informal, consisting of a first name or even a nickname. In business letters the written signature is often followed by a typed signature and an indication of the writer's position in the firm. Titles such as *Mr.* or *Dr.* are never written as part of a signature.

Additional letter parts, often found in business letters are (a) the subject line, (b) the attention line, (3) the identification initials. The subject line identifies the topic of the letter. The attention line (used only in letters addressed to a firm) directs the letter to a particular person within the firm, when the writer feels that the person has a special interest in the subject discussed. The identification initials indicate the person who dictated the letter and the secretary who typed it. The placement of these additional letter parts will be found in a letter model provided later.

Setup of the Letter

The informal social "duty" letter and the personal letter employ the same format with one exception: The date of the informal social "duty" letter may follow the signature, at the left margin.

Typed business letters are usually set up in a *block* format. Parts like the inside address are not staggered as they are in many handwritten letters.

Envelopes must always match letter pages in quality and color, and in style of addressing. In handwritten letters, the envelope address is usually indented. In business letters the envelope address is usually blocked, matching in detail the inside address. The return address is placed in the upper left corner of the envelope, following post office preference; but many writers of social and personal letters place the return address on the back flap of the envelope.

Forms of Address

PERSON	INSIDE ADDRESS	SALUTATION	COMPLIMENTARY CLOSE
President	The President The White House Washington, D.C.	Sir: *or* My dear Mr. President:	Most respectfully yours, *or* Respectfully yours,
Senator	The Honorable John Doe The United States Senate Washington, D.C.	Sir: *or* My dear Senator:	Very truly yours,
Congressman	The Honorable John Doe The House of Representatives Washington, D.C.	Sir: *or* My dear Mr. Doe:	Very truly yours,
Governor	The Honorable John Doe Governor of New York Albany, New York	Sir: *or* Dear Governor Doe:	Very truly yours,
Mayor	The Honorable John Doe Mayor of the City of Troy City Hall Troy, Colorado	Sir: *or* Dear Mayor Doe:	Very truly yours,
College Registrar	The Registrar Finn University Tobin City, N.J.	Dear Sir:	Very truly yours,
Rabbi	Rabbi John Doe	My dear Sir: *or* Dear Rabbi Doe:	Respectfully yours, *or* Very truly yours,
Protestant Clergyman	The Reverend John Doe	Reverend Sir: *or* My dear Mr. Doe:	Respectfully yours, *or* Very truly yours,
Priest	The Reverend John Doe	Reverend and dear Father: *or* Dear Father Doe:	Respectfully yours, *or* Very truly yours,
Nun	Sister Lioba, O.S.B.* . . . . (*Indicate order)	Reverend and dear Sister: *or* Dear Sister Lioba:	Respectfully yours, *or* Faithfully yours,
Woman Formally in a Business Letter	Miss Mary Doe *or* Mrs. John Smith	My dear Madam: *or* My dear Miss Doe:	Very truly yours,
Man Formally in a Business Letter	Mr. John Doe	My dear Sir: *or* My dear Mr. Doe:	Very truly yours,
Man or Woman in Less Formal Business Letters	Mr. John Doe *or* Miss Mary Doe	Dear Sir: *or* *more usually* Dear Mr. Doe: Dear Miss Doe:	Sincerely yours, *or* Sincerely,

PERSON	INSIDE ADDRESS	SALUTATION	COMPLIMENTARY CLOSE
Business Firm	Perfect Corporation	Gentlemen:	Very truly yours,
Man or Woman in a Social or Personal Letter	(No inside address needed, but be certain to use Mr., Mrs., Miss, Dr., or other title of courtesy before name on the envelope.)	Dear Mr. Jones, Dear Mrs. Doe, Dear Tom, Dear Jane, *or in friendly letters any familiar salutation in good taste*	Sincerely, *or any more intimate closing in good taste, such as* Affectionately yours, Lovingly,

SOLVING THE SEX QUESTION IN LETTER WRITING

With more and more women holding prominent career positions, the question constantly arises about the use of the traditional "Dear Sir" when the identity of the recipient of a business letter is unknown. Many sources suggest using "Dear Sir or Dear Madam," but this is cumbersome. The time-honored "Gentlemen" could be increased to "Gentlemen and Ladies" but this is stilted, and both retain the masculine precedence. A reversal of order might be employed.

However, a simpler solution is to use the title of the person addressed: "Dear Personnel Director"; "Dear Registrar"; "Dear Principal"; "Dear Public Service Commissioners." The same idea can be used in writing to a company: "Dear Jones Bookstore"; "Dear Executive Tax Service."

If it is known that the addressee is a woman, and her preference of titles is known, then address her as "Miss Mary Alston," or "Mrs. Joan Krantz," or "Ms. Sara Ledbetter." However, in many cases the correct choice is unknown and a wrong choice can sour a good relation before it has a chance to develop. If in doubt, simply write "Dear Eunice Reynolds." Or better still, incorporate her title in the salutation as "Dear Professor Caffey" or "Dear Director Smith."

With so many single parents these days, teachers have discarded the former "Dear Mother," in favor of "Dear Parent or Guardian."

COMMUNICATING IDEAS IN A LETTER

A successful letter is one that wins a favorable response. When you write a social "duty" letter, you seek a specific response–*I want Ann to realize how much I appreciate the silver tray she sent.* When you write a business letter, you also seek a specific response–*I want the bookkeeper at Greynolds, Inc., to understand that the 2% discount he took is not justified and that a check for $5.64 must be sent to me.* When you write a personal letter, you seek a much less tangible and much less specific response of friendship shared–*I want Tom to get pleasure and knowledge from the news I send and a deepened appreciation of our friendship.* In all of these types of letters, the success of the letter is judged by the response.

The Response Desired

So important is this response that the first principle of effective letter writing is: *Let the response you desire be your guide throughout the letter.*

A good practice is to pause a moment before beginning to write and answer the following questions:

Just why am I writing this letter?

Just how do I want my reader to feel when he finishes this letter?

In a particularly important letter, you may want to write out for yourself in a sentence or two the response you desire. But in most letters it will be enough if you get the response desired clearly in your own mind before you start writing.

The You-Attitude

When you have determined the desired response, you must next consider that goal from your reader's point of view. Imagine yourself the reader. Then select a plan for your letter, a set of ideas, a tone of approach, and a phrasing that would move *you* to the response desired.

This tactic of viewing a letter problem through the reader's eyes may be called the *you-attitude.* So important is the you-attitude that the second principle of effective letter writing is: *Let your reader's interests be your guide in the selection and phrasing of ideas.*

A letter which concentrates on the selfish interests of the writer is apt to be dull, and generally ineffective. Readers respond best when their own interests are being considered. In writing personal letters, you should stick to subjects that will give pleasure to your reader. Respond to the main points of his last letter to you. Involve him as much as possible in what you say. Instead of saying: "I found the view from the bridge over the rushing waters very impressive," say: "If only you could have shared that view from the dam with me. I know you would have thought, as I did, 'It's just like the Ausable River.' "

When you write business letters, you are always concerned with the advancement of some interest–getting a job, making a sale, collecting an account. Yet, these letters as well must be written with the you-attitude if they are to gain the response desired and win good will for the writer and his firm. A job applicant should tell how his training and experience will benefit the reader. The writer of a collection letter should stress the advantage his reader will gain through prompt payment–satisfaction in knowing his debts are paid or the protection of his credit standing.

Expression Skill

With the exception of formal correspondence, letters are best written in a natural conversational tone. After all, as already mentioned, the letter substitutes for a person-to-person meeting and should employ language appropriate to such meetings. Stilted language, artificiality, or phrases designed to impress have no place in a letter.

Writing skill, however, is very important to the letter writer. Actually, a letter is *not* a person-to-person meeting, and it requires skill to convey an idea and a set of feelings precisely and naturally through the written word.

The need to write well leads to a further principle of effective letter writing: *Let your ideas and feelings find expression in language that is clear, persuasive, natural, thoughtful, and interesting.*

The basic method of improving your ability to express yourself in writing is to read good writing and to practice as much writing as possible. As you read good writing notice how logical and constructive is the thought behind it. Notice how the writer phrases his ideas precisely. Notice how easily and naturally the writer expresses himself. Such attention to the techniques of skillful writing will enhance your own writing skill.

When you practice writing, concentrate on the ideas and feelings you want your writing to convey, rather than on techniques and style. Think hard until you have an idea worthy of expression. Make yourself feel the mood you want to convey–cheeriness, sympathy, friendliness, or whatever that mood may be. Concentrate on that idea and feeling until the right phrasing comes to you. With an increase of experience, you will discover that you are acquiring skill, that the right words and phrasing come more and more readily.

When you concentrate on the ideas and feelings you want to convey, language will begin to flow; the trick is to keep it flowing. Your first attempt to express a business-letter idea may be, "Please do something about this." Obviously, this idea needs more definite thought and expression. If you concentrate upon it, you will gain not only a clearer thought but also more precise expression of that thought, and you will be writing, "Please pick up the damaged table on Saturday morning."

You can speed up this skill-building process further if you bear in mind the writing principles discussed in other chapters of this book.

WATCH THESE EXPRESSIONS

accept, except Do not confuse. *I shall accept* (receive) *the letter. I shall except* (exclude) *this sum from the list.*

affect, effect Do not confuse. *The news will affect* (influence) *his mood. The manager will effect* (bring about) *a new schedule. The effect* (the noun form) *of television is obvious.*

busy In personal letters never write *I would have answered sooner but I was too busy* or any similarly rude expression.

beside, besides Do not confuse. *The wastebasket is beside* (alongside of) *the desk. Who is going besides* (in addition to) *you?*

due to Do not use *due to* in place of *because of* or *owing to. Due* is an adjective and makes a questionable preposition.

favor Do not refer to a letter as a *favor* in such trite expressions as *Your favor of June 1 received.*

good, well Do not use *good* as an adverb. *This program works well* (not *good*).

hoping Avoid such letter endings as *hoping to hear from you.*

I am, I remain Avoid these old-fashioned phrases in your letter closings.

its, it's Do not confuse. *Every machine has its* (possessive) *own cover. It's* (it is) *going to be warm today.*

said Avoid such expressions as *the said program* or *the said matter.*

thanking you Avoid such expressions as *thanking you for your interest* followed by a complimentary close.

AVOID THESE EXPRESSIONS

anticipating
as per, as regards
at your earliest convenience
awaiting, we await
beg
duly noted
esteemed
recent date
trusting that this is satisfactory
valued
we are, we remain
we trust
we wish to
with due regard
with reference to the matter
yours

THE LETTER OF APPLICATION

A particularly important kind of sales letter is the *letter of application,* the letter a job seeker sends to a prospective employer requesting a job interview. The application letter is apt to get attention when it is written or typed neatly upon good, white, bond paper and opens with a statement that is distinctive. Far too many application letters begin with a trite, "I am writing this letter to apply for the job advertised in today's *Herald.*" Much better would be an opening like the following:

> My basic training in computer programing and my two years of part-time experience in data processing are the work advantages I can best offer in a letter. But if I could call upon you, in response to your advertisement in today's *Herald,* I know that I could show you why I am the young man you need in your new automated division.

The application letter builds desire by outlining details of experience, education, and skill which will be useful in the job that is being sought. With desire built, the applicant can provide proof in the form of references and possibly samples of his work. Finally, the applicant moves his reader to action by requesting an interview, making himself available at any time convenient to the prospective employer.

Here are a few *do's* and *don'ts* on application letters:

DO'S

Write or type neatly on one side only of good quality, white paper.

Write large numbers of application letters. Write to firms that advertise, and write to firms that don't. Keep writing.

Learn as much as possible about your prospective employer and gear your letter to the way your education and experience will help him.

Exhibit confidence in your background and ability.

Request an interview at the end of the letter.

Write follow-up letters.

DON'TS

Don't write on letterheads of other business firms, hotel or club stationery.

Don't limit your job-seeking efforts to openings provided you by friends, relatives, and the local press. Don't wait for an answer from one firm before writing to another.

Don't make a vague offer to do anything.

Don't be timid and apologetic or conceited and boasting. Don't end vaguely at one extreme or attempt to pressure your reader into action at the other.

Don't neglect to thank the prospective employer for the courtesy of the interview he granted, even when you don't get the job.

How Businessmen Evaluate Applications

Today's business executive has very little time to read long letters. Most executives stress that they are more likely to reply to a short, well-written letter that makes the applicant's point quickly.

A vice president of a large chemical company submits the following letter as an example of a good application. It was received by his company in reply to a blind-box advertisement:

For your review I enclose a copy of my current resume which describes my qualifications for the position advertised in the March 25 issue of the New York Times.

My background and experience closely parallel the requirements outlined in your advertisement. I am, therefore, reasonably sure that I can make a valuable contribution to your company. Won't you call me at 586-3657 to arrange for an interview.

The vice president of a school-supply company received the following letter from a college student. He considers it to be an excellent letter of application:

In answer to my inquiry, the Atlanta Chamber of Commerce sent me your name as one of the firms in your city that hires college students for temporary summer work.

Although my home is San Francisco, and I attend Stanford University, I plan to take a one-day-a-week course at Georgia Tech this summer. This course will be given on Monday of each week and will run for six weeks.

It was a fortunate coincidence for me that your firm's name was submitted, because you are engaged in the type of business in which I hope to make my future.

At present, I am a sophomore at Stanford University, majoring in economics. Scholastically, I am in the top 10 per cent of my class, and I am a reporter on our college newspaper.

I realize that for the first six weeks of my twelve-week vacation, I will be able to work only four days a week. However, since I do not have to be back to school until the end of September, I will be able to work a full week for the last six weeks of my summer vacation.

I wish to learn every aspect of the writing-paper and school-supply business; therefore, I am willing to work in any phase of it–stockroom, manufacturing, sales, or office administration.

I will be in Atlanta on June 12. May I then call you and present myself for an interview?

Very truly yours,

The vice president of marketing of a business machine manufacturing company received the following letter, which accompanied a well-organized resume:

I am presently attending the University of Pennsylvania and will be graduated in June. I have decided that my educational background and experience in summertime and part-time employment is such that selling offers me the best opportunity for personal advancement and financial success. I have been impressed with your ads in recent issues of the Wall Street Journal *and I want to investigate the opportunities in your organization for a selling-trainee opening.*

Please write to me if I may phone for an interview.

Here's an example that the personnel manager of one of the largest merchandising corporations considers to be an effective letter-resume combination:

Your very fine company has impressed me for some time as the type of organization with which I would like to become associated. Your progressive merchandising policies and steady growth provide the type of opportunity I am seeking.

You will note from the attached resume that I am presently employed. I find working for my employer and my relationships with my associates most enjoyable. However, the firm is small and presents little in the way of opportunity for either personal growth or advancement.

I know I do not have much in the way of experience which could be utilized by a company such as Sears. However, I can assure you I would take an enthusiastic approach to learning. I would display mature judgment in viewing business problems after a limited amount of training. Above all, I have considerable ambition and am willing to sacrifice in order to obtain an opportunity.

My plans are such that I will be in Chicago the week of August 10, during which time I would like to have an interview at your convenience. May I call you for an appointment?

Very truly yours,

AN EMPLOYMENT RESUME

The employment resume is designed to introduce you to a prospective employer. You are looking for a job; he is looking for someone to fill the job; it goes without saying that you want the introduction to be a favorable one. So it is up to you to supply him, *briefly and clearly,* with the facts about yourself, your background, your education, and your work experience, in such a way that he will want to hire *you* instead of another applicant.

RULE NUMBER ONE: Be as brief as possible, yet include all pertinent facts.

RULE NUMBER TWO: Present yourself in the best possible light.

Some employment applicants have their employment resumes made up in quantity, either by mimeographing or multigraphing, and send them out with a covering letter to prospective employers. Some carry their resumes about with them when they go to answer advertisements that have appeared in newspapers or periodicals. Some resumes are supposed to be filled out on forms provided by the employment agency to which you have applied for help in finding a job. Whichever way your employment resume is used, it is obvious that it should present you most favorably. Use a typewriter and be sure the copy is letter perfect–no misspellings, no mistakes in grammar; also, no corrections, no strike-overs, no noticeable erasures. And see to it that your typewriter ribbon is dark and legible.

Most employment agencies will require you to fill out their form in ink while you are in their office. In such cases, before starting on the rounds of the agencies, take time and thought to prepare in advance, and to bring with you, a typed employment resume. Even if it is not possible for you to use this resume in its exact form, it is still likely that a great deal of what you have thought out can be used to good advantage.

In gathering material for this section, a number of employment agency directors were interviewed. Without exception they emphasized the point that the employment resume should be *brief, inclusive, and factual.* There is no place in an employment resume for attempts to be funny or clever.

Some employers will be interested in having, in addition, such personal information as:

Height
Weight
Marital Status
Number of Dependents
Military Experience
Present Military
  Status, etc.

A good resume has the following advantages over the overly comprehensive resumes so popular a number of years ago: It is brief, which assures that it will be read; it cites the essential information that the applicant wants the prospective employer to know at present; it shows, by its conciseness and organization, that the applicant is a methodical individual who knows how to bring out essential facts.

Below is an example of a resume described in the previous paragraph:

RESUME OF CHARLES DEERING, JR.

PERSONAL DATA: Married, One Child
Excellent Health

MILITARY SERVICE: U.S. Navy–Two years
Lt. Jr. Grade

EDUCATION: DePauw University, Indiana
B.A.–Economics (major)
Speech (minor)

PREVIOUS EXPERIENCE:

Trainee	One year
Merchandise and Operating Assistant Manager	One year

RETAIL EXPERIENCE:
Approximately two years experience in retail stores ranging in sales volume from $500,000 to $1,200,000. Responsibilities included department management, merchandising, advertising, personnel and operating assignments.

The Library: Indispensable Aid

A crucial skill for a literate person is the ability to use the library effectively. Not only is it essential for any organized research project, but it enhances the caliber of all other kinds of writing, and it provides a basis for the fullest enjoyment of pleasure reading.

Since the core of the library is the book collection, people need to know how to find and use books most effectively.

PARTS OF A BOOK: In addition to the main body of printed matter, each book contains some or all of the following parts. Every book has a *title page*, the right-hand page near the front on which are printed the title, the author, the publisher, and the place of publication. Sometimes there is a subtitle printed beneath the title which is added to give a better idea of the scope of the book.

The date on the title page may merely indicate when the book was printed, so the date on the reverse side of the title page is more important, as it tells the *copyright date,* near the time when the book was actually completed. The listing of more than one copyright date often means that additions or revisions were made to the original book. In a bibliography use the latest copyright date.

The *foreword* and *preface* are very similar. They tell something about the purpose of the book, how it can be used, or they acknowledge people who have helped prepare it. An *introduction,* written by the author or an authority on the subject, can summarize the book or introduce the subject.

The *Table of Contents* appears in the front and lists the chapters in order of their appearance, while the *index* is found on the last few pages and is an alphabetical arrangement listing specific persons, places, and topics with the exact page numbers where they are found.

Lists of maps, illustrations, charts are usually found immediately after the Table of Contents. Many books have an appendix near the back containing material that is not really part of the text but which is closely related to it. A United States history book, for example, may have in its appendix a copy of the Constitution.

Many books containing scientific, foreign, or other words that people may not understand have a *glossary* to define these terms.

TYPES OF BOOKS: To help people find books libraries classify, or arrange, books according to a clearly defined plan so that those which are similar in some way stand together on the shelves. They usually first divide the books into *fiction, biography,* and *non-fiction* categories. Fiction is a made-up story, although it can have much truth in it in the way of factual details, real-life characters, and actual settings. Novels such as *The Outsiders,* and short stories, are fiction.

A *biography* is the account of someone's life, and an *autobiography* is the account of one's own life. *Amos Fortune, Free Man* by Elizabeth Yates is a biography, while *The Story of My Life* by Helen Keller is an autobiography.

All other books in the library are usually designated non-fiction, or factual books, although this also includes such special types as folklore, mythology, poetry, drama, and essays.

DEWEY DECIMAL SYSTEM: In school and public libraries non-fiction is cataloged by the *Dewey Decimal System,* named for Melvil Dewey who in 1876 divided all knowledge into ten main classes and assigned numbers to each. Here is a listing of the Dewey class numbers:

CLASS NUMBER	MAIN CLASS
000—099	General Works
100—199	Conduct of Life (Philosophy)
200—299	Religion
300—399	Social Sciences
400—499	Language
500—599	Pure Sciences
600—699	Applied Science/Technology
700—799	Fine Arts and Recreation
800—899	Literature
900—999	History, Geography, Biography

Each of the main classes is subdivided into ten subdivisions. For instance, Pure Science is broken down this way:

510—Mathematics
520—Astronomy
530—Physics
540—Chemistry
550—Earth Sciences
560—Fossils
570—Biology
580—Botany
590—Zoology

Each subdivision is further broken down. For example, within the subclass 790—799 (Recreation), there is 796, outdoor sports; 797, water and air sports; 798, horse and other animal racing; 799, fishing. Further subdivision comes after the decimal. Thus 796.3 is for ball games, while 796.32 is for basketball; 796.33 is for football; 796.34 is for racquet games; and 796.35 is for baseball, etc.

CALL NUMBERS: In addition to the class number, each book also has an author designation which is placed under the class number. These two lines make up the call number which appears on the spine of the book and the catalog card. The call number for *The Many Faces of the Civil War* by Werstein:

973.7 = Dewey # for U. S. history, Civil War period
W498m = W498 for Werstein, the "m" for first word of title.

READING SHELVES: You "read" shelves of books just as you read pages in a book, left to right, line by line (or row by row), with shelf dividers setting off the different "pages." Dewey numbers range from lower numbers on the left to higher on the right, with authors alphabetized within the same number. This is the correct placement of books on a shelf:

155	155.03	155.1	155.1	155.12	155.22
N36g	B42k	M32q	N19h	K14b	A12n

CLASSIFYING FICTION/BIOGRAPHY: Although fiction can fall within the 800s of the Dewey system, and biography in the 900s, most school and public libraries pull these books out and arrange them separately. Fiction is arranged alphabetically by the author's last name. If two authors have the same last name, then the first name is alphabetized, so books by Elizabeth Allen come before those by Merritt Allen. Novels by the same author are alphabetized by title, so Stevenson's *Kidnapped* comes before his *Treasure Island.*

Many libraries give fiction an "F" classification for the first line of the call number, with an author code below it for the second line. A library might have this call number for *Little Women* and *Little Men,* both by Louisa May Alcott: F = Fiction
Alc = Alcott

Biographies are arranged alphabetically by *the person being written about,* so all the books about a person will stand together on the shelf. Often libraries give these books a "B" classification, or sometimes a 92 (part of the Dewey number for biographies.) Thus two biographies of Abraham Lincoln, one by Judson and one by Nolan, would have almost identical call numbers:

B B (The only difference is the author designation
L63j L63n at the end of the number representing Lincoln)

A collective biography, containing the lives of several people, is placed in the Dewey category for biography, 920—928, and has a regular author number.

SPECIAL COLLECTIONS: Sometimes there are other special collections that are housed separately. Short stories may be pulled out of their regular 800 number and put in a place designated S. C. (for story collection). Reference books are routinely shelved by themselves. Here is the call number for the reference book *Twentieth Century Authors* by Kunitz:

R
928
K96t

It is interesting how books from all these sections can be brought together for a special use. A teacher of American history preparing for a class unit on colonial life and the Revolution might go to the library and choose books from every single Dewey class number plus the other designations. Here are some books she might pick, with their broad class numbers: (Notice every class number is used.)

Subject	Class Number
Schools in colonial times	300
Signers of the Declaration (collected biography)	900
Development of constitutional government	300
Revolutionary war weapons	600
Sports and games in colonial days	700
A biography of George Washington	B
Johnny Tremain, a novel laid in Revolutionary days	F
The poem "Paul Revere's Ride"	800
How to embroider a sampler	700
A U. S. history book	900
Slavery	300
Tools used to build a log cabin	600
Foods and recipes	600
Story behind the song "Yankee Doodle"	700
Indian words adopted into our language	400
A description of Monticello, Jefferson's home	900
Colonial costumes	300
The founding of Pennsylvania by Quakers	200
Witchcraft in Salem village	100
Skits from American history	800
An encyclopedia article	000
Native birds painted by Audubon	500

LIBRARY OF CONGRESS CLASSIFICATION SYSTEM: Very large libraries or those with large collections of books on one subject find that the Library of Congress System suits their needs better because it can be divided into more precise categories than the Dewey Decimal System. Major classes are indicated by letters rather than by numbers, subdivided then by other letters and numbers. A book, *The Loch Ness Monster* by Cooke, would have the L.C. number QL89.C65, while its Dewey call number would be: 001.94
C7721

THE CARD CATALOG is the file for the library

containing alphabetized cards for every book in the library. For each book there is an author card, a title card, and as many subject cards as are necessary to cover the subjects dealt with in the book. Books of fiction have subject cards only if they contain authentic information about a location, a time period, specific events or people. Subject cards are distinguished because they are typed either in red or all capital letters. Here are examples of catalog cards.

USING THE CARD CATALOG: How do you look up a person in the card catalog? Do it as you do someone in the telephone book, last name first. This is true if the person is the author of a book or if the person is the subject of the book.

To find a title, look up the first word of the title unless the first word is "A," "An," or "The." If the first word is an article, go to the second word.

Numbers and abbreviations are filed as though they were spelled out.

Author Card

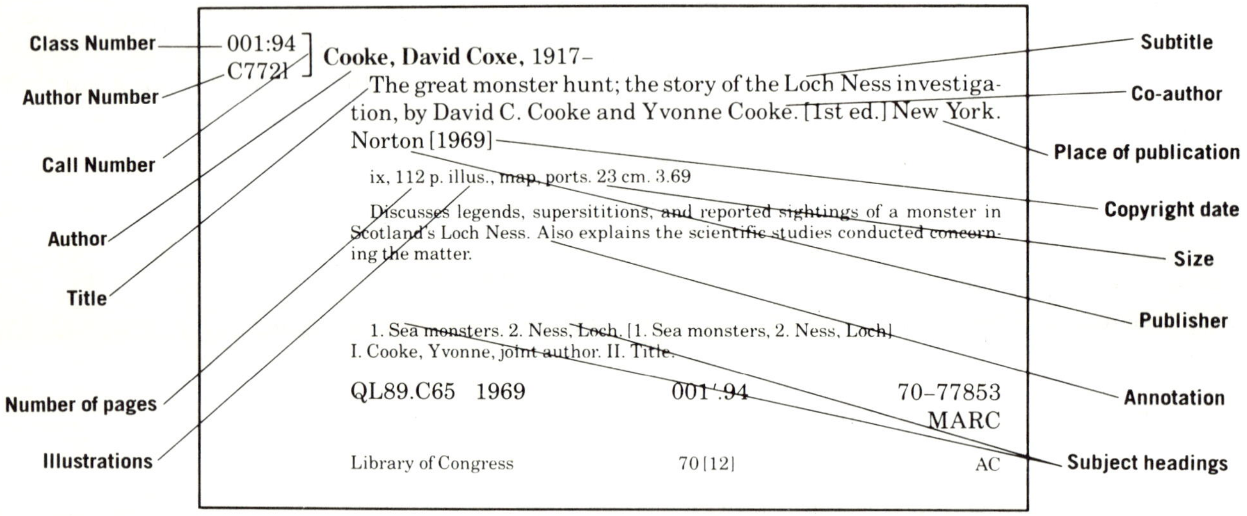

Title Card

The great monster hunt

001:94
C7721
Cooke, David Coxe, 1917–
The great monster hunt; the story of the Loch Ness investigation, by David C. Cooke and Yvonne Cooke. [1st ed.] New York. Norton [1969]

ix, 112 p. illus., map, ports. 23 cm. 3.69

Discusses legends, supersititions, and reported sightings of a monster in Scotland's Loch Ness. Also explains the scientific studies conducted concerning the matter.

1. Sea monsters. 2. Ness, Loch. [1. Sea monsters, 2. Ness, Loch]
I. Cooke, Yvonne, joint author. II. Title.

QL89.C65 1969 001'.94 70–77853
MARC
Library of Congress 70 [12] AC

Subject Card

Sea Monsters

001:94
C7721
Cooke, David Coxe, 1917–
The great monster hunt; the story of the Loch Ness investigation, by David C. Cooke and Yvonne Cooke. [1st ed.] New York. Norton [1969]

ix, 112 p. illus., map, ports. 23 cm. 3.69

Discusses legends, supersititions, and reported sightings of a monster in Scotland's Loch Ness. Also explains the scientific studies conducted concerning the matter.

1. Sea monsters. 2. Ness, Loch. [1. Sea monsters, 2. Ness, Loch]
I. Cooke, Yvonne, joint author. II. Title.

QL89.C65 1969 001'.94 70–77853
MARC
Library of Congress 70 [12] AC

All names beginning "Mc," "Mac," "M'" are filed as though they were spelled "Mac."

In parentheses are the first three letters of the word you would look behind for the following titles: *Mr. Roberts* (Mis); *McGregor Strikes Back* (Mac); *1001 Questions about Birds* (One); *A Moveable Feast* (Mov); *Jane Eyre* (Jan); *The Count of Monte Cristo* (Cou); *And Now Tomorrow* (And because the first word is not "An").

Cards for books by a person come before cards for books about that person: Irving, Washington (author of "Rip Van Winkle") precedes IRVING, WASHINGTON (subject of a biography).

Periods in history are arranged chronologically, factual books first, then fiction.

U. S.–History
U. S.–History-Revolution
U. S.–History-Revolution-Fiction
U. S.–History-Civil War
U. S.–History-Civil War-Fiction
U. S.–History-20th Century

ALPHABETIZING: Most people think they know how to arrange in correct alphabetical order, yet they still have trouble finding things in the card catalog. One reason is that there is more than one system of alphabetical arrangement. The library uses the "word-by-word" system, meaning alphabetizing by letters to the end of each word, short words before long words. The other system, used by many encyclopedias and people who index books, is the letter-by-letter system, which is a strict alphabetical arrangement of all letters disregarding the ending of words.

LIBRARY SYSTEM	OTHER SYSTEM
New Amsterdam	New Amsterdam
New Delhi	Newark
New Zealand	New Delhi
Newark	New Zealand

SUBJECT HEADING: The most difficult part of library research seems to be establishing the key word or phrase that will lead you to the information you seek—finding the right subject heading. This is true not only for the card catalog but also for any other index, in books, encyclopedias, the *Readers' Guide,* etc.

One help is the existence of cross references, "See" and "See also" cards. A "See" card means there is nothing here, that you must look elsewhere. A "See also" card means there is something here but the information you seek may be listed under another heading. For instance, if you look up "Child abuse," you may be told to see the correct subject heading which is "Cruelty to children." Or if you look up "Energy," there may be a "See also" reference which tells you that "Energy" is a valid subject heading (for books about the physics of force and energy) but if you want something about energy as a fuel you should "See also" the alternative heading, "Power resources."

Here are some questions to ask yourself if you are having trouble with subject headings:

* Is there a larger subject that might include it? (U. S.—History—Civil War, rather than Gettysburg, Battle of).

* Is there a smaller subject? (American poetry, rather than Poetry).

* Does your subject overlap another? (Are you searching for the entertainment or the electronics aspect of television?)

* Is there another way to spell it or say it? (Cookery, French vs. French cookery; or Balzac, Honoré de vs. de Balzac, Honoré).

* Does it have a prefix? (U. S. Supreme Court instead of just Supreme Court).

* If your topic is a person, where and when did he live? What was he famous for? (For a report on Michelangelo you would probably do much better not reading a full-length biography but using information under Art—History; European history; Painting—History; Renaissance; Sculpture.

OTHER SOURCES: While today's libraries still find books the most useful sources of information, do not overlook the many non-book materials in its collection. Catalog cards will direct you to recordings, tapes, filmstrips, microfilm, microfiche, pictures, etc. The Vertical File contains pamphlets, clippings, maps, and other materials arranged alphabetically by subject matter in a filing cabinet or pamphlet boxes.

OTHER INFORMATION RETRIEVAL SOURCES: We have discussed at length using the card catalog, for it is a comprehensive index to materials in the library. However, there are additional useful indexes to help you out. Indexes are lists (or catalogs) of subjects, authors, or titles with information about where to find more material.

*Computers, besides storing information, can tell where it is located, both within a library and in other places.

* Indexes to books and to encyclopedias are a useful aid to finding material in a book or encyclopedia. Too many people commonly ignore the index volume of an encyclopedia set (usually the last volume), but it is an invaluable tool, as it locates all the information in the entire set and often pinpoints where material is found that has no sepa-

rate article in the alphabetical listing. It can save time, also, as different encyclopedias head the same information differently, i.e. Man, Prehistoric; Prehistoric man; Fossil man; Evolution of Man.

Here is a typical index listing:

Newton, Sir Isaac (English physicist) N:306 with picture
Aerodynamics A: 78-79
Calculus (History) C:22
Color Ci:666
Dynamics D: 321
Gravitation G:320
(Specific information about Newton's Theory of Gravity will be found in volume G on page 320).

* Reference books, such as *Play Index, Short Story Index, Poetry Index* tell in which books specific plays, stories, and poems are located.

* Some magazines and newspapers, such as *National Geographic* and the *New York Times* have indexes to back issues of their publications. Larger libraries index the local newspaper and put it on microfilm or microfiche.

*One of the most valuable indexing tools is the *Readers' Guide to Periodical Literature,* which indexes almost two hundred magazines of general interest. Paperback supplements are published twice a month, which are combined into three-month supplements. Then a full year's guide is bound in a single hardcover volume. There is also an *Abridged Readers' Guide* covering fewer magazines. This service is especially useful for finding recent, current information. Here is a typical entry, with explanation:

Under "Libraries" there are four sub-heads in one issue: Automation; Circulation; Federal aid; and Fines. Under "Fines" is found this entry:

A librarian throws the book at overdue borrowers.
L. Giuliano. il por People Wkly 17:133 Ap 5 '82

This means L. Giuliano has written an article titled "A librarian throws the book at overdue borrowers," which is found in the magazine *People Weekly,* dated April 5, 1982, on page 133. The volume number for that issue is 17. The article also contains pictures (il) and a portrait (por).

A HOME REFERENCE LIBRARY: Reference books, which are usually expensive, are not intended for straight-through reading, but are designed to impart specific information quickly. The reference collection in a library is usually extensive and is not available to be checked out. Everyone should make a survey of what is available at their favorite library, but most people like to build a small home collection which can prove to be very useful at odd times of the day or night. Many of these books can be purchased in paperback so they fit into the average family's budget.

Indispensable in the home is a good *dictionary* which defines words, gives correct spelling and syllable division, and contains a great deal of additional front and back matter. An unabridged dictionary contains almost all the words in the language, while an abridged one is shortened.

Equally important for the home is a multi-volume general *encyclopedia* containing information about people, places, things, ideas, and events. Annual yearbooks keep it up-to-date. While a one-volume encyclopedia is ideal for quick reference, the more comprehensive multi-volume set is naturally better for detailed information such as school reports.

A handy tool is an *almanac,* such as the *World Almanac,* which is published yearly in paperback and is full of lists, tables, statistics, and all kinds of facts and figures.

For anyone who writes anything a *thesaurus* is most helpful. Also available in paperback, it is a dictionary of synonyms, to help the writer find the exact word needed.

Quotation books, again in paperback, allow the reader and writer to identify a quotation, to cite it in full, and to find an apt one on a particular theme.

Also useful in the home is an *atlas,* a book of maps, which is indispensable for planning trips as well as for obtaining information on political divisions, population, climate, resources, etc.

If a family has special hobbies or students pursuing special interests, there are innumerable handbooks covering single subjects and other reference books that could be purchased. It is always advisable to make friends with the local librarian, who can direct you to almost any information you seek.

Foreign Words and Phrases

In a language like English, whose vocabulary is at least 80 per cent borrowed from other language sources, it is not always easy to judge whether a word or expression should be considered as "foreign" or "naturalized." The choice is easier when it comes to full sentences and sayings. The chief sources of our foreign words and phrases are French and Latin. Other heavy contributors are Italian (particularly for musical terms), German, Greek, and Spanish. But English is a ready borrower and adapter, and we find in our list contributions from other European languages (Russian, Dutch, Scandinavian, Portuguese, etc.); from Semitic tongues, such as Hebrew and Arabic; from languages of Asia, such as Japanese, Chinese, Persian, and Turkish; from the tongues of the American Indians; and even from languages of the far Pacific, notably Hawaiian.

In each case, we have given the pronunciation of the word or expression with an approximation to the language of origin, even where usage has established a current English pronunciation; for instance, while there is a current English pronunciation of a Latin term like *bona fide,* our transcription approximates the sound of the original Latin because the current pronunciation is already commonly known.

The system of transcription is for the most part self-explanatory. Place the stress on the syllable that appears in capitals. Pronounce: AH like the *a* in *father;* EH like the *e* in *met;* EYE as in *eye;* OH like the *o* in *or;* OO as in *fool;* EE as in *seen;* OW as in *fowl;* ZH like the *s* in *pleasure;* AW as in *awe;* AY as in *lay.* In French words, ÃH, ẼH, ÃW, ŨH represent the four French nasal sounds of *an, vin, on, un,* respectively; shut off completely the passage between nose and mouth, so that your breath-stream is forced into the nose, and pronounce at the same time AH, EH, AW, UH. The transcription Ö represents a sound halfway between the *e* of *met* and the *o* of *or* (for which the French spelling is *eu* or *oeu*); the transcription Ü represents a sound intermediate between the *oo* of *fool* and the *ee* of *seen* (purse lips for *oo,* and try to say *ee*). In German words, KH represents the sound of *ch* in *ach,* Ç the sound of *ch* in *ich* (the nearest English approximation is the *h* of *huge).* Abbreviations for the names of the source language are as follows:

F	French	Jap	Japanese
L	Latin	Ch	Chinese
It	Italian	Du	Dutch
Sp	Spanish	Pers	Persian
G	German	Swed	Swedish
Pt	Portuguese	Yid	Yiddish
R	Russian	Arab	Arabic
Gk	Greek	Turk	Turkish
Sk	Sanskrit	Hind	Hindi
Heb	Hebrew	Norw	Norwegian

Other languages of rare occurrence (Hungarian, Irish, Welsh, Icelandic, Basque, Egyptian, Hawaiian, etc.) are left unabbreviated.

The translations given are sometimes literal, but more often aim at rendering the meaning of the foreign word or expression.

The italicized words and expressions are still considered "foreign." These words should be underlined in the original manuscript and italicized when printed. Not all authorities will agree with this list. When you "naturalize" a word or phrase, be prepared to defend your act. A quick rule to follow is: If the word or phrase does not appear in one of the major dictionaries, then it is still "foreign."

India—Hall of Special Audience in Red Fort, Delhi

A

ab initio (ahb ee-NEE-tee-oh), from the beginning (L)

à bon marché (a bãw mar-SHAY), cheap, a bargain (F)

ab ovo (ahb OH-woh), from the egg, from the very start (L)

absinthe (ap-SẼHT), wormwood, absinth (F)

a cappella (ah kahp-PEHL-lah), church style, without accompaniment (It)

accelerando (ah-chay-lay-RAHN-doh), with increasing speed (It)

Achtung (AKH-toong), attention (G)

adagio (ah-DAH-joh), slowly (It)

ad astra per aspera (ahd AH-strah pehr AH-speh-rah), to the stars through difficult places (L)

addendum (ahd-DEHN-doom) (pl. addenda, ahd-DEHN-dah), to be added (L)

Adeste Fideles (ah-DEHS-teh fee-DEH-lehs), Come, ye faithful (L)

ad hoc (ahd HOHK), for this, for this purpose (L)

adieu (a-DYÖ), farewell, good-bye (F)

ad infinitum (ahd een-fee-NEE-toom), to infinity, on and on (L)

adiós (ah-DYOHS), farewell, good-bye (Sp)

ad lib(itum) (ahd Lee-bee-toom), at pleasure (usually abbr. ad lib) (L)

ad nauseam (ahd NOW-seh-ahm), to the point of disgust (L)

ad valorem (ahd wah-LOH-rehm), in proportion to value or valuation (L)

affaire de coeur (a-FEHR duh KÖR), love affair (F)

affaire d'honneur (a-FEHR daw-NÖR), matter involving honor (F)

aficionado (ah-fee-thyoh-NAH-doh), fan, enthusiast (Sp)

a fortiori (ah fohr-tee-OH-ree), with greater reason, all the more (L)

agenda (ah-GHEHN-dah), things to be done (L)

agent provocateur (a-ZHÃH praw-vaw-ka-TÖR), one who provokes others into unlawful actions (F)

agio (AH-joh), ease; currency differential (It)

Agnus Dei (AHG-noos DEH-ee), Lamb of God (L)

agora (AH-goh-rah), marketplace (Gk)

aguardiente (ah-gwahr-DYEHN-teh), firewater, brandy (Sp)

aide-de-camp (EHD duh KÃH), field aide (F)

aigrette (eh-GREHT), egret, spray of feathers (F)

aiguillette (eh-ghee-YEHT), shoulder-knot (F)

à la (a la), in the–fashion (à la française, French style) (F)

à la carte (a la KART), according to the menu, picking out individual items (F)

alameda (ah-lah-MEH-dah), poplar grove (Sp)

à la mode (a la MAWD), in the fashion (F)

alcázar (ahl-KAH-thahr), fortress, fortified palace (Arab-Sp)

al fresco (ahl FRAYS-koh), in the open air (It)

alias (AH-lee-ahs), otherwise, at another time (L)

alibi (AH-lee-bee), elsewhere (L)

allegro (ahl-LAY-groh), quick, lively, merry (It)

alma mater (AHL-mah MAH-tehr), fostering mother, school or college (L)

aloha oe (ah-LOH-hah OH-eh), farewell to you (Hawaiian)

Alpenstock (AHL-pen-shtok), iron-tipped staff used in mountain climbing (G)

alpha-omega (AHL-fah OH-may-gah), beginning and end (Gk)

alter ego (AHL-tehr EH-goh), another I, close and inseparable friend (L)

alto (AHL-toh), low female voice (used for *contralto,* "counter high") (It)

alumnus, alumna (ah-LOOM-noos, ah-LOOM-nah), graduate of an institution (L)

amabile (ah-MAH-bee-lay), amiable, pleasing (It)

amanuensis (ah-mah-noo-EHN-sees), clerk, secretary (L)

amicus curiae (ah-MEE-koos KOO-ree-eye), friend of the court (L)

amour propre (a-MOOR PRAW-pruh), self-love, pride (F)

ancien régime (ãh-SYẼH ray-ZHEEM), old, prerevolutionary regime (F)

animato (ah-nee-MAH-toh), animated, with spirit (It)

anno Domini (AHN-nob DOH-mee-nee), in the year of our Lord (abbr. A.D.) (L)

Anschluss (AHN-shloos), annexation, union (G)

ante bellum (AHN-teh BEHL-loom), before the war (L)

ante meridiem (AHN-teh meh-REE-dee-ehm), before noon, morning (abbr. A.M.) (L)

antipasto (ahn-tee-PAH-stoh), appetizer, hors d'oeuvre (It)

apartheid (a-PART-hayt), South African policy of racial segregation (Du)

apéritif (a-pay-ree-TEEF), appetizer, before-meal drink (F)

aplomb (a-PLÃW), self-possession, poise (F)

a posteriori (ah pohs-teh-ree-OH-ree), with hindsight, reasoning backwards from observed facts (L)

appassionato (ahp-pahs-syoh-NAH-toh), passionately (It)

Après moi le déluge! (a-PREH MWAH luh day-LÜZH), after me the deluge, I don't care what happens after I'm gone (F)

a priori (ah pree-OH-ree), reaching conclusions before gathering facts (L)

apropos (a praw-POH), opportunely, by the way, with regard to (F)

aquavit (ah-kwah-VEET), brandy (Swedish, from Latin *aqua vitae,* water of life)

arbiter elegantiarum (AHR-bee-tehr eh-leh-gahn-tee-AH-room), arbiter of style or taste (L)

argot (ar-GOH), slang, thieves' cant (F)

argumentum ad hominem (ahr-goo-MEHN-toom ahd HOH-mee-nehm), diversion of a discussion to the personality of the opponent (L)

aria (AH-ryah), vocal solo passage in an opera (It)

arista (AH-rees-tah), the best, honors group in a high school (Gk)

arpeggio (ahr-PAY-joh), notes of chord played in harplike succession (It)

arrière-pensée (a-RYEHR pãh-SAY), mental reservation, afterthought (F)

arroz con pollo (ahr-ROHTH kohn POH-lyoh), chicken with rice and condiments (Sp)

ars amandi (AHRS ah-MAHN-dee), the art of loving (L)

ars gratia artis (AHRS GRAH-tee-ah AHR-tees), art for art's sake (L)

ars longa, vita brevis (AHRS LOHN-gah, WEE-tah BREH-wees), art is long, but life is fleeting (L)

attaché (a-ta-SHAY), diplomatic official attached to an embassy (F)

au courant (oh koo-RÃH), posted, informed (F)

auf Wiedersehen (owf VEE-duhr-zayn), good-bye, till we meet again (G)

France—The Sacré Coeur, Paris

au gratin (oh gra-TẼH), baked with crumbs or cheese on top (F)

au jus (oh ZHÜ), in its natural juice or gravy (F)

aurea mediocritas (OW-ray-ah meh-dee-OH-kree-tahs), the golden mean (L)

au revoir (oh ruh-VWAHR), good-bye, till we meet again (F)

auri sacra fames (OW-ree SAH-krah FAH-mehs), sacred lust for gold (L)

aurora borealis (ow-ROH-rah boh-ray-AH-lees), the northern lights (L)

Aut Caesar aut nullus (owt KEYE-sahr owt NOOL-loos), either everything or nothing (L)

Autobahn (OW-toh-bahn), automobile highway (G)

auto da fé (OW-toh dah FEH), burning at the stake on a charge of heresy (Pt)

Aux armes! (oh-ZAHRM), to arms! (F)

avant-garde (a-VÃH-GAHRD), in the van or forefront (F)

Ave atque vale! (AH-weh AHT-kweh WAH-leh), hail and farewell (L)

Ave Caesar, morituri te salutamus (AH-weh KEYE-sahr, moh-ree-TOO-ree teh sah-loo-TAH-moos), Hail, Caesar, we who are about to die salute you (L)

Ave Maria (AH-weh mah-REE-ah), Hail, Mary (L)

à votre santé! (a VAW-truh SÃH-tay), to your health! (F)

B

baba (bah-BAH), light cake (F)

babu (BAH-boo), gentleman, Mr. (Hindi)

babushka (BAH-boosh-kuh), scarf over the head, tied under the chin "little grandmother" fashion (R)

baklava (or *paklava*) (bah-KLAH-vah), Turkish pastry made with nuts and honey (Turkish)

bakshish (BAHK-sheesh), tip, money (Persian)

balalaika (buh-luh-LEYE-kuh), three-stringed triangular guitar (R)

bambino (bahm-BEE-noh), baby, child (It)

banderilla (bahn-deh-REE-lyah), dart with streamer used in bullfight (Sp)

banditti (bahn-DEE-tee), incorrect spelling for *banditi*, "bandits" (It)

banzai (BAHN-zeye), cheer or battle cry, "ten thousand years" (Jap)

bar mitzva (BAHR-MEETS-vah), confirmation ceremony (Heb)

baroque (ba-RAWK), irregular in shape, over-ornamental (F)

bas bleu (BAH BLÖ), blue-stocking, over-intellectual woman (F)

bas-relief (bah-ruh-LYEHF), sculpture with figures projecting from background (F)

basso profundo (BAHS-soh proh-FOON-doh), deep bass voice (It-L)

bathos (BAH-thos), false pathos; an anti-climax (Gk)

beau geste (BOH ZHEHST), fine gesture or deed (F)

beau monde (BOH MÃWD), high society (F)

beaux arts (BOH-ZAHR), fine arts (F)

béchamel (bay-sha-MEHL), rich white sauce (F)

beige (BEHZH), undyed, grayish tan (F)

Beiheft (BEYE-heft), supplement, supplementary volume (G)

bel canto (behl KAHN-toh), fine singing (It)

belladonna (behl-lah-DAWN-nah), lovely lady, poisonous plant, eye-drug (It)

belles-lettres (behl-LEH-truh), literature, the humanities (F)

Bel Paese (behl pah-AY-say), beautiful country, a creamy cheese (It)

berceuse (behr-SÜZ), cradle-song, lullaby (F)

béret (bay-REH), flat, round cap (F)

bête noire (BEHT NWAHR), black beast, pet abomination (F)

bêtise (beh-TEEZ), foolish act or word (F)

beurre noir (BÖR NWAHR), black butter sauce (F)

billet-doux (bee-YEH DOO), love note or letter (F)

bis (BEES), twice, encore (L)

bisque (BEESK), rich soup (F)

bistro (bee-STROH), cabaret, wine-shop (F)

blanc mange (BLÃH MÃHZH), white pudding (F)

blasé (bla-ZAY), jaded, satiated, bored (F)

blintzi (BLEEN-tsy), cheese or meat wrapped in pancake (R)

Blitzkrieg (BLITZ-kreek), lightning war; swift, sudden attack (G)

Blut und Boden (BLOOT unt BOH-duhn), blood and soil (G)

Blut und Eisen (BLOOT unt EYE-zuhn), blood and iron (G)

B'nai B'rith (BNEYE BREETH), sons of the covenant, Jewish service organization (Heb)

bocce (BAW-chay), an Italian bowling game (It)

boeuf á la mode (BÖF a la MAWD), larded and pot-roasted beef (F)

Boer (BOOR), peasant or settler in South Africa (Du)

Bohême (boh-EHM), gypsy-like, unconventional living (F)

bolero (boh-LEH-roh), a Spanish dance (Sp)

Bolsheviki (buhl'-shuh-vee-KEE), Maximalists, Lenin-led Communists (R)

bombe glacée (BÃWB gla-SAY), frozen dessert (F)

bona fide (BOH-nah FEE-day), in good faith (L)

bon ami (BÃW-na-MEE), good friend (F)

bonanza (boh-NAHN-thah), windfall, run of luck (Sp)

bonbon (Bãw-BÃW), candy (F)

bon gré mal gré (bãw-GRAY mal-GRAY), willy-nilly (F)

bon marché (baw mar-SHAY) (*see* à bon marché)

bon mot (bãw MOH), witticism (F)

bonne (BAWN), maid, nursemaid (F)

bonus (BOH-noos), extra payment (L)

bon vivant (bãw-vee-VÃH), one who likes to live well (F)

bon voyage (bãw-vwa-YAHZH), a happy trip (F)

borsch (BAWRSHCH), Russian beet soup, usually with sour cream (R)

boudoir (boo-DWAHR), lady's private sitting-room (F)

bouffant (boo-FÃH), puffed out, full (F)

bouillabaisse (boo-ya-BEHS), seafood soup (F)

bouillon (boo-YÃW), clear beef or chicken broth (F)

bourgeoisie (boor-zhwah-ZEE), middle class (F)

boutonnière (boo-taw-NYEHR), buttonhole, flower for a buttonhole (F)

bravo, brava (BRAH-voh, BRAH-vah), cry of approval; hired killer (It)

Brie (BREE), a creamy French cheese (F)

brio (BREE-oh), vivacity, liveliness (It)

brioche (bree-AWSH), bun, light roll (F)

Iran—Street Scene, Teheran

broccoli (BRAWK-koh-lee), green variety of cauliflower (It)

brochure (braw-SHÜR), pamphlet (F)

brut (BRÜ), raw, unadulterated (F)

Bund (BOONT), league; union, organization (G)

Bundesrepublik (BOON-duhs-reh-poo-bleek), West German Federal Republic (G)

burro (BOOR-roh), donkey (Sp)

bushido (BOO-shee-doh), code of honor of *samurai* class (Jap)

C

ca. See *circa*

cabala, kabala (kahb-ah-LAH), Hebrew occult religious philosophy (Heb)

cacciatora (kah-chah-TOH-rah), hunter style (It); more properly *alla cacciatora*

caciocavallo (kah-choh-kah-VAHL-loh), piquant Italian cheese (It)

cacique (kah-THEE-kay), American Indian chief, political leader (Carib-Sp)

caesura (keye-SOO-rah), break in line of poetry (L)

café (ka-FAY), coffee shop, saloon (F);—**au lait** (oh LEH), coffee with milk;—**noir** (NWAHR), black coffee

caffè espresso (kah-FEH ays-PREHS-soh), strong black coffee, machine-made (It)

Calvados (kal-va-DOHS), apple brandy from the French region of the same name (F)

camaraderie (ka-ma-rad-REE), loyalty, comradeship, good fellowship (F)

camarilla (kah-mah-REE-lyah), clique, group of special advisors (Sp)

Camembert (ka-māh-BEHR), a soft French cheese (F)

camino real (kah-MEE-noh reh-AHL), royal or main highway (Sp)

camorra (kah-MAWR-rah), Neapolitan secret society (It)

campanile (kahm-pah-NEE-lay), bell tower (It)

campo santo (KAHM-poh SAHN-toh), graveyard, cemetery (It)

canaille (ka-NA-yuh), rabble (F)

canapé (ka-na-PAY), open sandwich served as appetizer (F)

canard (ka-NAHR), duck, hoax (F)

canasta (kah-NAHS-tah), basket, card game (Sp)

can can (kāh-KĀH), kicking dance (F)

cannelloni (kahn-nayl-LOH-nee), large hollow macaroni stuffed with meat (It)

cantabile (kahn-TAH-bee-lay), singable, in singing style (It)

cantata (kahn-TAH-tah), musical composition for solos or choruses (It)

canton (kāh-TĀW), political subdivision of Switzerland (F)

cap-à-pied (ka-pa-PYEH), head-to-foot armor (F)

capias (KAH-pee-ahs), "you may take"; arrest warrant (L)

capriccio (kah-PREE-choh), free musical composition, caprice (It)

carabiniere (kah-rah-bee-NYEH-ray), Italian military policeman (It)

carioca (kah-RYOH-kah), native of Rio; Brazilian dance (Pt)

carpe diem (KAHR-peh DEE-ehm), "seize the day"; make hay while the sun shines (L)

carte blanche (KART BLĀHSH), free hand; authorization to act as one will (F)

cartel (kar-TEHL), monopoly trust; organized group of business interests (F)

Carthago delenda est (kahr-TAH-goh deh-LEHN-dah EHST), Carthage must be destroyed (L)

cartouche (kar-TOOSH), cartridge; oval space for inscription of name of Egyptian Pharaoh (F)

casserole (kas-RAWL), clay saucepan for cooking and serving; contents thereof (F)

casus belli (KAH-soos BEHL-lee), occurrence giving rise to war (L)

caudillo (kow-DEE-lyoh), chief, leader (Sp)

cause célèbre (KOHZ say-LEH-bruh), famous or sensational trial (F)

causerie (kohz-REE), chat, informal talk (F)

cavatina (kah-vah-TEE-nah), short song (It)

caveat (KAH-weh-aht), let (him) beware (L);—**emptor** (EHMP-tohr), let the buyer beware

cave canem (KAH-weh KAH-nehm), beware of the dog (L)

cello (CHEHL-loh); abbr. of *violoncello,* musical instrument (It)

certiorari (kehr-tee-oh-RAH-ree), "to be ascertained"; writ to procure records (L)

c'est-à-dire (seh-ta-DEER), that is to say (F)

c'est la vie (seh-la-VEE), that's life (F)

ceteris paribus (KEH-teh-rees PAH-ree-boos), other things being equal (L)

chacun à son goût (sha-KŪH a-sāw-GOO), everyone to his taste (F)

chacun pour soi (sha-KŪH poor SWAH), every man for himself (F)

chaise longue (SHEHZ LĀWG), reclining chair or sofa (F)

champagne (shāh-PA-nyuh), French sparkling wine (F)

champignon (shāh-pee-NYĀW), mushroom (F)

chanteuse (shāh-TÖZ), female singer (F)

chargé d'affaires (shar-ZHAY da-FEHR), minor government official temporarily replacing a higher diplomat (F)

charivari (sha-ree-va-REE), mock serenade or raucous music (F)

chasseur (sha-SÖR), hunter; light-infantryman; footman (F)

château (sha-TOH), castle, palace (F)

chef (de cuisine) (SHEF duh kwee-ZEEN), head cook (F)

chef d'oeuvre (SHEH DÖ-vruh), masterpiece (F)

Cherchez la femme! (shehr-SHAY la FAM), look for the woman in the case (F)

chérie (shay-REE), dearie, sweetheart (F)

chetnik (CHET-neek), Yugoslav resistance fighter (Serbo-Croatian)

chevaux-de-frise (shuh-VÖH duh FREEZ), barrier of spikes in timber (F)

chez (SHAY), at the home of (F)

Chianti (KYAHN-tee), Italian wine (It)

chiaroscuro (kyah-roh-SKOO-roh), light and dark effect (It)

chic (SHEEK), elegant, elegance (F)

chiffon (shee-FÃW), rag; silk crepe, whipped ingredients in pie (F)

chile con carne (CHEE-leh kohn KAHR-neh), Mexican dish consisting of kidney beans, ground meat, and red peppers (Sp)

chop suey (TSAH SOO-ee), Chinese-American dish of meat and vegetables (Ch)

chow mein (CHOW MYEHN), Chinese dish of fried noodles, with meat or vegetables (Ch)

Cid (THEED), chieftain, leader (Sp, from Arab *sayyid*)

ci-gît (see-ZHEE), here lies (F)

cinquecento (cheen-kway-CHEHN-toh), 16th century (It)

circa (KEER-kah), about, approximately; abbr. ca. (L)

Civis Romanus sum (Kee-wees roh-MAH-noos SOOM), I am a Roman citizen (L)

Civitas Dei (KEE-wee-tahs DEH-ee), the City of God (L)

clair de lune (KLEHR duh LÜN), moonlight (F)

claret (kla-REH), light red wine (F)

clef (KLAY or KLEHF), key (F)

cliché (klee-SHAY), stereotype; hackneyed expression (F)

clientèle (klee-ãh-TEHL), customers or patrons (F)

clique (KLEEK), set; group (F)

clôture (kloh-TÜR), closure of debate (F)

cocido (koh-THEE-doh), Spanish stew (Sp)

coda (KOH-dah), tail; concluding musical passage (It)

Code Napoléon (KAWD na-poh-lay-ÃW), code of civil law of France of 1804, applied with modifications in Louisiana (F)

codex (KOH-dehks), body of laws; manuscript on parchment (L)

Cogito, ergo sum (KOH-ghee-toh, EHR-goh SOOM), I think, therefore I exist (L)

cognac (kaw-NYAK), French brandy (F)

cognoscenti (erroneous for *conoscenti*, koh-noh-SHEHN-tee), experts (It)

coiffeur (kwa-FÖR), hairdresser (F)

coiffure (kwa-FÜR), hairstyle (F)

coloratura (koh-loh-rah-TOO-rah), embellishment in vocal music; soprano (It)

commando (koh-MAHN-doh), raiding troops (Du, from Pt)

comme ci, comme ça (kawm SEE, kawm SA), so-so (F)

comme il faut (kawm eel FOH), proper; properly; in the right fashion (F)

***commedia* dell'arte** (kohm-MEH-dyah dayl-LAHR-tay), guild players' comedy, often improvised (It)

commissar (kuhm-mee-SAHR), government official (R, from F *commissaire*)

commune (kaw-MÜN), self-governing town; French revolutionary movement (F)

communiqué (kaw-mü-nee-KAY), official statement or dispatch (F)

compote (kãw-PAWT), stewed fruit (F)

compte rendu (KÃWT rãh-DÜ), book review; report (F)

con amore (kohn ah-MOH-ray), lovingly (It)

concerto (kohn-CHEHR-toh), musical composition for solo instrument(s) with orchestral accompaniment (It)

concierge (kãw-SYEHRZH), janitor, superintendent (F)

concordat (kãw-kawr-DAH), pact, agreement (F from Latin *concordatus*)

condottiere (kohn-doht-TYEH-ray), Italian Renaissance leader of mercenary troops (It)

confer (KOHN-fehr), compare; see; abbr. cf. (L)

confetti (kohn-FEHT-tee), candies; plaster or paper imitations used at feasts (It)

confrère (kãw-FREHR), colleague; associate (F)

conga (KAWN-gah), Latin-American dance (Sp or Pt)

con moto (kohn MAW-toh), with movement; fast (It)

connoisseur (kaw-neh-SÖR), expert; one who knows (F)

conquistadores (kohn-kees-tah-DOH-rehs), conquerors (Sp)

console (kãw-SAWL), ornamental bracket for supporting shelf; table with ledges (F)

consommé (kãw-saw-MAY), concentrated meat broth (F)

consortium (kohn-SOHR-tee-oom), international finance control group (L)

contra (KOHN-trah), against (abbr. con; L)

contrabasso (kohn-trah-BAHS-soh), double-bass viol (It)

copula (KOH-poo-lah), connective; the verb "to be" or a similar verb (L)

coq au vin (KAWK oh VẼH), chicken braised in winc (F)

coquetterie (kaw-keht-REE), flirtatiousness (F)

coram populo (KOH-rahm POH-poo-loh), publicly (L)

cordillera (kohr-dee-LYEH-rah), mountain range (SP)

cornu copiae (KOHR-noo KOH-pee-eye), horn of plenty (L)

corona (koh-ROH-nah), crown (L)

corps de ballet (KAWR duh ba-LEH), ballet troupe (F)

corpus (KOHR-poos), body; collection (L)

corpus delicti (KOHR-poos deh-LEEK-tee), the body or tangible evidence of a crime (L)

corpus juris (KOHR-poos YOO-rees), the body of the law; collection of laws (L)

corrida (kohr-REE-dah), bullfight (Sp)

corrigenda (kohr-ree-GHEHN-dah), things to be corrected (L)

corsage (kawr-SAHZH), bodice; flowers worn on bodice (F)

cortège (kawr-TEHZH), procession (F)

corvée (kawr-VAY), forced labor (F)

cosi cosi (koh-SEE koh-SEE), so-so (It)

coterie (kawt-REE), small, intimate group or circle (F)

coup de grâce (KOO duh GRAHS), death-blow (F)

coup de main (KOO duh MĔH), sudden blow (F)

coup d'état (KOO day-TAH), seizure of government by sudden stroke (F)

couturier (koo-tü-RYAY), dressmaker (F)

crèche (KREHSH), crib, manger, public nursery (F)

credenza (kray-DEHN-tsah), small table or cupboard (It)

credo (KREH-doh), belief, article of faith, creed (L)

crème de menthe (KREHM duh MĂHT), peppermint liqueur (F)

crêpe (KREHP), thin cloth of silk, rayon, wool, etc. (F)

crêpe suzette (KREHP sü-ZEHT), thin pancake (F)

crescendo (kray-SHEHN-doh), gradual increase in loudness or intensity (It)

critique (kree-TEEK), criticism (F)

croissant (krwa-SĂH), crescent-shaped roll (F)

Croix de Guerre (KRWAH duh GHEHR), war cross, French military decoration (F)

croquette (kraw-KEHT), fried meat or fish, covered with bread crumbs (F)

croupier (kroo-PYAY), man who rakes in stakes at gambling table (F)

crux (KROOKS), cross; main point at issue (L)

cucaracha (koo-kah-RAH-chah), cockroach (Sp)

cui bono? (KOO-ee BOH-noh), to whose advantage? (L)

cuisine (kwee-ZEEN), cookery, cooking (F)

cul-de-sac (KÜL-duh-SAHK), blind alley, dead end (F)

cum grano salis (koom GRAH-noh SAH-lees), with a grain of salt (L)

cum laude (koom LOW-deh), with praise, with honor (L)

curé (kü-RAY), parish priest (F)

curriculum (koor-REE-koo-loom), year's course of studies (L);—**vitae** (WEE-teye), outline of one's life

czar (more precisely *tsar*, TSAHR), Russian emperor, autocrat (R)

czardas (more precisely *csárdás*, CHAHR- dahsh), Hungarian dance (Hungarian)

D

da capo (dah KAH-poh), from the start (It)

Dachshund (DAHKS-hoont), short-legged dog (G)

dal segno (dahl SAY-nyoh), from the sign (It)

data (DAH-tah) (sg. **datum**), information at one's disposal (L)

débâcle (day-BAH-kluh), disaster, collapse (F)

débris (day-BREE), wreckage, rubbish (F)

début (day-BÜ), coming out, first appearance (F)

débutante (day-bü-TĂHT), girl making first social appearance (F)

décolleté (day-kawl-TAY), low-necked (F)

décor (day-KAWR), stage setting, room setting (F)

de facto (deh FAHK-toh), in existence, in actuality (L)

deficit (DEH-fee-keet), amount less than what is needed (L)

de gustibus non est disputandum (deh GOOS-tee-boos nohn EHST dees-poo-TAHN-doom), there is no arguing about tastes (L)

Dei gratia (DEH-ee GRAH-tee-ah), by the grace of God (L)

déjeuner (day-zhö-NAY), lunch, breakfast (F)

de jure (deh YOO-reh), legally, legitimately (L)

dele (DEH-leh), erase, strike out, delete; abbreviation (L)

delenda est Carthago (deh-LEHN-dah EHST kahr-TAH-goh), Carthage must be destroyed (L)

delicatessen (day-LEE-kaht-EHS-suhn), prepared foods (G)

delirium tremens (deh-LEE-ree-oom TREH-mehns), alcoholic brain disease (L)

de luxe (duh LÜKS), luxurious, very fancy (F)

démarche (day-MAHRSH), diplomatic approach, step (F)

dementia praecox (deh-MEHN-tee-ah PREYE-kohks), adolescent mental illness (L)

demi-tasse (duh-MEE-TAHS), small cup of coffee (F)

demi-monde (duh-MEE-MAWD), fringe of society (F)

de mortuis nihil nisi bonum (deh MOHR-too-ees NEE-heel NEE-see BOH-noom), say nothing but good about the dead (L)

denarius (deh-NAH-ree-oos), Roman silver coin (L)

denier (duh-NYAY), small coin, unit of weight for hosiery (F)

dénouement (day-noo-MĂH), unraveling, solution of plot (F)

de novo (deh NOH-voh), anew, again from the start (L)

Deo volente (DEH-oh woh-LEHN-teh), God willing (L)

de profundis (deh proh-FOON-dees), out of the depths (L)

de rigueur (duh ree-GÖR), indispensable, required (F)

dernier cri (dehr-NYAY KREE), latest style, last word (F)

derrière (deh-RYEHR), back part, buttocks (F)

descamisado (dehs-kah-mee-SAH-doh), shirtless, follower of Evita Perón (Sp)

déshabillé (day-za-bee-YAY), in state of informal undress (F)

desideratum (deh-see-deh-RAH-toom; pl. **desiderata,** deh-see-deh-RAH-tah), what is desired (L)

détente (day-TÃHT), release of strained relations (F)

de trop (duh TROH), in excess, superfluous, not wanted (F)

deus ex machina (DEH-oos ehks MAH-kee-nah), outside intervention to solve a crisis (L)

Deus vobiscum (DEH-oos woh-BEES-koom), God be with you (L)

diaspora (dee-AHS-poh-rah), dispersion, scattering (particularly of Jews after destruction of Jerusalem) (Gk)

dictum (DEEK-toom), saying, pronouncement (L)

diminuendo (dee-mee-noo-EHN-doh), diminishing in volume (It)

Dirndl (DEERNDL), peasant-girl dress (G)

diseur (fem. diseuse; dee-ZÖR, dee-ZÖZ), monologist (F)

diva (DEE-vah), female opera singer (It)

divertissement (dee-vehr-tees-MÃH), lively piece between acts (F)

divide et impera (dee-WEE-deh eht EEM-peh-rah), divide and conquer (L)

doge (DAW-jay), medieval ruler of Venice (It)

dogma (DOHG-mah), belief, article of faith (Gk)

dolce far niente (DOHL-chay FAHR NYEHN-tay), sweet idleness (It)

dolce stil nuovo (DOHL-chay STEEL NWAW-voh), sweet new literary style of 14th century (It)

Dominus vobiscum (DOH-mee-noos woh-BEES-koom), the Lord be with you (L)

don (DOHN), tutor at English universities; Spanish and Italian title of respect; Mafia leader (It, Sp)

donna (DAWN-nah), lady, woman (It)

Doppelgänger (DOH-pehl-gheng-uhr), ghostly double (G)

dossier (daw-SYAY), file (F)

double entendre (DOO-blãh-TÃH-druh), expression with double meaning (F)

dramatis personae (DRAH-mah-tees pehr-SOH-neye), cast of characters (L)

droshky (DRAWSH-kee), cab, carriage (R)

duce (DOO-chay), leader (It)

dueña (DWEH-nyah), chaperone (Sp)

duomo (DWAW-moh), cathedral (It)

dybbuk (DEE-book), bewitched person; evil spirit entering living body (Heb)

E

eau de vie (OH duh VEE), brandy (F)

ecce homo (EHK-keh HOH-moh), behold the man (L)

échelon (aysh-LÃW), steplike formation of troops, any hierarchical arrangement (F)

éclair (ay-KLEHR), pastry filled with cream (F)

éclat (ay-KLAH), success, prestige (F)

Edda (EHD-dah), old Scandinavian poetry (Icelandic)

Edelweiss (AY-duhl-veyes), white Alpine flower (G)

editio princeps (eh-DEE-tee-oh PREEN-kehps), original edition (L)

eisteddfod (ay-STETH-vohd), musical or poetic contest (Welsh)

élan (ay-LÃH), sparkle, liveliness (F)

el dorado (ehl doh-RAH-doh), fabulous South American land of gold (Sp)

Eli (EH-lee), my God (Heb)

élite (ay-LEET), select few (F)

Elohim (eh-loh-HEEM), God, Supreme Being (Heb)

embarras du choix (ãh-ba-RAH dü SHWAH), trouble making up one's mind (F)

embonpoint (ãh-bãw-PWẼH), plumpness (F)

emeritus (eh-MEH-ree-toos), retired with honor (L)

émigré (ay-mee-GRAY), emigrated, exiled (F)

en bloc (ãh BLAWK), together; as a unit (F)

en brochette (ãh braw-SHEHT), on a skewer (F)

enceinte (ãh-SẼHT), pregnant, with child (F)

en coquille (ãh kaw-KEE-yuh), served in a shell (F)

encore (ãh-KAWR), again; repeat (F)

enfant gâté (terrible) (ãh-FAH gah-TAY, teh-REE-bluh), spoiled child, brat (F)

en masse (ãh MAHS), all together, in a mass (F)

ennui (ãh-NWEE), boredom (F)

en passant (ãh pa-SÃH), incidentally; by the way (F)

ensemble (ãh-SÃH-bluh), together, in a group (F)

entente (ãh-TÃHT), understanding; international agreement, alliance (F)

entourage (ãh-too-RAHZH), surrounding company (F)

entr'acte (ãh-TRAKT), between the acts (F)

entrée (ãh-TRAY), entrance; main dish (F)

entre nous (ãh-truh-NOO), between us (F)

entrepreneur (ãh-truh-pruh-NÖR), one who undertakes or manages (F)

envoi (ãh-VWAH), postscript (F)

épater le bourgeois (ay-pa-TAY luh boor-ZHWAH), to bedazzle and befuddle people (F)

epaulette (ay-poh-LEHT), shoulder piece (F)

e pluribus unum (eh PLOO-ree-boos OO-noom), one out of many (L)

ergo (EHR-goh), therefore, consequently (L)

Erin go bragh (EH-reen goh BRAH), Ireland forever (Ir)

errare humanum est (ehr-RAH-reh hoo-MAH-noom EHST), to err is human (L)

erratum (pl. **errata;** ehr-RAH-toom, ehr-RAH-tah), error, mistake (L)

ersatz (EHR-zatz), substitute, synthetic replacement (G)

escargots (ehs-kar-GOH), snails (F)

espada (ehs-PAH-dah), sword; the matador who kills the bull with a sword (Sp)

esprit de corps (ehs-PREE duh KAWR), spirit of loyalty to one's group (F)

et alii (eht AH-lee-ee); abbr. et al., and others (L)

Sweden—River front, Stockholm

et cetera (eht KEYE-teh-rah); abbr. etc., and others, and other things (L)

ethos (EH-thos), custom, national character (Gk)

et passim (eht PAHS-seem), abbr. et pass., and everywhere, scattered throughout a work (L)

et tu Brute? (eht TOO, BROO-teh), you, too, Brutus? (L)

étude (ay-TÜD), study; short musical composition (F)

et uxor (eht OOK-sohr); abbr. et ux., and wife (L)

eureka! (EH-OO-reh-kah), I have found it! (Gk)

ewig Weibliche (AY-vik VEYEB-li-çe), eternal feminine (G)

ex cathedra (ehks KAH-theh-drah), authoritatively, pontifically (L)

excelsior (ehks-KEHL-see-ohr), ever higher (L)

exempli gratia (ehk-SEHM-plee GRAH-tee-ah), abbr. e.g., for instance (L)

ex libris (ehks LEE-brees), from among the books of (L)

ex officio (ehks ohf-FEE-kee-oh), by virtue of his office (L)

exposé (ehks-paw-ZAY), statement, explanation, revelation (F)

ex post facto (ehks pohst FAHK-toh), after the fact (L)

extempore (ehks-TEHM-poh-reh), without previous preparation (L)

extra (EHKS-trah), beyond, in addition (L)

ex voto (ehks WOH-toh), as a vow; tablet or inscription recording an accomplished vow (L)

F

facsimile (fahk-SEE-mee-leh), exact reproduction (L)

fait accompli (FEH-ta-kolaw-PLEE), thing already done (F)

falsetto (fahl-SAYT-toh), excessively high tone (It)

fandango (fahn-DAHN-goh), Spanish dance (Sp)

farina (fah-REE-nah), flour or meal (L)

fatti maschi, parole femmine (FAHT-tee MAHS-kee, pah-RAW-lay FAYM-mee-nay), deeds are masculine, words feminine (It)

faute de mieux (FOHT duh MYÖ), for lack of anything better (F)

faux pas (FOH PAH), false step, blunder (F)

feis (FAYS), Irish song festival (Ir)

femme de chambre (FAM duh SHÃH-bruh), chambermaid (F)

femme fatale (FAM fa-TAL), enchantress, "vamp" (F)

festina lente (fehs-TEE-nah LEHN-teh), make haste slowly (L)

Festschrift (FEHST-shrift), memorial or commemorative volume (G)

fiacre (FYA-kruh), cab (F)

fiancé, fiancée (fyãh-SAY), betrothed (F)

fiasco (FYAHS-koh), failure (It)

fiat (FEE-aht), administrative order without legislative authorization (L)

fiesta (FYEHS-tah), festival (Sp)

filet mignon (fee-LEH mee-NYÃW), tenderloin steak (F)

financière (fee-nãh-SYEHR), spicy stew (F)

fin de siècle (FÊH duh SYEH-kluh), end of the century; decadence (F)

fine champagne (FEEN shãh-PAH-nyuh), brandy (F)

fines herbes (FEEN ZEHRB), minced chives, parsley, etc. (F)

finis (FEE-nees), end (L)

finocchio (fee-NAWK-kyoh), fennel (It)

fleur de lis (FLÖR duh LEE), lily emblem of France (F)

foie gras (FWAH GRAH), goose liver (F)

fondue (fãw-DÜ), melted cheese (F)

force majeure (FAWRS ma-ZHÖR), superior force (F)

fortissimo (fohr-TEES-see-moh), very loud (It)

foulard (foo-LAHR), neckerchief of silk fabric (F)

franc-tireur (frãh-tee-RÖR), sniper, guerrilla fighter (F)

frappé (fra-PAY), whipped, semifrozen (F)

Frau (FROW), lady, madam, Mrs. (G)

Fräulein (FROY-leyen), Miss, young lady (G)

fresco (FRAYS-koh), mural painting (It)

fricassé (free-ka-SAY), diced meat in thick sauce (F)

frijoles (free-HOH-lehs), kidney beans (Sp)

friseur (free-ZÖR), hairdresser (F)

fritos (FREE-tohs), fried potatoes, etc. (Sp)

fromage (fraw-MAZH), cheese (F)

Führer (FÜ-ruhr), leader (G)

G

gabelle (ga-BEHL), salt tax (F)

gaffe (GAF), bad blunder (F)

gala (GAH-lah), festive (It)

garbanzos (gahr-BAHN-thohs), chick-peas (Sp)

garçon (gar-SÃW), boy, waiter (F)
garni (gar-NEE), garnished (F)
gâteau (gah-TOH), cake (F)
gaucherie (gohsh-REE), awkward or tactless action (F)
gaucho (GOW-choh), South American cowboy (Sp)
gaudeamus igitur (gow-deh-AH-moos EE-ghee-toor), let us therefore rejoice (L)
Gauleiter (GOW-leye-tuhr), Nazi district leader (G)
gazpacho (gath-PAH-choh), Spanish cold soup (Sp)
gefilte fish (guh-FEEL-tuh FISH), stuffed fish (Yiddish)
geheime Staatspolizei (guh-HEYE-muh SHTATS-poh-lee-tseye), abbr. Gestapo, secret state police (G)
geisha (GAY-shah), Japanese professional girl entertainer (Jap)
Gemütlichkeit (guh-MÜT-liç-keyet), congeniality, coziness (G)
gendarme (zhãh-DARM), policeman, constable, state trooper (F)
generalissimo (jay-nay-rah-LEES-see-moh), general in chief (It)
genre (ZHÃHR), kind, sort, species (F)
Gestalt (guh-SHTAHLT), shape, form, pattern (G)
Gestapo (guh-STAH-poh), see geheime Staatspolizei
Gesundheit (guh-ZOONT-heyet), (good) health (G)
ghetto (GAYT-toh), restricted section for Jews or others (It)
gigolo (zhee-goh-LOH), man paid to be dancing partner or companion (F)
glacé (gla-SAY), iced, sugared (F)
Gleichschaltung (GLEYEÇ-shahlt-ung), coordination, assimilation (G)
glissando (glees-SAHN-doh), gliding (F-It)
Glockenspiel (GLOK-uhn-shpeel), carillon (G)
gloria in excelsis Deo (GLOH-ree-ah een ehks-KEHL-sees DEH-oh), glory to God on high (L)
gnocchi (NYAWK-kee), flour or potato small dumplings (It)
golem (GOH-lehm), robot created for an evil purpose (Heb)
goniff (GOH-nif), thief (Yiddish)
gorgonzola (gohr-gohn-TSAW-lah), Italian green mold cheese (It)
Gott mit uns! (GAWT mit OONS), God is with us! (G)
Gott sei dank! (GAWT zeye DAHNK), thanks be to God (G)
goulash (more properly *gulyás*, GOO-LYAHSH), Hungarian meat stew (Hungarian)
gourmet (goor-MEH), epicure, lover of good food (F)
goy (GOY), Gentile, non-Jewish (Heb)
Graf (GRAHF), count (G)
graffiti (grahf-FEE-tee) scratched inscriptions (It)
grande dame (GRÃHD DAHM), great lady (F)
grand prix (GRÃH PREE), first prize (F)
granita (grah-NEE-tah), ice pudding (It)
gratin (gra-TÊH), dish prepared with cheese or bread crumbs (F)
gratis (GRAH-tees), free, without charge (L)
gringo (GREEN-goh), U.S. American (Sp)
gruyère (grü-YEHR), Swiss cheese (F)
guerrilla (ghehr-REE-lyah), warfare by irregulars (Sp)
guru (GOO-roo), teacher (Hindi)
gusto (GOOS-toh), taste, enjoyment (It)

H

habeas corpus (HAH-beh-ahs KOHR-poos), you may have the body; writ to bring someone into court (L)
hacienda (ah-THYEHN-dah), plantation (Sp)
Hadassah (hah-DAHS-sah), Jewish women's organization (Heb)
hallelujah (hah-lay-LOO-yah), praise the Lord (Heb)
hanukkah (HAH-nook-kah), dedication, feast of lights (Heb)
hapax legomenon (HAH-pahks leh-GOH-meh-non), something said only once (Gk)
hara-kiri (HAH-rah-kee-ree), belly-cutting, ceremonial suicide (Jap)
haricots verts (ah-ree-KOH VEHR), green beans (F)
Hasenpfeffer (HAH-zehn-pfef-fuhr), marinated hare (G)
Hasidim (khah-SEE-deem), Jewish religious sect (Heb)
haute couture (OHT koo-TÜR), group of high class dress designers (F)
Heft (HEHFT), volume (G)
hegira (more properly *hijra*, HEEJ-rah), Mohammed's flight; escape; moving day (Arab)
Heimweh (HEYEM-vay), homesickness (G)
Heimwehr (HEYEM-vehr), home guard, militia (G)
Herrenvolk (HEHR-ren-folk), master race (G)
hetaira, **hetaera** (HEH-teye-rah), courtesan (Gk)
hiatus (hee-AH-toos), split, break in line, pause between vowels (L)
hic jacet (HEEK YAH-keht), here lies (L)
hidalgo (ee-DAHL-goh), nobleman, man of gentle birth (Sp)
hierba maté (YEHR-bah mah-TEH), Paraguayan tea (Sp)
hodie mihi, cras tibi (HOH-dee-eh MEE-hee, KRAHS TEE-bee), today to me, tomorrow to you (L)
hoi polloi (hoy pohl-LOY), the many, rabble (Gk)
homard (aw-MAHR), lobster (F)
hombre (OHM-breh), man (Sp)
homo homini lupus (HOH-moh HOH-mee-nee LOO-poos), man is a wolf to his fellow-man (L)
homo sapiens (HOH-moh SAH-pee-ehns), man as a thinking animal or as a genus (L)
honni soit qui mal y pense (aw-NEE SWAH kee MAHL ee PÃHS), evil to him who evil thinks (F)
honoris causa (hoh-NOH-rees KOW-sah), bestowed in recognition of merit (L)
horribile dictu (hohr-REE-bee-leh DEEK-too), horrible to relate (L)
hors de combat (AWR duh kõh-BAH), disabled, out of the fight (F)

hors d'oeuvres (AWR DÖ-vruh), appetizers, relishes (F)

hôtel de ville (hoh-TEHL duh VEEL), town hall (F)

houri (HOO-ree), Mohammedan nymph of paradise (Persian)

hukilau (hoo-kee-LAH-OO), feast (Hawaiian)

hula-hula (HOO-lah-HOO-lah), Hawaiian dance (Hawaiian)

humanum est errare (hoo-MAH-noom EHST ehr-RAH-reh), to err is human (L)

hybris (HOO-brees), transgression of moral law; act of defiance (Gk)

hysteron proteron (HOOS-teh-rohn PROH-teh-rohn), putting the cart before the horse (Gk)

I

ibidem (ee-BEE-dehm), abbr. ibid., in the same place (L)

idée fixe (ee-DAY FEEKS), preconceived notion (F)

id est (EED EHST), abbr. i.e., that is (L)

Iesus Nazarenus Rex Iudaeorum (YEH-soos nah-zah-REH-noos REHKS yoo-deye-OH-room), abbr. I.N.R.I., Jesus of Nazareth King of the Jews (L)

ignis fatuus (EEG-nees FAH-too-oos), will-of-the-wisp (L)

illuminati (eel-loo-mee-NAH-tee), enlightened ones, deep thinkers (L)

imbroglio (eem-BRAW-lyoh), mix-up, mess (It)

impedimenta (eem-peh-dee-MEHN-tah), baggage, hindrances (L)

imprimatur (eem-pree-MAH-toor), license to print, sanction (L)

in absentia (een ahb-SEHN-tee-ah), in one's absence (L)

in articulo mortis (een ahr-TEE-koo-loh MOHR-tees), on the point of death (L)

in camera (een KAH-meh-rah), in chambers; in private (L)

incognito (een-KAW-nyee-toh), in disguise, not revealing one's identity (It)

Japan—Ginza by night, Tokyo

incomunicado (een-koh-moo-nee-KAH-doh), cut off from communication with the outside (Sp)

index expurgatorius (EEN-dehks ehks-poor-gah-TOH-ree-oos), list of forbidden books (L)

in esse (een EHS-seh), in being, existing (L)

in extenso (een ehks-TEHN-soh), in full (L)

in extremis (een ehks-TREH-mees), on the point of death (L)

influenza (een-floo-EHN-tsah), respiratory disease, flu (It)

in folio (een FOH-lee-oh), once folded sheet of printing (L)

infra (EEN-frah), below (L)

ingénue (ẽh-zhay-NÜ), innocent feminine character (F)

in hoc signo vinces (een hohk SEEG-noh WEEN-kehs), in this sign you will conquer (L)

in loco parentis (een LOH-koh pah-REHN-tees), in the place of a parent (L)

in medias res (een MEH-dee-ahs REHS), into the thick of things, without introduction (L)

in memoriam (een meh-MOH-ree-ahm), in memory of (L)

innamorato (een-nah-moh-RAH-toh), lover (It)

innuendo (een-noo-EHN-doh), hint, insinuation (L)

in primis (een PREE-mees), among the first (L)

in quarto (een KWAHR-toh), printing sheet folded twice (L)

in re (een REH), in the matter of (L)

in rem (een REHM), proceedings against a thing rather than a person (L)

in saecula saeculorum (een SEYE-koo-lah seye-koo-LOH-room), for ever and ever (L)

insignia (een-SEEG-nee-ah), distinguishing marks (L)

insouciance (ẽh-soo-SYÃHS), indifference, studied carelessness (F)

intaglio (een-TAH-lyoh), decoration cut into a stone (It)

integer vitae scelerisque purus (EEN-teh-ghehr WEE-teye skeh-leh-REES-kweh POO-roos), upright in life and free of guilt (L)

intelligentsia (een-tehl-lee-GHEHN-tsyah), informed intellectual people collectively (R)

inter alia (EEN-tehr AH-lee-ah), among other things (L)

inter alios (EEN-tehr AH-lee-ohs), among others (L)

interim (EEN-teh-reem), meanwhile (L)

intermezzo (een-tayr-MEH-dzoh), music played during intermission (It)

inter nos (EEN-tehr NOHS), between us (L)

in toto (een TOH-toh), completely, entirely (L)

intra muros (EEN-trah MOO-rohs), within the walls (L)

in vino veritas (een WEE-noh WEH-ree-tahs), in wine is the truth (L)

ipse dixit (EEP-seh DEEK-seet), he himself said it; the master has spoken (L)

ipso facto (EEP-soh FAHK-toh), by the very fact (L)

item (EE-tehm), likewise (L)

ite, missa est (EE-teh, MEES-sah EHST), go, the service is finished (L)

izvestiya (eez-VYEHS-tee-yuh), news, information (R)

J

jai-alai (HAH-ee ah-LAH-ee), Basque ball game (Basque)

jardinière (zhar-dee-NYEHR), mixed vegetables; ornamental flower pot (F)

je ne sais quoi (zhuh nuh SEH KWAH), I don't know what (F)

jeu d'esprit (ZHÖ dehs-PREE), witticism (F)

jeunesse dorée (zhö-NEHS daw-RAY), gilded youth, elegant young people (F)

jihad (JEE-hahd), holy war (Arab)

jinni (JEEN-nee), supernatural being that can take human shape (Arab)

jinrickisha (JEEN-REEK-shah), mandrawn two-wheeled cab (Jap)

jodhpur (JOHD-poor), a kind of riding breeches (Hind)

joie de vivre (ZHWAH duh VEE-vruh), joy of being alive (F)

jongleur (zhaw̃-GLÖR), minstrel, juggler (F)

judo (JOO-doh), Japanese system of wrestling (Jap)

jujutsu (JOO JOO-tsoo), see judo (Jap)

junta (HOON-tah), administrative council or committee (Sp)

Jupiter Pluvius (YOO-pee-tehr PLOO-wee-oos), Jupiter of the rain (L)

jus gentium (YOOS GHEHN-tee-oom), law of nations, international law (L)

K

ka (KAH), the soul (Egypt)

kabuki (KAH-boo-kee), Japanese form of drama (Jap)

Kaddish (KAHD-deesh), prayer for the dead (Heb)

Kaffeeklatsch (kahf-FAY-klahtch), gathering for coffee and chatting (G)

kamikaze (KAH-mee-kah-zeh), divine wind; suicide dive bomber (Jap)

Kapellmeister (kah-PEHL-MEYE-stuhr), orchestra or chorus leader (G)

kaput (kah-POOT), finished, done for (G)

Katzenjammer (KAHT-suhn-yahm-muhr), hangover (G)

kibbutz (keeb-BOOTS), Israeli collective farm settlement (Heb)

kibitzer (KIB-its-uhr), onlooker at game, offering unwanted advice; meddler (Yid)

kimono (KEE-moh-noh), Japanese outer garment with sash and loose sleeves (Jap)

Kirschwasser (KEERSH-VAHS-suhr), cherry brandy (G)

Kismet (KEES-meht), fate, lot, will of Allah (Turk)

Knesset (KNEHS-seht), unicameral Israeli parliament (Heb)

koine (koy-NAY), language common to a large area (Gk)

koinos topos (koy-NOHS toh-POHS), commonplace (Gk)

kolkhoz (kuhl-KHAWS), collective farm (R)

Kol Nidre (KOHL NEE-dray), all vows; prayer of atonement; melody to which prayer is sung (Heb)

Kommandatura (kohm-mahn-dah-TOO-rah), command headquarters (G)

Komsomol (KOHM-suh-muhl), Communist youth organization (R)

Konzertmeister (kohn-TSEHRT-MEYE-stuhr), chief violinist of orchestra (G)

kopek (more properly *kopeika,* kuh-PYEY-kuh), small Russian coin (R)

kraal (KRAHL), South African village or enclosure (Du, from Pt *curral*)

Krasnaya Zvezda (KRAHS-nuh-yuh zviz-DAH), Red Star, Soviet Army organ (R)

Kremlin (more properly *kreml',* KRYEHML'), citadel of Moscow, seat of government (R)

Kriegspiel (KREEK-shpeel), war game (G)

kulak (koo-LAHK), fist, tight-wad, well-to-do peasant (R)

Kultur (kool-TOOR), civilization, culture German style (G)

Kulturkampf (kool-TOOR-KAHMPF), Prussia's struggle to dominate Catholic Church (G)

kummerbund (KUM-muhr-buhnd), man's sash for waist (Pers)

Kuomintang (GWOH-meen-tahng), national people's party (Ch)

L

la belle dame sans merci (la BEHL DAM SÃH mehr-SEE), the beautiful lady without mercy (F)

labor omnia vincit (LAH-bohr OHM-nee-ah WEEN-keet), labor overcomes everything (L)

lagniappe (la-NYAP), small present to purchaser with purchase (F from Sp from Quechua)

laissez faire (leh-SAY FEHR), let things alone, noninterference (F)

Landwehr (LAHNT-vehr), home guard, militia (G)

lapsus calami (LAHP-soos KAH-lah-mee), slip of the pen (L)

lapsus linguae (LAHP-soos LEEN-gweye), slip of the tongue (L)

largo (LAHR-goh), broad, slow tempo (It)

lasagne (lah-SAH-nyay), broad, flat macaroni (It)

laudator temporis acti (low-DAH-tohr TEHM-poh-rees AHK-tee), one who praises the good old days (L)

lb. (abbr. for *libra,* LEE-brah), pound (L)

Leben Sie wohl (LAY-buhn ZEE VOHL), good-bye, be well (G)

Lebensraum (LAY-buhns-rowm), living space (G)

legato (lay-GAH-toh), bound, with no pause between notes (It)

Légion d'Honneur (lay-ZHÃW daw-NÖR), military and civil order (F)

lei (LAY), wreath of flowers worn around the neck (Hawaiian)
leitmotiv (LEYET-moh-teef), guiding theme (G)
lento (LEHN-toh), slow tempo (It)
lèse-majesté (LEHZ-ma-zhehs-TAY), treason, offense against ruler (F)
l'état, c'est moi! (lay-TAH seh MWAH), *I* am the state! (F)
liaison (lyeh-ZǍW), linking, connection (F)
libido (lee-BEE-doh), psychic drive associated with the sexual instinct (L)
Liederkranz (LEE-duhr-krahnts), singing society; type of cheese (G)
Limburger (LEEM-boor-guhr), type of cheese (G)
lingerie (lĕh-zhuh-REE), women's underwear (F)
lingua franca (LEEN-gwah FRAHN-kah), international or common language in multilingual area (L or It)
lira (LEE-rah), Italian unit of currency (It)
literati (lee-teh-RAH-tee), educated or cultured people, literary men (L)
loggia (LAWJ-jah), portico projecting from a building (It)
logos (LOH-gohs), word (Gk)
luau (loo-AH-oo), Hawaiian banquet (Hawaiian)
Luftwaffe (LOOFT-vahf-fuh), German air force (G)
lycée (lee-SAY), high school (F)

M

macabre (ma-KAH-bruh), gruesome (F)
macédoine (ma-say-DWAHN), mixture of fruits or vegetables (F)
mademoiselle (mad-mwah-ZEHL), young lady, Miss (F)
Madonna (mah-DAWN-nah), my Lady; the Virgin Mary (It)
maestoso (mah-ays-TOH-soh), majestic (It)
maestro (mah-AYS-troh), master, teacher (It)
Mafia (MAH-fyah), Sicilian secret organization (It)
Magna Charta (MAHG-nah KAHR-tah), Great Charter; English Bill of Rights (L)
magna cum laude (MAHG-nah koom LOW-deh), with great praise or distinction (L)
magnifico (mah-NYEE-fee-koh), magnificent; great man (It)
magnum bonum (MAHG-noom BOH-noom), great good; great benefit (L)
magnum opus (MAHG-noom OH-poos), great work, masterpiece (L)
maharajah (mah-hah-RAH-jah), great king (Hind)
maharani (mah-hah-RAH-nee), great queen (Hind)
Mahatma (mah-HAHT-mah), great soul, teacher (Sk)
mais où sont les neiges d'antan? (MEH-ZOO săw lay NEHZH dăh-TĂH), but where are the snows of yesteryear? (F)
maître d'hôtel (MEH-truh doh-TEHL), head steward, head butler (F)
major domo (MAH-yohr DOH-moh), chief steward, head servant (L)
maladroit (ma-la-DRWAH), awkward, tactless (F)
malaria (mah-LAH-ryah), illness transmitted by mosquito bite (It)
mal de mer (MAL duh MEHR), seasickness (F)
malentendu (ma-lăh-tăh-DÜ), misunderstanding (F)
malgré lui (mal-GRAY LWEE), in spite of himself (F)
mañana (mah-NYAH-nah), tomorrow (Sp)
mandamus (mahn-DAH-moos), we order; legal writ (L)
manicotti (mah-nee-KAWT-tee), stuffed pasta rolls (It)
manifesto (mah-nee-FEHS-toh), declaration (It)
maquis (ma-KEE), French freedom fighters (F)
maraca (mah-RAH-kah), gourd used as musical instrument (Sp)
mardi gras (mar-DEE GRAH), Shrove Tuesday (F)
mare nostrum (MAH-reh NOHS-troom), our sea (L)
mariage de convenance (ma-RYAZH duh kăw-vuh-NĂHS), marriage of convenience (F)
marimba (mah-REEM-bah), wooden xylophone (Sp)
marina (mah-REE-nah), settled and landscaped seashore (It)
marrons glacés (ma-RŎH gla-SAY), candied chestnuts (F)
Marsala (mahr-SAH-lah), Sicilian sweet wine (It)
masseur, masseuse (ma-SÖR, ma-SÖZ), male, female massage expert (F)
matador (mah-tah-DOHR), bullfighter who kills bull with sword (Sp)
maté (mah-TEH), see hierba maté
materia medica (mah-TEH-ree-ah MEH-dee-kah), drugs, pharmacology (L)
matsoth (MAH-tsoth), Passover unleavened bread (Heb)
maxixe (mah-SHEE-shuh), Brazilian dance (Pt)
mazuma (mah-ZOO-mah), money (Yid)
mazurka (mah-ZOOR-kah), Polish dance (Pol)
mazzeltov (MAH-zuhl-tohv), good luck (Heb)
mea (maxima) culpa (MEH-ah MAHK-see-mah KOOL-pah), my (greatest) fault (L)
Meerschaum (MEHR-showm), mineral substance for making smoking pipes (G)
Mein Kampf (meyen KAHMPF), my battle, my struggle (G)
Meistersinger (MEYE-stuhr SING-uhr), master singer (G)
mélange (may-LĂHZH), mixture (F)
mêlée (meh-LAY), mix-up, fight, brawl (F)
memorabilia (meh-moh-rah-BEE-lee-ah), things worth remembering (L)
memorandum (meh-moh-RAHN-doom), something to be remembered, a note to that effect (L)
ménage (may-NAHZH), household (F)
Menorah (meh-NOH-rah), Jewish seven-candle candelabrum (Heb)

mens sana in corpore sano (MEHNS SAH-nah een KOHR-poh-reh SAH-noh), a sound mind in a sound body (L)

menu (muh-NÜ), bill of fare (F)

meringue (muh-RÊHG), beaten and baked egg whites (F)

mesa (MEH-sah), tableland, plateau (Sp)

mésalliance (may-za-lee-ÃHS), marriage with a person of inferior social position (F)

mestizo (mehs-TEE-thoh), half-breed (Sp)

métier (may-TYAY), trade, craft (F)

Métro (may-TROH), Paris subway (F)

mezzo (MEH-dzoh), half (It)

midi (mee-DEE), south (F)

migraine (mee-GREHN), headache (F)

miles gloriosus (MEE-lehs gloh-ree-OH-soos), braggart, swaggerer (L)

minestrone (mee-nehs-TROH-nay), vegetable soup (It)

mirabile dictu (mee-RAH-bee-leh DEEK-too), wonderful to relate (L)

mirabile visu (mee-RAH-bee-leh WEE-soo), wonderful to see (L)

mirabilia (mee-rah-BEE-lee-ah), wonderful things (L)

mise en scène (MEE-zãh-SEHN), stage setting (F)

miserere (mee-seh-REH-reh), have mercy (L)

modicum (MOH-dee-koom), proper or small measure (L)

modus operandi (MOH-doos oh-peh-RAHN-dee), way of working (L)

modus vivendi (MOH-doos wee-WEHN-dee), way of living (together) (L)

mores (MOH-rehs), customs, folkways, conventions (L)

mot juste (MOH ZHÜST), the right word for the occasion (F)

moue (MOO), pout, grimace (F)

mousse (MOOS), frozen whipped dessert (F)

Moyen Age (mwa-YÊH-NAHZH), Middle Ages (F)

mufti (MOOF-tee), civilian judge; civilian garb (Arab)

mutatis mutandis (moo-TAH-tees moo-TAHN-dees), with the appropriate changes (L)

muzhik (moo-ZHEEK), Russian peasant (R)

N

naive (na-EEV), innocent, guileless (F)

naïveté (na-eev-TAY), innocence, guilelessness (F)

née (NAY), born; having as a maiden name (F)

négligée (nay-glee-ZHAY), loose indoor robe for women (F)

ne plus ultra (neh PLOOS OOL-trah), no further (L)

nihil obstat (NEE-heel OHB-staht), there is no impediment (L)

nil admirari (NEEL ahd-mee-RAH-ree), be surprised at nothing (L)

nil desperandum (NEEL dehs-peh-RAHN-doom), never despair (L)

n'importe (nẽh-PAWRT), it doesn't matter (F)

Nirvana (neer-VAH-nah), extinction; oblivion; Buddhist paradise (Sk)

Nisei (NEE-say), second-generation Japanese-Americans (Jap)

nisi (NEE-see), unless (L)

noblesse oblige (naw-BLEHS aw-BLEEZH), high rank involves responsiblitity (F)

Noël (naw-EHL), Christmas (F)

nolle prosequi (NOHL-leh PROH-seh-kwee), I will prosecute no further (L)

nolo contendere (NOH-loh kohn-TEHN-deh-reh), no contest (L)

nom de guerre (NÕH duh GHEHR), pseudonym (F)

nom de plume (NÕH duh PLÜM), pen name (F)

non compos mentis (nohn KOHM-pohs MEHN-tees), insane, not sound in mind (L)

non sequitur (nohn SEH-kwee-toor), it does not follow; logical inconsistency (L)

nota bene (NOH-tah BEH-neh; abbr. n.b.), note well (L)

note verbale (NAWT vehr-BAHL), verbal communication on diplomatic matter (F)

novella (noh-VEHL-lah), short story (It)

nuance (nü-ÃHS), shade, delicate degree of difference (F)

nuncio (NOON-chyoh), Papal envoy (It)

O

obbligato (ohb-blee-GAH-toh), solo passage, not to be omitted (It)

obit (OH-beet), he died (L)

obiter dictum (OH-bee-tehr DEEK-toom), spoken incidentally (L)

objet d'art (awb-ZHEH DHAR), object of art (F)

odium (OH-dee-oom), hatred; blame (L)

olla podrida (OH-lyah poh-DREE-dah), stew, hodgepodge (Sp)

omnia mutantur, nos et mutamur in illis (OHM-nee-ah moo-TAHN-toor NOHS eht moo-TAH-moor een EEL-lees), all things change, and we change with them (L)

omnia vanitas (OHM-nee-ah WAH-nee-tahs), all is vanity (L)

omnia vincit amor (OHM-nee-ah WEEN-keet AH-mohr), love overcomes everything (L)

omnium gatherum (OHM-nee-oom-GA-ther-um), miscellaneous collection (L and mock L)

onus probandi (OH-noos proh-BAHN-dee), the burden of proof (L)

opera (OH-peh-rah), works (L); musical drama (It)

opéra bouffe (oh-pay-RAH BOOF), comic opera, musical comedy (F)

opera omnia (OH-peh-rah OHM-nee-ah), all the works (L)

operetta (oh-pay-RAYT-tah), light opera, musical comedy (It)

opus (OH-poos), work (L)

opus citatum (OH-poos kee-TAH-toom), abbr. op. cit.; the work previously cited (L)

ora et labora (OH-rah eht lah-BOH-rah), pray and work (L)

ora pro nobis (OH-rah proh NOH-bees), pray for us (L)

oratorio (Oh-rah-TAW-ryoh), musical drama on sacred topic (It)

osso buco (AWS-soh BOO-koh), marrow bone of veal (It)

o tempora! o mores! (OH TEHM-poh-rah OH MOH-rehs), O, times and customs! (L)

outré (oo-TRAY), extreme, excessive (F)

oyer and terminer (oh-YEHR tehr-mee-NEHR), higher criminal court (Old F)

oyez (oh-YEHTS), hear ye! (Old F)

P

paella (pah-EH-lyah), South Spanish dish of rice and meat or fish (Sp)

palette (pa-LEHT), artist's color-mixing board (F)

palio (PAH-lyoh), Siena horse-race (It)

pampa (PAHM-pah), grassy plain in Argentina (Sp, from Quechua)

panache (pa-NASH), plume (F)

panem et circenses (PAH-nehm eht keer-KEHN-sehs), bread and games (L)

Panzer (PAHN-tsuhr), armored car, tank (G)

papier-mâché (pa-PYAY-mah-SHAY), paper pulp, cardboard (F)

par excellence (pa-rehk-seh-LÃHS), to a superlative degree (F)

parfait (par-FEH), ice cream with syrup or fudge (F)

pariah (PAH-ree-ah), outcast, rejected (Tamil)

pari passu (PAH-ree PAHS-soo), side by side, evenly (L)

parmigiana (pahr-mee-JAH-nah), Parma style, with melted cheese and tomato (It)

parmigiano (pahr-mee-JAH-noh), Parma cheese, usually for grating (It)

parti pris (par-TEE PREE), preconceived idea (F)

paso doble (PAH-soh DOH-bleh), two-step; Spanish dance (Sp)

passacaglia (pahs-sah-KAH-lyah), slow Italian dance or music (It)

passim (PAHS-seem), abbr. pass.; scattered everywhere (L)

pasta (PAHS-tah), dough; any macaroni product (It)

pâté (pah-TAY), paste (F);—***de foie gras*** (duh FWAH GRAH), goose-liver paste

pater familias (pah-tehr-fah-MEE-lee-ahs), head of family (L)

Pater Noster (PAH-tehr NOHS-tehr), Our Father, Lord's Prayer (L)

pater patriae (PAH-tehr PAH-tree-eye), father of his country (L)

patio (PAH-tyoh), courtyard, inner courtyard (Sp)

pâtisserie (pah-tees-REE), pastry (F)

patois (pa-TWAH), local dialect (F)

Italy—Amphitheatre, Pompeii

pax romana (PAHKS roh-MAH-nah), Roman peace, enforced peace (L)

pax vobiscum (PAHKS woh-BEES-koom), peace be with you (L)

peineta (pay-NEH-tah), tall comb (Sp)

penchant (pã-SHÃH), leaning, inclination (F)

per annum (pehr AHN-noom), by the year (L)

per capita (pehr KAH-pee-teh), by the head, apiece (L)

per diem (pehr DEE-ehm), by the day (L)

per se (pehr SEH), in itself, inherently (L)

persona non grata (pehr-SOH-nah nohn GRAH-tah), not acceptable diplomatic representative (L)

Pesach (PAY-sakh), Passover (Heb)

peseta (peh-SEH-tah), Spanish coin (Sp)

peso (PEH-soh), Latin American unit of currency (Sp)

petit bourgeois (puh-TEE boor-ZHWAH), lower middle class (F)

petite (puh-TEET), small, trim in figure (F)

petitio principii (peh-TEE-tee-oh preen-KEE-pee-ee), begging the question (L)

petits fours (puh-TEE FOOR), little sponge or pound cakes (F)

petits pois (puh-TEE PWAH), green peas (F)

phobia (FOH-bee-ah), fear, hatred (Gk)

pianissimo (pyah-NEES-see-moh), very softly (It)

piano (PYAH-noh), softly (It)

pibroch (PEE-brokh), bagpipe (Gaelic)

picador (pee-kah-DOHR), mounted bullfighter with lance (Sp)

piccolo (PEEK-koh-loh), small flute (It)

pièce de résistance (PYEHS duh ray-zees-TÃHS), main course (F)

pilaf (pee-LOW), Oriental rice dish (Persian)

piroshki (pee-RAWSH-kee), stuffed puffcakes (R)

pirouette (pee-roo-EHT), spin on one foot or in air (F)

più (PYOO), more (It)

pizza (PEE-tsah), pie, pancake (It)

pizzicato (pee-tsee-KAH-toh), plucking the strings of a musical instrument (It)

placebo (plah-KEH-boh), pacifier, medicine of no efficacy (L)

plaza de toros (PLAH-thah deh TOH-rohs), bullring (Sp)

plus ça change, plus c'est la même chose (PLÜ sa SHĂHZH PLÜ seh la mehm SHOHZ), the more it changes, the more it's the same thing (F)

pogrom (puh-GRAWM), devastation, massacre (R)

point d'appui (PWĔH da-PWEE), fulcrum, support point (F)

polenta (poh-LEHN-tah), thick gruel of corn, chestnuts, etc. (It)

polka (POHL-kah), fast Slavic dance (Czech)

pollice verso (POHL-lee-keh WEHR-soh), thumbs down (L)

Poltergeist (POHL-tuhr-geyest), racketing or prank-playing ghost (G)

pommes frites (PAWM FREET), fried potatoes (F)

poncho (POHN-choh), blanket with opening for head (Sp)

pons asinorum (POHNS ah-see-NOH-room), bridge of donkeys; hard problem for beginners (L)

portico (PAWR-tee-koh), covered gallery open on one side (It)

portmanteau (PAWRT-măh-TOH), traveling bag (F)

posada (poh-SAH-dah), inn (Sp)

posse (comitatus) (POHS-seh koh-mee-TAH-toos), force of a county, sheriff and assistants (L)

post bellum (pohst BEHL-loom), after-war (L)

post hoc, ergo propter hoc (pohst HOHK EHR-goh PROHP-tehr HOHK), after, therefore in consequence of something else (L)

post meridiem (pohst meh-REE-dee-ehm), abbr. p.m., P.M.; after noon (L)

post-mortem (pohst MOHR-tehm), after death, autopsy (L)

post scriptum (pohst SKREEP-toom), abbr. P.S.; written after main letter (L)

potage (paw-TAHZH), soup (F)

potpourri (poh-poo-REE), mixture, medley (F)

pourparler (poor-par-LAY), talk, negotiations (F)

pravda (PRAHV-duh), truth (R)

préciosité (pray-syoh-zee-TAY), excessive refinement (F)

première (pruh-MYEHR), first showing (F)

première danseuse (pruh-MYEHR dăh-SÖZ), first female dancer (F)

prestissimo (prays-TEES-see-moh), very fast (It)

prima donna (PREE-mah DAWN-nah), female opera star; anyone who wants to be first (It)

prima facie (PREE-mah FAH-kee-eh), at first glance, on the face of it (L)

primus inter pares (PREE-moos EEN-tehr PAH-rehs), first among equals (L)

prix fixe (PREE FEEKS), fixed price (F)

pro bono publico (proh BOH-noh POO-blee-koh), for the public good (L)

pro et con(tra) (PROH eht KOHN-trah), for and against (L)

profanum vulgus (proh-FAH-noom WOOL-goos), the fickle crowd (L)

pro forma (proh FOHR-mah), as a matter of form (L)

propaganda (proh-pah-GAHN-dah), that which is to be spread (L)

pro rata (proh RAH-tah), in proportion, in accordance with fixed rate (L)

prosciutto (proh-SHOOT-toh), salted Italian-style ham (It)

prosit (PROH-seet), to your health or success (L)

protégé (praw-tay-ZHAY), one taken under another's sheltering wing (F)

pro tempore (proh TEHM-poh-reh), abbr. pro tem; temporarily (L)

provolone (proh-voh-LOH-nay), spicy Italian cheese (It)

puchero (poo-CHEH-roh), South American stew (Sp)

pudenda (poo-DEHN-dah), genital organs (L)

pueblo (PWEH-bloh), village, town (Sp)

puissance (pwee-SĂHS), power (F)

pulque (POOL-kah), alcoholic beverage of Mexico (Sp from Nahuatl)

pundit (PUN-deet), man of learning (Hind)

purdah (PUR-dah), veil, feminine seclusion (Hind)

purée (pü-RAY), thick cream soup (F)

Purim (POO-reem), Jewish feast of deliverance (Heb)

Putsch (POOCH), abortive revolutionary attempt (G)

Q

qua (KWAH), considered as, in the capacity of (L)

quantum (KWAHN-toom), how great, how much (L)

quasi (KWAH-see), as if, as though (L)

que será será (KEH seh-RAH seh-RAH), what will be will be (Sp)

quidnunc (KWEED-nunk), what now, gossip, newsmonger (L)

quid pro quo (KWEED proh KWOH), something in return for something else (L)

¿quién sabe? (KYEHN SAH-veh), who knows? (Sp)

qui s'excuse s'accuse (KEE sehks-KÜZ sa-KÜZ), he who excuses himself accuses himself (F)

qui vive (KEE VEEV), on the alert, watchful (F)

qui va là? (KEE va LA), who goes there? (F)

quod erat demonstrandum (KWOHD EH-raht deh-mohn-STRAHN-doom), which was to be proved (L)

quod vide (KWOHD WEE-deh); abbr. q.v.; which see (L)

quondam (KWOHN-dahm), former, formerly (L)

quorum (KWOH-room), majority of legislative body for voting purposes (L)

quot homines, tot sententiae (KWOHT HOH-mee-nehs TOHT sehn-TEHN-tee-eye), as many opinions as there are people (L)

quo vadis? (KWOH WAH-dees), where are you going? (L)

R

ragoût (ra-GOO), spicy stew (F)

raison d'état (reh-ZÖH day-TAH), reason of state (F)

raison d'être (reh-ZÕH DEH-truh), reason for existing (F)

rajah (RAH-jah), king, ruler (Sk)

rallentando (rahl-layn-TAHN-doh), slowing up (It)

rani (RAH-nee), queen (Sk)

rapprochement (ra-prawsh-MÃH), reestablishing of friendly relations (F)

rara avis (RAH-rah AH-wees), rare bird (L)

Rathskeller (RAHTS-KEHL-luhr), basement restaurant and bar (G)

ravioli (rah-VYAW-lee), dumplings stuffed with meat or cheese (It)

re (REH), in the matter of (L)

realia (reh-AH-lee-ah), materials for teaching foreign cultures (L)

Reconquista (reh-kohn-KEES-tah), reconquest of Spain from the Moors (Sp)

recto (REKH-toh), on the right-hand page (L)

regata (ray-GAH-tah), Venetian gondola race (It)

Reich (REYEÇ), German state; empire (G)

Reichstag (REYEKS-tahk), German Parliament (G)

rendezvous (rãh-day-VOO), appointment, assignation (F)

répondez s'il vous plait (ray-põh-DAY seel voo PLEH), abbr. R.S.V.P.; please reply (F)

requiem (REH-kwee-ehm), rest; prayer for dead (L)

requiescat in pace (reh-kwee-EHS-kaht een PAH-keh), abbr. r.i.p.; may he rest in peace (L)

residuum (reh-SEE-doo-oom), remnant, residue (L)

résumé (ray-zü-MAY), summary (F)

ricksha (REEK-shaw), see jinrickisha

ricochet (ree-kaw-SHEH), bounce, rebound (F)

ricotta (ree-KAWT-tah), soft white Italian cheese (It)

rigor mortis (REE-gohr MOHR-tees), stiffness of death (L)

Rinascimento (ree-nah-shee-MAYN-toh), rebirth (It)

ris de veau (REE duh VOH), sweetbreads (F)

Risorgimento (ree-sohr-jee-MAYN-toh), Italian movement for unity (It)

risotto (ree-SAWT-toh), Italian rice dish (It)

rissolé (ree-saw-LAY), golden brown (F)

ritardando (ree-tahr-DAHN-doh), slowing up (It)

robot (ROH-boht), automaton trained to do man's work (Czech)

rodeo (roh-DEH-oh), roundup (Sp)

Roma caput mundi (ROH-mah KAH-poot MOON-dee), Rome, head of the world (L)

Rosh Hashanah (ROHSH hah-shah-NAH), head of year, New Year's Day (Heb)

rota (ROH-tah), wheel, Papal court (L)

rôti (roh-TEE), roast (F)

rôtisserie (roh-tees-REE), grill restaurant (F)

rotunda (roh-TOON-dah), circular building with dome (L)

roulette (roo-LEHT), gambling wheel (F)

rubaiyat (ROO-beye-yaht), quatrains, poems (Arab)

Rucksack (RUK-zahk), knapsack (G)

rupee (ROO-pee) Indian currency (Hind)

S

sabotage (sa-baw-TAHZH), intentional damage to arrest production (F)

sabra (SAH-brah), native Israeli (Heb)

sachet (sa-SHEH), small bag of perfume (F)

safari (sah-FAH-ree), hunting trip in Africa (Arab)

sahib (SAH-heeb), sir, master, title of respect (Arab)

salaam (sah-LAHM), peace, form of greeting (Arab)

salame (sah-LAH-meh), spiced sausage (It)

salmagundi (sal-ma-GOON-dee), spicy mixture (doubtful origin)

salon (sa-LÃW), drawing room, exhibition room (F)

salus populi suprema lex (SAH-loos POH-poo-lee soo-PREH-mah LEHKS), the welfare of the people is the supreme law (L)

salve (SAHL-weh), hail (L)

samba (SAHM-bah), Brazilian dance (Pt. from Am. Indian)

samovar (suh-muh-VAHR), Russian tea urn (R)

samurai (SAH-moo-reye), Japanese feudal nobleman (Jap)

sanctum sanctorum (SAHNK-toom sahnk-TOH-room), holy of holies (L)

sangfroid (sãh-FRWAH), coolness in the face of danger (F)

Yugoslavia—Dubrovnik

sans façon (sãh fa-SA͂W), unceremoniously (F)

sans gêne (sãh ZHEHN), without embarrassment, nervy (F)

sans souci (sãh soo-SEE), carefree, free from worry (F)

sarape (sah-RAH-peh), Mexican blanket (Sp)

sari (SAH-ree), Hindu female costume (Hindi)

sartor resartus (SAHR-tohr reh-SAHR-toos), tailor retailored, tit for tat (L)

Saturnalia (sah-toor-NAH-lee-ah), Roman December festival (L)

Sauerbraten (ZOW-uhr-BRAH-tuhn), marinated roast (G)

Sauerkraut (ZOW-uhr-krowt), pickled cabbage (G)

sauté (soh-TAY), fried in small amount of fat (F)

sauve qui peut (SOHV kee PO), every man for himself (F)

savoir faire (sa-VWAHR FEHR), tact, ability to do the right thing (F)

savoir vivre (sa-VWAHR VEE-vruh), knowledge of how to behave and get along (F)

sayonara (SAH-yoh-nah-rah), good-bye (Jap)

scherzo (SKAYR-tsoh), lively, jesting musical composition (It)

schlemiel (shluh-MEEL), easy mark, dumbbell (Yid)

Schmalz (SHMAHLTS), fat; silly sentimentality (G)

Schnapps (SHNAHPS), brandy, whiskey (G)

Schnitzel (SHNIT-suhl), cutlet (G)

schnorrer (SHNOHR-ruhr), beggar (Yid)

Schrecklichkeit (SHREHK-liç-keyet), frightfulness, policy of deliberate atrocity (G)

scilicet (SKEE-lee-keht), that is to say, to wit (L)

séance (say-ÃHS), session, sitting (F)

sec (SEHK), dry (F)

Sehnsucht (ZEHN-zookht), longing, nostalgic feeling (G)

semper fidelis (SEHM-pehr fee-DEH-lees), forever faithful (L)

semper paratus (SEHM-pehr pah-RAH-toos), ever ready (L)

senatus populusque romanus (seh-NAH-toos poh-poo-LOOS-kweh roh-MAH-noos), abbr. S.P.Q.R., the Roman Senate and people (L)

se non è vero, è ben trovato (say nohn eh VAY-roh, eh behn troh-VAH-toh), if it isn't true, it's a good lie (It)

sforzando (sfohr-TSAHN-doh), with force or vigor (It)

shah (SHAH), king of Persia (Persian)

shalom (shah-LOHM), peace, form of Hebrew or Israeli greeting (Heb)

shashlik (SHAHSH-leek), meat on skewer (R)

sheikh (SHEYEKH), old man, religious leader (Arab)

shekel (SHEH-kehl), unit of weight or money (Heb)

shillalagh (shil-LAY-lee), cudgel (Irish)

Shinto (SHEEN-toh), way of the gods; Japanese religion (Jap)

shish kebab (SHEESH keh-BAHB), lamb on skewer (Turk)

sic (SEEK), thus, precisely as it appears (L)

sic semper tyrannis (SEEK SEHM-pehr tee-RAHN-nees), may it always go thus with tyrants (L)

sic transit gloria mundi (SEEK TRAHN-seet GLOH-ree-ah MOON-dee), thus passes away the world's glory (L)

Siglo de Oro (SEE-gloh deh OH-roh), golden century (Sp)

s'il vous plait (seel voo PLEH), please (F)

similia similibus curantur (see-MEE-lee-ah see-MEE-lee-boos koo-RAHN-toor), like is cured with like (L)

sine die (SEE-neh DEE-eh), without assigning a day (L)

sine qua non (SEE-neh KWAH NOHN), indispensable requisite or condition (L)

Sinn Fein (SHIN FAYN), we ourselves; Irish revolutionary movement (Irish)

si vis pacem, para bellum (see wees PAH-khem, PAH-rah BEHL-loom), if you want peace, prepare for war (L)

skoal (SKOHL), to your health (Norw)

slalom (SLAH-lum), downhill skiing race (Norw)

smörgasbord (SMOR-gus-boord), table of appetizers and other foods (Swed)

soi-disant (swah-dee-ZÃH), self-styled (F)

soirée (swah-RAY), evening gathering (F)

solfeggio (sohl-FAY-joh), singing by notes (It)

solitaire (saw-lee-TEHR), alone, single (F)

solo (SOH-loh), alone, musical piece for one person (It)

sombrero (sohm-BREH-roh), hat (Sp)

sotto voce (SOHT-toh VOH-chay), in an undertone (It)

soubriquet (soo-bree-KEH), nickname (F)

soufflé (soo-FLAY), puffed up, baked custard (F)

soupçon (soop-SA͂W), suspicion, dash, trace (F)

soviet (suh-VYEHT), council of delegates (R)

spa (SPAH), watering place (Belgian place name)

spoor (SPOHR), track of animal (Du)

Sprachgefühl (SHPRAHKH-guh-FUL), feeling for language (G)

spumone (spoo-MOH-nay), Italian ice cream (It)

sputnik (SPOOT-neek), co-traveler, space satellite (R)

staccato (stahk-KAH-toh), having short notes (It)

Stakhanovite (stuh-KHAHN-uhv), champion speed worker in USSR (R)

stanza (STAHN-tsah) room; subdivision of poem (It)

status quo (STAH-toos KWOH), existing or previously existing state of affairs (L)

stet (STEHT), let it stand; disregard correction (L)

Strudel (SHTROO-duhl), type of cake (G)

stucco (STOOK-koh), mixture of lime and pulverized stone (It)

Stück (SHTUK), piece; selection (G)

studio (STOO-dyoh), study; place for studying or working (It)

Sturm und Drang (SHTOORM oont DRAHNG), storm and stress (G)

sub judice (soob YOO-dee-keh), not yet decided (L)

Ireland—Ashford Castle, County Mayo

subpoena (soob-POY-nah), under penalty; required appearance in court (L)

sub rosa (soob ROH-sah), under cover; in secret (L)

succès d'estime (sük-SEH dehs-TEEM), favored by critics and experts, but not by mass (F)

sui generis (SOO-ee GEH-neh-rees), in a class by itself; unique (L)

sukiyaki (SKEE-yah-kee), Japanese dish of meat and vegetables (Jap)

summa cum laude (SOOM-mah koom LOW-deh), with the highest praise (L)

summum bonum (SOOM-moom BOH-noom), the supreme good (L)

suo nomine (SOO-oh NOH-mee-neh), in his own name (L)

sûreté (sür-TAY), security; French security police (F)

suum cuique (SOO-oom kwoo-EE-kweh), to each his own (L)

svaraj (SVAH-rahj), self-rule, independence (Sk)

T

table d'hôte (TA-bluh DOHT), regular menu, no choice (F)

tabula rasa (TAH-boo-lah RAH-sah), clean slate (L)

tamale (tah-MAH-leh), Mexican dish of corn, meat, and red pepper (Sp)

tant mieux (pis) (TÃH MYÖ PEE), so much the better (worse) (F)

tarantella (tah-rahn-TEHL-lah), swift Italian dance (It)

Te Deum Laudamus (TEH DEH-oom low-DAH-moos), hymn of thanksgiving (L)

tempo (TEHM-poh), time, rate, rhythm, beat (It)

tempus fugit (TEHM-poos FOO-gheet), time is fleeting (L)

terminus (a quo, ad quem) (TEHR-mee-noos ah KWOH, ahd KWEHM), limit or boundary from which or to which (L)

terra cotta (TEHR-rah KAWT-tah), baked clay, earthenware (It)

terra firma (TEHR-rah FEER-mah), solid ground, mainland (L)

terra incognita (TEHR-rah een-KOHG-nee-tah), unknown land (L)

tertium quid (TEHR-tee-oom KWEED), a third factor (L)

tête-à-tête (TEH-ta-TEHT), face to face; intimate conversation (F)

thé dansant (TAY dãh-SÃH), afternoon tea and dance (F)

thesaurus (teh-SOW-roos), treasure trove; idea dictionary (L)

timbale, timballo (teh-BAL, teem-BAHL-loh), baked in a mold (F, It)

timeo Danaos et dona ferentes (TEE-meh-oh dah-NAH-ohs eht DOH-nah feh-REHN-tehs), I fear the Greeks even when they bear gifts (L)

toga (TOH-gah), loose, flowing robe of Romans (L)

toreador, torero (toh-reh-ah-DOHR, toh-REH-roh), bullfighter (Sp)

torso (TOHR-soh), upper part of body without head (It)

Totentanz (TOH-tuhn-tahnts), dance of death (G)

touché (too-SHAY), touched; remark that strikes home (F)

toujours (too-ZHOOR), always, forever (F)

toupet (too-PEH), wig, false hair (F)

tour de force (TOOR duh FAWRS), special feat of dexterity (F)

tournure (toor-NUR), roundness, gracefulness of line (F)

tout de suite (TOO duh SWEET), at once (F)

tovarishch (tuh-VAH-reeshch), comrade (R)

traduttore, traditore (trah-doot-TOH-ray, trah-dee-TOH-ray), a translator is a traitor (It)

trauma (TROW-mah), blow, wound, injury (Gk)

tricolore (tree-kaw-LAWR), French Flag, red, white, and blue (F)

Trimurti (tree-MOOR-tee), Hindu trinity, Brahma, Vishnu, and Shiva (Sk)

trio (TREE-oh), group of three (It)

trivia (TREE-vee-ah), commonplace things (L)

troika (TROY-kuh), vehicle drawn by three horses (R)

troppo (TRAWP-poh), too much (It)

trouvère (troo-VEHR), minstrel (F)

tsar (see czar)

tu quoque (TOO KWOH-kweh), you, too (L)

tutti-frutti (TOOT-tee FROOT-tee), all fruits, mixed fruits (It)

U

ubique (oo-BEE-kweh), everywhere (L)

ukaze (oo-KAHS), imperial edict (R)

ukulele (oo-koo-LEH-leh), Hawaiian guitar (Hawaiian)

ultima Thule (OOL-tee-mah TOO-leh), faraway, mythical locality (L)

ultimo (OOL-tee-moh), last (month; abbr. ult.) (L)

ultra (OOL-trah), beyond, outside of (L)

ultra vires (OOL-trah WEE-rehs), beyond one's strength or capacity (L)

und so weiter (oont ZOH VEYE-tuhr), and so forth; etc. (G)

uno animo (OO-noh AH-nee-moh), with one mind (L)

Untergang des Abendlandes (OON-tuhr-gahng dehs AH-buhnt-LAHN-duhs), decline of the West (G)

urbi et orbi (OOR-bee eht OHR-bee), to the city and to the world (L)

ut supra (OOT SOO-prah), as above (L)

V

vade mecum (WAH-deh MEH-koom), a book carried as a constant companion, a handbook (L)

vae victis (WEYE WEEK-tees), woe to the vanquished (L)

vale (WAH-leh), good-bye, farewell (L)

valuta (vah-LOO-tah), currency, foreign exchange (It)

vaquero (bah-KEH-roh), cowboy (Sp)

Veda (VEH-dah), knowledge, book of knowledge (Sk)

veld (FEHLT), open grassy country (Du)

veni, vidi, vici (WEH-nee WEE-dee WEE-kee), I came, I saw, I conquered (L)

verbatim (wehr-BAH-teem), word for word (L)

verbum sat sapienti (WEHR-boom SAHT sah-pee-EHN-tee), a word to the wise is sufficient (L)

Verein (fehr-EYEN), union, club (G)

vermicelli (vayr-mee-CHEHL-lee), thin spaghetti (It)

versus (WEHR-soos), abbr. vs.; against (L)

veto (WEH-toh), I forbid; executive prohibition (L)

Via Crucis (WEE-ah KROO-kees), the Way of the Cross (L)

vibrato (vee-BRAH-toh), with vibration (It)

vice versa (WEE-keh WEHR-sah), the other way around (L)

vide (WEE-deh), see (L)

videlicet (wee-DEH-lee-keht), abbr. viz.; to wit, namely (L)

vignette (vee-NYEHT), illustration, short essay (F)

vinaigrette (vee-neh-GREHT), seasoned with vinegar (F)

vin ordinaire (VẼH nawr-dee-NEHR), common table wine (F)

viola da gamba (VYAW-lah dah GAHM-bah), large viol (It)

virtuoso (veer-too-AW-soh), master performer or singer (It)

vis-à-vis (vee-za-VEE), face to face (F)

vista (VEES-tah), view, panorama (It)

viva voce (WEE-wah WOH-keh), orally, by word of mouth (L)

vive (VEEV) long live (F)

vodka (VAWT-kuh), grain spirits (R)

volaille (vaw-LA-yuh), fowl (F)

vol-au-vent (VAW-loh-VÃH), large, light patty; baked pastry shell (F)

Volkswagen (FOHLKS-vah-guhn), people's car; German automobile (G)

volte-face (VAWLT-FAS), about face; reversal (F)

vomitorium (woh-mee-TOH-ree-oom), exit of large public building (L)

von (FUN), of, from, prefix to noble family name (G)

voortrekker (FOHR-TREHK-kuhr), early settler, pioneer (Du)

vox clamantis in deserto (WOHKS klah-MAHN-tees een deh-SEHR-toh), the voice of one shouting in the wilderness (L)

vox populi, vox Dei (WOHKS POH-poo-lee, WOHKS DEH-ee), the voice of the people is the voice of God (L)

vraisemblance (vreh-sãh-BLÃHS), likelihood, verisimilitude (F)

vulgo (WOOL-goh), commonly, popularly (L)

W

wagon-lit (va-GŌH-LEE), sleeping car (F)

wahini (wah-HEE-nee), woman (Hawaiian)

wanderlust (VAHN-duhr-loost), desire for travel (G)

Wehrmacht (VEHR-makht), armed forces (G)

Weinstube (VEYEN-SHTOO-buh), wine tavern (G)

Weltanschauung, Weltansicht (VEHLT-ahn-show-ung, VEHLT-ahn-ziçt), general outlook, conception of things (G)

Weltschmerz (VEHLT-shmehrts), sorrow for the world, pessimism (G)

wunderbar (VOON-duhr-bahr), wonderful (G)

Wurst (VOORST), sausage (G)

X

xenophobia (KSEH-noh-FOH-bohs), fear or hatred of the foreign (Gk roots)

Y

Yahweh (YAH-veh), Jehovah, God (Heb)

Yoga (YOH-gah), yoking; restraint; Indian philosophy (Sk)

Yogi (YOH-ghee), follower of Yoga (Sk)

Yom Kippur (YOHM keep-POOR), day of atonement, Hebrew holiday (Heb)

Z

zabaione (dzah-bah-YOH-nay), custard mixed with Marsala wine (It)

Zeitgeist (TSEYET-gheyest), spirit of the times (G)

zucchini (dzook-KEE-nee), green squash (It)

Zwieback (TSVEE-bahk), toasted biscuit (G)

Spain—Patio de la Acequia, Granada

CHAPTER THREE

READING SKILLS

It is important for student and nonstudent alike to be able to read well and quickly. Every student must be able to master without undue delay the contents of the textbooks or other materials that form a part of his course. The good student is an efficient reader. He reads rapidly with good comprehension, he is able to read critically, and he retains what he has read.

PREVIEWING

A good way for a reader to approach a new text is to devote a few minutes to *previewing* the material. This is a useful reading technique by which the reader familiarizes himself with the general contents of the text before he begins the actual reading. To preview a selection:

1. *Read the title and subtitles.* If the titles have been well prepared, they will indicate the main ideas of the material. The subtitles generally indicate the various points that go logically under the main idea. To read subtitles in order is apt to provide you with a good outline of the material.

2. *Examine the diagrams, charts, and other visual aids.* These visual aids are included to help explain difficult concepts or to repeat essential points.

3. *Pay attention to the length of paragraphs,* and let them determine the speed at which you will read the selection. Long paragraphs are apt to mean more detailed texts; short ones give fewer details and constitute easier texts. Read the long ones more slowly, the short ones more quickly.

Here is an example of the preview technique, making use of a feature story that appeared in a newspaper, with its headline, subheadline, and subtitles. Note that in textbooks, chapter titles and subtitles perform the same function.

Headline	KEY PROBLEMS IN FOREIGN POLICY
Subheadline	How can the President alert the nation to this many-angled crisis?
Subtitles	More "Fireside Chats" Reform of the Press Conference Continuation of the Forums Less Consideration of "World Opinion"

In its original form the story had additional subtitles, but it is apparent that the four subtitles listed are most pertinent. In a very short time the reader has learned the basic theme of the article and the various points the author suggests. The article goes into greater detail, but the preview has provided the reader, in a nutshell, with the essential points. Since the paragraphs in this particular selection are fairly long, the reader will do well to proceed with caution and allow sufficient time for the comprehension of the material.

It is a good idea to preview everything you read–textbooks, newspapers, magazines, technical journals, essays, and so on. This applies especially to material that has a title, subtitles, and visual aids. The few minutes it will take you will pay off in time saved and greater reading efficiency.

FINDING MAIN IDEAS

In presenting factual-type material, the author has set out to convey to you, the reader, in as logical and lucid a manner as possible, the ideas he wishes to impart. In a single paragraph he usually presents the one basic idea; this may be contained in a single sentence, or it may be implied in various sentences in the paragraph. Further, in any given paragraph, most sentences will contain details that explain, illustrate, amplify, or in some way develop the main idea.

You, as the reader, will want to command those skills that will help you to pick out as quickly as possible the central thought of a paragraph. This implies the ability to understand the relationship between the main idea and the supporting details.

Here are some guides to finding the main idea:

1. The main idea may be directly stated in the first sentence of the paragraph.

> *The President tells the visitor that he is giving three-fourths of his time to international affairs.* The White House staff works unclocked hours on problems ranging from Cambodia to the Common Market, from Mongolia to megatons. The foreign callers come to consult and to be feted in a seemingly endless procession–some, seventy-five times since the President took office.

Note the central thought in the first sentence; note also how the following sentences amplify the thought by providing examples of how the President devotes most of his time to the consideration of foreign affairs problems.

2. The main idea may be directly stated in the first sentence and repeated, for emphasis, in the last sentence of the paragraph.

> Many people think that whisky is a good cure for *rattlesnake bites, but scientists claim that whisky is the worst possible medicine.* It acts as a stimulant and therefore makes the heart beat faster. As a result, the heart pumps blood more rapidly all over the body. Rattlesnake poison is dangerous because it gets into the blood stream. If the blood is forced to travel rapidly over the body, then so does the rattlesnake poison that is in the blood. *"Send for the doctor–not for the whisky bottle" is good advice if you're bitten by a rattler.*

Note how the main idea is stated in the first sentence and repeated, for emphasis and as a summary, in the last. The remaining sentences *explain* the main idea.

The above-quoted paragraph illustrates another common technique for presenting the main thought of a paragraph. Often, as here, only a *part of a sentence* contains the main thought. Textbook writers, because paragraphs in textbooks are short, often employ this technique.

3. The main thought may be directly stated in a sentence located in the middle of a paragraph.

> In spite of the disapproval of a number of community organizations, New York State is considering undertaking vast fall-out shelter construction. State officials have been urging comparable projects for years. *However, opinion is divided over the necessity for fall-out shelters.* Local pacifist groups are condemning such projects. Many well-known scientists consider it futile. The federal government has condoned construction of shelters but has not taken positive steps to implement their construction.

Again, note how the main thought appears in a single sentence, and how the remaining sentences explain this main thought.

Of course, not all writers prepare their material in precisely this way. Individual styles of writing and the nature of the material often suggest other ways of presenting one's thoughts.

There may be paragraphs that contain sentences only *implying* the main thought; they do not specifically state it in any one sentence. Other paragraphs may be so short that it becomes difficult to determine the central thought. Or a paragraph may contain two equally important ideas.

Here is a suggestion for finding the main thought in a paragraph, regardless of the type of paragraph construction. Ask yourself two questions in regard to the paragraph; then put together the two answers to these questions into a single sentence. This sentence will provide the main idea. Thus:

a. Ask yourself who or what the paragraph is about.

b. Ask yourself what this paragraph says about the subject.

c. Combine the answers to these two questions into a single sentence, and you will have the main idea.

This technique can be applied whether the main idea is definitely stated, or whether it is implied. The same technique can be used in determining the basic theme of an essay, a chapter, or a short story.

Using this technique, see if you can find the main idea of the following paragraph:

> The room was entirely carpeted with a thick, soft rug. Drapes, spun of gold thread, bedecked the large picture windows. Sterling silver candlesticks flanked a gold clock on the mantelpiece. Crimson velvet covered the large sofa. A Steinway grand piano stood in the center of the room.

What is the subject? *A room.*

What is distinctive about this room? *It is richly or expensively decorated.*

The main idea: The room was expensively decorated.

In stressing main ideas, you are not to infer that they alone are important, and that the details are useless. The sentences containing the details often furnish the "substance" of the story. Details can provide nuances of meaning; they can involve the reader's imagination.

CRITICAL READING

Reading quickly with adequate comprehension is not enough. The efficient reader must also be able to read critically, to evaluate what he reads. Such critical reading is a refinement of skill in reading. It requires that the reader be aware of the sources of the author's information; that he recognize the possible use of propaganda techniques; that he be able to differentiate between fact and opinion. Once you realize you are reading an opinion, accord it only the value you consider it to be worth. This does not mean that all opinion should be arbitrarily dismissed. Not at all. But not all opinion is worth accepting. Before you accept an opinion, evaluate it.

First, consider the author. Who is he? Is he or is he not an expert on the subject he is dealing with? You would not be very likely to accept the opinion of your neighbor, a carpenter, if he were to write an article on the causes of heart disease. But the chances are that you would believe implicitly the statements on heart disease made by Dr. Paul Dudley White, the eminent cardiologist. The critical reader does not blindly accept what he reads without knowing something about the author and his qualifications.

Guard against accepting overgeneralizations. Remember, things are not all white or all black. Don't let yourself be taken in by language that is emotionally tinged.

RATE OF READING

Most readers can improve their rate of reading without losing the essential ability to comprehend. (Obviously, there is no value or virtue in speed without comprehension.) Let your rate be determined by the purpose for which you read, and by the difficulty of the material.

For difficult factual reading, a reader's rate should be only two-thirds as fast as his most rapid reading. It is all very well to race through a popular magazine article or a book of light fiction; in reading *Moby Dick* or *Macbeth,* you will have to go more slowly if you wish to explore the deep meaning of these classics and to enjoy the beauty of the language. Nor should the student try to rush through a chapter of his physics or history text. What he wants to do is to absorb and digest, and make a part of his mental make-up, every fact and idea he comes upon in his reading.

Some of the more important rate-of-reading skills are skimming, skim-reading, and reading for key words.

Skimming

Skimming and reading are not one and the same. Skimming is a subskill in the reading process. Most readers who claim that they can "read" five or ten thousand words an hour are probably skimming, not reading at all.

In skimming you leave out whole sentences, whole paragraphs, even whole pages. When you glance at the headlines and subheadlines of your morning newspaper, you are skimming, not reading. The basic rule is to *skim for a definite purpose.* You will skim for a specific answer to a question, and you will skim when you want to get a general idea of the contents of some printed material.

1. SKIMMING FOR AN ANSWER TO A QUESTION. It may be a telephone number, or some general's middle initial, or the birth date of a President. Here is what you do:

a. *Preview the material* to find the answer you are looking for.

b. *Use guide words or phrases* to help direct you to the answer. For example, for George Washington's date of birth, turn to "Washington, George" in the encyclopedia, almanac, or other source book. Try to locate the words *birth, birthday, born,* or the like.

c. In skimming, *let your eyes move rapidly and*

efficiently over the text. You will not be moving your eyes from left to right from line to line as you do in ordinary reading; instead, there are two different ways you can let your eyes move. When the printed column is narrow (as in most newspapers, some textbook chapters, some magazine articles, etc.), your eyes can follow a vertical path down the center of the column. They will be able to see words to the left and to the right. As soon as you come upon the guide word or words, stop and read carefully. Another procedure is to let your eyes move in a left-to-right, then a right-to-left progression, taking in two or three lines of print as you go along, somewhat like an automobile going downhill, careening from side to side and so on down the hill. You can with this procedure observe words near the center of the zigzag path your eyes are taking.

In skimming, speed is essential. Go ahead as fast as you can.

2. Skimming in order to get a general idea of the contents. This can be a valuable procedure, for most of us just do not have the time to read thoroughly every bit of reading material that comes to our attention. The procedure is simple: First *preview* the article; then *read* the *first paragraph;* next *read* the *first sentence* of each following *paragraph;* last, *read* the *last paragraph* thoroughly.

Skim-Reading

This is a combination of reading and skimming. You read the important sections and skim the less important ones.

You can increase your rate of reading by reading the key words in sentences. Utilizing what may be called the "telegram style," perhaps 50 percent or more of a sentence is left out, without the reader's losing the meaning of the sentence. In the following paragraph, the key words have been italicized. By reading them, and them only, the reader will get the sense of the material.

> Our *forefathers fought* bloody *wars* and *suffered torture* and *death* for the *right to worship God according* to the varied *dictates* of *conscience.* Complete *religious liberty* has been *accepted* as an unquestioned personal *freedom* since our *Bill of Rights* was *adopted.* We have insisted only that *religious freedom* may *not* be pleaded as an *excuse for criminal* or clearly *antisocial conduct.*

A word of caution: Such words as *no, not, only,* and *less* are extremely important; so watch out!

Finally, your attitude when reading is important. Don't be afraid of the printed page! With material that is not especially difficult or technical, read on just as fast as you can without losing comprehension. Enter every reading situation with confidence and enthusiasm, and you will find this frame of mind will be a great help.

For further material on reading skills, refer to the books listed below:

1. Liddle, William, *Reading for Concepts* (New York: McGraw-Hill, 1977). Books "A" through "H" of this series are designed for readers in the seventh through twelfth grades.
2. Pauk, Walter, *How to Read Factual Literature* (Chicago: Science Research Associates, 1970). This book was written for readers in the seventh and eighth grades.
3. Pauk, Walter and Wilson, Josephine M., *How to Read Creative Literature* (Chicago: Science Research Associates, 1970). This book was written for readers in the ninth grade through adult level.

CHAPTER FOUR

AUTHORS AND THEIR WORKS

A knowledge of literature is the greatest humanizing force available to man. It teaches him respect for segments of mankind with whom he can have no direct acquaintance. It obligates him to compare his standards with the aims and codes of others. It provides him with illustrations of exemplary conduct, as well as of behavior to be reprobated. And it assures him of the immortality of the works of man, if not of man himself. The following brief biographical and critical accounts of some of the world's most famous writers is provided for reference.

Aeschylus (525?–456 B.C.), the Greek poet, is thought to have written about sixty plays. Only seven of his plays, dealing with the relationships of man with the gods and filled with accounts of murder, torture, revenge, and punishment, survive in their entirety. They are: the *Persae, Seven Against Thebes,* the *Agamemnon,* the *Choephori,* the *Eumenides, Prometheus Bound,* and the *Suppliant Women.*

Aesop (fl. ca. 570 B.C.), throughout classical antiquity was looked upon as the master of fables. However, it is unlikely that he left any written works. The short animal fables for which he is famous were used by him to make his point in debating.

Greek authors who were the creators of fables before the time of Aesop and other examples of fables have been found in the wisdom literature of the Sumerians, Babylonians, and Assyrians. About two hundred and thirty fables credited to Aesop, but probably spurious, are in the *Augustana,* which was printed in 1812.

Alcott, Louisa May (1832–1888), United States author, best known for her autobiographical *Little Women* (1868–1869), one of the most popular books ever written for girls.

Other books, drawn from her early experiences, were: *An Old-Fashioned Girl; Aunt Jo's Scrap Bag,* 6 vols.; *Little Men; Jo's Boys.* Her *Hospital Sketches* (1863) is valued for its vivid account of a nursing experience in the Civil War.

Andersen, Hans Christian (1805–1875), Danish author of some of the world's best-known stories. In 1822, when Andersen was seventeen, his first book, *Ungdoms-Forsog* (*Youthful Attempts*), was published under the pen name Villiam Christian Walter. His first poem, "Det doende Barn" ("The Dying Child"), appeared in 1827; he became better known with the publication of *Fodreise fra Holmens Kanal til Østpynten af Amager* in 1829, the same year his first play was performed. *Improvisatoren* (1835), an autobiographical novel with an Italian setting, was his first and most successful novel. While this book was being printed, Andersen began to write the children's stories that were to bring him lasting fame. Such fairy tales as "The Tinderbox," "Little Claus and Big Claus," "The Princess and the Pea," "Little Ida's Flowers," "The Tin Soldier," and "The Emperor's New Clothes" have been translated into eighty languages and are known and loved the world over.

Anderson, Maxwell (1888–1959), United States playwright who contributed to the development of modern American drama. His plays, some of which are written in a form of blank verse, include comedy, historical drama, and political satire. The World War I comedy *What Price Glory?* (1924) was written in collaboration with Laurence Stallings. He turned to history for *Elizabeth the Queen, Mary of Scotland,* and *Anne of the*

Thousand Days (1947). The very successful *Both Your Houses* was awarded the Pulitzer Prize. With two poetic plays, *Winterset,* inspired by the Sacco-Vanzetti case, and *High Tor,* he expressed his displeasure with the materialism of the modern world. In 1955 he wrote *The Bad Seed.*

Anderson, Sherwood (1876–1941), United States author whose stories presented sympathetically the lives of Middle Western townspeople. His first novel was *Windy McPherson's Son;* his reputation was made by *Winesburg, Ohio* (1919), which he called "A Book of the Grotesque"; it is a fictional study of repressed characters in a country village. This and the short stories in *The Triumph of the Egg, Horses and Men,* and *Death in the Woods* are considered his best work. In *Poor White* he studied the effects of the change to industry on a small town and its inhabitants. *Dark Laughter* and *Kit Brandon* are others of his works.

Aquinas, Saint Thomas (1225?–1274), medieval Italian philosopher, theologian, and the greatest organizer of Roman Catholic thought. His writings include theological and philosophical commentaries, discussions of doctrine, several short treatises, and two famous summaries of doctrine. The *Summa Contra Gentiles,* a manual of Catholic doctrine, was intended for use by missionaries in Spain. The *Summa Theologiae,* a large theological synthesis, was left unfinished.

Aquinas had immense influence on later theological thought and his doctrine has been officially endorsed by two encyclicals–Leo XIII's *Aeterni Patris* (1879) and Pius XI's *Studiorem Ducem* (1923). His eucharistic hymns, especially the "Lauda Sion" and the "Pange Lingua," are classed with the great medieval Latin lyrics.

Archimedes (ca. 287?–212 B.C.), Greek mathematician and inventor, was the only one of his age to make any real contribution to the theory of mechanics and to hydrostatics. His *On the Equilibrium and the Center of Gravity of Planes* may be considered the foundation of theoretical mechanics. The endless screw and the Archimedes screw are among the inventions ascribed to him. His other works include *On the Sphere and Cylinder, The Measurement of the Circle, On Conoids and Spheroids, On Spirals, The Quadrature of the Parabola, On Floating Bodies, The Sand Reckoner, The Method,* and *A Collection of Lemmas.*

Aristophanes (ca. 450–ca. 388 B.C.), most famous of all Greek writers of comedy, is credited with having written fifty-four plays, of which only eleven are extant. Those belonging to his first writing period are *Acharnians, Knights, Clouds, Peace,* and *Wasps.* The *Clouds* (423 B.C.) attacks "modern" education and morals, as they were taught by the Sophists. In the play, which ridicules Socrates and his pupils, their school known as the *Phrontisterion* or "Thinking Shop" is burned to the ground. *Wasps* (422 B.C.) satirizes the Athenians' penchant for lawsuits. To the second period belong *Birds, Lysistrata, Thesmophoriazusae,* and *Frogs.* In these the political satire is milder; *Frogs* is a literary rather than a "social" comedy. *Ecclesiazusae* and *Plutus* are the last of Aristophanes' plays. In the former, the women of Athens, instead of the men, are in power and the communism of wealth, property, and sex which is introduced is strongly reminiscent of that in the fifth book of Plato's *Republic.*

Aristotle (384–322 B.C.), a Greek famous in the fields of philosophy, logic, morals, politics, psychology, biology, and literary criticism. His theory of reasoning was the first, with modern additions, to survive to the present day as deductive logic. His treatises are concerned chiefly with logic (analytics), rhetoric, poetics, physics, psychology, and biology. In the *Poetics* is stated his theory of catharsis: tragedy "by raising pity and fear, purges the mind of these passions." Among his well known works are the *Organon,* concerning science or scientific reasoning; *Physics,* on inorganic nature; *Parva naturalia,* on such subjects as sensation, memory, sleep, and dreams; *Historia animalium,* a record of natural history data. Other important works include the *Eudemian Ethics* and the *Nicomachean Ethics.*

Arnold, Matthew (1822–1888), English poet and critic. The undercurrent of sadness found in much of his poetry, as in "Dover Beach," reflects his feelings about the conflict between long-cherished beliefs and science. Other noted poems are the long narrative "Sohrab and Rustum" and "The Scholar Gypsy." Arnold's outstanding critical essays are *Essays in Criticism* (1865, 1888), a discussion of the scope and importance of criticism; *Culture and Anarchy* (1869), an attack on the smugness and money-worship of Victorian England; and *The Study of Poetry,* which presents the thesis that poetry will have to replace religion.

Arouet, François Marie (1694–1778), who wrote under the pen name of Voltaire, French philosopher and author. *Zaire* is possibly the best of his tragedies that follows along classical lines. It probably is one of the ten or twelve best plays of the French classical school. His *Letters Concerning the English Nation* profoundly influenced other writers.

His two great historical works were *Siècle de Louis XIV* and *Essai sur l'histoire générale et sur les moeurs et l'espirit des nations* (7 volumes) with special attention given to cultural and economic developments. His short "philosophical novels" are popular today, particularly *Candide* (1759), a masterpiece of saucy satire. Voltaire was a prolific writer, and his voluminous correspondence is very revealing about himself.

Austen, Jane (1775–1817), English novelist.

The writings that established Jane Austen's literary reputation were *Pride and Prejudice,* a gently humorous novel of conflict between the heroine and hero; *Emma,* whose heroine is an engaging personality in spite of her meddling with the lives of others; *Sense and Sensibility,* which presents two heroines, one practical, the other inclined toward the romantic. *Mansfield Park, Northanger Abbey,* and *Persuasion* are other popular novels. Most of her fame and popularity came after her death.

Bacon, Francis (1561–1626), English philosopher, statesman, and man of letters.

Among his greatest professional, philosophical, and literary works are *The History of Henry VII;* the *Essays* (1597), an indication of his complete thoughts; and *New Atlantis,* a philosophic romance. He is also noted for his plan to develop a system of inductive logic. Of his plans to reorganize knowledge, in a philosophical work, *Instauratio Magna,* he completed, *The Advancement of Learning* and *Novum Organum.*

Balzac, Honoré de (1799–1850), French novelist, one of the greatest and most productive writers of fiction of all time. His first success came with the publication of *Les Derniers Chouans* in 1829. He conceived the idea of presenting an all-inclusive picture of modern civilization in *La Comédie Humaine.* It includes partly interconnected novels which recreate French society and picture in exact detail individuals of all classes and professions. Among the best known of his 85 novels are *Eugénie Grandet, Le Père Goriot, La Cousine Bette, Le Cousin Pons, The Magic Skin,* and the Swedenborgian *Seraphita.*

Baudelaire, Charles Pierre (1821–1867), French poet and critic. He is noted mainly for *Les Fleurs du mal (Flowers of Evil),* a volume of verse condemned as obscene. He excelled in writing of the macabre and the morbid, and exhibited this talent in his sympathetic translations of Poe's works. His only novel was the autobiographical *La Fanfarlo.*

Bellamy, Edward (1850–1898), United States writer, best known for his idealistic romance, *Looking Backward* (1888). This described a coming Utopian society that stressed cooperation, brotherhood, and especially technological adjustment to the needs of humans in A.D. 2000. Several tales combined in *The Blindman's World and Other Stories* subtly criticized conventional America.

Benét, Stephen Vincent (1898–1943), United States poet, novelist, and short story writer, best known for *John Brown's Body,* a long narrative poem of the Civil War which was awarded the Pulitzer Prize in 1929. His work is notable for a sense of drama and patriotism. Other well-known poems are "The Portrait of a Southern Lady" and "Ballad of William Sycamore." "The Devil and Daniel Webster" is one of his most imaginative short stories.

Beyle, Marie Henri (1783–1842), French writer who used the pseudonym of Stendhal, was one of the most creative and distinguished of French essayists and novelists. Although almost unknown during his lifetime, Stendhal wrote masterpieces which, for their psychological analysis, are among the greatest novels of all times. *The Red and the Black* is a brilliant picture of an ambitious young Frenchman to whom his own country seems foreign. *The Charterhouse of Parma* is a colorful, delightful novel of amour and politics. *Lucien Leuwen* is an unusually realistic and revealing political novel which was published in the United States as two novels: *The Green Huntsman* and *The Telegraph.*

Boccaccio, Giovanni (1313–1375), Italian writer and humanist, one of the principal figures of the Italian renaissance. *The Decameron,* his most famous work, was probably written during the years 1348–1358. It is composed of 100 stories told during a ten-day period by seven ladies and three gentlemen who, in 1348, flee to the country from plague-stricken Florence. The plots of the stories are based on popular tales of that period, especially the fabliaux, which had come to Italy from France. The word *Decameron* means "ten days' work." Boccaccio's other works include *Filicolo, Filostrato,* and *Teseida.*

Boswell, James (1740–1795), Scotsman, friend and biographer of Samuel Johnson, and one of the world's greatest diarists. His first literary fame came from *An Account of Corsica, the Journal of a Tour to That Island* and from his *Memoirs of Pascal Paoli.* However, it is for the *Life of Johnson* (1791) that Boswell continues to retain his place in English letters.

Brecht, Bertolt (1898–1956), German poet and playwright. His early plays, *Baal* and *Trommeln in der Nacht* (1922), won the contemporary critics' acclaim. Both these and *Im Dickicht der Städte* were expressionist. Brecht used stark realism and simplicity of style, as he had also used them in his early lyrics and ballads, collected under the satirical title *Die Hauspostille (Book of Family Devotions).* Brecht's greatest theatrical success was his *Die Dreigroschenoper (The Threepenny Opera),* with music by Kurt Weill. It is an adaptation of Gay's *Beggars' Opera* and portrays human greed, indolence, and bewilderment.

Brecht's claim to fame is based on plays that deal with human issues from a Marxist point of view: *Mutter Courage und ihre Kinder,* a chronicle of the Thirty Years' War; *Leben des Galilei; Herr Puntila und sein Knecht;* and the dramatic parables, *Der gute Mensch von Sezuan* and *Der kaukasische Kreidekreis.*

Brontë, Charlotte (1816–1855), English novelist. Charlotte Brontë recorded her memories of the school she attended in *Jane Eyre* (1847), her most famous novel. It is a fascinating tale of wild melodrama. Her book *Shirley* is the first English regional novel. The three Brontë sisters–Charlotte, Emily, and Anne–collaborated on *Poems* in 1846.

Brontë, Emily (1818–1848), English novelist and poet. Her *Wuthering Heights* (1847) is an intensely dramatic, creative work of fiction, a tale of psychological horror, technically interesting for its narrative point of view.

Browning, Elizabeth Barrett (1806–1861), English poet, wife of the poet Robert Browning. She was born Elizabeth Barrett, under which name she wrote and published *Sonnets from the Portuguese* (1850). This is considered her best work–gentle, yet deeply sincere–and assures her of a permanent place among English poets. Other works include *Casa Guidi Windows* and a novel in verse, *Aurora Leigh.*

Browning, Robert (1812–1889), English poet. For some years Browning wrote verse-drama, including his popular *Pippa Passes.* He then turned to shorter poems, such as "Home Thoughts from Abroad," "The Pied Piper of Hamelin," and "Waring," but won his greatest fame with such dramatic monologues as "My Last Duchess," "Andrea del Sarto," and "The Bishop Orders His Tomb at Saint Praxed's Church." The most outstanding works of his last years included *The Ring and The Book,* his greatest poem (1868), and his long dramatic or narrative poems, *Fifine at the Fair, The Inn Album, Dramatic Idyls,* in two series, *Pauline,* and *Sordello.*

Buck, Pearl S. (1892–1973), United States novelist who won the 1938 Nobel Prize in Literature. Until 1934 she spent most of her life in China, where her parents and her first husband were missionaries. Her first novel, *East Wind: West Wind* (1930), was followed by *The Good Earth* (1931), which won the Pulitzer Prize. Her later books include *The Patriot, Dragon Seed,* and *Peony*. Her works are notable for the vivid descriptions of Oriental life and problems, and for their understanding of humanity.

Burke, Edmund (1729–1797), was born in Ireland but became a British political thinker, statesman, and parliamentary orator. He was outstanding in protests against the Crown in favor of the American colonies. Two speeches, *On American Taxation* and *On Moving His Resolutions for Conciliation with the Colonies,* expressed Burke's pro-American sentiments. Two others of Burke's well-known speeches were on affairs in India–*On Mr. Fox's East India Bill* and *On the Nabob of Arcot's Debts*. He was hostile to the French Revolution and wrote his *Reflections on the French Revolution* as a protest.

Burns, Robert (1759–1796), one of the greatest Scottish poets. His *Poems, Chiefly in the Scottish Dialect* won him immediate acclaim. Among his better known poems are "Holy Willie's Prayer," a satiric poem; "The Cotter's Saturday Night," and "Tam O'Shanter." His songs "O Wert Thou in the Cauld Blast," "Flow Gently, Sweet Afton," "Ae Fond Kiss," "Auld Lang Syne," and "Coming thro' the Rye" are well loved in all English-speaking parts of the world.

Byron, George Gordon, 6th Baron (1788–1824), English poet and satirist. *Childe Harold* (1812–1818) and *Don Juan,* long romances in verse, are autobiographical, as was his poetic drama *Sardanapalus*. Byron's *The Vision of Judgment* is a satire on Southey. His letters were conversational and witty. Many of them, first published in the twentieth century, have enhanced his literary reputation. Other long poems include *The Bride of Abydos, Manfred,* and *Mazeppa*. A shorter piece, *The Prisoner of Chillon* (set in the Fortress of Chillon in Montreux, Switzerland) is today one of his most familiar works.

Carlyle, Thomas (1795–1881), Scots essayist and historian. His translation in 1824 of Goethe's *Wilhelm Meister's Apprenticeship* is a masterpiece. His book *The French Revolution* (1837) is his greatest work. He saw the French Revolution as a judgment of monarchy. He expressed his preference for the Middle Ages over the present in *Past and Present*. Another important work is *Latter-Day Pamphlets*. *Sartor Resartus* expressed his views on British society.

Cather, Willa (1873–1947), United States novelist of the frontier. In her pioneer novels, adventure was replaced by ordinary daily living. *O Pioneers!* (1913) was her first great success and *One of Ours* (1922) won the Pulitzer Prize. Other outstanding novels of Willa Cather's were *My Antonia,* about the Nebraska girlhood of a Bohemian immigrant; *A Lost Lady,* which mourned the passing of the pioneer spirit of the Middle West; and *Death Comes for the Archbishop,* an account of the establishment of the Catholic Church in the Southwest.

Cato, Marcus Porcius [called **The Censor**] (234–149 B.C.), Roman statesman, orator, and first Latin prose writer of importance. He wrote the first history of Rome in Latin, the *Origines,* but it is now lost. His only surviving work is *De Re Rustica,* written about 160 B.C., which dealt with the production of wine, oil, and fruit, and with grazing. He compiled an encyclopedia and maxims, and works on medicine, military science, and law.

Catullus, Gainus Valerius (84?–54 B.C.), Roman lyric poet. His many poems, of which about one hundred or so survive, include satires, epigrams, and especially passionate lyric poems addressed to the lady Lesbia.

Cervantes Saavedra, Miguel de (1547–1616), Spanish novelist, playwright, poet, and creator of Don Quixote. In January, 1605, his immortal work, *El Ingenioso Hidalgo Don Quixote de la Mancha,* appeared in Madrid. It was a mad, kindly satire on the pretensions inspired by chivalry and romance. The second part of *Don Quixote* was not completed until 1615. Of the twenty to thirty plays he wrote, only two, *El Trato de Argel* and *La Numancia,* have survived. A pastoral novel, *La Galatea,* appeared in 1584; his twelve excellent short novels, *Novelas ejemplares,* in 1613. The following year *Viaje del Parnaso,* a burlesque poem, and the *Adjunta al Parnaso,* in prose, appeared. Shortly before his death, Cervantes returned to his first enthusiasm, drama, with the *Ocho comedias y ocho entremeses nuevos*. By virtue of *Don Quixote,* Cervantes ranks as one of the world's great writers.

Chaucer, Geoffrey (ca. 1340–1400), probably the greatest English poet before Shakespeare. *The Canterbury Tales* has always been the most popular of Chaucer's works. In it some 30 pilgrims are described on their travels from a suburb in London to Canterbury. The pilgrims, drawn from different classes and occupations, are treated with gentle irony and humor as they tell their tales. Others of Chaucer's outstanding works are *Troilus and Criseyde* and *The Legend of Good Women.* He also wrote short poems and addresses.

Chekhov, Anton Pavlovich (1860–1904), Russian playwright and short story writer. His works present a graphic picture of middle-class Russia at the turn of the century. There is also a quality of timelessness created by his heroes who struggle against static forces of almost overwhelming inertia. His first full-length play, *Ivanov* (1887), was followed by *The Wood Demon* and *The Seagull* (1896). The plays usually considered his masterpieces are *Uncle Vanya; The Three Sisters* (1901), which is his most profound dramatic work; and *The Cherry Orchard.*

The best and best known of his many short stories are "The Lady with the Dog," "In the Ravine," "The Chorus Girl," "A Woman's Kingdom," "Peasants," and "Three Years," a story of Moscow life which includes much autobiographical material.

Cicero, Marcus Tullius (106–43 B.C.), Roman statesman, orator, scholar, and writer. His correspondence reveals the political, social, literary, and economic life of Rome. His best-known poems (they survive only in fragments) were the epics *On His Consulship* and *On His Life and Times.*

Four collections of Cicero's letters–to Atticus, to his friends, to Brutus, and to his brother–form a revealing historical source of the ancient world of his time.

Clemens, Samuel Langhorne (1835–1910), who wrote under the pen name of Mark Twain, United States' most famous humorist and the author of popular and outstanding autobiographical works, travel books, and novels. One of Twain's best books, *The Adventures of Tom Sawyer* (1876), is certainly his best for young people. It takes place in the river town of Hannibal, Missouri, and is a contrast of boys' "orneriness" with their natural decency. By general agreement, *Huckleberry Finn* (1884) is Twain's finest book and an outstanding American novel. Huck wants to be "free and satisfied." The book runs the gamut from humor to drama. *The Prince and the Pauper* is a historical novel making use of the ancient artifice of exchanged identities. Another historical fiction is *A Connecticut Yankee in King Arthur's Court.* Other works include: *Life on the Mississippi, Innocents Abroad* (1869), *Roughing It, The Gilded Age, Pudd'nhead Wilson* (1894), and many short stories.

Coleridge, Samuel Taylor (1772–1834), English poet, lecturer, journalist, and critic of literature, theology, philosophy, and society. His best known poems are: "The Rime of the Ancient Mariner" (1798), a narrative tale showing the poet's insight into the sense of the Infinite, "Christabel," and "Kubla Khan." The "Ancient Mariner" remains outstanding among narrative poems in English. He and William Wordsworth published *Lyrical Ballads* in 1798. Later poems include *Sybilline Leaves* and the critique *Biographia Literaria.*

Congreve, William (1670–1729), English dramatist. In 1692 he published the delightful *Incognito,* or *Love and Duty Reconcil'd.* In 1693 he achieved fame with the staging of *The Old Bachelor. Love for Love* is best suited for the stage. A tragedy, *The Mourning Bride,* is now remembered for its lyrics "Music Hath Charms" and "Hell Hath No Fury." *The Way of the World,* which appeared in 1700, is considered to be Congreve's masterpiece.

Conrad, Joseph (1857–1924), British seaman and novelist, born in Poland and named Teodor

Jósef Konrad Korzeniowski. He became one of the greatest novelists and short story writers in the English language. Conrad's first novels, *Almayer's Folly* (1895) and *An Outcast of the Islands* (1896), were set in the East Indies. They were followed by *The Nigger of the "Narcissus," Lord Jim* (1900), and *Chance* (1914). When *Chance* became famous, readers rediscovered *Lord Jim. Nostromo* (1904), his most elaborate novel, is a story of revolution, politics, and graft in a South American republic and is considered Conrad's masterpiece.

Cowper, William (1731–1800), once one of the most widely read of English poets. In 1784 he wrote the ballad *The Diverting History of John Gilpin,* which was soon sung throughout London. In 1779 the *Olney Hymns,* a book of religious verse, appeared. *The Castaway* was one of his longer tragic poems.

Crane, Stephen (1871–1900), United States novelist, poet, and short story writer. His novel, *Maggie: a Girl of the Streets,* is a naturalistic study of life in a New York slum. *The Red Badge of Courage* (1895), his most famous work, is a Civil War novel exploring the fear, shame, disgust, and courage of a Union soldier. Its realistic descriptions of battle scenes have great verisimilitude. Crane was the author of two books of poems, *The Black Riders* and *War Is Kind.*

Cummings, e. e. (1894–1962), United States poet and artist, whose volume of *Collected Poems* is probably his best known; his work shows deep poetic insight, strongly expressed in unusual ways–he was most unorthodox in punctuation, including the use of small letters for capital letters. *Viva, No Thanks, One Times One,* and *95 Poems* are among his volumes of verse. One of the better World War I novels was Cummings' *The Enormous Room.*

Dana, Richard Henry (1815–1882), United States lawyer and author, whose literary fame rests on a single book, *Two Years Before the Mast* (1840). It describes a voyage he himself made around Cape Horn to California and back and presents "the life of a common sailor at sea as it really is."

Dante [full name **Dante Alighieri**] (1265–1321), the greatest poet of Italy, author of the allegorical Christian poem, the sublime *Divina Commedia* or *Divine Comedy.* His other works include the *Vita Nuova* and *Monarchia,* on world government. Among his unfinished works are *Convivio* and *De vulgari eloquentia.*

Darwin, Charles Robert (1809–1882), English naturalist. In 1859, Darwin published his great work *On the Origin of Species by Means of Natural Selection, or the Preservation of Favoured Races in the Struggle for Life.* As an explanation for evolution he gave first place to the "survival of the fittest."

Defoe, Daniel (1659?–1731), English novelist and political pamphleteer. His pamphlet, *The Shortest Way with the Dissenters* (1702), resulted in a fine and imprisonment at Newgate. On his release, he started the periodical *The Review,* incorporating commercial interests and domestic and political articles. Defoe's political and domestic writings are now all but forgotten. His fame rests largely on *The Review,* which is important in the history of journalism, and on two novels, *Robinson Crusoe* (1719), one of the most famous books ever written, and *Moll Flanders* (1722).

Demosthenes (384/383–322 B.C.), Greek statesman and orator. The contents of his speeches illuminate the political, social, and economic life of Athens in the fourth century B.C. Among the most famous of his orations are the *Olynthiacs,* occasioned by Philip of Macedon's attack on the state of Olynthus, and the *Philippics,* directed against Philip. Demosthenes' famous speech, *On the Crown,* was used to vindicate himself at a trial held in 330 B.C.

De Quincey, Thomas (1785–1859), English writer, author of *Confessions of an English Opium-Eater* (1822). Of De Quincey's works, the most important are his autobiographical writings, his literary criticism, and the unfinished *Suspiria de Profundis,* with its theme that grief and pain are essential to the development of the soul. In the *Autobiographic Sketches,* his objective is to trace the growth and development of his own mind. The "Daughter of Lebanon," found at the end of the *Confessions,* even though only a fragment, is a splendid example of De Quincey's prose.

Descartes, René (1596–1650), French philosopher and mathematician, who extended mathematical ideas and proofs to all facets of knowledge and to knowledge itself. Descartes' outstanding work is the *Discourse on the Method of Properly Guiding the Reason in the Search for Truth in the Sciences.* This book established as the basis for modern

rationalism, scientific doubt and mathematical logic. Part is titled *Also the Dioptric, the Meteors and the Geometry, which are Essays in this Method* (Leyden, 1637). Descartes thus, in addition to his theoretical studies, also presents fully worked-out examples of his method's application. Other philosophical works are *Meditationes de Prima Philosophia* (1641) and *Principia Philosophiae* (1644). The *Geometry* (1637) embodies his discovery and formulation of coordinate geometry; much of this work has now been adopted by modern textbooks.

Dickens, Charles (1812–1870), one of the greatest English novelists. Dickens' humanitarian novels describe vividly the scenes of the poor of his time, including the poorhouse and the debtors' prison. In *David Copperfield* (1849–1850) he uses incidents from his own bitter childhood. The *Pickwick Papers* charmingly recreates the life of stagecoach and country inn. *Hard Times* may be considered historically important as Dickens' most radical book. As in all the novels that follow, Dickens demands social reform and the regeneration of men. Other Dickens novels include *Little Dorrit; A Tale of Two Cities,* a historical romance of the French Revolution; *Great Expectations; Oliver Twist* (1837–1839); and *Martin Chuzzlewit.*

Dickinson, Emily (1830–1886), United States poet, considered one of the great women poets of the nineteenth century, only six of whose poems were published in her lifetime. Thomas Wentworth Higginson published 116 poems in 1890–1891, and other collections appeared at intervals. In 1945 over 600 new poems were presented in *Bolts of Melody.*

Donne, John (1573–1631), English cleric, poet, and prose writer. Donne's life reflected the device he used in his writing the *Paradox.* His sensual, witty *Elegies* and the caustic *Satires* are examples of his early poetry. In later life, when he had left Roman Catholicism and embraced the Church of England, becoming Dean of St. Paul's, his writings became devotional. His works include, among others, the lyric *The Songs and Sonnets* and the prose *Paradoxes and Problems.*

Dos Passos, John (1896–1970), United States novelist. Dos Passos won fame with his novel about World War I, *Three Soldiers* (1921). In 1925 *Manhattan Transfer* appeared. The book presented a view of New York life, using an experimental technique. This same "collage" technique was carried forward in the trilogy *U.S.A.,* an important record of the United States from 1900 to the 1930s. The trilogy contains his best-known novels–*The 42nd Parallel; 1919,* a story of the World War I years; and *The Big Money,* which dealt with the frantic money-making of the post-World War I period. Dos Passos' later works include such novels as *The Grand Design, The Great Days,* and *Midcentury* (1961), as well as travel books, historical studies, and documentaries.

Dostoevski, Fëdor Mikhailovich (1821–1881), Russian novelist whose first novel, *Poor Folk,* brought him quick recognition. Between 1861 and 1881, he wrote several long novels, the best known of which are *Crime and Punishment* and *The Brothers Karamazov. Crime and Punishment* is the story of the murder of an old woman by a half-starved student; *The Brothers Karamazov* relates the love of a father and son for the same girl, with the son murdering the father. Other novels are *The House of the Dead, The Idiot,* and *The Possessed.* Of his short novels, *Notes from the Underground* is considered the best.

A giant of literature, Dostoevski continues to be one of the most widely read novelists of all times as new editions of his greatest works keep appearing.

Doyle, Sir Arthur Conan (1859–1930), English novelist and historian. It was through his cycle of Sherlock Holmes stories that Conan Doyle gained fame. The ingenious methods he suggested in these stories for the detection of crime are said to have influenced law enforcement agencies in developing scientific methods of crime detection. Doyle's Sherlock Holmes stories have been made into movies, plays, radio, and television shows. The best-known Holmes stories are *The Hound of the Baskervilles, The Sign of the Four,* and *The Memoirs of Sherlock Holmes.*

Dreiser, Theodore (1871–1945), United States author, distinguished for his naturalistic novels. His first novel, *Sister Carrie* (1900), was a starkly realistic picture of the poor conditions under which factory girls worked. Practically suppressed by its publisher, it attracted little attention. *Jennie Gerhardt* (1911) was also controversial, but it won success. Only then was a new edition of *Sister Carrie* accepted on its merits. The next year Dreiser brought out *The Financier,* first of a trilogy about a businessman whose career in many respects resembled that of an actual financial magnate. The others in the series were *The Titan* and *The Stoic*. The best of his novels, *An American Tragedy* (1925), was based on an actual murder case and brought Dreiser worldwide recognition as a major novelist.

Dudevant, Amandine Lucile Aurore (1804–1876), née Dupin [also **Baronne Dudevant**], French novelist, who used the pseudonym George Sand. Among her best-known novels are *Indiana, La Mare au Diable (The Haunted Pool),* and *La Petite Fadette (Fanchon the Cricket). Elle et Lui* is her version of her affair with Musset; *Un Hiver à Majorque (A Winter in Majorca)* tells of her life on the island with Chopin. The dramatization of several of her plays met with some success—*Le Marquis de Villemer* was a triumph.

Dumas, Alexandre, the Elder, (1802–1870), French novelist and dramatist. He is known for his famous romances: *The Count of Monte Cristo,* an exciting story of melodramatic revenge, romance, and adventure, *The Three Musketeers, Twenty Years After,* and *The Vicomte de Bragelonne,* which depict French life under Louis XIII. His *Louis XIV et Son Siecle* is the most important of his historical works, and his best-known play is *La Tour de Nesle.*

Dumas, Alexandre, the Younger (1824–1895), French playwright and novelist, son of Alexandre Dumas, the Elder. His novel *La Dame aux Camelias (Camille)* won him immediate acclaim. He wrote many plays and novels about contemporary trends in politics, business, and romance which became the bases for successful stage plays. Verdi's *La Traviata* is based on Dumas' *Camille.*

Eliot, T. S. (1888–1965), American-born British poet, playwright, and critic. His first book of poems, *Prufrock and Other Observations,* appeared in 1917; the next volumes were *Poems* (1920), *The Waste Land,* and *Ash Wednesday.* In 1944, he published *Four Quartets,* a modern metaphysical poem. He received the Nobel Prize for Literature in 1948. He wrote two religious verse plays, *The Rock* and *Murder in the Cathedral,* and returned to the theater with *The Family Reunion, The Cocktail Party, The Confidential Clerk,* and *The Elder Statesman.*

Emerson, Ralph Waldo (1803–1882), United States essayist, poet, lecturer, and one of the most stimulating thinkers of the nineteenth century. His Phi Beta Kappa oration at Harvard in 1837, later known as *The American Scholar,* was called by Oliver Wendell Holmes our intellectual Declaration of Independence. Emerson's views on democracy, conformity, individual liberty, American customs of the time, and a host of other subjects, were delivered as lectures and subsequently were published under a variety of titles. Among them were *Essays: First and Second Series, Representative Men, Society and Solitude,* and *English Traits.* His best-known poems include "Brahma," "The Concord Hymn," "The Problem," "Ode to Beauty," and "The Rhodora." Emerson, a Protestant minister, gave up the pulpit because of his nonconformist views.

Epicurus (341–270 B.C.), Greek philosopher. Most of our information on Epicurus comes from other sources. His own observations are expressed in forty short, pithy statements in *Principal Doctrines* and in three letters: *To Herodotus, To Pythocles,* and *To Menoeccus.* Epicurus' great work *On Nature* (originally in 37 books) was found in the papyrus rolls discovered at Herculaneum in the years 1752–1754. The doctrines of Epicurus offer the human soul outlets for its anxieties and show how the simple fact of being can be the foundation for real happiness.

Euripides (ca. 485–407 B.C.), youngest of the three great Greek tragedians, following Aeschylus and Sophocles. Of his 19 surviving plays the best known are *Medea, Electra, The Trojan Women, Orestes,* and *Alcestis.* The struggle of the human will to overcome human passions is a central theme in many of Euripedes' plays, as in *Medea.* Medea was wronged by Jason, who owed his achievements and his life to her. When he cast her off to marry a Greek princess, she punished him by killing his wife and her own children by him, leaving him to grow old alone.

Evans, Mary Ann (1819–1880), who used the pen name of George Eliot, was one of the great English novelists of the Victorian age. Her early novels were based on her memories of life in the English countryside of Warwickshire; they are considered somewhat autobiographical. Her first was *Scenes of Clerical Life*. Then came *Adam Bede*, her first long novel, which she described as a "country story–full of the breath of cows and the scent of hay." In *The Mill on the Floss* she again turned to the scenes of her early life and her relations with her brother Isaac. *Middlemarch* is her most substantial work. In the classroom she is well known for her *Silas Marner,* the story of a weaver whose lost gold is replaced by a strayed child.

Faulkner, William (1897–1962), United States author. With his first novels about mythical Yoknapatawpha County, Mississippi, *Sartoris* and *The Sound and the Fury* (both 1928–1929), Faulkner began a series of books about social and racial problems in the South. Others in the series are *As I Lay Dying; Light in August; Absalom, Absalom!;* "The Bear" [in *Go Down, Moses and Other Stories*]; and *Intruder in the Dust* (1948). He was awarded the 1949 Nobel Prize in Literature.

Aside from the Yoknapatawpha series, a trilogy on the Snopes family, *The Hamlet, The Town,* and *The Mansion,* began brilliantly but slackened as it progressed. Faulkner's most ambitious work was the novel *A Fable,* which won the Pulitzer Prize in 1955.

Fielding, Henry (1707–1754), English jurist, novelist, and playwright, is best known for one of the greatest of realistic novels, which he wrote toward the end of his career. This novel is *Tom Jones, or the History of a Foundling,* the long and zestful story of a lively hero, richly filled with adventures and characters.

Fielding's numerous plays include *Love in Several Masques, The Author's Farce, Tom Thumb,* and *The Coffee House Politican.* Prior to *Tom Jones* he had written the novels *Joseph Andrews* and *Jonathan Wild.* His prolific pen also produced poetry, essays, and treatises. In addition to his literary writings, he produced two newspapers and was called to the bar. Fielding was influential on such writers as Dickens and Thackeray.

FitzGerald, Edward (1809–1883), English translator. In 1859 an anonymous translation from the Persian was published as *The Rubaiyat of Omar Khayyám.* The translation was by FitzGerald. Regardless of the merit of the *Rubaiyat,* the translation was recognized immediately as a literary work of consequence. FitzGerald produced translations of *Agamemnon* of Aeschylus, Oedipus tragedies of Sophocles, and some plays of Calderón.

Fitzgerald, F. Scott (1896–1940), United States novelist who captured the spirit of the 1920s. The first of his best works, *This Side of Paradise* (1920), largely autobiographical, was about the rebellious youth of the twenties. It was followed by two volumes of short stories, *Flappers and Philosophers* and *Tales of the Jazz Age,* and a second novel, *The Beautiful and the Damned,* which revolved around the revolt of sophisticated youth and the meaninglessness of life. *The Great Gatsby,* Fitzgerald's best-known book, satirized wealthy Long Island society in the 1920s and revealed his literary merit. Some of his finest short stories were included in *All the Sad Young Men,* and another novel, *Tender Is the Night,* exploits his own sadly tortured domestic situation. He died before completing *The Last Tycoon* (published posthumously in 1941).

Flaubert, Gustave (1821–1880), French novelist. Many French critics call *Sentimental Education* Flaubert's best work. It is about the disillusionment of a young Parisian through love. His *Salammbô* is a barbaric, colorful story of love and war in ancient Carthage. In *Madame Bovary,* sometimes called "the perfect novel," Flaubert took a run-of-the-mill story of adultery in a small French village and turned it into a work of enduring literary merit.

Freud, Sigmund (1856–1939), Austrian physician and author, was the founder of psychoanalysis, which began as a technique for the analysis and cure of mental illness. His psychoanalytic principles have influenced medicine, psychology, the arts, religion, education, and the social sciences. He is considered one of the outstanding thinkers of the twentieth century. Through his early work on the treatment

of hysteria by hypnosis he became aware of the importance of the unconscious in men's minds. Later he gave up the use of hypnosis, substituting for it the technique of "free association of ideas" for bringing unconscious memories and emotions into consciousness. Among his leading works are *Studies in Hysteria* (with Josef Breuer) (1895); *The Interpretation of Dreams* (1899); *Introductory Lectures on Psychoanalysis* (1916); *Beyond the Pleasure Principle* (1920); *The Future of an Illusion* (1927); *Civilization and Its Discontents* (1930); and *Moses and Monotheism* (1939).

Frost, Robert Lee (1874–1963), four times winner of the Pulitzer Prize in Poetry, United States poet of the people, of New Englanders, of New England itself, its hills, its hardships, its humor, and inverse tenderness. While his poetry has a regional quality, its real subject is human life and destiny. His works include *A Boy's Will, North of Boston, New Hampshire, West-Running Brook, A Witness Tree, A Masque of Mercy,* and *Complete Poems.* Among his latest poems are "The Gift Outright," the poem delivered at the inaugural of President John F. Kennedy, which was included in a volume of poetry published in 1962, entitled *In the Clearing.* As a distinguished man of letters he received many awards and honorary degrees.

Galsworthy, John (1867–1933), British playwright and novelist, winner of the Nobel Prize in Literature in 1932. Galsworthy attracted wide attention with his novels, *The Man of Property* in 1906 and *The Island Pharisees* in 1908. The former was the first of *The Forsyte Saga* series. *The Indian Summer of a Forsyte, In Chancery, Awakening,* and *To Let* were others in the series. In 1942 Galsworthy published *The White Monkey,* the first of a trilogy about London after World War I, of which *The Silver Spoon* and *Swan Song* were the other two. *The Silver Spoon* shows Galsworthy's rapport with youth and beauty. Among his plays are *Strife, The Silver Box, Justice,* and *The Forest.*

Germaine, Anne Louise (1766–1817), who used the pen name Madame de Staël, French novelist and writer, wrote two very successful novels, *Delphine* and *Corinne.* Her chief work was *De l'Allemagne,* which through its enthusiasm for German romanticism, strongly influenced French literature.

Gibbon, Edward (1737–1794), English historian. Gibbon's monumental six-volume *Decline and Fall of the Roman Empire* (1788) remains one of the outstanding achievements in all historical writing. It displays a mastery of the architectonics of English prose. The *Decline* covers the period A.D. 180–641 exhaustively; and the period A.D. 641–1453 in summary form. Gibbon also wrote his autobiography, *Memoirs of My Life and Writings.*

Goethe, Johann Wolfgang von (1749–1832), dramatist, novelist, the greatest of German poets. His *Kleine Blumen* and *Kleine Blätter* ushered in a new epoch in German lyric poetry. One of the most beautiful love stories in world literature is the idyll of Sessenheim in *Dichtung und Wahrheit.* The influence of Greek tragedy is found in the quiet beauty of his new iambic version of *Iphigenie auf Tauris;* Renaissance classicism runs throughout the drama of *Torquato Tasso. Wilhelm Meisters Lehrjahre* tells the history of a young man's apprenticeship in the theater. This novel proved to be an instant and enduring influence on German literature. In *The Sorrows of Young Werther* the hero commits suicide because his love is unrequited.

The crowning achievement of Goethe's career was *Faust,* a philosophical drama that is at once profound and exciting.

Gogol, Nikolai Vasilievich (1809–1852), Russian novelist and dramatist. His first success came with *Evenings on a Farm* and "Taras Bulba," the best known of the *Cossack Tales.* He also published *Arabesques,* a collection of essays and stories, and a number of other short stories, including *Old World Gentlefolks.* He is best known in the English-speaking world for the *Inspector-General* [in Russian the *Revizor*] and *Dead Souls.* The *Inspector-General* is about a simple Russian who is mistaken for a high Russian official. *Dead Souls* is the story of a Russian scoundrel who goes about the countryside buying up "dead souls" or dead serfs.

Goldsmith, Oliver (1728–1774), English poet, playwright, and novelist. Until the publication of his poem "The Traveler" Goldsmith had written considerable popular material, mostly unsigned or under a pseudonym. Most of this early work which would now be labeled "commercial" was written to sustain himself. "The Traveler" was the first to appear under his own name and at once became a success. Then followed the great *Vicar of Wakefield,* which still is required reading in many English literature courses. In 1773 Goldsmith's play *She Stoops to Conquer* was staged. This incomparable farce is a great stage success to this day. Other works include a poem, "The Deserted Village," and a children's classic, *Little Goody Two-Shoes.*

Gorky, Maxim (1868–1936), Russian author. Gorky's famous play is *The Lower Depths* (1902). "My Fellow Traveler" and "Twenty-six Men and a Girl" are the best of his early stories. An autobiographical trilogy was composed of *Childhood, In the World* (V. Lyndyakh), and *My Universities.* The trilogy, a volume of *Recollections,* and *Fragments from My Diary* constitute Gorky's best works.

Gray, Thomas (1716–1771), English poet, whose "Elegy Written in a Country Churchyard," one of his most familiar poems, expresses feelings that are common to most people. He was not a prolific writer, yet he published enough to be considered one of England's great poets. His love for the beautiful local countryside inspired his "Ode on the Spring."

Grimm, Jacob Ludwig Carl (1785–1863), and **Wilhelm (Carl)** (1786–1859), German folklorists and philologists. Together they were the collectors and editors of Grimms' *Fairy Tales* and were generally known as The Brothers Grimm; Jacob was the grammarian, and Wilhelm the literary scholar.

Jacob Grimm's *Deutsche Grammatik* (1819–1822) was the result of both brothers' previous philological work. In 1811 Jacob published a purely literary work, *Über den altdeutschen Meistergesang* and Wilhelm brought out his volume of translations *Altdänische Heldenlieder, Balladen und Märchen übersetzt.* In 1812 the brothers published the two ancient fragments of the *Hildebrandslied* and the *Weissenbrunner Gebet;* in 1812–1815 they jointly edited the first edition of the *Kinder-und Hausmärchen,* the *Fairy Tales,* which have penetrated practically every household of the civilized world, and became a basis for the scientific study of comparative folklore.

Hamsun, Knut (1859–1952), Norwegian author, winner of the Nobel Prize in Literature in 1920, is best known throughout the English-speaking world for three novels, *Hunger, Growth of the Soil,* and *The Woman at the Well.* His interests were centered around the psychological analysis of people with real and simple problems such as hunger.

Hardy, Thomas (1840–1928), English novelist and poet, whose first popular success was *Far from the Madding Crowd.* Then came, among others, *The Hand of Ethelberta,* subtitled a "Comedy in Chapters"; *The Return of the Native,* the most melancholy and perhaps the most powerful; *Two on a Tower,* a long ironic story; and Hardy's most famous novel, *Tess of the D'Urbervilles,* which was, like his other novels, a gloomy, naturalistic study of character and environment. Adverse criticism turned him to poetry in which he expressed his pessimism in such books as *Wessex Poems, The Dynasts,* and *Moments of Vision.*

Harris, Joel Chandler (1848–1908), United States author, whose "Tar Baby Story" (1879) started the vogue for a new and different kind of dialect literature. Harris wrote just as the plantation Negro talked, adding humor and descriptive narrative. *Uncle Remus, Nights with Uncle Remus, The Tar Baby* and *Brer Rabbit* are good examples of his style. He also wrote a series of children's books: *The Story of Aaron* and *Gabriel Tolliver. On the Plantation* was autobiographical.

Harte, Francis Brett (1836–1902), United States author who wrote under the name of Bret Harte. He created a new type of short story and a new movement in American literature–the "local color" school. His first story, "The Luck of Roaring Camp," a tale of life in a western mining town, appeared in the *Overland Monthly* in 1868 and made his reputation. It was followed by "The Outcasts of Poker Flat" and "Tennessee's Partner." Harte's reputation was further strengthened by "Plain Language from Truthful James" (better known as "The Heathen Chinee"), a poem that attracted national attention. His "An Ingenue of the Sierras" and "A Protégée of Jack Hamlin's" were written in 1893.

Harte's most successful books were *The Luck of Roaring Camp and Other Sketches* (1870) and *Tales of the Argonauts.* His best play was *Ah Sin,* written in collaboration with Mark Twain and based on Harte's famous poem, "Plain Language from Truthful James."

Hawthorne, Nathaniel (1804–1864), one of the greatest fiction writers in United States literature. *Twice-Told Tales,* his first collection of short stories, was published in 1837. *The Scarlet Letter* (1850) ranks among his finest works and is one of the great works of fiction in the English language. The theme of the book is the revelation of sin, but Hawthorne was not so much interested in this as in its psychological consequences. Some of his other major novels are *The House of the Seven Gables,* about sinister influences within an old New England family; *The Marble Faun,* concerning several characters in Italy; and a partly autobiographical novel, *The Blithedale Romance,* growing out of Hawthorne's participation in the Brook Farm experiment in socialism.

Hegel, Georg Wilhelm Friedrich (1770–1831), German philosopher. Although his essay on *The Spirit of Christianity* is one of Hegel's most remarkable works, it was unpublished until 1907. His first great work, the *Phenomenology of Mind* was finished and published in 1807.

After the publication of his *Philosophy of Right* he appears to have devoted himself to his lectures. These were published as *Aesthetics,* the *Philosophy of Religion,* the *Philosophy of History,* and the *History of Philosophy.* The *Philosophy of History* sees civilizations as a struggle toward rational freedom.

Heine, Heinrich (1797–1856), an outstanding satirist and publicist, and one of the greatest German lyric poets. His *Buch der Lieder* placed him among the world's great poets. His poems such as "Lorelei" are musical and have a folk-like quality; often they are sharpened by subtle irony or dissonant endings. He wrote the famous verse satires *Atta Troll, Deutschland,* and *Gedichte.* His *Harzreise,* one of his prose travel sketches, shows his lyric emotion and wit.

Hemingway, Ernest (1899–1961), United States novelist and short story writer, noted for his gift for dialogue and understatement. *The Sun Also Rises* (1926), a touching fictional reminiscence of the "lost generation" of expatriates after World War I, brought Hemingway his first notable success. His stature as a novelist was increased with the publication of *A Farewell to Arms* (1929), a deep love story of World War I, and *For Whom the Bell Tolls* (1940), a story of love and bravery in the Spanish Civil War. His short novel, *The Old Man and the Sea* (1952), is the heroin story of an old Cuban fisherman's expedition in search of and struggle for a great fish in the Gulf Stream north of the island. For it Hemingway was awarded the Pulitzer Prize in 1953, and in 1954 he received the Nobel Prize in Literature.

Herodotus (fifth century B.C.), Greek author of a single work, a history of the Persian Wars; probably the first real historian. In the *History,* his theme is the war between democratic Greece and totalitarian Persia. Not only is it, for all its mistakes and fantasies, an artistic masterpiece, but also a leading source book for Greek history of the particular period and for much of that of western Asia and Egypt. Divided into nine books, it is sometimes referred to as the "Histories."

Holmes, Oliver Wendell (1809–1894), United States poet and humorist, famous for poems such as "Old Ironsides," "The Chambered Nautilus," and "The Deacon's Masterpiece." Collections of his famous and popular sketches contain *The Autocrat of the Breakfast Table* and *The Poet at the Breakfast Table.* He also wrote *Elsie Venner,* which has been called the first American psychological novel.

Homer (seventh or eighth century B.C.), early Greek poet, credited with being the author of two masterpieces of world literature, the epic poems *The Iliad* and *The Odyssey. The Iliad* masterfully tells the story of the long siege of Troy by the Greeks; *The Odyssey* relates the ten-year struggle of Odysseus to return to Greece from Troy.

Horace [**Quintus Horatius Flaccus**] 65–8 B.C.), celebrated Roman poet, was a contemporary and friend of Virgil. His works are made up of short, thoughtful, personal poems, and longer verse-essays dealing in a worldly-wise way with everyday manners and moral philosophy and literary criticism.

Of Horace's works there are extant only 121 lyric poems, *Odes, Epodes,* and *Carmen saeculare,* and 41 verse essays, *Satires,* sometimes called *Sermones, Epistles,* and *Ars poetica.* The descriptive power of Horace's verse greatly influenced English poetry.

Howells, William Dean (1837–1920), United States novelist and critic, was the spokesman of realism in American fiction. Howells' strongest novel was *A Modern Instance,* a realistic study of an average couple and their marital difficulties. His best-known novel, *The Rise of Silas Lapham,* depicts the newly rich Lapham trying to rise into Boston society.

Hughes, Langston (1902–1967), black United States poet and novelist. Langston Hughes is best known for his poetry, much of which has been translated into many languages. His books of verse include *The Weary Blues, Shakespeare in Harlem,* and *Freedom Blows.*

Hugo, Victor Marie (1802–1885), French poet, novelist, and dramatist. His plays include *Cromwell, Le Roi s'amuse* (the basis of Verdi's *Rigoletto*), and *Ruy Blas. Les Orientales,* a series of poems about the Levant, was published in 1829. In 1831 he published his first novel, *The Hunchback of Notre Dame (Notre Dame de Paris),* a great historical novel laid in the fifteenth century. In 1862 he published the novel *Les Miserables,* in which the poor of post-Napoleonic France are portrayed with great pathos. *The Toilers of the Sea* is another of his great novels upon which his popularity in the English-speaking world is founded.

Hume, David (1711–1776), British (Scottish) philosopher, historian, economist, and essayist. His *History of England,* extending from Caesar's invasion to 1688, in six volumes, and his *Political Discourses* brought him fame in England and abroad. In *A Treatise of Human Nature,* commonly referred to as the *Treatise,* and in the *Enquiry concerning Human Understanding,* Hume stated his philosophical theories.

Huxley, Thomas (1825–1895), English biologist, whose researches and studies in philosophy and religion made him a strong supporter of agnosticism. His scientific writings, such as *Man's Place in Nature,* backing Darwin's theory of evolution, and *The Theory of the Vertebrate Skull,* are among his most famous works. His *Collected Essays* (in nine volumes) and *Life and Letters of Thomas Huxley* (in two volumes) report his scientific lectures and his reasons for supporting agnosticism.

Ibsen, Henrik Johan (1828–1906), Norwegian poet and dramatist. His most famous plays are *A Doll's House, The Wild Duck, Hedda Gabler, Ghosts,* and *The Master Builder.*

Two of Ibsen's most outstanding literary works, *Brand* and *Peer Gynt,* awakened the moral sense of all Scandinavia with their ethical lessons. Ibsen wrote many other plays, including *St. John's Night, The Vikings of Helgeland, The Pretenders, Little Eyolf,* and *John Gabriel Borkman.*

Irving, Washington [known also by a number of pseudonyms, including **Geoffrey Crayon** and **Diedrich Knickerbocker**] (1783–1859), has been called "first American man of letters," "dean," or "father of American literature," "inventor of the short story."

Irving won his greatest literary success with *The Sketch Book* (1819–1820) in which "Rip Van Winkle" and "Legend of Sleepy Hollow" are the best-known stories. *Diedrich Knickerbocker's History of New York* is a humorous history of Dutch rule, prefaced by a mock-learned account of the world from the beginning. Irving wrote three biographies: *Oliver Goldsmith, Mahomet and His Successors,* and *George Washington.* Other works include: *Bracebridge Hall* (1822), *Tales of a Traveller* (1825), and *The Alhambra* (1832).

James, Henry (1843–1916), prolific writer, and one of the most celebrated of United States novelists. Beginning in 1865, he produced brilliant literary reviews and short stories. Most famous for his novels–he was the recognized master of the psychological novel–James also wrote dramas, travel books, literary criticism, and autobiographical works which include *A Small Boy and*

Others. Such novels as *The American, The Portrait of a Lady* (1881), *The Wings of the Dove,* and *The Ambassadors* won him acclaim, but *Daisy Miller,* a novelette, surpassed all in popularity. His most famous short fiction, *The Turn of the Screw* (1898), a psychological ghost story, added further laurels.

Other works include *The Spoils of Poynton, What Maisie Knew, The Golden Bowl,* and *The American Scene,* the last-named remarkable for its prose picture of, and brooding concern with, the materialistic drift of American life.

Jonson, Ben (1573?–1637), English dramatist. In 1598 Ben Jonson produced one of the most famous English comedies, *Every Man in His Humour,* a play in which Shakespeare is said to have played. Two of his better plays are the comedies *Volpone,* whose theme is greed, and *The Alchemist,* which deals with quackery. *The Silent Woman* (1609) and *Bartholomew Fair* (1614) are considered his masterpieces. In his later years, he wrote two comedies, *The Magnetic Lady* and *The Tale of a Tub,* and some masques. His beautifully written pastoral drama, *The Sad Shepherd,* was left unfinished; it was published four years after his death.

Joyce, James (1882–1941), Irish writer, whose first publication, *Chamber Music,* a volume of poems, appeared in 1907. He is best known for the short stories in the *Dubliners,* and the novels, *Portrait of the Artist as a Young Man* (1917), *Ulysses* (1922), and *Finnegans Wake* (1939). Joyce rejected the accepted conventions of novel-writing. He developed the "stream-of-consciousness" technique, which reveals his characters' thoughts, experiences, and impressions and shows how these affect their lives and behavior. He also used language like music to convey thoughts and impressions which he felt could not be captured in conventional statement.

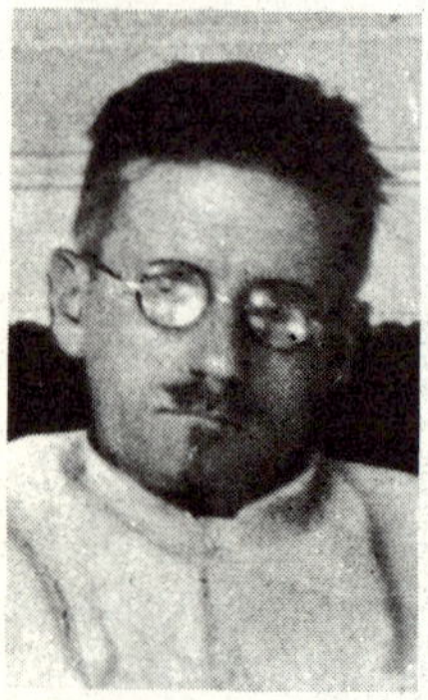

Jung, Carl Gustav (1875–1961), Swiss psychologist and psychiatrist, founder of analytic psychology (a name he preferred to *psychoanalysis*), was second only to Freud in the psychoanalytic field. Jung's works in English translation include: *Psychology of Dementia Praecox, The Theory of Psychoanalysis, Psychology of the Unconscious, Studies in Word Association, Psychological Types, Contributions to Analytical Psychology, The Secret of the Golden Flower,* with Richard Wilhelm, *Modern Man in Search of a Soul, Psychology and Religion, Integration of the Personality, Essays on Contemporary Events,* and *Essays on a Science of Mythology,* with C. Kerenyi. Jung first introduced the terms *extroversion* and *introversion.*

Kant, Immanuel (1724–1804), German philosopher, greatest of the idealists, and one of the most important thinkers of modern times. His classic, *The Critique of Pure Reason,* shows that human sensations and perceptual apparatus produce the immediate objects of perception. The three chief ideas of reason–God, freedom, and immortality–are developed in *Prolegomena, Groundwork to a Metaphysics of Morals,* and *Critique of Practical Reason.* In *Critique of Judgment,* Kant discusses the philosophical problems of aesthetics.

Keats, John (1795–1821), English lyric poet, whose great work *Endymion* tells the story of Endymion and the moon goddess. *Hyperion* is a blank verse epic. In "Lamia," the meter is rhymed heroics. It is in the great odes, new in form and spirit, that Keats pioneered. Of these, "Ode on a Grecian Urn" and "Ode to a Nightingale" are the best known, as is also the unfinished narrative *Hyperion.* Romantic medievalism is shown at its best in "The Eve of St. Agnes" and "La Belle Dame sans Merci."

Kipling, Rudyard (1865–1936), British author, whose collections of short stories, *Plain Tales from the Hills* (1888) and *Soldiers Three,* made his reputation in England. Two successful collections of poems, *Barrack Room Ballads* (1892) and *The Seven Seas,* followed. Kipling's two *Jungle Books* became generally familiar animals stories; he published *Kim* in 1901 and the classic children's book, *Just So Stories,* in 1902. His later works were *Puck of Pook's Hill, Rewards and Fairies,* and *Something of Myself* (1937), which was largely autobiographi-

cal. His patriotism is apparent in his writings; he also criticized some of the worst aspects of British colonialism. He received the Nobel Prize in Literature in 1907.

La Fontaine, Jean de (1621–1695), French poet. His most famous works are the *Contes* and the *Fables*. In the *Fables* he has adapted, to the not-too-nice world of Louis XIV, stories of all-too-human animals from Aesop and other sources. The child, the student, the man of the world–all find delight in these stories. The *Contes,* imitations in verse of Boccaccio and Ariosto, the *Cent Nouvelles, Nouvelles,* and others, illustrate La Fontaine's marvelous knack of saying shocking things in the most courteous and gentlemanly manner.

Lamb, Charles (1775–1834), English essayist and critic. In 1807 appeared *Tales from Shakespeare,* by Charles and Mary Lamb, in which Charles wrote about the tragedies and his sister Mary about the comedies. The following year, *Specimens of English Dramatic Poets who Lived about the Time of Shakespeare,* with short but suitable critical notes, established Lamb as a literary critic. His essays, despite their informal, familiar tone, placed him on a par with Montaigne, Steele, and Addison.

Lewis, Sinclair (1885–1951), United States novelist and social critic, who wrote several minor works before he won recognition with his *Main Street* (1920). This novel was the first in a series in which Lewis satirized the intolerance and materialism of American life. He also criticized the emptiness of the superficial intellectual who despised this kind of life but had nothing better to offer. *Babbitt* (1922), which added a new word to the English language, dealt with the complacent American, sucked dry of his individuality by the general pressure for conformity. *Arrowsmith,* for which Lewis refused a Pulitzer Prize, satirized the medical profession and emphasized the crushing of high scientific ideals. *Elmer Gantry* attacked ignorant, predatory religious leaders, and *Dodsworth* dealt with the European tour of a retired Midwestern manufacturer and his wife. Lewis was awarded the Nobel Prize in Literature in 1930, the first United States author to be so honored. His later works include *It Can't Happen Here, Cass Timberlane,* and *Kingsblood Royal.*

Lindsay, Vachel (1879–1931), United States poet, whose fame began with the publishing of his *General William Booth Enters into Heaven.* This type of poetry, based on the very heartthrob of American crowds and on camp-meeting rhythms, was widely acclaimed. The poems he recited and which his audiences continued to call for were "General William Booth," "The Congo," "Bryan, Bryan, Bryan," "Johnny Appleseed," and "The Santa Fe Trail." They have become a part of America's heritage. By 1920 Lindsay's best work was done. Lindsay's principal works include *General William Booth Enters into Heaven and Other Poems, Adventures While Preaching the Gospel of Beauty* (prose), *The Congo and Other Poems,* and *The Golden Whales of California, and Other Rhymes in the American Language.*

Livy [Titus Livius] (59 B.C.–A.D. 17), most famous of Roman historians. His *History of Rome* was originally in over 140 books and covered Roman history from the arrival of Aeneas in Italy to the death of Orusus, brother of the emperor Tiberius, in 9 B.C. Of this immense work only 35 books survive. Livy's history portrays Rome in the light of men and events, which he describes and interprets in universal terms.

Locke, John (1631–1704), English philosopher, one inspirer of the Age of Enlightenment and of Reason in England and in France. In 1690 Locke gave to the world *An Essay concerning Human Understanding,* which advanced an empirical theory of knowledge. Among Locke's posthumously published writings was *The Conduct of the Understanding,* which was very characteristic of his work. In *Two Treatises on Government,* he wrote in justification of constitutional monarchy, in essence a plea for the kind of democracy found in the United States Constitution. His last days were occupied in composing a *Fourth Letter on Toleration* which was never finished.

London, Jack (1876–1916), United States novelist, famous for his romantic tales of rugged adventure. Before turning to writing, he had worked as a sailor, trapper, and miner and found in these occupations material for his fiction. His first book, *The Son of the Wolf,* gained him a wide audience. *Martin Eden* (1909) is a partly autobiographical account of a struggle against

adverse economic and social conditions. *The People of the Abyss* is based on the time he spent in the London slums, and *The Cruise of the Snark* tells of his adventures sailing the South Pacific. Some of London's other outstanding works are *The Call of the Wild, White Fang, Burning Daylight, The Sea-Wolf, The Iron Heel,* and *The Valley of the Moon.*

Longfellow, Henry Wadsworth (1807–1882), the most popular United States poet of the nineteenth century. His book of poetry, *Ballads and Other Poems,* appeared in 1841 and was immensely popular. It included such well-known poems as "The Skeleton in Armor," "The Wreck of the Hesperus," "Excelsior," and "The Village Blacksmith." *Evangeline* (1847), a tale of the French exiles of Acadia, is one of his most popular poems. Others are *The Song of Hiawatha* (1855), *The Courtship of Miles Standish,* and *Tales of a Wayside Inn* which includes the national favorite, "Paul Revere's Ride." Longfellow translated Dante's *Divine Comedy.*

Lowell, Amy (1874–1925), United States poet, critic, and lecturer who was a major force in the Imagist movement. The characteristic qualities of her work include her mastery of the free verse technique, her brilliant use of sensuous impressions in describing the external world, and the restrained beauty of many of her shorter poems.

With her first volume, *A Dome of Many-Coloured Glass,* Amy Lowell was well on her way to fame. *Sword Blades and Poppy Seed* included her first poems in *vers libre* and "polyphonic prose." Other famous works include *Six French Poets; Men, Women and Ghosts; Tendencies in Modern American Poetry; Pictures of the Floating World,* which reflected her new interest in Oriental poetry; *Fir-Flower Tablets* (1921), with Florence Ayscough; A *Critical Fable;* a biography of John Keats; *East Wind;* and *Ballads for Sale.*

Lowell, James Russell (1819–1891), United States poet and critic, who became well known through his satiric *Bigelow Papers* (serialization begun in 1846), written in New England dialect. These charged that the Mexican War was an attempt to extend the area of slavery. "The Vision of Sir Launfal," with its theme that "the gift without the giver is bare," and the jolly and witty *Fable for Critics,* which measured very acutely some of his contemporaries, also brought fame to Lowell.

Partly through his co-editorship of the *North American Review* (1864–1872), Lowell published his critical essays on the great masters including Dante, Chaucer, Shakespeare, Cervantes, Milton, Fielding, Lessing, Wordsworth, Carlyle, Emerson, and many others. He was also the first editor of *The Atlantic Monthly.*

Lucretius [**Titus Lucretius Carus**] (earlier half of the last century B.C.), Latin poet and philosopher. His one celebrated poem of six volumes, *De rerum natura (On the Nature of Things)* presents in hexameter verse his appeals to man to be his own master, not to fear gods or death. Lucretius used Epicurus' atomic theory to convince man that the universe developed through the workings of natural laws in the combining of atoms.

Macaulay, Thomas Babington (1800–1859), English historian, poet, and essayist. Published in 1842, Macaulay's poetry, *Lays of Ancient Rome,* was very popular. In the following year he published his comprehensive collection of *Essays.* His *History of England from the Accession of James the Second,* in five volumes, was his major work, although he died before he could perfect the fifth volume.

Machiavelli, Niccolò (1469–1527), Italian statesman and writer. His most famous works, *The Prince* and *The Discourses,* use the life of Cesare Borgia to express his belief that such methods of conquest, the cementing of a new state out of scattered elements, and the dealing with false friends or doubtful allies, were worthy of commendation and imitation. *The Prince* is an analysis of the methods by which an ambitious man may rise to power. Machiavelli's other works include the *Mandragola,* a powerful play; lesser plays such as the *Clizia;* the *History of Florence;* and a novel, *Belfagor.*

Mann, Thomas (1875–1955), the greatest modern German novelist. His masterpiece, *Buddenbrooks* (1901), tells the story of a family much like his own, and follows its decline through four generations. A number of short novels next appeared, *Tonio Kröger, Tristan,* and *Death in Venice. The Magic Mountain* (1924), a study in microcosm of the forces which adversely influenced European society, won Mann the Nobel Prize in Literature in 1929.

The novels of Mann's exile included the biblical tetralogy, *Joseph und seine Brüder,* dealing with ancient Egypt and the biblical saga of Joseph; *Lotte in Weimar; Dr. Faustus* (1948); *Die Betrogene;* and the unfinished *Bekenntnisse des Hochstaplers Felix Krull,* a comic novel expanded from an early short story.

Maupassant, Guy de (1850–1893), French writer of short stories and novels. Of his almost 300 short stories, many are unsurpassed in style, craftsmanship, and psychological realism. Among these are "Boule de Suif" ("Tallow Ball"), "La Ficelle" ("The Piece of String"), and "Miss Harriet." Probably his most popular story is "The Necklace." His famous novels are *Bel-Ami,* in which a scoundrel succeeds because of his good looks, and *Une Vie (A Woman's Life),* which gives an analysis of a French woman's life and her frustration. Maupassant has had great influence on short story writing.

Melville, Herman (1819–1891), United States author whose first book, *Typee,* was based on his involuntary stay with a savage tribe in the South Seas. The adventures of the short voyage which followed furnished Melville with the ideas for his second and most humorous book, *Omoo.*

Melville began work on *Moby Dick,* his masterpiece, as a simple tale, a gusty account of a whaling voyage. Before he ended it, it had developed into an allegory, probing into the spiritual torments of a man who set himself the task of implacable vengeance. *Billy Budd, Foretopman,* a superb short novel, is Melville's most haunting sea story, published posthumously in 1924.

Menander (ca. 343/342–291/290 B.C.), Greek poet and outstanding representative of the comedy of his period. Only some fragments, and some of those of uncertain authorship, remain of Menander's work. The most important is the Cairo papyrus, discovered in 1905, containing 659 lines from *Epitrepontes,* 83 from *Heros,* 341 from *Samia,* 324 from *Perikeiromene,* and 61 from an uncertain play. In Menander's plays, as contrasted to Aristophanes', the chorus was not used, the debate type of speaking between two antagonists disappeared, and the theme changed from political or social philosophy to an everyday plot in Athenian life. *The Flatterer, The Superstitious Man,* and *The Lady from Andros* are good examples of Menander's new type of comedy.

Mencken, Henry Louis (1880–1956), United States editor, writer, and controversialist. For two decades the most ironic critic of American life and letters, Mencken often used literary criticism as a starting point for his ideas. He wrote enough reviews and miscellaneous essays to fill six volumes, aptly titled *Prejudices.* Many readers found it refreshing, after hearing others endlessly praise their nation, to find Mencken's description of the American people as "the most timorous, sniveling, poltroonish, ignominious mob of serfs and goosesteppers ever gathered under one flag in Christendom since the end of the Middle Ages." The famous platform for his ideas was the magazine *American Mercury,* which he helped found in 1924, after leaving the *Smart Set.*

His great work, *The American Language* (1918), brought together examples of American, not English, expressions and idioms. His autobiographical trilogy, *Happy Days* (1940), *Newspaper Days,* and *Heathen Days* (1943), deals largely with his experience in journalism.

Mill, John Stuart (1806–1873), British philosopher, economist, and reformer. Some of his essays written for journals were collected in the first two volumes (1859) of his *Dissertations and Discussions* and show wide interests. The twin essays on Bentham and Coleridge are perhaps his finest writings and show the new spirit he tried to inject into English radicalism. Among his important works are *System of Logic,* with its four canons of inductive method, published in 1843; *Principles of Political Economy;* and the brilliant essay "On Liberty" (1859).

Millay, Edna St. Vincent (1892–1950), United States poet. She first attracted attention with a long poem, "Renascence," written when she was only nineteen. This was later incorporated into a poetry volume, *Renascence and Other Poems.* She attracted a still larger audience with *A Few Figs from Thistles* and *Second April.* In 1921 she published three plays: *Two Slatterns and a King, The Lamp and the Bell,* and *Aria Da Capo. The Harp-Weaver and Other Poems* showed a new maturity; the title poem was awarded a Pulitzer Prize in 1922.

Milton, John (1608–1674), English poet. Milton's first great poem in English was "On the Morning of Christ's Nativity." Some of his other famous early works include *L'Allegro, Il Penseroso,* the masque *Comus,* and the elegy *Lycidas.* His *Areopagitica* was written in defense of the press; his *Of Reformation in England* had to do with church government. After Milton became completely blind, he dictated his famous and timeless epics, *Paradise Lost,* in which he tells of Satan's rebellion against God and the fall of man, and *Paradise Regained,* where Christ (the second Adam) gains back for mankind that which Adam and Eve lost. His *Samson Agonistes* is modeled after Greek drama.

Montesquieu, Charles Louis de Secondat (1689–1755), French political philosopher and man of letters, whose *Lettres Persanes* ("Persian Letters"), a satirical picture of European society, is a masterpiece of irony. His *Considerations sur les causes de la grandeur des Romains et de leur decadence.* ("Reflections on the Causes of Grandeur and Declension of the Romans") presents an interesting philosophy of history. His famous work, *The Spirit of the Laws,* is a study of comparative governments. Its checks and balances theory was incorporated into the Constitution of the United States. *Defense of the Spirit of the Laws* is the most brilliantly written of all his works.

Moore, Thomas (1779–1852), Irish poet whose *Irish Melodies* appeared in 1808, containing some of his best and most popular work, such as, "Believe Me If All Those Endearing Young Charms," and "Oft in the Stilly Night." *Lalla Rookh,* a poetic romance, was published in 1817 and became an immediate success. In 1831 Moore completed his *Life and Death of Lord Edward Fitzgerald,* probably his best piece of prose.

Nietzsche, Friedrich (1844–1900), German philosopher, one of the most influential thinkers of modern times. *Die Geburt der Tragödie* ("The Birth of Tragedy") was his first well-known work. His most perplexing work, and the most difficult to understand, *Also sprach Zarathustra* ("Thus Spake Zarathustra"), censures conventional Christian morality as something which the masses follow blindly; it preaches that superior to it is the morality of the natural aristocrats. According to Nietzsche, the will of man must create the superior man, the superman, who would rise above good and evil and be able to destroy deteriorating democracy. *Zarathustra* was Nietzsche's first attempt to systematize his thought. Then came *Jenseits von Gut und Böse* ("Beyond Good and Evil") and *Zur Genealogie der Moral* ("The Geneaology of Morals") which further presented his ideas. His last work was *Nietzsche contra Wagner,* slightly revised, a compilation of some parts of his earlier books. This is his briefest and probably his most beautiful book.

O'Neill, Eugene Gladstone (1888–1953), United States dramatist, the country's greatest playwright, and an artist of international renown.

O'Neill loved the sea and some of the best of his 47 plays *(The Moon of the Caribbees, The Long Voyage Home)* are salty as the sea. In 1920 O'Neill won a Pulitzer Prize with his first full-length play, *Beyond the Horizon,* a bitter domestic tragedy, written for the Provincetown Players. He won two more Pulitzer Prizes with *Anna Christie* and *Strange Interlude,*

and in 1936 became the second American (after Sinclair Lewis) to win the Nobel Prize in Literature. He thrilled theatergoers with tom-toms *(Emperor Jones)*, masks *(The Great God Brown)*, verbalized subconscious ideas *(Strange Interlude)*, and choral chants *(Lazarus Laughed)*. His great tragedy was *Mourning Becomes Electra. Ah, Wilderness* was the only comedy he wrote.

When O'Neill died he left at least three plays in manuscript, including the autobiographical *Long Day's Journey Into Night*. A fourth Pulitzer Prize, for *Long Day's Journey Into Night,* was awarded him posthumously in 1957.

Ovid [**Publius Ovidius Naso**] (43 B.C.–A.D. 18), Roman poet, famous for his love poems. Ovid's poems fall into three groups: erotic poems, such as *Art of Love;* mythological poems, particularly his greatest work in hexameters, *Metamorphoses* ("Transfigurations"); and poems of exile, of which *Tristia,* an autobiographical poem written during his years of exile, is a good example. This poem depicts the wretched life of his exile (for having written *Art of Love*) and pleads with Emperor Augustus for forgiveness.

Pascal, Blaise (1623–1662), French scientist and writer on religious subjects. The eighteen *Lettres écrites par Louis de Montalta à un provincial* (1656–1657), better known as *Les Provinciales,* help us to follow Pascal in his spiritual and theological beliefs and practices. Pascal's religious writings, which are mystical and in a pure literary style, are named *Pensées*. As a scientist, he is most famous for Pascal's law.

Pepys, Samuel (1633–1703), English diarist. Pepys was revealed as author and man about town in 1825 when his secret diary was published in part. The first entry was dated January 1, 1660, the last, May 31, 1669. The *Diary* (in six volumes) furnishes an invaluable picture of the Restoration period. During his lifetime Pepys' only known publication was the *Memoirs of the Royal Navy*.

Petrarch [**Francesco Petrarca**] (1304–1374), Italian poet, the first humanist and the first modern lyric poet, surpassed in Italian literature only by Dante. He adapted, among other things, the Ciceronian oration *Pro Archia,* that great declaration of the nature of poetry. Two of his ambitious and significant Latin works are *De viris* and the *Africa* (begun 1338 or 1339). He is honored for his Latin *Trionfi*. He also wrote *Bucolicum carmen, De vita solitairia,* and *De otio religioso*. His famous work *Canzoniere* contains songs and sonnets.

Pindar (ca. 522–443 B.C.), great lyric poet of ancient Greece. Forty-four complete odes and numerous fragments of his work still exist. Pindar's works are chiefly choral lyrics. He also developed the triumphal ode celebrating athletic victories, but generally having to do with myths. The Pindaric Ode influenced English verse form in the seventeenth and eighteenth centuries. *Epinicia* in ode form commemorates successes in the great athletic games.

Plato (428/427–348/347 B.C.), Greek philosopher who has deeply influenced Western thought for more than 2,400 years. His dialogues express his philosophy and are outstanding masterpieces of world literature through their beauty of style, depth, and range of thought. Among the dialogues are the early defense of Socrates in *Apology, Charmides, Phaedras,* with *Republic* perhaps the most noted. The world of Platonism is order, and all disorder is evil.

Plautus (254?–184 B.C.), comic dramatist of ancient Rome. His 21 surviving plays are vigorous portrayals of middle- and lower-class life. Plautus' plays are essentially translations of the Greek new comedy school of plays, but he was more than a translator; his command of Latin was such that his plays become originals. Among his extant plays are *Amphitruo, Asinaria, Captivi, Mercator, Miles Gloriosus, Pseudolus,* and *Stichus*.

Pliny, the Elder [**Gaius Plinius Secundus**] (A.D. 23 or 24–79), Roman savant and author. Pliny's *Natural History* is often inaccurate and most of the information in it is second-hand; but there are accounts of ancient arts and culture, such as sculpture and painting, which cannot be found in any other sources.

Pliny, the Younger [**Gaius Plinius Caecilius Secundus**] (61 or 62–ca. A.D. 113), Roman author and administrator, nephew of the elder Pliny. His official correspondence was an unusual collection, well written, portraying public and private life at the height of the Roman Empire. *The Letters* (in nine books) suggest a highly sophisticated poseur.

Plutarch (ca. A.D. 46–120), Greek biographer and writer. *Forty-six Parallel Lives* brought him fame and popularity. This series reflects Plutarch's learning and research in preparing the long lists of authorities to which he refers, and the comprehensive information on each person about whom he writes. Plutarch wrote a great deal, covering many topics. Some of his works, published under the title *Opera moralis,* include dialogues and essays on ethical, literary, and historical subjects.

Pope, Alexander (1688–1744), English poet, whose first publication was *Pastorals,* in 1709. His next publication, the *Essay on Criticism* (1711), was a poem outlining contemporary critical tastes and standards. His best-known work is *The Rape of the Lock.* For 12 years Pope worked on his translation of Homer. He also wrote *Elegy to the Memory of an Unfortunate Lady* and *Eloisa to Abelard.*

Poe, Edgar Allan (1809–1849), United States poet, critic, and short-story writer. In 1831 he brought out a first volume of *Poems.* His story, "A MS. Found in a Bottle," won a contemporary literary award. He also wrote "William Wilson" and "The Fall of the House of Usher," stories of supernatural horror, and published the first detective story, "The Murders in the Rue Morgue." In 1843 his "Gold Bug" also won a prize. His most famous poem, "The Raven" (1845), brought him national fame. Other well-known poems are "To Helen," "Israfel," and "The City in the Sea." *Tales of the Grotesque and Arabesque* comprise a collection of his short stories.

Porter, William Sidney (1862–1910), wrote under the pen name of O. Henry. This United States short-story writer saw and wrote about love, pathos, and small acts of heroism in the lives of ordinary people. Despite occasional clowning, his stories are artistically told and have social implications. His fame rests on his short stories *Bagdad on the Subway.* His first book, *Cabbages and Kings* (1904), portrayed unreal characters against strangely beautiful Honduran backgrounds. *The Four Million* revealed the lives of the people of New York City. *The Trimmed Lamp* and *Heart of the West* presented true and fascinating pictures of the Texas range.

Pound, Ezra Loomis (1885–1972), United States poet, translator, and critic. His major poems are *Homage to Sextus Propertius, Hugh Selwyn Mauberley,* and *The Cantos.* Some of his translations include the Anglo-Saxon *Seafarer,* the Chinese *Cathay,* and *Classic Anthology.* His *Letters* were published in 1950 and a selection of his *Literary Essays* in 1954.

Proust, Marcel (1871–1922), French novelist. *A la recherche du temps perdu (Remembrance of Things Past),* comprising seven novels, is Proust's outstanding work. In it he shows the many-sidedness of French society. The author takes the leading part, with musings and reverie as his method. The first part, *Du coté de chez Swann (Swann's Way),* shows the freshness and minuteness of recollections of childhood and is the best-known volume of the set.

Pushkin, Alexander (1799–1837), Russian poet. In 1825 Pushkin wrote his most outstanding work, the tragedy *Boris Godunov.* In 1829 *Poltava* appeared. The lyrics of his *A Voyage to Arzrum* are delightful. The *History of the Revolt of Pugachev* is a fine piece of historical writing. *The Captain's Daughter,* the one long novel he completed, is a good example of his prose. *Boris Godunov* and *Eugene Onegin* were used for operas by Mussorgsky and Tschaikovsky. Of Pushkin's short stories, "The Queen of Spades" is the most famous.

Rabelais, François (ca. 1495–1553), French author. The works that made Rabelais immortal were his history of the giant *Gargantua* and his history of the son of Gargantua, *Pantagruel.* These fabulous giant-heroes fight, eat, drink, and jest; besides, the story in each case reveals the education, politics, and philosophy of Renaissance France. The stories really are satires against the vulgarity and abuses of French society.

Racine, Jean (1639–1699), French tragic dramatist. *Andromaque,* a tragedy, was the first of many of his dramatic successes. Two of his masterpieces are *Phédre* and *Athalie. Athalie* was the means of introducing new ideas for plays, such as choruses. *Les Plaideurs* is a successful charming comedy. His tragedies were, *Britannicus, Mithridate, Iphigenie, Phédre,* and *Esther,* a masterpiece based on a biblical theme.

Robinson, Edwin Arlington (1869–1935), United States poet. Robinson's first success was *Captain Craig* (1902). He won three Pulitzer prizes in Poetry–*Collected Poems* (1921); *The Man Who Died Twice* (1924); and *Tristram* (1927). His forte was the short narrative poem, such as "Richard Cory" and "Miniver Cheevy." Three of his long poems, *Merlin, Lancelot,* and *Tristram* were taken from the King Arthur stories. His psychological studies found expression in *Avon's Harvest, Matthias at the Door,* and *Amaranth.*

Rolland, Romain (1866–1944), French novelist and biographer. The biographies include *Mahatma Gandhi,* an impassioned defense of the Indian leader; *Beethoven the Creator;* and books on Tolstoy and Michelangelo. His ten-volume novel, *Jean Christophe,* is the work upon which rests his fame. In this novel a musical genius battles poverty, attains success, and finally wins peace in death. Rolland's best-known play is *Les Loups (The Wolves).* He received the Nobel Prize in Literature in 1915.

Rossetti, Dante Gabriel (1828–1882), English painter and poet. In December, 1850, some of his most famous poems appeared, including "The Blessed Damozel." His *Ballads and Sonnets* contained much of his best work, including the completed *House of Life,* the great sonnet sequence, and the ballads, "Rose Mary," "The White Ship," "The King's Tragedy," and "Sister Helen."

Rostand, Edmond (1869–1918), French dramatist, the repeated production of whose comedy *Cyrano de Bergerac* continues to delight theatergoers to this day. In *L'Aiglon,* another famous play, Rostand's theme is the unhappy life of Napoleon II. *Chantecler,* the barnyard fable, was extremely successful. Besides plays Rostand also wrote patriotic verse.

Rousseau, Jean Jacques (1712–1778), French-Swiss moralist. Fame came to Rousseau through his essay, *Discours sur les sciences et les arts.* His *La Nouvelle Héloise,* a novel, was immediately and enormously popular. *Du Contract Social (The Social Contract)* was a French document of great influence for the French Revolution. The novel *Emile* expressed Rousseau's ideas on progressive education. Rousseau's autobiography, *Confessions,* is an uninhibited self-revelation anticipating the vogue for stark realistic descriptions in current literature. One of his last works was *Reveries d'un Promeneur Solitaire.*

Ruskin, John (1819–1900), English writer and critic. *Modern Painters* in five volumes and *The Seven Lamps of Architecture,* the latter appearing with Ruskin's own etchings, made a great reputation for him. Other works included *Ethics of the Dust,* and *The Crown of Wild Olive.* A more serious work was *Time and Tide,* a collection of "Thoughts" which gives a good picture of Ruskin's social and economic program. In 1871 Ruskin began *Fors Clavigera,* written for the English working man.

Sandburg, Carl (1878–1967), United States poet, historian, novelist, and folklorist. Sandburg was one of the group of writers who, in the days before World War I, brought about the "Chicago Renaissance" in letters. He later described his early years in his autobiography, *Always the Young Strangers.* His poems reflect industrial America. In 1914 a group of his *Chicago Poems* appeared in *Poetry;* later they were issued in book form. The favorable impression he made was strengthened with succeeding volumes–*Cornhuskers, Smoke and Steel,* and *Slabs of the Sunburnt West. The American Songbag* and *Carl Sandburg's New American Songbag* were collections of folk songs. Sandburg wrote one of the finest Lincoln biographies, *Abraham Lincoln: The Prairie Years* (2 volumes) and *Abraham Lincoln: The War Years* (4 volumes, which won the Pulitzer Prize for History, 1940). In 1948 he published a long novel, *Remembrance Rock,* dealing with the American experience from Plymouth Rock to

World War II. *Complete Poems* won him the Pulitzer Prize for Poetry in 1951.

Sappho (early sixth century B.C.), the greatest woman poet of Greece. Only eight books of her lyrical poems are known. The only complete collection of the known material is in *Sapphous Mele.* Her verse is a fine example of the "pure" love lyric, characterized by very strong expressions of passion and excellent control of meter. Simple language and deep feeling as well as perfect form are everywhere evident in her work.

Schopenhauer, Arthur (1788–1860), German philosopher, outstanding as a promoter of a metaphysical doctrine of the will as opposed to Hegelian idealism. His principal work is *Die Welt als Wille und Vorstellung (The World as Will and Idea).* His pessimism was clearly stated in both *Über den Willen in der Natur (On the Will in Nature)* and in *Two Essays.*

Scott, Sir Walter (1771–1832), Scottish poet and novelist. Scott is known for his narrative poems–*Lay of the Last Minstrel, Marmion,* and *The Lady of the Lake.* Of his novels, *Guy Mannering, The Heart of Midlothian,* and *The Bride of Lammermoor* are among the finest. *Ivanhoe* was the first of a long series of romances of British history, which included *Kenilworth, Quentin Durward,* and *The Talisman.* The splendid, heroic spirit of Scotland is found in his poems "Lochinvar" and "Proud Maisie."

Seneca, Lucius Annaeus (ca. 4 B.C.–A.D. 65), Roman philosopher, dramatist, and statesman. The most important of Seneca's works are his philosophical writings. These consist of a series of essays on practical ethics that preach Stoicism in a modified form, such as *De vita beata.* His nine tragedies, which include *Medea, Phaedra, Agamemnon, Oedipus,* and *Thyestes,* were most influential in Europe during and after the Renaissance.

Shakespeare, William (1564–1616), English poet and playwright. No one man in English literature–or for that matter in the literature of any language–has had his genius so universally acknowledged.

Today, more than 400 years after his birth, there is no country with even a single theatrical stage where his works are not produced at one time or another. There is no library where a copy or a translation of one of his books is not available. Every actor's ambition is to play Hamlet, and every actress hopes to play Juliet.

Of Shakespeare's poems the best-known are "Venus and Adonis", "The Rape of Lucrece," and "The Phoenix and the Turtle." Shakespeare's comedies and tragedies, written between 1589 and 1613, are given chronologically:

Henry VI (Parts 2 and 3), *Henry VI* (Part 1), *Comedy of Errors, Titus Andronicus, Richard III, Taming of the Shrew, Two Gentlemen of Verona, Love's Labour's Lost, Romeo and Juliet, Richard II, A Midsummer Night's Dream, King John, Merchant of Venice, Henry IV* (Parts 1 and 2), *Much Ado About Nothing, Henry V, Julius Caesar, As You Like It, Twelfth Night, Merry Wives of Windsor, Troilus and Cressida, All's Well that Ends Well, Hamlet, Measure for Measure, Othello, King Lear, Macbeth, Antony and Cleopatra, Coriolanus, Timon of Athens, Pericles, Cymbeline, Winter's Tale, Tempest, Henry VIII,* and *Two Noble Kinsmen.*

Shaw, George Bernard (1856–1950), Irish critic, pamphleteer, and playwright. His important plays include *Heartbreak House* (on World War I), *Back to Methuselah, Androcles and the Lion,* and *Saint Joan,* the latter about heroism and saintliness. Among his other plays are *Pygmalion, Candida* (on love as pity), *Arms and the Man* (a satire on the military profession), *The Doctor's Dilemma, You Never Can Tell, Man and Superman* (on eugenics), and *Fanny's First Play.* For a time he was a music critic and a dramatic critic and also wrote essays on a variety of subjects. He was awarded the Nobel Prize in Literature in 1925.

Shelley, Percy Bysshe (1792–1822), English poet. Shelley's chief works include the drama of *Hellas,* hoping for better things to come for mankind; *Alastor,* followed by *The Revolt of Islam* and *Julian and Maddalo;* the grand tragedy of *The Cenci;* and the sublime drama, *Prometheus Unbound.* The latter is his masterpiece and depicts the world moving from slavery

ever onward. *The Witch of Atlas,* the most perfect of Shelley's longer poems, is sheer imagination. *Adonais,* the elegy on Keats, followed in 1821. Shelley's letters to Thomas Love Peacock and others, and his incomplete *A Defence of Poetry,* are excellent prose. Of Shelley's lyrics some of the best loved are "Ode to the West Wind," "To a Skylark," and "The Indian Serenade."

Sinclair, Upton (1878–1968), United States author of the "muckraking" school, is noted for social protests. Sinclair's first recognition was won with *The Jungle* (1906), a realistic study of conditions among immigrants and in the Chicago packing houses where they worked. Sinclair continued to be a propaganda novelist with such works as *King Coal,* which took up the Colorado coal strike in 1913; *100%,* based on the Tom Mooney Preparedness Day bombing case; *Oil!,* an investigation of the Teapot Dome scandal, the film industry, and popular evangelism; and *Boston,* dealing with the Sacco-Vanzetti case. He also wrote nonfiction studies of such aspects of United States life as religion, journalism, and education.

In 1940 Sinclair began his popular series of contemporary historical novels, covering the period before and during World War II. The hero of the series, Lanny Budd, sees the rise of Nazism in Germany and later becomes a personal representative of President Franklin D. Roosevelt. Among the books included in the series are *World's End; Between Two Worlds; Dragon's Teeth* (1942 Pulitzer Prize for Fiction); *Presidential Agent; A World to Win; Presidential Mission;* and *O Shepherd, Speak!* In 1953 Sinclair published *The Return of Lanny Budd.*

Socrates (ca. 470 B.C.–399 B.C.), Athenian philosopher. There is no evidence that Socrates wrote anything. Information about his personality and doctrine is to be sought chiefly in the dialogues of Plato and the *Memorabilia* of Xenophon. Socrates dedicated himself to combating skepticism and arousing the love of truth and virtue. The Socratic method was to ask a question, then to show the inadequacy of the answer by further skillful questioning–all directed toward finding a sounder answer.

Sophocles (497–406 B.C.), one of the three great Greek tragic poets. His most famous play was *Oedipus Tyrannus (Oedipus Rex).* Other plays of Sophocles include *Antigone,* the *Trachiniae, Electra, Philoctetes, Oedipus at Colonus,* and *Ajax.* Besides these seven complete tragedies, there remain about four hundred lines of a satyr play, *The Ichneutai,* and several hundred fragments of plays.

Spenser, Edmund (1552–1599), English poet. Among his outstanding contributions were *The Shepheardes Calender,* consisting of 12 pastoral eclogues. Other works include *Astrophel, Amoretti,* which expresses wooing; and *Epithalmion,* which tells about Spenser's wedding. *The Faerie Queene,* Spenser's unfinished masterpiece (Books I–VI), is an allegory and expresses Spenser's beliefs in the areas of morals, religion, and politics.

Stein, Gertrude (1874–1946), United States author. A literary "cubist" who utilized her theories of abstract art in her writing, Gertrude Stein seemed to carry to extremes her unconventional, repetitious manipulation of words. One of her celebrated phrases is "a rose is a rose is a rose." In the very well done *The Autobiography of Alice B. Toklas,* Miss Stein, while seeming to write the life of her secretary and companion, actually wrote her own life. Among Miss Stein's better-known works is *Three Lives* (1908), a story of three women told in a unique style. Other works are a book of verse, *Tender Buttons;* a play, *Four Saints in Three Acts;* and *Everybody's Autobiography.*

Steinbeck, John Ernst (1902–1968), United States novelist and Nobel Prize winner in Literature. He is best known for his social novel, *The Grapes of Wrath,* which won the 1940 Pulitzer Prize. *The Grapes of Wrath* has remained an all-time best-seller and has been translated into many foreign languages.

Among other Steinbeck works are *Tortilla Flat* (1935), *In Dubious Battle, Of Mice and Men, The*

Moon Is Down, Cannery Row, The Winter of Our Discontent, and *Travels with Charlie in Search of America* (1962).

Sterne, Laurence (1713–1768), English humorist, who is mainly noted for *The Life and Opinions of Tristram Shandy, Gentleman (1860–1867),* and *The Sentimental Journey through France and Italy.* Sterne started the trend toward the sentimental novel.

Stevenson, Robert Louis Balfour (1850–1894), Scottish novelist, essayist, and poet. *Virginibus Puerisque* (1881) contains his best essays. Short stories and travel appear in books such as *Travels with a Donkey* and *Inland Voyage.* His popular books include *Treasure Island* (1883), a story of pirates and a cabin boy and their adventures with mutiny and buried gold; *Kidnapped,* a young Scot's romantic adventures on sea and land; and *A Child's Garden of Verses* (1885), an adult remembering his childhood. *The Strange Case of Dr. Jekyll and Mr. Hyde* (1886) is a psychological study of the struggle between right and wrong within man's soul.

Stowe, Harriet Beecher (1811–1896), United States writer, best known as the author of *Uncle Tom's Cabin; or Life Among the Lowly* (1852). Its publication in book form was an important factor in bringing to a head the antislavery sentiment in the North. She wrote a second antislavery novel, *Dred* (1856), and several books dealing with New England, such as *The Minister's Wooing* and *Oldtown Folks.*

Strindberg, August (1849–1912), Swedish playwright, novelist, short story writer, and poet. He is noted for his conception of "the war of the sexes." His first important work and the first living piece of modern Swedish drama was *Master Olaf,* completed in 1880. His first novel, *The Red Room,* an ironical account of the vagaries of Stockholm society, made him famous. His other plays include *Lucky Peter's Travels, The Dance of Death,* and *The Bridal Crown.* The best of his historical plays is *Gustav Vasa.* His short stories include the collection called *Married,* that led to a prosecution for blasphemy of which he was acquitted. In later life he acquired a new faith, with overtones of Swedenborgianism, which produced a drama in three parts, *The Road to Damascus.*

Swift, Jonathan (1667–1745), British satirist, a good example of whose satire was the *Argument to prove that the abolishing of Christianity in England, may, as things now stand, be attended with some inconveniences.* His best narrative poem was *Baucis and Philemon.* His most famous work was *Travels Into Several Remote Nations of the World,* in four parts, commonly known as *Gulliver's Travels* (1726). This story which delights children is actually a bitter attack on mankind.

Swinburne, Algernon Charles (1837–1909), English poet and critic. Probably his two most famous dramas are *The Queen Mother* and *Rosamond.* He is more famous for *Poems and Ballads,* a revolt against moral conventions. *Song of Italy* and *Songs before Sunrise* show Swinburne's enthusiasm for Mazzini's revolt in Italy. *Tristram of Lyonese,* a poetic drama, retells a medieval legend. *Atlanta in Calydon* is a poetic drama; "When the hounds of spring" is his best known chorus; and "The Garden of Prosperpine," one of his shorter poems, is a fine example of his masterly writing.

Tacitus, Cornelius (ca. 55–120), Roman historian. His works consist of the *Dialogue on Orators;* the *Life of Agricola; Germania (Germany),* an authentic account of the Germanic tribes; *Historiae (the Histories),* of which four books and a fragment survive, covering Galba's reign and the beginning of Vespasian's; and the *Annals,* of which twelve books survive, dealing with the reign of Tiberius and parts of the reigns of Claudius and Nero.

Tarkington, Booth (1869–1946), United States novelist and dramatist who wrote of Midwesterners in a satirical vein. The author of many kinds of writings, Tarkington won early recognition with his novel about political corruption, *The Gentleman from Indiana.* This was followed by the very popular romance *Monsieur Beaucaire,* which Tarkington later adapted for the stage. *The Conquest of Canaan,* a "problem" novel, was probably his most mature early work. His witty pictures of boyhood and adolescence, *Penrod* and *Seventeen,* enjoyed a considerable vogue. He was equally successful when he wrote about Midwestern life and character as shown by *The Turmoil* and *The Magnificent Ambersons* (Pulitzer Prize for Fiction, 1919). *Alice Adams* (Pulitzer Prize for Fiction, 1922), a deep character analysis of 22-year-old Alice and her problems, is perhaps his most polished novel.

Tennyson, Alfred, First Baron (1809–1892), English poet. The following won him wide acclaim: the volume of *Poems* which included "The Lady of Shalott," "The Dream of Fair Woman," "The Lotus Eaters," and "The Miller's Daughter," together with a score of other lyrics.

In Memoriam was published, in its original anonymous form, in 1850. Other famous works include "Ulysses"; *Tiresias and Other Poems; Jocksley Hall Sixty Years After;* "The Charge of the Light Brigade," a story of the Crimean War; *The Idylls of the King* (King Arthur), seven in number; *Enoch Arden;* and *Ballads and Other Poems,* which contains the gloomy and magnificent "Rizpah."

Thackeray, William Makepeace (1811–1863), English novelist. Thackeray's masterpieces are *Henry Esmond* (1852), a realistic story of Queen Anne's reign; *Pendennis,* a story of a selfish man; and *Vanity Fair* (1847), a comparison of a sweet, simple girl with a conniving, fascinating one. Some of his best essays are found in the *Roundabout Papers.*

Thibault, Jacques Anatole (1844–1924), French author and man of letters, who wrote under the pen name Anatole France, was awarded the Nobel Prize in Literature in 1921. His first novel, *Le Crime de Sylvestre Bonnard,* quickly won him literary acclaim. In forty years of writing France produced thoughtful, deep, lively, and beautifully written works. "Balthazar" and "L'Etui de Nacre" are fine examples of his keenly clever short stories. Among other works are *Le Puits de Sainte-Claire;* the thoughtful and critical books, *Les Opinions de Jérome Coignard* and *La Vie littéraire* (4 volumes); *La Rôtisserie de la Reine Pédauque,* a philosophical novel; and, a historical and philosophical work, *Thais,* set in Alexandria in the first century, in which a courtesan becomes a Christian through the efforts of a monk, but all for naught.

Thoreau, Henry David (1817–1862), United States writer, poet, and naturalist, whose greatest book is *Walden* (1854). In this, Thoreau, an individualist, wrote of his experiences while living alone with nature. Another well-known book is *A Week on the Concord and Merrimack Rivers.* His finest essays, *The Maine Woods, A Yankee in Canada,* and *Cape Cod,* contain his discoveries of what early America was like before civilization changed it. His essay *Civil Disobedience* inspired men such as Gandhi to try civil disobedience as a political tactic.

Thucydides (471?–400 B.C.), Greek historian. His great *History,* a recounting of the Peloponnesian War of 411 B.C., has been divided into eight books. It has no social and political references except as relating to the war and is noted for famous speeches, such as Pericles' funeral oration.

Thurber, James (1894–1961), United States writer and artist, considered by many the country's best humorist since Mark Twain. A serious writer as well as a comic artist, Thurber produced writings and drawings showing odd characters in surprising situations, humorous aspects of the war between men and women, and startling studies into the subconscious of unusual dogs and other animals, both real and imaginary. *My Life and Hard Times* is a hilarious autobiography. "The Secret Life of Walter Mitty" is his best-known short story. A successful stage play, *The Male Animal,* was written together with Elliott Nugent. While there is a satirical sense in many essays, parodies, and burlesques, a gentle humor is found in such fairy tales as *The Thirteen Clocks. The Years with Ross* is a witty record of associates on the *New Yorker* magazine.

Tolstoy, Leo Nikolayevich, Count (1828–1910), Russian novelist, playwright, and moral philosopher. His first story, *Childhood,* part of an autobiographical trilogy, was enthusiastically received. The ineffectualness, meanness, and crudeness of civilized man are revealed again and again in *Two Hussars, Lucerne, Three Deaths,* and *Kholstomer.* Tolstoy's philosophy found its full expression in the first of his great works, *War and Peace* (1863–1869). Considered one of the world's greatest novels, it traces the fortunes of two noble families and Russia's battles, defeat, and final victory over Napoleon. In 1873 he began *Anna Karenina,* a story of an adultery among the Russian nobility. *Resurrection* (1899–1900), a novel, tells of a Russian prince's seduction of a peasant girl and his repentance.

Tolstoy's plays include *The Power of Darkness,* a powerful drama of peasant life; *The Fruits of Enlightenment,* a light comedy satirizing the "fads" of society; and *The Living Corpse.*

Turgenev, Ivan Sergeyevich (1818–1883), Russian novelist generally contrasted with Flaubert, the naturalist, as the champion of realism. His first great success was *A Sportsman's Sketches.* Turgenev's masterpieces include short stories like "The Backwater," "Asya," "First Love," and the more complicated novels, *Rudin, A Nest of Gentlefolk, On the Eve,* and *Fathers and Sons* (1861). His best-known work in the United States is probably *Fathers and Sons.* Turgenev's last long works were *Smoke* and *Virgin Soil.*

Undset, Sigrid (1882–1949), Norwegian writer and Nobel Prize winner in Literature in 1928. Her most famous work, *Kristin Lavransdatter* (1920–1922) is a trilogy of Scandinavia. Mme. Undset's work demonstrates her ability to think in psychological terms and to judge the thinking and feelings of years gone by. Her work *Olav Amundsen* is a novel of the thirteenth century. Other books are *Jenny, Tree Marta Oulie, In the Wilderness, The Burning Bush, The Faithful Wife,* and *Men, Women, and Places,* an autobiography.

Villon, Francois (1431–ca. 1463), French poet, whose chief works took the form of mocking bequests to his family, friends, and particularly to his enemies. They were the *Petit Testament* and the *Grand Testament.* Throughout the *Grand Testament* are ballads and lyrics. The vainness of human life is the theme of all his poetry and is the very essence of his most famous and beautiful piece, the "Ballade des dames du temps jadis." His later poems include "The Ballad of the Hanged."

Virgil or **Vergil [Publius Vergilius Maro]** (70–19 B.C.), Roman poet. The *Eclogues,* the first of his certain works, is made up of ten pastoral poems that combine the beauty of nature with political life. This brought him recognition as one of Rome's leading poets. Then came the *Georgics,* four books on "tillage, trees, cattle, bees" showing that he was an expert on farming. Last came the *Aeneid,* a great national epic, which glorifies Rome, historically and culturally.

Wells, Herbert George (1866–1946), English novelist, journalist, and popular historian. His most popular work was *The Outline of History* (1920), a brief, clear history of mankind. The novels, *Kipps* and *Tono-Bungay,* exhibit his humor and social satire, both with a Dickensian touch. Wells also wrote a kind of science fiction to call attention to needed social reform. These works include *Men Like Gods, The Time Machine, The War of the Worlds,* and *The World Set Free.*

Whitman, Walt (1819–1892), United States poet. His *Leaves of Grass* (1855) demonstrated the inherent power of the free verse line, which he was the first to bring to perfection. His work revealed him as a mystic and a believer in pantheism, with high regard for all humanity. All of his works reflected his thinking and beliefs. Some of his poems, such as "Song of Myself" and "Out of the Cradle Endlessly Rocking," contain a spiritualized view of sex. Among his best poems are *Drum-Taps* and *Sequel to Drum-Taps,* containing the popular "When Lilacs Last in the Dooryard Bloom'd" and "O Captain! My Captain!" *Specimen Days* and *Democratic Vistas* are Whitman's chief prose works.

Whittier, John Greenleaf (1807–1892), United States poet and abolitionist. His best-known work is "Snowbound" (1866), an idyll of New England farm life. *Legends of New England,* a collection of short stories and poems, was his first book. He wrote in both prose and poetry–*Old Portraits and Modern Sketches, Literary Recreations and Miscellanies, Songs of Labor, The Chapel of the Hermits* and *Panorama,* the latter containing such favorites as "The Barefoot Boy" and "Maud Muller." *Home Ballads and Poems* contains "Telling the Bees," "My Playmate," and "Skipper Ireson's Ride." His best-known war

poem, "Barbara Frietchie" is found in *In War Time.*

Wilde, Oscar (1854–1900), English author. The outstanding works of Wilde are the novel, *The Picture of Dorian Gray,* and the clever, facetious plays, *The Importance of Being Earnest* and *Lady Windermere's Fan.* His powerful *Ballad of Reading Gaol* was published in 1898. His *Collected Poems* show that he might have made a considerable reputation as a poet had he not neglected this talent.

Wilder, Thornton (1897–1975), United States novelist and playwright. Wilder's novels, almost all historical, include *The Cabala, The Woman of Andros,* and *Heaven's My Destination. The Ides of March* is about the assassination of Julius Caesar. *The Bridge of San Luis Rey* is a novel showing that life may contain more design than is apparent. It won the Pulitzer Prize in 1928. His plays *Our Town, The Matchmaker,* and *The Skin of Our Teeth* (Pulitzer Prize, 1943) won both popular and critical acclaim.

Williams, Tennessee (1914–1983), United States author dramatist and the pen name of Thomas Lanier.

Williams' first public recognition came with the successful Broadway production of *The Glass Menagerie.* He won the New York Drama Critics' Circle Award three times–for *The Glass Menagerie, A Streetcar Named Desire,* and *Cat on a Hot Tin Roof*–and Pulitzer prizes for the latter two. Williams' characters all appear mentally sick. For such characters, no hope can be offered; but with his poetic language, Williams grants them sympathy. Other plays include *Summer and Smoke, The Rose Tattoo, Orpheus Descending, Suddenly Last Summer,* and *Night of the Iguana.*

Wolfe, Thomas Clayton (1900–1938), United States author. His novel *Look Homeward, Angel* (1929) has become an American classic. It is at the same time realistic and lyrical. It was followed by *Of Time and the River. The Web and the Rock* and *You Can't Go Home Again* were published after Wolfe's death. *You Can't Go Home Again* is considered the most mature of his autobiographical narratives. *The Hills Beyond* contains semibiographical stories somewhat like his novels.

Wordsworth, William (1770–1850), English poet. His collection of poetry in *Poems in Two Volumes* shows his extensive poetical power. His use of the sonnet and the ode give these poetic forms new vigor. *The Prelude,* the *Recluse,* and *Margaret, or the Ruined Cottage* place Wordsworth with the greatest poets.

Wright, Richard (1908–1960), black United States novelist. His most famous work, *Native Son* (1939), won the Springarm medal. Wright dealt with social problems in his novels, particularly those relating to black Americans. Other well known works include *Uncle Tom's Children, Black Boy,* and *White Man, Listen.*

Xenophon (ca. 430 B.C.–after 355 B.C.), Greek historian and man of letters. *Anabasis* is the most popular of Xenophon's writings. It tells about the military campaigns of Cyrus, the Persian king, and the withdrawal of the Greek hired soldiers to the Black Sea. The first two-thirds is a running narrative not too deep in thought, but vigorous, detailed, and exact. The *Hellenica* is the only history of this period (411–362 B.C.) written by a contemporary. The *Memorabilia* tells of the life and opinions of Socrates, with many of Xenophon's opinions included.

Yeats, William Butler (1865–1939), Irish twentieth-century poet, dramatist, and critic. First among Yeats' many poetic successes was *The Wanderings of Oisin. Purgatory* is a brief but important verse-drama. Other notable poetic dramas are *The Countess Cathleen, Cathleen Ni Houlihan, The Land of Heart's Desire,* and *Deirdre.* These plays established him as a stalwart of the Abbey Theatre in Dublin.

Yeats edited *The Oxford Book of Verse* and prefaced it with a long essay. He received the Nobel Prize in Literature in 1923.

Zola, Émile (1840–1902), French novelist. Zola wrote "scientific" novels in which the characters are governed by environment and heredity; of these his 20-volume series, *Les Rougon Macquart,* is an example. The series includes *Germinal* (1885), a clear, forceful account of an unsuccessful coal miners' strike and the misery of the children and adults who work in the mines; *L'Assommoir (The Dram-Shop),* a warning of the evils of alcohol; and *Nana,* an account of the crudeness of the demimonde of the Second Empire. *La Terre* is a powerful novel dealing with selfishness and brutality in peasant life. His *J'accuse* (1898) reflects his strong stand in the Dreyfus Affair. *Le Roman expérimental* states his theory of fiction and is the most widely known statement of naturalistic aims.

CHAPTER FIVE

WORLD HISTORY

CULTURE AND CIVILIZATION

Only man is capable of producing a culture and his history is inseparable from it. **Culture (in the broadest sense of the term) is the whole of social experience—the knowledges, technics, moral codes, customs and traditions that are transmitted by human groups from generation to generation. Each social group has a unique culture, but cultural anthropologists do distinguish these common elements in culture: the basic patterns are stable but with the years change in details; culture is conservative in its ends, but flexible in its means; it is greater and more enduring than any individual within it, but is realized only through individuals; and it is transmitted by symbols in the form of language, myth, art, religion, etc.** When does a "culture" become a "civilization"? The answer to this question is quantitative. **Culture becomes civilization when it produces an economic surplus, develops mastery over the environment, and has a relatively complex economic organization, a class-system, urban communities, recognized government, systematized law, a form of writing and elevated thought and esthetic patterns.**

Tool Culture. Cultural anthropologists have learned to make a virtue of necessity. The most numerous material remains of prehistoric cultures are the tools and weapons that prevailed. Considerable information about a culture can be derived from a tool. Nor can the importance of the tool in man's development be underestimated. It sharpened his cortico-motor reflexes, developed his sense of spatial relationships, increased his creative powers, extended his muscle power, introduced his first concepts of the possible mechanization of work, expanded his speech powers in order to transmit the tool-heritage and began the important process of division of labor and specialization of work. That this is no exaggeration can be judged by examining the importance of the tool or machine in our own civilization.

THE AGES OF MAN

Tools provide us with the basis for periodizing the cultural history of mankind.

The Eolithic or Dawn Stone Age. The **Eolithic** or Dawn Stone Age covered the first half million years of proto-human history. It was the time of Java or Peking Man. Its primary tool and weapon was a multiple-purpose ealith (a stone shaped by nature and unaltered by man) which fitted the hand and could be used to stab, cut or hack. In these first days the economy was **collectional**—the gathering of berries, roots, small animals and larvae for food. There is some evidence that spoken language and control of fire appeared at the end of Eolithic—but this is not certain. Nor is there any certainty about the grouping of men. It is assumed that the family was the basic unit of social organization and that kinship groups roamed as hunting packs or herds under the leadership of the strongest and craftiest. Nothing at all is known of the clothing or type of habitation used for shelter.

The Paleolithic or Old Stone Age. Since the **Paleolithic** or the Old Stone Age extended from ca. 500,000 B.C. to 10,000 B.C., and since material remains increase abundantly as times become more recent, it has been necessary to divide Paleolithic into **Upper** which ends about 130,000 B.C.,

Middle which ends about 70,000 B.C. and **Lower** which brought the age to an end about 10,000 B.C. While Java and Peking men may have continued on from Eolithic into Paleolithic, the epoch is predominantly that of Heidelberg and Neanderthal and Cro-Magnon men. Spurred by economic and defense needs, Paleolithic men invented the **manufactured tool.** Two types of stone-tool "industries" flourished during Lower and Middle Paleolithic—the "core" and the "flake." Core tools were produced by knocking chips off a large lump of flint or volcanic glass until it was reduced to a standard form, the *coup de poing* or "fist-hatchet." Flakes were produced by the Levalloisian technique: the shape of the tool desired was etched on the core; then, by either percussion or spatula-pressure, a flake was detached; the detached pieces were then shaped to desired sharpness by chipping. Earliest Paleolithic tools were undifferentiated. Over the years, however, the core tool became a primary one, that is, designed to produce secondary or specialized tools for perforating, chopping, cutting, scraping or sawing. By the time of Upper Paleolithic, highly specialized tools appeared and took the forms of bone needles, harpoons, pronged fishhooks, dart-throwers and bows and arrows.

Advances. Tooling revolutionized the food industry of primitive men. The mode of economy now became that of fishing and hunting. The fist-hatchet made the stalking and capture of animals safer and more certain. With the invention of the sling, the dart and the bow and arrow, man could capture animals at a distance; he was now provided with a relatively permanent food supply. With the further invention of the harpoon and fishhook, an increase in the food supply took place. Mastery of fire, moreover, gave Paleolithic men a varied food diet—as well as defense, heat and light. Now began an increase in creature comforts. Paleolithic men donned sewn clothing made from animal skins; they initiated the permanent residence, first in caves and then in crudely constructed shelters; and their men and women began to ornament themselves with beads, necklaces and pendants.

Cultural Advances. During Paleolithic, the family grouping of men expanded into larger kinship groups tracing their origin, either matri- or patrilinearly, from a common ancestor. Out of this kinship grouping came the first cultural institutions—economic, political, educational and religious. Men assumed all the duties of the hunt; women concerned themselves with the collectional and household manufacturing activities. Government was probably concerned with the maintenance of internal peace; and the mightiest hunters and the older men probably arbitrated conflicts, enforced taboos and distributed food equitably. Protection of the hunting lands turned the hunters, on occasion, into warriors. All strangers were, therefore, suspect. But good relations existed among neighboring groups of necessity. Often flint supplies gave out and had to be secured outside the locality by trade; or animals were forced by sudden climatic change to new grazing lands; or population decline caused by an imbalance of males and females may have threatened the survival of the group.

Education was for individual survival. Until puberty the child's education was in the hands of the women of the family. Thereafter, men took over the boy's training. He now underwent a severe initiation which included fasting, keeping long vigils and even mutilation; he was instructed in proper behavior to people and to things in the world about him; finally, he was taught to hunt safely and efficiently. Religious guidance was fundamental to the education of both girls and boys for there were many prescriptions and proscriptions to be heeded. Remains of burial and funerary practices make clear that late in Paleolithic men began to experience religious thought and feeling. It would seem that their religious outlook included concepts of a soul or spirit belonging to each individual, and of its persistence after death. Natural forces were regarded as being motivated by a mysterious, supernatural power or "mana." Later this undifferentiated supernatural force took the shape of spirits or ghosts present unseen, everywhere, and in all things in the universe **(animism)**. These spirits or ghosts were capable, as was perfectly obvious from the great insecurity in which men lived, of inflicting great harm unless propitiated. To placate these unseen powers, paleolithic men introduced religious rites. They carved female figurines as symbols of fertility with exaggerated sexual organs and worshipped them. They invented sympathetic magic or the practice of destroying an enemy by first mutilating his spirit resident in some effigy of him. They warded off evil by wearing amulets and talismans of beads or pendants. Finally, they created a class of professional religious practitioners called **shamans** who were possessed of powers of healing, divining and casting magical spells.

Though he accepted fully a supernatural explanation of the world of nature, paleolithic man was a close observer of things that mattered most to him. This was evident in his art work. For example, on the walls of caves he carved and painted reproductions of the animals which his band hunted—bison, mammoth, stags, reindeer, wolves. The realism, the naturalistic modeling, the use of light and dark masses, the employment of harmonious or agitated rhythms, the rigorous attention to detail, the ability to suppress detail to create a center of interest, the accuracy and sureness of drawing, the arresting of movement and action, the use of polychromatic effects—any or all of these characteristics of Cro-Magnon art establish the paleolithic artist as a very accomplished one. Nor was his skill limited to murals. He decorated his tools with small sculptures that never interfered with the function of the tool and made etchings that again illustrate his sense of realistic design. Paleolithic art was unquestionably functional in that it served the purposes of sympathetic magic; it was a form of religious ritual. But its esthetic values are timeless and universal.

The Neolithic or New Stone Age. Neolithic men exhausted the possibilities of stone technology. Since surface flint deposits were nearly depleted by 10,000 B.C., a mining industry was begun. Shafts were sunk and chalk veins were tapped with deerhorn picks for the flint they might yield. When required, Neolithic men burrowed long transverse tunnels in their mine pits. All tools were highly specialized now. In addition they were smoothed down to fine cutting edges on whetstones. Handles were attached to all chopping tools and they assumed distinctively modern appearances.

Toolmaking did not account for the profound revolution which occurred during the Neolithic Age. Discovery of agriculture and the domestication of animals did. When or how these two epoch-making discoveries took place is not known. There is some evidence for the prevailing belief that women first hit upon the art of cultivation; for many years it was they who farmed the land with picks, digging sticks and hoes while the men continued to hunt and fish. Domestication of animals lessened the need to hunt and fish and permitted the man to settle down as a cultivator.

What were the effects of this agricultural revolution? Permanent settlements along river valleys made their appearance; men experienced with new forms of durable housing—mud and thatch affairs or lake dwellings on high piles. Diets were enriched with large varieties of grains, fruits and vegetables; where rivers overflowed, large scale drainage and irrigation projects were begun; grain surpluses led to increased trade and this, in turn, effected a revolution in transportation on land and water—the wheeled vehicle and the sail were invented. Mankind developed new, civilized habits—a sense of property ownership, patience, industry and planning; soil-rootedness made him conscious of the seasons and the stars; new scientific curiosities led him to inventions such as pottery (for storage and cooking purposes) from baked clay, stone mills to grind grain, etc.

Animals continued, of course, to serve as sources of food, but they also provided man with a new source of motive power, new supplies of raw materials for textiles and a new means of transportation. Because of the availability of animals, plows and wheeled carts were invented; the textile industries of spinning and weaving took root. Civilization, clearly, was beginning to take shape.

Social reorganization followed upon economic revolution. Population increased rapidly and lived longer as the result of more abundant and more reliable food supplies. Though kinship grouping persisted in Neolithic times, it had become a fiction; the reality was the large tribe centered in a fixed locality. Tribal organization took on concrete form. Members of the tribe delegated to either strong men or elders authority to adjudicate an increasing number of disputes over property rights, to interpret tradition in changing circumstances, to defend the village against raids by hungry nomads, etc. This delegation of authority was the rudiment of formal government. Near the end of Neolithic times, representative governments gave way to absolute monarchies, out of necessity. An increase in the number, intensity and dire consequences of war was directly responsible. A lost war resulted in either annihilation, dispersal, subjugation or slavery. To prevent this, Neolithic groups submitted themselves to the authoritative leadership of war-chiefs.

Neolithic men carried religious belief forward from its state of a generalized animism to that of **polytheism.** The vague spirits of Paleolithic belief now became numerous specific gods possessing immortal but human or anthropomorphic personalities. These gods resided in stones, animals, springs, trees, caves and mountains. Methods for appeasing angry gods proliferated and took the forms of human sacrifice, animal slaughter, self-mutilation or torture, sacramental sexual relations or ritual cannibalism. Belief in an after-life also grew more concrete. Burials as a result became more elaborate: chambered tombs were constructed above the graves; into the tombs were piled furniture, weapons, clothing and food for the spirit of the departed. The first form of temple worship was that of worship at monumental stone structures—dolmens or trilithons (two upright stones with a covering slab, post-and-lintel style); or just megaliths, tremendous stones set individually in long rows (some were 70 feet high!); or cromlechs, like the famous one at Stonehenge, England, combining dolmens and megaliths in a circle.

Art declined during the Neolithic Age. Naturalism disappeared and was replaced by abstract representations of concentric lines, zigzags, spirals, dots and chevrons which were scratched or painted as decorative motifs on pottery.

ANCIENT EGYPT

The Land. As history recedes into the remoter past, geography emerges as a dominating, if not quite the dominant, factor. Ancient Egypt was, to a considerable extent, the product of a river, cataracts, delta and desert. "Egypt," said the Greek historian, HERODOTUS, "is the gift of a river." It lay along the Nile and annually that river overflowed to provide Egypt with the only moisture it had and with rich deposits of alluvial soil. Egypt proved equal to the challenge and evolved political, economic and social institutions that enabled her to capture, store and distribute the floodwaters. Canals, dikes and reservoirs appeared early in the history of civilization. The cataracts were in the southern Nilotic waters and created a natural boundary there which acted as a barrier both to expansion and invasion. The desert, too, was a formidable barrier. Geography kept Egypt at peace for centuries. The mouth of the Nile spread into a fertile delta; this region made Egypt the granary of the ancient world and gave her a valuable trading link to the Mediterranean world when she finally emerged from her isolation.

Predynastic Egypt. No written records exist from the period prior to the first families of **pharaohs** (called **dynasties**). Excavations reveal, however, that predynastic Egyptians had made important strides toward civilization. Stone was being abandoned for copper, and Egyptians had already mastered the art of smelting and casting this metal. As a people, the Egyptians were racially mixed, lived in villages as farmers and animal herders, fashioned stone, wood and copper tools, decorated pottery and wove linen goods. They had reclaimed swamplands and had begun local irrigation projects. Political units called **nomes** existed and were ruled by local nomarchs. Powerful nomarchs had effected early union of Upper and Lower Egypt. Some form of preternatural belief existed, for the dead were buried in graves along with their implements and with symbolic figurines.

THE PERSIANS

Persia lay on the Iranian plateau stretching eastward from the Tigris River to the Indus River. About 1800 B.C. an Aryan-speaking people occupied the northeastern edge of this plateau. For centuries they were subject to the rule of the Elamites; but Ashurbanipal, the Assyrian, devastated Elam and its capital at Susa (ca. 640 B.C.). When the Assyrians were destroyed in turn, the Medes under Cyaxeres (625–593 B.C.) took over the former Elamite Kingdom. But the Persians now made their bid for power. In 550 B.C. CYRUS THE GREAT took over the Median Kingdom and then continued westward to conquer Lydia and Chaldea. Cyrus's son, Cambyses (530–521 B.C.) added the Egyptian Empire to the Persian. At this point, the empire of the Persians was the largest of all those of the ancient world.

Darius I (521–485 B.C.) added little new territory to this vast empire but devoted his high intelligence to organizing it for efficient administration. His basic principle of organization was centralization through the monarch. Thus he built for himself four capitals with royal residences at Susa, Persepolis, Ecbatana and Babylon. These were interconnected with modernized highways over which flowed normal trade, postal communication and military patrols. The King made a regular circuit of his capitals and while in each he disposed of accumulated local problems. Reporting to him regularly were twenty *satraps* or governors appointed by and responsible solely to himself. (The empire had been divided into twenty *satrapies* or administrative divisions.) Each governor was responsible for the imperial tax and the army levies. In all other matters local autonomy was permitted and everywhere native cultures were tolerated. (Under the Persians, for example, the Hebrews were permitted to return from Babylon to Palestine.) But, to guarantee efficiency and to ward off the evils of bureaucratic corruption, the King appointed official spies known as "The King's eyes and the King's ears" who traveled about the empire incognito and reported back to the King the evils they observed or heard about. The Persian government itself was an absolute hereditary monarchy "by the grace of Ahura-Mazda." There were important limitations on the King's absolutism: he was expected to consult with the nobility, to base his law-making upon the Law of the Medes and the Persians and to be guided by precedents in the law. This was the empire that persisted in the Middle East until 333 B.C. It received its first important setback at the hands of the Greeks at the Battle of Marathon in 490 B.C.; and it was destroyed by Alexander the Great. Its influence, however, continued long after its demise.

CRETE

Between Persia and Ancient Greece lay the Aegean Sea and around that sea there flourished a number of civilizations which became transitional to the Greek. Earliest of these was the **Minoan** civilization which flourished on the island of Crete and which was revealed to the modern world by the brilliant excavations about 1900 (A.D.) of SIR ARTHUR EVANS. Knowledge of the Minoan civilization is still limited because its language is still undeciphered; what is known is due to archaeological discoveries. From these it is known that Minoan civilization flourished between 3000 and 1200 B.C. In this period, they dominated the Mediterranean sea with their trade and military power.

Their power was manifest in the mighty cities which they built at Cnossus and Phaestus on the island itself. Cnossus, for example, was dominated by the king's palace which was at least two stories high, contained a maze of living rooms, store rooms, workshops, offices, etc., was equipped with plumbing that provided running water and efficient sewage. Attached to the palace were factories which turned out articles for export—pottery, textiles and metal goods.

Unearthed figurines indicate that Minoan worship centered about a snake goddess, a symbol of fertility and of destruction. The dead were buried with their implements of war and livelihood; gods were appeased by sacrifice. There were, however, no temples. Minoan murals are exceptionally revealing: they show the people as unusually sports-loving and engaging in bull fights, boxing, races, etc. Women held an exceptionally high position; they play and work side by side with the men. All this is shown by the archaeological record. This record also reveals that about 1400 B.C. Minoan civilization took root in northwestern Asia Minor about the site of Troy and in a group of Greek islands centered about Mycenae on the mainland. Similar pottery, artistic design and "beehive" tombs prove this. Esthetic analysis of Mycenaean remains, however, shows that the creative flame was gone by 1400 B.C. Minoan art, at its height, is a rare combination of naturalism and spontaneity combined with exquisite delicacy; Mycenaean art is derivative and dull by comparison. The Minoan artist was master of the miniature: the figurine, the painted dagger, jewelry, inlay; Mycenaean is large and crude by comparison. The real influence of the Minoan Cretans was not upon the rough Trojans and Mycenaeans but upon those that conquered them, the ancient Greeks of Dorian and Ionian stock.

Greece

ORIGINS

Greek civilization did not spring full-blown from the soil of Greece. It took a millenium before the Greeks cast off their original barbarism. The earliest Greeks lived in the valley of the Danube; they spoke a common Indo-European tongue. By 2000 B.C., however, their language had become differentiated enough to enable us to divide them into Achaeans, Aeolians, Ionians, Illyrians, Boetians, Dorians, etc. About that time, too, they were uprooted from their homeland and began a folk-wandering southward into the Balkan peninsula; they came, that is, as conquerors.

The first to enter may have been the Achaean Hellenes (ca. 2000 B.C.). Over a period of 700 years these people filtered into central and southern Greece and then into the Aegean islands. They seem to have assimilated with the indigenous Greeks, and absorbed their superior culture; but they imposed upon them the Achaean language and rule. Ionians are found in western Greece as early as 1500 B.C. They, too, settled down, absorbed and assimilated with the natives. But about 1300 B.C. a barbarous tribe of Illyrians swept down into Thessaly and uprooted the Achaeans and the Ionians and forced them to scatter into the remoter regions of the peninsula and overseas to Asia Minor. It is quite likely that this upheaval, rather than the legendary kidnapping of Helen, brought the Achaeans under Agamemnon into collision with the Trojans in Asia Minor. This Illyrian conquest was followed by an even more devastating **Dorian invasion** which re-scattered the Achaeans and Ionians. After 1000 B.C. the invasions ended and Greece entered a period of incubation.

Invasion and dispersion were not without positive results. The decadent remnants of Minoan-Mycenean culture were destroyed, paving way for a new culture; the Greek nation differentiated into varied and conflicting types each occupying a fixed territory, and this spurred the growth of individualism; Greek culture became Mediterranean rather than Balkan; overseas, the Greeks came into contact with the civilizing ways of the Near East; and passage over the seas required that the Greeks become "maritime-minded" and oriented to a life of trade and commerce.

The Land. Trade and commerce were vital preconditions for the development of Greek civilization for the Balkan peninsula was a singularly barren land. Criss-crossing mountain ranges covered two-thirds of the land surface; arable plains made up a bare one-sixth. The rivers were non-navigable and varied between winter flood and summer dry-bed. Lakes were rare and inclined, because of poor drainage, to become malarial swampland. Scrubby pasture supported meager flocks of sheep and goats. Deforestation was acute; and there were only thin veins of metals basic to the ancient civilizations—gold, silver, lead, iron and copper. The historian HERODOTUS defined it accurately when he said that poverty was foster-sister to the Greeks. But while geography was, in the main, a barrier to civilization, it did open some opportunities. For example, there were rich deposits of stone and marble and potter's clay; natural harbors abounded along the eastern shore; the Aegean islands were natural stepping-stones to the Asiatic mainland and by occupying them, the Greeks made the Aegean Sea into a Grecian Lake.

The "Homeric" Greeks. Homer's *Iliad* and *Odyssey* are timeless masterpieces of epic poetry; they qualify as such by every standard of literary criticism—by clear, vivid and natural diction; by **epithets** that serve as haunting refrains and impress the *dramatis personae* upon the memory; by an **"heroic" meter, the hexameter;** by suspenseful beginnings *in media res* (in the middle of things) to avoid tedious or interruptive background material; by the music of their language; and by their wide range of human emotions, their varieties of style to fit the scenes, their plenitude of imagery and matchless rhetoric. They are "things of beauty," of "Attic shapes" in motion and as such their influence has not waned in the 2800 years of their lives. In a study of Greek and Roman influences on western civilization (*The Classical Tradition*), Gilbert Highet was compelled to make more than 250 references to Homer's epics. Here we can do no more than note Homer's literary impact. Our interest must be in what he revealed about the "dark age" in the preliterary history of Greece.

Homer's interest was in his own past; but he

was unable to escape his present. So, from between his lines, we are able to piece out that part of Greek history which is called the **"Homeric Age."**

Primitive Society. Homer's Greeks lived in a relatively primitive society. Their methods of wealth-gathering centered upon crude agriculture, herding and plundering on land and sea. Technologically they had passed from the Bronze to the threshold of the Iron Age. Some specialization of craft had begun for the epics speak of **freemen** who were smiths, potters, saddlers, masons, carpenters and cabinetmakers. Costlier goods, however—objects of art, weapons, fancy raiment and gold beakers—seen to have been imported. Trading was very limited and conducted by means of primitive barter. There was no coinage and wealth was estimated in flocks. The ox served as a medium of exchange. Most manufactured goods were produced in the home by slaves with the assistance of their masters and mistresses.

Private ownership, as an institution, had not yet appeared; landed property was owned by the family with the father as chief administrator. While the father could determine the use of the land, he could not sell it. He had to transmit it, by the common law of **primogeniture,** to his eldest son who became head of the household upon his father's death. The family unit was patriarchal; it was, in fact, a patriarchal despotism for the father could, if he wished, take concubines for himself or offer them to his guests, or commit infanticide, or slaughter his children as sacrifices to the gods. Fathers, however, rarely employed such practices. Homeric families are, for the most part, monogamous; intimacy and affection exist between husband and wife and between father and children; the position of the woman in the household is high and free even though marriage was by purchase. (Women were to lose this high status as Greek society developed.)

Homeric men could and did commit unspeakable barbarities upon one another; but concepts of a common humanity tempered their crudities. They are never far from tenderness, sentiment and tears; deep friendships are common; they show rare hospitality to strangers for they bathe them, clothe them, wine-dine-and lodge them, and then send them off with gifts; slaves have a rare position of equality in the household. On the other hand, they are never far from what we would consider immoralities either. Women are offered as prizes in athletic contests; wanton, cruel sacrifices are made upon funeral pyres; slavery and concubinage follow upon conquest; piracy is an honorable profession and pillage a necessary one; they admire unabashed lying, deceit and treachery. This was their response to an insecure world in which human life was cheap; to survive, a man must have the qualities of Ares, the God of War—strength, guile and deception. Fair was foul, and foul was fair. (These, in fact, are among Odysseus' most conspicuous traits.)

Politics. Political institutions were equally primitive though considerably advanced over Oriental forms as no divine-right absolute monarch existed in Homeric Greece. There was a **basileus or dynastic king** who served as commander in chief, high priest and chief justice. He was, however, a chief among equals. His equals were a landed aristocracy who claimed, as did the basileus, divine descent. They met on important occasions as a council and through this agency they checked any exercise of arbitrary power by the basileus. Within the council the nobility enjoyed complete freedom of speech. As a further check on absolutism there existed an assembly of all freemen who could, in a crisis of war or peace, approve or reject proposals made by the king or nobles. Government was completely decentralized; the power of the king extended, on a "feudal" basis, only as far as his noble retainers obeyed him. For example, while his anger was upon him and he did not choose to fight, Achilles ignored every demand and plea to do so made by King Agamemnon. There was no fixed law but custom; justice was administered by the family-feud—though there is some evidence that justice by trial was beginning to take root.

Religion. Homeric Greeks conceived the ideas that they lived on an earth that was a flat disk floating on Oceanus. Above them was the solid dome of heaven kept aloft by Atlas. Around them the seas abounded with marvels and foreign lands with freaks. Natural forces resulted from the actions of unseen gods who dwelt on Mt. Olympus. Gods were distinguished from men only by their immortality and their extraordinary powers; otherwise they had the shape of humans and all of the virtues and vices of mankind. They fought, feasted, made love, played tricks, lied, deceived, made music, roared with laughter, fell in love with mortals and produced thereby generations of illegitimate progeny. They were, indeed, a capricious lot and therefore had to be cajoled, persuaded or "bought off" by prayers, votive offerings and sacrifices. The head of each Greek family was qualified to conduct these religious rites and therefore there were, among the Homerics, no temples, no organized priesthood. Relations between these Greeks and their gods were earthbound for the Greeks seemed not to believe in underworld ghosts, or spirits, or, in fact, in any last judgment and afterlife punishment. Hence they had only the most rudimentary sense of sin. Life was to be lived on earth and religious devotion was centered upon extending it as long as possible with the aid of favoring gods or by outwitting unfavoring ones through developing the gift of prophecy or omen-reading.

THE WARS OF ANCIENT GREECE

The Greek nations were forced to fight their way to freedom because they were caught between the Persian Empire expanding westward from Asia Minor and Carthage expanding eastward from North Africa. The Persian menace first struck the Ionian Greeks who were resident in Asia Minor; by 546 B.C. Cyrus had subdued all the Greek cities there. Mainland Greece was now faced with the possibility that the Persians would cross over the Hellespont into Europe. Already the Persians were seeking to dominate the sea trade on the Mediterranean. When, therefore, Aristagoras in 499 B.C. led the Ionian cities in revolt against DARIUS, Athens risked the fury of the Persians by sending them naval assistance; Sparta refused to send aid. Darius gathered tremendous land and naval forces for an assault on Greece itself.

The Persians first landed at **Marathon** (490 B.C.). This direct threat to the independence of all the Greeks failed to unify them; the Athenian army was left to face the Persians alone. Under the military leadership of Miltiades and Callimachus the Persians were routed and driven into the sea. The results of this victory were immense: it showed that the Persians were not invincible; it delayed a second Persian attack for ten years; it began the Athenian leadership of Greece; it spelled the end of the tyranny as a form of government (for the Persians were fostering this form on the Ionian shore); it inspired the great classics of Aeschylus and Herodotus; it ensured that "western civilization" as opposed to "oriental civilization" would prevail in Europe. Of more immediate value, it forced the Greek cities to unite against the certainty of the second attack.

This attack came in 480 B.C. XERXES, the son of Darius, had gathered a force of 200,000 men for the attack and had selected **Thermopylae** as the battleground. LEONIDAS made his immortal stand against the Persians here and delayed them long enough to permit the evacuation of Athens. The Greeks were unable to prevent the destruction of Athens; nor did they make strenuous efforts to defeat the Persians on land. Greek strategy was to achieve a decisive victory on the sea. They met the Persians, as planned, at Salamis and wiped out the Persian fleet and army there. On the same day Persia's Carthaginian allies were routed. One year later, at Platea, the Persians were defeated on land and driven out of Europe.

The Peloponnesian Wars (431–404 B.C.) The unity finally achieved in the war against the Persians did not last. Capitalizing upon her leadership, Athens, in 478 B.C., organized the **Delian League,** a confederacy of about 200 city-states; then, led by Themistocles and Aristides, Athens converted this League into an imperialist grab-bag for herself. She intervened by occupation and threat of occupation in the internal affairs of the League members; she forced them to pay a tribute to Athens for "protection"; she dominated all their commercial activities. Athenian imperialism forced Sparta, in alliance with Corinth, to take steps against the possible loss of their own independence by strengthening the Peloponnesian League.

Thus matters stood when Pericles came to power in Athens. Democratic at home, Pericles pursued an aggressive imperialist policy abroad; he broke a long-standing alliance with Sparta; he allied with the enemies of Sparta and Corinth (Argos, the landed nobility of Thessaly, Megara, etc.); he helped a group of rebellious helots to colonize in Athenian territory; he began a policy to drive Corinthian trade out of the Aegean. Anticipating the reaction of the Spartans, Pericles completed the fortification of Athens by building the Long Walls connecting Athens with the port of Peiraeus, a distance of four and a half miles.

These preparations were made none too soon for in 431 B.C. Sparta and her allies declared war on Athens. The war lasted 27 years. It was featured, as Thucydides pointed out, by "calamities such as Hellas had never known."

After years of stalemate, the Athenians were

defeated at **Syracuse** in the west (413 B.C.) and ultimately at Athens in 404 B.C. The results of the Peloponnesian wars were calamitous in the extreme: the great age of Athens ended; Spartan hegemony was destroyed by the city-state of Thebes under the leadership of Epaminondas; war and confusion prepared the way for a new power rising in the north and readying itself to spring southward.

THE RISE OF MACEDONIA

Philip. At the beginning of the fourth century B.C. Macedonia was a semi-barbarian state on the northern fringe of Greece. PHILIP came to the Macedonian throne in 359 B.C. As a youth he had been taken as a hostage to Grecian Thebes; there he learned to hold Greek culture in great reverence and to disdain Greek politics, which had deteriorated.

Philip, it seems, determined to save Greece from itself by a liberating Macedonian conquest. He would unite her under his single rule and spread her culture abroad. His policy of conquest was to be by devious political fracturing of whatever Greek unity existed and then by direct military assault. With this goal before him, he developed a powerful army and seized the gold mines of Grecian Amphipolis. When the opportunity presented itself he entered a "sacred war" against Phocis on the side of ruling Thebes and this netted him Greek citizenship and a place on the Amhyctyonic Council.

At this time, only one Greek saw through Philip's maneuvering—DEMOSTHENES, and in his **"Philippics"** he warned of conquest to come and urged unity—military and political—upon the Greek city-states. His passionate and eloquent words went unheeded, even laughed at—Philip was such a cultured gentleman who lived so far away! With this advantage Philip defeated Olynthus and neutralized Athens herself. Against the advice of Demosthenes Athens permitted Macedonia to cooperate with her in a second "sacred war" against Amphissa. In the course of this campaign Philip took over all of central Greece. Thoroughly alarmed, Athens and Thebes permitted Demosthenes to organize a counter-Macedonian **Pan-Hellenic League**—which Philip crushed. He was now sole ruler in Greece. His policy toward the conquered Greeks was one of firm kindness; he even offered them an honored place in an expedition against the Persians that he was now planning. But in 336 B.C. he was murdered. His son Alexander succeeded.

Alexander. ALEXANDER THE GREAT was tutored by the great Greek philosopher Aristotle; and no more thoughtful world conqueror ever existed. Better than most, Alexander knew and appreciated the glory of Greek culture. But he knew that no Greek was safe from barbarian conquest until Greece had conquered all the world. He brought all his genius for military tactics, propaganda and political strategy to bear upon the realization of this goal.

First, Alexander crushed an uprising of Spartans in Greece itself; then, with half his army he went to meet the Persians in Asia Minor. He met them at Granicus in 334 B.C. and at Issus in 333 B.C. and routed them each time. Choosing not to pursue Darius, Alexander turned south and subdued the Phoenican coast; he then descended deeper into Egypt. Here his purpose was revealed fully for he launched a huge public works program to restore all things Egyptian and then recruited thousands of Greek intellectuals and workingmen to build for him a huge Greek city in Egypt itself; this city became **Alexandria,** the first cosmopolitan city in the world, a meeting-place for people from all over the world.

This done, Alexander now returned to meet Darius who had regrouped and enlarged his armed forces until they far outnumbered Alexander's; at Arbela, in 331 B.C., Darius was defeated again. Though Darius escaped, he was murdered by his own men; Alexander then assumed for himself the Persian title of the "Great King." He took over Persia's capitals and its treasuries; he assumed Oriental mannerisms and even his Macedonians had to now prostrate themselves before him. In pursuit of the murders of Darius Alexander now pushed on to conquer Bactria and India; but exhaustion had set in.

Alexander moved on to Babylon, where he contracted the swamp fever and died. He was thirty-three years old; but in his brief lifetime he had changed the face of the world. Alexander's empire died with him. PTOLEMY, a follower, seized Egypt and instituted a pharaonic rule; Seleucus took Syria and the lands of the Persian Empire; Greece degenerated into an internecine war between an Aetolian League and an Achaean League and Macedonia. The world awaited a new unifier and a new peace. In Italy one such was coming slowly to life and power.

Though chaos succeeded Alexander's efforts, what his conquest accomplished was incalculable. He broke down the barriers which had persisted for three millenia between Oriental and Occidental; out of the intermixture of cultures came a new, brilliant Hellenistic civilization; hieroglyphic and cuneiform fell to superiority of the Greek tongue; release of the Persian treasures stimulated trade and commerce to new heights; trade lanes now began to extend from the Pacific Ocean to the Atlantic; new cities grew up and old ones were revitalized all along the trade lanes. He had decisively altered his world.

Rome

THE BASES OF ROMAN CIVILIZATION

Geography. The mountains of Italy were not obstacles to political unification as were those of Greece; while precipitous, they terminated in the broad plains of Latium—large and fertile areas capable of intensive cultivation. The Appenines, however, forced the Romans to face westward, away from the civilizations of the eastern Mediterranean; and this gave the Romans the isolation they needed for independent development. Italy's peninsular form made it inevitable that, when able, the Romans would concentrate upon domination of the Mediterranean Sea. The open land areas, the easy invasion of Italy from northern lands and surrounding seas, forced the Romans on the defensive from their earliest days; militarism became synonymous with survival. Finally, the situation of Rome itself atop seven hills commanding the Tiber River gave her a powerful position on the peninsula.

People. The original Italian peoples are lost in the mists of the past. When the Romans emerged they were a linguistic, cultural and racial mixture of Samnites, Umbrians, Latins, Gauls, Greeks and Etruscans. Greek influence was particularly strong; but most profound was that of the **Etruscans,** an Oriental people whose high civilization was absorbed by the Romans. The earliest Romans were subject for many years to the overlordship of these Etruscans. Etruscan practices of many kinds seeped into Roman life and remained long after the Etruscans themselves had vanished.

Political Institutions. Because they began as a conquered people under absolute monarchy, the Romans created political institutions to defend themselves from the exercise of arbitrary power. When they became a free people, they placed supreme power in the hands of two political bodies —the **Assembly** and the **Senate.** The Assembly included all male citizens of military age. It was basically a ratifying body and as such had an absolute veto on executive decrees in matters of war, peace and justice. The Senate was a council of elders whose membership derived from traditional clans. Senators comprised, for the most part, a conservative, landowning aristocracy; they were charged with choosing successors to the monarchy and with safeguarding the **law of custom** from invasion by either the King or the Assembly. Such were the **checks and balances** that characterized the Roman government when it began its independent existence in 509 B.C.—the year the Etruscan kings were finally expelled.

Socio-Economic Institutions. The family was the basic unit in primitive Roman society. Its sole legal personality was the *pater* (father) who had the power of life and death within the family. Custom and the position of the Roman matron acted as restraints on the absolutism of this *paterfamilias.* The social group was separated by rigid class divisions: there were **patricians** or large landowners of noble birth, a privileged class who served in the Senate, monopolized army offices, and conducted public religious ceremonials. Then there were the **plebeians,** a free citizenry drawn from the the small farming and artisan classes. They served in the Assembly and enjoyed the right of trading, property holding, and judicial self-defense. But they were barred from entry into the Senate, they could not intermarry with the patricians, and had no recorded bill of rights. **Clients** or tenant farmers and slaves completed the class structure; they were without freedom or rights.

Religion. Religion cemented Romans of all classes. There were no priestly castes; religion was related to civic activities. However, specialists in religious knowledge did exist: *haruspices* who inspected the vital organs of sacrificed animals; *augurs* who interpreted omens.

Household and farm deities predominated: Janus, the Spirit of the Doorway; Vesta, The Spirit of the Hearth; the Penates, the Guardians of Household Stores; the Lares, The Guardians of Family Property; and the Genius or Guardian Spirit.

Religious devotion was quite materialistic: it was based on bargaining and contracting with the gods and such bargains and contracts were enforced by law, duty and taboo. Late in the monarchical period national gods made their appearance: **Jupiter,** the sky-god and chief over all; **Juno,** Jupiter's spouse and protector of matrons; **Minerva,** the artisan's divinity; and **Mars,** god of war. With national deities asserting themselves, the gods left the Roman household and entered into temples; worship became cultish.

The Roman Ideal. Where the Greeks found their ideal within themselves, the Romans looked back to their founding ancestors for theirs. For it seemed to Romans that these founders were worthy of worship. They had set the ideal of "sterling integrity, stern dignity, stoic endurance, rugged simplicity, hard economy and sturdy industry" for all posterity. They were unselfish patriots, austere puritans, practical utilitarians—without philosophy, imagination or culture.

FROM CITY-STATE TO NATION-STATE

From 509 to 265 B.C. the small city-state of Rome expanded its dominion until it was master of the whole Italian peninsula. This 250 year expansion was piecemeal and resulted from the efforts of the Romans to make themselves defensively secure against hostile neighbors and to solve their problem of a landless population at the expense of their neighbors.

The Fifth Century B.C. Etruscan power declined steadily during the fifth century B.C. and released a large number of Italian tribes for war and expansion. Rome was threatened by engulfment by any one or all of them. Cities in Latium had formed a **Latin League** and were pressing upon Rome. After many years of defensive battling, Rome brought the Latin League to terms by a tremendous victory at **Lake Regillus** (486 B.C.). Members of the Latin League were forced into an offensive-defensive alliance with Rome, an alliance that held for 150 years in wars against the Etruscans, the Aequi, and the Volsci. Aggressive advances by the northern Sabellians had set the Aequi and Volsci in motion against Rome. Under the leadership of CORIOLANUS the Aequi were vanquished; and under that of CINCINNATUS, the Volsci. Momentarily secure on her farther borders, Rome attacked and eliminated an Etruscan stronghold at Veli—twelve miles to her North across the Tiber. This latter victory enabled Rome to double her territory and to emerge as the leader of the Latin League.

The Fourth Century B.C. The fourth century B.C. opened with a disastrous invasion by barbarous **Gauls** which ended in the sack of Rome and the impoverishment of its people. Under Camillius the Romans painfully rebuilt their razed city, built strong walls around it, reorganized their army into more flexible units, introduced iron weapons, and revised their requirements for Roman citizenship.

Chastened and strengthened, the Romans were occupied for most of the rest of the century with eliminating the strong threat of the Samnites, war-like mountaineers who were threatening Rome's fertile lands in Campania. A victory over the Samnites had the effect of stirring Rome's allies in the Latin League to attack her; she was becoming too big and powerful for the security of other Italian states on the peninsula. But Rome defeated their combined effort. The Latin League was dissolved; its cities were isolated by separate treaties; some were made colonies; others were given a suffrageless Roman citizenship.

Rome became the capital of all Latium and the protector of all under her dominion. Colonies of Roman citizens were settled within the conquered territories to relieve the pressure of the landless upon Rome's land. The Samnites, defeated but not conquered, now (327 B.C.) attempted to organize all of the conquered people into a federation for independence. To meet this new threat, Appius

Claudius made further reforms in the army, built a navy, broadened the base for both military and tax levies, and constructed the first of the great Roman military highways (**The Appian Way**). The result was the complete defeat of the Samnites and their allies at the Battle of **Sentium** (296 B.C.). All Italy was within the grasp of the Romans.

The Conquest of Italy. The remainder of Italy was taken in the third century B.C. This was southern Italy where Greek cities predominated. When war between the Greek cities and Rome threatened, the city of Tarentum called upon King Pyrrhus of Epirus (in Greece) for aid. Pyrrhus responded and at Heraclea (280 B.C.) won a bitter and costly victory—hence the phrase "Pyrrhic victory." Pyrrhus's advantage came from the use of terror-spreading elephant cavalry. Rome now allied with her powerful North African neighbor, Carthage, in a defensive alliance against Pyrrhus. By 275 B.C. Pyrrhus was forced to leave Italy, and Tarentum fell; all of southern Italy now succumbed. Rome occupied Italy from the toe to the Po River.

Why Rome Conquered. Many reasons are given for Rome's success. Her enemies were disunited and Rome's policy of divide and rule was effective; Rome's allies were weakened by continual wars with *Rome's* enemies; Roman statesmen kept internal strife at a minimum by generous land grants, liberal division of the spoils of war and extension of democratic rights. Rome's victims were forced to place their armies at her disposal. Highway trunklines were built with each new conquest, colonies and garrisons were placed at all strategic outposts, bilateral treaties militated against new combinations against Rome.

Most important, however, was the use made of Roman citizenship.

Conquered peoples fell into four classes: **citizens, municipia, Latin Allies** and **Italian Allies.**

Roman citizens had full rights and privileges of citizenship.

Municipia had Roman citizenship *without* suffrage rights; they enjoyed local autonomy and the rights of trade; they served in the army and paid taxes.

The Latin Allies had no citizenship but still enjoyed the rights of trade; they furnished Rome with foreign legions and had some local autonomy.

The Italian Allies were Roman protectorates; they sent troop levies to Rome, levies that were supported at Roman expense and shared in the war booty.

Though the bulk of the Italians thus lost their independence, were bound to do Roman military service and had to pay numerous special taxes to their Roman rulers, Roman rule brought them many advantages: a *pax Romana* (Roman peace), an end to inter-tribal warfare, defense against external aggression, partial freedom and the possibility of full citizenship, economic unity, the use of Roman public works (aqueducts, roads, bridges, etc.) and a share in the new prestige that Rome had won for Italy.

Effects on Rome—Military, Economic, Cultural. The Roman army took on permanent form. It was a paid, national militia based on universal conscription of all property holders for service at home or abroad. The military unit was the phalanx of heavy and light infantry; the sub-unit was the centuriate (100 men). During the fourth century a more flexible form of legion (4000 infantry) was adopted. It was divided into 120 maniples for maneuverability. Larger units of cavalry were added and by the middle of the fourth century the Romans had a navy as well.

The Italian conquest extended the importance of agriculture in Rome's economy, since large tracts of arable soil were added to her holdings. Labor power for these expanded estates was provided by the slaves who were taken as war-prisoners. From the conquered people new techniques of farming were borrowed and applied (particularly in wine and olive production). War profits increased the demand for foreign luxury goods; trade expanded and with trade there came a money economy. Trade brought the trader—a new class of rich men that began to press for a larger share in government.

Latin translations of Greek works began to spread through Italy. Greek gods were adopted and given Roman "citizenship." Hellenistic philosophies began to capture the imagination of the intellectuals and to undermine the traditional beliefs.

THE ROMAN EMPIRE

Rise. Caesar had willed his rule to his nephew OCTAVIUS. Octavius had to fight for his bequest against MARC ANTONY and LEPIDUS—both Caesar's friends and both commanding effective military power. All three, however, had a common enemy in the republican forces led by Cassius and Brutus. A **Second Triumvirate** was therefore formed which consisted of Octavius, Antony and Lepidus. At **Philippi** the republicans were overwhelmed. Antony moved on to Egypt and to Cleopatra while Octavian (Octavius) returned to Rome to consolidate his position. When Antony divorced Octavia (Octavian's sister) to marry Cleopatra, Octavian declared war. At the **Battle of Actium,** 39 B.C., his fleet won a decisive victory over Antony and Cleopatra. Octavian was now without opposition.

The Principate. Julius Caesar had sought to transform Roman society; Octavian sought to reestablish it — within a new order. Octavian, for example, forced Caesar's appointees from the Senate if they were not descended from the highest Roman nobility. He decreed that no Roman citizen could marry a freeman, or outside his rank. Old Temples were restored—in marble. Republican forms were scrupulously observed. When Octavian acted it was *through* the Senate and Assembly. In 27 B.C. Octavian laid down all his extraordinary powers and it was the Senate that granted them to him anew by popular acclaim. Thus by senatorial proclamation Octavian became

Princeps—the head of the Senate and first citizen of the State

Imperator Caesar Divi filius—commander-in-chief of the armed forces and son of the Divine Julius (hence he could become the object of religious worship)

Augustus—restorer and augmenter of the state (a title formerly bestowed on certain gods).

In these bestowals the Senate recognized that the old order was gone; new times, new governmental forms. After a century of civil war the great desire of all Romans was peace and order. And Augustus Caesar was the one to give it to them.

Reforms. Augustus brought the *Pax Romana* to the Romans and to the world. The Roman army, recruited from the ranks of Roman citizens and officered by men from the aristocratic classes, stood guard at all the frontiers and within all troubled areas in the Empire. In Rome Augustus kept for himself a small praetorian guard. A standing navy was added to the armed forces. Military affairs were made the exclusive perogative of Augustus himself. Competence over the provinces was divided: those pacified and near at home were granted to the Senate; others were administered by the Imperator.

Within all provinces Augustus decided upon all military matters. To meet the rise in state expenditures for the military, for public works, for grain distribution and the like, Augustus made tax collection a state function; taxes were now collected efficiently and new import taxes were introduced. To keep expenses down, no new foreign conquests were undertaken—particularly after the resounding defeat suffered by the Romans under Varus at the hands of Arminius, a Germanic barbarian.

Height. Augustus died in 14 A.D. and his stepson TIBERIUS was nominated by the Senate as his successor. Tiberius abolished the *comitia tributa,* transferred certain provinces from the Senate to himself in order to reform them, suppressed two great mutinies in the ranks of the legionnaires and many personal plots against himself. He died unpopular in 37 A.D.

CALIGULA (37–41 A.D.) who succeeded him was insane and managed to dissipate the treasury in drunken revels and bizarre celebrations. The Praetorian Guard disposed of him. It was they who named Claudius as successor.

CLAUDIUS (41-54 A.D.) ruled well. He reoccupied Britain; reformed the bureaucracy by instituting special divisions; he completed the construction of two aqueducts and improved the great harbor at Ostia. Because she plotted against him, Claudius had his wife, Messalina, executed. He then married his niece, Agrippina, who bore him a son Nero. Agrippina then disposed of Claudius by poisoning him.

NERO (54-70 A.D.) was probably insane. His administration was filled with plot and counterplot, with assassination and execution, with persecution of the Christians who were made the scapegoat for a fire that swept Rome in 64 A.D., and with border revolts extending from Britain to Judea. When the Senate finally condemned Nero, he committed suicide.

VESPASIAN (70-79 A.D) proved a wise choice: he reformed the tax structure, recovered large tracts of public lands from extortionists, introduced rigid governmental economy, increased the income of the state, restored discipline in the ranks of the army and kept the peace. His successor, TITUS, ruled for two years only (79-81 A.D.) and was followed by Domitian.

DOMITIAN (81-96 A.D.) built the lines of forts between the Germanic and Roman lands where no natural boundaries existed. This established peace in the northeast. Murder and assassination, including his own, featured Domitian's rule.

NERVA'S (96-98 A.D.) brief rule produced an interesting agricultural scheme: to encourage agriculture in Italy a revolving fund was set up by the state; farmers could borrow from the fund at low interest rates; upon repayment, the principal was returned to the fund, and the interest was used for relief for indigent widows and orphans. Nerva began the adoptive system of imperial succession when he adopted Trajan as his son and successor.

TRAJAN (98-117 A.D.) was the first provincial to become an emperor. He was a brilliant military commander and during his rule he brought the Roman Empire to the Tigris and Euphrates Rivers—its widest extent. He also made important reforms in the imperial administration. He adopted Hadrian as his son.

HADRIAN (117-138 A.D.) was a most unmilitary ruler. His interests were in languages, literature, philosophy and art. To avoid the bother of empire, he ceded Mesopotamia and Assyria to the Parthians; granted independence to Dacia; completed the northern forts; built a wall in Britain between Roman and Celtic lines; destroyed Jerusalem and scattered the Jews far and wide through the Empire. Internal administration was reformed and the praetorian edicts were codified. Hadrian's Tomb (The Castle of Saint Angelo) on the banks of the Tiber is a most fitting memorial of this most esthetic of the Roman emperors.

ANTONINUS PIUS (139-161) ruled long and peacefully; his successor MARCUS AURELIUS (161–180) ruled long, was a man of peace, but lived through troubled times. There were local wars against the Parthians, Germanic tribes and others; there were severe persecutions of the Christians. These external exertions were in direct contradiction to the inner life of Marcus who, in his famous *Meditations,* a treatise on Stoicism, revealed himself as simple, conscientious, retiring, philosophical and ascetic.

COMMODUS (180-192) was a true son of Marcus Aurelius, at least in the flesh. The spirit of Commodus—cruel, sensuous and cowardly—was far removed from that of his father. With Commodus begins the decline of Rome.

THE DECLINE OF ROME

Rome's decline extended over centuries; it had no sudden fall. Many factors contributed to the decline. Science and technology did not keep pace with Roman expansion and Romans found that they were unable to handle efficiently the food, tools and transport problems that arose. The immense size of the empire was also a factor. It was impossible for the best-intentioned emperor to cope with the ceaseless problems of rising nationalisms, border attacks, graft and corruption in the provinces, inefficient bureacracy, gross waste of limited resources. The drain on the public treasury was continuous. The wider the empire became, the less intense became the degree of patriotism; loss of patriotism engendered corrupt political behavior. The army was sensitive to the decline particularly as it lost its Roman character and became increasingly provincial. With decline in emperor character, the army became a prime political force. It began to make and unmake emperors so frequently that one can say accurately that between the rule of Commodus (d. 192 A.D.) and the rise of DIOCLETIAN (284 A.D.) military anarchy prevailed in the Empire.

Political decline hastened the factors making for economic decline. Small farmers, the backbone of the Roman Republic, virtually disappeared or rather were absorbed into the immense estates as semi-slaves. The purchasing power represented by these small farmers disappeared and helped to ruin the city artisans who had produced manufactured goods for sale to the small farmers; besides, an important source of tax revenue also disappeared. With the ruin of the small farming and artisan classes, the state became the primary producer of goods, a factor which destroyed the initiative of the Romans. Resulting shortages of goods produced a steady inflation. Coinage began to disappear; what remained was debased and became worthless. The result was a reversion to barter. This had a tremendous impact upon the trading or middle classes who had become the backbone of the Empire. Foolish imperial decrees hastened the decline of this group. They were made responsible for the collection of taxes in the municipalities. Whatever they did not raise of the quota assigned them, they had to pay out of their own pockets. They could not meet their quotas because the artisans had been ruined with the decline of the small farmers. Soon the middle class followed the artisans into ruin.

Some social factors entered the picture too. Population declined all during the imperial period. War, epidemic and plague were chiefly responsible; and, as times grew harder, natural birth rates declined among the poor as well as the rich. Of equal importance was the failure of nerve which accompanied physical decline. This was revealed in the search for security above enterprise, in the widespread superstitions that developed, in the rush to join mystical cults that guaranteed, at least, some reward in the hereafter, in the loss of patriotism, in the wild and bestial indulgences of the rich, etc.

The Fall. Several strenuous efforts were made to halt the decline of the empire. Most notable was that of DIOCLETIAN (284-305 A.D.). Diocletian tried to augment the powers of the Emperor by introducing Oriental features of absolutism into his rule. He reformed the army; tried to halt inflation by instituting both price and wage controls; and made significant changes in imperial administration. This latter was most important for the future of European history. The Empire was divided in two, a western and eastern half and Diocletian ruled from the east. This division became permanent when CONSTANTINE (306-337) made Constantinople into a second Rome. When the fall came, it was the western half that collapsed; **the eastern half continued for more than a thousand years to preserve and disseminate the culture of the Roman Empire.**

The Foundations of Medieval Civilization

The **Medieval** or **Middle Ages** of European History are those that lie between the Greco-Roman Age and the Age of the Renaissance—approximately from 476 A.D. to about 1350. These Middle Ages reached their height between the 11th and 13th centuries. Our concern in this chapter is with Medievalism at its height and with only the broadest aspects of its civilization and culture.

FEUDALISM

A distinguishing feature of the Middle Ages was the **Feudal System,** a system that pivoted upon a **personal, contractual relationship** between two nobles—**a lord and a vassal.** A nobleman became a **lord** when he made a grant of a **fief** (a section of land with its peasant inhabitants) to another nobleman in exchange for the latter's services, chiefly military. A nobleman became a **vassal** when he accepted the fief and swore homage and fealty to his lord. It is important to remember that both the lord and the vassal were noblemen and freemen.

Origins of the Feudal System. Both Roman and German influences contributed to the creation of the Feudal System. It was not unusual in Roman times for a freeman to attach himself to a wealthy or influential man as a "client." In exchange for services, the client received protection. In more troubled times the practice of **commendation** arose. A client would "commend" both himself and his land to a patron in exchange for protection. In reverse, it was also a common practice for a wealthy landed patron to grant a client a *precarium* (land with precarious or uncertain tenure) ; in time this became a *beneficium* or a grant of land for a fixed period of time, say, a lifetime or two generations, in exchange for services. This land-services practice became merged with the Germanic practice of establishing a personal military relationship between a chief and his freeman-warriors. The Germans also introduced a practice of "immunity-grants" whereby powerful noblemen were granted free, unsupervised sovereignty over fixed territorial areas.

The Fief. In the tenth century the practice became fixed to **invest** a warrior-vassal with a fief. The fief might be a single, small holding or an entire duchy of many holdings. It was an *hereditary* holding and was transmitted by succession through the eldest son. Within the boundaries of the fief the vassal exercised sovereign rights: he collected taxes, coined money, exploited the resources, raised armies, provided for the public defense, administered justice, established and regulated markets and the like. The investiture of a fief was often recorded in a written contract. In the written contract was also included a listing of the services which the vassal would render to his lord. A fief could be *sub-infeudated* or divided among sub-vassals.

The Services of the Vassal. The basic obligation of the vassal to his lord was military service; in time this came to be limited to about forty days of military action. The number of fully equipped men that each vassal contributed depended upon the number of sub-vassals that he controlled. Vassals were also expected to help garrison the lord's fortress or castle and to engage in administrative activities. A vassal, then, might be chief administrative agent of fief and household; a constable or commander of the castle; a marshal or supervisor of the horses; a butler or supervisor of the wine supplies. Vassals were expected to attend the lord's court and to serve as judges in inter-vassal disputes, thus giving rise to a "trial by one's peers."

Feudal aids or monetary payments accompanied the personal services of the vassal; occasions for such payments were numerous. If the lord was captured in battle, the vassal had to contribute to ransom him back; if the lord planned an expensive undertaking in the nature of a pilgrimage or crusade, the vassal had to provide monetary assistance; if a vassal died, the inheriting son had to pay an inheritance tax. To protect himself against the possibility that an enemy would take legal possession of a fief, the lord secured the right to himself to veto a marriage proposal made to the vassal's daughter or widow; to assign custody over minors, who had inherited a fief, to a male regent. If a vassal failed to deliver his services, he could be forced to forfeit his fief and if he died without an heir, the fief would revert to the lord.

Feudal Hierarchy. Medievalism was patterned on the needs of these broad social groups: the peasants, the military nobility, and the clergy. These three groups formed **estates** and the first was the clergy, the second, the nobility, and the third, the peasantry and other producers (the townsmen did not fit easily into this medieval pattern—as we shall see).

In theory, the feudal hierarchy was carefully pyramided. At the top, as lord of all vassals, was the king; counts, dukes, and viscounts followed; beneath them were the barons or seignors; and knights or chevaliers made up the lowest rank. The Church held a special position in the hierarchy. In the 9th and 10th centuries many churchmen gave military service for feudal allotments and when this was prohibited on moral grounds, church fiefs were usually sub-infeudated among lay knights who could fulfil by proxy the Church's military duties.

Within the hierarchy, the king was potentially powerful but actually limited in his power to his own estate. Theoretically he owned all the land; in reality it was in the inalienable possession of the powerful nobility. Theoretically—as in Germany—the king ruled by divine right (The Holy Roman Emperor); in reality, he was an *elective* monarch chosen by the nobility and the clergy. Theoretically, the king commanded the allegiance of all his subjects; in reality, they obeyed him to the extent of their oath of allegiance and feudal contract. The point of this comparison is that the seeds of royal absolutism were buried in the medieval order and could be released the moment the power of the feudality weakened. This is precisely what happened by the 15th century.

Feudal Life. While feudalism prevailed, violence and turbulence characterized the life of the nobility as they contended over matters of inheritance and succession, of lay and ecclesiastical supremacy, of infractions of the feudal contract and the like. With war as an almost constant condition, feudal lords were forced to convert their homes into fortresses. The castle was a fortress. Its thick walls, crenelated towers, deep donjons, inner and outer battlements, surrounding moat, iron-toothed portcullis and drawbridge made it virtually unassailable by feudal armies except by seige and starvation.

The state of permanent war conditioned the education of youth. Feudal youth were trained to become knights or warriors. Like his Spartan prototypes, the feudal youth was removed from parental care at the age of seven or eight and sent to another feudal household for upbringing. He served as a page until he was sixteen and as a squire until he was twenty-one. Throughout these early years, he was made to live a hard life in the course of which he was taught the use and care of arms and horses. When he was battle-ready, he became a knight. This occasion was an impressive religio-feudal ceremony during which the knight-to-be knelt before another knight and received an *accolade* which was originally a sharp blow with the flat of a sword intended to knock the initiate out but was later modified to a slight tap on the head or shoulder. Once knighted, the warrior spent his time in war or warlike games which took the forms of hunting and tournaments or jousts.

ENGLAND

England was brought into the compass of European civilization by the Romans. In the fifth century A.D., however, the Romans had to retire before the onslaughts of the barbarian Angles, Saxons, Jutes and Frisians. The chaos which resulted was brought into some kind of order as a result of the missionary work of the Irish and Roman clergy. In 664, at the Synod of Whitby, Roman Catholic Christianity was officially adopted by the ruling tribes.

These tribes were divided into seven kingdoms, the so-called **Heptarchy.** By the ninth century, the kingdom of Wessex rose to power and produced one of England's great leaders, ALFRED THE GREAT (871-901). Alfred was able to establish a working relationship with the Danes who were threatening Anglo-Saxon England with extinction and then to initiate in England something of a "renaissance" of learning. He established schools and fostered the translation of Latin classics (e.g., Boethius' *Consolation of Philosophy,* Venerable Bede's *Ecclesiastical History of the English Nation*). He himself helped produce the *Anglo-Saxon Chronicle* and inspired the work of CAEDMON and CYNEWULF, founders of English literature. By codifying the laws and by remarkable defense of his realm, Alfred gave the English a tradition of strong kingship that soon became legendary. His work was undone by weak successors and by the conquest of England by KING CANUTE, the Dane (1016-1035). Canute's invasion forced many of the Anglo-Saxon nobility to flee to Normandy in France.

William the Conqueror. One such who fled was EDWARD THE CONFESSOR who in 1042 returned from Normandy to the throne of England. Edward brought with him many Norman advisers. Great rivalry developed between the Anglo-Saxon earls and these Norman nobles. When Edward died, the Witan (Council) selected Harold the Saxon (of Wessex) as king. WILLIAM, DUKE OF NORMANDY opposed this selection saying that Edward had promised the kingdom to him. In 1066 William invaded England and at the **Battle of Hastings** defeated Harold and his Anglo-Saxon forces. All of England fell as a feudal fief to the Conqueror.

Showing rare wisdom, William kept the government institutions he found in England and infused them with a new life. William destroyed the Anglo-Saxon earldoms, dividing them into smaller administrative units; over them he placed officials directly responsible to himself. Thus he merged Anglo-Saxon institutions with Norman institutions.

William's intention was to build a strong, centralized monarchy in England. His position was unique for he held all of England as a fief and could therefore make every landholder his vassal; every landholder had to serve in William's army. To further strengthen his position William kept a private standing militia for his use and prohibited private warfare. He issued a uniform royal currency. Even more remarkable for his time, William based his taxation upon the Domesday Survey (1085-1086), a national census of property holders and property! To defend his realm, William built castles everywhere and armed them with his own retainers.

Henry I (1100-1135). When William died the nobles tried to disrupt his plans for centralization. HENRY I consolidated his position by creating a permanent council of advisers—a bureaucracy of professional civil servants—and a group of "circuit" judges who traveled about the kingdom bringing the king's justice to all parts.

Henry II (1154-1189). Following Henry I's death, feudal and civil wars reduced England to a state of anarchy. Order was eventually restored by HENRY II, one of the greatest of all English kings. Henry was founder of the **Plantagenet dynasty** and ruled a land that extended from Scotland to the Pyrenees; his wife was the brilliant Eleanor of Aquitaine.

During the course of his reign, the English monarchy was considerably strengthened, particularly in the arena of judicial control. Henry's judicial reforms entered not only into the blood stream of the English nation, but into that of the United States as well. In the Assize of Clarendon of 1166 Henry did more than strengthen the king's justice. He initiated the participation of the people in the law-making process. The Clarendon Assize established the circuit judge as a permanent part of the English judicial system. When the circuit came to town, it was the duty of the sheriff to call up witnesses to give the judges information of existing wrongs. This practice created the **grand jury** which made "presentments" to the judges. In time these presentments were turned over to a **petit jury** ("twelve good men and true") to hear the presentments and pass judgment. He enlarged the jurisdiction of the King's Bench by permitting—contrary to feudal practice—civil as well as criminal cases to come before the circuit judges. This reduced considerably the power of the local, feudal baronial court.

Henry also resolved to reduce the power of the church courts by limiting the claim of "benefit of clergy" to major officials of the church. In this he was opposed by THOMAS A BECKET, the Archbishop of Canterbury. When Henry promulgated in 1164 the **Constitutions of Clarendon** which ordered that church officials accused of a crime should be taken before a royal court, Becket ordered churchmen to ignore the decree. After six years of dispute, at Henry's instigation a group of his followers murdered Becket.

The church and baronial courts having been curbed, the king's justices were free to consolidate English law and practice and out of their procedures there grew up the great system of **English Common Law.** Unlike Roman Law, the Common Law was never codified; it consisted of **customs and precedents.** In spite of this, it is wholly proper to call Henry II the "English Justinian."

Magna Carta (1215). Centralization of monarchical power suffered greatly under the rules of RICHARD THE LIONHEARTED and KING JOHN. Richard spent his father's bequest fighting as a knight errant in the Holy Land. John, whose goals of a centralized monarchy were consistent with Henry's but whose abilities and character were far inferior, became involved in a war with the feudal nobility and in a terrible quarrel with Pope Innocent III. As a result of his quarrel with Innocent, he lost all of his kingdom to the pope as a fief; and as a result of his war with the nobility, having been defeated in the **Battle of Runnymede,** he was compelled to sign the **Magna Carta** which placed severe restrictions on the power of the king in matters of taxation and judicial trial. At the time it was signed, Magna Carta served the interests of the feudal system. Only later did it become the **"charter of English liberties."** To cap this sad climax to the efforts of Henry II to establish the royalty in England, John proceeded to lose all of England's French possessions.

Edward I (1272–1307). When he came to the throne, EDWARD I resumed the reforms that were begun by the two Henrys. He further weakened the baronial and church courts; he strengthened the civil service; he gave strong impetus to a new institution, the English Parliament; he began the union of all the British Isles under one crown by conquering Wales (and creating a post of Prince of Wales as successor to the Crown) and Ireland. His work with Parliament deserves special mention since herein was the "wave of the future."

The Development of Parliament. Parliament is traced to the Anglo-Saxon Witan, a council of prominent nobles. William the Conqueror converted this into a Grand Council of nobles which served him in a judicial and advisory capacity.

Parliaments became popular in Europe during the second half of the thirteenth century as kings sought for revenues outside feudal dues to carry out their programs of national aggrandizement. It became customary to convene an assembly of three "estates," the lords, the clergy and townsmen (bourgeoisie) as a means of raising money. Spain had its **cortes,** France its **Estates General,** Germany its **diet** and England its **Parliament.** In 1265 SIMON DE MONTFORT had convened, on behalf of the feudal lords, the first British Parliament. But it was Edward I who convened the "Model Parliament."

Edward's purpose was to reduce his dependence upon the nobility for moneys and he therefore agreed, in 1297, that certain taxes would be levied only with the consent of Parliament. By the 14th century, this Parliamentary "power of the purse" was ingrained in English practice—to the considerable regret of the monarchs who followed Edward. Not only had this custom begun to prevail, but it also became a custom for the lords temporal and lords spiritual to sit together as the House of Lords, while the others sat separately as the House of Commons.

Furthermore, when Parliament met, it became the practice of the House of Commons to submit to the king a "list of grievances" which had to be taken care of before any money was voted. When England became involved in the Hundred Years War, and the financial drain became severe, the House of Commons began to insist on directing how the funds should be spent. For this to be legal, it became further necessary for the Commons to draw up a law which stipulated the way the money should be spent. Thus, in the Middle Ages, grew up one of the primary forms of modern democracy.

The Hundred Years War (1337–1450). The wars between England and France in the years between 1337 and 1450 were largely inspired by the desire of the kings of England who followed Edward to repossess their French holdings. As a result of these wars, England was driven permanently off the continent and forced to concentrate upon the British Isles. British kings became more and more independent in such matters as freedom of Parliamentary debate, extension of suffrage for Parliamentary members, the right of all money bills to originate in the House of Commons and not the House of Lords. The kings' power having been weakened by war and parliament, the power of the nobility rose.

The Wars of the Roses (1453–1485). The English baronial class split into two factions, **Lancaster** and **York**—Lancaster of the "Red Rose," and York of the "White Rose." (their emblems). Both factions struggled for control of the monarchy and of Parliament. The result was a lengthy civil war known as the **Wars of the Roses** (celebrated in Shakespeare's History Plays). As a result of this civil war, the feudal nobility virtually exterminated one another and permitted Henry VII of the **House of Tudor** to gain power. With Henry VII, England moves from the Middle Ages to modern history.

THE HOLY ROMAN EMPIRE

While other European nations took the path of national unity, Germany and Italy did not become united nations until the nineteenth century. The reasons for this failure were numerous. German emperors dissipated their energies in an effort to unite Germany and Italy, a policy that was opposed, as we have seen, by the papacy and the powerful Italian towns. The popes were particularly effective in preventing this union. They openly interfered in imperial elections within Germany and kept that nation split in perpetual war between Guelph and Ghibelline, they used their extensive powers of excommunication and interdict against such strong rulers as Barbarossa, Henry VI and Frederick II, and, when these failed, they invited foreigners like Charles of Anjou (1265) to make war on the Germans.

The Germans themselves made a unified nation nearly impossible by measures continually adopted to weaken the Emperor. For five hundred years thereafter there was no Germany—just a series of archduchies, margravates, counties, duchies and free cities known as the Germanies.

Italy suffered the same fate. The lead in preventing the unification of the Italian states was taken once more by the popes who feared for their vast possessions in Italy and by the short-sighted Italian cities. Constant invasion plagued the Italians as well. Following the decline of the Carolingian power Italy was invaded by the Normans who settled in Sicily. The Normans provided Italy with models of intelligent rule: laws were codified; a parliament was created (1225); trade and commerce were fostered. Because it threatened their power, the popes invited the French Angevins into Italy as conquerors. So bitter was the Italian resentment against the French that in 1282 at Palermo they rose up, at the house of vespers, and murdered every Frenchman they could find. (This massacre is known in history as the "Sicilian Vespers.") When the French left it became the turn of the Spaniard Alfonso of Aragon to conquer Sicily and Naples (1443). In 1494 Charles the VIII of France invaded Italy . . . but by this time Italy's will to exist as a nation was destroyed.

Out of this failure in government a new state was born—Switzerland. While Frederick II was King he permitted two Swiss cantons to become self-governing—subject to his overlordship. A habit of independence was born. When in 1291 Rudolph of Hapsburg, the German ruler decided to remove their independent rights, the Swiss cantons formed a Perpetual Compact or alliance directed against Rudolph. Their resistance was successful. In 1315 the frustrated Hapsburgs moved an army against the Swiss and were soundly beaten by boulders rolled down the declivities of the cantons. Their success encouraged the Swiss to organize a confederation. In 1394 the Hapsburgs compromised with necessity and recognized Swiss independence. Out of this struggle came the legend of **William Tell.**

The Economic Transition to Modern Times

THE COMMERCIAL REVOLUTION

Statistics of the growth of European commerce between 1350 and 1650 are not available; but some indication of the growth is reflected in the fact that by the latter date there were an estimated 2,000,000 tons of shipping afloat. We are concerned with this fact because with each increase in Europe's trade **the power and position of the middle class grew.** Fixed capital such as landed property began to take second place to fluid capital in the form of money. Manufacturing was becoming a competitor of agriculture for available investment capital. There still were many medieval shackles upon the free flow of trade—feudal tolls and tariffs, religious prohibitions, guild restrictions, and the like. But these were being shaken loose by the rise of **national states** under *national* monarchies, by the wave of humanism and new learning sweeping Europe, and by the religious reformation. Taking advantage of these dissolvents of the medieval order, the middle class began to develop forms of manufacturing that evaded the boundaries set down by the guilds. In the mainstream of all these charges, however, was the revolution in commerce that made itself felt by the fifteenth century.

Trade and Commerce. By 1400 European markets were no longer restricted to the luxury trade from the Near East. These still commanded an imposing position in the trade picture, but trading was as much concerned now with new European foodstuffs, textiles, shipbuilding materials and tools. Markets were no longer restricted to a few favored areas since goods could now travel along the king's roads protected by the king's police and the king's courts. The supply of money had increased; European deposits of gold and silver were dug with intensified fervor and North African mineral sources were tapped. When the Americas were discovered—just as European deposits were almost exhausted—a flood of gold and silver bullion re-entered the trade stream.

Manufacturing. Traders clamored for manufactured products to be sold abroad in exchange for luxury goods and for foodstuffs. Throughout these early years, in fact, the drain of gold and silver out of Europe was very heavy. Europe suffered from an almost continual unfavorable balance of trade which kept her prices low (deflation) and her debts high. When the political power of the guilds declined, entrepreneurs (early capitalists) appeared who discovered and invested in a new mode of production of manufactured goods, the **domestic** or "putting out" system.

Under this system the entrepreneur contracted with many craftsmen to supply them with raw materials and to pay them for the goods they manufactured out of the raw materials. The entrepreneur then disposed of the manufactured goods in the local or international market. This was a very attractive offer to the craftsman. He already owned his own tools, he could do the work at home (hence domestic), he did not have to worry about purchasing raw materials and selling his products, he could keep a garden patch and do some farming to supplement his income from manufacture.

To the entrepreneur this system was still not ideal: the cost was high since the craftsman made the whole product and insisted in producing quality goods, the entrepreneur depended upon the craftsman who owned the tools, the small number of craftsmen kept wages high, production was limited, invention of new tools was discouraged since craftsmen could not afford to finance them, etc. Over the years, the attractiveness of the craftsman's position brought many new workers into the field. Entrepreneurs took advantage of this situation by lowering wages considerably. The lowering of wages had the effect of increasing the dependence of the craftsman upon the entrepreneur. To get more money, the craftsman had to give up his farming and put his wife and children to work. Under pressure to make more, the craftsman became less concerned with the quality of the product. The entrepreneur, in turn, got poorer goods and found it increasingly difficult to supervise many workers in their homes. The time soon came when a more radical innovation in manufacturing processes would have to be made. For this period, however, the domestic system served admirably to build up the quantity of trade, the wealth of the entrepreneurs and to destroy effectively the power of the guilds.

Finance. Financing by means of money grew side by side with commerce and manufacturing.

Professional money lending was an old practice by 1400. As early as the 10th century monasteries began to engage in extensive money lending, generally to local peasants and landlords. Political loans were on occasion made to Emperors, Popes and high feudal lords. Later, the knightly orders (Templars, Hospitalers, etc.) played the part of kings of finance and supplied credit needs.

In the medieval cities the role of professional lenders fell to the Lombards, Jews and money changers. Medieval Jews, prohibited from becoming farmers or artisans, had been among the first to engage in commerce. The rise of Christian merchants forced them out of this business and into the business of money-lending since they were not subject to church prohibitions and money-lending was a necessary function in an expanding economy. Christians permitted them to settle in specified areas *only if they would make loans;* Jews paid with their lives *if they refused to make a loan when security was offered.* Jews, then, won "toleration" so that Christians might evade the church's prohibition of "usury"—though the latter of course reaped the rewards of usury.

Soon, however, the Italian Lombards became active competitors of the Jews. Their loans went out to the urban merchants, feudal lords and handicraftsmen. The Lombards discovered that they might lend out more money than they had (since some was always being paid back)—but not safely. Therefore, they began to solicit interest-bearing deposits (a practice forbidden to the Jews). This was the origin of commercial banking. Other methods—such as bills of exchange, bank drafts and bank acceptances—were soon instituted.

Business Organization. Forms of **partnership,** family and non-family, had developed in the Middle Ages and were continued into the modern period. So too was the **regulated company**—an association of merchants created to monopolize and exploit some branch of trade. It received its charter from the government. Each associated merchant worked as an individual entrepreneur but contributed to a common treasury to finance a central body which maintained foreign trade centers, gave protection to the membership and laid down the rules for the proper conduct of business.

But the most modern of the forms developed in this period was the **joint stock company.** The others were a union of persons; this was a union of capital. A number of investors put their money into a venture and then chose a board of directors to conduct the venture; they then shared the profits and the risks.

When joint stock companies came to be linked to regulated companies, they were called **chartered commercial companies.** A good example of one such was the famous English **East India Company.** Its capital was derived from shareholders but it did more than engage in commercial ventures. Its charter granted it monopoly rights to trade anywhere in the Pacific and Indian Oceans; to buy land in unlimited quantity; to deal with foreign potentates; to wage war and to make peace treaties. With these freedoms permitted to it, chartered companies began to colonize the world on behalf of the mother country.

DISCOVERY AND COLONIZATION

Colonization was first attempted, unsuccessfully, by the Crusaders. The germ of the colonial concept was also present in the trading posts which were set up in Europe and the Near East by the Venetians and the Hanseatic League in the 13th and 14th centuries. But these ventures were in relatively settled and civilized areas. Modern colonization began when a vast new world of either sparsely settled or barbarous regions were suddenly discovered, explored and found more than useful. The first burst of such exploration and discovery came in the half century between 1450 and 1500. Why at that time?

Causes. Many factors combined to produce the burst of overseas exploration in 1450–1500. Nations along the Atlantic coast were growing desperate for gold and silver with which to offset the unfavorable balance of trade with the Near East. They resented more and more bitterly the stranglehold which the free cities of Italy had upon that area and upon the Mediterranean Sea. Momentarily the Italian monopoly had been threatened when the Ottoman Turks in 1453 had captured Constantinople and overthrown the Byzantine Empire. (Indeed, they had advanced deep into Europe itself and had overrun Serbia, Wallachia, Bosnia and Greece.) The Turks, however, anxious to keep the favorable balance of trade with Western Europe, had renewed Venice's privileges in the Near East. Even had there not been this political domination of the Near East, the price of Far

Eastern commodities was extremely high since the price reflected the great distances by sea and overland that the goods had to come, the tariff that had to be paid en route, the brigandage that lined the whole trade route, etc. It was clear to thoughtful merchants that there was but one answer to this distressing problem: some all-water route to the Far East—either around Africa or by a westward sailing.

Successes. MARCO POLO and other travelers had returned to Europe with the news that Far Eastern lands were washed by some mighty water. Why could it not be the same mighty water that washed the Atlantic shores of Europe? Europeans became convinced that it was and began the systematic conquest of this water—which held so many terrors for the uninformed.

By 1450 improvements in seafaring were far advanced. The magnetic compass was in general use; the astrolabe to measure latitude out at sea was perfected; new scientific maps were in circulation; shipbuilding had advanced toward larger and more powerful vessels. With the invention by JOHANN GUTENBERG of the printing press, geographical, maritime and astronomical information was diffused over wide areas. In particular it became better and better known that the earth was a sphere and that one could reach east by sailing west.

Southward and westward sailing were in the minds of many men by 1450. National states were well advanced by that time and the monarchs hungered for more revenue with which to counter the feudal nobility; dispossessed nobles hungered for a new chance to recoup their fortunes. Individuals stirred by the Renaissance stress on man sought new adventures and new glories. Men looked to Africa and to the Far East as vast potential fields of conquest.

Now Europe needed bold and fearless navigators to try the dangers of the unknown sea. One who did not fear the sea was Prince HENRY THE NAVIGATOR, son of King John I of Portugal. Motivated by a zealot's hatred for the Moslems and a desire to conquer them by outflanking them in the south of Africa, Henry organized a navigational center on the southern tip of Portugal facing the Atlantic. Here captains were trained in the making of maps, the reading of them, the use of navigational instruments, etc.

Their training completed, Portuguese navigators began to edge cautiously down the western coast of Africa. In 1488 (twenty years after Henry's death) BARTHOLOMEW DIAZ reached the Cape of Good Hope. Ten years later VASCO DA GAMA sailed around Africa to India. The southward route had been breached. Six years before da Gama's feat, however, the Western route was opened by the world-shaking voyage of CHRISTOPHER COLUMBUS (1492). Some years had to pass before Europeans came to realize that Columbus had discovered a huge continent that blocked the way to the Far East. The first to see the ocean on the other side of the New World was VASCO NUNEZ DE BALBOA; and the first to circumnavigate the globe by sailing westward was FERDINAND MAGELLAN and his crew (Magellan having been killed in the Philippines). By 1522 the Mediterranean Sea route to the luxury items of the Far East had been circumvented in two directions. Hegemony over Far Eastern Trade now passed to the nations on the Atlantic shores. The Commercial Revolution was complete.

The Renaissance

For many years historians took their understanding of the historical period known as the **Renaissance** from a book written by the great Swiss historian, JAKOB BURCKHARDT—*The Civilization of the Renaissance in Italy.* According to Burckhardt, the Renaissance was a spontaneous creation of the Italian people in the fifteenth century (the quattrocento); it was something new that had no roots in the past. From nowhere came a new birth of individuality; from nowhere, an outburst of genius that took the forms of great art and literature. Several concepts distorted Burckhardt's view of the Renaissance: he was primarily concerned with culture and ideas; he, therefore, paid insufficient attention to other factors—religious, political, social or economic; he believed in the "great man theory of history" which blinded him to large movements involving lesser people. In spite of these weaknesses, Burckhardt's study remains a major classic of historical research.

Historians still do not agree on all that the Renaissance was, but most will accept the statement that it was not a "rebirth" so much as a **transitional period between medieval and modern times.** As a transitional period the roots of the Renaissance derive from the medieval outlook; its tentacles stretch toward the dawning era of modern science; in itself it was neither medieval nor modern. Because it was an in-between period it was characterized by criticism of the *status quo*, by restless curiosity about all things, by the raising of questions rather than the answering of them. Such intellectual attitudes inevitably led the men of the Renaissance to place man himself under more intensive examination and it was out of this emphasis upon *man* that the distinctive features of the Renaissance emerged. In this matter, Burckhardt cannot be denied; the Renaissance did burst with creativity and the artists of that period were great men even if they were not the *sole* determinants of the course of history during the Renaissance.

Renaissance Versus Medievalism. There was much in medieval life that Renaissance men openly rejected or disagreed with. While medieval men revered some of the Greco-Roman classics, Renaissance men hailed them all, no matter how pagan, how un-Christian. They made war against medieval Latin and 14th century vernacular and sought to return to the "pure Latin" of Cicero—a virtually unknown tongue. They were optimistic, worldly, and individualistic. They rejected "Gothic" architecture as "barbaric"; they no longer gave unthinking credence to Ptolemaic astronomy which placed man at the center of the universe; they pursued knowledge for knowledge's sake without fearing for their faith; they mocked at chivalry, scholastic philosophy, medieval economics; in short, they affirmed life with enthusiasm and joy.

Causes of the Renaissance. What forces accelerated this drive toward a "new birth?" Many of them lay in earlier developments: contact with Moslem and Byzantine civilizations; the Commercial Revolution with its interchange of goods and ideas; the new learning of the thirteenth century that flowered in scholasticism; the rise of national monarchies bolstered by the Bolognese revival of Roman law; the spread of universities; the near-scientific emphasis of the Nominalist movement within scholasticism; the growth of a wealthy, leisured middle-class seeking prestige as patrons of the arts. These might very well be designated **fundamental causes.** (It is worth reemphasizing that most of these causes lay, chronologically, *within* the medieval period.) For the more immediate causes, we must turn to the history of Italy in the fourteenth and fifteenth centuries.

IDEAS OF THE RENAISSANCE

The rise of the Renaissance dictators was accompanied by a rationalization of their activities and behavior. One such rationalization was the ideal of *virtù*. A man was to be judged by the bravery and skill with which he achieved his personal goals and by the subtlety and finesse of the means he employed. In pursuit of virtù, conscience was irrelevant. So wrote MACHIAVELLI in *The Prince.*

Machiavellanism. Machiavelli wrote *The Prince* out of a deep sense of frustration with the political condition of Italy—its helplessness before the might of Spanish and French invaders, its lack of patriotism, its dependence upon mercenary soldiers, its state of warring disunity. His dream was of a unified Italy, completely sovereign, untrammeled by church, religion or morals, free to undertake whatever was necessary to bolster its unlimited sovereignty over the lives of its subjects. The end of unity could only be achieved by a patriotic and ruthless prince, possessed of virtù, who by craft and force would reduce the peninsula of Italy to a single sway.

Such a prince, thought Machiavelli, was CESARE BORGIA. Why was Cesare qualified? He took the world as it was and men for what they were—as motivated primarily by evil purposes. He therefore planned to make evil his ally. He did not scruple to break his word when his promise no longer served his purpose; he strove to make himself both loved and feared by giving the appearance of being virtuous but doing all the evil required to maintain himself in power. All means are justified, argued Machiavelli, that serve the end of attaining and retaining political power. Ruse, cunning, artifice, conspiracy—these were the methods of the prince with grandeur of soul, strength of body and mind. Poison to the prince were such Christian ideals as humility, lowliness and contempt of worldly objects.

Such goals were not confined during the Renaissance to princes alone. They can be seen operating in the interesting lives of such Renaissance figures as Pope Alexander VI, Machiavelli, himself, the utterly unscrupulous critic Pietro Aretino, the adventurer Castagno, the braggart Benvenuto Cellini and even in the youth of Leonardo da Vinci.

The Perfect Courtier. The ideal of the "very perfect knight" of chivalry had decomposed by the time of the Renaissance; in its place appeared the ideal of the "very perfect gentleman." BALDASSARE CASTIGLIONE (1478–1529) established this ideal in his book *Il Cortigiano* (*The Courtier*). Who was the gentleman? He was born to a family of good manners or gentility, artistocrats in mind and body, standards and taste. In such an environment he would grow up skilled in sport and the use of arms, a graceful dancer and skilled musician, a master of several languages including Latin, familiar with great works of literature and art, and completely at ease in the company of accomplished women.

Women, said Castiglione, are a necessary part of the environment that makes the gentleman for they refine whatever brute instincts are the natural endowment of man. But women have to be trained in their role of complement to the gentleman and the first requirement was to be feminine in carriage, manners, speech and dress. To be the conversational equals of men, women, too, must undergo the studies that would provide them with ideas on literature, art and statecraft, with facility in many languages. Compared, then, with the medieval ideal of womankind, Renaissance woman was a real woman—rather than an ethereal ideal—and was celebrated as such in paintings of artists like Raphael and Andrea del Sarto both of whom used *live* models for their Madonnas. Gentlemen and gentlewomen, pursuing the ideal of *cortesia* (gentility) inevitably became patrons of the arts.

Art Patronage. Responding to the heightened interest in the remains of classical antiquity, the nobility and wealthy merchants began to collect antiques, to finance projects designed to spread classical, learning, and to give support to local, native artists who possessed unusual talent. The Medici, for example, built a museum for the study of antique art, financed diggings among Etruscan and Roman ruins, invited and supported artists like Bertoldo, Michelangelo, Leonardo and Verrochio to work in the museum on original projects. Lorenzo de Medici was himself exceptionally gifted as a poet and composer.

Artistic Individualism. While the artists appreciated these endowments and made much use of them, they resisted all efforts to form them into guilds or corporations so characteristic of the medieval outlook. The earliest of the great artists worked in guild workshops under the usual guild regulations and restrictions. Gradually the cult of individualism developed; artists of genius established themselves in individual studios and assumed an independent role. They still depended on commissions from the aristocracy and the church, but the subject matter and form of the artwork was to be exclusively their own. The result was that fine art was separated from the crafts; painting, sculpture and architecture became individual liberal arts, each with its own esthetic, or canons of taste and judgment.

As individual artists became recognized, there flocked about them groups of worshipping and imitating students. To bring some kind of order into art instruction, some of the masters began to organize art academies. From the art academies sprang the various schools of art which characterized the Renaissance.

The Protestant Reformation

FUNDAMENTAL CAUSES

Between 1517 and 1648 the "universality" of the Roman Catholic Church was shattered beyond repair. Roman Catholicism now had to share its leadership of Christians with a large number of national churches and private sects, each with its dogma, doctrine, ritual and sacramental acts. This momentous schism began as a reformation within the Roman Church but ended as a series of transformations outside it. The political, economic, social and cultural consequences of this schism in Christian thought and practice were explosive in the days of its origin and remain so in our own day, 300 years later. Reform movements within the Catholic fold had occurred previously, as we have seen; they were part of the evolution of the church's structure to meet changing social conditions. Why, then, should the reform inaugurated by MARTIN LUTHER have had such drastic consequences?

Church abuses. The number of church abuses had multiplied, but not significantly, over those that existed at the time of the Cluniac Reform. Many clergymen were ignorant and ineffective as priests; many led scandalous lives and in so doing broke their vows of poverty and chastity. The papal office was held by a number of Renaissance popes notorious for their loose and indulgent living and who were incredibly corrupt. They made a business out of the sale of religious offices and benefices; church offices and dispensations were placed on the auction block and those who won the bids and became church officers got their money back by charging outrageous fees for priestly services.

Still other venerated church practices were converted into profit-making enterprises. Two that figured largely in Luther's protest were the sale of relics and the sale of indulgences. Relics were objects believed to have been used by Christ, the Virgin and the saints and therefore possessed of miraculous power to cure the afflicted and to protect the threatened. Unrestrained and unreproved, relic-hawkers traveled through Europe selling unlimited quantities of holy splinters from the "true" cross or from the "bones" of saints. When the fantastic proportions reached by this traffic were exposed by the Humanists, a great revulsion followed. Even more controversy centered about the sale of indulgences.

An indulgence was a remission of all or part of the punishment for sinning in this life; it was effective in purgatory but not in hell. The practice was an ancient one and in the beginning granted after works of charity, fasting and the like. Church teaching held that Christ and the saints had accumulated a large "treasury of merit" while they were on earth; this treasury was deposited in heaven and the Pope, possessed of "the power of the keys and the authority to bind and loose," could draw upon the treasury to remit punishment both on earth and in purgatory. No indulgence was valid unless the recipient was truly contrite, confessed his sins and was absolved. Since canonical penalties often inflicted hardships and inequities upon helpless people, the church began the practice of commuting penalties into almsgiving. From almsgiving to the sale of indulgences was a natural step for the Renaissance popes who cared little for the spiritual significance of the indulgence and much for its possibilities for fund-raising. In fact, one of the popes turned over the traffic in indulgences to a banking firm which collected one-third of the "take" as their share of the "profits." When exposed, this, too, caused great indignation among the faithful.

All these things had been before and had brought on reform movements; why should these series of abuses have brought on a schism? The reason must lie deeper. Old abuses gather new force when they occur in a changed environment.

Waves of Doctrine. Disgust with the Pope's exercise of temporal power had stirred JOHN WYCLIFFE (1324?–1384) to denounce it, and to follow this denunciation with demands that the Scriptures be elevated above papal power, and that the clergy be permitted to live secular lives (marriage, etc.) to reduce the amount of corruption that prevailed among them. He thought, too, that the Bible ought to be translated into the vernacular so that all who could would read it.

The fall of the papacy into the "Babylonian Exile" revived Wyclifism after it had been suppressed and found an eloquent spokesman and martyr in the person of JOHN HUS (1369-burned 1415). Humanism added to the amount, not the depth, of anti-clericalism for it did so from within the church. Valla, Mirandola, Le Fevre, Colet, Reuchlin, von Hutten and Erasmus were merciless in their exposure of hair-splitting scholasticism, monkish practices of celibacy, poverty and obedience, church practices like worship of saints and relics, confession and absolution (on the ground that research did not reveal these practices among the first Christians). Humanists generally favored a return to a simpler form of Christian practice.

What the Humanists favored the Mystics in the Church (Thomas à Kempis, Meister Eckhart, Heinrich Suso, Johann Tauler, and others) practiced. In "imitation of Christ" they rejected mechanical schemes of salvation for more direct and personal ones. By contemplation, prayer and fasting they tried to come into direct communion with God without any intermediary—that is, without the church. These men were placing considerable reliance upon justification by faith alone and not upon St. James's, doctrine of "good works." Emphasis upon man's corruptibility and his need of faith caused a revival of interest in the epistles of St. Paul; Jacques Le Fevre made a translation of them into Latin and John Colet delivered a popular series of lectures upon them. The very bases of church practice were being challenged.

Religion and Nationality. While the Church's power prevailed, criticism had, perforce, to be cautious; why did it suddenly become bold and clamorous? When church critics found secular powers to support them by force of arms, they ceased to be fearful and did not hesitate to draw the conclusions from their criticisms.

Everywhere in Europe, save Germany and Italy, new national states had arisen and were making a strong assertion of secular sovereignty. In France, by the Pragmatic Sanction of Bourges (1438) and the Concordat of Bologna (1516), the kings succeeded in winning for themselves the right to dictate ecclesiastical appointments, jurisdiction and tax levies; by the Statute of Provisors (1351, 1390) and the Statute of Praemunire (1353, 1390), the English kings had made a similar assertion; nor were the Spanish kings far behind the French and English in their demands. These gains against the church stimulated rather than appeased royal appetites. They eyed enviously the vast domains of the church; and they resented the flow out of their countries of vast sums collected by the church in the form of annates, "Peter's Pence," indulgence fees, church court fines, income from vacant benefices, fees for bestowing the pallium upon bishops, etc. They felt that every effort of the church to excommunicate or to interdict was a violation of their sovereignty; they even turned hostile eyes upon the presence in their lands of church courts sharing judicial power with royal courts.

The bourgeoisie (middle class) fully supported the kings, for different reasons. They viewed the vast church holdings as immobilized capital that, if freed, could be used as a base for a great credit expansion; and they bitterly resented being deprived of the fluid capital they had in the form of countless payments to the church. And, since the chief burden of payment fell upon the lowly backs of the peasantry, they, too, echoed the bitter resentment of the kings and the bourgeoisie.

In such an atomosphere, church abuses became the sparks of a revolutionary movement to transform the church. This movement found its voice in Martin Luther whose career is a clear illustration of the causes at work in the Protestant Reformation.

The French Revolution

Revolution is a product of national paralysis. Between 1788 and 1789 the French monarchy entered into a period of crisis, chiefly financial. War, royal extravagance, reckless borrowing, inefficient taxation and the short-sighted inflexibility of the ruling groups had emptied the royal treasury; existing revenues were inadequate to meet obligations of the national debt; existing taxes on the peasantry and bourgeoisie were already crushing.

Potentially prosperous, the French nation was experiencing widespread poverty. Prices had risen because of crop failures; wages lagged far behind prices; business failures were increasing as a result of a British invasion of the French markets; large numbers of wage earners (which included part-time peasant workers) were unemployed. Economists like Turgot, Necker and Calonne, called in to solve the financial crisis did their best to delay collapse by minor economies and major loans. Each realized that France's salvation lay in opening the untaxed wealth of the privileged classes to taxation as the only solution; and for recommending this as national policy, each was dismissed.

At Calonne's suggestion, Louis XVI convened in 1787 an Assembly of Notables. These privileged groups were asked to tax themselves. They refused but did suggest that an Estates General or parliament of the three estates (clergy, nobility and the Third Estate) be called to consider the matter of taxation. The current finance minister, Archbishop de Brienne, coldly dismissed the suggestion of the Notables and undertook to float a new loan.

Popular Reaction. Encouraged by vocal popular support, the *parlement* (court) of Paris (on whose bench sat spokesmen for the bourgeoisie) refused to register de Brienne's new loan, or any loan or tax, unless it was approved by an Estates General. This was subversion and the king moved against the court with troops. But the soldiers refused to arrest the judges and in this act they were supported by menacing mobs in Paris. Uncomprehending and bewildered, Louis was compelled to summon the Estates General. Neither he, nor any Frenchman, foresaw the consequences of this act.

The Estates General. In 1789 the Estates General was only an historical memory since it had not met since 1614. At that time it consisted of three estates—the clergy, the nobility and the Third Estate, each meeting and voting as separate bodies. The least of the three had been the Third Estate. That this was no longer possible was clearly stated in an influential pamphlet written by the Abbé Sieyès. "What is the Third Estate?" asked the Abbé. And he answered: "It is everything. What has it been hitherto in the political order? Nothing! What does it desire? To be something!" Advisers of Louis accepted the truth of the Abbé's formulation and in assigning delegates, the Third Estate was permitted to choose 600 out of a total of 1200.

Elections were held in the early months of 1789 on the basis of almost universal male suffrage. In the course of electoral gathering local communities drew up *cahiers*—lists of grievances which the delegates were instructed to correct. It is interesting to note how un-revolutionary national sentiment was on the eve of the Revolution. The cahiers almost universally proclaimed the delegates loyal to the king and to the idea of hereditary succession. But they did propose hundreds of reforms. In general these reforms centered upon limiting by constitution the powers of the king and the bureaucracy; upon no taxation without representation; upon increased elective local autonomy; upon *universal* taxation; upon humane reformation of the criminal law and its procedures; upon immediate relief of the economic crisis.

Paralysis and Revolution. On May 5th the delegates gathered into a temporary structure called (ironically) the Hall of the (King's) Lesser Pleasures. The first important dispute was on a procedural question: How should the delegates vote? The first two estates insisted on each estate casting a single vote, as in the traditional manner. Realizing that this would place them at the mercy of the privileged groups, the Third Estate insisted on voting by head (one delegate—one vote) in a single body. Third Estate strategy rested on the knowledge that some nobility and many parish priests would vote with the Third Estate to give it a majority.

The result was a temporary paralysis; the first two estates met as separate orders and organized for action; the Third Estate refused to organize until its demands for meeting as a single body were met. The impasse lasted for five weeks. Then, on June 12, the Third Estate organized itself and invited the others to join it. To distinguish itself from the others, the Third Estate, on June 17, assumed the title of **National Assembly** and declared that it had sovereign power to act for the nation. The king's government was set aside. The Revolution had begun.

The National Assembly. On the same day (June 17) the National Assembly began quietly but ominously to reform the state of France. All of the royal taxes were abolished; committees were created to draw up a reformed financial structure and to take steps to relieve the distress among the poor. Louis had not yet acted. On the 20th of June Louis suspended the sessions of the Estates General. The Third Estate, in the form of the National Assembly, withdrew to a neighboring tennis court and there took an oath (The "Tennis Court Oath") not to disband until France had a constitution. This was done with great confidence because by this time many of the parish priests and nobility had joined the National Assembly.

On the 27th of June, Louis seemed to capitulate to the National Assembly by ordering the first two estates to sit with it; he began, however, to gather mercenary troops and to station them in Paris for a showdown. With each new detachment of troops, popular indignation and violence grew. It came to a head when, on July 14, the populace stormed and took the Bastille. Violence now rolled out of Paris into the countryside as enraged peasantry attacked the chateaux of the landed nobility. By the late summer of 1789, France was in the hands of the people; the authority of the crown had vanished. All eyes were turned to the National Assembly which in August had begun to reform France.

The Reforms of the National Assembly. Abolition of feudal privileges. In abolishing the survivals of the feudal past, the nobility in the National Assembly itself took the leadership. One after another the nobles rose to propose destruction of such privileges as exemption from taxation, collection of feudal taxes, monopoly rights, distinctions of rank, vested interests, hunting and fishing rights and the like.

The Declaration of the Rights of Man. Taking its lead from the example of the American Revolution, the French Revolutionists turned to a statement of general principles as a guide to further and more permanent reform. They drew up a **Declaration of the Rights of Man and of the Citizen.**

Three pillars of freedom were erected in the ideological structure. One was **property rights**: men were to be protected in their right to private ownership of property; no one could be deprived of property except in case of public necessity; anyone deprived of property had a basic right to compensation. A second was **personal rights**: these included the basic freedoms; religious toleration; equality before the law; due process of law . . . and the like. A third was **democracy**: sovereignty resided with the people; only the people could delegate sovereignty to government; and the people reserved the right of revolution against tyranny.

Secularization of the church. Church lands were confiscated and were sold in parcels to impoverished peasantry and were also used as backing for a new currency issued to meet the financial crisis. A Civil Constitution of the Clergy was then drawn up which made the priesthood elective civil servants of the state. All clergy were forced to take an oath of allegiance to the state to qualify for the priesthood. The Pope, of course, condemned this feature and prohibited oath-taking. The result was that the French clergy were divided into those who did (juring) and those who did not (nonjuring) take the oath.

The Constitution of 1791. To complete their essentially conservative revolution, the French Revolutionists drew up a constitution for France which established a limited monarchy on the principle of the separation of powers. A Legislative Assembly was created with full power to make the law; it was to be indirectly elected by electoral colleges. The executive power was given to the king. As a check upon absolutism the king was shorn of control of the army, church and local government and was removed from the legislative process by being given a veto that could be overridden by the Legislative Assembly.

The Radical Phase. By 1791 the conservative phase of the Revolution was complete. Events soon propelled the Revolution into a more radical phase. To begin with, the economic demands of the impoverished wage-earners were not met; if anything, the situation grew worse due to a currency inflation. Restless, hungry workers had become organized mobs directed by leaders of radical clubs which had begun to flourish in Paris. These clubs reflected the political spectrum which early made its appearance in the National Assembly. Conservatives, those who favored a status quo, concentrated in the **Girondist Party**; Radicals, those who favored complete abolition of the monarchy and a sharp limitation on the rights of the bourgeoisie as well as the clergy and nobility, gravitated to the **Jacobin Party.**

Emigres—those who managed to flee from France to the more hospitable lands of Prussia and Austria and England—had created enough anxiety there to cause the monarchs of these countries to issue an ultimatum to the French Revolutionists to desist in their persecution of church and nobility. National irritation with this unwarranted interference resulted in a declaration of war by the Legislative Assembly on Prussia and Austria. Invasion of France by these two nations created a national emergency. National mobilization of a citizen army to meet the threat of foreign invasion followed. The king and queen actively cooperated with the emigres abroad and, on one occasion, even attempted escape. To the Radicals in France, it seemed that the very Revolution was at stake. In 1792 they moved to take over the government.

THE RADICAL PHASE OF THE FRENCH REVOLUTION

Terror. The radical phase of the French Revolution was distinguished by increased use of terrorization as political policy. "Madame Guillotine" became the symbol of this period. Under the loose designation of "enemies of the people" thousands of people were slaughtered. Some were, of course, guilty of treasonable activity, of conspiracy with the emigres abroad and the instigators of civil war at home; some were guilty of no more than association by birth with suspected elements in the population; others were victims of spite, revenge, rivalry and the like. Terror, like power, corrupts; and corruption was no more evident than in the popular jubilation which attended the ceremonies of execution.

Those who used terror were themselves victimized by it. In January 1793 Louis XVI and Marie Antoinette were executed. Only the Girondists opposed this decision. DANTON and ST. JUST, by brilliant oratory, turned the National Convention to this decision. It was not long before the Girondists were made the victims of the terror by the Jacobins led by Danton, ROBESPIERRE and others. This done, it was Danton's turn and he was executed because he felt that it was time to call halt to the terror. Under Robespierre, the guillotine was employed with increasing frequency. But in 1794 he too lost his head though he was almost dead of bullet wounds.

Dictatorship. In September 1792 the monarchy was deposed and the First French Republic declared. An election was then held for a National Convention to frame a new constitution. In 1793 the constitution was published. It was democratic to the core and provided for universal male suffrage, an elected legislature, an executive elected by the legislature, annual elections and the like. But it was not put into effect.

Arguing that the national situation of civil war, foreign war and economic depression was too dire to permit the processes of democracy, the Jacobins set aside the constitution and created instead a dictatorial Committee of Public Safety composed of nine members. This Committee assumed all the powers of government; it sent its agents abroad to check on the loyalty of Frenchmen and to negotiate with foreign governments; it created revolutionary tribunals with virtually unlimited power to try and execute "enemies of the people"; it raised armies and fought the foreign enemies; it nationalized economic enterprise much more effectively than the absolute monarchs of France. For two years there was little but the outer trappings to distinguish Robespierre from Louis XVI.

The fall of Robespierre brought a reaction to terror and dictatorship (the **Thermidorean Reaction**). A new constitution was written in 1795 which returned France to a moderate course. Power was divided between a bicameral legislature and a Directory or executive of five members. Voting was restricted to property owners; age-limits for holding office were raised; two-thirds of the membership of a new legislature had to be chosen from the old. Terror had made men suspicious of democracy.

Reforms. Under the dictatorship some permanent reforms were effected. Price controls stopped the inflation; the metric system was adopted; a commission to revise the law code of France began its work by providing for prison reforms, abolition of imprisonment for debts, abolition of slavery in the colonies; public education was expanded with the creation of Normal schools and Polytechnical institutes; a national library was set up; confiscated land was sold to peasants and made France into a nation of small farmers. Above all, the civil war was suppressed and foreign enemies were forced into signing the peace treaties of 1795 which declared an end to foreign efforts to suppress the French Revolution and French efforts to spread it abroad. These accomplishments left permanent effects.

Not so were the efforts of the radical Jacobins to abolish *Monsieur* and *Madame* in favor of *Citizen;* to introduce a new calendar with 1792 as the Year I and with the months renamed to celebrate nature and her wonders; to institute and enforce the worship of the goddess Reason; to inaugurate an official Reign of Virtue and the like.

NAPOLEON BONAPARTE

The Directory ruled France for four years (1795–1799) and then succumbed to a bloodless *coup d'état* unleashed by NAPOLEON BONAPARTE who then ruled France until 1815.

In those five years the Directory so alienated the affections of the French people that they accepted Napoleon as their savior. The Directory was unable to cope with renewed inflation; when it issued a new currency, it could not force popular acceptance of it. Nor could it cope with increasing pressure by the clergy, widely supported by the people, for some restoration of their property and rights. Unbelievable corruption characterized the Directors, each of whom ruled for a price. Peace had been concluded with Prussia, Holland and Spain; but negotiations with England and Austria had fallen through because the Directory insisted upon an extension of France's boundaries to the Rhine.

On October 5, 1795 a Paris mob attacked the Directory and only the quick and ruthless wit of an artillery officer named Napoleon Bonaparte, a Corsican, saved it. On this "whiff of grapeshot" Napoleon marched into history as the prototype of the modern dictator.

What Makes A Dictator? No man in history has been more analyzed than Napoleon, who rose from complete obscurity to become European conqueror. A boundless ambition seems a first requirement. Napoleon had this in abundance.

Recognition of opportunity or rank opportunism coupled with unscrupulous and amoral actions speeded him. He did not hesitate to use artillery against an unarmed crowd, or to enter into a loveless marriage for advancement or to cajole the support of any group that could be useful to him. He permitted himself loyalty to no man; he was his own cause; and this limitless egotism seems a requisite for the temperament of a dictator. Ability, too, is needed; genius is preferable. Napoleon had both military and administrative genius.

The Rise To Power. Having saved the Republic and won the hand of Josephine Beauharnais who had great influence in the Directory, Napoleon in 1796 secured command of the Army of Italy; his instructions were to use his ragged force of 30,000 men to divert the Austrians from the south while the main thrust was made in the North. Napoleon turned this diversionary movement into a major thrust and virtually marched north on Vienna. The Austrians were forced to sue for peace. Acting on the principle that what is done can often not be undone, Napoleon, *without consent of the Directory,* negotiated the Treaty of Campo Formio which forced Austria to recognize French claims to the Rhine, to release her Italian possessions and to surrender Lombardy and Belgium to the French.

This done, Napoleon proceeded with political reorganization of the Italian states into the Cisalpine and Ligurian Republics. He announced himself as the liberator of Italy, the son of the French Revolution and imposed "liberty and equality" on the occupied lands. Beneath this role of liberator lay the more obvious role of terrorist; opposition to French booty-taking was punished with shocking brutality. Napoleon returned to Paris as a conquering hero. What could the Directory do? The army worshipped their commander.

The Egyptian Maneuver. It was clear to Napoleon that the Directory could not long survive. He, Napoleon, must not lend his strength to support their weakness. With keen political astuteness Napoleon therefore proposed that he undertake an Egyptian Campaign as a first step to deprive England of her life-line to Italy. Anxious to get rid of this rising menace, the Directory gave its ungrudging consent to the campaign. In July of 1798 Napoleon evaded the watchful British navy led by Admiral Nelson and landed in Egypt. In the Battle of the Nile, Nelson destroyed Napoleon's fleet and trapped him inside Egypt. Though Egypt fell an easy prey, Napoleon was unable to remove his army from Egypt. He therefore deserted it when news came that France was his for the taking.

A new coalition of powers (England, Russia, Austria, Portugal, Turkey and Naples) had been formed for an attack on France; along the Rhine and in the Italies the French armies were steadily being pushed back. Leaving his scruples in Egypt to follow his star, Napoleon barely evaded Nelson's fleet and returned to Paris as the conqueror of Egypt, as another Caesar. A conspiracy to overthrow the Directory was effected with the aid of three directors and the upper house of the legislature. On November 9, 1799 Napoleon's armed force took possession of the state.

Dictators prefer to act constitutionally. Having seized power, Napoleon wrote a new constitution establishing an elected **Consulate** with himself as First Consul. He created a legislative apparatus but made it impotent. By 1802, Napoleon was ready to throw off the disguise of democracy. He was elected consul for life. Two years later he became Emperor of the French with rights to hereditary succession.

Wherever possible he remained close to popular acceptance. After each coup he submitted the accomplished fact to a popular vote. Since these votes were conducted without free discussion, with no possible alternatives and under army rule, they were overwhelmingly for each of Napoleon's acts. (There is little doubt, on the other hand, that as long as he was successful, Napoleon did command the loyalty of the French people.)

Conqueror. In 1810 Napoleon ruled France, the eastern half of Italy, Belgium, Holland, the Rhineland—directly; indirectly he controlled the vast Confederation of the Rhine (the Germanies), the Grand Duchy of Warsaw (Poland), the Kingdom of Italy, the Kingdom of Naples, Switzerland and the Kingdom of Spain. Within the French orbits lay Denmark and Norway, Prussia and Austria. This overlordship was achieved by conquest in war.

Napoleon's victories at Ulm, Austerlitz, Jena, Friedland are classics of military strategy and are still studied in military academies. His military principles included: simplicity, rapidity, superiority of forces in localized areas, concentration, quick decision on the spot, meticulous study of positions and alternatives, keen perception of the psychology of the opponent, judicious use of all information, material and moral, attention to the most insignificant of details, obedient officers who took no initiative, rigid discipline and self-confidence. Yet, within five years of his position in 1810, his armies were defeated and his kingdom gone. What brought this conqueror so low?

Decline and Fall. Many factors served to bring about the collapse of Napoleon. None was more important than England's dogged resistance and her command of the seas and her ability to inspire and to supply opposition to Napoleon. England's chief weapon was her shops and her chief warrior shopkeepers who produced manufactured goods that were far more durable and cheap than any produced on the continent.

Napoleon hoped to choke off all British trade with the continent. By a series of decrees he placed a paper blockade around Europe and around England; no English ship could deliver goods to Europe; and no non-English ship could deliver goods to England. England retorted with her own blockade on French ships and on foreign ships trading with the French. Europeans felt severely the prohibition on entry into Europe of British goods and evaded Napoleon's **Continental System** by widespread smuggling.

It was the Continental System that led to Napoleon's disastrous Spanish campaign and march into Russia. In Spain Napoleon had to fight a species of guerilla warfare that drained men and supplies and could not be brought to a decision. In Russia he encountered similar warfare accompanied by a "scorched earth" policy and then by bitter winter fighting for which the French were unprepared. Half-a-million men were lost in the **Russian Campaign of 1812.** Moreover, willingness to fight the French resulted from the insurgence of nationalism that arose out of disillusionment with Napoleon's promises of liberation and out of national humiliation resulting from constant defeat at Napoleon's hands. Freedom proved a double-edged sword for the conqueror.

So, too, did Napoleon's efforts to unify such countries as Italy, Germany and Poland. Napoleon's aim was efficiency in French domination. But having tasted the sweets of unification, these countries now demanded the fruits—independence from French domination.

Finally, continual war exhausted the French materially and spiritually. Only a few Frenchmen reaped the benefits of war profits; on most fell the burdens of French taxation and the loss and mutilation of their loved ones. All of these factors collected at Leipzig in 1814 and in the **Battle of Nations** Napoleon suffered total defeat. He was sent to **Elbe** in exile but escaped and for "100 Days" gave Europe a fright until in 1815 he was finally destroyed at **Waterloo.** Once more he was sent into exile on the island of **St. Helena** in the mid-Atlantic. There he "ruled" until he died on May 5, 1821.

The Industrial Revolution

The Industrial Revolution spread out of England slowly; in 1850 the primary productive pattern in the western world was still agriculture and it was not until 1870 that manufacturing began to overtake agriculture.

There are many explanations for this slow progress. Europe, for example, spent the first quarter of the 19th century recovering from the Napoleonic Wars. Many of the countries lacked some one or more of the basic factors required for industrial progress. Social or cultural lag existed in mental outlook and educational system. In the United States wide stretches of free or almost free land acted as a deterrent and prevented large capital accumulation. England's initial superiority gave her a competitive advantage that handicapped other nations. In spite of these many handicaps, however, the Industrial Revolution spread into Europe, particularly into France, Belgium and Germany; Italy and Russia lagged until the very end of the 19th century.

Stages In The Industrial Revolution. Primary concentration in the first stage (ca. 1750–1850) was upon elaboration of the productive process: discovery of required raw materials, refinement of processes in the extraction of raw materials, extensions of the uses of the steam engine, construction of factories and the development in workers of factory discipline, laying the groundwork for an improved system of transportation and solving the problem of maximizing profits (capital accumulation).

In the second stage of the Industrial Revolution (1850–1900) productive inventiveness continued at a rapid pace; but the other factors of labor, distribution and exchange became the center of concentration. To reduce labor costs and the growing "threat" of labor organization, manufacturers began to invest in machines that would break down production into minute processes and destroy the basis of skilled labor. Symbolic of this trend was the work of the American, FREDERICK WINSLOW TAYLOR (1856–1915), in the field of scientific management. Taylor began experimental studies ("time-and-motion" studies) to set standards of efficient working performance. During this period the corporative form of business organization was elaborated as was the relation of business to banking.

In the field of invention a revolution was effected in transportation and communication. By 1850 the railroad had proved its effectiveness and a rush was begun in all countries to lay track. Problems involved in railroad transport were soon overcome by invention of high powered locomotives, air brakes, standard gauges, signal systems, refrigeration cars, sleepers and the like. Steamboating kept pace with railroading.

More and more industrialism, in this period, began to rely upon pure science. This was nowhere more true than in the field of communications. Out of the work of such men as Franklin, Galvani, Volta, Ampere, Ohm, Maxwell and Faraday came the possibility of communication by electrical impulses. An electric telegraph was invented independently by Carl Steinheil, a German, Charles Wheatstone, an Englishman, and Samuel Morse an American. The telegraph, however, was landbound until Cyrus W. Field solved the oceanographic problems required to lay a trans-Atlantic cable; this was accomplished in 1866.

Important advances were registered, too, in the field of lighting. The kerosene lamp was perfected in 1784. More useful, however, was the gaslighting device perfected by Murdock, Bunsen and Welsbach in the mid-nineteenth century. Toward the end of this period, electric lighting made its appearance as a result of the researches of Davy, Marks, Edison and many others.

The third stage of the Industrial Revolution had little unity—expansion occurred in every imaginable direction. Invention itself was systematized and accelerated through creation of subsidized laboratories. Of special note was the rise of the chemist as an adjunct to industry. Upon him fell the responsibility of discovering new uses for old resources and the manufacture of synthetic resources as substitutes for natural products.

Out of the invention of the internal combustion engine and the electric motor whole new worlds appeared: the automobile industry, the industries of radio and television, great hydroelectric plants, the airplane industry and the like. Of equal importance was the development of the precision instrument—a development that gave to the physicist the same status as the chemist in the industrial world. The engineer, of course, became a key figure as the demand for roads, bridges, communications, building structures, electrical appliances and the like rose.

Mass production became a startling reality when the factory was rationalized through use of assembly lines and standardized parts. Of primary importance was the distribution of this mass production. Problems of transport were solved through further developments of railroad and steamship and the introduction of trucks and airplanes. But the sale of goods required the transformation of advertising into a national industry. This in turn put pressure on the creation of mass media of communication. The linotype machine, typewriter, and rotary press accommodated this need; radio and television enhanced it. Along with the revolution in advertisement of products, came a revolution in the financing of the purchase of goods—installment buying. With exhaustion of resources at home began a worldwide search for raw materials such as rubber, tin, nitrates, manganese, magnesium, chromium, nickel, lead, copper, hardwoods, etc.

With the discovery of thermonuclear power a new and fourth stage in the Industrial Revolution loomed. This stage brought the physicist to the fore. It is too early to project the transformations that will be made as a result of this discovery of a new power-source. The peaceful uses of atomic energy have been probed—chiefly in the areas of medical research, agricultural production, new sources of power and the like. The world is waiting for a new dawn.

RESULTS OF THE INDUSTRIAL REVOLUTION

General. In essence, the Industrial Revolution was a transfer from hand tool to machine process; from muscle-wind-and-water power to steam-gas-electricity-and-atomic power. Manufacturing became a way of life emphasizing compulsory centralization of the labor force around the machine, complete dependence of the labor force upon the machine for a livelihood, impersonalization of the relations between worker and employer and regimentation of the life of the worker to the demands of production. From the factory flowed ever-increasing production and this was reflected in expanding commerce, accumulated capital, national and international corporations, business combinations in the forms of merger, trust, holding company, interlocking directorates, cartels and the like. Increased standards of living resulted and this was followed by rapid increases of population for the most part gathered into urban areas where cultural life blossomed on the nurture provided by increased educational facilities. But culture, too, followed the pattern of standardization; mass media threatened to produce mass minds, mass behavior.

Machine Culture. Mankind came to depend upon invention for innovation; progress was equated with multiplication of gadgets. There was no limit to inventiveness. In the wake of the mechanization of society came many problems affecting human welfare: overcrowded cities, indebtedness, increasing destructiveness of wars, labor-management conflict, and the like.

The Workingman. The brunt of the inhumanity in the machine civilization fell upon the workingman. Skilled workers of the late 18th and early 19th centuries resented and resisted the introduction of the factory system; they became, in fact, "machine-wreckers." Factory processes reduced the workingman to a mechanical unit engaged in some small specialized task that produced fatigue and boredom.

Moreover, in the early period of capital accumulation working conditions were abominable. Factories were hastily and cheaply built; no provisions were made for the health or safety of the employees in matters of ventilation, lighting or provisions for creature comforts. Child labor was brutally exploited in the form of pauper apprentices. Hours of work ranged between 14 and 16 a day. Wages were miserably low.

From impoverished conditions in the factory, workers moved to even worse conditions at home. Slums made up the bulk of dwelling quarters in factory towns. Crime and epidemic disease were the consequences of these miserable hovels in which workers dwelt. Added to these inadequate conditions of work was the continuous insecurity that hung over the heads of the working people. They were completely unprotected in the face of unemployment produced by technological change or depressions, of illness and accident for which there was no compensation, and of old age—a variable figure depending on the supply of workers available. This, then, was the social lag behind industrial progress.

Overcoming The Social Lag. To overcome the social lag to industrial progress, a humanitarian revolution in the minds of the rulers of mankind had to be effected. Horrible conditions had first to be seen as horrible, and felt as such. This required intensive education through propaganda and agitation, a campaign that was launched by workers' organizations, philosophers like Jeremy Bentham and William Godwin, poets like Shelley and Thomas Hood, novelists like Charles Dickens and George Eliot and politicians like Benjamin Disraeli, William Gladstone, Otto von Bismarck, Andrew Jackson. These men helped to transform the problem of working conditions into a *moral* question.

The result of all this agitation and propaganda was a series of social laws passed by interested governments which set out to reform the conditions under which men labored in factories and mines. In England, for example, between 1802 and 1860, a large number of factory acts were passed. These had the effect of reducing by law the number of hours of work, of discouraging the employment of child labor, of limiting the employment of women, of compelling the introduction of health, sanitation and safety devices in factories. Later legislation in England (1870–1920) freed workers to organize into labor unions and to strike for increased wages and improved working conditions.

Germany, under OTTO VON BISMARCK, took the leadership in framing the first social security laws, laws providing for workman's compensation in the event of accident on the job, for old age pensions, for sickness and unemployment insurance. These laws were eventually introduced into all the industrialized nations of the world.

The Capitalist System. Capitalism came to full growth under the impetus of the Industrial Revolution. It was the primary agency in the transformation of society from a low-producing to a high-producing level. In the course of its development, capitalism moved through several stages. The earliest was the stage of industrial capitalism—where individual capitalists owned the factories as single proprietorships or as partnerships. To a great extent these capitalists relied upon their own resources for expansion. As business grew, however, the single proprietorship and partnership proved to be inadequate as financial vehicles. The result was that capitalists began to depend more and more on the corporation—and the sale of stocks and bonds—as a means for gathering in wealth. Increasingly, in this second stage of capitalist development, industrialists began to turn to the banks for loans for expansion.

This led to the third stage, that of finance capitalism. In this stage industrial and banking elements in the economic process merged to provide industry with a virtually unlimited capital expansion base. In this area, as in the area of mechanization, a social lag appeared.

Ownership and management were divorced, a divorce that produced the possibilities of mismanagement. Mismanagement resulted in practices which strangled free competition by monopolization; which defrauded stockholders through issuance of "watered" stock, or failure to declare dividends; which practiced fraud on consumers through price fixing, adulteration of product and the like; which encouraged corrupt political practices like bribery of legislators. The social lag was somewhat remedied in most countries by government intervention that resulted in anti-trust laws, laws regulating the issuance of corporate securities, pure food and drug laws, income and corporate tax laws and the like.

Abandonment of Laissez Faire. Government intervention in the economic process is the antithesis of laissez faire, the system of ideas under which capitalism grew to maturity. As taught by Adam Smith in his *Wealth of Nations*, the doctrine of laissez faire assumed that there were rational, natural laws that governed economic behavior. Men left alone to pursue selfish ends in the use of their capital and labor would ultimately produce social good. The laws of free trade and of competition, of supply and demand, would determine success and failure in the economic struggle for existence; but the end result would be an increase in the total national wealth.

Smith founded the school of liberal or **classical economists,** members of which searched for "natural laws" in the economy of capitalism. Thus THOMAS MALTHUS proposed an "iron law" of population and demonstrated that famine, war, disease and population control are advantageous since population increases geometrically while food supply increases arithmetically. DAVID RICARDO "proved" that wages sink to the mere level of subsistence. Nassau Senior "demonstrated" that hours of work could not be lowered without disastrous consequences to profits. McCulloch "proved" on the basis of and existing "wages-fund" that wage increase to one group had to result in wage decrease for another.

All of this theorizing resulted in a pattern of beliefs that called for abolition of tariffs and subsidies, free contracting, treatment of labor organization as conspiracy, free competition, and no government restraint upon economic free choice. Between 1800 and 1860 the English government, for example, followed this doctrine to the letter. The "corn laws (tariffs)" were repealed, mercantilist regulations concerning the granting of monopolies were removed from the legislative books, laws protecting apprentices were abrogated. We have seen the abuses that followed upon this adoption of the complete policy of laissez faire. (There is little doubt that if we ignore humanitarian considerations, laissez faire did accomplish miracles in production at a time when the resources for such productive effort were limited.)

No country followed England in its application of the policy of laissez faire. From their inception, the classical economists were challenged on theoretical lines. From America and Germany came economic doctrines defending protectionism as a means for hastening industrial advance. Population theorists challenged Malthus when it became obvious that the industrial revolution would extend to the farm and result in fabulous increases in food production. The most serious challenge, however, came from the "socialists" who took the abuses of the capitalist as their starting point and ignored the many efforts being made by governments to correct these abuses.

Socialism. Socialism was as much an *ethical* as an economic discipline; its theories were in part formed out of a preconceived utopian dream in which all men were economically equal and lived in the midst of abundance.

Early socialists like SAINT-SIMON (1760–1825), FOURIER (1772–1837) and ROBERT OWEN (1772–1858) were labelled "Utopians" by later socialists like KARL MARX (1818–1883). This derogatory label was not directed against the ultimate plans of the Utopians, for these plans envisaged the abolition of the capitalist class and the substitution of some form of workingclass ownership and control of the means of production (as socialism is defined). Derogation was directed against the means by which these theoreticians proposed to eliminate the capitalist class.

Saint-Simon hoped to bring socialism by the arts of persuasion and appeal to Christian doctrine; Fourier proposed that workers and others form voluntary socialist societies which he called "phalanxes" where all would work for all; Owen hoped to convince capitalists by his own example to build model socialist communities with their capital. (Fourierism caught on somewhat in the United States in the 1830's and '40's where experiments like Brook Farm and Oneida were tried and failed. Owen went bankrupt after his ventures in capitalist socialism at New Harmony, Indiana.) LOUIS BLANC (1813–1882)—an influential figure in the Revolution of 1848 in France—advanced the concept of government financed socialist communities, a scheme for turning over factories to workers and financing them until they were able to stand on their own feet. In practice this system turned out to be a huge financial dole that almost bankrupted the government.

Karl Marx (author of *Capital* and co-author with Frederick Engels of *Communist Manifesto*) condemned all of these efforts and proposed instead his own brand of "scientific" socialism. He advocated both peaceful and violent waging of a "class war" to overthrow capitalism. His followers, who believed in peaceful "class war" became latter-day socialists; those who favored force and violence to establish a "dictatorship of the proletariat" became communists. Marxism, then, was both a theory about capitalist society and a blueprint for its replacement.

Imperialism and World War I

IMPERIALISM

About 1875 territorial aggrandizement became the dominant drive of the large European powers, and of the United States of America. No one cause can account for this phenomenon. The Industrial Revolution was certainly a most important factor. As industry expanded so did the need for raw materials, many of them unavailable in the industrialized lands. This caused a search for basic materials, particularly for such materials as rubber, tin, petroleum, tungsten, etc.

As mass production mounted, nations began to seek potential "outlets" for surplus goods; colonies could be excellent dumping grounds for these goods and in many cases imperialized markets were the "margin of profit" for manufacturers. Similarly with surplus capital that now began to accumulate. Investments at home rarely brought the rate of return that could be gained by investment in colonial areas where labor was cheap and monopoly assured by government fiat.

Accompanying these economic motives for imperialism were equally strong political, social, psychological and religious ones. Nationalism virtually dictated that each nation should seek some "place in the sun"; national pride was fostered by each new splatter of color on the map that showed national expansion; national propaganda led to widespread belief that each nation was engaged in a civilizing mission. Very popular, though little founded in fact, was the prevailing argument that all nations, riding the crest of tremendous population increases, needed outlets for "surplus" population. Enough people did emigrate to the colonies to make this fiction seem a fact. Also there was the revival in this period of missionary activities that opened wide new worlds to the West.

Finally, imperialist expansion was strongly advocated by military leaders in all nations as the best means for securing naval bases and an adequate supply of strategic raw materials. To the support of these military men came the geographers who developed anew the doctrines of geopolitics, the science of national security that determined what heartland and fringelands were vital to "defense"—even though they were inhabited by other peoples. Geopolitics became power-politics, politics supported by military force. In reality, it was a "scientific" rationale for world conquest or domination.

Methods and Forms of Imperialism. International trade, investments and loans are not imperialistic but are part of a normal process of international intercourse. They become imperialistic when they are used as excuses for territorial conquest or for establishing exclusive economic control. During the late nineteenth century it often happened that rulers of undeveloped areas borrowed heavily from the investment bankers of the west. In exchange for such loans favored concessions were made to European investors. If such rulers defaulted on their debts or were unable to protect the investments in railroads, mines, etc., it often happened that the rulers of the powerful investor nations sent troops into that area to "protect" the lives and property of their nationals. It was at this point that imperialism began. Under foreign control these areas lost their political freedom and the right to exploit their own national wealth.

Out of this pattern emerged four forms of imperialist control: the **colony** or direct political control where the powerful nation openly ruled the undeveloped area as a possession; the **protectorate** or indirect political control where the powerful nation ruled the undeveloped area through a native puppet; the **concession** or exclusive direct control over some particular resource; and the **sphere of influence** or indirect economic control over the whole of the undeveloped area. These basic forms intermingled freely. The imperialist test for any of them was the degree of freedom retained by the undeveloped area.

THE FIRST WORLD WAR

The basic causes of the first World War were the rival imperialist ambitions among the western powers, their excessive nationalistic pride, the armaments race that developed in the face of political and economic rivalry, the struggle of suppressed peoples for independence, the geopolitical drive to reach "natural boundaries" and the absence in the world of any effective world organization that might have prevented war through peaceful settlement of disputes. These fundamental causes worked themselves out in a series of international events the primary effect of which was to create two great systems of alliances that opposed each other in a menacing **balance of power.**

The Triple Alliance vs. The Triple Entente. The **Triple Alliance** of Germany, Austria-Hungary and Italy (and allied satellites) was born from Bismarck's desire to isolate France so that she could never wage a war of revenge against Germany after her ignominious defeat in the Franco-Prussian War. By promise and perfidy Bismarck secured a secret defensive alliance with Austria-Hungary, a "gentleman's agreement" with Russia, an alliance with Italy directed against France, English neutrality, Serbian and Rumanian allegiance, and Turkish friendship.

To each of these nations Germany promised diplomatic support for nationalist aspiration—no matter how contradictory these promises were. Thus Russia and Austria-Hungary were bitter rivals in the Balkans as were Serbia and Austria-Hungary; Italy had many grievances against Austria-Hungary with respect to *Italia Irridenta;* Rumania and Turkey could not be friends. Yet Bismarck accomplished the impossible as long as Germany pursued a non-imperialist policy of its own. When William II overrode Bismarck and began an aggressive policy of imperialism, economic rivalry and arms supremacy, the grand alliance fell apart. Out of its pieces was born the **Triple Entente.**

Russia was the first to leave and to join France in a Dual Alliance in 1894. When Germany rejected Russia's request for large modernization loans, France granted them in exchange for a military convention that amounted to a defensive alliance. (This agreement, incidentally, was as much directed against England as against Germany, for England was threatening France in the Sudan and Russia in Persia and the Far East.)

By 1900 a number of factors compelled England to reconsider her policy of "splendid isolation" from continental affairs. Germany had begun to construct a formidable navy and to challenge England's markets in all parts of the world. She was the chief obstacle to the union of British territories in east Africa. Now she proposed to construct a Berlin to Baghdad Railroad through Turkey which would possibly destroy England's trade advantage in the Near East and India. The result was the **Entente Cordiale** with France (1904), a settlement of all territorial differences and an implied defensive alliance. Russian-English differences over Persia and the Far East were finally settled in an entente that settled differences in Persia and Afghanistan by division of those territories. By 1907 the Triple Entente was complete and faced the Triple Alliance in a delicate balance of power.

International Crises. War approached by a series of international crises in North Africa and the Balkans. In 1905 France began a series of familiar maneuvers westward from Algeria into Morocco, an area that Germany had selected as her own hunting grounds. The Kaiser promised the Moroccan ruler support if he resisted French overtures and then went on to demand that the "Moroccan Question" be submitted to an international conference. Such a conference was held in 1906 at Algeciras and Germany forced through a policy of the "open door" in Morocco to France's chagrin.

In 1911 an uprising in Morocco gave the French an excuse to move in with troops. The Germans sent the "Panther," a gunboat, to challenge French occupation. War hung in the balance. At that moment English warships began to maneuver around the "Panther," and Germany decided that the time was not ripe for a challenge. In exchange for a part of the French Congo Germany gave France a "free hand" in Morocco.

Attention was now focused on the Balkans. In 1908 a group of humiliated **Young Turks,** resentful of the slow disintegration of the Turkish Empire, undertook a revolution. Austria-Hungary took advantage of this situation to annex Balkan territory. Russia, fearful of Austro-Hungarian moves, had secured a promise from her that she would support Russian moves in the Dardenelles area in exchange for Russian support for Balkan seizures by Austria-Hungary. This was the infamous "Buchlau Bargain."

Austria-Hungary violated the bargain by annexing Bosnia and Herzegovina without support for Russia's territorial ambitions. Russia was infuriated and resolved to make war on the first occasion that presented itself. She began to provoke Serbia into anti-Austrian activities. At the same time Russia continued maneuvering against Turkey by organizing a Balkan League (Montenegro, Serbia, Bulgaria and Greece) for an assault on Turkey. This assault came in 1912 and 1913 in two Balkan Wars. Once again Austria frustrated Russian ambitions by creating the buffer state of Albania. Europe became a "powder magazine."

The spark that blew it up occurred in Sarajevo, Bosnia when the Austrian Archduke Ferdinand was assassinated by a member of a secret society for the creation of a greater Serbia. Austria delivered an ultimatum to Serbia to stop all anti-Austrian propaganda, to suppress all anti-Austrian publications, to dismiss Serbian officials implicated in the assassination plot, to permit Austrian police forces to enforce the ultimatum. Serbia temporized and on July 28, 1914 Austria declared war on Serbia. On July 30 Russia mobilized. On July 31 Germany warned Russia to cease mobilizing; Russia refused. On August 1 Germany declared war on Russia and sent an ultimatum to France to remain neutral. France temporized. On August 3 Germany declared war on France and began to pass through Belgium whose neutrality had been guaranteed by all the European powers. On August 4, when Germany refused to respect Belgian neutrality, England declared war. The holocaust was on. Who was responsible?

The Military Phase. From 1914 to 1918 the greatest war in history to that date was fought. Before it was over, thirty nations had become participants, 65,000,000 men bore arms, 8,500,000 soldiers were killed, 29,000,000 were wounded, an inestimable number of civilians were destroyed and some $200,000,000,000 had been expended.

After initial German successes, the war settled down to a stalemate fought in "no-man's lands" from fixed trenches along the western front. Following an initial push to Paris, the Germans were stopped at the Marne; thereafter they were held in spite of such mighty pushes as the one at Verdun.

Allied counter-attacks came similarly to grief. Efforts of the Allies to take Turkey in the Gallipoli campaign were repulsed. The Austrians were checked in the Balkans. Italy deserted the Triple Alliance for the Allied cause but proved more of a handicap than an aid particularly following her defeat at Caporetto. In only one direction did the war move to a completion, that of Germany's assault on Russia. Then came the Russian revolution, and the Bolsheviks, who seized power from the democratic liberals in November of 1917, decided to seek peace. In 1918 they signed the **Treaty of Brest-Litovsk** which ceded Poland, Lithuania, Courland, Bessarabia, the Caucasus, Finland, Estonia, Latvia and the Ukraine to the Central Powers.

Germany did not win the war chiefly as a result of the entry of the United States in 1917. Provoked by unrestricted submarine warfare, sabotage, plots with Mexico and German sabre rattling, and led by economic stakes in the Allied cause and effective Allied propaganda in the United States, America declared war on April 6, 1917, resolved to make the world safe for democracy and to fight a war to end all wars. So did Woodrow Wilson frame the goals of the Allied cause. Entry of men and material from America in 1918 gave the Allied powers the strength to mount a final offensive in 1918, one that broke through German lines and forced the Germans to sue for peace on November 11, 1918.

The Versailles Treaty. Vision and reality met in battle on January 18, 1919 when the victorious powers met to determine the fate of their conquered enemies. The vision was in the person of Woodrow Wilson, President of the United States, who had boldly announced in January 1918 his **Fourteen Points** for an enduring peace. Wilson foresaw a post-war world where secret diplomacy would be outlawed; where the seas would be free; where all economic barriers to international trade would be removed; where armaments races would end; where imperialism would be eliminated on moral grounds; where national aspirations would be respected; where closed waters, such as the Dardenelles, would be forever open; and where a league of nations would be established to settle once for all all international disputes by conciliation, arbitration and judicial settlement. It was a splendid vision, one that captured the imagination of people all over the world.

The reality was in the persons of LLOYD GEORGE of England, CLEMENCEAU of France and ORLANDO of Italy who comprised a "Big Three" determined to make the Peace of Versailles a vengeful and profitable one at the expense of the conquered nations. What emerged was in the nature of a compromise between the vision and the reality.

Germany, Austria-Hungary, Turkey and Bulgaria were punished. Germany ceded Alsace-Lorraine back to France, Eurpen and Malmedy to Belgium and a corridor through West Prussia for Poland to reach the sea. Schleswig was returned to Denmark; Lithuania secured Memel; Danzig became an internationalized "free city"; the Saar was placed under the political control of the League of Nations and the economic control of France for fifteen years after which there was to be a plebiscite held in which the Saarlanders could vote for a permanent political settlement of their fate. Germany lost all of her Pacific holdings to the League of Nations which received them as "mandates" and which distributed them to the victorious powers for education and eventual release as independent states. (Such was Wilson's plan for the eventual elimination of imperialism.)

Germany was then stripped of all military power—armed forces, navy, fortifications—and had to submit to occupation of her territory to ensure enforcement of the terms of the treaty. At the same time, Germany was declared to be guilty of having provoked the war and was therefore made to bear the expense of repairing the damage. Reparations costs ran to some sixty billion dollars. As immediate payments on this reparations bill, Germany was stripped of railroads, capital equipment, livestock and coal. Out of the treaties of St.

Germain, Neuilly and Serves with Austria, Hungary and Turkey respectively came the birth of many new nations and additional mandated territories to be granted to the victorious powers.

The League of Nations. In exchange for many concessions to the nationalist and imperialist aims of the victorious allied powers, Wilson demanded that as Article I of the Versailles Treaty appear a covenant for a League of Nations to which all the victorious powers would belong and which would be given sufficient power to end all future wars.

To some degree this was accomplished. An international organization was framed which would include an Assembly of all the member nations, each with a single vote; an executive Council of permanent big-power members and non-permanent elected members to enforce decrees of the Assembly; a World Court for the judicial settlement of disputes; a Secretariat for arranging meetings and recording results. The covenant also provided for a mandate system to eliminate imperialism. It was projected, too, that the League would form committees to alleviate some of the basic economic, health, education and communication problems of the world.

That there would be an end to war seemed a realizable hope in the year 1919. Countries were already projecting a series of disarmament conferences that would reduce the burden of maintaining powerful armed forces. Nationalism had been satisfied in the creation of the "succession states" of Poland, Czechoslovakia, Austria, Hungary, Yugoslavia and others. Imperialism would end as mandatory nations fulfilled their obligations to their territories and prepared them for the status of independent nations who would then join the League. International anarchy was to end with the establishment and growth in the power of the League of Nations and the World Court. International cooperation was to replace economic rivalry. What causes for any future war were possible?

But twenty years later came a second, and even more terrible, war. What went wrong with the vision?

The Shaping of the Modern World

SOVIET RUSSIA

In March 1917 the Tsar was overthrown and a liberal democratic state set up under the leadership of Prince Lvov and Professor Miliukov. Instrumental in this overthrow were the numerous "soviets" or local government that had made their appearance during the stages of the first revolution. In the elected Soviets the Bolsheviks (communists) led by Lenin had no control.

In the first All-Russian Congress of Soviets held in June of 1917 Kerensky Social Revolutionaries and Menshevik socialists-groups favoring democratic processes of government—were voted control of the government. Even after the Bolsheviks had seized control of the government of Petrograd in November 7th they could not secure approval from a constitutional assembly called in January 1918 to confirm the seizure. This constitutional assembly was freely and democratically elected. However, when it voted down Bolshevik proposals with respect to making peace, distributing land and disarming all of the Russians but the workers, it was abruptly dismissed and in its place was created a dictatorship under the leadership of Nicolai Lenin, Leon Trotsky and Joseph Stalin.

Many circumstances played into the hands of the Bolsheviks to enable them to maintain and to consolidate their power. They voluntarily signed the Treaty of Brest-Litovsk with Germany in which they surrendered a considerable portion of European Russia. Moreover, they published secret treaties that revealed many of the imperialist aims of the warring allied powers.

Frightened by the success of the Bolsheviks, the Allied powers dispatched an international force to aid the "White Russians" in their effort at a counter-revolution. Since these "White Russians" contained many of the elements of the hated Old Regime the Allied intervention was strongly opposed.

Meanwhile, the Bolsheviks set up the Cheka—

secret police and revolutionary tribunals—which destroyed not only elements of the old regime but *all* opposition to Bolshevism. At the same time, to give meaning to their "socialist" revolution, the Bolsheviks temporarily turned factories over to workers' committees, distributed land to the peasants, as much as each could work, nationalized all industry without compensation, confiscated all Tsarist obligations to domestic and foreign lenders and removed money as a means of exchange.

Consolidation. In 1919 a Supreme Economic Council was created to make plans for the eventual creation of complete state ownership and operation of the means of production. The productive system collapsed and in 1921 there was desperate poverty.

In 1921, therefore, Lenin ordered a "new economic policy" to be instituted. The base of the new economic policy was state ownership of about 85 per cent of the means of production. In the remaining 15 per cent the Communists permitted foreign investors to invest funds at high rates of interest. Opposition abroad was considerably disarmed by this maneuver; Western nations were led to believe that Russia would some day return to the family of capitalist nations. In 1924 Communist Russia was officially recognized by Great Britain, France and Italy. Not until 1934 did the United States follow suit.

The "Plan" was fulfilled in a series of "five-year plans" launched by JOSEPH STALIN in 1928. All foreign influence in Russian industry was abolished. A state planning commission drew up goals for a five-year increase in industrialization, mechanization and electrification of state owned industries. Every type of incentive was used to increase worker productivity; this was needed, for productivity increase was linked to a decrease in consumption—the surplus being used to purchase basic machinery abroad. Meanwhile, the process of forcible collectivization of farms was begun.

Thus straitjacketed the Russian economy did move into the high gear of production. Opposition to collectivization was so strong, however, that Russia suffered another severe food famine in 1934. A second five-year plan eased the consumption picture somewhat; a third was just begun when Russia was attacked by the Nazi forces. Her industrialization, considerably aided by American "lend-lease," stood her in good stead and enabled her to make a rapid recovery after the war.

Dictatorship. Protest in Russia could find no effective means of expression once the Bolsheviks had imposed their dictatorship. All political opposition was suppressed. The "purge" and staged trials became an institution by which Joseph Stalin periodically eliminated potential rivals.

Yet the Communists could not forever ignore the need for some form of national consent. In 1936 they granted a constitution which constructed a tremendous facade of republican institutions that were designed to conceal the dictatorship. A bicameral legislature representing all the people and their nationalist divisions was created; an elective ministry headed by a premier was set up as executive. An extensive "bill of rights" was added. But the realities in these political forms are evident in the facts that in Soviet elections only one party is permitted, that only members of the Communist Party may hold high office, in the control which the state holds over all means of communication, in the secret police, in the use of secret trials and summary executions, in the absence of all debate at the meetings, when called, of the legislature, in the rigid control of ingress and egress from Russia itself, in antireligious official attitudes and propaganda, in the strict control of education.

FASCIST ITALY

BENITO MUSSOLINI, founder of Italian Fascism, came to power by a coup d'etat on October 28, 1922. He and his "Black Shirts"—a private army—"marched on Rome" and took possession of the state apparatus. Only the complete breakdown of the democratic apparatus of the Italian government could have permitted this to take place. This breakdown was due to Italy's multi-party system that, at the crucial moment, was unable or unwilling to form a government to counteract this coup. A breakdown in government was the result of accumulating difficulties resulting from widespread postwar depression, unemployment, radical efforts to seize factories, peasant revolts, etc.

Once in power, Mussolini destroyed all opposition and civil liberty, ruled by terror and secret police, resorted to political assassination and prepared Italy for a series of wars that would make the Mediterranean an Italian lake. Both industry and labor were harnessed to state purposes. Industrialists had no choice but to produce what the state required; labor was denied every form of free action on its own behalf. Both were organized into "corporations" (hence the "corporate state") and these were directed by state-appointed bureaucrats. Propaganda and militarization took the place of education. From earliest age, the youth were organized as military cadres and taught implicit obedience to the dictates of *Il Duce* ("The Leader").

The economy felt the artificial stimulation of increased war production and Mussolini was able to secure a surplus which enabled him to make Italy somewhat more self-sufficient by the draining of marshes, improvement of railroads, large hydroelectric and reclamation projects, subsidies for overseas trade, construction of a merchant marine, etc. But the intent of this program of reform was war and renewed imperialistic attacks on those powers which held territories overseas particularly England and France.

NAZI GERMANY

ADOLPH HITLER'S coup came in January 1933. As in Italy, the normal process of democratic government had broken down when the major parties in the Reichstag were unable to agree on a government bloc. Few governments were more democratically oriented than Germany under the Weimar Republic, a government created to replace that of the German Kaiser. When faced with large scale unemployment and dissatisfaction resulting from the world depression in 1933, the radical and liberal parties were unable and unwilling to combine to suppress the threat of the author of *Mein Kampf* and his private army of Brown Shirts.

Adolph Hitler was a master of vicious propaganda; he exploited every grievance of the Germans by centering them upon a few scapegoats —the Treaty of Versailles, the Jews, the German need for *lebensraum* (living space). To justify the use of these scapegoats, he constructed out of a long history of racist theorizing (DE GOBINEAU, HOUSTON STEWART CHAMBERLAIN) the doctrine of the racial superiority of the German Nordic. He convinced the German people by ceaseless dinning through every means of communication that they were the only source of civilization, that they stood in dread danger of corruption and bestialization through intermingling with inferior race, that they must save the world by conquering it for humanity and civilization, etc.

At best one might say that the German people had little inkling—though the unspeakable brutality of the Nazi Storm Troopers must have been evident to them from the day Hitler took power—that these false and vicious doctrines were soon to be translated into furnaces that would burn up more than 6,000,000 people whose only crime was that they were of different religions and nationalities from the ruling German cliques.

After 1934 Hitler became *Der Führer* ("the Leader"). The German state was completely totalitarianized. Industry and labor were organized in similar fashion to that of Mussolini. Capitalism was retained but placed at the beck and call of state needs. War production was immediately begun in preparation for a series of adventures to test the democracies' will to resist and eventually for a bid for world conquest. German freedom disappeared and the Gestapo and the Storm Troopers combined to produce absolute terror.

THE WEAKENING OF THE DEMOCRACIES

World War I proved to be empty victories for the democracies. In 1921 and again in 1931 they suffered depressions of unparalleled dimensions. England, in particular, found that economically she was slipping into the place of a second rate power in the face of American and Japanese competition. Unemployment, exhaustion of native resources, mounting taxes which destroyed considerable investment capital, the failure of Germany to produce any sizeable reparations, widespread strikes among the transport workers and coal miners—all of these factors helped keep successive British governments reeling. In 1923 the first Labor government, under Ramsey Macdonald, was elected; but it was no more able to manage the various crises than the Conservatives.

With the onset of the Great Depression England experimented with a coalition government of Conservative and Laborites. The great achievement of this government was the final abandonment of England's free trade policy for a policy of imperial preference and the Statute of Westminster. The latter was virtually a declaration of independence for all British dominions. It created the British Commonwealth of Nations for the dominions, a system which permitted any dominion to leave the Empire when it wished and if it stayed within the Empire to enjoy absolute local autonomy. (No dominion has left the Commonwealth except Ireland, which in 1922 became Eire, a free state without any political ties to England.)

As the Fascist menace rose to challenge England's position, England began a rearmament program that stimulated the economy to slow revival. Out of the general feeling of helplessness that England felt, however, was generated her policy of "appeasement"—a policy associated particularly with Prime Minister Neville Chamberlain. This policy had as its central aim the strengthening of Fascism to a point where it could successfully attack Communism. In the struggle which ensued, England hoped, both would destroy each other.

French difficulties were similar to those of England with this addition—under the impact of economic crisis the normally unstable French Governments became even more so. France felt keenly Germany's inability to meet her reparations payments since France had been the chief sufferer among the western powers of the first World War. High taxes and shortages of goods produced an astronomical inflation in France in 1926. Unemployment, loss of foreign markets, colonial difficulties and the threat of both Germany and Italy to her security kept France off balance throughout the two decades and made her a leading exponent of appeasement. She, more than any, sought to direct Hitler's power eastward toward Russia.

Finally, the United States withdrew completely from the arena of international responsibility. She rejected the League of Nations, refused to enter the World Court and adopted a series of neutrality laws that were designed to remove her physically from direct or indirect participation in any future European conflict. The world depression of 1931 struck the United States with especial force. Unemployment mounted to 16,000,000, factory production fell by fifty per cent, emergency relief drained the treasury and forced the policy of government borrowing that was to become the greatest government debt in history following the second world war. These difficulties intensified America's desire to remove itself from the arena of world affairs and to concentrate upon her own revival.

Finally, the hope of the democracies resided in the League of Nations; but it proved to be a weak vessel. Weakened by the requirement of unanimity for any decisive action, by the provision in the convenant permitting an aggressor to leave the League after two years' notice, by the absence from the membership rolls of both the United States and the Soviet Union—the League had proved itself incapable of coping with any threat to the peace involving a major power. Its successes were on the fringes of international politics.

Lack of confidence in the League was reflected in the successive disarmament conferences that were held outside League auspices. Though none of these conferences was an unqualified success, the earliest ones—particularly the Washington Arms Conference of 1921–1922—did manage to provide for a cessation in the armaments race for a ten-year period. Japanese ambitions in the Far East were effectively curbed by a Nine-Power Treaty and a Four-Power Treaty which made her sign support for the open door policy, for preservation of China's territorial integrity and for the integrity of the Pacific island possessions of the western powers. (Japan freely violated all these commitments since no effective check was provided for to ensure that she fulfilled them.) Even the idealist Kellogg-Briand Peace Pact which "outlawed war" was negotiated by America and France outside the League. Moreover, both France and England placed their reliance on the construction of a wide system of security alliances (the Little Entente, the Locarno Pacts, etc.) rather than on the force of the League. International anarchy was as prevalent with the League as in the days before the League. With this state of affairs in the world there was no reason for the aggressive fascist nations to hesitate in their new imperialist policy . . . the second factor leading to World War II.

THE NEW IMPERIALISM

The old imperialism was, for the most part, directed against helpless, undeveloped areas; the new imperialism unleased by the powers of the Rome-Berlin-Tokyo Axis was directed against strong, advanced nations. In 1931 Japan began what she called a punitive expedition against Chinese bandits, an expedition that ended with the conquest of all of Manchuria. When the League investigated this aggression through the Lytton Commission and condemned the actions of Japan, Japan left the League, and converted Manchuria into the puppet state of Manchukuo. From this as a base, Japan in 1933 spilled over into the province of Jehol.

It was now Hitler's turn. In 1935, Hitler ordered general conscription and then marched his troops into the Rhineland. Both these actions had been forbidden in the Treaty of Versailles. The French met this threat with the construction of an "impassable" Maginot Line; Hitler built the "Siegfried Wall" opposite it.

In 1936, Generalissimo Francisco Franco, aided and equipped by both Mussolini and Hitler, began an assault on the Spanish Republic with the avowed purpose of setting up a fascist regime in Spain. Spain became an experimental laboratory for the use of Axis weapons and troops; pursuing the policy of "non-intervention" the democratic nations stood aside while these tactics were being employed. After a gallant but hopeless defense, the Spanish Republic collapsed in 1939. Once again the democracies gave evidence that they would not resist fascist aggression until it was directed against themselves.

In 1936, Mussolini began his assault on Ethiopia to revenge the defeat at Adowa and to outflank England on the east coast of Africa. Worried now, England attempted to force the League to adopt sanctions against Italy, particularly sanctions on the sale of oil. But United States oil companies took this as an opportunity to capture the Italian market. As a result, Italy proceeded unchecked until Ethiopia was hers.

Meanwhile, Hitler's "Fifth Column" of Nazi Austrians had begun to agitate for *anschluss* (union) of Germany and Austria. The Austrian Chancellor Schussnigg resisted Hitler's demands. As European eyes focussed on this crisis, the Japanese, in 1937, began their plunge into the deep south of China, a plunge that Chiang Kai shek—China's President and Generalissimo—could do no more than delay. With attention shifted to the Far East, Hitler on March 11, 1938, simply walked in and took over Austria without a struggle. Within weeks Austria was nazified by the well-organized fifth column which had been in secret preparation for many years.

A few months later Hitler, at a Nuremberg Conference, began agitating for the Sudetenland of Czechoslovakia—a section of Czechoslovakia that contained many German-speaking people. This demand led to a remarkable series of meetings in which England's Chamberlain and France's Daladier granted to Hitler his demands upon Czechoslovakia because this was the only way to achieve "peace in our time" and because this was to be Hitler's "last request!" In the face of this complete acquiescence, Hitler took over all of Czechoslovakia and permitted Poland and Hungary small slices bordering their lands.

Italy, early in 1939, took over Albania. This was no sooner done, than Hitler began to agitate for a return of the Polish Corridor to Germany. This was absolutely his last demand. But in August of 1939 came a "diplomatic revolution" that changed the international situation overnight.

THE SECOND WORLD WAR

Poland was crushed by Hitler in five weeks; the Nazis unleashed the *Blitzkreig* tactic, a combined bombing and armored vehicle attack that was both mobile and paralyzing. Poland's allies lent her no assistance. Russia now moved to collect its dividends on the Nazi-Soviet pact. Lithuania, Latvia, Estonia, the Rumanian provinces of Bessarabia and Bukowina, and (1940) Finland were conquered by the Red Army.

In April 1940 the Nazis overran Denmark and Norway. British failure forced Chamberlain out of office and Winston Churchill became Prime Minister on May 10, 1940. On that very day came the Nazi attack on the Low Countries and France. France fell in one of the most ignominious defeats in military history on June 21, 1940. Collaborationists like Laval set up a new French government at Vichy; Italy formally entered the war by an assault on British positions in North Africa; England was without allies; the United States began to drop its aloofness as Roosevelt began his campaign to win Americans to the support of England. Such were the consequences of the fall of France.

Germany now began its air assault on England and against meager opposition. Hitler's air blitz on England failed. The small Royal Air Force proved marvelously effective and destroyed 3,000 German planes; British morale grew sturdier with each attack; supplies, protected by the British navy, began to pour in; American aid grew mountainously especially after the passage of the Lend-Lease Act; Hitler was forced to pull his Italian ally out of difficulties in North Africa and the Balkans and this diverted his energies eastward.

In June 1941 Hitler attacked Russia without warning in a hope to break through the Caucusus into India and to join there with the Japanese who had already advanced far into Southeast Asia in the direction of eastern India. Initial successes brought the Nazis to the gates of Moscow and far south to the city of Stalingrad. On December 7, 1941, Japan attacked the U.S. naval base at Pearl Harbor. America now entered the conflict.

In 1942 the counteroffensive against the Axis powers began. Russia destroyed the Nazi army at Stalingrad and began an offensive that carried her to Berlin in 1945. England defeated the Nazi-Fascist forces deep in Egypt at El Alemain and took the offensive that ended only when the British met the American forces who had landed in western North Africa to spring a trap on the Nazis. The U.S. began its island-hopping campaign that brought her to the perimeter of the Japanese Islands. No assault had to be made on these islands for the dropping of atom bombs on Hiroshima and Nagasaki convinced the Japanese military that further resistance was useless. Russia completed the demolition of the Japanese by destroying its Manchurian armies.

From North Africa Anglo-American forces crossed over to Italy and began a northward assault on German-held positions. But the greatest water-borne assault in history came on D-day—June 6, 1944—when Anglo-American forces invaded Normandy and continued rolling until all of western Germany had fallen. Victory in Europe came on May 7, 1945; Victory in Japan came on August 14, 1945. The most devastating war in the history of mankind was over. Its total cost in money, lives, disease, broken bodies, broken minds will probably never be fully calculated; its effects upon the political, social, economic, psychological and cultural institutions of the civilized world are as yet incalculable. Yet it, more than any other phenomenon, shaped the frame and features of the world today. We can do no more than indicate some of the vectors that have revealed themselves since 1945 and wait for their unraveling in the future.

THE POST-WAR WORLD

"One World." World War II was fought on a high ideological level. In August 1941 Churchill and Roosevelt met to frame the "Atlantic Charter." The nobility of the cause of the united nations was framed in the words of this document, words that bear repetition especially today. The allied nations agreed that

- they will seek no aggrandizement, territorial or otherwise;
- territorial changes will be made in accord with the freely expressed wishes of the people concerned;
- people will choose the form of government under which they will live;
- they will see to it that people who have forcibly lost their self-government will get it back;
- with due respect for existing obligations, they will see to it that all States have access, on equal terms, to the trade and raw materials of the world;
- they will get all nations to collaborate to improve labor standards, economic advancement, and social security;
- they will establish a peace in which men may live out their lives free from fear and want;
- they will assure freedom of the seas; and
- they will disarm aggressors and will remain armed themselves until permanent security is established.

Out of this drive for world peace came the United Nations organization.

THE UNITED NATIONS

A United Nations Organization had been projected simultaneously with the issuance of the Atlantic Charter. At the Moscow Conference—and other military meetings during the war—the need for such an organization was officially proclaimed and the basic principle of the equality of states was announced (1943).

At Teheran (1943) a planning committee was projected. It met at Dumbarton Oaks (1944) and consisted of the Big Four—the United States, the United Kingdom, the Soviet Union and China. Ninety percent of the Charter of the United Nations was hammered out at Dumbarton Oaks. The remainder was completed at Bretton Woods (N.H.) where an International Bank for Reconstruction and Development and an International Monetary Fund to stabilize world currencies were set up; at Yalta where the formula on the voting procedures in the Security Council was agreed upon and each of the great powers was granted an absolute veto on all matters except procedure; and at San Francisco (April-June 1945) where the addition of the important Article 51 was made, the article that provided for regional pacts for individual or collective self-defense pending action by the Security Council.

Purposes. Article I of the Charter of the UN sets forth its major goals: "To maintain international peace and security, and to that end: to take effective collective measures for the prevention and removal of threats to the peace . . ."; and "To achieve international cooperation in solving international problems of an economic, social, cultural or humanitarian character . . ."

Membership. All independent, peace-loving nations are eligible if they accept the obligations of the UN and are willing and able to carry them out. On January 1, 1957 there were over eighty member nations.

Structure. There are six main organs of the UN: **The General Assembly** composed of all member states. Each state may send five delegates but each state is entitled to only one vote. On most matters a two-thirds vote prevails. The Assembly must meet at least once a year but may meet in special session. After the creation in 1947 of an interim committee called the "Little Assembly" one may now say that the General Assembly is in continuous session.

The Security Council. This was to have been the leading organ of the UN. It consists of eleven members, five (U.S., U.K., USSR, France and China) with permanent seats and six elected by the General Assembly for two-year terms. It is in continuous session and has the primary responsibility for maintaining peace and security; all other members of the UN are bound to carry out its decisions. But its decisions have been few since each of the permanent members has an absolute veto on all substantive matters. Its *potential* power remains virtually limitless.

The Economic and Social Council (ECOSOC). ECOSOC's 18 member council is chosen for staggered three-year terms by the General Assembly. It is charged with carrying out programs of international and social improvement. The most spectacular accomplishments of the UN have been in the work of this organ through its many specialized agencies whose titles clearly indicate their functions: The International Labor Organization (ILO), the Food and Agricultural Organization (FAO), the United Nations Educational Scientific and Cultural Organization (UNESCO), the International Civil Aviation Organization (ICAO), The International Bank for Reconstruction and Development (IBRD), the International Monetary Fund (IMF), the International Telecommunications Union (ITU), the World Health Organization (WHO), the International Trade Organization (ITO). Through these organizations particularly does the light of "one world" shine through.

The Trusteeship Council. This organ supervises territories previously administered by the League of Nations as mandates as well as such territories that nations have voluntarily placed under trusteeship with the UN. Six UN members are at present charged with advancing the political and economic development of 20,500,000 people in eleven African and Pacific areas. The Council sends out questionnaires, hears reports, listens to complaints from natives and sends out on-the-spot investigating committees—unless the trust-holding power designates its trust territory as "strategic."

U.N. Successes and Limitations. Since 1945, the United Nations has scored many successes. It caused Russian withdrawal of troops from Iran (1946); it halted Civil War in Greece and set up the U.N. Balkan Commission; it created the independent states of Israel, Indonesia and Libya; it fought the Korean War to a truce; it halted intense religious battles between India and Pakistan over the disputed territory of Kashmir; it halted similar strife in the Israeli-Arab War of 1948–9; it stopped a tripartite invasion of Egypt by England, France and Israel in 1956 (caused these nations to withdraw from Egyptian territory). In 1948, the General Assembly adopted the Declaration of Human Rights, a world charter of human civil liberty; and in the same year approved the Genocide Convention to protect any ethnic group from extinction. The U.N. sponsored GATT., a general agreement on tariffs and trade to limit world economic nationalism.

U.N. limitations, however, were evident in the rapid increase of regional agreements for collective security (NATO and the WARSAW PACT); the constant use of the veto power by the Soviet Union in the Security Council; inability of the U.N. to establish a permanent international armed force; existence within the U.N. of political blocs (American, Soviet, Afro-Asian), inability to act on such matters as suppression of the Hungarian revolt, etc.

THE COLD WAR

Communist Imperialism. By 1947, the "One World" built during the war was replaced by a so-called Cold War between two power blocs: a Western bloc headed by the United States and an Eastern bloc headed by the Soviet Union. Conflicting military and economic goals were the basic causes of the Cold War. Russian satellite states were created in Albania, Bulgaria, Hungary, Rumania, Czechoslovakia, Poland and East Germany. Yugoslavia, under Marshall Tito, broke from her satellite status but retained a Communist form of government. Estonia, Latvia, Lithuania, the Karelian Isthmus of Finland, Finnish Petsamo, Bessarabia and the eastern provinces of Poland were absorbed into the U.S.S.R. itself. The Chinese Communists drove Chiang Kai shek off the mainland on to Taiwan (Formosa) and assumed control of China; later, the Chinese Communists conquered Tibet. Chinese Communists aided in the formation of Communist North Korea. In each of these conquered or absorbed territories, the Communists instituted political dictatorship and economic totalitarianism modeled after the Soviet state. Efforts at protest or revolt in Czechoslovakia, Poland, East Germany, Hungary and Tibet were crushed. The Communists inspired hostilities in Greece, the Philippines and Malaya; and major wars in Korea and Indo-China. They were constantly active in the Middle East and Latin America, and important inroads were made in Indonesia and Africa. Meanwhile Russia's military power was enhanced by the successful firing of a thermonuclear bomb and by the launching of a 3000-pound space missile. Soviet diplomats combined the diplomacy of threat with an increased program of foreign aid to backwood nations. Through shipments of military equipment, Communist prestige increased in the Middle East and in Africa.

Counterattack. The Western counterattack to Soviet-bloc expansion evolved with events and took three forms.

Containment. In 1947, President Truman called for an end to Communist expansion and in the **Truman Doctrine** offered American military, economic and financial aid to any nation under attack or threat of attack by Communist-bloc nations. Subsequently, the United States intervened directly and unilaterally to counter Communist attacks or threats in Greece, Turkey, Korea, Indo-China, the Philippines and Malaya. This was followed by the formation of a series of defensive military alliances designed to "contain" Communist expansion.

On April 4, 1949, the North Atlantic Treaty Organization (NATO) was formed. Original members included Belgium, Canada, Denmark, France, Greenland, Iceland, Italy, Luxemburg, the Netherlands, Norway, the United Kingdom and the United States; subsequently Greece, Turkey and West Germany were added to the alliance to form a community embracing more than 400,000,000 people. NATO, located in Paris, is composed of a ruling Civilian Council and a Military Council, with a Supreme Commander who controls motorized infantry divisions, air and naval fleets, complex and instantaneous communication systems, suppliers and, of course, conventional and atomic weapons. In its first decade NATO was able to overcome difficulties created by the failure of member nations to meet personnel quotas, forces withdrawn from non-NATO operations (French withdrawal of troops for use in Indo-China and Algeria), competition among members for favored posts and commands and non-NATO rivalries among members (England vs. Greece vs. Turkey over Cyprus; England vs. Iceland over North Atlantic fisheries). The most serious threat to NATO, however, was the demand by President De Gaulle of France for complete parity with the United States and England in Mediterranean commands and over control of atomic weapons (the latter forbidden by the United States without the consent of Congress). As a result, the United States was forced to move all its French-based atomic equipment to other sites.

Less effective than NATO was the alliance formed in Southeast Asia (SEATO) among Australia, New Zealand, Pakistan, the Philippines, Thailand, France, England and the United States. This alliance is purely consultative and it suffers considerably from the absence of India, Burma, Indonesia, Taiwan (the Republic of China) and Japan.

Least effective is the Middle East Treaty Organization (METO) organized by England but financed by the United States. It includes only Turkey, Iran, Pakistan and England (Iraq having dropped out in 1959) and is merely consultative; moreover, Egypt and the Arab League are violently opposed to it. Because these multilateral alliances have been strengthened by bilateral agreements between the United States and countries across the world, American troops are provided with military bases along the fringe of the Communist world. That the United States has not abandoned unilateral action is evident in the 1957 adoption of the **Eisenhower Doctrine** which provides for armed assistance to repel Communist aggression in the Middle East, if requested by a Middle Eastern nation.

Strengthening Europe's Economic Defenses. The United States launched its Marshall Plan (1948–1952) to remove the ruins of war, to rebuild Europe's economy and to reduce the effectiveness of the Communists throughout Europe. This economic and financial aid was distributed in Europe by the **Organization of European Economic Cooperation** (OEEC). European cooperation within the OEEC was the first step in a move toward European integration. In 1946 Belgium, the Netherlands and Luxemburg organized a tariff union (Benelux) within the OEEC. In 1949 a Council of Europe was formed to examine the possibilities of political unity of the OEEC powers. Then in 1952, France, Italy, West Germany and the Benelux nations adopted the Schuman Plan which integrated the economies of these six countries into a coal and steel community under a unified high authority which planned the production, the distribution and the labor forces available for the making of steel. In 1957, Euratom was created to promote common production of nuclear energy; and in 1959, the Schuman Plan nations began Euromarket designed to eliminate all tariffs within the community and to adopt a common tariff against all nations outside the community. England proposed a wider free-trade area to embrace all Western Europe. Finding no approval for this plan by Euromarket, England began to organize its own free-trade area to include itself, Sweden, Norway, Denmark, Austria, Switzerland and Portugal.

Strengthening Non-European Economic Defenses. To offset Communist inroads into the more backward areas of the world, the United States and its allies have begun large-scale programs of economic aid to these areas. Technical assistance to improve control over natural resources was made available under President Truman's Point Four program and a similar United Nation's project. Loans and grants-in-aid were provided for Southeast Asia in the British-sponsored and American-financed Colombo Plan; and to all the rest of the world in the United States' **Development Loan Fund** and **Agricultural Trade and Development Loan Funds** (which distributes America's farm surpluses to needy nations). Other sources of loans for approved projects were the **American Export-Import Bank** and the **International Bank for Reconstruction and Development.** Billions of dollars and pounds poured into these backward areas have successfully halted important Communist gains, and have kept the governments of these nations, generally inclined to Communism, on a neutral path.

Support for Former Enemies. Since enemies of Communism are not necessarily friends of democracy, the Western powers have taken active steps to obtain necessary allies. Thus, Marshall Tito, heading a Communist state in Yugoslavia, was aided by loans and military support to defy the Soviet bloc and retain his independence; Generalissimo Franco, heading a Fascist state in Spain, was encouraged to be friendly to the Western powers by a defense agreement with the United States in which air bases were exchanged for military and economic aid. Similarly, Japan, having been effectively democratized, was permitted to rearm, admitted to the United Nations, granted large sums of rehabilitory aid, and made a defense bastion in the Far East. Most significant, however, was the treatment accorded to Germany.

The Yalta and Potsdam agreements of 1945 provided that both Germany and its historic capital, Berlin, were to be partitioned until the country was completely demilitarized, denazified and democratized. When this was accomplished Germany was to be reunited as a minor power. Unilateral Russian action, however, in changing Germany's boundaries within the eastern zone, in blockading Berlin, and in converting the Russian zone into the satellite nation of East Germany, caused the Western powers to take positive steps. West Germany became an independent state; the German General Staff was recreated; West Germany was militarized and admitted to NATO. The Western powers maintained their position in West Berlin despite the efforts of Russian Premier Khrushchev who threatened to turn West Berlin, located well within the territory of the East German state, over to East Germany, and conclude a separate peace treaty with East Germany.

East and West met at the conference table at Geneva in 1959 in an attempt to solve the problem of a united Berlin and a united Germany.

Decade of Turmoil. The 1960s brought internal strife to many countries of the world as new political groups fought to gain more personal freedoms.

Civil war gave birth to several new nations in Africa, while others claimed their independence from the rule of Great Britain and France. Military leaders vied for control of Greece, Portugal, and a number of countries in Latin America.

The National Association for the Advancement of Colored People (NAACP) led by Roy Wilkins and the Southern Christian Leadership Conference (SCLC) led by Martin Luther King, Jr., championed the cause of racial equality in the United States. Their protest marches and boycotts in the early 1960s won some changes in the law. Later more radical groups stirred up violent riots in the large urban areas, reacting against the bitter plight of blacks and similar minorities.

In Northern Ireland the age-old conflict between (middle-class) Protestants and (lower-class) Catholics erupted again when Catholics called for total independence from Great Britain. Tempers flared and terrorist groups roamed the streets, frightening and murdering their opponents in the cause. The conflict worsened as the decade rolled on.

In Czechoslovakia the democratic policies of President Alexander Dubcek earned the scorn of nearby Russia. To make sure the reforms didn't spread to other Communist satellites, the Soviet government sent its army into Czechoslovakia in August 1968 to sweep Dubcek from power.

Military Challenges. During the 1960s the powers of East and West tested their strength in several crucial showdowns.

When Cuban Premier Fidel Castro brought Russian missiles onto his island fortress in 1962, President John F. Kennedy placed a naval blockage against the shipments. He said Castro and his Russian partners had violated the Monroe Doctrine–the policy which President James Monroe laid down over a hundred years earlier, when he declared that the United States would not allow foreign powers to stake new claims in the Western Hemisphere.

In Southeast Asia, Communist super-powers supported the government of North Vietnam as it tried to take South Vietnam. The United Nations sent military advisors to South Vietnam, then troops. The conflict spread to the neighboring countries of Cambodia, Laos, and Thailand. The United States pledged to defend South Vietnam if the conflict became a full-scale war; Russia and China did the same for North Vietnam. But both sides wanted to keep the conflict from growing into another world war. The United States committed over 500,000 soldiers to the contest, but by the end of the sixties most American leaders knew the effort would fail. At home, college students demonstrated against America's role in Asia and many young men burned their draft cards to show their contempt for what they called an "immoral war."

DÉTENTE

Richard M. Nixon took office as President of the United States in 1969 with two goals for his administration: (1) to settle the unrest in America's streets, and (2) to establish a more peaceful climate on the world scene. He knew the first goal depended on reaching the second. He also realized that if America was to find world peace, it had to melt the ice of its "cold war" with the Communist powers. Mr. Nixon called this process *détente,* using a French term that means "to relax tension."

The United States began a round of Strategic Arms Limitation Talks (SALT) with the Soviet Union. At these conferences the diplomats from both nations agreed to limit the number of new weapons they made–especially atomic weapons. At the same time the United States invited Chinese athletes to visit North America for what newspaper columnists jokingly called "ping-pong diplomacy." Relations grew more friendly between the two nations and climaxed with President Nixon's courtesy trip to China in early 1972. A treaty between the United States and North Vietnam ended the long stand-off in Southeast Asia with American troops leaving the area at the end of 1972. In April 1973, North Vietnamese troops took the last major cities in South Vietnam and united the country with their own.

Economic Problems. Israel and its Arab rivals called for military aid in their long-time dispute, but the spirit of *détente* led major world powers to keep "hands off." Arab nations banded together to resist this policy, and in the fall of 1973 they refused to ship oil to the United States. They ended the boycott several months later, but the Arab-controlled group of Oil Producing and Exporting Countries (OPEC) doubled the price of crude oil. This triggered a new surge of inflation in the United States and other Western countries. China, Russia, and most Communist countries in Eastern

Europe produced enough oil for their own needs, so the price hike did little to harm their economies.

By the time James Earl (Jimmy) Carter became President in 1977, the cost of living in the United States was rising by about eight percent each year. The United States imported much more than it sold to other nations, and had to borrow billions of dollars' worth of credit to cover the difference. This **balance of payments deficit** loomed as a primary concern of the Western world. It meant that the American dollar was worth less than it was a year earlier–or even a month earlier. Because the United States was so active in the business of the Western world, its growing debt threatened to disrupt international economy. President Carter proposed new programs to make the United States able to produce more of its own energy. In early 1978 he met in Munich, West Germany with other Western leaders to seek ways of strengthening the international system of trade. Ironically, by this time the European continent and Japan had bounced back from World War II even better than the United States and Great Britain.

Détente seemed threatened by President Carter's demand for human rights in Communist countries. He cited the Helsinki pact of 1973, in which the Soviet Union pledged to give its citizens freedom of speech, freedom of worship, and other concessions. Carter and his aides criticized the Soviet Union for putting political and religious dissenters on trial: the Soviet government warned the United States to stop meddling in Russia's domestic affairs.

Yet the period of *détente* had real benefits. Because of easing tensions in the Middle East, President Carter could invite President Anwar Sadat of Egypt and Prime Minister Menachem Begin of Israel to a summit conference at Camp David, in the Maryland hills near Washington, D.C. On September 17, 1978, the three men signed a "Framework for Peace in the Middle East," which outlined steps for ending the 30-year dispute between Israel and its Arab neighbors.

With his election to the presidency in 1980, Ronald Reagan began to work toward a decrease in the federal deficit, with an economic program including the largest budget and tax cuts in United States history. Though unemployment reached a 9.7% rate in 1982 (the highest since 1941), by 1984 interest rates and inflation had declined. The country's approval of President Reagan's economic policies was reflected in his landslide victory in 1984 to a second term.

Reagan's foreign policies were based on a strong anti-communist stance. In 1983 he sent a task force to Grenada and later joined three European countries in sending a "peacekeeping" force to Beirut, Lebanon. During his term the White House continued to push for aid to anti-communist forces in Central America. Reagan's belief in a strong defense system was reflected throughout his administration in increased defense spending.

CHAPTER SIX

AMERICAN HISTORY

Origins

The origins of American history may be found in developments in Europe. The fourteenth and fifteenth centuries saw extraordinary developments taking place in Europe. These included the rise of a middle class, the appearance of independent nations, the growth of industry and commerce, the invention of printing, a new interest in science, the development of religious conflict. These changes led Europeans to explore the world. Columbus' discovery of America in 1492 was but one of many attempts on the part of Europeans to find an all-water route to the Far East.

A year after Columbus' first voyage on behalf of Spain, the Pope gave Spain title to all of the New World, with the exception of the eastern part of South America, known today as Brazil, which was awarded to Portugal. Spain ruled her vast empire despotically. There was no religious freedom, Indians were treated harshly, and self-government was denied to the colonists.

In 1608, the French founded Quebec. For a century afterward, they continued to explore North America, following the great waterways of the continent–the St. Lawrence River, the Great Lakes, and the Mississippi River. However, by 1750 only about 80,000 settlers had come to New France. Like Spain, France denied her colonies the right of self-government. Furthermore, since France was interested mainly in the fur trade, settlers who wished to farm the land were discouraged from migrating to the colonies.

In 1607, the English founded Jamestown in Virginia, and in 1620, what was to become Plymouth in Massachusetts. In 1664, they forced the Dutch to surrender their colony of New Netherlands, which included what is now New York, New Jersey, Pennsylvania, and Delaware. The English flag now floated from Maine to the border of Florida. The English colonies, unlike those of Spain and France, attracted large numbers of settlers. By 1750 there were nearly 1,500,000 people living in the thirteen colonies strung along the Atlantic coast.

These settlers had come for many reasons. Some hoped to find religious freedom; some sought political liberty; others hoped to improve their economic lot. The prospect for the small farmer was far brighter in the English colonies because land ownership was widespread, especially in New England and in the middle colonies. England granted more political, religious, and economic freedom than either Spain or France.

English colonists came to believe that all men were equal and should have equal opportunities. They insisted that the political rights won by their fellow countrymen in England over the centuries were also rightfully theirs. Building upon their heritage of the Magna Charta (1215), the Petition of Rights (1628), and the Bill of Rights (1689), the English colonists developed their own democratic institutions. In Virginia the House of Burgesses, established in 1619, was the first elected legislature in the New World. In 1639, Connecticut drew up the Fundamental Orders, the first written constitution in America. New England town meetings involved the participation of qualified citizens in making local decisions and choosing their officials. By 1750 most of the colonial legislatures had some measure of control over the royal governors by virtue of "the power of the purse," that is, the right to grant or withhold taxes.

Religious freedom also developed in the English colonies. Roger Williams founded Rhode Island as a colony affording complete religious freedom for all, with separation of church and state. Maryland's Act of Toleration granted freedom of worship to all Christians. William Penn, in 1682, granted religious freedom in Pennsylvania.

Beginning in 1689, England and France were engaged in a worldwide struggle for colonies and commerce. In 1754, the fourth and most decisive of these wars broke out. In the New World it was known as the French and Indian War. Its outcome was a complete defeat for the French. The Treaty of Paris (1763) gave to England Canada and all of the French territory east of the Mississippi, with the exception of New Orleans.

The victory proved to be a mixed blessing for England. Before 1763, she had paid little attention to the colonies which had had virtual self-government. The Navigation Acts, which had been designed to compel the colonies to trade almost entirely with the mother country, in accordance with the mercantilist theory, had not been enforced. After the French and Indian War, England's attitude changed. To protect the colonists from Indians, England needed an army of 10,000 in the colonies, at a cost of one million dollars a year. Added to this sum was the huge debt with which the English were saddled as a consequence of the war. She determined to make the colonies pay part of the cost of maintaining the army as well as the interest on the war debt. Furthermore, British officials began to collect customs duties, which had long been evaded by colonial smugglers.

There followed a series of British enactments which became increasingly objectionable to the colonists. The lands west of the Appalachians were closed to colonial settlers. The Sugar Act, the Stamp Act, and the Townshend Acts, all designed to increase revenue for Britain, aroused anger among the colonists. Committees of Correspondence succeeded in organizing opposition to Britain, coordinating the efforts of patriots in the various colonies.

On April 19, 1775, fighting broke out at Lexington, Massachusetts. The news spread quickly. Harsh measures by the British convinced many colonists that independence was the next logical step. On July 4, 1776, the Second Continental Congress adopted the Declaration of Independence, written chiefly by Thomas Jefferson, which expressed the democratic ideals of the American Revolution.

The war between England and her American colonies was a long and a bitter one. Under the inspiring leadership of George Washington, the colonists, with the help of France, scored a series of remarkable victories. The Treaty of Paris (1783) ended the war, granting full independence to the colonies.

Once free, the colonies became thirteen independent states, loosely bound together under the Articles of Confederation. The period from 1781 to 1789 has been called the Critical Period, because it seemed that the weak central government would fail to solve its economic and political problems. In 1787, the representatives of twelve of the thirteen states met in Philadelphia to strengthen the powers of the central government. Instead of merely revising the Articles of Confederation, however, they drew up an entirely new plan of government for the nation and wrote a new constitution. This document, the Constitution of the United States, has remained the basis of our federal system of government.

A task which was uppermost in the minds of the representatives was the prevention of tyranny. They agreed with the famous French philosopher Montesquieu that there could be no liberty when the powers to make the laws and to enforce the laws were given to the same person or group or when the power of judging was not separated from legislative and executive powers. Accordingly, they decided to set up a system in which no one person or agency could make a law, arrest a violator, find him guilty, and punish him.

In the section "American Government," we shall examine the three main branches of our Federal Government in order to understand the responsibilities of each, as well as the relationships among the branches.

Development

During the quarter century between the inauguration of President Washington and the end of the War of 1812, the new nation achieved maturity and general recognition from the international community.

It was first necessary to learn whether the Constitution could adequately provide guidance in transforming the sovereign states into a federal nation. Some leaders were at least as strongly devoted to their state–Jefferson always called Virginia his "country"–as to the Union. Others considered that the United States relegated the states to subdivisions. This division appeared to some extent in the platforms of political leaders and, as they developed, of political parties. As the nation evolved, the aggregation of states, the region–New England, the South, the West–tended to replace the state in its capacity to attract primary loyalties, especially when the region could be identified with a minority position. Nevertheless, political regionalism invariably was disguised as the doctrine of states' rights, because under the Constitution the state was a political entity that had specific rights, whereas the region had no standing of any kind.

POLITICAL PARTIES

Nor did the Constitution recognize the existence of political parties, or factions (the term in vogue in the eighteenth century), and all the Constitution-builders professed an aversion to factionalism. At first only one's opponents were described as forming a faction. Those who favored the strengthening of the new central government described themselves as Federalists. Their opponents, who preferred minimal government administered locally, were therefore dubbed Antifederalists, or simply Antis. But the latter, choosing to emphasize positive concepts, such as liberty, professed to see a trend toward monarchism among the Federalists, and so called themselves Democratic-Republicans, soon shortened to Republicans. With polarization, the factional names acquired symbolic value, and by the time John Adams became President a two-party system was operative.

It then became necessary for that system to develop effective mechanisms. The election in 1796 of an Executive team of antithetical politicians, the Federalist President John Adams and the Republican Vice President Thomas Jefferson, disclosed the absurdity and the need for reform. When the electoral process in the election of 1800 returned a tie vote for two Republican candidates, Jefferson and Aaron Burr, that was resolved under Constitutional procedures only after 36 ballots in Congress just a week before inauguration day, reform became imperative. The result was the Twelfth Amendment, ratified in 1803 and operative in 1804, which required a separate ballot for the President and Vice President.

Once the legitimacy of party organization was accepted, the Congressional members of the several parties (known as *caucuses*) assumed the prerogative of selecting candidates. Federal caucuses nominated John Adams, Charles Pinckney, DeWitt Clinton, and Rufus King in the elections from 1800 through 1816, while Republican caucuses named Thomas Jefferson, James Madison, and James Monroe. After three successive two-term Republican administrations, the Federalist Party ceased to exist nationally in 1820. Four years later the Republican Party, lacking external opposition, was internally in turmoil. Only one-third of the Republicans in Congress attended the caucus that named William Crawford to run for the Presidency. Three competitors found it expedient to announce their candidacies through the sponsorship of state legislatures: Andrew Jackson, John Quincy Adams, and Henry Clay. When the two-party system began to function once more in the 1830s, the caucus had lost its nominative function. It was replaced by the party convention, which had nominated candidates for state office since the 1790s. The first Democratic national convention met in 1832, but two minor parties, the Anti-Masonic and National Republican parties, nominated Presidential candidates in 1831.

FOREIGN RELATIONS

The confrontation between Federalists and Republicans had been well defined during President Washington's Administration, from 1789 to 1797, when Alexander Hamilton and Thomas Jefferson

THE UNITED STATES

After Treaty of Sept. 3, 1783

The Resignation of George Washington (detail).

were their recognized spokesmen. Both foreign and domestic policy were matters of partisan controversy. The French Revolution and the Napoleonic Wars had an impact because interested parties abroad sought support within the United States.

The Republicans considered the early phases of the French Revolution a continuation of the American Revolution. Thomas Paine, Thomas Jefferson, and James Monroe were ardent advocates of the French republic, whereas such Federalists as Alexander Hamilton, John Adams, and John Jay supported a counterrevolutionary backlash. Washington was initially neutral, but gradually turned toward the Federalist position. As the Terror of 1793 was succeeded by the general warfare of the Napoleonic period, even the Republicans were disillusioned.

The break in the alliance between France and the United States was a direct result of the "XYZ Affair" of 1797, a demeaning and unsuccessful attempt by the French Directory to browbeat President Adams' administration by insulting American negotiators. A state of undeclared war in 1798 was accompanied by the establishment of an American navy, while France under Napoleon embarked on full-scale war against Great Britain and neighboring European countries. As the tempo of the European war accelerated, the two major belligerents alternately wooed and abused the United States. Under such conditions, Napoleon unexpectedly sold Louisiana to the United States in 1803. American merchant shipping throve on risky but profitable wartime ventures. After 1805 the attempts of three American Presidents to enforce neutrality through "nonintercourse" and embargoes aroused resentment on the part of American commercial interests and retaliation at the hands of the belligerents. The practice that most outraged Americans was that of "impressment"–removing sailors from United States ships under the pretext that they were British deserters, as was often the case.

THE WAR OF 1812

The years of frustration ultimately played into the hands of a new generation of political leaders from the West, who welcomed an excuse to advocate an offensive foreign policy. Known as the War Hawks, they proposed to smite the Spanish in the Floridas and the British in Canada, to secure the southern and northern borders of the United States. The ensuing War of 1812 proved militarily indecisive, despite moments of naval glory and the spectacular victory for the United States at New Orleans. The political significance of the war makes the Treaty of Ghent, signed in 1814, a landmark in United States history. The world was impressed that a hitherto untried nation could hold to a standstill Europe's foremost naval power, the conqueror of Napoleon.

The development of American internal politics was no less dramatic. The Republicans in 1798 and 1799 had sponsored the Kentucky and Virginia Resolutions, proclaiming the concept that the Union was a revocable compact among sovereign states. Now they had become a nationalist party of militant expansionists. The Federalists, on the other hand were virtually insulated in New England. They compromised their original position by considering, at the Hartford Convention of 1814, whether their region might not be more prosperous outside than within the Union. The Treaty of Ghent made such notions irrelevant, and enabled the country to devote its full energies to the consolidation of the vast territories it now controlled.

ORGANIZING AN EMPIRE

The United States had undergone a remarkable physical change between the treaties of 1783 and 1814. At the end of the Revolutionary War, the thirteen original states claimed a hinterland extending to the Mississippi, with undefined and insecure borders south and north. Spain claimed the entire Gulf coast. British troops continued to occupy strategic points that admittedly belonged to the United States, pending France's fulfillment of all the terms of the Treaty of Paris. Jay's Treaty of 1794 with Great Britain settled some of the disputes with Britain, and Thomas Pinckney's Treaty of San Lorenzo with Spain in 1795 gave Georgia a disputed strip in the hinterland of Florida. These were holding operations, maintaining instability.

Meanwhile, Congress under the Articles of Confederation and later under the Constitution established a pattern of organization for the trans-Appalachian territories. Georgia west of the Chattahoochee was ceded to the Federal Government in 1802 and became Mississippi Territory. The Territory Southwest of the River Ohio, originally the western sections of Virginia and North Carolina, became the states of Kentucky and Tennessee in 1792 and 1796 respectively. The Territory North of the River Ohio (Northwest Territory for short) was organized in 1787 with the provision that it would be formed into states, each of which would be admitted to the Union upon attaining a population of 60,000. A further provision prohibited the institution of slavery throughout the entire area. The authority of the Federal Government to organize and legislate for territories that would be guaranteed statehood was thus established even before the Constitution was ratified.

THE NEW WEST

In 1803, Ohio–the first state carved out of the Northwest Territory–was admitted to the Union. That same year, the total area of the United States was doubled by the acquisition of Louisiana. This vast tract extended the sovereignty of the United States west to the Rocky Mountains. Some questioned the authority of the Federal Government to acquire territory by purchase (as in this instance) or by conquest; but Jefferson set a precedent that met with general approval. The Louisiana Purchase–soon renamed Missouri Territory–was expected to evolve into states and be added to the Union. However, it was not so generally conceded that the Federal Government could legislate concerning the extension of the institution of slavery into the Missouri Territory.

It was anticipated that this territory would be settled mostly by small farmers, who would adhere to the Republican ideals of Jefferson. Within the agrarian South itself, however, planters already prevailed over yeomen, and cotton plantations were taking the place of tobacco plantations to such an extent that the region had virtually developed a one-crop economy: cotton was "king." This resulted in the rejuvenation of the institution of slavery, the narrowing of trade relations to the

The Aaron Burr—Alexander Hamilton Duel (detail)

A cartoon satirizes the 1836 presidential election campaign.

Another cartoon looks at the presidential campaign of 1856.

export of cotton, and the substitution of South Carolina for Virginia as the regional headquarters. Nor were the interests of the cotton South identical with those of the new West on such questions as the protective tariff (which the South abhorred) or the need to build roads or canals.

THE CHANGING EAST

The East–or the North, by which was meant New England and the Middle states–was also changing, largely as a result of the War of 1812 and the introduction from England of the technology of the Industrial Revolution. Commerce and finance, including speculation, had accounted for the earlier prosperity of the East and its prevailing political pattern of Federalism. But now the country had abandoned colonial habits and discovered the function of new devices behind which a manufacturing industry could flourish. While traders needed a strong navy and merchant marine, favored commercial treaties with foreign countries, and valued an expanding hinterland for its investment possibilities (especially in cheap land), manufacturers needed sources of raw materials, markets for finished goods, treaties that would permit selective import discrimination, and a strong and controlled financial structure. The West needed ample credit, free or cheap land for those who would live on it, internal improvements to assure access to and from markets, a militia to control or expel the Indians, and removal of property restrictions on the exercise of the franchise.

Expansion before the Civil War (1814-1861)

Three regional patterns were taking form. The South and the East were in competition for an alliance with the new West. The South and West shared an essentially agrarian base and trust in local rather than in central government; but only central government could provide roads and canals and organize effective armed forces for security against Indians, the Spanish, or the British. Both the East and the West wanted the National Road and the Erie Canal, and tariff schedules to protect the crops of the farmers and the manufactures of the townsmen; but they parted company on the issue of the Bank of the United States. Borrowing homesteaders hated it, while the rising tycoon depended on it. The West could accept neither the Southern version of Republicanism nor the Eastern brand of revived Federalism. Henry Clay, a true son of the West, offered his "American system" that combined roads and canals, protective tariffs, and a strong financial structure, but he never gained the political following of two other Westerners, Andrew Jackson and John C. Calhoun.

JACKSONIANS AND WHIGS

After a period of fluidity two new major parties emerged. One, a Jacksonian (not Jeffersonian) version of Republicanism, became the Democratic Party from 1828 to the eve of the Civil War. This movement was supported generally in the West and among the disfranchised in the East, particularly the emerging urban working class. Jackson's enemies tried to insult him by calling him "King Andrew," and by depicting the Democrats as American-style Tories. In the current jargon, the converse of a Tory was a Whig, and this was the name adopted by the anti-Jacksonians. They included followers of Calhoun, who switched his allegiance from West to South; devotees to Clay's American system; and ex-Federalists who aligned themselves with Daniel Webster of New England, spokesmen for the merchant and manufacturing class. The Whigs, a coalition in the guise of a party, had no platform. Webster supported the protective tariff, but Calhoun didn't. Calhoun reformulated the concept of nullification, while Webster demanded loyalty to the Union. The Whigs finally elected a President after the issueless campaign of 1840. He was the picturesque but nonpolitical William Henry Harrison, who died within a month and was succeeded by an anti-Jacksonian Democrat, John Tyler.

THE ISSUE OF SLAVERY

One issue that did not appear crucial to the major political figures in the decades after the War of 1812 was that of slavery, although such discerning experts as Jefferson and John Quincy Adams suspected its potential gravity early on. The point became controversial in national politics rather indirectly, in connection with the procedure for admitting new states. Eight of the 16 states that comprised the Union in 1803 were "slave" states; that is, their economy significantly depended on the use of slave labor. They shared power in the Senate with an equal number of "free" states, while in the House of Representatives the ratio of delegates was 49 "slave" to 57 "free." However, some of the slave-state Congressmen held office only because the Constitution gave every five blacks as much representation in the House of Representatives as every three whites (although the blacks had no other political existence). Whatever resentment the North felt against this advantage exercised by the slave interests was mitigated by the fact that only three more territories open to slavery remained east of the Mississippi, whereas at least four territories would be formed out of the Northwest Territory, where slavery was prohibited under the Ordinance of 1787. In spite of an initial proslavery handicap, the slave power would soon inevitably be a minority in both Houses.

The trans-Mississippi acquisition postponed the doom of the slave power. In 1820 the 22 states then in the Union were evenly divided, and the "slave" minority in the House had slipped only from 44 percent to 42 percent. The pending admission of Missouri as a slave state would tip the balance against the free-soil power. Henry Clay, known as a compromiser, proposed that the District of Maine in Massachusetts, having long sought statehood, should be matched with Missouri to maintain equilibrium. He also proposed that henceforth a line be extended westward along Missouri's southern border, north of which slavery would be banned just as it had previously been banned in the Northwest Territory. This Missouri Compromise of 1820 was forthwith adopted, and a crisis was averted for a decade or so. But the South did not fail to observe the shape of the remaining territory, of which only a relative sliver remained potential slave territory. The only solution for the slave power was to annex additional land south of the slave-free border: the Spanish Southwest.

ANNEXATION, SOUTH AND NORTH

The notion of annexing contiguous territory was neither novel nor unexplored. As soon as it had become clear that the Louisiana deal did not include any part of Spanish Florida, frontiersmen began to infiltrate their neighbor's domain. West Florida between the Mississippi and Pearl rivers was occupied in 1810 and two years later was annexed to the new state of Louisiana. The process–settlement of Americans on foreign territory, liberation of the area, annexation–was to be repeated on almost every occasion, from Texas to Hawaii. In Florida, the next step was the invasion of Mobile and the extension of American claims eastward to the Perdido in 1813. The rest of Florida was bought in 1819 for a minimal price from Spain, which was in no position to defend its holdings; for much of Spanish America was authentically in a state of revolution. The Adams-Onís Treaty of 1819 not only added Florida to the United States; it also defined for the first time the southern border of the Louisiana Purchase.

Meanwhile, the northern border was also subject to negotiation. There was no question that the United States had hoped to annex part of Canada during the War of 1812. The Treaty of Ghent with Great Britain ended this prospect, and a series of agreements culminated in the Convention of 1818, which made the forty-ninth parallel the permanent boundary between the United States and British North America from the Lake of the Woods to the Rocky Mountains. Between the Rockies and the Pacific Ocean, north of the present northern border of California and south of the still undefined Russian border, was a vast tract known as the Oregon country, still the preserve of fur traders and mountain men. British and American claims to Oregon remained unresolved by mutual agreement, and the region was in effect open to all.

THE MONROE DOCTRINE

These border problems having been settled, the United States asserted a sphere of influence. As the Spanish possessions in South America became independent during the years 1810 to 1825, they sought approval and recognition from the United States. Until pending disputes between the United States and Spain were resolved, these appeals from South America were ignored, but with the ratification of the Adams-Onís Treaty in 1821, the United States took steps to enter into relations with the ex-colonies. When it appeared that a league of European powers (the Holy Alliance) proposed to help Spain recover these colonies, President James Monroe proclaimed his doctrine: "The American continents . . . are henceforth not to be considered as subjects for future colonization by any European powers."

THE MEXICAN WAR

This proclamation, which in fact required the British navy for its enforcement, was not a self-denying ordinance. For an American colony had already infiltrated Spanish Mexico in 1821, and continued to enlarge after Mexico had achieved its independence. The initial step toward acquiring the Mexican state of Texas was undertaken by President Jackson in 1829. Thereafter it was only a matter of time until the sequence of revolution, liberation, and annexation was pursued. This time it required a full-scale war between the United States and Mexico to confirm the objective, but in 1848, under the terms of the Treaty of Guadalupe Hidalgo, the Mexican territories became the American Southwest, adding New Mexico and California to the already admitted state of Texas. In 1846 an agreement had been concluded with Great Britain that extended the forty-ninth parallel westward from the Rocky Mountains through the Oregon country. The ultimate shape of the United States was virtually attained, fulfilling the dogma of Manifest Destiny "to overspread the continent allotted by Providence for the free development of our yearly multiplying millions"–which by 1848 exceeded 20 million.

COMPROMISE OF 1850

The organization of all this territory again raised the problem that had vexed the country in 1820 and had brought about the Missouri Compromise. The Presidential election of 1848 was the first in which the question of slavery, or at least its extension into the territories, was the principal issue. During the Mexican War, the House of Representatives had passed the Wilmot Proviso that would have excluded slavery from any ceded territory, but the South mustered enough support in the Senate to beat back this offensive. In 1848 both parties were split on the question of slavery extension. In the very week during which Wisconsin's admission restored a balance of 15 states on each side, the Democrats picked Lewis Cass for their Presidential candidate. Cass had developed the concept of "popular sovereignty." He wanted to discard the old principle of a demarcation between free and slave territories; he believed that the settlers should vote their preferences on the issue. Inasmuch as hardly any of the remaining unorganized territory would support the use of slave labor, the North could accept popular sovereignty in principle. The South might well endorse a pro-

The U.S. Capitol, ca. 1858

gram that would remove the thorny issue from Congress, where they could no longer hope to break even.

The Whigs again nominated a nonpolitical general, Zachary Taylor, taking no stand on the crucial questions–and won. Their victory was made possible, however, by the swing vote of the Free-Soil Party, composed of antislavery Democrats and Whigs, who won enough votes in New York to deprive Cass of the Presidency.

The gold rush that swelled the population of California indirectly canceled the truce, for it was imperative to provide law and order on the West Coast. California applied for immediate statehood in 1849 under a free-soil constitution, although most of the proposed state was on the "slave" side of the Missouri Compromise line. Congress delayed the admission of California despite President Taylor's plea for prompt action, and the Californians set up "vigilantes" to assume the police role. In 1850 Clay again came to the rescue with a compromise. Its basic elements were (for the North) the admission of a free-soil California and (for the South) a strict law enforcing the return of fugitive slaves to their masters. Moreover, two other proposed territories (Utah and New Mexico) north and south of the line of demarcation would be organized under the concept of popular sovereignty. The Compromise of 1850 was unenthusiastically adopted.

THE FAILURE OF COMPROMISE

The nation now attempted to consolidate its acquisitions. During the next decade there was a great leap forward of immigration, homesteading, railroad building. The peopling of the Great Plains inevitably hastened the development of territories into states, and again the slavery issue appeared. In 1854 the Kansas-Nebraska Bill proposed to apply the principle of popular sovereignty to the next tier west of Iowa and Missouri, extending from British North America south to the territory reserved for the Indians, and west to Utah and New Mexico. Under the Missouri Compromise, these territories were both destined for free soil; the new dispensation would give the slave power a chance. Once the bill was signed, partisans with strong convictions and guns were sent into the territories to frame constitutions.

The pro-slavery forces showed special capacity for organization in Kansas Territory (where rival constitutions appeared), accompanied by terrorist campaigns that gave rise to the popular allusion to "bleeding Kansas." By the time of the election of 1856, a national Republican Party had succeeded the transitory Free-Soilers. It held its first convention and nominated John C. Frémont for President. Frémont, with 33 percent of the popular vote, brought the Republicans to the rank of a major party. The Whigs joined the Federalists in the archives of history.

The stroke that ended all possibility of compromise on slavery was applied by the U.S. Supreme Court. The judiciary, under the brilliant and durable guidance of Federalist John Marshall, had established beyond question its role as stabilizer and sustainer of balance between the Executive and Legislative branches. Often upholding the Federal government against the states, sometimes protecting states' rights, only once had the Supreme Court (in *Marbury v. Madison* in 1803) declared an act of Congress unconstitutional. Now, more than half a century later (in *Dred Scott v. Sandford* in 1857), the Court declared that no legislature–national, state, or territorial–could prohibit the institution of slavery. Where the Kansas-Nebraska Act had removed the thorny controversy from Congress to territorial conventions, the Court now forced it to the battlefield. The moderates who had hoped to contain the institution or to control its spread, were driven from contention, leaving as contestants only those who refused to limit slavery or those who would abolish it.

As so many grave issues had taken on the aspect of a clash between Federal and states' rights, so the issue of slavery was transformed into a contest between (1) those who would secede rather than compromise on slavery and (2) those who identified hostility toward slavery with loyalty to the Union. Their predicament was personalized by the Republican candidate for the Presidency in 1860, Abraham Lincoln. Within a few years, on taking office and under the stress of Civil War, Lincoln passed from a free-soil to an abolitionist position. The war was essentially a defense of the Union, as Lincoln and most in the North understood it. But in Southern eyes it was a defense not only of the right of states to leave the Union, but a defense of an institution vital to the economy of the South.

Jefferson Davis

Thomas J. ("Stonewall") Jackson

The Civil War—Black Union soldiers

THE CIVIL WAR

The population of the United States at the outbreak of the Civil War was about thirty-one million, of whom more than 60 percent lived in the North. One-third of the Southern minority were slaves. The economy of the South had long since ceased to compete with that of the North. The South was in effect a colonial supplier of cotton to British and Northern factories. The North, on the other hand, had embraced industrialization and was capable of supplying the potential market of the West and drawing upon its untapped resources. The West had already received more free immigrants than the entire servile labor force of the South. An economic alliance between the West and the North awaited only the building of railroads to link the two regions.

Under these circumstances, few people could expect the South to stave off the Northern military offensive for more than four years. Even during the Civil War, the Union lacked actual unity. The exigencies of war brought a boom to Western farmers, fortunes to profiteers, and a decline in the real income of workers and artisans. It irreversibly altered the economy of the nation.

Readjustment and Reconstruction (1864–1876)

The first postwar decade was devoted to Reconstruction. The Federal Government had to restructure the relationships between the states of the defeated Confederacy and the triumphant Union. President Lincoln and (after his assassination) President Andrew Johnson proposed to bind the nation's wounds by restoring autonomy to the South consistent with the termination of slavery, as formulated in the Thirteenth Amendment ratified in December 1865. This charitable policy would have to be achieved at the expense of the ex-slaves.

THE SOUTH IS READMITTED

A spate of "black codes" enacted by the first popular legislatures throughout the South angered the Republicans who controlled Congress. A Freedmen's Bureau, with the function of protecting the interests of the blacks, had been set up temporarily in March 1865, and was given permanent status over Johnson's veto in July 1866. Inasmuch as the Southern representation in the House of Representatives would increase when the blacks achieved full (rather than three-fifths) representation, Congress refused to readmit the former states until they accepted the Fourteenth Amendment, which spelled out the civil rights of blacks. When all of the "sinful ten" states had "flung back into our teeth the magnanimous offer of a generous nation" (in the words of Congressman James A. Garfield), Congress passed in March 1867 a Reconstruction Act that instituted martial law throughout the South.

By the end of 1869 most of the Southern states were in the fold and the Fifteenth Amendment ratified in March 1870 gave voting privileges to all male blacks, North and South. For the next five or six years the Republican Party closely supervised the legislatures of the Southern states, imposing civil rights through a series of so-called Force Acts. Under this umbrella a combination of freedmen, white Republicans of Northern origin (derisively called "carpetbaggers"), and white Southern Republicans (who were ridiculed as "scalawags") enacted social legislation that was unacceptable to the white supremacists. When the Northern Republicans chose to relax their supervision, the unreconstructed Southern whites resumed their opposition to blacks, both through the underground Ku Klux Klan and an official Democratic Party. Around this party a political structure known as the "solid South" was firmly established.

THE NEW NORTH

The same administration that presided over Reconstruction in the South was responsible for the transformation of the North. There the main drive of the Republican Party was to serve the industrialists and financiers who were building railroads, operating steel mills, mining coal, iron, and the recently discovered petroleum, and in general developing an industrial plant suitable for a powerful modern nation. The legislation to encourage these activities, forming the essential Republican platform, included high tariffs and sound currency. Other ingredients that did not appear in party manifestoes included subsidies for the railroads, relaxation of free enterprise in favor of various patterns of monopoly, and tolerance of corruption. In this era politicians such as William Tweed were able to plunder cities of millions of dollars, slums appeared in large urban centers, and scandals on a large scale demeaned the Presidency.

The first railway from New York to Chicago had been completed in 1865, and four years later the Union Pacific and Central Pacific met in Utah Territory. Railroads had given the Union the edge in the Civil War, and they determined which communities in the West would survive to become cities. In earlier times, commerce and enterprise exemplified in the career of John Jacob Astor had built the great fortunes, but the capital accumulation that followed the Civil War was in the hands of such pioneers as the railroad builder, Cornelius Vanderbilt. Railroads also introduced coolie labor to the United States, and the first serious confrontation between capital and labor alarmed the nation when the railroad workers of the Baltimore and Ohio struck in 1877. Finally, in reaction against the ruthless power exercised in rural areas by the railroads, the Grange (a farmers' social and welfare society) turned toward lobbying for antirailroad legislation on a state level.

The Urbanization of America (1876–1917)

The Reconstruction program formally ended as a result of the Presidential election of 1876. A depression in 1873 and 1874, revulsion against the spread of corruption, firm resistance to civil rights in the South, and even the humiliating defeat of General George Custer by the Sioux in Montana Territory combined to bring about a state of general discontent. The time had come for an understanding between the Democrats (who wished to assume political jurisdiction in the South) and the Republicans (who were frightened when the Democrats gained control of the House of Representatives in 1874, for the first time since the Civil War). In 1876 the Democratic Presidential candidate, Samuel J. Tilden, won a popular majority but was one vote short in the electoral college. A deal was made whereby the Democrats would deprive Tilden of the Presidency in favor of the Republican candidate, Rutherford B. Hayes, if Hayes would withdraw Federal troops from the South. Immediately after the withdrawal the Democrats took over the state governments in the former Confederacy, and within a few years the blacks were tenant farmers, or sharecroppers. They were excluded by economic pressure and by force from exercising civil and political rights they had briefly acquired. The economy of the South continued to produce mainly cotton, recovering from wartime collapse but remaining outside the mainstream of postwar prosperity.

END OF THE FRONTIER

In the North and in the West that prosperity was neither under control nor equitably distributed. At the beginning of this period, which comprised the last quarter of the nineteenth century, about one-fourth of the population lived in communities exceeding twenty-five hundred inhabitants. The total population rose, with the help of some nine million immigrants, from about fifty million in 1880 to about seventy-five million in 1900. Most of the newcomers settled in rural areas and the West was settled so thoroughly that no discernible frontier existed after 1890. The plains proved as fertile as anticipated, once the range was largely enclosed and made arable; and crops were so abundant that their prices fell steadily and farmers could not live on what they produced.

PROBLEMS OF RISING REVENUES

At the same time huge fortunes were accumulated, private enterprise was short-circuited to permit the reckless manipulation of public resources. Financial crises (called "panics") recurred and credit was kept tight. Small entrepreneurs found it difficult to finance a grubstake, but magnates such as John D. Rockefeller and Andrew Carnegie organized industrial empires. The accumulation of private capital was exceeded only by that in the United States Treasury. With revenues constantly exceeding expenditures, the Federal Government no longer needed high tariffs to provide income. Tariffs favored manufacturers and made manufactured goods expensive for farmers and workers, so tariff reduction became a perennial slogan of reformers. Another catchphrase was "cheap money," which usually meant the coinage of silver, a metal increasingly produced in the West and therefore a significant commodity. Groups in every part of the country were for or against high tariffs or free coinage, and geographical sectionalism was giving way to confrontations between the Establishment–big business and big politics–and its victims.

THE 1880s AND 1890s

In three consecutive Presidential elections, 1880 through 1888, the Democratic and Republican candidates evenly shared the electorate, with less than one percentage point separating their popular votes. The Democrat, Grover Cleveland, won the Presidency in 1884. The prize went to Republicans James A. Garfield and Benjamin Harrison respectively in the preceding and following campaigns. But issues played a negligible role in each instance. During the 1890s, however, the monetary system and tariffs began to arouse interest and as tariffs rose, so did passion concerning the imposition of the "cross of gold." After the McKinley Tariff of 1890 and the Panic of 1893, the fervor of the cheap-money partisans was expressed when an eloquent Democratic politician, William Jennings Bryan, reminded the urban gold advocates "that the great cities rest upon our broad and fertile prairies."

LABOR UNIONS

Both workers and farmers attempted to organize in the late nineteenth century. The unions, speaking for an abused minority, were suppressed or controlled by the most powerful segments of society. The mushroom growth of the Knights of Labor in the 1880s was stifled by the thrust of the American Federation of Labor as organization by craft, a narrow but more intensive base, proved more successful than organization by class. After several violent confrontations between labor and management in this period, notably at Haymarket Square in Chicago in 1886 and at the Homestead, Pennsylvania, plant of the Carnegie corporation in 1892, unionism made little progress before the turn of the century.

FARM ORGANIZATIONS

The farmers who were an abused majority, made impressive political progress. Within the Democratic Party, the Farmers' Alliances that developed from the Grange elected nine Congressmen and two Senators in 1890 and began to consider forming an independent party. The convention of the People's Party in 1892 picked a Presidential candidate who won 8.5 per cent of the popular vote and the ballots of 22 electors from four states. Their platform was based on the free coinage of silver, national ownership of rail, telegraph, and telephone facilities, a graduated income tax, an eight-hour day, and the popular election of Senators–several of which proposals were eventually adopted by the traditional parties and enacted into law. The Populists increased their strength in 1894, but in 1896 they were persuaded to endorse the Democratic candidate, Bryan. His defeat terminated third-party efforts for many decades and prolonged the ascendancy of the Republican alliance with big business.

The Spanish-American War—The Battle of Manila Bay, Philippine Islands, May 1898

THE NATION REACHES FULL GROWTH

Through a combination of aggressive enterprise, indulgent government, enormous resources, and geographical isolation, the United States emerged into the twentieth century as a major power. The gold standard and a record tariff were on the books. Farm production began to satisfy an expanding domestic market. The United States produced more steel than any country in the world. For a quarter-century the trade balance was increasingly favorable, and soon after the turn of the century the United States became a creditor rather than a debtor in the international market. The circumstances favored a new manifestation of expansionism, which had been almost dormant in the second half of the nineteenth century; only the purchase of Alaska from the Russians in 1867 significantly added to the national domain. Just before the end of the century the contagion of European imperialism spread to the Western Hemisphere. The vigorous economy would soon require new markets, new sources of raw material, new fields for the investment of capital.

THE SPANISH-AMERICAN WAR

In such an environment, the plight of the offshore island of Cuba proved to be a catalyst. The drive to annex Cuba to the United States had diminished once the island was no longer potential slave territory. But Spain's poor administration of Cuba, in which American capital was heavily invested after the Civil War, provided a reason for intervention. More dramatic justification developed–according to some sources, was provided–when the U.S. battleship *Maine* was blown up in Havana harbor in February 1898. The Spanish-American War began in April; by August, Spain sought peace; and the treaty signed in Paris in December transferred to the United States possession of the Philippine Islands, Puerto Rico, and Guam, as well as the mandate of Cuba. In that year the annexation of the Hawaiian Islands, governed as a "republic" by Americans since 1893, was also consummated. Thus the United States found itself responsible for the administration of widely scattered dependencies inhabited by large populations whose integration into the existing American system was not contemplated.

The Spanish-American War—Wreck of the *Maine*

Portrait by Gilbert Stuart

GEORGE WASHINGTON

Very little is known of the boyhood of George Washington. He was born on February 22, 1732 into a family of moderately prosperous Virginia planters. His father, Augustine Washington, died when George was 11.

Washington's military career began in late 1752 when he secured an appointment as a district adjutant for the Virginia militia. Washington played an important role in the French and Indian War.

Near the end of the war, Washington resigned from the military with the rank of colonel, and on January 6, 1759 married Martha Dandridge Custis, a wealthy widow with two children. For the next 15 years Washington pursued the role of a prosperous Virginia planter. He joined in issuing the call for a Continental Congress and attended the first meeting of that body in September of 1774 at Philadelphia as a representative from Virginia. The Second Continental Congress elected him commander-in-chief of the armed forces.

Fighting came to an end in 1781 with Washington's capture of Cornwallis and his forces at Yorktown. Washington's reputation as a war hero was of such magnitude that some of his friends planned to make him king of the emerging nation. But Washington rejected the idea.

Washington resigned his command and returned home to Mount Vernon. But the new government was too weak to deal with factional rivalries. At first Washington felt that Congress could strengthen the Articles of Confederation, but later he joined a convention to overhaul the entire system.

At the convention in Philadelphia in May of 1787, Washington was unanimously elected its president. He later secured ratification of the new Constitution by the states. When the electoral college met in New York City in February of 1789, he was unanimously elected the first President of the United States.

Washington brought to the Presidency the cautious judgment, intelligence, and resourcefulness that characterized his entire life. He was persuaded to stand for reelection and won.

Refusing a third term, Washington retired to Mount Vernon where he died on December 14, 1799 at the age of 67.

Portrait Attributed to Edgar Parker

JOHN ADAMS

John Adams lacked the personal grace and magnetism which so marked his predecessor, George Washington. Born in Braintree (now Quincy), Massachusetts on October 30, 1735, Adams gave thought to entering the ministry, but four years at Harvard College changed his mind. After graduation he taught school at Worcester, Massachusetts. Then he studied law, and in 1758 was admitted to the bar.

In 1764 he wed Abigail Smith and began a long and fullfilling marriage. They had five children, including John Quincy Adams, sixth President of the United States. Intelligent, intense, and ambitious, Adams came to public attention in 1765 when he wrote a position paper for the town of Braintree against the Stamp Act. He represented Massachusetts at both the First and Second Continental Congress. He was one of the first to call for drafting the Declaration of Independence.

Heading the Federalist slate, Adams was elected President in 1796 by a margin of only three electoral votes over his Democratic-Republican opponent, Thomas Jefferson, who became Vice-President. Adams defied popular sentiment by refusing to go to war when France insisted that the United States abrogate the Jay Treaty of 1794. However, Adams did call for the establishment of a navy and waged a brief, undeclared war against French ships. Adams' decision to avoid full-scale war proved sound. When Napoleon took over France, good relations between the two countries were soon restored.

Adams ran for a second term as President, but lost to Thomas Jefferson. He retired to his home at Quincy, Massachusetts, where he died on July 4, 1826, the 50th anniversary of the Declaration of Independence.

Portrait by Rembrandt Peale

THOMAS JEFFERSON

Born April 13, 1743 at Shadwell, Virginia, Thomas Jefferson was the third in a family of ten children and the son of a prominent plantation owner. As the oldest son he inherited his father's substantial estate. An excellent student, Jefferson graduated from the College of William and Mary in 1762. He studied law and established a successful legal practice. In 1772 Jefferson married Martha Wayles Skelton.

Elected to the Virginia House of Burgesses in 1769, Jefferson expressed colonial grievances against Great Britain. He was a delegate from Virginia to the Second Continental Congress. In June of 1776 he wrote the basic draft of the Declaration of Independence, which was little changed when adopted by Congress on July 4, 1776.

Jefferson spent the years from 1784 to 1789 in Europe, mostly in France, where he succeeded Benjamin Franklin as minister.

Shortly after returning to the United States in 1789, he became Secretary of State in Washington's cabinet. He resigned this post in 1793 and spent the next three years at his Monticello (Virginia) estate. His supporters promoted his Presidential candidacy in 1796. Jefferson did little campaigning, but polled almost as many electoral votes as Adams and thus became Vice-President.

By 1800 much of the country had turned against Federalist policies. Jefferson was elected the nation's new Chief Executive. The Louisiana Purchase of 1803 went far beyond Jefferson's strict interpretation of the Constitution, but he signed the measure and arranged for the Lewis and Clark Expedition to explore the region. Jefferson won reelection in 1804 by a wide margin.

One of the most intelligent and broadly cultivated men ever to serve as President, Jefferson retired to his home at Monticello. He died on July 4, 1826.

Portrait by John Vanderlyn

JAMES MADISON

Slight of build, delicate of health, mild in manner, James Madison was more a social scientist and philosopher than a politician. Known as the Father of the Constitution, he completed his work on the Constitution and the Bill of Rights years before he became President.

Madison was born at Port Conway, Virginia, on March 16, 1751. He enrolled at the College of New Jersey (now Princeton) and distinguished himself in debate. He graduated in 1771.

Despite his studious nature, Madison found himself caught up in the revolutionary fervor. In 1776 he was sent to a state convention where he assisted in drafting a new constitution for Virginia. In 1779 the Virginia legislature elected him to a term in the Continental Congress, and he became one of the first delegates to push for strengthening the powers of the Federal Government. Madison returned to Virginia in 1783 and the following year won election to the state legislature.

Madison advocated a convention to draw up a new framework of Union. By the time such a convention met at Philadelphia in 1787, Madison had prepared the so-called Virginia Plan, which served as a model for the new Constitution.

Madison threw all his energy into securing ratification of the Constitution. With Jay and Hamilton, he authored *The Federalist*, a series of influential pro-Constitution essays.

While still in Congress, Madison married Dolley Todd, a young widow who was later much admired for the role she played as First Lady. In 1801 he became Secretary of State under Thomas Jefferson, his friend and mentor for a quarter of a century.

In 1808 Jefferson announced his retirement, and Madison ran for the Presidency on the Democratic-Republican ticket, easily defeating his Federalist opponent. He was elected to a second term in 1812.

Madison retired to Montpelier, his estate in Virginia. He enjoyed a long and active retirement editing his papers and occasionally taking part in public affairs. He died at the age of 85 on June 28, 1836.

Portrait Attributed to Samuel F. B. Morse

JAMES MONROE

Born in Westmoreland County, Virginia, April 28, 1758, James Monroe was a son of prosperous planters. At the age of 16 he enrolled at the College of William and Mary, but two years later left to fight in the Revolution.

In 1782, Monroe won election to the Virginia legislature and the following year was elected to represent Virginia at the Congress of the Confederation, where he served until 1786. He opposed the Constitution, finding it a threat to Virginia's sovereignty. In 1790 the Virginia legislature appointed him to fill an unexpired term in the U.S. Senate.

President Washington selected Monroe to represent the United States in France in 1794. Washington hoped that Monroe would be able to ease the tensions between the two countries, but Monroe was recalled in 1796. After serving as governor of Virginia (1799–1803) he returned to France at the request of Thomas Jefferson to negotiate the purchase of New Orleans. Monroe arranged for the purchase of the entire Louisiana Territory, which doubled the size of the United States. He returned to Virginia to resume his law practice in 1807, and in 1811 again won election to the governorship. He resigned the same year to become Secretary of State in Madison's cabinet, a post which he held until becoming President himself in 1817.

As Monroe ascended to the Presidency, the country entered a period of peace, economic growth, and continued expansion. Credit for this "Era of Good Feeling" fell to Monroe, and he was reelected President in 1820. Monroe approved the Missouri Compromise, added Florida to the United States, and agreed with Great Britain to remove troops from the United States–Canadian border. In 1823 he warned European nations not to interfere with the newly liberated countries of the Western Hemisphere. (A policy now known as the Monroe Doctrine).

Most of his retirement was spent on his estate in Virginia. He died in New York City on July 4, 1831.

Portrait by C. P. A. Healy

JOHN QUINCY ADAMS

The only son of a president to achieve that high office also, John Quincy Adams was much like his father. Lacking in personal magnetism, he was nevertheless a brilliant public speaker, which earned him the nickname, "Old Man Eloquent."

Born at Braintree (now Quincy), Massachusetts, on July 11, 1767, Adams received much of his formal education in Europe, where he accompanied his father on a series of diplomatic missions. Adams returned to the United States in 1785, graduated from Harvard in 1787, and in 1790 gained admission to the bar.

Massachusetts elected him to the U.S. Senate in 1803. He vigorously supported Jefferson's Embargo Act of 1807, despite its unpopularity in his home state. The move cost Adams his Senate seat, and he believed his political career finished. However, in 1809 President Madison made him U.S. Minister to Russia. He participated in negotiating the Treaty of Ghent and later became U.S. Minister to Great Britain. In 1817 he returned to the U.S. to serve as Secretary of State under President Monroe, until becoming President himself in 1825. Since no candidate had a majority in the election of 1824, the election was decided in the House of Representatives. Henry Clay threw his support (and the election) to Adams.

Adams suffered from being a minority President. Carefully refusing to play politics, he lost the election of 1828 to Andrew Jackson.

He returned home to Braintree, but in 1830 was elected to the House of Representatives. Adams spent the last 17 years of his life in the House, where he is best remembered for his long and successful struggle to repeal the House gag rule, a device used to prevent debate on the slavery issue.

Suffering a cerebral stroke, Adams died on February 23, 1848 in the Speaker's room of the House of Representatives.

Portrait by John Wesley Jarvis

ANDREW JACKSON

Born in a frontier settlement in the Carolinas on March 15, 1767, Andrew Jackson was the first President to come from truly humble beginnings. His formal education was interrupted when he joined the militia to fight in the Revolution. Captured by the enemy in 1781, Jackson received a saber slash on the face for refusing to clean the boots of a British officer. He taught school briefly, read law, and was admitted to the North Carolina bar in 1781.

When the War of 1812 was declared, Jackson offered his services to the Federal Government. A victorious campaign against the Creek Indians enabled Jackson to secure much of what is now Georgia and Alabama. Jackson's most famous victory, however, came in January of 1815 when he defeated the British at New Orleans. Called back into service in 1818, he defeated the Seminole Indians in Florida.

In 1823, Jackson won election to the U.S. Senate from Tennessee, and in 1824 ran for President. He got a plurality of the popular and electoral votes. However, the election was thrown into the House of Representatives where Jackson lost to Adams.

Resolved to defeat Adams in the next election, Jackson resigned his Senate seat and returned to Tennessee. Campaigning as "the people's candidate," Jackson won an easy victory over Adams in the election of 1828. He was reelected in 1832 by an equally safe margin.

Jackson called for the election of the President by popular vote and for the sale of Federal land to settlers. He fought bills to aid special-interest groups.

Leaving the Presidency to Martin Van Buren, Jackson retired in 1837 to his estate in Tennessee, where he continued to play a backstage role in national affairs. He died on June 3, 1845 at the age of 78.

Portrait by G. P. A. Healy

MARTIN VAN BUREN

Born at Kinderhook, New York, on December 5, 1782, Van Buren was the third of five children in a farming family. Talented and ambitious, Van Buren engaged in local politics. In 1812 he was elected to the state senate, where he served until 1820.

In 1821 the state legislature chose Van Buren to fill a vacant seat in the U.S. Senate. In the Senate he worked to curtail the spread of slavery.

In the election of 1828 he won the governorship of New York. He resigned this position after only two months to accept appointment as Secretary of State in Jackson's cabinet. Van Buren reopened British West Indian ports to American trade. He also obtained France's promise to pay for damage to American shipping dating back to the Napoleonic Wars.

In 1831 he resigned as Secretary of State to become U.S. Minister to Great Britain, but enemies in the Senate blocked his confirmation. The following year President Jackson supported Van Buren's nomination as his running mate.

With Jackson's help he was nominated for the Presidency by the Democrats in 1836, easily defeating a divided opposition. The major event of Van Buren's Administration was the Panic of 1837, just two months after he took office. Banks around the nation were forced to close or suspend payment. Van Buren did not believe that the government should stimulate the economy or alleviate the problems.

Renominated by the Democrats in 1840, Van Buren was badly defeated. He tried to recapture the Presidency in 1844 and 1848, but met with failure both times. He died at his home in Kinderhook at the age of 79 on July 24, 1862.

Portrait by E. F. Andrews

WILLIAM HENRY HARRISON

Like so many Presidents before him, William Henry Harrison was the son of a prominent Virginia planter. Born on February 9, 1773, Harrison studied briefly to be a doctor. In 1791 he dropped his studies to become an ensign in the Army at Ft. Washington (later Cincinnati). In 1796, while still in the Army, Harrison married Anna Symmes.

After resigning from the army in 1798, Harrison was appointed secretary of the Northwest Territory by President Adams. The following year he was elected to represent the territory in Congress. Harrison authored and successfully pushed through Congress the Land Law of 1800. Known as the Log Cabin Act, it provided for the sale of smaller parcels of Government land.

In 1800 he accepted appointment by President Adams as governor of the recently created Indiana Territory, a post at which he remained for 13 years. Much of his activity in this position involved securing Indian land for the United States. In 1811, Harrison won his famous battle against the Indians at Tippecanoe.

As the War of 1812 broke out, Harrison was put in charge of all American troops in the Northwest. He scored a notable victory over the British at the Battle of the Thames.

After the war, Harrison became active in politics. In 1828 he served briefly as U.S. Minister to Colombia.

Harrison was one of several candidates to oppose Martin Van Buren in the election of 1836. He lost, but in 1840 was again nominated by the Whigs. This time the party managers groomed Harrison's image to appeal to the common man.

Harrison died of pneumonia on April 4, 1841, a month after his inauguration. He was the first President to die in office.

Portrait by G. P. A. Healy

JOHN TYLER

John Tyler became President by accident when William Henry Harrison died one month after his inauguration. Tyler had been tacked on to the Whig slate in 1840 in the hope of attracting Southern votes.

Born on March 29, 1790 in Virginia, Tyler studied law under his father and entered the bar in 1809. He served in the Virginia state legislature from 1811 to 1816, and in the U.S. House of Representatives from 1817 to 1821.

Tyler became governor of Virginia in 1825. He resigned the governorship in 1827 to run for the U.S. Senate, where he served until 1836.

Tyler opposed Jackson's decision to remove Federal funds from the Bank of the United States. In 1836 the Virginia legislature ordered Tyler retract his comments about Jackson's policy from the Senate records; Tyler resigned his seat rather than comply.

The Whigs nominated him as Harrison's running mate. Aware of the differences between himself and the victorious Whigs, Tyler wanted to maintain a low profile as Vice-President. His elevation to the Presidency created tremendous party discord. After twice vetoing legislation for a new national bank, President Tyler was expelled from the Whigs.

Neither the Democrats nor the Whigs would support Tyler in the election of 1844. He withdrew from the race and supported Polk's candidacy.

Tyler spent the next 15 years at his estate in Virginia and did not hold public office. During the Civil War he threw his support to the South and was elected a member of the Confederate Congress. He died on January 18, 1862 at Richmond, Virginia.

Portrait by G. P. A. Healy

JAMES K. POLK

Born on November 2, 1795, on a farm in Mecklenburg County, North Carolina, James Polk was the son of Scotch-Irish immigrants. In 1806 he accompanied his family as they resettled in the frontier state of Tennessee.

Polk turned his attention to politics as well as the law, speaking out often on public issues. In 1823 he was elected to the Tennessee House of Representatives, where he worked to improve the educational system, limit land speculation, and lower taxes.

In 1824, Polk was elected to the U.S. House of Representatives, where he served until 1839. Polk was closely identified with the Jackson Administration. He supported lower tariffs, opposed the Bank of the United States, and called for the election of the President by popular vote. He won the governorship of Tennessee in the election of 1839, but he lost in the subsequent elections of 1841 and 1843.

Despite these two defeats, Polk was still considered a strong vote-getter. When delegates to the 1844 Democratic convention became deadlocked over a Presidential candidate, they turned to Polk on the ninth ballot.

By coming out squarely in favor of the annexation of Texas and by suggesting that the United States should possess the whole Oregon Territory, Polk appealed to popular sentiments. He won the election by a small margin.

Polk lowered tariffs and revived the independent treasury system. In late 1845, Congress admitted Texas to the Union as a state. A boundary dispute led to war with Mexico, which ended in complete victory for the United States. Mexico gave up its claims to Texas, California, and almost all of the Southwest for $15,000,000.

Polk returned to his home in Tennessee when his term expired in March of 1849. Stricken by cholera, he died on June 15, 1849.

Portrait by Unknown Mid-19th-Century Artist

ZACHARY TAYLOR

Born on November 24, 1784, Zachary Taylor was still an infant when his family moved to the Kentucky frontier. Taylor received a minimum of formal education. In 1810 he married Margaret Smith, with whom he had six children.

In 1808, Taylor was commissioned as an officer in the Army. He gave distinguished service in the War of 1812, the Black Hawk War of 1832, and the Seminole Indian War of 1836.

After the annexation of Texas in 1845, he was sent to secure the Texas border. A number of skirmishes with Mexican troops led to a formal declaration of war against Mexico on May 13, 1846. Taylor's military victories came in quick succession, and he became a national hero. His life had been fairly removed from politics, and Whig leaders felt this would make him invulnerable to criticism. As a plantation owner and slaveholder, he could appeal to Southern voters. Taylor won the election of 1848 by a small margin.

President Taylor relied on his advisors in running the government. But in matters of conscience Taylor was entirely his own man. When California applied for admission to the Union as a non-slave state, a passionate debate brought the nation to the brink of civil war. Although a slaveholder himself, Taylor believed that California should be admitted.

Taylor's attitude might have led to war had he not died on July 9, 1850, after a brief illness diagnosed as cholera.

Portrait by G. P. A. Healy

MILLARD FILLMORE

Millard Fillmore was born in a log cabin on January 7, 1800 at Locke in western New York State.

Fillmore excelled at the little formal education to which he was exposed. At the age of 14 he became an apprentice to a clothmaker, but then decided to study law. He moved to Buffalo and worked in a law office. In 1823 he was admitted to the bar.

In 1832 he won election to the U.S. House of Representatives on an anti-Jackson platform. Joining the Whig party, he served three more terms in the House. In his last term, Fillmore was chairman of the House Ways and Means Committee.

At the Whig convention of 1848 Fillmore was nominated for Vice-President on Taylor's ticket. His nomination was an attempt to mollify northern Whigs, who were opposed to Taylor. As it turned out, northern Whigs found greater support in President Taylor than in Vice-President Fillmore; Taylor stood with the antislavery forces and refused to compromise with the South. Fillmore urged compromise. Elevated to the Presidency when Taylor died in July of 1850, Fillmore appointed a new cabinet. Within three months, five separate bills (collectively known as the Compromise of 1850) had become law.

After his term ended, Fillmore returned to his law practice in Buffalo. He ran for President in 1856, but finished a poor third. He died on March 8, 1874, one month after suffering a paralytic stroke.

Portrait by G. P. A. Healy

FRANKLIN PIERCE

A dark-horse candidate, Franklin Pierce defeated his better-known rival, General Winfield Scott, in the Presidential election of 1852. But the Presidency proved no blessing for Pierce.

Born November 23, 1804 at Hillsboro, New Hampshire, Pierce was admitted to the bar in 1827. His father, Benjamin Pierce, served as governor of New Hampshire.

Pierce was elected in 1829 to the New Hampshire legislature, later serving as Speaker of that body. In 1832 he was elected to the U.S. House of Representatives, and later to the U.S. Senate.

In 1842, Pierce returned to New Hampshire. However, he soon was offered several important positions, including that of Attorney General in President Polk's cabinet. Instead, Pierce enlisted in the army at the outbreak of the Mexican War in 1846.

After the war, Pierce attended the 1852 Democratic national convention as New Hampshire's favorite son, not expecting to win the Presidental nomination. But the delegates became deadlocked over more popular candidates, and they gave him the nomination.

Few critical issues were raised in the campaign. But Pierce's personality, his campaign style, and the fact that the South felt uneasy about Scott combined to give Pierce the election.

Pierce appointed an exceptionally able cabinet. He supported the Gadsden Purchase of 1853 and planned to build a transcontinental railway. He also fully obtained Senate ratification of a trade agreement with Japan.

Pierce was not renominated by the Democrats in 1856. After his term he spent several years in Europe and then returned to Concord, where he died on October 8, 1869.

Portrait by William M. Chase

JAMES BUCHANAN

Born in a log cabin in southern Pennsylvania on April 23, 1791, James Buchanan was admitted to the bar in 1813.

After brief service in the War of 1812, Buchanan served in the Pennsylvania legislature from 1814 to 1816. In 1820 he was elected to the first of five consecutive terms in the U.S. House of Representatives. In 1831, Jackson appointed Buchanan as U.S. Minister to Russia, where he served two years and arranged an important trade agreement.

In 1834, Buchanan was picked to fill a vacant seat in the U.S. Senate. After President Polk took office, Buchanan became Secretary of State. He convinced President Polk to accept the 49th parallel as a compromise boundary with Canada for the Oregon Territory.

In the election of 1856 Buchanan's chief opponent, John C. Frémont, vigorously opposed slavery. Buchanan stressed the importance of preserving the Union. Though he believed that slavery was wrong, he said he would not impose Federal control where it existed. By carrying the South and five Northern states, Buchanan won the election.

As President, Buchanan tried to stay on middle ground concerning slavery. But his support of the Dred Scott Decision and his attempt to have Kansas admitted to the Union as a slave state led Northerners to believe that he favored the South.

With much of his support gone, Buchanan did not run for reelection in 1860. The Democratic party split into Northern and Southern wings, which ensured the victory of the Republican candidate, Abraham Lincoln. Many Southerners believed the Republican Party wanted to destroy the South. Thus seven Deep South states withdrew from the Union during the final months of Buchanan's term.

When his term of office ended in March 1861, Buchanan returned to his home near Lancaster. The Republicans scorned him as a Southern collaborator and a chief cause of the Civil War. He died on June 1, 1868.

Portrait by G. P. A. Healy

ABRAHAM LINCOLN

Born on February 12, 1809, in Hardin County, Kentucky, Abraham Lincoln was the second child of Thomas and Nancy Hanks Lincoln. Young Abe had less than a year's formal schooling.

The Lincolns moved to southern Indiana and then to the Illinois wilderness. In the village of New Salem, young Lincoln worked as a clerk, postmaster, and assistant surveyor.

Lincoln was elected to the state legislature in 1834. Meanwhile he studied law and was licensed to practice in 1836.

In 1846, Lincoln was elected to the U.S. House of Representatives as a Whig. His party opposed the war against Mexico. This position was unpopular in Illinois, so Lincoln resumed his law practice in 1849.

Lincoln's interest in politics revived when Congress repealed the Missouri Compromise in 1854. Lincoln took the position that slavery must be tolerated in the states where it existed, but prevented from spreading beyond them. The repeal left the decision to the settlers. Lincoln campaigned against Senator Stephen A. Douglas in 1854, and a third candidate won the election. But Lincoln established his reputation as a popular leader.

After several other campaigns, Lincoln won the Republican nomination as President in 1860. Four candidates contended, but none won a majority of the popular vote; Lincoln led with 40 percent. A clear majority of the electoral college made him President.

When Lincoln was inaugurated, seven Southern states had already seceded from the Union. On his 39th day in office he was confronted with the attack on Fort Sumter; he called up troops, and the Civil War began. In the course of the war he opposed slavery more vigorously. He proclaimed freedom for all slaves in the war zone.

He was reelected in 1864 but faced opposition from Northern leaders of Congress who wanted to punish the South for the war. Only five days after General Robert E. Lee surrendered, an assassin killed the President who had preserved the Union.

Portrait by E. F. Andrews

ANDREW JOHNSON

Born on December 29, 1808 at Raleigh, North Carolina, Andrew Johnson was a self-made man who rose from poverty to hold the nation's highest office.

When Johnson was three years of age, his father died. His mother supported the family with menial jobs. As a tailor's apprentice, Johnson learned a trade and taught himself to read in spare moments. In 1826 he opened a tailor shop at Greeneville, Tennessee, and the following year he married Eliza McCardle. She taught her husband writing and arithmetic and eventally bore him five children.

By 1843, Johnson had emerged as a dominant force in eastern Tennessee politics and was elected to the U.S, House of Representatives. His raucous manner alienated the well-to-do, but he had the support of laborers, small farmers, and mountain people.

In 1857, Johnson was elected to the U.S. Senate. As the Civil War approached, Johnson supported the view that slavery was protected by the Constitution both where it existed and in the territories. However, he also felt that the Union was more important than slavery. He was the only Senator from the South who remained in Congress, refusing to join the Confederacy. As a result, Lincoln appointed him military governor of Tennessee, where he served from 1862 to 1864. In the election of 1864, the Republicans joined the "War" Democrats to form the Union party, and nominated Johnson as Lincoln's Vice-Presidential running mate.

Lincoln would have had a difficult time persuading the so-called Radical Republicans to adopt his policies of peaceful reconciliation toward the South. Then he was murdered, and the task fell to Johnson.

Angered by Johnson's policies, the Radical Republicans in the House passed a resolution to impeach the President on 11 counts. Fortunately, when the case went to the Senate, Johnson was acquitted by one vote.

Johnson did not receive the Democratic nomination for President in 1868. He returned to Tennessee where he won election to the U.S. Senate in 1874. He had served only a few months of his term when he died on July 31, 1875 of a paralytic stroke.

Portrait by Henry Ulke

ULYSSES S. GRANT

The military hero of the Civil War, Ulysses S. Grant, was born on April 27, 1822 at Point Pleasant, Ohio. While still an infant, he moved with his parents to Georgetown, Ohio. He was educated locally until age 14 and was then sent to a nearby academy. In 1839, he obtained an appointment to West Point, where he distinguished himself as a horseman rather than a scholar.

Grant graduated from West Point in 1843 and spent his next two years with the infantry in Missouri and Louisiana. During the Mexican War he served under Taylor and Scott and was twice cited for bravery.

With the outbreak of the Civil War, Grant volunteered his services to the Union Army. The governor of Illinois put him in charge of a state regiment; a brief and successful campaign against Confederate irregulars in Missouri earned him the rank of brigadier general. Fearless in battle, Grant soon distinguished himself as a military leader.

Grant continued to score victories, and he was soon put in charge of all Union forces in the West. In 1864 Lincoln put him in charge of all U.S. troops. After a costly campaign, Lee surrendered to Grant on April 9, 1865; Grant became an undisputed national hero.

After the war Grant supported mild reconstruction, but later he joined with the Radical Republicans to impose harsh penalties on the South. In 1868, Grant was nominated for the Presidency on the first ballot at the Republican convention and won a decisive victory in the election.

Grant was a fine soldier, but a failure as President. Nonetheless, he was reelected to a second term in 1872 by an even greater margin than his previous victory. Many of his subordinates and men he trusted were corrupt. His reconstruction policies alienated the South from the rest of the nation.

In 1880, he failed to secure the Republican nomination by a small margin. A series of investments left Grant almost penniless during his final years. He died on July 23, 1885, shortly after completing his *Personal Memoirs*.

Portrait by Daniel Huntington

RUTHERFORD B. HAYES

Rutherford B. Hayes was born at Delaware, Ohio, on October 4, 1822. He attended private schools and later graduated from Kenyon College in Ohio at the top of his class. He studied law at Harvard and entered the Ohio bar in 1845. In 1853, Hayes married Lucy Webb, who as First Lady was admired as a fine hostess. The couple had eight children.

Hayes' law practice grew steadily. He became active in the Republican party and defended a number of fugitive slaves in court. In 1858, he was elected city solicitor for Cincinnati. When the Civil War broke out, Hayes became a major in an Ohio volunteer infantry. He served four years and was wounded several times. In 1864, while still on active duty, he was nominated and elected to the U.S. House of Representatives. But Hayes resigned from the army only at the end of the war.

At the Republican convention of 1876, Hayes was Ohio's favorite-son candidate for the Presidential nomination. A deadlock between candidates resulted in the convention's turning to Hayes and giving him the nomination on the seventh ballot.

In the election, Democrat Samuel J. Tilden received a plurality of more than a quarter of a million votes. However, the electoral votes from four states–Florida, Louisiana, South Carolina, and Oregon–were in dispute. A special commission set up by Congress resolved the matter by giving these votes (and the election) to Hayes, whose margin of victory was one electoral vote. Southern Democrats, angered at the prospect of another Republican Administration, were promised that all remaining Federal troops would be withdrawn from the South. Hayes carried out that promise.

Hayes' Administration attempted to reform civil service and resumed paying government employees in cash, which had been halted during the Civil War. When riots broke out in several states as a result of the railroad strike of 1877, Hayes sent Federal troops to restore order.

When his term of office expired in 1881, he devoted himself to a variety of good works, including prison reform, aid to black people, and public education. He died on January 17, 1893 at his home in Fremont, Ohio.

Portrait by Calvin Curtis

JAMES A. GARFIELD

Born November 19, 1831 in a log cabin at Orange, Ohio, James A. Garfield was raised by his mother, who ran the family farm after the death of her husband in 1833. Garfield attended Western Reserve Eclectic Institute (now Hiram College) in Hiram, Ohio, and eventually graduated from Williams College in Williamstown, Massachusetts.

Garfield returned to Ohio, where he taught at the Eclectic Institute (serving as its President from 1857 to 1861), studied law, and became active in the Republican party.

With the outbreak of the Civil War, Garfield was commissioned a lieutenant colonel of Ohio volunteers. In 1862, while on active duty, his home district elected him to the U.S. House of Representatives. He served nine consecutive terms.

Garfield sided with the Radical Republicans in Congress. After the death of President Lincoln he voted for the Reconstruction Acts and the impeachment of President Johnson.

A shadow was cast over Garfield's distinguished career when he was accused of taking bribes for political favors. Garfield denied the charges, which were never conclusively proven.

In January of 1880, Garfield was elected to the U.S. Senate by the Ohio legislature. When the Republicans met at Chicago that year to nominate a Presidential candidate, they reached a deadlock between former President Grant and James G. Blaine. Eventually, the delegates turned to Garfield, giving him the nomination on the 36th ballot.

Fortunately for Garfield, the country was prosperous. President Hayes had lifted the pall of corruption from the Grant Administration. Garfield won a small plurality at the polls and a somewhat safer margin in the electoral vote.

Garfield might have made an excellent President. Unfortunately, four months after his inauguration he was shot by a disappointed office seeker. Garfield died 79 days later at Elberon, New Jersey, where he had been taken to escape the summer heat in Washington, D.C.

Portrait by Daniel Huntington

CHESTER A. ARTHUR

Born October 5, 1830 at Fairfield, Vermont, Chester A. Arthur was the son of a Baptist minister. At the age of 15 he attended Union College at Schenectady, New York, graduating in 1848. He completed his legal education at a New York City law office and in 1854 was admitted to the bar.

In 1859, Arthur married Ellen Lewis Herndon, who died shortly before Arthur became President. The couple had three children, but one did not survive infancy.

Arthur was very active in local politics. He helped to assure the Presidental nomination of Grant in 1868, and eventually became the number-two man in the state Republican party.

At the Republican convention of 1880, Arthur again supported the nomination of Grant. When the nomination went instead to James A. Garfield, Arthur was given the second spot on the ticket.

Arthur became President on September 20, 1881, after the death of President Garfield. Many wondered if this man of machine politics could provide effective leadership for a nation torn by factional rivalry. However, Arthur conducted himself as President in an exemplary manner. Ignoring political advantage, he filled Federal appointments with men of merit.

Further, he called for legislation to reform the civil service and signed the Pendleton Civil Service Act of 1883. Supporting what he felt were the best interests of the nation, he vetoed a large rivers-and-harbors bill. However, the bill was passed over his veto.

Arthur hoped to run for President in his own right in 1884, but he failed to win the nomination. When his term expired he returned to New York City, where he died on November 18, 1886, of a kidney condition.

Portrait by Eastman Johnson

GROVER CLEVELAND

Born on March 18, 1837 at Caldwell, New Jersey, Grover Cleveland was the only President to serve two non-consecutive terms in the White House. Cleveland grew up in western New York state and eventually settled in Buffalo. Here he worked as a law clerk, studied law, and was admitted to the bar in 1859.

In 1881, Cleveland was elected mayor of Buffalo. His reputation for integrity and business-like efficiency attracted the attention of state Democratic leaders seeking a candidate to run against the scandal-ridden Republican administration in Albany. Cleveland brought to the state government the same honest, efficient administration he had demonstrated during his brief tenure as mayor of Buffalo.

With such a record, Cleveland appealed to the Democrats as the ideal candidate for President. He was given the nomination on the second ballot at the party convention in July of 1884, despite the opposition of old-line Democrats from New York. Cleveland won a narrow victory over James G. Blaine.

During his first term, Cleveland supported a strict gold standard and lower tarriffs, but met with an unsympathetic Congress in both areas. He supported further civil service reform. But he also bowed to his political supporters and many Democrats in positions under his immediate control. He vetoed the Dependent Pension bill of 1887, believing it an unjust raid on the public treasury by veterans' groups.

In the election of 1888, Cleveland won a plurality of the popular vote, but lost the election to Benjamin Harrison in the electoral vote. Cleveland returned to New York and prepared for the next election. Running against Harrison and a strong third-party candidate (James B. Weaver of the Populists), Cleveland won a plurality at the polls and a substantial victory in the electoral vote.

By 1896, many Democrats had gone over to an easy-money, free-silver policy; Cleveland found himself with scant influence in the party. After his term, he retired to Princeton, New Jersey and became a trustee and lecturer at Princeton University. He died on June 24, 1908.

Portrait by Eastman Johnson

BENJAMIN HARRISON

Born on August 20, 1833 at North Bend, Ohio, Benjamin Harrison was a grandson of William Henry Harrison, ninth President of the United States. Harrison attended Farmer's College near Cincinnati, and later Miami University, where he graduated in 1852.

Harrison was admitted to the bar in 1854 after two years of legal training with a Cincinnati law firm. He moved to Indianapolis, where he enjoyed reasonable success at the practice of law until the Civil War. He joined the new Republican party, worked for Frémont's election in 1856, and in 1859 was elected Indianapolis city attorney. In 1862 Harrison took command of an Indiana volunteer infantry regiment which engaged in heavy fighting during the latter stages of the Civil War.

After the war Harrison's reputation as an attorney grew swiftly, as did his participation in the state Republican party. From 1879 to 1881 he led the Indiana delegation to the Republican convention of 1880, where he helped swing the nomination to Garfield.

Elected by the Indiana legislature to the U.S. Senate in 1881, Harrison refused an offer to join Garfield's cabinet.

In 1887, Harrison lost his bid for reelection to the Senate. However, the following year the Republicans nominated him for the Presidency when James G. Blaine decided not to run. In the election, Harrison trailed Cleveland by a small margin at the polls but carried the electoral vote, 233 to 168.

With the support of a Republican Congress during his first two years in office, Harrison was able to enact much of his legislative program.

But opposition to his high tariffs and labor problems combined to defeat Harrison in the election of 1892.

Harrison's first wife died in October 1892, shortly before he was defeated in his try for a second term. In 1896, he married Mary Scott Lord Dimmick, with whom he had one child. Harrison died on March 13, 1901 at Indianapolis.

Portrait by Harriet Murphy

WILLIAM McKINLEY

Born on January 29, 1843 in the small town of Niles, Ohio, William McKinley was the seventh of nine children and the son of an iron founder. At 17 he entered Allegheny College at Meadville, Pennsylvania, but illness interrupted his education.

He was admitted to the bar in 1867 and set up a law practice at Canton, Ohio. He became active in the Republican Party and in 1869 won elective office as prosecuting attorney for Stark County. In 1871, he married Ida Saxton.

Elected to the U.S. House of Representatives in 1876, McKinley served in that body until May of 1884. McKinley's Democratic opponent in the election of 1882 challenged the results of the election and the Democratic majority in the House voted to unseat McKinley. However, he was soon back in Congress, winning the next three elections.

With the assistance of Mark Hanna, a Cleveland industrialist and skilled political manager, McKinley resolved to win the Republican Presidential nomination in 1896. In fact, McKinley won the nomination on the first ballot. Running against Democrat William Jennings Bryan, McKinley came out strongly in favor of sound money and the gold standard.

Elected by a large plurality, the new President called a special session of Congress early in 1897 and fulfilled a campaign promise to raise tariffs yet higher.

It was McKinley's foreign policy, however, which won the attention of his countrymen. With the public enraged by the sinking of the battleship, *Maine*, McKinley called for war against Spain on April 11, 1898. The conflict lasted less than four months. Cuba was freed, and the United States took possession of Puerto Rico, Guam, and the Philippines.

Eagerly renominated by the Republicans in 1900, McKinley stayed home in Ohio during the campaign. The return of prosperity and the popularity of McKinley's foreign policy combined to give him a healthy victory, with a plurality of over 800,000 votes.

While shaking hands with a crowd in Buffalo, New York, just six months after his second inauguration, McKinley was shot by an assassin. The President died a few days later on September 14, 1901.

Portrait by John Singer Sargent

THEODORE ROOSEVELT

Born in New York City on October 27, 1858, Theodore Roosevelt was the second of four children in a well-to-do family. A sickly child, he overcame his weakness and was an advocate of the vigorous, outdoor life. He graduated from Harvard in 1880. The same year he married his first wife, Alice Hathaway Lee, who died in 1884 after giving birth to a daughter. His mother died soon thereafter.

Roosevelt quit politics, bought land in the Dakotas, and lived the life of a rancher and cowboy for the next few years.

In 1895, Roosevelt became president of the New York City Board of Police Commissioners and worked diligently to end corruption. In the Spanish-American War he gained tremendous fame by leading the Rough Riders up San Juan Hill.

Buoyed by his war record, Roosevelt won election to the governorship of New York. Two years later (1900) he accepted second place on McKinley's ticket and was nominated by acclamation at the Republican convention. Roosevelt feared that the Vice-Presidency might be a political dead end. But then McKinley died from an assassin's bullet.

Elevated to the White House at the age of 42, Roosevelt brought tremendous vision and energy to the presidency. He believed the chief executive should take an active role in seeking out and correcting national problems. Nicknamed the "Trust Buster," he initiated law suits against numerous large corporations accused of anti-competitive practices.

In 1904, Roosevelt was unanimously nominated by the Republicans for a second term. He won election in his own right by a record plurality of over 2,500,000 votes.

Roosevelt left the Presidency to his hand-picked successor, William H. Taft, in 1909 and was off on an extended safari to Africa. Upon returning to the United States, Roosevelt formed the Bull Moose party and ran for President in 1912, but was defeated. He died suddenly of a blood clot on January 6, 1919 at his home at Oyster Bay, New York.

Portrait by Anders L. Zorn

WILLIAM H. TAFT

Born in Cincinnati, Ohio on September 15, 1857, William H. Taft was the son of Alphonso Taft, a cabinet member under President Grant and later a U.S. ambassador. Taft graduated from Yale in 1878 (second in his class) and from Cincinnati Law School in 1880.

In 1881, Taft was appointed assistant prosecuting attorney for Hamilton County, Ohio. He later served briefly as a Federal tax collector, traveled to Europe for several months, and worked for his father's law firm for four years. In June of 1886, he married Helen Herron, with whom he had three children.

In 1900, Taft was appointed by President McKinley to head the U.S. Philippine Commission and the next year was appointed the first civil governor of the Philippines.

In 1904, Taft accepted an offer from President Roosevelt to become Secretary of War. Admitting that he had "no aptitude for managing an army," Taft acted more like a Secretary of State than a Secretary of War, traveling widely on behalf of the President.

Taft saw himself nominated for President on the first ballot at the Republican convention in June 1908. Few important issues were at stake in the campaign. Aided by the popularity of the Roosevelt years and his own reputation, Taft won a substantial victory over Democrat William Jennings Bryan.

Before the end of Taft's term Progressive Republicans felt that he had become too closely allied with the conservative wing of the party. They began a movement to make former President Roosevelt the Republican nominee in 1912. When Roosevelt's supporters were unable to overthrow Taft at the Republican convention, they organized the Progressive (Bull Moose) party. This split the Republican vote and ensured the victory of Woodrow Wilson.

Taft chose to teach law at Yale University for the next eight years. During World War I, he presided over the National War Labor Board for 14 months. In 1921, President Harding named him chief justice of the Supreme Court, where he remained until one month before his death on March 8, 1930.

Portrait by F. Graham Cootes

WOODROW WILSON

Scholar, reformer, and peacemaker, Woodrow Wilson was born December 28, 1856 at Staunton, Virginia. He grew up at Augusta, Georgia, witnessed the Civil War as a child, attended Princeton University, and graduated in 1879.

In June of 1885, Wilson married Ellen Louise Axson, with whom he had three daughters. She died when Wilson was President in 1914, and the following year he married Mrs. Edith Bolling Galt, a widow.

Wilson taught briefly at Bryn Mawr College, and later at Wesleyan University. In 1890, he accepted a professorship at Princeton University. Here Wilson achieved a measure of fame for his writings and his classroom lectures, and was elected president of Princeton in 1902.

In 1910, Wilson resigned from Princeton to run for the governorship of New Jersey as a Democrat. He won a sizable victory at the polls.

By 1912, Wilson's reputation among progressive Democrats made him a front runner for the Presidential nomination. Wilson benefited from the split in the Republican party and won 435 electoral votes of a total 531.

President Wilson went to Congress with a long list of precisely worded legislative proposals and soon secured passage of the Federal Reserve Act, the Federal Trade Commission Act, and the Clayton Antitrust Act, as well as a reduction of tariffs. In foreign affairs, Wilson attempted to repair and maintain friendly relations with a variety of nations. After the Germans promised to cease submarine attacks on neutral ships, Wilson entered the Presidential election of 1916 with the slogan, "He kept us out of war." Wilson won a close victory.

German submarines resumed their attacks on U.S. ships soon after the election. On April 2, 1917, Wilson asked Congress for a declaration of war against Germany. At the end of the war in 1918, he participated in the peace talks and pushed for the establishment of the League of Nations.

A paralytic stroke in the fall of 1919 forced Wilson to spend his remaining 17 months as President in bed. Still partially paralyzed after the completion of his term he died on February 3, 1924 at Washington, D.C.

Portrait by E. Hodgson Smart

WARREN G. HARDING

Warren G. Harding was born November 2, 1865 near present-day Blooming Grove, Ohio. He graduated from Ohio Central College in 1883, and later studied law. Then he went to work for a newspaper in Marion, Ohio. In 1884, with two partners, he paid $300 for the dying *Marion Star*. He soon bought out his partners, ran the paper virtually single-handed, and saw it prosper. In 1891, he married Florence Kling De Wolfe, the ambitious daughter of a Marion banker.

Harding became active in Republican politics. In 1909, he ran for governor of Ohio, but was badly defeated. Nevertheless, he was the victorious Republican candidate for the U.S. Senate four years later.

Harding reluctantly decided to try for the Republican Presidential nomination in 1920. Harry M. Daugherty, a skillful strategist who had managed Harding's political campaigns in Ohio, swung the Republican convention to Harding when the delegates became deadlocked.

Promising a "return to normalcy," Harding campaigned from his home at Marion. Harding's landslide victory in November probably reflected the national reaction against Wilson's policies during his last years in office. As President, Harding did not lead the way in legislation as did his predecessor.

Some of Harding's appointees were men of the highest integrity and ability; but most were merely personal friends or those to whom the President owed a political debt. The government was soon awash in corruption. The extent to which Harding was personally involved in the scandals remains unclear. Some historians view him as an honest man betrayed by his closest friends.

In any case, Harding died suddenly on August 2, 1923, shortly after returning from a trip to Alaska. Because Harding's wife refused to allow an autopsy, even the cause of his death remains a mystery.

Portrait by Charles S. Hopkinson

CALVIN COOLIDGE

Calvin Coolidge was born on July 4,1872, at Plymouth, Vermont. He attended Amherst College, graduated in 1895, and later studied law. Establishing a legal practice at Northampton, Massachusetts, Coolidge was elected to the city council in 1898.

In 1906 Coolidge was elected to the lower house of the Massachusetts legislature. In 1916 he began the first of three consecutive terms as lieutenant governor of Massachusetts. In 1918 he was nominated by the Republicans for the governorship of the state, winning the election by a slight margin.

As governor, Coolidge attracted national attention in September of 1919, when the Boston police went on strike. Riots erupted in the city, and Coolidge sent in the state militia to restore order.

Later that year, Coolidge was reelected governor by a far greater margin than in the previous election. The following year (1920), Coolidge was nominated for the Vice-Presidential spot on the Republican ticket.

Carried into office along with President Harding on the anti-Wilson tide, the new Vice-President set about his duties in his characteristically diligent manner. After the death of Harding, Coolidge was sworn into office by his father, a notary public, whom Coolidge had been visiting in Vermont.

Coolidge did much to salvage the dignity of the presidency and the esteem of the Republican party. He forced the resignation of Harding's attorney general, Harry Daugherty, and set up a commission to investigate the Teapot Dome oil lease. He then appointed Owen J. Roberts and Harlan F. Stone as special prosecutor and attorney general, saying, "Let the guilty be punished."

Fifteen months after taking office, Coolidge was elected President in his own right, easily defeating a badly divided Democratic Party. His popular vote exceeded by 2,500,000 the combined total of his two opponents, Robert La Follette and John W. Davis.

Coolidge chose not to seek another term. He died of a heart attack on January 5, 1933 at his home at Northampton.

Portrait by Elmer W. Greene

HERBERT C. HOOVER

Born on August 10, 1874 at West Branch, Iowa, Herbert Hoover was the son of a blacksmith. He worked his way through Stanford University and graduated in 1895 with an engineering degree. In 1897, he was placed in charge of a gold-mining operation in Australia. In the following years, Hoover traveled throughout the world as a mining consultant and engineer.

In London at the outbreak of World War I, Hoover chaired a committee that distributed almost a million dollars' worth of food and supplies to the needy of Belgium and northern France. With the entry of the United States into the war, Hoover was appointed U.S. food administrator. He returned to Europe after the armistice to take charge of Allied relief efforts.

In 1928, Hoover was nominated by the Republicans for the Presidency. Aided by the prosperity which had accompanied eight years of Republican Administration, he won a landslide victory over Democrat Alfred E. Smith. Hoover saw a need for reform in the Government and in the social and business life of the nation.

Unfortunately, Hoover was unable to foresee the Depression, which began with the stock market crash in October of 1929. As businesses failed and millions lost their jobs, Hoover began new public works projects to provide employment. He created the Reconstruction Finance Corporation to make loans to industry, banks, farm organizations, and state and local governments. He hoped that such money would stimulate the economy and "trickle down" to the unemployed in the form of new jobs.

Badly defeated in his try for a second term, Hoover retired from office in March of 1933 and devoted himself to writing. He helped with relief efforts after World War II and headed "Hoover Commissions" for President Truman and President Eisenhower to study the efficiency of the Federal Government. He died on October 20, 1964 at New York City.

Portrait by Frank O. Salisbury

FRANKLIN D. ROOSEVELT

Born January 30, 1882 at his family's estate at Hyde Park, New York, Franklin D. Roosevelt was the son of a wealthy financier and railroad executive. Roosevelt attended private schools and graduated from Harvard University in 1903. He attended Columbia Law School and passed the bar exam in 1907. In 1905 he married a distant cousin, Eleanor Roosevelt.

Roosevelt's name, his ties to the Wilson Administration, and the reputation he had built during the war gave him the Vice-Presidential spot on the Democratic ticket in 1920. Although defeated in the election, Roosevelt became leader of the Democratic Party. In August of 1921, he was stricken with polio, from which he never fully regained the use of his legs.

Nominated for President by the Democrats in 1932, Roosevelt won a sweeping victory over Hoover. Faced with a dismal economic picture, the new President acted decisively. He declared a bank holiday and took measures to restore confidence in the banking system. Calling Congress into special session for what became known as the "Hundred Days," Roosevelt obtained passage of relief and reform legislation unrivaled in U.S. history. It expanded the powers and responsibilities of the Federal Government on an unprecedented scale.

Although the Roosevelt program did not end the Great Depression, it pleased the majority of Americans who reelected Roosevelt President for second, third, and fourth terms. His consummate skill and innovative flair no doubt added to his reelection victories and to his ability to implement his programs.

Roosevelt supported the Allied cause and led the nation through World War II. He died suddenly and unexpectedly on April 12, 1945 at Warm Springs, Georgia, shortly before the final victory of World War II.

Portrait by Martha G. Kempton

HARRY S. TRUMAN

Born at Lamar, Missouri on May 8, 1884, Harry S. Truman was the oldest in a family of three children. After graduating from high school in 1901, Truman held a series of jobs. During World War I he commanded an artillery battery in several campaigns and by the time of his discharge in 1919 had won promotion to major.

In 1934, Truman was elected to the U.S. Senate where he vigorously supported the New Deal. Reelected in 1940, Truman was one of the first to call for a special Senate committee to oversee the nation's vast defense expenditures.

Truman's reputation in the Senate secured him the Vice-Presidential spot on the Democratic ticket in 1944. He had served as Vice-President only 83 days when Roosevelt died. Truman became the nation's new Chief Executive. Within the next few months both Germany and Japan surrendered.

The first years of Truman's Administration were marked by the problems of returning to a peacetime economy, labor unrest, and the start of the cold war. Truman formulated the "Fair Deal," which included proposals for additional Social Security benefits, protection of minority employment rights, and new Federal power projects. But most of the program was blocked in Congress. In foreign affairs, Truman implemented the Marshall Plan, which helped rebuild Europe, and outlined the Truman Doctrine, which guided U.S. foreign policy for the next 25 years.

Nominated by the Democrats in 1948, Truman defeated Republican candidate Thomas E. Dewey. His second term was marked by the signing of a public housing act, the only major piece of Fair Deal legislation to get past Congress. Abroad, Truman won a round with the Russians when they ended the Berlin blockade. In June of 1950, Truman sent U.S. forces to the aid of South Korea, and later recalled General MacArthur to keep him from attacking China.

Announcing that he would not stand for reelection, Truman retired to his home at Independence, Missouri, at the end of his term in January of 1953. He remained a strong influence in the Democratic Party until he died on December 26, 1972 at Kansas City, Missouri.

Portrait by J. Anthony Wills

DWIGHT D. EISENHOWER

Dwight D. Eisenhower was born at Denison, Texas, on October 14, 1890. He grew up in Abilene, Kansas, where his family moved not long after his birth. Eisenhower won an appointment to West Point, from which he graduated in 1915. A series of routine military assignments followed.

With the outbreak of World War II, Eisenhower was called to Washington, D.C., to help plan U.S. military strategy. In June of 1942, he was sent to London to command all U.S. forces in the European theater. He led the Allied invasions of North Africa, Sicily, and Italy. These successes led to appointment as commander of the combined Allied force for the invasion of France. The success of this mission on D-Day (June 6, 1944) and the surrender of the German regime made Eisenhower an international hero.

In November of 1945, General Eisenhower was appointed Army chief of staff, in which role he helped to establish the U.S. Department of Defense. In June of 1948, he became the president of Columbia University. Two years later, President Truman made him commander of NATO forces in Europe.

Eisenhower was nominated for the Presidency in 1952 by the Republicans, who hoped that he could end the 20-year Democratic hold on the White House. He was elected overwhelmingly. Four years later he was reelected President by an even greater margin, despite concern for his health.

Eisenhower's foreign policy was dramatic. He ended the war in Korea, helped establish SEATO, and engaged in summit diplomacy. Led by his Secretary of State, John Foster Dulles, Eisenhower made atomic weapons the cornerstone of U.S. defense strategy. He sent military aid to Lebanon and Formosa when those countries appeared threatened by Communist aggression.

After his term expired in January of 1961, Eisenhower retired to his farm at Gettysburg, Pennsylvania, where he worked on the memoirs of his Presidency. He died on March 28, 1969 after a prolonged illness.

Portrait by Aaron Shikler

JOHN F. KENNEDY

John F. Kennedy was born on May 29, 1917 at Brookline, Massachusetts. His father, Joseph P. Kennedy, once served as U.S. Ambassador to Britain. Kennedy majored in government and international relations at Harvard University and graduated with honors in 1940. Kennedy then enlisted in the Navy. Placed in command of a PT boat in the Pacific, he was decorated for his heroism.

In 1946, Kennedy was elected U.S. Representative from Massachusetts. After two terms in the House, Kennedy was elected to the U.S. Senate in 1952.

In 1953, Kennedy married Jacqueline Lee Bouvier. The couple had three children, but one died shortly after birth.

An overwhelming reelection to the Senate in 1958 boosted Kennedy's prestige and made him a chief contender for the Democratic Presidential nomination in 1960. Kennedy was able to secure the nomination on the first ballot at the Democratic convention. Criticizing the lack of progress under the Republican Administration and calling for a "New Frontier," he won a narrow victory over Republican candidate Richard Nixon. At age 43, Kennedy was the youngest man elected President.

Kennedy's foreign policy was often the focus of world attention. Relations between the United States and Soviet Union were marred by the ill-fated Bay of Pigs invasion of Cuba, the rekindling of the Berlin issue, and the resumption of atmospheric testing of nuclear weapons. Tension reached a climax in October of 1962, when the United States discovered that the Soviets had been installing long-range missiles in Cuba. Kennedy placed a U.S. naval blockade around Cuba, forcing Soviet Premier Khrushchev to remove the missiles from the island.

The Kennedy Administration came to an abrupt end on November 22, 1963. Riding in a motorcade in Dallas, Texas, Kennedy was shot. He was the fourth U.S. President to be assassinated.

Portrait by Elizabeth Shoumatoff

LYNDON B. JOHNSON

Born August 27, 1908, at Stonewall, Texas, Lyndon B. Johnson was the son of a teacher and Texas state legislator. In 1930, he graduated from Southwest Texas State College.

Johnson soon turned to politics, assisting in the successful Congressional campaign of Richard M. Kleberg, who then took Johnson to Washington as his staff secretary.

In 1935, Johnson was named administrator for Texas of the National Youth Administration. Two years later, he won a seat in the U.S. House of Representatives. Johnson was reelected five times, serving in the House through 1948.

In 1948, Johnson made his second attempt to win a seat in the U.S. Senate. He captured the Democratic primary runoff by a margin of only 87 votes (out of almost 900,000 cast). He easily defeated the Republican candidate in the general election, and in 1954 was overwhelmingly reelected to a second term.

Johnson hoped to win the Democratic Presidential nomination in 1960, but that prize went to John F. Kennedy. Johnson accepted Kennedy's offer of the second spot on the ticket. He became one of the nation's most active Vice-Presidents, serving as a member of the National Security Council, attending cabinet meetings, and fulfilling numerous special assignments. Kennedy's assassination on November 22, 1963 elevated Johnson to the presidency. A year later, he was elected to the office in his own right.

During Johnson's first two years in office he obtained passage of the remaining items of the Kennedy program, including a tax reduction and a civil rights act. His landslide election victory in November of 1964 helped to increase the Democratic majority in Congress. This allowed Johnson to secure approval of many of his own "Great Society" programs, including medical care for the aged, a voting rights bill, and various antipoverty measures. However, he was sharply criticized for pulling the nation deeper into the costly and fruitless Vietnam conflict.

After his term, Johnson retired to his ranch at Johnson City. He died of a heart attack on January 22, 1973.

Official White House Photograph by Ollie Atkins

RICHARD M. NIXON

Richard M. Nixon was born January 9, 1913 at Yorba Linda, California. An excellent student, Nixon graduated from Whittier College in 1934. He won a scholarship to Duke University School of Law, from which he graduated third in a class of 44 in 1937. Nixon joined the Navy and served in the Pacific as an aviation ground officer in World War II. He was elected to Congress in 1946 and reelected in 1948. He was instrumental in obtaining the Alger Hiss perjury conviction. In 1950, he was elected to the U.S. Senate by a margin of almost 700,000 votes and two years later was nominated by the Republicans as Eisenhower's running mate.

As Vice-President during the eight-year Eisenhower Administration, Nixon achieved considerable prominence. In 1960, Nixon was nominated for the Presidency. However, he lost the election to John F. Kennedy by a small margin.

Early in 1968, Nixon announced his intention to run again for the Presidency. Having won Republican primaries in six states, he secured the nomination on the first ballot at the party's convention in August and later defeated Hubert H. Humphrey by a slender margin. Four years later he won a landslide reelection victory over Democratic Senator George McGovern.

The single greatest problem facing the new President was the Vietnam War. While pressing ahead with peace negotiations, Nixon began withdrawing U.S. troops and increasing the use of U.S. air power. Early in his second term, a ceasefire agreement was finally signed and all remaining U.S. forces were withdrawn from Vietnam.

Men working for President Nixon's reelection campaign committee were caught breaking into Democratic headquarters in the Watergate complex in Washington, D.C. Investigation of the incident revealed high-level Administration involvement in this crime and a host of others. After a protracted battle between the President and Congress, Nixon released evidence, that clearly indicated his participation in a cover-up of the Watergate affair. Facing almost certain impeachment and conviction, Nixon resigned his office on August 9, 1974.

Official White House Photograph by David Kennerly

GERALD R. FORD

Born July 14, 1913 at Omaha, Nebraska, Gerald Ford was originally named Leslie Lynch King, Jr., after his father. While Ford was still an infant, his parents divorced and his mother moved to Grand Rapids, Michigan, where she married Gerald Rudolph Ford. The future President was adopted by his stepfather and given his name.

An excellent student and athlete, Ford graduated from the University of Michigan in 1935. Turning down a chance to play professional football, Ford entered Yale Law School. He graduated in 1941 and returned to Grand Rapids to open a law practice. Ford enlisted in the Navy during World War II and saw action in the Pacific aboard the U.S.S. *Monterey*.

In 1948 he was elected to the first of 13 consecutive terms in the U.S. House of Representatives. He performed his Congressional responsibilities with diligence.

On October 10, 1973, Vice-President Spiro Agnew resigned his office. Two days later, President Nixon nominated Ford to succeed Agnew. Congress overwhelmingly approved him for the Vice-Presidency on December 6, 1973. On August 9, 1974, hours after the Nixon resignation, Ford was sworn in as the nation's thirty-eighth Chief Executive.

Ford's most serious domestic problem was the economy. He stressed voluntary programs to control inflation. In early 1975, with the recession worsening, he received Congressional approval of a tax cut in order to stimulate the economy.

Ford ran for the Presidency in his own right in the 1976 election, but lost.

Official White House Photograph by Karl Schumacher

JIMMY CARTER

James Earl ("Jimmy") Carter was born at Plains, Georgia on October 1, 1924. The young man preferred to be known as Jimmy. He was the first in his family to finish high school. In order to qualify for the U.S. Naval Academy, he first spent two years at Georgia colleges.

After graduating from Annapolis in 1946, he spent five years in the Navy in an atomic submarine program. He supplemented his training in nuclear physics by attending Union College in Schenectady, N.Y., at night.

When James Earl Carter, Sr., died in 1953, Jimmy Carter abandoned a naval career to assume responsibility for family affairs in Plains. He was active in the community and was twice elected to the state senate. In 1970, he won the governorship of Georgia.

In 1975, Carter decided to run for the Presidency. He defeated the top contenders in a series of state primaries, and the Democratic convention unanimously chose Carter as their nominee on the first ballot.

Carter's campaign was energetic, but it left many unsure of his stand on basic issues. He received an electoral college margin of 56 votes. The first President to be elected from the Deep South since the Civil War, Carter won his own region mainly because of black support, and the labor vote was decisive in the North.

Soon after taking the oath of office, Carter emerged with a distinct personal style. He honored his campaign promise to pardon Vietnam "draft dodgers," proposed tax and electoral reforms, and prepared a plan for reorganization of the executive branch. He took steps toward a reconciliation with Vietnam, Angola, and Cuba. But his most characteristic contribution in foreign policy was his insistence that all nations honor basic human rights.

Official White House Photograph by Michael Evans

RONALD WILSON REAGAN

At age 69, Ronald Reagan became the oldest person ever elected President. In robust health, he survived an assassin's bullet fired as he left a Washington, D.C. hotel after he had been in office only seventy days.

Reagan was born on February 6, 1911, in Tampico, Illinois. His father was a shoe salesman. An avid athlete, Reagan played football in high school and college. He graduated from Eureka College in Illinois in 1932.

As a young man, Reagan dreamed of becoming a movie star. After graduation, he worked as a radio sportscaster, first in Davenport, and later in Des Moines, Iowa. He signed his first movie contract in 1937.

During World War II, Reagan served as a captain in the United States Army Air Forces. After the war, he resumed acting and became president of the Screen Actors Guild.

Reagan married Jane Wyman in 1940. They had two children, Maureen and Michael, but divorced in 1948. In 1952 Reagan married Nancy Davis. The couple had two children, Patricia and Ronald.

Reagan broke into politics in 1964, when he switched parties and began campaigning for conservative Republican Barry Goldwater for President. Encouraged by his success as a speaker, Reagan ran for governor of California in 1966. He won, and was reelected in 1970.

Reagan sought the Republican bid for President in 1976 but lost to incumbent Gerald Ford. Four years later, after a nationally televised debate, Reagan won a landslide victory over Jimmy Carter.

As President, Reagan faced high unemployment, rising interest rates, and runaway inflation. One of his first acts as President was the elimination of draft registration, honoring his commitment to cut federal spending.

In foreign affairs, he voiced strong opposition to organized terrorism. His election also marked the end of detente and arms control. Determined to contain Soviet military aggression, he pledged to increase U.S. defenses and aid countries threatened by communist take-over.

Reagan worked to reduce taxes, federal payrolls, and government interference in people's lives.

ASSASSINS AND THE PRESIDENCY

Eight United States Presidents have been targets of assassinations. Four were killed. Three escaped harm. In the most recent attempt on a President's life, Ronald Reagan was shot in the chest as he left a Washington, D.C. hotel. He later recovered.

His assailant, John W. Hinckley, Jr., 25, who was later declared innocent by reason of insanity, opened fire as Reagan stepped from the Washington Hilton on March 30, 1981. Three other men were wounded, including Reagan's press secretary, James Brady. It was the first attack on a President since two women tried to kill President Gerald Ford in separate incidents in northern California in September of 1975.

Ford escaped injury when Lynette Alice Fromme, 26, one of murderer Charles Manson's followers, pulled a 1911 Colt .45 pistol from her purse and aimed it at the President as he shook hands in a Sacramento crowd. Three weeks later, Sara Jane Moore, 45, fired a revolver at Ford from across a street in San Francisco. A bystander grabbed her arm as the gun went off. No one was hurt. Both women were sentenced to life in prison in Alderson, West Virginia. They were the first persons convicted under a 1965 ruling that makes an assassination attempt on a President or Vice-President a federal crime.

President John Kennedy was cut down by a sniper's bullet in November of 1963 in Dallas. Lee Harvey Oswald, 24, was accused of the assassination, but was shot and killed by an enraged nightclub owner, Jack Ruby, on November 24, 1963, while in police custody. Though he never stood trial, Oswald, an ex-Marine and self-proclaimed communist, was declared the killer by the Warren Commission. Ruby died in prison before the Oswald shooting was resolved.

On November 1, 1950, President Harry Truman was the target of an assassination attempt by two Puerto Rican nationalists. The men attempted to shoot their way into Blair House in Washington, where the President was staying while the White House underwent remodeling. Truman was unharmed, but one guard was killed and three others wounded.

An assassin's bullet missed President-elect Franklin D. Roosevelt at a political rally in Miami on February 15, 1933. The bullet was fired by bricklayer Joseph Giuseppe Zangara, an anarchist who said he wanted to kill the head of a capitalistic state. Zangara was electrocuted on March 20, 1933.

A saloonkeeper opposed to Former President Theodore Roosevelt shot him in the chest on October 14, 1912 in Milwaukee. A glasses case in Roosevelt's pocket deflected the bullet. Wounded, Roosevelt insisted on giving his 50-minute stump speech before going to the hospital. His assailant, John N. Schrank, died in an insane asylum forty-one years later.

William McKinley was shot twice as he worked his way through a reception line at an international exposition in Buffalo, New York, on September 6, 1901. He died eight days later. His assassin, Leon Czolgosz, an anarchist factory worker, was electrocuted on October 29, 1901.

President James Garfield was on his way to a college reunion when he was shot as he stood in the railroad station. His assassin, Charles J. Guiteau, was hanged in 1882. Although fatally wounded, Garfield remained in office until his death on September 19, 1881, two months after the shooting.

On Good Friday, April 15, 1865, Abraham Lincoln was shot in the head while watching a play at Ford's Theater in Washington. His killer, actor John Wilkes Booth, jumped from the President's box to the stage, shouting, "Sic semper tyrannis" (Thus always to tyrants), the motto of Virginia. Lincoln was carried unconscious to a nearby house, where he died the next morning.

President Andrew Jackson was the first target of an assassination in the United States. In 1835, while attending a congressman's funeral, he was fired upon by a deranged house painter. The assailant, who fired two pistols from less than six feet from Jackson, missed. He was later found insane.

In recent years, even those running for political office have risked assassination. Robert Kennedy, President Kennedy's brother, was slain in June, 1968, as he left a campaign rally in Los Angeles. His attacker, Sirhan B. Sirhan, is serving life in prison.

Former Alabama Governor George C. Wallace was shot and paralyzed from the waist down as he campaigned in a Laurel, Maryland shopping center in 1972. His attacker, Arthur Bremer, a Milwaukee busboy, was sentenced to sixty-three years in prison for the attempt. Bremer, 21 at the time, told police he had wanted to kill Richard Nixon.

Emergence as a World Power (1896–1917)

The United States adopted its colonial role vigorously. The attempt by the Filipinos to assert their independence from foreign dominion was suppressed over a period of two years. Cuba was recognized as sovereign only after accepting a constitution that permitted arbitrary American intervention and after ceding Guantánamo for use as a United States military base. In the Insular Cases of 1901, the U.S. Supreme Court ruled that the acquisitions from Spain were not part of the United States, but were to be administered without representation. Hawaii, on the other hand, became a territory and received as its first governor Sanford B. Dole, its erstwhile president. The interests of the United States in China were safeguarded by the unilateral declaration of the Open Door Policy, which won international acceptance in 1900. The United States, in turn, participated in the joint effort by Western powers to suppress the Boxer Rebellion against the Chinese government.

THE BIG STICK

Assured of its status as a Caribbean and Pacific power, the United States planned to protect its interests by building a canal across Central America between the Caribbean Sea and the Pacific Ocean. This was made possible in 1903 when the province of Panama withdrew from Columbia, under the protection of the U.S. Navy. The new republic of Panama then leased a canal zone to United States in perpetuity. United States armed forces were used to protect the interests of businessmen and investors in Santo Domingo in 1905, in Cuba from 1906 through 1909, in Nicaragua in 1909, and in Haiti in 1915.

Perhaps more significant than the establishment of Caribbean protectorates was the extension of the Monroe Doctrine by the so-called Roosevelt Corollary of 1904, which proclaimed the intention of the United States to intervene anywhere in Latin America when local authorities appeared incapable of maintaining law and order. Mexico was a target of this policy during its revolution that began in 1911. President Wilson announced that he would recognize only a chief executive who had been legally elected. In 1914 he dispatched a force to seize Veracruz on a pretext. When Francisco Villa, one of the generals contending for the Mexican presidency, led raids across the border in 1916 to retaliate against the incursion into his country, Wilson sent an American contingent on a counterraid that provoked the indignation of Villa's opponent, President Venustiano Carranza.

PROGRESSIVE POLITICS

The display of energy in foreign policy during the first decade of the twentieth century was matched by a zeal to loosen the ties between big business and the government. The change in policy was a reaction to abuses by such tycoons as J. P. Morgan, John D. Rockefeller, and the railroad magnates James J. Hill and E. H. Harriman, all of whom combined to create a massive trust known as Northern Securities. The Progressive movement led by Congressman Robert M. La Follette weakened monopolies on the state level, and national leaders presented themselves as enemies of corporate arrogance. In 1902 President Theodore Roosevelt used the Sherman Antitrust Act to break up Northern Securities, which gave him the reputation of a "trust-buster." Other accomplishments of his Administration included regulative agencies and legislation, such as the Interstate Commerce Commission and the Pure Food and Drug Act, both in 1906. The succeeding Administration of William Howard Taft attempted to stem the Progressive trend in the Republican Party, driving Roosevelt into opposition.

The political feud within the Republican camp gave the Presidency in 1912 to Woodrow Wilson, the first Democrat other than Cleveland to achieve that office since the Civil War. Wilson rode the Progressive tide under the slogan of the New Freedom. The major domestic achievement during his first term was the ratification in 1912 of the Sixteenth Amendment, which imposed an income tax and thus met a major objective of the Populist movement. Wilson convinced Congress to strengthen the drive against monopoly in 1914 by passing the Clayton Antitrust Act, which specifically exempted trade unions from classification as a "trust," and by creating the Federal Trade Commission. Other reforms and changes in direction under Wilson's purposeful leadership included reorganization of the banking system under the Federal Reserve Act of 1913. Wilson provided Federal aid in the building of highways in 1916 as it became evident that the automobile was here to stay.

DRIFT TOWARD WAR

The course of developing the New Freedom was interrupted by events in Europe, where rival blocs were competing for control of the world's markets. In the approaching showdown between the long-established colonial powers–Great Britain, France, and Russia (the Allies) and the less stable empires of Germany and Austria-Hungary (the Central Powers)–the United States had little interest. But as in the nineteenth-century contest between Great Britain and Napoleonic France, neutrality was difficult to maintain. British conduct toward neutral shipping was often as high-handed as that of the Germans, yet the German embargo of the British Isles threatened the flourishing commerce between Great Britain and the United States. Britain's status as a major customer made it possible for the United States to overlook minor breaches. On the other hand, the Germans had no weapons other than submarines to enforce its blockade, so it inevitably brought about innocent American deaths on the high seas. This swept the United States into the camp of the Allies. Wilson, who was reelected in 1916 because "he kept us out of war," asked Congress for a declaration of war in April 1917; and the United States entered the First World War–not as an "ally," but as an "associated power."

FIRST WORLD WAR

The nation met its responsibilities as a belligerent with efficiency; it accepted unprecedented restrictions on its economy and liberty. The War Industries Board concentrated the forces of industry, agriculture, and manpower. Civilians were conscripted into the armed forces, and the Committee on Public Information mobilized public opinion. Once the war was over, the American people found them so uncomfortable that they rallied around the slogan of a "return to normalcy."

World War I—Maneuvers

World War I—U.S. soldiers going over the top

World War I—U.S. soldiers with gas masks in the trenches

World War I—Capt. Eddie Rickenbacker and his Spad Airplane

Between World Wars (1918–1945)

Nevertheless the First World War transformed the United States into a world power, and President Wilson became for a season the hero of the victorious Allies. The Fourteen Points proposed by Wilson to Congress in January 1918 as a peace platform became the framework for peace negotiations in which he participated personally at Versailles in 1919, winning the Nobel Prize for peace en route. He was responsible for formulating a Covenant for a League of Nations that was incorporated into the proposed peace treaty. Its purpose was to set up a forum where a stabilized world could conduct international business without recourse to arms. When the treaty, with its Covenant, was brought to the Senate for ratification in March 1920, it was passed by a majority short of the required two-thirds. Wilson was unable to convert either the Senate or the electorate to his vision. The United States recoiled from the possibility of compromising a particle of its sovereignty. In 1921 a relatively unknown Republican Senator, Warren G. Harding, became the first "dark horse" of the century to achieve the Presidency in the first election in which women were eligible to vote. The country turned back to business as usual.

DECADE OF PROSPERITY

The relaxation of discipline was sudden. The armed forces were demobilized, the railroads were returned to private control, tariffs were raised to peak levels and extended to protect industries that had not existed in prewar days and crops never before shielded. Taxes that confiscated fortunes

The *Question Mark*, a Fokker C-2, with the help of a refueling plane sets an endurance record of almost 151 hours in 1929.

were repealed and monopolistic practices were revived. These changes brought a decade of unprecedented prosperity. Among the contributing factors were a population of well over one hundred million, more than half of whom were urban; advances in technology, particularly in chemistry and the use of electric power; above all the development of the automobile, which paralleled in its economic and social influence the development of the railroad in the mid-nineteenth century. Just as the automobile increased the mobility of persons and goods, so the new medium of radio increased the spread of information. The broadcasting network exemplified the complex modern enterprise, just as the marketplaces of the land were being forged into linked chains. Transportation, communications, and merchandising assumed their modern characteristics, and in turn stimulated such industries as steel, glass, rubber, oil, and advertising. Only the liquor industry was depressed, for during the war the temperance movement convinced the American people of the evils of alcohol. Prohibition became effective one year after the ratification of the Eighteenth Amendment in January 1919.

DRIFT TOWARD DEPRESSION

The United States did not cut itself off entirely from the world. The nation's role on the world stage required its involvement in international trade. Although production and credit were expanding rapidly within the United States after the war, these activities were disrupted on the world scene by maneuvers around the war debt and reparations. Perhaps the inequitable distribution of wealth aggravated the difficulties. In any case, the world's consuming market could no longer profitably absorb the abundance produced. A panic in the stock exchange in September and October 1929, preceded a rapid decline in business activity and employment. The ensuing depression spread from the United States throughout the world. Its effects were profound. It altered the course of American economy and internationally contributed to the political circumstances that led directly to the Second World War.

The Wall Street "crash" occurred seven months after President Herbert Hoover's inauguration, at which he predicted the final victory over poverty. The remainder of Hoover's Administration was engaged in an effort to achieve recovery in a manner consistent with Republican policies. Government could intervene in the private economy sector only if it benefited business, for prosperous industry was considered the prerequisite to general prosperity. Accordingly, the Reconstruction Finance Corporation (RFC) was created in January 1932, with the mission of distributing Federal funds where they would presumably do the most good. Banks and big business received help. Direct relief to victims of the economic disaster was not within the jurisdiction of the RFC.

THE NEW DEAL

This program did not appeal to the stricken electorate. They returned the Democratic Party to power by voting for Franklin D. Roosevelt as President. The crisis of bank failures in 1933 coincided with his inauguration, but Roosevelt told his countrymen that they had "nothing to fear but fear itself." In this spirit of indomitable optimism, a series of bold, innovative measures were directly addressed to the catastrophe. Roosevelt's program, known as the New Deal, included relief for the farmer in the Agricultural Adjustment Act (AAA), for small as well as big business in the National Industrial Recovery Act (NIRA), for the youthful unemployed in the Civilian Conservation Corps (CCC) and the National Youth Administration (NYA), and for jobless adults in the Public Works Administration and successively in the Civil Works, Works Progress, and Work Projects administrations (CWA, WPA). Insurance against bank failures was guaranteed by the Federal Deposit Insurance Corporation (FDIC); and insurance against the effects of severed income was provided in the Social Security system, which also fostered the passage of state unemployment insurance laws. Collective bargaining between management and labor was encouraged by the National Labor Relations Act. The proliferation of what became known as "alphabet agencies" continued. Most of them survived the constitutional test, although the Supreme Court struck down NIRA and AAA. This led to a logistic attack against the Court by Roosevelt, usually referred to as "packing" the Court. Although neither the Constitution nor tradition limited the number of Justices, Roosevelt's lunge proved unpopular. After a series of Court rulings more favorable to the New Deal, the "packing" attempt was abandoned.

At first the business community supported the New Deal. But when the safety of the capitalist system was assured, Roosevelt began to lose business approval. On the other hand, a powerful new labor organization, the Committee for (later Congress of) Industrial Organization (CIO), arose within the established American Federation of Labor (AFL). The CIO organized workers by industry rather than according to craft in the AFL tradition. Spurred by favorable legislation and a friendly government, the unions almost tripled their membership in the eight years after 1933, and could be numbered safely in the Democratic fold. Most of the voting blacks were in Northern working-class precincts and were likely to find more in common with the party of Roosevelt than with the Republicans, whose ties with Lincoln appeared tenuous. Additional support for Roosevelt was gained when, in 1933, the Twenty-First Amendment repealed Prohibition; this reform had been in the Democratic platform. The Depression lingered on despite the best efforts of the first two Administrations of Franklin Roosevelt; yet the New Deal remained popular and even the Republican candidate in 1940, Wendell Willkie, did not attack it in principle. Roosevelt easily won an unprecedented third term. To a great degree, however, his foreign policy accounted for his victory in 1940. The Second World War was already under way, sending shock waves across both oceans. The American people felt it was no time to change leadership.

WAR CLOUDS AGAIN

During the first two Roosevelt Administrations, Adolf Hitler had risen to power over Europe and made a partnership in an anticommunist axis with

World War II—A montage of photographs depicting the attack of Pearl Harbor

imperial Japan and fascist Italy. This aroused mixed reactions among Americans. Antipathy toward communism prevailed in the United States, which waited 16 years to recognize the obviously stable government of the Soviet Union. However, few Americans considered the dictators of Italy and Germany and the martial emperor of Japan champions of enlightened capitalism. They observed with distaste the ruthless treatment of Jews and dissidents in Germany, Italy's conquest of Ethiopia, the cynical participation of Italian and German troops in Spain's civil war, and the even more cynical absorption of Austria and Czechoslovakia by Hitler. On the other hand, sentiments of neutralism were strong. This caused the United States to play an ambiguous role toward Spain, to abstain from participation in the League of Nations, and to observe with aloofness the Japanese aggression against China. The Soviet Union, perhaps aware that anticommunist Europe was willing to support Hitler in an eastward drive, formed an alliance with Hitler in 1939. Most of Western Europe was overrun by the Nazis in 1940, and the United States prepared to face the imminent danger, adopting peacetime conscription for the first time in September 1940. Modest aid was tendered to Great Britain. The neutrality laws were revised. And in anticipation of the approaching Presidential campaign, Roosevelt named Republicans to the sensitive Navy and War posts in his cabinet.

SECOND WORLD WAR

Only after the Hawaiian Islands were directly attacked by the Japanese on December 7, 1941, did the United States enter the Second World War. The nation immediately became the "arsenal of democracy," and its contribution of goods and personnel undoubtedly assured the reversal of Axis aggression. Once more the entire economy was geared to a single task, this time under the Office of War Mobilization. The vast production capacity was now fully utilized, bringing an end to the Depression and even restoring prosperity to the farmers, who had languished since the end of the First World War in near-poverty. Organized labor, committed to abstain from striking for the duration, enrolled members at an accelerating pace. Among these were large numbers of women and black ex-sharecroppers who had found factory jobs in Northern cities. The prosecution of the war was conducted with enthusiasm. President Roosevelt, elected to a fourth term in 1944, maintained active leadership, attending countless conferences. These began in August 1941, with a secret meeting between Roosevelt and British Prime Minister Winston Churchill on the high seas to formulate the Atlantic Charter. This document became the basis of the United Nations Declaration of January 1942. Summit meetings of the allied leaders continued in 1943 at Casablanca, Cairo, and Teheran. The meeting at Yalta in February 1945, was

World War II—"D" Day, U.S. troops land on a beachhead in Northern France.

World War II—U.S. 3rd Infantry Division passes the shattered remains of a German convoy.

World War II—Nagasaki, Japan, following the explosion of the second U.S. atomic bomb.

World War II—Japanese Foreign Minister Mamoru Shigemitsu signs surrender terms on board the U.S.S. *Missouri.*

World War II—U.S. military personnel gather in Paris to celebrate the end of the war.

the last attended by Roosevelt, whose death in April placed his Vice-President, Harry S. Truman, in charge of the peacemaking activities.

THE BOMB AND THE UNITED NATIONS

Before the war was concluded, President Truman made the fateful decision to drop the first atomic bombs in history, over the Japanese cities of Hiroshima and Nagasaki, on August 6 and 9, 1945. This event occurred three months after the Germans had surrendered and a few days after the conclusion of the Potsdam Conference, at which the organization of the postwar world was discussed by those who would be in charge.

Meanwhile, from April to June 1945, the United States hosted a meeting in San Francisco of the nations which had signed the 1942 declaration concerning war aims. These nations now signed a charter establishing a new international organization to "maintain international peace and security," to "develop friendly relations among nations," and in general to reincarnate the League of Nations in the coming era. The United States was a charter member of this organization, the United Nations. The prospects for the international community after the Second World War seemed more promising than those for the peoples of the world after the First World War.

The Cold War (1946–1972)

Before the surrender of Japan on September 2, 1945, the friendship among the allies began to fray, revealing a schism between its communist and anticommunist members. It soon became apparent that the powers would divide into two blocs, led by the surviving superpowers, the United States and the Soviet Union. All the nations were weary of war and no power on earth would dare provoke the United States to demonstrate once more that its nuclear monopoly could bring intolerable destruction. The Soviet Union, however, chose not to relinquish this unique opportunity to establish a tier of buffer states around its heartland. Therefore, there ensued a condition between belligerency and amity between the two major powers that came to be known as "cold war."

TRUMAN DOCTRINE AND MARSHALL PLAN

Each bloc attempted to blame the other for the onset of this unwelcome atmosphere. In one version, the declaration of this "war" was attributed to Churchill, who made a speech at Fulton, Missouri, on March 5, 1946. There he described an "iron curtain" stretching across Europe from the Baltic to the Adriatic, dividing the contending camps. A year later the United States opened what may be viewed as an offensive in the contest–the proclamation of the Truman Doctrine, in the tradition of the Monroe Doctrine and the Roosevelt Corollary. President Truman declared in March 1947 (on the occasion of providing aid to the Greek government against communist insurgents) that it would be "the policy of the United States to support free peoples who are resisting attempted subjugation by armed minorities or by outside pressures." This formula was soon abbreviated to the concept of "containment" of communism. In June 1947, Secretary of State George Marshall proposed a plan to provide economic aid to the devastated countries of Europe, without discrimination. The Soviet government refused aid on behalf of its client states. Certain beneficiaries of the Marshall Plan banded together in 1949 as the North Atlantic Treaty Organization (NATO), which functioned as the military arm of the anticommunist bloc in Europe.

The first overt clash between the blocs in Europe occurred over Berlin, a disputed enclave geographically within the communist-occupied sector of

Germany. The United States supported the besieged city with an impressive airlift in 1948 and 1949. As a result, each bloc took control of a part of the former capital, and before the end of 1949 two Germanies were established as independent countries.

KOREA AND INDOCHINA

The decisive military superiority of the anticommunist camp ended when the Soviet Union demonstrated its own atomic capacity in 1949. In the same year communist power expanded with the military victory of the forces of Mao Tse-tung in China. In 1950 the communist North Koreans attacked the anticommunist South Koreans. Although the military defense of the anticommunist cause was undertaken by the United Nations (during a brief boycott of the organization by the Soviet Union), the actual conduct of the ensuing Korean War was led by the United States. China became involved and the fighting ended in a truce in 1953 that restored the lines breached in 1950.

General Dwight D. Eisenhower, supreme Allied commander in Europe during the Second World War and more recently supreme commander of the NATO forces in Europe, was elected President in 1953 to succeed Truman. One of his preelection promises was to end the war in Korea. He kept this promise. He also restrained his Secretary of State, John Foster Dulles, from providing the French in Indochina with more than economic aid in their effort to regain their colony in that area. When the French were expelled in 1954, however, Eisenhower was convinced that the Indochinese independence movement with headquarters in Hanoi was completely under communist control. During his Administration an anticommunist regime was established in Saigon with United States help. This regime proved unstable, but its maintenance as an anticommunist nucleus was considered essential. It received ever-increasing military and economic aid and finally the reinforcement of manpower. The Southeast Asia Treaty Organization was set up in 1954 in the NATO pattern. Its futility was matched only by the so-called Eisenhower Doctrine in support of any nation in the Middle East that should request aid "against armed aggression from any country controlled by international communism." In 1961 President John F. Kennedy inherited not only a bellicose policy against the communist bastion in Cuba, but also the execution of an ill-conceived military expedition against Cuba. In 1962 Kennedy compelled the Soviet Union to desist from its projected buildup of missiles in Cuba.

The Korean War—U.S. paratroopers descend on a designated location.

The Korean War—A railroad depot in North Korea minutes after being bombed by U.S. planes

BALANCE OF POWER

As the scope of the cold war widened and confrontations increased, both camps became aware of their roles. The communists, in a mirror image of the Truman Doctrine, declared that they would aid any war of "national liberation." Although nuclear war was intolerable, conventional (or "brushfire") wars could be waged. Meanwhile, both camps were subject to internal stress. Two of the anticommunist powers, France and Great Britain, joined Israel in attempting to seize the Suez Canal in 1956. The United States and the Soviet Union joined to support the United Nations' condemnation of the aggression against Egypt. On the other hand, a rift developed and widened between the Soviet and Chinese communists. Each of these major sections of the communist camp competed for goodwill within the Third World, as the uncommitted or unaligned nations–many of them liberated ex-colonies–came to be called. Finally, in the 1960s, the growing stability of China and its potential capacity to wield atomic warfare began to alter the polarity of the contest, and a triangular balance of power began to emerge. This fluid situation was of little advantage to the United States. After decades of costly effort in Indochina, the United States was left with only the certainty of defeat and diminished status.

The United Nations constantly admitted members of the Third World who tended to drift toward one of the communist groupings and almost never were attracted to the anticommunist camp. The United States found itself in the unaccustomed role of spokesman for a minority. The Nixon and Ford Administrations looked to Secretary of State Henry Kissinger as the architect of their foreign policy. They sought to adjust to the situation by establishing a détente with the Soviet Union and initiating modified diplomatic relations with China. This reversal of policy was exemplified by the admission of the People's Republic of China to the United Nations in 1971 and by an agreement with the Soviet Union in 1972 to limit the use of strategic missiles.

The Korean War—U.S. troops in action

SPACE RACE

The competition between the Soviet Union and the United States for political power on earth was paralleled by a race for the exploitation of space. The development of missiles led directly to the production of artificial satellites. The Soviet Union sent the first satellite into orbit on October 4, 1957, and less than four months later the United States sent its first satellite around the earth. The Soviet Union first made physical impact on the moon in 1959 and first sent a man into orbit in 1961, but the United States was the first to land a man on the moon's surface in 1969. The rivalry was officially terminated by a joint manned space mission in July 1975. But the competitors still covet the military and intelligence by-products that continue to accrue.

THE HOME FRONT HEATS UP

The cold war had a pronounced effect on the domestic affairs of the United States, from the Truman through the Nixon Administrations. So Under the cloak of anticommunism, dissidence of every sort was repressed. Landmark events were the "loyalty" check of government employes instituted in 1947 by Truman, the indictment of communists under the Smith Act in 1949, the enactment of the Subversive Activities Control Act and the Internal Security Act in 1950, and the series of investigations conducted or inspired by Senator Joseph McCarthy from 1950 to 1954.

Several minority groups–particularly blacks –crusaded for more civil rights in the 1950s and 1960s. The Supreme Court decision of 1954, *Brown v. Board of Education of Topeka,* reversed the 1896 ruling of *Plessy v. Ferguson* by declaring unconstitutional the segregation of blacks in public schools. This was followed by a vigorous movement to enforce and amplify the full exercise of black citizenship. The Montgomery, Alabama bus boycott began in 1955 to assert the right of blacks to equal public accommodations. It was the opening skirmish on behalf of civil rights led by the Reverend Martin Luther King, Jr., and his Southern Christian Leadership Conference. The struggle against segregation continued in its nonviolent phase as Freedom Riders tested the manner in which legal victories were translated into practice. This phase reached its climax in a mass march on Washington in 1963. A more militant phase of the movement attempted to enforce the political rights of blacks, culminating in a spectacular march from Selma to Montgomery, Alabama in 1965.

Simultaneously resistance to the war in Indochina began to peak. The antiwar and civil rights movements merged, resulting in the so-called "revolt on the campus" and the street tumult coinciding with the 1968 Democratic national convention in Chicago. Both President Lyndon Johnson and President Richard Nixon were disturbed by the rising discontent.

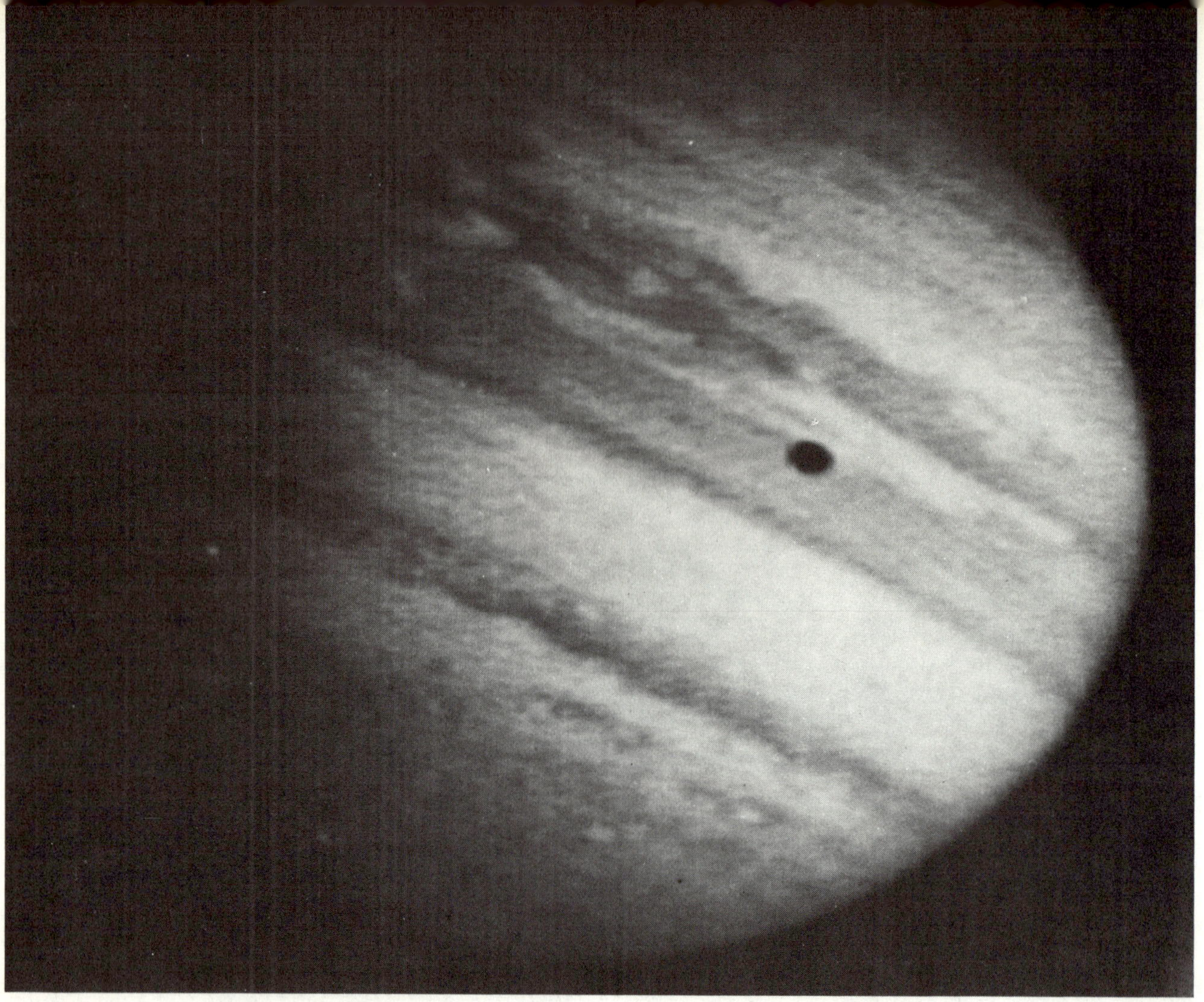

Jupiter's red spot and a shadow of the moon as photographed by *Pioneer 10*

Civil Rights Demonstration
Montgomery, Alabama, March 17, 1965

Dr. Martin Luther King, Jr.

Astronaut Edwin E. Aldrin, Jr. stands alongside the U.S. flag deployed by him and Astronaut Neil A. Armstrong after they landed on the moon in *Apollo 11.*

The *Apollo 11* Lunar Module ascent stage on its way to a docking rendezvous prior to returning to earth.

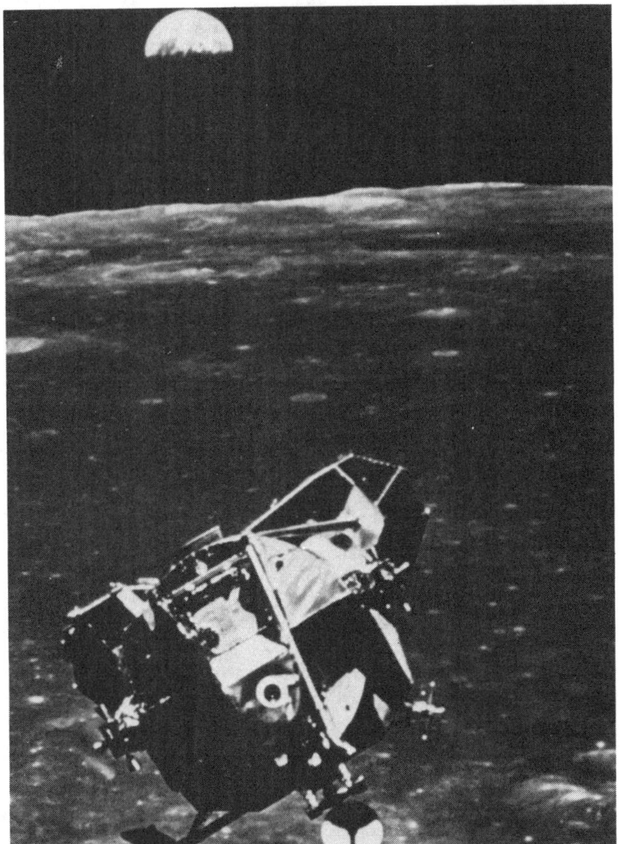

An *Apollo 12* astronaut examines the TV camera on the surface of the moon. The Lunar Module is in the background.

Apollo 15 Astronaut James B. Irwin rides on the surface of the moon in the Lunar Rover.

The Skylab II Space Station, photographed from the Command Module.

Profile of a Superpower Since 1955

After the Second World War, the United States recovered economically far more robustly than in the period after the First World War. Following an interval of mild recession and readjustment, an upswing began during the first Eisenhower Administration with the end of the Korean War. The real gross national product in 1955 was more than twice that of 1929, and the Federal balance for fiscal 1955 and 1956 showed a surplus. Eisenhower warned of the rise of a "military-industrial complex." He was succeeded in 1961 by John F. Kennedy, whose ambitious domestic program included considerable social legislation, conservation, and accelerated space exploration. Alhough the Mercury, Gemini, and Apollo projects were virtually completed in the Kennedy and Johnson Administrations, the struggle in Indochina depleted the resources of the country at the expense of the social reforms. It so undermined the "war on poverty" declared in 1964 by President Johnson that the "great society" had to be aborted.

In November 1967, the population of the United States reached 200 million. This was double the population during the First World War, when the country first became predominantly urban. By 1967 about three-fourths of the population lived in cities. An unusually large proportion of the population were immigrants or offspring of recent immigrants, who tended to settle in urban areas. Of the 32 million immigrants who arrived in the United States by 1920, those who came before 1900 were mostly from the countries of northern Europe, but thereafter an increasing proportion came from southern and eastern Europe and were considered less capable of being assimilated. A similar attitude toward the influx of Chinese and Japanese unskilled labor in the second half of the nineteenth century resulted in discriminatory immigration laws and even total exclusion. An immigration act of 1924 restricted the proportion of south and east Europeans who could acquire permanent residence. This policy was reversed in 1965, essentially by altering the primary basis of admission from country of origin to the skill of the immigrant.

TECHNOLOGICAL INFLUENCES

At the turn of the century the highway began to take the place of the railroad as the principal mode of transport. After the Second World War, passengers and freight began to take to the air. In the aerospace age, automation was augmented by computer technology. Mobility increased and the population dispersed geographically. As manufacturing had previously gained at the expense of agriculture, now the service industries and the government bureaucracies began to draw workers away from the farms, mines, and factories. The surplus of products required new markets, either at home or abroad, while personal income failed to keep pace. Government intervention attempted to cushion the effects of inflation and a rising rate of unemployment.

POLITICAL CHANGES

The increasing role of the Federal government and tension between the executive and legislative branches of government became controversial during the third quarter of the twentieth century. The spectrum in both political parties ran from liberal to conservative; each party had a contingent favoring the reduction of government power, whether in central or local sphere. Services were expected from government, but they were costly and offered excessive opportunity for corruption. Conservatives generally proposed that the Federal Government shed its bureaucracies and allow local communities to monitor their own affairs. Liberals preferred to make sure that hard-won benefits would not be lost. Many sought a balance between laissez faire and the welfare state, and debated whether to entrust significant areas of administration to city hall, the state house, or the District of Columbia. "Strong" Presidents were somewhat out of favor, largely because of the abuse of power revealed in the aftermath of the Watergate scandal of Nixon's Administration. However, few believed that Congress could pro-

Vietnam War—U.S. troops guard captured Vietcong soldiers.

Vietnam War—U.S. troops move into action.

A caisson bearing the body of the assassinated black leader, Martin Luther King, Jr.

vide the world's most powerful and richest country with the leadership demanded by the contemporary situation.

CONSTITUTIONAL CHANGES

During the twentieth century, flaws in the political process were corrected several times by amendments to the Constitution, a procedure that had already rationalized the mode of Presidential elections with the Twelfth Amendment. The Seventeenth Amendment, ratified in 1913, required direct popular election of Senators instead of their selection by state legislatures. This reform was adopted after 29 of the 48 states had already passed laws compelling their legislatures to do this. In 1967 new procedures for Presidential succession in an emergency were incorporated in the Twenty-fifth Amendment. The heart attacks of President Eisenhower (during which Vice-President Nixon had tentatively assumed Executive authority) and the lingering disability of Presidents Garfield and Wilson stimulated the reform. The amendment defined the circumstances under which Presidential duties may be assumed by the Vice-President, and also prescribed the filling of a Vice-Presidential vacancy. An occasion for utilizing the Twenty-fifth Amendment occurred in 1973, when a criminal indictment forced Vice-President Spiro Agnew to resign. Nixon then appointed Congressman Gerald Ford to replace Agnew. In 1974, President Nixon also resigned and Ford succeeded to the Presidency; he in turn appointed Nelson Rockefeller to the Vice-Presidency. Thus from 1974 through 1976 the executive branch was headed by unelected but duly constituted chiefs.

TEST OF MATURITY

In general, the Constitutional procedures served well. The black population gained appropriate political power largely in the courts and by using the rights to petition, assemble, and speak freely. It took the Twenty-fourth Amendment in 1964 to eliminate the poll tax, long an instrument for denying the franchise. The threat of impeachment forced President Nixon to resign when his role in obstructing justice was established. Convictions were handed down against some of Nixon's most powerful associates in the Watergate affair. This proved to many Americans that the Constitutional process works creditably. Others, however, were so disgusted by the deeds of recent Administrations that they shunned politics altogether.

The United States entered its bicentennial year soberly, knowing that the fate of the Western world depended on the kind of example it could provide. Its economy was faltering but did not appear likely to disintegrate. Its enemies were divided; its friends were critical but could be rallied; its own population was frustrated but capable. At the nation's two-hundredth birthday the United States faced inexorable tests of its maturity.

Thus it seemed quite appropriate that 1976 should be an election year. After a hotly contested round of primaries, Georgia's Governor James Earl ("Jimmy") Carter emerged as the Democratic presidential choice. The Republicans rallied around Gerald Ford, hoping that his experience in the White House would earn official sanction at the ballot box. Carter promised to reduce unemployment and turn back the tide of inflation. He pledged to bring Washington a government that was "as good, decent, and honest as the American people themselves"–an appeal to the voters disgruntled by Watergate. On the other hand, Ford proposed to continue the policy of détente with the Soviet Union, and he predicted that the economic problems at home would take care of themselves as America developed more of its own energy resources.

Carter won the election, but soon discovered how hard it was to deliver what he'd promised. The high cost of oil, a long miners' strike in the coal industry and a series of harsh winters pushed inflation ahead. The Carter Administration created thousands of new public-service jobs, but not enough to absorb the growing number of unemployed people. Congress balked at the President's proposal to streamline the Federal government. Labor unions rejected his pleas to soften their wage demands. The public reacted skeptically to the Administration's treaty with Panamanian President Omar Trujilos, which would give the Canal Zone back to Panama by the year 2000. (The treaty passed Congress by a slim margin.) All in all, Carter fared poorly during his first year in the White House.

As time went on, Carter made better progress in foreign affairs. In a surprise move, he invited Egyptian President Anwar Sadat and Israeli Prime Minister Menachem Begin to a summit conference at Camp David in September 1978. There they drafted a "Framework for Peace in the Middle East" and vowed to sign a formal peace treaty within three months. American envoys met Soviet negotiators for a second series of Strategic Arms Limitation Talks (SALT), to hammer out an agreement on sophisticated new weapon systems.

Meanwhile, President Carter bargained with Japanese and Arab leaders in an effort to right America's balance of trade. Economic problems became a major concern of the Carter administration, in both the domestic and foreign arenas.

A group of Iranian students seized the United States embassy in Tehran on November 4, 1979, beginning one of the most tense confrontations of Carter's Administration. The students held 50 hostages for several months, ignoring the pleas of the United Nations and the new Islamic government of Iran.

Five divisions of Soviet troops invaded Afghanistan on January 3, 1980 to replace the socialist government of President Hafi-zulla Amin with leaders who would be more responsive to Russia's directives. The United States protested the invasion.

In 1980 Carter again ran for office but was defeated in a landslide victory by the former governor of California, Ronald Reagan. A leading spokesman for the conservative wing of the Republican Party, Reagan was a popular candidate because of his fiscal policies and winning speaking ability. Faced with high unemployment, interest rates, and inflation, the American people viewed economic concerns at the forefront of the campaign. By 1982 signs of economic recovery began to appear, but the president's position in foreign affairs seemed to be faltering.

After a resounding defeat in 1984 of Democratic challenger Walter Mondale, President Reagan sought to strengthen his role in foreign policy. Under attack for the continued presence of 1,500 U.S. Marines in Lebanon, he announced their withdrawal in early 1984. The role of the United States in Central America continued as a source of contention between Congress and the president. Congress also forced Reagan to reduce his requested increase for defense spending.

While the economy began to improve, the federal deficit continued to increase. Attacking the deficit became a major focus of the second term of Reagan's presidency.

AMERICAN GOVERNMENT

The U.S. Constitution separates the powers of government as a safeguard against dictatorship. You will note that Article I of the Constitution begins with the phrase: "All legislative powers herein granted shall be vested in a Congress . . . ." Article II begins with a parallel phrase: "The executive power shall be vested in a President . . . ," while Article III states: "The judicial power of the United States shall be vested in one Supreme Court, and in . . . inferior courts. . . ." Each of these branches is independent of the others.

THE EXECUTIVE BRANCH

The office of the President has developed over the years. Many changes have taken place in the method of electing the President. The authors of the Constitution wanted to avoid having the President chosen directly by the people; they feared the public would not know the qualifications of the candidate and might choose unwisely. Consequently, they provided that every four years each state should select "electors" equal in number to the total number of the state's representatives and senators in Congress. These presidential electors would use their own judgment in electing a President and Vice-President, voting as they saw fit. Groups of electors (known as "electoral colleges") would meet in the capitals of their respective states and cast their ballots for President and Vice-President, writing two names on each ballot. The votes of the electoral colleges would then be sent to the president of the Senate, who would open and count the votes. The candidate who received a majority of all of the electoral votes cast would be declared the President-elect; the candidate with the next highest number would be the Vice-President-elect.

This system was soon changed. By 1800 two political parties had grown up, each putting forth its own candidates for office. Electors were pledged to one of these parties. They became "rubber stamps" who cast the state's electoral vote for the candidate of the party they represented. Today each party chooses a slate of electors; most voters in the state don't know them. On Election Day, voters continue to choose electors, convinced that the elector will vote for the candidate whom the voter wants. However, in the elections of 1948, 1956, 1960, 1968, and 1972 a few electors exercised their constitutional rights and voted for candidates of their own choice rather than that of the voters.

Political parties brought another important change in the method of electing the President. In 1796, John Adams became our second President because he had received the largest number of electoral college votes. Thomas Jefferson became the Vice-President, even though he and Adams were of different political parties. Furthermore, if each elector wrote on his ballot the names of the two candidates of his political party, a tie for first place might easily result. (This actually happened in 1800. The election went to the House of Representatives, where Thomas Jefferson was chosen on the thirty-sixth ballot.)

To remedy these defects, Amendment XII was added to the Constitution in 1804. It provided that the President and Vice-President be chosen on separate ballots.

Many voters dislike the electoral college system because it can elect a "minority President" who has not received even 50 percent of the popular vote. Each state's entire electoral vote goes to the candidate who polls the most votes in the state, no matter how narrow the margin of victory over his opponent. Consequently, a candidate can receive a majority of the popular vote and yet fail to win the election. This happened in 1888, when Grover Cleveland had clear majority over Benjamin Harrison, yet Harrison became President because he had more of the electoral college votes. Harrison carried the states with a large electoral vote, while Cleveland carried the states with a small electoral vote.

Reformers have often tried to make the method of electing a President more democratic. One proposal is to elect the President directly by popular vote, abolishing the electoral college. Another has been to divide each state's electoral vote among the candidates according to the popular vote.

Powers of the President

On the White House desk of President Harry S. Truman was a small sign that read, "The buck stops here." This meant that the President had to make the final decisions about a tremendous number of problems which arose each day. The Presidency has been called "the world's biggest job." As a matter of fact, it is really six different jobs:

1. The President as Chief Administrator. The Constitution states: "The executive power shall be vested in a President of the United States of America." This includes primarily the job of enforcing the laws. However, this duty is so great that the President must delegate some of this power. The President is the head of nearly two and a half million federal employees who run the approximately 2,200 government departments, bureaus, boards, and other administrative agencies.

Directly under his command is the executive office of the President. Included in this office are several staff agencies. The White House office itself includes the President's press secretary, a legal counsel, a correspondence secretary, an appointments secretary, and a number of political, legislative, and administrative aides.

The President's chief lieutenants are the eleven members of his cabinet, who head the Departments of State; Treasury; Defense; Justice; Interior; Agriculture; Commerce; Labor; Health, Education and Welfare; Housing and Urban Development; Transportation.

Four presidential staff agencies work closely with the President:

A. *Office of Management and Budget.* The director of the budget advises the President on the fiscal requirements of the many government agencies. The Bureau advises him about legislation that concerns the costs of operating these agencies. The Office of Management and Budget has been called "Chief Housekeeper," since it tries to improve the efficiency of the Administration.

B. *Council of Economic Advisors.* This board is made up of three members who advise the President concerning economic trends. It also suggests new laws regarding the economy of the nation and helps the President prepare reports on the economic state of the nation.

C. *National Security Council.* This is an important agency concerned with national defense. It includes the Secretary of State, Secretary of Defense, director of the Central Intelligence Agency, and the director of the Office of Emergency Preparedness. It is the nation's top strategy planning body, meeting weekly with the President and Vice-President.

D. *Office of Emergency Preparedness.* This staff agency advises the President on the status of our country's raw materials, manpower, industry, military and civilian defense. It also coordinates, directs, and plans all civil and defense mobilization.

In addition to these agencies and departments, a number of others work closely with the President. These include the United States Information Agency, the Veterans' Administration, the Small Business Administration, and others.

Lastly, there are the many so-called independent agencies created by Congress. These include the Civil Aeronautics Board, the Atomic Energy Commission, the Interstate Commerce Commission, and the Federal Power Commission. These are formally part of the executive branch. (In theory, the constitution was designed to prevent executive, legislative, and judical power from being concentrated within any one of our three branches. However, these agencies do function in all three areas. They make rules, judge offenders, and execute their own laws.)

2. The President as Legislator. In spite of the separation of powers, our Chief Executive has important law-making powers. The Constitution states that the President "shall from time to time give to the Congress information on the State of the Union, and recommend to their consideration such measures as he shall judge necessary and expedient." This is how the President plays a major note in shaping national legislation. The President appears before Congress and urges legislation he considers important. The Constitution gives him the power to veto bills of which he does not approve. Congress usually cannot muster the two-thirds vote necessary to pass a bill over the President's veto. So Congress usually writes a bill to be in line with what the White House will accept.

3. The President as Chief Diplomat. In today's troubled world, the conduct of foreign relations may well be the President's most vital role. He appoints United States diplomats to their overseas posts, with the advice and consent of the Senate. The Constitution gives him also the responsibility of receiving foreign ambassadors. This involves the important power to recognize foreign governments. After the Communist revolution in 1917, Presidents Coolidge and Hoover refused to receive a Russian ambassador, thus refusing to recognize the Soviet government. Furthermore, the President has the power to make treaties, which must be approved by two-thirds of the Senate. However, he can also make executive agreements which do not require Senate approval. In 1939, for instance, President Roosevelt traded fifty United States destroyers to Great Britain for island bases without the Senate's approval.

4. The President as Chief of State. Unlike members of Congress, the President represents all Americans rather than those of a particular section. He appears at important public ceremonies. He is in a unique position to help mold public thinking, through press conferences, radio, and television. Presidents Franklin D. Roosevelt and Jimmy Carter, for example, used "fireside chats" to help gain the nation's support for their programs.

5. The President as Commander in Chief. The Constitution places the President at the head of all of the armed forces of the United States. He must approve all military promotions and is responsible for the nation's defense and military preparedness. Although the Constitution gives Congress the power to declare war, the President may determine whether or not a state of war exists. President Truman, for example, ordered United States troops into Korea in 1950, although Congress had not formally declared war. Once war comes, the President decides when, where, and how our military power will be used.

6. The President as Party Chief. Although political parties are not mentioned in the Constitution, the President is the head of his political party. He is responsible for choosing the party's national chairman. As chief executive he can award hundreds of government jobs in Washington and throughout the country, a power known as "patronage." Often, he uses these positions to reward loyal members of the party. The President often uses his prestige to support some of his party's candidates in Congressional or state elections.

Presidential Succession

John Adams, the first Vice-President of the United States, once remarked that an appropriate title for the Vice-President would be "Your Superfluous Excellency." He referred to the fact that the main responsibility of the office was to preside over the Senate. In that position, the Vice-President does not even have the privilege of voting, except in case of a tie.

Yet the constitutional qualifications for the Vice-President are the same as for the Presidency. The history of our nation has given ample evidence that this was a wise precaution. Eight of our presidents have died in office, four of them by assassination. If the President dies, the Vice-President takes office. The Constitution did not say he would necessarily become President in name. It provided that the *duties* of the chief executive would be performed by the Vice-President in case of the President's "death, resignation, or inability to discharge the duties" of his office.

While Dwight D. Eisenhower was President, he suffered two serious illnesses. The public became aware of the fact that the Constitution, in the phrase quoted above, left unanswered two important questions: (1) Who determines whether the President is incapable of serving as chief executive? (2) What happens if a President is declared unable to serve, and then recovers his health and capacities?

In 1965, Congress proposed the Twenty-fifth Amendment to the Constitution. Ratified on February 10, 1967, this amendment provides that in the event of death, resignation, or impeachment of the President, the Vice-President actually becomes the President; he does not simply perform the duties of the Chief Executive. He appoints a new Vice-President, who must be confirmed by a majority vote of Congress. Further, the amendment details the procedures to be followed if the President becomes temporarily or permanently incapacitated and unable to serve.

Presidential Tenure

How long can a President serve in office? The Constitution did not limit the number of terms of office a President might serve. Both Washington and Jefferson, however, decided that two terms were sufficient. This remained an "unwritten precedent" until 1940. In that year Franklin D. Roosevelt ran for reelection to a third term. Because he was so popular, and because World War II had broken out in Europe, the voters gave him an easy victory. In 1944, he was chosen again for a fourth term.

Many people felt that no man should be permitted to serve for so long a period. They led a movement which resulted in the adoption of the Twenty-second Amendment, which went into effect in 1951. This Amendment forbids any person from serving as President for more than two full terms. A person who has come to the Presidency from the Vice-Presidency as the result of the death of the President is considered to have had a "full term" if he holds office for over two years.

THE LEGISLATIVE BRANCH

Of the three branches of the Federal Government, the legislative branch is the only one elected *directly* by the people. The Constitution granted the power of making all federal laws to Congress, composed of the Senate and the House of Representatives.

The House of Representatives

Representation in the House is based upon population, each state being guaranteed at least one representative. There are 435 members. Most representatives are elected from a congressional district, whose area is determined by the state legislature. Some states also have Congressmen-at-large, elected by the voters of the entire state. Members of the House of Representatives serve for two years.

In addition to the law-making powers which it shares with the Senate, the House of Representatives has three special powers. It has the sole power to initiate revenue bills. It alone has the power to impeach the President or any other civil officer of the United States for "Treason, Bribery, or other high Crimes and Misdemeanors." Lastly, the House of Representatives elects the President if the electoral college fails to do so. This happened in 1800 and 1824.

The Senate

The Constitution provided that the Senate be made up of two senators from each state. Hence all states, regardless of their size or population, have an equal voice in the Senate. All senators are elected for six years. Since one-third of the Senate comes up for election every two years, the Senate never changes more than one-third of its membership at any time, as the House of Representatives may.

The Senate has three special powers, which permit it to check the power of the President. Its approval is needed for Presidential appointments to cabinet posts, ambassadorships, and other high offices. The two-thirds vote of the Senate required for ratification of treaties has given it a significant role in foreign relations. Finally, the Senate sits as a court of trial in impeachment cases, a two-thirds vote being necessary for conviction. (The Senate also has the power to elect the Vice-President when the electoral college fails to do so. However, this power has been used only once, in the election of 1836.)

The Powers of Congress

Most of the legislative powers granted to Congress are found in Article I, Section 8. In addition to granting 17 specific powers to Congress, this section also contains the so-called *elastic* clause. This provides that Congress shall have the power "to make all laws which shall be necessary and proper for carrying into execution the foregoing powers. . . ." This clause has made possible a tremendous growth of the Federal Government.

Although Congress's powers are vast, it does not have the power to legislate as it sees fit. Article I, Section 9, and the first ten Amendments (The Bill of Rights) limit the right of Congress in many ways. For example, Congress may not tax exports, appropriate money for the Army for a period of over two years, suspend the privilege of the writ of *habeas corpus,* or grant a title of nobility.

How a Bill Becomes a Law

A bill must be introduced by a member of Congress, in either one of the two houses (except for bills for the raising of revenue, which must originate in the House of Representatives). Thousands of bills are introduced in each session of Congress. Out of this number, fewer than one thousand become laws. The process by which a bill becomes a law is often long and complicated.

1. *The bill is introduced.* In the Senate, a sponsor introduces the bill from the floor, usually without discussion. In the House of Representatives, a sponsor of the bill drops it into a box known as the "hopper" at the desk of the Speaker of the House. (The Speaker is chosen at the start of each new Congress from the majority party. He ordinarily votes on issues only in case of a tie.)

2. *A committee studies the bill.* Because of the thousands of bills which are introduced during a session of Congress, the committee system was set up. In the House of Representatives there are 19 "standing" or regular committees; in the Senate there are 15. Large committees are generally broken down into subcommittees, each responsible for part of the parent committee's work. Each committee is made up of members from both political parties. Generally, the committee reflects the relative party strengths in the particular house of

Congress, so that the majority party controls each committee.

Seniority determines who will be chairman of the committee. That is, the position is usually held by a member of the majority party who has had the longest period of service on the committee.

In the House of Representatives, the Speaker assigns the bill to the appropriate committee. Senators state their choice of committee on all bills they introduce.

The committee may announce public hearings, at which supporters and opponents of the bill may appear and state their positions. At the close of the hearings, the committee decides whether to report the bill favorably or to pigeonhole it–that is, not report it at all. Over 90 percent of all bills introduced in Congress are killed in committee.

Most committee hearings are for the purpose of examining bills introduced. However, Congress also has the power to use committee hearings to "investigate," in order to see how well the laws of Congress are being executed and to find out whether new legislation is needed. In recent years, investigatory hearings into crime, Communism, and corruption have attracted widespread public attention.

3. *Bills reach the floor.* After the committee has reported a bill favorably, the bill goes on the calendar of the house to which the committee belongs. Some bills are considered more important than others. In the House of Representatives the Rules Committee may decide when a bill shall be called up. Some bills may never be reached at all if this committee places them at the bottom of the list. In the Senate, the policy committee of the majority party determines priorities.

The members debate the bill on the floor. In the House, the large membership has made it necessary to limit the time each member is allowed to speak. But in the Senate there is unlimited debate. A Senator or group of Senators can try to "talk a bill to death" to prevent its being brought to a vote. This strategy is called a "filibuster."

Each house may revise or amend the bill in the course of debate. The vote is finally taken. If a majority approves, the bill is sent to the other house for consideration. There the entire process starts all over again. The bill may be pigeonholed in committee, defeated on the floor, or approved. (Sometimes the procedure is speeded up by having similar bills start at the same time in both houses.)

4. *A conference committee may consider the bill.* In the course of its travel through both houses, the bill may have been changed considerably, so that the House version and the Senate version differ in details. In such a case, a conference committee, made up of members of both houses, meets to adjust these differences. The bill is then sent back to both houses for final approval.

5. *The bill goes to the President.* The bill becomes law after receiving the President's signature. If he holds it for a period of ten days (Sundays excepted) while Congress is in session, it also becomes law. (If Congress is not in session and the President holds the bill for ten days, it is automatically killed. This is called a "pocket veto.") If the President disapproves of the bill, he returns it to the house in which it started, with a statement of his objections, called a "veto message." If two-thirds of each house again vote for it, it becomes a law in spite of his veto.

THE JUDICIAL BRANCH

The judicial branch can be understood better if we contrast it with the legislative and executive branches. The primary function of Congress is to make laws. The primary function of the executive branch is to carry these laws into effect. The courts settle legal disputes in terms of existing law.

In the United States the courts have a particularly important role to play. Our Constitution is based upon the idea of limited government. The judicial branch has been given a major responsibility for seeing that government does not exceed the powers the people have given it.

How Federal Courts Are Organized

In Article III, Section 1, the Constitution provides for a Supreme Court and ". . . such inferior [lower] courts as the Congress may from time to time ordain and establish." In accordance with this, Congress created the Federal court system, consisting of three types of courts (and one special court, the Court of Claims).

1. *Federal District Courts.* At the base of the Federal court system are the 84 District Courts. Since these are the first to hear most cases, they are said to have *original* jurisdiction. Only one judge ordinarily sits on a case, although three may sit as a court in special circumstances. Like all other federal judges, District Court judges are appointed for life by the President, subject to the advice and consent of the Senate. In the District

Courts are tried most cases of crime against the United States and suits between individual citizens of different states.

2. *The United States Courts of Appeals.* Immediately above the District Courts are the eleven Courts of Appeals. These are ordinarily three-judge courts. Since they hear cases on appeal from the District Courts, they are said to have appellate jurisdiction. They are concerned primarily with questions of law rather than with findings of fact. Thus they relieve the Supreme Court of some of the tremendous burden of appellate work.

Usually, the decision of a Court of Appeals is final. Unless a case involves an extremely complex and important point of law, the Supreme Court would not have time to review it. Only a small fraction of cases go from the Courts of Appeals to the United States Supreme Court.

3. *The Court of Claims.* The Court of Claims was created in order to handle debt claims against the United States Government. Most of these claims arise out of government contracts. The Court of Claims has five judges.

4. *The Supreme Court of the United States.* The nation's highest tribunal consists of nine judges. Since the Constitution does not specify the number of judges, Congress decides this by law. (At first the Supreme Court had six judges. Congress has set the number at as many as ten and as few as five.)

One of the judges is designated as the chief justice. His decisions, however, have no more legal weight than those of his fellow justices. The Court ordinarily hears arguments for two weeks and then recesses for two weeks to reach decisions and write opinions. Cases are decided by a majority vote of the justices. (Many important cases have been decided by a five-to-four vote.) In addition to the majority decision, there may be a *dissenting,* or minority, opinion. In case a justice agrees with the majority decision but differs with the reasoning behind it, he may write a *concurring* opinion.

The Supreme Court has wide discretion to decide which cases it will hear on appeal from lower courts and which it will refuse to hear. In general, the Court will hear cases that have been decided differently in two or more lower courts. You will recall that unless there is a real constitutional issue or an important point of federal law involved, the Court will usually decline to hear an appeal. Thus, out of about 1,500 cases, the Court will hear only about 200.

In addition to the cases brought to the Supreme Court on appeal, the Court has original jurisdiction in certain cases. These cases are prescribed by the Constitution and are relatively rare. They include cases involving foreign diplomats and suits brought by one state against another.

Our Dual Court System

It should be noted that each of the states has its own court system. Since the United States Consitution is the supreme law of the land, any case involving federal law or the federal Constitution is heard in a United States court rather than in a state court. The Supreme Court of the United States exercises the power to void laws passed by state legislatures and to overrule decisions of state courts, when it deems these laws or decisions to be in conflict with federal law or the United States Constitution.

CHECKS AND BALANCES

We have examined the responsibilities of each of the three main branches of our government. The Constitution provided a system of checks and balances to prevent any branch from invading the rights of the others. There have been occasions in our history, however, when conflict arose because one of the branches considered that its independence was being threatened. Let us review the important checks and balances and note some of the notable instances of conflict among the three branches.

Congress and the President

As noted above, the President may check Congress by using his veto power over legislation. He may also call Congress into special session and recommend legislation to Congress. Through the prestige of his office, he can exert great influence on public opinion and on Congress.

Meanwhile, Congress can check the President by the use of its constitutional powers. The administration must depend upon Congress for money. If Congress refuses to appropriate funds the President needs to enforce a law, it can tie his hands. Furthermore, although the President is commander in chief of the armed forces, Congress determines the size and equipment of those forces. Both houses may override the President's veto by two-thirds vote. In addition, the Senate may check the President by refusing to approve his appointments or by refusing to ratify treaties. The Constitution provides that the House of Representatives may bring impeachment charges against the President, and the Senate has the power to try him on these charges.

Conflict between the executive and legislative branches has been a part of our history since the days of George Washington. In 1789, President Washington tried to hasten the Senate's ratification of an Indian treaty by going to the Senate with his advisors to answer any questions the Senators had. The Senators sat in silence, resenting what they considered to be an intrusion on their powers. Washington walked out, vowing never to set foot in the Senate chamber again. No President did, in fact, until President Wilson appeared before the Senate 130 years later. Washington's successor, John Adams, remarked that Congress and the President were "natural enemies."

During the Civil War, Abraham Lincoln not only used the constitutional powers of the President but also some that belonged to Congress. According to the Constitution, only Congress may "raise and support armies," yet Lincoln issued a call for volunteers, declared martial law, and ordered the Treasury to pay funds for military purposes. He waited until Congress had adjourned to issue his Emancipation Proclamation. He said, "I felt that measures, otherwise unconstitutional, might become lawful by becoming indispensable to the preservation of the Constitution . . ." After Lincoln's assassination, Andrew Johnson continued to insist upon the powers of the President. His conflict with Congress was climaxed by his impeachment trial, which failed of conviction by just one vote.

Woodrow Wilson believed strongly that the President must give legislative leadership to Congress. He insisted upon appearing in person before Congress on major proposals for legislation. When the Senate refused to allow the United States to join the League of Nations after World War I, he "went to the people." On a cross-country tour he urged the voters to make Congress vote for his measure.

In 1933, Franklin D. Roosevelt continued the Wilson pattern of Presidential leadership in legislation. He spoke to Congress of "building a strong and permanent tie between the legislative and executive branches of the government." When he felt that an individual Senator failed to support his program, he did not hesitate to go into the Senator's home state to campaign against his reelection.

Conficts between the legislative and executive branches have also arisen out of the activities of congressional committees. Congressional investigations have often served useful purposes, such as the uncovering of the Teapot Dome scandal during the administration of President Harding and the revelation of corruption in the Internal Revenue Department during the 1950s. However, important questions concerning the independence of each branch arise out of these hearings. How far may a committee go in requiring officials of the executive branch to appear before it and testify? The President clearly may not be so forced, but what of cabinet officers? May the President order his subordinates not to give information to a congressional committee? These and other questions arose during the hearings on the role of communism in the government and the army conducted by Senator Joseph McCarthy in 1953–1954, and the Senate investigation into campaign wrongdoings in 1973.

The Supreme Court and the Other Branches

The Constitution provides for checks by the President on the judicial branch. He has the power to appoint new Supreme Court judges and other federal judges to fill vacancies. Furthermore, he may grant pardons and reprieves, except in cases of impeachment. The Senate checks on the courts by its power to refuse to ratify Presidential appointments. Impeachment charges against federal judges are brought by the House of Representatives and tried by the Senate.

The Supreme Court, on the other hand, exercises a tremendously important check upon the other two branches. It may set aside any law passed by Congress and approved by the President if a majority of the Court's members find that the law violates any part of the Constitution. Furthermore, it may also declare any actions of the executive branch unconstitutional.

This power, known as *judicial review,* is not expressly granted to the Supreme Court by the Constitution. In 1803 Chief Justice John Marshall first declared an act of Congress unconstitutional, in the celebrated case of *Marbury* v. *Madison.* In his decision, Marshall declared: "It is emphatically the province and duty of the judicial department to say what the law is. . . . A law repugnant to the Constitution is void. . . ."

This power of judicial review has been a major

source of conflict. Thomas Jefferson strongly criticized the doctrine as making the Constitution "a mere thing of wax in the hands of the judiciary, which they might twist, and shape into any form they please." He insisted that each branch should have the authority to interpret its own powers. Andrew Jackson is reported to have said about a decision with which he disagreed: "John Marshall has made his decision, now let him enforce it!" Few decisions in our nation's history have been as unpopular as the Court's ruling in the Dred Scott case, in 1857, that Congress lacked the power to exclude slavery from the territories.

The argument over the power of judicial review reached a climax in the 1930s, when the Supreme Court held so many New Deal laws unconstitutional that President Franklin D. Roosevelt proposed to Congress that he be allowed to "pack" the Court by making as many as six new appointments to the Court. In this way, he hoped to get more favorable decisions. Congress refused to support him in his effort, however.

In 1952, President Harry S. Truman, in order to forestall a steel strike which he felt would imperil national defense at a time when the country was engaged in the war in Korea, ordered his Secretary of Commerce to seize and operate the steel mills. The Supreme Court held his action to be unconstitutional. It argued that the President normally has only those powers specifically granted to him by the Constitution and the laws. In grave emergencies, however, he may exercise powers beyond these *if Congress agrees*. Here we see a basic role of the Court: to act as the "guardian of the Constitution" by curbing the power of the other branches.

The Constitution of the United States

WE THE PEOPLE of the United States, in Order to form a more perfect Union, establish Justice, insure domestic Tranquility, provide for the common defence, promote the general Welfare, and secure the Blessings of Liberty to ourselves and our Posterity, do ordain and establish this CONSTITUTION for the United States of America.

ARTICLE I.

SECTION 1. All legislative Powers herein granted shall be vested in a Congress of the United States, which shall consist of a Senate and House of Representatives.

SECTION 2. [1] The House of Representatives shall be composed of Members chosen every second Year by the People of the several States, and the Electors in each State shall have the Qualifications requisite for Electors of the most numerous Branch of the State Legislature.

[2] No person shall be a Representative who shall not have attained to the Age of twenty five Years, and been seven Years a Citizen of the United States, and who shall not, when elected, be an Inhabitant of that State in which he shall be chosen.

[3] [*Representatives and direct Taxes shall be apportioned among the several States which may be included within this Union, according to their respective Numbers, which shall be determined by adding to the whole Number of free Persons, including those bound to Service for a Term of Years, and excluding Indians not taxed, three fifths of all other Persons.*]* The actual Enumeration shall be made within three Years after the first Meeting of the Congress of the United States, and within

NOTE.–This text of the Constitution follows the engrossed copy signed by Gen. Washington and the deputies from 12 States. The superior number preceding the paragraphs designates the number of the clause; it was not in the original. Spelling and punctuation in the Constitution are set according to copy supplied by the United States Government Printing Office; 88th Congress, 1st Session; House Document No. 112.

* The part included in heavy brackets was changed by section 2 of the fourteenth amendment.

every subsequent Term of ten Years, in such Manner as they shall by Law direct. The Number of Representatives shall not exceed one for every thirty Thousand, but each State shall have at Least one Representative; and until such enumeration shall be made, the State of New Hampshire shall be entitled to chuse three, Massachusetts eight, Rhode-Island and Providence Plantations one, Connecticut five, New-York six, New Jersey four, Pennsylvania eight, Delaware one, Maryland six, Virginia ten, North Carolina five, South Carolina five, and Georgia three.

[4] When vacancies happen in the Representation from any State, the Executive Authority thereof shall issue Writs of Election to fill such Vacancies.

[5] The House of Representatives shall chuse their Speaker and other Officers; and shall have the sole Power of Impeachment.

SECTION 3. [1] The Senate of the United States shall be composed of two Senators from each State, [chosen by the Legislature thereof,] * for six Years; and each Senator shall have one Vote.

[2] Immediately after they shall be assembled in Consequence of the first Election, they shall be divided as equally as may be into three Classes. The Seats of the Senators of the first Class shall be vacated at the Expiration of the second Year, of the second Class at the Expiration of the fourth Year, and of the third Class at the Expiration of the sixth Year, so that one third may be chosen every second Year; [*and if Vacancies happen by Resignation, or otherwise, during the Recess of the Legislature of any State, the Executive thereof may make temporary Appointments until the next Meeting of the Legislature, which shall then fill such Vacancies*]. **

[3] No Person shall be a Senator who shall not have attained to the Age of thirty Years, and been nine Years a Citizen of the United States, and who shall not, when elected, be an Inhabitant of that State for which he shall be chosen.

[4] The Vice President of the United States shall be President of the Senate, but shall have no Vote, unless they be equally divided.

[5] The Senate shall chuse their other Officers, and also a President pro tempore, in the Absence of the Vice President, or when he shall exercise the Office of President of the United States.

[6] The Senate shall have the sole Power to try all Impeachments. When sitting for that Purpose, they shall be on Oath or Affirmation. When the President of the United States is tried, the Chief Justice shall preside: And no Person shall be convicted without the Concurrence of two thirds of the Members present.

[7] Judgment in Cases of Impeachment shall not extend further than to removal from Office, and disqualification to hold and enjoy any Office of honor, Trust or Profit under the United States: but the Party convicted shall nevertheless be liable and subject to Indictment, Trial, Judgment and Punishment, according to Law.

SECTION 4. [1] The Times, Places and Manner of holding Elections for Senators and Representatives, shall be prescribed in each State by the Legislature thereof; but the Congress may at any time by Law make or alter such Regulations, except as to the Places of chusing Senators.

[2] The Congress shall assemble at least once in every Year, and such Meeting shall [*be on the the first Monday in December,*] *** unless they shall by Law appoint a different Day.

SECTION 5. [1] Each House shall be the Judge of the Elections, Returns and Qualifications of its own Members, and a Majority of each shall constitute a Quorum to do Business; but a smaller Number may adjourn from day to day, and may be authorized to compel the Attendance of absent Members, in such Manner, and under such Penalties as each House may provide.

[2] Each House may determine the Rules of its Proceedings, punish its Members for disorderly Behavior, and, with the Concurrence of two thirds, expel a Member.

[3] Each House shall keep a Journal of its Proceedings, and from time to time publish the same, excepting such Parts as may in their Judgment require Secrecy; and the Yeas and Nays of the Members of either House on any question shall, at the Desire of one fifth of those Present, be entered on the Journal.

[4] Neither House, during the Session of Congress, shall, without the Consent of the other, adjourn for more than three days, nor to any other Place than that in which the two Houses shall be sitting.

---

* The part included in heavy brackets was changed by section 1 of the seventeenth amendment.

** The part included in heavy brackets was changed by clause 2 of the seventeenth amendment.

*** The part included in heavy brackets was changed by section 2 of the twentieth amendment.

SECTION 6. [1] The Senators and Representatives shall receive a Compensation for their Services, to be ascertained by Law, and paid out of the Treasury of the United States. They shall in all Cases, except Treason, Felony and Breach of the Peace, be privileged from Arrest during their Attendance at the Session of their respective Houses, and in going to and returning from the same; and for any Speech or Debate in either House, they shall not be questioned in any other Place.

[2] No Senator or Representative shall, during the Time for which he was elected, be appointed to any civil Office under the Authority of the United States, which shall have been created, or the Emoluments whereof shall have been encreased during such time; and no Person holding any Office under the United States, shall be a Member of either House during his Continuance in Office.

SECTION 7. [1] All Bills for raising Revenue shall originate in the House of Representatives; but the Senate may propose or concur with Amendments as on other Bills.

[2] Every Bill which shall have passed the House of Representatives and the Senate, shall, before it become a Law, be presented to the President of the United States; If he approve he shall sign it, but if not he shall return it, with his Objections to that House in which it shall have originated, who shall enter the Objections at large on their Journal, and proceed to reconsider it. If after such Reconsideration two thirds of that House shall agree to pass the Bill, it shall be sent, together with the Objections, to the other House, by which it shall likewise be reconsidered, and if approved by two thirds of that House, it shall become a Law. But in all such Cases the Votes of both Houses shall be determined by Yeas and Nays, and the Names of the Persons voting for and against the Bill shall be entered on the Journal of each House respectively. If any Bill shall not be returned by the President within ten days (Sundays excepted) after it shall have been presented to him, the Same shall be a Law, in like Manner as if he had signed it, unless the Congress by their Adjournment prevent its Return, in which Case it shall not be a Law.

[3] Every Order, Resolution, or Vote to which the Concurrence of the Senate and House of Representatives may be necessary (except on a question of Adjournment) shall be presented to the President of the United States; and before the Same shall take Effect, shall be approved by him, or being disapproved by him, shall be repassed by two thirds of the Senate and House of Representatives, according to the Rules and Limitations prescribed in the Case of a Bill.

SECTION 8. [1] The Congress shall have Power To lay and collect Taxes, Duties, Imposts and Excises, to pay the Debts and provide for the common Defence and general Welfare of the United States; but all Duties, Imposts and Excises shall be uniform throughout the United States;

[2] To borrow Money on the credit of the United States;

[3] To regulate Commerce with foreign Nations, and among the several States, and with the Indian Tribes;

[4] To establish an uniform Rule of Naturalization, and uniform Laws on the subject of Bankruptcies throughout the United States;

[5] To coin Money, regulate the Value thereof, and of foreign Coin, and fix the Standard of Weights and Measures;

[6] To provide for the Punishment of counterfeiting the Securities and current Coin of the United States;

[7] To establish Post Offices and post Roads;

[8] To promote the Progress of Science and useful Arts, by securing for limited Times to Authors and Inventors the exclusive Right to their respective Writings and Discoveries;

[9] To constitute Tribunals inferior to the supreme Court;

[10] To define and punish Piracies and Felonies committed on the high Seas, and Offenses against the Law of Nations;

[11] To declare War, grant Letters of Marque and Reprisal, and make Rules concerning Captures on Land and Water;

[12] To raise and support Armies, but no Appropriation of Money to that Use shall be for a longer Term than two Years;

[13] To provide and maintain a Navy;

[14] To make Rules for the Government and Regulation of the land and naval Forces;

[15] To provide for calling forth the Militia to execute the Laws of the Union, suppress Insurrections and repel Invasions;

[16] To provide for organizing, arming, and disciplining the Militia, and for governing such Part of them as may be employed in the Service of the United States, reserving to the States respectively, the Appointment of the Officers, and the Authority of training the Militia according to the discipline prescribed by Congress;

[17] To exercise exclusive Legislation in all Cases whatsoever, over such District (not exceeding ten Miles square) as may, by Cession of particular States, and the Acceptance of Congress, become the Seat of the Government of the United States, and to exercise like Authority over all Places purchased by the Consent of the Legislature of the State in which the Same shall be, for the Erection of Forts, Magazines, Arsenals, dock-Yards, and other needful Buildings;–And

[18] To make all Laws which shall be necessary and proper for carrying into Execution the foregoing Powers, and all other Powers vested by this Constitution in the Government of the United States, or in any Department or Officer thereof.

SECTION 9. [1] The Migration or Importation of such Persons as any of the States now existing shall think proper to admit, shall not be prohibited by the Congress prior to the Year one thousand eight hundred and eight, but a Tax or duty may be imposed on such Importation, not exceeding ten dollars for each Person.

[2] The Privilege of the Writ of Habeas Corpus shall not be suspended, unless when in Cases of Rebellion or Invasion the public Safety may require it.

[3] No Bill of Attainder or ex post facto Law shall be passed.

*[4] No Capitation, or other direct, Tax shall be laid, unless in Proportion to the Census or Enumeration herein before directed to be taken.

[5] No Tax or Duty shall be laid on Articles exported from any State.

[6] No Preference shall be given by any Regulation of Commerce or Revenue to the Ports of one State over those of another: nor shall Vessels bound to, or from, one State be obliged to enter, clear, or pay Duties in another.

[7] No Money shall be drawn from the Treasury, but in Consequence of Appropriations made by Law; and a regular Statement and Account of the Receipts and Expenditures of all public Money shall be published from time to time.

[8] No Title of Nobility shall be granted by the United States: And no Person holding any Office of Profit or Trust under them, shall, without the Consent of the Congress, accept of any present, Emolument, Office, or Title, of any kind whatever, from any King, Prince, or foreign State.

*See also the sixteenth amendment.

SECTION 10. [1] No state shall enter into any Treaty, Alliance, or Confederation; grant Letters of Marque and Reprisal: coin Money; emit Bills of Credit; make any Thing but gold and silver Coin a Tender in Payment of Debts; pass any Bill of Attainder, ex post facto Law, or Law impairing the Obligation of Contracts, or grant any Title of Nobility.

[2] No State shall, without the Consent of the Congress, lay any Imposts or Duties on Imports or Exports, except what may be absolutely necessary for executing it's inspection Laws: and the net Produce of all Duties and Imposts, laid by any State on Imports or Exports, shall be for the Use of the Treasury of the United States; and all such Laws shall be subject to the Revision and Controul of the Congress.

[3] No State shall, without the Consent of Congress, lay any Duty of Tonnage, keep Troops, or Ships of War in time of Peace, enter into any Agreement or Compact with another State, or with a foreign Power, or engage in War, unless actually invaded, or in such imminent Danger as will not admit of delay.

ARTICLE II.

SECTION. 1. [1] The executive Power shall be vested in a President of the United States of America. He shall hold his Office during the Term of four Years, and, together with the Vice President, chosen for the same Term, be elected as follows

[2] Each State shall appoint, in such Manner as the Legislature thereof may direct, a Number of Electors, equal to the whole Number of Senators and Representatives to which the State may be entitled in the Congress: but no Senator or Representative, or Person holding an Office of Trust or Profit under the United States, shall be appointed an Elector.

[*The Electors shall meet in their respective States, and vote by Ballot for two Persons, of whom one at least shall not be an Inhabitant of the same State with themselves. And they shall make a List of all the Persons voted for, and of the Number of Votes for each; which List they shall sign and certify, and transmit sealed to the Seat of the Government of the United States, directed to the President of the Senate. The President of the Senate shall, in the Presence of the Senate and House of Representatives, open all the Certificates, and the Votes shall then be counted. The Person having the greatest*

Number of Votes shall be the President, if such Number be a Majority of the whole Number of Electors appointed; and if there be more than one who have such Majority, and have an equal Number of Votes, then the House of Representatives shall immediately chuse by Ballot one of them for President; and if no Person have a Majority, then from the five highest on the List the said House shall in like Manner chuse the President. But in chusing the President, the Votes shall be taken by States, the Representation from each State having one Vote; A quorum for this Purpose shall consist of a Member or Members from two thirds of the States, and a Majority of all the States shall be necessary to a Choice. In every Case, after the Choice of the President, the Person having the greatest Number of Votes of the Electors shall be the Vice President. But if there should remain two or more who have equal Votes, the Senate shall chuse from them by Ballot the Vice President.]*

3 The Congress may determine the Time of chusing the Electors, and the Day on which they shall give their Votes; which Day shall be the same throughout the United States.

4 No Person except a natural born Citizen, or a Citizen of the United States, at the time of the Adoption of this Constitution, shall be eligible to the Office of President; neither shall any Person be eligible to that Office who shall not have attained to the Age of thirty five Years, and been fourteen Years a Resident within the United States.

5 In Case of the Removal of the President from Office, or of his Death, Resignation, or Inability to discharge the Powers and Duties of the said Office, the Same shall devolve on the Vice President, and the Congress may by Law provide for the Case of Removal, Death, Resignation or Inability, both of the President and Vice President, declaring what Officer shall then act as President, and such Officer shall act accordingly, until the Disability be removed, or a President shall be elected.

6 The President shall, at stated Times, receive for his Services, a Compensation, which shall neither be encreased nor diminished during the Period for which he shall have been elected, and he shall not receive within that Period any other Emolument from the United States, or any of them.

Before he enter on the Execution of his Office, he shall take the following Oath or Affirmation:–"I do solemnly swear (or affirm) that I will faithfully execute the Office of President of the United States, and will to the best of my Ability, preserve, protect and defend the Constitution of the United States."

SECTION 2. 1 The President shall be Commander in Chief of the Army and Navy of the United States, and of the Militia of the several States, when called into the actual Service of the United States; he may require the Opinion, in writing, of the principal Officer in each of the executive Departments, upon any Subject relating to the Duties of their respective Offices, and he shall have Power to grant Reprieves and Pardons for Offences against the United States, except in Cases of Impeachment.

2 He shall have Power, by and with the Advice and Consent of the Senate, to make Treaties, provided two thirds of the Senators present concur; and he shall nominate, and by and with the Advice and Consent of the Senate, shall appoint Ambassadors, other public Ministers and Consuls, Judges of the supreme Court, and all other Officers of the United States, whose Appointments are not herein otherwise provided for, and which shall be established by Law: but the Congress may by Law vest the Appointment of such inferior Officers, as they think proper, in the President alone, in the Courts of Law, or in the Heads of Departments.

3 The President shall have Power to fill up all Vacancies that may happen during the Recess of the Senate, by granting Commissions which shall expire at the End of their next Session.

SECTION 3. He shall from time to time give to the Congress Information of the State of the Union, and recommend to their Consideration such Measures as he shall judge necessary and expedient; he may, on extraordinary Occasions, convene both Houses, or either of them, and in Case of Disagreement between them, with Respect to the Time of Adjournment, he may adjourn them to such Time as he shall think proper; he shall receive Ambassadors and other public Ministers; he shall take Care that the Laws be faithfully executed, and shall Commission all the Officers of the United States.

SECTION 4. The President, Vice President and all civil Officers of the United States, shall be removed from Office on Impeachment for, and Conviction of, Treason, Bribery, or other high Crimes and Misdemeanors.

*This paragraph has been superseded by the twelfth amendment.

ARTICLE III.

SECTION 1. The judicial Power of the United States, shall be vested in one supreme Court, and in such inferior Courts as the Congress may from time to time ordain and establish. The Judges, both of the supreme and inferior Courts, shall hold their Offices during good Behaviour, and shall, at stated Times, receive for their Services a Compensation, which shall not be diminished during their Continuance in Office.

SECTION 2. [1] The judicial Power shall extend to all Cases, in Law and Equity, arising under this Constitution, the Laws of the United States, and Treaties made, or which shall be made, under their Authority;–to all Cases affecting Ambassadors, other public Ministers and Consuls;–to all Cases of admiralty and maritime Jurisdiction;–to Controversies to which the United States shall be a Party;–to Controversies between two or more States;–between a State and Citizens of another State;*–between Citizens of different States;–between Citizens of the same State claiming Lands under Grants of different States; and between a State, or the Citizens thereof, and foreign States, Citizens or Subjects.

[2] In all Cases affecting Ambassadors, other public Ministers and Consuls, and those in which a State shall be Party, the supreme Court shall have original Jurisdiction. In all the other Cases before mentioned, the supreme Court shall have appellate Jurisdiction, both as to Law and Fact, with such Exceptions, and under such Regulations as the Congress shall make.

[3] The Trial of all Crimes, except in Cases of Impeachment shall be by Jury; and such Trial shall be held in the State where the said Crimes shall have been committed; but when not committed within any State, the Trial shall be at such Place or Places as the Congress may by Law have directed.

SECTION 3. [1] Treason against the United States, shall consist only in levying War against them, or in adhering to their Enemies, giving them Aid and Comfort. No Person shall be convicted of Treason unless on the Testimony of two Witnesses to the same overt Act, or on Confession in open Court.

[2] The Congress shall have Power to declare the Punishment of Treason, but no Attainder of Treason shall work Corruption of Blood, or Forfeiture except during the Life of the Person attainted.

ARTICLE IV.

SECTION 1. Full Faith and Credit shall be given in each State to the public Acts, Records, and judicial Proceedings of every other State. And the Congress may by general Laws prescribe the Manner in which such Acts, Records and Proceedings shall be proved, and the Effect thereof.

SECTION 2. [1] The Citizens of each State shall be entitled to all Privileges and Immunities of Citizens in the several States.

[2] A Person charged in any State with Treason, Felony, or other Crime, who shall flee from Justice, and be found in another State, shall on Demand of the executive Authority of the State from which he fled, be delivered up, to be removed to the State having Jurisdiction of the Crime.

[3] [*No Person held to Service or Labour in one State, under the Laws thereof, escaping into another, shall, in Consequence of any Law or Regulation therein, be discharged from such Service or Labour, but shall be delivered up on Claim of the Party to whom such Service or Labour may be due.*]**

SECTION 3. [1] New States may be admitted by the Congress into this Union; but no new State shall be formed or erected within the Jurisdiction of any other State; nor any State be formed by the Junction of two or more States, or Parts of States, without the Consent of the Legislatures of the States concerned as well as of the Congress.

[2] The Congress shall have Power to dispose of and make all needful Rules and Regulations respecting the Territory or other Property belonging to the United States; and nothing in this Constitution shall be so construed as to Prejudice any Claims of the United States, or of any particular State.

SECTION. 4. The United States shall guarantee to every State in this Union a Republican Form of Government, and shall protect each of them against Invasion; and on Application of the Legislature, or of the Executive (when the Legislature cannot be convened) against domestic Violence.

* This clause has been affected by the eleventh amendment.

** This paragraph has been superseded by the thirteenth amendment.

ARTICLE V.

The Congress, whenever two thirds of both Houses shall deem it necessary, shall propose Amendments to this Constitution, or, on the Application of the Legislatures of two thirds of the several States, shall call a Convention for proposing Amendments, which, in either Case, shall be valid to all Intents and Purposes, as Part of this Constitution, when ratified by the Legislatures of three fourths of the several States, or by Conventions in three fourths thereof, as the one or the other Mode of Ratification may be proposed by the Congress: Provided, [*that no Amendment which may be made prior to the Year One thousand eight hundred and eight shall in any Manner affect the first and fourth Clauses in the Ninth Section of the first Article; and*] * that no State, without its Consent, shall be deprived of its equal Suffrage in the Senate.

ARTICLE VI.

1 All Debts contracted and Engagements entered into, before the Adoption of this Constitution shall be as valid against the United States under this Constitution, as under the Confederation.

2 This Constitution, and the Laws of the United States which shall be made in Pursuance thereof; and all Treaties made, or which shall be made, under the Authority of the United States, shall be the supreme Law of the Land; and the Judges in every State shall be bound thereby, any Thing in the Constitution or Laws of any State to the Contrary notwithstanding.

3 The Senators and Representatives before mentioned, and the Members of the several State Legislatures, and all executive and judicial Officers, both of the United States and of the several States, shall be bound by Oath or Affirmation, to support this Constitution; but no religious Test shall ever be required as a Qualification to any Office or public Trust under the United States.

ARTICLE VII.

The Ratification of the Conventions of nine States, shall be sufficient for the Establishment of this Constitution between the States so ratifying the Same.

DONE in Convention by the Unanimous Consent of the States present the Seventeenth Day of September in the Year of our Lord one thousand seven hundred and Eighty seven and of the Independence of the United States of America the Twelfth IN WITNESS whereof We have hereto subscribed our Names,

G° WASHINGTON—
Presid^t. and deputy from Virginia.

[Signed also by the deputies of twelve States.]

New Hampshire.
JOHN LANGDON,
NICHOLAS GILMAN.

Massachusetts.
NATHANIEL GORHAM,
RUFUS KING.

Connecticut.
WM. SAML. JOHNSON,
ROGER SHERMAN.

New York.
ALEXANDER HAMILTON.

New Jersey.
WIL: LIVINGSTON,
DAVID BREARLEY,
WM. PATERSON,
JONA: DAYTON.

Pennsylvania.
B FRANKLIN,
ROB^T MORRIS,
THOS. FITZSIMONS,
JAMES WILSON,
THOMAS MIFFLIN,
GEO. CLYMER,
JARED INGERSOLL,
GOUV MORRIS.

Delaware.
GEO: READ,
JOHN DICKINSON,
JACO: BROOM,
GUNNING BEDFORD, jun,
RICHARD BASSETT.

Maryland.
JAMES MCHENRY,
DAN^L CARROLL,
DAN OF S^T THOS. JENIFER.

Virginia.
JOHN BLAIR—
JAMES MADISON Jr.

* Obsolete.

North Carolina.
WM. BLOUNT,
HU WILLIAMSON,
RICH'D DOBBS SPAIGHT.

South Carolina.
J. RUTLEDGE,
CHARLES PINCKNEY,
CHARLES COTESWORTH PINCKNEY,
PIERCE BUTLER.

Georgia.
WILLIAM FEW,
ABR BALDWIN,
Attest: WILLIAM JACKSON, *Secretary.*

ARTICLES IN ADDITION TO, AND AMENDMENT OF, THE CONSTITUTION OF THE UNITED STATES OF AMERICA, PROPOSED BY CONGRESS, AND RATIFIED BY THE LEGISLATURES OF THE SEVERAL STATES PURSUANT TO THE FIFTH ARTICLE OF THE ORIGINAL CONSTITUTION

ARTICLE [I] *

Congress shall make no law respecting an establishment of religion, or prohibiting the free exercise thereof; or abridging the freedom of speech, or of the press, or the right of the people peaceably to assemble, and to petition the Government for a redress of grievances.

ARTICLE [II]

A well regulated Militia, being necessary to the security of a free State, the right of the people to keep and bear Arms, shall not be infringed.

ARTICLE [III]

No Soldier shall, in time of peace be quartered in any house, without the consent of the Owner, nor in time of war, but in a manner to be prescribed by law.

* Only the 13th, 14th, 15th, and 16th articles of amendment had numbers assigned to them at the time of ratification. Articles of amendment that did not have numbers assigned to them at ratification are shown here in proper order with the corresponding number placed in light brackets.

ARTICLE [IV]

The right of the people to be secure in their persons, houses, papers, and effects, against unreasonable searches and seizures, shall not be violated, and no Warrants shall issue, but upon probable cause, supported by Oath or affirmation, and particularly describing the place to be searched, and the persons or things to be seized.

ARTICLE [V]

No person shall be held to answer for a capital, or otherwise infamous crime, unless on a presentment or indictment of a Grand Jury, except in cases arising in the land or naval forces, or in the Militia, when in actual service in time of War or public danger; nor shall any person be subject for the same offence to be twice put in jeopardy of life or limb, nor shall be compelled in any criminal case to be a witness against himself, nor be deprived of life, liberty, or property, without due process of law; nor shall private property be taken for public use without just compensation.

ARTICLE [VI]

In all criminal prosecutions, the accused shall enjoy the right to a speedy and public trial, by an impartial jury of the State and district wherein the crime shall have been committed; which district shall have been previously ascertained by law, and to be informed of the nature and cause of the accusation; to be confronted with the witnesses against him; to have compulsory process for obtaining Witnesses in his favor, and to have the Assistance of Counsel for his defence.

ARTICLE [VII]

In Suits at common law, where the value in controversy shall exceed twenty dollars, the right of trial by jury shall be preserved, and no fact tried by a jury shall be otherwise reexamined in any Court of the United States, than according to the rules of the common law.

ARTICLE [VIII]

Excessive bail shall not be required, nor excessive fines imposed, nor cruel and unusual punishments inflicted.

ARTICLE [IX]

The enumeration in the Constitution, of certain rights, shall not be construed to deny or disparage others retained by the people.

ARTICLE [X]

The powers not delegated to the United States by the Constitution, nor prohibited by it to the States, are reserved to the States respectively, or to the people.

ARTICLE [XI]

The Judicial power of the United States shall not be construed to extend to any suit in law or equity, commenced or prosecuted against one of the United States by Citizens of another State, or by Citizens or Subjects of any Foreign State.

ARTICLE [XII]

The electors shall meet in their respective states and vote by ballot for President and Vice-President, one of whom, at least, shall not be an inhabitant of the same state with themselves; they shall name in their ballots the person voted for as President, and in distinct ballots the person voted for as Vice-President, and they shall make distinct lists of all persons voted for as President, and of all persons voted for as Vice-President, and of the number of votes for each, which lists they shall sign and certify, and transmit sealed to the seat of the government of the United States, directed to the President of the Senate;–The President of the Senate shall, in presence of the Senate and House of Representatives, open all the certificates and the votes shall then be counted;–The person having the greatest number of votes for President, shall be the President, if such number be a majority of the whole number of Electors appointed; and if no person have such majority, then from the persons having the highest numbers not exceeding three on the list of those voted for as President, the House of Representatives shall choose immediately, by ballot, the President. But in choosing the President, the votes shall be taken by states, the representation from each state having one vote; a quorum for this purpose shall consist of a member or members from two-thirds of the states, and a majority of all the states shall be necessary to a choice. [*And if the House of Representatives shall not choose a President whenever the right of choice shall devolve upon them, before the fourth day of March next following, then the Vice-President shall act as President, as in the case of the death or other constitutional disability of the President.*]* The person having the greatest number of votes as Vice-President, shall be the Vice-President, if such number be a majority of the whole number of Electors appointed, and if no person have a majority, then from the two highest numbers on the list, the Senate shall choose the Vice-President; a quorum for the purpose shall consist of two-thirds of the whole number of Senators, and a majority of the whole number shall be necessary to a choice. But no person constitutionally ineligible to the office of President shall be eligible to that of Vice-President of the United States.

ARTICLE XIII

SECTION 1. Neither slavery nor involuntary servitude, except as a punishment for crime whereof the party shall have been duly convicted, shall exist within the United States, or any place subject to their jurisdiction.

SECTION 2. Congress shall have power to enforce this article by appropriate legislation.

ARTICLE XIV

SECTION 1. All persons born or naturalized in the United States, and subject to the jurisdiction thereof, are citizens of the United States and of the

---

* The part included in heavy brackets has been superseded by section 3 of the twentieth amendment.

State wherein they reside. No State shall make or enforce any law which shall abridge the privileges or immunities of citizens of the United States; nor shall any State deprive any person of life, liberty, or property, without due process of law; nor deny to any person within its jurisdiction the equal protection of the laws.

SECTION 2. Representatives shall be apportioned among the several States according to their respective numbers, counting the whole number of persons in each State, excluding Indians not taxed. But when the right to vote at any election for the choice of electors for President and Vice-President of the United States, Representatives in Congress, the Executive and Judicial officers of a State, or the members of the Legislature thereof, is denied to any of the male inhabitants of such State, being twenty-one years of age, and citizens of the United States, or in any way abridged, except for participation in rebellion, or other crime, the basis of representation therein shall be reduced in the proportion which the number of such male citizens shall bear to the whole number of male citizens twenty-one years of age in such State.

SECTION 3. No person shall be a Senator or Representative in Congress, or elector of President and Vice-President, or hold any office, civil or military, under the United States, or under any State, who, having previously taken an oath, as a member of Congress, or as an officer of the United States, or as a member of any State legislature, or as an executive or judicial officer of any State, to support the Constitution of the United States, shall have engaged in insurrection or rebellion against the same, or given aid or comfort to the enemies thereof. But Congress may by a vote of two-thirds of each House, remove such disability.

SECTION 4. The validity of the public debt of the United States, authorized by law, including debts incurred for payment of pensions and bounties for services in suppressing insurrection or rebellion, shall not be questioned. But neither the United States nor any State shall assume or pay any debt or obligation incurred in aid of insurrection or rebellion against the United States, or any claim for the loss or emancipation of any slave; but all such debts, obligations and claims shall be held illegal and void.

SECTION 5. The Congress shall have power to enforce, by appropriate legislation, the provisions of this article.

ARTICLE XV

SECTION 1. The right of citizens of the United States to vote shall not be denied or abridged by the United States or by any State on account of race, color, or previous condition of servitude.

SECTION 2. The Congress shall have power to enforce this article by appropriate legislation.

ARTICLE XVI

The Congress shall have power to lay and collect taxes on incomes, from whatever source derived, without apportionment among the several States, and without regard to any census or enumeration.

ARTICLE [XVII]

The Senate of the United States shall be composed of two Senators from each state, elected by the people thereof, for six years; and each Senator shall have one vote. The electors in each State shall have the qualifications requisite for electors of the most numerous branch of the State legislatures.

When vacancies happen in the representation of any State in the Senate, the executive authority of such State shall issue writs of election to fill such vacancies: *Provided,* That the legislature of any State may empower the executive thereof to make temporary appointments until the people fill the vacancies by election as the legislature may direct.

This amendment shall not be so construed as to affect the election or term of any Senator chosen before it becomes valid as part of the Constitution.

ARTICLE [XVIII]

[*SECTION 1. After one year from the ratification of this article the manufacture, sale, or transportation of intoxicating liquors within, the importation thereof into, or the exportation thereof from the*

United States and all territory subject to the jurisdiction thereof for beverage purposes is hereby prohibited.

[*SECTION 2. The Congress and the several States shall have concurrent power to enforce this article by appropriate legislation.*

[*SECTION 3. This article shall be inoperative unless it shall have been ratified as an amendment to the Constitution by the legislatures of the several States, as provided in the Constitution, within seven years from the date of the submission hereof to the States by the Congress.*]*

ARTICLE [XIX]

The right of citizens of the United States to vote shall not be denied or abridged by the United States or by any State on account of sex.

Congress shall have power to enforce this article by appropriate legislation.

ARTICLE [XX]

SECTION 1. The terms of the President and Vice-President shall end at noon on the 20th day of January, and the terms of Senators and Representatives at noon on the 3d day of January, of the years in which such terms would have ended if this article had not been ratified; and the terms of their successors shall then begin.

SECTION 2. The Congress shall assemble at least once in every year, and such meeting shall begin at noon on the 3d day of January, unless they shall by law appoint a different day.

SECTION 3. If, at the time fixed for the beginning of the term of the President, the President elect shall have died, the Vice-President elect shall become President. If a President shall not have been chosen before the time fixed for the beginning of his term, or if the President elect shall have failed to qualify, then the Vice-President elect shall act as President until a President shall have qualified; and the Congress may by law provide for the case wherein neither a President elect nor a Vice-President elect shall have qualified, declaring who shall then act as President, or the manner in which one who is to act shall be selected, and such person shall act accordingly until a President or Vice-President shall have qualified.

SECTION 4. The Congress may by law provide for the case of the death of any of the persons from whom the House of Representatives may choose a President whenever the right of choice shall have devolved upon them, and for the case of the death of any of the persons from whom the Senate may choose a Vice-President whenever the right of choice shall have devolved upon them.

SECTION 5. Sections 1 and 2 shall take effect on the 15th day of October following the ratification of this article.

SECTION 6. This article shall be inoperative unless it shall have been ratified as an amendment to the Constitution by the legislatures of three-fourths of the several States within seven years from the date of its submission.

ARTICLE [XXI]

SECTION 1. The eighteenth article of amendment to the Constitution of the United States is hereby repealed.

SECTION 2. The transportation or importation into any State, Territory, or possession of the United States for delivery or use therein of intoxicating liquors, in violation of the laws thereof, is hereby prohibited.

SECTION 3. This article shall be inoperative unless it shall have been ratified as an amendment to the Constitution by conventions in the several States, as provided in the Constitution, within seven years from the date of the submission hereof to the States by the Congress.

ARTICLE [XXII]

SECTION 1. No person shall be elected to the office of the President more than twice, and no person who has held the office of President, or acted as President, for more than two years of a term to which some other person was elected President

*Repealed by section 1 of the twenty-first amendment.

shall be elected to the office of the President more than once. But this article shall not apply to any person holding the office of President when this Article was proposed by the Congress, and shall not prevent any person who may be holding the office of President, or acting as President, during the term within which this Article becomes operative from holding the office of President or acting as President during the remainder of such term.

SECTION 2. This article shall be inoperative unless it shall have been ratified as an amendment to the Constitution by the legislatures of three-fourths of the several States within seven years from the date of its submission to the States by the Congress.

ARTICLE [XXIII]

SECTION 1. The District constituting the seat of Government of the United States shall appoint in such manner as the Congress may direct:

A number of electors of President and Vice-President equal to the whole number of Senators and Representatives in Congress to which the District would be entitled if it were a State, but in no event more than the least populous State; they shall be in addition to those appointed by the States, but they shall be considered, for the purposes of the election of President and Vice-President, to be electors appointed by a State; and they shall meet in the District and perform such duties as provided by the twelfth article of amendment.

SECTION 2. The Congress shall have power to enforce this article by appropriate legislation.

ARTICLE [XXIV]

SECTION 1. The right of citizens of the United States to vote in any primary or other election for President or Vice-President, for electors for President or Vice-President, or for Senator or Representative in Congress, shall not be denied or abridged by the United States or any State by reason of failure to pay any poll tax or other tax.

SECTION 2. The Congress shall have the power to enforce this article by appropriate legislation.

ARTICLE XXV

SECTION 1. In case of removal of the President from office or of his death or resignation, the Vice-President shall become President.

SECTION 2. Whenever there is a vacancy in the office of the Vice-President, the President shall nominate a Vice-President who shall take office upon confirmation by a majority vote of both Houses of Congress.

SECTION 3. Whenever the President transmits to the President pro tempore of the Senate and the Speaker of the House of Representatives his written declaration that he is unable to discharge the powers and duties of his office, and until he transmits to them a written declaration to the contrary, such powers and duties shall be discharged by the Vice-President as Acting President.

SECTION 4. Whenever the Vice-President and a majority of either the principal officers of the executive departments or of such other body as Congress may by law provide, transmit to the President pro tempore of the Senate and the Speaker of the House of Representatives their written declaration that the President is unable to discharge the powers and duties of his office, the Vice-President shall immediately assume the powers and duties of the office as Acting President.

Thereafter, when the President transmits to the President pro tempore of the Senate and the Speaker of the House of Representatives his written declaration that no inability exists, he shall resume the powers and duties of his office unless the Vice-President and a majority of either the principal officers of the executive department or of such other body as Congress may by law provide, transmit within four days to the President pro tempore of the Senate and the Speaker of the House of Representatives their written declaration that the President is unable to discharge the powers and duties of his office. Thereupon Congress shall decide the issue, assembling within forty-eight hours for that purpose if not in session. If the Congress, within twenty-one days after receipt of the latter written declaration, or, if Congress is not in session, within twenty-one days after Congress is required to assemble, determines by two-thirds vote of both Houses that the President is unable to discharge the powers and duties of his office, the Vice-President shall continue to discharge the same as Acting President; otherwise, the President shall resume the powers and duties of his office.

ARTICLE XXVI

SECTION 1. The right of citizens of the United States, who are eighteen years of age or older, to vote shall not be denied or abridged by the United States or by any State on account of age.

SECTION 2. The Congress shall have power to enforce this article by appropriate legislation.

ARTICLE XXVII

This Article had not completed ratification by the end of 1979, and Congress extended the term for ratification to 1982.

1. Equality of rights under the law shall not be denied or abridged by the United States or by any State on account of sex.
2. The Congress shall have the power to enforce, by appropriate legislation, the provisions of this article.
3. This amendment shall take effect two years after the date of ratification.

CHAPTER SEVEN

STATES AND COUNTRIES

The Fifty States of the United States

From the original 13 colonies, the United States has grown to the present 50 states. It is not unreasonable to assume that the number may still grow, now that the non-contiguous territories of Alaska and Hawaii have become states. Of course, this growth cannot be at the nineteenth-century rate because the possessions are now limited.

This section gives a brief history of each state including government and economy, and at the end of the next section there is a table with statistics related to the states.

ALABAMA

Alabama advertises itself as "The Heart of Dixie." It is, indeed, one of the original "Cotton Belt" states of the Old South. The first settlement in what is now Alabama was made by the French on Mobile Bay, in 1702. The French lost control of the area to the British in 1763. At the end of the War for Independence, all of the present state except the Mobile area was ceded to the United States. Mobile was then ceded to Spanish Florida, but regained by the United States in 1813.

Alabama was set up as a territory in 1817. It was then reorganized and admitted into the Union on December 14, 1819, as the twenty-second state. Alabama seceded from the Union on January 11, 1861, and joined the Confederate States of America. The first Confederate capital was located at Montgomery, Alabama. With the surrender of Mobile after the Battle of Mobile Bay in 1865, the defeat of Alabama was completed. Devastation due to the war was less severe than in other states of the South, but the economy of the state was wrecked and industry almost ceased. The state was readmitted in 1868, but federal troops were not withdrawn until four years later.

With the antebellum pattern of life destroyed, years of confusion and slow rebuilding followed. The economy revived somewhat in the eighties when steel production began in the Birmingham area. Other industries began to expand rapidly. A great industrial boom has taken place in Alabama during the twentieth century. This rapid industrial growth, combined with a revitalized agriculture that is no longer dependent solely upon cotton, has brought about vigorous change and revolutionary progress in "The Heart of Dixie."

Government. The state constitution dates from 1901. The state sends two senators and seven representatives to the U.S. Congress. The legislature consists of a senate of 35 members and a house of representatives of 106 members. The state is divided into 67 counties; in 1970 there were 35 cities with a population of more than ten thousand.

Economy. Major resources include iron, coal, limestone, and the "black soils" for agriculture. The great TVA projects that have arisen along the Tennessee River have brought extensive industrial expansion to northern Alabama. The presence of iron, coal, and limestone (all of which are major components of steel-making) in the same area of north-central Alabama has made Bir-

Alabama—Bellingrath Gardens near Mobile

mingham the leading iron and steel center of the South.

Alabama is also one of the leading lumber-producing states. Over 634,000 acres of national forests existed in Alabama in 1970. The chief crops grown in Alabama are cotton, corn, peanuts, and oats. Special crops include tung oil and pecans, both derived from nut trees. The raising of cattle and hogs is becoming significant in the state's economy.

ALASKA

Alaska was discovered in 1741 by Vitus Bering, a Danish explorer in the service of Russia. Russian fur traders and trappers followed the explorers. In 1784 they founded the Kodiak settlement and Sitka, the capital of Russian America, in 1799. On March 30, 1867, Alaska was sold to the United States by Czar Alexander II to prevent its capture by the British, with whom Russia was then at war. The United States paid $7,200,000, or less than two cents per acre!

President Andrew Johnson and Secretary William H. Seward were derided for making what was thought to be a useless purchase. The area of the present state was set up as a district and governed under the general laws of Oregon, although it was not governed by that state itself. After a series of gold discoveries in the district, Alaska was organized into a territory on August 24, 1912. The development of salmon fisheries, copper mining, and the growth of a tourist industry during the twenties and thirties strengthened the economy of the territory and generated a strong campaign for statehood. During World War II the statehood issue was set aside. The territory's strategic location and its natural wealth attracted the Japanese. They attempted an invasion in 1942 and managed to occupy Attu and Kiska islands in the Aleutian Archipelago of Alaska. The United States poured millions of dollars into Alaskan defenses, and in 1943 the Japanese were expelled.

The postwar economy was strengthened by further heavy defense spending, with the consequent expansion of industry and population. A renewed campaign for statehood resulted in victory on January 3, 1959, when Alaska entered the Union as the forty-ninth state.

Government. Alaska's executive branch consists of 20 departments under the governor's office. The legislature consists of a senate of 20 members and a house of representatives of 40 members. The state sends two senators and one representative to Congress. There are no counties in Alaska, but a system of boroughs performs the same functions. There were five cities in 1970 with a population of over 10,000.

Economy. Much economic activity centers around fishing, forestry, and the tourist industry. It is now fairly certain that Alaska's Kenai Peninsula and the Arctic Slope form two of the world's major petroleum areas, and someday may rival or even surpass production in the Middle East. An 800-mile trans-Alaska pipeline was completed in 1977 to carry oil from the North Slope to the Gulf of Alaska in the south.

Agriculture is well developed in the Matanuska Valley of southern Alaska and in the interior around Fairbanks. Hay, potatoes, wheat, and rye are the major crops. Some dairying and ranching is carried on near Anchorage, the state's largest city. Sawmills and canneries are concentrated in the panhandle.

The state's transportation system includes one railroad, 470 miles long, serving the interior between Fairbanks and Anchorage. Travel to Alaska is possible by automobile on the Alaska Highway,

Alaska—Mt. McKinley

1,523 miles long. This road lies mostly in Canada, and extends from Dawson Creek in British Columbia, to Fairbanks, Alaska, with several spur routes in both Alaska and Canada.

ARIZONA

Many of the Indians that live in Arizona today are the descendants of two highly advanced cultures that developed there in prehistoric times. Abandoned cliff-cities and other ruins scattered over Arizona belonged to the famous Basket-Maker people and their successors, the Pueblo people. A great 30-year drought during the thirteenth century is thought to be the chief cause of the abandonment of most of the cliff-cities. The descendants of the cliff-dwellers were found living in fortified towns and mesas, or near watercourses when Coronado's Spanish expedition entered the region in 1540.

Spanish settlement began in 1752, although Spanish missionaries had been active in Arizona since the end of the sixteenth century. Arizona became a part of independent Mexico in 1821. Most of the present state was ceded to the United States in 1848 by the Treaty of Guadalupe Hidalgo. That part lying south of the Gila River formed part of the Gadsden Purchase that was added in 1854 (*see also* New Mexico). Arizona was organized as a territory in 1863 and entered the Union as the forty-eighth state on February 14, 1912.

Government. The state constitution dates from 1910. The legislature consists of a senate of 30 members and a house of representatives of 60 members. The state sends to the national Congress two senators and four representatives. Arizona is divided into fourteen counties, and in 1970 there were 13 cities with a population of more than ten thousand.

Economy. The state's greatest resource is copper, and 40 to 50 percent of the entire United States production is mined in Arizona. Silver, uranium, zinc, molybdenum, gold, and other minerals are mined. Tourists, attracted by the healthful dry climate and many great natural wonders, provide a major source of revenue.

Water is always a precious mineral, and particularly so in Arizona, where it is in short supply. Four major dams on the Colorado and two on the Salt and Gila rivers provide water for irrigation and other uses. Through irrigation, deserts give way to fields of lettuce, cantaloupe, cotton, and citrus trees. Hoover Dam (formerly Boulder Dam), on the Colorado River in the northwest, is the

Arizona—Petrified Forest and Teepee Formations

highest in the U.S. and one of the highest in the world. It forms Lake Mead, which is shared with Nevada. Generators at the dam supply a large percentage of the electric power that is used in Arizona. Over one million acres of land are under irrigation in the state.

The most important crops are cotton, grain sorghums, and barley. Pasturing of sheep is heavy but diminished from earlier years.

ARKANSAS

The area of the present state of Arkansas was visited by Hernando de Soto in 1541–1542. It was claimed for France in 1682 by Sieur de La Salle as a part of the Mississippi drainage area. The French yielded the region to Spain in 1762 but it was given back to France in 1800. (French trappers established the first permanent settlement within the present state in 1686 and called it Arkansas Post. It was located at the confluence of the Arkansas River with the Mississippi River.) The region became a part of the Louisiana Purchase in 1803 and came under the American flag. Arkansas Territory was organized in 1819 from a part of Missouri Territory. It assumed its present boundaries (by excluding what is now Oklahoma) and was admitted to the Union as the twenty-fifth state on June 15, 1836.

Arkansas—Observation Tower, Hot Springs Mountain

The people of Arkansas were seriously divided on the issue of slavery and secession, but on May 6, 1861, the state voted to secede and join the Confederate States of America. Union forces won a costly battle at Pea Ridge in northwestern Arkansas in 1862, and captured Little Rock the following year. In 1868 Arkansas was readmitted to the Union.

Government. The legislature of Arkansas is called the General Assembly (*see* Colorado) and is composed of a senate of 35 members and a house of representatives of 100 members. The governor and lieutenant governor are elected for two years. Arkansas is represented in Congress by two senators and four representatives. The state is divided into 75 counties, and in 1970 there were 25 cities and towns with a population of more than ten thousand.

Economy. Arkansas is an agricultural state. Cotton is the chief crop; and rice, soybeans, wheat, fruit, and sweet potatoes are grown in significant amounts. The state ranks fifth in the production of cotton. Erosion is a serious problem in the state.

Large portions of the state's land is thought to require drastic corrective measures. Forests cover three-fifths of the state and hardwood timber forms the basis for most of the state's manufacturing.

Mineral production centers around bauxite, an ore of aluminum. Most of this (97 percent of the U.S. domestic supplies) is taken from mines just southwest of Little Rock. Titanium, lead, oil, natural gas, and coal are also mined. The tourist industry has developed greatly in recent decades. Numerous springs, caves, cool highlands, and scenic spots, along with the great many lakes, have attracted vacationers and sightseers in large numbers.

CALIFORNIA

The name *California* was first used in a book published in 1510 by Garcia Ordoñez de Montalvo. The first European known to have seen California was Juan Rodriguez Cabrillo, who passed up the coast of the present state in 1542. San Diego and Monterey were settled in 1769 and 1770, respectively, as fortified outposts and missions. It was in 1823 that Mexico achieved independence and came into possession of California. There were 21 missions in the state, strung along the coast about a day's journey apart.

San Francisco was founded in 1776 and was called Yerba Buena until 1847. Los Angeles was founded in 1781 as Neustra Señora la Reina de Los Angeles, (city of Our Lady, Queen of the Angels). By 1844 all the missions were broken up or sold by the Mexican government to private interests.

Relations with Mexico were altered in 1838 when that government recognized the separate existence of California within the Mexican Union. A final attempt to install a Mexican governor was thwarted in 1845. About this time, Americans began settling in the state, especially in the Great Central Valley, around Sacramento. In June 1846, John C. Fremont challenged Mexican authority by capturing Sonoma and setting up the famous "Bear Flag Republic." This movement was at first disavowed by the United States Government, but the onset of war between Mexico and the United States led to the recognition of Fremont's Bear Flag revolt. Fremont was persuaded to place his troops under the command of Commodore John D. Sloat, and the United States then proceeded to occupy California. In 1848 Mexico surrendered all claims to California and on September 9, 1850, California was admitted to the Union as the thirty-first state. Two years earlier, James Marshall, a lumberjack, found gold nuggets while building a sawmill for John Sutter on the American River. This started the famous "Forty-niner" gold rush and the rapid development of the state's natural resources.

Government. The legislature consists of a senate of forty members and an assembly of eighty members. The governor and lieutenant governor are elected for four years. The state sends two senators and 43 representatives to the U.S. Congress. The state is divided into 58 counties. San Bernardino County, covering 20,131 square miles, is the largest county in the United States. In 1970, there were 288 cities and towns in California with a population of more than ten thousand.

Economy. California's economic activities are as

California—San Francisco

varied as are the climate and landforms. The state leads in the total value of farm products. In the agricultural picture, specialty crops and fruits are especially important. In addition, cotton, wheat, barley, rice, poultry, and vegetables are grown in large quantities. The chief specialty crops are raisin and wine grapes, plums, prunes, apricots, citrus fruits, including oranges, lemons, and grapefruit, nuts, and dates. California produces 85 percent of the nation's wine.

California ranks second in the nation in cotton production and leads all states in sugar beets, fishery products, persimmons, seed crops, lemons, walnuts, almonds, apricots, avocados, figs, grapes, olives, peaches, pears, plums, prunes, artichokes, cantaloupes, carrots, strawberries, dates, asparagus, green limas, broccoli, cauliflower, and celery. The specialty crops and fruit are grown mainly in the Great Central and the Imperial valleys, largely on irrigated lands.

The principal mineral is petroleum, in the production of which California regularly ranks third, after Louisiana and Texas. Other major minerals mined are gypsum, mercury, natural gas, tungsten, lead, zinc, copper, and iron ore. The state was fifth in the production of gold in 1960. Only Texas outranks California in total mineral production. In lumber production, California ranks second to Oregon.

However large other industries of the state are, most of California's income is derived from manufacturing. The state ranks first in slaughtering of cattle, in value of processed foods, and in the production of wine and olive oil. Iron and steel production is centered in the Los Angeles area, while shipbuilding is concentrated in San Francisco and San Diego. Palo Alto is the center of the electronics industry and of aircraft building.

Outstanding natural features such as waterfalls, canyons, and desert scenery, have been enclosed or preserved within both state and federal parks and monuments, providing the basis for a large tourist industry. In addition, sport centers, winter and summer resorts are located all over the state. Several million persons visit California every year as tourists or vacationers.

COLORADO

Spanish explorers had visited Colorado during the sixteenth and seventeenth centuries. However, it was not until 1706 that Juan de Uribarri took formal possession of the region for Spain, despite a claim by France originating with Sieur de La Salle in 1682. The eastern part of the present state eventually was included in the Louisiana Purchase and came under the American flag in 1803. The remainder of Colorado passed into United States possession in 1848 as a part of the Mexican cession.

Zebulon M. Pike explored Colorado in 1806, discovering the peak now named for him. Between 1820 and 1850 Major Stephen Long and John C. Fremont explored parts of the present state. The discovery of gold at Cherry Creek in 1858 attracted settlers; the first settlement was made at Auraria (now part of Denver). Colorado was organized as a territory in 1861. Movements for statehood failed on several occasions, but were successful in 1876 when Colorado was admitted to the Union as the thirty-eighth state. In 1906, the United States mint opened at Denver, and Mesa Verde National Park was established to preserve abandoned cliff-cities of a former Indian civilization (*see* Arizona).

Government. The state's legislative body is called the General Assembly (in other states this

Colorado—Mesa Verde National Park

name is often applied to the lower legislative chamber). It consists of a senate of 35 members and a house of representatives of 65 members. The governor and lieutenant-governor are elected for four years. The state sends two senators and five representatives to Congress. Colorado is divided into 63 counties, and in 1970 there were 26 cities and towns having a population of more than ten thousand.

Economy. More than 250 different minerals are mined in Colorado, the major ones being coal, oil, molybdenum, zinc, lead, vanadium, and uranium. Colorado has huge reserves of oil in the form of oil shales, but their mining awaits fuller development of methods to extract the oil from the shale.

Colorado is a leading sheep-raising state, and Denver is said to be the world's largest sheep-marketing center. The state's agriculture relies heavily upon irrigation and more than 20 percent of the crop lands are seriously eroded. Nevertheless, the state ranks first in the production of broomcorn, second in sugar beets, second in onions, fourth in beans, and eighth in barley. In addition, Colorado is a leading producer of celery, potatoes, wheat, peaches, cherries, and cattle feed. National forests cover nearly fourteen million acres. Tourism is a large industry, based chiefly on the big game for hunters and the Rocky Mountain scenic and ski areas.

CONNECTICUT

Connecticut is one of the 13 original states. A Dutch navigator named Adraen Block discovered and explored the Connecticut River in 1614. A Dutch trading post, established at Hartford in 1633, was replaced by an English settlement in 1635. Windsor and Wethersfield were founded in 1634. The Dutch attempted to expel the English but failed. In 1639 the three towns drew up a constitution which governed them until Charles II granted a charter in 1662. This famous charter served the colony and then the state of Connecticut until 1818. In 1687 King James II of England called upon Connecticut to surrender the charter. The colonists refused and hid it in an oak tree. However, the existing government was dissolved and the colony was despotically ruled until the overthrow of King James II in 1689. The famous Charter Oak is shown on a United States postage stamp, issued in 1935 to commemorate the three-hundreth anniversary of the state.

The charter struggle and other events in Connecticut were closely observed by other colonies and had a strong influence in arousing public opinion against England. Connecticut contributed large amounts of supplies to the Continental Army. It was the only colony in which the British governor supported the Colonists and continued in office during the Revolution. Fifteen percent of the population participated in the war. Nathan Hale, a Connecticut schoolteacher, was hanged as a spy by the British in 1776. Connecticut joined the Union as the fifth state on January 9, 1788.

Government. Our present system of representation in Congress was proposed by the Connecticut delegation to the Constitutional Convention in 1787. It was adopted and is called the Connecticut Compromise. Connecticut's legislative body is called the General Assembly (*see* Colorado); it consists of a senate of 36 members, and a house of representatives of 177 members. The governor and lieutenant-governor are elected for four years. The state sends two senators and six representatives to the U.S. Congress. County government, established in 1666, was formally abolished by the General Assembly in 1960. The eight former counties remain only as geographical subdivisions. In 1970,

Connecticut—Nathan Hale Schoolhouse, East Haddam

there were 78 cities and towns in Connecticut with a population of more than ten thousand. (For a note on New England towns, *see* Massachusetts.)

Economy. Only three minerals (mica, beryl, and feldspar) are of economic importance. The chief industry of Connecticut is manufacturing. In 1970 the state ranked thirteenth in the nation in value added by manufacturing. It was a leader in the production of hats, firearms, clocks, watches, aircraft engines, needles, pins, nails, and hardware.

A high-quality leaf tobacco is grown in Connecticut, and the Connecticut Valley is a major fruit-growing region.

DELAWARE

Delaware is one of the 13 original states. The first attempted settlement, made near Lewes by the Dutch in 1631, was destroyed by the Indians. In 1638 the Swedes established a successful colony at Fort Christina, now Wilmington. This colony, called New Sweden, prospered until it was overwhelmed by a Dutch invasion in 1655. Nine years later (1664), the Dutch were conquered by the British.

The colony was deeded to William Penn in 1682. However, the area remained a distinct unit within Penn's territory and was called the "Three Lower Counties." A long dispute between William Penn and the Baltimores (proprietors of the Maryland colony) was settled when Mason and Dixon surveyed the region in 1763.

Delaware—Caesar Rodney Statue, Rodney Square, Wilmington

The same governor and General Assembly served both colonies until 1704 when a dispute over defense caused the Three Lower Counties to form their own General Assembly. The two colonies continued to share the same governor until the War for Independence.

In 1776 the Three Lower Counties became "Delaware State," and joined with 12 other colonies to prosecute the war with the British. The first star in the American flag represents Delaware State, because it was the first to ratify the new federal constitution creating the United States, on December 7, 1787. In 1792 a new state constitution changed the name "Delaware State" to "State of Delaware." Delaware remained in the Union throughout the Civil War (1861–1865).

Government. The legislature of Delaware is called the General Assembly and consists of a senate of 19 members and a house of representatives of 39 members. The state has one representative-at-large and two senators in the U.S. Congress. The state is divided into three counties. Delaware is the only state today that subdivides the counties into "hundreds." The hundred is an ancient unit, meaning originally a piece of land that could provide 100 men for use in time of war. It was once used in Delaware as the basis for representation in the General Assembly, but today is used only for tax and other minor purposes.

Economy. Delaware is mainly an industrial state. Wilmington is one of the chief chemical manufacturing centers of the world. Textiles rank next to chemicals, followed by leather-making. Shipbuilding is also important. Wilmington is the chief industrial and urban complex. Commercial fishing centers around Lewes, a port on the Atlantic Ocean. Wilmington and New Castle are major seaports. The Chesapeake and Delaware Canal, completed in 1829 and widened in 1919, provides a shortcut between Delaware Bay and Chesapeake Bay through the Delmarva Peninsula.

Excellent highways cross Delaware in all directions. Surf bathing and harness racing attract many visitors and vacationers to the state.

FLORIDA

Florida was visited twice from 1513 to 1521 by Ponce de Leon, a Spanish adventurer. He named the country Florida. Hernando de Soto marched through the interior of the Florida Peninsula in 1539.

A settlement of French Huguenots, established in 1564 at Fort Carolina on the St. John's River, was wiped out by the Spanish in 1565. In the same year the first permanent white settlement in what is now the United States was founded at St. Augustine by Spanish colonists.

Spain ceded Florida to the English in 1763, but a fierce three-way war broke out among the English, the Indians, and the Spanish colonists. This war merged into the American Revolution. Florida was used as a base for raids on Carolina and Georgia towns. In 1783 the British gave Florida back to Spain, and in 1795 Spain sold a part of Florida on the gulf coast to France. The United States occupied that part in 1812, claiming that France had included it in the sale of Louisiana to the United States in 1803.

In the War of 1812, the British captured Pensacola but were driven out by Andrew Jackson. He abandoned it and had to recapture it in 1818. In the following year Spain sold all of Florida to the United States for five million dollars.

In 1835, war broke out between the United States and the Seminole Indians. The Seminole War was merely a more serious phase of a war that had been going on since Andrew Jackson invaded Florida in 1818.

After more than a thousand Seminoles and their allies had been rounded up and sent west of the Mississippi (*see* Oklahoma), a treaty of peace was concluded in 1839. But sporadic fighting continued until 1842. On March 3, 1845, Florida was admitted to the Union as the twenty-seventh state. Florida seceded from the Union on January 10, 1861, and was readmitted on February 6, 1868.

Florida—Miami

Government. The legislature of Florida consists of a senate of 48 members and a house of representatives of 119 members. The state has no lieutenant-governor. Florida sends two senators and 15 representatives to the U.S. Congress. There are 67 counties, and in 1970 there were 87 cities and towns with a population of more than ten thousand.

Economy. The great citrus fruit belt for which Florida is so famous lies in the highland section of the peninsula, among the lakes. Grapefruit and oranges are the leading citrus crops. Florida is the leading state in the production of oranges, grapefruit, and limes. Tobacco, cotton, peanuts, and sugar cane are other major crops in the state.

The state has rich mineral deposits. Three-fourths of phosphate mined in the United States comes from Florida. Fuller's earth, uranium (recovered from phosphate deposits), ilmenite and rutile (ores of titanium) are also mined in Florida.

Industrial growth has been rapid in recent years, chiefly in processed foods. The greatest industry of Florida is tourism. The long beaches, pleasant climate, and the tropical Everglades are contributing factors in the fame of Florida as a vacation land.

GEORGIA

Georgia is one of the original 13 states, and it was the last English colony to be established in what is now the United States. Before the white settlers came, Creek Indians lived on the southern plains and lowlands while the Cherokees inhabited the highlands.

Hernando de Soto visited the region in 1540 and French explorers followed a few years later. The English claimed the region in 1629 as part of the Carolina grant made by King Charles I, but did not attempt to plant a colony there until 1732. In that year, George II deeded the region to a group led by General James Oglethorpe, and Oglethorpe landed the first settlers the following year. Georgia ratified the U.S. Constitution on January 2, 1788, and in 1802 the state sold all of its claims west of the Chattahoochee River. In 1832, the Creek Indians in the state were deported westward, followed by the Cherokees in 1838. Georgia seceded from the Union on January 19, 1861.

Georgia suffered heavily in the Civil War. Several of the engagements in the state were bitterly

Georgia—Fort Pulaski Moat

fought and costly in terms of men and material. Toward the end of the war, General Sherman's troops burned Atlanta and marched toward the sea, causing such great destruction through fire and looting that the line of march is still discernible from the air. Georgia was readmitted to the Union in 1868, but expelled in 1869 and again readmitted in 1870.

Government. The constitution of 1945 is the eighth one adopted in Georgia. The Georgia legislature consists of a senate of 24 members and a house of representatives of 195 members. The minimum voting age is 18. Georgia has two senators and ten representatives in the U.S. Congress. The state is divided into 159 counties, the largest number of counties in any state except Texas. In 1970, there were 39 cities and towns with a population of more than ten thousand.

Economy. Georgia furnishes 78 percent of the nation's kaolin, or china clay. Gold was discovered in 1828 and until 1849 most of the gold in the United States came from Georgia. The quarrying of granite and marble is an important industry. Iron and coal are mined in the Appalachians. Forests cover about two-thirds of the state, and Georgia leads in the production of turpentine and resin, both derived from the sap of trees. The principal agricultural crops are cotton, peanuts, hogs, tobacco, and poultry. The state is the largest producer of sea island cotton. Georgia leads the nation in pecan and peanut production.

HAWAII

The Hawaiian Islands, formerly called the Sandwich Islands, were discovered in 1778 by Captain James Cook. Cook returned to the islands the following year after exploring the coast of North America (*see* Oregon). He was killed on the main island of Hawaii as he tried to retrieve a stolen boat.

Between 1795 and 1819, the island archipelago was united into a kingdom by Kamehameha I. Christian missionaries began working there in 1820. The kingdom adopted its first constitution in 1840. Immigration from Asia and Europe in large numbers began with Chinese in 1852, followed by Polynesians from other Pacific islands in 1859, Portuguese in 1878, Japanese in 1886, and Filipinos in 1906.

The pineapple industry was established by Captain John Kidwell in 1882, using plants imported from Jamaica. By 1893, American owners of the sugar cane and pineapple industries formed the strongest groups in the islands. The instability of the kingdom and the desire of the growers to export under more favorable conditions led to a revolt in 1893, and the establishment of a Hawaiian Republic under Sanford B. Dole.

American businessmen managed to get the islands annexed to the United States in 1898. The Territory of Hawaii was organized on June 14, 1900. A plebiscite for statehood was not held until 1940. Japanese forces attacked Pearl Harbor on December 7, 1941, forcing the United States into World War II. A constitution was adopted in 1950

Hawaii—Mauna Loa

and statehood was achieved on August 21, 1959. Thereby, Hawaii became the fiftieth state.

Government. The legislature consists of a senate of 25 members and a house of representatives of 51 members. The governor and lieutenant-governor are elected for four years. The state sends two senators and two representatives to the U.S. Congress. Hawaii is divided into five counties. There are 34 municipalities having more than 2,500 inhabitants (1970). Nine of these had a population of more than ten thousand in 1970.

Economy. The mainstays of the state's economy are military expenditures, agriculture, and tourism. Plantation agriculture is highly developed with sugar cane the most important crop. Crops vary with altitude zones. Sugar grows in the lowlands. Pineapples, the second largest crop, grow on the terraced uplands. The plantations of Hawaii are outstandingly efficient and some are highly mechanized. The people enjoy a high standard of living. Some diversified agriculture is beginning to be practiced.

IDAHO

The early history of Idaho is that of the Oregon country, especially with regard to the Oregon boundary dispute, the explorations of Lewis and Clark, and other explorations (*see* Oregon). After 1853, however, what is now Idaho became a part of the new Washington Territory. The region of Idaho became known to white men after the discovery of gold in 1859 near the present Lewiston. By 1862 there were thirty thousand white people in the region. In March 1863, Idaho was organized into a territory, with the capital at Lewiston. It included Montana until 1864, and Wyoming until 1868. These separations reduced the territorial limits to about what they are today. However, errors in earlier surveys of boundaries necessitated changes at various times.

Serious Indian troubles developed between 1877 and 1879, in which many settlers and soldiers were killed. The Snake River Valley was opened by the laying of tracks for the Oregon Short Line Railroad in 1880. Idaho was admitted to the Union on July 3, 1890 (forty-third state). Labor trouble in the Coeur d'Alene area led to rioting and the blowing up of a mill. In 1905 Governor Steunenburg was assassinated. This resulted in the famous trial of a member of the western Federation of Miners, who was sentenced to life imprisonment.

Government. Idaho is governed under its original constitution of 1889. The legislature consists of a senate of 35 members and a house of representatives of 70 members. The governor and lieutenant-governor are elected for four years. The state is represented in the U.S. Congress by two senators and two representatives. Idaho is divided into 44 counties, and in 1970 there were nine cities and towns with a population of more than ten thousand.

Economy. Silver, lead, zinc, and antimony are the chief minerals mined in Idaho. The state ranks high in the mining of antimony, lead and cobalt, and it produces 44 percent of the domestic silver. Other major minerals produced are phosphate rock, garnet, nickel, columbium, tantalum, copper, gold, and mercury. Beryllium has been recently discovered, and other minor minerals are produced.

Although large areas are arid, agriculture is a leading industry in Idaho. Irrigation is widely practiced and there are over three million acres under irrigation in the state. The most important cash crops are cereals, over 50 percent of which is wheat. The growing of hops, a new industry, is spreading. Other crops include sugar beets, potatoes, oats, barley, beans, apples, and prunes.

Idaho—Craters of the Moon National Monument

Illinois—Chicago

ILLINOIS

Illinois was discovered in 1673 by the French explorers Father Jacques Marquette and Louis Joliet.

The early history of the state is that of French exploration and settlement. Sieur de LaSalle several times crossed Illinois between Lake Michigan and the Mississippi River by using the historic portage route to the Illinois River, and thence down that river to the Mississippi. La Salle built Fort Crevecoeur near the present Peoria. In about 1700 two settlements were established near the mouth of the Illinois River. They were Kaskaskia and Kahokia. Both were settled by missionaries, traders, and Indians.

In 1717 these settlements were called the Illinois District and were annexed to the French province of Louisiana. By 1720 there were three additional villages in the district. In 1763 France ceded the district to the British, who annexed it to Quebec in 1774.

George Rogers Clark led a military expedition of Virginians into the Illinois country (1778–1779). Largely because of this expedition, the entire region was ceded to the United States in 1783. When Indiana Territory was set up in 1800 (*see* Indiana), Illinois was a part of it. In 1809 Illinois Territory was organized with the seat of government at Kaskaskia. Illinois was admitted to the Union as the twenty-first state on December 3, 1818.

Government. The Illinois legislature consists of a senate of 58 members and a house of representatives of 177 members. The governor and lieutenant-governor are elected for four years. The state sends two senators and 24 representatives to the United States Congress. The state is divided into 102 counties. In 1970 there were 147 cities and towns in Illinois with a population of more than ten thousand. Chicago is the second largest city in the United States and the thirteenth largest in the world.

Economy. Illinois is mainly an agricultural state despite the fact that it ranks fourth in value added by manufacturing. The state ranks fourth in the nation in cash receipts from farming. Nineteen percent of the total value of all farm commodities is from corn, and 16 percent of the remainder is from soybeans. Other major crops include wheat and oats. Over seven million hogs are raised every year in Illinois.

Illinois ranks eleventh among the states in mineral production; it is a leading producer of fluorspar and tripoli; and it ranks high in building stone and coal.

Chicago is the key city of the second largest manufacturing region in the United States. The Chicago area is the machinery-making center of the nation, and northern Illinois is one of the fastest growing industrial districts.

Chicago's leadership in meat-packing has been lost to such cities as Omaha and Kansas City. Some of the world's largest printing establishments and food processing plants are located in Chicago. Heavy industry, including great steel mills and oil refineries extend southeastward from Chicago and into Indiana along Lake Michigan. The great inland seaport of Indiana Harbor also serves Chicago and parts of Illinois.

INDIANA

Indiana is one of the states that formerly comprised the old Northwest Territory. The region was inhabited mainly by the Potawatomi and Miami Indians when French explorers visited there in 1679. After several unsuccessful trips, the French were able to establish a permanent settlement in 1732, at the present city of Vincennes. However, only 31 years later the entire area of the present Indiana was lost to the British. The British were driven out by Americans under George Rogers

Clark in 1779. The territory northwest of the Ohio River was organized into the Northwest Territory in 1787. Indiana Territory—an area comprising all of the present Indiana, Illinois, Wisconsin, and parts of other states—was carved out of the Northwest Territory in 1800. William Henry Harrison, later the ninth President of the United States, became the territorial governor, with his capital at Vincennes. Harrison was forced into a showdown fight with the Prophet, a famous Indian leader. At the Battle of Tippecanoe on November 7, 1811, Indian power in the Territory was broken. Congress formally admitted Indiana into the Union on December 11, 1816, as the nineteenth state. However, its area was greatly reduced from the original extent of Indiana Territory.

Government. The state's legislative body is called the General Assembly. It consists of a senate of 50 members and a house of representatives of 100 members. The state is represented in Congress by two senators and eleven representatives. Indiana is divided into 92 counties. In 1970 there were 53 cities and towns that had a population of more than ten thousand.

Economy. This is a major manufacturing state, ranking eighth in the nation; but it is also a "Corn Belt" prairie state, ranking tenth in cash income from sale of agricultural crops.

The metal industries employ six of every ten persons engaged in manufacturing. The state ranks third in steel production, provides 80 percent of all limestone used in the nation, and makes 12 percent of all household furniture. Other large industries include brick and tile making, rubber processing, the manufacture of prefabricated houses, and automotive parts.

Corn is the major farm crop, but most of it is marketed as livestock feed, mainly for hogs. Indiana is third in the nation in production of soybeans, third in corn, and third in hogs.

Indiana—St. Mary's College for Girls, South Bend

IOWA

Iowa was a part of the original Louisiana Purchase territory. Father Marquette and Louis Joliet visited the area of the present state in 1673, stopping at the mouth of the Des Moines River. The first settlement was made in 1785 by Julien Dubuque near the city that now bears his name. He was attracted by the lead deposits nearby.

In 1763, the entire region of Louisiana was ceded to Spain, and returned to France in 1800. In 1803, the United States purchased Louisiana. After the state of Louisiana took this name and entered the Union in 1812, the name of the entire region north of the new state of Louisiana was changed to Missouri. In 1821, the state of Missouri came into existence, leaving Iowa without a name or a government. In 1834, it became a part of Michigan Territory and then a part of Wisconsin Territory. Iowa was established as a territory in 1838 and separated from Wisconsin Territory. At that time it embraced the greater part of Minnesota and all of the two Dakotas. On December 28, 1846, Iowa was admitted to the Union as the twenty-ninth state. During the Civil War Iowa remained loyal to the Union and furnished nearly eighty thousand men to the federal armies.

Government. The legislature is called the General Assembly and consists of a senate of 50 members and a house of representatives of 100 members. The governor and lieutenant-governor are elected for two years. The state is represented in the U.S. Congress by two senators and six representatives.

Iowa is divided into 99 counties. Most of the county lines meet at right angles, forming tiers and rows of squares, with county seat towns nearly in the center of the square counties. These counties also contain neat rows and tiers of townships, at least twelve to a county. Nearly every community

Kansas—State House, Topeka

in Iowa is an incorporated place, but in 1970 only 27 of them had a population of more than ten thousand.

Economy. Iowa is the richest state in agriculture, with nearly 96 percent of the state under cultivation. Iowa leads all states except California in cash receipts from farming. Although it is only one-third the size of California, Iowa has almost the same amount of land as California under cultivation (36 million acres).

Corn grows on about one-third of the farm acreage of the state, and Iowa leads all other states except Illinois in corn growing. In oats Iowa leads all states. Other major crops are sugar beets, wheat, barley, buckwheat, flax, rye, alfalfa, soybeans, and red clover.

Iowa ranks thirty-first in mining, but is third in the mining of gypsum. Coal underlies large areas of the state. Meat packing leads all other manufacturing industries. Cedar Rapids has the largest cereal mill in the world.

KANSAS

The first white men to gaze upon the wide prairies of Kansas were the Spanish explorers led by Coronado in 1541. All but the southwestern section was included in the Louisiana Purchase of 1803. The southwestern area was a part of Texas until 1850 when it was turned over to the United States and became a part of the Missouri Territory. The name *Missouri* had been adopted in 1812 as the name of the remaining part of the Louisiana Purchase after the state of Louisiana had entered the Union (*see* Louisiana).

Kansas was separated from Missouri Territory and organized into a territory under provisions of the Kansas-Nebraska Bill of 1854. Immigrants from both slave and free areas further east began to pour into Kansas. Serious political conflict soon arose between pro-slavery and anti-slavery groups.

A pro-slavery government, set up in 1855, expelled anti-slavery supporters from the legislature. Free-state factions organized a new government, declaring the existing government to be illegal. Violence attended these actions. The town of Lawrence was destroyed twice, and other towns were burned in attacks and reprisals. The pro-slavery faction drew up another constitution at Lecompton and presented it to the voters, who defeated it in 1858. Thereupon the "Wyandotte" constitution, drawn up by free-state groups, was passed and adopted by large majorities. On January 29, 1861, Kansas was admitted to the Union as the thirty-fourth state. However, guerilla warfare broke out and the conflict merged with the greater war being fought in the east. Quantrill's raiders and other groups devastated large areas of Kansas before the Confederacy was defeated in 1865.

Government. The legislature consists of a senate of 40 members and a house of representatives of 125 members. The governor and lieutenant-governor are elected for two years. Kansas sends two senators and five representatives to the United States Congress. The state is divided into 105 counties, and in 1970 there were 34 cities and

Iowa—The Capitol Building, Des Moines

towns with a population of more than ten thousand.

Economy. Kansas is the nation's number one wheat producer, and the state is primarily agricultural. Kansas is second in sorghums, and ranks fourth in the number of cattle. Corn, hay, soybeans, barley, oats, and sugar beets are also major crops. In industry, the manufacture of transportation equipment (including aircraft) has become important in recent years. This industry group is especially prominent in Wichita and Kansas City. Kansas ranks fifteenth in mining. Petroleum, natural gas, and zinc are the principal minerals.

KENTUCKY

Kentucky's recorded history began, as did that of many other states, with the journeys of great French explorers. Robert Cavelier, Sieur de La Salle (1648–1687), considered the greatest of them, passed down the Ohio River (Kentucky's northern boundary) in 1669. The French claimed the region until they released it to Spain in 1762, despite a standing British claim. France dispatched at least one expedition to the present Kentucky to police Indian attempts to reclaim the area. The English entered Kentucky as early as 1750, when it formed a part of Virginia, but were driven out by the Indians.

A group of settlers from Pennsylvania managed to establish Harrodsburg on the Kentucky River in 1775. In the following year, Daniel Boone led colonists through historic Cumberland Gap and founded Boonesboro as a fort and settlement. Violence began immediately, for even chance encounters between Indians and white people generally resulted in bloodshed. Boonesboro was attacked several times, but withstood the sieges.

Through the efforts of George Rogers Clark, hero of the Revolutionary War in the west, Kentucky was established as a county of Virginia in 1776. It had been divided into three counties by 1780 and a statehood movement was growing. Virginia refused to consent to statehood until after 1789. On June 1, 1792, Kentucky was admitted to the Union as the fifteenth state.

During the War of 1812, the threat to New Orleans (the chief port for Kentucky goods) aroused Kentuckians to take a leading part in Andrew Jackson's campaign to defend New Orleans against the British. Kentuckians helped explore and settle the newly acquired Louisiana region. Even the restless Daniel Boone moved westward (he died in Missouri in 1820 at the age of 86, less than a year before that state entered the Union).

Kentucky—Mammoth Cave National Park

Government. The legislative body of Kentucky is called the General Assembly and consists of a senate of 38 members and a house of representatives of 100 members. The governor and lieutenant-governor are elected for four years. The state sends two senators and seven representatives to the U.S. Congress. Kentucky is divided into 120 counties. In 1970 there were 37 cities and towns having a population of more than ten thousand.

Economy. Kentucky is an agricultural state. The chief crop is tobacco (the state ranks second to North Carolina). Corn, apples, strawberries, popcorn, fescue seed, bluegrass seed, hay, and soybeans are also major crops. The state is acclaimed as the home of the world's finest race horses, most of which are raised in the Bluegrass region around Lexington.

Coal is the principal mineral of Kentucky, and chiefly because of it, the state ranks ninth as a mineral producer.

LOUISIANA

Hernando De Soto entered what is now Louisiana in 1541, claiming it as a part of Spanish Florida. In 1682 the entire Mississippi and Missouri valley region was claimed for France by La Salle, and named Louisiana. In order to strengthen her claim, France sent Iberville to found the first settlement at Mobile (see Alabama). The first settlement in the present Louisiana was made at Natchitoches, on the Red River, in 1714. Bienville founded New Orleans in 1718 and in 1722 it became Louisiana's capital.

The entire region was ceded to Spain in 1762, but by the Treaty of San Iledefonso in 1800, it was returned to France. On April 30, 1803, Napoleon sold all of Louisiana to the United States for 15 million dollars, at a rate of about four cents per acre. That part lying west of the Mississippi was organized into the Territory of Orleans in 1804. Shortly afterwards the area east of the Mississippi was added and the combined areas were admitted to the Union under the name of Louisiana on April 30, 1812. The state seceded January 26, 1861. In 1862 New Orleans was captured by federal forces and occupied until the end of the war. The state was readmitted to the Union in 1868 and federal troops were withdrawn in 1877.

Government. The legislature consists of a senate of 39 members and a house of representatives of 105 members. Both governor and lieutenant-governor are elected for four years. The state sends two senators and eight representatives to the U.S. Congress. Louisiana is divided into 64 parishes that correspond to counties in other states. In 1970 there were 37 cities and towns with a population of more than ten thousand.

Economy. About one-third of the state is composed of rich delta land. Louisiana produces most of the cane sugar and rice grown in the United States. Forests cover about 56 percent of the state and lumbering is an important industry. Louisiana is second only to Texas in petroleum output. The largest oil refinery in the United States is at Baton Rouge. The state is the second largest producer of sulphur. The port of New Orleans is second only to New York in tonnage handled. It is the chief port of entry for Latin American products. Baton Rouge and Lake Charles are also major ports. Aside from New Orleans, Shreveport in the northwest is the chief industrial and trade center.

Louisiana—Mississippi River loading dock, Baton Rouge

MAINE

Giovanni da Verrazano is credited with having discovered the coast of Maine in 1524. However, it was not until a century later that systematic exploration of Maine began. One of the first explorations was that of John Smith in 1614. Temporary settlements were made in 1604 (Neutral Island), 1607 (Sabino Point), 1608 (Mount Desert Island), and 1623 (Monhegan Island). The first permanent settlement was made at Pemaquid in 1625.

Various grants of land in the region were confusing and led to disputes that lasted for two centuries. Massachusetts disputed all claims and completed the possession of Maine by 1691.

Maine's association with Canada has often been bitter. New Brunswick and Maine fought a war over their boundaries until settlement was made in 1842 by the terms of the Ashburton Treaty.

For a long time Maine was restless under the government of Massachusetts. Opportunity for separation came from the growing slavery question. Missouri had applied for admission to the Union as a slave state. This led to the famous Missouri Compromise in which a free state (in this case, Maine) was to be admitted along with Missouri, a slave state. Maine was separated from Massachusetts and entered the Union on March 15, 1820, as the twenty-third state.

Maine—Coastline at Schoodic

Government. The legislature consists of a senate of 32 members and a house of representatives of 151 members. The constitution of statehood (1820) is still in force. The governor is elected for four years. There is no office of lieutenant-governor. Maine has an Executive Council of seven members to advise the governor. Massachusetts and New Hampshire are the only other states that have executive councils. Maine sends two senators and two representatives to the U.S. Congress. The state is divided into 16 counties.

Many of the functions that are performed by counties in other states are performed by "towns" in Maine (*see* Massachusetts; Connecticut). The "town" of New England is roughly equivalent to "township" in other states except Wisconsin. The New England word "town" should *never* be confused with "town" as popularly used for any small community (as it is used in the next sentence.) In 1970, there were 18 cities and towns with a population of more than ten thousand.

Economy. Maine is a leading state in the manufacture of paper and other wood products. The chief types of trees used commercially are spruce, fir, beech, cedar, hemlock, white pine, birch, maple, and aspen. Nearly half the communities are engaged in wood products industries of one kind or another. There are numerous plants making paper, some of which are among the largest in the world. Maine is the second leading producer of potatoes in the United States. Granite is another major product of the state. Fishing is a major industry. Clams (soft-shell), lobsters, scallops, sardines, cod, haddock, and mackerel are the chief kinds of fish caught. Portland and Rockland are the chief fishing ports.

MARYLAND

Maryland is one of the 13 original states. The grant of the present state was made in 1632 by Charles I to George Calvert, first Lord Baltimore. Lord Baltimore's purpose in acquiring the grant was to establish a refuge for persons of the Catholic faith who were at that time being persecuted.

About two hundred colonists landed in Maryland in 1634, and founded the settlement of St. Mary's. The young colony experienced setbacks from several quarters and for a time (1645–1646) St. Mary's was occupied by dissident groups. In 1649 the famous Toleration Act was passed. This document guaranteed the freedom of worship to all Christians. However, several Puritan (Protestant) groups continued to be hostile, and took up separate settlements in Maryland. The Puritans revolted and held the province from 1654 to 1657. In 1657, Lord Baltimore was restored to control of Maryland. In 1692 Maryland was converted to a royal colony directly under the King of England. In 1715 the Baltimores regained possession of the

Maryland—Hampton House "Ghost Room"

colony and retained it until the Revolutionary War. A 50-year dispute with Pennsylvania was finally settled by the surveys of Mason and Dixon (the Mason-Dixon Line) from 1763 to 1767. The city of Baltimore was founded in 1730. Maryland took an active part in the struggle for independence. Congress met at Annapolis in 1783. Maryland ratified the Constitution on April 28, 1788 (seventh state).

During the War of 1812, rioting occurred in Baltimore and the city was under siege by British ships. Fort McHenry withstood the siege, an event commemorated by Francis Scott Key in our national anthem. Maryland was divided in sympathy during the Civil War, but remained loyal to the Union. In September 1862, the fierce battle of Antietam (Sharpsburg) was fought in Maryland.

Government. The legislative body is called the General Assembly and consists of a senate of 43 members and a house of delegates of 142 members. The governor is elected for four years. There is no office of lieutenant-governor. The state sends two senators and eight representatives to the U.S. Congress.The United States capital is located in the District of Columbia, which forms an enclave in Maryland and has no connection whatever with the state. Maryland is divided into 23 counties, and in 1970 there were 57 cities and towns with a population of more than ten thousand. Baltimore, the state's largest city, has the status of a county and is an enclave in Baltimore County but not a part of the county. Baltimore is the seventh largest city in the United States.

Economy. Manufacturing industries form the major part of the economy. Aluminum, chemicals, ships, missiles, clothing, rubber, and machinery are manufactured. Baltimore is a leading port, commercial and trade center. It is also a major steel center. The seafood industry is of major importance; and Maryland is a leader in its catch of striped bass, soft-shell clams, and oysters.

MASSACHUSETTS

Massachusetts is one of the 13 original states. A Protestant group in England, at first called "Separatists," and later "Pilgrims," sought refuge from religious intolerance in Holland (The Netherlands), and then set sail for North America in 1620. They established the first permanent white settlement within the present Massachusetts, at Plymouth in December 1620. They also instituted a form of democratic government in accordance with terms they had drawn up among themselves before landing—the historic Mayflower Compact. Others, seeking religious freedom, began to found settlements all along the coast, and in 1630 the Massachusetts Bay Colony was chartered to unify the settlements. Boston was settled in 1630, and Massachusetts was made a royal colony in 1691.

The people of Massachusetts were foremost in the movement that brought about a break with England and the independence of the United States. The movement began with rioting and boycotts that eventually led to the Boston Massacre of March 5, 1770, when British soldiers fired into a crowd of colonists. In 1773, cargoes of tea were dumped into Boston Harbor by a group disguised as Indians and led by Samuel Adams. In retaliation, Boston was occupied and the port closed. Patriots then called the First Continental Congress, which ordered a general boycott of all English goods. The siege of Boston followed the first engagements of the War for Independence at Lexington and at Concord Bridge. George Washington took command of the Continental Army at Cambridge on July 3, 1775. The Battle of Bunker Hill, March 17, 1776, led to the British evacuation of Boston, to which the British were never able to return. Following the end of the war, a period of economic depression set in, which lasted until Massachusetts adopted the federal Constitution on February 6, 1788.

Massachusetts—Paul Revere Statue, Boston

Government. The legislative body of the state is called the General Court of the Commonwealth and consists of a senate of 40 members and a house of representatives of 240 members. Both governor and lieutenant-governor are elected for four years. The state sends two senators and twelve representatives to the U.S. Congress in Massachusetts. As in other New England states, the "town" (roughly similar to the "township" in other states) is of greater significance in local government than is the county. There are over 300 towns within the state. In addition, there are 152 cities with a population of more than ten thousand.

Economy. Massachusetts is overwhelmingly a manufacturing state, and is the nation's oldest manufacturing region. Textiles have usually been prominent, but the state is known for the great variety of its manufactured products. Few minerals or other raw materials for industry originate within the state.

More than half of the state's population lives in the metropolitan area of Boston. The city is a major world seaport, the largest fishing port in the nation, as well as one of the leading manufacturing centers. Research is a major industry in Massachusetts. Some 338 research laboratories employing numerous scientists, engineers, and technicians are located in the state.

MICHIGAN

The French explorer Étienne Brulé (who met a tragic death as a sacrificial victim among his former friends, the Huron Indians) may have been the first white man to see what is now the state of Michigan in 1610. Jesuit missionaries and French explorers gradually opened up the region, and Father Marquette founded the first settlement at Sault Sainte Marie in 1668. Detroit was founded in 1701. After the French and Indian War, the British came into control of Michigan, annexing it to Canada in 1774. By the Treaty of Paris (1783) it was ceded to the United States. In the following years British agents stirred up Indian trouble for the settlers. Organized Indian forces defeated General Saint Clair but met disastrous defeat at the hands of General "Mad" Anthony Wayne at Fallen Timbers in 1794 (*see* Ohio).

In 1805 Michigan Territory was organized, embracing the lower peninsula and with a southern boundary farther south than at present. In 1834, the territory was expanded to include the entire region between Lake Erie and the Missouri River. The opening of the Erie Canal brought commerce and a rapid increase in population. A serious boundary dispute known as the "Toledo War" (*see* Ohio) was settled, resulting in the moving of the southern boundary northward. As compensation, Michigan was given the entire upper peninsula. The peninsula turned out to be a hidden treasure of copper, iron, and other valuable resources. Michigan was reduced to its present size by 1837 and admitted to the Union on January 26 of that year as the twenty-sixth state.

Government. The legislature consists of a senate of 38 members and a house of representatives of 109 members. The governor and lieutenant-governor are elected for four years. The state sends two senators and 19 representatives to the U.S. Congress. Michigan is divided into 83 counties. In 1970 there were 78 cities with a population of more than ten thousand. Detroit is the fifth largest city in the United States, behind Philadelphia and ahead of Houston (1970).

Economy. The state has well-diversified and highly-developed agricultural industries, including dairying. The principal crops are plums, peaches, cherries, honey (a by-product of the fruit-growing industry), apples, corn, hay, oats, winter wheat, and sugar beets.

Michigan—Isle Royale National Park

Despite its agricultural wealth, Michigan is predominantly an industrial state. The manufacture of automobiles is by far the leading industry, employing more than half the industrial workers of the state. Iron ore is the chief mineral mined in Michigan, most of it coming from the upper peninsula. Copper, petroleum, natural gas, salt, and limestone (some of the largest quarries in the world) are also mined in the state. The Great Lakes are ice-free from April to November, and they form the busiest waterway in the world. The famous Soo Canal between Lake Superior and Lake Huron handles twice as much tonnage annually as does the Panama Canal, even though the latter is open all year.

MINNESOTA

French fur traders came to Minnesota by way of the Great Lakes in about 1658. Little was known of the region until Jesuit missionaries penetrated Minnesota in 1680. Father Hennepin traveled up the Mississippi River in that year and discovered the Falls of St. Anthony, which he named (located in present-day Minneapolis). The French claimed the region east of the Mississippi River but ceded it to England in 1763. In 1783 the United States acquired this part, and the remainder of the future state was acquired as a part of the Louisiana Purchase of 1803. Zebulon Pike (*see* Colorado) traced the Mississippi's upper course to Cass Lake in 1806. Henry R. Schoolcraft traced the great river to its source in 1832, and found it to be in Lake Itasca in northcentral Minnesota.

The first settlement was made in 1819 at Fort St. Anthony (name changed to Fort Snelling in 1824). Eastern Minnesota became a part of the Northwest Territory, set up by Congress in 1787. Minnesota then became successively a part of Indiana, Illinois, Michigan, and finally Wisconsin Territories. Western Minnesota, acquired in 1803, was at first a part of Louisiana, then of Missouri, Michigan, Wisconsin, and Iowa Territories. In 1849 the two sections were at last put together to form Minnesota Territory. Minnesota became the thirty-second state on May 11, 1858.

While the Civil War was on, the Sioux Indians started a war of their own, nearly succeeding in driving white people out of southern Minnesota. Five hundred white settlers died in the Sioux War, and damage ran into millions of dollars. The war ended with the defeat of the Indians at Wood Lake (1862).

Minnesota—Minneapolis

Government. The legislature consists of a senate of 67 members and a house of representatives of 133 members. The governor and lieutenant-governor are elected for four years. The state sends two senators and eight representatives to the U.S. Congress. Minnesota is divided into 87 counties, and in 1970 there were 54 cities and towns with a population of more than ten thousand. The city of Minneapolis ranks thirty-second in the nation, while St. Paul ranks forty-sixth.

Economy. Agriculture, mining, and manufacturing are all chief industries in the state. Manufacturing is chiefly in the south and in the Duluth area around Lake Superior. The state consistently ranks first in creamery butter, oats, turkeys, and sweet corn. Other major crops are corn, soybeans, and green peas. Minnesota's principal mineral is iron ore, most of it coming from three major mining districts in the northeast. The iron is taken mainly by rail to the Lake Superior ports of Duluth and Two Harbors, where it is loaded on ore boats and sent to the great steel mills and furnaces in the lower Great Lakes region (Cleveland, Lorain, Gary, Pittsburgh, and Buffalo). The city of Duluth itself is also a steel-making center. The state supplies more than half of the nation's iron ore. The great new ore deposits of Quebec and Venezuela now pose serious competition to Minnesota iron ore.

MISSISSIPPI

Spanish explorers led by Hernando de Soto were the first white men to enter what is now Mississippi. De Soto discovered the Mississippi River in 1541. The first permanent settlement in the state was made by the French on the Gulf Coast of the future state in 1699. Natchez was settled in 1716 in an attempt by the French to secure a more firm control of the Mississippi Valley. But they lost the region to the British in 1763. After the independence of the United States, Mississippi was ceded to the United States by England. However, it was still claimed by Spain. The treaty of San Lorenzo in 1795 secured the area to legal United States control. Mississippi Territory was organized in 1798. The boundaries were extended in 1804 and in 1812 by the addition of parts of the Louisiana Purchase. On December 10, 1817, Mississippi was admitted to the Union as the twentieth state.

Mississippi seceded from the Union on January 8, 1861, the second state to do so. The chief struggle during the war that followed was for control of the Mississippi River. The siege of Vicksburg, a vital port on the river, became one of the most critical battles of the war. When Vicksburg fell on July 4, 1863, the fate of the Confederacy was sealed, although other engagements were fought in the state before the end came. Mississippi was readmitted to the Union in 1870.

Government. The legislature consists of a senate of 52 members and a house of representatives of 140 members. The governor and lieutenant-governor are elected for four years. The state is represented in the U.S. Congress by two senators and five representatives. Mississippi is divided into 82 counties. In 1970, there were 24 cities having a population of more than ten thousand.

Mississippi—D'Evereux Home

Economy. Mississippi's greatest resources are her soils and forests. Cotton is the major crop; the state ranks third in the production of that commodity. The state leads in the output of tung-oil nuts. Other major crops include pecans, sweet potatoes, corn, rice, wheat, oats, sugar cane, and sorghum. The state ranks eighth in broiler-chicken production. It is also the tenth ranking oil producer in the nation. Mississippi is one of the major lumbering states, and about 58 percent of its area is covered by forests, including over a million acres in national forests. Shrimp fishing is important on the Gulf Coast at Biloxi and Gulfport.

MISSOURI

The Southern part of what is now the state of Missouri was visited by De Soto in 1541 when he crossed the Mississippi River near Memphis. On the basis of the explorations of Marquette, Joliet, and La Salle, the region was claimed by France. In 1705, a party of French explorers ascended the Missouri River to the present site of Kansas City. The territory, then called Louisiana, was ceded to Spain in 1763 and given back to France in 1800 (*see* Louisiana). The United States came into possession of the area in 1803 as a part of the Louisiana Purchase. When the state of Louisiana entered the Union in 1812, the name Missouri became applied to the remainder of the Purchase, which included the entire Missouri River Valley. Daniel Boone (*see* Kentucky) moved into Missouri in 1795 and was an active agent in the state's development. Under terms of the Missouri Compromise, the state of Missouri entered the Union on August 10, 1821 (*see* Maine). The boundary was much the same as today except for a small area that was added in the northwest in 1837. The remainder that was once called Missouri Territory gradually became organized into smaller units, taking on names that had already been growing in popularity or had already existed, such as Dakota, Nebraska, and Kansas.

Missouri—The climatron, Missouri Botanical Garden, St. Louis

Government. The legislative body is called the General Assembly and consists of a senate of 34 members and a house of representatives of 163 members. The governor and lieutenant-governor are elected for four years. The state sends two senators and ten representatives to the U.S. Congress. Missouri is divided into 114 counties. In 1970 there were 54 cities and towns with a population of more than ten thousand. St. Louis has the status of a county and is separate from St. Louis County (*see* Maryland for a similar condition). In 1970 St. Louis was the eighteenth largest city in the United States and Kansas City was the twenty-sixth.

Economy. Missouri is a leading livestock-raising state, ranking fourth in number of hogs and sixth in cattle. The chief crops are soybeans, wheat, corn, and clover. Missouri mines about 45 percent of the United States' lead. Other major minerals mined are barite, lime, iron, copper, and coal. Missouri's largest manufacturing industries are in transportation equipment and food processing. A unique industry in the state is the making of corncob pipes (mainly at the town of Washington). Kansas City (not to be confused with Kansas City, Kansas) and St. Louis have two-thirds of the state's total number of factories. The making of shoes and leather products are also important industries in Missouri.

MONTANA

About a third of the present Montana was included in the original Oregon country, while the remainder formed part of the Louisiana Purchase. The region was explored in 1742–1743 by Sieur de la Verendrye, a French explorer. In 1805 the Lewis and Clark expedition crossed the region. A fort was built at the mouth of the Big Horn River in 1807. The first settlements were made between 1809 and 1829. Jesuit missionaries established missions among the Flathead Indians in 1841.

The discovery of gold on Hell Gate River in 1852 and 1857 was the real beginning of Montana's modern history. Mining settlements sprang up, attracting trade, exploration, and industry.

Conflict with the Indians culminated in the disastrous battle of the Little Big Horn River on June 25, 1876, in which General George Armstrong Custer and his entire force were wiped out by Sioux Indians under Sitting Bull.

Copper and silver mining in the 1880s resulted in rapid development of the region. Montana became a state on November 8, 1889, the forty-first (six days after the two Dakotas).

Government. The Montana legislature consists of a senate of 50 members and a house of representatives of 100 members. The governor and lieutenant-governor are elected for four years. The state is

Montana—Custer's Last Stand (Marker)

represented in the U.S. Congress by two senators and two representatives. Montana is divided into 56 counties, and in 1970 there were eight cities and towns with a population of more than ten thousand.

Economy. Irrigation plays a significant part in agriculture. Montana is a major producer of wheat, barley, sugar beets, and potatoes. Cattle and sheep are also important. Forests cover nearly twenty million acres, or about one-fourth of the state.

Montana is the third-ranking copper producer, and is the number one producer of vermiculite and chromite. (Vermiculite is a form of mica and is used for heat insulation. Chromite is the ore of the metal chromium.) The state also ranks second in the mining of zinc, silver, and fluorspar. Montana is also a large producer of crude petroleum.

NEBRASKA

Nebraska's wide prairies were first seen by Europeans when Coronado reached the region in 1541. As a part of the Louisiana region, it was ceded by France to Spain in 1763. Spain returned it to France in 1800, and the area was sold by Napoleon to the United States in 1803. The explorers Lewis and Clark crossed the future state in 1804. The first settlement was made at Bellevue in 1823, although trading posts had been set up by fur traders as early as 1810. It is estimated that between 1840 and 1866 over two and one-half million people crossed Nebraska on the Overland Trail to California. Settlers began squatting on Indian lands during those years, until in 1854 the entire region (known as Missouri Territory) was opened to settlement. The Kansas-Nebraska Bill of 1854 divided Missouri Territory into Nebraska Territory and Kansas Territory.

With the breaking of ground for the Union Pacific Railroad in 1863, a period of Indian warfare ensued that lasted until the 1870s. Nebraska became a state on March 1, 1867, the thirty-seventh state. In 1882 it annexed part of Dakota Territory and in 1908 received another piece of territory from South Dakota.

Government. By an amendment to the 1875 constitution, Nebraska adopted a single-house legislature, the only state with such a body. This

Nebraska—Chimney Rock located on U.S. Highway 26

legislature consists of 49 members, elected for two years. The governor and lieutenant-governor are elected for two years. Nebraska is represented in the U.S. Congress by two senators and three representatives. Although there are a total of 536 incorporated villages and cities in the state, only 12 of them had a population of more than ten thousand in 1970.

Economy. Three-fourths of the population live in the eastern third of the state. Agriculture is the chief industry, although the processing of meats and other farm products are large industries that are dependent upon the rich farm lands. Farming provides 80 percent of the state's income. The state is third in number of cattle.

Oil and natural gas have been discovered in the western part of Nebraska. Other minerals mined include potash, pumice, gypsum, salt, shale, and clay. Omaha, on the Missouri River, is one of the largest livestock markets in the world and the largest meat-packing center in the United States. The city ranks second in frozen-food production.

NEVADA

Nevada was first visited by Europeans in 1738 when Franciscan friars crossed the state. Peter Ogden of the Hudson's Bay Company discovered the Humboldt River in 1825. John C. Fremont led an exploring party through the region (1843–1844). The first settlement was made by Mormons in 1849 in the valley of the Carson River. The area had become a part of the United States one year earlier, with the Mexican Cession. Nevada became a part of Utah Territory in 1850, but a separate government was soon established and requested annexation to California. The request was turned down, and the area was then organized into Nevada Territory (1861). The state was admitted to the Union on October 31, 1864. In 1866, a section of land was added to the state from Arizona.

The discovery of silver in the Comstock Lode region in 1859 initiated the rapid development of the state. A decline set in when the Comstock worked out, but a revival was made with the discovery of gold southeast of the Comstock region, early in the twentieth century.

Government. The legislature consists of a senate of 20 members and an assembly of 40 members. The governor and lieutenant-governor are elected

Nevada—Hoover Dam

for four years. Carson City, the capital, is the smallest capital city in the United States. Nevada sends two senators and one representative to the U.S. Congress. The state is divided into 17 counties. Nye County (18,064 square miles) is the third largest county in the nation. Elko (17,126 square miles) is fourth. In 1970 there were nine cities and towns with a population of more than ten thousand. (Compare this with 288 such cities and towns in California.)

Economy. Despite its dry climate, Nevada is covered with 20 million acres of forests. However, only a small amount of this is commercial timber. Ranching is the main agricultural concern. Alfalfa is raised. Some irrigation is practiced. Other crops include wheat, barley, oats, and potatoes.

Nevada has rich mineral resources, and these form the mainstay of the state's economy. Mercury, manganese, copper, tungsten, gold, uranium, and barite are the chief minerals mined. The state currently ranks fourth in copper production. Gambling and tourism also bring dollars to the state.

NEW HAMPSHIRE

New Hampshire is one of the 13 original states. The area of the present state was first explored in 1603 by Sir Martin Pring. John Smith explored the coastline in 1604. The region was originally a part of the First Charter of Virginia of 1606, but was given to the Plymouth Company in 1620. In 1629, Captain John Mason secured a claim to all the

New Hampshire—Dartmouth College

land between the Piscataqua and the Merrimack rivers, extending northward to Lake Champlain. This he called New Hampshire, for his native district of Hampshire, England. The first permanent settlement was made at Little Harbor in 1623 by David Thompson.

Upon the death of Mason the colony was placed under the protection of Massachusetts (1641). New Hampshire was made a royal colony in 1679. Boundaries were disputed by the Mason family, and they remained to plague the colony and later the state of New Hampshire. Controversy between New Hampshire and New York developed over the land between the Connecticut River and Lake Champlain, north of Massachusetts. Eventually New York won, but the citizens of the disputed area revolted and declared themselves to be the independent state of "New Connecticut" (*see* Vermont).

Early in 1775, New Hampshire declared for independence and was the first to draw up a new constitution. In the war, a notable victory was achieved by New Hampshire and Vermont troops at Bennington (August 16, 1777). New Hampshire ratified the federal Constitution (the ninth state) in 1788.

Government. The legislature consists of a senate of 24 members and a house of representatives whose membership is restricted to from 375 to 400 members. The governor and five administrative officers (called councilors) are elected for two years. There is no office of lieutenant-governor. The state sends two senators and two representatives to the U.S. Congress. The state is divided into ten counties, but they are not as important governmentally as are the cities and towns located in them (*see* Massachusetts.) In 1970, there were 13 cities having a population of more than ten thousand.

Economy. Location, resources, and the traditions of the people have combined to make the state a land of small farms and small towns. The chief field crops are hay, potatoes, and vegetables. Granite is quarried in several places and is the chief mineral of the state. Manufacturing is concentrated in the larger cities and towns of the south and east.

NEW JERSEY

New Jersey is one of the original 13 states. It was first settled by the Dutch, who built a trading post at Bergen on the Hudson River in 1618. In 1664, the area of the present state was taken from the Dutch by the English. The Duke of York, brother of Charles II, King of England, gave the state its identity in 1664, when he granted the land between the Hudson and Delaware rivers to Lord John Berkeley and Sir George Carteret. Today, the boundaries of New Jersey are exactly those set by the Duke of York in his original deeds of lease. However, from 1674 to 1702 the state was divided into the two colonies of East New Jersey and West New Jersey. On April 17, 1702, Queen Anne reunited the two Jerseys into one royal colony.

The people were divided in feelings during the War for Independence. Those favoring independence won out when a new constitution was adopted in 1776. Because of its strategic location between New York City and Philadelphia, New Jersey became a major battleground. Washing-

New Jersey—Morven, The Executive Mansion of New Jersey at Princeton

ton's Continental Army spent a large part of its time in the state, including three winters at encampments. Nearly one hundred battles were fought by the forces of the Continental Army on New Jersey soil. New Jersey became the third state to ratify the Constitution of the United States, on December 17, 1787.

Government. The legislative body is called the Legislature and is composed of a senate of 40 members and a General Assembly of 79 members. New Jersey is represented in Congress by two senators and 15 representatives. The governor is elected for a four-year term. There is no lieutenant-governor. New Jersey is divided into 21 counties. In 1970, there were 177 cities having a population over ten thousand.

Economy. After tourism, manufacturing is the largest industry. The state ranks seventh in manufacturing in the nation. Manufacturing in the state is concentrated in a 15-mile-wide corridor between Philadelphia and New York. The state is the "core" area of research and science laboratory work in the United States, with more than four hundred research laboratories in the area. Heavy industry in the corridor is concentrated along the Delaware River and in the northeastern counties, opposite New York City.

A favorable climate and almost an unlimited market have given rise to large gardening and dairying industries. The principal farm crops are corn, wheat, potatoes, cranberries, and apples. The chief minerals of New Jersey are stone, glass sand, gravel, iron ore, and clay.

NEW MEXICO

Because of the high level of culture reached by the ancient cliff-dwellers and their descendants, the Pueblo Indians, the pre-Columbian history of New Mexico becomes a significant part of the state's heritage. Most of the larger ruined cities are enclosed within state and national parks and monuments. Many of these sites have museums and collections that portray the everyday life and cultural contributions of the past civilization in what is now New Mexico.

The earliest white explorers were Spaniards who governed the region. Cabeza de Vaca, Coronado, and Nuño de Guzman were the principal explorers. Juan de Oñate conquered the region (1588–1599) and founded the first settlement at San Gabriel. By 1630, Franciscan friars had established about fifty missions throughout New Mexico. Santa Fe was founded in 1605 or 1606 . In 1680 a great Indian revolt expelled all the Spanish from the region and it was not reconquered until 1692.

In 1821, the area became a province of the Republic of Mexico under the name of New Mexico. This entire province was ceded to the United States under terms of the Treaty of Guadalupe Hidalgo, after Mexico's defeat in the Mexican War of 1846–1848.

New Mexico—Acoma Mission

In 1850, all of the land west of Texas and east of California was organized into New Mexico Territory. These limits were changed by the addition of the Gadsden Purchase (*see* Arizona) in 1854, by the transfer of the northeastern corner to Colorado in 1861, by the transfer of the northwestern corner to Nevada in 1866, and by the organization of the western half into Arizona Territory in 1863.

Statehood was hotly debated for more than sixty years, but on January 6, 1912, New Mexico became the forty-seventh state. (Arizona followed about a month later.)

Government. The legislature consists of a senate of 42 members and a house of representatives of 70 members. The governor and lieutenant-governor are elected for four years. The state is represented in the U.S. Congress by two senators and two representatives. New Mexico is divided into 32 counties. In 1970, there were 15 cities and towns with a population of more than ten thousand.

Economy. Agriculture is a major industry in New Mexico. Irrigation is extensively practiced. The chief crops are lint cotton, cottonseed, sorghums, hay, and vegetables.

New Mexico is at present the largest domestic source of uranium, with about 66 percent of the total reserves of that metal. Petroleum, natural gas, copper, zinc, and perlite are other major minerals produced in the state. Lumbering is also important in the state's economy.

NEW YORK

New York is one of the original 13 states. Giovanni da Verazzano, sailing for France, discovered New York harbor and the lower Hudson River in 1524. In 1609, Henry Hudson explored the river that is named for him, and his voyage was the basis for the Dutch claim to all the region drained by the river. Permanent settlements were made near the present Albany in 1624, and on Manhattan Island (now a part of New York City) in the same year. The entire Dutch-settled region was called New Netherland. The chief towns were Fort Orange, now Albany, and New Amsterdam, now New York City.

Dutch rule, lasting fifty years, was notable for the famous "Patroonship" system, designed to encourage further settlement. This was the giving of feudal rights, including perpetual land tenure, to the "Patroons" who purchased land from the Indians.

In 1664, the English seized the colony. They renamed Fort Orange, Albany and changed New Amsterdam to New York, both in honor of the Duke of York and Albany.

During 110 years of British rule, many events occurred that contributed to the founding of the United States. The trial of John Peter Zenger in 1735 led to an early victory for freedom of the press in the colonies. A plan proposed in 1754 by Benjamin Franklin for the federal union of the colonies was the forerunner of the Declaration of Independence. The Stamp Act Congress, organized to protest British taxes, met in New York City in 1765.

New York's strategic location as a middle colony with a major trade route (the Hudson-Mohawk route) made it one of the most important battlegrounds during the War for Independence. In 1776 the British fleet took possession of New York City and retained it throughout the war, despite American efforts to capture the city. Washington was able, however, to draw large quantities of supplies from the free area of the colony. In 1777, a British campaign to split the 13 colonies by a three-way drive on Albany was defeated at Saratoga, in one of the world's most decisive battles. Contributing to this victory was the heroic stand made by General Herkimer at Oriskany, preventing the British from uniting their invading forces.

Washington fortified the lower Hudson in 1778, and the Iroquois Indians' alliance with the British was broken in western New York in the following year. General Washington established the Continental Army headquarters in April 1782, at Newburgh on the Hudson River, and it remained there until the end of the war. The last battle of the war was fought at Johnstown, N.Y., on October 25, 1781. After the reoccupation of New York City by the American Army in 1783, Washington bade farewell to his officers at Fraunces Tavern. Six years later he returned to the city (the first capital of the United States under the Constitution) for his inauguration as the first president of the nation. New York had entered the Union on July 26, 1788, as the eleventh state.

New York—The United Nations Building

Government. The legislative power of the state is vested in a two-house legislature. It consists of a senate of 58 members and an assembly of 150 members. Both the governor and the lieutenant-governor are elected for four years. The state sends two senators and 39 representatives to the U.S. Congress. New York is divided into 62 counties, five of which are within the city of New York. In 1970 there were 158 cities and towns with a population of more than ten thousand. New York City is the largest in the United States and third largest in the world (after Tokyo and London). Buffalo, the state's second largest city, ranks twenty-eighth in the nation.

Economy. New York has been the nation's leading state in the value of manufactured products since 1830. It also outranks all other states in the variety and extent of manufacturing.

Apparel is the largest single industry in the state. About 36 percent of all apparel produced in the nation comes from New York State. Ranking next in terms of employment are machinery, printing, and publishing. One-fourth of the printing in the United States is done in the state. The manufacture of paper, pulp, and paperboard is concentrated in the north and northwest. Instrument industries in New York employ 29 percent of the nation's workers in this field, and the photographic industry employs two-thirds of all the nation's workers in that field.

New York is not often thought of as a mineral-rich state, yet it leads the nation in the mining of industrial talc, garnet, wollastonite, emery, and titanium. It is a major producer of zinc, gypsum, salt, sand and gravel, and mines about 5 percent of the iron ore in the United States. New York leads all states in the utilization of radioactive materials in medical research, diagnosis, and treatment.

It is well to note that fully 25 percent of all the people in the United States live within a 250-mile radius of New York City, so New York State ranks unusually high as a wholesale market region. The state leads all others in both retail and wholesale activities. In banking and finance, New York is also the leader, having 518 banks with resources amounting to 78 billion dollars. This makes the state, and in particular, the city of New York, the financial center of the world (New York City is also the largest insurance center in the nation).

The Port of New York has about 600 miles of piers and handles about 24 percent of the waterborne foreign trade in the country. The Port of New

York Authority is a bi-state agency of New York and New Jersey, set up to develop and promote this port district.

The Port of Buffalo is the largest state port on the Greak Lakes, in terms of value and in tonnage. The city has 37 miles of waterfront on Lake Erie. The opening of the St. Lawrence Seaway in 1959 provided a new seacoast for ocean commerce along the river and the Great Lakes. This project stimulated plans for deep-water ports by Massena, Ogdensburg, Oswego, Rochester, and other cities in the state.

Dairying is the largest agricultural industry, and the state is second in the nation in the number of dairy cows and in the production of milk. Other major agricultural crops include grapes, apples, peaches, potatoes, maple syrup, and buckwheat. The state ranks fourth in total vegetable production and second in the production of cheese and ice cream.

North Carolina—Wright Monument in Wright Brothers National Memorial near Kitty Hawk

NORTH CAROLINA

North Carolina is one of the 13 original states. The first English attempts to establish settlements in what is now the United States were made in North Carolina in 1584, 1585, and 1587. In the year 1587, Roanoke Island became the site of a colony, established by Sir Walter Raleigh, in which the first white child was born in America. Her name was Virginia Dare. This was the famous "Lost Colony." Its disappearance was so complete that the only clues ever found were the word *Croatoan* (the name of another island) and a few pieces of armor. The state was not permanently settled until 1663.

In 1629, King Charles I of England granted what is now North and South Carolina to Sir Robert Heath. In 1663 King Charles II gave the area to a group of "proprietors." In 1710 North and South Carolina were separated. Beginning in 1712, each had a separate capital and governor. In 1729, North Carolina became a royal colony (the King having bought out the proprietors). North Carolina entered the Union on November 21, 1789, the twelfth state to ratify the new federal Constitution.

North Carolina was the last state to secede from the Union. It did so on May 20, 1861, and was readmitted in July 1868.

Government. The state legislature consists of a senate of 50 members and a house of representatives of 120 members. The governor may not succeed himself, and has no veto power. The state sends two senators and 11 representatives to the U.S. Congress. North Carolina is divided into 100 counties. In 1970 there were 41 cities and towns having a population of more than ten thousand.

Economy. The state is rich in natural resources. Its climate and soil permit a wide range of economic activities.

North Carolina's Piedmont region is dotted with the world's largest concentration of textile, tobacco, and furniture factories. The state leads the nation in all three. Value added by manufacturing is the largest in the South and fourteenth in the nation.

In agriculture, North Carolina is the number one producer of tobacco in the United States. Other major cash crops are corn, soybeans, cotton, and peanuts. Also grown extensively are wheat, oats, barley, sweet potatoes, hay, peaches, and apples. North Carolina is first in the country in farm population and eleventh in farm production. Its timber covers 20 million acres, and furnishes about 7 percent of the total value of the state's farm products.

An astounding variety of minerals are found in North Carolina. There are 300 types, leading all states in variety. The state produces 74 percent of all the sheet mica in the United States. The state is also a leading producer of feldspar, kaolin clays, talc, and stone (chiefly granite).

NORTH DAKOTA

Most of North Dakota lies in the drainage basin of the Missouri-Mississippi system which was claimed by Sieur de La Salle for France in 1682. This claim was transferred to Spain in 1762. The British obtained title to part of the state in the north and east in 1763. The United States received all but the British-claimed area in 1803, as a part of the Louisiana Purchase. In 1818, the British-claimed area was formally ceded to the United States, although French and English fur traders continued to explore the region.

Lewis and Clark crossed North Dakota on their famed journey of exploration (1804–1806). David Thompson, the great English geographer, had explored and mapped the Souris and Missouri river basins in 1797.

Attempts at settlement occurred in the early nineteenth century at Pembina in the northeast, but the present state remained virtually unoccupied except for Indians and trading posts until the 1850s. In 1829, the American Fur Company built Fort Union at the mouth of the Yellowstone River. In 1857 the first military outpost was established at Fort Abercrombie on the Red River of the North. By 1860 regular steamboat service was available on both the Missouri and Red River of the North. Dakota Territory was organized in 1861 and included both North and South Dakota, plus parts of Wyoming and Montana.

North Dakota—Theodore Roosevelt National Memorial Park

Dakota Territory was opened for homesteading in 1863. Railroads began to cross the territory in 1871. In 1889 the Dakota Territory was divided into two territories. The division was made along the seventh standard parallel. North Dakota and South Dakota were admitted to the Union on November 2, 1889. President Benjamin Harrison apparently never revealed which statehood bill he signed first, so that it will never be known which of the two sister states was the first to be admitted to the Union. North Dakota is generally given as the thirty-ninth state only because of its alphabetical position, but either state could be placed thirty-ninth or fortieth.

Government. The present constitution dates from statehood. The law-making body is called the Legislative Assembly and consists of a senate of 50 members and a house of representatives of 108 members. The governor and lieutenant-governor are elected for four years. The state is represented in the U.S. Congress by two senators and one representative. North Dakota is divided into 53 counties. There are 356 municipalities, of which 10 had a population of more than ten thousand in 1970.

Economy. Agriculture is the chief industry. Large-scale mechanized farms are common. The state leads in the production of barley, ranks second in rye, and second in wheat. Other important crops include flax seed, potatoes, hay, oats, and corn.

North Dakota is the newest oil-boom state, and petroleum is the most valuable mineral found there. The state ranks ninth in reserves. The major fields are located around Williston. Refineries are located at Dickinson, Williston, and Mandan.

OHIO

The first recorded inhabitants of Ohio were the Mound Builders, prehistoric Indians. Those living in Ohio left more than ten thousand burial and ceremonial mounds. Most of the Mound Builders of Ohio belonged to the Hopewell culture. Artifacts found in the mounds indicate advanced cultural progress and social life.

Early in the seventeenth century Jesuit priests and French explorers began entering the region.

Moravian missionaries founded a settlement which they called Schoenbrunn in eastern Ohio in 1772. This settlement was destroyed in 1776. Marietta on the Ohio River was founded in 1788, becoming the first permanent town in the future state.

After the Revolutionary War the British continued to encourage the Indians to violence in the region north of the Ohio River. The new federal Government was determined to put an end to the Indian troubles and sent General "Mad" Anthony Wayne to deal with the situation. In 1794, Wayne brought a disastrous defeat upon the Indians at Fallen Timbers, near present Toledo. In 1795, Wayne secured the Greenville Treaty, bringing about peace in Ohio.

New towns began to spring up soon after the treaty was signed. In 1796, the famous Western Reserve surveys began. Ohio became the first state to be carved out of the old Northwest Territory. It unofficially entered the Union as the seventeenth state on February 19, 1803. The entrance was made official on August 8, 1853, retroactive to the original 1803 date. A serious border dispute between Ohio and Michigan in 1835 resulted in the "Toledo War." Ohio was awarded the disputed area and Michigan was given what proved to be a tremendous bargain–the copper-rich Upper Peninsula.

Government. The legislative body of Ohio is called the General Assembly. It consists of a senate of 33 members and a house of representatives of 99 members. The governor and lieutenant-governor are elected for four years. Ohio sends two senators and 23 representatives to the U.S. Congress. The state is divided into 88 counties, and in 1970 there were 153 cities and towns with a population of more than ten thousand. Cleveland ranks tenth in the nation, and Columbus ranks twenty-first.

Ohio—University of Cincinnati campus

Economy. Although Ohio ranks third among the states in manufacturing, it is also a major farming state, ranking eighth in gross value of farm production. Agriculture in the state is varied, including even greenhouse farming, the largest such industry in the nation. Along Lake Erie is a major fruit-growing region, aided by the lake's influence on the climate. In addition, the state ranks fifth in corn, first in timothy seed, fifth in oats, third in popcorn, and sixth in hogs.

Iron and steel products are the largest group of manufactured products. Steel mills and blast furnaces are concentrated along Lake Erie, especially at Cleveland and Lorain. Ohio ranks first in business machines, clay products, electrical machinery, tires and tubes, and machine tools.

Cleveland, Toledo, Lorain, Ashtabula, and Sandusky now rank as seaports since the completion of the Great Lakes-Saint Lawrence Seaway (*see* New York). In fact, Toledo has a substantial foreign trade zone, and is the world's greatest coal-shipping port. The chief minerals mined in Ohio are coal, clay, lime, and salt.

OKLAHOMA

The recorded history of Oklahoma began in 1541 when De Soto visited the eastern part of the region and the Spanish Coronado expedition crossed central Oklahoma. The section was not known as Oklahoma until 1866, and then not officially until 1890. Little was known of the area until it became a part of the Louisiana Purchase in 1803. American explorers then made maps of the region.

Oklahoma early became a refuge for Indians who were driven from east of the Mississippi, and this role shaped the destiny of the future state. Between 1820 and 1840, Indian treaties were signed with Cherokee, Choctaw, Chickasaw, Seminole, and Creek tribes. These five tribes were allotted areas for settlement and were given land by the Government. They eventually set up their

Oklahoma—Travertine Creek, Platt National Park

own governments and became autonomous areas with their own capital cities. The Five Nations were divided on the issues of the Civil War, and considerable internal strife resulted.

Cattle drives northward through the Indian country required many grazing leases on Indian lands. The railroads brought an influx of white people to the country. After the Civil War, Creek and Seminole peoples ceded large areas in the central part of the future state to the United States. These lands were opened for white settlement on April 22, 1889. On opening day, fifty thousand people were on hand. By nightfall, tent cities had sprung up and six counties had been created. The following year Oklahoma was designated a territory. By 1895 all of southwestern Oklahoma had been opened to white settlement.

The Indians struggled to remain independent of Oklahoma Territory. They attempted to become a separate state in 1905, but were defeated. In 1906 President Theodore Roosevelt joined the white and Indian territories into a single state. Oklahoma was declared the forty-sixth state on November 16, 1907.

Government. The state has a senate of 48 members and a house of representatives of from 120 to 123 members. The governor and lieutenant-governor are elected for four years. The state is represented in Congress by two senators and six representatives. Oklahoma is divided into 77 counties. In 1970, 30 cities and towns had a population of more than ten thousand.

Economy. Agriculture is the major industry of Oklahoma. However, soil erosion is a serious problem because the state lies in a region of erratic rainfall, some years being rainy and others being too dry. Farmers in the state are often faced with the problem of protecting topsoils either from severe drought or severe flooding. The most important crop is wheat and production is the second-highest in the United States. Other crops include cotton, grain, sorghums, and broomcorn.

Oklahoma ranks fourth in the production of petroleum. Natural gas, coal, gypsum, zinc, and salt are also produced. Petroleum refining is the chief nonagricultural industry.

OREGON

The name *Oregon* was originally applied to the whole region of what is now the Pacific Northwest and includes Oregon, Washington, parts of Idaho, Montana, and Canada's British Columbia. Discovery and exploration were first carried out by sea voyages along the coast. Spanish sailors from Mexico, in 1543, were the first white men to see the Oregon country. Spanish claims were challenged by the British after the visits of Sir Francis Drake in 1579, and especially after the voyages of exploration of Captain James Cook (1778), and George Vancouver (1792). The Russians, too, claimed the region as a result of their fur-trading expeditions in the latter part of the eighteenth century. American interest was stimulated by the overland expedition of Lewis and Clark in 1804–1806, and by the sea voyage to the coasts by Captain Robert Gray in 1791 and 1792.

Russian and Spanish claims lapsed by agreement, but British and American rivalry in the fur trade and between settlements brought about serious conflicts. An agreement made in 1818 for joint occupancy was finally terminated by treaty in 1846, after the so-called Oregon Question threatened to involve the United States in war with Great Britain. The original American demand was "Fifty-Four Forty or Fight," but the forty-ninth parallel of latitude was finally accepted as the boundary between the United States and British-controlled Canada.

Settlement began when the Pacific Fur Company established Astoria in 1811. In 1813 Astoria was sold to the Northwest Company. That company was then absorbed by the Hudson's Bay

Oregon—Ice Lake, Wallowa Mountain

Company, which actually governed the region of present Oregon until the treaty in 1846. Settlements were established in 1829 in the Willamette River valley. American settlers formed a provisional government in 1843 and Oregon Territory was organized in 1848. Oregon was admitted to the Union on February 14, 1859, as the thirty-third state.

Government. The present constitution of Oregon dates from statehood. The legislative body is called the Legislative Assembly and consists of a senate of 30 members and a house of representatives of 60 members. The governor is elected to a four-year term. There is no lieutenant-governor. The state is divided into 36 counties. Harney County (10,131 square miles) is the eighth largest of the more than three thousand counties in the United States. In 1970 there were 24 cities and towns with a population of more than ten thousand.

Economy. Nearly 30 million acres of standing forests blanket the state, and Oregon leads the nation in lumbering. Oregon produces annually nearly eight million board feet of lumber, or about 25 percent of the total United States' production. Agriculture is another major industry. The state is a leading producer of peppermint, filberts, black raspberries, beans, beets, lily bulbs, holly, and seedling root stocks. The most productive farm land lies in the Willamette Valley between Portland and Eugene.

Manufacturing ranges from lumber products through aluminum, textiles, and fertilizers. Mining includes gold, silver, mercury, copper, and nickel. Oregon is one of the few states with commercial deposits of quicksilver and chromite ores, and one of two states producing nickel.

Fishing is important along the coast and on the Columbia River; salmon, trawl fish, clams, crabs, and tuna are the chief kinds taken.

PENNSYLVANIA

Pennsylvania is one of the 13 original states. William Penn (1644–1718), an English Quaker, received the grant of Pennsylvania from Charles II in 1681. It has been said that the immediate purpose of Charles' act was to get rid of "the troublesome Quakers." If so, he must have been roundly satisfied, because the Quakers flocked to Pennsylvania in the first few years. Penn himself came in 1682, and Philadelphia was laid out in the same year.

Penn set about concluding a number of treaties with the Lenni-Lenape and other tribes of Indians. His work saved years of bloodshed during the opening up of the land for settlement. Penn's domain was enlarged in 1682 by the grant of the "Three Lower Counties," which were retained as a nominal part of Pennsylvania until 1776 (*see* Delaware). The constitution devised in 1701 lasted until the Revolution.

Pennsylvania was often involved in long disputes over the colony's boundaries, and later over state lines. Some of these led to violence, as in the "Pennamite" and "Yankee" wars. The last change in the boundary was the adding of a triangle in 1792 to give the state an outlet on Lake Erie in the west.

Pennsylvania took a leading part in the Revolution. The Declaration of Independence was signed at Philadelphia in 1776. During a large part of the war, Pennsylvania served as Washington's base of operations. Except for a brief period when Philadelphia was occupied by the British, the city was the seat of the Continental Congress. Winter quarters were established at Valley Forge by the Continental Army during the winter of 1777–1778. The state ratified the federal Constitution on December 12, 1787, the second state to do so (following Delaware).

Government. Pennsylvania's legislative body is called the General Assembly and consists of a senate of 46 members and a house of representatives of 202 members. The governor and lieutenant-governor are elected for four years. The state sends two senators and 25 representatives to the U.S. Congress. Pennsylvania is divided into 67 counties (including the city of Philadelphia, whose boundary includes all of Philadelphia County). Philadelphia is the fourth largest city in the United States. Pittsburgh ranks twenty-fourth in the nation. In 1970 there were 101 cities and towns with a population of more than ten thousand.

Economy. Despite a varied agriculture and some of the richest soils in the nation, Pennsylvania is predominantly an industrial state. However, the state ranks second in the nation in egg production and fifth in dairying. The chief farm crops are corn, wheat, tobacco, and potatoes. Pennsylvania ranks second (to West Virginia) in coal mining. The principal coal seams are those of hard coal (anthracite) in the northeastern counties, and soft coal (bituminous) in the southwest. Half of the world's supply of anthracite coal comes from Pennsylvania. The state also ranks fourth in kaolin and second in limestone. Petroleum and natural gas are produced in large quantities. The state leads the nation in the production of iron and steel. Heavy industry is concentrated in the Pittsburgh and Philadelphia areas. Seventeen million tons of iron and steel come from the blast furnaces of Johnstown, Pittsburgh, Morrisville, Bethlehem, Steelton, and Coatesville each year. Most of the iron ore used comes from Minnesota over the Great Lakes route. Textile manufacturing is also a large industry, concentrated mainly in Philadelphia, Allentown, and Reading. The world's largest knitting mill is located at Reading (pronounced "Redding").

Pennsylvania—Memorial Chapel, Valley Forge

RHODE ISLAND

Rhode Island is one of the 13 original states. Rhode Island and Providence Plantations (still the official name of the state) was founded by Roger Williams in 1636. Williams had been exiled from Massachusetts for his religious beliefs. He persuaded several settlers to go with him into exile, and obtained land near the present Providence by purchase from the Indians of the Narragansett Bay region. The town of Newport was founded in 1639.

The New England Confederation, which had been formed for defensive purposes in 1643, threatened the little colony along Narragansett Bay. This prompted Roger Williams to hurry off to England where he got a charter for his colony (1652). This charter remained the governing law of Rhode Island until 1842. During the colonial period Rhode Island became a principal refuge for those who were persecuted because of their political beliefs. It was one of the first colonies to resist British oppression by burning the British cruiser *Gaspée.* Nathaniel Greene, a leading hero of the war, led a thousand Rhode Island men to Boston upon the outbreak of war.

Rhode Island was suspicious of the larger states throughout the early years of independence, and was at first fearful of joining a stronger union in which the small states could be trampled upon. Threats of annexation and of cutting off trade forced Rhode Island into ratifying the federal Constitution as the thirteenth state on May 29, 1790.

Government. The legislative body is called the General Assembly and consists of a senate of 50 members and a house of representatives of 100 members. The governor and lieutenant-governor are elected for two years. Rhode Island is represented in the U.S. Congress by two senators and two representatives. The state has five counties, but they have no political functions whatever. The town and city are the major units of local government. Of the 43 towns and cities in 1970, 27 had a population of more than ten thousand.

Economy. Rhode Island's larger cities are still the stronghold of the textile industries which have been on the decline elsewhere in New England. Woolens and worsteds are the leading textiles manufactured. Machinery, fabricated metal products, and jewelry are other leading industries. Agriculture and mining in Rhode Island are not important on a national level.

Rhode Island—Kitchen of James Mitchell Varnum House, East Greenwich

South Carolina—Fort Sumter, Charleston

SOUTH CAROLINA

South Carolina is one of the original 13 states. Spanish explorers visited the area as early as 1520. However, England claimed the future South Carolina along with the entire North American coast on the basis of the voyages of discovery of John and Sebastian Cabot. In 1629, Charles I granted the region to Sir Robert Heath, who made no attempt to establish settlements. In 1663, Charles II made a second grant of the same area (which included the present North Carolina) to eight "proprietors." This colony was called Carolina. The first settlement was made in 1670 at Charlestown. This settlement was later moved and renamed Charles Town (changed to Charleston in 1783). In 1729, Carolina was divided into North Carolina and South Carolina (although actually there always had been two separate governments).

During the Revolutionary War, South Carolina contributed more money to the cause than any other state except Massachusetts. The colony had been prosperous from the very beginning, and for a time Charleston was a leading center of wealth and culture in North America. However, the state of South Carolina suffered heavily in the war. Charleston was besieged and forced to surrender. Much of the war was waged in guerrilla fashion by such leaders as Francis Marion ("Swamp Fox"), Sumter, and Pickens. South Carolina ratified the federal Constitution on May 23, 1788, the eighth state to sign.

The Civil War began in South Carolina after that state seceded from the Union on December 20, 1860. The bombardment of Fort Sumter in Charleston Harbor were the opening shots of the war (April 12–13, 1861). Tremendous damage was inflicted on the state, especially along the route of General Sherman's army in the famous march to the sea (*see* Georgia). At the close of the war a military government was imposed upon the state for twelve years. On June 25, 1868, the state was readmitted to the Union but was one of the worst sufferers during the period of Reconstruction.

Government. The legislative body is called the General Assembly. It consists of a senate of 46 members and a house of representatives of 124 members. The governor and lieutenant-governor are elected for four years. The state sends two senators and six representatives to the United States Congress. South Carolina is divided into 46 counties, and in 1970 there were 20 cities with a population of more than ten thousand.

Economy. South Carolina is an agricultural state. The principal crops are tobacco, corn, lint cotton, soybeans, and peaches. Of the minerals, large reserves of rare-earth minerals exist, although the state now ranks only forty-first in the value of minerals produced. The state ranks second in kaolin and kyanite clays. The state has a trend toward metals manufacturing, but textiles are by far the leading manufacture.

SOUTH DAKOTA

South Dakota was a part of the Louisiana Purchase of 1803. The state was first explored in 1743, mainly by the Verendrye brothers, who were French explorers from Canada. They buried a lead plate to serve as proof of their visit and of the claim of France to the region. The plate was found in 1913. The Lewis and Clark Expedition passed through the state in 1804 and 1806. Fort Teton (Fort Pierre) was established as a trading post in 1831. Steamboat service on the Missouri started the following year. Fort Pierre became a United States military post in 1855, and Sioux Falls was founded in 1857. South Dakota was successively placed under the governments of Missouri Territory (1812), Michigan Territory (1834), Wisconsin Territory (1836), Iowa Territory (1838), Minnesota Territory (1849), and then a part became part of Nebraska Territory in 1854. Dakota Territory was organized in 1861 and until 1863 included parts of Montana and Wyoming. Railroad construction initiated rapid settlement and development of the state. On November 2, 1889, South Dakota became either the thirty-ninth or the fortieth state (*see* North Dakota). A great land rush ensued when nine million acres of former Sioux Indian lands were sold in 1892.

South Dakota—Mount Rushmore

Government. The legislature consists of a senate of 35 members and a house of representatives of 75 members. The governor and lieutenant-governor are elected for two years. South Dakota is divided into 67 counties (Armstrong County was abolished in 1959). The state sends two representatives and, of course, two senators to the Congress. Three counties remain unorganized and without government functions. In 1970 there were eight cities and towns with a population of more than ten thousand.

Economy. South Dakota is a farming state, and the farms are generally large (averaging over 800 acres) and highly mechanized. The state is a major producer of wheat, barley, oats, corn, rye, and flaxseed.

The state leads in the mining of gold (the Homestake Mine), although South Dakota ranks only forty-second in the value of minerals produced. Beryllium and mica are also mined in large quantities.

TENNESSEE

In April 1541, De Soto reached the present Memphis, Tennessee area and crossed the Mississippi there into what is now Arkansas. Early in 1682 Sieur de La Salle built Fort Prud'homme. A French trading post was established near Nashville in 1714 and French settlers founded Fort Assumption. The English settled at Fort Loudoun near Knoxville in 1756. This fort was captured by the Cherokees in 1760 and the garrison was massacred. A series of permanent settlements were established in the valleys of the Holston and Watauga rivers in 1769 by colonists from Virginia and North Carolina.

A number of pioneers, including Daniel Boone, founded the state of Transylvania. They drew up a form of government in 1780 and founded a settlement at Nashville. However, Virginia refused to sanction the new state. John Sevier founded another state that was called Franklin. This time North Carolina refused to sanction the state and regained control over the territory in 1788.

After North Carolina and Virginia had given up their claims to Tennessee, the region was organized as "Territory South of the Ohio," but this did not include Kentucky (which was a Virginia County at that time). Statehood came on June 1, 1796, when Tennessee became the sixteenth state (four years after Kentucky had entered the Union).

The Tennessee people took a leading part in exploring and settling the American Southwest. In the war with Mexico, Tennessee became known as the "Volunteer State" because 30,000 soldiers volunteered for the war when only 2,800 had been called for.

Next to Virginia, Tennessee was the main battleground in the Civil War. Shiloh and the engagements around Chattanooga were bloody and crucial battles in the war. Tennessee had withdrawn from the Union on June 24, 1861, and was readmitted on July 24, 1866.

Government. The legislative body is called the General Assembly and consists of a senate of 63 members and a house of representatives of 99 members. The governor is elected for a four-year term. There is no office of lieutenant-governor. Tennessee sends two senators and eight representatives to the U.S. Congress. The state is divided into 95 counties, and in 1970 there were 32 cities and towns with a population of more than ten

Tennessee—Confederate Monument, Fort Donelson

thousand. The largest city is Memphis, which ranks seventeenth among the United States cities in population.

Economy. The chief crops of Tennessee are cotton, tobacco, soybeans, and corn. Coal fields cover over 5,000 square miles of the state, and Tennessee is a leading producer of coal. Tennessee leads in the mining of zinc and is second in phosphate rock. The state ranks twenty-eighth in mineral production; about 30 different minerals are mined commercially. Chemicals, iron, and steel products are the chief manufactures. Memphis is Tennessee's major port. Oak Ridge was founded by the U.S. Government in 1942 for atomic energy development and research in nuclear physics.

TEXAS

The Spanish initiated the exploration of Texas in 1519, when Alonso Álvarez de Peñeda was sent out to explore and map the coast along the Gulf of Mexico. Cabeza de Vaca added to European knowledge of the region by spending six years with the Indians there. In 1685, the French began exploring Texas. Thus, the claims of France and Spain overlapped until the defeat of France in 1763 by the British. Texas was then Spanish until it passed to an independent Mexico in 1821. During the Spanish period, missions and forts were established throughout the region. The first settlement in Texas dates from 1686.

American settlers, led by Moses Austin and later by his son, Stephen F. Austin, established homes in Texas while it was governed by Mexico. A flood of American settlers soon ran into conflict with Mexican sovereignty. In 1835, the colonists revolted against Mexico and set up a provisional government. Santa Anna, the Mexican general who had already overthrown his own government, set out to crush the revolt. Texans captured San Antonio in December 1835, but were crushed when Santa Anna's superior forces overwhelmed the small garrison in the Alamo, the chapel of an old Spanish mission, on March 6, 1836. There were no survivors; all died fighting, including Davy Crockett, Jim Bowie, and William Travis.

After the fall of the Alamo, Santa Anna was caught by surprise at San Jacinto. Forces under Sam Houston annihilated the Mexican Army and captured Santa Anna. This ended Mexican sovereignty over Texas. The Texas Republic came into existence on March 2, 1836 and lasted until the state entered the Union voluntarily on December 29, 1845, as the twenty-eighth state. Texas seceded from the Union in 1861 and was readmitted March 30, 1870.

Government. The present constitution dates from 1876. The Texas legislature consists of a senate of 31 members and a house of representatives of 150 members. The governor and lieutenant-governor are elected for two years. Texas sends 24 representatives besides the two senators to the Congress. Texas is divided into 254 counties, the largest number of counties in any state. In 1970 there were 125 cities and towns with a population of more than ten thousand.

Economy. Texas leads all states by a wide margin in the production of petroleum and helium. The total value of minerals is 22 percent of the United States total. More than three-fifths of all natural gas used in the country comes from Texas. Other minerals include sulphur, salt, gypsum, asphalt, and magnesium (from seawater).

Great chemical industries have grown up in the Houston area. The Port of Houston is connected to the Gulf of Mexico by the Houston Ship Canal (57.3 miles long). Houston itself is the largest inland cotton market in the world.

Texas ranks as one of the leading agricultural states. Large farms dominate the state's agriculture. Texas leads in the production of cotton and grain sorghum. Other important crops include pecans, corn, winter wheat, oats, rice, castor beans, potatoes, sweet potatoes, peanuts, and grapefruit.

Texas—The Alamo

The state also leads in the livestock industry. It has more cattle and sheep than any other state. Tourism is an important industry in southern and western Texas.

UTAH

The first white men to see Utah were Spanish explorers and the Franciscan friars. Captain James Bridger discovered Great Salt Lake in 1825. The first settlement was made at Salt Lake City in July 1847, by a group of about 150 Mormon settlers.

The Mormon Church (properly called the Church of Jesus Christ of Latter-Day Saints) was founded at Fayette, New York, in 1830 by Joseph Smith. Persecution and opposition forced the Mormons to move westward. Brigham Young joined the group after it had reached Kirtland, Ohio (near Cleveland) in 1832. They were driven from Ohio and then from Missouri. In 1840, they were at Nauvoo, Illinois; by 1844 Nauvoo had become the largest town in Illinois because of the influx of converts and settlers. Joseph Smith and his brother Hyram were jailed and then shot by a mob on June 27, 1844. The charter of Nauvoo was revoked and the Mormons were again forced to flee westward. They reached the Great Salt Lake and founded Salt Lake City in 1847. Mormons attempted to enter the Union as the State of Deseret; they were finally admitted as the Territory of Utah in 1850.

Utah early came into conflict with federal authorities over the practice of polygamy, which had been outlawed by the United States in 1862. The Edmunds Bill took citizenship away from polygamists, and in 1890 the court declared their church property forfeited. This forced the Mormons into accepting monogamist laws. Thereupon Utah was admitted to the Union as the forty-fifth state, on January 4, 1896.

Government. The Utah legislature consists of a senate of 28 members and a house of representatives of 69 members. The governor is elected for four years. There is no office of lieutenant-governor. Utah is represented in the U.S. Congress by two senators and two representatives. The state is divided into 29 counties, and in 1970 there were 15 cities and towns with a population of more than ten thousand.

Utah—Temple Square in Salt Lake City

Economy. The raising of sheep and the production of wool are a leading agricultural industry. Most farming in Utah is done by irrigation, although some dry farming is practiced. Utah is primarily a mining state, ranking sixteenth in the nation. The state is second in asphalt production, and also in copper, gold, silver, molybdenum, and vanadium; third in uranium, lead, and potassium salts; fourth in iron ore.

VERMONT

Samuel de Champlain was the first European to see Vermont. He discovered Lake Champlain in 1609. The first settlement was made by the French on La Motte Island in Lake Champlain in 1666. Fort Dummer (now Brattleboro) was the site of the first English settlement, established in 1724 by colonists from Massachusetts.

The early history of Vermont centers on the disputes over the Mason Land Grants and the earlier charter grants by both England and France. Later, the charters of both New Hampshire and Massachusetts included parts of the present Vermont. This conflict was settled in favor of New Hampshire in 1740. But the New Hampshire colony inherited a dispute with New York that had been in progress over the eastern boundary of New York. The king was asked to decide and did so—in favor of New York. The latter colony ignored the claims and rights of settlers who had purchased their lands from New Hampshire. Armed conflict resulted, especially at Bennington (now in Vermont).

In 1775, a convention met at Westminster and declared for independence, and a second convention declared for an independent state to be called New Connecticut. A third convention in 1777 changed the name of the region to Vermont. Be-

Vermont—The State House, Montpelier

cause of bitter opposition from New York and New Hampshire, Vermont was denied statehood for 14 years. The Vermonters were finally able to settle claims of both the other states and on March 4, 1791, Vermont became the first state to be admitted to the Union after the original 13 states had ratified the federal Constitution. During the War for Independence, Vermont fought independently and was for a time seeking an independent peace. But eventually it joined the other former colonies in the peace negotiations. The capture of Fort Ticonderoga (in New York) by Vermont hero Ethan Allen and his Green Mountain Boys was one of the major events of the war.

Government. The state legislature consists of a senate of 30 members and a house of representatives of 150 members. Vermont sends two senators and one representative to the U.S. Congress. The state is divided into 14 counties and 246 towns and cities (*see* Maine for a note on "town" and on New England counties). In 1970 there were eight cities with a population of more than ten thousand, and 47 cities and towns with a population of more than twenty-five hundred.

Economy. Manufacturing is the principal industry, although tourism and recreation have become much more important in recent years. Vermont leads in maple syrup production. Other crops grown are potatoes, oats, apples, and hay. Granite is the principal mineral produced, although the state is the number one producer of asbestos.

VIRGINIA

Virginia is one of the 13 original states. It was settled under a charter issued in 1606 by King James I. The first permanent settlement (at Jamestown in 1607) was established only after several unsuccessful attempts (*see* North Carolina).

The first legislative assembly in the Western Hemisphere, the House of Burgesses, convened in Jamestown in 1619. In 1622, Indians massacred nearly one-third of the settlement's inhabitants. In 1624, Virginia was made a crown colony.

After a revolution in England had overthrown the king and Cromwell had assumed the powers of government, Virginia obtained a new charter of self-government. However, the colony reverted to the crown when Charles II came to power. An era

Virginia—Houdon Statue of George Washington, in the State Capitol, Richmond

of prosperity in Virginia ensued, based mainly on the growing of tobacco on the Tidewater plantations, using slave labor.

The Navigation Acts of 1660 and 1663 ushered in a period of remonstrance and protest that foreshadowed the Revolution which came a century later. The Navigation Acts imposed unwanted restrictions upon Virginia's trade. Soon after, Governor Sir William Berkeley placed drastic limitations upon democratic government and the House of Burgesses. This led to Bacon's Rebellion of 1676. Savage reprisals and brutal hangings by Berkeley ended the rebellion. In 1699, during the reign of William and Mary in England, the Virginia capital was removed to Middle Plantation, and that town's name was changed to Williamsburg. Williamsburg became one of the great social, cultural, and political centers of American life. The city declined after removal of the capital to Richmond in 1780. In 1927 the restoration of Williamsburg to its original condition was begun and has been nearly completed at a cost, so far, of more than sixty-eight million dollars.

By 1763, Virginia was moving toward revolution and independence. Virginians disputed the Hillsborough Proclamation of 1763, prohibiting settlement of Virginians beyond the crest of the Allegheny Mountains in the west. England asserted Parliament's right to legislate for the colonies. This brought a series of events that led to war.

Virginia took the lead among the colonies and provided most of the leaders in the war that resulted. The rise of Virginia politicians and farmers to the status of great American statesmen was exemplified in the careers of Jefferson, Richard Henry Lee, Patrick Henry, Madison, Pendleton, Randolph, Mason, Washington, and others. The Colonial Assembly adjourned on June 20, 1775, and never met again.

The Second Continental Congress elected George Washington commander in chief on June 14, 1775. He proceeded to Cambridge, Massachusetts, to take control of the army (*see* Massachusetts).

Virginia's second governor, Thomas Jefferson, wrote the Declaration of Independence for the colonies. George Mason drafted the Declaration of Rights—the model for the Bill of Rights that was later added to the United States Constitution. "Light Horse Harry" Lee, Daniel Morgan, John Paul Jones, George Rogers Clark, and George Washington all took leading parts in fierce battles that led to victory. Virginia became the tenth state on June 25, 1788. The state gave up its claims to the vast region west of the mountains and north of the Ohio River.

Upon the outbreak of the Civil War in 1861, Virginia decided upon secession. Again the state provided great leaders in such men as Robert E. Lee, "Stonewall" Jackson, J. E. B. Stuart, and Joseph E. Johnston. The critical battles of the war were fought in Virginia, and the capture of Richmond (the Confederate capital from April 1861) was the primary object of the boldest strikes made during the war by Union commanders. Virginia was the battlefield upon which the South's greatest victories were won. But it was also at Appomattox, Virginia that General Lee was forced to surrender, ending one of the bloodiest wars in the history of the world up to that time.

Government. In 1776, the House of Burgesses was converted into the General Assembly of two houses, the senate, presently made up of 40 members, and the house of delegates, now having 100 members. The governor and lieutenant-governor are elected for four years. The state sends two senators and 10 representatives to the U.S. Congress. As of 1963, the state was divided into 96 counties and 35 independent cities which have the status of counties. In 1970 there were 29 cities and towns having a population of more than ten thousand.

Economy. Coal is the most important mineral, including high-grade coking coal. Lead, stone, gypsum, manganese, lime, and titanium are also produced. The state has diversified agriculture, but livestock-raising and tobacco-growing are leading activities. Tobacco is the leading cash crop today, just as it was in colonial times.

WASHINGTON

The early history of Washington is that of the Oregon country (*see* Oregon). American interests grew strong and came in conflict with those of the British after the overland expedition of Lewis and Clark (1804–1806). An agreement between England and the United States in 1818 allowed both nations to occupy the region. The United States advanced its claim to the Columbia River basin during the presidential campaign of James K. Polk in 1844. The dispute was arbitrated in 1846 and a treaty was signed, establishing the boundary of Oregon on the forty-ninth parallel of latitude, which is the present international boundary. Later, a dispute over the San Juan Islands was also arbitrated and settled.

In 1848, Oregon Territory was formed, and it included the present state of Washington. In 1853, Washington Territory was separated and organized. Agitation for statehood began in 1876 and ended when Washington was admitted to the Union as the forty-second state on November 11, 1889.

Washington—Olympic National Park

Government. The legislature consists of a senate of 49 members and a house of representatives of 99 members. The governor and lieutenant-governor are elected for four-year terms. Washington sends two senators and seven representatives to the U.S. Congress. The state is divided into 39 counties, and in 1970, there were 39 cities and towns with a population of more than ten thousand. The city of Seattle, largest in the state, ranks twenty-second in the nation.

Economy. Because the state has the greatest potential power supplies, the aluminum industry was attracted there. Vast forests of principally hemlock, fir, and pine make the forestry industries among the largest in the nation. The manufacture of wood products, including paper and pulp, is the largest single industry in Washington, and the state ranks third in this field. Agriculture is also a major industry, with much of it practiced on irrigated lands. Western Washington has large dairy farms and berry fields, while in the east the growing of wheat and ranching are the chief agricultural industries. Washington leads all states in the production of apples, hops, mint; ranks second in Bartlett pears, filberts, apricots; fourth in winter wheat.

WEST VIRGINIA

West Virginia is the youngest state east of the Mississippi River. It was originally a part of Virginia. But when that state seceded from the Union in 1861, the western counties (most of the present state of West Virginia) seceded from Virginia. By a proclamation of President Lincoln on June 20, 1863, these counties were admitted to the Union as the thirty-fifth state.

West Virginia—Capitol Building, Charleston

Government. West Virginia is governed by a senate with 34 members and a house of delegates with 100 members. The state sends two senators and four representatives to the U.S. Congress and has six electoral votes in federal elections. There is no lieutenant-governor. The major unit of local government is the county. West Virginia is divided into 55 counties.

Economy. Coal underlies nearly two-thirds of the state. West Virginia has led the nation in the mining of coal since 1936. Over a hundred million tons are mined every year, accounting for 80 percent of the state's total mineral production. Other minerals produced include petroleum, natural gas, salt, and limestone.

Although there are about seven million acres of farm land, only about one million acres are in crops. Sixty-five percent of the state is in woodlands, including nearly a million acres of national forests. The chief crops grown in West Virginia include tobacco, fruit, wheat, corn, oats, and potatoes. The eastern panhandle is a noted apple-growing region.

Manufacturing in West Virginia is centered in the valley of the Kanawha River and along the Ohio River. The Kanawha Valley is one of the major chemical-producing areas of the United States.

WISCONSIN

Wisconsin was explored by the French from bases in Canada. Jean Nicolet visited eastern Wisconsin in 1534. A fuller exploration was conducted by the traders Radisson and Groseilliers (1658–1659). Father Allouez established a mission near the present Green Bay in 1665. The first permanent settlement was made near the same place in 1670. The entire state was a part of New France until the French defeat in 1763. The sympathies of the early settlers were generally with the English, and they retained this allegiance during the Revolutionary War.

The United States acquired Wisconsin as a result of the Treaty of Paris in 1783, ending the war and establishing American independence. The region was included in the Ordinance of 1787, establishing the Northwest Territory. When Indiana

Territory was separated from this in 1800, Wisconsin was included in Indiana. In 1805, it became a part of Michigan Territory, and from 1808 until 1818 it was a part of Illinois Territory. Wisconsin was again transferred to Michigan Territory after Illinois became a state in 1818, and there it remained until 1836. In that year Wisconsin Territory was organized, thus ending a complicated series of changes in government. At that time Wisconsin Territory included parts of Minnesota, Iowa, and the Dakotas. Iowa was separated in 1838. On May 29, 1848, Wisconsin became the thirtieth state and was reduced to its present boundaries.

Government. The law-making body is called the Legislature, as in most states, and consists of a senate of 32 members and an assembly of 100 members. The governor and lieutenant-governor are elected for four years. The state sends two senators and nine representatives to the U.S. Congress. Wisconsin is divided into 72 counties (Menominee became the seventy-second county in 1961). In 1970 there were 52 cities and towns with a population of more than ten thousand. Milwaukee, the state's largest city, ranks twelfth in the nation.

Economy. Wisconsin is famous for its dairy products, but agriculture has recently been surpassed in importance by the rising industrial complexes centering around Milwaukee and the southeast. Although the state has little coal, about 85 percent of the nation's iron ore is within easy reach in the Greak Lakes area and the lakes themselves form a major transportation route for incoming raw materials and outgoing finished products. The fabrication of iron and steel products is the largest industry. Textiles, footwear, furniture, chemicals, and shipbuilding are other major manufactures. In agriculture, the dairying industry is concentrated in the southern counties. In 1970 the state ranked first in milk and cheese and second in creamery butter. The principal crops are those used in feeding cattle, such as corn, oats, and hay. The best cash crop is potatoes, grown mainly in northern Wisconsin.

Wisconsin—Ancient quartzite cliffs overlooking Devils Lake, Baraboo

WYOMING

Chevalier de la Verendrye, a member of a remarkable family of Canadian explorers passed through the Wyoming Wind River region in 1743–1744. Wilson Hunt explored the Powder River on his way to Oregon in 1811. John Colter spent the winter of 1806–1807 in Wyoming, and discovered the Yellowstone region. In 1842 John C. Fremont ascended Fremont Peak in Wind River Range, accompanied by Kit Carson. The first white settlement in Wyoming was made in 1834 at Fort William (later changed to Fort Laramie) by William Sublette and Robert Campbell. This post was sold to the United States government in 1849. Part of the Mormon migration to Utah (*see* Utah) stopped in Wyoming and settled at Fort Bridger in 1853.

Wyoming came to the United States in three sections. The greater part was included in the Louisiana Purchase of 1803. More was added by the settlement of the Oregon dispute in 1846, and Mexico ceded the remainder in 1848 as a result of the Treaty of Guadalupe Hidalgo.

The discovery of gold in 1867 and the completion of the Union Pacific Railroad in Wyoming in 1868 caused a wave of settlement. The Territory of Wyoming was organized in 1868 from parts of Utah, the Dakota Territory, and Idaho Territory. The great natural wonders of the Yellowstone region were set aside as a national park in 1872 (the oldest national nature park). Wyoming became the forty-fourth state on July 10, 1890.

Government. The legislature consists of a senate of 30 members and a house of representatives of 61 members. The governor is elected for a four-year term. There is no office of lieutenant-governor in Wyoming. The Territory of Wyoming was the first government under the American flag to guarantee equal suffrage to women (in 1869). The state sends two senators and one representative to the U.S. Congress. Wyoming is divided into 23 counties, and in 1970 there were five cities with a population of more than ten thousand.

Economy. Many of the soils of the state are very fertile and produce well when water is provided. About two million acres of land are already under irrigation, and more is planned to be placed under irrigation. Wyoming's agriculture revolves around the cattle industry and sheep-raising. The chief mineral produced is oil. Natural gas is also found in large quantities and uranium has recently become a major mineral product.

Wyoming—Thousands of Oregon Trail travelers carved their names on Register Cliff near Guernsey (Inset shows actual names)

Districts, Commonwealths, Possessions, and Trust Areas Of the United States

Besides the District of Columbia and the Commonwealth of Puerto Rico, this section includes lands and peoples associated with the United States in the form of possessions, territories, or trust areas. At some time in the future these areas may become one of the United States.

DISTRICT OF COLUMBIA

The District of Columbia is the seat of government and the location of the federal capital of the United States. It is limited to the city of Washington.

Rivalry developed between northern and southern congressmen over the location of the nation's capital. The institution of slavery was one issue in the arguments. Finally, in 1790, Alexander Hamilton and Thomas Jefferson worked out a compromise.

The District of Columbia was organized from lands ceded by Maryland and Virginia. The District then was a perfect square, measuring ten miles along each of the four sides. However, in 1846 the part ceded originally by Virginia and lying across the south bank of the Potomac River was returned to Virginia, and now forms Arlington County of that State.

In 1791, President Washington chose the exact site for the Capitol Building and the city of Washington. He then commissioned Pierre L'Enfant, a French engineer, to design a layout for the city of Washington. L'Enfant's ideas for wide avenues and streets were considered wasteful by many, but Washington approved the plans himself and laid the cornerstone of the Capitol Building on September 18, 1793. President John Adams, Washington's successor, was the first President to serve the nation from the new capital. He moved from Philadelphia to Washington on June 3, 1800. The city of Washington was incorporated in 1802.

The original Capitol Building was burned (along with the White House) by the British during the War of 1812. Both the present White House and Capitol Building date from 1818. The Capitol was not actually completed until 1863.

The White House is the official residence of the President. The cornerstone of the original building was laid by Washington on October 13, 1792. Extensive alterations have been made, in 1902–1903 under President Theodore Roosevelt and in 1948–1952 under President Truman. A major redecorating project was carried out under Jacqueline Kennedy in 1963.

The Capitol is one of the chief attractions of the District of Columbia. It crowns the summit of Capitol Hill, 88 feet above the level of the Potomac River. It covers four acres and its height is 287 feet, 5.5 inches. The original plan was drawn by Dr. William Thornton of the Virgin Islands. Benjamin Latrobe and Charles Bulfinch had charge of repair and reconstruction after the British burning of the building in 1814. The present Senate and House wings were added in 1851. The bronze statue of Freedom on top of the great dome is 19.5 feet tall, and weighs 15,000 pounds. The rotunda is 180 feet high and has a diameter of 97 feet.

Government. The city of Washington (District of Columbia) is governed by a mayor, an assistant, and a 13-member city council elected by the district's voters. The district has one Delegate to the House who may vote in committees but not on the floor. Amendment Twenty-three to the Constitution of the United States gave the citizens of the District the right to vote in national elections. This amendment was ratified by the requisite number of states and became law in 1961.

Buildings and Monuments. The Lincoln Memorial in West Potomac Park was dedicated in 1922. Its famous statue of President Lincoln was the work of Daniel Chester French. The memorial is of Colorado-Yule marble. The wells are enclosed by a colonnade of 38 Doric columns. Inside are three memorials—a seated figure of Lincoln, a passage from Lincoln's Second Inaugural Address, and his Gettysburg Address.

The Thomas Jefferson Memorial was dedicated in 1943. Its central circular chamber is occupied by a huge statue of Jefferson. The building incorporates pantheonic design of Vermont and Georgia marble.

The Washington National Monument is an obelisk of white marble 555.5 feet tall. It was

District of Columbia—Capitol Building, Washington, D.C.

begun in 1848 and completed in 1885. An elevator takes visitors to the 500-foot level.

Other famous buildings and monuments in the District include the National Archives, Smithsonian Institution, the National Geographic Society, the Folger Shakespeare Library, and the National Gallery of Art. In nearby Arlington are the Pentagon, the Iwo Jima Memorial, the Tomb of the Unknown Soldier, and the Custis-Lee Mansion (the last two are in Arlington National Cemetery).

Economy. Most of the people either work for the federal Government or are in wholesale and retail businesses. There are six hundred manufacturing firms in the District. Printing and publishing is the largest single industry.

Outlying U.S. Areas

AMERICAN SAMOA

These comprise the seven eastern islands of the Samoa group in the South Pacific, 2,300 miles southwest of Hawaii. They became a United States territory in 1900. The larger islands of the Samoan group (Western Samoa) form an independent nation. Administered by the Interior Department, American Samoa elects its own governor, bicameral legislature and a non-voting delegate to Congress. Chief port is Pago Pago (pronounced "Pango Pango") but the seat of government is the nearby town of Fagatogo on the Island of Tutuila.

The islands are of volcanic origin; they have a mild climate with a distinct dry season, and are heavily forested. The people are Polynesians. The chief exports are canned fish, *copra* (dried coconut), cocoa, and handicrafts.

COMMONWEALTH OF PUERTO RICO

(Estado Libre Asociado de Puerto Rico)

The spelling *Porto Rico* is today unacceptable, having been replaced by *Puerto Rico* by an Act of Congress in 1932. Columbus discovered Puerto Rico in 1493. The famous Ponce de León (*see* Florida) founded San Juan in either 1506 or 1508. The chief purpose was to protect Mona Passage, which at that time was the principal gateway to the Spanish possessions that lay in and along the Caribbean Sea.

San Juan was fortified early because of raids and sieges by English buccaneers. Dutch warships also attacked the town and destroyed a large part of it in 1625. La Fortaleza, El Morro, and San Cristóbal are three fortresses that were built at various times as a means of defense. Puerto Rico remained a Spanish possession until 1898.

The Treaty of Paris in 1898 ended the Spanish-American War and ceded Puerto Rico (along with Guam and the Philippines) to the United States. The troops led by General Nelson Miles had captured the island without serious fighting on July 25, 1898.

The territorial status of Puerto Rico was determined by the Jones Act of 1917; this status was retained until July 25, 1952, when the Commonwealth of Puerto Rico was proclaimed.

Government. The commonwealth form of government is defined as a "compact," establishing an association between the United States and Puerto Rico. The electorate chooses a delegate (resident commissioner) who sits in the U.S. House of Representatives, but has no vote. The citizens of Puerto Rico are citizens of the United States and subject to most of the same national laws, except the internal revenue statutes. Puerto Rico is not subject to United States taxes, including income tax.

The commonwealth is autonomous in local government. The executive power is vested in a governor, elected for four years. The Council of Secretaries (10 members) advises the governor. The legislature consists of a senate of 27 members and a house of representatives of 51 members. Spanish is the mother language, but English is widely spoken and its use is growing. All instruction below high-school level is given in Spanish.

Economy. Manufacturing is the leading industry. Textiles and apparel, plastics and chemicals, and electronic equipment are among the leading products. The processing of sugar cane is still an important industry but the income from dairy and livestock products is now greater. Tourism is also a large revenue producer.

San Juan is the chief port of entry by both air and water. The city is the governmental, cultural, and industrial heart of Puerto Rico. The chief agricultural crop is sugar cane; coffee, tobacco, and pineapples are next in importance, in that order. Eighty-seven percent of all trade is with the United States mainland.

GUAM

This is the largest and southernmost island of the Marianas group, located south of Japan and east of the Philippines. The island is not a part of the United States Trust Territory of the Pacific Islands, but serves as headquarters for the administration of that territory. One of the largest United States military installations in the Pacific is located on Guam. Under the administration of the Interior Department, Guam elects its own governor, legislature, and one delegate to the United States House of Representatives who can vote in committee but not on the floor. Residents who are American citizens cannot vote in presidential elections. It was discovered by Magellan in 1521 and acquired by the United States in 1898 as a result of the Spanish-American War. It was captured by the Japanese in 1941 but was regained after bitter fighting in 1944. It was then used as a base for B-29 bomber raids against Japan.

NORTHERN MARIANAS

Extending in a 500-mile arc east of the Philippines and southeast of Japan, the Mariana islands (with the exception of Guam, which is separate) are in process of becoming a United States commonwealth like Puerto Rico. They were formerly part of the United States Trust Territory of the Pacific Islands but they have already elected their own governor and legislature. Military bases on the islands are important for United States defense.

TRUST TERRITORY OF THE PACIFIC ISLANDS

Assigned to United States administration by the United Nations, this group of almost 2,000 islands, 98 of them inhabited, is scattered over three million square miles in the western Pacific Ocean. Often called Micronesia, they consist of the Caroline and Marshall islands, including some noted for World War II battles (Truk, Enewetak, and Kwajalein) and as nuclear testing sites (Bikini). Negotiations are underway for full self-government, with the United States retaining responsibility for defense. When this happens the UN will end the trusteeship of the United States.

UNINCORPORATED TERRITORIES

Howland, Jarvis, and Baker Islands are south of Hawaii, uninhabited since World War II, and are under the Interior Department.

Johnston Atoll, southwest of Hawaii, is operated by the Nuclear Defense Agency. It has a population of 300 on one square mile. An atoll is an island formed by coral deposits.

The Midway islands consist of two coral atolls at the northwestern end of the Hawaiian chain of islands. They served as a "China Clipper" transoceanic flight base before World War II. During the war the Japanese were defeated in the great Battle of Midway in June 1942. Consisting of two square miles, with a population of 2,256, they are administered by the United States Navy.

Wake Island, the scene of a great World War II

battle in 1945, is on a direct route from Hawaii to Hong Kong. With its sister islands of Wilkes and Peale, it is administered by the United States Air Force.

VIRGIN ISLANDS

The United States' group comprise about 50 islands in the West Indies just east of Puerto Rico. They were discovered by Columbus in 1493, and acquired by the United States from Denmark in 1917. The people, mainly of African origin, have been United States citizens since 1927. St. Croix, the largest island, has a jet airport. St. Thomas Island is the site of the capital. Tourism is the most important industry. The making of rum, raising of cattle, and growing of sugar cane are also important. The chief export is rum. A 1972 law allows the people to elect one delegate to the United States House of Representatives who can vote in committee but not on the floor.

CANAL ZONE

The Canal Zone is no longer an outlying territory of the United States. Two treaties signed by the United States and the Republic of Panama in 1978 dealt with the operation and defense of the Canal Zone until 1999 and with the guarantee of its permanent neutrality. At that time Panama assumed general territorial jurisdiction over the former Canal Zone. The United States maintains control over the land, water and installations of the canal itself, including military bases necessary to operate and defend the zone, until December 31, 1999. Until 1990 the canal administrator is a United States citizen with a Panamanian deputy. After that, until 1999, the administrator will be a Panamanian with the deputy being a United States citizen.

The building of the Panama Canal was one of the greatest engineering projects in all history. Plans for a canal across the Isthmus of Panama had been put forward even before Columbus died. Plans were made on several occasions, down to the nineteenth century.

It remained for the French to actually begin the work. Ferdinand de Lesseps headed the construction of the Suez Canal, which opened in 1869. He was a national hero in France because of his success, and when he proposed the Panama project he received enthusiastic support.

The problems in Panama were vastly more difficult to overcome than in the Suez project. The French effort ended after an expenditure of 300 million dollars. The De Lesseps project began on New Year's Day, 1880, and ended in bankruptcy in 1888.

In 1903, the United States signed a treaty with Colombia to acquire land and construction rights in the Isthmus of Panama, which was a part of Colombia at that time. However, Colombia balked at the terms of the treaty, which led to a local revolution against Colombia. A treaty with an independent Panama was then signed, granting the United States sovereignty over a Canal Zone. In 1921, Colombia accepted 25 million dollars as compensation for the loss of Panama, and established relations with the new republic in 1924 (see Panama).
tion for the loss of Panama, and established relations with the new republic in 1924 (*see* Panama).

The United States began construction in 1904, using some of the partially excavated route of the French project. However, the cost ran to almost 400 million dollars. The canal was opened to traffic on August 15, 1914.

Statistics for the United States

NAME OF STATE (ZIP CODE ABBREVIATION) NICKNAME	POPULATION RANK IN POP. AREA (SQ. MI.) RANK IN AREA	CAPITAL* LARGEST CITY	BIRD FLOWER	DESCRIPTION OF FLAG
Alabama (AL) Heart of Dixie Cotton State	3,990,000 22 51,609 29	Montgomery* 178,157 Birmingham 284,413	Yellowhammer Camellia	A crimson St. Andrew's cross on a square white field
Alaska (AK) No official nickname	500,000 50 586,412 1	Juneau* 19,528 Anchorage 173,017	Willow ptarmigan Forget-me-not	A deep blue field with seven gold stars in the shape of the Big Dipper constellation at the left and a single gold star representing Polaris in the upper right-hand corner.
Arizona (AZ) Grand Canyon State	3,053,000 29 113,909 6	Phoenix* 764,911	Cactus wren The blossom of the saguaro cactus	The lower half is a blue field; the upper half is composed of red and yellow rays, emanating from a large, copper-colored five-pointed star superimposed on the center of the flag.
Arkansas (AR) Land of Opportunity	2,349,000 33 53,104 27	Little Rock* 158,461	Mockingbird Apple blossom	A white diamond outlined in blue centered on a red field; twenty-five white stars arranged around the blue border of the diamond indicate Arkansas' position as the twenty-fifth state to enter the Union; within the white diamond are four large blue stars and the word "Arkansas"; three of these stars, placed below "Arkansas," signify the three nations of Spain, France, and the United States, to which Arkansas successively belonged; the star above "Arkansas" commemorates the Confederacy, and the diamond itself signifies that Arkansas is the only diamond-producing state in the Union.
California (CA) Golden State	25,622,000 1 158,693 3	Sacramento* 275,741 Los Angeles 2,966,763	California valley quail Golden poppy	A California grizzly bear set in the center of a white field; at the top left is a red star; below the bear the words "California Republic" appear above a broad red stripe. Known as the Bear Flag.
Colorado (CO) Centennial State	3,178,000 27 104,247 8	Denver* 491,396	Lark bunting White and lavender Rocky Mountain columbine	Three equal stripes, two of which are blue, representing the sky, and one white, representing snow-capped mountains; on the left is a red "C" encircling a disk of yellow.
Connecticut (CT) Constitution State Nutmeg State	3,154,000 26 5,009 48	Hartford* 136,392 Bridgeport 142,546	Robin Mountain laurel	A blue background with a white shield bearing the state seal in the center; beneath the shield is the state motto; the flag is bordered with a gold fringe.
Delaware (DE) First State Diamond State	613,000 47 2,057 49	Dover* 23, 512 Wilmington 70,195	Blue hen chicken Peach blossom	A buff-colored diamond bearing the state seal is placed in the center of a blue field; below the diamond are the words "December 7, 1787," the date when Delaware ratified the Constitution of the United States.
Florida (FL) Sunshine State	10,976,000 7 58,560 22	Tallahassee* 81,548 Jacksonville 540,898	Mockingbird Orange blossom	The state seal lies in the center of a white field, crossed by diagonal red bars, which stand for the bars of the Confederate flag.
Georgia (GA) Empire State of the South Peach State	5,837,000 12 58,876 21	Atlanta* 425,022	Brown thrasher Cherokee rose	A combination of an earlier flag with a field of blue containing the state seal, and the battle flag of the Confederacy with its field of red containing crossed blue bars and thirteen white stars.
Hawaii (HI) The Aloha State	1,039,000 39 6,450 47	Honolulu* 365,048	Nene (Hawaiian goose) Hibiscus	Eight horizontal stripes which, from the top, are alternately white, red, and blue; in the upper left-hand corner is the British Union Jack.
Idaho (ID) Gem State	1,001,000 40 83,557 13	Boise* 102,451	Mountain bluebird Syringa	A dark-blue field bordered by a gold fringe; in the center is the state seal; below this a red band contains the words "State of Idaho" in gold.
Illinois (IL) The Inland Empire	11,511,000 5 56,400 24	Springfield* 99,637 Chicago 3,005,072	Cardinal Violet	In the center of a white field fringed in gold is a symbol based on the state seal.
Indiana (IN) Hoosier State	5,498,000 14 36,291 38	Indianapolis* 700,807	Cardinal Peony	A flaming torch in gold against a blue field surrounded by a circle of thirteen stars; below is a semicircle of five stars; above the torch is a larger star and the word "Indiana."

NAME OF STATE (ZIP CODE ABBREVIATION) NICKNAME	POPULATION RANK IN POP. AREA (SQ. MI.) RANK IN AREA	CAPITAL* LARGEST CITY	BIRD FLOWER	DESCRIPTION OF FLAG
Iowa (IA) Hawkeye State	2,910,000 28 56,290 25	Des Moines* 191,003	Eastern goldfinch Wild rose	A white field bordered on the staff end by a blue band and on the opposite end by a red band: centered in the white field is an eagle bearing the state motto.
Kansas (KS) Sunflower State	2,438,000 32 82,264 14	Topeka* 115,266 Wichita 279,272	Western meadowlark Sunflower	The flag has a wreath above the seal to represent the Louisiana Purchase. The yellow sunflower stands for the state's prairies and for the golden future.
Kentucky (KY) Bluegrass State	3,723,000 23 40,395 37	Frankfort* 25,973 Louisville 298,451	Cardinal Goldenrod	The center of the state seal on a field of blue; the words "Commonwealth of Kentucky" appear in gold around the top half of the seal, and a garland of goldenrod is below the seal; the flag is fringed in gold.
Louisiana (LA) Pelican State	4,462,000 18 48,523 31	Baton Rouge* 219,486 New Orleans 557,482	Brown pelican Magnolia	In the center of a blue field is a white pelican feeding its young; beneath the pelican is a white ribbon inscribed in blue with the state motto.
Maine (ME) Pine Tree State	1,156,000 38 32,215 39	Augusta* 21,819 Portland 61,572	Chick-a-dee Pine cone and tassel	The state seal lies in the center of a blue field.
Maryland (MD) Old Line State Free State	4,349,000 19 10,577 42	Annapolis* 31,740 Baltimore 786,775	Baltimore oriole Black-eyed Susan	Bears the coats of arms of the Calvert and Crossland families, Crossland being the maiden name of the wife of the first Lord Baltimore. The Maryland flag is the only state flag embodying recognized armorial bearings.
Massachusetts (MA) Bay State Old Colony	5,798,000 11 8,257 45	Boston* 562,994	Chick-a-dee Mayflower (ground laurel or trailing arbutus)	One side bears the state coat of arms on a white field; the reverse has a white field in the center of which is a blue shield bearing a green pine tree.
Michigan (MI) Great Lake State Wolverine State	9,075,000 8 58,216 23	Lansing* 130,414 Detroit 1,203,339	Robin Apple blossom	The symbols of the state seal appear on a dark-blue field.
Minnesota (MN) North Star State Gopher State	4,162,000 21 84,068 12	St. Paul* 270,230 Minneapolis 370,951	Loon Pink and white lady's-slipper	The state seal is placed in the center of a blue field.
Mississippi (MS) Magnolia State	2,598,000 31 47,716 32	Jackson* 202,895	Mockingbird Magnolia	In the upper left-hand corner is a Union Jack with a ground of red and saltier of blue bearing thirteen white stars; the remainder of the flag is divided into three horizontal bars of equal width, the upper blue, the center white, and the lower red.
Missouri (MO) Show Me State	5,000,000 15 69,686 19	Jefferson City* 33,619 St. Louis 453,085	Bluebird Hawthorn	Three horizontal bands of equal width, the top one of red, the center one of white, and the bottom one of blue; in the middle is the state seal surrounded by a band of blue bearing twenty-four white stars.
Montana (MT) Treasure State	824,000 44 147,138 4	Helena* 23,938 Billings 66,798	Western meadowlark Bitterroot	The state seal is centered on a bright blue field; gold fringe borders the upper and lower edges.
Nebraska (NE) Cornhusker State	1,606,000 35 77,227 15	Lincoln* 171,932 Omaha 311,681	Western meadowlark Goldenrod	The state seal is gold and silver against a blue field.
Nevada (NV) Sagebrush State Battle Born State	911,000 43 110,540 7	Carson City* 32,022 Las Vegas 164,674	No official state bird; however, the mountain bluebird is used. No official flower; however, the sagebrush is sometimes used.	Two sprays of green sagebrush with stems crossed at the bottom to form a half-wreath in the upper left-hand corner of a field of cobalt blue; above, and completing the circle, is a yellow scroll bearing the words "Battle Born"; centered in the circle is a five-pointed star surrounded by the word "Nevada."

NAME OF STATE (ZIP CODE ABBREVIATION) NICKNAME	POPULATION RANK IN POP. AREA (SQ. MI.) RANK IN AREA	CAPITAL* LARGEST CITY	BIRD FLOWER	DESCRIPTION OF FLAG
New Hampshire (NH) Granite State	977,000 42 9,304 44	Concord* 30,400 Manchester 90,936	Purple finch Purple lilac	A blue field on which is centered the state seal surrounded by laurel leaves interspersed with nine stars.
New Jersey (NJ) Garden State	7,515,000 9 7,836 46	Trenton* 92,124 Newark 329,248	Eastern goldfinch Purple violet	The state seal is centered on a buff-colored field.
New Mexico (NM) Land of Enchantment	1,424,000 37 121,666 5	Santa Fe* 48,899 Albuquerque 331,767	Roadrunner Yucca flower	A field of gold with the ancient Zia Sun symbol in red in the center.
New York (NY) Empire State	17,735,000 2 49,576 30	Albany* 101,727 New York 7,071,030	Bluebird (unofficial) Rose	The state seal lies in the center of a dark-blue field.
North Carolina (NC) Tar Heel State Old North State	6,165,000 10 52,586 28	Raleigh* 149,771 Charlotte 314,447	Cardinal Dogwood	At the right are two horizontal stripes, one red and one white; on the left is a vertical blue stripe; at the top of the vertical stripe is a gold scroll inscribed with the date "May 20 1775" commemorating the Mecklenburg Declaration of Independence; at the bottom, in another golden scroll is the date "April 12th 1776," commemorating the Halifax Resolves, which instructed North Carolina's delegates to the Continental Congress to vote for independence; in the center, between these two scrolls, are the initials "N" and "C" separated by a white star.
North Dakota (ND) Sioux State Flickertail State	686,000 46 70,665 17	Bismarck* 44,485 Fargo 61,308	Western meadowlark Wild prairie rose	On a field of blue a bald eagle with widespread wings holds a group of arrows in its left claw and an olive branch in its right claw; in its beak is a scroll that reads "*E Pluribus Unum*"; beneath the eagle on a red scroll are the words, "North Dakota"; above the eagle is a double semicircle of stars representing the original thirteen states.
Ohio (OH) Buckeye State	10,752,000 6 41,222 35	Columbus* 564,871 Cleveland 573,822	Cardinal Scarlet carnation	A swallow-tailed pennant bearing three red and two white horizontal stripes; on the left is a blue union, on which seventeen stars are disposed about a white "O" centered on red.
Oklahoma (OK) Sooner State	3,298,000 25 69,919 18	Oklahoma City* 403,213	Scissor-tailed flycatcher Mistletoe	In the center of a blue field is the buckskin shield of an Osage Indiana warrior; the shield is decorated with six painted crosses; seven eagle feathers form a fringe at the bottom; a peace pipe crossed by an olive branch appears on the face of the shield.
Oregon (OR) Beaver State	2,674,000 30 96,981 10	Salem* 89,233 Portland 366,383	Western meadowlark Oregon grape	A navy blue field bearing the shield of the state seal in gold, supported by thirty-three gold stars and topped by the words "State of Oregon"; the reverse shows a gold beaver.
Pennsylvania (PA) Keystone State	11,901,000 4 45,333 33	Harrisburg* 53,264 Philadelphia 1,688,210	Ruffed grouse Mountain laurel	The state shield, with eagle and wreath, supported by two harnessed draft horses; streamers below the state motto; the field is dark blue.
Rhode Island (RI) Little Rhody Ocean State	962,000 41 1,214 50	Providence* 156,804	Rhode Island Red Violet (unofficial)	In the center of a white field is a gold anchor; beneath the anchor on a blue ribbon is the motto "Hope"; all this is surrounded by a circle of thirteen gold stars; the flag is edged with a yellow fringe.
South Carolina (SC) Palmetto State	6,165,000 24 31,055 40	Columbia* 99,296	Carolina wren Carolina jessamine	A field of blue with a white palmetto tree in the center and a white crescent in the upper corner near the staff.
South Dakota (SD) Coyote State Sunshine State	706,000 45 77,047 16	Pierre* 11,973 Sioux Falls 81,343	Ring-necked pheasant Pasqueflower	On a field of blue is a blazing sun surrounded by the words "South Dakota, The Sunshine State"; on the reverse is the state seal.
Tennessee (TN) Volunteer State	4,717,000 17 42,244 34	Nashville* 455,651 Memphis 646,356	Mockingbird Iris	In the center of a crimson field is a circle of blue with a rim of white; in the center of the circle are three white stars; on the edge are two vertical bars—one blue and one white.

NAME OF STATE (ZIP CODE ABBREVIATION) NICKNAME	POPULATION RANK IN POP. AREA (SQ. MI.) RANK IN AREA	CAPITAL* LARGEST CITY	BIRD FLOWER	DESCRIPTION OF FLAG
Texas (TX) Lone Star State	15,989,000 3 267,338 2	Austin* 345,496 Houston 1,594,086	Mockingbird Bluebonnet	A blue vertical stripe next to the staff and two horizontal stripes, the upper white and the lower red; a white star is in the center of the blue stripe.
Utah (UT) Beehive State	1,652,000 36 84,916 11	Salt Lake City* 163,033	Sea gull Sego lily	Within a gold circle in the center of a blue field is the state seal; the flag is fringed in gold.
Vermont (VT) Green Mountain State	530,000 48 9,609 43	Montpelier* 8,241 Burlington 37,712	Hermit thrush Red clover	The state coat of arms against a field of blue; the coat of arms contains a shield bearing a landscape scene with pine tree, cow, and sheaves of grain; a buck's head as the crest; a badge of crossed pine branches; and a red scroll bearing the state motto and the word "Vermont."
Virginia (VA) Old Dominion	5,636,000 13 40,817 36	Richmond* 219,214 Norfolk 266,979	Cardinal American dogwood	The state seal in the center of a deep blue field; a white fringe borders the edge farthest from the flagstaff.
Washington (WA) Evergreen State	4,349,000 20 68,192 20	Olympia* 27,447 Seattle 493,846	Willow goldfinch Rhododendron	A dark green field with the state seal in the center.
West Virginia (WV) Mountain State	1,952,000 34 24,181 41	Charleston* 63,963	Cardinal Rhododendron maximum (big laurel)	The state coat of arms (the central scene from the state seal) in a field of white bordered by a strip of blue; above the coat of arms is a ribbon bearing the words "State of West Virginia" and below is a wreath of rhododendron maximum.
Wisconsin (WI) Badger State	4,766,000 16 56,154 26	Madison* 170,616 Milwaukee 636,212	Robin Wood violet	The Wisconsin coat of arms is centered on a field of dark blue, the edges of which are trimmed with a knotted fringe of yellow silk.
Wyoming (WY) Equality State	511,000 49 97,914 9	Cheyenne* 47,283 Casper 51,016	Meadowlark Indian paintbrush	A white silhouetted buffalo in the center of the blue field with a border of white and an outer border of red; the state seal appears on the buffalo's side.
District of Columbia (DC)	631,000 67			

Statistics for Outlying United States' Areas

NAME OF OUTLYING AREA ZIP CODE ABBREVIATION	POPULATION	CAPITAL* LARGEST CITY	AREA (SQ. MI.)
American Samoa (AS)	32,297	Fagatogo* Island of Tutuila	76
Commonwealth of Puerto Rico (PR) (Estado Libre Asociado de Puerto Rico)	3,196,520	San Juan* 434,849	3,435
Guam (GU)	106,000	Agana* 4,180 Dededo 23,644	209
Johnston Atoll	300	None	1
Midway Islands	2,256	None	2
Northern Mariana Islands (CM)	16,758	None	181.9
Trust Territory of Pacific Islands (TT)	116,149	None	533
Virgin Islands (VI) (St John, St. Croix, St. Thomas)	96,569	Charlotte Amalie* on St. Thomas 11,671	133
Wake Island	300	None	3

Countries of the World

This section contains a brief history of each country of the world. Statistics will be found in the tables at the end of the section.

AFGHANISTAN

The history of Afghanistan is that of a succession of foreign conquests, by the Persians under Cyrus the Great in 516 B.C., and by Alexander the Great around 334 B.C. In the tenth century, the Turks, who brought Islamic culture with them, gained control. The Mongol hordes of Genghis Khan invaded and remained in power for two centuries. Later, another Mongol, Tamerlane, seized control.

In the seventeenth century, Afghans began a series of uprisings against foreign domination, and for centuries there was unrest in the country. An Anglo-Indian army invaded Afghanistan, precipitating the First Afghan War, lasting from 1838 to 1842, in which the Afghans were defeated. The British re-invaded the country in the Second Afghan War, in which the Afghans were again defeated. A new ruler stabilized the country, concluded treaties of demarcation with India and Russia, and curbed the power of tribal chiefs.

In 1919, while Britain was having difficulties with the liberation movement in India, Afghanistan seized the opportunity to declare war on England. Britain soon recognized Afghan independence. The country remained neutral in both world wars, and was admitted to the United Nations on November 19, 1946.

After a Soviet-backed coup in 1979, Babrak Kamal, a pro-Soviet leader, became Revolutionary Council President for the country. Since the coup, an estimated 60,000–100,000 Soviet troops continue to occupy the country, participating in guerrilla warfare.

ALBANIA

Albania occupies the region that the classical Greeks called Illyria. The Greeks were never able to conquer all of Illyria, but the Romans succeeded in doing so in the second century A.D. In later centuries, their control was never firmly established. The region of present Albania fell under the control of successive invaders, including Byzantines, Bulgars, Normans, Venetians, Neapolitans, and finally the Turks. Turkish control lasted from 1479 until 1912.

Independence movements began in 1878 and ended in 1912 when, after the First Balkan War, Albania was established as a nation. After World War I, the country gradually became an Italian protectorate. A threat to partition Albania resulted in the establishment of a republic under Ahmed Zog, who proclaimed himself king in 1928. In 1939 Italy annexed Albania.

During World War II, Albania became the base for an Italian invasion of Greece. Communist-led guerrillas under Enver Hoxha freed Albania with Allied assistance. In 1946 the country was declared a People's Republic. Relations with Yugoslavia became strained and were broken in 1948.

Albania's relations with the Soviet Union deteriorated until they were broken completely in 1961. Albania was admitted to the United Nations on December 14, 1955. In 1971, the country renewed diplomatic ties with Greece and Yugoslavia.

ALGERIA

The coast of North Africa was first colonized in historic times by Phoenicians from the Mediterranean coast of Asia. Carthage, one of the Phoenician cities, controlled the entire coast until the city's destruction by Rome in 146 B.C. Romans called the region Numidia. Roman culture and economic activity progressed in Numidia until it became a wealthy cultural center of the Roman world. Invasions by Vandals and revolts by the native inhabitants (Berbers) brought an end to Roman rule in the fifth century.

The Arab conquest took place in A.D. 637, and successive waves of Arabs swept over Algeria until after the eleventh century. The Berbers gradually accepted Islam but retained their own customs and language. Spain occupied parts of the coast in the sixteenth century but a Turkish pirate named Horuk Barbarossa expelled the Spaniards. Thereafter, piracy developed along the "Barbary Coast," as the region was called after the sixteenth century. Turkish control of the region was carried out

Algeria—The Harbor, Algiers

by a series of officials known according to their rank as beylerbeys, pashas, aghas, and deys. In the seventeenth century, the city of Algiers became the chief center of piracy and the strongest state of the Barbary Coast.

Algiers began to defy even the Turkish (Ottoman) emperors in the eighteenth century and piracy thrived as never before. Early in the nineteenth century a United States fleet, and later a combined Dutch and British fleet, smashed the major strongholds along the Barbary Coast. In 1830 France invaded Algeria and took over complete control. The name Al-Jazair, the Arabic name, was changed to Algérie in French and after 1838 this became the general name for the region.

Throughout the nineteenth century movements for either independence or greater autonomy resulted in several revolts against the French. It was not until after World War II that a strong movement for independence or assimilation developed. Guerrilla warfare, initiated by an organization known as Front de Libération Nationale (FLN), eventually caused the fall of the Fourth French Republic. General Charles de Gaulle was called in to lead the Fifth Republic and to solve the Algerian crisis. He offered Algeria self-determination and a cease-fire agreement was signed in 1962.

In the meantime, many French settlers in Algeria revolted against France. The French Army in Algeria waged a heavy campaign against the rightist group among the settlers. On April 8, 1962, Algeria gained its independence, thus ending 132 years of French rule. It was admitted to the United Nations in October of the same year. Alge-

In 1967 Algeria severed ties with the United States, declared war on Israel, and moved toward a stronger relationship with the USSR.

ANDORRA

Andorra is a co-principality, and the official long form of the name is *Valls d'Andorra* ("Valleys of Andorra" in the Catalan language). The country dates from the time of Charlemagne. The counts of Foix of France and the Spanish Bishop of Urgel were the original inheritors of the principality. When Henry II of Navarre ascended the French throne, he was established along with the Bishop of Urgel as co-prince of Andorra. It has remained a co-principality to this day, except for a brief interlude of occupation by the French (1793–1806). The president of France is now co-prince with the Bishop of Urgel.

The people are mainly pastoral, but iron and lead are mined. Smuggling activities have long been associated with Andorra.

ANGOLA

The Portuguese colonized Angola in 1574. Luanda, the present capital, was founded in 1575. The Portuguese kept full possession of the huge region except for a brief occupation by the Dutch from 1641 to 1648.

Pro-independence forces have been active in Angola since World War II. In 1962 the United Nations General Assembly voted to condemn Portugal's "colonial war" against the people of Angola. In 1974 a revolution in Portugal resulted in that country's withdrawal from its African colonies. Angola was declared independent on November 11, 1975. The three main Angolan groups which had fought against the Portuguese could not agree to form a coalition government, and civil war broke out. Financial aid from Russia and about fifteen thousand Cuban troops helped the Popular Movement win most of the country in May 1977. Russian influence continued strong in 1985.

ARGENTINA

The name *Argentina* is derived from the Latin word for silver. The Spanish explorers referred to the region as *Plata,* or "silver," because they saw Indians using silver and assumed that there were rich mines in the region.

Juan Diaz de Solis was the first European to visit what is now Argentina. The first permanent settlement was made in 1553 at Santiago del Estero by colonists from Chile. Buenos Aires was founded in 1536, but was wiped out by the Indians and was reestablished in 1580.

The early settlements were ruled from Bolivia and Peru. It was not until 1776 that the huge region achieved the status of a viceroyalty in the Spanish Empire. In 1810, revolution broke out against Spanish authority. José de San Martín led the revolt that ended in independence in 1817. Soon after, San Martín collected an army and crossed the Andes to liberate Chile and Peru from Spanish rule.

The country got off to a bad start as a nation. Internal strife, combined with a series of dictatorial regimes, characterized Argentina until 1853. The War of the Triple Alliance occurred between 1856 and 1870. In this war Argentina, Brazil, and Uruguay joined to fight Paraguay.

In 1943, a pro-Axis government installed itself to prevent Argentina from joining the Allies in World War II. Colonel Juan D. Perón became president in 1946 and large-scale reforms were enacted. In 1955 Perón was overthrown by a military junta. He returned in 1973 to be elected president once again, but died 10 months later. His wife Isabel then became president. After several years of terrorism and kidnappings, the country came under the control of another military junta in 1976, when Mrs. Perón was ousted.

In 1982 Argentine troops sought to win control of the British-held Falkland Islands, located 250 miles off the Argentine coast. England and Argentina had claimed sovereignty over the islands since 1833. After two months the Argentines surrendered the islands to British control.

AUSTRALIA

Many Europeans believed in the existence of a great southern continent long before it was discovered. On old maps this supposed continent was named *Terra Australis Incognita* ("Unknown Southern Land").

In 1606, a Dutch navigator named Jansz sighted what is now Cape York Peninsula. Another Dutch navigator, Dirck Hartog, landed on the west coast in 1616. Dirck Hartog Island is named in his memory. In 1642 the explorer Abel Tasman discovered Tasmania (the Tasman Sea is also named for him) and New Zealand. None of the early explorers and navigators made any attempt to claim the land or even to ascertain how large it was. That was left for the greatest navigator in English history—Captain James Cook (1728–1779).

Australia—Aerial view of Sydney

Captain Cook's first voyage (he made three to the South Pacific region) was made to observe the transit of the planet Venus from below the equator. From Tahiti (where he made the observation) he traveled westward, circled New Zealand, and then passed up the eastern coast of Australia, mapping it with remarkable precision. Cook took possession of the land for Britain. The first settlement was made in 1788 by Captain Arthur Phillip, at what is now Sydney. He landed a total of 1,030 men, of whom 736 were convicts. (Many were political prisoners with education and talent, whose offenses would today be considered misdemeanors only. All penal settlements were abolished by 1868.)

The discovery of gold in 1851 made Australia famous in a short time. The population grew quickly and railroads began to open up the interior to farming. Wool and wheat were two of the commodities that helped to develop Australia. A flock of only 105 sheep in 1792 has grown to 150,000,000

The present Australian states were originally British colonies. New South Wales was founded in 1786; Tasmania in 1825; Western Australia in 1829; South Australia in 1834; Victoria in 1851; and Queensland in 1859.

On January 1, 1901, the above colonies were federated under the name Commonwealth of Australia, and the term *colony* was replaced by *state*. Northern Territory was established in 1911, the same year that the Australian Capital Territory was acquired from New South Wales. The capital was moved there in 1927. In recent times a number of dependencies were acquired. The most important of these is the Trust Territory of New Guinea which Australia first occupied in 1914. Australia was confirmed as trustee by the League of Nations in 1921 and by the United Nations in 1946. Australia became a member of the United Nations on November 1, 1945.

During World War II, Australia was threatened with invasion by the Japanese. However, the Japanese were turned back in the Solomon Islands engagements and in the famous naval battles of the Coral Sea. Japan is now Australia's most important trade partner.

AUSTRIA

The Austro-Hungarian monarchy had its origins in the eighth century under Charlemagne. After the Napoleonic Wars, the Congress of Vienna in 1815 left Austria as the dominant power on the continent. In 1919 after World War I, the monarchy was dissolved. There followed years of chaos. The Social Democrats introduced important economic reforms, which were checked by an army-supported dictatorship. After Adolf Hitler came to power in Germany, Austria was occupied by the Nazis and forcibly annexed to Germany in March 1938.

After World War II, the United States and Great Britain declared the Austrians a "liberated" people, although the country was occupied by foreign troops until 1955. Austria was admitted to the United Nations on December 14, 1955. The Socialist Party dominates Austria's government.

BAHAMA ISLANDS

The Bahama Islands, or Bahamas, are the site of Columbus' first landfall in the New World on October 12, 1492. The British have controlled the islands since the seventeenth century. At first they were merely the base for pirates; but under royal governors, appointed after 1717, the pirates were driven out. The islands became a crown colony in 1767, after many Loyalists from the Thirteen Colonies settled there. The slaves were emancipated in 1838.

In 1964, the Bahamas were granted autonomy. The population (mostly black) achieved independence on July 10, 1973, and the Commonwealth of the Bahamas was admitted to the United Nations on September 18, 1973. Banking and tourism are the major business activities.

BAHRAIN

Bahrain is one of the Persian Gulf states. It comprises several islands close to the mainland of Saudi Arabia. It is governed by an amir, whose ancestors concluded a treaty in 1882 giving the United Kingdom control over the nation's foreign affairs. On August 15, 1971, Bahrain declared its independence. On September 21, 1971, it became a member of the United Nations. Its first parliament convened in 1973.

Bahrain is one of the countries that declared an oil embargo against the United States and other nations in 1973–1974.

Austria—Ringstrasse with the Parliament, City Hall, and Votive Church, Vienna

BANGLADESH

Originally a part of British India, the territory of the present republic of Bangladesh became the eastern part of Pakistan in 1947, when the British withdrew from the subcontinent. East Pakistan was separated from West Pakistan by a thousand miles of Indian territory. Although both parts of Pakistan shared a common religion, Islam, East Pakistan, with the larger population and more advanced industry, resented the political control maintained by West Pakistan.

An independence movement, led by Sheikh Mujibur (Mujib) Rahman, culminated in a bloody revolution in December 1971. With the help of the Indian army, East Pakistan defeated the troops of West Pakistan.

The country declared its independence and adopted a parliamentary democracy on December 16, 1972, remaining part of the British Commonwealth, under the name of Bangladesh. It was admitted to the United Nations on September 17, 1974. In January 1975, Mujibur Rahman was made president of a one-party republic. He was executed during a coup on August 15, 1975. A new government came to power in 1977.

Other coups ensued, and in 1982 the Army took over and placed the country under martial law.

BARBADOS

The island of Barbados in the Caribbean Sea was occupied by the British in 1627. It remained a British crown colony for almost 340 years. In 1652, it elected its own assembly. In 1834, the slaves on Barbados were freed.

Barbados achieved autonomy in 1961, and its prime minister, Sir Grantley Adams, a black Barbadian, became prime minister of the short-lived West Indies Federation. On November 30, 1966, Barbados was made independent, and remained within the Commonwealth. The island was admitted to the United Nations on December 9, 1966.

In 1982, President Reagan became the first United States president to visit the island.

BELGIUM

The name of the country is derived from the Belgae, an ancient people who were conquered by the Romans under Julius Caesar in about 50 B.C. The present area of Belgium was a Roman province until overrun by the Germanic Franks in the fifth century A.D.

After the decline of Frankish rule under Charlemagne and his successors, the region became broken up into a series of duchies. Flanders arose as a power in the fourteenth century, united with Burgundy, and as a result of a series of princely marriages became part of the possessions of the House of Hapsburg. Charles of Hapsburg, a native of Ghent, inherited this entire region, known as the Netherlands (or Low Countries), as well as Spain and the Spanish possessions in America. In 1519 he also became Holy Roman Emperor. The

Bahamas—The Sheraton British Colonial Hotel, Nassau

present Belgium, then the southern Netherlands, was then the most prosperous part of Europe. His son, Philip II of Spain, ruled the Netherlands as a Spanish dependency. In 1568, the Netherlands revolted and in 1579 the northern provinces became the Dutch Republic.

The southern provinces remained in Hapsburg control, first ruled by Spain, after 1713 by the Austrian branch of the family. In the French revolutionary and Napoleonic periods, the Austrian Netherlands were annexed by France. From 1815 to 1830 this region was reunited with the provinces to the north as the Kingdom of the Netherlands. The southern provinces, which differed in language, religion, and culture from those in the north, revolted in 1830 and declared their independence. Prince Leopold of Saxe-Coburg became the king of the new Kingdom of Belgium.

Belgium's neutrality was guaranteed by neighboring powers. Despite this, the German armies overran Belgium during World War I. Again, during World War II, Belgium fell under German occupation.

After the war, Belgium became part of an economic union with the Netherlands and Luxembourg called Benelux.

In 1984 Prime Minister Wilfried Martens introduced a severe three-year austerity budget to reduce unemployment and the national debt.

BELIZE

Formerly known as British Honduras, this British colony in Central America was settled by Jamaicans in the seventeenth century and was made a dependency of Jamaica in 1862. By 1884 it had become a separate colony.

British Honduras was given self-government in 1964. As an indication of its intention to seek independence, the local government changed the name of the colony to Belize, which is also the name of its largest city and former capital. Belmopan is now the capital.

Guatemala, which borders Belize to the west, has long claimed the region. The claim is based on the fact that the region was part of the Spanish captaincy-general of Guatemala when the Central American nations became independent. The inhabitants of British Honduras rejected a proposal made in 1968 by a mediator that they enter into a close relationship with Guatemala. Great Britain sent troops to Belize in 1977 to help keep peace with Guatemala.

The country achieved independence September 21, 1981.

BENIN

Formerly called Dahomey, this West African country is made up of several small native kingdoms, and its boundaries were formed through the political conflicts attending French and English territorial rivalry. However, the Portuguese were the first Europeans to explore and establish trading posts in what is now Benin. They founded Porto-Novo, the present capital. The French gradually pushed the English aside in the region, and the present boundaries took shape at the end of the nineteenth century. The area became a colony and part of the loose federation of French West Africa in 1904. In 1946 it became an overseas territory of France.

On December 4, 1958, Dahomey established its National Constituent Assembly and proclaimed the Republic of Dahomey as a member of the French Community. It became independent on August 1, 1960. It was admitted to the United Nations on September 20, 1960. Col. Ahmed Kerekou, who took power in 1972, declared the country a socialist state governed by Marxist-Leninist principles. On December 1, 1975, Dahomey changed its name to Benin.

BERMUDA

Bermuda was named for Juan de Bermúdez, who discovered the islands in 1500. Colonization began with the shipwrecked survivors of the *Sea Venture* in 1609. Until 1684 Bermuda was a part of the Virginia Company's grants. Hamilton became the capital in 1815. The United States built air and naval bases there during World War II.

Bermuda is a British dependency with semi-representative government. Its parliament, established in 1620, is the oldest British parliament outside Britain.

BHUTAN

Little is known of Bhutan before the conquest of the region by a Tibetan warlord in the sixteenth century. With Tibet, Bhutan fell under Chinese control in the eighteenth century. The British sought trade privileges in Bhutan, and by 1910 they were able to win control over Bhutan's foreign policy in return for a subsidy. India succeeded Britain in 1947 as protector of Bhutan.

Bhutan became a hereditary monarchy in 1907. The present constitutional monarchy was instituted in 1967. Bhutan was admitted to the United Nations on September 21, 1971.

BOLIVIA

Bolivia was the site of two Indian civilizations of a high level in pre-Columbian times. The first was that of the Tiahuanaco people that arose on the shores of Lake Titicaca in about A.D. 600 and lasted until A.D. 900. These people were noted for their great stone buildings, statues, and elaborate art work in pottery. The second civilization was that of the Quechua Inca Empire that spread down into Bolivia from the north. The empire developed in about A.D. 1200. Under the leaders Pachacuti and his son Topa (1471–1493) the empire expanded to include the present Ecuador, Peru, Bolivia, and part of Chile, plus other areas.

The Incas were noted for great works in stone set without mortar, and so precisely set that the blade of a knife cannot be inserted between stones. They also farmed by irrigation, built great highways with retaining walls, fabricated colorful costumes and had an elaborate government, religion, and social life. The Inca Empire was split and weakened before the coming of the Spanish. It is possible that Pizarro, the Spanish conquistador, would not have been able to conquer the empire, had not a civil war been in progress when he came in 1532.

In 1539, the town of La Plata (later changed to Sucre) was founded and became the capital of Alto Peru, the early name of the region that is now Bolivia. In 1559, it became a vice-royalty of Spanish Peru. The Indians rebelled several times in later centuries but were crushed. Spain held on to Alto Peru until 1824, when Antonio Jośe de Sucre, one of Simón Bolivar's generals, marched in and captured the region. In 1825 Bolivia declared its independence and took its name from the great South American liberator, Simón Bolivar.

A war with Chile, called the War of the Pacific, broke out over nitrate deposits, and because Bolivia was seeking an outlet to the Pacific Ocean. Bolivia was aided by Peru, but Chile defeated both and seized the province of Atatcama and part of southern Peru. Ever since, Bolivia has remained a landlocked nation.

Bolivia became a member of the United Nations on November 14, 1945. In 1967 Bolivian soldiers captured and executed Che Guevara, a naturalized Cuban Communist and guerrilla leader.

After a series of coups and revolts, a military regime took control of Bolivia in 1974 and banned all civilians from public office. The military officers resigned in October 1982, allowing a congress elected by the people to take over and elect a president. Bolivia had the highest rate of inflation worldwide in 1985. Two unsuccessful coups and a general strike plagued the government.

BOTSWANA

Formerly known as Bechuanaland, this country wedged between Rhodesia and South Africa was made a British protectorate in 1885 at the request of its Bantu inhabitants, who feared the advance of the Boers from the Transvaal. In 1895, its southern part was annexed to Cape Colony (now part of South Africa), but the larger northern part of Bechuanaland remained a protectorate.

On September 30, 1966, the protectorate became the independent republic of Botswana, part of the Commonwealth. It remained economically dependent, however, on South Africa. Botswana has a one-chamber assembly, which is also advised by a council of chiefs of the principal tribes.

BRAZIL

The first European to visit Brazil was the Spanish navigator Vincent Yañez Pinzón, who landed near Recife in January 1500. By the terms of the Treaty of Tordesillas, Brazil was granted to Portugal, and Pedro Alvarez Cabral formally claimed the land for Portugal on Easter Sunday, 1500. Cargoes of dyewood called *pau brasil* had been obtained along the coast by early navigators. The name Brazil was derived from the name of this wood, although Cabral had named the region Terra de Vera Cruz.

The first settlement was made in 1532 at São Vicente. A French colony was established at Rio de Janeiro in 1555. It was abolished in 1567 with the founding of the present city of Rio de Janeiro by the Portuguese on the same spot. From 1578 to 1640, Brazil was under Spanish rule. Dutch settlements were expelled in 1654. The discovery of gold in 1693, and of diamonds in 1729, brought fresh waves of immigrants.

In 1808, the royal family of Portugal was driven out by Napoleon; they took refuge in Brazil. Don

João VI opened Brazil to foreign commerce and removed other restrictions, which helped bring about greater prosperity and economic activity. Dom João returned to Portugal in 1821, but left his son to rule. The prince opposed his father and declared himself Dom Pedro I, Emperor of Brazil. Thereafter, Brazil's history is separate from that of Portugal.

The new empire plunged deep into internal troubles soon after independence. In 1831 Dom Pedro abdicated in favor of his son Dom Pedro II, who was not crowned until 1840 because of his youth. His reign lasted until he was desposed in 1889. The nation was then organized into the United States of Brazil with a constitution modeled after that of the United States of America.

The early years of the republic were marked by repeated revolts. However the nation adjusted nearly all its boundaries with neighboring states between 1900 and 1928. The disputed boundaries had resulted in major wars with Argentina in 1852, and with Paraguay in 1856–1870.

Brazil joined the Allies in World War I and again in World War II. In the latter war, Brazilian troops fought in Europe. The long regime of Getulio Vargas (1937–1945) improved Brazil's economic situation somewhat, but the loss of her rubber monopoly and the overproduction of coffee after World War II left Brazil with serious internal weaknesses.

Two ambitious projects were undertaken after the war. One was the building of the new capital city, Brasília, which was begun in 1957. Three years later it was officially designated the capital, and by 1975 it had a population of more than half a million. The other project was the construction of the Trans-Amazon Highway from the Atlantic Ocean to the border of Peru, a distance of more than 3,000 miles. It was complete in 1974. Meanwhile, the phenomenal growth of the city of São Paulo occurred without plan. It is now the largest city in South America.

Brazil became a member of the United Nations on October 24, 1945. In recent years, the country has been beset by economic troubles. In the early '80s it had huge oil debts and 95 percent inflation. In 1985 the foreign debt grew to $100 billion, making it the largest in the world.

BRITISH ANTARCTIC TERRITORY

The British Antarctic Territory is a crown colony, formed in 1962 from parts of the Falkland Islands and dependencies. It comprises all British-administered, claimed, or held territories south of latitude 60° South. The chief units of the colony are South Shetland Islands (1,800 square miles) and Antarctic Peninsula.

The Falklands remain a British dependency, although Argentina, which calls them *Islas Malvinas,* claims them also. When Argentina invaded them April 2, 1982, Britain sent a task force to the area and forced an Argentine surrender.

BRITISH INDIAN OCEAN TERRITORY

A group of islands in the Indian Ocean that were formerly dependencies of Seychelles Or Mauritius were formed in 1965 into a separate British colony. They included the Chagos Archipelago and the islands of Aldabra, Farquhar, and Desroches.

Brazil—Palácio da Alvorada, Brasília

In 1973, one of the Chagos group, Diego Garcia was turned over to the United States, which two years later began building a naval base there.

BRUNEI

Brunei was once (sixteenth century) a powerful state that controlled all of the large islands of Borneo, plus parts of the Sulu and Philippine islands. But today, Brunei consists of two small enclaves on the north coast of Borneo in southeast Asia. Brunei is surrounded by the Sarawak section of the Federation of Malaysia.

The government is supported mainly by revenues from oil wells in the state. Oil production, though very large, has passed its peak. The island of Labuan lies just off the coast of Brunei but is not now a part of it. Brunei became self governing in 1971 and achieved independence January 1, 1984.

BULGARIA

The Bulgars were a tribe who migrated from central Asia in A.D. 679. They mixed with the Slavic peoples already there to form the modern Bulgarians. The Bulgars founded an empire in the seventh century, but declined under pressure from the Byzantine Empire. A second empire grew up under Semeon II (893–927), but was conquered again by the Byzantines.

Bulgaria was conquered by the Turks in 1396. In 1876 the Bulgarians revolted, and with the aid of Russia, gained their independence. The Kingdom of Bulgaria that was established included all of the present Bulgaria plus Macedonia and most of what is now European Turkey. In 1885, the region of Rumelia was added.

The Bulgarian struggle to get or to keep a coastline on the Aegean Sea (and hence on the Mediterranean Sea) involved the country in the Balkan Wars, World War I, and World War II. The nation allied itself with Nazi Germany in World War II and withdrew too late to prevent a Russian invasion and an eventual Communist-backed revolution that destroyed the monarchy (1944–1946).

The country is now known as the People's Republic of Bulgaria. Admitted to the United Nations on December 14, 1955, it is a close ally of the Soviet Union. Charges by the U.S. and Italy that the Bulgarian secret police were instrumental in the 1981 shooting of Pope John Paul II caused Bulgaria's image to suffer in the mid-80's.

BURMA

Burma first became a united country in 1044 when Anawrahta founded a kingdom that was to last for two hundred years. Five hundred years of disunity followed, ending in 1754, when Alaungpaya established another kingdom over nearly all of the present Burma. British conquest began in 1824 and was completed with the annexation of Burma to the empire in 1886.

Burma gradually regained self-government, starting with a legislative council in 1897. Further steps toward political independence were taken in 1937. The long fight for independence ended in 1948 when the Union of Burma became a reality under the leadership of U Nu. In 1962, a socialist revolution deposed U Nu and General Ne Win became the head of a new government, proclaimed as the Socialist Republic of the Union of Burma in 1974. At that time Burma left the Commonwealth.

Burma was the scene of heavy fighting during World War II. The famous Burma Road led across great mountains from Lashio in Burma to southern China, and was used by the Allied armies to supply Chinese resistance forces in the war with Japan.

BURUNDI

The Watutsi, or Tutsi, people came to the area of the present Burundi in the fifteenth century. They gradually subjugated the Bahutu, or Hutu peoples. This was the situation when Germany, during the nineteenth century, established a zone of influence in the region.

After World War I, the League of Nations mandated the portion of German East Africa known as Ruanda-Urundi to Belgium. It was attached, for administrative purposes, to the Belgian Congo (now Zaire), but the ancient indigenous monarchies of Ruanda and Urundi were maintained.

Ruanda-Urundi became a Belgian trust territory under United Nations auspices after World War II. In 1960 separate elections were held in each of the kingdoms, and two years later they became independent as the republic of Rwanda and the kingdom of Burundi, refusing to reunite.

Both were admitted to the United Nations on September 18, 1962. In 1966 the premier of Burundi declared that country a republic and he became its president. Burundi has no constitution.

CAMBODIA

For almost a thousand years, from the sixth to the fifteenth century, the strongest power in southeastern Asia was the Khmer Empire. The magnificent ruins of Angkor are the remains of monuments that were constructed between the ninth and thirteenth centuries, at the height of that empire. It succumbed to attacks from the Thais, one of its vassal peoples, from the Annamese, and from the Mongols. After several centuries, the remnants of the Khmer Empire, the present Cambodia, became a French protectorate in 1863.

France ruled Cambodia, while maintaining its royal house in nominal authority, until after World War II. The nationalist movement that emerged under the Japanese occupation rode on the coattails of the more aggressive movement in adjoining Vietnam (Annam and Tonkin), and Cambodia was given its independence in 1949 as an "associated state of the French Union."

The Vietnamese nationalists, under the leadership of Ho Chi Minh, attempted to involve Cambodia in total repudiation of French rule, especially after the Vietnamese defeat of the French at Dien Bien Phu in 1954. The anticommunist Southeast Asia Treaty Organization, on the other hand, unilaterally guaranteed Cambodian independence.

King Norodom Sihanouk abdicated his throne in March, 1955, was elected premier in September, and withdrew Cambodia from the French Union. On December 14, 1955, Cambodia was admitted to the United Nations.

As head of state, Prince Norodom Sihanouk steered his country on a neutralist course to avoid being involved in the armed struggle under way in Vietnam.

In 1970, a pro-Western coup by Lon Nol deposed the prince, and the United States and South Vietnamese forces bombed and sent troops into Cambodia to drive out the North Vietnamese forces that were based there.

A civil war developed between the Lon Nol Government and insurgents known as the Khmer Rouge. In April 1975, Lon Nol fled from Cambodia and the Khmer Rouge forces took over the country and immediately named Norodom Sihanouk chief of state for life, although his authority was entirely honorary. He resigned in 1976.

The Khmer Rouge government kept the nation's activities a secret, but refugees said that hundreds of thousands were killed in a post-war purge. The communist regime renamed the nation "Democratic Kampuchea," but the traditional name of Cambodia is still commonly used.

In January 1979, communist troops from Vietnam seized control of the country. China protested this action, because the Soviet Union had supported the new take-over, and the Chinese feared that the Soviets would use Cambodia as a base of operations against them. Clashes between Vietnamese and anti-Communist forces continued in 1983. By 1985 the Vietnamese forces had overrun all major Khmer Rouge bases.

CAMEROON

The Cameroon region was visited late in the fifteenth century by the Portuguese. Trading posts were established there in the seventeenth century. From 1888 to 1914, Germany occupied Cameroons. The territory was invaded by French and British troops during World War I.

After the defeat of Germany, the region was divided into a western Cameroons under British control and a larger eastern Cameroons under French control.

The portion assigned to France obtained internal autonomy in 1959 and complete independence in 1960. The part under British control consisted of two parts. The northern part decided by plebiscite in February 1961 to join the Federation of Nigeria. At the same time a plebiscite was held in the southern part and as a result that section united with the former French area, all of which became the Federal Republic of Cameroon in 1961. In 1972 a unitary state was instituted. In 1985 an attempted coup by the Republican Guards was crushed.

CANADA

Both France and Great Britain based their claims to Canadian territory on the landings of explorers: that of John Cabot on Cape Breton Island for England in 1497; and that of Jacques Cartier on the Gaspé coast of Quebec for France in 1534. But neither the British nor the French tried to take permanent physical possession of any part of the territory before the seventeenth century.

The French explorer Samuel de Champlain tried unsuccessfully to establish a station in the vicinity of the Bay of Fundy in 1604 and 1605. In 1608 he was able to locate the first permanent post at

Canada—Parliament Buildings, Ottawa

Quebec. In 1610, Henry Hudson sailed into the bay named after him, still seeking a water route to Asia. On the basis of Hudson's voyage, Charles II of England granted the entire northeastern wilderness to a private trading corporation, the Hudson's Bay Company.

The French government chartered private trading companies to exploit New France for more than a half-century. Their settlements were persistently harassed by the English. A post set up by Champlain at Port Royal was destroyed by a Virginia raiding party in 1613 and twice thereafter; eventually it became British in 1713 as Annapolis Royal in Nova Scotia. Quebec was subject to a series of similar raids.

Louis XIV declared New France—the combined settlements of Acadia in the Bay of Fundy area and Canada in the St. Lawrence valley—to be a Crown colony in 1663. He appointed a governor to act as chief of state. For a century New France developed under this regime, although in the early stages of the French and Indian Wars much of Acadia was lost to the British.

The colonial wars in North America ended in 1763 with the total cession of New France to Great Britain.

But in 1774, the former New France was reorganized as an extended province called Quebec. Parliament hoped that the Quebec Act would preserve the overwhelmingly French character of the recently conquered territory, lest the French colonists find common cause with disaffected settlers

William Lyon Mackenzie.

to the south. The statute only further outraged the English-speaking colonists.

The decade following the Quebec Act was critical. English-speaking refugees from the rebellious lower colonies began to populate widely separated areas of Nova Scotia and Quebec, laying the foundation for the emerging provinces of New Brunswick, Prince Edward Island, and Upper Canada (Ontario).

In the next generation some of the ideas associated with Jacksonian democracy in the United States began to penetrate the Canadian border. Such influences inspired the uprisings of 1837, led by Louis Papineau in Lower Canada and by William Lyon Mackenzie in Upper Canada.

The Earl of Durham was sent to British North America to study the situation. He recommended the adoption of representative government for the two Canadas. Since many of the colonists were moving West, he also urged that the two provinces be reunited to guarantee a minimum French impact once the democratic regime was instituted. In 1840 Parliament created the province of Canada (in which two districts, Canada West and Canada East, were recognized). But only after Nova Scotia was granted representative government in 1848 was the same privilege extended to Canada.

The British Parliament was apprehensive of the increasing power of the United States in the second half of the nineteenth century. The British government was able to resolve several border disputes: In 1818 the forty-ninth parallel became the line of demarcation from the Lake of the Woods to the Rocky Mountains; a controversial border between Maine and New Brunswick was peaceably settled in 1842; and in 1846 the dangerous Oregon question was resolved when the forty-ninth parallel was extended almost to the Pacific Ocean. But some leaders in the United States pressed for more acquisition of British American territory. Parliament feared that British recognition of the Southern Confederacy during the American Civil War

Louis Joseph Papineau.

might serve as a pretext, following Union victory, for hostile movements across the border, and so Parliament encouraged the provinces to consolidate their powers. This was the reasoning behind Parliament's British North America Act of 1867. The Dominion of Canada was created by this act. It was a confederation of British colonies under the authority of the British Parliament. Its original members were two of the Atlantic provinces, Nova Scotia and New Brunswick, and the two sections of the province of Canada—Ontario and Quebec. The act provided for the eventual admission of all British North America.

The Hudson's Bay Company returned its holdings to Great Britain, which immediately ceded them to the Dominion of Canada. They became the Northwest Territories in 1870. The only settled district within the Territories was organized within the year as the fifth province of Canada, under the name of Manitoba. In 1871 the colony of British Columbia agreed to join the Dominion as a sixth province if a railway would be constructed to link it with the eastern provinces. Prince Edward Island became the seventh province in 1873.

The last years of the nineteenth century brought a spectacular westward shift in Canada's population. In 1898, Yukon Territory was detached from the Northwest Territories adjoining Alaska. By 1905 settled sections of the Territories between Manitoba and British Columbia were organized into the new provinces of Saskatchewan and Alberta. Except for Newfoundland (which became part of Canada in 1949), the Dominion attained its ultimate territorial extent and virtually its final political organization by 1905.

Government. The trend in Great Britain was to relax its tight control over its possessions and to encourage them to run their own affairs. The power of the Crown was vested in an appointed governor-general and in appointed lieutenant-governors of each province. Most law-making powers were assigned to a Senate, whose members were appointed for life. (Those appointed after 1965 must retire at the age of 75.) The Canadian House of Commons was, like that of the United Kingdom, elective and based on population. While the provinces have their own constitutions, which they alone may amend, they have authority only over their internal affairs to the degree authorized under the constitution. This document, the British North America Act, specifies the powers granted to the provinces. Powers not so enumerated are to be exercised by the federal government. (This is the reverse of the system in the United States, where the specified authority of the federal government is defined and residual powers are granted to the states.)

Although not quite a nation, the Dominion was admitted to the League of Nations and independently participated in foreign affairs. Great Britain called an imperial conference in 1926, at which it declared that the dominions were autonomous and equal members of a Commonwealth of Nations, headed by a single sovereign. This concept was formalized by the British Parliament in 1931 as the Statute of Westminster. Under this statute Canada formally attained sovereignty and nationhood.

Perhaps the most significant subsequent constitutional development was the ruling in 1949 that Canadian citizens could no longer appeal the decisions of the Supreme Court of Canada to the British Privy Council. In the same year the British Parliament passed the second British North America Act, which made it clear that amendments to the first British North America Act could not be made without the participation of the Canadian Parliament.

Canada's international role has been distinctive. Its national policy is independent of the United States, despite strong economic pressures. In its internal policies, however, Canada suffers from chronic controversy concerning the balance between federal and provincial authority. A cohesive and articulate French minority comprises a majority within the province of Quebec. The French nationalist movement is itself divided into factions, one of which agitates for separation and sovereignty. The use of the French language has parity throughout Canada and supersedes the English language within the province of Quebec.

Economy. Canada proved to be a late bloomer. The first years of the twentieth century saw the anticipated development of agriculture, mining, and industry. The United States had already peopled its West, and the Canadian prairies received the overflow—not only from the states, but from every part of Europe and even from the Orient. At first Canadians feared direct economic encroachment from the United States, and a policy of trade protectionism was adopted. But capital investment from the United States has become sufficiently dominant to appear as a possible menace to many Canadians.

Cape Verde Islands—Cape Verdeans display portraits of two leaders of their country.

CAPE VERDE ISLANDS

An archipelago about 375 to 525 miles west of Senegal in Africa was discovered by the Portuguese sailor Diogo Gomes in 1460. Two years later Portuguese settlers and their African slaves populated the uninhabited islands. They were transferred to the Portuguese crown in 1495 and a century later the first governor was appointed.

In modern times the Cape Verde Islands were made an overseas province of Portugal. The leaders of the independence movement in Portuguese Guinea (now Guinea-Bissau) were mostly from Cape Verde. When the Portuguese withdrew from their African colonies, both the mainland and the islands became independent. Cape Verde became a republic on July 5, 1975. On September 16, 1975, the country was admitted to the United Nations.

CAYMAN ISLANDS

These coral islands in the Caribbean Sea south of Cuba were discovered by Columbus in 1503 and were colonized from nearby Jamaica.

Until 1959, the Caymans were administered as a dependency of Jamaica. In 1962, they were given self-government as a separate colony with a partly elected legislature. Emperor Bokassa was ousted in a coup in 1979 and replaced by his cousin, David Dacko. Dacko's reign ended abruptly in 1981, when he was replaced by a military general.

CENTRAL AFRICAN EMPIRE

During the last decade of the nineteenth century, the French explored what is now the Central African Empire. In 1894, the Territory of Ubangi-Shari was established, and was merged in 1905 with Chad to form Ubangi-Shari-Chad. In 1910, Gabon and Middle Congo were added to this group to form French Equatorial Africa.

That loose federation came to an end when the constituent states chose to become autonomous states within the French Community of Nations in 1958. On December 1, 1958, the Ubangi-Shari section became the Central African Republic and was proclaimed an independent nation two years later. It was admitted to the United Nations on September 20, 1960. In 1976 President Jean-Bedel Bokassa changed the country's name to Central African Empire and declared himself its first emperor.

The Central African Empire exports diamonds, uranium, textiles, and other goods. It has not been able to develop many of its natural resources because it is cut off from the major trade routes.

CHAD

Arabs visited this general area in Africa many centuries ago, but it was not explored until late in the nineteenth century. Various African tribes inhabited the region, alternately warring and living in some sort of peace. Slave traders scoured the territory for their exports of human beings to Egypt and the Near East, while other traders sought ostrich feathers and ivory.

The French helped put an end to the slave trade in the Chad area, and by 1910 it had become part of French Equatorial Africa. In 1920 it was given separate administration and it became an autonomous member of the French Community in 1958. It declared its independence on August 11, 1960, and was admitted to the United Nations on September 20, 1960.

Chad suffered from conflicts between the Moslem, pro-Arab, and conservative population of the north and the black, more progressive population of the south. Years of scanty rainfall have also been destructive.

Chad has consistently tried to africanize its proper names. President François Tombalbaye change his first name to Ngarta. The capital, Fort Lamy, was renamed N'Djamema. After fifteen years in the presidency Tombalbaye was killed in a military coup in 1975.

Libya took advantage of the confusion in Chad's government to annex 37,000 square miles of territory in northern Chad in 1976. In 1981 Libya and Chad announced plans to unite though several African countries and France denounced the proposal. Libyan troops were withdrawn that year. In 1983 some 3000 French troops were sent to Chad Habre to oppose Libyan-backed rebels. By 1984 troops were withdrawn.

CHANNEL ISLANDS

William the Conqueror, of Normandy, who invaded England in A.D. 1066 and became king of England, was already ruler of the Channel Islands. They have remained a territory of the English Crown ever since.

CHILE

Chile—University of Concepcion

In 1520, during his epic voyage around the earth, Ferdinand Magellan landed on an island near a region of South America called "Tchili" by the natives of the area. This was the first visit by Europeans to what is now called Chile. In 1535, Diego de Almagro was sent to explore the land to the south of Peru. He was not successful in the venture, but five years later Pedro Valdivia annexed the present-day Chile down to the Maipú River, near where Santiago, the capital of Chile, now stands. The chief obstacles to Spanish conquest were the fierce Araucanian Indians, who continued to resist long after Chile had become an independent nation.

In 1810, Chile declared its independence, and the war that followed with Spain was fought by Chileans under the leadership of Bernard O'Higgins and José de San Martín. The Spanish were finally driven from the country in 1818.

Chile passed through a turbulent and unstable period after independence. By 1837 the nation fought a bitter war that destroyed a Peruvian-Bolivian confederation against her. Again in 1879–1883, Chile fought the War of the Pacific against the combined armies of Peru and Bolivia, and won. In that war Bolivia lost its outlet to the sea to Chile (the Atacama region). Chile was admitted to the United Nations on October 24, 1945.

Among South American nations, Chile has a reputation for political stability. The accession by normal political processes of a Marxist president, Salvador Allende Gossens, in 1970 was unprecedented. However, the country was disunited. Foreign influence, including that of the United States, was brought to bear. In 1973, Allende was deposed by a military junta and murdered. The succeeding administration reversed Allende's policies.

Repressive government tactics continued in spite of protests through 1984.

CHINA
(People's Republic of China)

The Chinese state has existed without interruption for over four thousand years. The Chinese were experiencing one of their periods of cultural and intellectual Golden Ages when Europe was still in the Stone Age. The original home of the Chinese people appears to have been in the valley of the Wei River in the present Shensi Province area. In about the twenty-eighth century B.C. a loose empire appeared under the Hsia dynasty. This was the first recorded state. Its successor, the Shang dynasty, left written records about the first important cultural development (1750–1122 B.C.).

The period of the Chou dynasty (1122–221 B.C.) was a great feudal period. About 770 B.C., the capital was moved from Sian to Loyang on the Yellow River. The period of the new state, called the Eastern Chou dynasty, was the time when the great philosophers Confucius and Lao-tzu lived. It was a classical age in literature and art.

From 221 to 206 B.C. one of the notable men in world history was the ruler of China. His name was Shih Huang-ti and his dynasty was known as Ch'in or Chin, from which the word *China* was derived. He left the Great Wall as one of his legacies, and is the founder of modern China.

The Han dynasty (206 B.C.–A.D. 220) followed. The classics were restored, Buddhism was introduced, sculpturing as a fine art began, and paper was invented. The Han rulers expanded the Chinese Empire westward into the heart of Asia. They established contact with the Roman Empire in the west. The Han rulers began the system of civil service examinations that lasted to 1911.

The Grand Canal, another spectacular feat of Chinese workmanship, was begun under the Sui (A.D. 581–618) and T'ang (618–907) dynasties. The T'ang dynasty is usually considered the most splendid in Chinese history. Under Emperor Tai Tsung (627–649) China became powerful. A great system of roads was built from Sian, the capital. Handicrafts and arts flourished as never before. China reached its greatest area in 650. At that time it included all of today's China, plus southeast Asia and other areas. Printing was invented, the use of silk developed, and poetry and painting advanced. The invention of movable type, gunpowder, and the magnetic compass followed.

The Mongols crashed through the Great Wall in the thirteenth century, at the same time that they were invading western Europe. Genghis Khan established the Mongol dynasty and extended his rule as far south as the present Fukien province. Chinese civilization persisted, as was witnessed by Marco Polo who visited China during the short period of Mongol domination. During the reign of the Manchu emperors (1644–1911), the last dynasty, China declined rapidly. In the nineteenth century, rebellion weakened the ruling Manchus (Ming dynasty) and foreign interference developed. The Portuguese had reached China in 1516, the Spanish in 1557, the Dutch in 1606, and the English in 1637. Western governments supported the Manchus in the Taipeng Rebellion (1850–1864) in order to get access to Chinese commerce and trade privileges. The Boxer Rebellion (1900) was put down by foreign troops, including those of the United States. China suffered heavy losses and was further weakened in a war with Japan (1894–1895). The imperial government was finally overthrown in 1911.

Sun Yat-sen, the founder of the Republic of China (1912), lost control to a group of military chiefs or warlords. Chiang Kai-shek gained control and was for a time allied with the Communists. A split developed in 1927 between Chiang Kai-shek and the Communists. Japan, taking advantage of disunity, occupied Manchuria in 1931. The Sino-Japanese War began in 1937 and merged into World War II. During the war, American aid reached China mainly over the Burma Road and by air. By 1945 the Japanese were completely expelled. The Communist forces had been attacked by Chiang Kai-shek in 1936, and had transferred their center of power to Shensi in northern China, by means of a great land journey known as the "Long March." Their strength had been greatly reduced, but by the end of World War II, the Communist movement was again threatening Chiang Kai-shek.

Although supported by the United States, Chiang Kai-shek steadily lost ground in the civil war that erupted after World War II. By 1949 the Nationalist forces had been expelled from the mainland, and took refuge on Taiwan (Formosa).

The People's Republic of China was proclaimed in 1949 by the Communists under Mao Tse-tung. In 1950 China retrieved Tibet, which had broken away in the fall of the Manchu dynasty. For many years the Peking regime was denied membership in the United Nations, where China's seat was held by representatives of the government on Taiwan that called itself the Republic of China. In 1971 the United Nations voted to expel the dele-

U.S. President Richard M. Nixon is greeted on Feb. 21, 1972 by Chairman Mao Tse-tung of the Peoples Republic of China.

gates from Taiwan and to seat those of the People's Republic. The United States had long opposed this move, and continued to withhold full diplomatic recognition of the Peking regime. But the animosity was dissipated after President Richard Nixon visited Peking in 1972 and met with Chinese leaders Mao Tse-tung and Chou En-lai. In December 1978, President Jimmy Carter's administration announced plans to establish formal diplomatic ties with the People's Republic of China. The Reagan administration continued the good will policy toward both China and the Republic of China on Taiwan.

In 1984 China announced widespread changes to reduce government control over the economy. These policies introduced elements of capitalism without eliminating the Communist theory.

CHINA
(Republic of China)
See **Taiwan**

COLOMBIA

Columbus explored the northern coast of what is now Colombia in 1502 on his last voyage to the New World. The city of Bogotá, deep in the interior, was founded in 1538. Shortly after this, the region began to be called New Granada. It included the present Colombia, Panama, Ecuador, and Venezuela. The state was ranked as a viceroyalty within the Spanish American empire.

A war for independence was begun in 1810 and continued until 1819, when Bolivar and Santander won the Battle of Boyaca. From 1819 to 1830 Colombia was a part of Bolivar's Gran Colombia that included nearly the same area as did the old Spanish viceroyalty. By 1832, Ecuador and Venezuela had seceded from Gran Colombia. The remainder changed its name to Colombia and became a republic. During the turbulent nineteenth century in Colombia no less than ten different constitutions were promulgated.

In 1903, the country lost Panama to a United States-instigated revolt which established the Republic of Panama. The first seven decades of Colombia's twentieth-century history have been relatively more peaceful and accompanied by considerable economic and social progress. The nation has been experiencing severe economic and political difficulties in the past few years.

COMORO ISLANDS

The Comoro archipelago was acquired by France in 1886, although the island of Mayotte had been occupied since 1843. In 1912, the archipelago was declared a colony and attached to Madagascar (now the Malagasy Republic) for administration. Upon the latter's independence, the Comoro group became an overseas territory of France.

When the inhabitants voted for independence in 1974, France did nothing to impede their desire, although Mayotte had voted against independence. On July 6, 1975, the Comoro legislature declared their independence. Mayotte again voted to remain French in a 1976 referendum. A leftist regime which had seized power in 1975 was overthrown in a pro-French coup in 1978.

CONGO

A Portuguese navigator, Diego Cam, discovered the mouth of the Congo (Zaire) River in 1484. Thereafter, exploration was mainly done by French missionaries and slave-traders. In the nineteenth century Henry M. Stanley (in the service of Belgium) and Pierre Savorgnan de Brazza (in the service of France) opened up the country to European penetration and established claims to the region. The French claims to what is now the Republic of Congo were recognized at the Congress of Berlin in 1855. In 1903, the territory was organized into Moyen (Middle) Congo, and it became a part of French Equatorial Africa (a loose federation) in 1908. On September 28, 1958, Middle Congo became the Republic of Congo, an autonomous member of the French Community. It remained in the Community when it became an independent nation on August 15, 1960, as the Republic of Congo. It was admitted to the United Nations on September 20, 1960. In 1970, it changed its name to the People's Republic of the Congo.

This country should not be confused with Zaire, known from 1960 to 1971 as the Democratic Republic of Congo. During those years Zaire was called "Congo (Kinshasa)" to distinguish it from the country by the same name north of the Congo River, known as "Congo (Brazzaville)."

Communistic influence in Congo has been strong since 1963.

COSTA RICA

Costa Rica was discovered in 1502 by Christopher Columbus. It was conquered by the Spanish and made a royal province before the middle of the sixteenth century.

In 1821, Costa Rica declared its independence, but was annexed by Mexico. From 1823, when the Mexican Empire broke up, until 1839, Costa Rica was a member of a loose federation called the United Provinces of Central America.

The country became wholly independent in 1840, and proclaimed itself a republic in 1848. Many boundary disputes were settled, including one with Nicaragua and another with Panama.

Up to 1948, Costa Rica had enjoyed internal peace. In that year, a disputed presidential election resulted in new elections and a new constitution in 1949. Unrest continued to plague the country, and terrorist activity went on for several years. In 1954 Costa Rica charged Nicaragua with meddling in its internal affairs. The dispute ended in an agreement by both countries to curb terrorist activity. Costa Rica was admitted to the United Nations on November 2, 1945.

CUBA

The island of Cuba was discovered by Christopher Columbus on his first voyage in 1492. Santiago de Cuba was founded in 1514 by Diego Velásquez and was the capital until 1589. Cuba was the base for the historic expeditions of Cortés to Mexico and of De Soto to Florida. Havana was founded in 1519, captured by the British in 1762, and returned to Spanish control the following year.

Unsuccessful revolts occurred in 1868, in 1875, and in 1895. In the latter part of the nineteenth century the brilliant leader, José Martí, was mainly responsible for the development of national consciousness in Cuba.

The United States declared war against Spain after the sinking of the American battleship *Maine* in Havana harbor on February 15, 1898. The slogan, "Remember the Maine," aroused a patriotic sentiment in the United States for war against Spain. The land battles of ElCaney and San Juan Hill and the naval battle at Santiago resulted in Spain's loss of Cuba. By the terms of the Platt Amendment to the new Cuban constitution of 1901, Cuba became virtually a protectorate of the United States and was occupied by the United States Marines on three occasions. In 1934 the Platt Amendment was repealed but the United States kept its Guantanamo naval base.

A military dictatorship was inaugurated in Cuba in 1952 by Fulgencio Batista. In 1953, opposition to the Batista regime developed into a large-scale revolt. The leader of the rebel group was Fidel Castro, who operated mainly from fortified positions in the Sierra Maestra (mountains) in eastern Cuba. Several unsuccessful revolts were staged before 1958, when full civil war developed. Batista fled to exile in the Dominican Republic and Castro's rebels took over the government. At first Castro was on friendly terms with the United States, but in 1960 his government began seizing the properties of United States companies.

The United States severed diplomatic relations in 1960, and Cuba increasingly turned toward the Soviet Union for support and aid. In April 1961, a United States-sponsored invasion force landed on the Bay of Pigs at the south coast of Cuba, but was defeated in 72 hours with a loss of 1,200 prisoners. In October 1962, United States high-altitude photographs showed Soviet missiles in Cuba. The discovery nearly precipitated a war between the United States and the Soviet Union. After the United States threw up a naval blockade of Cuba, the Soviet Union withdrew.

Tension between the United States and the Soviet Union eased considerably, but Cuba-United States relations continued strained. Since 1975, Cuba, with considerable encouragement from the Soviets, has continually expanded its revolutionary operations in Africa and more recently in Latin America.

As a result of the U.S.-led invasion of Grenada in 1983, twenty-four Cubans died and seven hundred were captured (later repatriated).

CYPRUS

Cyprus was famous in the ancient world for its rich copper deposits. The word *copper* is derived from the name *Cyprus*. The Egyptians occupied the island until 1450 B.C., and the Greeks came in 1400 B.C. Between 500 B.C. and A.D. 1562, Phoenicia, Egypt, Persia, Greece, Rome, the Byzantine Empire, Venice, and finally the Ottoman Empire (Turks) all held Cyprus.

The United Kingdom administered Cyprus after 1878, and in 1914 the British annexed the island. In modern times Greek Cypriots have often attempted to unite Cyprus with Greece. Although the Greeks form a majority of the population, a large Turkish minority always opposed such a move. Violence broke out in 1955 between the two groups. Civil war developed and ended only after an unexpected proposal for an independent Cyprus was suddenly accepted by the Greek Cypriots. On August 16, 1960, Cyprus became an independent republic. The country was admitted to the United Nations on September 20, 1960.

Tension between the Greek and Turkish populations of Cyprus continued to flare into open clashes, particularly in 1964. In 1974 an advocate of *enosis* (union with Greece) tried to seize control of the island. This was followed by a Turkish invasion. Finally the two groups reached a truce. The Turks maintained an enlarged sector in the northeast and refused to accept any alternative to a federal state. United Nations peace-keeping forces were sent to prevent further violence until an agreement among the Cypriots could be reached. However, the peace talks failed and fighting broke out again. The Turks enlarged the territory under their control, and on June 8, 1975, they voted to form a separate Turkish state.

In 1983 a declaration of independence was announced, but the new state named the Turkish Republic of Northern Cyprus, was not recognized by other nations.

CZECHOSLOVAKIA

Czechs and Slovaks settled in the present region before the sixth century ended. The Slovaks were conquered by the Magyar people and for a thousand years had no independent existence. The Czechs, however, formed the Kingdom of Bohemia in the tenth century.

Bohemia had a golden age of cultural growth in the fourteenth century that lasted until 1620. Prague, its capital, became a great center of Latin learning. In 1526, Bohemia came under Hapsburg rule and the Czech population was subjected to German and Austrian influences. The revolt of 1618 ended disastrously at the Battle of White Hill (White Mountain) in 1620, which crushed Czech national aspirations until the mid-nineteenth century.

The breakup of the Austro-Hungarian Empire presaged a serious move for independence during World War I. A Czech state came into existence on October 28, 1918. Two days later the Slovak National Council indicated its desire to unite with the Czechs in a single state. The Republic of Czechoslovakia was declared on November 14, 1918.

Czechoslovakia became a victim of Nazi expansionist aims in 1938. The republic was dismembered and abolished in 1939. A German-sponsored Slovak state was not recognized by the Allies, who supported a government-in-exile led by Dr. Eduard Beneš in London. Czechoslovakia regained its territory in 1944, and all severed sections were eventually reunited, except for part of Ruthenia.

Czechoslovakia moved in two stages into a Communist form of government. In February 1948, Beneš had to accept Clement Gottwald, a Communist, as Prime Minister, after the Communists had taken over control of much of the machinery of government. In June 1948, President Beneš was forced to resign after an election in which the people were permitted to vote only for candidates on a slate approved by the Communists. Czechoslovakia became a member of the United Nations on October 24, 1945.

Alexander Dubček became the leader of Czechoslovakia's Party in early 1968 and announced new liberal policies for the nation. Russia and other Warsaw Pact nations invaded the country on August 20, 1968 to halt Dubček's reforms.

Despite the activity of intellectuals and liberals, Russia has continued to keep a tight rein on the country.

DENMARK

Recent excavations from Danish peat bogs have provided proof that man lived in the Jutland region of Denmark at least eleven thousand years ago.

In ancient times Jutland was colonized by Norway, which lies to the north across the Skagerrak (strait). People from Denmark invaded England in the ninth century after Christ, Harald "Bluetooth" united Denmark for the first time in the tenth century and his son Sweyn conquered England.

During these centuries the Danish Vikings took part in raids along the shores of Western Europe. During the reign of Canute the Great (1014–1035), England, Denmark, and Norway were united. During the next three centuries, Denmark continued to expand, and under the reign of Valdemar II (1202–1241) it became the leading power of northern Europe. In the reign of Margarethe (1387–1412), Denmark, Sweden, and Norway were united. This union was dissolved in 1532, but Norway remained a part of the Crown of Denmark until 1814.

Danes settled Greenland in 1721. Serfdom was abolished in 1788. In the mid-nineteenth century, Denmark lost territory on the south of the Jutland

Peninsula to Prussia. In 1918, the independence of Iceland was recognized. Germany attacked the kingdom on April 9, 1940, conquering it in a few hours. However, the conquest was costly to maintain because the Danes became expert saboteurs and the Danish fleet was scuttled by its own officers in the harbor of Copenhagen. The nation was liberated on May 5, 1945. Denmark became a member of the United Nations on October 24, 1945. Severe labor strife afflicted the country in 1985.

DJIBOUTI

This nation on the northeast coast of Africa was formerly French Somaliland. It was taken by France in the late nineteenth century. The country held a strategic location at the strait leading to the Suez Canal, and for many years it was Ethiopia's only link with the sea.

In 1967, the people voted to remain under French control, and the region became known as the Territory of the Afars (related to the Ethiopians) and the Issas (related to the Somalis). Immigrants from both countries kept pouring into the area and bitter fighting flared up between them. On June 27, 1977, the territory proclaimed its independence from France and adopted the name of Djibouti, the capital city. Ethiopia and Somalia have renounced their claims to the area. French aid is a mainstay to the economy.

Denmark—Tivoli Gardens, Copenhagen

DOMINICAN REPUBLIC

The island of Hispaniola, on which the present Dominican Republic is located, was discovered and named by Christopher Columbus during his first voyage in 1492. The city of Santo Domingo was founded by his brother, Bartholomew Columbus, in 1496. The island became a base for Spain's discovery and exploration of the New World. The Spanish lost Hispaniola to the French in 1697, but regained the eastern two-thirds of the island in 1809. The remainder of the island became the independent Haiti, now the Republic of Haiti.

A revolt by Dominicans in 1821 freed the country from the Spanish, but in 1822 Haiti occupied Santo Domingo (the name of the former Spanish-held area at that time). Haitians remained until expelled by another revolt in 1844, and the name was changed to the Dominican Republic. Independence was short-lived, however, because Spain regained the country in 1861. The Spanish withdrew in 1865.

The next half-century was one of corrupt rule, confusion, and dictatorship for Santo Domingo. In 1907, the United States undertook control of the country's finances; and in 1915, the U.S. Marines occupied the country. They remained until 1924. In 1930, Rafael Leonidas Trujillo Molina assumed power. He and members of his family maintained a tight control until he was assassinated in 1961. The Dominican Republic was admitted to the United Nations on October 24, 1945.

After Trujillo's assassination, Joaquin Balaguer resigned as president; and in 1962, the first real election in almost forty years returned Juan Bosch to the presidency. Bosch was deposed in a coup the next year, and civil turmoil continued. In 1965 the United States sent in Marines to protect American lives and property, and to prevent the possibility of a government of the Castro type. In the first election after the troops were withdrawn, Balaguer defeated Bosch, and was reelected in 1970 and 1974.

EAST GERMANY

For the history of Germany prior to the provisional partition in 1945, see West Germany (Federal Republic of Germany). The failure of the Allies to agree upon the future disposition of defeated Germany after World War II resulted in the formal division of Germany into an eastern and a western section. In June 1948, the Russians instituted a series of unilateral changes, including the use of a new currency in the eastern zone. They also blockaded Allied traffic into the western section of Berlin. That city was forced to rely upon airlifted supplies until the blockade was broken. Five months after the Federal Republic of Germany had been established in the western zone, the German Democratic Republic was organized by the Russians in the eastern zone on October 7,, 1949.

The Democratic Republic was maintained largely under Soviet protection. It seemed that the unification of Germany was not imminent, and the two Germanies began to deal with one another. They finally signed their first treaty in May 1972. Both were admitted to the United Nations on the same day, September 18, 1973.

ECUADOR

The area of what is now Ecuador became a part of the great South American empire of the Inca Indians a few years before the voyages of Columbus to the New World.

The Spanish Conquistador Francisco Pizarro began the conquest of the Inca Empire in 1530. One of Pizarro's men founded Quito (the present capital of Ecuador) in 1534. Spanish colonial domination lasted until 1822. In that year the revolutionary generals Simón Bolívar and José San Martín met at Guayaquil, Ecuador, to decide on the future of the liberated regions of northern South America. The result of this meeting was the formation of Gran Colombia, which included the present states of Venezuela, Colombia, Panama, and Ecuador. This union collapsed in 1830 and Ecuador became an independent republic.

Petroleum exports have provided the basis for the economy since 1972. A declining oil market since 1982 has caused severe economic shortages.

EGYPT

The civilization of ancient Egypt arose in the lower valley of the Nile River over five thousand years ago. By 3200 B.C. the land of Egypt was unified by King Menes, who ruled as "King of Upper and Lower Egypt." The use of writing developed in Egypt at this time. From small beginnings a mighty empire and a high civilization arose, led mainly by priest-kings and kings who called themselves gods. Their civilization

Egypt—Sphinx and Pyramids

flourished for 2,500 years. The Egyptians built great cities, temples, pyramids, and statues; they opened sea and land routes of trade, and their armies commanded respect throughout the world.

In 1150 B.C., civilized peoples elsewhere discovered iron and how to use it. Egypt had no iron resources, and this contributed to the decline of its power. The history of ancient Egypt came to an end with the conquest by Alexander the Great in 332 B.C.

In 30 B.C., Roman legions entered Egypt. It became the chief source of grain in the Roman world. Byzantine (Eastern Roman Empire) rule began in A.D. 395 and lasted until the Arab conquest in A.D. 600. Egypt gradually developed into a Moslem nation with a strong Arabic culture. Arabic rule lasted to the sixteenth century and then gave way to a long period of Turkish (Ottoman Empire) rule.

In 1881, a revolution against the Turkish authorities resulted in French and British intercession. Egypt became a British protectorate in 1882. The protectorate ended in 1922, and Egypt became a self-governing kingdom in 1936. In 1951, an army junta overthrew the monarchy; and in 1956 Egypt nationalized the famous Suez Canal, over the objections of many foreign powers.

A short war between Egypt and Israel broke out in October 1956, in which the United Kingdom and France joined in attacking Egypt. It was ended when the United Nations interceded. In 1958, Egypt and Syria united to proclaim a United Arab Republic. In 1961, Syria withdrew from the union, but the name United Arab Republic was retained by Egypt as the nation's official title until 1971. Then the official designation of the country became Arab Republic of Egypt. Under one name or another, Egypt has been a member of the United Nations since it was first admitted on February 1, 1958.

Egypt sought with varying degrees of zeal to act as the spokesman of the Arab world, particularly in its relations with Israel. Hostility between Israel and Egypt developed into active warfare in June 1967. Israel emerged after six days of combat with total victory. Israel occupied Egypt's Sinai Peninsula and a truce continued until 1973. In October of that year, Egypt took the offensive, and forces of each country were able to cross the Suez Canal to establish beachheads on the other's territory. In the ensuing negotiations, Israel withdrew from the west bank of the canal and from a strip along its east bank, and Egypt reopened the canal for the first time in eight years.

El Salvador—The National Palace in the city of San Salvador

In the late '70s, Egypt's president, Anwar Sadat, emerged as a leading figure for world peace, with special attention to the Middle East. His efforts ended with his assassination October 6, 1981.

EL SALVADOR

The history of El Salvador began in 1524 with its conquest by the Spanish conquistador Pedro de Alvarado. San Salvador was founded in 1528 at its present location. Throughout the Spanish colonial period the area of the present republic formed two provinces of the captaincy-general of Guatemala.

Independence from Spain was achieved as a part of Guatemala in 1821. In 1824, the area became a part of the United Provinces of Central America, a federation of Central America that lasted until 1839. El Salvador became a separate nation on January 1, 1841. The Organization of Central American States (ODECA), formed in 1951, includes El Salvador. The capital of this loose association of states is at San Salvador. The political history of El Salvador during the past century has been marked by violence and rapid changes in government. El Salvador became a member of the United Nations on October 24, 1945.

During the early '80s, El Salvador became a battleground for competing ideologies, with the United States supporting the government and Russia and Cuba backing the leftist guerrillas seeking its overthrow. In 1983 extreme right-wing death squads were accused of killing more than 1,000 leftists.

EQUATORIAL GUINEA

Equatorial Guinea is the former Spanish

Guinea. It consists of Río Muni (an enclave on the equatorial coast of West Africa) and two islands in the Gulf of Guinea. One of these islands, formerly called Fernando Póo and renamed Macias Nguema (after the first president of the country), is about 20 miles offshore. The other, formerly named Annobón and renamed Pigalu, is about four hundred miles to the southwest. All were acquired by Spain in 1778. The islands were used as stations in the slave trade. No attempt to occupy Río Muni was made until the last quarter of the nineteenth century.

In 1959, the territories were designated as two provinces of Spain. In 1963, they were granted a degree of autonomy and called Equatorial Guinea. A referendum concerning independence was held in 1968, and on October 12, 1968, full independence was granted. The country was admitted to the United Nations on November 12, 1968.

ETHIOPIA

In ancient times the power of Egypt's pharaohs extended southward into what is now Ethiopia and along the headwaters of the Nile River. By the eleventh century before Christ, Ethiopian rulers had turned the tables and ruled mighty Egypt for a few centuries. During this period of expansion the Ethiopians absorbed much Egyptian culture. Christianity was introduced in about A.D. 330.

In the following centuries Ethiopia continued as a powerful state, although it ceased to rule Egypt. Through contacts with foreign regions, trade and immigration expanded. By the fifteenth century, however, Ethiopia had become divided into many small kingdoms.

Modern Ethiopia dates from the time of Menelik I (1844–1913) who pieced the country back together again. It grew into an empire, but the former kingdoms that made up the empire now form mere provinces in modern Ethiopia.

The Italian occupation and colonization of parts of Ethiopia began in the late nineteenth century. Italian expansion culminated in a full-scale invasion and conquest of the empire in 1935.

In 1941, during World War II, British and Ethiopian troops reconquered the country. Ethiopia became a member of the United Nations on November 13, 1945. In 1952, the former Italian colony of Eritrea was made an autonomous part of Ethiopia; but in 1962, it was reduced to the status of a province. A movement for the secession of Eritrea erupted into armed clashes by 1970.

After his appearance in defense of Ethiopia before the League of Nations in 1936, the Emperor Haile Selassie became an international figure. He was deposed by a military junta in 1974, after a reign of 44 years, and the monarchy was abolished in 1975. The capital of Ethiopia, Addis Ababa, is the headquarters of the Organization of African Unity, established there in 1963. The new government signed a pact with Russia in 1977. The following year, Cuba sent 20,000 troops in to help repulse an attack by Somali forces.

An extended drought in Ethiopia in 1984 brought worldwide aid to millions who faced starvation.

FAROE ISLANDS

About A.D. 1000, the Vikings came to the Faroe Islands from Norway. At first a Norwegian dependency, they were attached to the Danish Crown, along with Norway, in 1380. In 1709, they became a part of the Danish kingdom. In 1814, when Norway was ceded to Sweden, the Faroes remained with Denmark, along with Iceland and Greenland.

In 1940, when the Nazis invaded Denmark and the Low Countries, the British sent forces to secure the islands from German occupation; at the end of the war they withdrew. A plebiscite for self-determination resulted in such a close vote (5,660 for independence, 5,499 against) that the Danish government declared the voting indecisive. Renewed negotiations led to a degree of autonomy, especially in economic matters. The islands acquired their own currency, which had to be covered by the Danish kroner, and the right to fly their own flag at sea.

FIJI

The Fiji Islands were discovered by Abel Tasman in 1643 and were visited by Captain James Cook in 1774. Captain William Bligh was the first to describe Fiji to any extent. Missionaries came to the islands in 1835 and helped to eradicate cannibalism.

The islands were annexed by Great Britain in 1874 and were administered by the colonial office until 1970, when a parliamentary system was set up and Fiji became an independent nation. It was admitted to the United Nations on October 13, 1970.

Finland—Helsinki

FINLAND

The Finnish people came originally from the Volga region of what is now the Soviet Union. They arrived in the present area of Finland sometime during the seventh century A.D. The Swedes began to penetrate Finland in the twelfth century. Swedish invasions took the form of religious crusades to convert the people to Christianity. This struggle against pagan Finns lasted two hundred years, ending with the complete conquest of Finland by the Swedes in 1293.

Russia annexed parts of Swedish-held areas in 1721, and the remainder of Finland in 1809. Finland was a grand duchy of the Russian Empire until 1917. The revolution in Russia gave the Finns a chance to proclaim independence.

In the great civil war that followed the Bolshevik victory in November 1917, Germany intervened on behalf of Finland and secured the *de facto* separation from Russia, but intended to establish a German-controlled government. However, after Germany's defeat, Finland emerged in 1919 as a parliamentary republic.

The Aland Islands were secured from Sweden in 1921. In 1939, the Soviet Union and Finland broke relations and two short wars followed that merged with World War II. Finland was defeated and had to pay, both in money and in the loss of some territory. Finland paid her reparations by 1952 and the Soviet Union abandoned the Porkkala naval base, returning it to Finland. However, parts of Karelia and the Petsamo region are apparently permanently lost. Finland was admitted to the United Nations on December 14, 1955.

FRANCE

Classical Greek colonies were founded on the Mediterranean coast of what is now France as early as 600 B.C. However, very little was known of the region until Julius Caesar began his conquests in 58 B.C. The Celtic tribes who lived in the present France were called "Gauls" by the Romans. Gallic legends, traditions, and influence have remained an integral part of French culture. Gallic France achieved a high order of civilization. The region was richly endowed with prosperous cities, a thriving trade, and with great works of both Roman and Gallic engineering and architecture.

After A.D. 180, Gaul experienced violent invasion and wholesale destruction. Visigoths, Ostrogoths, Vandals, Lombardi, Alemanni, Burgundians, and many other invaders passed through Gaul, or conquered parts of it.

In A.D. 476 the Western Roman Empire came to an end and Gaul was left to fend for itself. The Franks, a Germanic tribe, entered Gaul and by A.D. 486 had united under Clovis, who became a convert to Christianity in 496. The Franks gradually conquered most of Gaul, but their Merovingian dynasty was unable to maintain control over large areas.

Under the later Merovingians, power passed to the mayors of the palace. Eventually these mayors took over the kingship titles, and in this way the

France—Paris

Carlovingians became the ruling dynasty of the region that was beginning to be called "France."

Charlemagne (768–814), also called Charles the Great, raised the Frankish people to the height of power in western Europe. Charlemagne ruled not only what is now France, but most of Germany and Italy as well. He had a difficult task in defending his realm from the Vikings and hundreds of other great and small groups. France became one great battlefield.

Huge castles rose over the ashes of formerly beautiful Roman cities. People locked themselves into these bastions for defense against the rising violence and lawlessness that gradually pervaded all western Europe. The population sold its freedom for protection, and serfdom became an established institution—the Age of Feudalism had come to France.

After his death the empire of Charlemagne fell apart. What was left of the once-great empire—a small area centered around Paris—went to Hugh Capet, who founded the third dynasty of French kings. His family was to rule France for 800 years.

The Capetian kings gradually expanded their authority and began to establish order in the lands they controlled. The fashioning of a new France by the Capetian kings was done at the expense of feudal elements and with the aid of a rising new middle class of merchants and nonfeudal groups.

Louis IX (1226–1270) overcame the feudal nobility by making the kingship popular to all groups—even to the peasantry. He outlawed a number of feudal practices and his capital became the intellectual center of Europe. Louis IX died while on a Crusade to the Holy Lands.

The Crusades began in 1096 and lasted until the fourteenth century. Most of the leaders in the first four Crusades were of the French nobility. France learned many lessons in warfare, and received from the Crusades the benefits of greater commerce and quickened industrial activity. These things stimulated a Renaissance in France and helped to lift Europe out of the "Dark Ages."

French power and the Capetian dynasty itself were challenged from England, first by Henry II (1154), and then by Henry's sons, Richard and John. The French kings were able to hold most of their territory in this first great encounter with English power.

In 1328, Edward III again challenged the right of the Capetian house to the French throne. The fighting began in 1337 and lasted for over one hundred years. It was during this "One Hundred Years' War" that Joan of Arc inspired French arms and helped to crown Charles VII king of France. Joan was captured and burned at the stake as a witch, but French armies advanced and by 1461 had driven the English out of France.

It should be noted that French-speaking nobility fought on both sides in this war. Yet France came out of the war more united than ever before. The next two centuries saw discord once more, but this time the conflict was a religious one.

The Protestant Reformation did not have as strong an effect on France as it did on other countries. But large areas of the population that did become Protestant were persecuted by the Catholics.

Under Louis XIV (1643–1715) kingship reached its greatest heights. The Sun King built a magnificent court and did much to make France the center of Western civilization.

The splendor of monarchial France did not last. The end came during the reign of Louis XVI, when a revolution overturned the throne in 1789. The

French Revolution abolished the divine right principle, replacing it with political authority. The bloody civil war that ensued ended only when Napoleon Bonaparte took control. Napoleon led the French nation in conquests and empire-building that ended in his defeat at Waterloo (a town in present Belgium).

The First Empire was succeeded by a monarchy (1814–1848) and the Second Republic (1848–1852). Memories of Napoleon were revived during the short Second Empire that lasted from 1852 to 1870, led by Napoleon III. After 1870, France blundered into a conflict with a newly united Germany. She was beaten, and then revolution overthrew the Empire, creating the Third Republic (1875).

A chance for revenge against German came in 1914. In that year World War I began and France became the main battlefield. Although victorious, France was greatly weakened.

World War II began in 1939 and again German armies crossed the frontiers of France. This time the nation's resistance against a large German army lasted only six weeks. A government was established to administer the German occupation. An "unoccupied" zone was governed from Vichy. Meanwhile, a government-in-exile functioned from London under the leadership of General Charles de Gaulle. French guerrilla fighters (the Resistance) worked closely with the De Gaulle headquarters and the Allies. Following the invasion by the Allies, France was liberated by October 1944.

De Gaulle retired in 1946. The Fourth Republic that governed from 1946 to 1958 lost major French colonies, including those in the Middle East, Indochina, Tunisia, and Morocco. But it made a bitter and vain effort to retain Algeria. Recalled to take the leadership of the Fifth Republic, De Gaulle granted independence to this colony in 1962. Although he resigned once more in 1969, many of his policies were continued by his successor, Georges Pompidou.

France was a charter member of the United Nations on October 24, 1945. The country also joined the North Atlantic Treaty Organization; but in that alliance French policy was independent and unpredictable.

While France has resisted communism, it has drifted toward socialism, culminating with the election May 10, 1981, of Francois Mitterrand, a socialist candidate, over Giscard D'Estaing. Mitterrand proceeded to nationalize five major industries and most banks.

FRENCH GUIANA

French Guiana was settled in 1604 and has been a French possession since 1667. It was long the site of a penal colony named Devil's Island, but the last prisoners were removed in 1945. In 1946, French Guiana became an overseas department of France. It is the last European dependency on the mainland of South America.

FRENCH POLYNESIA

The Overseas Territory of French Polynesia was formerly called French Settlements in Oceania. The major island groups that comprise the territory were made protectorates of France in 1844 and colonies in 1880. The Marquesas and Gambier groups were annexed in 1881. The entire region became a member of the French Community in 1958.

FRENCH SOUTHERN TERRITORIES

This Overseas Territory of France includes: (1) the Kerguelen Archipelago of three hundred islands, discovered in 1772 by Yves de Kerguelen. With an area of 2,700 square miles, they are located in the Indian Ocean southeast of Madagascar and used mainly in scientific research; (2) the Crozet Archipelago, discovered in 1772 by Marion-Dufressne. These 15 islands in the Indian Ocean, with an area of 193 square miles, are uninhabited; (3) St. Paul, an uninhabited island of 3 square miles south of Madagascar in the Indian Ocean; (4) New Amsterdam, an island of 19 square miles, discovered in 1522 by Magellan's ships. It is located in the south Indian Ocean and used as an administrative center; and (5) the Adelie Coast (Terre Adèlie) of the Antarctic continent, an estimated 150,000-square-mile area, discovered in 1840 by Dumont d'Urville.

In 1960, other islands were added to the territory. These include Europa, Juan de Nova (Saint-Christophe), Bassas-de-India, and the Glorioso Islands, all located in Mozambique Channel and having a total area of 23 square miles.

GABON

In the mid-nineteenth century, the region of

Gabon and the city of Libreville, together with other African republics of today, were established under French control and lumped together under the name of "French Equatorial Africa." In 1910, the colony of Gabon was officially organized as part of that region.

In 1946, the French Union was established and Gabon became an overseas territory. In 1960, it became completely independent within the French Community. Gabon was admitted to the United Nations on September 20, 1960.

GAMBIA

An enclave within Sierra Leone on the coast of West Africa is the tiny nation of Gambia, the smallest on the African mainland. It was formed out of the colony and protectorate of the same name. Great Britain acquired both in the seventeenth century and usually administered them from Sierra Leone.

In 1963, Gambia was given autonomy, and on February 18, 1965, it was made a member of the Commonwealth. On September 21, 1965, Gambia became a member of the United Nations. In 1970 the Gambians voted to become a republic, but to retain Commonwealth membership.

Gambia has a treaty with Senegal to form a confederation called Senegambia, although each country will retain its sovereignty.

GHANA

The first authenticated landing of Europeans in this region of Africa was that of some Portuguese in 1470. The first British trading expedition came in 1553. Over the centuries Danes, Dutch, Germans, Portuguese, and British controlled parts of what was then called the Gold Coast.

During the eighteenth century slave trade developed, and by 1821 the British won increasing control of the region. The Crown took over the private trading-post settlements. In time the Danish forts were purchased by Britain. The Fanti chiefs approved a pact that allowed British agents to participate in administering justice.

Ghana was granted autonomy in 1951 and independence on December 12, 1956. It remained within the Commonwealth, became a member of the United Nations on March 8, 1957, and became a republic within the Commonwealth on July 1, 1960. The presidency was abolished in 1972. Three additional coups to overthrow the government occurred in 1978, 1979, and 1981.

GIBRALTAR

Located on a peninsula jutting out from Spain's southern coast, and guarding the Mediterranean Sea, the rock of Gibraltar was captured by England from Spain in 1704. It has been a British colony ever since, despite frequent Spanish protests. It was granted local autonomy in 1969.

GILBERT AND ELLICE ISLANDS (TUVALU)

A group of archipelagoes in the Pacific Ocean comprise the British colony of the Gilbert and Ellice Islands, formed in 1915. It includes the Gilbert Islands on each side of the Equator, whose inhabitants are Micronesians; the Ellice Islands, south of the Equator, whose inhabitants are Melanesians; and several other islands. The colony was granted self-government in 1971. At the end of 1975, the Ellice Islands separated from the others and renamed itself the territory of Tuvalu.

GREECE

Historians regard the ancient Greeks as the founders of Western civilization. The Greeks were the first to develop the concept of democracy. They became Western civilization's first great dramatists, philosophers, scientists, doctors, geographers, orators, and poets. After two thousand years, the Greek world passed its vast heritage on to Rome. In a real sense, Greek civilization did not die; it merely moved to Rome, changed its form, and then brought forth a new civilization—that of modern times.

The recorded story of Ancient Greece began on the island of Crete, which lies on the southern limits of the Aegean Sea south of the mainland of the Greek peninsula. The Cretan civilization, also known as the Minoan, developed about 3000 B.C. It flourished until about 1600 B.C., when it was overpowered by an invasion from the mainland.

The mainland Greeks then developed the Mycenaean civilization on the mainland. By this time Greeks had entered the Bronze Age. They built fortified cities and ships that crossed the Mediterranean Sea to carry on trade with other peoples. Finally they developed a written language (deciphered in 1953). Mycenae in southern

Greece—The Acropolis, Athens

Greece was the central city of this civilization. Mycenaean civilization produced the events described in the *Iliad* and the *Odyssey*.

The Mycenaeans were eventually overwhelmed by invaders from the north. The invaders came in three separate waves, each wave displacing earlier ones. The invasions ended about 1000 B.C. All four groups (including the original Mycenaeans) settled down, intermingled, and finally created the Greek Golden Age.

About 750 B.C., Greeks began to establish colonies along the Mediterranean coast. Some of the more famous colonies were Lisbon, Marseille, Odessa, Naples, Pompeii, and Syracuse. During the Golden Age (480–399 B.C.) there were more than 150 Greek states and colonies strung along the Mediterranean and Black Seas from Spain in the West to the Caucasus, on the edge of Asia in the East.

The first coinage in the Western world appeared in Asia Minor (Kingdom of Lydia) as a result of the rise of Greek trade and commerce there. The coins of Athens became world famous for their reliability, and those of Syracuse were of unsurpassed workmanship and design.

Invasions by Persians from the east (Asia Minor) stirred the Greek world into a movement to unify the scattered states for defensive purposes. The Persian invasions were halted in a series of great battles by the Greeks. A united Greek army crushed the Persians at Platea in 479 B.C. It was at the end of the Persian Wars that the Golden Age flourished.

Athens was the center of Greek intellectual and artistic ferment during this period. The greatest works of sculpture, architecture, drama, and history were produced at Athens at that time. However, nearly all the Greek states shared in the Golden Age. As the power of Athens grew, so did the jealousies of her neighbors. In particular, Sparta became the bitter enemy of Athens. Sparta was a militaristic, highly disciplined, and regimented state. The wars that followed between Athens and her enemies were won by Sparta and the Golden Age came to an end.

Sparta was herself defeated soon after, and all Greece lay weakened by warfare—the ripe fruit for any determined conqueror. Alexander the Great seized the opportunity and in 338 B.C. conquered all of Greece.

Alexander the Great spread Greek culture and ideas throughout the known world. However, his great empire crumbled after his death in 323 B.C.

The Roman army easily conquered a divided Greece in 197 B.C. and again in 167 B.C. Greece became a mere province in the Roman Empire. It was called Achaea. The name *Greek* was first used by the Romans. The classical Greeks called themselves "Hellenes" and their land "Hellas."

After the fall of Rome, Greece became part of the Byzantine, or Eastern Empire. After A.D. 1261, a group of independent states arose and flourished until all were conquered by the Turks in 1460. Some of the islands remained in the possession of Venice until the eighteenth century.

In the nineteenth century the spirit of national independence was reawakened. Following an unsuccessful attempt in 1770, the Greeks proclaimed an independent state in 1821. Their independence was supported by Britain, France, and Russia, and was defended by those powers in 1827. The London Protocol of 1830 secured international recognition of the Greek state.

Greece became a monarchy—first under a Bavarian royal house, then under a Danish prince, who took the throne as George I in 1863. As the result of several wars, Greece acquired Crete, parts of Macedonia and Thrace, and parts of European Turkey. This led to a disastrous war with Turkey, after which some two million Greeks were exchanged for more than a million Turks living in Greece.

During World War II, Greece was under German occupation. The monarchy found exile in Cairo, while the resistance forces fought on in Greece. After the war, the resistance (which included communists) tried to seize power. But a plebiscite in 1946 accepted the monarchy.

A military junta took power in 1967 and forced Constantine, the last king, to flee. The dictatorship was overthrown in 1973, and a parliamentary republic was restored by referendum in 1974.

In 1981, Andres Papandreou of the Panhellenic Socialist Movement was elected prime minister. Greece is a member of the NATO military alliance.

GREENLAND

The huge island of Greenland was discovered and colonized at the end of the tenth century by Eric the Red. Two centuries later it was claimed by Norway, but thereafter the colony was neglected. Although many explorers passed the west coast of Greenland, only traces of the old colony remained when the island was revisited in 1721 by Danish missionaries.

Greenland was again colonized, receiving only enough aid to support the missions and provide a base for explorations.

After the Napoleonic Wars, Denmark and Norway were separated, and Greenland remained with Denmark. In 1979 it was granted home rule, electing a socialist-dominated legislature. It also translated its official name into the Greenlandic language, Kalaallit Nunaat.

GRENADA

The most southerly of the British Windward Islands, Grenada was discovered by Columbus in 1498. It was held alternately by the French and British until 1784. The Windward Islands were given autonomy in 1967, with the status of associated states in the British Commonwealth, and it declared its independence in 1974.

In 1983, acting on intelligence reports of a buildup by Soviet and Cuban operatives, the United States sent in a military detachment to secure the island. American troops were withdrawn in 1985.

GUADELOUPE

Guadeloupe was discovered by Columbus in 1493. It was colonized in 1635 and became a French possession in 1674. It was made an overseas department of France in 1946. Its dependencies include Marie Galante, Les Saintes, Désirade, St. Barthélemy, and part of St. Martin.

GUATEMALA

The ancestors of modern-day Guatemalans were the Mayan peoples who developed a remarkable civilization between A.D. 300 and 900. The Maya were a short, stocky people who lived originally in what is now Mexico, Guatemala, Honduras, British Honduras, and El Salvador. The classic civilization (ca. A.D. 350 to 600) may have included two million people. The Maya developed mathematics, a 365-day calendar, ideographic writing, sculpture, music, and literature. Their great cities now lie abandoned.

The Spanish conquest began in 1524 and was completed by 1550. The capital was established at Guatemala City in 1776. In 1821, all the Central American colonies declared their independence of Spain and joined the Mexican Empire. Soon they withdrew to form the United Provinces of Central America. This union was weak and collapsed in 1939, and Guatemala the same year became a republic. Its government has been among the least stable in Central America. Guatemala was admitted to the United Nations on November 21, 1945.

Since 1945 the government has seen a shift toward socialism; assassinations and political violence have wracked the country. Founded in 1975, the Guerrilla Army of the Poor has stepped up their military offensive by attacking army posts. In 1982 a military coup seized power; a second military coup occurred in 1983.

GUINEA

European penetration and exploration of what is now Guinea began in the fifteenth century under the Portuguese. France began to trade and acquire territory there early in the seventeenth century. France administered all her Guinea region as a part of Senegal until 1845. Resistance to French rule was bitterly carried out by Samory Touré, who fought the French from 1882 until he was captured in 1898. The boundaries of Guinea were established in 1882.

In 1946, Africans in Guinea became French citizens and a territorial legislature was organized. At that time it became a part of the loose federation of French West Africa. In 1958, Guinea was given the choice of becoming an independent nation, either in the French Community or outside it. Guinea chose independence without association with the Community. It was admitted to the United Nations on December 12, 1958.

After the 1984 death of Sekou Toure, who had been at the country's helm since 1958, the military took control of the country.

GUINEA-BISSAU

Located on the West African coast between the former French colonies of Senegal and Guinea, this region belonged to Portugal since Bissau was set up as a Portuguese post in 1687. Before that, since its discovery by Nuno Tristão in 1446, this part of Guinea was active in the slave trade. Its status as a Portuguese colony was settled by an agreement with France in 1886. Initially administered from Cape Verde, Portuguese Guinea became a separate colony in 1879. In 1951, it was designated an overseas territory. Its independence was recognized by Portugal on September 7, 1974, and ten days later Guinea-Bissau was admitted to the United Nations. A coup in 1980 placed Joao Bernardo Vieira in absolute power.

GUYANA

The westernmost of the three European colonies known as the Guianas, this area was first colonized by the Dutch. It was traded to the British after the Napoleonic era.

The three settlements of Berbice, Essequibo, and Demerara were combined in 1831 to form British Guiana, and became a crown colony in 1928. Local autonomy was introduced in 1953, and a contest developed between the black and East Indian inhabitants for control. The black faction prevailed, and on May 22, 1966, the independence of the country was recognized. On September 20, 1966, Guyana was admitted to the United Nations.

HAITI

That portion of the island of Hispaniola that is now the Republic of Haiti was ceded to France in 1697. It became known as St. Domingue, while the Spanish portion of Hispaniola was called Santo Domingo.

French control was swept away by a revolution in 1803. Jean Jacques Dessalines named the country Haiti, and was proclaimed emperor. He was assassinated in 1806. From that date until 1820, Haiti was divided into a kingdom and a republic. Haiti was reunited in 1822 by Jean Pierre Boyer, who also seized Santo Domingo. He ruled the entire island of Hispaniola until 1844. The future Dominican Republic withdrew in that year.

From 1915 to 1934, Haiti was occupied by the United States. It became a member of the United Nations on October 24, 1945.

In 1957 Dr. Francois Duvalier ("Papa Doc") was voted president; in 1964 he was named president for life. Upon his death in 1971, his son, Jean-Claude, became successor to the office.

Early in 1986 Jean-Claude Duvalier fled the country with his family to France. A six-man junta stepped into power.

HONDURAS

In 1502, Christopher Columbus discovered the region that is now Honduras. The Spanish explorer Hernan Cortés made the first settlement there in 1524 and claimed the land for Spain.

Honduras remained under the rule of Spain until 1821, when the country revolted and was annexed to Mexico. From then on, Honduras' history includes a series of alliances and wars with neighboring countries. Starting in 1883 and continuing for twenty years, Honduras was in continuous revolt and civil disorder. In 1911 the United States intervened in the strife between Honduras and Guatemala. Civil war followed World War I. The United States intervened again in 1915, and the 1930s were turbulent.

Honduras was admitted to the United Nations on December 17, 1945.

An Army coup in 1975 ousted Gen. Oswalado Lopez Arellano, who had been president during most of the years from 1963–75. Arellano held the office through one election and two coups. An elected civilian government took office in 1982. The United States provided economic and military aid in 1984.

HONG KONG

Hong Kong was occupied in 1841 by the British. In 1860, the Kowloon peninsula was added. Additional territory was added by a lease agreement in 1898. Hong Kong is a crown colony, administered by a governor assisted by an executive council. In 1984 China and Great Britain signed an agreement to transfer Hong Kong from British to Chinese control in 1997.

HUNGARY

Within historic times the area of the present Hungary was a part of the Roman provinces of Pannonia and Dacia. Germanic tribes displaced the Romans in the second century A.D., and were, in turn, conquered by Attila the Hun in the fifth century.

The Magyars (Hungarians) were originally located in what is now central Russia. They invaded and occupied the lands between the Tisza and Danube rivers in A.D. 895.

The Magyars fought wars on all sides. Their greatest period of expansion was during the reign of Louis the Great (1342–1382) which was after the country had been overrun by the Mongols (1235–1270) from Asia. Hungarian power was broken by the Turks in 1526. Thereafter, the nation was split into several petty baronies and duchies.

The Hapsburg kings of Austria defeated the Turks and gradually united the Magyar people under Austrian control. Hungary was finally driven to revolt by the repressive policies of Prince Metternich in 1848. The revolt was crushed in 1849. Austria was gradually weakened by war with Prussia, and was forced to give in to Hungarian national aspirations in 1867. In that year a dual monarchy was established, called Austria-Hungary.

Austria-Hungary expanded into the Balkans in the twentieth century. The assassination of the heir to the throne of Austria-Hungary in 1914 pre-

Hong Kong—General view of Victoria Island

cipitated World War I, in which the dual monarchy entered on the side of Germany. After the war, the dual monarchy collapsed.

Hungary was separated from Austria and stripped of nearly two-thirds of its territory. In 1920, it became a kingdom, but without a king. In the hope of retrieving lost territory, Hungary in World War II joined the Axis powers and was again defeated along with Germany. She again lost territory, this time what had been acquired after 1937.

In 1948, the Hungarian Workers party (Communist) seized control and established the one-party (Communist) People's Republic of Hungary. A revolt occurred in 1956 which was directed against the Communist regime. After temporary success, the revolt was crushed with the aid of military forces from the U.S.S.R. Hungary was admitted to the United Nations on December 14, 1955.

By the late 1970s, Hungarian laws had relaxed to allow more personal freedoms than most other communist nations. Many Hungarians who fled the country in 1956 have returned to their homeland.

ICELAND

Iceland was settled shortly before A.D. 900, mainly by Norsemen. Christianity appeared at the beginning of the twelfth century, and with it certain reforms which helped to stablize the various fighting clans. In the mid-thirteenth century, both sides in a civil war appealed to Norway for intervention; the result was unification with that country in 1262–1264.

Then followed a succession of events which nearly wiped out the island: harsh Norwegian rule, volcanic eruptions, and bubonic plague. Iceland passed into Danish hands in 1483 when the king of Denmark came to the Norwegian throne.

With the decline of the monarchs, Iceland began its struggle for freedom, and in 1874 won limited home rule. By 1918, it had become a sovereign nation under Denmark's crown. On June 17, 1944, Iceland became a completely independent republic. The Althing, or assembly, is the world's oldest surviving parliament.

During World War II, Iceland served as an important naval station for United States warships. In 1972, Iceland banned foreign fishing fleets from within 200 miles of its shores.

INDIA

The earliest civilization known to have existed on the subcontinent of India developed in the Indus River valley of what is now Pakistan about five thousand years ago. The ruins at Mohenjodaro indicate a very high degree of civilization.

Mystery surrounds the fate of that civilization. The Aryan invasions began about four thousand years ago, and their influence gradually spread throughout India. They established Hinduism, the family pattern of India, and the caste system. Alexander the Great came to India by way of the Khyber Pass in 326 B.C., but Greek influence was not felt east of the Indus valley. The Maurya Empire arose after Alexander's visit. Under Asoka (273–232 B.C.), India was finally united into one state. It included nearly all of the present India, Pakistan, and other parts of southern Asia. After Asoka, India was subdivided into many competing states. The Gupta rulers became the first Hindu kings and brought about a "golden age" of Sanskrit learning. Rich cities and great universities were founded. By about A.D. 1000, the Hindu period had reached its peak. Many of the great works of art and architecture in India that still survive date from this period.

The next age of flourishing civilization was initiated by the Moslem invaders who had gradually spread their power and influence throughout northern India from the eighth to the sixteenth century. The unification of India began again in 1526. Babar, Akbar, Shah Jahan, and Aurangzeb established the Mogul Empire and caused the rise of a new and even richer civilization in India. Aurangzeb, the last of the great emperors, tried to convert the people to Islam by force. This, together with the extravagance of the Mogul rulers, led to the downfall of Mogul power. Their demise made it easier for the Europeans to obtain a foothold on the subcontinent.

Vasco da Gama (Portuguese) reached Calicut (on the west coast of India) in 1498. Thereafter the Portuguese, English, and French began a mad scramble for spheres of trade and colonies. The British eventually won. By the middle of the nineteenth century they controlled most of India in one form or another. British withdrawal was sudden and decisive in 1947. India was then a single independent nation, but was still divided in many other ways.

The most serious division was between Hindu and Moslem. Bloodshed and civil war resulted

India—Golden Temple of Amritsar

when the Moslem state of Pakistan was proclaimed upon the date of Indian independence. Other serious problems that still plague the Indian nation are the many language and ethnic barriers; the system of caste and other religious issues; the poverty of the masses; and the lack of a national tradition and spirit.

India has attempted to remain neutral between communist and capitalist nations. She tried to defend her borders against Chinese claims and invasions. India also was engaged in a serious dispute over Kashmir. Kashmir is divided between India and Pakistan, and only an armed truce prevents warfare along that frontier. India has been trying to lessen the linguistic differences and problems by establishing states on the basis of language or of national ethnic minorities.

Elected as prime minister in 1966, Indira Gandhi was the second successor to Jawaharal Nehru, the prime minister from 1947 to 1964. She held a second term from 1980 to 1984, when she was assassinated by Sikh extremists. Her son, Rajiv, replaced her as prime minister.

INDONESIA

According to Indonesian history, the people of the original archipelago were overwhelmed by countless migrations from the Asian mainland. Some two thousand years ago, Hindu traders introduced their religion and culture. Then followed Indian Buddhists who also greatly influenced the natives. The Islamic religion entered at the end of the fifteenth century and gained a firm foothold.

Portuguese traders came next. They were soon pushed out by the Dutch, under whom the islands became a highly important colony until World War II. From the beginning of the nineteenth century on, the Dutch rulers put down several attempts at revolution. World War II ended the Japanese occupation, and the Dutch attempted to return to power. A self-proclaimed independence followed, with both open and guerrilla warfare. At the end of 1949, the Dutch officially relinquished sovereignty. On September 28, 1950, Indonesia became a member of the United Nations.

A dispute with the Netherlands arose over the disposition of Dutch New Guinea, which Indonesia claimed as her province of West Irian. In 1963, West Irian was turned over to Indonesia by the United Nations. Meanwhile, the parliamentary system was changed to an authoritarian regime, based on the slogan of "guided democracy." A military coup in 1965 suppressed the strong communist faction of Indonesia. In 1967, it deposed President Sukarno. The leader of the junta, Suharto, became president and prime minister. Indonesia, which had been a charter member of the United Nations, withdrew from the organization in January 1965. But she resumed membership on September 28, 1966.

IRAN

Iran was called Persia until 1935. The history of Persia dates back to the time of the Medes, a people who settled in what is now Iran in 1500 B.C. The Medes dominated the Persians until the time of Cyrus the Great. In about 549, Cyrus conquered the Medes and extended his Persian kingdom. Persia conquered Babylonia, restoring Jerusalem to the Jews in 538 B.C. Persia failed to capture the Greek city-states in 490 and 480 B.C., and was itself defeated by Alexander the Great in 331 B.C.

The Parthians prevented the Romans from conquering Persia. They controlled the area until the third century A.D., and were followed by the Sassanians, who ruled for another four centuries.

The Arabs brought Islam to Persia in the seventh century A.D., and for centuries afterward religious caliphates ruled in Persia. The Mongols invaded in A.D. 1250. After the defeat of the caliphate in 1502, Persia was ruled by a shah (king). A constitution was granted in 1906. The period following was marked by attempts of foreign powers to gain spheres of influence in Persia. During World War II, Iran was occupied by the Allies to prevent German access to the rich Iranian oil fields. The sovereignty of Iran was reaffirmed by the Allies at the Tehran Conference in 1943. Iran joined the United Nations on October 24, 1945.

Iran is now one of the largest exporters of oil in the world. Its income allows the nation to invest in a wide variety of foreign enterprises. Iran is purchasing nuclear power plants from France and the United States; and in 1974, it loaned money to Great Britain to shore up the British economy.

Popular protests forced the shah of Iran to leave the country in January 1979. Religious leader Ayatollah Khomeini seized control and shortly thereafter the American Embassy was stormed with 90 persons captured. Among them were 52 Americans who were held for 444 days before being released unharmed January 20, 1981.

(See section on Iraq for Iran-Iraq warfare since 1980.)

IRAQ

Modern Iraq occupies the area the ancient Greeks called Mesopotamia, one of the cradles of modern civilization. As such, the history of Iraq extends back to the very beginning of writing, about 4000 B.C., and archaeologically even farther.

Eridu, Ur, Nineveh, and Babylon were among the earliest cities in human civilization. The Sumerian culture developed in about 3000 B.C. and later influenced the culture of Egypt, and the rising new civilizations of Greece and Crete.

The Sumerians were succeeded by Akkadians, Assyrians, Scythians, Persians, and finally Romans. The Arabs conquered Iraq in A.D. 637. Baghdad became a brilliant center of cultural and intellectual life.

The Mongol invasions of the thirteenth century ended the prosperity, destroyed the remarkable irrigation system, and turned the land of former greatness into a desert. The Ottoman Turks swept into Iraq in 1638 and maintained their control until, during World War I, British troops wrested it from them. The League of Nations established a British mandate over Iraq, and a monarchy was established in 1921. The mandate was terminated in 1932. The monarchy was overthrown in 1958, shortly after Iraq and Jordan had joined in a federation. The federation was terminated and Iraq was declared a republic.

Hostilities between Iraq and Iran flared into open warfare in September 1980. The border war centered around disputes over the Shatt al-Arab waterway; fighting continued through 1985.

IRELAND

Recorded Irish history begins with the arrival of St. Patrick on the Emerald Isle in the fifth century. Christianity spread rapidly thereafter and Ireland became dotted with great monasteries that were centers of learning and of Gaelic and Latin culture. The Viking invasions of the eighth century nearly put an end to Irish learning, but Viking power was finally broken at the Battle of Clontarf in 1014.

Anglo-Norman invasions began soon after. For 800 years, Ireland grappled with neighboring Britain for a separate and independent existence. Successive British monarchs attempted to control, cajole, or colonize Ireland, but usually ended up persecuting the inhabitants, either for religious or political reasons. Rebellions during the nineteenth century were fair warning that Irish nationalism was growing strong and ever more resentful of English control.

A civil war and political turmoil marked the period of 1916–1921 that ended with the establishment of the Irish Free State with dominion status in the British Commonwealth of Nations. In 1937, a further change came about when the

Ireland—Glendalough

British governor-general was replaced by a president. The name was then changed to Ireland (in Gaelic, *Eire*). In 1948, Ireland withdrew from the Commonwealth and on April 15, 1959 became a republic. The republic became a member of the United Nations on December 14, 1955.

Protestant and Catholic groups still wage a sporadic war of terrorism against one another.

ISLE OF MAN

The Isle of Man has been attached to the Crown of England since 1346. It is administered under its own laws and form of government consisting of legislative council, governor, and the Court of Tynwald. The people are Celtic in origin, and are called Manx, or Manxmen. Manx and English are spoken.

ISRAEL

Israel is the collective name that was applied to the descendants of Jacob, those Hebrew peoples who migrated under Abraham from Mesopotamia to Canaan sometime during the twentieth century before Christ.

The Israelites conquered most of the Canaanites, adopted their language and some of their culture. Later, some of the remaining Canaanites became known as Phoenicians. The land of Canaan is now called Palestine, part of which forms modern Israel.

In about 1100 B.C., the Israelites formed a loose organization of tribes. A united kingdom was established by Saul (1010 B.C.–970 B.C.). It became the heart of a great Hebrew civilization that flourished under David and his son, Solomon. After the death of Solomon, the kingdom split into two parts. In 722 B.C., northern Israel was conquered by the Assyrians. The southern part, Judea, held out until 586 B.C., when the Babylonians captured Jerusalem and exiled the Jews. Judea arose again after 538 B.C. and continued to flourish until A.D. 70, when Roman legions captured Jerusalem, bringing an end to ancient Israel.

The Arabs seized Palestine (the Roman name for Canaan) in A.D. 636. Four hundred years of Moslem rule followed, in which Christians and Jews were tolerated. The Turks seized the region in 1065, and the Crusades were begun in order to free the Holy Land of Christendom. Successive waves of invasions continued after the Crusades, and the Turks managed to recapture or retain most of Palestine until 1917. Jews began to return to Palestine in 1878. Britain occupied it from 1917 until 1948.

Zionism is the name of the national movement for the restoration of Palestine to the world's Jews. The Balfour Declaration of Britain (1917) supported the idea behind Zionism. Under the United Kingdom's mandate, Jewish immigrants arrived in large numbers, particularly under Nazi persecution of the European Jews and during World War II. Jews attempted to find refuge in Palestine, which they considered their historic homeland (Zion); their hopes collided with the aspirations of some Arabs, who wanted to establish independent Arab states in the area. Britain, caught between conflicting pressures, restricted Jewish immigration to Palestine. Eventually, Britain therefore precipitously abandoned the mandate, leaving the United Nations to provide a solution.

The solution proposed was the creation of a Jewish state and an Arab state in Palestine. On May 14, 1948, the Jews proclaimed their state, which they called Israel. The states of the Arab League immediately attacked Israel, were beaten off, and signed an armistice in 1949. However, no peace was established.

The Israeli government was forced to protect its population from constant sporadic attacks from all sides. The Palestinian Arabs either fled or accepted minority status within Israel. The issue of the displaced Palestinians became a critical factor in the Middle East question, along with the issue of Arab recognition of the state of Israel.

Warfare broke out in 1956, when Israel invaded Egypt and defeated the Egyptian army. The intervention of French and British forces on their behalf brought about a settlement by the United Nations. In 1967, Egypt took the offensive and was decisively defeated within six days. In 1973, Egypt forcibly recovered part of the territory occupied since 1967 by Israel. In all these conflicts Syria and other Arab states participated against Israel. On numerous occasions the issue was brought before the United Nations (to which Israel was admitted on May 11, 1949). After the acquisition of Arab territory in the 1967 war, most United Nations resolutions were unfavorable to Israel. The forging of peaceful relations between Israel and her Arab neighbors remained a major international problem.

ITALY

The roots of Italian history lie in the Roman period, and the history of Rome rested upon Greek and Etruscan civilizations.

Roman civilization began as an offshoot of that of the Etruscans whom the early Romans conquered about 200 B.C. Etruria (modern Tuscany) lay in the north-central part of the Italian peninsula. The Etruscan civilization spread into the Po River valley and reached its greatest development about 600 B.C. Etruscan control over Latium (Rome) lasted to about 500 B.C., and over southern Italy for another hundred years. Their influence upon Roman civilization is seen through the development of urban centers, large public works, maritime commerce, and in art forms. The Etruscans borrowed from Greece, and probably also from Lydia in Asia Minor.

When Rome conquered the Etrurian states in Southern Etruria in about 400 B.C., the Greek states and colonies in that area collapsed. By 272 B.C., the entire Italian peninsula had come under Roman rule.

The period of unification was followed by overseas expansion. Three wars were fought for control of the Mediterranean Sea with the Phoenician city of Carthage (near present-day Tunis in Africa). After one hundred years of war, Carthage was overwhelmed in 146 B.C.

Rome had been a republic since its founding, but because of the wars of conquest and expansion, an imperial form of government was established in 27 B.C. The first 200 years of the empire were marked by a golden age of peaceful development, prosperity, and progress in literature, the arts, engineering, architecture, and government. Despite the personal rule of some incompetent emperors, the Roman Empire flourished primarily through efficient administrative machinery, and through the occasional genius of such emperors as Augustus (27 B.C.–A.D. 14), Trajan (98–117), Hadrian (117–138), and Marcus Aurelius (161–180).

The empire eventually became too large and troublesome for the personal rule of one emperor. It was split in A.D. 395 into the Eastern Roman Empire with the seat of government at Constantinople (the present Istanbul) and a Western Roman Empire whose capital remained at Rome. Following the death in 337 of Emperor Constantine, who ruled both empires, open rebellions broke out. Spain, Gaul (France), and all the African territories had already been lost when

Italy—Milan Cathedral

Odoacer, a German prince, established a kingdom in the Italian peninsula in A.D. 476. The Western Roman Empire had ended. The Eastern Roman Empire survived and flourished until 1453, when the Turks overran it and captured Constantinople.

From the sixth century down to the thirteenth, Italy suffered from invasions—including those of the Lombards, Franks, Saracens, and Germans. From the tenth to the fourteenth century the Holy Roman Empire of German kings and the Christian Church, centered in Rome, became the leading contenders for power in the Italian peninsula. However, the rise of small city-states with powerful maritime interests upset the balance between papal and German rule. The south became united in the Kingdom of Naples, and the Papal States were established in central Italy; and most of the city-states were located in the north and along the coasts of both the Adriatic and Tyrrhenian seas.

Beginning in the thirteenth century, a revival of trade, commerce, and learning spread out from the main centers of both the Byzantine and the Western Christian world. This was stimulated, to a large degree, by the Crusades of Europeans against Moslem control of the Holy Lands of Christendom.

Modern Italian history dates from the rise of the new commerce, trade, and industrial centers of the Italian peninsula during and after the great Crusades. The Italian peninsula emerged as the heart of an unparalleled surge in art, music, literature, science, and philosophical movements. Industry, trade, commerce, farming, and orderly government revived. Milan, Florence, Genoa, Pisa, Lucca, Venice, and Bologna vied with one another for leadership in the Renaissance of the Western world.

In later centuries the Italian city-states were overwhelmed by other European powers. Venice, Milan, and the Kingdom of Piedmont (in the northwest) managed to keep alive ideas of national unity and their own independence.

Modern Italian national consciousness was greatly influenced and strengthened by the "Resorgimento" movement, led by Giuseppe Mazzini and Count Camillo Cavour, in the nineteenth century. The Kingdom of Piedmont and its ruling House of Savoy served as the rallying point for Italian unification. Giuseppe Garibaldi initiated a series of military adventures that helped lead to a united Italy in 1870. Rome became the capital of the kingdom in that year, but the Roman Catholic Church continued in bitter opposition to unification for another 60 years.

Italy suffered heavy losses during World War I. This setback, combined with a severe economic depression, ushered in a Fascist dictatorship led by Benito Mussolini in 1922. During World War II, Italy joined Hitler's Nazi regime in Germany. The nation became a major battlefield of the war and was devastated by land invasion and air attack. Mussolini's Fascist empire collapsed near the end of the war; and in 1945, the Italian Social Republic was set up. In 1946, this was transformed into a constitutional republic. The reign of the House of Savoy came to an end. Italy became a member of the NATO alliance in 1949 and a member of the United Nations on December 14, 1955.

The Italian constitution does not allow the reorganization of the Fascist Party, but it does allow the Communist Party to take an active role in government. Inflation and uneasy labor relations have brought down a number of Italian premiers in recent times.

IVORY COAST REPUBLIC

Portuguese navigators first landed in the late fifteenth century in what is now the Ivory Coast Republic. For the next 200 years, European traders dealt extensively in ivory and slaves taken from the region. French missionaries established themselves there in 1687, and at the beginning of the eighteenth century a trading post was set up by the French near Abidjan. Additional settlements by the French were established in the nineteenth century.

On March 10, 1893, the Ivory Coast became a French colony and later was consolidated with other French-controlled regions to form French West Africa. The colony was designated a territory within the French Union in 1946. On August 7, 1960, the Ivory Coast became an independent republic associated with the French Community. It was admitted to the United Nations on September 20, 1960.

JAMAICA

Columbus discovered Jamaica in 1494 on his second voyage. The island was colonized by the Spanish in 1523. The British captured it in 1655, and it was formally ceded by Spain in 1670. Jamaica acquired internal self-government in 1944 and cabinet government was introduced in 1953.

Jamaica joined a British-sponsored Federation of West Indies in 1958. However, the island withdrew in 1961 and became an independent nation on August 6, 1962. Jamaica was admitted to the United Nations on September 18, 1962.

In 1974, the Jamaican government took half ownership in American companies that have Jamaican mines for bauxite (aluminum ore).

In recent years, Jamaica's relations with the United States under the leadership of Prime Minister Seaga have improved. The country severed relations with Cuba in 1981 and President Reagan visited Jamaica in 1982. Jamaica participated in the 1983 invasion of Grenada.

JAPAN

According to legend, the Japanese Empire was founded in 660 B.C. The first capital was at Nara and was removed to Kyoto in A.D. 784. Buddhism and Chinese culture entered Japan during the Nara period. The Chinese influences were molded and changed to suit native forms. The shogunate form of government (in which real power lay not with the emperor but with military leaders called "shoguns") began in 1192 and continued until 1867.

The first contacts with the West occurred when Portuguese traders arrived in southern Japan in 1543. However, Japan remained generally sealed off to Westerners except for a few Dutch and Chinese merchants until the coming of Commodore Matthew C. Perry from the United States in 1853. The signing of a treaty of peace and friendship with the United States caused turmoil among the ruling forces and eventually led to the destruction of feudalism in Japan. In 1867, the emperor won back full control of the throne from the feudal shoguns.

The opening up of Japan to Western influence also ushered in a period of Japanese expansion. Japan defeated China in 1895, Russia in 1905, and Korea in 1910. By 1922, Japan was the third naval power of the world and one of the five "great powers." Military factions dominated Japan after 1926, and events that led up to World War II began with an invasion of China in 1931. By 1936, the military were in full control. Manchuria (a region of China) had been conquered and organized into a puppet state called Manchukuo. In 1936, Japan withdrew from the League of Nations and set up close relations with the Axis Powers (Germany and Italy).

Japan launched a full-scale invasion of China in 1937. The United States was sympathetic to China and extended her credit, placing embargoes on the shipping of aircraft and other war materials to Japan. Japan retaliated with a sneak attack on the United States Pacific naval base at Pearl Harbor, Hawaii, on December 7, 1941. This was the beginning of World War II in the Pacific area. (The war had been under way in Europe since 1939, when Germany invaded Poland.)

The Pacific war was marked by a series of great naval battles. On land it was a bitter jungle war and a series of beachhead landings from island to island. The Japanese reached the Coral Sea off Australia in May 1942, where they were stopped in the great Battle of the Coral Sea. Their eastward move was halted at Midway Island in June 1942, and in Alaska at the same time. Thereafter, the war went against Japan, as Allied strength began to build up. The most decisive battle was probably Leyte Gulf (October 23, 1944), the biggest naval battle in history. The Japanese fleet was crushed and Japanese aircraft resorted to suicide "Kamikaze" dives on American ships. By October 26, the Japanese fleet no longer existed as a force.

The final blow was an atomic bomb attack launched by the United States against Hiroshima on August 6, 1945, and against Nagasaki on August 9, 1945. Japan surrendered, signing the terms on August 14 aboard the battleship *Missouri* in Tokyo Bay. The Japanese people participated enthusiastically in the great changes that transformed Japan from a feudal militaristic empire into a progressive and democratic nation.

Japanese economic recovery was phenomenal,

Japan—Nijubashi Bridge, main entrance to Imperial Palace

but also important were the basic changes made in the life and culture of Japan. The new Japan has become a Westernized nation in many of its social patterns. Japan became a member of the United Nations on December 18, 1956.

In September 1972, Japan broke its diplomatic ties with the Chinese government-in-exile on Taiwan and restored friendly relationships with mainland China. The United States has withdrawn most of its military forces from Japan and has given virtually all of its bases there to the Japanese government.

In its rise to leadership among industrial nations of the world, Japan has become a fierce competitor to the United States in the manufacture of automobiles, electronics, computers and many other products. The rivalry has resulted in some modifications of Japan's trade policies and the imposition of some sanctions by the United States.

An agreement to increase the importation of citrus fruits and beef was signed with the United States in 1984.

JORDAN

The nation is named for the famous river of Jordan whose valley forms one of the earliest sites of human civilization. Excavations at Jericho, near the Dead Sea, reveal a Neolithic culture eight thousand years old. The history of western Jordan is much the same as that of Palestine (*see* Israel). However, Jordan's history has one other chapter not included in that of Palestine. This is the era of the Nabataeans, a mysterious Arabic people who built one of the finest of all ancient cities in the desert of what is now southern Jordan. The ruins of Petra, the capital city, were discovered in A.D. 1812. The Nabataeans controlled the trade routes between the Dead Sea and Red Sea. Their empire developed an alliance with Rome that could have changed the history of the world, had it lasted. Petra developed a unique Arabic-Greco-Roman culture. The kingdom was annexed by the Romans in the second century after Christ.

The great northward invasion of the Arabs in A.D. 633 brought Islam to the region. From the twelfth century until the Ottoman conquest in 1517, the area was controlled by Christian Crusaders from Europe. The Ottoman Turks ruled this entire part of southwestern Asia until 1917, when T. E. Lawrence (known as Lawrence of Arabia) led Arab troops against the Turks to a decisive victory. As a result, an Arab state was set up in the eastern part of Britain's Palestinian mandate.

In 1921, Abdullah ibn Hussein (head of the Hashemite family of Arabia) was installed by the British as king of the new state, which was known as Transjordan because it was on the far side of the river. In 1927, it was recognized as a state under British protection. The mandatory power signed a treaty with Abdullah in 1946 recognizing him as ruler of the Hashemite Kingdom of Transjordan. Two years later the Palestinian mandate ended, Israel was formed under United Nations auspices in western Palestine, and Transjordan joined with other Arab states in a military attack on Israel. Much Palestinian territory west of the Jordan was annexed to Abdullah's kingdom, which then changed its name to Jordan. Part of the city of Jerusalem thus fell to Jordan. The state was admitted to the United Nations on December 14, 1955.

Under Abdullah's grandson, Hussein, Jordan continued to oppose Israel along with Egypt and other Arab states. During the Arab-Israeli War of 1967, Israel captured Jordan's west-bank territory. The continued occupation of the west bank became a major obstacle to peace in the Middle East. Jordan became more moderate in her relations with Israel than the Palestinians did. In fact, the Palestinians almost seized control of Jordan's kingdom, and were forced to transfer their bases to Syria in 1970. Hussein joined the other Arab states in the attack on Israel in 1973.

Jordan initiated the severance of diplomatic ties with Egypt after the Israeli-Egyptian peace treaty of 1979. Relations were resumed in 1984.

KENYA

Settlements of Arabs from nearby Zanzibar were established in what is now Kenya as early as the seventh century A.D. After the fifteenth century, the Portuguese competed with the Arabs for control of the coast. After 1740, the sultanate on Zanzibar Island became the ruler of most of eastern Kenya until 1887. Zanzibar then came under British influence and other opportunities, and the British East Africa Protectorate was created in 1895. Britain then induced Europeans to settle in the region, which was valued as a gateway to Uganda. Most of the usable land was occupied by Europeans, and the local tribesmen were driven to the least desirable locations. In 1920, Kenya became a colony.

A movement for African control and for independence began within the decade. The tribes organized in a guerrilla strike force known as the Mau Mau, and eventually brought self-government by stages. Jomo Kenyatta became a member of the colonial cabinet in 1962 and was prime minister when Kenya became independent on December 12, 1963. Four days later the country was admitted to the United Nations.

KUWAIT

In 1716, settlements were established in Kuwait by migrants from the neighboring Arabian Desert. The present ruling dynasty dates from 1756. British protection was extended upon the invitation of the Sheikh Mubarak al-Sabah (1896–1915), to prevent occupation by the Turks. After World War I Kuwait became independent, but remained under the protection of the British Crown. On June 19, 1961, that protection was terminated by mutual consent.

On May 14, 1963, the United Nations admitted Kuwait to membership. Kuwait exercises a great influence on Middle East and world affairs because of her enormous oil resources, which were largely developed by American companies since World War II. The country consistently supports the Arab anti-Israeli position.

Friction with Iran resulted in an Iranian air attack of two Kuwaiti oil tankers in the Persian Gulf in 1984.

LAOS

In the thirteenth century the Thai (Siamese) people migrated southward from China into Indochina, where they organized Lao tribes into a powerful kingdom that reached its peak in the seventeenth century, with its capital at Vientiane. The decline of this kingdom was complete with the fall of Vientiane to the Thais in 1827. The French, who had acquired a foothold on the Indochinese coast (in Annam and Tonkin, now North Vietnam), attached Laos to their Union of Indochina in 1893. In 1899 Laos became a French protectorate.

Japan occupied Indochina in World War II. Upon their withdrawal, resistance movements arose in all the Indochinese states. The most influential movement was that of the Vietminh, led by Ho Chi Minh in Vietnam. In 1949, a Laotian monarchy was reinstated and its government was recognized as independent within the French Union; but a dissident faction, the Pathet Lao, arose in 1953. Generally sympathetic with the Vietminh, the Pathet Lao participated at times in government with the monarchy. The kingdom of Laos became a member of the United Nations on December 14, 1955, and was assured of the protection of the anticommunist Southeast Asia Treaty Organization.

As the Pathet Lao accepted more and more aid from North Vietnam, it was inevitable that the Indochina War would involve Laos. One of the main routes used by North Vietnamese forces to reach their targets in South Vietnam passed through eastern Laos. In 1970, United States and South Vietnamese forces made a brief and unsuccessful incursion into southern Laos. With the victory of the communist forces in Indochina in 1975, the coalition and the monarchy yielded to Pathet Lao control.

LEBANON

The name *Lebanon* is derived from a great mountain range that extends through the country. The history of Lebanon has been associated with that of Syria since Phoenician times. Tyre, Sidon, and Byblos were famous Phoenician trade centers which sent colonists to found Carthage, Marsailles, Cádiz, and other cities along the Mediterranean Sea. Syria and Lebanon were united under Alexander the Great, under Rome, and later under the Arabs and Turks. Christians from Syria sought refuge in Lebanon, and the Druze sect of Islam also escaped to the Lebanese mountains and forests for protection. The Crusaders controlled parts of Lebanon in the thirteenth century, and left descendants there.

Modern Lebanon dates only from the 1860s, when France intervened in the Turkish rule of Lebanon in order to protect Maronite Christians who had revolted against the Druzes. From 1864 until World War I, the Turks ruled Lebanon under an agreement that permitted Christian freedom. During the war, France and Britain came to an agreement concerning the postwar division of the Middle East. Syria and Lebanon were allotted to France, and this change was approved by the League of Nations in 1923. At this time the state of Greater Lebanon was created, with a population about evenly divided between Moslems and Christians. The constitution of 1926 provided that the division would be reflected in the political institutions. This originated the tradition that the president should be a Christian and that he appoint a Moslem prime minister. As the Moslem population began to outnumber the Christians, this failed to be reflected in the legislature.

Plans for Lebanese independence were suspended by the conditions of World War II, when the Vichy French who controlled Lebanon were displaced in 1941 by the Free French. In 1945, the independence of Lebanon was recognized, and the country was admitted to the United Nations on October 24, 1945.

The government was fairly stable and the country was the most prosperous in the Arab world. In the conflict between the Arab states and Israel, Lebanon sided with the Arabs. The possibility of Communist influence in 1958 led President Dwight D. Eisenhower to send a large contingent of American troops to Lebanon, but they were not used in combat.

In the 1970s, the Palestinian Arabs used Lebanese soil to establish bases for raids on Israel, and this resulted in Israeli raids on Lebanon. A civil war broke out in 1975, with the Christian minority arrayed against a combination of Palestinians and Lebanese Moslems. The principal issue appeared to be the inequity of Moslem representation in Lebanese government.

The problem has been seriously exacerbated by the action of neighboring Mideast nations to protect their own interests, among them Israel and Syria. In 1982, the United States, France and Italy sent in a "peacekeeping force" that failed in its objective.

Civil strife continued to disrupt the country in 1984; in addition, heavy fighting erupted in 1985 between Shiite militiamen and Palestinian guerrillas.

LEEWARD ISLANDS

The most northerly group of islands in the Lesser Antilles of the British West Indies is called the Leeward Islands. They were discovered by Columbus in 1493, and they all have had a great degree of autonomy under British administration.

The British Virgin Islands may be considered part of this group. They were acquired in 1666 and never formed part of the West Indies Federation that existed from 1958 to 1962. All the other Leeward Islands did belong to this federation.

Antigua and Barbuda, St. Kitts-Nevis, and Anguilla are now independent nations.

LESOTHO

A small enclave within South Africa, the kingdom of Lesotho is administered under its own constitution by a hereditary monarchy. Its people, however, depend for their livelihood on the economy of the surrounding republic. The Basutos, a

Lebanon—Temple of Bacchus (or Venus), Baalbek

Lesotho—Women building a road

Bantu people, sought British aid against the threatened encroachments of the Boers in 1867. In 1868, the area was acquired by Britain, and three years later it was annexed to Cape Colony (now Cape Province of South Africa). After a revolt of the Basutos, their territory became the crown colony of Basutoland in 1884. It was excluded from South Africa when the Union was formed in 1909.

When the Union became the Republic of South Africa in 1961, the continued separation of Basutoland was reconsidered. The British had permitted the Basuto monarchy to function, and the republic chose not to challenge the tradition. On October 4, 1966, Basutoland became the independent country of Lesotho. It was admitted to the United Nations on October 17, 1966. It chose to remain within the British Commonwealth.

After the government of Prime Minister Chief Leabua Jonathan lost an election in 1970, Jonathan suspended the constitution and parliament and the king was forced to flee from Lesotho. In 1973, Jonathan promised that a constitutional system would be reinstated.

LIBERIA

Liberia was founded in 1822 by the American Colonization Society. It was designed to promote the establishment of a country for free American blacks. The first settlement was made near the present city of Monrovia (named for James Monroe, fourth President of the United States). Immigration by blacks continued even after the American Civil War.

In 1847, the Republic of Liberia was established. Before it became well established, it lost a considerable amount of territory to French and British colonies. The United States aided in the country's finances, military organization, and in settling boundary disputes.

Liberia joined the United Nations on November 2, 1945.

LIBYA

Phoenician and Greek states competed for the control of the fertile Mediterranean coast of what is now Libya from 500 B.C. to 250 B.C. Romans replaced the Greeks in the third century before Christ. During the Phoenician, Greek, and Roman periods, some of the most prosperous and beautiful cities in the ancient world flourished along the coast.

Beginning with Vandal invasions in the fourth century A.D., Libya (the Greek name for the region) was looted and the cities were ruined. The region was then ruled in succession by the Byzantines, Arabs, and Turks (Ottoman Empire) down to the nineteenth century. It became part of the Barbary Coast of pirate strongholds, ruled by feudal deys. Between 1802 and 1805, the United States fought the pirates of Tripoli. United States Marines stormed the city in 1805. (Tripoli in Libya should not be confused with the ancient Tripoli in Lebanon).

Italy occupied Libya in 1911, but was unable to secure full control until the defeat of the Sanusi movement in 1931. In World War II, Libya became a major battlefield between the British Eighth Army and Field Marshal Rommel's German Africa Corps. Fierce tank battles developed as Rommel advanced along the coast to threaten Egypt. The battle of El Alamein in Egypt, in June 1942, was one of the critical engagements of World War II. It resulted in the defeat of Rommel, his long retreat westward back through Libya, and his final expulsion from Africa (*see* Tunisia).

Libya was not returned to Italy, which had sided with the Axis powers in the war. After a brief period of British and French control, the United Nations recognized the independence of the country under a monarchy.

With the discovery of oil in Libya and the rising resentment against remnants of British and American control, an insurrection occurred in 1969, led by a military junta. Its principal leader, Muammar al-Qadaffi, became dictator.

Libya began buying jet fighters and other advanced weapons from France and the Soviet Union. In 1977, the Libyan army fought several border battles with Egypt, and Chad accused Libya of invading its northern uranium fields.

Deterioration of relations between the United States and Libya led to the closing on May 6, 1981, by the United States of the Libyan mission in Washington. Later that year the United States shot down two Libyan jets in the Gulf of Sidra. In 1985 evidence of opposition to Qadaffi became apparent within the country.

LIECHTENSTEIN

The history of Liechtenstein dates back to 1342. Its present boundaries were fixed in 1434. Liechtenstein is a sovereign European state, described as a constitutional monarchy and ranked as a principality. It consists of two counties (Vaduz and Schellenberg); it is bordered on the east by Austria, on the west by Switzerland.

LUXEMBOURG

The present Duchy of Luxembourg was originally a part of Roman-held territories called Belgica, from which the name Belgium was derived. It became a part of Charlemagne's empire from A.D. 800 until A.D. 963.

Luxembourg was founded in 963 by Count Sigefroid, a son of Charlemagne. The territory was greatly enlarged under Countess Ermesinde (1196–1247). Charles IV (1346–1378) became also emperor of the Holy Roman Empire, and it was he who made Luxembourg a duchy. After 1443, the duchy remained under foreign control for four hundred years.

The duchy was awarded to the Netherlands' king as a grand duchy in 1815; and in 1839, it lost more than half of its territory to the new Kingdom of Belgium. By the Treaty of London in 1867 Luxembourg was declared an independent state under the protection of the Great Powers.

The duchy was overrun in World Wars I and II, but in each case its territory was restored after the war. Luxembourg was admitted to the United Nations on October 24, 1945.

MACAO

Located on the coast of China southwest of Hong Kong, Macao was acquired by the Portuguese in 1557 and remained in their hands by an agree-

Libya—Theatre Sabratha near Tripoli

ment with the Chinese Empire in 1887. The Communist Chinese made no attempt to recover the peninsula and two small islands.

Macao, previously an overseas province of Portugal, was given increased autonomy in 1976 when it was redesignated a territory. Statutes passed by its assembly became as binding as laws, rather than as provisional decrees subject to Portuguese approval, and the territory was made responsible for its own defense and security.

MALAGASY REPUBLIC (MADAGASCAR)

The name *Madagascar* is applied generally to the large island off Africa's east coast, but it is often also used as an alternate name of the Malagasy Republic. The culture and language of the Malagasy people reveal a clear relationship with Indonesian peoples, and it has been established that the island was first colonized by Indonesians before the Christian era. Arabs, Phoenicians, and Chinese have also visited Madagascar in historic times. The Portuguese were the first Europeans to sight the island (1500). French, Dutch, and British competed in the seventeenth century for trading rights on the island.

The French gradually won out but had to deal with strong native kingdoms and were expelled for a time (1672) in an uprising of the native peoples. The French maintained a tenuous control until the twentieth century. In 1896, they made Madagascar a colony, and achieved military supremacy over the natives. National feelings continued to run high after the conquest.

France gradually permitted internal self-government. In 1947, rebellion broke out and thousands died in the year of fighting that followed. In 1958, Madagascar voted to join the new French Community of Nations. The Malagasy Republic was established in 1959 and became a sovereign state on June 26, 1960. It was admitted to the United Nations on September 20, 1960.

A coup in 1972 threw out the French-supported government in favor of a new socialist regime. The Malagasy leaders closed down French businesses and a United States satellite-tracking station. They turned to Communist China for financial aid. Several Arab business concerns have opened offices on the island.

MALAWI

Formerly known as Nyasaland, the area west and south of Lake Nyasa was crossed by David Livingstone in 1859. It became a British protectorate (British Central Africa) in 1891, and was renamed Nyasaland in 1907. In 1953, the protectorate was joined with Northern and Southern Rhodesia to form the Central African Federation, but nine years later Nyasaland withdrew from the federation, which was dissolved in 1963. On July 6, 1964, Nyasaland became the independent state of Malawi, and on December 1, 1964, it became a member of the United Nations. In 1966, Malawi decided to become a republic, although it remained within the British Commonwealth.

MALAYSIA

The Peninsula of Malaya lies across the Strait of Malacca from the island of Sumatra. For centuries it has been a land bridge between the Asian continent and the South Pacific islands. By the thirteenth century, Indian, Chinese, and Islamic cultures had reached and mingled here. Europeans entered Malaya during the fifteenth and sixteenth centuries (first the Portuguese, then the Dutch). British influences appeared in the eighteenth century, when Britain took Malacca from the Dutch. They also leased Penang Island; and in 1819, they acquired Singapore at the tip of Malaya.

The opening of the Suez Canal and the introduction of rubber trees from South America changed the economy of Malaya. By the end of the first decade of the twentieth century, Britain had treaty relationships with rulers of all the Malay states. Japan occupied the area during World War II. In 1946, these protectorates were formed into a Union and two years later into the Federation of Malaya, which also absorbed from the former crown colony of the Straits Settlements both Penang and Malacca (Singapore having been made a separate colony). The Federation of Malaya was granted independence within the British Commonwealth on August 31, 1957. And on September 17, 1957, it joined the United Nations. On September 16, 1963, two British Colonies in Borneo—Sarawak and North Borneo (renamed Sabah—and the independent state of Singapore joined the Federation, which changed its name to Malaysia. In 1965, Singapore withdrew to become an independent country once more.

Malaysia—Town of Lota Kinabalu, capital of Sabah

MALDIVE ISLANDS

This group of coral islands lies some four hundred miles south of Sri Lanka (formerly Ceylon). They were a protectorate of Ceylon after the seventeenth century; when the British acquired Ceylon, they also took over the protectorate. The islands served as a British military base until 1976.

With the independence of Ceylon in 1948, British protection was maintained. On July 26, 1965, the Maldives became independent. The country was admitted to the United Nations on September 21, 1965, and became a republic in 1968.

MALI

A great Moslem empire named Mali flourished in the western Sudan during the early part of the fourteenth century. Its ruler, Mansa Musa, conquered Timbuktu (now Tombouctou) and became legendary in African history. The empire disintegrated long before the French reached the region in the late nineteenth century. They established French West Africa in 1904, and within it the territory called French Sudan, east of Senegal.

After World War II, the French Sudan became an overseas territory; and in 1957, it was granted the right to rule itself. In 1958, the Sudanese Republic was formed within the French Union. In 1959, this republic joined with its neighbor, Senegal, as the Federation of Mali.

Senegal withdrew from the federation the next year, and the independent Republic of Mali emerged on September 22, 1960. Six days later Mali became a member of the United Nations. The constitutional regime endured until 1968, to be replaced by a military dictatorship.

MALTA

Malta has been under the rule of Phoenicians, Greeks, Carthaginians, Romans, and Arabs. In A.D. 1090, it became a part of Sicily; and in 1530, it was taken by the Knights of St. John. It was ruled by them until Napoleon captured it in 1798. After the defeat of Napoleon in 1814, the island was annexed to the British Crown.

Because of its strategic location between Sicily and North Africa, Malta has always been of great military importance. It was so useful to the British during World War II that its people were given a unique unit citation, the George Cross, for their contribution. The Maltese were accustomed to considerable local self-government, but British international policy slowed down the drive toward genuine autonomy. When the State of Malta was officially created in 1961, defense and external affairs were kept in British hands.

Following a referendum on the island, Malta acquired its independence on September 21, 1964. It remained within the Commonwealth, but chose to become a republic in 1974. It became a member of the United Nations on December 1, 1964.

MARTINIQUE

Martinique was discovered by Columbus in 1502 and colonized by the French in 1635. It has remained a French possession since 1815, first as a colony and since 1946 as an overseas department.

MAURITANIA

Like other North African countries, the territory of Mauritania derives its name from its Moorish population. However, the modern Mauritania has no other relationship to ancient Mauretania.

European traders were attracted to this barren region of northwest Africa as early as the fifteenth century, because it produced the valuable commodity called "gum arabic." The Berbers brought Islam to the region in the eleventh century, and they were in turn supplanted by Arabs. But enduring European control was imposed by the French, who set up French West Africa in 1904, including the protectorate established the preceding year over Mauritania. The colony of this name was organized in 1920, and it became an overseas territory in 1946.

On November 28, 1960, independence was granted to the Islamic Republic of Mauritania. On October 27, 1961, the country was admitted to the United Nations. In 1975, Mauritania annexed the southern part of the former Spanish Sahara, but Saharan guerrillas resisted the change. In 1980 Mauritania renounced its claim to the Spanish Sahara.

MAURITIUS

An uninhabited island in the Indian Ocean east of Madagascar attracted Dutch colonists early in the seventeenth century. They named the island for Prince Maurice, son of William of Orange. African slaves were imported by the next owners of the land, the French; and after the British seized it in 1810, they brought in laborers from India, who became a majority of the island's dense population.

On March 12, 1968, Mauritius became an independent state within the British Commonwealth. She joined the United Nations on April 24, 1968.

MEXICO

The pre-Columbian history of Mexico is that of three related civilizations that grew up in the Valley of Mexico and the Yucatan region. Two of these civilizations were the most advanced cultures in pre-Columbia America. The first was the Mayan, described elsewhere (*see* Guatemala). The great cities of Chichen Itza, Mayapan, and Uxmil were located in present-day Mexico, in the Yucatan region. The Mayan civilization flourished from the third century B.C. until about the thirteenth century A.D. The Nahua group of people, which includes the Toltecs and the later Aztecs, developed a high culture in the Great Valley of Mexico about the tenth century A.D. The Aztecs, who conquered the Toltecs, built the brilliant culture that Cortés found and destroyed in A.D. 1519. The Spanish brought their Catholic religion, legal and economic systems, and imposed them upon the Aztecs, enslaving part of the population.

Mexico—Metropolitan Cathedral, Mexico City

The Spanish gradually extended their control outward from the Valley of Mexico until their possessions extended as far north as northern California and as far south as Guatemala. A movement for independence developed after the Napoleonic occupation of Spain had weakened the Spanish monarchy and imperial control over outlying areas. In 1810, a revolt broke out, led by a priest, Miguel Hidalgo, and later by another priest, José Maria Morelos. Finally, in 1821, Mexican independence was achieved under Vicente Guerrero and Agustin de Iturbide.

Mexico became a republic in 1823. But between 1834 and 1849 the government was controlled by dictators. Texas seceded in 1835 and joined the United States. The subsequent war between the United States and Mexico ended in defeat for Mexico and the loss of its northwestern region.

A reform government was inaugurated in 1855, but France invaded Mexico in 1861. Archduke Maximilian of Austria was placed on the throne of a French puppet state. The Mexicans revolted, executed Maximilian, and restored the republic in 1867.

In the twentieth century, Mexico has become a powerful nation, playing a leading role in Latin American affairs. Its abundant oil supply gave its economy a boost during the height of the oil shortage of the '70s but inflation and the drop in oil prices caused an economic crisis. The peso was devalued and private banks were nationalized. The U.S. maintains friendly ties with the "south of the border" country.

MONACO

Monaco dates from A.D. 1338 when the principality was established. In 1815 it was placed under the protection of the Kingdom of Sardinia (now part of Italy). It was at that time larger than it is today. It lost territory to Sardinia and France in 1848 and 1861.

In 1861, Monaco became a protectorate of France but remained otherwise independent. It is a favorite resort area.

MONGOLIA

Mongolia is an ancient land, the original center of a powerful empire that extended from the Pacific Ocean to the Danube. The most famous Mongol khan was Genghis, who led the invasion of India and Russia in the thirteenth century. More enduring empires were formed by the Golden Horde in Russia, by the Tartars in southern Asia, and by Kublai, who founded a Chinese dynasty that lasted nearly a century (1279–1368). Later, India was ruled by Mongols (known as Moguls), and Tamerland threatened Europe with a Mongol invasion.

In modern times Mongolia refers to a region north of China. The Manchus brought some of the Mongols under their control in the seventeenth century. The rest of the Mongols were not subjugated until the eighteenth century.

In 1911, the Manchu dynasty of China was overthrown, and the area known as Outer Mongolia declared its independence, while Inner Mongolia was incorporated into China. Outer Mongolia was ruled by the so-called "Living Buddha," who died in 1924. During the Russian Revolution, anticommunist ("white") Russians seized control of the region until communist forces defeated them in 1921. The communists allowed the monarchy to remain until 1924, when the Mongolian People's Republic was established in the Soviet image. This republic was not recognized by China until 1946. It was admitted to the United Nations on October 28, 1961. Treaties between Mongolia and the Soviet Union in 1966 and 1976 have brought large numbers of Russian troops to the country.

MOROCCO

The Phoenicians discovered and colonized the coast of what is now Morocco in about 1200 B.C. The Carthaginians later established control and expanded their area. Roman legions took over after the fall of Carthage in 146 B.C. The region was called Mauretania by the Romans (not to be confused with the modern republic of Mauritania).

As the Roman Empire disintegrated, northern Africa was subjected to invasions. The Vandals crossed from Spain to conquer the region early in the fifth century and were not expelled until the middle of the sixth century by the Byzantine general Belisarius. Arabs brought the religion of Islam as they swept westward across Africa in the seventh century. They united with the native Berbers in a dynasty that consolidated a great empire in what is now Morocco, Spain, Portugal, Algeria, Tunisia, and Libya. This empire flourished under the Almorovids, Almohades, Marinids, and finally the Sa'adi dynasties. The last dynasty brought about the great golden age of Moroccan history. Vast treasures in gold and ivory were amassed in the magnificent capital of Marrakech. This dynasty fought fierce wars with the Great Mali Empire and captured Timbuktu (Tombouctou) in 1591 (*see* Mali). The present dynasty of Morocco was established in 1649, and still occupies the throne.

Morocco was drawn into European conflicts chiefly because of its strategic location in Africa. France had conquered neighboring Algeria in 1832 and also became interested in Morocco. The French defeated a combined Algerian and Moroccan army in 1844. Thereafter French influence began to grow in the country.

Spain invaded northern Morocco in 1860. The next 50 years were marked by rivalry between France and Spain for control of Morocco. This rivalry almost caused a world war until the Treaty of Algeciras settled the rivalry in favor of France. Spain retained the "Rif" region of northern Morocco until expelled in the Rif War of the 1930s that helped bring on the Spanish Civil War (*see* Spain). In 1912, Morocco became officially a protectorate of France. In 1923, Tangier was separated and established as an international trading and financial zone.

In 1953, the French tried to overcome the movement toward independence by deposing the Sultan Mohammed V. On March 2, 1956, France acknowledged the independence of Morocco. On April 7, 1956, Spain followed suit. Tangiers was turned over to Morocco on October 29, 1956, and the country was admitted to the United Nations on November 12, 1956. Only the so-called Spanish presidios within Morocco remained under Spanish rule. In 1975, Spain allowed Morocco to acquire the northern part of its former colony of Spanish Sahara.

After years of fighting, Morocco controls the urban areas, but the guerrilla forces—the Polisario Front—move about freely in the vast deserts.

MOZAMBIQUE

Mozambique was discovered by Vasco da Gama for Portugal in 1498 and was colonized by the Portuguese in 1505. The boundaries became fixed at the end of the nineteenth century. It generally became known as Portuguese East Africa. In 1951, Mozambique was designated an overseas province of Portugal. In 1962, some inhabitants of the province formed the Mozambique Liberation Front, or *Frelimo,* to win independence. The Portuguese revolution of 1974 resulted in the victory of Frelimo in Mozambique, for independence was granted on June 25, 1975. The country became a member of the United Nations on September 16, 1975.

NAMIBIA

In 1884, Germany was given control of the region known as South-West Africa. The Germans turned the area over to South Africa in 1915, and it was governed under supervision of the League of Nations. The United Nations tried to assume this advisory role, but South Africa rejected its instructions.

In May 1968, the United Nations formed a council to plan the liberation of South-West Africa. The UN renamed the area "Namibia" and criticized South Africa for claiming the land. Marxist groups have begun raids on South African strongholds in Namibia, in an effort to force the country's independence.

A severe drought caused famine and many deaths in 1984.

NAURU

A tiny island in the Pacific Ocean, northeast of the Solomons, Nauru was annexed by Germany in 1888. After World War I, it was mandated to Australia. After World War II, Australia continued to administer Nauru under United Nations auspices. On January 31, 1968, Nauru became an independent republic with a special relationship with the British Commonwealth.

NEPAL

Little was known about the land until the fourteenth century A.D., when a Rajput ruler established a dynasty which lasted into the eighteenth. Later, Gurkhas and Chinese invaded and occupied the land.

The nineteenth century brought more conflict. As a result of border disputes, British-Nepalese relations deteriorated and the war of 1814 followed, with Britain victorious. During World War I, Nepal aided British forces and was granted independence in 1923. In World War II, Nepal was again on the Allied side.

An attempt to institute parliamentary government failed in 1959. Nepal was admitted to the United Nations on December 14, 1965. The nation has forged closer links with India and Communist China in recent years.

NETHERLANDS

Recorded history in the Netherlands began with the conquest by Julius Caesar in 55 B.C. The end of Roman rule triggered clashes between Saxon and Frankish forces over control of the region. (Christianity was introduced about A.D. 800.) Charlemagne and the Franks won control, but after his death the area of the present Netherlands became a part of the Holy Roman Empire.

The seeds of capitalism and individual enterprise were being sown at the same time. This was evident in the towns where a craftsman and merchant group began to challenge the ruling nobility, even during the Middle Ages. The country had several small, competing duchies and other feudal units.

Netherlands—Harbor of Rotterdam

In 1477, the Spanish branch of the Hapsburg family acquired control of the Netherlands. By 1549, the Netherlands, Spain, and Austria were united under Hapsburg rule.

Soon thereafter the Dutch people began to revolt. By 1581, they had established a new republic, called United Provinces. In the seventeenth century, the United Provinces became one of the world's leading maritime and commercial powers. Rivalry with Britain wore down the republic's strength, however, and it succumbed to Napoleon's great invasion of 1795. The Netherlands were reestablished by the Congress of Vienna (1815), and remained independent until they were overwhelmed by the German blitzkrieg ("lightning war") invasion of 1940. After World War II, the rich Dutch East Indies were lost in a revolt which led to the creation of the Republic of Indonesia. The Netherlands joined the United Nations on December 10, 1945.

NETHERLANDS ANTILLES

Two groups of islands in the Caribbean Sea constitute the Dutch dependency of the Netherlands Antilles.

The Leeward group, off the coast of Venezuela, comprises the islands of Curaçao, Aruba, and Bonaire, each of which is represented in the legislature. Discovered in 1499, they have been under Dutch control since 1634.

The Windward group, east of Puerto Rico, was first settled in the seventeenth century by Europeans. It is much smaller and is represented by a single legislator. The islands in this group are Saba, St. Eustachius, and Sint Maarten (the southern half of an island shared with France).

NEW CALDEDONIA

New Caledonia was discovered in 1768 by Louis Antoine de Bougainville. Captain James Cook named the island when he landed there in 1774.

New Caledonia became a French possession in 1853. It was long used as a penal colony. It became an overseas territory of France in 1946.

NEW HEBRIDES

These islands were discovered in 1606 and have been administered jointly by the United Kingdom and France. The people of the islands are mainly Melanesians.

The New Hebrides consist of 12 large islands and about 60 smaller islands. The group is located roughly 500 miles west of Fiji and 250 miles northeast of New Caledonia, in the South Pacific Ocean.

NEW ZEALAND

The Polynesian Maori people in the fourteenth century invaded the islands that now comprise modern New Zealand. The Dutch navigator Abel Tasman discovered New Zealand for Europeans in 1642. In 1769, Captain James Cook sailed around the island to determine its size. New Zealand was largely ignored thereafter until the nineteenth century when Britain took formal possession (1840).

New Zealand—Wellington City and Harbor from Tinakori Hills

Colonization resulted in conflict with the native Maoris, and war with them continued until 1864. In 1867, Maoris were granted their own representatives in government. With the introduction of refrigeration, in 1882, New Zealand became a leading world exporter of dairy produce and meat. From then on economic development became rapid.

New Zealand became a colony in 1852, a dominion in 1907, and a sovereign state within the British Commonwealth in 1947. It was admitted to the United Nations on October 24, 1945.

NICARAGUA

Columbus discovered the coast of Nicaragua and landed there in 1502. The Spanish founded Granada and León in 1524. Throughout most of the colonial period the entire region was ruled by the Spanish from bases in Guatemala. The Central American areas of the Spanish Empire declared their independence on September 15, 1821. The United Provinces of Central America, a federation, was established in 1823, and Nicaragua was a part of it. Nicaragua withdrew from the federation in 1838 and became a republic.

During the nineteenth century Nicaragua was often considered as a possible site for a transcontinental canal. In the end, the canal was built across the Isthmus of Panama. Conditions in Nicaragua became unstable, and the United States occupied the country from 1912 to 1925, and from 1926 to 1933.

Marxist rebels began a round of terrorist murders and kidnappings in the early 1970s, and President Anastasio Somoza imposed martial law. The guerrillas, led by the Marxist Sandinista, invaded Nicaragua May 29, 1979, and the Somoza government toppled seven weeks later. The United States has since actively supported the anti-Sandinista (contras) rebels and imposed trade restrictions on Nicaragua's sugar exports.

In June, 1985, Congress voted to provide $27 million in aid to Nicaragua.

NIGER

The first European explorers to enter the region that is now the Republic of Niger arrived in the mid-nineteenth century. In 1890, the French began to settle in the area, and its status progressed from military territory in 1900, to autonomous territory in 1922, to overseas territory in 1946. On August 3, 1960, Niger became an independent country. It was admitted to the United Nations on September 20, 1960.

NIGERIA

The eastern Guinea coast of Africa was first visited by the Portuguese in 1472. All of the maritime nations of Europe participated thereafter in its lucrative slave trade.

Britain abolished this trade and began to promote trade in palm oil in its place. To protect this interest, the British seized the town of Lagos in 1851. In 1861, the surrounding area was annexed as a colony. In 1888, the Yoruba country in the interior was also brought under British protection, a claim that won international recognition.

In 1900, the protectorate of Southern Nigeria was formed; and in 1906, it became the Colony and Protectorate of Southern Nigeria. Simultaneously, Britain increased her control of the hinterland. Northern Nigeria became a protectorate and was combined with Southern Nigeria in 1914. A threefold division was made: the Lagos region became the Colony of Nigeria, while the remainder became the Eastern and Western provinces of the protectorate. In 1954, the Federation of Nigeria was formed under a single administration. The Eastern and Western regions were granted autonomy in 1957, the Northern in 1959. On October 1, 1960, the Federation of Nigeria became an independent state. It joined the United Nations six days later. In 1963, it became a republic.

The geographical divisions concealed a significant disunity within Nigeria, based on tribal allegiances—particularly involving the Hausa and Fulani in the north, the Yoruba in the west, and the Ibo in the east. This caused a savage civil war from 1967 through 1970, during which the Ibo attempted to form a separate state of Biafra. This disaster cost over a million casualties.

Calm settled over the nation with the restoration of civilian government in 1979 following 13 years of military government.

A military coup in 1983 ousted the democratically-elected government.

NORTH KOREA

Korea was recovered from Japanese occupation at the end of World War II. An administrative dividing line was established at the thirty-eighth parallel, pending an agreement between the Soviet Union and the United States liberation forces. Negotiations failed, but the division between the northern and southern parts of the country remained. North Korea was organized on May 1, 1948 on the Soviet model.

In 1950, North Korean forces invaded South Korea. The border war lasted three years and ended in a truce, with no territorial change. (For the history of Korea, *see* South Korea.)

NORWAY

The recorded history of Norway began during the eighth century, when a series of small kingdoms were established along the rocky coasts and deep inlets (called *fjords*) of Norway. The people who established these kingdoms were called Vikings.

The Viking period of Norwegian history lasted from about A.D. 800 to about A.D. 1050. In these years, the Vikings sailed sturdy longboats over the North Atlantic, reaching Ireland, the Hebrides, and southern Europe. They also sailed westward to Iceland, Greenland, and North America. Recent evidence has been found in Canada that proves Vikings spent some time there in about A.D. 1024. The Vikings also colonized Iceland, Greenland, and parts of western Europe. One of their most famous colonies was on the coast of northwestern France; this colony became Normandy, and the Vikings there became known as Normans. Their descendants conquered England and Ireland.

Norway was united for the first time in A.D. 860 by Harold the Fairhaired. King Olaf I introduced Christianity. After the close of the Viking period, Norway was weakened by the loss of trade to Hanseatic League cities and by internal dissension.

Norway lost its independence in 1380 when King Haakon of Denmark inherited the Norwegian kingdom. Denmark and Norway were united for more than four hundred years, and Norway was little more than a province in the Danish kingdom. Sweden was a part of this union from 1397 to 1523.

Denmark sided with Napoleon in the early years of the nineteenth century. As a result of Napoleon's defeat, Denmark was forced to give up Norway, which was then united with the Crown of Sweden. Denmark retained the former island colonies of Norway (Greenland, Iceland, and the Faroe Islands) that had come to be administered by Denmark during the union of the two countries.

Sweden and Norway remained united until 1905. Norway became a major maritime nation and selected King Haakon VII to be its king, despite Swedish opposition. The Swedes later recognized Norwegian independence.

Norway was neutral during World War I but was overrun by the Nazis during World War II. King Haakon and the government escaped to England. After the war, Norway joined NATO and abandoned her former neutral position. The kingdom was admitted to the United Nations on November 27, 1945.

OMAN

Oman is the southeastern part of the Arabian Peninsula, extending along the Arabian Sea. It is under the control of an Arab sultan whose forebears came from Yemen in 1744 and expelled the Persians. In 1798, the descendants of this Yemenite conqueror obtained protection from the British and succeeded in building an empire (called Muscat and Oman) that included Zanzibar and part of the East African coast, as well as a coastal section of Baluchistan. Only in 1958 did the small empire give its last enclave in Baluchistan back to Pakistan. In 1965, the United Nations recommended that Britain end its protectorate, but no formal action was taken. The sultan who seized the throne from his father in 1970 changed the country's name to Oman. On October 7, 1971, Oman was admitted to the United Nations.

PAKISTAN

The religion of Islam spread rapidly over southern Asia after the eighth century. In the tenth century a Moslem warrior group swept into India by way of the Khyber Pass in the west. Moslem power and influence moved eastward along the Ganges Plain and southward in the valley of the Indus River. By the sixteenth century it had reached Bengal on the far eastern edge of the Indian subcontinent and included most of the lower Ganges and Bengal regions.

Under British influence during the eighteenth and nineteenth centuries, the Moslem position was threatened by the rise of Hindu patriotism. In

1906, the All-India Moslem League was founded to help create a Moslem state.

The Moslem leader Mohammed Ali Jinnah invented the name *Pakistan* (from the first letters of "Punjab," "Afghan," and "Kashmir," and the remainder from "Baluchistan"). The Dominion of Pakistan came into existence amid riots and bloodshed in 1947. On March 3, 1956, Pakistan was proclaimed the Islamic Republic of Pakistan, but retained full membership in the British Commonwealth of Nations. The constitution proved unsatisfactory and was abolished within two years. A new constitution in 1962 provided for two provinces—West Pakistan and East Pakistan—each with its own legislature. This arrangement also proved unworkable, for the Bengalis of East Pakistan felt they were at a disadvantage. Again the constitution was abolished in 1969, and in the elections of 1971 the East Pakistan voters exerted their full powers.

When the president of Pakistan delayed convening of the legislature, East Pakistan declared itself independent. A rebellion broke out, and it was only with the aid of India that East Pakistan was able to defeat West Pakistan late in 1971. As a result, East Pakistan became the independent state of Bangladesh, and only West Pakistan remained to bear the name of the country. Once more a constitution was framed, and the country adopted the name of the Islamic Republic of Pakistan. But this time it withdrew from the Commonwealth, in which Bangladesh chose to remain.

Pakistan—Badshahi Mosque at Lahore

Pakistan's proximity to Afghanistan has made it a refuge for Afghans fleeing the Russian invasion of their country. The United States began sending economic and military aid to Pakistan in 1981.

PANAMA

The Isthmus of Panama was first seen by white men in 1501 when the Spaniard Rodrigo de Bastides landed near the present Portobelo. Columbus saw the isthmus the following year and claimed it for Spain. Balboa crossed the isthmus in 1513 and discovered the Pacific Ocean (which he named). Balboa also became the first governor of the region.

When the Spanish conquistadores began their conquest of the fabulous Inca Empire in South America, they used the Isthmus of Panama to carry supplies, soldiers, and captured treasures. British buccaneers made daring raids against strong points in Panama and against Spanish galleons that sailed to and from Panama, laden with gold and other loot from the Inca Empire.

In 1739, Panama was attached to the viceroyalty of New Granada that included the present Colombia, Panama, and Venezuela. In 1821, Panama became a part of the independent Gran Colombia, a new state that comprised the present Colombia, Venezuela, Ecuador, and Panama. Upon dissolution of Gran Colombia in 1830, Panama remained a part of Colombia. With the help of the United States, it was separated from Colombia in 1903 to facilitate the building of a projected canal across the isthmus. From time to time, Panama demanded that the zone (leased in perpetuity to the United States) be restored to Panamanian sovereignty. The United States signed a treaty to that effect in 1978.

(For updated information on the Canal Zone, see page 344.)

PAPUA NEW GUINEA

New Guinea is an island north of Australia, also known as Papua or Irian. Its western half was once Netherlands New Guinea and was annexed in 1963 by Indonesia. The eastern half of New Guinea is itself divided into two portions, the most northerly of which was known as German New Guinea from 1884 to 1914. It was captured during World War I by Australia and became an Australian mandate, the Territory of New Guinea, in 1920. The southeastern quarter of the island was seized in 1883 by the British colony of Queensland (Australia). It was annexed by Great Britain as the colony of British New Guinea in 1888, and handed over to Australia in 1906 to become the Territory of Papua.

None of these incursions by Europeans profoundly involved the native population, which is largely Melanesian or black. The Territory of New Guinea has been administered by Australia since 1949. With the gradual increase of self-government, Papua New Guinea became capable of achieving independence, which was granted on September 16, 1975. Papua New Guinea was admitted to the United Nations on October 10, 1975.

PARAGUAY

The region of present Paraguay was first visited by Europeans in the expedition of Juan de Salazar that founded Asunción in 1537. The Jesuits came later and gathered together the Guaraní Indians to build a remarkable series of prosperous Guaraní communities in the region. Spanish colonists initiated a campaign of slander against the Jesuits that led to the destruction of the mission communities. The Guaraní were eventually destroyed as a people.

The Spanish ruled Paraguay as a part of the viceroyalty of Peru and then as part of La Plata. La Plata declared independence from Spain in 1810. After the expulsion of the Spanish, Uruguay and Paraguay then fought Argentina, which was attempting to annex them.

Nearly all of Paraguay's history since that time has been concerned with wars and dictatorial rule. The War of the Triple Alliance (1865–1870) was the bloodiest in the history of Latin America. It was fought by Brazil, Uruguay, and Argentina against Paraguay. Paraguay was crushed, her economy completely ruined; she has never recovered from this disaster. In 1932, a long dispute between Paraguay and Bolivia erupted into another war that lasted until 1938. Economic difficulties and dictatorial rule have continued in the post-World War II period. Paraguay became a member of the United Nations on October 24, 1945.

Paraguay has joined its modernized neighbor, Brazil, in a series of projects to aid the economies of both. They have built a highway linking the two countries; and in 1974, they signed a pact to build the world's largest electric generator on the Paraná River.

PERU

The Inca civilization that developed in pre-Columbian Peru arose slowly from a nucleus in the Cusco Valley about A.D. 1200. In 1438 the empire began to expand under Pachacuti and his son Topa Inca. At its height, the empire had about twelve million people and included most of what is today Peru, Bolivia, Chile, Ecuador. The Incas built great palaces, irrigation works, highways, and cities. Arts, handicrafts, and agriculture were developed to a degree equalled only by the Mayan people of Mexico and Guatemala.

Francisco Pizarro brought down the empire in 1532 and 1533. In 1535, the city of Lima was founded. It became the capital of a wealthy Spanish empire in America. Treasures of gold and silver poured a veritable flood into the Spanish treasury. Indians were enslaved to work the gold mines. The Spanish treasure galleons bound from Peru became the favorite target of English "sea dogs."

Simón Bolívar and José de San Martín landed in Peru in 1820 and by 1824 (Battle of Ayacucho) had destroyed the Spanish Empire in America. Peru thereafter was a republic, but experienced harsh rule under a rigid militarist group until the twentieth century. Peru lost a nitrate-rich region to Chile, in the War of the Pacific (1879–1884). Then Peru became a relatively stable country, with a constitution. In 1980 the country returned to democratic leadership after twelve years of military rule. It became a member of the United Nations on October 31, 1945.

Peru—San Martín Square, Lima

PHILIPPINES

The Philippines were discovered by Ferdinand Magellan while on his epic voyage around the world in 1521. The Spanish were able to retain control over the Philippines until the end of the nineteenth century. The islands were named for Philip II, King of Spain.

Revolutions in Central and South America stimulated an independence movement in the Philippines. A Filipino doctor named Emilio Aguinaldo stirred up a revolt in 1896 which merged with the Spanish-American War.

After the war ended, Aguinaldo demanded independence. The Americans refused. In 1941, Japanese forces captured the Philippines. The fall of the Corregidor fortress in the harbor of Manila was a major event of World War II. Americans under Douglas MacArthur returned to the Philippines with a massive invasion force on October 20, 1944. Fighting had to be waged from island to island throughout the huge archipelago.

On July 4, 1946, the Philippines were granted independence. Aguinaldo, who was nearly one hundred years old, saw his dream realized. The Philippines were admitted to the United Nations on October 24, 1946.

At first the Philippines was a republic; but in 1973, President Ferdinand Marcos instituted a parliamentary dictatorship. Martial law existed from 1972 until 1981. Marcos relinquished some of his legislative power and was again elected to a six-year term. Internal strife prompted demonstrations for Marcos' resignation. After an embittered election in early 1986, Marcos claimed victory. As a result of demonstrations and widespread resistance throughout the Philippines, Marcos was forced to concede the presidency to Aquino and flee the country.

Philippines—Maranao Dance by Maranao natives

PITCAIRN

Pitcairn was discovered by Philip Carteret in 1767. In 1790, the island was occupied by nine mutineers from the British ship the *Bounty*, who brought with them 12 Tahitian women. Nothing more was heard of the island until the visit of an American ship in 1808. It was learned then that all the men had killed each other, except John Adams, who ruled the colony. In 1838, Britain took formal possession of the island. In 1856, all of the colonists were removed. Forty of them later returned, but the population never exceeded one hundred. The colony is administered from New Zealand.

POLAND

Poland dates from the unification of several small Slavic states in the tenth century. In A.D. 966, Christianity was introduced. Boleslaus the Brave (992–1025) made Poland an independent kingdom.

In 1241, the Mongols invaded Poland. The Teutonic knights helped to expel the Mongols, but remained to threaten Poland's independence. For centuries Poland has contended with German pressure from the west. Poland reached the height of her power from the fourteenth to sixteenth centuries under the Jagellon dynasty of rulers. She defeated the German Tannenberg order in 1410 and annexed Lithuania in 1569.

Polish power declined under German (Prussian), Swedish, and Russian invasions. The country eventually was divided among neighboring powers.

Napoleon's Grand Duchy of Warsaw partially revived Poland, but the revival ended in 1815 when Napoleon was defeated. Revolts in 1830, 1831, and 1863 were crushed. After the Allied victory in World War I, Poland became a republic in 1918. It was divided between Germany and the Soviet Union in 1939. The Nazi invasion of Poland was the opening phase of World War II. The Poles fought fiercely, especially around Warsaw, which was nearly destroyed. After Germany's invasion of the Soviet Union, Poland's forces fought their way back into German-occupied Poland.

After World War II, Poland was reconstituted with new borders. She gained territory from Germany and yielded territory to the Soviet Union; thus the entire country shifted toward the west. As the result of an election in 1947, a procommunist government was formed, which framed a constitution of the Soviet type in 1952.

Militant labor activists led a movement that culminated in 1980 with the government's granting workers the right to form independent trade unions and to strike. Further demands by the principal trade union, Solidarity, led the government to declare martial law. The United States imposed economic sanctions, and martial law was lifted in December 1982. Meanwhile, the government arrested Lech Walesa and other Solidarity leaders, who had called for a nationwide strike that did not materialize, but they were later released.

PORTUGAL

The Iberian Peninsula was wrested from Carthage by Roman armies in about 138 B.C. The section now known as Portugal was then called Lusitania. Starting in the fifth century A.D. and continuing until 711, Portugal was overrun by a succession of invaders, including Alans, Suevi, Visigoths, and Celtic peoples. In 711, the Arabs conquered the region, but Ferdinand of Castile regained it in 1139. By the thirteenth century, the boundaries of the nation were established and Lisbon was the capital.

During the reign of John (João) I (1385–1433), the Portuguese defeated the Spanish and began a period of growth and progress. Portuguese explorations of unknown regions began under John, who founded a school for navigation. A series of brilliant navigational exploits resulted in the establishment of a Portuguese Empire by the sixteenth century. Bartholomew Diaz rounded the Cape of Good Hope in Africa (1486), discovering a new route to India. Vasco da Gama made the voyage to India in 1497, and Portuguese navigators discovered Brazil in 1500.

In 1580, Spain took over Portugal and its empire, but sovereignty was restored by a rebellion in 1640. A long war ensued. In 1668, Spain recognized Portugal's independence. Brazil was lost by Portugal in 1822, and the Bragança royal house was overthrown by a revolution in 1910. But instability plagued the nation until the rise of António de Oliveira Salazar, who became prime minister in 1932. He established a conservative dictatorship. In 1974, his successor, Marcello Caetano, was overthrown by a military junta. The administration wavered in its domestic policies, but abandoned the colonial empire that it was incapable of preserving. All the overseas territories of Africa became independent in 1974 and 1975, and Macao became an autonomous territory.

QATAR

On a peninsula jutting into the Persian Gulf, west of the United Arab Emirate is Qatar, formerly a British protectorate. It ended this relationship when it declared its independence on September 1, 1971. Admission to the United Nations followed in twenty days.

Qatar exports about one hundred seventy-eight million barrels of crude oil each year. The income from oil gives Qatar the second highest income per capita of any nation in the world.

Portugal—The Parque Eduardo VII, Lisbon

RÉUNION

The largest island of the Mascarene group in the Indian Ocean was discovered by a Portuguese navigator in 1528, claimed by the French in 1638, and colonized by them in 1662. It was named Ile de Bourbon until after the French Revolution, when it was renamed La Réunion. In 1946, it became an overseas territory of France.

RHODESIA (Zimbabwe)

Cecil Rhodes, who organized the British South Africa Company in 1889, was responsible for the northward expansion of British holdings from Cape Colony at the tip of South Africa. By 1895, the Zambesi region was named Rhodesia, after Rhodes. The company administered the area under a British charter until the European settlers voted in 1923 to accept self-government, rather than join the Union of South Africa.

Meanwhile, the company had expanded its operations further north. These holdings were designated Northern Rhodesia in 1911, so the autonomous portion became known as the colony of Southern Rhodesia.

Government leaders were unable to bring the two regions together because Southern Rhodesia was controlled by its minority of white settlers, a prospect inacceptable to the black population of Northern Rhodesia. Nevertheless, the British government decided in 1953 to form a federation to include the two Rhodesias and adjoining Nyasaland. The federation was dissolved in 1963.

By this time, Southern Rhodesia had adopted a new constitution and committed itself against extending powers of government to its black majority. Great Britain disapproved this policy. So the government of Southern Rhodesia (which was renamed Rhodesia in 1964) declared its independence on November 11, 1965.

The United Nations asked all its members to impose economic sanctions against Rhodesia. Only Portugal and South Africa ignored the resolution. Rhodesia prospered as an independent nation and declared itself a republic in 1970.

Guerrilla forces began raiding government outposts to try to press the white leaders into a compromise. But peace talks failed, and the bush war spread into Mozambique. In 1977, the United States stopped buying chrome from Rhodesia to protest that government's hard line against black rule. Early in 1979, the white Rhodesians voted to relinquish their control of the government in coming years.

Elections were held and the country achieved independence on April 18, 1980.

ROMANIA

Most of the present Romania became a part of the Roman province of Dacia after Emperor Trajan conquered the Dacians in the fierce campaign of A.D. 101–106. Roman influence remained even after numerous invasions by other peoples in later centuries. The Dacians gradually emerged as the Vlachs or Wallachians who were converted to Christianity during the eleventh century.

Wallachia and another state called Moldavia developed in the region late in the thirteenth century. Wallachia was seized by the Turks in 1476 and Moldavia was taken over in 1513.

The Ottoman Empire's control over both areas was challenged from time to time by Russia. The latter took Bessarabia from Moldavia in 1812, and Austria seized Bucovina from Wallachia in 1775. The Russians invaded both areas in 1828, but released them in 1834.

The Congress of Paris established Wallachia and Moldavia as separate states, and they were united under Alexander Cuza in 1859. The resulting new nation was called Romania or Rumania.

During World War I, Romania joined the Allies, but was defeated by Germany early in 1918. Later that year Romania came back into the war on the Allied side. After the war Romania received the regions of Bucovina, Bessarabia, Transylvania, and Banat.

King Carol II, who had renounced the throne in 1925, was returned in 1930. Romania was caught in a series of threats and power moves by Russia, Germany, and Italy. King Carol abdicated and the country entered an alliance with the Axis powers on the side of Germany.

King Michael (son of Carol II) engineered a coup d'état in 1944. Romania then entered the war on the Allied side.

The communists gained election victories in 1947, and King Michael was forced to resign. Romania was then proclaimed a people's republic (in 1965 changed to "socialist republic"). It became a member of the United Nations on December 14, 1955.

RWANDA

The history of Rwanda is closely associated with the Tutsi (Watutsi) and Hutu Bahutu peoples. (The latter are a Bantu group.) The Tutsi early managed to become the ruling tribe and the Hutu became the feudal lower "caste." These conditions failed to change even when the white men came. Germany was awarded the country along with Urundi (the future Burundi) in 1884, and relations were peaceful with the native ruling Tutsi people. During World War I, Belgium occupied both Ruanda (the future Rwanda) and Urundi. The League of Nations attached both countries to the Belgian Congo in 1920. After World War II, Ruanda and Urundi (then called Ruanda-Urundi) became a single trust territory of the UN.

In 1959, clashes erupted between the Tutsi and the Hutu, the latter demanding basic freedoms. Tensions mounted until the United Nations called for popular elections, which abolished the monarchy in Ruanda. The UN hoped that the two sections would become a single independent state. However, internal differences prevented their unification. On July 1, 1962, Rwanda (with a slight change in spelling) became an independent nation. It was admitted to the United Nations on September 18, 1962.

ST. HELENA

The Portuguese discovered St. Helena in 1502. It has belonged to the United Kingdom since 1673.

St. Helena is a crown colony with several dependencies: Ascension Island, 700 miles to the northwest (administered with St. Helena since 1922), and the Tristan da Cunha archipelago, far to the south (so administered since 1938).

ST. PIERRE AND MIQUELON

These small islands lying ten miles south of Newfoundland are all that remain of the once-great French empire in North America. First settled by the French in 1604, they have been permanently French since 1816. The colony was given autonomy in 1935 and made an overseas territory in 1946.

SAMOA

This group of islands is located in the South Pacific, just east of Fiji and north of Tonga. It was a German colony from 1899 to 1914, when New Zealand landed troops on the main island and seized control. The League of Nations allowed New Zealand to administer the government of Samoa; and in 1945, the United Nations affirmed New Zealand's responsibility for the area.

The Samoans elected their own government in October 1959. The country became an independent monarchy on January 1, 1962, although New Zealand continues to give financial aid.

SAN MARINO

San Marino is the oldest republic in the world. According to tradition, it was founded in the fourth century by a Christian refugee from persecution. Its monastery has been occupied since A.D. 885. A tiny district in the midst of Italy's Apennine Mountains, San Marino preserved its independence throughout the Middle Ages and modern wars. A republic, it has a trade treaty with Italy.

SÃO TOMÉ AND PRÍNCIPE

São Tomé and Príncipe were discovered in 1471 and have been Portuguese territory since 1522. The islands became an overseas province in 1951 and were granted independence on July 12, 1975. Admission to the United Nations followed on September 16, 1975.

A severe drought in 1984 affected agricultural production, a mainstay of the economy.

SAUDI ARABIA

Saudi Arabia was founded by Abdu-l-Aziz ibn Sa'ud (1880–1953). However, the history of Saudi Arabia is closely associated with that of the Arabian peninsula, of which it occupies the greater part. (*See also* Kuwait and Yemen).

The Arabian peninsula has been inhabited throughout historic times by Semitic peoples, but unified states were not formed until the arrival of

Mohammed (A.D. 570–632), who founded Islam. Through Islam, the land of Arabia became famous throughout the world. Mohammed and his successors led the Arabians out of Arabia and spread their religion from the Atlantic Ocean to the borders of China and the Pacific Ocean. The Arabian language and culture became nearly as widespread as the religion of Islam.

The puritanical Islamic sect of Wahhabism was fused with the Sa'udi family in the eighteenth century, thus leading to the beginnings of the present kingdom of Saudi Arabia. By 1830, the Sa'udi family controlled Nejd, Hasa, and Oman. Setbacks occurred in the following years; but in 1901, Abdu-l-Aziz resumed his conquest of all Arabia. In 1906, he broke the power of the leading competing tribes. He captured Mecca in 1924, the Kingdom of Hejaz in 1926, and the Kingdom of Nejd in 1927. British recognition was accorded in 1927.

When Abdu-l-Aziz ibn Sa'ud died in 1953, he left a state that was largely his own creation. Arabia became a member of the United Nations on October 24, 1945.

King Faisal led the development of Saudi Arabia's crude oil reserves. The nation took control of the Arabian American Oil Company between 1973 and 1976, then launched a massive economic development program. Saudi Arabia gave financial aid to Egypt and other Arab countries in their conflict with Israel. Then King Faisal stopped oil shipments to the United States and other nations in 1973–1974 to protest American military aid to Israel.

Faisal was assassinated in March 1975, and Crown Prince Khalid became the new king.

Following Khalid's death, Fahd became king in June 1982. The United States has maintained friendly relations with the Saudis, who have exercised a moderate position in meetings of OPEC.

SÉNÉGAL

Prior to the coming of white men, Sénégal was at various times a part of the famous ancient empires of Ghana and of Mali. The Portuguese visited the present Sénégal in the fifteenth century. The French established Saint-Louis as a trading post at the mouth of the Sénégal River in 1659. From about 1870 to the end of the century, France secured Sénégal and consolidated its control.

The colony was transformed into a territory in 1946 and became autonomous in 1958. In January 1959, Sénégal and Sudan (the future Mali) joined in the Federation of Mali, but the federation broke up shortly after it became independent. Sénégal proclaimed its independence on August 20, 1960, and remained within the French Community of Nations. The country was admitted to the United Nations on September 28, 1960.

In 1981 Senegal signed an agreement with Gambia for confederation of the two countries under the name Senegambia. While maintaining individual sovereignty, the two countries adopted joint monetary and defense policies.

SEYCHELLES

The Seychelles archipelago was colonized by the French in the eighteenth century. The islands were captured by the British in 1794, included as a part of Mauritius in 1814, and organized as a colony in 1888. They became a crown colony in 1903, and were granted independence as of June 29, 1976. In 1979 the country became a one-part state under a new constitution.

SIERRA LEONE

Little is known of the history of Sierra Leone before its discovery by Europeans. About 1460, a Portuguese adventurer named Pedro da Cintra visited the region and gave it the present name. Some hundred years later an Englishman, Sir John Hawkins, landed an expedition to obtain slaves. Other slave traders followed.

During the seventeenth and eighteenth centuries, Sierra Leone was a pirate haunt. Around 1787, English abolitionists succeeded in having the government declare Sierra Leone to be the home for England's freed slaves.

By 1808, Sierra Leone was made a British colony with a Crown-appointed governor and advisory council. Schools were founded, frontiers with Liberia were agreed upon, and Africans were appointed to the executive council in an unofficial capacity. It was a long and slow, but orderly process.

In April 1961, Sierra Leone became independent and a member of the British Commonwealth of Nations. It maintains close ties with Great Britain. Sierra Leone was admitted to the United Nations on September 27, 1961.

SINGAPORE

A small island at the tip of the Malay Peninsula, Singapore, was founded by Sir Stamford Raffles in 1819. It was a trading post controlled by the British East India Company. Along with Penang and Malacca, it was designated as the colony of the Straits Settlements in 1867.

In 1946, Singapore became a separate crown colony and was given autonomy in 1959. Singapore joined the Federation of Malaysia in 1963, but chose to secede and become an independent republic on August 9, 1965. Shortly thereafter it joined the British Commonwealth, having already become a member of the United Nations on September 21, 1965.

SOLOMON ISLANDS

East of New Guinea is an archipelago, the Solomon Islands, that came under British protection in the last decade of the nineteenth century. They were the scene of heavy naval fighting during World War II. After a period of self-government beginning in 1976, the islands attained independence in 1978.

Not to be confused with this British protectorate (which includes such large islands as Guadalcanal and New Georgia) are a smaller chain of Solomon Islands to the west. This chain, including Bougainville, is part of the state of Papua New Guinea.

SOMALIA

The name *Somalia* is used here as the short form for the Somali Republic and should not be confused with the region of Somalia or Somaliland, of which it is only a part. The region includes parts of what are now Ethiopia, Kenya, and the Territory of Afars and Issas (former French Somaliland).

The former Somaliland protectorate was under Egyptian control until it was acquired by Britain in 1884. It was administered as a dependency of India from Aden, until the Italians occupied it during World War II.

The colony of Italian Somaliland was established in 1889 south of the British protectorate, on a coast previously belonging to Zanzibar and to Kenya. During the war with Ethiopia in 1934, Italy added the Ethiopian province of Ogaden to its Somali colony. This colony became known as Italian East Africa; it was taken over by Britain during World War II. In 1950, the United Nations returned the former Italian Somaliland to Italy under mandate.

In June 1960, the British and Italian lands became independent and merged to form the Somali Republic on July 1. The country joined the United Nations on September 20, 1960. In 1970, a military coup changed the name to the Democratic Republic of Somalia. The new government permitted Soviet military bases to be built on Somali territory.

SOUTH AFRICA

Portuguese sailors rounded the Cape of Good Hope in 1488. One of them, Vasco da Gama, discovered the Natal coast in 1497. The first European settlement in the region was made by the Dutch at the Cape of Good Hope in 1652. Primitive Bushmen and Hottentots were the principal peoples that the white settlers found in southern Africa. They soon, however, came into contact with migrating Bantu peoples from the north. As settlement increased, conflict with Bantus arose in four separate wars, that occurred between 1779 and 1812.

The British occupied the Cape in 1795. As a result of the Napoleonic Wars, the entire colony was ceded to Great Britian in 1815. British settlers came in 1820 and slavery was abolished in 1834. The descendants of the Dutch became known as Afrikaners. Disputes with British policies led to the "Great Trek," a migration by the Afrikaners in 1836. They settled in Natal and north of the Vaal River (Transvaal). The British extended their control into those regions by the middle of the century, beginning with the annexation of Natal in 1843. By 1897, all of southern Africa, except the Orange Free State and the Transvaal, was under British rule of one form or another.

Meanwhile conflict with Africans resulted in the establishment of various *apartheid* projects, in which separate white and nonwhite settlements were developed. Nonwhite labor was essential to the economy, so *apartheid* could go only so far. The discovery of gold and diamonds brought an influx of immigrants and, with them, rising conflict between Afrikaners and the British government.

The conflict centered on the Afrikaner-controlled regions of Transvaal and the Orange

Free State. The latter had been independent since 1854, and the former since 1877.

The unsuccessful Jameson Raid of 1895 was followed by the Boer War of 1899–1902. (The descendants of the first Dutch settlers were also called Boers.) This war was between the British and an alliance of the Orange Free State and Transvaal. The two Boer republics lost their independence. In 1909 four states in southern Africa were combined to form the Union of South Africa, which was accepted as a member of the British Commonwealth of Nations (1926).

After World War II the Afrikaner segment of the population gained political control and legislated the separation of races. South Africa withdrew from the Commonwealth in 1960 and became a republic the following year.

South Africa became a member of the United Nations on November 7, 1945. Within the organization, she has been criticized by an increasing number of member states, partly because of her policy of *apartheid.*

In 1963, South Africa began setting up separate units for its black population known as *Bantustans.* Within a decade or so, most of the projected "homelands" were well under way. This segregationist action is one of many of South Africa's racial policies which have produced widespread anti-apartheid protests in the United States against this nation.

SOUTH KOREA

The recorded history of Korea began with the migration of Tungusic people into northern Korea from Manchuria about four thousand years ago. At the beginning of the Christian era there were three kingdoms in Korea. One of these (the Silla dynasty) united all Korea in A.D. 669.

For many centuries thereafter, Chinese, Japanese, and Mongolians fought for possession of Korea. After the empire of Mongols fell in the thirteenth century, their power in the peninsula of Korea disappeared. In 1392, the strong Yi dynasty assumed the reins of government. A brilliant age of cultural development followed, in which the Korean alphabet was introduced and arts flourished.

A great war of survival against Japan broke out in 1592. Korea won the war but the country was left in a weakened condition.

The United States opened relations with Korea in 1882. Japan invaded Korea in 1904 and annexed the country in 1910, naming it Chosen. After the defeat of Japan in World War II, Korea was divided temporarily at the thirty-eighth parallel between Soviet and United States jurisdictions, according to agreements made at Potsdam. When the two liberating nations failed to agree, separate regimes were set up at Pyongyang and at Seoul. The former organized a procommunist government (*see* North Korea) and the latter formed the Republic of Korea, usually known as South Korea, on August 15, 1948.

On June 25, 1950, a North Korean army struck across the border without warning. Within two days, and with United Nations authorization, the United States ordered its armed forces to protect South Korea against the aggressors. Several other countries supplied small contingents to fight under the United Nations command. Seoul, the capital of South Korea, fell to the North Koreans, who advanced almost to the southern tip of the peninsula. After United States forces landed at Inchon, the North Koreans were driven back almost to their border with China. This brought the Chinese Communists into the war, and the United Nations forces retreated to the thirty-eighth parallel. In July 1953, an armistice was signed. No significant territorial change occurred.

During the intervening 30-plus years, an uneasy peace has existed between the North and South Koreans existing on either side of a demilitarized zone (DMZ). Numerous clashes have occurred during this time.

Although the two nations had agreed in 1972 to move toward reunification, no sign of this effort was seen until 1985 when the two countries agreed to discuss economic issues.

SOUTH YEMEN

This name is generally used for an independent state that is officially called the People's Republic of Yemen. Although its population is largely Arab, it must not be confused with its neighbor to the north, the Yemen Arab Republic, generally known as Yemen.

The ancient port of Aden at the southwest corner of Arabia was acquired by Britain in 1839. Its strategic importance was increased with the opening of the Suez Canal. Long a dependency of British India, it became a crown colony in 1937. Surrounding the colony were a number of Arab sultanates that Britain loosely organized in 1937 under a protectorate. Between 1959 and 1962 the protectorate was transformed into a Federation of South Arabia, to which the colony of Aden was attached in 1963. A period of civil warfare ended when South Arabia declared its independence as the Southern Yemen People's Republic on November 30, 1967. Under that name, Southern Yemen joined the United Nations on December 14, 1967. On November 30, 1970, it assumed its present name.

SPAIN

The recorded history of Spain began about 1100 B.C. with the Phoenician colonies. The present city of Cádiz, on the southwest coast, founded by Phoenicians in 1130 B.C., may be the oldest city in Europe. Carthage also planted colonies along the coast of Spain, beginning about 500 B.C. The present city of Barcelona began as a Carthaginian colony.

Rome sought the Iberian peninsula mainly for its rich gold and silver mines. Spain was called Hispania by the Romans, who conquered it from Carthage during the Second Punic War (218–200 B.C.). Roman Hispania became a rich and prosperous center of Roman culture. Several great Roman writers (such as Seneca and Quintilian) and even some of the emperors (including Trajan and Hadrian) came from Roman Spain. Large cities, highways, aqueducts, and other great engineering works dotted the land.

In the fifth century a series of invasions ended the prosperity of Spain. The Moorish invasions from Africa, beginning in A.D. 711, had a lasting effect upon the future of the Iberian Peninsula. Moorish domination throughout most of what is now Spain continued from 711 until 1492.

Moorish Spain left a rich heritage, including prosperous cities, great philosophers, a distinctive architecture, fine craftsmanship in design and art work, and brilliant writers and physicians. The Moors introduced an efficient irrigation system that still serves Spanish farmers in some areas. The Moorish occupation left Spain with a higher civilization than that of most of Europe at the time.

In 1479, the kingdoms of Aragon and Castile were united. Granada, the last of the Moorish states, fell before the armies of King Ferdinand and Queen Isabella in 1492. This period of Spanish history was noted for the cruelty of the Inquisition, which tortured any group standing in the way of royal power. It was also the period during which Spain began her rise to world power through voyages of exploration and discovery.

The Spanish golden age came during the sixteenth century, when the treasures from her colonial empire began pouring into the country. The armies of Spain were the strongest of Europe, and on the high seas only the English pirates and buccaneers presented serious difficulties.

The beginning of decline in Spanish power dates from the defeat of the Armada that King Philip II sent in 1588 to punish England's Queen Elizabeth I. The great fleet of over one hundred thirty warships was wiped out by a combination of storm and the smaller, more maneuverable English ships. Wars sapped the strength of the empire. By the time Napoleon had come to power in France, Spain was on the verge of internal collapse. Joseph Bonaparte, brother of the Emperor, was proclaimed King of Spain. However, a Spanish revolt restored the Bourbon's throne (1816).

Spain grew still weaker, losing nearly all her American colonies to independence movements early in the nineteenth century. In 1898, the United States crushed the Spanish Empire by capturing the Philippines, Puerto Rico, and Guam, and by freeing Cuba in a short war.

Spain chose to remain neutral during World War I. The African colony of Morocco revolted in 1921 and the Spanish army was overwhelmed by Moroccan soldiers. This was the signal for a reform movement in Spain.

General Miguel Primo de Rivera made himself dictator in 1923. However, in 1930, he was overthrown and the monarchy was reestablished. In 1931, a republic was proclaimed.

In 1936, an election gave the leftist parties a strong majority. Army officers revolted later that year, setting off a violent civil war that lasted until the victory of General Francisco Franco in 1939. In the civil war, the Republican group was opposed by a rightist Nationalist group that included Fascist elements. Germany tested many of her World War II weapons by turning them over to the Nationalists while the Soviet Union contributed weapons to the Republican group.

Franco's victory resulted in the formation of a "corporative republic." Spain then proceeded to aid the Nazis during World War II, though refraining from active participation in the war. As a result of her stand, Spain was isolated diplomatically after the War. Spain was admitted to the United Nations in 1955.

The dictatorship established after the civil war endured through Franco's lifetime. He named as his successor the son of the Bourbon pretender to the throne. In November 1975, Juan Carlos de Bourbon, grandson to the previous king, was restored to the monarchy. Despite an attempted coup in 1981, the army remained loyal to the king.

SRI LANKA

For nearly two thousand years, Sinhalese kings ruled Ceylon with only occasional interruptions. Many wars were fought against invaders from southern India and China. Early in the sixteenth century the Portuguese established relations with Ceylon and began a conquest of the island. By the end of the century they had gained control. The Dutch supplanted them in the middle of the seventeenth century. In 1796, the British expelled the Dutch and annexed their settlements to one of their administrations in India. In 1802, Ceylon was constituted a crown colony.

The British firmly suppressed attempted native rebellions; they introduced tea and rubber plantations, importing Tamils as laborers. Internal struggles broke out between Buddhists and Moslem traders. In addition, the inhabitants strove constantly for a voice in their own government.

On February 4, 1949, Ceylon became a Dominion within the British Commonwealth. On December 14, 1955, the country became a member of the United Nations. It changed from a monarchy to a republic on May 22, 1972, and at that time also chose to use its Sinhalese name, Sri Lanka. A shift from a prime minister to a presidential form of government occurred in 1978.

SUDAN

The region known as Nubia was invaded by Egyptians around 3000 B.C.; and Egypt ruled it continuously until the eighth century B.C., when the Sudanese defeated and subjugated the Egyptians.

Gradually the country became Christianized. It was invaded in the sixteenth century by Arabs from the north and Moslem blacks from the Blue Nile Valley.

In the nineteenth century, Egypt, then a Turkish province, launched a successful invasion that made Sudan an Egyptian province. The region remained under Egyptian-Turkish rule for 60 years, a period marked by native unrest. A series of revolts beginning in 1880 smashed Egyptian rule but brought little improvement in conditions. Constant wars of expansion were waged against neighboring tribes, and an attempted conquest of Egypt in 1889 ended in disaster.

Following this debacle, French influence began to spread in the Sudan. Alarmed at growing French power, Britain sent a joint British-Egyptian force into the region and won a complete victory. In 1899, Britain and Egypt assumed joint control in Sudan.

Following World War II, Egypt became dissatisfied with the joint arrangement and demanded British withdrawal. An agreement was finally reached that provided for Sudanese independence. After an election, Sudanese officials took office in 1954 and began the process of replacing all foreigners in government and military positions. On January 1, 1956, the Republic of Sudan was established.

Sudan has found itself in the midst of recent terrorist revolts in the Arab world. In March 1973, eight Palestinian rebels murdered the American ambassador, a Belgian diplomat, and the French *chargé d'affaires* in Khartoum. The Sudanese government released the terrorists to another revolutionary group in Egypt.

Large numbers of refugees have aggravated the economic problems of Sudan in recent years. In 1985 the government of President Nimeiry was overthrown in a military coup.

SURINAM

In 1667, the Dutch acquired Surinam from the British in exchange for New Netherland (an area that now includes New York) in North America. It remained a colony called Netherlands Guiana (or Dutch Guiana) until 1954, when it was given the status of a dependency of the Dutch crown. The home government was more than willing to grant this country its freedom. Most of the population of Surinam are East Indians or descendants of slaves brought over from Africa. The republic of Surinam was proclaimed on November 25, 1975, and it was admitted to the United Nations on December 4, 1975. In 1982 the National Military Council took control of the government.

SWAZILAND

The Swazis, a Bantu people in southern Africa, gradually bargained away their resources to the

British and Boer colonists who were their neighbors at the end of the nineteenth century.

Sobhuza II became king of Swaziland in 1921. He remained king after Swaziland became an independent state within the British Commonwealth on September 6, 1968. Swaziland was admitted to the United Nations on September 24, 1968. A parliamentary system installed in 1967 was discarded by King Sobhuza in 1973.

A parliamentary form of government was restored in 1979, although political parties are forbidden.

SWEDEN

The first mention of the Swedes by Europeans was made by the Roman historian Tacitus in about A.D. 100. He described them as having "mighty ships and arms." Uppsala was founded about A.D. 500.

Swedes explored interior Russia. Rurik (probably a Viking from Sweden) founded the Russian State (*see* U.S.S.R.).

A long series of wars against Finland began in 1157, ending with the conquest and Christianization of Finland in 1293. In 1319, Norway and Sweden were united; and in 1397, all of Scandinavia was united under Queen Margarethe of Denmark.

Sweden broke away in 1523 and elected Gustavus Vasa (Gustaf I) as king. Gustavus freed the country from the rule of Danish nobles and the Hanseatic League cities. By 1560, Sweden was the strongest power in northern Europe. Between 1611 and 1718 Sweden expanded to be the foremost Protestant power.

Sweden declined through internal dissension and the combined efforts of Prussia, Russia, and Hanover. The last war ever fought by Sweden was against Napoleon in 1814. Norway was united to Sweden (taken from Denmark) between 1814 and 1905. Sweden gradually became a democratic nation as the king handed over more and more power to the Riksdag (Parliament). Sweden has mantained strict neutrality since 1814, but joined the United Nations on November 19, 1946.

SWITZERLAND

When Julius Caesar set about his conquest of self by the Latin name of *Helvetia* on postage stamps. The area came under the control of various Germanic peoples in the fifth century A.D. It was part of Charlemagne's Frankish domain in the eighth century and part of the Holy Roman Empire by the eleventh century. In the thirteenth century it came under Hapsburg rule.

Oppressive rule by the Hapsburgs led to an "eternal alliance" between the cantons of Schwyz (the name from which "Switzerland" is derived), Uri, and Unterwalden in 1291. This was the first step toward a Swiss nation. In 1315, the Swiss defeated the Hapsburgs at Morgarten Pass. Thereafter the Swiss became renowned throughout Europe as great fighters and tough soldiers. Other countries hired Swiss mercenaries to do their fighting. The Swiss defeated Charles of Burgundy in 1477. The number of cantons in the alliance had grown to eight by then. Four more victories over Austria followed within a century. The country secured complete independence from the Holy Roman Empire at Basel in 1499.

The confederation had grown to 13 (plus some allied cantons) by 1513. Then the Reformation troubles began. The conflict between Catholic and Protestant in Switzerland plagued the federation until 1847. A number of rebellions occurred, but were unsuccessful. Switzerland was occupied by Napoleon's forces for a time; but it was restored with its 22 cantons in 1815 by the Congress of Vienna.

Since 1874 Switzerland has operated under an enlarged federal authority, with a constitution similar to that of the United States. The nation has managed to remain neutral in all wars since 1815. At the same time, it has been a refuge for exiles and has offered Swiss services to international organizations. Switzerland was the headquarters of the League of Nations, and the Swiss also offered the city of Geneva as the site of the United Nations. However, Switzerland is not a member of the United Nations.

Long known as a banking center, Switzerland offers a stable currency and attracts foreign investments. In 1984 a proposal to open bank records to foreign authorities for investigation was rejected.

SYRIA

Syria is the name of an ancient region that included the present Syria, Lebanon, Israel, and Jordan. In 1471 B.C., Egypt conquered ancient Syria. Successive invasions by Babylonia, Assyria, Persia, and Macedonia eventually destroyed the outline of Syria.

The region of the present-day Syria, centered around the city of Damascus (reputedly the oldest inhabited city in the world), became a notable trading area. Famous caravan routes between the Persian Gulf and the Mediterranean Sea passed through Palmyra and Damascus. In A.D. 105, the entire region came under Roman rule. Palmyra rose to great fame under Queen Zenobia, but was destroyed by the Roman Emperor Aurelian in A.D. 273. In A.D. 637, Damascus became the capital of a large Arab empire called the Caliphate of Omayyad, which extended all the way to India. The Christian Crusaders invaded Syria in the twelfth century. A series of small Crusaders' states grew up in Syria that lasted until the coming of the Ottoman Empire in the sixteenth century. Ottoman rule continued until after World War I. After the war, the League of Nations gave Syria the control of France. The Syrians were dissatisfied with the mandate and demanded home rule. Rebellions were crushed by the French in 1925 and 1927.

In 1941, Syria was proclaimed an independent republic. The Arab League was formed in 1945 with Syria as a member. The French withdrew in 1946, and Syria joined the Arab League to resist the formation of Israel. Syria was defeated, along with the Arab League, and an internal struggle developed. In 1958, Syria joined with Egypt to form the United Arab Republic, which was dissolved in 1961. When Syria entered the war against Israel in 1967, she lost her southwestern corner (the Golan Heights) to Israel. Syria continued to allow guerrilla units to stage raids on Israel from her territory. She refused to negotiate peace with Israel until the Golan Heights were restored and the issue of the Palestinian refugees was settled.

Syria has been the most militant of the Arab countries and has engaged in every conflict that has occurred in the Middle East over the past 30 years. In 1984, Syrian forces were in the thick of the fighting in Lebanon.

TAIWAN

This large island 110 miles east of the Chinese mainland probably received Chinese immigrants during the Tang Dynasty (A.D. 618–907), but it was not part of the Chinese Empire until the end of the seventeenth century. The Portuguese first saw the island in 1544 and named it *Formosa* ("beautiful"). By 1624, there were Dutch forts on the island; but Chinese refugees drove out the Dutch, even before others came from the mainland to conquer the island in 1662.

After the Japanese victory in her war with China in 1895, Taiwan was ceded to Japan. It remained Japanese for half a century, during which its economy was improved but its culture was blighted. It was restored to Chinese control after World War II. Within a few years, the Taiwanese began to revolt against the Chinese government. At this time, the Chinese government was being driven out of the mainland by the Chinese Communists; so the anticommunist or Nationalist governments took refuge on Taiwan, which became the official seat of administration for Nationalist China.

The Nationalist administration tried to bring peace and order to its new home, from which it expected to launch a reconquest of the mainland. It improved the economy of the island and represented China in many world capitals. It was a member of the United Nations from October 24, 1945 until 1971, when the organization voted to transfer the Chinese seat to the representatives of the People's Republic of China.

The main support of the Nationalist government was the United States. Even after 1971 the United States continued to recognize the Nationalists while negotating with the People's Republic. Both Chinese governments agreed in principle that Taiwan is part of China.

TANZANIA

The name of this republic was coined from that of its two component units, Tanganyika and Zanzibar, which had separate histories before their merger in 1964.

Vasco da Gama was the first modern European to visit the east coast of Africa in 1498. He found the Arabs entrenched there, and they remained in control as slave traders, despite Portuguese efforts to gain a foothold. In the early eighteenth century, the dominant power was that of the sultan of Muscat and Oman, whose headquarters were on the offshore island of Zanzibar (*see* Oman).

In 1884, the coast became part of German East Africa. This colony was split after World War I, and the bulk of it was mandated in 1922 to Britain under the name of the large lake on its west border, Tanganyika. It became a United Nations trust territory in 1946. After achieving local autonomy in 1960, Tanganyika became independent on December 9, 1961. Five days later it became a member of the United Nations. On its first anniversary, Tanganyika became a republic within the British Commonwealth.

Meanwhile, Zanzibar and the nearby island of Pemba acquired a population from southern Asia, and its Arab masters were supplanted by Portuguese, who dominated during the sixteenth and seventeenth centuries. In 1699, the Portuguese were driven out by Arabs from Oman. Zanzibar became one of the leading slave trading centers in eastern Africa.

British interest required the ban of this commerce with her colonies; and in 1822, the Imam of Oman signed a treaty with Britain containing this provision. Thus began an era of British protection that continued when Zanzibar was separated from Oman in 1856. The region became a colony of Great Britain during World War I. Autonomy was granted in 1963; and on June 24 of that year, the sultanate became independent. On January 12, 1964, the sultan was deposed and the People's Republic of Zanzibar was proclaimed.

Zanzibar had been admitted to the United Nations on December 16, 1963. But on April 26, 1964, Zanzibar and Tanganyika united to form a single republic. Thereafter only one membership was retained in the United Nations. The name was changed on October 29, 1964 to United Republic of Tanzania.

THAILAND

Tribes of Indochina began a migration during the sixth century B.C. into the area now called Thailand. In the middle of the fourteenth century, a unified Thai kingdom was established. It expanded over the centuries by wars of conquest against neighboring small states. It continued for 400 years. By the sixteenth century, contact with Europeans had been established, and Thailand enjoyed a flourishing trade with various Asian and European countries.

There were intermittent wars with Burma until 1764. Then Thailand was invaded by the Burmese and the Thai capital was destroyed. Shortly afterward, the Thais succeeded in driving out the Burmese and established a new capital at Bangkok.

Late in the nineteenth century, Thailand engaged in a boundary dispute with the French, who at that time controlled Indochina. France sent troops and warships that forced Thailand to give up territorial rights in Cambodia. Later, the Thais gave up additional territory to France and Great Britain.

Thailand was an absolute monarchy until 1932, when a revolt set up a representative government with universal suffrage. In 1939, the country (which had until then been known as Siam) officially changed its name to Thailand.

While France was embroiled in World War II, Thailand demanded that territory taken from it be returned. Japan mediated the dispute; this strengthened relations between Thailand and Japan. Immediately after the attack on Pearl Harbor, Japan was granted the right to move troops across Thai territory to the Malay area. In January 1942, Thailand declared war against the Allies. The pro-Japanese government was overthrown in 1944, and the new leaders expressed sympathy for the Allied cause. However, Japan remained in control of Thailand until the war ended. Thailand was admitted to the United Nations on December 16, 1946.

After World War II, the country generally sided with the anticommunist powers in the Cold War. During the war in Indochina, Thailand became a staging area for United States air forces that raided Indochina. Thailand was one of the few Asian members of the Southeast Asia Treaty Organization. Its government was overthrown by a military junta in 1971, which was in turn succeeded by a constitutional government in 1973. In 1975, the first elections ever held in Thailand returned a coalition government, but the military regained power in a coup in 1976.

Another military coup in 1977 installed Kriangsak Chomanan as prime minister, although he resigned in 1980. The military continues at the nation's helm.

TOGO

Togo should not be confused with Togoland, a term formerly used for a political unit which no longer exists. Togo was originally colonized by the Ewe people, who now form part of the population in Togo and in neighboring Ghana. The Portuguese began taking slaves from the Togo region in the fifteenth and sixteenth centuries. After competing with both France and Britain for control, Germany established a formal protectorate over the area in 1894.

The original region of which Togo now forms a part was called Togoland. It was held by the Germans until after World War I. In 1919, Togoland was divided into British-administered Togoland and French-administered Togoland, both under trusteeship. Trusteeship was continued under the United Nations after World War II. In 1956, the people of British-held Togoland voted to join the Gold Coast Colony, which became Ghana. British Togoland then ceased to exist.

In 1956, the French-held area voted to terminate trust status, but the vote was not accepted by the United Nations. In April 1958, elections were held under United Nations supervision; this time Togo was given permission to negotiate with France for independence. Full independence was granted on April 27, 1960, and the country was admitted to the United Nations on September 20, 1960.

TONGA

The archipelago of Tonga in the Pacific Ocean has been ruled by a monarchy that is at least 900 years old. The Dutch were the first Europeans to visit the islands, but it was Britain that signed a treaty establishing her protectorate in 1900. By a similar agreement, the islands regained their independence on June 4, 1970, and became a member of the British Commonwealth.

TRINIDAD AND TOBAGO

The islands of Trinidad and Tobago were discovered by Christopher Columbus in 1498, on his third voyage to the New World. The original inhabitants (Carib and Arawak Indians) were killed off or enslaved by the Spanish. The Spanish at first used both islands as centers for the expeditions of discovery and conquest in what is now Latin America.

Colonization of both islands began in the sixteenth century. Tobago was colonized by English settlers from nearby Barbados, and eventually changed hands between the Spanish and English many times before finally becoming a British colony in 1814.

Trinidad is much larger and richer in resources than Tobago. It was colonized by Spanish immigrants, who were later augmented by colonists from other lands. Slaves were introduced early to work sugar cane plantations. During the last half of the nineteenth century many people from South Asia came as laborers in the fields and forests of Trinidad. Trinidad was captured by the British in 1797.

Both islands were at first ruled as separate colonies. Trinidad became a crown colony in 1802, and Tobago was administered as a part of the Windward Islands until 1877, when it also became a crown colony. However, Trinidad and Tobago were united in 1888.

The Federation of West Indies was created in 1958 and included as one of its members a combined Trinidad and Tobago. On February 6, 1962, the British government dissolved the federation. Trinidad and Tobago were then united into an independent nation on August 31, 1962. The new nation became a member of the United Nations on September 18, 1962 and a republic in 1976.

TUNISIA

The ancient city of Carthage was founded in 850 B.C., not far from the present city of Tunis. Following the destruction of Carthage in the Punic Wars, the region came under the domination of various peoples (including the Romans, Byzantines, Vandals, Arabs, Spanish, Turkish, and French). Relics of all these civilizations are still to be found throughout the country; the strongest imprint was left by the Arab-Moslem culture.

Under the Husseinite dynasty, which began early in the eighteenth century, a major source of revenue was piracy. In the nineteenth century, United States naval forces destroyed pirate bases along the so-called Barbary Coast and made the high seas safe for shipping.

In 1881, the French entered Tunisia from Algeria and forced it to become a protectorate, a status which lasted well into the twentieth century. Important World War II battles were fought in Tunisia.

After achieving autonomy, the Tunisians declared their independence on March 20, 1956. Ignoring the monarchy, they instituted a republic on July 25, 1957. Tunisia became a member of the United Nations on November 12, 1956.

TURKEY

About 1900 B.C., the Hittite people invaded Asia Minor from either Europe or Central Asia. Their language and customs persisted for 700 years in Asia Minor. Greeks from the west and Assyrians from the east eventually destroyed their empire, and they gradually disappeared from history.

From about 1000 B.C., the Greeks, Lydians, and others dominated Asia Minor. The Greeks became the most influential people and established great centers of classical Greek culture at such cities as Ephesus, Pergamum, Miletus, and Halicarnassus.

The Persians overran most of Greek-controlled Asia Minor, but all of it was recaptured by Alexander the Great in 333 B.C. The Romans conquered Asia Minor in 63 B.C.

The Byzantine or Eastern Roman Empire continued Roman rule until the Seljuk Turks (a Moslem people from central Asia) invaded and conquered the area in the eleventh century. These Seljuks were the ancestors of the present-day Turks. The Crusades by Western Europeans were directed at the Seljuks. But they were conquered instead by the Mongolians of Central Asia. Turkish power revived under the Ottoman Turks after the Mongol invasions receded. The Ottoman Empire expanded at the expense of Christian and other Moslem states. Constantinople, the last Christian imperial capital in eastern Europe, fell in 1453. The city was made the Ottoman capital under the name *Istanbul.*

The history of modern Turkey begins with the decline of the Ottoman power that started in 1529, when the Ottomans failed to take Venice in a bloody siege. Throughout the later centuries, the Ottoman Empire fought defensive wars and continued to lose them. It became derisively known as the "Sick Man of Europe." The Greeks regained their independence in the 1820s. The North African territories—Egypt, Algeria—were detached. Serbia was removed from Turkish control, even after a Turkish victory in the Crimean War. The Balkans became the target of European power grabs, while Turkey was left with only a small enclave around Istanbul as a souvenir of her European holdings.

These territorial losses and the despotic domestic policy aroused patriots within the country (known as Young Turks) to force the sultan to establish a constitutional monarchy in 1909. Italy took Libya from the Turks in 1911. In a gamble to recover some power in Europe, Turkey allied herself with Germany in World War I, and lost her Middle East possessions. Out of the ruins came a revolution headed by Kemal Ataturk, who drove the Greeks out of Asia Minor and proclaimed a republic on October 29, 1923.

Turkey remained neutral throughout World War II, joining the victorious Allies only in February 1945, in time to participate as a belligerent in the peace negotiations. Turkey joined the United Nations on October 24, 1945. In 1950, Turkey sent a token contingent to fight in Korea; and in 1952, she became a signatory of the North Atlantic Treaty Organization. Relations with Greece were strained in 1974 because of the dispute over Cyprus. The Turkish invasion of Cyprus resulted in an arms embargo by the United States. Turkey ordered the United States to leave its Turkish military bases; but in 1976, they signed a new treaty that allowed the Americans to stay.

Turkey signed a non-agression pact with Russia in 1978.

A military takeover in 1980 yielded power to an elected parliament in 1983. Martial law, in effect since 1978, was lifted in 1984.

TURKS AND CAICOS ISLANDS

The Turks and Caicos, discovered by Ponce de León in 1512, are geographically a part of the Bahama Islands group in the West Indies. They were administered as part of Jamaica from 1848 until Jamaica became independent in 1962. After that, the Turks and Caicos became a British dependency.

TUVALU

(See Gilbert and Ellice Islands)

UGANDA

Arab and English immigration into this region of Africa began about the middle of the nineteenth century. The British established a protectorate in 1894. Progress toward self-government was begun in 1920.

On October 9, 1962, Uganda became an independent nation within the British Commonwealth. Sixteen days later, Uganda became a member of the United Nations; and in 1967, the nation became a republic. Its government lacked stability until Idi Amin seized the presidency in 1971 and established a dictatorship. He aroused ill will in Europe and the United States by expelling the large Asian population of Uganda in 1972. The United States cut off economic aid in 1973, and Amin called for Soviet help. He was driven into exile in 1979. Since Amin's flight, the country has been in social and economic upheaval.

UNION OF SOVIET SOCIALIST REPUBLICS

The region that now comprises the heart of the U.S.S.R. (also called the Soviet Union) was known as Scythia to the ancient Greeks. The people were called Scythians. Greek colonies were established along the northern shores of the Black Sea in Scythia about 1000 B.C.

The modern history of the Soviet Union is largely that of the Russians (also called Great Russians to distinguish them from Ukrainians, or Little Russians, and Byelorussians, or White Russians).

The first state in the region of the present European Soviet Union was founded by three Scandinavian brothers named Rurik, Sineus, and Truvor. Their seat of government became the Slavic city of Novgorod (New Town) in A.D. 862. Novgorod (also called Novgorod the Great) seems to have had a long previous association with bands of Vikings, and it is possible that the three brothers were Vikings. Rurik (from whose name the word *Russia* may have been derived) eventually became the sole ruler of Novgorod. After Rurik's death in A.D. 879, the center of political power gradually shifted southward to Kiev on the Dnieper River in the present Ukraine.

Novgorod and Kiev were growing political centers in the ninth century. They were trading posts and commercial centers on the famous trade route across Europe that has since become known as the "Water Road." The Water Road was a wilderness system of river, lake, and portage routes that connected the Baltic and Black seas through what is now the western part of European Russia.

Russia—Nevsky Prospect, Leningrad

Several princely states gradually grew up along the Water Road, but Novgorod and Kiev remained the leading centers until the coming of the Mongol invaders during the thirteenth century. Between 879 and 1242, Kiev expanded and grew to become the "mother" of Slavic culture and chief seat of learning.

The death blow to Kiev as a national center came early in the thirteenth century when the Mongol invasions began. The Mongols (called Tatars by Russians) swept over southern Russia, toppling one princely state after another. Many of the leaders, including those from Kiev, fled to the great forest where they established new cities and prepared for defense against the oncoming Mongolian armies. Kiev was overpowered and ruined by the Mongols in 1240.

Soon all the Russian states were paying tribute to the Mongols—all but Novgorod, which withstood the attacks. Alexander Nevsky, the first great Russian national hero, became the ruler of free Novgorod in 1240 and of Vladimir in 1252. In 1240, he defeated an invasion by Swedes and then crushed the Teutonic Knights on frozen Lake Peipus (Chudskoye) in 1242. However, he was no match for the "Golden Horde," and soon even Novgorod was paying taxes to the Mongol princes.

It should be noted that the Mongols did not destroy the Orthodox Church, nor did they disrupt the system of government by "Grand Princes" that had prevailed in Russia before the invasion. They simply exacted taxes from the ruling princes.

A century after the invasions, Moscow began to rise as a religious and political center. Ivan (Russian for John) Kalita, "The Purse," ruler of Moscow from 1328–1340, persuaded the head of the Christian Church to move from Vladimir to Moscow. Ivan then had himself crowned "Grand Prince of Vladimir and all Rus." This was the beginning of Muscovite expansion.

Mongol power was broken under the steady fighting of Muscovite princes. Ivan III (1462–1505) finally freed Russia from Mongol domination. Ivan also put an end to the independence of Novgorod the Great, although that city is still a prosperous industrial center of the Soviet Union.

A series of powerful rulers, including Ivan IV ("the Terrible"), continued to expand the Muscovite state. They crushed all opposition to autocra-

CONDENSED WORLD GAZETTEER

Keyed to the Quick Reference World Map (next two pages)

Latest Estimated Population Figures

AFGHANISTAN (E-23) Republic. Area 252,000 sq. mi. Pop. 19,800,000. Capital Kabul.

ALBANIA (D-20) People's Republic. Area 11,000 sq. mi. Pop. 2,550,000. Capital Tirane.

ALGERIA (E-19) People's Republic. Area 896,593 sq. mi. Pop. 17,300,000. Capital Alger (Algiers).

ANDORRA (D-19) Co-Principality. Area 179 sq. mi. Pop. 26,560. Capital Andorra la Vella.

ANGOLA (J-20) People's Republic. Area 481,350 sq. mi. Pop. 5,800,000. Capital Luanda.

ARGENTINA (L-14) Federal Republic. Area 1,072,163 sq. mi. Pop. 25,720,000. Capital Buenos Aires.

AUSTRALIA* (K-3) Federal Parliamentary State. Area 2,967,900. sq. mi. Pop. 13,640,000. Capital Canberra.

AUSTRIA (D-19) Federal Republic. Area 32,375 sq. mi. Pop. 7,510,000. Capital Wien (Vienna).

BAHAMAS* (F-14) Parliamentary State. Area 5,382 sq. mi. Pop. 210,000. Capital Nassau.

BAHRAIN (F-22) Independent Monarchy (Emirate). Area 256 sq. mi. Pop. 260,000. Capital Al Manama.

BANGLADESH* (F-1) Republic. Area 55,126 sq. mi. Pop. 76,820,000. Capital Dacca.

BARBADOS* (G-15) Parliamentary State. Area 166 sq. mi. Pop. 250,000. Capital Bridgetown.

BELGIUM (C-19) Constitutional Monarchy. Area 11,782 sq. mi. Pop. 9,890,000. Capital Bruxelles (Brussels).

BELIZE* (G-13) United Kingdom Colony. Area 8,866 sq. mi. Pop. 140,000. Capital Belmopan.

BENIN (DAHOMEY) (H-19) Military. Area 43,475 sq. mi. Pop. 3,200,000. Capital Porto Novo.

BHUTAN (F-1) Monarchy. Area 18,000 sq. mi. Pop. 1,035,000. Capital Thimphu.

BOLIVIA (J-14) Military Dictatorship. Area 424,165 sq. mi. Pop. 5,790,000. Capital La Paz and Sucre.

BOTSWANA* (K-20) Republic. Area 222,000 sq. mi. Pop. 690,000. Capital Gaborone.

BRAZIL (J-15) Military Dictatorship. Area. 3,286,488 sq. mi. Pop. 109,180,000. Capital Brasília.

BRUNEI* (H-2) Sultanate. (United Kingdom Prot.) Area 2,226 sq. mi. Pop. 147,000. Capital Bandar Seri Begawan.

BULGARIA (D-20) People's Republic. Area 42,823 sq. mi. Pop. 8,760,000. Capital Sofiya (Sofia).

BURMA (F-1) Socialist Republic. Area 261,789 sq. mi. Pop. 30,830,000. Capital Rangoon.

BURUNDI (I-20) Dictatorship. Area 10,747 sq. mi. Pop. 3,860,000. Capital Bujumbura.

CAMBODIA (G-2) People's Republic. Area 69,898 sq. mi. Pop. 8,350,000. Capital Phnom Penh.

CAMEROON (H-19) Republic. Area 179,558 sq. mi. Pop. 6,530,000. Capital Yaoundé.

CANADA* (B-12) Federal Parliamentary State. Area 3,851,809 sq. mi. Pop. 22,990,000. Capital Ottawa.

CANAL ZONE (H-13) U.S. Terr. Area 647 sq. mi. Pop. 45,200. Capital Balboa Heights.

CAPE VERDE (G-16) Independent Republic. Area 1,557 sq. mi. Pop. 300,000. Capital Praia.

CENTRAL AFRICAN REPUBLIC (H-20) Military Dictatorship. Area 241,305 sq. mi. Pop. 2,610,000. Capital Bangui.

CHAD (G-20) Republic. Area 495,750 sq. mi. Pop. 4,120,000. Capital N'Djamena.

CHILE (L-14) Military Dictatorship. Area 292,258 sq. mi. Pop. 10,450,000. Capital Santiago.

CHINA (E-2) People's Republic. Area 3,691,500 sq. mi. Pop. 852,130,000. Capital Peiping (Peking).

COLOMBIA (H-14) Republic. Area 439,737 sq. mi. Pop. 24,370,000. Capital Bogotá.

COMOROS (J-21) Independent State. Area 863 sq. mi. Pop. 310,000. Capital Moroni.

CONGO (I-19) Dictatorship. Area 132,046 sq. mi. Pop. 1,390,000. Capital Brazzaville.

COSTA RICA (H-13) Republic. Area 19,652 sq. mi. Pop. 2,010,000. Capital San José.

CUBA (F-13) Communist Dictatorship. Area 42,827 sq. mi. Pop. 9,330,000. Capital Habana (Havana).

CYPRUS* (E-21) Republic. Area 3,572 sq. mi. Pop. 700,000. Capital Nicosia.

CZECHOSLOVAKIA (D-20) Federal Socialist Republic. Area 49,374 sq. mi. Pop. 14,200,000. Capital Praha (Prague).

DENMARK (C-19) Constitutional Monarchy. Area 16,630 sq. mi. Pop. 5,070,000. Capital Köbenhavn (Copenhagen).

DJIBOUTI (G-21) Republic. Area 8,900 sq. mi. Pop. 300,000. Capital Djibouti.

DOMINICAN REPUBLIC (G-14) Republic. Area 18,658 sq. mi. Pop. 4,840,000. Capital Santo Domingo.

ECUADOR (I-13) Dictatorship. Area 109,484 sq. mi. Pop. 7,310,000. Capital Quito.

EGYPT (F-20) Republic. Area 386,900 sq. mi. Pop. 38,070,000. Capital Cairo.

EL SALVADOR (G-13) Republic. Area 8,124 sq. mi. Pop. 4,120,000. Capital San Salvador.

EQUATORIAL GUINEA (H-19) Republic. Area 10,830 sq. mi. Pop. 320,000. Capital Malabo.

ETHIOPIA (H-21) Military Dictatorship. Area 471,800 sq. mi. Pop. 28,680,000. Capital Addis Ababa.

FIJI* (J-6) Independent Parliamentary State. Area 7,055 sq. mi. Pop. 580,000. Capital Suva.

FINLAND (B-20) Republic. Area 130,129 sq. mi. Pop. 4,730,000. Capital Helsinki.

FRANCE (D-19) Republic. Area 210,039 sq. mi. Pop. 52,920,000. Capital Paris.

FRENCH GUIANA (H-15) Overseas Department. Area 34,750 sq. mi. Pop. 58,000. Capital Cayenne.

GABON (I-19) Dictatorship. Area 103,347 sq. mi. Pop. 1,530,000. Capital Libreville.

GAMBIA, THE* (G-17) Republic. Area 4,467 sq. mi. Pop. 540,000. Capital Banjul.

GERMANY, EAST (C-19) People's Republic. Area 41,650 sq. mi. Pop. 17,000,000. Capital East Berlin.

GERMANY, WEST (C-19) Federal Republic. Area 95,985 sq. mi. Pop. 60,000,000. Capital Bonn.

GHANA* (H-18) Military Dictatorship. Area 92,100 sq. mi. Pop. 10,310,000. Capital Accra.

GIBRALTAR* (E-18) United Kingdom Colony. Area 2.25 sq. mi. Pop. 29,400. Capital Gibraltar.

GREECE (E-20) Republic. Area 50,960 sq. mi. Pop. 9,170,000. Capital Athinai (Athens).

GREENLAND (A-16) Danish Colony. Area 840,000 sq. mi. Pop. 100,000. Capital Godthaab.

GRENADA* (G-15) Parliamentary State. Area 133 sq. mi. Pop. 106,200. Capital Saint George's.

GUAM (G-4) U.S. Terr. Area 209 sq. mi. Pop. 110,300. Capital Agana.

GUATEMALA (G-12) Republic. Area 42,042 sq. mi. Pop. 6,260,000. Capital Guatemala.

GUINEA (G-18) Republic. Area 94,926 sq. mi. Pop. 4,530,000. Capital Conakry.

GUINEA-BISSAU (G-17) Republic. Area 13,948 sq. mi. Pop. 530,000. Capital Bissau.

GUYANA* (H-15) Republic. Area 83,000 sq. mi. Pop. 780,000. Capital Georgetown.

HAITI (G-14) Dictatorship. Area 10,714 sq. mi. Pop. 4,670,000. Capital Port-au-Prince.

HONDURAS (G-13) Dictatorship. Area 43,277 sq. mi. Pop. 3,140,000. Capital Tegucigalpa.

HONG KONG* (F-2) United Kingdom Colony. Area 403 sq. mi. Pop. 4,366,600. Capital Victoria.

HUNGARY (D-20) People's Republic. Area 35,920 sq. mi. Pop. 10,600,000. Capital Budapest.

ICELAND (B-17) Republic. Area 39,769 sq. mi. Pop. 220,000. Capital Reykjavik.

INDIA* (F-24) Federal Republic. Area 1,269,420 sq. mi. Pop. 610,080,000. Capital New Delhi.

INDONESIA (I-2) Republic. Area 782,663 sq. mi. Pop. 139,620,000. Capital Jakarta.

IRAN (PERSIA) (E-22) Islamic Republic. Area 636,000 sq. mi. Pop. 33,900,000. Capital Tehran.

IRAQ (E-21) Military Dictatorship. Area 168,928 sq. mi. Pop. 11,510,000. Capital Baghdad.

IRELAND (EIRE) (C-18) Republic. Area 27,136 sq. mi. Pop. 3,160,000. Capital Baile Atha Cliath (Dublin).

ISRAEL (E-21) Republic. Area 7,992 sq. mi. Pop. 3,540,000. Capital Jerusalem.

ITALY (D-19) Republic. Area 116,313 sq. mi. Pop. 56,190,000. Capital Roma (Rome).

IVORY COAST (H-18) Republic. Area 123,484 sq. mi. Pop. 5,020,000. Capital Abidjan.

JAMAICA* (G-13) Parliamentary State. Area 4,244 sq. mi. Pop. 2,060,000. Capital Kingston.

JAPAN (E-4) Constitutional Monarchy. Area 145,747 sq. mi. Pop. 112,770,000. Capital Tokyo.

JORDAN (F-21) Constitutional Monarchy. Area 36,832 sq. mi. Pop. 2,780,000. Capital Amman.

KENYA* (H-21) Republic. Area 224,961 sq. mi. Pop. 13,850,000. Capital Nairobi.

KOREA, NORTH (D-3) People's Democratic Rep. Area 46,800 sq. mi. Pop. 16,250,000. Capital Pyongyang.

KOREA, SOUTH (E-3) Republic. Area 38,130 sq. mi. Pop. 35,860,000. Capital Seoul.

KUWAIT (F-22) Independent Emirate. Area 6,880 sq. mi. Pop. 1,030,000. Capital Al Kuwait.

LAOS (G-2) People's Democratic Republic. Area 91,400 sq. mi. Pop. 3,380,000. Capital Vientiane.

LEBANON (E-21) Republic. Area 3,950 sq. mi. Pop. 2,960,000. Capital Bayrut (Beirut).

LESOTHO* (K-20) Constitutional Monarchy. Area 11,720 sq. mi. Pop. 1,040,000. Capital Maseru.

LIBERIA (H-18) Republic. Area 43,000 sq. mi. Pop. 1,750,000. Capital Monrovia.

LIBYA. (F-20) Socialist Republic. Area 675,000 sq. mi. Pop. 2,440,000. Capital Tripoli.

LIECHTENSTEIN (D-19) Constitutional Monarchy. Area 62 sq. mi. Pop. 24,700. Capital Vaduz.

LUXEMBOURG (D-19) Constitutional Monarchy. Area 999 sq. mi. Pop. 360,000. Capital Luxembourg.

MACAO (F-2) Port. Overseas Province. Area 6 sq. mi. Pop. 257,000. Capital Macao.

MADAGASCAR (J-22) Republic. Area 226,658 sq. mi. Pop. 8,011,000. Capital Antananarivo.

MALAWI* (J-21) Republic. Area 45,747 sq. mi. Pop. 5,180,000. Capital Lilongwe.

MALAYSIA* (H-2) Federal Constitutional Monarchy. Comprises West Malaysia and East Malaysia (Sarawak and Sabah). Area 127,316 sq. mi. Pop. 12,300,000. Capital Kuala Lumpur.

MALDIVES (H-23) Republic. Area 115 sq. mi. Pop. 120,000. Capital Male.

MALI (G-18) Military Dictatorship. Area 478,822 sq. mi. Pop. 5,840,000. Capital Bamako.

MALTA* (E-19) Republic. Area 122 sq. mi. Pop. 318,000. Capital Valetta.

MAURITANIA (G-18) Republic. Area 398,000 sq. mi. Pop. 1,320,000. Capital Nouakchott.

MAURITIUS* (K-22) Parliamentary State. Area 787.5 sq. mi. Pop. 870,000. Capital Port Louis.

MEXICO (F-12) Federal Republic. Area 761,604 sq. mi. Pop. 62,330,000. Capital Mexico City.

MONACO (D-19) Sovereign Principality. Area 0.73 sq. mi. Pop. 30,000. Capital Monaco-Ville.

MONGOLIA (D-1) People's Republic. Area 604,000 sq. mi. Pop. 1,490,000. Capital Ulaanbaatar (Ulan Bator).

MOROCCO (E-18) Constitutional Monarchy. Area 177,117 sq. mi. Pop. 17,830,000. Capital Rabat.

MOZAMBIQUE (J-21) People's Republic. Area 308,642 sq. mi. Pop. 9,440,000. Capital Maputo.

NAMIBIA (SOUTH-WEST AFRICA) (K-20) South Africa Terr. Area 318,261 sq. mi. Pop. 862,000. Capital Windhoek.

NAURU* (I-6) Republic. Area 8.2 sq. mi. Pop. 7,128. Capital Yaren.

NEPAL (F-24) Constitutional Monarchy. Area 54,362 sq. mi. Pop. 12,860,000. Capital Kathmandu.

NETHERLANDS (C-19) Constitutional Monarchy. Area 15,892 sq. mi. Pop. 13,770,000. Capital Amsterdam.

NEW ZEALAND* (M-6) Parliamentary State. Area 103,747 sq. mi. Pop. 3,140,000. Capital Wellington.

NICARAGUA (G-13) Republic. Area 50,000 sq. mi. Pop. 2,230,000. Capital Managua.

NIGER (F-19) Military Dictatorship. Area 489,000 sq. mi. Pop. 4,730,000. Capital Niamey.

NIGERIA* (H-19) Military Dictatorship. Area 356,699 sq. mi. Pop. 64,750,000. Capital Lagos.

NORWAY (B-19) Constitutional Monarchy. Area 125,053 sq. mi. Pop. 4,030,000. Capital Oslo.

OMAN (F-22) Independent Sultanate. Area 82,000 sq. mi. Pop. 790,000. Capital Masqat (Muscat).

PAKISTAN (F-23) Federal Republic. Area 307,374 sq. mi. Pop. 72,370,000. Capital Islamabad.

PANAMA (H-13) Military Dictatorship. Area 29,209 sq. mi. Pop. 1,720,0000. Capital Panama.

PAPUA NEW GUINEA (I-4) Republic. Area 178,260 sq. mi. Pop. 2,830,000. Capital Port Moresby.

PARAGUAY (K-15) Republic. Area 157,048 sq. mi. Pop. 2,720,000. Capital Asuncion.

PERU (I-13) Military Dictatorship. Area 496,224 sq. mi. Pop. 16,090,000. Capital Lima.

PHILIPPINES (G-3) Republic. Area 115,800 sq. mi. Pop. 43,750,000. Capital Manila.

POLAND (C-20) People's Republic. Area 120,725 sq. mi. Pop. 34,360,000. Capital Warszawa (Warsaw).

PORTUGAL (E-18) Republic. Area 35,383 sq. mi. Pop. 9,450,000. Capital Lisboa (Lisbon).

PUERTO RICO (G-14) U.S. Commonwealth. Area 3,421 sq. mi. Pop. 3,045,000. Capital San Juan.

QATAR (F-22) Independent Emirate. Area 4,400 sq. mi. Pop. 100,000. Capital Doha.

RHODESIA (J-20) Republic. Area 150,875 sq. mi. Pop. 6,530,000. Capital Salisbury.

ROMANIA (D-20) People's Republic. Area 91,700 sq. mi. Pop. 21,450,000. Capital Bucuresti (Bucharest).

RWANDA (I-20) Republic. Area 10,169 sq. mi. Pop. 4,290,000. Capital Kigali.

SAN MARINO (D-19) Republic. Area 24 sq. mi. Pop. 20,000. Capital San Marino.

SÃO TOMÉ AND PRÍNCIPE (H-19) Democratic Republic. Area 372 sq. mi. Pop. 80,000. Capital São Tomé.

SAUDI ARABIA (F-21) Monarchy. Area 865,000 sq. mi. Pop. 9,240,000. Capital Riyadh.

SENEGAL (G-18) Republic. Area 78,685 sq. mi. Pop. 5,110,000. Capital Dakar.

SEYCHELLES* (I-22) Military Dictatorship. Area 107 sq. mi. Pop. 60,000. Capital Victoria, Mahé.

SIERRA LEONE* (H-18) Republic. Area 27,925 sq. mi. Pop. 3,110,000. Capital Freetown.

SINGAPORE* (H-2) Republic. Area 227 sq. mi. Pop. 2,280,000. Capital Singapore.

SOMALIA (H-22) Military Dictatorship. Area 246,300 sq. mi. Pop. 3,260,000. Capital Mogadishu.

SOUTH AFRICA (K-20) Republic. Area 471,445 sq. mi. Pop 26,130,000. Capitals Pretoria and Cape Town.

SPAIN (D-18) Monarchy. Area 194,885 sq. mi. Pop. 35,970,000. Capital Madrid.

SRI LANKA (CEYLON)* (H-24) Republic. Area 25,332 sq. mi. Pop. 14,270,000. Capital Colombo.

SUDAN (G-20) Military Dictatorship. Area 967,500 sq. mi. Pop. 16,130,000. Capital Khartoum.

SURINAM (H-15) Independent Republic. Area 70,060 sq. mi. Pop. 440,000. Capital Paramaribo.

SWAZILAND* (K-21) Parliamentary Monarchy. Area 6,704 sq. mi. Pop. 500,000. Capital Mbabane.

SWEDEN (B-20) Constitutional Monarchy. Area 173,732 sq. mi. Pop. 8,220,000. Capital Stockholm.

SWITZERLAND (D-19) Federal Republic. Area 15,943 sq. mi. Pop. 6,350,000. Capital Bern.

SYRIA (E-21) Republic. Area 71,498 sq. mi. Pop. 7,600,000. Capital Dimashq (Damascus).

TAIWAN (FORMOSA) (F-3) Republic. Area 13,893 sq. mi. Pop. 16,050,000. Capital Taipei.

TANZANIA* (I-21) Republic. Area 364,943 sq. mi. Pop. 15,610,000. Capital Dar es Salaam.

THAILAND (SIAM) (G-1) Constitutional Monarchy. Area 198,500 sq. mi. Pop. 42,960,000. Capital Krung Thep (Bangkok).

TOGO (H-19) Republic. Area 21,925 sq. mi. Pop. 2,280,000. Capital Lomé.

TONGA* (K-7) Independent Monarchy. Area 225 sq. mi. Pop. 90,000. Capital Nuku'alolfa.

TRINIDAD-TOBAGO* (H-14) Parliamentary Monarchy. Area 1,980 sq. mi. Pop. 1,080,000. Capital Port of Spain.

TUNISIA (E-19) Republic. Area 63,379 sq. mi. Pop. 5,740,000. Capital Tunis.

TURKEY (E-21) Republic. Area 300,948 sq. mi. Pop. 40,160,000. Capital Ankara.

UGANDA* (H-21) Military Dictatorship. Area 93,104 sq. mi. Pop. 11,940,000. Capital Kampala.

UNION OF SOVIET SOCIALIST REPUBLICS (C-22) Federal Socialist Republic. Area 8,600,340 sq. mi. Pop. 257,900,000. Capital Moskva (Moscow).

UNITED ARAB EMIRATES (F-22) Federation. Area 32,300 sq. mi. Pop. 230,000. Capital Abu Dhabi.

UNITED KINGDOM (GREAT BRITAIN and NORTHERN IRELAND)* (C-18) Constitutional Monarchy. Area 94,217 sq. mi. Pop. 55,930,000. Capital London.

UNITED STATES (E-12) Federal Republic. Area 3,615,122 sq. mi. Pop. 220,100,000. Capital Washington, D.C.

UPPER VOLTA (G-18) Military. Area 105,869 sq. mi. Pop. 6,170,000. Capital Ouagadougou.

URUGUAY (L-15) Military Dictatorship. Area 68,536 sq. mi. Pop. 3,100,000. Capital Montevideo.

VATICAN CITY (D-19) Independent Sovereignty. Area 108.7 acres. Pop. 1,000.

VENEZUELA (H-14) Republic. Area 352,144 sq. mi. Pop. 12,360,000. Capital Caracas.

VIETNAM (G-2) People's Republic. Area 130,653 sq. mi. Pop. 46,500,000. Capital Hanoi.

WESTERN SAMOA* (J-7) Republic. Area 1,133 sq. mi. Pop. 160,000. Capital Apia.

YEMEN (G-21) Military Dictatorship. Area 77,200 sq. mi. Pop. 6,870,000. Capital San'a.

YEMEN, PEOPLE'S DEMOCRATIC REPUBLIC OF (G-22) Socialist Republic. Area 111,074 sq. mi. Pop. 1,633,000. Capital Aden.

YUGOSLAVIA (D-20) Federal Socialist Republic. Area 98,766 sq. mi. Pop. 21,560,000. Capital Beograd (Belgrade).

ZAIRE (I-20) Republic. Area 905,365 sq. mi. Pop. 25,630,000. Capital Kinshasa.

ZAMBIA* (J-20) Republic. Area 290,586 sq. mi. Pop. 5,140,000. Capital Lusaka.

**Member British Commonwealth of Nations.*

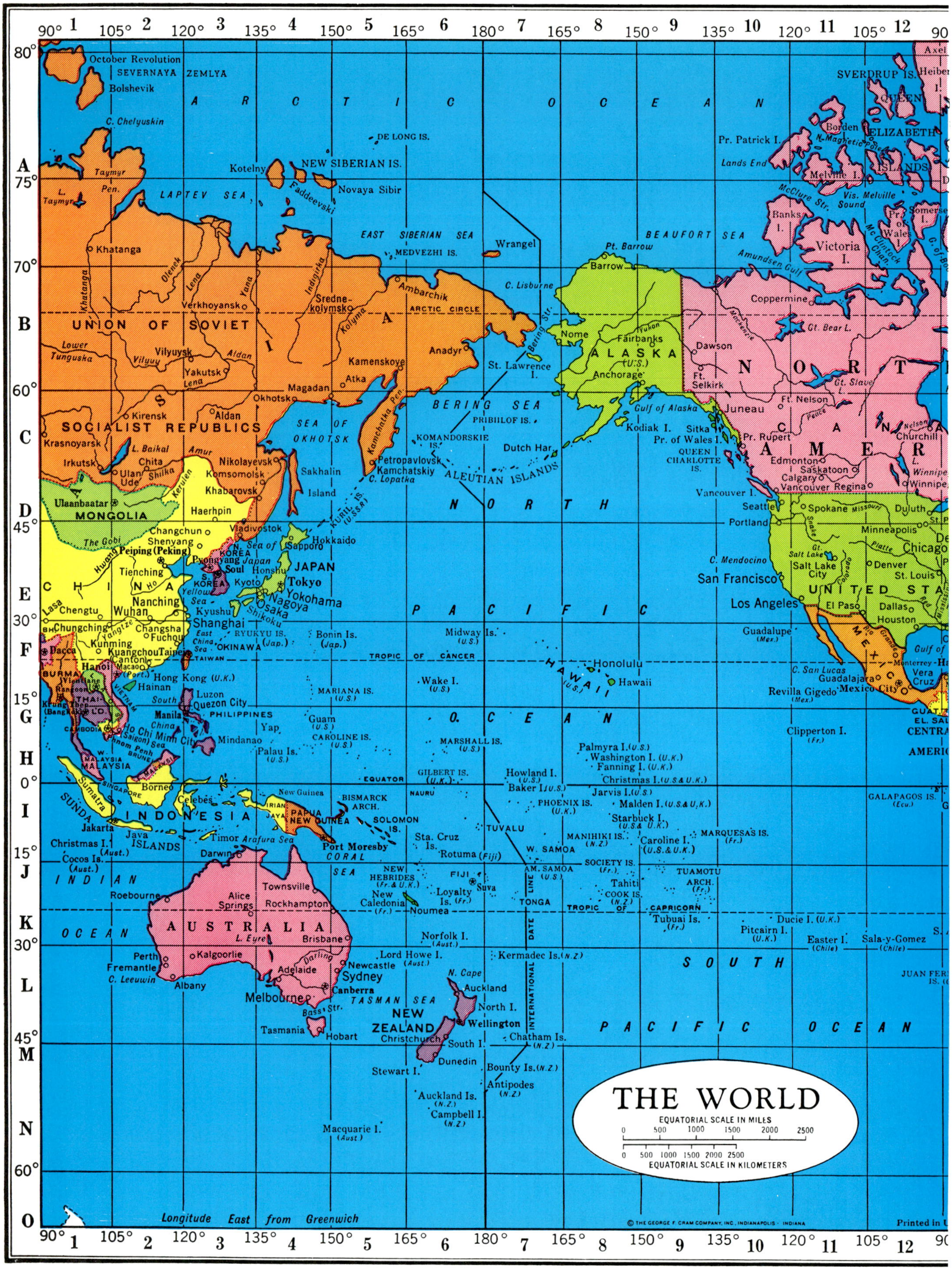
THE WORLD
EQUATORIAL SCALE IN MILES
0 500 1000 1500 2000 2500
0 500 1000 1500 2000 2500
EQUATORIAL SCALE IN KILOMETERS
© THE GEORGE F. CRAM COMPANY, INC. INDIANAPOLIS · INDIANA
Printed in U
Longitude East from Greenwich
90° 1 105° 2 120° 3 135° 4 150° 5 165° 6 180° 7 165° 8 150° 9 135° 10 120° 11 105° 12 90
80° A 75° 70° B 60° C D 45° E 30° F 15° G H 0° I 15° J K 30° L 45° M N 60° O
A R C T I C O C E A N
October Revolution
SEVERNAYA ZEMLYA
Bolshevik
C. Chelyuskin
Taymyr Pen.
L. Taymyr
LAPTEV SEA
Kotelny
NEW SIBERIAN IS.
Faddeevski
Novaya Sibir
DE LONG IS.
EAST SIBERIAN SEA
MEDVEZHI IS.
Wrangel
Khatanga
Olenek
Lena
Yana
Indigirka
Kolyma
Verkhoyansk
Sredne-kolymsk
Ambarchik
ARCTIC CIRCLE
UNION OF SOVIET SOCIALIST REPUBLICS
Lower Tunguska
Vilyuy
Vilyuysk
Aldan
Yakutsk
Kamenskoye
Anadyr
Atka
Magadan
Okhotsk
Kirensk
Aldan
Krasnoyarsk
L. Baikal
Amur
Irkutsk
Chita
Ulan Ude
Shilka
Nikolayevsk
Komsomolsk
Khabarovsk
Kamchatka Pen.
SEA OF OKHOTSK
Sakhalin Island
Petropavlovsk Kamchatskiy
C. Lopatka
KURIL IS. (U.S.S.R.)
BERING SEA
St. Lawrence I.
Bering Str.
C. Lisburne
PRIBILOF IS.
KOMANDORSKIE IS.
Dutch Har.
ALEUTIAN ISLANDS
Ulaanbaatar
MONGOLIA
The Gobi
Kerulen
Haerhpin
Changchun
Shenyang
Vladivostok
Peiping (Peking)
Huang Ho
Tienching
N. KOREA
Pyongyang
S. KOREA
Soul
Sea of Japan
Hokkaido
Sapporo
JAPAN
Honshu
Tokyo
Yokohama
Nagoya
Kyoto
Osaka
Shikoku
Kyushu
C H I N A
Yellow Sea
Lasa
Chengtu
Wuhan
Nanching
Shanghai
Chungching
Changsha
Fuchou
Yangtze
Kunming
Kuangchou
Canton
Taipei
East China Sea
RYUKYU IS. (Jap.)
OKINAWA
Bonin Is. (Jap.)
TAIWAN
Dacca
BURMA
Hanoi
Vientiane
Rangoon
THAILAND
Bangkok
LAOS
CAMBODIA
VIETNAM
Macao (Port.)
Hong Kong (U.K.)
Hainan
South China Sea
Luzon
Quezon City
Manila
PHILIPPINES
Ho Chi Minh City
Mindanao
MALAYSIA
BRUNEI
SINGAPORE
Borneo
Celebes
Sumatra
SUNDA
Jakarta
Java
INDONESIA
ISLANDS
Timor
Arafura Sea
Christmas I. (Aust.)
Cocos Is. (Aust.)
MARIANA IS. (U.S.)
Guam (U.S.)
Yap
CAROLINE IS. (U.S.)
Palau Is. (U.S.)
EQUATOR
New Guinea
IRIAN JAYA
PAPUA NEW GUINEA
BISMARCK ARCH.
SOLOMON IS.
Port Moresby
CORAL SEA
Darwin
Townsville
Rockhampton
Alice Springs
AUSTRALIA
L. Eyre
Brisbane
Roebourne
INDIAN OCEAN
Perth
Fremantle
C. Leeuwin
Kalgoorlie
Albany
Adelaide
Darling
Newcastle
Sydney
Canberra
Melbourne
Bass Str.
Tasmania
Hobart
TASMAN SEA
Lord Howe I. (Aust.)
Norfolk I. (Aust.)
NEW ZEALAND
N. Cape
Auckland
North I.
Wellington
South I.
Christchurch
Dunedin
Stewart I.
Chatham Is. (N.Z.)
Bounty Is. (N.Z.)
Antipodes (N.Z.)
Auckland Is. (N.Z.)
Campbell I. (N.Z.)
Macquarie I. (Aust.)
Kermadec Is. (N.Z.)
NEW HEBRIDES (Fr. & U.K.)
New Caledonia (Fr.)
Noumea
Loyalty Is. (Fr.)
FIJI
Suva
Rotuma (Fiji)
Sta. Cruz Is.
TONGA
TUVALU
NAURU
GILBERT IS. (U.K.)
MARSHALL IS. (U.S.)
Wake I. (U.S.)
Midway Is. (U.S.)
TROPIC OF CANCER
TROPIC OF CAPRICORN
INTERNATIONAL DATE LINE
P A C I F I C
NORTH
O C E A N
HAWAII (U.S.)
Honolulu
Hawaii
Howland I. (U.S.)
Baker I. (U.S.)
PHOENIX IS. (U.K.)
W. SAMOA
AM. SAMOA (U.S.)
MANIHIKI IS. (N.Z.)
Palmyra I. (U.S.)
Washington I. (U.K.)
Fanning I. (U.K.)
Christmas I. (U.S. & U.K.)
Jarvis I. (U.S.)
Malden I. (U.S. & U.K.)
Starbuck I. (U.S. & U.K.)
Caroline I. (U.S. & U.K.)
MARQUESAS IS. (Fr.)
SOCIETY IS. (Fr.)
Tahiti
COOK IS. (N.Z.)
TUAMOTU ARCH. (Fr.)
Tubuai Is. (Fr.)
Pitcairn I. (U.K.)
Ducie I. (U.K.)
Easter I. (Chile)
Sala-y-Gomez (Chile)
JUAN FER IS.
S O U T H
P A C I F I C O C E A N
GALAPAGOS IS. (Ecu.)
Clipperton I. (Fr.)
Revilla Gigedo (Mex.)
Guadalupe (Mex.)
BEAUFORT SEA
Pt. Barrow
Barrow
Nome
Yukon
Fairbanks
ALASKA (U.S.)
Anchorage
Gulf of Alaska
Kodiak I.
Sitka
Juneau
Pr. of Wales I.
QUEEN CHARLOTTE IS.
Pr. Rupert
Vancouver I.
Seattle
Portland
C. Mendocino
San Francisco
Los Angeles
SVERDRUP IS.
QUEEN ELIZABETH ISLANDS
Borden
N. Magnetic Pole
Pr. Patrick I.
Lands End
Melville I.
McClure Str.
Vis. Melville Sound
Banks I.
Pr. of Wales I.
Victoria I.
McClintock Chan.
Amundsen Gulf
Coppermine
Gt. Bear L.
Mackenzie
Dawson
Ft. Selkirk
Gt. Slave L.
Ft. Nelson
Peace
NORTH AMERICA
Churchill
Edmonton
Saskatoon
Calgary
Vancouver
Regina
Winnipeg
Spokane
Missouri
Duluth
Snake
Minneapolis
Platte
Chicago
Gt. Salt Lake
Salt Lake City
Colorado
Denver
St. Louis
UNITED STATES
El Paso
Dallas
Houston
MEXICO
Gulf of Mexico
C. San Lucas
Guadalajara
Mexico City
Monterrey
Vera Cruz
CENTRAL AMERICA
EL SAL
GUAT

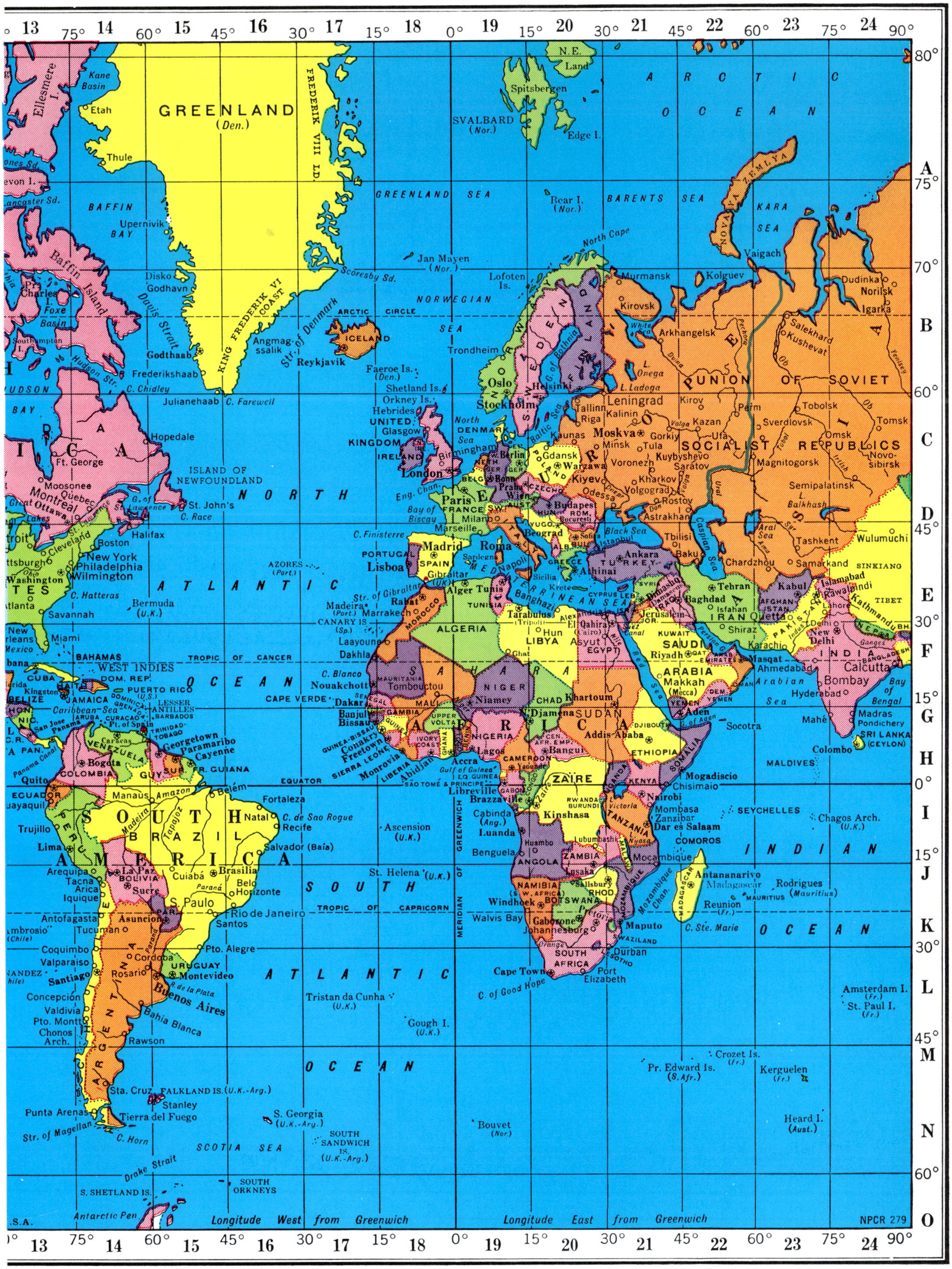
GREENLAND
(Den.)
ARCTIC OCEAN
GREENLAND SEA
BARENTS SEA
KARA SEA
NORWEGIAN SEA
SVALBARD
(Nor.)
Spitsbergen
N.E. Land
Edge I.
Bear I.
(Nor.)
Jan Mayen
(Nor.)
North Cape
BAFFIN BAY
Baffin Island
Davis Strait
Ellesmere I.
Kane Basin
Etah
Thule
Upernivik
Disko
Godhavn
Godthaab
Frederikshaab
C. Chidley
Julianehaab
C. Farewell
Angmagssalik
KING FREDERIK VI COAST
FREDERIK VIII LD.
Str. of Denmark
Scoresby Sd.
ARCTIC CIRCLE
ICELAND
Reykjavik
Faeroe Is.
(Den.)
Shetland Is.
Orkney Is.
Hebrides
UNITED KINGDOM
IRELAND
Glasgow
Birmingham
London
Eng. Chan.
Bay of Biscay
Paris
FRANCE
Marseille
Milano
Roma
Madrid
SPAIN
PORTUGAL
Lisboa
Gibraltar
Str. of Gibraltar
C. Finisterre
Trondheim
Oslo
Stockholm
Helsinki
Lofoten Is.
Murmansk
Kirovsk
Arkhangelsk
L. Onega
L. Ladoga
Leningrad
Kalinin
Tallinn
Riga
Kaunas
Moskva
Minsk
Gorkiy
Tula
Kazan
Kirov
Perm
Ufa
Kuybyshev
Saratov
Voronezh
Kharkov
Kiyev
Odessa
Volgograd
Rostov
Astrakhan
Gdansk
Warzawa
Berlin
Praha
Wien
Budapest
Beograd
Bucuresti
Black Sea
Istanbul
Ankara
TURKEY
Athinai
Krete
Sicilia
Sardegna
Napoli
MEDITERRANEAN SEA
CYPRUS
Tbilisi
Baku
Caspian Sea
Aral Sea
Tashkent
Samarkand
Chardzhou
Tehran
IRAN
Isfahan
Shiraz
Baghdad
Damascus
Jerusalem
Suez Canal
KUWAIT
SAUDI ARABIA
Riyadh
Makkah
(Mecca)
Red Sea
Persian Gulf
YEMEN
Aden
G. of Aden
Socotra
Arabian Sea
Masqat
Karachi
Quetta
Kabul
AFGHANISTAN
PAKISTAN
Islamabad
Rawalpindi
Lahore
New Delhi
INDIA
Ahmedabad
Bombay
Hyderabad
Calcutta
Bay of Bengal
Madras
Pondichery
SRI LANKA
(CEYLON)
Colombo
MALDIVES
Mahé
Kathmandu
TIBET
SINKIANG
Wulumuchi
Semipalatinsk
L. Balkhash
Magnitogorsk
Sverdlovsk
Tobolsk
Omsk
Novosibirsk
Tomsk
Salekhard
Kushevat
Vaigach
Kolguev
NOVAYA ZEMLYA
Dudinka
Norilsk
Igarka
UNION OF SOVIET SOCIALIST REPUBLICS
ALGERIA
Alger
Tunis
TUNISIA
Rabat
MOROCCO
Marrakech
Madeira
(Port.)
CANARY IS.
(Sp.)
Laayoune
Dakhla
Tarabulus
(Tripoli)
LIBYA
Hun
Ghat
El Qahira
(Cairo)
Asyut
EGYPT
SAHARA
NIGER
Niamey
CHAD
Ndjamena
SUDAN
Khartoum
ETHIOPIA
Addis Ababa
DJIBOUTI
SOMALIA
Mogadiscio
KENYA
Nairobi
Mombasa
Zanzibar
Dar es Salaam
TANZANIA
RWANDA
BURUNDI
ZAIRE
Kinshasa
Brazzaville
Lubumbashi
Cabinda
(Ang.)
Luanda
Benguela
ANGOLA
Huambo
ZAMBIA
Lusaka
Salisbury
RHOD.
MALAWI
MOZAMBIQUE
Moçambique
Mozambique Chan.
COMOROS
MADAGASCAR
Antananarivo
Reunion
(Fr.)
MAURITIUS
Rodrigues
(Mauritius)
SEYCHELLES
Chagos Arch.
(U.K.)
NAMIBIA
(S.W. AFRICA)
Windhoek
Walvis Bay
BOTSWANA
Gaborone
Johannesburg
Pretoria
Maputo
SWAZILAND
LESOTHO
Durban
SOUTH AFRICA
Cape Town
C. of Good Hope
Port Elizabeth
MAURITANIA
Nouakchott
Tombouctou
MALI
Dakar
Banjul
Bissau
GAMBIA
GUINEA
GUINEA-BISSAU
Conakry
Freetown
SIERRA LEONE
Monrovia
LIBERIA
IVORY COAST
Abidjan
UPPER VOLTA
GHANA
Accra
NIGERIA
Lagos
CAMEROON
Yaounde
CEN. AFR. EMP.
Bangui
Gulf of Guinea
EQ. GUINEA
SÃO TOMÉ & PRINCIPE
Libreville
GABON
CAPE VERDE
C. Blanco
AZORES
(Port.)
NORTH ATLANTIC OCEAN
SOUTH ATLANTIC OCEAN
TROPIC OF CANCER
EQUATOR
TROPIC OF CAPRICORN
MERIDIAN OF GREENWICH
Ascension
(U.K.)
St. Helena
(U.K.)
Tristan da Cunha
(U.K.)
Gough I.
(U.K.)
Bouvet
(Nor.)
S. Georgia
(U.K.-Arg.)
SOUTH SANDWICH IS.
(U.K.-Arg.)
SOUTH ORKNEYS
S. SHETLAND IS.
SCOTIA SEA
Drake Strait
Antarctic Pen
FALKLAND IS. (U.K.-Arg.)
Stanley
Tierra del Fuego
Str. of Magellan
C. Horn
Punta Arenas
Sta. Cruz
INDIAN OCEAN
Pr. Edward Is.
(S. Afr.)
Crozet Is.
(Fr.)
Kerguelen
(Fr.)
Heard I.
(Aust.)
Amsterdam I.
(Fr.)
St. Paul I.
(Fr.)
C. Ste. Marie
HUDSON BAY
Hudson Str.
Foxe Basin
Southampton I.
Ft. George
Hopedale
Moosonee
Québec
Montreal
Ottawa
G. of St. Lawrence
St. John's
C. Race
ISLAND OF NEWFOUNDLAND
Halifax
Boston
New York
Philadelphia
Wilmington
Washington
Cleveland
C. Hatteras
Bermuda
(U.K.)
Savannah
Miami
New Orleans
BAHAMAS
WEST INDIES
CUBA
HAITI
JAMAICA
Kingston
DOM. REP.
PUERTO RICO
(U.S.)
LESSER ANTILLES
BARBADOS
TRINIDAD-TOBAGO
Pt. of Spain
Caribbean Sea
Panama Canal
VENEZUELA
Caracas
Georgetown
Paramaribo
Cayenne
FR. GUIANA
GUYANA
SURINAM
Bogota
COLOMBIA
Quito
ECUADOR
Guayaquil
PERU
Trujillo
Lima
Arequipa
Tacna
Arica
Iquique
Antofagasta
BOLIVIA
La Paz
Sucre
PARAGUAY
Asunción
Tucuman
Coquimbo
Valparaiso
Santiago
Concepción
Valdivia
Pto. Montt
Chonos Arch.
CHILE
ARGENTINA
Cordoba
Rosario
Buenos Aires
R. de la Plata
URUGUAY
Montevideo
Bahia Blanca
Rawson
SOUTH AMERICA
BRAZIL
Manaus
Amazon
Belém
Fortaleza
Natal
C. de Sao Rogue
Recife
Salvador (Baía)
Cuiabá
Brasilia
Belo Horizonte
S. Paulo
Rio de Janeiro
Santos
Pto. Alegre
Longitude West from Greenwich
Longitude East from Greenwich
NPCR 279

ARCTIC OCEAN
GREENLAND
(DENMARK)
CANADA
ALASKA
YUKON TERRITORY
NORTH WEST TERRITORIES
MACKENZIE
KEEWATIN
FRANKLIN
BRITISH COLUMBIA
ALBERTA
SASKATCHEWAN
MANITOBA
ONTARIO
QUEBEC
NEWFOUNDLAND
LABRADOR PENINSULA
HUDSON BAY
BAFFIN ISLAND
VICTORIA ISLAND
BANKS I.
DEVON I.
PARRY ISLANDS
QUEEN ELIZABETH ISLANDS
SOUTHAMPTON ISLAND
BAFFIN BAY
DAVIS STRAIT
DENMARK STRAIT
BEAUFORT SEA
BERING STRAIT
LONG STRAIT
ASIA
SIBERIA
GULF OF ALASKA
PACIFIC
WASHINGTON
OREGON
IDAHO
MONTANA
WYOMING
NORTH DAKOTA
SOUTH DAKOTA
MINNESOTA
WISCONSIN
MICHIGAN
IOWA
NEW YORK
PENNSYLVANIA
MAINE
NEW BRUNSWICK
NOVA SCOTIA
MOUNT
Lake Superior
Lake Michigan
Lake Huron
L. Ontario
L. Erie
Hudson Strait
Arctic Circle
Edmonton
Calgary
Winnipeg
Regina
Montreal
Quebec
Toronto
OTTAWA
Vancouver
Seattle
Portland
Minneapolis
St. Paul
Chicago
Milwaukee
Detroit
Cleveland
Buffalo
Boston
New York
Halifax
Thule
Yellowknife
Churchill
Thunder Bay

NORTH AMERICA
MILES
0 100 200 300 400 500 600
0 100 200 300 400 500 600
KILOMETERS
Copyright by
The George F. Cram Company, Inc.
Atlas Headquarters Since 1867
Indianapolis · Indiana
UNITED STATES
MEXICO
CENTRAL AMERICA
WEST INDIES
SOUTH AMERICA
ATLANTIC OCEAN
PACIFIC OCEAN
GULF OF MEXICO
CARIBBEAN SEA
Bay of Campeche
TROPIC OF CANCER
GREATER ANTILLES
BAHAMA ISLANDS
BAHAMAS
CUBA
HABANA
JAMAICA
KINGSTON
HAITI
DOMINICAN REPUBLIC
SANTO DOMINGO
PUERTO RICO
SAN JUAN
GUATEMALA
BELIZE
BELMOPAN
HONDURAS
SALVADOR
SAN SALVADOR
NICARAGUA
MANAGUA
COSTA RICA
PANAMA
COLOMBIA
BOGOTA
VENEZUELA
ECUADOR
QUITO
PERU
CALIFORNIA
NEVADA
UTAH
COLORADO
ARIZONA
NEW MEXICO
TEXAS
OKLAHOMA
KANSAS
MISSOURI
ARKANSAS
LOUISIANA
MISSISSIPPI
ALABAMA
GEORGIA
FLORIDA
TENNESSEE
KENTUCKY
NORTH CAROLINA
SOUTH CAROLINA
VIRGINIA
WEST VIRGINIA
OHIO
ILLINOIS
INDIANA
BAJA CALIFORNIA
SONORA
CHIHUAHUA
COAHUILA
NUEVO LEON
TAMAULIPAS
DURANGO
SINALOA
ZACATECAS
JALISCO
MICHOACAN
GUERRERO
OAXACA
CHIAPAS
YUCATAN
CAMPECHE
QUINTANA ROO
MEXICO CITY
San Francisco
Los Angeles
San Diego
Denver
Dallas
Houston
San Antonio
El Paso
New Orleans
Jacksonville
Tampa
Miami
Atlanta
St. Louis
Kansas City
Memphis
Nashville
Pittsburgh
Cincinnati
Columbus
Guadalajara
Monterrey
Veracruz
Merida
Acapulco
Galveston
Key West
C. Canaveral
BERMUDA (U. K.)
CLIPPERTON I. (FR.)
REVILLAGIGEDO IS. (Mexico)
LAS TRES MARIAS IS.
Longitude West from Greenwich
120 110 100 90 80 70
NPCR 279
PRINTED IN U.S.A.
WESTERN EXTENSION OF ALASKA SHOWING THE
ALEUTIAN ISLANDS
BERING SEA
ALEUTIAN ISLANDS
PACIFIC OCEAN
EASTERN EXTENSION OF THE
WEST INDIES
LESSER ANTILLES
CARIBBEAN SEA
—EXPLANATION—
National Capitals are shown in capital letters WASHINGTON
Capitals of States and Provinces are shown underlined Madison
Population of Cities and Towns is indicated by symbols thus:
1,000,000 or over
250,000 to 1,000,000
100,000 to 250,000
50,000 to 100,000
25,000 to 50,000
Less than 25,000

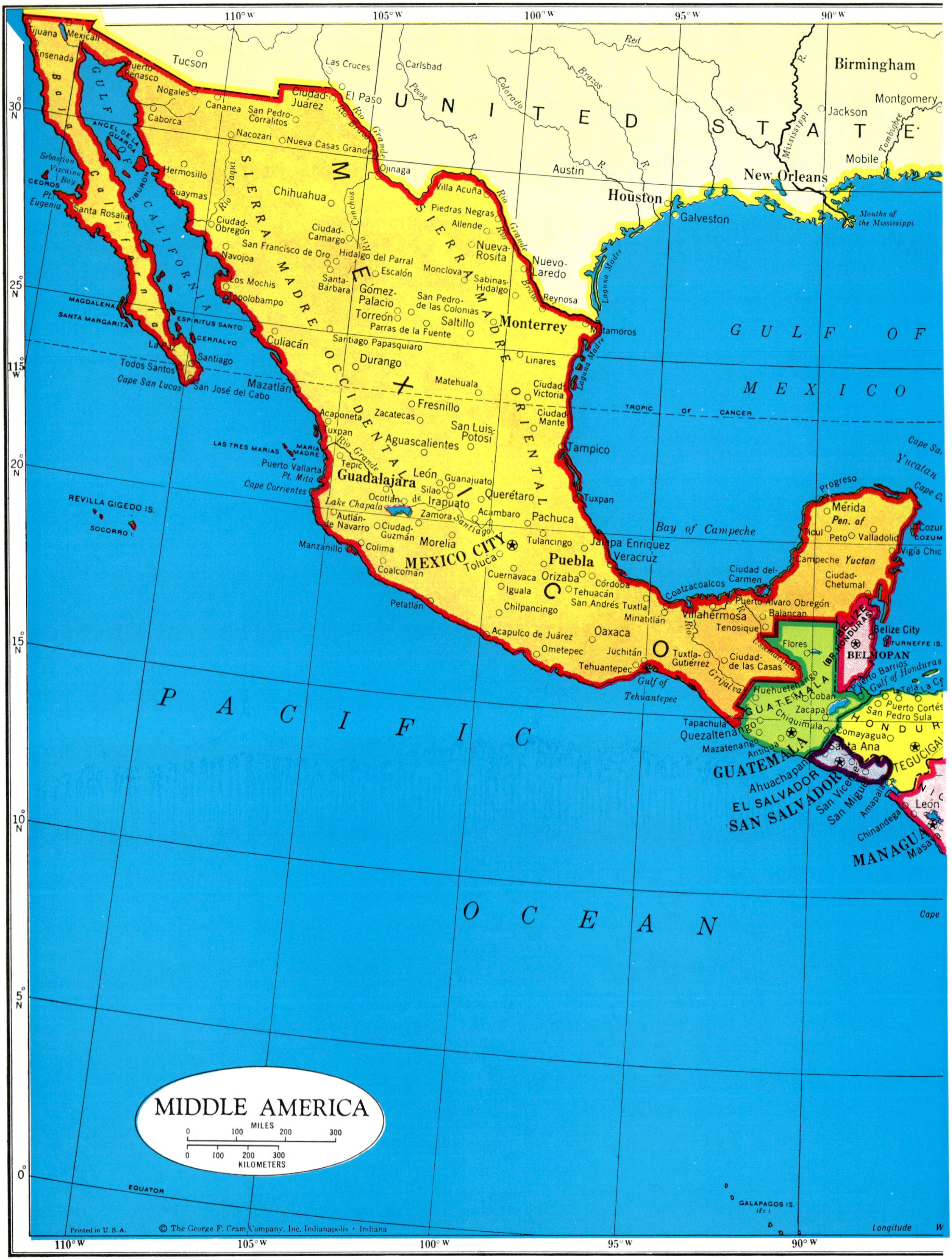
MIDDLE AMERICA
MILES
0 100 200 300
0 100 200 300
KILOMETERS
110° W
105° W
100° W
95° W
90° W
30° N
25° N
20° N
15° N
10° N
5° N
0°
115° W
UNITED STATES
MEXICO
GULF OF MEXICO
PACIFIC OCEAN
GULF OF CALIFORNIA
Baja California
SIERRA MADRE OCCIDENTAL
SIERRA MADRE ORIENTAL
TROPIC OF CANCER
EQUATOR
Bay of Campeche
Gulf of Tehuantepec
Gulf of Honduras
Pen. of Yucatan
Yucatan
MEXICO CITY
Tijuana
Mexicali
Ensenada
Tucson
Puerto Peñasco
Nogales
Cananea
Caborca
Nacozari
Hermosillo
Guaymas
Santa Rosalia
Ciudad-Obregón
Navojoa
Los Mochis
Topolobampo
La Paz
Todos Santos
Santiago
Cape San Lucas
San José del Cabo
Sebastian Vizcaino Bay
CEDROS
Pt. Eugenia
ANGEL DE LA GUARDA
TIBURON
MAGDALENA
SANTA MARGARITA
ESPIRITUS SANTO
CERRALVO
Ciudad-Juárez
El Paso
San Pedro-Corralitos
Nueva Casas Grandes
Ojinaga
Chihuahua
Ciudad-Camargo
Hidalgo del Parral
San Francisco de Oro
Escalón
Santa-Barbara
Gómez-Palacio
Torreón
San Pedro-de las Colonias
Parras de la Fuente
Saltillo
Monterrey
Monclova
Sabinas-Hidalgo
Nueva-Rosita
Piedras Negras
Allende
Villa Acuña
Nuevo-Laredo
Reynosa
Matamoros
Linares
Culiacán
Santiago Papasquiaro
Durango
Mazatlán
Acaponeta
Tuxpan
Tepic
Matehuala
Fresnillo
Zacatecas
Aguascalientes
San Luis-Potosí
Ciudad-Victoria
Ciudad-Mante
Tampico
Tuxpan
Guadalajara
León
Guanajuato
Silao
Irapuato
Querétaro
Ocotlán
Lake Chapala
Zamora
Acambaro
Pachuca
Autlán-de Navarro
Ciudad-Guzmán
Morelia
Colima
Manzanillo
Coalcomán
Toluca
Tulancingo
Jalapa Enriquez
Veracruz
Puebla
Orizaba
Córdoba
Tehuacán
Cuernavaca
Iguala
Chilpancingo
Petatlán
Acapulco de Juárez
Oaxaca
Ometepec
Juchitán
Tehuantepec
San Andrés Tuxtla
Minatitlán
Coatzacoalcos
Villahermosa
Tenosique
Tuxtla-Gutiérrez
Ciudad-de las Casas
Tapachula
Ciudad del-Carmen
Campeche
Mérida
Progreso
Ticul
Peto
Valladolid
COZUMEL
Vigía Chico
Ciudad-Chetumal
Puerto Alvaro Obregón
Balancan
Puerto Vallarta
Pt. Mita
Cape Corrientes
LAS TRES MARIAS
MARIA MADRE
REVILLA GIGEDO IS.
SOCORRO I.
Rio Grande
Rio Bravo
Rio Yaqui
Conchos
Pecos R.
Colorado R.
Brazos R.
Red R.
Mississippi R.
Tombigbee R.
Laguna Madre
Rio Santiago
Grijalva
Usumacinta
Carlsbad
Las Cruces
Austin
Houston
Galveston
New Orleans
Mouths of the Mississippi
Birmingham
Montgomery
Jackson
Mobile
GUATEMALA
Flores
Huehuetenango
Cobán
Zacapa
Chiquimula
Quezaltenango
Mazatenango
Antigua
BELIZE
(BR. HONDURAS)
Belize City
BELMOPAN
TURNEFFE IS.
Puerto Barrios
Puerto Cortés
San Pedro Sula
Tela
Comayagua
HONDURAS
TEGUCIGALPA
EL SALVADOR
SAN SALVADOR
Ahuachapán
Santa Ana
San Vicente
San Miguel
Amapala
Chinandega
León
MANAGUA
Masaya
GALAPAGOS IS. (Ec.)
Cape
Longitude W
Printed in U. S. A.
© The George F. Cram Company, Inc. Indianapolis • Indiana

85° W
80° W
75° W
70° W
65° W
60° W
30° N
25° N
20° N
15° N
10° N
5° N
0°
ATLANTIC
OCEAN
Columbia
Atlanta
Charleston
Tallahassee
Jacksonville
Cape Canaveral
Lake Okeechobee
West Palm Beach
Miami
Key West
FLORIDA KEYS
DRY TORTUGAS
Straits of Florida
BERMUDA IS. (U.K.)
BAHAMA ISLANDS
BAHAMAS
LITTLE BAHAMA BANK
GRAND BAHAMA
GREAT ABACO
N.W. Providence Channel
N.E. Providence Channel
NASSAU
NEW PROVIDENCE
ANDROS ISLAND
ELEUTHERA I.
CAT I.
SAN SALVADOR
RUM CAY
GREAT EXUMA
Exuma Sound
LONG I.
CROOKED ISLAND
Crooked Island Passage
ACKLINS I.
MAYAGUANA
LITTLE INAGUA
GREAT INAGUA
CAICOS IS. (U.K.)
TURKS IS. (U.K.)
TROPIC OF CANCER
WEST INDIES
HABANA
Marianao
Matanzas
Cárdenas
Pinar del Rio
CUBA
Jovellanos
Sagua la Grande
Santa Clara
Cienfuegos
Trinidad
Sancti Spiritus
Moron
Ciego de Avila
Camaguey
Gibara
Holguin
Guantanamo
Baracoa
Manzanillo
Santiago de Cuba
I. PINOS
CAYO LARGO
Old Bahama Channel
BAHAMA BANK
Windward Passage
GREATER ANTILLES
CAYMAN ISLANDS (U.K.)
GRAND CAYMAN
JAMAICA
Montego Bay
Falmouth
St. Ann's Bay
Port Maria
Port Antonio
Savanna-la-Mar
KINGSTON
Spanish Town
HAITI
Port de Paix
Cap Haitien
Gonaives
G. of Gonaives
GONAVE
Jérémie
Les Cayes
PORT-AU-PRINCE
DOMINICAN REPUBLIC
Monte Cristi
Puerto Plata
San Francisco de Macoris
Samaná
Bani
SANTO DOMINGO
San Pedro de Macoris
Barahona
I. BEATA
HISPANIOLA
SAONA
Mona Passage
MONA (P.R.)
PUERTO RICO (U.S.)
SAN JUAN
Arecibo
Mayagüez
Ponce
Caguas
Guayama
CULEBRA
VIEQUES
CHARLOTTE AMALIE
ANEGADA
VIRGIN IS. (U.S.&U.K.)
ST. THOMAS (U.S.)
ST. CROIX (U.S.)
ANGUILLA (U.K.)
ST. MARTIN (Fr.&Neth.)
ST. BARTHELEMY (Fr.)
BARBUDA (U.K.)
St. John's
ANTIGUA (U.K.)
ST. KITTS
NEVIS
MONTSERRAT
GUADELOUPE (Fr.)
POINTE-A-PITRE
MARIE GALANTE (Fr.)
DOMINICA
ROSEAU
LEEWARD IS.
LESSER ANTILLES
MARTINIQUE (Fr.)
FORT de FRANCE
Castries
ST. LUCIA (U.K.)
WINDWARD IS.
BARBADOS
BRIDGETOWN
ST. VINCENT (U.K.)
THE GRENADINES
ST. GEORGE'S
GRENADA
TOBAGO
TRINIDAD & TOBAGO
PORT OF SPAIN
San Fernando
CARIBBEAN SEA
SWAN IS. (Hond.)
BAY IS.
SERRANILLA BANK (Col.)
SERRANA BANK (Col.)
QUITA SUENO BANK (Col.)
RONCADOR (Col.)
I. PROVIDENCIA (Col.)
I. SAN ANDRÉS (Col.)
LITTLE CORN I.
GREAT CORN I. (Nic.)
Trujillo
Caratasca Lagoon
Rio Patuca
Rio Coco
Cape Gracias a Dios
Puerto Cabezas
Matagalpa
NICARAGUA
Granada
Bluefields
Lake Nicaragua
San Juan de Norte
COSTA RICA
Puntarenas
SAN JOSÉ
Cartago
Limon
Coronado Bay
Pt. Burica
Bocas del Toro
Colón
Pt. San Blas
Gulf of Mosquitos
CANAL ZONE (U.S.)
PANAMA
David
Penonome
Chitré
Las Tablas
I. COIBA
Pt. Mariato
PERLAS IS.
Gulf of Panama
La Palma
Gulf of Darien
ARUBA (Neth.)
CURACAO (Neth.)
BONAIRE (Neth.)
WILLEMSTAD
LOS ROQUES
ORCHILLA
MARGARITA
TORTUGA
Pt. Gallinas
Guajira Pen.
Gulf of Venezuela
Santa Marta
Barranquilla
Cartagena
Maracaibo
Lake Maracaibo
Mompos
Magangue
Monteria
Coro
Tucacas
Puerto Cabello
La Guaira
CARACAS
San Felipe
Maracay
Valencia
Barquisimeto
La Ceiba
Trujillo
Valera
Guanare
Encontrodos
Mérida
San Cristóbal
San Fernando
Rio Apure
Rio Arauca
Carúpano
Cumaná
Barcelona
Maturín
Tucupita
Orinoco
Ciudad Bolivar
El Callao
Tumeremo
Rio Caura
Rio Caroni
Santa Elena
Puerto Paez
VENEZUELA
GUYANA
Cucuta
Bucaramanga
Rio Magdalena
Rio Cauca
CORDILLERA OCCIDENTAL
CORDILLERA CENTRAL
CORDILLERA ORIENTAL
Medellin
COLOMBIA
Manizales
Tunja
BOGOTA
Armenia
Ibague
Villavicencio
Rio Meta
Neiva
Buenaventura
Cali
Popayán
Rio Guaviare
Tumaco
Pasto
Mitú
San Carlos
Boa Vista
Rio Branco
BRAZIL
EQUATOR
Santa Isabel
Rio Negro
ECUADOR
West from Greenwich
LR 279

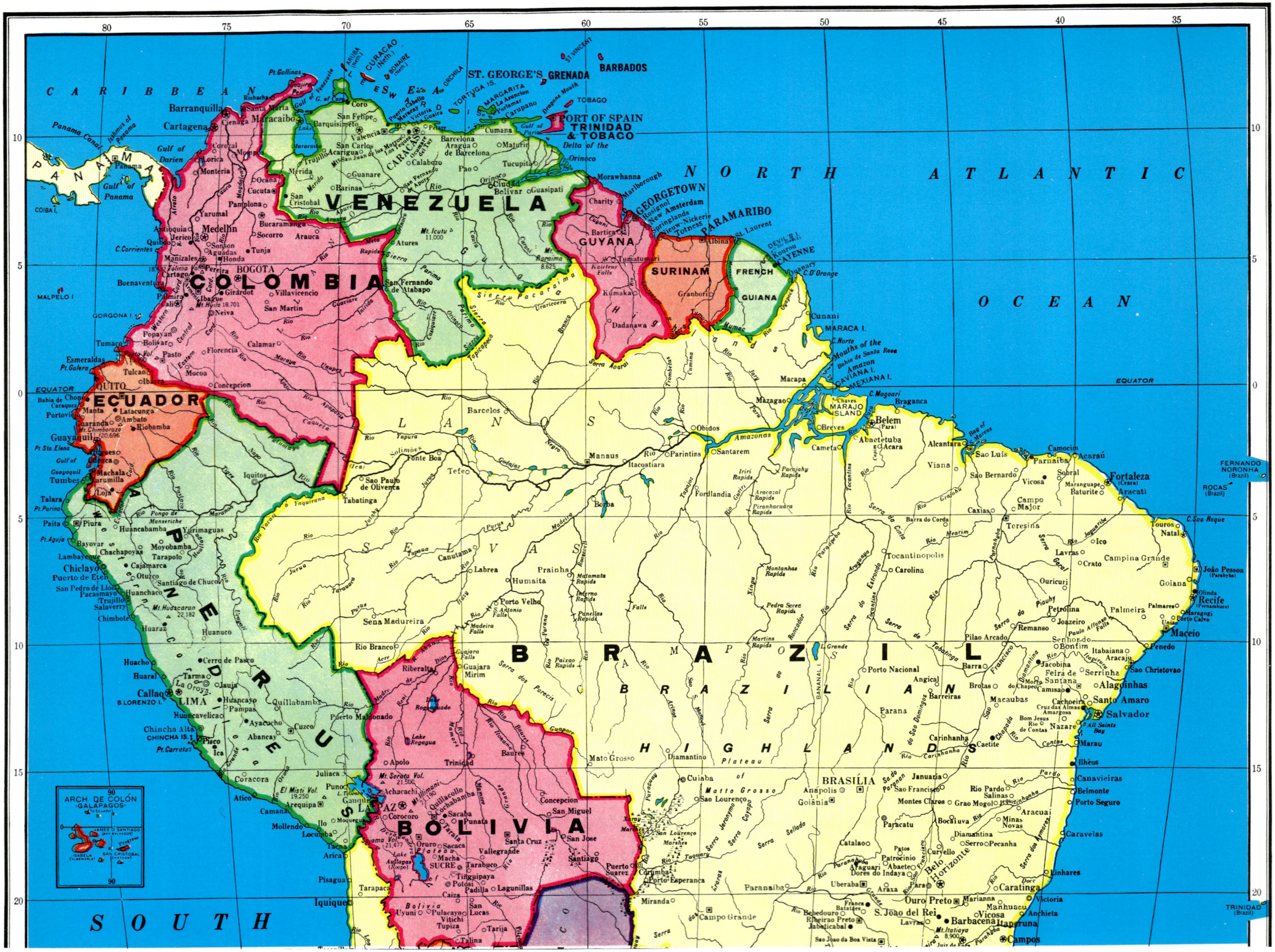

CARIBBEAN
NORTH ATLANTIC OCEAN
SOUTH
EQUATOR
VENEZUELA
COLOMBIA
ECUADOR
PERU
BOLIVIA
BRAZIL
GUYANA
SURINAM
FRENCH GUIANA
PANAMA
TRINIDAD & TOBACO
PORT OF SPAIN
BARBADOS
ST. GEORGE'S GRENADA
GEORGETOWN
PARAMARIBO
CAYENNE
CARACAS
BOGOTA
QUITO
LIMA
LA PAZ
SUCRE
BRASILIA
BRAZILIAN HIGHLANDS
ARCH. DE COLÓN (GALAPAGOS)

SOUTH AMERICA
PACIFIC OCEAN
SOUTH ATLANTIC OCEAN
ARGENTINA
PARAGUAY
URUGUAY
CHILE
BUENOS AIRES
MONTEVIDEO
SANTIAGO
ASUNCION
Rio de Janeiro
Sao Paulo
Cordoba
Rosario
Mendoza
Bahia Blanca
FALKLAND ISLANDS (Arg.-U.K.)
SOUTH GEORGIA (Arg.-U.K.)
Cape Horn
TROPIC OF CAPRICORN
Longitude West from Greenwich
MILES
KILOMETERS
Copyright by
The George F. Cram Company, Inc.
Atlas Headquarters Since 1867
Indianapolis · Indiana
—EXPLANATION—
Capitals are shown thus: CAPITAL
Populations of Cities, Towns, Etc., are indicated by symbols thus:
250,000 or over
100,000 to 250,000
50,000 to 100,000
25,000 to 50,000
15,000 to 25,000
Less than 15,000
NPCR 279
Printed in U.S.A.

EUROPE
MILES
0 100 200 300 400 500
0 100 200 300 400 500
KILOMETERS
Copyright by
The George F. Cram Company, Inc.
Atlas Headquarters Since 1867
Indianapolis · Indiana
A T L A N T I C
O C E A N
ARCTIC OCEAN
NORWEGIAN SEA
ARCTIC CIRCLE
NORTH SEA
BALTIC SEA
Denmark Strait
ICELAND
FAEROERNE
SHETLAND IS.
ORKNEY IS.
BRITISH ISLES
UNITED KINGDOM
SCOTLAND
ENGLAND
WALES
IRELAND
NORWAY
SWEDEN
FINLAND
DENMARK
OSLO
STOCKHOLM
KØBENHAVN
HELSINKI
LONDON
PARIS
FRANCE
SPAIN
PORTUGAL
MADRID
LISBOA
BERLIN
EAST GERMANY
WEST GERMANY
POLAND
WARSZAWA
CZECHOSLOVAKIA
PRAHA
AUSTRIA
WIEN
HUNGARY
BUDAPEST
SWITZERLAND
BERN
ITALY
ROMA
YUGOSLAVIA
BEOGRAD
ALBANIA
GREECE
BULGARIA
SOFIYA
ROMANIA
BUCURESTI
LITHUANIA
LATVIA
ESTONIA
NETHERLANDS
AMSTERDAM
BELGIUM
BRUXELLES
English Channel
Bay of Biscay
Strait of Gibraltar
BALEARIC ISLANDS
CORSE (CORSICA)
SARDEGNA (SARDINIA)
SICILIA (SICILY)
MALTA VALETTA
TYRRHENIAN SEA
ADRIATIC SEA
Ionian Sea
M E D I T E R R A N E A N
A F R I C A
SAHARA ATLAS MTS.
EXPLANATION
Capitals are shown in capital letters thus: PARIS
Population of Cities and Towns is indicated thus:
1,000,000 or over Glasgow
250,000 to 1,000,000 Lyon
100,000 to 250,000 Zürich
50,000 to 100,000 Koblenz
25,000 to 50,000 Cherbourg
Less than 25,000 Gaeta
Longitude West from Greenwich
Longitude East from Greenwich

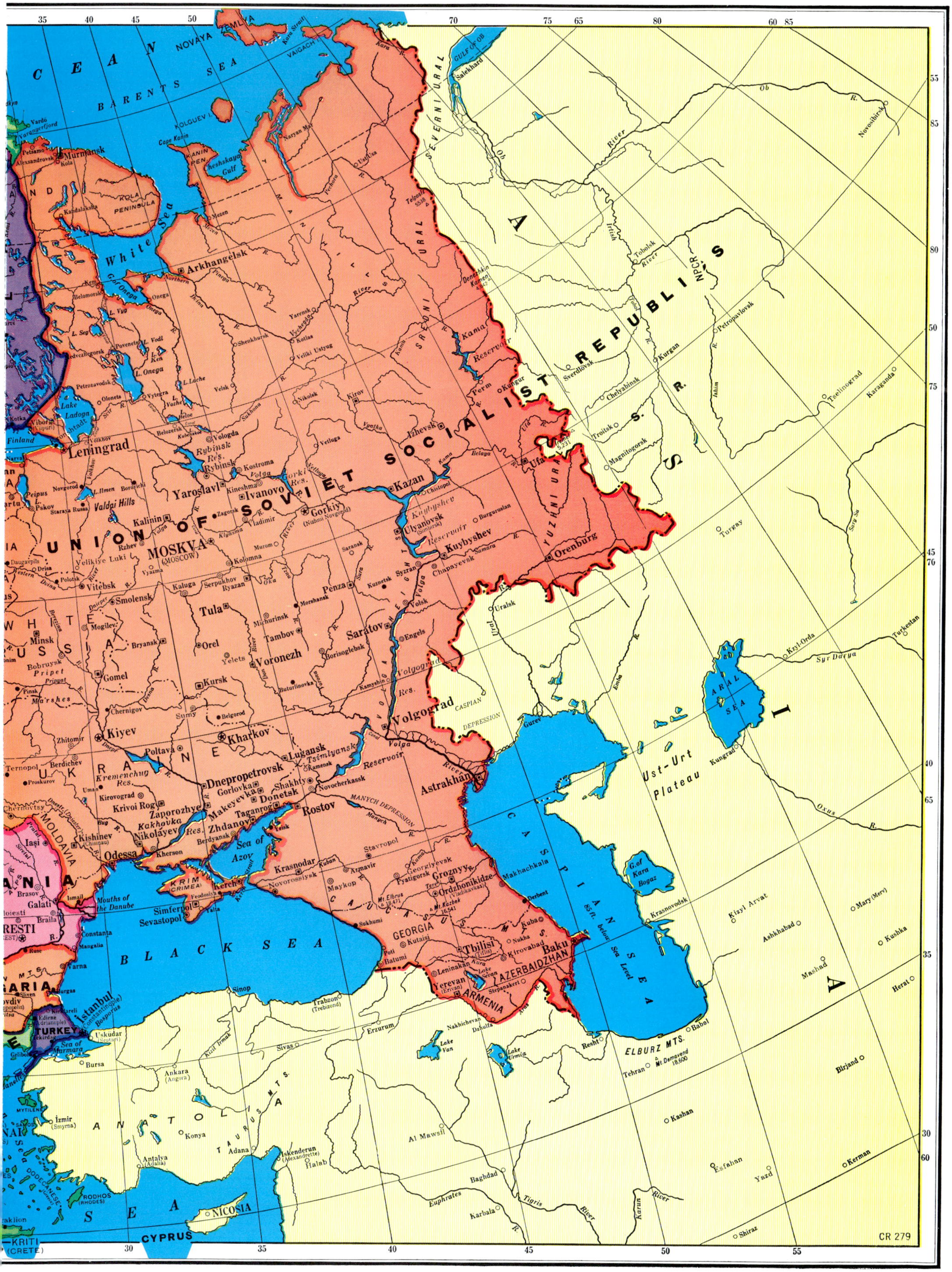

UNION OF SOVIET SOCIALIST REPUBLICS
U. S. S. R.
A S I A
BARENTS SEA
NOVAYA ZEMLYA
KOLGUEV I.
KOLA PENINSULA
White Sea
Murmansk
Arkhangelsk
Leningrad
Lake Ladoga
L. Onega
Finland
Valdai Hills
Kalinin
Yaroslavl
Ivanovo
Gorkiy
MOSKVA (MOSCOW)
Vologda
Rybinsk Res.
Kazan
Kirov
Izhevsk
Perm
Ufa
Kama Reservoir
Kuybyshev
Ulyanovsk
Orenburg
Penza
Saratov
Volgograd
Astrakhan
CASPIAN DEPRESSION
Smolensk
Vitebsk
Minsk
WHITE RUSSIA
Gomel
Tula
Orel
Kursk
Voronezh
Tambov
Kharkov
Kiyev
UKRAINE
Poltava
Dnepropetrovsk
Zaporozhye
Donetsk
Lugansk
Rostov
Zhdanov
Odessa
MOLDAVIA
Kishinev
Nikolayev
Sea of Azov
KRIM (CRIMEA)
Simferopol
Sevastopol
Kerch
Krasnodar
Stavropol
MANYCH DEPRESSION
CAUCASUS MTS.
Mt. Elbrus 18,471
Mt. Kazbek 16,541
Groznyy
Ordzhonikidze
Makhachkala
GEORGIA
Tbilisi
Batumi
ARMENIA
Yerevan
AZERBAIDZHAN
Baku
BLACK SEA
CASPIAN SEA
85 ft. below Sea Level
ARAL SEA
Ust-Urt Plateau
Gurev
Uralsk
Sverdlovsk
Chelyabinsk
Magnitogorsk
Kurgan
Tobolsk
Petropavlovsk
Tselinograd
Karaganda
Novosibirsk
Turgay
Kzyl-Orda
Turkestan
Syr Darya
Oxus R.
Krasnovodsk
Kizyl Arvat
Ashkhabad
Mary (Merv)
Kushka
Mashad
Herat
Tehran
Mt. Demavend 18,600
ELBURZ MTS.
Kashan
Esfahan
Yazd
Kerman
Birjand
Shiraz
Baghdad
Karbala
Al Mawsil
Euphrates
Tigris River
Lake Van
Lake Urmia
TURKEY
Istanbul (Constantinople)
Bosporus
Sea of Marmara
Ankara (Angora)
Bursa
Izmir (Smyrna)
Konya
Adana
ANATOLIA
TAURUS MTS.
Sivas
Trabzon (Trebizond)
Erzurum
Sinop
Iskenderun (Alexandrette)
Halab
CYPRUS
NICOSIA
RODHOS (RHODES)
DODECANESE
KRITI (CRETE)
SEA
Constanta
Varna
Galati
Iasi
Mouths of the Danube
Ural R.
Volga
URAL MTS.
CR 279

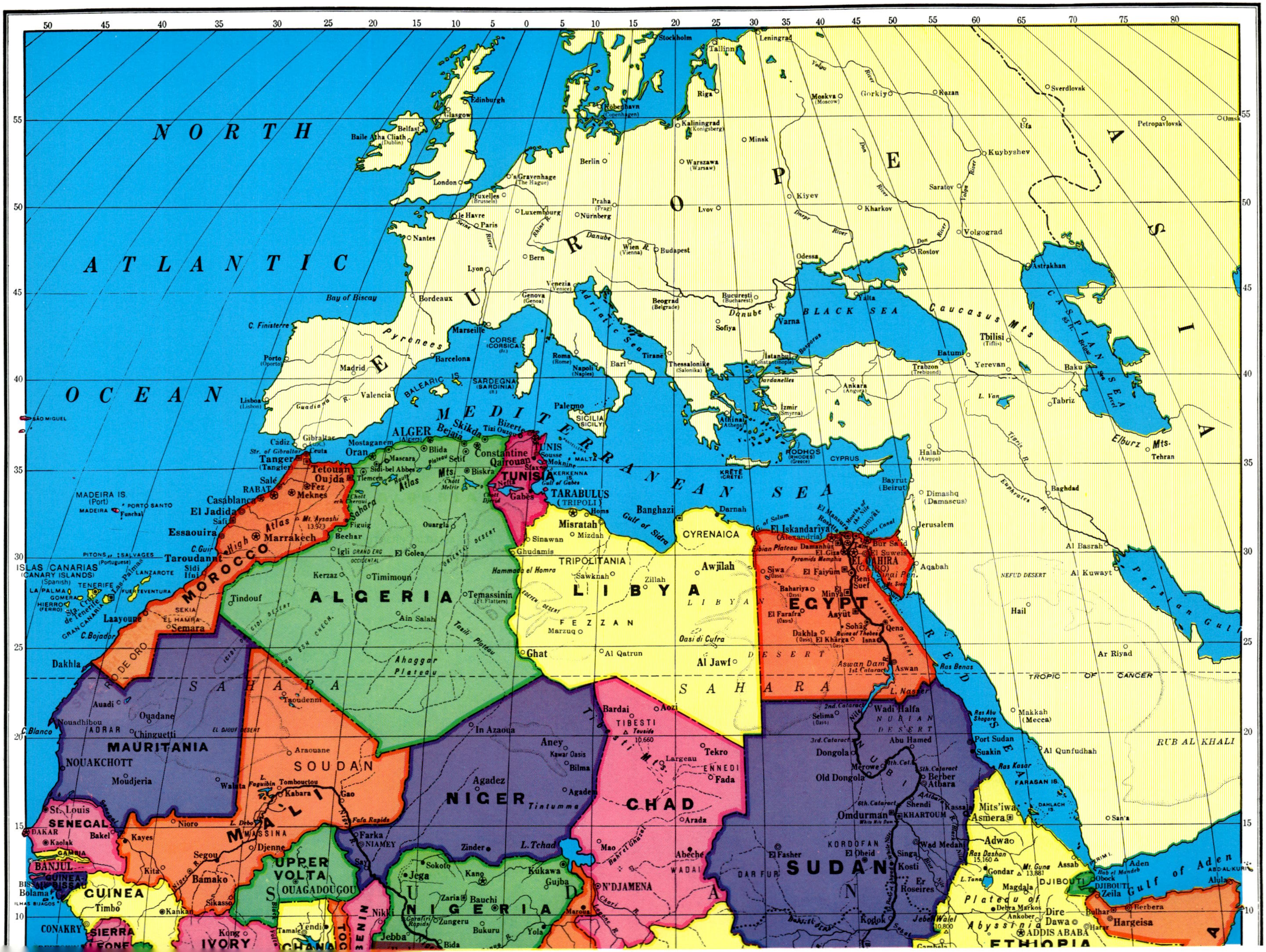
NORTH ATLANTIC OCEAN
EUROPE
ASIA
MEDITERRANEAN SEA
BLACK SEA
CASPIAN SEA
Persian Gulf
RED SEA
Gulf of Aden
Bay of Biscay
Adriatic Sea
Gulf of Sidra
SAHARA
TROPIC OF CANCER
RUB AL KHALI
NEFUD DESERT
LIBYAN DESERT
NUBIAN DESERT
Caucasus Mts
Elburz Mts.
Pyrenees
Atlas
High Atlas
Ahaggar Plateau
Tassili Plateau
TIBESTI
ENNEDI
FEZZAN
CYRENAICA
TRIPOLITANIA
KORDOFAN
DAR FUR
WADAI
MOROCCO
ALGERIA
TUNISIA
LIBYA
EGYPT
SUDAN
CHAD
NIGER
MALI
MAURITANIA
SENEGAL
GUINEA
UPPER VOLTA
NIGERIA
ETHIOPIA
DJIBOUTI
RIO DE ORO
MADEIRA IS.
ISLAS CANARIAS (CANARY ISLANDS)
CORSE (CORSICA)
SARDEGNA (SARDINIA)
SICILIA (SICILY)
CYPRUS
BALEARIC IS.
KRÉTÉ (CRETE)
RODHOS (RHODES)
Stockholm
Leningrad
Tallinn
Riga
Moskva (Moscow)
Gorkiy
Kazan
Sverdlovsk
Petropavlovsk
Omsk
Kuybyshev
Ufa
Saratov
Volgograd
Rostov
Astrakhan
Kharkov
Kiyev
Minsk
Kaliningrad (Königsberg)
Warszawa (Warsaw)
Lvov
Berlin
Praha (Prag)
Nürnberg
Wien (Vienna)
Budapest
Beograd (Belgrade)
Bucuresti (Bucharest)
Sofiya
Odessa
Yalta
Varna
Istanbul (Constantinople)
Ankara (Angora)
Izmir (Smyrna)
Athinai (Athens)
Thessaloniki (Salonika)
Tirane
Bari
Roma (Rome)
Napoli (Naples)
Palermo
Venezia (Venice)
Genova (Genoa)
Bern
Luxembourg
Bruxelles (Brussels)
's Gravenhage (The Hague)
London
Edinburgh
Glasgow
Belfast
Baile Atha Cliath (Dublin)
København (Copenhagen)
Paris
Le Havre
Nantes
Lyon
Bordeaux
Marseille
Barcelona
Madrid
Valencia
Porto (Oporto)
Lisboa (Lisbon)
Gibraltar
Cadiz
Ceuta
Tanger (Tangier)
Tetouan
Oujda
Fez
Meknes
RABAT
Salé
Casablanca
El Jadida
Safi
Marrakech
Essaouira
Taroudannt
Sidi Ifni
Layoune
Semara
Dakhla
Tindouf
Oran
Mostaganem
ALGER (Algiers)
Blida
Bejaia
Skikda
Constantine
Setif
Biskra
Tlemcen
Sidi-bel-Abbes
Bechar
Ouargla
El Golea
Timimoun
Kerzaz
Ain Salah
Temassinin
Tamanrasset
Bizerte
TUNIS
Sousse
Kairouan
Sfax
Gabes
TARABULUS (TRIPOLI)
Homs
Misratah
Banghazi
Darnah
Sinawan
Mizdah
Ghudamis
Ghat
Marzuq
Sawknah
Zillah
Awjilah
Al Jawf
Al Qatrun
Oasi di Cufra
El Iskandariya (Alexandria)
Bur Said
El Suweis
EL QAHIRA (CAIRO)
El Faiyum
Siwa
Asyut
Qena
Aswan
Wadi Halfa
Dongola
Old Dongola
Abu Hamed
Berber
Atbara
KHARTOUM
Omdurman
El Obeid
El Fasher
Kosti
Wad Medani
Port Sudan
Suakin
Kassala
Asmera
Gondar
Addis Ababa
Dire Dawa
Harar
Hargeisa
Berbera
Zeila
Aden
Jerusalem
Bayrut (Beirut)
Dimashq (Damascus)
Halab (Aleppo)
Baghdad
Al Basrah
Al Kuwayt
Ar Riyad
Makkah (Mecca)
Al Qunfudhah
Hail
Aqabah
Tbilisi (Tiflis)
Yerevan
Baku
Tabriz
Tehran
Batumi
Trabzon (Trebizond)
Aney
Bilma
Agadez
Agadem
Zinder
In Azaoua
Bardai
Aozi
Tekro
Fada
Largeau
Abeche
Mao
N'DJAMENA
Arada
NIAMEY
Gao
Tombouctou
Kabara
Djenne
Segou
Bamako
Nioro
Kayes
Kita
Sikasso
Araouane
Taoudenni
OUAGADOUGOU
Kano
Sokoto
Zaria
Bauchi
Kukawa
Gujba
Jega
Zungeru
Bukuru
Yola
Jebba
Bida
NOUAKCHOTT
Moudjeria
Chinguetti
Ouadane
Atar
Nouadhibou
St. Louis
DAKAR
Kaolak
BANJUL
Bakel
Timbo
CONAKRY
Kankan
SIERRA LEONE
IVORY
GHANA
TOGO
BENIN
Funchal
Stockholm

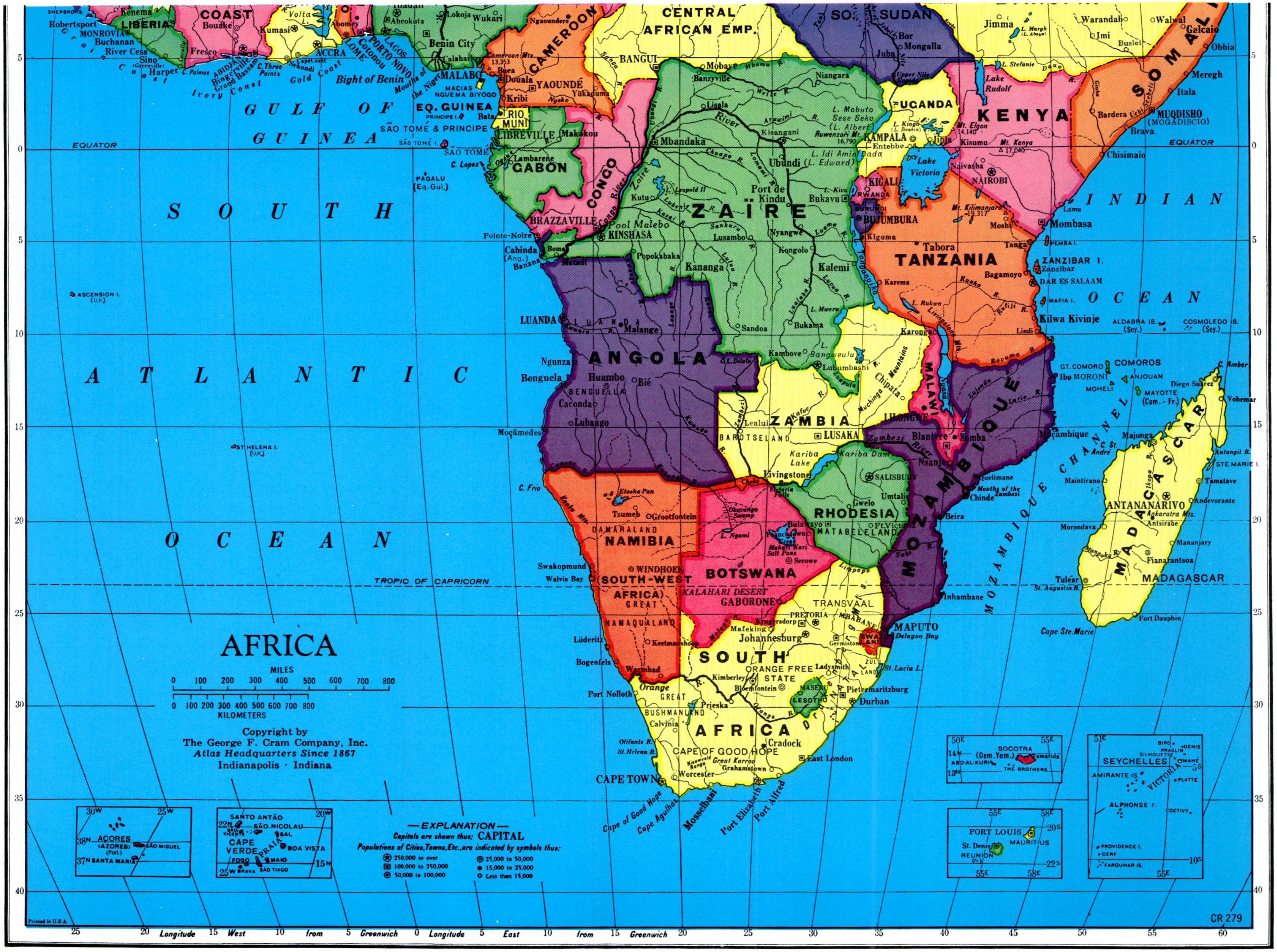
AFRICA
MILES
0 100 200 300 400 500 600 700 800
KILOMETERS
0 100 200 300 400 500 600 700 800
Copyright by
The George F. Cram Company, Inc.
Atlas Headquarters Since 1867
Indianapolis · Indiana
—EXPLANATION—
Capitals are shown thus: CAPITAL
Populations of Cities, Towns, Etc., are indicated by symbols thus:
250,000 or over
100,000 to 250,000
50,000 to 100,000
25,000 to 50,000
15,000 to 25,000
Less than 15,000
CR 279
Printed in U.S.A.
SOUTH ATLANTIC OCEAN
INDIAN OCEAN
GULF OF GUINEA
MOZAMBIQUE CHANNEL
EQUATOR
TROPIC OF CAPRICORN
Longitude West from Greenwich
Longitude East from Greenwich
LIBERIA
COAST
CENTRAL AFRICAN EMP.
SUDAN
CAMEROON
EQ. GUINEA
RIO MUNI
SÃO TOMÉ & PRINCIPE
GABON
CONGO
ZAÏRE
UGANDA
KENYA
SOMALIA
RWANDA
BURUNDI
TANZANIA
ANGOLA
ZAMBIA
MALAWI
MOZAMBIQUE
RHODESIA
NAMIBIA
(SOUTH-WEST AFRICA)
BOTSWANA
SOUTH AFRICA
LESOTHO
SWAZILAND
MADAGASCAR
COMOROS
KINSHASA
BRAZZAVILLE
LIBREVILLE
YAOUNDÉ
MALABO
BANGUI
KAMPALA
NAIROBI
MUQDISHO (MOGADISCIO)
KIGALI
BUJUMBURA
DAR ES SALAAM
LUANDA
LUSAKA
LILONGWE
SALISBURY
WINDHOEK
GABORONE
PRETORIA
MASERU
MBABANE
MAPUTO
CAPE TOWN
ANTANANARIVO
MORONI
ACCRA
LOMÉ
PORTO NOVO
LAGOS
MONROVIA
ASCENSION I. (U.K.)
ST. HELENA I. (U.K.)
PAGALU (Eq. Gui.)
ALDABRA IS. (Sey.)
COSMOLEDO IS. (Sey.)
Lake Victoria
Cape of Good Hope
Cape Agulhas
AÇORES (AZORES) (Port.)
CAPE VERDE
SOCOTRA (Dem. Yem.)
PORT LOUIS
MAURITIUS
REUNION (Fr.)
SEYCHELLES
VICTORIA
AMIRANTE IS.
ALPHONSE I.

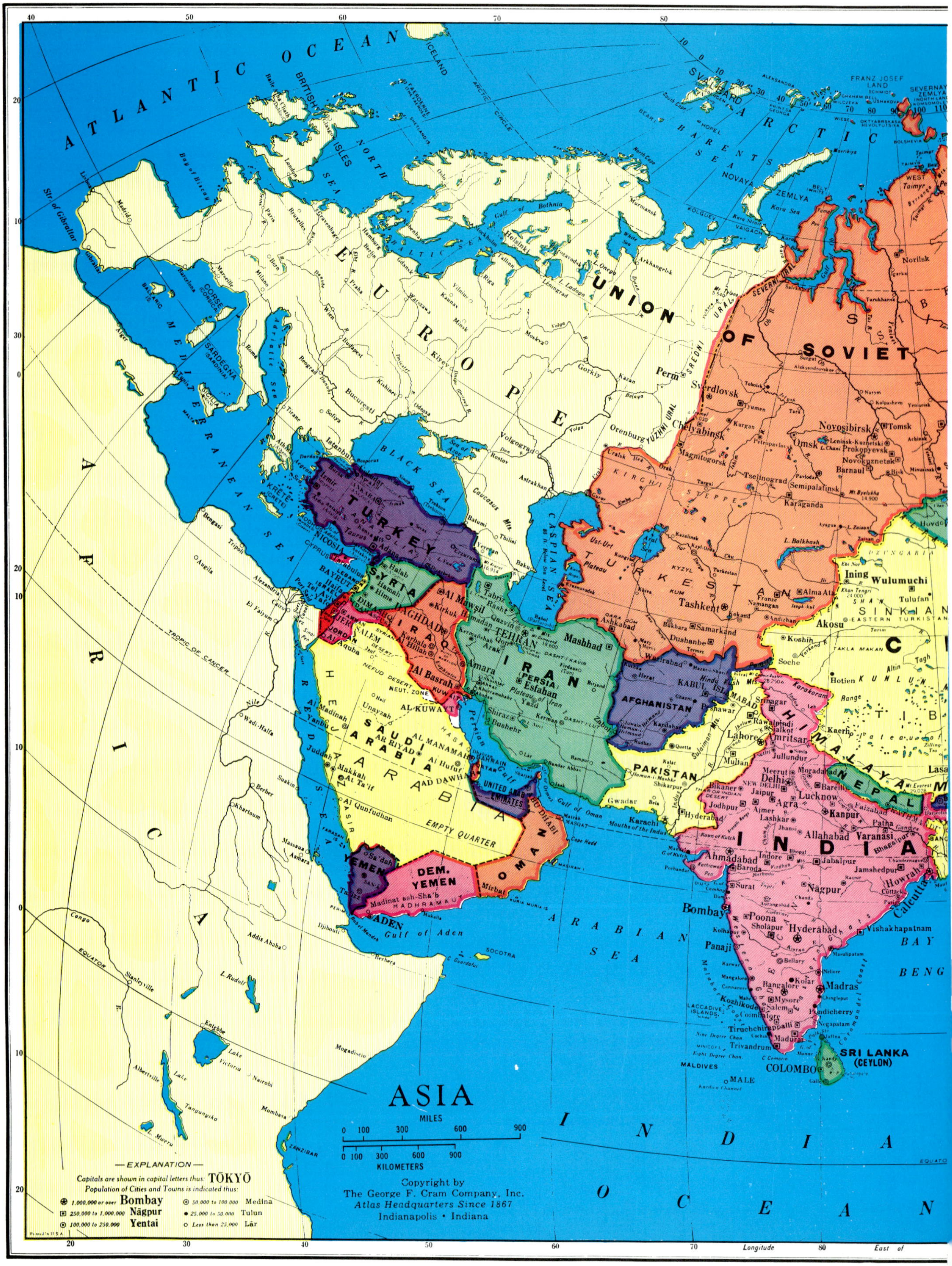
ASIA
MILES
0 100 300 600 900
0 100 300 600 900
KILOMETERS
—EXPLANATION—
Capitals are shown in capital letters thus: TŌKYŌ
Population of Cities and Towns is indicated thus:
1,000,000 or over Bombay
250,000 to 1,000,000 Nāgpur
100,000 to 250,000 Yentai
50,000 to 100,000 Medina
25,000 to 50,000 Tulun
Less than 25,000 Lār
Copyright by
The George F. Cram Company, Inc.
Atlas Headquarters Since 1867
Indianapolis • Indiana
Printed in U.S.A.
ATLANTIC OCEAN
ARCTIC
BARENTS SEA
NORTH SEA
EUROPE
UNION OF SOVIET
MEDITERRANEAN SEA
BLACK SEA
CASPIAN SEA
AFRICA
TURKEY
SYRIA
IRAQ
IRAN
AFGHANISTAN
PAKISTAN
INDIA
NEPAL
HIMALAYA
SAUDI ARABIA
YEMEN
DEM. YEMEN
OMAN
UNITED ARAB EMIRATES
SRI LANKA (CEYLON)
COLOMBO
MALDIVES
ARABIAN SEA
INDIAN OCEAN
TROPIC OF CANCER
EQUATOR
Longitude East of

SOCIALIST
REPUBLICS
MONGOLIA
GOBI DESERT
INNER MONGOLIA
MANCHURIA
CHINA
NORTH KOREA
SOUTH KOREA
JAPAN
SEA OF JAPAN
SEA OF OKHOTSK
BERING SEA
ALEUTIAN IS.
SAKHALIN
HOKKAIDO
HONSHU
SHIKOKU
KYUSHU
TOKYO
Yokohama
Sendai
Nagoya
Osaka
Hakodate
Sapporo
Vladivostok
Khabarovsk
Harbin
Chilin
Changchun
Shenyang
Anshan
PEIPING
(PEKING)
Tienching
Taiyuan
Tsinan
Chingtao
YELLOW SEA
EAST CHINA SEA
Shanghai
Nanching
Wuhan
Hangchou
Ningpo
Wenchou
Fuchou
Changsha
Chengtu
Chungching
Kueiyang
Kunming
Kuangchou
(Canton)
Victoria
Hsiamen
Shantou
Nanning
Hsian
Lanchou
Chengchou
Kaifeng
Hsüchou
TAIWAN (FORMOSA)
Kaohsiung
RYUKYU
PHILIPPINE SEA
PHILIPPINES
LUZON
MANILA
Quezon City
MINDANAO
Davao
SAMAR
LEYTE
HAINAN
VIETNAM
HANOI
Da Nang
Ho Chi Minh City
(Saigon)
CAMBODIA
PHNOM PENH
LAOS
VIENTIANE
THAILAND
(SIAM)
KRUNG THEP
(BANGKOK)
Gulf of Thailand
BURMA
Mandalay
RANGOON
SOUTH CHINA SEA
MALAYSIA
WEST MALAYSIA
KUALA LUMPUR
SINGAPORE
EAST MALAYSIA
SABAH
SARAWAK
BORNEO
INDONESIA
SUMATRA
JAVA
JAKARTA
Surabaya
Bandung
CELEBES
CELEBES SEA
SULU SEA
BANDA SEA
FLORES SEA
TIMOR
HALMAHERA
IRIAN JAYA
NEW GUINEA
PAPUA NEW GUINEA
PORT MORESBY
SOLOMON IS.
BISMARCK ARCHIPELAGO
CORAL SEA
ARAFURA SEA
AUSTRALIA
CAROLINE ISLANDS
MARIANA ISLANDS
MARSHALL ISLANDS
PACIFIC OCEAN
TROPIC OF CANCER
EQUATOR
STANOVOY RA.
Verkhoyansk Mts.
Krasnoyarsk
Irkutsk
L. Baikal
ULAANBAATAR
Hami
Tibet
Greenwich
LR 279

VIETNAM
CAMBODIA
MALAYSIA • LAOS • THAILAND
SINGAPORE
0 50 100 150 MILES
0 50 100 150 KILOMETERS
95° E
100° E
105° E
110° E
20° N
15° N
10° N
5° N
0
Longitude East from Greenwich
B U R M A
C H I N A
L A O S
THAILAND
(SIAM)
KRUNG THEP
(BANGKOK)
CAMBODIA
PHNOM PENH
VIETNAM
HANOI
Haiphong
Nam Dinh
Hue
Da Nang
Ho Chi Minh City
(Saigon)
WEST MALAYSIA
KUALA LUMPUR
SINGAPORE
EAST MALAYSIA
SARAWAK
Kuching
BORNEO
Pontianak
Mandalay
Bassein
RANGOON
Moulmein
Nanning
(Yungning)
Hopu
Chanchiang
Haikou
HAINAN
GULF OF TONKIN
GULF OF MARTABAN
GULF OF THAILAND
ANDAMAN SEA
SOUTH CHINA SEA
MERGUI ARCHIPELAGO
STRAIT OF MALACCA
SUMATRA
Medan
Banda Aceh
Pinang
Taiping
Ipoh
Melaka
NATUNA ISLANDS
ANAMBAS IS.
TAMBELAN IS.
RIOUW ARCHIPELAGO
Isthmus of Kra
Vientiane
Chiang Mai
Nakhon Ratchasima
Battambang
Kompong Cham
Tonle Sap
Kampot
PHU QUOC
POULO CONDORE
Cape Bastion
EQUATOR
CR 279
Printed in U.S.A.
© The George F. Cram Company, Inc.
Indianapolis · Indiana

tic rule and established serfdom. Peter the Great (1682–1725) founded St. Petersburg (now Leningrad) in 1703 as a glittering European capital city. After Peter, Russia began to accept Western Europe's culture, fashions, and science. The rules of Peter, Elizabeth, and Catherine the Great added Ukraine, Byelorussia (White Russia), Bessarabia, Crimea, and other areas to the growing empire. Siberia, Central Asia, and Alaska were added by Catherine the Great and Tsars Alexander I and Nicholas I.

Petty wars, heavy taxation, and repression gradually brought on a crisis in the empire. The crisis began with the Pugachev Revolt in 1773 and continued until the overthrow in 1917. Serfs had been freed in 1861 by Tsar Alexander II, who tried to stem the tide of demands by granting several reforms. (It was this Alexander who sold Alaska to the United States in 1867.) Alexander was assassinated in 1881.

World War I found Russia on the Allied side. But the war brought only defeats and privations for the Russian army. The army was finally unable to get supplies or to get clear decisions from the head of government. In March 1917, a moderate government took over upon the abdication of Tsar Nicholas II, who was no longer able to control the government. In November 1917, the moderate government was overthrown by a revolutionary Marxist group called the Bolsheviks. All authority for government was then handed over to councils of workers and peasants (the word for council in Russian is *soviet*). All major industrial and commercial activities were nationalized. A great civil war followed. Despite foreign intervention, the Bolsheviks were victorious by 1921.

The creation of the Soviet Union was the greatest act in the long career of V. I. Lenin, revolutionary leader and Marxist philosopher. After the death of Lenin in 1924, factional disputes arose. These took the form of purges and finally the redirection of state power toward the building of heavy industry. Communist leaders abandoned the idea of the world Marxist movement for immediate revolution and internal growth. Joseph Stalin ushered in a period when the Soviet Union consolidated its power internally. Heavy industry was planned and activated at the expense of consumer products and agriculture. The Stalin group laid heavy hands upon the freedom of the Russian people.

The Soviet Union was invaded by German forces in June 1941. The resulting battles on Russian soil were among the bloodiest ever fought. German armored divisions succeeded in reaching the Volga River at Stalingrad (now Volgograd), where they besieged the city for two months. This action marked the turning point in the war. United States military assistance reached the Soviet Union chiefly through the northern sea route and over the southern land route.

After the war and the death of Stalin (1953), the Soviet Union changed directions in political, social, and economic matters. A more relaxed attitude toward other nations began to appear. When Nikita Khrushchev assumed power in 1956, he denounced Stalinist excesses and tensions began to ease. The so-called Cold War between Western democracies and the Soviet Union tapered off.

The Soviets never let up, however, in their relentless effort toward world conquest. Massive military and economic help in Indo-China and aid to African and Latin American countries helped in the ideological war against the free world; and the success of their efforts is beyond question.

Khrushchev was deposed in 1964. His successor was Leonid Brezhnev who died in 1982 to be succeeded by Yuri Andropov, who died in 1984. Konstantin Chernenko was chosen his successor. President Andrei Gromyko became head of state in July, 1985.

UNITED ARAB EMIRATES

Along the south coast of the Persian Gulf between Qatar and Oman are seven Arab sheikhdoms, whose main resource is oil.

In earlier times their principal activity was piracy. In the nineteenth century, they came under British influence and signed a truce to abstain from such violations of international law. This gave them the name of the Trucial States, and they became a collective British protectorate while their sheikhs maintained their local power. On December 2, 1971, the states became the United Arab Emirates and signed a treaty with Britain as an independent country. A week later the United Arab Emirates became a member of the United Nations. In 1975 they were fully nationalized.

UNITED KINGDOM

The full form of the name is the United Kingdom of Great Britain and Northern Ireland. This name evolved slowly, beginning in 1707. At that time the Crowns of England and Scotland were united to form the Kingdom of Great Britain. The name was correctly used for both the island and the kingdom. In 1801, the name *Ireland* was added as a result of the union of Ireland with the Crown. The last change occurred in 1927, when Ireland withdrew from the union of kingdoms, leaving behind the six counties of Ulster. These became Northern Ireland, which replaced "Ireland" in the full name of the United Kingdom.

The island of Great Britain was inhabited in pre-Roman times by Celtic peoples who lived mainly in the southern part. The chief tribe was the Briton, from which the name *Britain* is derived.

Julius Caesar was unable to conquer the island during his expedition of 54 B.C. However, the island was conquered by the Roman Emperor Claudius in A.D. 43, and Roman rule was gradually extended northward. The Romans built a great wall (part of which still stands) to mark the northern limits of their government and to keep out the warlike Picts of present-day Scotland. Roads were built. Christianity was introduced; many cities and towns were founded during the Roman period. The Romans withdrew gradually as pressure mounted from invading forces of Nordic peoples. By A.D. 410, they had left the island to the invaders.

A period of confusion and invasion followed. After the Roman departure, Danes, Saxons, Angles, and Jutes gained territory in Britain. The Celtic peoples gradually withdrew deeper into the secluded forests and uplands of what is now Wales and Scotland. The Welsh people are largely the descendants of the ancient Celts who first inhabited Britain.

England—Westminster, Big Ben, and the Houses of Parliament, also showing Westminster Abbey

Many small kingdoms developed, especially in the southern part of Britain. Some of them were united to form larger kingdoms; by the eighth century, Wessex had become the strongest. Its greatest leader was Alfred the Great (849–899), who defeated the Danes. However, Danish rule was reinstituted in 954. From 1017 to 1035, most of what is now England was united to the Crown of Denmark under King Canute.

The modern history of Britain began in 1066 when William the Conqueror, himself the descendant of Norse (Norman) invaders of France, invaded and defeated the last Saxon king at Hastings. William built a strong government. French was introduced as the language of the nobility. Under William and his descendants, the English language began to take form. This is called the Norman period (William was also king of Normandy, a region in France). In 1154, the Plantagenet family of kings introduced further refinements in government, including the jury system. Repressive taxes caused the nobility to revolt. In 1215, King John was forced to sign the Magna Charta, or Great Charter, that established several basic limits in government. The beginnings of a parliamentary system were made under Edward I (1272–1307). The "model parliament" of 1295 included clergymen and townspeople, as well as lesser nobility. It established a trend toward democracy in government.

The Hundred Years' War represented for Britain and France the final flowering of feudalism and the end of the Middle Ages. The use of gunpowder signaled the end of the armored knight on horse, as well as the great castle bastions of feudal times. A trend toward strong central government began in Britain. Trade and commerce revived, along with the beginnings of competition for markets and colonies outside Britain. As an island kingdom with a long seafaring tradition, Britain was well prepared to compete with the Dutch, Spanish, French, and others for the control of newly discovered lands.

The reign of Elizabeth I (1558–1603) initiated the golden age of British culture and history. The flowering of art, drama, and literature went hand-in-hand with expansion overseas. British power eventually gained an empire that spread over the known world and was the largest empire in history. Britain achieved supremacy in commerce and trade, as well as in naval and military power.

A period of absolute monarchy after Elizabeth I was followed by the outbreak of civil war in 1642. When monarchy was restored in 1688, it was no longer under the "divine right" concept. Parliament passed a "Bill of Rights" in 1689, which has served as a model for many other nations of the world.

After the wars with France in the seventeenth and eighteenth centuries, the British Empire had reached its greatest extent. The Industrial Revolution reached Britain and an era of political and social reform followed. The Victorian period under Queen Victoria (1837–1901) saw the rise of great parliamentarians and the beginning of the colonial movement for self-government or independence. The empire began to break up, often with violence. But in some cases, the colonies made a peaceful transition from empire to the new "commonwealth" concept. The American colonies were lost in 1783; Canada became a dominion (an associated state) in 1867; New Zealand, Australia, and South Africa, at the beginning of the twentieth century; Ireland withdrew in 1922, and Egypt in 1936. India gained her independence in 1947.

The Commonwealth of Nations, formerly called the British Commonwealth, is a loose association of Great Britain and about 35 countries which were her former colonies, although not all chose to be included. Heads of these nations meet at intervals to discuss mutual goals and problems.

The United Kingdom in the twentieth century has engaged in two world wars. The most critical of these was World War II, in which Britain was severely bombed and 360,000 British service men lost their lives.

The British of recent years have been preoccupied with problems such as the struggle in Northern Ireland; inflation and high unemployment; and the invasion in 1982 by Argentina in the Falkland Islands. Prime Minister Margaret Thatcher's handling of that situation and her program to get the country back on a sound financial footing helped her win reelection in 1983. Britain has profited from huge oil discoveries in the North Sea. The United Kingom continues as one of the United States' staunchest allies.

Diplomatic ties with Libya ceased in 1984 when a policewoman was killed and ten Libyan demonstrators were wounded in front of the Libyan embassy in London.

UNITED STATES OF AMERICA

(See Pages 201–348)

UPPER VOLTA

The history of Upper Volta until the end of the nineteenth century A.D. was that of the empire-building Mossi people. Their origin is somewhat obscure, but they probably came from eastern Africa sometime in the eleventh century A.D. They first established small kingdoms in the region of the present Ghana and then spread out northward along the Black, Red, and White Volta rivers.

The original empire was centered on the present city of Ouagadougou. It persisted down to modern times. The Mossi people sacked the city of Timbuktu (Tombouctou) in 1333. They also fought the Mali and Songhai peoples that were near neighbors. Mossi power declined after the eighteenth century.

By 1896, the empires of the region were weak and the French were able to establish a protectorate. In 1919, the former kingdoms were united into a territory called Upper Volta, and were added to the French West African group of colonies. In 1932, Upper Volta was dismembered and abolished. However, on September 4, 1947, the Territory of Upper Volta was reestablished with the 1932 boundaries. This was done to avoid political conflict. On December 11, 1958, Upper Volta became the autonomous Voltaic Republic. In 1959, the name was changed back to Upper Volta. Upper Volta became an independent nation on August 5, 1960. It was admitted to the United Nations on September 20, 1960.

URUGUAY

Juan de Solis discovered the Uruguay region in 1516. Colonia del Sacramento was founded by the

Uruguay—Montevideo

Portuguese as a rival to Spanish Buenos Aires, located just a few miles away (across the Río de la Plata estuary). Rivalry between the Portuguese in Uruguay and the Spanish in Argentina continued until the Uruguay region was annexed to the viceroyalty of Buenos Aires. Uruguay revolted against Spain in 1810. It had to fight not only the Spanish, but also Brazil and Argentina, both of which tried to annex the country. Independence was achieved in 1825 from Argentina and in 1828 from Brazil. Uruguay became a republic.

During the rest of the nineteenth century, Uruguay had mostly unstable governments; but in 1903, President José Batlle y Ordónez initiated a series of reforms that made Uruguay one of South America's most progressive democracies. It became a member of the United Nations on December 18, 1945.

In 1952, the presidential system was abandoned and the executive power was shared by a board of nine members—six from the majority and three from the minority party. The presidential system was restored in 1957, then again abrogated in 1973 for a military dictatorship. In 1985 a civilian form of government was restored.

VATICAN CITY

The Vatican City is an independent state located in Italy, within the city of Rome.

The state's modern history dates from February 11, 1929, when the Lateran Treaty was signed between Italy and His Holiness, the Supreme Pontiff (pope) of the Roman Catholic Church. The treaty established the boundaries and guaranteed the independence of the state. Vatican City issues its own coins and stamps and maintains diplomatic relations with about 70 nations, the United States becoming one in 1984.

VENEZUELA

Venezuela was discovered by Columbus in 1498, but until Caracas was founded in 1567 there were no important settlements. As part of New Granada (*see* Colombia) it participated in the revolt led by Simón Bolívar and Francisco de Miranda in 1810 and 1811, and after independence was won in 1821 remained part of the new state of Gran Colombia. But this state disintegrated; and in 1830, Venezuela became independent. Throughout the nineteenth century, and until the presidency of Romulo Betancourt in 1958, a succession of dictators ruled Venezuela. The constitution of 1961, and reforms of succeeding presidents, apparently made democracy work in Venezuela. The country became a member of the United Nations on December 18, 1945.

Assisting in the founding of the Organization of Petroleum Exporting Countries (OPEC) in 1976, Venezuela financed a $150 billion development plan for 1981–85 for domestic improvements.

VIETNAM

The history of Vietnam can be traced back to the fourth century B.C., when a group of people called

Venezuela—Ciudad Universitaria, Caracas

the Viets entered the Tonkin Gulf area of Southeast Asia. They conquered and intermarried with the local people. About 200 B.C., they set up the kingdom of Nam-Viet, which was later conquered by Chinese armies.

The Chinese ruled Nam-Viet until A.D. 938, when Viet leaders expelled them and planted the new kingdom of Vietnam. France captured Vietnam in the eighteenth century and set up a protectorate there in 1884.

Japan took control of the country in World War II and established the puppet state of Bao Dai. In 1946, Communist forces known as the Vietminh overthrew the Bao Dai. They refused to accept French rule, and France launched a full-scale attack on the country. The French forces were defeated at Dien Bien Phu in 1954.

A peace conference in Geneva divided the country into North and South Vietnam to separate the pro-communist and and anticommunists forces until elections could be held in 1956. But the elections were never held, and the two nations remained hostile toward one another.

In 1963, a guerrilla movement emerged in South Vietnam to overthrow the South Vietnamese government. A series of military chiefs held the presidency of South Vietnam, but each failed to quash the Vietcong guerrillas. The United States poured money and troops into the conflict, to no avail. South Vietnam fell to the communist forces in the spring of 1975, after more than a million Vietnamese civilians and over 200,000 Vietnamese soldiers had been killed. More than 47,000 American soldiers also died in the war.

The country was officially reunited on July 2, 1976. It adopted the flag, capital, and government of the former North Vietnam. In 1977, the United States agreed to allow Vietnam to join the United Nations. Since then, Vietnam troops have engaged troops in neighboring Cambodia, Thailand, and China.

WALLIS AND FUTUNA

The islands were ruled by kings and as a protectorate of France from 1842 until 1961, when they became an overseas territory of France. The territory is located in the South Pacific Ocean.

WESTERN SAMOA

Western Samoa was made a German protectorate in 1900. It became a League of Nations mandated territory of New Zealand in 1920. Partial self-government was achieved in 1947. By 1961, the islands were ready for full independence, which had been pledged to them by New Zealand in 1946. Independence was granted on January 1, 1962.

WEST GERMANY

The Romans used the name *Germania* to designate an area that was almost the same as that of modern Germany. The inhabitants of Germania were described as being divided into classes of noblemen, freemen, vassals, and slaves. The Romans waged war against various tribes that came from this region, beginning with Cimbri and Teuton peoples in the second century A.D. In later centuries German peoples came over to the Roman areas peacefully and often joined up with the legions of Imperial Rome. Still later, they began to invade Roman provinces, and finally aided in the destruction of the Roman world.

The rise of Frankish power and the establishment of a Frankish empire under Merovingians marked the beginning of a long series of unification attempts in what is now Germany. Charlemagne inherited the region from the Merovingians. His Frankish empire included what is now France, Germany, and part of Italy. Upon his death the empire dissolved. Germany was again united in the Holy Roman Empire that was set up in 962. The Holy Roman Empire dominated Central Europe until the Reformation. The empire crumbled from lack of a steady central authority and from internal dissension. The rise of national kingdoms and prosperous trading cities also helped destroy the effective authority of the empire. The Thirty Years' War of 1618–1648 split Germany and the Holy Roman Empire into a maze of fragments, including over three hundred separate states and independent cities.

The rise of Prussia under Frederick II (1740–1786) once again presented an opportunity for the establishment of a German nation. German nationalism asserted itself during the French Revolution and the Napoleonic era. A successful movement for unification came into being under the leadership of Otto von Bismarck, Chancellor of Prussia. Rivalry between Prussia and Austria for the control of Germany developed into a series of wars (1864–1871) which Prussia won, assuming the position of the leading economic and military power on the Continent. An intricate system of alliances established a delicate balance of political power in Europe. This balance was finally upset in the Balkans by the 1914 murder of the heir to the throne of the Austro-Hungarian Empire, which led to World War I.

World War I ended in the defeat of Germany and the destruction of the German Empire. In the social disorder that followed, National Socialism, or Nazism, gained a powerful following under the leadership of Adolf Hitler. In 1933, Hitler converted the Weimar Republic of Germany into the German Third Reich, a Nazi dictatorship.

Expansionist policies, the persecution of political minorities, and the execution of plans to exterminate the Jewish population of Germany marked the Nazi regime. In 1938, Hitler annexed Austria and then Czechoslovakia. World War II was precipitated by the sudden German invasion of Poland on September 1, 1939. The Soviet Union had signed a nonaggression pact with Hitler and had helped in the partition of Poland. Yet German forces invaded Russia in a lightning-like stroke on June 22, 1941. On December 7, 1941, Japan, which had become allied with Germany, without warning attacked Pearl Harbor. While the Americans adopted a holding action in the Pacific, they planned, along with the Allies, an invasion of Europe. The German armies, in the meantime, pushed further into Russia and were finally halted at Stalingrad (*see* U.S.S.R.). The allied invasion began in Africa in November 1942, and continued in Sicily and Italy, gradually splitting the Axis forces and sapping German military strength. On June 1, 1944, a great Allied invasion force landed on the coast of Normandy in France. The Nazi military machine was crushed. On May 8, 1945, Germany surrendered.

On June 5, 1945, Germany was divided into four zones of occupation. The four occupation powers (the United Kingdom, France, the Soviet Union, and the United States) set up an Allied Control Council for the government of the German capital city of Berlin, which became an island in the Soviet Union's zone of occupation.

The failure of the Allies to agree upon procedures and upon the future disposition of defeated Germany ended the policy of cooperation and brought about the demise of the Allied Control Council for Berlin. In 1949, Germany was formally divided into western and eastern sections. The western part became the Federal Republic of Germany with a provisional capital at Bonn, on the Rhine River in Westphalia. Territories in the east that included East Prussia were partitioned by Poland and the Soviet Union. Berlin, originally di-

West Germany—The Lukaskirche, Protestant Church, Munich

vided into four zones of occupation, eventually consisted of only two zones—West Berlin, which was associated with the Federal Republic, and East Berlin, which was under the administration of the German Democratic Republic (the Soviet zone). The Saar region was formally united to the Federal Republic after agreement between France and the Federal Republic, after free elections had been held.

Since World War II, West Germany has become one of the leading industrial nations of the world and, like Japan, a keen competitor with U.S. auto makers. Its agreement to allow the deployment of nuclear missiles within its borders sparked huge demonstrations in 1983 but government leaders reaffirmed their determination to stick to their decision.

WINDWARD ISLANDS

The more southerly group of islands in the Lesser Antilles of the British West Indies is called the Windward Islands. They comprise, from north to south, Dominica, St. Lucia, St. Vincent, and Grenada. They were members of the West Indies Federation that existed from 1958 to 1962. Discovered by Columbus and often in dispute between the French and English, while the indigenous Carib Indians fiercely resisted conquest by Europeans, these islands were before 1958 organized as the colony of Windward Islands and in 1967 were made associated states. As such, they had maximum self-government short of independence. In 1974, Grenada declared its independence (*see* Grenada), but the others remained associated states.

Yemen—View of Sana'a, the capital

YEMEN

Yemen is the heart of the famous "Arabia Felix" of ancient times. It was the site of the Kingdom of Saba (950–115 B.C.), supposedly ruled for a time by the great Queen of Sheba.

The Yemen region was conquered by the Ottoman Turks in 1517 and remained under their loose control until they were expelled by the British in World War I (1918). Turkish control had been only nominal after 1913. Yemen became a member of the United Nations on September 30, 1947.

The ruler of Yemen was the heredity imam until military forces proclaimed the Yemen Arab Republic on September 18, 1962. Today two countries are recognized, North Yemen or the Yemen Arab Republic, and South Yemen or the People's Democratic Republic of Yemen. The People's Republic of Yemen went to war with Yemen in 1979. The war was short-lived and a mutual withdrawal of forces was agreed to.

YUGOSLAVIA

The South Slavs migrated to the Balkans from the east and north during the sixth century A.D. and later. Most of them were converted to Christianity during the eighth and ninth centuries, but under later Turkish rule many became Moslems. Of the many attempts to form lasting states, only the Serbians were partially successful.

In the second half of the nineteenth century, the South Slavs consisted of Serbians, Slovenes, Croatians, Bosnians, Macedonians, and Montenegrins. In 1878, Serbia achieved independence. The Balkan Wars of 1911–1913 led to a series of events that eventually became the immediate cause of World War I. After the war a unified Slavic state emerged, comprising Serbia, Croatia, Bosnia and Herzegovina, Slavonia, and Dalmatia. This new state was called the Kingdom of the Serbs, Croats, and Slovenes. The state

U.S. Secretary of State, Henry Kissinger (left) with President Josip Broz Tito of Yugoslavia (right) during the former's visit to Yugoslavia in November 1974. (With them is an interpreter.)

proved unstable, and the king declared himself dictator in 1929 and renamed the country Yugoslavia.

During World War II pressure was used by both the Axis and Allied powers to secure Yugoslav support. The Germans invaded the country in April 1941, and the king thereafter ruled from exile in London. Several resistance groups emerged within Yugoslavia, the most enduring of which was led by Tito, a communist, who was eventually supported by the Soviet Union, the British, and the Americans. Yugoslavia was a charter member of the United Nations on October 24, 1945.

On November 29, 1945, Yugoslavia was proclaimed a republic, and the constitution of 1946 made it a federal republic. The leader in the Soviet-type government was Tito, although he did not become president until 1953, when a new constitution provided for that office. By this time, relations between the Soviet Union and Yugoslavia had deteriorated. The differences between two communist countries revealed for the first time that nations could belong to the communist camp and yet not be "satellites" of the Soviet Union. Yugoslavia became a leader of the so-called unaligned bloc.

Under the constitution of 1963, the official name was changed to the Socialist Federal Republic of Yugoslavia.

Following Tito's death in 1980, a rotating system of succession was established among members representing each republic and autonomous province.

ZAIRE

This name is an African equivalent of Congo, and was adopted by the government formerly known as Republic of the Congo, with its capital at Kinshasa, both for itself and for the river. An even earlier name of this state was Belgian Congo, before independence was achieved.

The mouth of the Congo River was discovered by the Portuguese explorer Diego Cam. Exploration into the interior began when David Livingstone and Henry Stanley, in the nineteenth century, followed the Congo through the great rain forest. Stanley was in the service of Belgian King Leopold II who subsidized several of Stanley's expeditions. Conflicts between European nations over the Congo area were prevented by the Berlin Conference of 1884, which established the Belgian king's claims to the main basin of the Congo River.

The personal rule of the king ended in 1908 when the Congo region was organized into the colony of Belgian Congo. Serious movements toward independence did not occur until 1959. Belgium agreed to grant independence on June 30, 1960.

No sooner had the nation become independent than its army mutinied. The national army then became an uncertain and undisciplined force that supported various leaders at different times. Katanga province, rich in minerals, seceded from the republic. A special United Nations force tried to maintain some semblance of order but failed. The nation's first prime minister was murdered under

President Joseph Mobutu of Zaire (right) with U.S. heavyweight challenger Muhammad Ali. The latter was in Zaire for a title bout with George Foreman.

mysterious circumstances; and in 1961, the Congolese Parliament convened under United Nations auspices and protection. The central government tried to negotiate with the secessionist Katanga Province, but its leader, Moise Tshombe, refused to carry out agreements. UN Secretary-General Dag Hammarskjöld was killed in a plane crash while flying into Katanga Province in order to secure an agreement. A new constitution was drafted in 1962 but led to still another secessionist movement, in Kasai Province. By the latter part of 1963, both secessions had ended, and United Nations supervisory forces were able to leave the country by the end of June 1964.

The constitution in effect was superseded by another imposed in 1966 by President Joseph Mobutu. He remained in that office under a new constitution adopted by referendum in June 1967. As part of the africanization program, he changed his name to Mobutu Sese Seko, and that of the country to Zaire, in 1971.

Most foreign business owners sold their interests to native operators in 1974, but the government of Zaire asked them to return. Low copper prices hurt the economy of the country; and in 1977, a force of Cuban-trained guerrillas invaded Zaire from Angola. Troops and planes from Morocco, Egypt, and France helped President Mobutu repel the attack. Another invasion was attempted in 1978 but without success.

ZAMBIA

After the federation of Rhodesia and Nyasaland was dissolved on the last day of 1963, the British protectorate of Northern Rhodesia was given autonomy. (For the history of Northern Rhodesia, see Rhodesia.) On October 24, 1964, the protectorate was given its independence within the Commonwealth, as the republic of Zambia. On December 1, 1964, it joined the United Nations. Relations between black-ruled Zambia and her white-ruled neighbor, Rhodesia, continued to be unfriendly; and for a time in 1973, their borders were closed. An alternate link to the coast was provided by the building of a highway and railroad through Tasmania to the port of Dar es Salaam.

ZIMBABWE (See Rhodesia)

The main street of Lusaka, Zambia.

Statistics for Countries of the World

NAME OF COUNTRY	POPULATION	CAPITAL* LARGEST CITY	AREA (SQUARE MILES)	GOVERNMENT	MAJOR LANGUAGES
Afghanistan Democratic Republic of Afghanistan	15,100,000	Kabul* 891,750	251,773	Military government, U.S.S.R. control	Pushtu, Persian
Albania People's Socialist Republic of Albania	2,800,000	Tirana* 198,000	11,100	1 party, Communist state	Albanian
Algeria Democratic and Popular Republic of Algeria	21,351,000	Algiers* 2,200,000	919,595	Presidential regime	Arabic, French
Andorra Principality of Andorra	45,000 (scattered through 7 small villages)	Andorra la Vella* No population figure available	188	Co-principality, France and Spain, Council of 24 members	Catalan
Angola People's Republic of Angola	7,770,000	Luanda* 475,300	481,353	1 party, committee rule	Portuguese, Bantu
†Antigua and Barbuda	80,000	St. John's* 25,000	171	2 party, parliamentary government	English
Argentina Argentine Republic	30,097,000	Buenos Aires* 2,922,800	1,065,189	Federal republic. Long under military control, but Oct., 1983, defeat of Peronists gave civilian control.	Spanish
†Australia Commonwealth of Australia	15,462,000	Canberra* 246,100 Sydney 3,231,700	2,966,200	Multi-party, democratic federal state system, parliamentary government	English
Australian External Territories:					
Norfolk Island	1,800		13½		
Coral Sea Island			1		
Territory of Ashmore and Carter Island			2		
Cocos (Keeling) Island	569		5½		
Christmas Island	3,184		52		
Australian Antarctic Territory			2,472,000		
Austria Republic of Austria	7,600,000	Vienna* 1,504,200	32,374	Multi-party, federal republic	German
†The Bahamas Commonwealth of the Bahamas	260,000	Nassau* 138,000	5,380	Independent within British Commonwealth, multi-party, parliamentary government	English
Bahrain State of Bahrain	409,000	Manama* 300,000	258	No parties, traditional Emirate	Arabic
†Bangladesh People's Republic of Bangladesh	99,585,000	Dacca* 3.4 million (metropolitan area)	55,598	Military rule	Bengali, English
†Barbados	300,000	Bridgetown* 7,600	166	Independent sovereign state within British Commonwealth; multi-party, parliamentary government	English
Belgium Kingdom of Belgium	9,900,000	Brussels* 1,000,221 (metropolitan area)	11,779	Multi-party, parliamentary democracy under constitutional monarch	Flemish French
†Belize	158,000	Belmopan* 2,932 Belize City 39,887	8,867	2 party, parliamentary government	English, Spanish, Indian languages
Benin People's Republic of Benin	3,910,000	Porto-Novo* 123,000 Cotonou 215,000	43,475	No political parties, Marxist-Lenist military government	French, Fons, and Adjas

NAME OF COUNTRY	POPULATION	CAPITAL* LARGEST CITY	AREA (SQUARE MILES)	GOVERNMENT	MAJOR LANGUAGES
Bhutan Kingdom of Bhutan	1,417,000	Thimphu* 10,000	17,800	No political parties, absolute monarch	Dzong Ka, Nepali, others
Bolivia Republic of Bolivia	6,037,000	Sucre (legal)* 63,259 LaPaz (de facto)* 881,400	424,165	Multi-party, centralized republic	Spanish, Aymara Quechua
†Botswana Republic of Botswana	1,038,000	Gaborone* 59,000	224,600	Multi-party, parliamentary democracy	English, Tswana, and other Bantu languages
Brazil Federative Republic of Brazil	134,380,000	Brasilia* 411,305 Sao Paulo 7 million	3,286,470	2 party, military government	Portuguese
Brunei	218,000	Bandar Seri Begawan*	2,226	Sultanate	English, Malay
Bulgaria People's Republic of Bulgaria	8,969,000	Sofia* 1,056,900	42,823	Communist state	Bulgarian
Burma Socialist Republic of the Union of Burma	37,100,000	Rangoon* 2,186,000	261,288	1 party, socialist republic	Burmese, Shan, others
Burundi Republic of Burundi	4,691,000	Bujumbura* 200,000	10,759	1 party, presidential regime	Kirundi, French, others
**Cambodia (Kampuchea) Cambodian People's Republic	6,300,000	Phnom Penh* 500,000	69,900	1 party, communist state	Khmer, French Annamese
Cameroon United Republic of Cameroon	9,506,000	Yaounde* 400,000 Douala 500,000	179,558	1 party, presidential regime	French, English, others
†Canada	25,142,000	Ottawa* 695,000 Montreal 2,800,000	3,851,809	Multi-party, confederation with parliamentary democracy.	English, French
**Cape Verde Republic of Cape Verde	340,000	Praia* 36,600 Mindelo 40,000	1,557	1 party, constitutional assembly	Portuguese, Bantu
Central African Republic	2,585,000	Bangui* 367,100 (metropolitan area)	240,324	Military government	French, Sangho, others
Chad Republic of Chad	5,116,000	N'Djamena* 303,000 (metropolitan area)	495,755	1 party, military government	French, Arabic, Sara, others
Chile Republic of Chile	11,655,000	Santiago* 3,448,700	292,135	Political activity suspended, military government	Spanish
**China People's Republic of China	1,034,907,000	Peking* 8,500,000 Shanghai 12,000,000	3,691,521	1 party, communist state	Chinese
China (Taiwan) Republic of China	18,500,000	Taipei* 2,298,000 (metropolitan area)	13,814	Multi-party, presidential regime	Chinese
Colombia Republic of Colombia	28,248,000	Bogota* 4,486,200	440,831	Multi-party, parliamentary government	Spanish
Comoros Federal Islamic Republic of the Comoros	445,000	Moroni* 22,000 (metropolitan area)	838	Military rule	Malagasy, French
Congo People's Republic of the Congo	1,745,000	Brazzaville* 200,000 (metropolitan area)	132,046	1 party, military government	French, Kongo, Batéké, M'Bochi

NAME OF COUNTRY	POPULATION	CAPITAL* LARGEST CITY	AREA (SQUARE MILES)	GOVERNMENT	MAJOR LANGUAGES
Costa Rica Republic of Costa Rica	2,693,000	San Jose* 867,800	19,653	Multi-party, federal republic	Spanish
Cuba Republic of Cuba	9,995,000	Havana* 1,008,500	44,218	1 party, communist state	Spanish
**†Cyprus Republic of Cyprus	662,000	Nicosia* 121,500	3,572	Multi-party, parliamentary government	Greek, Turkish
Czechoslovakia Czechoslovak Socialist Republic	15,466,000	Prague* 1.1 million	49,365	1 party, communist state	Czech, Slovak
Denmark Kingdom of Denmark	5,112,000	Copenhagen* 654,437	16,633	Multi-party, parliamentary constitutional monarchy	Danish
Greenland (Kalaallit Nunaat*) *official name now	51,000	Nuuk* 9,717	840,000	Formerly an integral part of Denmark, it was granted home rule in 1979; has socialist-dominated legislature	Greenlandic, Danish
Djibouti Republic of Djibouti	500,000	Djibouti* 200,000 (metropolitan area)	8,996	Multi-party, parliamentary government	French, Somali
†Dominica Commonwealth of Dominica	82,000	Roseau* 20,000	290	Parliamentary	English
Dominican Republic	6,416,000	Santo Domingo* 1.3 million	18,704	Multi-party, centralized republic	Spanish
Ecuador Republic of Ecuador	9,091,000	Quito* 918,900 Guayaquil 1,278,900	108,624	Multi-party, republic	Quechau, Spanish, Jivaroan
Egypt Arab Republic of Egypt	47,000,000	Cairo* 5,084,463	385,201	Presidential regime	Arabic
El Salvador Republic of El Salvador	5,100,000	San Salvador* 400,000	8,124	Military-dominated	Spanish
Equatorial Guinea Republic of Equatorial Guinea	300,000	Malabo* 25,000	10,832	Military regime	Spanish, English, Fang
Ethiopia Socialist Ethiopia	31,998,000	Addis Ababa* 1,200,000	472,400	Military regime	Amharic, others
†Fiji Dominion of Fiji	700,000	Suva* 64,000	7,056	Parliamentary democracy	English, Fijan, Hindustani
Finland Republic of Finland	4,873,000	Helsinki* 490,204	130,119	Multi-party, parliamentary government	Finnish, Swedish
France French Republic	54,872,000	Paris* 2,296,945	210,040	Multi-party, Republic	French
French Overseas Departments:					
French Guiana	73,022		32,252		
Guadeloupe	314,800		687		
Martinique	328,566		425		
Mayotte	53,000		144		
Reunion	515,814		969		
St. Pierre and Miquelon	6,300		93		
French Overseas Territories:					
French Polynesia comprises 130 islands administered from Tahiti, including Society Islands, Windward and Leeward islands, Marquesas Islands, the Tuamotu Archipelago including the Gambler Islands, and the Austral Islands.	160,000		1,544		

NAME OF COUNTRY	POPULATION	CAPITAL* LARGEST CITY	AREA (SQUARE MILES)	GOVERNMENT	MAJOR LANGUAGES
France–continued					
French Southern and Antarctic Lands comprises Adelie Land and island groups in Indian Ocean, Kerguelen Archipelago, and Crozet Archipelago.					
New Caledonia	142,500		8,548		
Wallis and Futana Islands	11,943		106		
Gabon Gabonese Republic	958,000	Libreville* 225,200	103,347	1 party, presidential regime	French, Fange, Omyere
†The Gambia Republic of The Gambia	695,886	Banjul* 40,000	4,361	Republic	English, Mandinka, Wolof
Germany, East German Democratic Republic	16,718,000	East Berlin* 1,145,743	41,825	1 party, communist state	German
Germany, West Federal Republic of Germany	61,700,000	Bonn* 289,400 Berlin 2 million	96,011	Multi-party, federal republic	German
†Ghana Republic of Ghana	13,804,000	Accra* 998,800	92,098	Military government	English, Twi, Fanti, Ga
Greece Hellenic Republic	9,884,000	Athens* 3,300,000 (metropolitan area)	50,962	Multi-party, parliamentary government	Greek
†Grenada State of Grenada	113,000	St. George's* 30,813	133	After the U.S. invasion, Oct., 1983, government administered by a British Governor and a 9-man council until new elections could be held, presumably under a democratic constitution	English, French-African patois
**Guatemala Republic of Guatemala	7,956,000	Guatemala City* 1,307,300	42,042	Military government	Spanish, Indian languages
Guinea People's Revolutionary Republic of Guinea	5,579,000	Conakry* 575,000	94,925	1 party, presidential regime	French, Fulani
Guinea-Bissau Republic of Guinea-Bissau	842,000	Bissau* 109,500	13,948	Revolutionary council	Portuguese, Criouio
†Guyana Cooperative Republic of Guyana	900,000	Georgetown* 170,000	83,000	Multi-party, presidential regime	English, Hindi, Portuguese, Negro patois
Haiti Republic of Haiti	6,100,000	Port-au-Prince* 745,700	10,714	1 party, presidential regime	French, French-Creole
Honduras Republic of Honduras	4,424,000	Tegucigalpa* 472,700	43,277	Strong military influence	Spanish, Indian languages
Hungary Hungarian People's Republic	10,700,000	Budapest* 2,085,615	35,919	1 party, communist state	Hungarian
Iceland Republic of Iceland	239,000	Reykjavik* 84,600	39,769	Multi-party, parliamentary government	Icelandic, Danish
**India Republic of India	746,388,000	New Delhi* 5.2 million Calcutta 9.1 million	1,269,420	Multi-party, parliamentary government	Hindi, Urdu, English, and others
Indonesia Republic of Indonesia	169,442,000	Jakarta* 5,500,000	741,101	No parties, military government	Bahasa Indonesian (Malay), Javanese
Iran Islamic Republic of Iran	43,280,000	Teheran* 4,496,159	636,363	Islamic republic	Farsi Persian Kurdish
Iraq Republic of Iraq	15,000,000	Baghdad* 3,205,645	168,928	1 party, military government	Arabic, Kurdish
Ireland Irish Republic	3,575,000	Dublin* 525,360	27,137	Multi-party, parliamentary government	English, Gaelic

NAME OF COUNTRY	POPULATION	CAPITAL* LARGEST CITY	AREA (SQUARE MILES)	GOVERNMENT	MAJOR LANGUAGES
Israel State of Israel	4,100,000	Jerusalem* 398,000	8,219	Multi-party, parliamentary government	Hebrew, Arabic
Italy Italian Republic	57,400,000	Rome* 2.9 million	116,303	Multi-party, parliamentary government	Italian
Ivory Coast Republic of Ivory Coast	9,178,000	Abidjan* 1,686,100 (metropolitan area)	124,503	1 party, presidential regime	French, Mande languages
†Jamaica	2,388,000	Kingston* 671,000	4,244	2 party, parliamentary government	English
Japan	119,896,000	Tokyo* 8.2 million	145,809	2 party, parliamentary constitutional monarchy	Japanese
Jordan Hashemite Kingdom of Jordan	2,689,000	Amman* 684,600	37,297	1 party, constitutional monarchy	Arabic
Kenya Republic of Kenya	19,362,000	Nairobi* 959,000 (metropolitan area)	224,081	1 party, presidential regime	Swahili, Kikuyu, English, others
Kiribati Republic of Kiribati	61,000	Tarawa* 22,148	266	Parliamentary	English, Gilbertese, Ellice
Korea, North Democratic People's Republic of Korea	19,630,000	Pyongyang* 1,283,000	47,077	1 party, communist state	Korean
Korea, South Republic of Korea	41,999,000	Seoul* 8,000,000	38,211	Military rule	Korean
Kuwait State of Kuwait	1,758,000	Kuwait* 60,400 Hawalli 152,300	6,532	No political parties, constitutional monarchy	Arabic
Laos Lao People's Democratic Republic	3,732,000	Vientiane* 200,000	91,428	1 party, communist state	Lao, French, others
Lebanon Republic of Lebanon	2,700,000	Beirut* 1,100,000	3,950	Multi-party, parliamentary government	Arabic, French
Lesotho Kingdom of Lesotho	1,474,000	Maseru* 75,000	11,716	Multi-party, constitutional monarchy	English, Sesotho
Liberia Republic of Liberia	2,180,000	Monrovia* 306,000	38,250	Political activity suspended, military rule	English, African languages
Libya Socialist People's Libyan Arab Jamahiriya	3,684,000	Tripoli* 858,500	679,536	1 party, military government	Arabic
Liechtenstein Principality of Liechtenstein	27,000	Vaduz* 5,000	62	2 party, hereditary constitutional monarchy	German
Luxembourg Grand Duchy of Luxembourg	400,000	Luxembourg* 80,000	1,034	Multi-party, constitutional monarchy	French, German, Luxembourgian
Madagascar Democratic Republic of Madagascar	9,645,000	Antananarivo* 600,000	226,658	Political activity suspended, military government	French, Malagsy
Malawi Republic of Malawi	6,829,000	Lilongwe* 75,000 (metropolitan area)	45,747	1 party, presidential regime	English, Nyanja
Malaysia	15,330,000	Kuala Lumpur* 1,081,000 (metropolitan area)	127,316	Parliamentary democracy under a constitutional monarchy	Malay, English, Chinese, Dayak
†Maldives Republic of Maldives	173,000	Male* 32,000	115	Parliamentary government, limited democracy	Divehi
Mali Republic of Mali	7,562,000	Bamako* 620,000 (metropolitan area)	478,841	1 party, military government	French, Mande languages

NAME OF COUNTRY	POPULATION	CAPITAL* LARGEST CITY	AREA (SQUARE MILES)	GOVERNMENT	MAJOR LANGUAGES
†Malta	400,000	Valletta* 14,000	122	Multi-party, parliamentary government	Maltese, English, Italian
Mauritania Islamic Republic of Mauritania	1,700,000	Nouakchott* 250,000	398,000	Military government	Arabic, French
Mauritius	1,018,000	Port Louis* 146,884	787	Multi-party, parliamentary democracy under a constitutional monarchy (Queen Elizabeth)	English, French, Creole
**Mexico United Mexican States	77,659,000	Mexico City* 15 million	761,604	1 party, federal republic	Spanish, Indian languages
Monaco Principality of Monaco	28,000	Monaco-Ville* 1,700	0.73	1 party, constitutional monarchy	French
Mongolia Mongolian People's Republic	1,860,000	Ulaanbaatar* 435,400	604,247	1 party, communist state	Khalkha, Mongolian
Morocco Kingdom of Morocco	23,565,000	Rabat* 435,510 (Rabat-Sale) Casablanca 1,371,330	171,117	Multi-party, constitutional monarchy	Arabic, French, Spanish, Berber
Mozambique People's Republic of Mozambique	13,413,000	Maputo* 755,300	308,769	Marxist one-party state, committee rule	Portuguese, Bantu
†Nauru Republic of Nauru	8,000	Yaren* (no population figure available)	8	2 party, parliamentary government	Nauruan, English
Nepal Kingdom of Nepal	16,578,000	Kathmandu* 125,000	56,136	No political parties, monarchy	Nepali, others
Netherlands Kingdom of the Netherlands	14,437,000	Amsterdam* 712,294	16,464	Multi-party, parliamentary democracy under a constitutional monarchy	Dutch
Netherlands Antilles	253,300	Willemstad* On Curacao 50,000	385	Constitutionally on level of equality with the Netherlands within the Kingdom	
Curacao, Aruba, Bonaire, St. Eustatius, Saba, St. Maarten					
†New Zealand	3,238,000	Wellington* 342,000 Auckland 818,000	103,883	2 party, parliamentary government	English, Maori
**Nicaragua Republic of Nicaragua	2,914,000	Managua* 552,900	57,000	Five-member junta	Spanish
Niger Republic of Niger	6,284,000	Niamey* 300,000	490,100	Political activity banned, military government	French, Hausa
†Nigeria Federal Republic of Nigeria	88,148,000	Lagos* 1,404,000	356,700	Multi-party, federal republic	English, Housa, Ibo, Yoruba
Norway Kingdom of Norway	4,145,000	Oslo* 452,023	125,057	Multi-party, parliamentary constitutional monarchy	Norwegian
Oman Sultanate of Oman	1,009,000	Muscat* 50,000	115,800	No political parties, absolute monarchy	Arabic
Pakistan Islamic Republic of Pakistan	96,628,000	Islamabad* 201,000 Karachi 3,498,634	307,374	Military rule	Urdu, English, others
Panama Republic of Panama	2,101,000	Panama* 655,000	29,762	Military-dominated	Spanish, English
†Papua-New Guinea	3,353,000	Port Moresby* 116,900	178,704	Parliamentary government	English, Papuan

NAME OF COUNTRY	POPULATION	CAPITAL* LARGEST CITY	AREA (SQUARE MILES)	GOVERNMENT	MAJOR LANGUAGES
Paraguay Republic of Paraguay	3,623,000	Asunción 481,706	157,047	Presidential dictatorship	Spanish, Guarani
Peru Republic of Peru	19,157,000	Lima* 3.1 million	496,222	Multi-party, republic	Spanish, Quechua, Aymara
Philippines Republic of the Philippines	55,528,000	Quezon City* 1.1 million Manila is defacto capital 1.6 million	115,831	Multi-party, presidential regime	Tagalog, English, Spanish, others
Poland Polish People's Republic	36,887,000	Warsaw* 1.5 million	120,727	1 party, communist state	Polish
Portugal Republic of Portugal	10,045,000	Lisbon* 812,400	35,516	Multi-party, parliamentary government	Portuguese
Qatar State of Qatar	276,000	Doha* 190,000	4,247	No political parties, traditional Emirate	Arabic
Romania Socialist Republic of Romania	22,683,000	Bucharest* 1,861,007	91,699	1 party, communist state	Romanian
Rwanda Republic of Rwanda	5,836,000	Kigali* 156,650	10,169	No political parties, military government	Kinyawanda, French
St. Kitts-Nevis	52,000	Basseterre* 14,725	101	Multi-party, parliamentary government	English
†Saint Lucia	124,000	Castries* 45,000	238	Parliamentary government	English
†Saint Vincent and the Grenadines	138,000	Kingstown* 23,200	150	Multi-party, parliamentary government	English
San Marino Most Serene Republic of San Marino	23,000	San Marino* 3,000	24	Multi-party, parliamentary government	Italian
Sao Tomé and Principe Democratic Republic of Sao Tome-Principe	100,000	Sao Tome 25,000	372	1 party, republic	Portuguese, Bantu
Saudi Arabia Kingdom of Saudi Arabia	11,100,000	Riyadh* 1,793,000	830,000	No political parties, absolute monarchy	Arabic
Senegambia	6,700,000	Dakar* 978,553	79,750	Multi-party, parliamentary government created in 1982 from union of Senegal and Gambia; cabinets function separately.	French, English, Wolof, Mande
†Seychelles Republic of Seychelles	67,000	Victoria* 23,000	171	Single party, republic	Creole, English, French
†Sierre Leone Republic of Sierra Leone	3,805,000	Freetown* 500,000	27,699	1 party, presidential regime	English, African languages, Creole
†Singapore* Republic of Singapore	2,531,000	Singapore* 2,334,400	239	Multi-party, parliamentary government	English, Malay, Chinese, Tamil
†Solomon Islands	263,000	Honiara* 19,200	10,640	Multi-party, parliamentary government. Within the Commonwealth of Nations	Pidgin English, English
Somalia Somali Democratic Republic	6,393,000	Mogadishu* 400,000	246,300	No political parties, military government	Somali, Italian, Arabic
South Africa Republic of South Africa	31,698,000	Cape Town* (legislative) 213,830 Pretoria* (administrative) 528,407 Bloemfontein* (judicial) 230,688	435,868	2 party, parliamentary government (limited to white adults)	English, Africaans, Shosa, Zulu, Sotho

NAME OF COUNTRY	POPULATION	CAPITAL* LARGEST CITY	AREA (SQUARE MILES)	GOVERNMENT	MAJOR LANGUAGES
Namibia (South-West Africa)	1,038,000	Windhoek* 64,095	318,827	On Jan. 18, 1983, South Africa dissolved the Namibian General Assembly and assumed direct control of the territory	
**Spain Spanish State	38,435,000	Madrid* 3,520,320	194,885	Multi-party, parliamentary monarchy	Spanish
The Balearic and the Canary Islands are provinces of Spain					
†Sri Lanka Democratic Socialist Republic of Sri Lanka	15,925,000	Colombo* 585,776	25,332	Multi-party, parliamentary government	Sinhalese, Tamil, English
Sudan Democratic Republic of the Sudan	21,103,000	Khatoum* 333,921	966,757	1 party, presidential regime	Arabic, English, African languages
Suriname	420,000	Paramaribo* 67,700	63,037	Military government	Taki-Taki, Dutch, Spanish, others
†Swaziland Kingdom of Swaziland	651,000	Mbabane* 33,000	6,704	No political parties, constitutional monarchy	English, siSwati
Sweden Kingdom of Sweden	8,335,000	Stockholm* 1,386,980	179,896	Multi-party, parliamentary constitutional monarchy	Swedish
Switzerland Swiss Confederation	6,500,000	Bern* 145,000 Zurich 375,000	15,941	Multi-party, parliamentary government	German, French, Italian, Romansch
Syria Syrian Arab Republic	10,075,000	Damascus* 1,142,000	71,498	Multi-party, presidential regime	Arabic, Kurdish, Armenian
†Tanzania United Republic of Tanzania	21,202,000	Dar-es-Salaam* 700,000	364,886	1 party, presidential regime	Swahili, English
Thailand Kingdom of Thailand	51,725,000	Bangkok* 4.7 million	198,500	Political activity suspended, military government	Thai, Chinese, English, others
Togo Republic of Togo	2,926,000	Lomé* 283,000	21,853	1 party, presidential regime	French, African languages
†Tonga Kingdom of Tonga	106,000	Nuku'alofa* 19,900	270	No political parties, constitutional monarchy	Tongan, English
†Trinidad and Tobago Republic of Trinidad and Tobago	1,168,000	Port-of-Spain* 250,000 (metropolitan area)	1,970	2 party, parliamentary government	English, Creole
Tunisia Republic of Tunisia	7,202,000	Tunis* 1,000,000	63,378	1 party, presidential regime	Arabic, French
Turkey Republic of Turkey	50,207,000	Ankara* 1,877,755 Istanbul 2,772,708	300,948	Military rule	Turkish, Kurdish, Arabic
†Tuvalu	9,000	Funafuti* 2,200	10	Parliamentary government	English, Samoan, Gilbertese
†Uganda Republic of Uganda	14,268,000	Kampala* 458,000	91,104	Presidential regime	English, African languages
Union of Soviet Socialist Republics	272,500,000	Moscow* 8.2 million	8,649,490	1 party, communist state	Russian, and other languages
United Arab Emirates	1,523,000	Abu Dhabi* 449,000	32,000	Federal system, monarchs rule member states	Arabic
United Kingdom of Great Britain and Northern Ireland	56,100,000	London* 6,696,008	94,222	Multi-party, parliamentary constitutional monarchy	English, Welsh, Gaelic
British possessions: Channel Islands	130,000		75	Separate legal existence, lieut. gov. named by Crown	
Isle of Man	61,000		227	Lieut. gov. named by Crown	

NAME OF COUNTRY	POPULATION	CAPITAL* LARGEST CITY	AREA (SQUARE MILES)	GOVERNMENT	MAJOR LANGUAGES
Gibraltar	30,000			A dependency	
British West Indies:					
Montserrat	11,600		32	Possession	
Anguilla	7,000		35	Autonomous elected government	
Cayman Islands	18,000		102	Dependency	
Turks and Caicos Islands	7,000		193	Separate possessions	
Bermuda	54,893		21 (360 small islands)	A dependency	
South Atlantic Dependencies:					
Falkland Islands	1,800		4,700		
St. Helena	5,300		47		
Tristan da Cunha	262		40		
Ascension	1,179		34		
Asia and Indian Ocean Colony					
Hong Kong	5,287,000		35½	A Crown colony	
Pacific Ocean Colony					
Pitcairn Island	61		18	A colony	
**United States of America (For information on U.S. Possessions see pp. 341-344)	236,413,000	Washington, DC* 3,060,922 (metropolitan area) New York 9,120,346 (metropolitan area)	3,628,150	2 party, federal republic	English
Upper Volta Republic of Upper Volta	6,700,000	Ouagadougou* 200,000	105,869	Military junta	French, Mande, Voltaic languages
Uruguay Oriental Republic of Uruguay	2,934,942	Montevideo* 1,260,600	68,037	Political activity banned, military government	Spanish
†Vanuatu Republic of Vanuatu	130,000	Vila* 15,100	4,707	Multi-party, parliamentary government	English, French
Vatican State of Vatican City	1,000	Vatican City	108.7 acres	No parties, papal state	Latin, Italian
Venezuela Republic of Venezuela	18,700,000	Caracas* 2,700,000	352,143	Multi-party, federal republic	Spanish
Vietnam Socialist Republic of Vietnam	59,030,000	Hanoi* 2 million Ho Chi Minh City 3.5 million	127,207	1 party, communist state	Annamese, Chinese, French
Western Samoa	162,000	Apia* 33,400	1,101	2 party, parliamentary constitutional monarchy	Samoan, English
Yemen, North Yemen Arab Republic	5,500,000	Sanaa* 277,800	77,200	No parties, military government	Arabic
Yemen, South People's Democratic Republic of Yemen	2,147,000	Aden* 264,326	130,541	1 party, presidential council	Arabic
Yugoslavia Socialist Federal Republic of Yugoslavia	22,997,000	Belgrade* 1,300,000	98,766	1 party, communist state	Slovene, Macedonian, Serbo-Croat
Zaire	32,158,000	Kinshasa* 3,000,000	905,063	1 party, presidential regime	French, Swahili, Lingala
†Zambia Republic of Zambia	6,554,000	Lusaka* 538,000	290,586	1 party, presidential regime	English, Bantu
†Zimbabwe	10,500,000	Harare* 657,000 (metropolitan area)	150,873	Multi-party, parliamentary government	English, Shona, Sindebele

† (Before name of country) means it belongs in the Commonwealth of Nations formerly called the British Commonwealth. Some have monarchs other than Queen Elizabeth II, some are dictatorships, etc. The Commonwealth is simply a loose association of self-governing nations plus some colonies and protectorates.

** Some countries described as one-party or two-party systems may actually have more legal political parties, but they are not viable politically, i.e. Mexico has five, but only one has governed since 1929. Also, in the U. S. other parties come and go, but there are only two major parties.

Population figures in most cases are 1985 estimates.

The United Nations

The United Nations does not represent the first attempt at world cooperation. After World War I, President Wilson and others conceived the idea of a League of Nations, an organization devoted to the settlement of disputes and the prevention of war. The main defect of the League was that it had no independent strength with which to punish aggressor nations or to enforce the peace. The League's failure during the 1930s to stop Japan from attacking Manchuria and Italy from attacking Ethiopia and its inability to stop World War II marked the demise of this well-intentioned organization.

Throughout World War II, a realization was growing that a more effective international body would have to be created. The Atlantic Charter, signed in 1941 by President Roosevelt and British Prime Minister Churchill, stressed the concept of full cooperation between nations. Later twenty-six countries signed the Declaration of the United Nations which reasserted this concept. Conferences held in 1943 at Moscow and Tehran paved the way for an organization "... for the maintenance of international peace and security." Still later, representatives of the United States, the United Kingdom, China, and the Soviet Union met at Dumbarton Oaks, near Washington, D.C., to work out a more detailed blueprint for the new world organization, which they agreed to call the United Nations.

On April 12, 1945, one of the chief architects of the United Nations, Franklin D. Roosevelt, died. Two weeks after his death the San Francisco Conference met at the Opera House in that city. After eight weeks of hard work, delegates from fifty countries approved the Charter of the United Nations. The solemn signing took eight hours.

THE BASIC STRUCTURE OF THE UNITED NATIONS

"We the peoples of the United Nations determined to save succeeding generations from the scourge of war, which twice in our lifetime has brought untold sorrow to mankind ... do hereby establish an international organization to be known as the United Nations."

These are the words of the Preamble of the Charter of the United Nations. The Charter goes on to state the purposes of the organization and to describe its organization.

Purposes. The Charter sets forth three basic purposes:

1. To maintain international peace and security by preventing aggression and settling disputes peacefully.
2. To develop friendly relations among nations based on respect for equal rights and self-determination of peoples.
3. To achieve international cooperation in solving economic, social, cultural, and humanitarian problems and in promoting respect for human rights and fundamental freedoms for all.

In accordance with these purposes, all members agree to (1) settle disputes peacefully, (2) to refrain from threat or use of force against another state, and (3) to assist the United Nations in its undertakings and not to aid any state against which the United Nations is acting.

Bearing in mind the arguments which helped keep the United States out of the League of Nations, the Charter specifically states that there is to be no intervention in matters essentially within the domestic jurisdiction of any state.

Any amendment to the Charter must be approved by a two-thirds vote of the General Assembly and ratified by two-thirds of the members of the United Nations. The first amendments were ratified in 1965 and became effective on January 1, 1966. They increased the number of members of the Security Council and the Economic and Social Council.

Membership. The Charter provides that membership shall be "open to all ... peace-loving states which accept the obligations contained in the present Charter and which, in the judgment of the organization, are able and willing to carry out these obligations." Members are admitted by vote of the General Assembly upon recommendation of the Security Council.

As will be explained later, the permanent members of the Security Council have a veto. During the first ten years, the Soviet Union vetoed for membership every country it considered too favorable to the West, including Italy, South Korea, and Japan. At the same time, when the Soviet Union

United Nations—The San Francisco Conference, June 26, 1945

put up Hungary, Romania, and Bulgaria for membership, the majority on the Security Council voted them down as being "satellite states" under Soviet domination. In 1955, however, a "package deal" was arranged, and sixteen nations came in together. Since then a number of other nations, including the new nations of Africa, have been admitted, making a total membership of well over 140 nations.

THE GENERAL ASSEMBLY

The central body of the United Nations is the General Assembly. All member states are members of the Assembly, each having one vote, although each nation may send up to five representatives. Often called "the Town Meeting of the World," the General Assembly meets in annual, regular sessions, although special sessions can be called by the Secretary-General at the request of the Security Council or of a majority of the members of the United Nations.

The General Assembly can discuss and make recommendations on all matters within the scope of the Charter, except that it may not discuss issues which are at that time on the agenda of the Security Council. However, at the time of the Korean conflict in November 1950, the General Assembly adopted the "Uniting for Peace" resolution. This greatly increased the power of the General Assembly. It provided that if the Security Council should, because of the use of the veto by one of its permanent members, fail to act in a situation threatening international peace, then the General Assembly might hold an emergency session within twenty-four hours and recommend collective action, including the use of armed force. You may recall that it was the failure of the Council of the League of Nations to take action to halt aggression which weakened that organization's efforts. The

United Nations—Eighteenth Regular Session of the General Assembly

"Uniting for Peace" resolution was designed to prevent a repetition of that failure.

Decisions of the General Assembly on important matters, such as those involving the maintenance of peace, the admission of members, and the election of the nonpermanent members of the Security Council, are decided by a two-thirds majority. Other less important matters are decided by a simple majority.

THE SECURITY COUNCIL

The Charter places "the primary responsibility for the maintenance of peace and security" on the Security Council. It has fifteen members including five permanent members—China, France, the Union of Soviet Socialist Republics, the United Kingdom, and the United States—and ten nonpermanent members. Each year, the General Assembly elects five nonpermanent members for a two-year term. These nonpermanent members are not eligible for immediate reelection to the Security Council.

Although the Security Council meets periodically, it is set up so as to be able to function at any time. It is said to be "in continuous session," because each member is always represented at UN Headquarters.

Each member of the Security Council has one vote. Routine, or "procedural" matters, as the Charter says, are decided by an affirmative vote of any nine of the fifteen members. However, in all other cases, the five permanent members must either cast affirmative votes or abstain. The Security Council may not take action if any permanent member casts a negative vote on a substantive matter.

The power of veto in the Security Council means that no enforcement action will be taken against any permanent member, for no nation is likely to vote against itself. The veto was written into the Charter at the insistence not only of the Soviet Union, but of the United States as well, because of the fear that otherwise the United States Senate might not ratify the Charter.

The argument against the veto power is that its abuse by the Soviet Union has weakened the ability of the United Nations to act effectively. However, the "Uniting for Peace" resolution, as we have seen, provides a method by which the General Assembly can undertake to solve a problem when a veto in the Security Council blocks action.

It is important to remember that the main aim of the United Nations is not to fight any of its members but rather to provide machinery for peaceful settlement of disputes. Hence, the Security Council may call upon disputing nations to settle their dispute by such means as negotiation or by settlement by the International Court of Justice (see below). If the dispute is not settled, the Security Council may itself recommend a settlement.

The Council is given the authority, if all attempts at a peaceful settlement fail, to call upon the members of the United Nations, who are pledged to make armed forces available to the Security Council for land, sea, and air forces to use in blockades or "other operations" against the nation whose action is threatening the peace.

THE ECONOMIC AND SOCIAL COUNCIL

The founders of the United Nations were convinced that part of the job to be done by the international organization was the improvement of living conditions all over the world. Chapter IX of the Charter states that "the United Nations shall promote higher standards of living, full employment, conditions of economic and social progress . . . international, cultural, and educational cooperation . . . universal respect for . . . human rights and fundamental freedoms for all without distinction as to sex, race, language, or religion."

In accordance with these objectives, the Economic and Social Council (ECOSOC) was provided for. ECOSOC has members, elected annually for three-year terms in groups of eighteen by the General Assembly. The Council meets as often as necessary to perform its duties, usually for two sessions a year.

The functions of the Economic and Social Council are to make studies on international health, social, economic, cultural, and educational problems, and to make recommendations to the General Assembly on the basis of these studies. It may call international conferences on matters related to these fields. In connection with these very broad areas of interest, the Council often calls upon the cooperation of private organizations and experts to help in its work. The Specialized Agencies, which will be discussed in detail later, are brought into relationship with the United Nations through the Economic and Social Council.

United Nations—Trusteeship Council concludes examination of conditions in Tanganyika, July 13, 1961.

THE TRUSTEESHIP COUNCIL

When World War I ended, Germany's colonies were taken from her and handed over to various other nations for administration as "mandates." This meant that they were no longer to be considered colonies. Instead, the administering countries promised to rule them fairly and to report regularly to the League of Nations. After World War II, most of the mandates were transferred to the United Nations, whose Charter established a Trusteeship Council to supervise the governing of trust territories. The goal is to advance these territories to the point where they will be able to govern themselves or achieve complete independence.

Trust territories include, in addition to those formerly held as mandates under the League of Nations, territories taken from Axis powers after World War II and dependent territories voluntarily turned over to trusteeship by the nations controlling them.

The Trusteeship Council is made up of those United Nations members which administer trust territories and an equal number of those which do not. Included in the number, however, must be the five permanent members of the Security Council. The Trusteeship Council holds two regular sessions a year, as well as special sessions which may be required. Decisions are made by a simple majority vote.

As the number of trust territories gaining their independence has increased, the work of the Trusteeship Council has lessened. The members are charged with taking an active part in the governing of the remaining trust territories. Each year, the administering government has to report to the Council about economic, political, and educational progress made in the trust territory during the year. Thousands of petitions and complaints are received by the Council from people in trust territories all over the world. Special missions are sent out to territories to investigate conditions. The Council reports to the General Assembly on developments in the trust territories.

THE INTERNATIONAL COURT OF JUSTICE

The principal judicial organ of the United Nations is the International Court of Justice. It is the successor of the Permanent Court of International Justice, often called the World Court. Located at The Hague, Netherlands, it has fifteen judges, no two from any one nation. They are chosen by the Security Council and the General Assembly for nine-year terms. All members of the United Nations are automatically associated with the Court. Other nations may join upon the consent of the General Assembly and the Security Council.

The function of the Court is to decide points of international law over which a dispute may arise between nations. Only nations, not individuals, may bring a case before the Court. All United Nations members undertake to obey the Court's decisions. If a nation should fail to do so, an appeal may be made to the Security Council, which may take any action it sees fit. A nation may, if it wishes, promise in advance that it will always be ready to submit to the Court's decision in certain types of cases, provided the opposing nation does the same. The United States reserved the right to decide in each specific case whether it would allow

United Nations—Security Council meets on the Cypress Question, March 3, 1964.

the matter to come before the Court. The International Court of Justice may also give advisory opinions on legal questions which the other organs of the United Nations may submit to it.

The services of the Court have been extensively used by the members of the United Nations. Cases have involved disputes between Albania and the United Kingdom over damage to British warships by mine explosions in the Corfu Channel, between the United States and France over the rights of Americans in Morocco, between Cambodia and Thailand over ownership of a holy temple, and many others.

THE SECRETARIAT

The day-to-day work of the United Nations is entrusted to a staff known as the Secretariat. About four thousand people from all over the world make up the Secretariat. They do not represent their own nations but are bound by the Charter to serve as international public servants.

Members of the Secretariat make the arrangements for conference, draft reports, and collect information for use by the delegates. Skilled interpreters sit in soundproof boxes overlooking meetings of various UN bodies and provide simultaneous translations for transmission by the language earphones that are provided at every seat on the floor. No matter what language is being spoken, a delegate can hear a translation in English, French, Spanish, Russian, or Chinese.

At the head of the Secretariat is the Secretary-General. He is elected by the General Assembly on the recommendation of the Security Council for a five-year term. As the chief administrative officer of the United Nations, he serves all the main organs of the world organization except the Court. He reports annually to the General Assembly. He supervises the staff of the Secretariat, assisted by under-secretaries and other officials.

One of the most important roles of the Secretary-General arises out of his right to go before the Security Council at any time and call its attention to a situation which he regards as a threat to world peace. This places the Secretary-General at the center of most international disputes, in a position to exercise tremendous influence in world affairs. In 1960, for example, the Security Council passed a resolution giving Secretary-General Dag Hammarskjöld, who had succeeded Trygve Lie in the post, full authority for organizing a force to secure peaceful conditions in the newly independent Congo. On September 18, 1961, while he was en route to a meeting in Africa to strengthen peace efforts, Hammarskjöld was killed when his plane crashed in flames. His successors, U Thant of Burma and Kurt Waldheim of Austria, have continued to stress the fact that the Secretary-General must take the initiative in attempting to bring about permanent peace.

SPECIALIZED AGENCIES

Associated in a close relationship with the United Nations are agencies of various kinds that are not actually part of the world organization but are related to it by special agreements through the Economic and Social Council. These agencies are called the "Specialized Agencies" because each one has a special field of work, such as education, health, or finance. Although these agencies report regularly to the United Nations through ECOSOC, they are largely independent, each having its own membership, officers, treasury, and budget. Membership in the Specialized Agencies is not dependent upon United Nations membership. Consequently, the number of nations participating is not necessarily the same as the number of nations belonging to the United Nations.

About four billion people are in the world. It has been estimated that more than half of them are ill-fed or underfed or both. These are, in the main, the people of Asia, the Middle East, much of Africa, and large areas of Latin America. Much of the problem is due to primitive and unscientific methods of farming.

Nepal—Workers at Government Forest Nursery at Thankot

The problem of food shortages is not a new one. However, it has been complicated by the so-called "population explosion." The number of people in the world is increasing faster than ever before. In 1900, the population of the world was about one and a half billion people. Today, as we have seen, it is four billion. It is estimated that by the year 2000 there will be more than six billion people in the world.

The Food and Agriculture Organization is an agency concerned with improving the production, distribution, and consumption of food from agriculture and fisheries. Its work falls into three main classes: (1) collecting and distributing information from all over the world, (2) meetings and conferences of experts to discuss ways of solving the problem of food shortages, (3) sending experts to countries whose governments ask for help in developing food resources.

FAO's varied activities have been worldwide in scope. Fishermen in Chile have been helped to discover better fishing grounds. Farmers in Ethiopia have learned to fight animal diseases and those in the Middle East, to fight desert locusts. Sri Lanka was aided in the setting-up of timber mills. Tough grasses and hardy trees have been planted in the deserts of North Africa. Israeli farmers have been taught new methods of dairy farming.

It has been estimated that fully half of the people in the world are suffering from diseases that are preventable by knowedge, skills, and techniques already at hand. The problem is to find a way of bringing the knowledge to the place where it is needed. The World Health Organization was created to direct and coordinate health work in order to raise the health standards of people all over the world.

WHO sends public health experts and demonstration teams for disease control to countries requesting this service. It helps to train health workers of all kinds and provides hundreds of fellowships for doctors and nurses to study abroad.

The results of its efforts have been very impressive. In 1950, Indonesia asked for help against yaws, a crippling disease of which there were ten million victims in Indonesia. In four years, medical teams trained by WHO had cured 1,300,000 cases. Egypt has been helped in the fight against bilharziasis, a disease which used to cause one out of every five deaths in that country. Malaria-

Peru—A census-taker in the village of Chinchera

control teams have worked in all corners of the globe and millions of people have been vaccinated against a variety of dread diseases including polio, diphtheria, and yellow fever. WHO has also worked to encourage medical research into such areas as cancer and heart disease.

World War II resulted in the destruction of schools and colleges all over Europe. Even before the war ended, representatives of various nations met to make plans for rebuilding their educational systems after the war. An agency to coordinate this effort was to be set up. However, the idea of an agency devoted only to rehabilitation gradually changed to the notion that a permanent educational and cultural organization should be set up under the United Nations.

The preamble to UNESCO's constitution expresses the basic aim of the agency: "Wars begin in the minds of men, and it is therefore in the minds of men that the defenses of peace must be constructed." The idea has been put in another way: "One idea is worth more than a hundred thousand bayonets."

At present, there are six main items in UNESCO's program: (1) compulsory primary education, (2) scientific research for the improvement of living conditions, (3) the elimination of racial and social tensions, (4) the development of mutual appreciation by peoples all over the world of the culture of other peoples, (5) the growth in freedom of information, and (6) "fundamental education," meaning learning to live properly as regards diet and health, as well as to read and write.

In recent years UNESCO has engaged in several major projects. Latin American governments have been helped to increase primary education for the children of their countries. Scientific research for the development of natural resources in the arid zone from Morocco to India has been encouraged. Appreciation of Asian and Western cultural values, primarily through international visits and exchange of ideas, literature, and art, has been promoted. Teams of experts have gone out to India, Mexico, and Egypt to set up teacher-training institutes. An extensive fellowship program has been organized to promote the exchange of students and teachers. The first committee of the International Geophysical Year was organized with the help of UNESCO. An extensive survey of the Indian Ocean has been made in an effort to provide new sources of food for much of the world's population.

The International Labor Organization was founded in 1919 as part of the League of Nations. Its aim is ". . . universal and lasting peace . . . based upon social justice." It strives to persuade nations to improve labor conditions and living standards. It is made up of representatives of employers, labor, and the governments of the member nations. Its headquarters are in Geneva, with branch offices around the world.

A major part of ILO's work is the development of "Conventions" (or treaties) dealing with such matters as safety and health for workers, minimum age for employment, collective bargaining, and equal pay for equal work. These conventions are the product of long study and debate. They are submitted to the member governments for ratification. A country that ratifies binds itself to report each year on what progress it has made toward putting into effect the laws recommended by the Convention.

ILO also conducts training courses, does research, and publishes many economic and statistical reports. It cooperates with other Specialized Agencies in the task of raising living standards through advice on how to produce more and better goods. Recent studies by ILO have dealt with automation and its effects, protection of workers against radiation, and discrimination in employment.

In 1946, a new kind of bank was ready for business. Its aim was to help nations to finance the rebuilding of areas devastated by war and to aid underdeveloped nations. It was named the International Bank for Reconstruction and Development, with headquarters in Washington, D.C. Member nations bought stock in the Bank. Each has a representative on the Board of Directors, which meets once a year, and passes on all loans. The Bank lends money to member governments or to private enterprises where payment is guaranteed by the government. It will provide funds, however, only where it is reasonably sure that the loan can be paid back with interest and where private banks will not handle the loan. The Bank obtains funds not only from the sale of its stock but also by issuing bonds, which are bought by private investors in various countries.

The effects of the Bank's activities have been felt all over the world. The Pacific Railroad of Mexico was modernized with a very large loan. Through the Bank, Colombia added 190 miles of railway and Sri Lanka was able to build hydroelectric installations. India built a power plant near Bombay. Peru was helped to irrigate 125,000 acres of land. A loan helped Israel develop the Dead Sea Potash Works.

In 1960, a new agency, affiliated with the International Bank for Reconstruction and Development, was established. It was the International Development Association, set up to help finance economic growth to the less-developed countries. Its loans are made on very flexible terms, with long periods of repayment, low rates of interest, or no interest at all.

Another agency affiliated with the Bank is the International Finance Corporation. Like IDA, it is concerned with helping less-developed countries build dams, schools, hospitals, and roads. IFC aids economic development by encouraging productive private enterprise, in association with private investors, without requiring government guarantee of repayment. It has assisted in the development of private enterprises in Brazil, Chile, Pakistan, and Australia.

The International Monetary Fund works in close association with the Bank. In fact, a government must be a member of IMF in order to join the Bank. The Fund's purpose is to help a nation which is temporarily short of gold or foreign currency because its exports are not earning enough to pay for its imports. In such a case, the nation may buy the necessary foreign money from IMF, which has available the currency of all member nations. The Fund also provides technical assistance by sending experts who advise governments on monetary questions.

The basic aim of the International Civil Aviation Organization is to make flying from one country to another safer and easier. Its headquarters are in Montreal, but it holds regional meetings all over the world.

ICAO has drafted a set of rules and regulations to standardize international air operations, and immigration, customs, and health procedures at international airports. ICAO experts make recommendations to member governments regarding suitable airport sites and the improvement of weather information and of search and rescue operations. Much of its work is directed toward meeting new requirements for jet operations. Nations with inadequate roads or railways are helped to improve air service for quick and easy transportation.

The Universal Postal Union was set up in 1874 in Berne. It is now part of the United Nations. As a result of its work, several billion pieces of mail are carried safely from one country to another. The Union guarantees the delivery of mail under the established rates throughout the world and its return to place of origin, if it cannot be delivered.

Similar to the UPU is the International Telecommunication Union, which dates back to 1865. Although in its early days it was concerned largely with improving international telegraph service, today much of its work involves radio broadcasting. If stations in different countries were to broadcast on any wave length they wished to, radio communications among nations would be extremely difficult, since there would be a great deal of interference. To prevent this, ITU records the frequency assignments made by individual nations and tries to persuade them to agree on an orderly sharing of radio frequency bands.

The scientific study of weather conditions has become increasingly important in the age of the airplane, television, and radio. The World Meteorological Organization, with headquarters in Geneva, aims to collect and exchange, among weather stations all over the world, accurate meteorological information. It also provides technical assistance to member nations to improve

Bangladesh—Dacca, Bengali women learning to cut cloth and sew

weather forecasting services. It has recently added to its work the spreading of information based upon the observations of weather satellites.

In 1957, the International Atomic Energy Agency was established in order to help put the power of the atom to work for peaceful uses. Its headquarters are in Vienna. Unlike the other Specialized Agencies, IAEA is an intergovernmental agency which makes an annual report directly to the General Assembly.

IAEA supplies advice to nations wishing help in establishing atomic installations for peaceful purposes, and arranges for the exchange of atomic materials.

The Intergovernmental Maritime Consultative Organization (IMCO) began operations in 1958 with headquarters in London. It seeks to promote cooperation in regard to the regulation of ocean shipping and the improvement of safety at sea.

In force since 1948, the General Agreement on Tariffs and Trade seeks to reduce barriers to international trade. To aid developing countries, GATT set up the International Trade Center in 1964.

THE UNITED NATIONS IN ACTION

One evaluation of the work of the United Nations ended with this comment: "To measure the UN's contribution, one need only ask how much meaner and poorer, how much less touched by hope or reason, would be the world scene if it suddenly ceased to exist."

Since its establishment, the United Nations has done much to provide hope for people all over the world. In 1953, the United Nations Children's Fund, known as UNICEF, was set up as a permanent agency. It works with WHO and other Specialized Agencies to help children grow strong and healthy. UNICEF is supported by contributions from governments and from private persons and organizations.

Another program which coordinates the work of various Specialized Agencies is the Expanded Program of Technical Assistance (EPTA). A Technical Assistance Board, composed of the Secretary-General of the United Nations or his representative and the heads of the cooperating agencies, administers a special fund, which it distributes to be used for work that no agency by itself is equipped to undertake. By coordinating the work of WHO, WMO, ILO, FAO, and other agencies, TAB has provided training for doctors, nurses, and nutritionists, with the host government providing the hospitals and Specialized Agencies of the UN providing expensive equipment. Other projects have included providing engineers and other experts to help in town planning, in building dams and hydroelectric projects, and in setting up fisheries. In 1959, a new program called the Special Fund was established. It concentrates on a few large projects which are considered to be especially urgent. It is hoped that the success of these projects will open the way for investment of much larger sums by private business in countries that badly need new enterprises.

At its first meeting in 1946, the Economic and Social Council elected a Commission on Human Rights to draw up an international bill of rights for all people. On December 10, 1948, the Universal Declaration of Human Rights was unanimously adopted by the General Assembly. It proclaims that all people are born free and equal and are entitled to life, liberty, and security of person, the right to travel freely and live where they please, and freedom of speech, press, assembly, and worship.

ECOSOC has also worked for human welfare in other ways. Its Commission on the Status of Women has made a number of studies and recommendations to insure equality of rights and duties between men and women. Another commission of the Council is the Commission on Narcotic Drugs which works to strengthen control over international traffic in drugs.

A special committee of ECOSOC drafted the Genocide Convention, which the General Assembly adopted in 1958. This Convention is designed to outlaw the crime of *genocide,* defined as an attempt to destroy "a national, ethnical, racial, or religious group as such." A year later the Assembly unanimously adopted a Declaration of the Rights of the Child, which asserts the right of every child to be given proper food, shelter, medical care, and education, the right to play, and to be taught the spirit of universal brotherhood.

Another problem with which the United Nations has concerned itself has been aid to refugees. The UN Office of the High Commissioner for Refugees gives international protection to people driven out of their homelands. Refugees from Communist China, Morocco, Tunisia, Hungary, Israel, and East Germany have been given emergency relief and have been aided in finding homes and employment.

THE U.N. MEETS MANY CRISES

The United Nations has faced many serious crises, several of which could have resulted in a major war and in the destruction of the UN itself. The UN did not succeed in reaching a settlement in every one of these crises. It is important to remember, however, that a successful settlement depends upon the willingness of governments to cooperate in order to avoid war.

CHAPTER EIGHT

PHYSICS

Matter and Energy

When we look around us and examine the objects found in our homes, in the streets, in stores and factories, and in Nature everywhere, we realize that the things with which we are surrounded are made of a great variety of materials. Chemists have found that all complex substances—wood, steel, glass, plastics, even the waters of the ocean and the air we breathe—are mixtures of chemical **compounds.** Nearly a million compounds have been identified, and these, in turn, are merely different combinations of only about a hundred chemical **elements** known to science.

THREE FORMS OF MATTER

Some of the substances we meet are **solids,** such as iron or stone. Others are **liquids,** such as oil or water. Still others are **gases,** such as air or steam. These three conditions—solid, liquid and gas—are called the three **physical states** of matter. A solid object can be thought of as one that tries to keep a definite shape and a definite bulk, or volume. A liquid also has a definite volume, because it is almost impossible to pack it into any smaller space. But a liquid will take on the shape of *any* container into which it is poured (see Fig. 1). A gas, on the other hand, has neither a definite shape nor a definite volume: If some air is let into a chamber that was previously pumped out, this quantity of air will fill the whole space uniformly. Unlike water in a jar, a gas does not have a distinct surface.

Some common substances are mixtures of matter in several states. Fine sand or silt mixed with water will not settle out. It forms a **colloidal suspension**—a stable mixture of a solid and a liquid. Ink is another example. Milk is an **emulsion** —globules of one liquid (fat) suspended in another (water). **Foam** is a gas suspended in a liquid.

FIGURE 1. (Left) Definite volume, definite shape (Center) Definite volume, no definite shape (Right) No definite volume, no definite shape

Often, we know a single kind of matter in all three principal states. Water is a common example. Ordinarily, water is a liquid, but at low temperatures it goes into its solid state (called ice), and at higher temperatures it becomes steam, which is the name for the gaseous state of water. We usually think of air as a gas, but at about 300 degrees below zero it turns into a bluish liquid. Iron, commonly seen in the solid state, becomes a liquid in a foundry and is a gas in the sun and in the stars, where the temperature is many thousands of degrees. These are all **physical changes,** and the material keeps its identifying characteristics all the while. But when wood burns or cement hardens or cream turns sour there is in each case a more permanent change and new substances are formed. These are examples of **chemical change.**

GENERAL CHARACTERISTICS OF MATTER

In studying physics, we are not especially interested in the *special* properties of the many kinds of matter; this is the business of the chemist. What we do want to find out about are the *general* characteristics common to all kinds of matter. One of these is *permanence.* Experience shows that we can neither manufacture nor destroy matter. All we can do is to change it from one form to another by chemical processes like those mentioned.

Another general fact about matter is the obvious one that it *takes up space.* No two things can occupy the same space at the same time. A boat pushes aside the water as it passes and a chisel forces apart the fibers of a block of wood. Even air acts to keep other intruding material out, as you can see by performing a simple experiment:

EXPERIMENT 1: Float a small cork on water in a basin and push the open end of a tumbler down over it. The water surface inside the glass is found to be pushed down, as shown by the change in position of the cork. The same principle applies to the air pumped into the suit of a deep-sea diver or into a caisson used in underwater construction projects.

Sometimes we meet situations where two pieces of matter *do* seem to occupy the same space:

EXPERIMENT 2: Fill a glass brim full of water. Add salt, from a shaker, a little at a time. With care, a considerable amount of salt can be put in without making the water overflow.

The explanation here is that water—in fact, any substance—is not *continuous* matter; there are spaces between the water molecules, into which other molecules such as those of the salt can enter.

Another general property of material bodies that we shall have more to do with later on is called **inertia.** In some respects, this is the most fundamental of all the attributes of matter. It can best be described as the tendency for any object to stay at rest if it is at rest now, or—if in motion—to continue moving as it is now. When a car in which you are sitting starts up suddenly, you find yourself falling back into your seat. Nothing actually pushed you backward—your body merely tried to stay at rest, as it was originally. If, after getting under way the brakes are quickly applied, you pitch forward; your body obviously tries to persist in its previous motion.

EXPERIMENT 3: Place a heavy rock or a bucket of sand on a board resting on two pieces of pipe, which act as rollers. Tie one end of a piece of heavy cord to the weight and wrap the other end a few times around a short stick, to act as a grip (Fig. 2). A gentle pull on the string will make the board and its load glide along easily, and once in motion it will tend to keep going; but a *sudden* sharp jerk will break the string while hardly moving the weight at all.

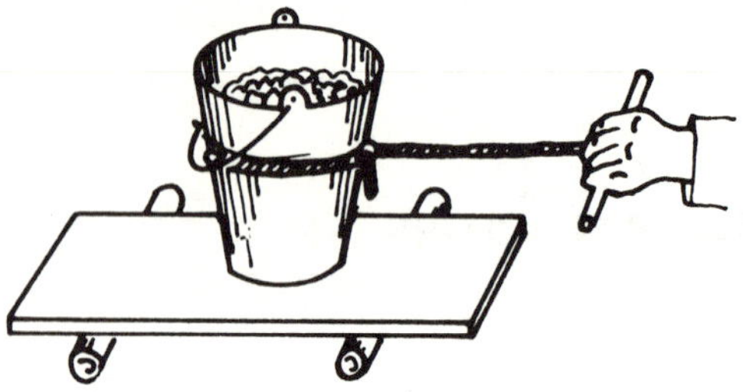

FIGURE 2.

Once in motion, the weight had a tendency to keep moving, but when at rest it strongly opposed any attempt to get it into motion.

MASS AND WEIGHT

Our experience points to the fact that the heavier a body is, the more it shows this property of inertia. Now what we call the **weight** of a body is simply the amount of the pull of the earth's gravity on it. This means that a body has weight only because it happens to be near a very large object like the earth. If a standard one-pound weight is moved farther from the earth's surface it weighs less—the earth does not pull it quite so hard. But if you think about the last experiment and others of a similar kind, you see that they would work equally well if the whole set-up were far away from the earth, so these inertia effects cannot depend directly on the *weight* of a body as such. They are found to depend only on the amount of matter in the body, and this is called its **mass.** In other words, the weight of a body depends on how near to the earth it is, while its mass would be the same anywhere in the universe, provided only that nothing is taken away from it or added to it.

For example, two bricks together have twice the mass of a single brick, but if the pair of bricks could be put on a spring scale at rest 1,600 miles above the earth's surface, their weight would be found to be only about that of a single brick at sea level.

And finally, the inertia of a body depends only on its mass, or how much material there is in it.

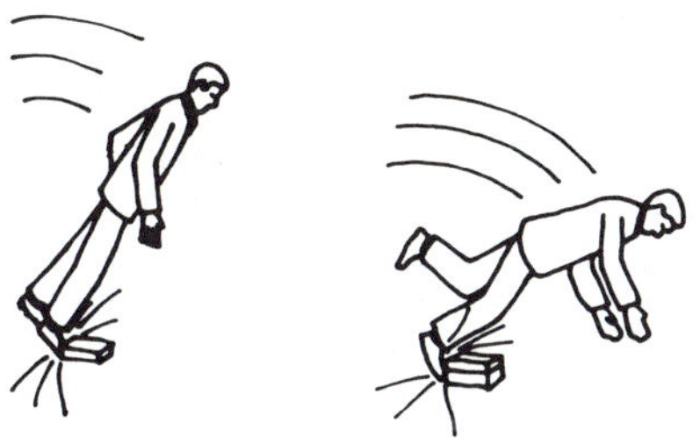

FIGURE 3. The greater mass has greater inertia

FORMS OF ENERGY

Besides matter, there are other things that we deal with in physics—things like electricity, light, sound, and heat. These are not kinds of matter, for they neither take up space nor have weight, in the usual sense. They are forms of **energy.** Energy is something that produces changes in matter. You saw that heat can change water from a liquid to a gas, for example. Light from the sun can fade the dye in cloth or form an image on a film in your camera. **Electrical energy** can turn a motor, put silver plating on a spoon, or send your voice over thousands of miles of space. **Chemical energy** heats your home and runs your car, and the action of atomic energy is known to everybody.

Probably the most familiar energy effects are the ones that are able to make bodies move or change their motion. This so-called **mechanical energy** has been called the "go" of things. A machine of any kind, whether it is a simple hand tool or a printing press or airplane, puts mechanical energy to work. Later you will learn how physicists measure energy exactly. But before we can measure anything as intangible as energy, we must find out how to measure some simpler things.

Systems of Measurement

Physics is known as an exact science, and this means that it is possible to make precise measurements of the things we talk about; we must not only know how to describe events and things but also be able to answer the question, "How much?" concerning them. From earliest times, people have found ways of specifying quantities such as the distance between towns, the interval of time between important events or the amount of goods bought and sold. To do this, they set up systems of measurement, based on convenient units of measure.

There are many types of measurement. Some are very direct and simple, others require great care and the use of highly complex instruments. But whatever it is that you wish to measure, you can do so only in terms of some chosen unit. And the unit must be the same *kind* of thing as the quantity that is to be measured.

MEASUREMENT OF LENGTH

For example, take the simplest kind of measuring operation—finding the *length* of an object. Before you can express the result, you must have a length **unit,** such as the inch, yard or mile. The size of the unit is arbitrary. You may choose it any way you like, but once you select it, you must stick to it as a standard. Historians are not absolutely certain how the Standard Yard was originally selected, but that is not important. In the English system of measure, which is used in civil affairs in all English-speaking countries, the Standard Yard is taken to be the distance between the end marks on a certain bronze bar kept in a vault at the Office of the Exchequer in London. It is assumed that all goods sold by length are measured by a stick or tape that has been marked off according to the Standard Yard through copies that are kept in the bureaus of standards of the various countries.

In the last paragraph, inches, yards and miles were mentioned. Why have more than one length unit? Simply for convenience in measuring things of very *different* lengths. To express the length of a pencil, the inch would be the most suitable unit; to give the distance between two cities, you would use the mile. The pencil *could* be measured in miles, but the number you would get would be ridiculously small. Similarly, expressing the distance between towns in inches would lead to an inconveniently large number. Always try to choose a unit that is not too different in order of magnitude from the thing you are measuring.

THE METRIC SYSTEM: THE METER

The sizes of the various length units in the English system do not seem to be related in any simple way. They are arbitrary, and it is necessary to remember that there are 12 inches in one foot, 3 feet in a yard, 5,280 feet in a mile, and so on. This makes it difficult to change a measurement from one unit to another; it would be much simpler if we had a system where all conversions went by *multiples of ten.* Then, in order to change units you would only have to move the decimal point the proper number of places. Such a scheme was set up about 150 years ago and is called the **Metric system.** It is now the accepted system of measure in all scientific work in all countries.

The fundamental length unit in the Metric system is the **standard meter.** It is the distance between the ends of a certain bar of platinum alloy kept at the International Bureau of Weights and Measures in France. Copies of this bar are carefully kept in other countries. The meter is a little longer than the yard—39.37 inches, to be precise.

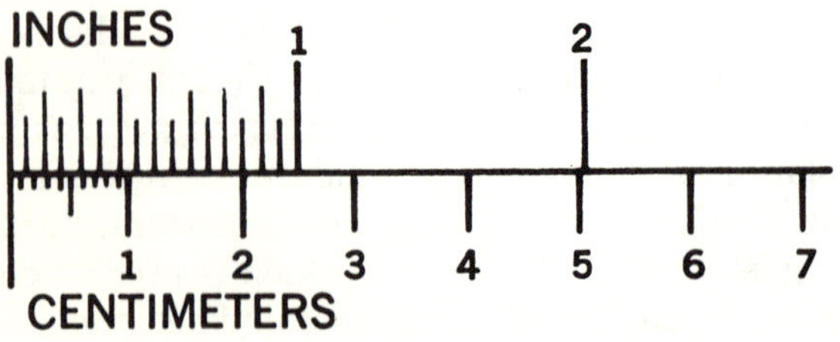

FIGURE 4.

The following table gives the most commonly used Metric units of length. Notice that the name of each is formed by putting a distinguishing prefix to the word "meter." For instance, a centimeter is 0.01 meter, and a kilometer is 1,000 meters. The standard abbreviations and the relations to the English system are also given.

TABLE 1
METRIC UNITS OF LENGTH

1 kilometer (km)	= 1,000 meters
1 METER (m)	= PRIMARY UNIT
1 centimeter (cm)	= 0.01 meter
1 millimeter (mm)	= 0.001 meter

1 km = 0.621 mile; 1 m = 39.4 in.;
2.54 cm = 1 in.

EXAMPLE 1: The table shows how easy it is to change from one length unit to another in the Metric system. Suppose a rug was measured as 0.0012 km long. This is a small decimal, and it would be easier to judge the size of the result if it were written in terms of a smaller unit, say the centimeter. Since there are 100 cm in a meter and 1,000 m in a kilometer, there will be 100 × 1,000, or 100,000 cm in a kilometer. Then our 0.0012 km will amount to 0.0012 × 100,000, or (moving the decimal point five places to the right to multiply by 100,000), 120 cm. Equally well, we could write it as 1.20 m.

By comparison, see how much more arithmetical work is needed to change, say, 1.47 miles to inches: There are 12 in. to 1 ft and 5,280 ft in a mile, so we will have to multiply all three numbers together to get the result: 12 × 5280 × 1.47 = 93,100 in.

Notice, incidentally, that while actual multiplication gives us 93,139.2 we rounded off to 93,100. This is because the 1.47 is given only to 3 **significant digits,** so it would be meaningless to write the final result to any more than this number. This remark applies regardless of where the decimal point happens to come in a final result.

EXPERIMENT 4: Measure the thickness of a single page of this book by finding how many sheets are needed to extend ½ inch along the edge of a ruler. In order to count the sheets, make use of the page numbering. If you start at page 1, the last page number in the stack will be the number of sheets making up a 1-inch thickness.

MEASUREMENT OF AREA AND VOLUME

In order to measure area (or surface) we need an arbitrary unit that is itself an area. It is simplest to choose this area to be a square, and we can avoid introducing anything really new by making the side of this square equal in length to one of our previous length units. Thus for area measurement we have square inches, square feet, square centimeters, square kilometers, etc. To write abbreviations for the area units we use *exponents* as a shorthand notation. Square centimeters is written cm^2, square inches is in^2, and so on, but these abbreviations are still to be read aloud as "square centimeters" and "square inches."

EXAMPLE 2: How many square centimeters are there in a rectangular strip of film $1\frac{1}{8}$ in. wide and 40 in. long?

SOLUTION: The area of the film, in square inches, is $1\frac{1}{8} \times 40 = 45\ in^2$. According to Table 1, 1 in = 2.54 cm, so $1\ in^2 = 2.54 \times 2.54 = 6.45\ cm^2$. Multiplying 45 by 6.45 gives the result $290\ cm^2$. (Are you perfectly clear as to why the two numbers had to be *multiplied* together to get the result?)

Bulk or **volume** requires a cubical unit for its measurement. Thus there are cubic centimeters (cm^3), cubic feet (ft^3), etc. In all, volume measurement goes very much like length and area measurement. There is a special name given to a Metric unit of volume equal to $1{,}000\ cm^3$. It is called a **liter** (pronounced "leeter"), and is just larger than a U.S. liquid quart.

MEASURING MASS AND WEIGHT

The fundamental Metric standard of mass is the **kilogram,** a cylinder of platinum alloy kept at the International Bureau of Weights and Measures. The kilogram was set up to be the mass of 1,000 cm^3 of water, thus referring the standard of mass to the standard of length through the choice of a standard substance, water. As in the case of length measure, additional units are specified, differing from each other by powers of ten. Table 2 gives the commoner Metric mass units, their abbreviations, and how they are related to the English units:

TABLE 2
METRIC UNITS OF MASS

1 metric ton	= 1,000 kilograms
1 KILOGRAM (kg)	= PRIMARY UNIT
1 gram (gm)	= 0.001 kg
1 milligram (mg)	= 0.001 gm

1 kg = 2.2 lb   454 gm = 1 lb   1 oz = 28.4 gm

When we weigh an object, we balance it against copies of the standard mass units. What we are doing, fundamentally, is comparing the mass of the object with that of the standard, using the earth's attraction (weight) to do so. If we use a spring scale instead of a balance scale, both weighings must be made at the same place. Since weighing is a convenient method of comparing masses, both the weight of an object and its mass may be represented by the same number and in the same units.

TIME

All events that happen in Nature involve the idea of time, so we must also have a way of measuring this quantity. Fortunately, both the English and Metric systems use the same fundamental time unit, the **second.** Basically, time is measured by the turning of the earth, and clocks are merely devices made to keep step with this motion. The time of a complete turn, one **day,** has been divided into 24 hours, each containing 60 minutes and each minute containing 60 seconds. That is, there are $24 \times 60 \times 60 = 86{,}400$ seconds in one day. Additional units differing from the second by powers of ten are not in general use.

More recently, the second has been rigorously defined in terms of the motion of the earth in its orbit around the sun. For practical purposes, the difference can be ignored.

DERIVED UNITS; DENSITY

Up to this point you have become acquainted with units for measuring length, mass and time. These are sometimes called **fundamental units** because the great variety of other quantities that we meet in physics can be expressed as combinations of them. We already had two kinds of **derived units**—area and volume, which are both based on simple combinations of the length unit.

As a further example, let us have a look at a useful quantity called **density.** Everybody realizes that a given volume of one material has, in general, a different weight than the same volume of some other material. For instance, we ordinarily say that iron is "heavier" than wood. More exactly, we should say that *any given volume* of iron is heavier than *the same volume* of wood. To make the comparison exact, we can weigh a certain volume of iron, say 1 cubic foot. When this is done, the weight is found to be about 490 lb. By comparison, the weight of a cubic foot of pine wood is around 30 lb. We say that the density of iron is 490 pounds per cubic foot (written lb/ft^3), while that of the wood is 30 lb/ft^3. The density of water in these units turns out to be 62.4. In the Metric system, because one kilogram was chosen to be the mass of 1,000 cm^3 of water, the density of water is 1,000 gm per 1,000 cm^3, or simply 1 gm/cm^3. This is equivalent to 1,000 kg/m^3.

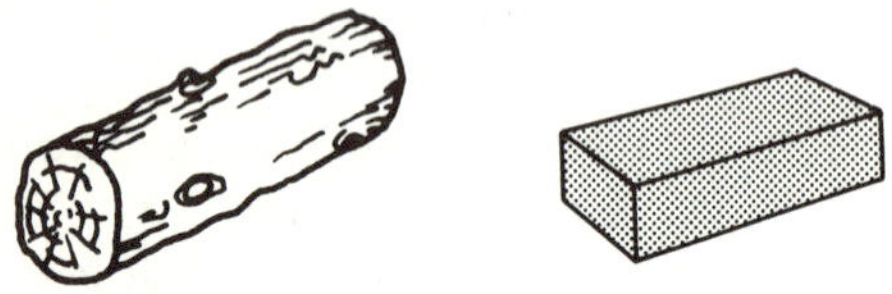

FIGURE 5. The log weighs twice as much as the brick, although brick is over three times as dense as wood

In general, then, the **density** of a substance is the **weight** (or, numerically, **mass**) of any portion of it **divided by** the **volume.** Stated as a formula,

$$D = \frac{M}{V},$$

where D stands for density, M for mass and V for volume. Of course this equation may be solved for either M or V as well:

$$M = DV, \qquad \text{or} \qquad V = \frac{M}{D}.$$

TABLE 3
DENSITIES OF SEVERAL MATERIALS

Substance	*D, lb/ft³*	*D, gm/cm³*
Aluminum	170	2.7
Iron	490	7.9
Lead	700	11.3
Gold	1200	19.3
Limestone	200	3.2
Ice	57	0.92
Wood, pine	30	0.5
Gasoline	44	0.70
Water	62.4	1.00
Sea Water	64	1.03
Mercury	850	13.6
Air*	0.08	0.0013
Hydrogen*	0.0055	0.00009

EXAMPLE 3: What is the weight (mass) of a block of ice measuring $1 \times 1\frac{1}{2} \times 3$ ft?

SOLUTION: From these dimensions, the volume of the block is 4.5 ft^3. The table gives the density of ice as 57 lb/ft^3. Then, using $M = DV$ we get $M = 57 \times 4.5 = 256$ lb.

EXPERIMENT 5: Find the density of a stone from its weight and volume. First weigh the stone on a household scale or postal scale and record the weight in pounds. Then put some water in a straight-sided jar or glass, mark the level on the side, carefully put the stone into the water, and mark the new water level (Fig. 6). The volume of the stone will be the same as the volume of the displaced water. You can compute this, because the volume is that of a cylinder whose base is the cross-section of the jar, and whose height is the rise in water level. Measure the rise and also the inside diameter of the jar in inches. The volume, in *cubic feet,* is given by

$$\frac{\pi\,(\text{diameter})^2\,(\text{height of rise})}{4 \times 12^3},$$

where $\pi = 3.14$. Finally, divide the weight of the stone, in pounds, by the last result to get the density in pounds per cubic foot.

FIGURE 6.

*Measured at standard temperature and pressure

Liquids

Many familiar devices and machines make use of physical principles applying to liquids.

LIQUID PRESSURE

A liquid, such as water, pushes on the sides as well as on the bottom of the container in which it rests. A wooden barrel or water tank has to be reinforced with hoops to resist the sidewise force, and the sides of a cardboard carton of milk bulge out. But it is also true that a liquid at rest presses *upward* on anything placed in it:

EXPERIMENT 6: Push the closed end of a tumbler or empty tin can beneath the surface of water in a bowl and you will actually feel the upward thrust of the water on the bottom.

Here we talk for the first time about **force.** What is a force? It is quite correct to say that a force is a push or a pull, but we want some way of measuring the *amount* of push or pull. Suppose a ten pound weight is resting on a table. Then it is reasonable to say that this object is *exerting a downward force of 10 lb* on the table top. This means that we can measure forces, at least downward ones, in *weight units,*—in pounds or grams, in kilograms or even in tons. And by means of simple arrangements such as strings and pulleys, or even liquids themselves, we can use weights to exert measured amounts of force in any direction we wish. Such devices will be described later.

The next question is, "What is pressure?" In everyday affairs, the terms "pressure" and "force" are used loosely to mean the same thing; here we must be a little more careful. **Pressure** is measured by the **force** divided by the **area** of the surface on which it acts. For example, if the ten pound weight mentioned above has a bottom area of 5 in^2 (square inches) and makes even contact with the table top all over this face, then the pressure between it and the table amounts to $10 \text{ lb}/5 \text{ in}^2 = 2 \text{ lb/in}^2$ (pounds per square inch). If the weight were standing on another one of its faces, say one that had an area of only 2.5 in^2, the pressure would then be $10 \text{ lb}/2.5 \text{ in}^2$, or 4 lb/in^2—twice as much as before, because the same force is spread over only half the area (see Fig. 7). In general, we can say

$$p = \frac{F}{A},$$

where p is the pressure, F the force and A the area. Notice that pressure is an example of a derived quantity. It is a combination of the weight unit and the length (area) unit. Pressure can also be measured in lb/ft^2, kg/cm^2, etc.

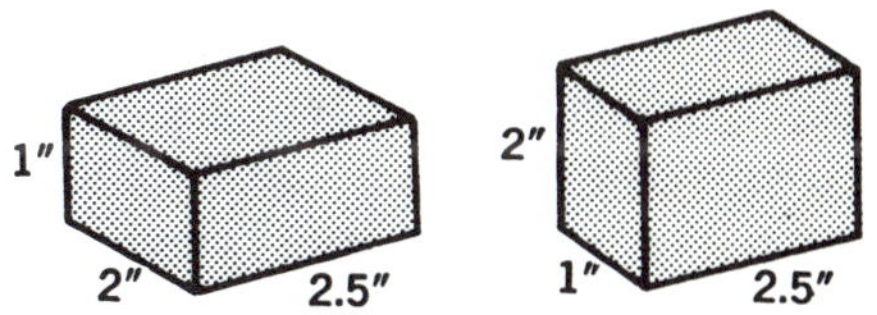

FIGURE 7. Pressure depends on area of contact

Pressure Depends on Depth

At any point within a liquid that is at rest, the pressure is the same in all directions—up, down or sidewise. This is obvious, because if you think of any interior drop of liquid, it is at rest and so must be pushed equally from all sides by the surrounding liquid.

Furthermore, the amount of pressure at any point in a liquid standing in an open vessel increases with the depth of that place beneath the top surface. Prove this by an experiment:

EXPERIMENT 6a: Punch several clean nail holes at various heights along the side of a tall can or milk carton, put the container in a sink and fill it with water. A curved stream comes from each opening, but those from the lower holes extend straighter, showing that the water pressure is greater lower down.

Think of a tall, tubular jar whose cross-section area is just 1 in^2. If you pour a given amount of water into it, say 1 lb, the force on the bottom will be just 1 lb. Since the bottom area is 1 in^2, the pressure will amount to 1 lb/in^2. Now pour another pound of water in. The liquid is twice as deep as before. The bottom now supports 2 lb of liquid, so the pressure on it is 2 lb/in^2. Reasoning this way, we see that the **pressure** at any point in a free-standing liquid **is directly proportional to the depth** below the surface. This means that if you go twice as far beneath the surface, the pressure becomes exactly twice as great as before; if you go three times as deep it becomes three times as great, and so on.

The depth referred to is the depth measured *straight down* from the level of the free surface of the liquid to the level of the place in question. Even if the vessel or pipe slants, this is the way the depth is to be taken. In the vessel shown in Fig. 8, the free surfaces in the two tubes stand at the same level, because pressure depends only on vertical depth and not on the size or shape of the container. Since no water flows one way or the other at the place where the tubes join, the pressure there must be the same from both sides, and so must the depth. For the same reason, the water stands at the same level in a teapot and in its spout (Fig. 1), even though there is much greater *weight* of water in the pot than in the spout.

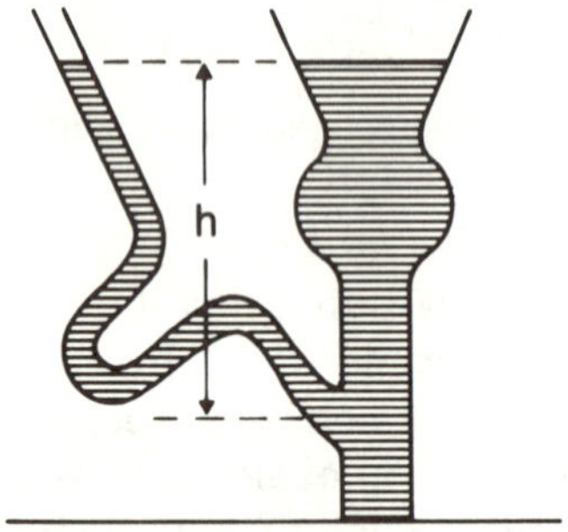

FIGURE 8.

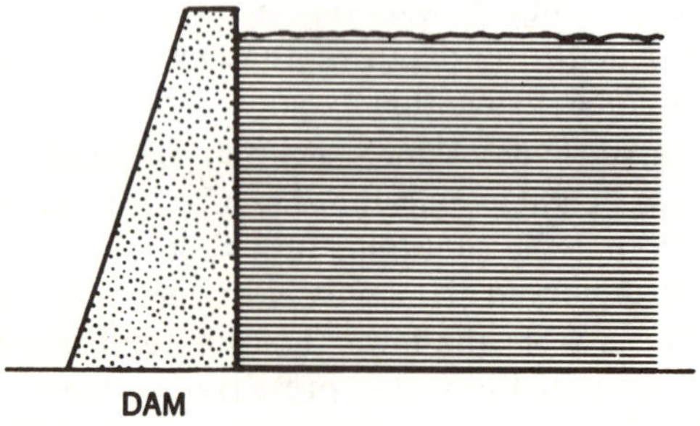

FIGURE 9.

If there is a small hole in a dike at a point 10 ft below the water surface, does it take a greater force to keep the hole closed if the body of water is the Atlantic Ocean than it does if it were a small pond? Why?

COMPUTING THE PRESSURE

There is a simple way to get a formula for figuring the amount of pressure at any point in a liquid. You already know that the pressure is proportional to the depth. It must also be proportional to the density of the liquid. This is because pressure is caused by the weight of the liquid, and doubling the density would double the weight of any column of liquid. So we get the result that

$$p = hD,$$

where p is the pressure at any point in the liquid, h is the depth of that place below the surface, and D is the density of the liquid.

EXAMPLE 4: What is the pressure on the side of a dam at a point 20 ft vertically below the water surface?

SOLUTION: In the formula $p = hD$ we put $h = 20$ ft and (from the table on p. 21), $D = 62.4$ lb/ft^3, getting $p = 20 \times 62.4 = 1{,}248$ lb/ft^2. Notice that since h was given in feet, we had to use the density in corresponding units, that is, in pounds per cubic *foot*. The result is then in pounds per square foot. Now that we have the answer, we are at liberty to change it to any other units we like. Very often, pressure in the English system is given in pounds per square *inch*. Since there are 144 square inches in a square foot, we can change our result to these units by dividing by 144. Then we have $p = 1{,}248/144 = 8.67$ lb/in^2.

EXAMPLE 5: What is the *total force* on the bottom of a swimming pool 80 ft long and 25 ft wide, filled to a depth of 5 ft? What is the force on one of the sides?

SOLUTION: The total force is the pressure (force per unit area) multiplied by the area on which it acts. Then $F = hDA$, or $F = 5 \times 62.4 \times 80 \times 25 = 624{,}000$ lb, or 312 tons. The pressure on a side will vary from zero at the surface to its greatest value at the bottom. To get the total force on a side, we must then use the *average* pressure, or the pressure *half way down*. In this case, we must take $h = 2.5$ ft. Then $F = 2.5 \times 62.4 \times 80 \times 5 = 62{,}400$ lb $= 31.2$ tons.

Applications of Fluid Pressure

The water supply for a town is often pumped from a lake or reservoir to a *standpipe* (Fig. 10), from where it flows down to the water in the mains and is distributed to the houses. The height of the water in the standpipe produces the pressure that moves the water along the piping and delivers it to the places where it is used. If a building is taller than the standpipe level, there must be an auxiliary pump to supply water to the upper floors.

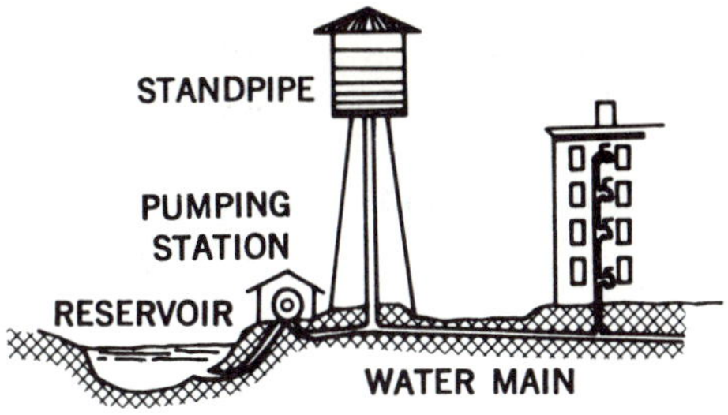

FIGURE 10

Some of the most important applications of liquid pressure use the pressure of confined liquids, rather than merely the weight of a liquid with a free surface. Any extra pressure applied to a confined liquid will be transmitted to all parts of the container. This is the principle of the **hydraulic press** (Fig. 11). Pressure is applied mechanically to a small piston, and this same amount of pressure then acts on every part of the inside surface of the system, including the large piston. But if the area of the larger piston is, say, 100 times that of the smaller one, the total force on the large one will be 100 times whatever force is applied to the small piston. Such presses are used in making bricks, glassware or metal parts and in stamping out automobile bodies. Large machines of this kind may be capable of exerting forces of 10,000 tons or more. The **car lift** used in a greasing station and the barber chair are other examples of the hydraulic press. In the car lift the pressure source is a tank of compressed air, while in the barber chair it is a small pump operated by a foot pedal.

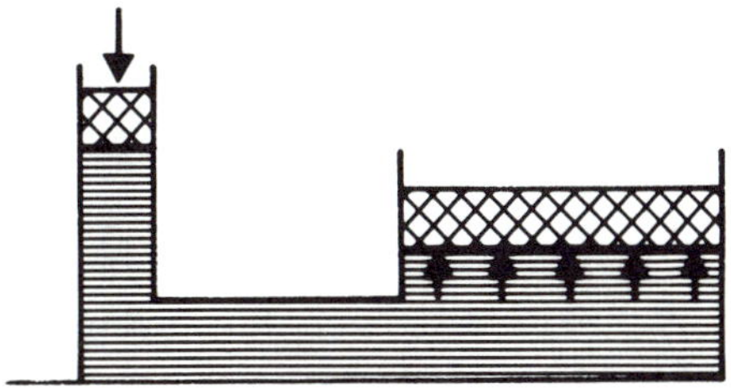

FIGURE 11. Hydraulic press

BUOYANCY AND FLOTATION

We saw that, at any place, a liquid exerts pressure equally in all directions, even pushing upward on the bottom of an object immersed in it. Think of a brick-like body hung in water, its sides being in a vertical position (Fig. 12). First of all, the pairs of pressure forces on the opposite sides cancel out. Also, since pressure increases with depth, the upward force on the bottom of the brick will be greater than the downward force on the

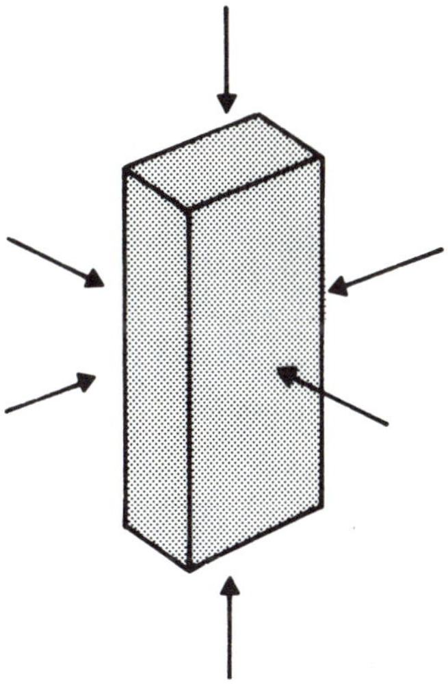

FIGURE 12

top. This means that there is a net *lifting* force—the brick is *lighter* when in water than it would be out in the air. This is true, of course, for an object of any shape immersed in any liquid.

The existence of such a lifting force is referred to as **buoyancy.** A large rock is easily lifted from the bottom of a pond, but becomes heavy the moment it clears the surface of the water. Sitting in a well-filled bathtub, you can support your whole weight by means of your fingertips. Nearly twenty-two centuries ago the Greek philosopher Archimedes discovered, in just this way, the scientific law governing buoyancy: **Any object immersed in a liquid appears to lose an amount of weight equal to that of the liquid it displaces,** or pushes aside. For instance, a stone having a volume of one-half cubic foot will displace 0.5 ft^3 of water, which weighs $\frac{1}{2} \times 62.4$, or 31.2 lb. Under water, then, this stone will weigh 31.2 lb less than when out of water. If a body is able to *float* in water, it means that the buoyant force is equal to the *whole* weight of the body. In this instance, the object seems to have lost its entire weight.

EXPERIMENT 7: Weigh an empty, corked bottle. Also weigh a pie tin. Put a pot in the pie tin and fill the pot brim full of water. Now lower the bottle carefully into the water, letting it float there. Remove the bottle, then the pot, and weigh the pie tin along with the water that overflowed into it. You will find the weight of water equal to the weight of the bottle, proving Archimedes' law for floating bodies.

It turns out that a body will float if its density is less than that of the liquid, otherwise it will sink. By looking at Table 3, you will then understand why wood, ice and gasoline can float on water, while iron, stone and mercury sink.

EXPERIMENT 8: A fresh egg does not float in water, because its overall density is greater than that of water. Dissolve 2 tablespoonfuls of salt in a glassful of water and the egg will now float because dissolving the salt increased the density of the liquid, making it greater than that of the egg.

Long ago, the suggestion to build ships of iron was ridiculed because everybody knew that "iron is heavier than water." Actually, the overall density of a steel ship—its total weight divided by its total volume—is less than that of water, because the interior is hollow and largely empty. The total weight of a ship is called its **displacement,** because we have seen that its weight must be just equal to that of the water displaced, or pushed aside by it.

EXAMPLE 6: A ship has a volume of 230,000 ft^3 below the water line. What is its displacement?

SOLUTION: It will displace $230{,}000 \times 64 = 14{,}720{,}000$ lb, or 7,360 tons of salt water.

EXAMPLE 7: A rectangular block of wood measures $20 \times 20 \times 5$ cm. When floated flatwise, it is found that 3 cm of the short side is under water. What is the density of the wood?

SOLUTION: The block will sink until it just displaces its own weight of the liquid. The weight of water displaced will be $20 \times 20 \times 3$, or 1,200 gm, since water has a density of 1 gm/cm^3. Then the density of wood will be this weight divided by the volume of the whole block, or $1{,}200/20 \times 20 \times 5$, which comes out equal to 0.6 gm/cm^3. We sometimes use the term **specific gravity** to indicate the density of a material relative to water. Since the density of water is 1 gm/cm^3, this is numerically the same as the specific gravity; but in the English system, the density must be divided by 62.4 to get the specific gravity.

Applications of Flotation

When the lungs are filled with air, the human body has a slightly smaller overall density than water, and so can float. But, as every swimmer knows, the body must be almost completely immersed in order to displace a large enough weight of water.

A submarine can be made to descend or rise by pumping water into or out of its ballast tanks.

EXPERIMENT 9: Get a tall jar with a flexible metal screw top and fill it with water. Fill a small glass vial about two-thirds with water, close the end with the thumb, and invert into the jar of water. Adjust the amount of water in the vial very carefully, drop by drop, until it just floats. At this stage the slightest downward push should send it to the bottom momentarily. Now fill the jar to the brim and screw the cap on tightly. When you push down on the cover with your thumb, the vial will sink to the bottom: release the pressure and it comes to the top. The explanation of the action of this miniature submarine is that pressure applied to the lid is transmitted to the water, forcing slightly more water into the vial. Its overall density is then just greater than that of water, and it sinks. Releasing the pressure allows the air in the top of the vial to push the extra water out again and the vial rises.

According to an old sailors' superstition, a sinking ship will not go all the way to the bottom but will remain suspended somewhere in the depths. This is false, because when enough water has entered the hull to make the overall density of the ship greater than that of water, it keeps sinking until it hits the bottom. If it is denser than water when at the surface, it must continue to be so even at great depths, since water is practically impossible to compress. Even at the deepest spot in the ocean, where the water pressure is almost 8 tons per square inch, water is compressed by only about 3 percent of its bulk.

The depth to which a floating body immerses itself in a liquid can be used as a measure of the density of the liquid. A tall stick or tube, with one end weighted so that it floats upright, can have a scale marked on its side to read the density directly. This is a **hydrometer,** familiarly used to measure the density of the solution in car batteries (the density is a measure of the condition of charge of the battery).

The Air and Other Gases

Although we are not generally aware of it, air has mass. This can be checked directly by weighing a closed bottle of air, then pumping it out and weighing again. For a 1-liter bottle, the difference amounts to more than a gram.* The fact that air has mass becomes quite evident when it is in rapid motion, as you will find out later in this chapter.

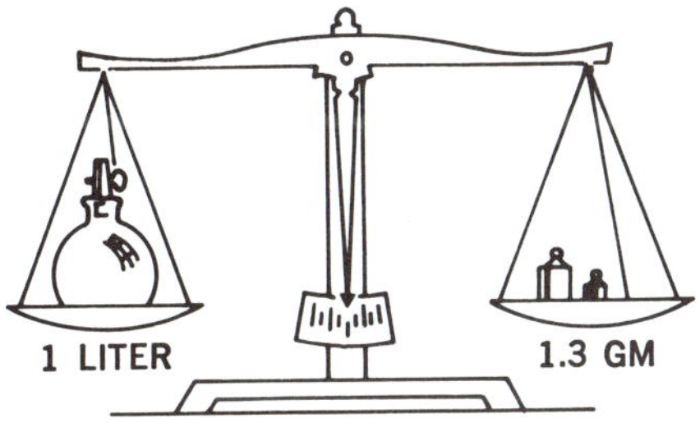

FIGURE 13. Weighing air

AIR PRESSURE

Since the air weighs something, it exerts pressure on anything immersed in it, including your own body. The reason you do not feel this pressure is that it is counterbalanced by an equal pressure from the inside—there is air in the body cavities and in the tissues and fluids. At the earth's surface, air pressure amounts to about 14.7 lb/in^2 (1,034 gm/cm^2). This is over a ton per square foot.

EXPERIMENT 10: The existence of air pressure can be shown by removing the air from one side of an exposed surface. Get a tin can that has a tight-fitting cover or an opening provided with a screw cap. Put a little water in the can, stand it in a pan of water and boil it vigorously, with the cover removed, in order to drive out the air by means of the escaping steam. Weight the can down if it tends to upset. While still boiling, close the cap tightly, quickly transfer the can to a sink and run cold water over it to condense the steam inside. Outside air pressure will crush the vessel in a spectacular way.

The condensing (turning to liquid) of some of the steam in the last experiment left a partial **vacuum** inside the can. A vacuum is simply a place not occupied by matter, or an empty space. For a long time, people believed that a vacuum had the mysterious power of "sucking" things into it. But how does the vacuum you create when you sip a soda succeed in getting a grip on the liquid in order to pull it up into your mouth?

THE BAROMETER

In the seventeenth century, the Duke of Tuscany decided to have a deep well dug. To his surprise, no pump was able to raise the water more than about 34 feet above the level in the well. The great scientist Galileo became interested in the question and suggested to his friend and pupil, Torricelli, that he make experiments to test "the power of a vacuum." Torricelli reasoned that if a 34-foot height of water was needed to satisfy a vacuum a much shorter column of mercury would be sufficient. Mercury is 13.6 times as dense as water, so a height of only 34/13.6, or 2½ feet, should be enough. He tried an experiment: A glass tube about a yard long, sealed at one end, was completely filled with mercury. The other end was held closed with the thumb. Then the tube was turned over and the open end set in a large dish of mercury. When the thumb was removed, the mercury dropped away from the sealed end until its upper surface came to rest about 30 inches above the liquid in the dish (Fig. 14). The mer-

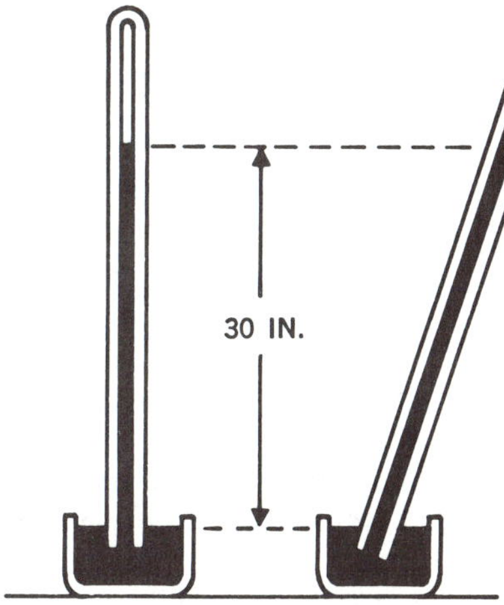

FIGURE 14. Mercury tube barometer

* Can you tell why, from the Table 3?

cury, in descending from the top of the tube, left a vacuum behind it, and it seemed that this vacuum was able to hold up a 30-inch column of mercury. Torricelli concluded that the liquid is supported not by any mysterious sucking action of the vacuum, but by the outside air *pressing* on the mercury in the open dish.

To complete the argument, other people carried such instruments up the side of a mountain, where the air pressure is less. Surely enough, it was observed that the mercury in the tube now stood lower, but regained its former height when brought back to the valley. Here, then, is an instrument that can be used to measure changes in air pressure. It is called a **barometer.** A more compact and convenient form of this instrument is the **aneroid** barometer (Fig. 15). It consists of a sealed metal can from which most of the air has been pumped. Changes in outside air pressure make the flexible cover bend in and out very slightly, and the motion is magnified by a lever system, moving a pointer over a scale from which the air pressure can be read off directly.

One important use of the barometer is to determine altitude. Once we know how the pressure of the air depends on altitude, we can use the barometer readings to give our height. An aneroid barometer with the scale marked directly in height units forms the **altimeter** of an airplane.

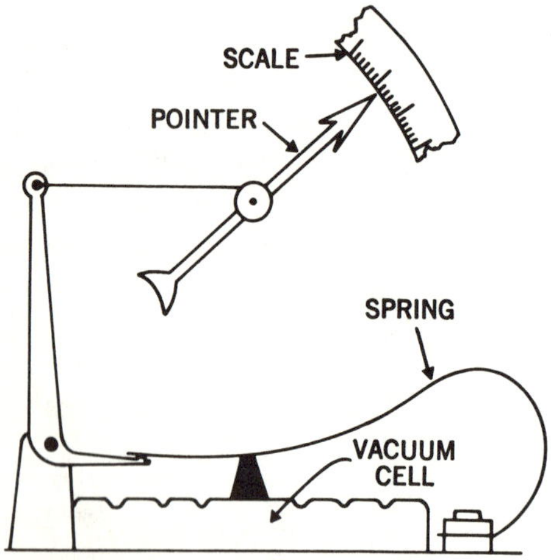

FIGURE 15. Aneroid barometer

The other main use of the barometer is in forecasting weather conditions. Contrary to general belief, moist air is *less* dense than dry air, water vapor itself being only around 5/8 as dense as dry air. Since it is less dense, moist air exerts less pressure, and so in moist weather the barometer falls. This gives us a way of predicting what kind of weather we will have in the immediate future. A steady, high barometer indicates fair weather; a rising barometer means fair or clearing weather conditions; and a rapidly falling barometer means a storm is approaching. By combining information obtained at stations all over the country, the Weather Bureau is able to prepare and distribute maps from which forecasts can be made at any locality.

THE ATMOSPHERE

The **atmosphere** is the name we give to the whole body of air surrounding the earth. If it were not for the earth's gravity, this layer of gas would escape out into the vacuum of interplanetary space. As mentioned above, it is the weight of the air that causes it to exert pressure. But there is one important difference between the pressure due to the weight of a liquid, as discussed in the previous chapter, and the pressure of the air: Liquids are virtually incompressible, and this leads to the simple proportion between pressure and depth. But gases, such as air, are fairly easy to compress. The weight of the upper layers compresses the lower ones, with the result that the density and pressure both fall off in a more complicated way as we go upward from the surface of the earth. In going up one mile from sea level, the height of mercury in the barometer falls about 5½ inches, but in going up an additional mile from a 10 mile height, it falls only a little over ½ inch. The *rate* of falling off is a constantly decreasing one (see Fig. 16).

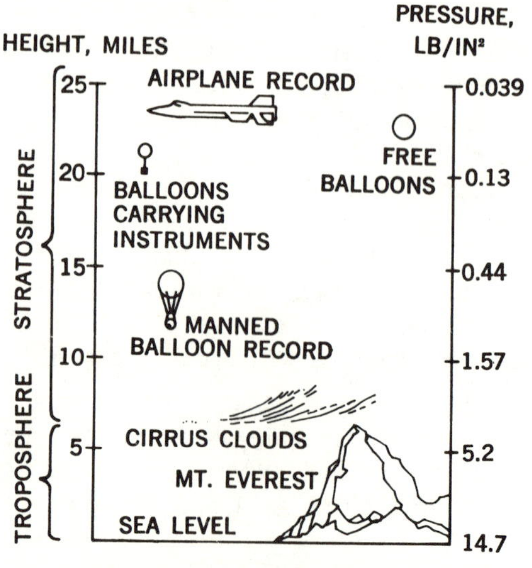

FIGURE 16. The lower atmosphere

The part of the atmosphere above about 6.5 miles is called the **stratosphere.** It is a relatively cold and calm region in which no clouds form. It has been explored to some extent by free-sailing balloons carrying instruments and, more recently, by high-altitude rockets and radar. The atmosphere continues to thin out with increasing height, and apparently has no sharp boundary. Air can still be detected at heights of several hundred miles.

GAS VOLUME: BOYLE'S LAW

When air is pumped into an automobile tire, a large volume of outside air is forced into the relatively small space inside the tube. All gases, including air, are compressible; and in order to force a gas into a small space, extra pressure must be applied to it. The greater the applied pressure, the smaller the space occupied by the gas. In the seventeenth century, Robert Boyle, an Irish scientist, discovered by experiment the exact relationship that holds: **If the temperature of the gas is kept constant,** then **the volume will be inversely proportional to the pressure.** This means that if the pressure is doubled, the volume becomes half as much; if the pressure is tripled, the volume becomes one-third of what it was, etc. In the form of an equation,

$$\frac{V_1}{V_2} = \frac{p_2}{p_1}$$

where p_1 and V_1 are, respectively, the pressure and the volume in one case and p_2 and V_2 are the values in another. In the formula, notice that on the left, the numerator has the "1" and the denominator has the "2", while on the right, it is just the other way around. This is characteristic of *inverse* proportion.

EXAMPLE 8: The air pressure in a tire is to be 30 lb/in^2 as read on an ordinary tire gauge, and the inside volume of the tube, assumed constant, is 0.95 ft^3. What volume of outside air is needed to fill the tube to this pressure on a day when the barometric pressure is 15 lb/in^2?

SOLUTION: A tire gauge reads the pressure *above* atmospheric, so the total pressure on the air in the tube is 30 + 15, or 45 lb/in^2. Then, if V_1 is the volume that this amount of air occupies outside, we can make the proportion

$$\frac{V_1}{0.95} = \frac{45}{15};$$

cross multiplying:

$$V_1 = \frac{0.95 \times 45}{15} = 2.85 \text{ ft}^3.$$

Buoyancy in Gases

Archimedes' law of buoyancy also holds for gases. In making very accurate weighings, the difference in the weight of air displaced by the object and by the metal weights must be taken into account. But air has such low density compared with solids, this effect can usually be neglected. A large, hollow body, such as a balloon, can displace more than its own weight of air, and so can float in air. Since the air is less dense higher up, a balloon will rise only to the level where the weight of the displaced air becomes equal to its own weight. Balloons are usually filled with hydrogen or helium. These gases are the lightest known, and provide a large lifting force.

Uses of Air Pressure

There are many uses for compressed air: It is utilized in inflating tires, in operating air brakes and tools such as the riveting hammer, and in keeping water out of underwater workings (see Experiment 1).

Low pressures have their uses, too. The vacuum cleaner is a familiar example. In making electric lamps, radio and television tubes and X-ray tubes it is extremely important to be able to remove as much air as possible. Modern pumps can reduce the air pressure in a tube to less than one-billionth of normal atmospheric pressure. Special methods can attain a billionth of this.

AIR RESISTANCE

So far, the discussion has been about air at rest. When air moves, even with moderate speed, important new forces come into play. These forces are responsible for the operation of sailboats, atomizers, parachutes, airplanes, etc. The most evident effect is the resistance that the air offers to the movement of objects through it. Hold your hand out the window of a moving car and you feel the resistance force directly. The car itself experiences such a force. At usual driving speeds, more than half the power delivered by the engine may be used up in working against air resistance.

The actual resistance force increases with the *cross-section area* of the moving body and especially with its *speed* of motion. In addition, the *shape* of the object is of great importance. What we call **streamlining** a body means giving it a suitable shape so that it will offer a minimum of opposition to the flow of air past it. This means eliminating all sharp corners and projections, approaching the general "tear-drop" shape shown in Fig. 17a. Contrary to what you might expect, the front of the body is broader than the rear. But if the body is to be a high-speed jet plane or rocket traveling faster than sound, a sharp-nosed shape gives best performance (Fig. 17b).

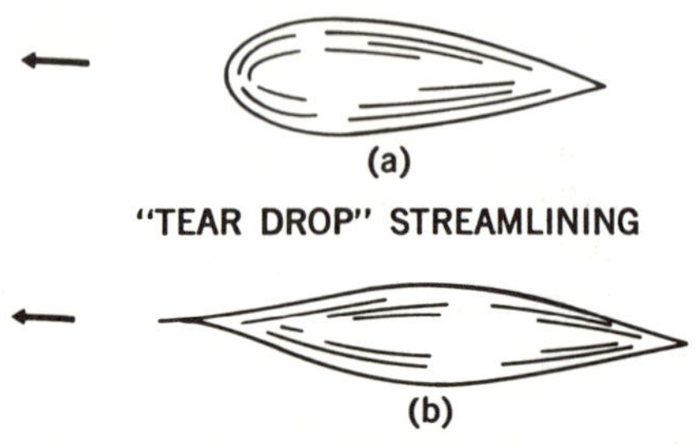

FIGURE 17.

Fig. 18 shows the comparative resistance, of (a) a streamlined rod, (b) a round rod and (c) a flat plate of the same cross-section and all moving at a given speed. The air flow around each is also pictured. Behind the round and flat objects, the stream lines break up into whirls, whose effect is to retard the movement of the body. The tapered tail of (a) fills in this region, allowing the flow to join smoothly at the rear.

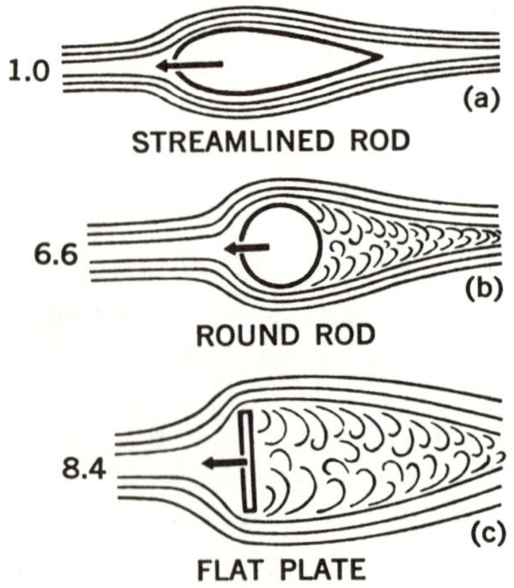

FIGURE 18. Relative resistance

Bodies falling through the air are retarded by air resistance. If not for this effect, all objects, regardless of difference in weight, would fall at the same rate.

EXPERIMENT 11: Drop a coin and a sheet of paper from shoulder height at the same instant. The coin quickly reaches the floor, while the paper flutters down slowly. To show that this result is not due to their difference in weight but only to the difference in air resistance, repeat the trial after first wadding the paper up into a small ball. This time both will be seen to hit at the same instant.

THE AIRPLANE; BERNOULLI'S LAW

Of the many applications of the physics of the air, the one that has had the greatest impact on civilization is, of course, the airplane. At the very beginning we may well ask, "What keeps an airplane up?" The answer is not at all obvious. We know that a plane must be moved rapidly through the air in order to sustain itself, and that it must have a large, slightly inclined surface—a wing—to furnish the supporting force. Seen from the moving airplane, the surrounding air streams backward, over and around it. The tilted wing surface deflects some air downward, and as a result the plane is literally "knocked" upward. But this is responsible for only a small effect. Actually, it is the flow of air around the curved *upper* surface of the wing that accounts for most of the lift. To see how this works, try an experiment:

EXPERIMENT 12: Hold one edge of a piece of letter paper against your chin, just below your lower lip, with the paper hanging over and down (Fig. 19). If you now blow above the paper, it will rise to a horizontal position as if pulled upward into the air stream.

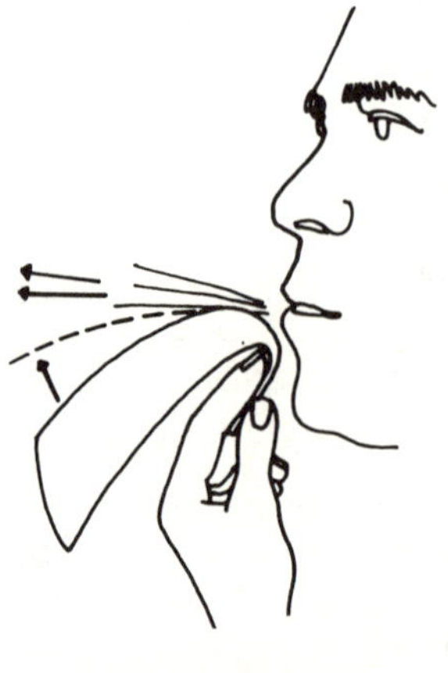

FIGURE 19.

This action is an instance of a general law discovered by the eighteenth century Swiss scientist Daniel Bernoulli: A moving stream of gas or liquid exerts less sidewise pressure than if it were at rest. The result is that things seem to be drawn into such a stream; they are really *pushed* in by the greater pressure from outside.

Bernoulli's principle gives us a way of understanding the action of air on a wing. In a properly designed wing, the airstream separates at the front of the wing and rejoins smoothly at the rear (Fig. 20). Since the air that flows over the upper surface has to travel a greater distance its average speed must be greater than that below, and so the decrease in pressure is greater on the top side, resulting in a lifting force on the entire wing. The forces on the upper side of a wing may account for over four-fifths of the whole lift.

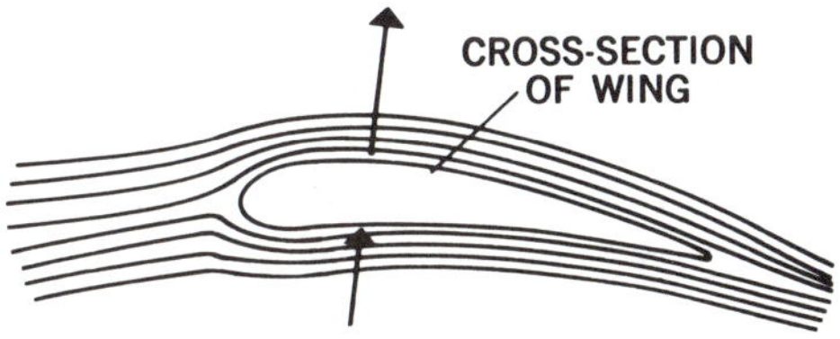

FIGURE 20. Airplane wing

The control surfaces of the airplane, as well as the propeller that moves it through the air, operate on this same principle. In the **helicopter** the airflow over the wing surfaces is produced by whirling the rotating wings, rather than by rapid motion of the whole plane through the air. As a result, a helicopter can hover over one spot on the ground, or even move in the backward direction.

Other Applications

A number of familiar observations and devices can be described in terms of Bernoulli's law. In an **atomizer** (spray gun), a stream of air is blown across the end of a small tube that dips into the liquid (Fig. 21). The decreased pressure at the side of the air stream allows normal air pressure, acting on the surface of the liquid in the bottle, to push the liquid up the tube. Here the moving air breaks it up into small drops and drives it forward. The **carburetor** of an auto works in the same way.

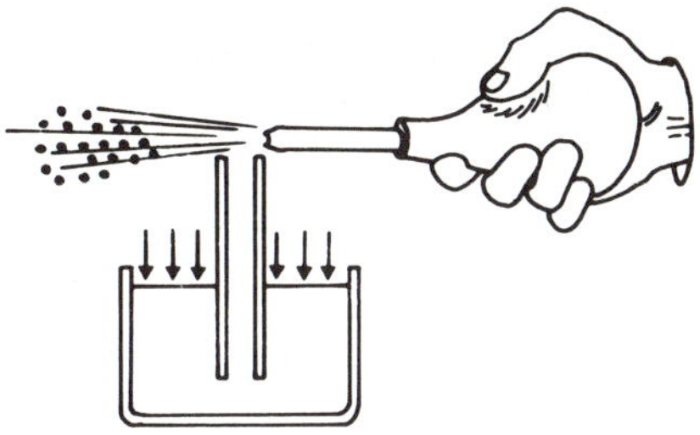

FIGURE 21. Atomizer (spray gun)

Two cars, passing each other at high speed, are in danger of sideswiping because of the decrease in air pressure in the space between them. A strong gale is capable of lifting the roof off a house. An amusing experiment shows the same effect:

EXPERIMENT 13: Lay a dime about half an inch from the edge of a table and place a saucer a few inches beyond. With your mouth at the level of the table top, blow a sudden strong breath across the top of the dime (as if whistling) and it will jump into the dish.

The curving of a baseball or of a "sliced" golf ball is explained by Bernoulli's principle. Some air is dragged around by the spin of the ball (Fig. 22). At "A" this air is moving *with* the stream of air caused by the ball's moving along, while at "B" the two *oppose* each other. The greater relative air speed at "A" makes the ball veer to that side.

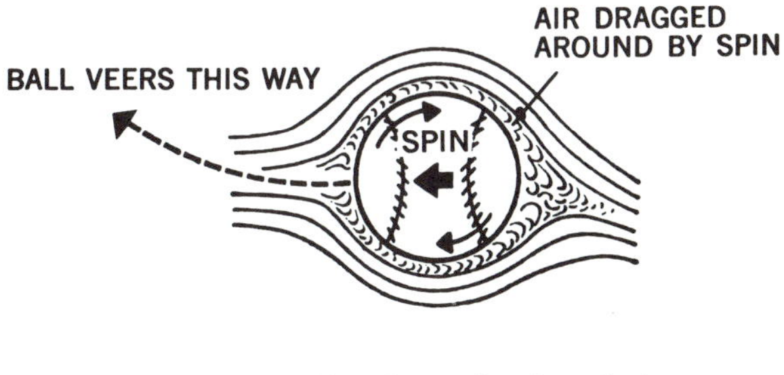

FIGURE 22. Curving of a baseball

Forces

We have described a force as a push or a pull—something that would produce the same effect as the direct action of your muscles. It was also pointed out that forces can be measured in ordinary weight units, such as grams, pounds, etc. We shall now have a closer look at forces and find out how, under certain conditions, they are capable of holding an object in balance.

REPRESENTATION OF FORCES; VECTORS

In most of the practical situations we deal with, not one but a number of forces act on the body in question. There is a simple and convenient way of representing the forces and of finding their net effect. In the first place, in order to describe a force completely, we must specify not only its *amount* (say, in pounds) but its *direction* in space; obviously it makes a difference whether a force acts to the left or to the right, or whether it acts upward or downward.

A force acting at a given point is pictured by a line drawn outward from that point in the given direction, and the *length* of the line is made to represent the *strength* of the force.

Besides forces, there are other physical quantities, to be discussed later, that have both magnitude and direction. Such a quantity is called a **vector.** Any vector may be represented by a directed line segment.

In Fig. 23 A stands for a force of 5 lb acting toward the northeast. The scale chosen for this drawing is "¼ in = 1 lb," and so the line, drawn in the proper direction, is made 5 quarter-inches long. An arrow is placed at the end of the line to give its sense of direction. In the same way, B is an eastward force of 9 lb acting at the same point. Any convenient scale may be used in these drawings, as long as we stick to the same scale throughout the problem.

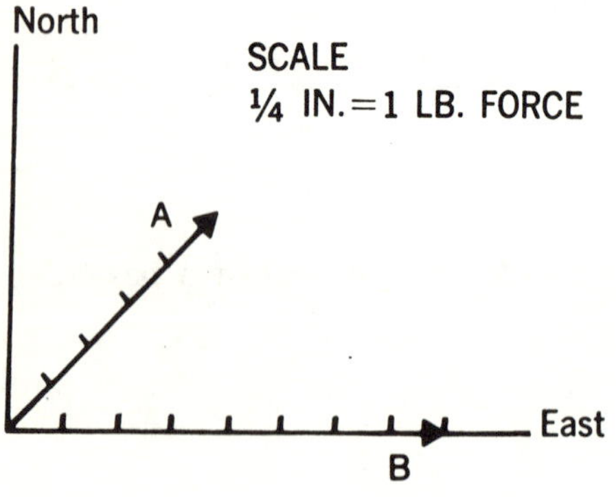

FIGURE 23. Representing force vectors

RESULTANT OF A SET OF FORCES

It is found by experience that when a number of forces act on a body they can always be replaced by a single force having a definite amount and direction. This single force, which replaces the effect of all the others, is called their **resultant.** There is a simple way of finding it by means of a drawing: Draw all the forces, end to end, until they have all been put down (the order in which you pick them off from the original drawing does not matter). Then, if you draw a line out from the starting point to the end of the last force, this line will correctly represent the resultant as to direction and amount.

EXAMPLE 9: Three forces act at a point. One is 4 lb straight down, another is 11 lb to the right and the third is 9 lb upward and to the left at an angle of 45 degrees. Find their resultant.

SOLUTION: Fig. 24 shows these forces, drawn to

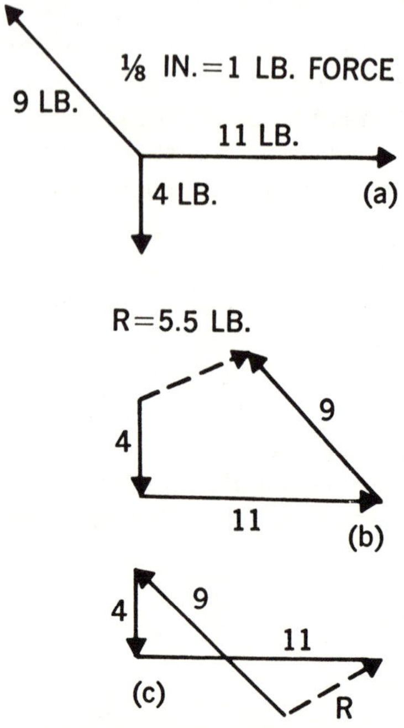

FIGURE 24. Combining vectors

scale. Now, keeping the same length and direction for each force, lay them off end to end, as in (b). Then the resultant is gotten by drawing a line from the starting point out to the end of the last force. This line, when measured, turns out to be 11/16 in. long. Therefore the resultant amounts to 11/16 divided by ⅛, or 5.5 lb, and has the direction shown. In (c) the forces have been laid off in a different order, but the resultant has the same size and direction as before.

Notice that the size (length) of the resultant is, in general, *not* equal to the sum of the magnitudes of the separate vectors. The actual value will depend on their relative positions.

If all the acting forces are in a single line (such as east-west), the magnitude of the resultant is simply the sum of all those acting to one side less the sum of all those acting toward the other. As an example, suppose a man can pull with a force of 100 lb, while a boy can pull only 70 lb. If they both pull toward the east, the combined effect is 170 lb force; if the man pulls westward and the boy eastward, the resultant is a 30 lb force toward the west (the direction of the larger force).

Another case where the resultant can easily be calculated rather than measured from a scale drawing is that of two forces at right angles to each other (Fig. 25). The resultant is the hypotenuse of a right triangle and its amount may be computed by the right triangle rule.

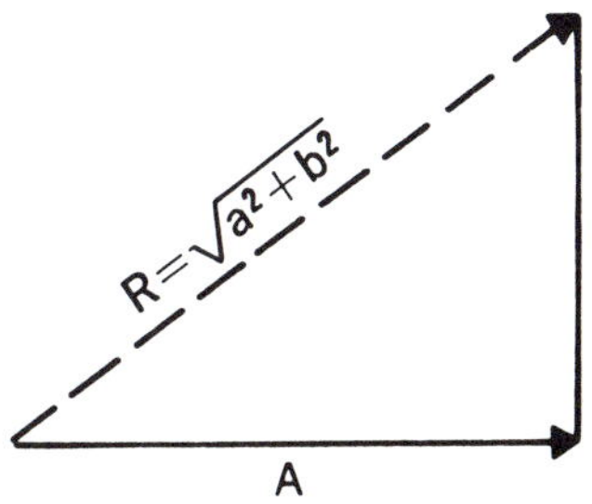

FIGURE 25. Forces at right angles

EQUILIBRIUM OF FORCES

One of the most important mechanical situations that engineers and designers must deal with is that in which all the forces acting on a body just hold it at rest. This balancing-out of the applied forces will occur if the **resultant** of all of them is **zero.** When this happens, the body is said to be in **equilibrium.** Conversely, if a body is observed to remain at rest, we know that the resultant of all the acting forces must be zero. This fact can be used to find the values of some of the forces. An example will show how:

EXAMPLE 10: A wire-walker at the circus weighs 160 lb. When at the position shown in Fig. 26, what is the stretching force in each part of the wire?

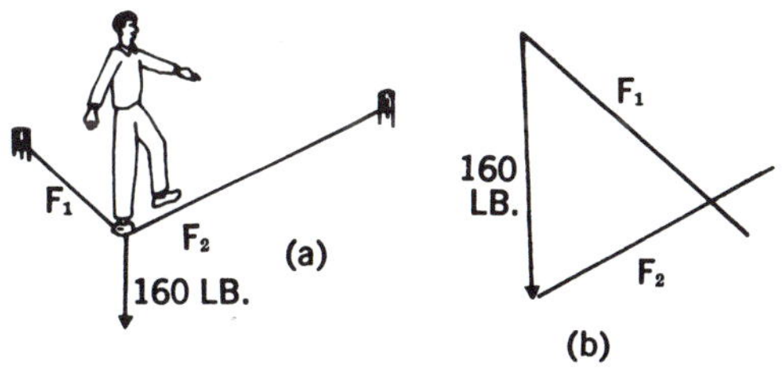

FIGURE 26. Tensions in a wire

SOLUTION: First we note that the point *B* is the place where the forces in question meet. One of them is the man's weight. We sketch it in the downward direction from *B* as shown and label it "160 lb." Acting from *B* along the left-hand portion of the wire is some force—call it F_1—whose value is still unknown. As yet, we can only sketch it in, but do not know how long to make it. Likewise, F_2 is the force in the other part of the wire. In general F_1 and F_2 will be different.

Since the three forces hold the point *B* in equilibrium, they must form a *closed triangle* by themselves (zero resultant). Off to one side, Fig. 26b, draw the weight force to scale. From the tip of this force, draw a line in parallel to BC. We do not know how long to make this force; however, if we did, we would then proceed to draw the third force from its end, heading parallel to the wire AB, and should have to land at the starting point of the weight force. It is clear what we now have to do: Simply begin at this point and draw a line back in the proper direction until it crosses the line of F_2. This crossing point fixed the lengths (or amounts) of the two forces. The force lines can now be measured, using the same scale that was employed in drawing the 160-lb weight, and so the magnitudes of F_1 and F_2 can be found. In this example they turn out to be about 165 lb and 135 lb, respectively. Try a construction like this yourself, using a weight and direction of your own choosing.

CENTER OF GRAVITY

In most of the cases we meet in practice, the forces acting on a body are not all applied at a single point, but at several different places. The weight of a body is a good example. The earth's gravity pulls downward on every particle of a material body with a force equal to the weight of that particle, as pictured in Fig. 27. However, we can replace all these separate forces by a single

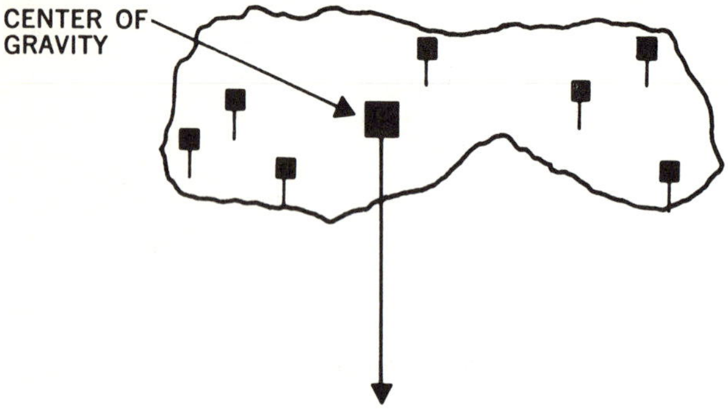

FIGURE 27.

one, equal to the entire weight of the object. This force must be considered to act at a given place called the **center of gravity** of the body. There is such a point for every object. If the body is made of uniform material and has a simple shape, such as a sphere, cube, straight rod, etc., the location of the center of gravity is obvious (Fig. 28a). The position of the center of gravity of an irregular object may be found by trial, by seeing where it will balance without any tendency to rotate in any direction (Fig. 28b).

FIGURE 28. Locating the center of gravity

If a body is supported at any point other than its center of gravity, it will try to move until its center of gravity is as low as possible. This explains, for instance, why it is impossible to balance a pencil on its point.

EXPERIMENT 14: Fasten a weight to the inner edge of a flat cylindrical box (Fig. 29). Placed on a sloping board, it will mysteriously roll *up* the slope when released. Notice that the center of gravity is very near the position of the concealed weight, and that while the box goes up the hill, the center of gravity goes *down,* as it must.

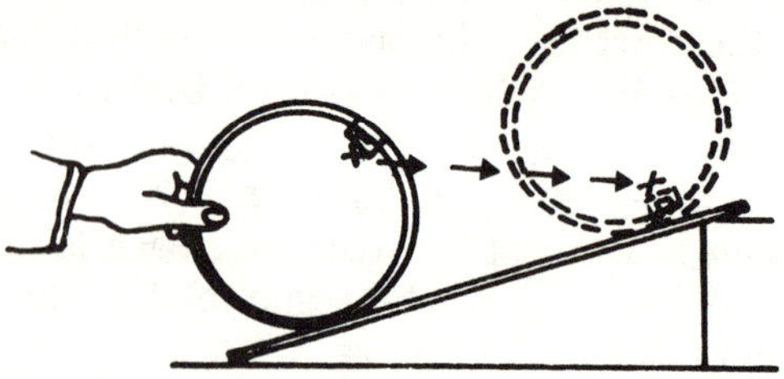

FIGURE 29. The mystery cylinder

TORQUE AND ROTATION

In general, if the forces applied to a body do not all act at a single point, there is the possibility that the body will rotate. How can we measure the ability of a force to produce rotation? Think of the example of pushing a revolving door (Fig. 30). If you want to turn the door most effectively, you push with your hand near the edge of the door rather than near the hinge. It is found that the **turning effect** of any force is given by multiplying the **amount of the force** by the **distance from the pivot** point to the line of the force. This turning effect of a force is called the **torque,** and

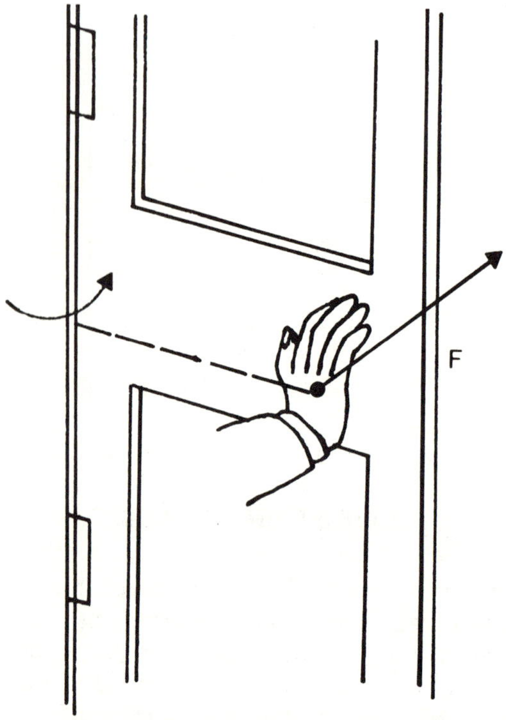

FIGURE 30. Revolving door

the distance mentioned is the **torque arm.** In symbols,

$$T = Fh$$

where T is the torque, F the force and h the torque arm. Notice what the units are for T: If F is in pounds and h is in feet, the units for T will be **foot pounds.** Here again we have an example of a derived quantity (p. 451).

If the body in question is not to rotate, then the net torque must be zero, that is, **the sum of all torques that tend to turn the body in one direction must be equal to the sum of all those tending to turn it in the opposite direction.** The word "direction" here refers to the sense of rotation—**clockwise** (in the direction turned by the hands of a clock), or **counterclockwise.**

In figuring the torques, we may take any point as a prospective center of turning—it need not be the place where the actual pivot or axle is located.

EXAMPLE 11: How big a downward force must be applied to the end of the crowbar shown in Fig. 31 in order just to lift the 200-lb weight? Neglect the weight of the bar itself.

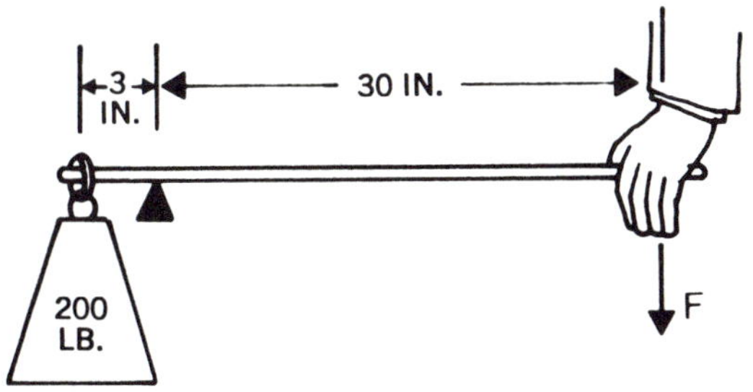

FIGURE 31. Lifting by means of a crowbar

SOLUTION: Taking the torques about the pivot point, the one due to the weight will be 200×3, or 600 in.lb. If we call the applied force F, in pounds, it will have a torque around this point of amount $30F$ in.lb. These two torques are in opposite directions: The latter one is clockwise, the other is counterclockwise. Setting the two equal, $200 \times 3 = 30F$, or $F = 20$ lb force.

EXAMPLE 12: A 5-ton truck stands 30 ft from one pier of a uniform bridge 100 ft long weighing 20 tons (Fig. 32). Find the downward force on each pier.

SOLUTION: First we must put down all the forces acting *on* the bridge: A 5-ton downward force at C; a 20-ton downward force at G, the center of gravity of the bridge structure; and at the piers, upward forces F_A and F_B whose values are

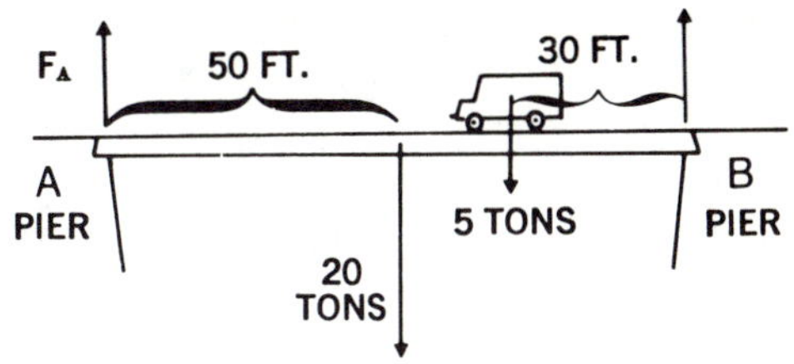

FIGURE 32. Downward force on the piers of a bridge

to be found. Take torques around A. The two weight forces tend to turn the bridge clockwise about A, and their torques amount to $20 \times 50 + 5 \times 70$, or 1,350 ft-tons. The only counter-clockwise torque is that of F_B, amounting to $100F_B$. Notice that F_A does not contribute any torque, since it has no torque arm around A. Setting the torques in the two directions eqqual, $100\ F_B = 1{,}350$, $F_B = 13.5$ tons force. We could now repeat the process, taking torques around, say, the point B; but there is a simpler way to find the remaining force F_A: From the fact that the resultant of all the acting forces must be zero (p. 463) we have, simply because all the forces in this problem are either upward or downward, $F_A + 13.5 = 20 + 5$, so that $F_A = 11.5$ tons. So we see that by using the two equilibrium conditions that state (1) the resultant of all the forces must be zero and (2) the torques around any point must balance, we can work out any equilibrium problem.

GRAVITATION: NEWTON'S LAW

One of the greatest scientific achievements of all time was Newton's discovery of gravitation, around the middle of the seventeenth century. Earlier, the astronomer Kepler had found certain regularities about the motion of the plants around the sun. Newton, trying to explain these rules, decided that the planets must move in the observed way because they are pulled by a force exerted by the sun. He concluded that this force of gravitation exists not only between the sun and the planets but between *any* two objects in the universe, and he worked out the factors on which the amount of force depends. This is stated by his **Law of Gravitation: Any two bodies in the universe attract each other with a force that is directly proportional to their masses and inversely**

proportional to the square of their distance apart. This may be stated as a formula:

$$F = \frac{Gm_1m_2}{d^2}$$

where F is the force of attraction, m_1 and m_2 are the two masses, and d is their distance apart. G is a constant, whose value is fixed once we have chosen our units for F, m and d. If F and m are measured in pounds and d in feet, the value of G is 0.000 000 000 033. Because G is so small, the attraction between ordinary objects is very weak, but when the bodies concerned are very massive, the force may be extremely large. Thus, the attractive force between the earth and the moon amounts to about 15 million trillion tons.

The gravitational force of the earth for objects on it—what we have been calling **gravity**—is responsible for their weight. The attraction of the moon for the waters of the ocean is a main cause of the **tides.**

Notice that while Newton's law allows us to calculate the amount of the attraction in any case, it does not tell us what gravitation is, nor why such a force exists. These are philosophical rather than scientific questions!

Motion

In the world about us, everything moves. This may seem to contradict the discussion where we talked about bodies at rest. But a body at rest on the ground is really moving with the rotation of the whole earth, and the earth in turn moves in its path around the sun, and so on. Rest and motion are relative terms. We will now find out how to measure the motions of bodies, and how the forces acting on them determine the way in which they move.

SPEED AND VELOCITY

In any kind of motion—for example, in making a trip—two things are of interest: What is the *rate* of motion and in what *direction* does it take place? Rate of motion is what we call **speed.** It is measured by the distance covered divided by the elapsed time. In symbols,

$$v = \frac{d}{t},$$

where d stands for the distance, t is the time required and v is the speed. Speed is a derived unit, and we are at liberty to use any distance unit and any time unit for this purpose. Table 4 gives convenient factors for changing from one common speed unit to another.

TABLE 4

CONVERSION FACTORS FOR SPEED UNITS

To change from a unit given at the side to one given at the top, multiply by the factor in the appropriate square. Thus 100 cm/sec = 100 × 0.0328 = 3.28 ft/sec.

	mi/hr	ft/sec	cm/sec	knots*
mi/hr	—	1.47	44.7	0.868
ft/sec	0.682	—	30.5	0.592
cm/sec	0.0224	0.0328	—	0.0194
knots*	1.15	1.69	51.5	—

Even where the rate of motion is not constant over the whole journey, the above formula has a meaning: it gives the **average speed** for the entire trip. For instance, if a car travels to a city 90 miles away in a total time of 3 hours, the average speed will be 90 mi/3 hr = 30 mi/hr. But no trip of this kind is made at constant speed; there may have been times when the car was going much faster or much slower than this, as indicated by the speedometer.

When the directional aspect is combined with

*1 knot = 1 nautical mile per hour.

the speed we have the **velocity** of motion. Velocity, like force, is a vector (p. 462), and so an arrowed line can be used to stand for a velocity. A body can have several velocities at the same time. A ball rolled across the floor of a moving railroad car (Fig. 33) has the common forward velocity of everything in the train, plus the crosswise velocity with which the ball is rolled. The **resultant velocity**

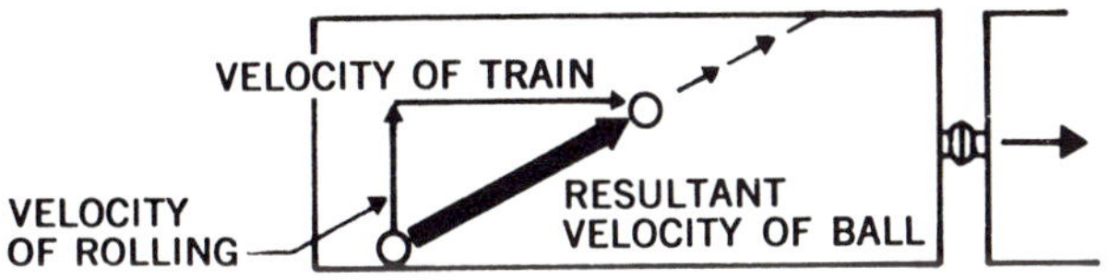

FIGURE 33. Combination of velocities

—how the ball would appear to move as seen by someone on an overhead bridge—is given by the same construction we used before. The actual path is the straight line indicated.

ACCELERATION

In most of the motions we commonly observe, the speed is not at all constant, whether it is the flight of a bird, the swinging of a pendulum or the fall of a stone. Any motion in which the speed or direction are variable is called **accelerated motion.** The **acceleration** is defined as the **rate of change** of the **velocity,** that is, the change in velocity divided by the time it takes to make that change. For instance, if a car going 25 ft/sec picks up speed until, 5 sec later, it is going 60 ft/sec, its rate of pick-up will be 60—25, or 35 ft/sec in 5 sec. Dividing, this amounts to 7 ft/sec/sec ("feet per second per second"). This means only that the car increased its speed at an average rate of 7 ft/sec *each second.* Instead of writing "ft/sec/sec," we recognize that the time unit comes in *twice* as a factor in this derived unit, and we write "ft/sec^2" and read it "feet per second squared."

Motion with Constant Acceleration

One kind of motion that is readily described and computed is that where the amount of the acceleration is *constant.* This holds, for a limited time at least, when a train is gathering speed, or when it is being brought to rest by the brakes. In the latter case, the speed is *decreasing,* and this is sometimes called decelerated motion. However, no special name is really needed; this can be taken care of merely by putting a *minus* sign in front of the value for the acceleration.

EXAMPLE 13: A car going 30 ft/sec is brought to rest by its brakes at the uniform rate of 5 ft/sec^2. How long must the brakes be applied?

SOLUTION: Saying that the braking acceleration amounts to -5 ft/sec^2 means that the car will lose speed at the rate of 5 ft/sec each second. To take away all the initial speed of 30 ft/sec will then require 30/5 or **6** sec.

How *far* will a constantly-accelerating object move in a given time? To answer such a question, you must remember that the speed of motion is changing all the while. But we can find out what is happening by making use of the *average* speed; and here, since the speed changes at a uniform rate, the average speed will be half way between the speed at the beginning and the speed at the end of the interval. The next example will show how we can compute the distance in a specific case:

EXAMPLE 14: A car going 26 ft/sec begins to accelerate at the rate of 2 ft/sec^2. How fast will it be going after 8 sec, and how far will it go in this time?

SOLUTION: In 8 sec, the total gain in speed will be $8 \times 2 = 16$ ft/sec, so the final speed will be 24 + 16, or 42 ft/sec. To find the distance traveled, we note that the speed at the beginning of the acceleration period was 26 and at the end was 42 ft/sec, so that the average speed over this interval is $\frac{1}{2}(26 + 42) = 34$ ft/sec. Going, in effect, 34 ft/sec for 8 sec, the car would cover a distance of 34×8, or 272 ft.

Falling Motion; Projectiles

The ancient Greek philosopher Aristotle described the motion of a freely falling body by saying that the heavier the body, the faster it would fall. This does, at first thought, seem true, but you have already performed an experiment (Experiment 11) that throws some doubt on this conclusion. In the latter part of the sixteenth century, the great Italian scientist Galileo tried some experiments that convinced him that it is merely the disturbing effect of air resistance that ordinarily makes a light object fall more slowly than a heavy one. In a vacuum, all bodies fall at the same rate.

Galileo went on to find just how a falling body

moves. He found that, when the effects of the surrounding air can be neglected, a falling body has a constant acceleration—the kind of motion we have been discussing above. This acceleration is called the **acceleration due to gravity,** and is denoted by the symbol g. Its value changes slightly from place to place on earth, and especially with height, but the standard value is close to

$$32 \text{ ft/sec}^2, \text{ or } 980 \text{ cm/sec}^2.$$

Knowing the value of g, it is not difficult to calculate the motion of a falling body. The results will be quite accurate for compact solid objects falling moderate distances. The case of a body falling great distances in air is, in general, too complicated for computation.

EXAMPLE 15: A small stone is dropped from the roof of a tall building and is seen to hit the ground 7.0 sec later. Neglecting air resistance, find the height from which the stone fell and how fast it was going when it hit the ground.

SOLUTION: In the stated time, the stone, starting from rest, picks up a speed of $7 \times 32 = 224$ ft/sec, which is its speed just before hitting the ground. Its *average* speed for the whole trip is half the sum of the speed at the start and at the finish, or $\frac{1}{2}(0 + 224) = 112$ ft/sec. Going at this speed for 7 sec, a body would cover a distance of $112 \times 7 = 784$ ft, which is the distance of fall.

A **projectile**—a thrown stone or a bullet—is really a falling body. If shot upward at an angle, it immediately begins to *fall* short of the direction of fire, just like any falling object. It continues to fall in this way while moving forward, and so follows the observed curved path. Since bullets travel at high speed, the results may be somewhat altered by air resistance.

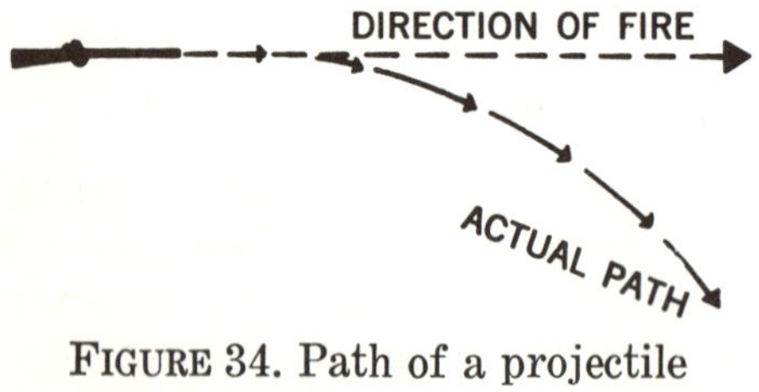

FIGURE 34. Path of a projectile

EXPERIMENT 15: Place two coins at the very edge of a table, one on top of the other. A sharp blow with a knife blade held flat against the table will send the lower coin off like a projectile, while the upper one will fall almost straight down. In spite of this difference in path, both will be heard to strike the floor at the same time, since both really *fall* the same distance.

FORCE AND MOTION

In the preceding pages you learned how to describe certain types of motion, such as motion with constant speed or motion with constant acceleration, and how to figure out times, distances, etc. Now we take up the more involved question of what *causes* and *maintains* the motion of an object—that is, the relation of force to the motion it produces.

MOTION: NEWTON'S LAWS

The general answer to such questions was given by the brilliant work of Newton in the form of his **Three Laws of Motion.** These principles form the basis of the whole subject of Mechanics.

The First Law: Inertia

The First Law is called the **Law of Inertia.** Inertia was described as one of the fundamental properties of matter. Although the general idea was anticipated by Galileo, Newton succeeded in putting it into precise form:

Every body remains in a state of rest or of uniform motion in a straight line unless acted upon by forces from the outside.

This law states that motion is as natural a condition as rest. A car going along a straight, level road at constant speed is in equilibrium: The weight of the car is balanced by the supporting force of the pavement, and the forward pull of the engine counterbalances the retarding forces of friction and air resistance. The resultant force is zero, and the car is in equilibrium just as truly as if it were at rest.

Centripetal Force; Satellites

If the car comes to a curve, the pavement must furnish, through friction with the tires, an additional force to swerve the car from its natural straight path and enable it to round the curve. If the road is slippery, this force will be lacking and the car will continue straight ahead, tending to skid off the road.

The force required to hold a moving object in a circular path is called **centripetal*** force.

Many situations arise in practice where centripetal force must be taken into account. The curves

* The word means "toward the center."

FIGURE 35. Not enough centripetal force; the car continues along its "natural" straight path

on a road or on a bicycle racetrack are "banked," or raised at the outer edge to furnish such a force. Mud flying from the wheel of a car leaves the wheel in a straight line—it "flies off on a tangent." Laundries make use of centrifugal ("away from the center") dryers in which the wet clothes are whirled in a wire basket. Chemists and biologists use a **centrifuge** to separate suspended solid matter from a liquid. When the mixture is whirled rapidly, the difference in centripetal force on the solid material and on the less dense liquid causes the solids to collect at the outer rim. Using special arrangements, the centripetal force on a particle can be made to exceed 100 million times its weight.

A satellite following an orbit around a planet or a planet going around the sun is held in orbit by the centripetal force furnished by gravitational attraction.

The Second Law: Acceleration

Newton's First Law is limited in its usefulness, since it tells what happens only in the case where there is *no* resultant force. In the majority of actual situations, outside forces do act; the Second Law tells what can be expected under such circumstances.

In order to see what is involved, consider the particular case of a hand truck which can be pushed along on a level floor. If the truck is standing still to begin with and nobody pushes on it, it will remain at rest (First Law). What happens, now, if it is pushed in such a way that the force acting on it is kept constant? An actual trial shows that the truck will move forward with *constant acceleration.* In general, we find that a constant force acting on a given body that is free to move will give it a constant acceleration in the direction of the force.

If we were to double the amount of force, we would find that the acceleration would become just twice as great as before. On the other hand, if the mass of the car were doubled and the same force used as before, the acceleration would be just half of its earlier value. From experiments such as these, we conclude that the acceleration is proportional to the force divided by the mass (Fig. 36).

We are now able to state the **Second Law: A body acted upon by a constant force will move with constant acceleration in the direction of the force; the amount of the acceleration will be directly proportional to the acting force and inversely proportional to the mass of the body.**

Newton's Second Law can be put into a useful form by remembering what happens to any given object when it falls under gravity: Here the acting force is equal to the weight of the body, and the acceleration is, in every case, that of gravity, g. Making a direct proportion between force and acceleration, we can write

$$\frac{F}{W} = \frac{a}{g}$$

where W is the weight of the body, F is any applied force and a is the acceleration that this force will give to the body. F and W are to be measured in the same units, and a and g are to be measured in the same units.

EXAMPLE 16: A car weighing 3,200 lb accelerates at the rate of 5 ft/sec^2. Neglecting friction, what is the effective forward force exerted by the engine?

SOLUTION: The proportion gives $F = W\ (a/g)$. Substituting the numbers, $F = 3200 \times 5/32 = 500$ lb force.

The Third Law; Action and Reaction

Newton's Third Law deals with the observed fact that it is not possible to exert a force on a

FIGURE 36. A constant force produces a constant acceleration

body without exerting a force in the opposite direction on some other body or bodies. There are many common illustrations of this: If you jump from a rowboat to a pier, the boat is thereby shoved backward. A gun "kicks" when the bullet goes forward. A ship's propeller can drive it forward only because it continually throws water backward.

Newton defined what is called the **momentum** of a body. It is the **mass multiplied by the velocity.** In symbols

$$M = mv,$$

where M is the momentum, m is the mass and v the velocity of the body. M is a derived quantity and any appropriate units may be used for m and v. The **Third Law** makes a simple statement about momentum. It says that **when any object is given a certain momentum in a given direction, some other body or bodies will get an equal momentum in the opposite direction.**

EXAMPLE 17: A gun has a mass of 2,500 gm and the bullets each have a mass of 100 gm. If a bullet leaves the gun with a speed of 800 meters/sec, with what speed will the gun start back?

SOLUTION: The momentum of the bullet will be 100×800 gm m/sec (gram meters per second). Calling the recoil speed of the gun V, its momentum just after firing will be $2500V$. Setting the two momenta equal, $2500\ V = 100 \times 800$, so that $V = 32$ m/sec. V comes out in m/sec because the speed of the bullet was given in these units.

If the gun and bullet were subject to no other forces after firing, the two would go in opposite directions, each continuing to move with its own constant speed forever (First Law). This would nearly be the case, for example, if the gun were fired far out in space where friction and gravitational forces are negligible. If the gun were fixed in the ground rather than free to recoil, the reaction would be transmitted to the whole earth instead of to the gun alone. Because of the earth's enormous mass, its resulting motion would be far too small to be detectable.

A jet engine or rocket gets its propelling force from the reaction of the gases discharged toward the rear at high speed. Even though the mass of gas shot out each second is not very large, its high speed makes the product mv very large. The jet plane or rocket gets an equal momentum in the forward direction. A rocket will work perfectly well in the vacuum existing in interplanetary space, provided it carries its own fuel and the oxygen needed to burn it.

EXPERIMENT 16: The reaction principle can be demonstrated by making a rubber-band slingshot on a board resting on rollers (Fig. 37). Tie the band back by means of a string and place a fairly massive stone in firing position. Release the stretched band by burning the thread and observe the recoil of the board as the stone goes forward.

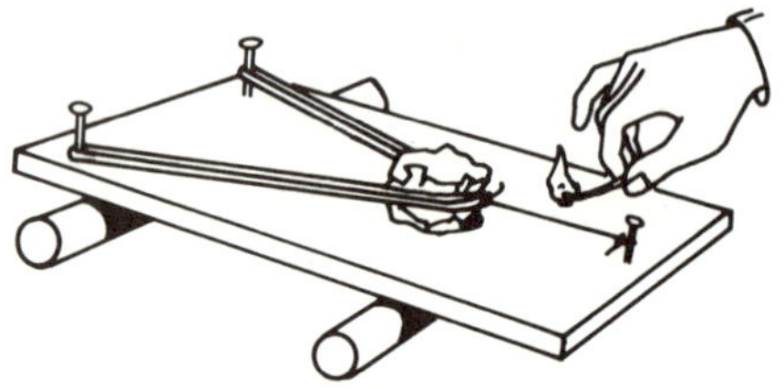

FIGURE 37. Recoil

ROTATIONAL INERTIA

Newton's laws apply to rotation as well as to the forward motion of an object as a whole. A body that is set spinning has a tendency to keep spinning—**rotational inertia.** The purpose of a heavy flywheel on an engine is to smooth out the separate power thrusts by means of its great rotational inertia.

A massive rotating wheel also has a tendency to keep its axis in a constant direction in space. This is the principle of the **gyroscope,** a rapidly rotating wheel mounted in a pivoted frame, so that the axis may hold its direction in spite of any motion of the mounting. The ability to keep its direction constant makes the gyroscope useful in the construction of several aircraft instruments, such as the turn indicator, artificial horizon, gyrocompass and automatic pilot.

CHAPTER NINE

CHEMISTRY

Matter

Strike a match. Any kind of match will do. Watch it carefully. What do you see? What did you hear? What did you smell? What do you feel? Blow it out. Did it go out completely? Try it again, this time holding the match in a horizontal position. Notice the shape of the flame. Do you see the liquid creeping just ahead of the flame? Light a wooden toothpick with the match, and then blow them both out. Blow harder on the toothpick. Blow it again. What happens? Do you have any evidence that match manufacturers are safety conscious? What differences in the properties of the match before and after burning can you find? Can the charred remnants of the match still be called a match?

A tremendous amount of chemistry has been illustrated by the phenomena which you have just observed. You will notice that in making observations we use not only our eyes, but also our other senses. The more senses we can employ in observation, the more thorough will be our findings. We will use these observations in becoming acquainted with some of the fundamental terms and ideas of chemistry. The observations will help us visualize chemical ideas and give meaning to the explanation of other phenomena of Nature.

PROPERTIES OF MATTER

We distinguish one form of matter from another by its **properties.** When you were asked to handle the match and the toothpick, you knew just what was meant because you were familiar in a general way with the properties of those objects. You are aware, of course, that a wooden match has more properties in common with a toothpick than a paper match. The wood gives the two objects a common substance. A **substance** is a definite variety of matter, all specimens of which have the same properties. Aluminum, iron, rust, salt, and sugar are all examples of substances. Notice that they are all homogeneous, or uniform in their makeup. Granite or concrete cannot be called substances because they are not homogeneous. They are made up of several different substances.

Substances have two major classes of properties: physical and chemical. **Physical** properties describe a substance as it is. **Chemical** properties describe the ability of a substance to change into a new and completely different substance.

Physical Properties

Substances have two kinds of physical properties: specific and accidental. **Specific physical properties** include those features which definitely distinguish one substance from another. Some of the important specific physical properties are:

1. Density—the weight of a unit volume of a substance. This is usually expressed as g./cc. in the metric system, or lbs./cu. ft. in the English system. Since 1 cc. of water weighs lg., its density is 1 g./cc. A cubic foot of water weighs 62.4 lbs. The density of water in the English system is 62.4 lbs,/cu. ft. Multiplying a metric density by 62.4 gives the English density of the substance. Table I lists densities of some common substances.

2. Specific Gravity—The ratio of the weight of a given volume of a substance to the weight of the same volume of water at the same temperature. Since 1 cc. of water weighs 1 g., specific gravity is numerically equal to the metric density of a substance. Both density and specific gravity have to do with the "lightness" or "heaviness" of a substance. Aluminum is "lighter" than lead. Water is "lighter" than mercury. Density is used more with solids, while specific gravity is used more with liquids or solutions (acid in the battery of your car, or alcohol or glycol in the radiator of your car).

TABLE I
DENSITY OF SUBSTANCES

Substance	*g./cc.*	*lb./cu. ft.*
Aluminum	2.7	168.5
Brass	8.6	536.6
Copper	8.9	555.4
Cork	0.22	13.7
Diamond	3.5	218.4
Gold	19.3	1204.3
Ice	0.917	57.2
Iron	7.9	493.2
Lead	11.3	705.1
Magnesium	1.74	108.6
Mercury	13.6	849.0
Rust	4.5	280.8
Salt	2.18	136.0
Sugar	1.59	99.0
Steel	7.83	488.8
Sulfur	2.0	124.9
Water, fresh	1.0	62.4
Water, sea	1.025	64.0
Zinc	7.1	443.0

3. Hardness—Ability of the substance to resist scratching. A substance will scratch any other substance which is softer. The **MOH Hardness Scale** is used as a basis for comparing the hardness of substances. This scale is made up of various minerals of different hardness (Table II), but since so few of these minerals are commonly known, Table II also gives the approximate hardness of some familiar substances. Low hardness numbers indicate soft substances, and the higher the number, the harder the substance.

4. Odor. Many substances have characteristic odors. Some have pleasant odors, like methyl salicylate (oil of wintergreen); some have pungent odors, like ammonia or sulfur dioxide (a gas which forms when the head of a match burns); some have disagreeable odors, like hydrogen sulfide (a gas which forms in rotten eggs).

5. Color. You are familiar with the color of such substances as gold or copper. White substances are usually described as colorless.

Normally it takes a combination of several specific physical properties to identify a given substance. A single property identifies a substance **only if the property is unique in Nature.** Thus, hardness serves to identify the diamond because diamond is the hardest known substance. The color of gold, however, is not unique as many prospectors unfortunately found out. Their "strike" of "fool's gold" looked like gold, but turned out to be pyrite, a far less valuable substance also known as iron sulfide.

Accidental physical properties are such features as *weight, dimensions,* and *volume.* They have nothing to do with the nature of the substance, but they enable us to find out how much of a given substance we have. **Objects,** particularly manufactured objects, may possess similar accidental properties, but these are in no way fundamentally related to the substances which make up the objects. Thus, matches and toothpicks are objects. Each is made according to a pattern of accidental properties. But toothpicks may be made of wood or of plastic, two completely different substances with totally different specific physical properties.

TABLE II
HARDNESS

MOH Scale		*Other Substances*	
Talc	1	Graphite	0.7
Gypsum	2	Asphalt	1.3
Calcite	3	Fingernail	1.5
Fluorite	4	Rock Salt	2.0
Apatite	5	Aluminum	2.6
Feldspar	6	Copper	2.8
Quartz	7	Brass	3.5
Topaz	8	Knife Blade	5.4
Corundum	9	File	6.2
Diamond	10	Glass	6.5

Chemical Properties

The chemical properties of a substance describe its ability to form new substances under given conditions. A change from one substance to another is called a **chemical change,** or a **chemical reaction.** Hence, the chemical properties of a substance may be considered to be a listing of all the chemical reactions of a substance and the conditions under which the reactions occur.

In the striking of a match, several chemical

properties of the substances in a match are illustrated. Examine Figure 1 carefully. Notice the

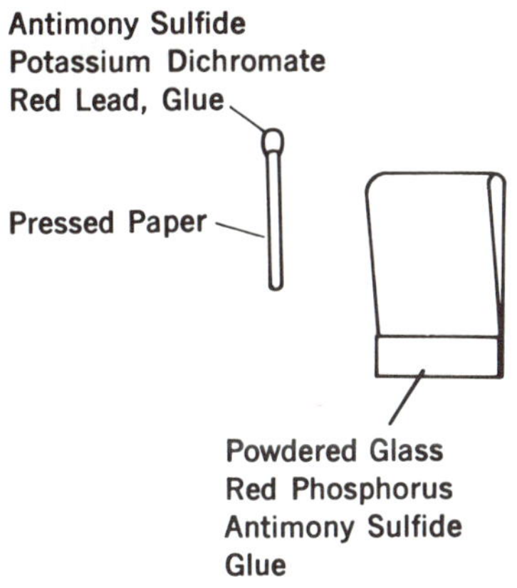

"SAFETY" MATCH

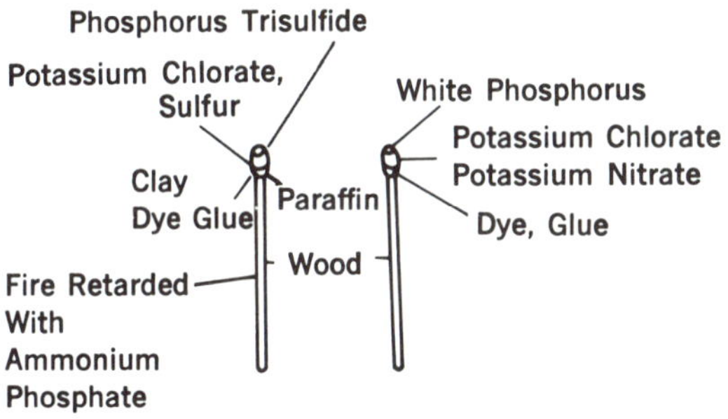

MODERN BANNED "STRIKE ANYWHERE"

FIGURE 1.

various substances present in each type of match. When you strike a "safety" match, the heat of friction of the head of the match rubbing on the glass is sufficient to cause the phosphorus on the scratching area to burn. This then generates enough heat to cause the substances in the head of the match to ignite. The burning of these, in turn, produces the heat necessary for the match-stick to catch fire. Notice that all of these substances burn (chemical property) but each does so at successively higher temperatures (conditions). None of the substances burns at room temperature! Since the phosphorus is contained only on the scratching area of the box or cover of the matches, they can be "struck" only on this area. (Occasionally safety matches can be struck on glass or linoleum where rubbing produces sufficient heat to cause the head to start burning.)

The phosphorus trisulfide in the tip of the "strike anywhere" match is very sensitive to heat. Rubbing this tip on almost any moderately hard surface will produce sufficient frictional heat to cause this substance to burn. The other substances in the tip, and finally the match-stick are then ignited as the temperature rises. White phosphorus was formerly used in the tip of this type of match. This substance likewise bursts into flame at temperatures slightly above room temperature. However, the men who worked with white phosphorus and inhaled its fumes contracted a disease known as "phossy jaw" which caused their jaw bones to rot. When laws were passed prohibiting the use of white phosphorus, the company owning the patents on phosphorus trisulfide voluntarily opened them to free public use.

The charred remnants of the match-stick and toothpick consist principally of carbon, one of the new substances formed when wood or paper burn. The "after-glow" you observed in the toothpick is a chemical property of carbon. You have seen the same phenomenon in a charcoal fire. The match-stick exhibited no after-glow because it had been treated with a solution of a *fire-retardant* substance which soaked into the wood. Borax was formerly used for this purpose, but ammonium phosphate is generally considered to be more effective for this purpose and is now widely used, not only in match-sticks, but also in drapes, tapestries, and other types of decorations.

KINDS OF MATTER

As you look at the different objects about you, you are perhaps impressed by the almost endless variety of matter. Classification of the kinds of matter into fundamental groups was an impossible task until chemists began to probe into the **composition** of matter. Knowledge of composition quickly led to the discovery that all matter is made up of either pure substances or mixtures of pure substances. Substances, in turn, are of two types, either elements or compounds. Figure 2 diagrammatically shows the kinds of matter on the basis of composition.

Elements

Elements are the basic constituents of all matter. An element is the simplest form of matter. It

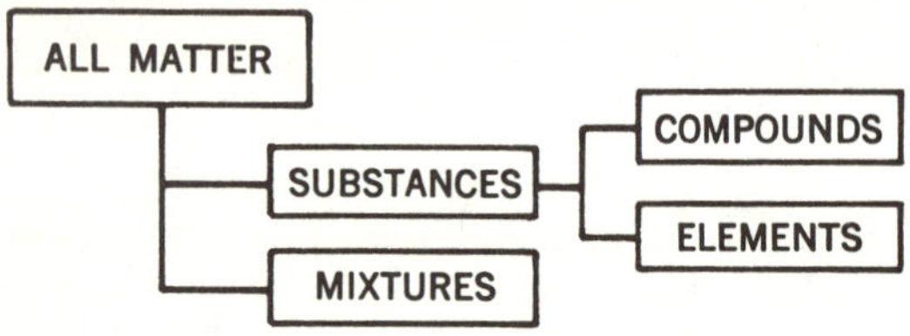

FIGURE 2.

cannot be formed from simpler substances, nor can it be decomposed into simpler varieties of matter. Some elements exist free in Nature; others are found only in combination. Free or combined, they are the building blocks which make up every different variety of matter in the universe. Table III is a list of the more commonly known elements together with their chemical **symbols.**

How many of these have you seen? How many of them have you heard of? A complete list of the 103 elements known at this time is found in Table VI.

TABLE III

Element	*Symbol*	*Element*	*Symbol*
Aluminum	Al	Neon	Ne
Argon	A	Nickel	Ni
Arsenic	As	Nitrogen	N
Bromine	Br	Oxygen	O
Calcium	Ca	Phosphorus	P
Carbon	C	Platinum	Pt
Chlorine	Cl	Plutonium	Pu
Copper	Cu	Potassium	K
Fluorine	F	Radium	Ra
Gold	Au	Silicon	Si
Helium	He	Silver	Ag
Hydrogen	H	Sodium	Na
Iodine	I	Sulfur	S
Iron	Fe	Tin	Sn
Lead	Pb	Uranium	U
Magnesium	Mg	Zinc	Zn
Mercury	Hg		

In general, the symbols are made up of the principal letter or letters in the name of the element. The symbols of elements known in antiquity are taken from their Latin names: Copper (Cuprum) Cu; Gold (Aurum) Au; Iron (Ferrum) Fe; Lead (Plumbum) Pb; Mercury (Hydrargyrum) Hg; Potassium (Kalium) K; Silver (Argentum) Ag; Sodium (Natrium) Na; Tin (Stannum) Sn. Symbols are quite important in chemistry, for they represent more than merely the name of an element.

If all matter were to be broken down into the elements which form it, the percentage of each element in Nature would be as shown in Figure 3.

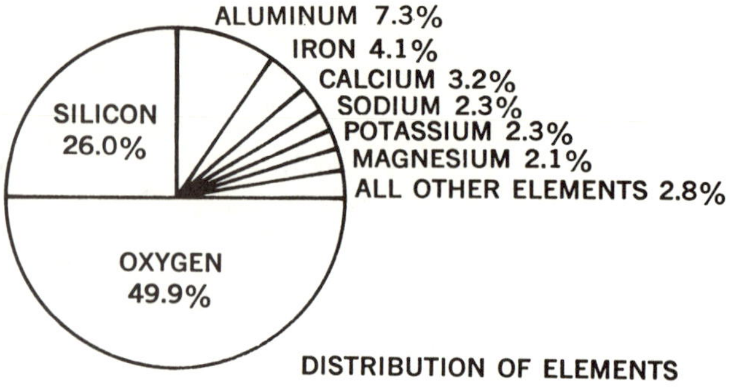

FIGURE 3.

The elements in your body can easily be remembered from the advertising sign shown in Figure 4. The symbols of the most common body elements are contained in it. Use Table III to look up the names of the twelve elements represented in the figure. The last two symbols in the sign, NaCl, stand for ordinary table salt.

Compounds

A compound is a pure substance made up of elements which are chemically combined. They are perfectly homogeneous and have a definite composition regardless of origin, location, size, or shape. A compound can be decomposed into its elements only by some type of chemical change. The elements cannot be separated in a compound by any physical means.

Compounds are much more abundant than elements. Many thousands of compounds are known. Water, sand, rust, ammonia, sugar, salt, alcohol, and benzene are all examples of familiar compounds. It is important to bear in mind that when elements combine to form compounds, the elements lose all of their properties, and a new set of properties unique to the compound are created. For example, if you were to eat any sodium or inhale any chlorine, you would quickly die, for both of these elements are poisonous. But when these two elements combine, they form a compound

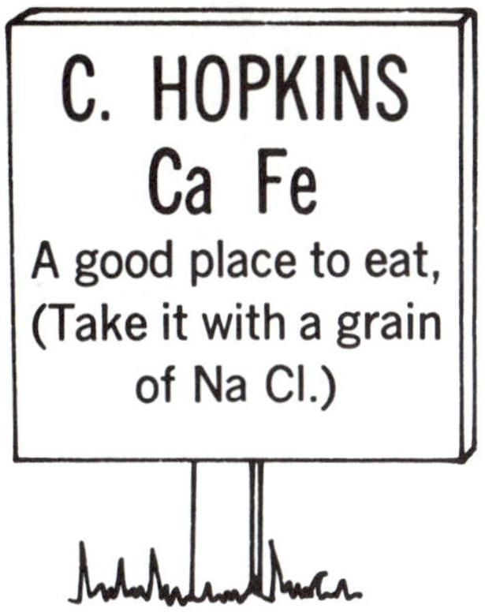

FIGURE 4.

called sodium chloride, which is ordinary table salt, a substance we must eat as part of our regular diet to maintain good health.

Mixtures

Most natural forms of matter are mixtures of pure substances. A mixture is a combination of substances held together by physical rather than chemical means. Soil and most rock, plants and animals, coal and oil, air and cooking gas, rivers and oceans, these are all mixtures. Mixtures differ from compounds in the following ways:

The ingredients of a mixture retain their own properties. If you examine a fragment of concrete you will observe that the grains of sand or gravel held together by the cement retain their identity and can be picked free. Their substance has not been changed in the formation of the concrete.

Unlike compounds which have a definite, fixed composition, **mixtures have widely varying composition.** Thus, solutions are mixtures. An infinite number of different salt water solutions can be made simply by varying the amount of salt dissolved in the water.

Mixtures can be separated into their ingredients by physical means, that is, by taking advantage of the differences in the physical properties of the ingredients. No matter how completely you mix or grind salt and pepper together, the salt can be separated from the pepper by dissolving it in water. The insoluble pepper will remain unaffected. The separation is completed by straining or **filtering** the liquid through a piece of cloth which will retain the pepper, and then evaporating the liquid **(illustrate)** to dryness of recrystallize the salt.

Perhaps you would like to try this separation for yourself. Read the following procedure fully and gather your materials before you start. Then proceed with the experiment.

EXPERIMENT 1: Mix a quarter teaspoon of salt and about half that much pepper (ground black) in a small drinking glass. Stir until a good mixture is obtained. Add about a half glass of water and stir until the salt is dissolved. Place a handkerchief or small piece of cloth loosely over the top of a small sauce pan. Filter the liquid into the pan. Notice that all the pepper remains on the cloth and that the salt solution in the pan is perfectly clear. Taste the clear filtrate to see if the salt is really there. Over a very low heat boil away the water in the pan. Be sure to remove the pan just as the last bit of liquid disappears. The white sediment is the recrystallized salt. Taste it to make sure.

The separation of mixtures into ingredients is an important operation. Almost every industry that uses natural products as raw materials employs one or more of the basic methods of separating mixtures. All of the methods take advantage of differences in physical properties of the ingredients. Some of the important methods of separating mixtures are:

Sorting. This involves a selection of the desired ingredient from the waste product in a fragmented mixture. It may be done by hand or by machine. The mining of coal is an example of this process. Here the coal is blasted loose from the inside of the earth and is then separated by sorting from the rock which accompanies the coal.

Magnetic Separation. Some iron ore is magnetic. This ore is scooped up in giant shovels from the earth, crushed, and poured on to a magnetized belt as shown in Figure 5. The non-magnetic waste ma-

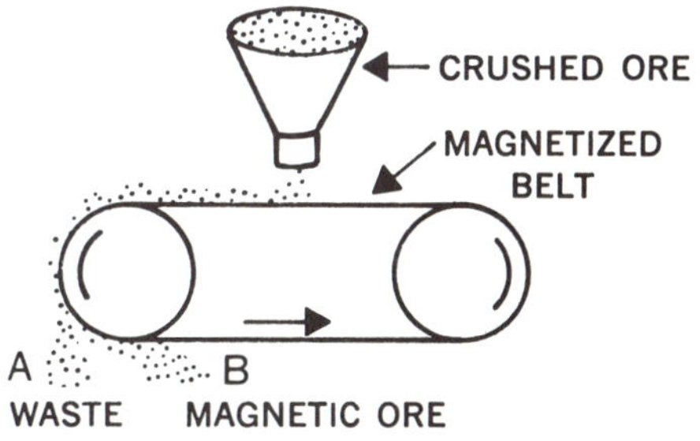

FIGURE 5.

terial drops off the belt at A, but the magnetic ore clings to the belt until it reaches B, and is thus separated.

Distillation. This process takes advantage of the difference in temperature of boiling **(boiling point)** between the ingredients of a solution. The ingredient with the lowest boiling point boils away first, leaving the higher boiling residue behind. The low boiling ingredient is said to be more **volatile** than the residue. The ingredient which boils off as a gas is then **condensed** back to a liquid by cooling and is collected in a new container.

EXPERIMENT 2: Dissolve a teapoon of sugar in a cup of water and place the solution in a tea kettle. Taste the solution to be sure it is sweet. Heat the solution to boiling. Hold a large plate vertically with the far edge just in front of the spout of the kettle so that the steam strikes it. (See Fig. 6.) Let the condensed moisture **(condensate)** run down the plate into a cup. Taste the condensate. Is it sweet? Where is the sugar? Which is more volatile, water or sugar? Remove the kettle from the burner before the solution boils completely to dryness.

FIGURE 6.

Simple distillation effectively separates water and sugar because the boiling points of these two substances are relatively far apart. When the boiling points of ingredients to be separated are close together, a process known as **fractional distillation** is used. In this process, a large tower or column is erected above the boiling pot and fitted with cooling coils, or a cooling jacket (See Fig. 7). This provides efficient condensation of the less volatile ingredient and permits the more volatile one to escape to a new container. The separation of crude petroleum into such products as gasoline, lubricating oil, and fuel oil is accomplished by fractional distillation of the petroleum.

Extraction. The process of extraction involves the dissolving out of an ingredient from a mixture

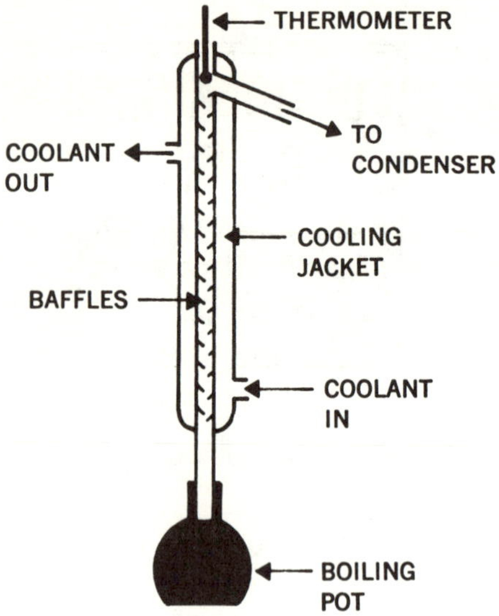

FIGURE 7. Fractional Distillation Column

with a suitable **solvent.** Water was the solvent used to extract salt from the salt and pepper mixture in Experiment 1. Water is also used to extract the flavor of coffee from ground coffee beans in your coffee maker. Alcohol is used to extract vanillin, vanilla flavor, from vanilla beans. Other solvents like benzene, carbon tetrachloride, ether, and acetone are used to extract stains from your clothing.

Gravitation. This process takes advantage of differences in density or specific gravity of the ingredients in a mixture. In the panning of gold, the gold grains settled to the bottom of the pan because of their high density, and the lighter rocks were washed over the edge of the pan with water. In wheat harvesting, the light chaff is blown away from the denser wheat grains. The cleansing action of soap is also based upon this process. Soap bubbles surround the dense dirt particles on your skin or clothing and float the particles away.

PHYSICAL CHANGE

A physical change involves the alteration of the properties of a substance without affecting the substance itself. Hammering a piece of metal will modify its shape and increase its hardness, but the substance of the metal will remain unchanged. Freezing water to ice or boiling it to steam causes a thorough change in physical properties, but the substance remains water.

CHEMICAL CHANGE

Chemical change involves such a thorough change in a substance that an entirely new substance is formed in the process. The new substance created has its own set of properties, so physical change accompanies chemical change. Do you remember how completely the match was transformed as it burned? That was a chemical change. All burning involves chemical change. So does the rusting of iron, the toasting of bread, the drying of ink, the taking of a photograph, and the digestion of food. Chemical change is a common occurrence.

There are four principal types of chemical change: combination, decomposition, replacement, and double displacement. All chemical changes involve one or a combination of these basic varieties. Let us examine each type more carefully.

1. Combination. Combination is the direct joining of two or more simple substances, either elements or simple compounds, to form a more complex compound. For example, copper will join with oxygen in the air when heated to form a compound, copper oxide.

EXPERIMENT 3: Remove about 2 inches of insulation from a 6-inch length of copper wire. Clean the exposed metal with sandpaper to a bright copper color. Heat the copper to redness in the upper part of a gas flame for about one minute. Permit the wire to cool. Notice the black coating on the copper. This is copper oxide. Scrape it off with a knife. This exposes copper metal once more as indicated by the color. Repeat this experiment until you are satisfied that the copper is really **oxidizing** in the flame.

The reaction involved in Experiment 3 can be stated in words thus:

Copper	+	**Oxygen**	=	***Copper oxide**
An element		*An element*		*A compound of the two elements*

2. Decomposition. Decomposition is the breaking down of a compound into simpler compounds or into its elements. For example, hydrogen peroxide decomposes in strong light or on contact with skin or other living tissue. Hydrogen peroxide is a compound of hydrogen and oxygen. It decomposes into water, a simpler compound of hydrogen and oxygen, and into oxygen, an element.

EXPERIMENT 4: Pour a small amount of hydrogen peroxide solution into the palm of your hand. Watch the solution closely. The bubbles which form are bubbles of oxygen gas. The rest of the peroxide forms water.

The reaction in Experiment 4 may be stated thus:

Hydrogen peroxide	=	**Oxygen**	+	**Water**
A compound		*An element*		*A compound*

3. Replacement. Replacement involves the substitution of one element for another in a compound. For example, if a piece of iron were to be dropped into a solution of sulfuric acid (the solution present in the battery of your car), hydrogen gas would be observed bubbling out of the solution. Sulfuric acid is a compound of hydrogen, sulfur, and oxygen. The iron replaces the hydrogen, liberating it as an element, and forms a new compound, iron sulfate (iron, sulfur, and oxygen), in solution. This reaction may be stated thus:

Iron *An element*	+	**Sulfuric Acid** *A compound*	=
Hydrogen *An element*	+	**Iron sulfate** *A compound*	

4. Double Displacement. In double displacement reactions, two compounds react to form two new compounds by exchanging parts. To observe a reaction of this type we need a special solution. Let us make it first.

EXPERIMENT 5: Phenolphthalein is the active ingredient of many common laxatives. It can be extracted from them as follows. Crack and peel off the sugar coating from two Feen-a-mint* tablets, taking care to disturb as little as possible the yellow powder just under the coating. Place the two tablets in a small cup and add one tablespoon of rubbing alcohol. Stir until the yellow phenolphthalein is dissolved from the gum, forming a pale yellow solution.

Keep this phenolphthalein solution in a stoppered

* The equal sign (=) indicates that the substances on the left are transformed into the substance on the right during chemical change. As we will see later, the total weight of substances combining on the left must precisely equal the total weight of products formed on the right. The equal sign emphasizes this quantitative nature of the science of chemistry. Furthermore, many chemical changes are reversible, which means that the substances on the right can be induced to re-form the substances on the left.

* Trade Name.

bottle. An old well-rinsed nose-drop bottle would be excellent. We will use this solution several times. Phenolphthalein has the property of turning red in solutions of alkalis, but is colorless in acid solutions. An **alkali** is a compound which is the opposite of an **acid.** An alkali **neutralizes** an acid to water and salt solution. Such a reaction is a double displacement type. Let us observe one.

EXPERIMENT 6: Dissolve a few crystals of lye (sodium hydroxide) in one quarter cup of water. Add 2 or 3 drops of phenolphthalein solution prepared in Experiment 5. The red color shows that sodium hydroxide is an alkali. Add vinegar (acetic acid) drop by drop with stirring to the sodium hydroxide solution. When the phenolphthalein becomes colorless, the reaction is completed.

All of the substances involved in the reaction in Experiment 6 are compounds. The reaction may be stated thus:

Sodium Hydroxide	+	**Acetic Acid**	=	**Sodium Acetate**	+	**Water**
An alkali		*An acid*		*A salt*		

In every chemical change, energy is either given off or absorbed. **Energy** is the ability to do work. Heat, light, sound, and electricity are some of the many forms of energy. Fuel oil burns to produce heat. Magnesium burns in a flash bulb to produce light. Dynamite explodes to produce sound and shock. On the other hand, water decomposes into its elements, hydrogen and oxygen, by absorbing electrical energy. A photograph is made by the absorption of light by the chemicals in the film.

It is important not to confuse the energy change in a reaction with the conditions under which a reaction occurs. Wood burns to produce heat, but not at room temperature. The wood must first be heated to a point considerably above room temperature before it will begin to burn. The high initial temperature is a condition under which the reaction of burning takes place. The production of heat by burning wood is a result of the reaction itself.

Many reactions take place only in the presence of a **catalyst.** A catalyst is a substance which alters the speed or rate of a chemical without becoming permanently changed itself. A catalyst which speeds up a reaction is called a **negative catalyst.** Water is a catalyst for many reactions. Perfectly dry iron will not rust in dry air. Dry crystals of acetic acid will not react as in Experiment 6 with dry crystals of sodium hydroxide.

EXPERIMENT 7: With a match, try to burn a cube of sugar. Notice that the sugar melts but does not burn. Dip the other end of the sugar cube into some cigarette or cigar ashes. *Bear in mind that these ashes have already been burned!* Apply a flame to the ash-covered end of the cube. It now burns because of the presence of a catalyst.

Structure of Matter

We have seen that chemical change involves a complete transformation of one substance into another. Early chemists reasoned that such a thorough change must in some way be related to the way matter is constructed. They sought to find out the nature of the building blocks which made up the different varieties of matter. They hoped that once they could create some sort of "model" of the fundamental particles of matter, they could then explain not only the various ways that matter was constructed, but also the behavior of substances during the process of chemical change.

As early as 450 B.C. the Greek philosophers reasoned that all matter was built up of tiny particles called **atoms.** Development of this idea was slow, but in 1802 DALTON suggested that all matter could be broken down into elements, the smallest particles of which he referred to as atoms. By 1895, the theory that atoms existed was extended to account for particles of matter even smaller than atoms. By 1913, evidence of the presence of several subatomic particles had been gathered. The work of probing into the structure of matter continues at the present moment. We have not yet learned the full story, and many features of the behavior of matter are still unexplained. There is much room in the field of science for young people with talent.

From a chemical point of view an atomic model has been developed which is quite satisfactory. We will use it to explain all common phenomena. We will also look at some of its weaker points in order to show that science is not cut and dried, but rather is constantly changing as men of science progress toward a better understanding of Nature.

ATOMS

If we were to take a strip of aluminum or a piece of copper (elements) and subdivide them into smaller and smaller pieces, we would eventually come to a tiny particle which, if further subdivided, would no longer show the properties of the element. We call the smallest particle of an element which has all the properties of the element an **atom.** Atoms are really quite small, too small to be seen with the most powerful microscope yet developed. It would take about 100 million atoms to make a line one inch long. You can thus see that a one inch cube would contain a fantastic number of atoms. The important thing is that atoms are both small and numerous.

ATOMIC STRUCTURE

In 1913 NEILS BOHR, a Danish scientist, suggested an atomic model which serves chemists well to the present day. He pictured the atom as consisting of three basic kinds of particles: **electrons, protons,** and **neutrons.** The electron is a particle possessing a negative (−) electrical charge. The proton is a particle consisting of a positive (+) electrical charge equal in magnitude (but opposite in type) to the charge on the electron. The neutron is a particle with no electrical charge. The proton and neutron have essentially the same weight. A weight of one unit has been assigned to each. The electron is much smaller, weighing about 1/1848 times as much as either of the other two. From a chemical point of view, we can consider the weight of the electron to be zero. Table IV summarizes the properties of these three particles which make up an atom.

TABLE IV

Particle	*Charge*	*Weight*
Electron	−1	0
Proton	+1	1
Neutron	0	1

In the Bohr model of the atom, protons and neutrons are considered to be packed together in the center of the atom to form what is known as the **nucleus.** Electrons travel about this nucleus in orbits which are at relatively large distances from the nucleus. The average nucleus occupies about one-ten thousandth of the total volume of an atom. The situation is quite similar to the planets revolving about the sun in our solar system.

At this point, three important characteristics of atoms can be stated:

1. Despite the presence of electrically charged particles in atoms, all elements are observed to be electrically neutral. Therefore, the number of positive protons in the nucleus of an atom must be equal to the number of electrons surrounding the nucleus.

2. Since elements differ from one another, their atoms must differ structurally. Each element has an **atomic number.** The atomic number is more than just a catalog number. It is a special characteristic of each element. In the Bohr model, the atomic number is equal to the number of electrons revolving about the nucleus of the atom. Thus, each atom of hydrogen (atomic number 1) has a single electron spinning about the hydrogen nucleus. Each atom of uranium (atomic number 92) has 92 electrons spinning about the uranium nucleus. Since atoms are electrically neutral, the atomic number also equals the number of protons present in the nucleus of an atom.

3. Equal numbers of atoms of different elements weighed under the same conditions have a different weight. Therefore, the atoms of different elements have different atomic weights. The **atomic weight** of an **atom** is equal to the sum of the number of protons and the number of neutrons in the nucleus of the atom. Thus, all of the weight of an atom comes from its nucleus. Atomic weights are relative, which is to say they do not give the number of grams or pounds that an atom weighs, but they merely tell how much heavier or lighter an atom of one element is than another. For example, the atomic weight of oxygen is 16 and the atomic weight of helium is 4. This means that each atom of oxygen weighs 16/4, or 4 times as much as each atom of helium.

These three atomic characteristics are summarized in Table V.

It may be well to pause here to see how our atomic model is shaping up. Can you visualize a nugget or kernel like a popcorn ball with tiny specks of dust spinning round and round it? Perhaps the popcorn ball also has peanuts in it, giving it two different kinds of particles. We can think of the popcorn as protons and the peanuts as neu-

TABLE V

Characteristic	*Structural Explanation*
Neutral atoms	Number of electrons = Number of protons
Atomic Number	Number of electrons = Number of protons = atomic number
Atomic Weight	Number of protons + Number of neutrons = atomic weight

trons, all tightly held together in the nucleus. The specks of dust spinning around would be the electrons, equal in number to the pieces of popcorn. The specks of dust would contribute practically nothing to the total weight of our imaginary atom. A model of hydrogen would consist of a single piece of popcorn with a single speck of dust spinning around it. A uranium model would contain quite a lot of popcorn (92 pieces) and many peanuts (146). It would also be quite dusty (92 specks). The sum of the particles in the uranium nucleus is 238, which is the atomic weight of uranium. Figure 8 gives us another picture of our model.

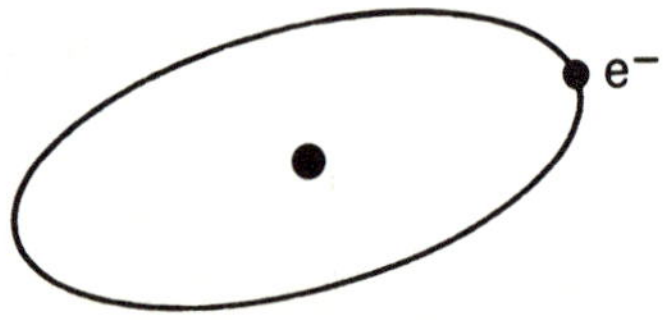

HYDROGEN
At. No. 1
At. Wt. 1

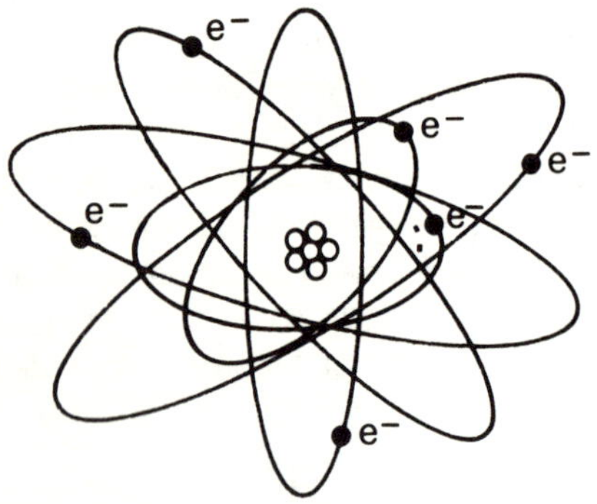

CARBON
At. No. 6
At. Wt. 12

FIGURE 8.

Distribution of Electrons

Our model of an atom is still incomplete. The electrons which revolve about the nucleus do so according to a definite pattern. Groups of electrons maintain definite average distances from the nucleus, thereby forming what may be called **shells** of electrons surrounding the nucleus. Each shell is capable of containing a definite number of electrons, the number increasing as the distance from the nucleus increases. The shells are designated by letters—k, l, m, n, o, p—starting with the shell nearest the nucleus. The k-shell can contain up to 2 electrons, the l-shell up to 8, the m-shell up to 18, and the n-shell up to 32. The maximum number of electrons in any shell can be calculated from the relationship:

$$\text{Number} = 2\,s^2 \qquad (1)$$

where:

Number = maximum number of electrons possible in the shell.
s = the number of the shell (k = 1, l = 2, m = 3, etc.).

The distribution of electrons by shells for the atoms of each element is given in Table VI. As you read through this list starting with element number 1, hydrogen, be sure to notice the following points:

1. In the first 18 elements the new electron is always added in the outermost shell until the shell is filled. Then a new shell is started.
2. In the higher numbered elements there can be 2 or even 3 unfilled shells of electrons.
3. Eight electrons temporarily fill each of the shells beyond the m-shell, and a new shell must be started before more electrons can be fitted into the temporarily filled shell.

TABLE VI
DISTRIBUTION OF ELECTRONS

At. No.	Element	k	l	m	n	o	p	q
1	Hydrogen	1						
2	Helium	2						
3	Lithium	2	1					
4	Beryllium	2	2					
5	Boron	2	3					
6	Carbon	2	4					
7	Nitrogen	2	5					
8	Oxygen	2	6					
9	Fluorine	2	7					
10	Neon	2	8					
11	Sodium	2	8	1				
12	Magnesium	2	8	2				
13	Aluminum	2	8	3				
14	Silicon	2	8	4				
15	Phosphorus	2	8	5				
16	Sulfur	2	8	6				
17	Chlorine	2	8	7				
18	Argon	2	8	8				
19	Potassium	2	8	8	1			
20	Calcium	2	8	8	2			
21	Scandium	2	8	9	2			
22	Titanium	2	8	10	2			
23	Vanadium	2	8	11	2			
24	Chromium	2	8	13	1			
25	Manganese	2	8	13	2			
26	Iron	2	8	14	2			
27	Cobalt	2	8	15	2			
28	Nickel	2	8	16	2			
29	Copper	2	8	18	1			
30	Zinc	2	8	18	2			
31	Gallium	2	8	18	3			
32	Germanium	2	8	18	4			
33	Arsenic	2	8	18	5			
34	Selenium	2	8	18	6			
35	Bromine	2	8	18	7			
36	Krypton	2	8	18	8			
37	Rubidium	2	8	18	8	1		
38	Strontium	2	8	18	8	2		
39	Yttrium	2	8	18	9	2		
40	Zirconium	2	8	18	10	2		
41	Niobium	2	8	18	12	1		
42	Molybdenum	2	8	18	13	1		
43	Technetium	2	8	18	14	1		
44	Ruthenium	2	8	18	15	1		
45	Rhodium	2	8	18	16	1		
46	Palladium	2	8	18	18	0		
47	Silver	2	8	18	18	1		
48	Cadmium	2	8	18	18	2		
49	Indium	2	8	18	18	3		
50	Tin	2	8	18	18	4		
51	Antimony	2	8	18	18	5		
52	Tellurium	2	8	18	18	6		
53	Iodine	2	8	18	18	7		
54	Xenon	2	8	18	18	8		
55	Cesium	2	8	18	18	8	1	
56	Barium	2	8	18	18	8	2	
57	Lanthanum	2	8	18	18	9	2	
58	Cerium	2	8	18	20	8	2	
59	Pra'mium	2	8	18	21	8	2	
60	Neodymium	2	8	18	22	8	2	
61	Promethium	2	8	18	23	8	2	
62	Samarium	2	8	18	24	8	2	
63	Europium	2	8	18	25	8	2	
64	Gadolinium	2	8	18	25	9	2	
65	Terbium	2	8	18	27	8	2	
66	Dysprosium	2	8	18	28	8	2	
67	Holmium	2	8	18	29	8	2	
68	Erbium	2	8	18	30	8	2	
69	Thulium	2	8	18	31	8	2	
70	Ytterbium	2	8	18	32	8	2	
71	Lutetium	2	8	18	32	9	2	
72	Hafnium	2	8	18	32	10	2	
73	Tantalum	2	8	18	32	11	2	
74	Tungsten	2	8	18	32	12	2	
75	Rhenium	2	8	18	32	13	2	
76	Osmium	2	8	18	32	14	2	
77	Iridium	2	8	18	32	17	0	
78	Platinum	2	8	18	32	17	1	
79	Gold	2	8	18	32	18	1	
80	Mercury	2	8	18	32	18	2	
81	Thallium	2	8	18	32	18	3	
82	Lead	2	8	18	32	18	4	
83	Bismuth	2	8	18	32	18	5	
84	Polonium	2	8	18	32	18	6	
85	Astatine	2	8	18	32	18	7	
86	Radon	2	8	18	32	18	8	
87	Francium	2	8	18	32	18	8	1
88	Radium	2	8	18	32	18	8	2
89	Actinium	2	8	18	32	18	9	2
90	Thorium	2	8	18	32	18	10	2
91	Pr'tinium	2	8	18	32	20	9	2
92	Uranium	2	8	18	32	21	9	2
93	Neptunium	2	8	18	32	22	9	2
94	Plutonium	2	8	18	32	23	9	2
95	Americium	2	8	18	32	24	9	2
96	Curium	2	8	18	32	25	9	2
97	Berkelium	2	8	18	32	26	9	2
98	Californium	2	8	18	32	27	9	2
99	Einsteinium	2	8	18	32	28	9	2
100	Fermium	2	8	18	32	29	9	2
101	Mendelvium	2	8	18	32	30	9	2
102	Nobelium	2	8	18	32	31	9	2
103	Lawrencium							

4. **There are never more than 8 electrons in the outermost shell.**

On the basis of the distribution of electrons we can detect four different structural types of atoms in Table VI. These are:

1. **Inert elements**—Those with all shells filled. (These are underlined in Table VI.)
2. **Simple elements**—Those with only one unfilled shell.
3. **Transition elements**—Those with two unfilled shells.
4. **Rare earth elements**—Those with three unfilled shells.

At first glance, this whole problem of the distribution of electrons in our atomic model might appear to be quite imposing. Actually it is not as hard as it may seem. Remember that we want a model which is useful in explaining chemical change. Two vitally important points are basic in relating chemical change with atomic structure. These are:

Only electrons are involved in chemical change. The nuclei of atoms are in no way altered during chemical change.

In particular, **the electrons in the outermost shell are affected during chemical change.** Occasionally electrons from the second outermost shell may be affected in some of the higher numbered elements, but the influence of chemical change never penetrates the atom deeper than the second outermost shell.

ISOTOPES

Evidence is available to show that not all of the atoms of a given element are identical. They may vary in atomic weight. Atoms of an element with different atomic weights are called **isotopes** of the element.

Examine Figure 9. This shows three different kinds of hydrogen atoms. The first has an atomic weight of 1, the second has an atomic weight of 2, and the third has an atomic weight of 3. Notice that the only structural difference is the number of neutrons in the nucleus of each isotope. All three isotopes have but one electron because all are atoms of hydrogen and have atomic number 1. Similarly, all three isotopes have a single proton in the nucleus because each must remain electrically neutral. Isotopes, then, are atoms of the same element possessing different numbers of neutrons in their nuclei.

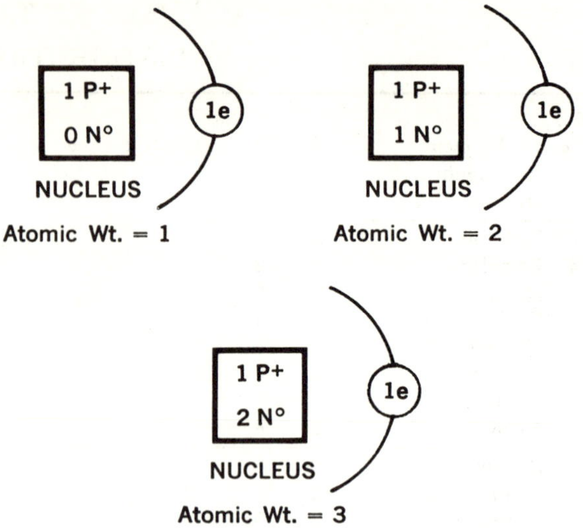

FIGURE 9. The 3 Isotopes of Hydrogen

ATOMIC WEIGHTS

Almost all of the elements have isotopes. The relative abundance of each isotope of a given element in Nature varies considerably. For example, the element chlorine has two principal isotopes, one of atomic weight 35 and one of atomic weight 37. If you were to pick up a container of chlorine, about 75% of the chlorine atoms in the container would have atomic weight 35, and the other 25% would have atomic weight 37. The average weight of all the atoms in the container would then be about 35.5. The listed atomic weight of chlorine can be found in the table on page 484. You will find it to be 35.457. This number is the average atomic weight of all the atoms present in a sample of natural chlorine. The listed **atomic weight** of any **element** is the average of the atomic weights of the isotopes of the element, taking into account the relative abundance of each isotope in a natural sample.

On a practical basis, the average atomic weight of an element is measured by comparing the weight of a given number of atoms of the element to the weight of the same number of atoms of oxygen. The weight of oxygen is taken as 16. How chemists know when they are dealing with a given number of atoms will be described later.

SYMBOLS

In Table III the symbols of some of the more common elements were given. These symbols are very important in chemistry for they represent three things:

1. The name of an element.
2. One atom of an element.
3. A quantity of the element equal in weight to its atomic weight.

For example, when we write the symbol O, we mean not only the name, oxygen, but we also represent a single oxygen atom with this symbol. What is perhaps most important of all, since oxygen has an atomic weight of 16, the symbol O stands for 16 units of weight of this element. This may be 16 grams, or 16 pounds, or 16 tons. We can select any system of weight units we need when we use symbols to indicate quantities of elements. This idea will be developed further in the next section.

THE BOHR MODEL

Our atomic model, as created by BOHR, is now sufficiently developed to explain chemical phenomena. It contains a nucleus composed of positive protons and neutral neutrons which supply the weight of the atom. Surrounding the nucleus are shells of electrons carrying sufficient negative charge to offset the positive charge on the nucleus. Figure 10 is a diagram of the atomic structure of an isotope of phosphorus of atomic weight 31. It shows the number of protons and neutrons in the nucleus, and the number and distribution of electrons in the shells. The atomic weight is the sum of the number of protons and neutrons in the nucleus. The atomic number is the sum of the electrons in the shells.

If you are familiar with the properties of electricity, you know that opposite charges attract one another and like charges repel one another. As you look at Figure 10, two questions might be raised.

Why aren't the negative electrons attracted into the positive nucleus, causing our model to collapse? The answer to this is in the idea that the electrons are spinning about the nucleus. If you tie a piece of string to a ball and whirl it around, the string will get tight. The whirling motion of the ball causes it to want to fly away from your hand, but the string holds it back. In our atom, the electrical attraction of the positive nucleus and the negative electron just balances the tendency of the whirling electron to escape from the nucleus.

A second question suggested by Figure 10 is:

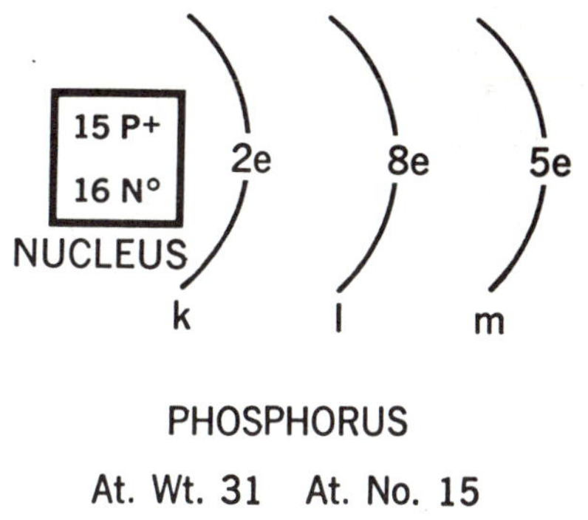

FIGURE 10.

Why doesn't the nucleus fly apart as a result of the repulsion of the protons on each other? In answer to this we can merely state that there is some sort of packing energy holding nuclei together. This energy is not always 100% efficient, because we know that some nuclei do break apart in a process known as **radioactivity.** This will be described later. The exact nature of the packing energy is not yet understood. At this moment scientists all over the world are at work trying to solve this secret of Nature.

THE PERIODIC TABLE

On the basis of electronic distribution, all of the elements have been arranged in a table called the **Periodic Table.** Figure 11 gives this arrangement, showing the atomic number, symbol, and atomic weight of each element. Where atomic weights have not yet been accurately measured, the approximate value is given in brackets.

The vertical columns are called **groups.** All of the elements in a group have the same electronic structure in their outermost shell. For example, all of the elements in Group I have 1 electron in the outermost shell (Check this with Table VI). Elements in Group II have 2 outermost electrons, elements in Group III have 3 outermost electrons, and so on. The inert elements at the far right of the table have 8 outermost electrons. The transition elements may be thought of as arranged in **sub-groups,** and all of these have 2 outermost electrons with the exception of the Copper-Silver-Gold subgroup which has only 1 outermost electron.

The horizontal rows of elements are called **periods.** All the elements in a given period have the same number of shells of electrons. For example, the elements in Period 1 have but one shell

PERIODIC TABLE OF ELEMENTS

PERIODS	GROUP I	GROUP II											GROUP III	GROUP IV	GROUP V	GROUP VI	GROUP VII	INERT Elem.
1	1 H 1.008																	2 He 4.003
2	3 Li 6.940	4 Be 9.02											5 B 10.82	6 C 12.010	7 N 14.008	8 O 16.000	9 F 19.00	10 Ne 20.183
3	11 Na 22.997	12 Mg 24.32	TRANSITION ELEMENTS										13 Al 26.97	14 Si 28.06	15 P 30.98	16 S 32.06	17 Cl 35.457	18 A 39.944
4	19 K 39.096	20 Ca 40.08	21 Sc 45.10	22 Ti 47.90	23 V 50.95	24 Cr 52.01	25 Mn 54.93	26 Fe 55.85	27 Co 58.94	28 Ni 58.69	29 Cu 63.57	30 Zn 65.38	31 Ga 69.72	32 Ge 72.60	33 As 74.91	34 Se 78.96	35 Br 79.916	36 Kr 83.7
5	37 Rb 85.48	38 Sr 87.63	39 Y 88.92	40 Zr 91.22	41 Nb 92.91	42 Mo 95.95	43 Tc [99]	44 Ru 101.7	45 Rh 102.91	46 Pd 106.7	47 Ag 107.88	48 Cd 112.41	49 In 114.76	50 Sn 118.70	51 Sb 121.76	52 Te 127.61	53 I 126.92	54 Xe 131.3
6	55 Cs 132.91	56 Ba 137.36	57 La 138.9 58 I 71	72 Hf 178.6	73 Ta 180.88	74 W 183.92	75 Re 186.31	76 Os 190.2	77 Ir 193.1	78 Pt 195.23	79 Au 197.2	80 Hg 200.61	81 Tl 204.39	82 Pb 207.21	83 Bi 209.00	84 Po [210]	85 At [210]	86 Rn [222]
7	87 Fr [223]	88 Ra 226.05	89 Ac [227] 90 I 103															

LANTHANIDE SERIES	57 La 138.92	58 Ce 140.13	59 Pr 140.92	60 Nd 144.27	61 Pm [145]	62 Sm 150.43	63 Eu 152.0	64 Gd 156.9	65 Tb 159.2	66 Dy 162.46	67 Ho 163.5	68 Er 167.2	69 Tm 169.4	70 Yb 173.04	71 Lu 174.99
ACTINIDE SERIES	89 Ac [227]	90 Th 232.12	91 Pa 231	92 U 238.07	93 Np 237	94 Pu [242]	95 Am [243]	96 Cm. [243]	97 Bk [245]	98 Cf [246]	99 Es [254]	100 Fm [255]	101 Md [258]	102 No [253]	103

RARE EARTH ELEM. 1

FIGURE 11.

of electrons. Those in Period 2 have 2 shells, and so on. It is important to note that the last element of each period is an inert element. The lanthanide series of rare earth elements is part of Period 6, and the actinide series of rare earth elements is part of Period 7.

All four structural types of elements are shown in the table. The inert elements form a group at the extreme right. The simple elements are found in Groups I through VII. The transition elements are at the center. The rare earth elements are extracted from the table and listed at the bottom.

It has been pointed out that the chemical behavior of elements is based upon the electronic structure of their atoms, particularly the structure of the outer shell. Since each *group* of elements has the same structure in the outer shell, we can expect the members of a group to show similar chemical behavior. For this reason we can expect to find much use for the Periodic Table as we explore the chemical behavior of elements.

Compounds

Elements in the free or uncombined state make up only a small fraction of matter. Most of matter occurs as compounds or mixtures of compounds. Let us now put our Bohr model of the atom to the test to see whether it is useful in explaining how elements can combine to form all the various compounds.

THE INERT ELEMENTS

Take another look at Table VI. Pay special attention to the elements which are just above the separating lines. Notice that except for helium, all of these elements have eight electrons in the **outermost shell.** Then notice that the next element in each case has one electron in a new shell. Why doesn't this new electron go into one of the existing shells? The answer is that it simply doesn't fit, which is another way of saying that the shells of electrons in the elements just above the separating lines are, for the moment at least, filled up or saturated with electrons.

Now look up each of the elements just above the separating lines in the Periodic Table (Fig.

TABLE VII
PROPERTIES OF INERT ELEMENTS

Property	Helium He	Neon Ne	Argon A	Krypton Kr	Xenon Xe	Radon Rn
Atomic Number	2	10	18	36	54	86
Atomic Weight	4.003	20.183	39.944	83.7	131.3	222
Density, g/cc.	0.00018	0.0009	0.00179	0.00374	0.0058	0.0099
Solubility, ml/100 ml. of water	1.49	1.5	5.6	6.0	28.4	0.000002
Parts in Million parts of dry air	4	12.3	9400	0.5	0.06	——
Boiling Point, °F.	−452.2	−410.8	−302.4	−243.4	−161.0	−79.5
Melting Point, °F.	−458.1	−416.6	−308.7	−250.8	−170.0	−96.1

11). You will find all of them in the column at the far right under the heading: Inert Elements. Each of them occurs at the end of a period. Eventually, in subsequent periods in our atmosphere, the outermost shells may consist of more than eight electrons.

These inert elements all have one chemical property which is: they have no chemistry! They combine with nothing. They form no compounds either among themselves or with other elements. They are indeed chemically inert. All of these elements are gases at room temperature, and all except radon are present in inert elements; their electronic configuration obviously represents a temporarily saturated state.

You might ask why we should bring up this group of elements which form no compounds in a section devoted to the formation of compounds. Well, these elements possess a structure so stable that they resist compound formation. All the other elements are less stable since they do form compounds. It is suggested that when active elements combine to form compounds, they undergo a rearrangement of their electronic structures in order to gain an electronic configuration similar to that of a nearby inert element. Such a rearrangement causes the active elements to become structurally more stable.

VALENCE

The tendency of elements to form compounds through a shift of electronic structure is known as **valence.** Actually the term valence may be used to indicate two different things. One is **valence mechanism,** that is, the manner in which elements attain a stable electronic distribution. The other is **valence number,** that is, the number of electrons of an element involved in forming a compound. Let us examine first the valence mechanism, the process by which compounds are formed.

Electrovalence

Consider for a moment the structure of an atom of sodium. It has one electron in its outermost shell and eight electrons in its next outermost shell. If the lone electron were to be removed from the sodium atom, the remaining electronic structure would be identical to the structure of neon, an inert element which immediately precedes sodium in the Periodic Table. The removal of the electron would change the nature of the particle by causing it to have one excess positive charge. It would no longer be a sodium atom for, although its nucleus is still that of sodium, it would possess an insufficient number of electrons to be a sodium atom. Nor would it be neon, for its nucleus has too many protons. An electrically charged particle of the type described is called an **ion.** The one being considered is a sodium ion. Ions possess properties which are totally different from the atoms from which they come.

The idea of forming an ion from an atom is reasonable enough, but where can the electron go? The elements near sodium in the Periodic Table, like potassium or calcium or magnesium, would not accept an additional electron, for it would not bring them nearer a stable electronic configuration. But over near the other end of the Periodic Table are elements like chlorine. Chlorine has seven electrons in its outermost shell. The addition of one or more electrons would give it the same stable configuration as argon, another inert element. The addition of the electron to the chlorine atom would form a particle with one excess negative charge. It would be neither a chlorine atom nor an argon atom. It would be a **chloride ion.** Once the electron has been transferred from the sodium atom to the chlorine atom, we then have oppositely charged ions which are capable of attracting one another electrically. They do so to form the familiar compound, sodium chloride, which is ordinary table salt. Figure 12 shows the formation of this compound. The process of forming a compound through the **transfer of electrons** is called **electrovalence.**

A careful consideration of the Periodic Table will lead to the discovery of the elements which show electrovalence. Elements in Groups I, II, and III give up 1, 2, or 3 electrons respectively to form positive ions. These elements are said to exhibit **positive valence.** Elements in Groups V, VI, and VII accept 3, 2, or 1 electron respectively to form negative ions. These elements are said to exhibit **negative valence.** Table VIII gives the symbols for typical ions formed by elements in each of these groups.

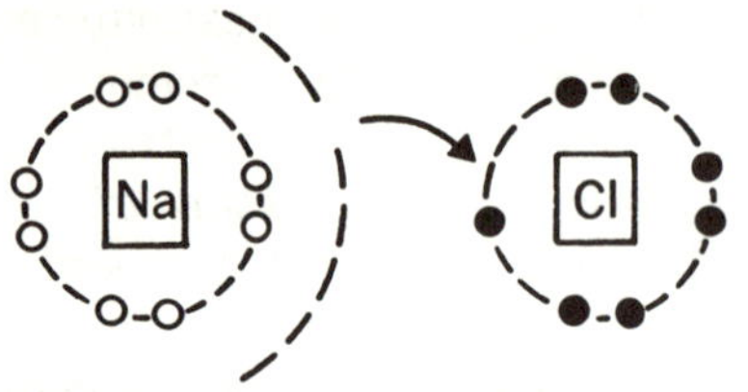

FIGURE 12. Electrovalence

Theoretically, the elements in Group IV can form ions either by gaining or by losing electrons.

It is not difficult to see that it takes energy to remove an electron from a sodium atom, or to force an electron into a chlorine atom. Similarly it seems reasonable that it takes more energy to strip the 2 electrons from a magnesium atom than to remove the 1 electron from a sodium atom. The ease with which an element loses or gains electrons is a measure of its **activity.** On the basis of energy considerations we may state the following. Elements in Groups I and VII are more active than those in Groups III and V. Only elements near the bottom of Group IV form ions. Thus, it can be seen that activity decreases as we consider elements toward the center of the Periodic Table.

Within a given Group, there is also a range of chemical activity. Considering Group I, the negative electron to be removed from the hydrogen atom is much closer to the positive nucleus than the electron to be removed from the cesium atom. Thus it can be seen that it takes less energy to form a cesium ion than to form a hydrogen ion. Therefore, cesium is much more active than hydrogen. On the other hand, in Group VII, similar reasoning tells us that it will require more energy to force an electron into a bromine atom where the positive nucleus is buried within a cloud of negative electrons, than to force an electron into a fluorine atom where the positive nucleus is relatively close to the outermost shell and can help attract the extra electron in. On the basis of energy considerations we may state that the most active electrovalent elements are to be found in the **lower left** and **upper right** areas of the Periodic Table.

The transition and rare earth elements also form ions. However, because both their outermost and second outermost shells are unfilled, they give up not only their outermost electrons to form ions, but they may also give up some electrons from their second outermost shell as well. Thus it is common to find these elements forming two or more different positive ions.

The compounds formed by electrovalence, then, really consist of oppositely charged ions packed and held together by electrical attraction. Such compounds are called **ionic agglomerates.**

Covalence

On the basis of electrovalence, we would expect an element like carbon, which is in Group IV, to be fairly inert and form few compounds. Yet this element forms more compounds than all the other elements put together. Obviously, then, there must be some other valence mechanism.

Carbon has four electrons in its outermost shell. Hydrogen has one electron in its only shell. Suppose that four hydrogen atoms were to approach

TABLE VIII
SYMBOLS OF TYPICAL IONS

Group	*I*	*II*	*III*	*V*	*VI*	*VII*
Ionic Symbols	Na^{+}	Ca^{++}	Al^{+++}	N^{---}	O^{--}	F^{-}
	K^{+}	Mg^{++}			S^{--}	Cl^{-}

a carbon atom very closely, so closely that the shell of each hydrogen atom penetrated into the outermost shell of the carbon atom. The electrons in these interpenetrated shells would then be influenced by the nuclei of both types of atoms. Both atoms would, in a sense, be sharing electrons. What would be the net effect? Figure 13 shows us. The electron of each hydrogen atom is indicated by an x, and the carbon electrons are indicated by dots (the inner carbon atoms are not shown). We can see that two electrons are now associated with each hydrogen atom giving them the stable helium configuration, and eight electrons are associated with the carbon atom giving it the stable neon configuration. Both types of atoms have attained stable structures through this sharing

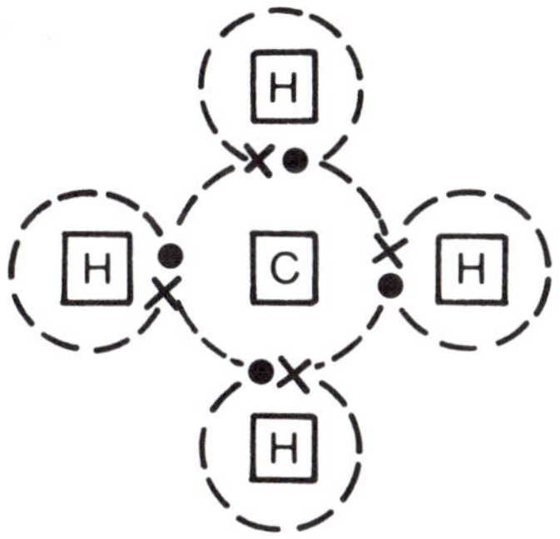

FIGURE 13. Covalence

process. The compound described is methane, the principal ingredient of natural gas used in cooking. The process of forming a compound through the sharing of pairs of electrons is called **covalence.**

A pair of electrons shared between two atoms is often called a **bond.** In methane, carbon is united to four hydrogen atoms by single bonds. Many compounds exist in which two or even three pairs of electrons are shared by two atoms. Figure 14 shows the bonding in carbon dioxide, a gas which bubbles out of carbonated water, and of acetylene, a gas commonly used in welding. Two pairs of electrons are shared between each oxygen atom and the central carbon atom in carbon dioxide, forming eight electrons around each of the three atoms present. Three pairs of electrons are shared between the two carbon atoms in acetylene, and a single pair is shared between the carbon and hydrogen atoms. Carbon dioxide is said to have two **double bonds,** and acetylene is said to have a **triple bond** between its two carbon atoms.

The net effect of covalence is to form tiny particles of compounds containing a definite number of atoms. These discreet, individual particles which possess all the properties of the compound

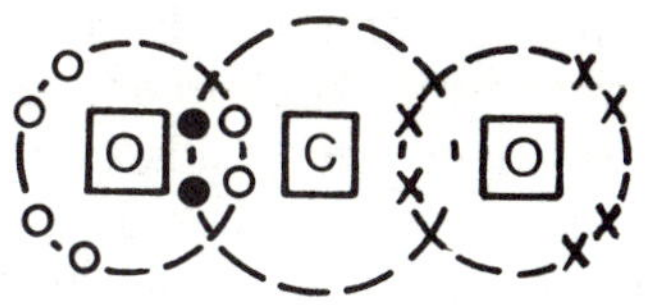

CARBON DIOXIDE

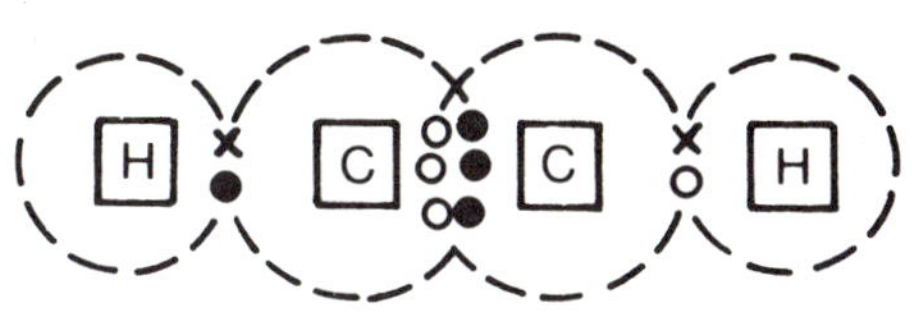

ACETYLENE

FIGURE 14.

are called **molecules.** Molecules are present only in covalent compounds. Electrovalent compounds do not have molecules, but rather, are made up of ions packed together. Table IX summarizes the differences between electrovalence and covalence.

VALENCE NUMBER

The **valence number** of an element is the number of electrons of the element involved in the formation of a compound. Since free elements are

TABLE IX

VALENCE MECHANISMS

Mechanism:	*Electrovalence*	*Covalence*
Process:	Complete transfer of electrons	Sharing of pairs of electrons
Via:	Formation of ions	Interpenetration of atoms
Product:	Ionic agglomerates	Molecules

not combined with other elements, **elements in the free state have a valence number of zero.** Most elements exhibit a variety of valence numbers depending upon the particular compound they happen to be part of. To help you determine the valence number of an element in a compound, the following general rules are given:

1. Elements of Group I of the Periodic Table normally have a valence of +1.
2. Elements of Group II normally have a valence number of +2.
3. Elements of Group VII normally have a

valence number of −1 in **binary compounds** (compounds which contain only 2 elements).

4. In electrovalent compounds in general:
    a. The valence number of an ion is numerically equal to the charge on the ion.
    b. Positive ions have positive valence numbers.
    c. Negative ions have negative valence numbers.
5. In covalent compounds in general:
    a. The valence number of an atom in a covalent compound is numerically equal to the number of its electrons shared with atoms different from itself. For example, referring again to Figure 14, the carbon atom in carbon dioxide shares all four of its outermost electrons with oxygen atoms, so its valence number is 4. But in acetylene, three carbon electrons are shared with another carbon atom while one electron is shared with a hydrogen atom. The carbon-to-carbon bonds don't count, so the valence number of carbon in acetylene is 1.
    b. Oxygen always has a valence number of −2 in its compounds (except peroxides, where its valence number is −1).
    c. Elements like carbon, silicon, nitrogen, phosphorus, sulfur, and chlorine, when they are centrally located in covalent molecules, normally have positive valence numbers.
6. The net sum of all the valence numbers exhibited in a given compound must be zero.

These rules generally apply in most chemical compounds. Where exceptions occur, they will be pointed out.

FORMULAS

The **formula** of a compound is a ratio of the number of atoms of each element present in the compound. In electrovalent compounds, the formula gives the simplest ratio of constituents in whole numbers. In covalent compounds, the formula gives the exact number of atoms of each element present in a molecule of the compound.

The symbols of the elements present are used in writing formulas. If more than one atom of an element is required in the formula, a subscript numeral is written behind the symbol of the element to indicate the number of its atoms in the formula. For example, the formula for water is H_2O. This means that in every molecule of water there are two atoms of hydrogen and one atom of oxygen. Note that when only one atom of an element is present in the formula, the subscript 1 is understood and not written. The formula for sodium chloride, NaCl, tells us that this compound contains equal numbers of sodium and chlorine atoms. We know from previous discussions that in this compound the atoms are actually present as ions. A formula gives no indication as to whether a compound is electrovalent or covalent. This characteristic must be ascertained from the properties of the compound.

FORMULAS AND VALENCE

If we know the valence of each element in a compound, we can easily write its formula. Let us look at a few examples.

EXAMPLE 1: A compound consists solely of magnesium and chlorine. What is its formula?

SOLUTION: Mg, a Group II element, has a valence number of +2. Cl, a Group VII element, has a valence number of −1.

Therefore, to form a compound in which the sum of the valence numbers is zero, it will take two chlorine atoms to nullify each magnesium atom. The formula of this compound must therefore be:

$$MgCl_2.$$

The name of this compound is magnesium chloride. The suffix, **-ide**, is used with the root of the name of the negative element in binary compounds. The terms *oxide, sulfide, nitride, phosphide, carbide, fluoride, bromide,* and *iodide* appear in the names of compounds in which these negative elements are combined with one other positive element to form a binary compound.

Look carefully at the formula of magnesium chloride, $MgCl_2$. Behind Mg, the subscript 1 is understood. Behind Cl is the subscript 2. Do you see that the valence number of each element has been criss-crossed and written as a subscript behind the symbol of the other element? Let us try this idea with another example.

EXAMPLE 2: What is the formula of aluminum oxide?

SOLUTION: Al, a Group III element, has a valence

number of +3. O, a Group VI element, has a valence number of −2.

Criss-crossing the valence numbers and using them as subscripts, we have the formula:

$$Al_2O_3.$$

Note that the sign of the valence numbers is ignored when we write formulas.

Does this formula for aluminum oxide satisfy the rule of zero net valence for compounds? Let's check it.

$$\text{For Al: } 2 \times (+3) = +6.$$
$$\text{For O: } 3 \times (-2) = -6.$$
$$\text{Net valence (sum)} = 0.$$

EXAMPLE 3: What is the formula of calcium sulfide?

SOLUTION; Ca, a Group II element, has a valence number of +2. S, a group VI element, has a valence number of −2. Criss-crossing the valence numbers and writing them as subscripts, we have the formula:

$$Ca_2S_2.$$

However, this is not the simplest formula for this compound. This formula tells us that the ratio of calcium to sulfur atoms is 2:2. This, of course, is the same as a ratio of 1:1. Therefore, to write this formula in its simplest form, we reduce the subscripts to 1, and the formula becomes:

$$CaS.$$

Now let's look at the relationship between formulas and valence the other way. Suppose we are given the formula of a compound and we have to find the valence numbers of the elements present. Let's look at some examples.

EXAMPLE 4: What are the valence numbers of the elements in sulfur dioxide, SO_2?

SOLUTION: Our rules tell us that oxygen has a valence number of −2. Since there are 2 oxygen atoms in our formula, the total negative valence is then −4. Therefore, to satisfy the rule of zero valence in the compound, the valence number of S in SO_2, must be +4.

EXAMPLE 5: What are the valence numbers of the elements in sulfuric acid, H_2SO_4?

SOLUTION: O always has a valence number of −2. H, a Group I element, has a valence number of +1. The 4 O atoms give us a negative valence of $4 \times (-2) = -8$. The 2 H atoms give us a positive valence of $2 \times (+1) = +2$. Therefore, in order to make the net valence of the compound zero, S in H_2SO_4 has a valence number of +6.

RADICALS

In many chemical compounds there are clusters of elements which behave as if they were a single element. Such a group of elements is known as a **radical.** Consider the following series of compounds.

Series A

Sodium chloride	$NaCl$
Sodium hydroxide	$NaOH$
Sodium nitrate	$NaNO_3$

Series B

Sodium sulfide	Na_2S
Sodium sulfate	Na_2SO_4
Sodium carbonate	Na_2CO_3

In series A, the hydroxide (OH) and the nitrate (NO_3) groups have behaved toward sodium in exactly the same way as a single chlorine atom. Similarly, in series B, the sulfate (SO_4) and carbonate (CO_3) groups have behaved toward sodium in exactly the same way as a single sulfur atom. All of these groups are radicals.

The atoms within a radical are held together by covalent bonds, but in each case, they contain either an excess or a deficiency of electrons, causing the radical to possess an electrical charge. Thus, radicals are really complex ions. They then combine as a unit with other ions to form electrovalent compounds.

Radicals possess a net valence number equal in magnitude and sign to the net charge on the radical, just like any other ion. Table X gives the names, formulas, and valence numbers of the common radicals.

TABLE X

RADICALS

Valence Number + 1	Valence Number − 2
Ammonium NH_4^+	Carbonate CO_3^{--}
	Chromate CrO_4^{--}
Valence Number − 1	Dichromate $Cr_2O_7^{--}$
Acetate $C_2H_3O_2^-$	Sulfate SO_4^{--}
Bicarbonate HCO_3^-	Sulfite SO_3^{--}
Chlorate ClO_3^-	
Hydroxide OH^-	***Valence Number − 3***
Cyanide CN^-	Phosphate PO_4^{---}
Nitrate NO_3^-	
Nitrite NO_2^-	
Permanganate MnO_4^-	

Since ammonium is a positive radical, it will form

compounds with all the negative radicals. Notice how the formulas of these compounds are written.

Ammonium acetate	$NH_4C_2H_3O_2$
Ammonium carbonate	$(NH_4)_2CO_3$
Ammonium phosphate	$(NH_4)_3PO_4$

Note that it takes two ammonium ions to satisfy the valence of the carbonate ion, and three ammonium ions to satisfy the valence of the phosphate ion. (Remember ammonium phosphate from the match stick?)

Look carefully at the names and formulas of the radicals. The suffixes **-ite** and **-ate** occur repeatedly. The suffixes are used only with radicals containing oxygen atoms. Notice that "-ite" radicals contain less oxygen than "-ate" radicals. For example:

Sulfite, SO_3	Sulfate, SO_4
Nitrite, NO_2	Nitrate, NO_3

Note also that there is no definite number of oxygen atoms in either type. The formulas of each radical must be learned individually through repeated use.

FORMULA OR MOLECULAR WEIGHTS

Just as symbols represent more than just the name of an element, so formulas stand for more than merely the name of a compound. A formula stands for three things:

1. The name of a compound.
2. One molecule of the compound (if it is covalently bonded).
3. A quantity of the compound equal in weight to its **formula weight.**

This concept of the formula weight of a compound is one of the most important ideas in chemistry. Its definition is very simple. **The formula weight of a compound is the sum of all the atomic weights of the elements present in the formula of the compound.** The formula weight of sodium chloride, NaCl, is found as follows:

Atomic weight of Na	22.997
Atomic weight of Cl	35.457
Formula weight of NaCl	58.454.

Similarly, the formula weight of water, H_2O, would be found thus.

Atomic weight of H (× 2)	2.016
Atomic weight of O	16.000
Formula weight of H_2O	18.016.

Since the formula of a covalent compound represents the constituents of a molecule of the compound, the formula weight is usually referred to as the **molecular weight** of the compound. As a matter of fact, since a formula gives no indication as to the type of bonding present in a compound, the term **molecular weight** is commonly used even with electrovalent compounds, even though no molecule is present in these compounds. Thus, in usage, the terms formula weight and molecular weight are completely interchangeable.

A quantity of a compound equal in weight to its formula weight is called a **mole.** For example, 18.016 units of weight of water is one mole of water. 18.016 grams of water would be one **gram-mole**; 18.016 pounds of water would be one **pound-mole**; etc. Any quantity of a given compound can be expressed in terms of the number of moles of the compound present. The number of moles of a compound is found by using the following expression:

$$\frac{\textbf{Actual weight}}{\textbf{Formula weight}} = \textbf{Number of moles.} \qquad \textbf{(1)}$$

We will begin to see in the next section how fundamentally important the concept of the mole is in the science of chemistry.

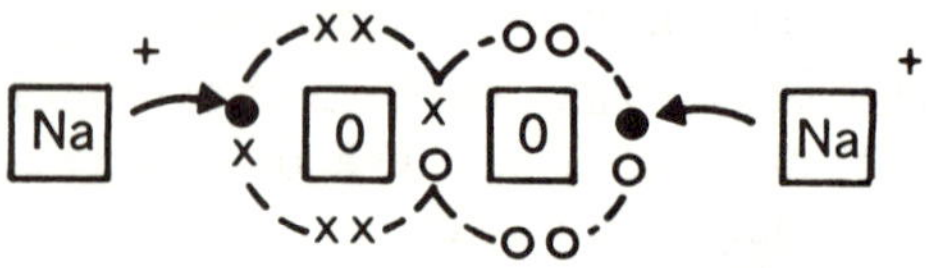

FIGURE 15.

Laws of Chemistry

We have seen how our model of an atom has given us a reasonable explanation of how atoms are combined in compounds. Now we want to look at some of the basic laws of chemistry. These laws were discovered only after years of painstaking observation of the behavior of Nature. It should be kept in mind that *they were all known before our atomic model was created.* Each contributed to the development of our model. However, our primary concern now with these laws is with the assistance they can give us in understanding chemical change.

CONSERVATION OF MATTER

The Law of Conservation of Matter states that matter is neither created nor destroyed during chemical change. This means that the sum of the weights of the substances entering a chemical change must be precisely equal to the sum of the weights of the substance formed as a result of chemical change. This law has been verified by repeated study of chemical changes using delicate balances to measure the weights of **reactants** and **products.**

As we have seen, chemical change involves a **redistribution** of electrons, either by transfer or by sharing, but no new electrons are formed in chemical change, nor are any destroyed. The nuclei of atoms, which possess all the weight, remain unchanged and are carried along into new combinations solely as a result of the redistribution of electrons. Thus, our atomic model is consistent with the Law of Conservation of Matter.

DEFINITE PROPORTIONS

The Law of Definite Proportions states that a given compound always contains the same elements combined in the same proportions by weight. The decomposition of a compound into its elements for the purpose of finding out how much of each element is present is known as **analysis** of the compound. Repeated analysis of a compound always shows that it contains the same elements in the same weight proportions.

For example, water always contains 8 parts by weight of oxygen to 1 part by weight of hydrogen. Let us see if these results are consistent with our concepts of atomic structure and compound formation. Oxygen, with atomic weight 16.0, has 6 electrons in its outermost shell. Hydrogen, with atomic weight 1.0, has 1 electron in its shell. Oxygen needs 2 electrons to fill its outermost shell. Our concept of compound formation tells us that 2 hydrogen atoms are required to provide sufficient electrons to fill the outer shell of oxygen. Furthermore, this gives us a weight proportion of 16 parts by weight of oxygen (1 atom) to 2 parts by weight of hydrogen (2 atoms), which is consistent with the 8 to 1 proportion always found in the analysis of water.

The Law of Definite Proportions has further significance. The process of causing elements to combine to form compounds is known as **synthesis** of compounds. The Law of Definite Proportions dictates that a compound formed by synthesis must contain the same weight proportions of its elements as any other samples of this compound. Thus, water produced in a laboratory by combining oxygen and hydrogen must contain 8 parts by weight of oxygen to 1 part by weight of hydrogen, the same as any other water sample. Now suppose that one took 8 parts by weight of oxygen and 2 parts by weight of hydrogen and attempted to combine them. What would happen? Well, it can be seen that there is too much hydrogen. The 8 parts of oxygen would combine with 1 part of hydrogen, and the rest of the hydrogen would remain unchanged. In this case the oxygen is said to be the **limiting reactant,** for the amount of water formed is based upon the amount of oxygen present. Likewise, in this case, there is said to be an excess of hydrogen present, for there is more present than oxygen can combine with.

In similar fashion, if one were to begin with 10 parts by weight of oxygen and 1 part by weight of hydrogen, 8 parts of oxygen would combine with the 1 part of hydrogen to form water, and the rest of the oxygen would be left unchanged. Here, the hydrogen is the limiting reactant and an excess of oxygen is present. This concept of limiting and excess reactants is very important, for in all chemical changes that involve two or more reactants, one of the reactants will always be the limiting reactant, and the others will be in excess.

AVOGADRO'S HYPOTHESIS

Avogadro's Hypothesis states that equal volumes of gases measured at the same temperature and pressure contain equal numbers of molecules. All gases exist as molecules. By finding the ratio of weights of equal volumes of various gases, we can find the ratio of their molecular weights. For example, let us consider again the compound water, and its elements hydrogen and oxygen. We can easily convert water to a gas (steam) and weigh a given volume of it. Likewise, the same volume of hydrogen and oxygen, both gases, can be brought to the same temperature as the steam and weighed. The weight ratios found by this procedure always turn out to be as follows:

Hydrogen	1 part	by weight
Oxygen	16 parts	by weight
Water	9 parts	by weight

The sample of oxygen weighs 16 times as much as the sample of hydrogen, and the sample of steam weighs 9 times as much as the hydrogen. Since, by Avogadro's Hypothesis, each of these samples contains the same number of molecules, the individual molecules of each of these substances must possess these same weight proportions. Now we know the weight of one of these molecules. The formula of water is H_2O, and its molecular weight, obtained by adding the atomic weights in the formula, is 18. Recalculating our weight ratio found above to a basis of 18 for water we get:

Hydrogen	2 parts	by weight
Oxygen	32 parts	by weight
Water	18 parts	by weight

Since this ratio is a ratio of molecular weights, and since the actual molecular weight of water is 18, the actual molecular weight of hydrogen must be 2, and the actual molecular weight of oxygen must be 32.

Therefore, the molecular of hydrogen gas must contain 2 atoms of hydrogen, because the atomic weight of hydrogen is 1. Similarly the molecule of oxygen must contain 2 atoms of oxygen, because the atomic weight of oxygen is 16, one half of the molecular weight. The formula of hydrogen gas is therefore written H_2 to indicate the 2 atoms in the molecule. The formula for oxygen gas is O_2. Both of these molecules are covalently bonded.

Avogadro's Hypothesis is thus very useful in finding the molecular weight and formula of a gaseous substance, provided that its weight can be compared with the weight of a substance whose formula is known. Experimental and mathematical studies of Avogadro's Hypothesis have indicated its accuracy beyond reasonable doubt.

EQUATIONS

An equation is simply a statement of a chemical change using chemical symbols. When sulfur, or any other substance, burns, in air, it is combining with oxygen in air to produce an oxide. Let us look at this reaction in the form of a chemical equation.

S	+	O_2	=	SO_2
Sulfur		*Oxygen*		*Sulfur dioxide*

Examine the equation closely. Is it consistent with the Law of Conservation of Matter? In other words, are there equal numbers of each type of atom on each side of the equation? Yes, we see that this is so. This equation, therefore, is said to be **balanced.** An equation is meaningless unless it is balanced.

This equation tells us more than merely that sulfur combines with oxygen to produce sulfur dioxide. It has quantitative significance just as symbols themselves do. It tells us that one atomic weight's worth of sulfur reacts with one molecular weight's worth of oxygen to produce one molecular weight's worth of sulfur dioxide. If units of grams are used, this would be:

S	+	O_2	=	SO_2
32.1 g.		32 g.		64.1 g.

In other words, this equation tells us that one mole of sulfur combines with one mole of oxygen to produce one mole of sulfur dioxide.

Let us look at another reaction. You will recall that when copper is heated in air, black copper oxide is formed. This reaction is indicated as follows:

Cu	+	O_2	=	CuO
Copper		*Oxygen*		*Copper oxide*

What about our Law of Conservation of Matter now? Do you see that we have apparently destroyed some oxygen? This equation is not balanced. It is called a **skeleton equation,** for it indicates only the names of the substances involved.

This equation would be balanced if we could put a subscript 2 behind the O of CuO to make it CuO_2. But this would violate the Law of Definite Proportions, because black copper oxide always has the formula CuO. In balancing equations, **the subscript in the formulas of compounds may not be changed.**

A skeleton equation is balanced by placing numbers, called **coefficients,** in front of the formulas of the substances in the reaction. Look again at our skeleton equation. An even number of oxygen atoms appears on the left side of the equation. By placing the coefficient 2 in front of CuO, we would have two oxygen atoms on each side of the equation, for the coefficient multiplies all the symbols in the formula immediately behind it. This would change our equation to read:

$$Cu + O_2 = 2CuO.$$

Now we have too much copper on the right. This

can be remedied by placing another coefficient 2 in front of the Cu, giving us the following.

$$2Cu + O_2 = 2CuO.$$

Now the equation is balanced. We have 2 copper atoms and 2 oxygen atoms on each side of the equation. The balanced equation now reads, 2 moles of copper combine with 1 mole of oxygen to produce 2 moles of copper oxide. The following expression shows how the weights of each of the substances in the balanced equation may be indicated:

$2Cu$	$+ O_2 =$	$2CuO$
2×63.6	32	$2(63.6 + 16)$
127.2	$+32 =$	159.2

So, 127.2 units of weight of copper combine with 32 units of weight of oxygen to form 159.2 units of weight of copper oxide. These units of weight may be grams, pounds, tons, etc., just so long as all three weights are expressed in the same units. This weight relationship also tells us that copper and oxygen combine in a weight ratio of 127.2 parts by weight of copper to 32 parts by weight of oxygen. Similarly, 159.2 parts by weight of copper oxide are formed for every 32 parts by weight of oxygen or every 127.2 parts by weight of copper.

Let us look at one more example. Butane gas (C_4H_{10}) is commonly used as a bottled gas in rural areas. It burns with oxygen to form carbon dioxide and water. The skeleton equation is:

$$C_4H_{10} + O_2 = CO_2 + H_2O.$$

Let us balance this skeleton equation using the "even numbers" technique described in the previous example.

1. Starting with oxygen, we see an even number of oxygen atoms on the left, and an odd number on the right. The CO_2 has an even number of oxygen atoms, so we have to work with the H_2O. Let's try a coefficient of 2. This would give us:

$$C_4H_{10} + O_2 = CO_2 + 2\ H_2O.$$

This gives us an even number of oxygen atoms, but we need 10 hydrogen atoms and this gives us only 4 (2×2). Therefore we need a larger coefficient.

2. A coefficient of 5 would give us the right amount of hydrogen, but 5 is an odd number, so we must go to the next even multiple of 5 which is 10. This will do, but it gives us 20 hydrogen atoms on the right. By placing another coefficient of 2 in front of the C_4H_{10} we would also have 20 hydrogen atoms on the left. This gives us:

$$2\ C_4H_{10} + O_2 = CO_2 + 10\ H_2O$$

Now our hydrogen is balanced and we have an even number of oxygen atoms on each side.

3. Now we look at the carbon. We have 8 carbon atoms on the left, so we need a coefficient of 8 in front of the CO_2 to balance the carbon. This gives us:

$$2\ C_4H_{10} + O_2 = 8\ CO_2 + 10\ H_2O.$$

We still have an even number of oxygen atoms on each side.

4. Now we are finally ready to balance the oxygen. There is a total of 26 oxygen atoms on the right side of the equation. A coefficient of 13 in front of the O_2 will give us 26 oxygen atoms on the left side. Now our equation is balanced and looks like this:

$$2\ C_4H_{10} + 13\ O_2 = 8\ CO_2 + 10\ H_2O.$$

This equation reads: 2 moles of butane combine with 13 moles of oxygen to produce 8 moles of carbon dioxide and 10 moles of water. The weight proportions involved are:

Reactants:	Butane:	$2(48 + 10)$	$= 116$	
	Oxygen:	$13(32)$	$= 416$	532
Products:	Carbon Dioxide:	$8(12 + 32)$	$= 352$	
	Water:	$10(2 + 16)$	$= 180$	532

The characteristics of a balanced equation may be summarized as follows:

1. It obeys the Law of Conservation of Matter.
2. It obeys the Law of Definite Proportions.
3. Its coefficients give the molar proportions of reactants and products involved in the reaction.

Symbols, formulas, and equations all have definite quantitative meanings. We are now ready to look at some numerical applications based upon these ideas.

PERCENTAGE COMPOSITION

If we know the formula of a compound, we can easily find the percentage by weight of each element present. A statement of the percentage of each element present in a compound is called its **percentage composition.** In chemistry, this composition is always on a weight basis unless specifically stated otherwise. Sometimes the composition of mixtures of gases is given on a volumetric basis.

The computation of percentage composition from the formula of a compound is based upon the meaning of symbols and formulas. Each symbol stands for one atomic weight's worth of the element it represents, and each formula stands for one molecular weight's worth of the compound it represents. Let us see how percentage composition calculations are carried out.

EXAMPLE 6: What is the percentage composition of water, H_2O?

SOLUTION:

	No. of Atoms	*Atomic Weight*	*Total Weight*
Hydrogen:	2	1.0	2.0
Oxygen:	1	16.0	16.0
Molecular weight of H_2O:			18.0

$$\text{Percentage of hydrogen} = \frac{2.0}{18.0} \times 100 = 11.1\%$$

$$\text{Percentage of oxygen} = \frac{16.0}{18.0} \times 100 = 88.9\%.$$

Note that the percentage of each element is found from the expression:

$$\frac{\textbf{Total wt. of element present}}{\textbf{Molecular wt. of compound}} = \textbf{\% of element.}$$

EXAMPLE 7: What is the percentage composition of sulfuric acid, H_2SO_4?

SOLUTION:

	No. of Atoms	*Atomic Weight*	*Total Weight*
Hydrogen:	2	1.0	2.0
Sulfur:	1	32.1	32.1
Oxygen:	4	16.0	64.0
Molecular weight of H_2SO_4:			98.1

$$\text{Percentage of hydrogen} = \frac{2.0}{98.1} \times 100 = 2.0\%$$

$$\text{Percentage of sulfur} = \frac{32.1}{98.1} \times 100 = 32.7\%$$

$$\text{Percentage of oxygen} = \frac{64.0}{98.1} \times 100 = 65.3\%$$

EXAMPLE 8: Find the percentage of oxygen in calcium nitrate, $Ca(NO_3)_2$.

SOLUTION:

	No. of Atoms	*Atomic Weight*	*Total Weight*
Calcium:	1	40.1	40.1
Nitrogen:	2	14.0	28.0
Oxygen:	6	16.0	96.0
Molecular weight of $Ca(NO_3)_2$:			164.1

$$\text{Percentage of oxygen} = \frac{96.0}{164.1} \times 100 = 58.5\%.$$

Note particularly how the number of atoms of each element was obtained.

EXAMPLE 9: An iron ore field contains ferric oxide, Fe_2O_3, also known as **hematite,** mixed with rock which bears no iron. Naturally, both hematite and rock are scooped up in the giant shovels used in mining the ore. Samples taken at various spots in the ore field show that the field contains 80% hematite and 20% rock. Find the weight of pure iron in one ton of this ore, and the percentage of iron in the ore field.

SOLUTION: (1) Wt. of Fe_2O_3 per ton of ore:
$2{,}000 \times 0.80 = 1600$ lbs. of Fe_2O_3 per ton of ore.

(2) Percentage of Fe in Fe_2O_3:

	No. of Atoms	*Atomic Weight*	*Total Weight*
Iron:	2	55.9	111.8
Oxygen:	3	16.0	48.0
Molecular weight of Fe_2O_3:			159.8

$$\text{Percentage of Fe} = \frac{111.8}{159.8} \times 100 = 70\%$$

(3) Wt. of Fe per ton of ore:
$1600 \times 0.70 = 1120$ lbs. of Fe per ton of ore.

(4) Percentage of Fe in the field:

$$\frac{1120}{2000} \times 100 = 56.0\% \text{ Fe in the ore field.}$$

Example 9 shows how percentage composition problems may be a part of many different varieties of practical problems. Such fields as analytical chemistry, metallurgy, mining, mineralogy, and geology all make use of calculations of this type.

COMPUTATION OF FORMULAS

If we know the percentage composition of a compound, we can compute the **simplest formula** of the compound. As we have seen, a formula is a ratio of the number of atoms of each element present in the compound. The simplest formula gives this atomic ratio in terms of the smallest whole numbers of each type of atom present. For example, the true formula of hydrogen peroxide is H_2O_2. Its simplest formula would be HO. In general, the simplest formula is the true formula for all electrovalent compounds. In covalent compounds, where the formula represents the composition of the molecule of the compound, the true formula is either the same as the simplest formula, or it is some whole number multiple of it. We will learn how to calculate true formulas later, but for now, let us concentrate on finding the simplest formula of a compound.

EXAMPLE 10: A compound is analyzed and found to contain 75% carbon and 25% hydrogen. Find its simplest formula.

SOLUTION: Since each different type of atom contributes to the total weight of the compound **in parcels of weight** equal to its own atomic weight, we can divide the weight percent of a given element by its atomic weight to get the relative number of atoms of the element contributing to the total weight percent. For the compound under consideration this would be:

$$\text{Carbon:} \quad \frac{75}{12} = 6.25$$

$$\text{Hydrogen:} \quad \frac{25}{1} = 25.0$$

Thus we have 6.25 carbon atoms for every 25 hydrogen atoms in this compound. To reduce these numbers to the simplest whole numbers, we divide each by the smaller. The entire calculation would then be as follows:

$$\text{Carbon:} \quad \frac{75}{12} = 6.25; \quad \frac{6.25}{6.25} = 1.$$

$$\text{Hydrogen:} \quad \frac{25}{1} = 25; \quad \frac{25}{6.25} = 4.$$

Therefore, the simplest formula of this compound is CH_4.

EXAMPLE 11: A compound contains 21.6% sodium, 33.3% chlorine, and 45.1% oxygen. Find its simplest formula.

SOLUTION:

$$\text{Sodium:} \quad \frac{21.6}{23.0} = 0.95; \quad \frac{0.95}{0.94} = 1.$$

$$\text{Chlorine:} \quad \frac{33.3}{35.5} = 0.94; \quad \frac{0.94}{0.94} = 1.$$

$$\text{Oxygen:} \quad \frac{45.1}{16.0} = 2.82; \quad \frac{2.82}{0.94} = 3.$$

Therefore, the formula of this compound is $NaClO_3$.

EXAMPLE 12: Some crystalline solids have molecules of water forming part of their crystal structure. Such solids are known as hydrates. Ordinary household washing soda, made up of sodium carbonate and water, is a typical hydrate. The percentage of water present can be found by measuring the loss in weight of a hydrate sample dried in a hot oven. A 20.00 g. sample of washing soda is dried in an oven. After drying it is found to weigh 7.57 g. Compute:

(a) The percentage of water in washing soda.
(b) The formula of washing soda.

SOLUTION:

(a) $\text{Percentage } H_2O = \frac{\text{loss in wt.}}{\text{original wt.}} \times 100 =$

$$\frac{20.00\text{–}7.57}{20.00} = 62.15\%.$$

(b) The percentage of Na_2CO_3 is 100% − 62.15% = 37.85%

$$Na_2CO_3\text{:} \quad \frac{37.85}{106} = 0.357; \quad \frac{0.357}{0.357} = 1.$$

$$H_2O\text{:} \quad \frac{62.15}{18.0} \times 3.45; \quad \frac{3.45}{0.357} = 10.$$

(to the nearest whole number)

Therefore, the formula of washing soda must indicate 1 part of Na_2CO_3 and 10 parts of H_2O. Its formula is written as follows: $Na_2CO_3 \cdot 10H_2O$. This is the standard method of writing the formula of a hydrate. It indicates that the crystal contains 10 moles of water for every mole of sodium carbonate. Note particularly that since a molar ratio of constituents was sought, the molecular weights of each constituent were used in finding the molar ratio.

WEIGHT RELATIONSHIPS IN EQUATIONS

We have seen that chemical equations tell us the number of moles of each substance involved in a given reaction. For example, the equation for the rusting of iron,

$$4\ Fe + 3\ O_2 = 2\ Fe_2O_3,$$

tells us that iron combines with oxygen in a ratio of 4 moles of iron to 3 moles of oxygen, and that 2 moles of iron oxide are produced for every 4 moles of iron entering the reaction.

These molar ratios, in turn, indicate the ratio of weights of each substance involved. The equation tells us that iron and oxygen combine in a ratio of (4×55.9) parts by weight of iron to (3×32) parts by weight of oxygen, and that (2×159.8) parts by weight of iron oxide are thereby produced in this reaction. When we multiply the coefficient of a substance in a balanced equation by the formula weight of the substance, we obtain a quantity known as the **equation weight** of the substance. **The actual weight of substances involved in a chemical reaction are in the same ratio as their equation weights.**

Therefore, if we know the balanced equation for a reaction, and the actual weight of any one substance involved in the reaction, we can find the actual weight of any other substance participating in the reaction from the following proportion:

$$\frac{\textbf{Actual wt. of one substance}}{\textbf{Its equation weight}} = \frac{\textbf{Unknown actual weight}}{\textbf{Its equation weight}}$$

Let us look at an example involving the finding of actual weights.

EXAMPLE 13: 27.95 g. of iron are oxidized completely.

(a) What weight of oxygen combined with the iron?

(b) What weight of iron oxide was produced?

SOLUTION: First we write the balanced equation for the reaction and place the equation weight of each substance involved below its formula as follows:

$$\begin{array}{ccccc} 4\ Fe & + & 3\ O_2 & = & 2\ Fe_2O_3 \\ 4 \times 55.9 & & 3 \times 32 & & 2 \times 159.8 \end{array}$$

Part a: Substituting in the expression above to find the actual weight of oxygen we have: (Let x represent the unknown wt.)

$$\frac{27.95}{223.6} = \frac{x}{96}$$

$$x = \frac{27.95 \times 96}{223.6}$$

x = 12.0 g. of oxygen.

Part b: Substituting in the expression above to find the actual weight of iron oxide we have:

$$\frac{27.95}{223.6} = \frac{x}{319.6}$$

$$x = \frac{27.95 \times 319.6}{223.6}$$

x = 39.95 g. of iron oxide.

The steps, then, in solving this type of problem are:

1. Write the **balanced** equation for the reaction.
2. Find the equation weights of the substances concerned.
3. Equate the ratios of actual weights to equation weights for each of the substances, and solve for the unknown actual weight.

EXAMPLE 14: Sodium hydroxide, NaOH, may be prepared by treating sodium carbonate, Na_2CO_3, with calcium hydroxide, $Ca(OH)_2$, according to the following equation (skeleton):

$$Na_2CO_3 + Ca(OH)_2 = NaOH + CaCO_3.$$

What weight of NaOH can be produced from 74.2 g. of Na_2CO_3?

SOLUTION: Balanced equation:

$$\begin{array}{ccccccc} Na_2CO_3 & + & Ca(OH)_2 & = & 2\ NaOH & + & CaCO_3 \\ 1 \times 106 & & & & 2 \times 40 & & \end{array}$$

Therefore:

$$\frac{74.2}{106} = \frac{x}{80}$$

$$x = \frac{74.2 \times 80}{106}$$

x = 56 g. of NaOH.

Notice that it is assumed that there is sufficient calcium hydroxide present to react with all of the sodium carbonate. If any excess calcium hydroxide is used, it will remain unchanged, for the sodium carbonate is the limiting reactant in this case.

CHAPTER TEN

ASTRONOMY

A Brief History

The history of astronomy may be conveniently divided into three periods: the geocentric, the galactic, and the universal. The first had its beginnings in ancient history, and came to a close in the sixteenth century. The second extends from the seventeenth through the nineteenth centuries. And the third began and continues in the present century.

THE GEOCENTRIC PERIOD

Early astronomers believed the earth to be in the center of the universe; and assumed that the sun, moon, and stars revolved about that stationary earth. Their interest, hardly scientific in our sense of the term, was mainly in practical matters, in the real and supposed relation of celestial events to those on the earth; in searching the skies for clues to good and evil omens.

Even so, remarkable discoveries were made then. The calendar was developed with great accuracy. The apparent path of the sun among the stars—the ecliptic—was carefully defined. The complete cycle of solar and lunar eclipses was determined. And as early as the second century B.C., the motion of the earth's axis was well understood.

The great figure of Nicolaus Copernicus (1473–1543) is closely associated with the end of the primitive geocentric period in the sixteenth century.

THE GALACTIC PERIOD

Modern astronomy can be said to have begun in this period. Copernicus demonstrated that the earth, far from being the center of the universe, was merely one of the planets revolving about the central sun. Hardly unique, the earth was found to be a quite ordinary planet, going through ordinary motions in an ordinary way.

Indeed the central sun itself was realized to be merely one star among the multitudes in the heavens, one among billions of similar stars in every direction about us—some larger, some smaller, some heavier, some lighter than our sun.

In this period the approach became increasingly scientific, motivated largely by the desire to know, to understand the basic laws governing the motion of heavenly bodies, to explain what the eye saw.

Progress from the sixteenth through the nineteenth centuries resulted from the effective combination of extended observation, improved instruments, and the work of scientific genius.

Observation. Great quantities of data of fundamental importance were painstakingly gathered by careful observers, chief among whom is the great name of Tycho Brahe (1546–1601).

Instruments. The introduction of the telescope in 1610 by Galileo Galilei (1564–1642) was, of course, a milestone in the development of the science of astronomy; as was the later invention and introduction of the spectroscope. The two instruments complement one another: the telescope permits us to see the stars more clearly; the spectroscope analyzes stellar light, furnishing us with much information about the stars.

Genius. Like every science, astronomy requires for its advancement the labors of great minds that are able to apply to the observed data insight, imagination, intuition, as well as great learning.

Such minds were Johannes Kepler (1571–1630) and Sir Isaac Newton (1642–1727): Kepler by the discovery of the laws of planetary motion and Newton by the discovery of the Universal Law of Gravitation.

THE UNIVERSAL PERIOD

Now it became apparent that the galaxy of stars to which our sun belongs is merely one of many galaxies—some larger, some smaller than ours. To these much of the astronomical research of the last half century has been devoted, in an effort to achieve a "complete" picture of the universe. To aid this research ever greater optical telescopes, as well as gigantic radio telescopes, have been constructed.

The great theoretical genius associated most closely with this period in the public mind (although he was primarily a physicist and mathematician) is the late Dr. Albert Einstein (1879–1955). Cosmology and astrophysics depend more and more on his theory of relativity.

This is the astronomic period in which we live. And it is far from concluded.

The Universe

INTRODUCTION AND DEFINITIONS

For as long as man has been conscious of himself and the universe he inhabits, he has regarded the sky with awe and wonder—a source of constant and compelling fascination. Awe and wonder generate study and science; man seeking ceaselessly to conquer ignorance and solve mysteries, thus developing finally into the science of astronomy.

Astronomy is the science of the positions, motions, constitutions, histories, and destinies of celestial bodies. In the course of its development as a science, it has already discovered many of the basic laws governing those bodies. But it is the nature of scientific investigation that its work is never done—and here, as elsewhere, immense labors remain to be performed.

THE STUDY OF ASTRONOMY?

We study astronomy because the intelligent, inquiring mind must ask questions and seek answers; must know "Why?" and discover "How?" And from the beginning, whenever man has looked up, there was the sky—always confronting him with seemingly imponderable problems, always challenging him to solve its mysteries.

On one level, man has stated his reaction in magic and mythology, and this has been expressed in the world's art, literature, and religions. On another level, he has attempted to explain the celestial phenomena perceived by his senses in scientific terms—and these explanations are the subject matter of the science of astronomy.

THE COMPONENTS

The earth we live on is a planet—one of a number of planets that revolve about the sun. The unassisted eye is capable of detecting the sun, several planets, one satellite (our moon), several thousands of stars, shooting stars (meteors), and once in a great while a comet.

These celestial bodies are the components that constitute the universe, in much the same way that homes, churches, hospitals, and parks are components of a community.

To the best of our knowledge, the **universe consists of stars** (billions and billions of these), nebulae, planets, planetoids, satellites, comets, etc.

STARS

Stars are large globes of intensely heated gas, shining by their own light. At their surface, they reach temperatures of thousands of degrees; in their interior, temperatures are much higher.

At these temperatures, matter cannot exist either in solid or in liquid form. The gases constituting the stars are much thicker than those on the earth usually are. The extremely high values of their density are due to enormous pressures which prevail in their interior.

Stars move above in space, although their motion is not immediately perceptible. No change in their relative position can be detected in a year. Even in a thousand years, the stars will seem not to have moved substantially. Their pattern now is almost exactly that of a thousand years ago. This seeming fixedness is due to the vast distance separating us from them. At these distances it will take many thousands of years for the stellar pattern to undergo a noticeable change: This **apparent** constancy of position accounts for the popular name "fixed stars."

NEBULAE

A **nebula is a vast cloud composed of dust and gas.** The gases which compose it are extremely thin and of low temperature. Nebulae do not shine by their own light, but are made visible by the light of neighboring stars. When they are so visible, they appear to the unaided eye not unlike a fuzzy star. Their actual size and structure, however, can be determined only with the aid of a telescope. Other nebulae are dark and obscure the stars beyond them.

PLANETS

The planets that revolve around our sun are large, solid, nearly spherical masses. The best known to us is, of course, our own earth. All of them are relatively cool and are made visible by reflected sunlight; several can be seen at one time or another by the unaided eye. Three planets, however, can be seen only with the aid of a telescope. At first glance, planets look very much like the multitude of stars that glitter in the sky; but an observer can identify a planet by one or more of the following characteristics:

A. Planets shine with a **steady** light, while stars do not. The light reaching our eyes from stars seems to change rapidly in both color and brightness. These changes in color and brightness cause the **twinkling** of the stars.

B. Planets **wander** in the heavens: A planet which at one time was close to one star may later be observed close to another star. Stars, on the other hand, seem to keep the same positions relative to one another. See Fig. 1. The very word "planet" is derived from a Greek word meaning "wanderer."

C. Planets, when observed through telescopes, appear as **small disks** of light. The greater the magnification, the larger will be the diameter of the disk. Stars, even with the largest telescope, appear only as points of light. Even in the 200-inch telescope, they appear as mere points, having no measurable diameter.

D. Planets may be found **only in a narrow strip** in the sky. Their motions are limited to the boundaries of this strip. Stars, of course, may be found in any part of the sky.

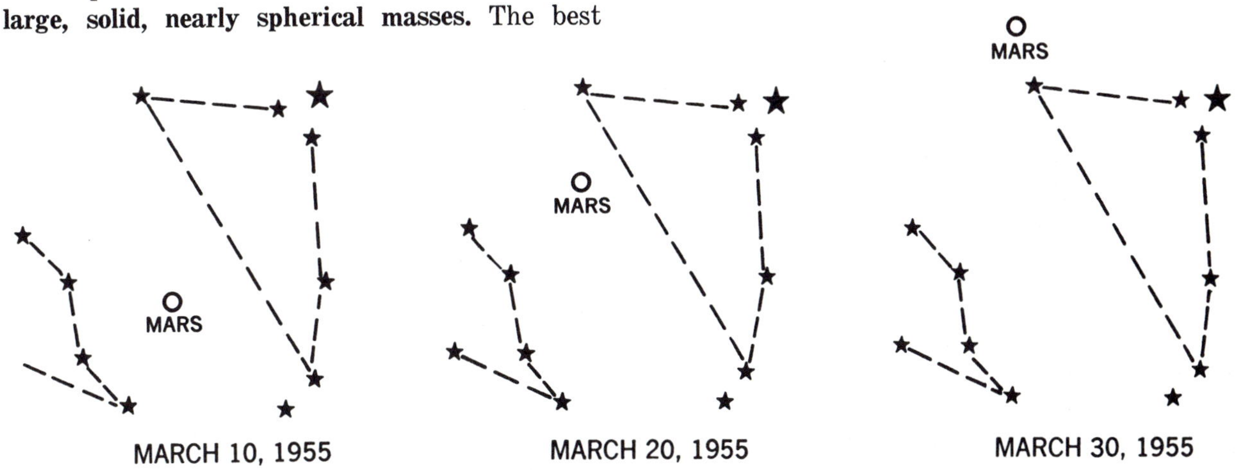

FIGURE 1. Views of the same part of the sky on three different dates, March 10, March 20, and March 30, 1955. Note that the stars maintain the same relative position. The planet (Mars) has wandered considerably in that time.

PLANETOIDS

Planets are small, irregularly shaped solid bodies revolving, like the major planets, about the sun, and differing from planets primarily in size. They are also known either as asteroids or as minor planets. The largest planetoid, Ceres, has a diameter of 480 miles; but many of them have a diameter of only two miles. The first planetoid was discovered on January 1, 1801; many more have since been discovered. It is estimated that more than 100,000 planetoids can be photographed with one of the large telescopes.

They, too, shine by reflected sunlight; however, because of their small surface, the amount of reflected light is very small. They cannot be seen without the aid of a telescope.

SATELLITES

Six of the nine major planets have one or more moons revolving round them. These are called satellites. The earth has only one moon (satellite), while the planet Jupiter, for example, has fourteen. To date, thirty-four satellites have been discovered, the last as recently as 1975.

COMETS

Comets are celestial bodies of unique form and large size which appear from time to time. A typical comet consists of a luminous sphere, or head, connected to a long, tenuous cylinder, or tail. The head may seem as large as the sun; the tail describes an arc in the sky.

To the naked-eye observer a comet appears as motionless as the moon. Actually it moves at speeds of hundreds of miles per second. The exact speed can be determined from its changing position relative to the fixed stars.

There are less than seven hundred known comets, and several new ones are discovered every year.

The vast majority are too faint to be visible to the naked eye. Fairly great comets are rather rare; these appear, on the average, once or twice in a lifetime.

Of the 625 or so known comets, more than 259 are known to move in "closed orbits"—that is, in more or less elongated, cigar-shaped paths. The fact that the orbit is "closed," has no beginning or end, is of great importance. Comets moving in them go round the same path continuously; many of them have been observed several times during their returns to the vicinity of the earth.

The orbits of the other 368 comets are either parabolic or hyperbolic. They very likely made only one appearance in the vicinity of the earth, coming, probably, from outer space, making a U-turn, and then left, never to be seen again.

METEOROIDS

Meteoroids are usually tiny (about the size of the head of a pin), solid objects traversing through space. Occasionally a group of meteoroids is attracted to the earth and becomes entangled in its atmosphere. The heat resulting from this encounter consumes the object; the dust resulting from this cremation falls to the earth. Hundreds of tons of meteoric dust descend each year. On rare occasions large meteoroids manage to reach the earth before they are consumed. **The light phenomenon which results from the entry of the meteoroid into the earth's atmosphere is called meteor, or "shooting star,"** the glow of which may persist several seconds.

The universe is composed of stars, nebulae, planets, comets, and other celestial bodies. Here, the components are assembled to form the design of the universe.

The planets, planetoids, satellites, comets, and meteorites revolve about a single star: the star we call the sun. Together they form the Solar System. The sun, and billions of other stars, form the community of stars known either as Our Galaxy, or the Milky Way Galaxy. The universe contains many such stellar communities, or galaxies.

Stellar distance is of an order of magnitude entirely different from that of planetary distance: the former is enormously greater than the latter.

Distances between galaxies are still greater than distances between stars. In attempting to comprehend such extraordinary distances it is essential to use a scale. The plan of the universe on such a scale is given later in this section.

THE SUN

Although it may not seem so, the sun is just an ordinary star, similar to numerous other stars that we see in the sky.

The sun appears large to us because it is, relatively speaking, near to us. All other stars appear as small points of light in the sky because they are far away. See Figs. 2a and 2b. Our interest in this star (the sun) derives from the fact that the earth receives from it both heat and light—energy of

FIGURE 2a. The sun is just an ordinary star. All the other stars look tiny, as they are so remote that we see them only as mere points of light.

FIGURE 2b. Other objects, too, appear smaller with increasing distance. Note the apparent size of the distant tree.

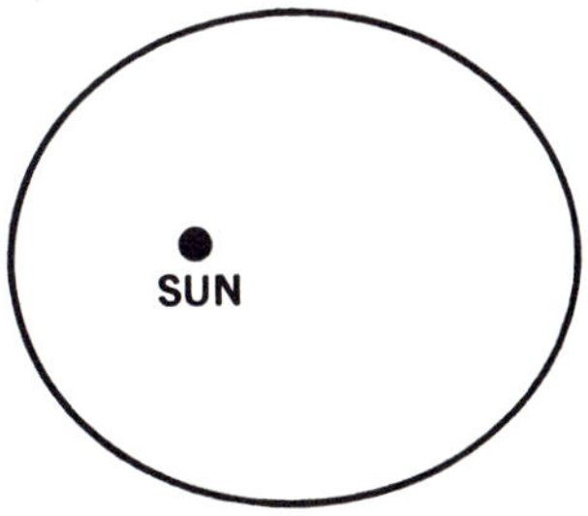

FIGURE 2c. The oval curve suggests the circumference of the whole universe. The dot represents the location of the sun.

fundamental importance in maintaining life. The oval curve in Figure 2c represents the universe and the dot the position of the sun within the universe. (Note that Fig. 2c, as well as Figs. 3, 4, and 5, are symbolic representations and not figures drawn to scale.)

PLANETS

There are nine planets revolving about the sun: Mercury, Venus, Earth, Mars, Jupiter, Saturn, Uranus, Neptune, and Pluto. Mercury is closest to the sun, and at a somewhat greater distance is Venus; then, the earth; and the farthest known planet from the sun is Pluto.

The earth is 93 million miles from the sun. **This distance is often referred to as an Astronomical Unit.** Mercury is only four tenths the earth's distance from the sun. Pluto, the most distant planet, is forty times the earth's distance. The distance of Pluto can be stated as forty times 93 million miles, or simply as forty astronomical units.

A reducing scale may help to visualize these distances. The scale that is commonly used represents the sun-earth distance as one foot long:

93 million miles equal 1 foot; or,

1 astronomical unit equals 1 foot.

On this scale, Mercury is fourth tenths of a foot; Venus is seven tenths; and the earth is one foot away from the sun. The farthest planet is forty feet from the sun. A circular box of forty-foot radius could accommodate all the planets. The box could be quite shallow, as all the planets move approximately in the same plane.

THE SOLAR SYSTEM

The sun and the planets are the major components of the solar system. Other members of this system are:

1. the host of smaller planets known as planetoids or asteroids
2. the several moons, known as satellites, that revolve about six of these planets;
3. comets that appear from time to time;
4. the vast number of meteoroids.

The circle around the dot in Figure 3 represents the entire solar system.

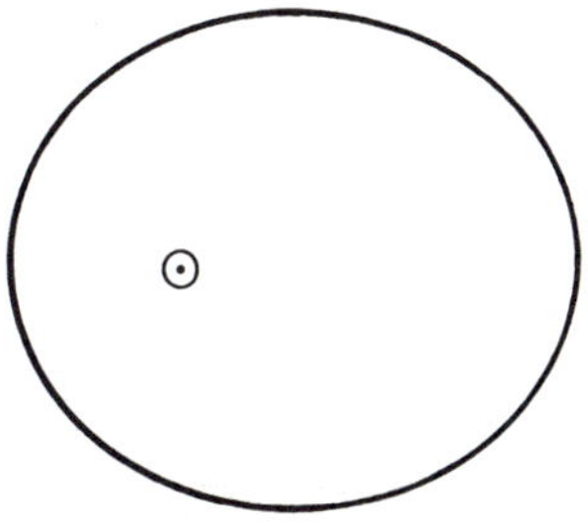

FIGURE 3. The oval curve suggests the circumference of the whole universe. The dot and the small circle represent the sun and the solar system, respectively.

THE STARS

Distances to stars are immensely greater than distances to planets. Even the star nearest our own sun is at a distance of 270,000 astronomical units. Using the scale (one foot equals one astronomical unit, or 93 million miles), the star closest to our sun would be at a distance of fifty miles.

The two units should be carefully noted. Distances between planets are stated in **feet,** while those between stars are stated in **miles.** A mental picture might help to visualize this distinction. The sun, and all the planets, could be accommodated in a circular house of forty foot radius. The closest star, by our scale, would be in a house fifty miles away. Other stars, by our scale, are at scale distances of thousands and hundreds of thousands of miles from the sun.

OUR GALAXY

These stars form a large community called Our Galaxy or the Milky Way Galaxy. It is estimated that the number of stars in our galaxy is close to a hundred billion—otherwise stated as 100×10^9, or a hundred thousand million.

The outer surface of the galaxy is often compared either to a grindstone or to a lens.

A top view of the galaxy would reveal its circular shape as well as the spiral design formed by the stars. A side view would suggest its similarity to a lens, namely, that it is thick in the center, and thins out toward the edges.

Again using the one foot scale, the diameter of the circle would be close to a million miles, while the maximum thickness is only about one sixth of the diameter.

Our galaxy is represented in Figure 4.

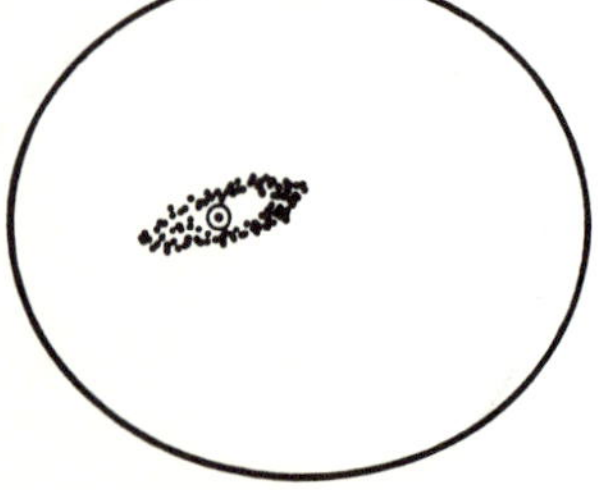

FIGURE 4. The oval curve represents the circumference of the universe. Our galaxy is indicated inside the oval. The dot and the circle represent the sun and the solar system, respectively.

OTHER GALAXIES

Ours is not the only galaxy in the universe: many have been discovered in recent years, strikingly similar to our own. The scale distances between them are from ten to twenty million miles. A highly simplified picture of the universe is shown in Figure 5.

OUTLINE OF THE UNIVERSE IN TERMS OF ACTUAL DISTANCES

The distance to the sun is 93 million miles; the distance to our nearest star, Alpha-Centauri, is 25,000,000,000,000 miles, or 25 million million miles. Distant stars are inconceivably more remote.

FIGURE 5. The "complete" universe consists of many galaxies. One, containing the sun, is known as our galaxy, the galaxy, or the Milky Way galaxy.

The mile unit is of no use in dealing with the distances of stars and galaxies—instead, astronomers use the unit "light-year": one light-year is the distance that a beam of light travels in one year. The distance covered by a beam of light in one second is 186,000 miles; hence:

One light-year =

$$186{,}000 \times 60 \left(\frac{\text{seconds}}{\text{minute}}\right) \times 60 \left(\frac{\text{minutes}}{\text{hour}}\right)$$

$$\times 24 \left(\frac{\text{hours}}{\text{day}}\right) \times 365\tfrac{1}{4} = 5{,}880{,}000{,}000{,}000 \text{ miles}$$

or 6 million million miles, approximately.

The star nearest the solar system is 4.3 light-years away. The diameter of our galaxy is about 100,000 light-years; its maximum thickness is 15,000 light-years. An average distance between galaxies would be approximately a million light-years.

The sun is only a minute fraction of a light-year from the earth. The distance to the sun may be stated as 8 light minutes.

Distances to heavenly bodies, when stated in terms of light, have an added meaning—for the sun, it implies that it takes a beam of sunlight 8 minutes to reach the earth.

So for the stars. A ray of light from Alpha-Centauri reaches the earth 4⅓ years after leaving the star.

The most distant object seen by the unaided eye is the Andromeda galaxy—2 million light-years away. The light entering the observer's eye has been en route for that time.

A BRIEF HISTORY OF THE UNIVERSE

The most tenable theory to date for the history of the universe is the one known as the "big bang theory." According to that theory, all the matter and all energy that is present in the universe was once concentrated in a small, enormously hot, preposterously dense ball.

Then 10, or more, thousand million years ago the ball exploded (big bang!), sending into space torrents of gas (primarily protons, neutrons, electrons, and some alpha particles), immersed in a vast ocean of radiation.

As time went on, concentration of matter formed in that turbulent gas—each concentration contracting in response to its own gravitational field, while moving outward in the ever-expanding universe.

These concentrations of gas (also known as nebulae) became galaxies when they fragmented into massive blobs to form protostars (masses of gas that in due course of time are destined to become stars).

Many of these protostars, while shrinking and flattening under influence of their own gravitational and centrifugal forces, became unstable, causing smaller masses of gas to break away and form protoplanets; and the protoplanets similarly produced protosatellites.

The protostars eventually became stars; the protoplanets and protosatellites, after proper cooling, condensing, and contracting, became planets and satellites.

To the best of our knowledge, the transition of our sun from a protostar to a star took place some 5 billion years ago. The planets and the satellites of the solar system were formed shortly thereafter.

UNAIDED OBSERVATION

On a clear night far away from city lights, the naked eye can see

A. Some 2,000 to 3,000 stars in each hemisphere of the sky. Some of these are only a few light-years away, others at distances of many hundreds of light-years.

> NOTE: To the human eye, all of these stars appear equally distant and it is helpful to imagine that all these stars are attached to the inside of an imaginary large sphere called the celestial sphere. See Fig. 6.

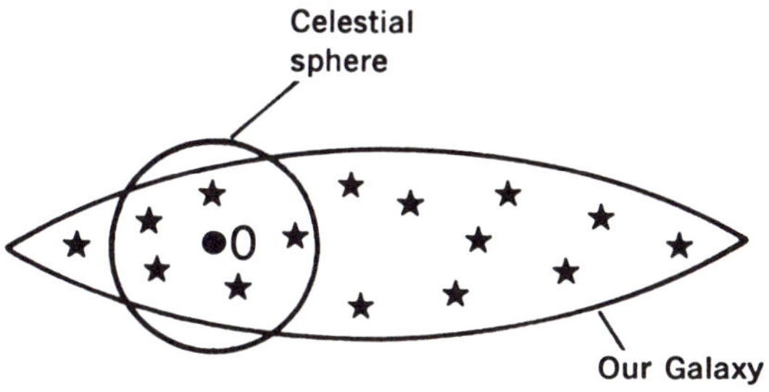

FIGURE 6. The celestial sphere is an imaginary spherical projection screen, upon which the observer, situated at the center, "sees" the stars and other celestial bodies.

B. Several planets traveling among the stars, each planet at its own characteristic velocity.

C. Meteors, five or ten every hour, each streaking across the sky and leaving a flash of light in its wake.

D. Comets, really bright ones—once or twice in a lifetime.

E. Nebulae—e.g., the great emission nebula in Orion or the dark Horsehead Nebula (also in Orion).

F. The Milky Way. An irregular belt describing a complete circuit of light on the surface of the celestial sphere. The belt varies from 5° to 50° in width. The light is due to the combined radiation emitted by the billions of stars along the long dimension of our flattened galaxy (lines AB in Figure 7). This band contrasts with the relative darkness (due to the paucity of stars) along the narrow dimension (lines AC) of the galaxy.

G. Other galaxies—e.g., the galaxy in Andromeda, that can be seen in northern latitudes and the two galaxies known as Magellanic Clouds in southern latitudes.

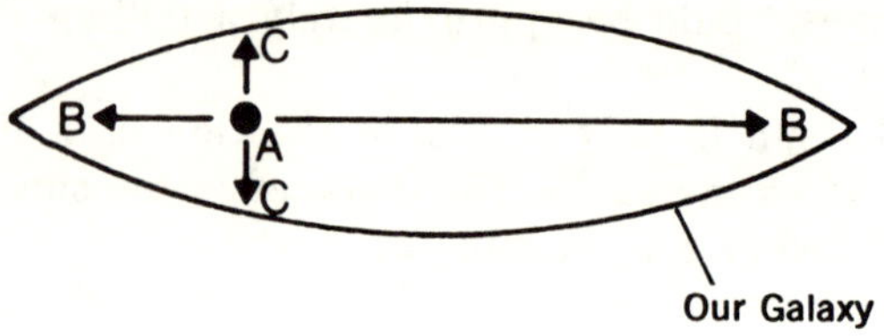

FIGURE 7. An observer at point A sees the merging light from billions of stars along lines AB. This forms the Milky Way. There are much fewer stars along lines AC, hence comparative darkness.

Identifying and Locating Stars Without a Telescope

Astronomy is one of the several sciences engaged in the study of nature. Much remains to be learned, and many important discoveries can still be made without the use of any equipment. The sky is the laboratory. The time is any fine, clear evening. The place is outdoors, preferably away from city lights, with an unobstructed view of the sky.

The brighter stars appear on the celestial sphere in groups known as constellations.

The names of forty-eight constellations are listed in a catalog published as long ago as A.D. 150.

The ancients either imagined that the groups formed pictures of gods, heroes, animals, etc., or they wanted to honor their gods, heroes, animals, etc., and named the constellations accordingly.

Modern astronomy recognizes eighty-eight constellations, each with its own clearly defined boundaries and each bearing the name originally given to it. The eighty-eight areas completely cover the celestial sphere.

NOTE: Celestial objects outside our own galaxy are also identified with the constellation in which they are seen. Hence the names "galaxy in Andromeda" or "galaxy in Ursa Major."

In this chapter, we shall pay particular attention to some thirty well-known constellations, such as Orion, the Big and Small Dippers, Cassiopeia, and so on, and we shall begin with the group that is probably easiest to identify—the Big Dipper. As its name implies, the stars form the outline of a dipper. It is important to become familiar with that group of stars as it is with reference to it that the locations of other constellations are most often determined. The Big Dipper can be seen every clear evening in most of the northern hemisphere. This section deals primarily with the stars of that constellation.

THE STARS OF THE BIG DIPPER

Seven bright stars form the pattern of the Dipper. The four forming the "bowl" are known as Dubhe, Merak, Phecda, and Megrez, all Arabic names: Dubhe means "bear," Merak "loin," Phecda and Megrez, "thigh" and "the root of the bear's tail," respectively.

The stars forming the "handle" of the Dipper are known as Alkaid, Mizar, and Alioth, also Arabic names, meaning "the chief," and "the apron"; the precise meaning of the name "Alioth" is still disputed.

Close to Mizar is the small star Alcor. The Arabs called these two stars "the Horse and the Rider." The star Alcor was used by them in a test for good eyesight. See Fig. 8.

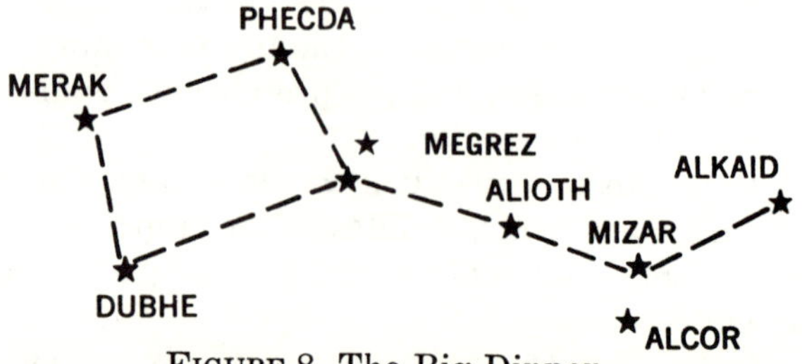

FIGURE 8. The Big Dipper.

SCALE OF ANGULAR DISTANCES

Locations of stars are stated in terms of angles or arcs. The angular distance, measured in degrees, is the angle or arc, subtended by these stars at the vantage point of the observer.

FIGURE 9. The angular distance of the full moon is about half a degree.

It is of importance to be able to gauge small angles in the sky. The diameter of the full moon is about half a degree, otherwise stated more formally as: The angle, or arc, subtended at our eye by the diameter of the full moon is .5°. See Fig. 9.

Another angular distance often used is the one between Dubhe and Merak—close to five degrees.

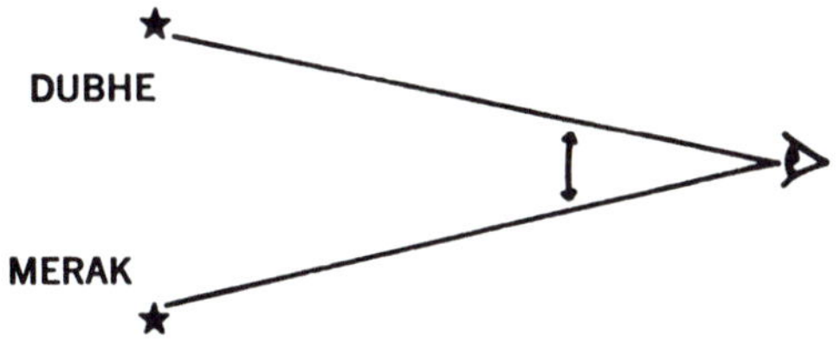

FIGURE 10. The angle subtended by Dubhe and Merak at the eye of a terrestial observer is close to 5°.

Ten moons could be placed side by side in the distance between these two stars. See Fig. 10.

PROBLEM 1:

Estimate the angular distance between Dubhe and Megrez.

Answer: 10°, approximately.

LEGENDS

One of the early names given to this constellation was the "Great Bear" and the Arabic names meaning "thigh," "loin," etc., describe parts of the bear. See Fig. 11.

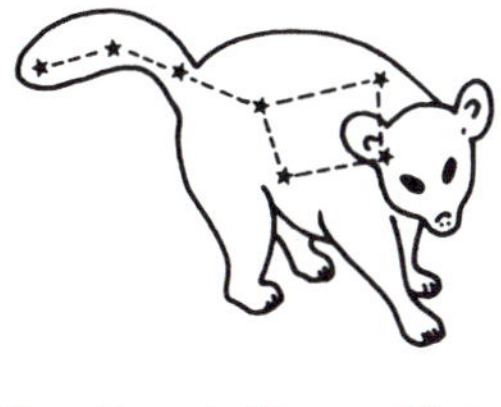

FIGURE 11. The Great Bear. Note the position of the Big Dipper.

The reason for this is not known, as an observer can scarcely imagine the outline of a bear or any other animal in that constellation.

An ancient legend held that the Bear represented Callisto, a daughter of the King of Arcadia, beloved of Jupiter, who, in order to protect her, changed her into a Bear and transferred her to the skies.

Another legend held that the Great Spirit purposely put the Great Bear in the sky to act as a "calendar" for earthly bears. During the half year when the Great Bear is low in the sky, all earthly bears stay in their dens and keep warm. When the Bear is high in the sky, bears leave their dens, for summer has begun.

OTHER NAMES

The names Great Bear and Big Dipper are still in common use. The scientific name for the constellation is the Latin translation of Great Bear—Ursa Major. In England, the constellation is known as the Plough, or the Wain (for wagon).

NOTE: To be accurate, the term Big Dipper should be used to refer to the seven bright stars and the term Great Bear or Ursa Major to refer to all the stars in the constellation. Often, however, these terms are used interchangeably.

APPARENT BRIGHTNESS OF STARS

The seven stars of the Big Dipper differ materially in apparent brightness. The brightest star is Alioth; the faintest, Megrez.

Technically this is stated in terms of apparent magnitude. Alioth has the smallest apparent magnitude (1.7); Megrez, the largest (3.4).

HIPPARCHUS' CLASSIFICATION OF STARS ACCORDING TO BRIGHTNESS

The ancient Greek astronomers classified the visible stars according to their apparent brightness, into six classes. This basic classification, in the main, is still valid. To Hipparchus, who lived on the island of Rhodes in the second century B.C., goes the credit for this classification. The twenty brightest stars known to him were arbitrarily designated as stars of the **first magnitude**; and the next fifty in order of apparent brightness were designated as stars of the **second magnitude**; and so on. The designation of **sixth magnitude** was given to several hundred stars barely visible to the normal human eye. See Fig. 12. Thus a completely

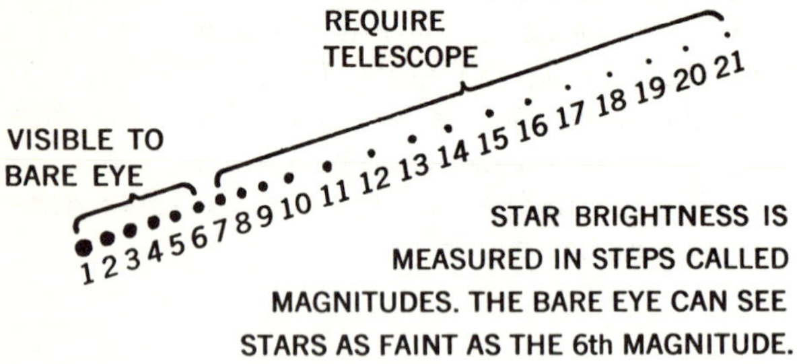

FIGURE 12. The relationship between brightness and magnitude.

arbitrary classification of stars, according to their brightness, was obtained. These magnitudes are, however, only *apparent* magnitudes. Some stars are actually bright, but appear faint because of their great distance.

DECIMAL DIVISION OF APPARENT MAGNITUDES

In the nineteenth century, the decimal division was introduced. In this classification, a star of magnitude 5.5 has an apparent brightness halfway between that of a star of magnitude 5.0 and that of a star of magnitude 6.0. Similarly, to state that the North Star (Polaris) has a magnitude of 2.1 signifies that its apparent brightness is only slightly less than the brightness of a star of magnitude 2.0. Increasingly, the decimal method of denoting magnitudes has been applied more extensively and made more precise.

RELATION BETWEEN APPARENT MAGNITUDE AND APPARENT BRIGHTNESS

There is a simple relationship between the apparent magnitude and apparent brightness.

This is based on a psychophysical law that states that if a stimulus, e.g., brightness, increases in a geometric progression, such as 1,2,4,8,16, etc., the sensation resulting from it increases in an arithmetic progression 1,2,3,4,5, etc.

From that law it was determined empirically that magnitude 2 stars are 2.5 (more precisely, 2.512) times brighter than magnitude 3 stars. Similarly, magnitude 3 stars are 2.512 times brighter than magnitude 4 stars, and so on.

PROBLEM 1:

The star Dubhe in the constellation Ursa Major has an apparent magnitude of 2.0 An unknown star, X, had an apparent magnitude of 4.0. How much brighter is Dubhe than star X?

Solution: A decrease in one order of magnitude corresponds to an increase of 2.5 times in apparent brightness. A decrease of two orders of magnitude is the same as an increase of $2.5 \times 2.5 = 6.25$ times in apparent brightness.

Answer: To the eye, Dubhe will appear more than six times brighter than the star X.

Stars down to magnitude 19 are visible with the 200-inch Mount Palomer telescope, and stars as dim as magnitude 24 can be photographed (long exposure) with that telescope. Even fainter stars can be photographed with the aid of image tubes.

ZERO AND NEGATIVE VALUES OF APPARENT MAGNITUDE

The twenty stars originally designated as first magnitude stars were subsequently regrouped. This was necessary because some of the stars were much brighter than others. The brighter stars of this group were designated as having magnitudes of .9, .8, .7, etc., through .0 to negative numbers. The star with the greatest apparent brightness at night is Sirius. Its apparent magnitude is -1.6. On the same scale, the apparent magnitude of our sun is immensely greater: -26.7.

DETERMINING APPARENT MAGNITUDES

The method of determining the magnitude of stars by observation is rather simple. With practice, fairly accurate results (an accuracy of .1 of a magnitude) can be obtained. The method was used extensively by the German astronomer Friedrich Argelander (1799–1875) and his associates in the preparation of the great star catalog, the "B.D. Catalog." (B.D. is the abbreviation of the German title of the catalog, *Bonner Durchmusterung*—"Bonn Catalog.") By this method, the observer compares the apparent brightness of a star with two or more neighboring stars of known magnitudes. Thus, a star that appears somewhat fainter than a neighboring star of 2.4 magnitude and somewhat brighter than another neighboring star of 2.6 magnitude, will be designated as having a magnitude of 2.5. In using this method it is advisable to make sure that:

A. The star to be measured and the known magnitude stars should be at about the same distance above the horizon.
B. The known magnitude stars should be as close as possible to the star to be measured.
C. One of the known magnitude stars should be somewhat brighter and the other somewhat fainter than the star to be measured.

The following table contains a list of stars of known apparent magnitude. These can be used for the determination of magnitude of many other stars.

Star	*Constellation*	*Apparent Magnitude*
Alpheratz	Andromeda	2.2
Schedar	Cassiopeia	2.5
Diphda	Cetus	2.2
Achernar	Eridanus	.6
Hamal	Aries	2.2
Acamar	Eridanus	3.1
Aldebaran	Taurus	1.1
Rigel	Orion	.3
Capella	Auriga	.2
Bellatrix	Orion	1.7
Canopus	Carina	− .9
Sirius	Canis Major	−1.6
Procyon	Canis Minor	.5
Pollux	Gemini	1.2
Regulus	Leo	1.3
Dubhe	Ursa Major	2.0
Acrux	Crux	1.1
Arcturus	Boötes	.2
Zubenelgenubi	Libra	2.9
Shaula	Scorpius	1.7
Nunki	Sagittarius	2.1
Markab	Pegasus	2.6

NOTE: On maps these figures are rounded off to the nearest integer.

PROBLEM 2:

Determine which of the two is the brighter star, Alkaid or Merak.

Answer: Alkaid is the brighter one. The apparent magnitude of Alkaid is 1.9; that of Merak, 2.4.

PROBLEM 3:

Find three stars in the Big Dipper that appear to be of equal brightness.

Answer: Mizar, Merak, and Phecda have almost the same apparent brightness. Precisely, they are designated as being 2.4, 2.4, and 2.5 magnitude stars, respectively. Phecda is by a very slight degree fainter than the other two.

PROBLEM 4:

Determine the apparent magnitude of the North Star (Polaris).

Answer: Polaris is but slightly brighter than Merak, and slightly fainter than Dubhe. It is usually designated as a 2.1 magnitude star.

Note again, this refers to **apparent** magnitudes. Actually, Polaris is much brighter than our sun —in fact, nearly 1,500 times brighter. The great distance accounts for its being only a magnitude 2.1 star. Stated in terms of time, it takes light, traveling at the speed of 186,000 miles per second, 8⅓ minutes to reach earth from the sun; and 400 years to reach earth from Polaris.

APPARENT DAILY MOTIONS OF STARS

It is common knowledge that the sun seems to rise in the east, describe an arc in the sky, and set in the west.

The stars, too, seem to move in arcs in the sky —also from the eastern to the western part of the horizon. A complete revolution takes 23 hours, 56 minutes and 4.09 seconds. This can very easily be approximately verified any clear evening with the aid of a good watch.

PROBLEM 5:

Object: To verify a complete revolution of a star. (This period is known as a "sidereal" day, or a "starday.")

Equipment: A good watch.

Procedure:

a. Note the time at which some bright star appears just above the eastern horizon.

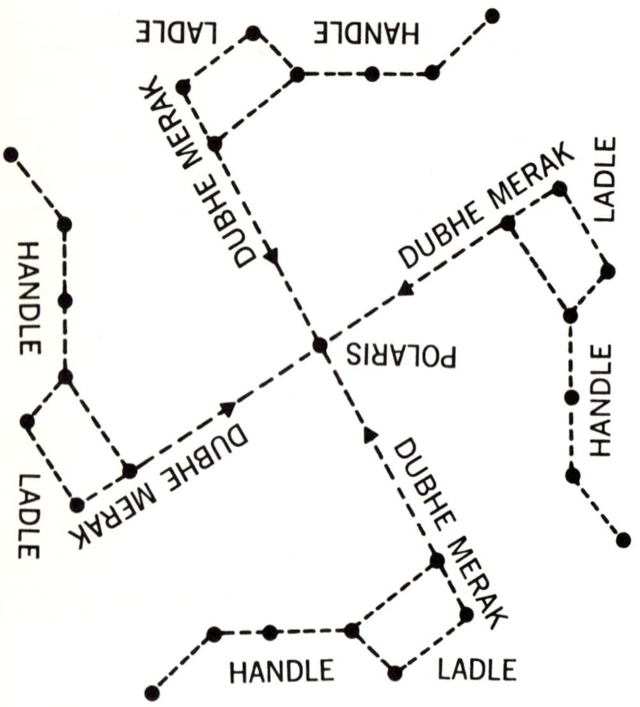

FIGURE 13. In the course of approximately 24 hours, the Big Dipper completes one revolution in the sky. Only part of that circle can actually be observed, as sunlight makes it impossible to observe the stars during the daytime. This figure shows the Big Dipper at 6-hour intervals.

b. The next day repeat the procedure under (a).

Results: The experiment demonstrates that every star completes one apparent revolution in 23 hours, 56 minutes and 4 seconds.

The term "apparent" is often repeated here for good reason. The motion is really *only* apparent; it may even be considered an optical illusion. Actually it is the earth, spinning on its axis in the opposite direction, that causes the stars to seem to move as they do.

This daily rotation can also very effectively be observed by watching a constellation, such as Ursa Major.

If, when first observed, the constellation appears level with the bowl on the right:

Six hours later it will appear with the handle pointed downward;

Twelve hours after the original observation, the Big Dipper will appear with the open part of the bowl pointing downward;

Eighteen hours after the original observation, the Big Dipper will appear to have the handle pointing upward.

In any 23 hours, 56 minutes and 4 seconds, the Big Dipper can be seen in any one of those positions.

During part of that time, the sun will interfere with the observations. The faint starlight cannot be discerned in the bright sky of day.

THE APPARENT ANNUAL MOTION OF THE STARS

The fact that stars complete a revolution in less than twenty-four hours is of great importance. It signifies, of course, that the stars make more than one revolution in a 24-hour period.

The difference between 24 and the period of revolution is:

	24 hours
−	23 hours, 56 minutes, 4 seconds
	3 minutes, 56 seconds.

Thus, the stars begin the next revolution in the remaining 3 minutes and 56 seconds. This can be verified by observation.

A star that appears on the horizon, say, at eight o'clock on a Sunday evening will be slightly **above** the horizon the following evening at eight o'clock. Tuesday evening at eight o'clock, the star will be still further above the horizon and a month later at eight o'clock in the evening, the star will be substantially above the horizon.

After three months, at eight o'clock in the evening, the star will be a quarter of a circle away from the eastern horizon. At the end of a year, the star will have completed an apparent circle.

This movement of a star is also an *apparent* movement. It is due to the **real** movement of the earth about the sun. The earth completes a revolution around the sun in 12 months.

This apparent annual movement of stars obtains for constellations as well.

Thus Ursa Major at eight o'clock in the evening in October is close to the horizon with the bowl opening upward.

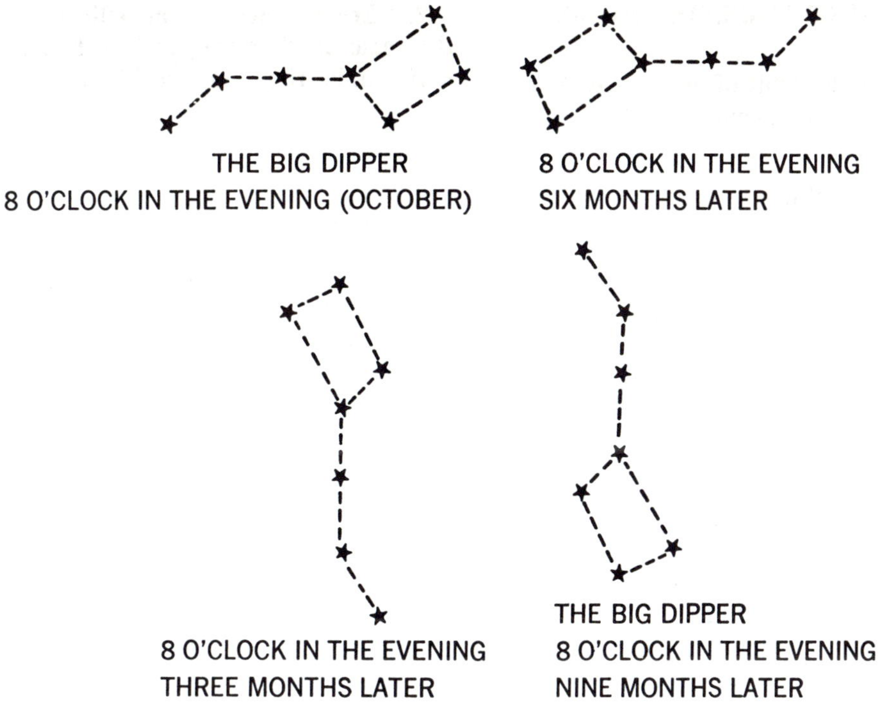

FIGURE 14.

Three months later at the same time in the evening, the handle will point downward.

In April at the same time of the evening, the Big Dipper will be high above the horizon and will appear with the bowl to the left.

In July at the same time of the evening, the Big Dipper will appear with the bowl at the bottom.

Thus in a period of 365¼ days, the Big Dipper completes 366¼ apparent revolutions: 365¼ of them are due to the rotation of the earth on its axis, and one is due to the revolution of the earth about the sun.

The Mechanics of the Solar System

INTRODUCTION

The solar system consists of the sun; the planets and their satellites; the planetoids, comets, meteorites, and dust. Both the adjective "solar" and the noun "system" are appropriate.

"Solar" indicates that the sun governs: it contains nearly 99.9 per cent of all the matter in the system. (The mass of all the planets, satellites, etc. comprises the other .1 or 1 per cent.) As a result of this division of mass, the "massive" sun is nearly stationary while all the "lighter" bodies revolve around it.

The word "system" implies that all the bodies observe great regularity in their motions. The laws governing these motions have been known for several centuries. Of great importance among the several laws are the three that are known by the name of their discoverer (Johannes Kepler) and the Universal Law of Gravitation (first stated by Isaac Newton).

KEPLER'S FIRST LAW OF PLANETARY MOTION

This law states that the orbit of every planet is an ellipse which has the sun as one of its foci.

DEMONSTRATION:

Object: To draw an ellipse.

Equipment: Pencil, piece of string, two thumbtacks, paper.

Procedure:

1. Place string to form an angle, ABC.
2. Fix the ends A and C with the thumbtacks, and place the pencil at B.
3. Keeping the string taut, move the pencil around to form the oval curve. See Fig. 15.

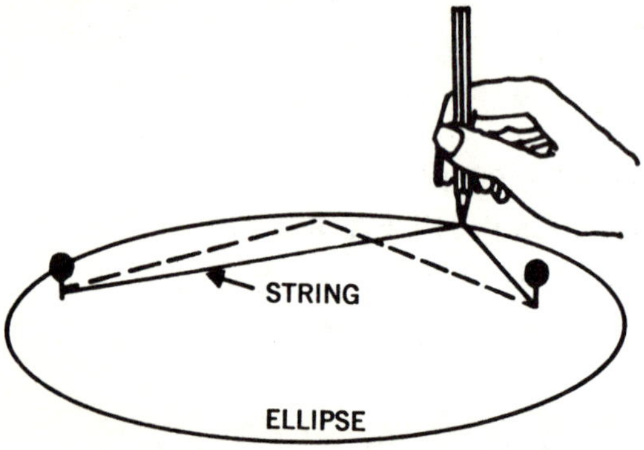

FIGURE 15. Drawing of an ellipse. Fix the end of the string at points A and C. Stretch the string to form the angle at B. Keeping the string taut at all times move the pencil about to form the oval curve. A is one focus of this ellipse. C is the other.

Result: The curve described by the pencil is an ellipse. The two points that were kept fixed by the thumbtacks are called the foci of the ellipse (sing. focus).

PROBLEM 6:

Given an ellipse. Its major axis is 5 inches long, its minor axis is 3 inches long.

Find: 1. The distance between the foci; 2. the eccentricity of the ellipse.

Solution: 1. The major axis, the minor axis, and the distance between the foci are related by a simple formula. If the length of the major axis is denoted by a; if the length of the minor axis is denoted by b; and the distance between foci is denoted by c; the formula is:

$$b^2+c^2=a^2 \text{ or } c=\sqrt{a^2-b^2}.$$

In this case, $c=\sqrt{5^2-3^2}=4$ inches. The distance between the foci is 4 inches. See Fig. 16.

2. **"Eccentricity" of an ellipse is defined as the ratio of distance between foci to length of major axis.** It is denoted by e.

$$e=\frac{c}{a}$$

This ratio, in the case of an ellipse, is always larger than 0 and less than 1. It indicates how "eccentric," compared with a circle, the ellipse is. When the ratio is small, say .1, the ellipse is very little eccentric. It is almost circular. When the eccentricity is large, say .8, the ellipse is highly elongated. In this problem the eccentricity is given by:

$$e=\frac{4}{5}=.8$$

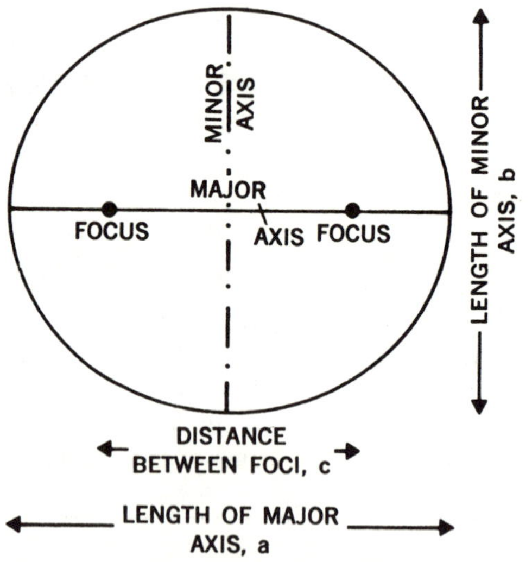

FIGURE 16. In an ellipse the length of the major axis, a, the length of the minor axis, b, and the distance between the foci, c, are related by the formula—

$$b^2+c^2=a^2$$

Planets move in nearly circular orbits. The eccentricities of Venus and of the earth are .01 and .02, respectively.

Comets move in elongated orbits. The orbit of Halley's Comet is an ellipse, with an eccentricity of .97.

KEPLER'S SECOND LAW OF PLANETARY MOTION

This law deals with the speed of the planets in their respective orbits. The speed is not constant, the planets moving faster the closer they are to the sun. The maximum speed of any planet is attained when it is closest to the sun, the minimum when it is farthest. The point on the orbit closest to the sun is known as perihelion, the farthest, aphelion.

Though the speeds of the planets in their orbits are not constant, another feature closely connected with speed *is* constant—namely, the speed with which the line connecting the sun and any particular planet passes over areas.

This is expressed in the formal version of Kepler's second law: **The radius vector of each planet passes over equal areas in equal intervals of time.**

The radius vector is an imaginary line that connects the sun with a planet—short at the perihelion and long at the aphelion.

The second law indicates that at aphelion, the planet moves slower than at perihelion in order to pass over equal areas of the ellipse. See Fig. 17.

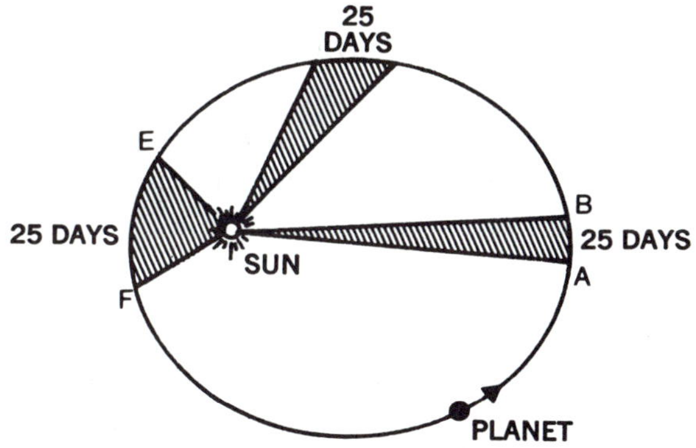

FIGURE 17. Kepler's second law of planetary motion. The radius vector would cover equal areas (three such areas are shown here shaded) in equal times (25 days).

At aphelion the planet moved relatively slowly to get from A to B. At perihelion the planet had to move at a relatively high speed to cover the distance from E to F.

The term radius vector used in the formal version of the law is an imaginary line joining the sun with the planet. The line connecting the sun to A, or the sun to B, or the sun to D, etc., is a radius vector.

The earth's average velocity along its orbit about the sun is 18.5 miles per second. Since the orbit is almost a circle, its speed does not vary materially along the path. At aphelion, the earth moves only by ½ a mile per second slower than at perihelion.

In the case of highly eccentric orbits, such as those pursued by comets, the orbital speed varies greatly. Halley's Comet, when at perihelion, has a speed of 100 miles per second; and at aphelion, of less than 1 mile per second.

KEPLER'S THIRD LAW OF PLANETARY MOTION

The third law deals with the relationship between the period of a planet and its mean distance from the sun.

The "period" is the time that it takes a planet to complete one revolution about the sun. For the earth, this is 365.26 days; for the planet Mercury, only 88 days; for Pluto, the farthest planet, 248 *years.*

Kepler's third law states that **the squares of the periods of any two planets are proportional to the cubes of their mean distances to the sun.**

This can be stated as an algebraic equation: Let the two planets be designated as A and B.

$$\frac{(\text{period of A})^2}{(\text{period of B})^2} = \frac{(\text{mean distance of the sun to A})^3}{(\text{mean distance of the sun to B})^3}$$

If the known data for the earth are used for one of these planets, say B, the equation becomes:

$$\frac{(\text{period of A})^2}{(365.26)^2} = \frac{(\text{mean distance of the sun to A})^3}{(93{,}000{,}000)^3}$$

This equation has two variables: the period of a planet and its mean distance. If one of these is obtained by observation, the other can be computed algebraically.

PROBLEM 7:

The period of the planet Mars is 687 days. Compute the mean distance of Mars from the sun.

Solution: Inserting the given data in the equation:

$$\frac{(\text{mean distance of Mars from sun})^3}{(93{,}000{,}000)^3} = \frac{(365)^2}{(687)^2}$$

Answer: The distance of Mars from the sun is 142,000,000 miles.

NOTE: Kepler's third law is not quite complete. The complete form was evolved by Newton. In the complete form, "the squares of the periods" have to be multiplied by the combined mass of the sun and the planet. The corrected equation reads:

$$\frac{(\text{period of A})^2(\text{mass of sun \& planet A})}{(\text{period of B})^2(\text{mass of sun \& planet B})} = \frac{(\text{mean dist. of A})^3}{(\text{mean dist. of B})^3}$$

EVALUATION OF KEPLER'S THREE LAWS

The discovery of these laws was a milestone, not only in the history of astronomy, but also in the history of science in general. It is an eternal monument, not only to the brilliance of Kepler, but also to his devotion to science, to which he committed infinite patience and labor.

There was one shortcoming to these laws, however—a very important shortcoming. Kepler's laws did not explain the behavior of the planets, why they move in elliptical orbits, or why their speeds change as they do.

The answers were soon forthcoming in Sir Isaac Newton's epoch-making book, *Mathematical Principles of Physics*. There, Newton showed that the planets behave as they do because of a most fundamental universal law—the law of gravitation; and that Kepler's three laws are merely consequences of that universal law.

NEWTON'S UNIVERSAL LAW OF GRAVITATION

The law, dealing with forces between material objects, states that every particle of matter attracts every other particle of matter with a force, depending on three factors:

A. Mass of one object.
B. Mass of the other object.
C. The distance between the objects.

These factors are often denoted as M, m, and r, respectively.

The formal statement of the law is: **Every particle of matter in the universe attracts every other particle with a force that is proportional to the product of their masses, and inversely proportional to the square of the distance between them.**

The law can also be expressed as an algebraic equation:

$$FG = (\text{force of gravity}) \times \frac{Mm}{r^2}$$

G is known as the universal gravitational constant. Its value is 6.7×10^{-8} if M and m are expressed in grams, r in centimeters, and F in dynes. The formula for the Universal Law of Gravitation will then be:

$$F = 6.7 \times 10^{-8} \frac{Mm}{r^2}$$

PROBLEM 8:

A mass of 2,000 grams, about 4.4 pounds, is at a distance of 2.54 centimeters (about 1 inch) from another mass of 5,000 grams. Find the force of attraction between these two bodies.

$$F = 6.7 \times 10^{-8} \frac{2000 \times 5000}{(2.54)^2} = .1 \text{ dyne}$$

Answer: The force with which each mass attracts the other is .1 dyne.

A dyne is an extremely small force, much smaller than a pound of force. Approximately 500,000 dynes are equal in value to one pound of force.

APPLICATION OF THE LAW OF GRAVITATION

The law was of enormous aid in solving a host of problems. Chief among these are:

A. Freely falling bodies. Any body not properly supported, will fall toward the center of the earth.
B. Ocean tides and tides in the atmosphere.
C. Motion of comets.
D. Precession of equinoxes.
E. Motion of planets. If the gravitational force between the earth and the sun ceased to operate, the earth would go off on a tangent. It is the direct result of this law that planets revolve about the sun as they do. This result is shown in Figure 18.

The nine planets move in elliptical orbits at various distances from the sun, counterclockwise.

Although gravitation applies, of course, to the stars and galaxies as well, its effect is easier to see in the case of planets because of the presence of *one* large mass (the sun) acting on several close, smaller masses (the planets). The perturbation on these motions by distant stars is extremely small.

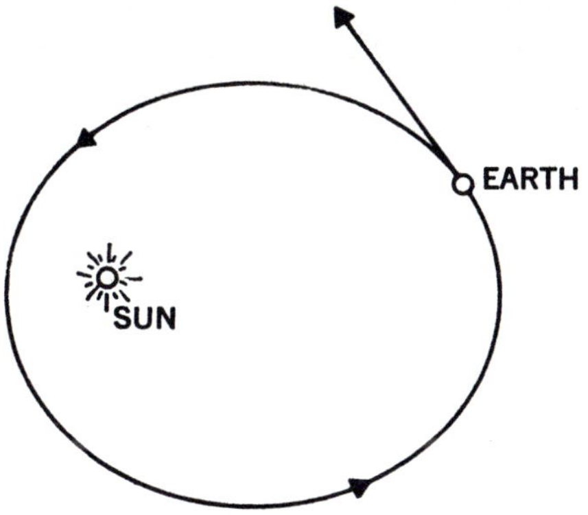

FIGURE 18. Effect of gravitational attraction. It is due to the gravitational attraction of the sun that the earth continues to move in its orbit.

In the absence of this attraction the earth would leave its elliptical orbit and go off on a tangent, such as at point A, farther and farther away from the sun.

APPARENT MOTION OF PLANETS AS SEEN FROM THE EARTH

The true motion of the planets cannot be observed from the earth, because the earth itself is constantly in motion. Observations indicate only the motion of the planets relative to that of the earth. At times a planet's relative velocity, with respect to the earth, is greater than its true velocity, as when the earth and the planet move in opposite directions; at other times the planet's relative velocity is less than its true velocity, as when a planet and the earth move in the same direction.

Of particular interest in the apparent motion of planets is the retrograde phase in which planets seem to move in a direction opposite to their normal one. See Figure 19.

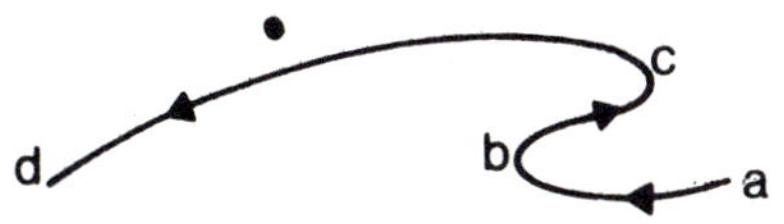

FIGURE 19. Retrograde motion. As seen against the background of the celestial sphere the planet was moving at A in the normal direction (this is called "direct motion"), and continued to do so until point B. From B to C the motion is in a direction opposite to normal (retrograde motion). At point C, the planet makes a U-turn and continues in direct motion.

The backward or retrograde motion of several of the planets puzzled astronomers for many centuries, until finally it was explained by Copernicus. An example is of great aid in visualizing the apparent retrograde motion.

Let the inner circle in Figure 20 represent the orbit of the earth around the sun. Let the large circle represent the orbit of Mars. The earth, being closer to the sun, moves faster than Mars. Let the top of the figure represent part of the celestial sphere. The sphere serves as a background upon which the movements of Mars are observed.

When the earth is in position 1, Mars will be seen in place 1 on the celestial sphere. Several weeks later, both the earth and Mars will have moved in their orbits. Mars is now at point 2. As the earth moves through positions 3 and 4, the line described by Mars on the celestial sphere will be of a body in retrograde motion.

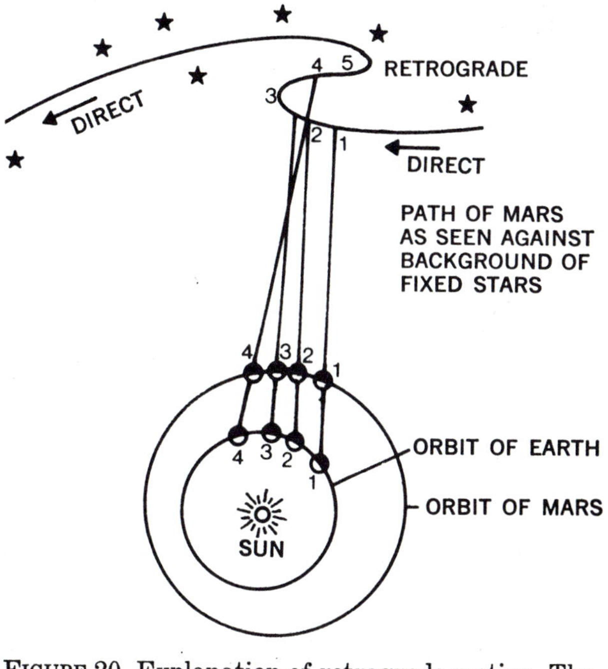

FIGURE 20. Explanation of retrograde motion. The earth, being closer to the sun than Mars, moves faster than Mars (the earth completes its circle in 365 days, Mars 687). At point 1, Mars is "ahead" of the earth; its motion is direct. At point 4 the earth is "ahead" of Mars, and the latter seems to retrograde.

SIDEREAL AND SYNODIC PERIOD OF A PLANET

In connection with planets, there are two definitions of period: (A) sidereal period; and (B) synodic period. These differ in length due to the motion of the earth.

A. Sidereal Period is the time it takes the planet to complete one revolution in its orbit. Another way of saying the same thing is: It is the time required by a planet to complete a circle on the celestial sphere, **as seen from the sun.**

B. The Synodic Period, which involves the motion of the earth, is the interval between one time that the sun, the earth, and planet are aligned and the next time. Since both the earth and the planet are in motion, the synodic period differs materially from the sidereal.

Thus, the sidereal period of Mars is 687 days; its synodic period is 780 days.

In the case of Saturn, the sidereal and synodic periods are 29.5 years and 378 days, respectively. The former signifies that it takes Saturn nearly 30 years to complete its orbit about the sun; the latter that every 378 days, the sun, the earth, and Saturn are situated along a straight line. This is shown in Figure 21.

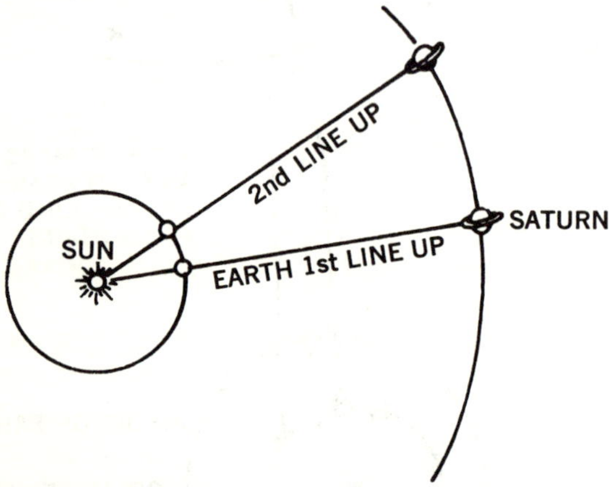

FIGURE 21. The synodic period of Saturn. This period is the interval of time between one lineup of sun-earth-Saturn to the next time these planets form a straight line. The synodic period of Saturn is 378 days. It consists of 365 days for a complete revolution of the earth plus 13 days needed for the earth to catch up with Saturn, which in the meanwhile has moved on to a new position.

The 378 days are composed of (a) 1 revolution of the earth about the sun (365 days); and (b) 13 days to catch up with Saturn which, in the meanwhile, has moved to a new position in its orbit.

There are two simple formulas to compute the synodic periods of planets. One formula is to be used for inferior planets, the other for superior.

Mercury and Venus are Inferior Plants. They are closer to the sun than the earth.

The orbits of the superior planets are outside the earth's orbit. See Figure 22.

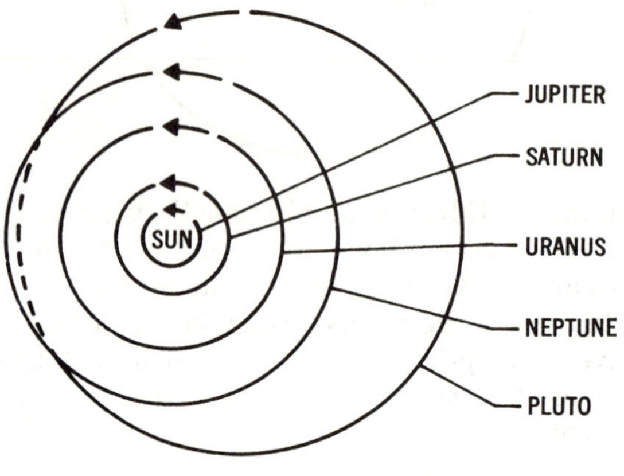

FIGURE 22. Orbits of five superior planets. The orbits are ellipses of small eccentricity, hence closely resemble circles. All the planets move in a counterclockwise direction, as shown by the arrows. The length of the arrow indicates the distance the planet travels in one year. The four other planets (not shown) move along orbits inside the orbit of Jupiter.

The formula for an inferior planet is:

$$\text{Synodic period of planet} = \frac{360}{P-E}$$

P is the number of degrees of arc that a planet moves in its orbit in one day; E is the number of degrees that the earth moves in its orbit in one day.

For Mercury,

$$P = \frac{360}{88}$$

$$E = \frac{360}{365\frac{1}{4}}$$

Substituting these numbers in the formula, we then get:

$$\text{Synodic period of Mercury} = \frac{360}{\frac{360}{88} - \frac{360}{365\frac{1}{4}}}$$

$$= 116 \text{ days}$$

For a superior planet, the formula is:

$$\text{Synodic period of superior planet} = \frac{360}{E-P}$$

where E and P have the same meaning as in the previous formula.

The proof of this second formula is fairly simple. The denominator $E-P$ stands for the number of degrees that the earth gains on a planet in *one* day. But in a synodic period, the earth gains a complete revolution (360°) on the planet; hence, that period is equal to the number of times $(E-P)$ is contained in 360.

PROBLEM 9:

Compute the synodic period of Mars.

Given: The sidereal period of the earth is $365\frac{1}{4}$ days, or $E = \frac{360}{365\frac{1}{4}}$; and the sidereal period of Mars is 687 days, or

$$P = \frac{360}{687}$$

Answer: 780 days.

Basic Planetary Data

INTRODUCTION

For each planet there is now available a large number of data. These include dimensions as well as other physical and orbital data.

The methods used to obtain several of these values are indicated in this part.

DISTANCE TO SUN

One fairly accurate way to determine the mean distance of a planet to the sun makes use of Kepler's third law.

If distances are measured in astronomical units and sidereal periods in years, the third law can be written as

$$(\text{period of a planet})^2 = (\text{mean distance of planet to sun})^3$$

PROBLEM 10:

The sidereal period of the planet Mars is 687 days. Find the mean distance of Mars from the sun.

Solution: Changing days into years and inserting in above formula,

$$\left(\frac{687}{365.25}\right)^2 = (\text{mean distance of Mars to Sun})^3$$

The answer for mean distance is 1.52 astronomical units, or (multiplying 1.52 by 93,000,000) 142,000,000 miles.

ECCENTRICITY

The eccentricity of a planet's orbit can be found

A. By determining the distance of the planet from the sun at different times of the year.

B. By plotting a graph of date versus distance from the sun. The graph will be an ellipse.

C. By computing the eccentricity e, using the formula $e = \frac{c}{a}$ where c is the distance from either focus (the sun is at one of the foci) to the center of the ellipse and a is the length of half of the major axis.

NOTE: Computing actual (as opposed to mean) distances from the sun for a planet other than the earth is a more arduous task.

INCLINATION OF ORBIT TO ECLIPTIC

This is obtained from observations on the celestial sphere. The inclination is equal to the maximum angle the planet reaches above or below the ecliptic.

PERIOD OF ONE REVOLUTION, SIDEREAL

The sidereal period can be obtained by using the formulas given on page 514 and the observed synodic period.

PERIOD OF ONE REVOLUTION, SYNODIC

The synodic period is obtained by noting the interval of time between two successive conjunctions of the planet with the sun, i.e., two successive times that the planet is on the line that joins the sun and the earth.

ORBITAL VELOCITY

This is obtained by dividing the length of the circumference by the time it takes to cover that distance, i.e., by the sidereal period.

DISTANCE OF A PLANET FROM EARTH

One method that can be used to determine the distance of a planet from the earth is triangulation. In this method a line of position, say, 1,000 km long, is established on earth. The angles from both ends of the line to the planet are measured. Standard formulae from elementary trigonometry are used to find the distance to the planet.

Another method is to measure the time elapsed for a radar signal to make a round trip to the planet. The distance to the planet is obtained by multiplying half the time for the round trip by the velocity of light.

PROBLEM 11:

A radar signal was sent to the planet Venus early in 1958. The round trip took about 5 minutes (300 seconds). Find the distance to the planet at that time.

Solution: Since the velocity of light, or the velocity of radar, is 186,000 miles per second, then

$186{,}000 \times 150 =$ approximately 28,000,000 miles.

ANGULAR DIAMETER

The anglar diameter of a planet is determined by

A. Sighting through a telescope one limb of the planet.

B. Rotating the telescope to the other limb.

The angle through which the telescope has been rotated is equal to the angular diameter of the planet.

LINEAR DIAMETER

The linear diameter of a planet is obtained by multiplying the angular diameter (in radians) by the distance to the planet. The formula is:

Linear diameter = angular diameter $\times$ distance to planet

The angular diameter in this formula has to be in radian units. (A radian is an angle that subtends an arc of a circle equal to the radius of that circle; 1 radian is slightly more than 57°.) The rate of conversion from degrees to radians is 1 radian $= \frac{360°}{2\pi}$. The diameter will be in the same unit as that used for distance to the planet.

VOLUME

Assuming that the planet is a sphere, the geometrical formula for volume of a sphere can be used:

$$\text{Volume} = \frac{4}{3}\pi \times \text{the radius}^3$$

where π has a value of 3.14.

MASS

The mass of a planet that has a satellite orbiting around it is obtained from Kepler's third law as amended by Newton (see note following Problem 7).

One form of this amended law is

$$P^2 = \frac{4\pi^2 a^3}{G(M_1+M_2)}$$

where
P is the sidereal period of the satellite
a is the distance from center of satellite to center of planet
G is the universal gravitational constant (in the meter-kilogram-second system $G=6.7\times 10^{-11}$ newtons$\times$meters$^2\times$kilograms^{-2}).
M_1 and M_2 are the masses of the planet and the satellite, respectively. The mass of the satellite (M_2) is usually so much smaller than the mass of the planet (M_1) that it may be omitted from the formula.

PROBLEM 12:

Find the mass of Mars, given that its satellite Phobos is at a distance of 5,820 miles=9,400 km=9.4×10^6 meters and it orbits the mother planet in 7 hours 39 minutes=27,500 seconds.

Solution: Using meters for the unit of distance and seconds for the unit of time, then

$$M_1 = \frac{4\pi^2 \times (9.4\times10^6)^3}{6.7\times10^{-11}\times27{,}500^2} = 7\times10^{23} \text{ kg, ap-}$$

proximately, for the mass of Mars, or about 11 per cent the mass of the earth.

The mass of planets that do not have natural satellites (e.g., Venus) is obtained by the use of either (A) an artificial satellite that orbits the planet or (B) determining the perturbation exerted by the planet on a close passing planetoid or spacecraft.

DENSITY

Mean density of a planet is obtained by dividing the mass by the volume. The value of a density is often stated in terms relative to the density of the earth.

SURFACE GRAVITY

The acceleration due to gravity at the surface of a planet is derived from Newton's Universal law of gravitation with M being the mass of the planet and m=1. In the gravity formula is $F=6.7\times10^{-8}\frac{M}{r^2}$. In the meter-kilogram-second system, the formula is $F=6.7\times10^{-11}\frac{M}{r^2}$. r is the radius of the planet proper units.

VELOCITY OF ESCAPE

The speed that an object must acquire in order to escape from the gravitational field of a planet is obtained from

$$V=\sqrt{2}\,\frac{Gm}{r}$$

In the centimeter-gram-second system, $G=6.7\times 10^{-8}$ the mass has to be stated in grams, and the distance of the object from the center of the planet in centimeters. The escape velocity will be in units of centimeters per second.

PERIOD OF ROTATION ABOUT AXIS

The period of rotation of planets that have identifiable features (e.g., Mars) is determined by timing a complete rotation of such a feature.

The Doppler shift in radar waves between the approaching limb and the receding limb of a planet is used to determine the period for planets that do not have identifiable features.

INCLINATION OF PLANET'S EQUATOR TO ORBIT

This is usually derived from the study of an arc described by a surface marking on the planet.

ALBEDO

Albedo pertains to the ability of an object to reflect light. Some objects—e.g., tops of clouds—reflect most of the light falling upon them; others absorb most of the light, reflecting little. Stones, rocks, and soil are poor reflectors of light.

Albedo is defined as the ratio of the quantity of light reflected to the light received by the object.

In reference to the planets, albedo is equal to the ratio:

$$\frac{\text{light reflected by the planet}}{\text{sunlight falling on the planet}}$$

The denominator can be computed from the known value of the sun's luminosity and the planet's distance from the sun. The numerator is derived from the intrinsic brightness of the planet.

CHAPTER ELEVEN

GEOLOGY

Introduction

Derived from the Greek *geo,* "earth," plus *logos,* "discourse," geology is the science which deals with the origin, structure, and history of the earth and its inhabitants as recorded in the rocks.

To the geologist, the earth is not simply the globe upon which we live—it is an ever present challenge to learn more about such things as earthquakes, volcanoes, glaciers, and the meaning of fossils. How old is the earth? Where did it come from? Of what is it made? To answer these questions, the earth scientist must study the evidence of events that occurred millions of years ago. He must then relate his findings to the results of similar events that are happening today. He attempts, for example, to determine the location and extent of ancient oceans and mountain ranges, and to trace the evolution of life as recorded in rocks of different ages. He studies the composition of the rocks and minerals forming the earth's crust in an attempt to locate and exploit the valuable economic products that are to be found there.

In pursuing his study of the earth the geologist relies heavily upon other basic sciences. For example, **astronomy** (the study of the nature and movements of planets, stars, and other heavenly bodies) tells us where the earth fits into the universe and has also developed several theories as to the origin of our planet. **Chemistry** (the study of the composition of substances and the changes which they undergo) is used to analyze and study the rocks and minerals of the earth's crust. The science of **physics** (the study of matter and motion) helps explain the various physical forces affecting our earth, and the reaction of earth materials to these forces.

To understand the nature of prehistoric plants and animals we must turn to **biology,** the study of all living forms. **Zoology** provides us with information about the animals, and **botany** gives us some insight into the nature of ancient plants. By using these sciences, as well as others, the geologist is better able to cope with the many complex problems that are inherent in the study of the earth and its history.

The scope of geology is so broad that it has been divided into two major divisions: **physical geology** and **historical geology.** For convenience in study, each of these divisions has been subdivided into a number of more specialized branches of subsciences.

PHYSICAL GEOLOGY

Physical geology deals with the earth's composition, its structure, the movements within and upon the earth's crust, and the geologic processes by which the earth's surface is, or has been changed.

The broad division of geology includes such basic geologic subsciences as **mineralogy,** the study of minerals, and **petrology,** the study of rocks. These two branches of geology provide us with much-needed information about the composition of the earth. In addition, there is **structural geology** to explain the arrangement of the rocks within the earth, and **geomorphology** to explain the origin of its surface features.

These branches of physical geology enable the

geologist to make detailed studies of all phases of earth science. The knowledge gained from such research brings about a better understanding of the physical nature of the earth.

CASUAL OBSERVATION

How can we learn more about this fascinating earth and the stories to be read from its rocks? Actually it is very simple, for geology is all around us. The geologist's laboratory is the great outdoors, and each walk through the fields or drive down the highway brings us in contact with the processes and materials of geology.

For example, pick up a piece of common limestone. There are probably fossils in it. And these fossils may well represent the remains of animals that lived in some prehistoric sea which once covered the area.

Or maybe you are walking along a river bank. Notice the silt on the bank after the last high water stage. This reminds us of the ability of running water to deposit **sediments**—sediments that may later be transformed into rocks. Notice, too, how swift currents have scoured the river banks. The soil has been removed by **erosion,** the geologic process which is so important in the shaping of the earth's surface features.

Perhaps you see a field of black fertile soil supporting a fine crop of cotton or corn. It may surprise you to learn that this dark rich soil may have been derived from an underlying chalky white limestone—still another reminder of the importance of earth materials in our everyday life.

EARTH AS A PLANET

The earth is one of nine planets comprising the solar system. It is the largest of the four planets of the inner group (Mercury, Venus, Earth, and Mars) and is third closest to the sun (Fig. 1).

Shape of the Earth. The earth has the form of an **oblate spheroid.** That is, it is almost ball-shaped, or spherical, except for a slight flattening at the poles. This flattening, and an accompanying bulge at the equator, are produced by the centrifugal force of rotation.

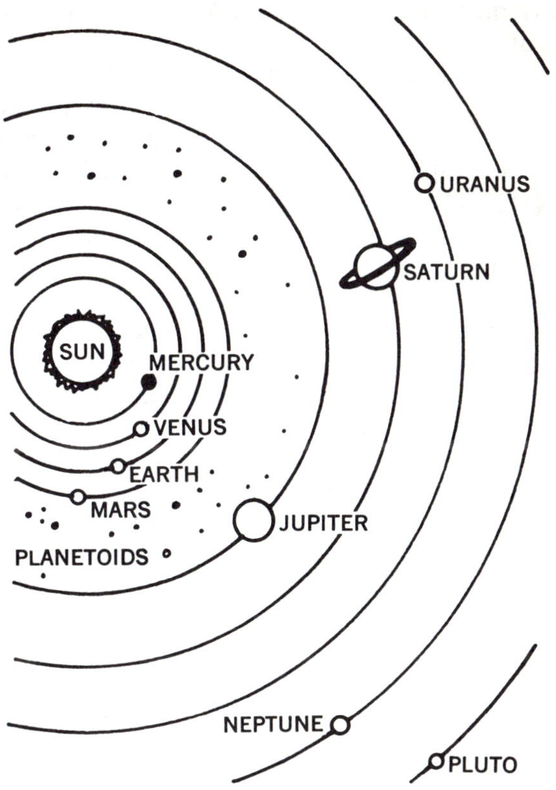

FIGURE 1. Planets of the solar system and their relation to the sun.

Size of the Earth. Although the earth is of great size, Jupiter, Saturn, Uranus, and Neptune all have greater equatorial diameters. Earth has a polar diameter of about 7900 miles (the equatorial diameter is approximately 27 miles greater because of the bulge described above). The circumference of the earth is about 24,874 miles, and the surface area comprises roughly 197 million square miles, of which only about 51 million square miles (29 per cent) are surface lands. The remaining 71 per cent of the earth's surface is covered by water.

Earth Motions. We have already learned that each of the planets revolves around the sun within its own orbit and period of revolution. In addition to its trip around the sun, the earth also rotates.

Rotation of the Earth. The earth turns on its axis (the shortest diameter connecting the poles), and this turning motion is called *rotation.* The earth rotates from west to east and makes one complete rotation each day. It is this rotating motion that gives us the alternating periods of daylight and darkness which we know as day and night.

As it rotates, the earth has a single wobble. This has to do with the fact that the earth's axis is tilted at an angle of 23½ degrees. However, this wobbling motion is so slow that it takes approximately 26,000 years to complete a single wobble. The tilting of the earth's axis is also responsible fcr the seasons.

Revolution of the Earth. The earth revolves around the sun in a slightly elliptical **orbit** approximately once every 365¼ days. During this time (a solar year), the earth travels at a speed of more than 60,000 miles per hour, and on the average, it remains about 93 million miles from the sun.

In addition to rotation, revolution, and the wobbling motion, our entire solar system is heading in the general direction of the star Vega at a speed of about 400 million miles per year.

PRINCIPAL DIVISIONS OF THE EARTH

The earth consists of air, water, and land. We recognize these more technically as the **atmosphere,** a gaseous envelope surrounding the earth; the **hydrosphere,** the waters filling the depressions and covering almost three-fourths of the land; and the **lithosphere,** the solid part of the earth which underlies the atmosphere and hydrosphere.

The Atmosphere. The atmosphere, or gaseous portion of the earth, extends upward for hundreds of miles above sea level. It is a mixture of nitrogen, oxygen, carbon dioxide, water vapor, and other gases (see Table 1).

GAS	PER CENT BY VOLUME
Nitrogen	78.084
Oxygen	20.946
Argon	.934
Carbon dioxide	.033
Neon	.001818
Helium	.000524
Methane	.0002
Krypton	.000114
Hydrogen	.00005
Nitrous oxide	.00005
Xenon	.0000087

TABLE 1. Analysis of gases present in pure dry air. Notice that nitrogen and oxygen comprise 99 per cent of the total volume of atmospheric gases.

Of great importance to man, the elements of the atmosphere make life possible on our planet. Moreover, the atmosphere acts as an insulating agent to protect us from the heat of the sun and to shield us from the bombardment of meteorites, and it makes possible the evaporation and precipitation of moisture. The atmosphere is an important geologic agent (see Chapter 9) and is responsible for the processes of weathering which are continually at work on the earth's surface.

The Hydrosphere. The hydrosphere includes all the waters of the oceans, lakes, and rivers, as well as **ground water**—which exists within the lithosphere. As noted earlier, most of this water is contained in the oceans, which cover roughly 71 per cent of the earth's surface to an average depth of about two and a half miles.

The waters of the earth are essential to man's existence and they are also of considerable geologic importance. Running streams and oceans are actively engaged in eroding, transporting, and depositing sediments; and water, working in conjunction with atmospheric agents, has been the major force in forming the earth's surface features throughout geologic time. The geologic work of the hydrosphere will be discussed in some detail in later chapters of this book.

The Lithosphere. Of prime importance to the geologist is the lithosphere. This, the solid portion of the earth, is composed of rocks and minerals which, in turn, comprise the continental masses and ocean basins. The rocks of the lithosphere are of three basic types, **igneous, sedimentary,** and **metamorphic.** Igneous rocks were originally in a molten state but have since cooled and solidified to form rocks such as granite and basalt. Sedimentary rocks are formed from sediments (fragments of pre-existing rocks) deposited by wind, water, or ice. Limestone, sandstone, and clay are typical of this group. The metamorphic rocks have been formed from rocks that were originally sedimentary or igneous in origin. This transformation takes place as the rock is subjected to great physical and chemical change. Marble, which in its original form was limestone, is an example of a metamorphic rock.

Most of what we know about the lithosphere has been learned through the study of the surface materials of the earth. However, by means of deep bore holes and seismological studies, geologists have gathered much valuable information about the interior of the earth. Additional geologic data are derived from rocks which were originally buried many miles beneath the ground but have been brought to or near the surface by violent earth movements and later exposed by erosion.

MAJOR PHYSICAL FEATURES OF THE EARTH

The major relief features of the earth are the **continental masses** and the **ocean basins.** These are the portions of the earth which apparently remained stable throughout all of known geologic time.

The Continental Masses. The continents are rocky platforms which cover approximately 29 per cent of the earth's surface. Composed largely of granite, they have an average elevation of about three miles above the floors of the surrounding ocean basins and rise an average of one-half mile above sea level (Fig. 2). The seaward edges of the continental masses are submerged and these are called the **continental shelves.**

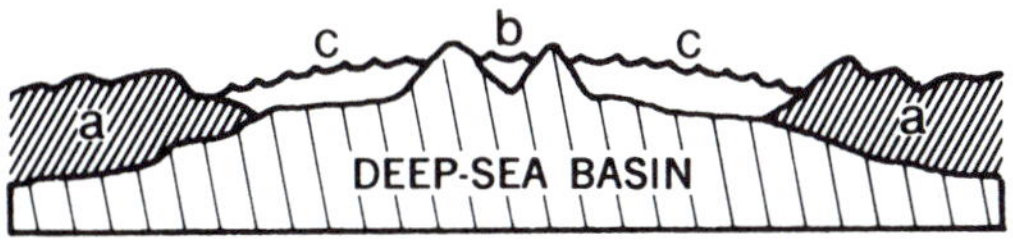

FIGURE 2. Relation between continents and ocean basins.
a—Continents.
b—Volcanic islands.
c—Sea level.

Although the continental surfaces appear to be very irregular to man, the difference in elevation between the highest mountain (Mount Everest—more than 29,000 feet above sea level) and the deepest part of the ocean (more than 35,000 feet deep, south of the Mariana Islands in the Pacific) is inconsequential when considered in relation to the size of the earth.

The Ocean Basins. The ocean basins contain the greatest part of the hydrosphere and cover more than 70 per cent of the earth's surface. The floors of the oceans were originally believed to be quite flat and featureless, but recent oceanographic studies indicate that this is not so. The surface of the ocean floor possesses as many irregularities as the land and includes deep trenches, canyons, and submarine mountain ranges.

Of the five oceans, Arctic, Antarctic, Atlantic, Indian, and Pacific, the latter is deepest (about 35,000 feet) and largest, covering almost half of the earth. The bottoms of the deepest parts of the oceans are composed of basalt, a rather dense, dark, igneous rock. In many places the basaltic bottom is covered by layers of marine sediments.

The origin of the continents and ocean basins and their relationship to each other are discussed in later sections.

GEOLOGIC FORCES

Geologic investigation of almost any part of the earth's surface will reveal some indication of great changes which the earth has undergone. These changes are of many kinds and most have taken place over millions of years. They are, in general, brought about by the processes of **gradation, tectonism,** and **volcanism.**

Gradation. The surface rocks of the earth are constantly being affected by gradational forces. For example, the atmosphere attacks the rocks, weathering them both physically and chemically. In addition, the rivers and oceans of the hydrosphere are continually wearing away rock fragments and transporting them to other areas where they are deposited. Gradation, then, includes two separate types of processes: **degradation,** which is a wearing down or destructive process, and **aggradation,** a holding up or constructive process.

Degradation, commonly referred to as erosion, results from the wearing down of the rocks by water, air, and ice. Here are included the work of atmospheric weathering, glacial abrasion, stream erosion, wind abrasion, etc.

Aggradation, known also as deposition, results in the accumulation of sediments and the ultimate building up of rock strata. The principal agents depositing these sediments are wind, ice, and water. The work of each of these geologic agents is discussed elsewhere in this book.

Tectonism. This term encompasses all the movements of the solid parts of the earth with respect to each other. Tectonic movements, which are indicative of crustal instability, produce **faulting** (fracture and displacement), **folding, subsidence,** and **uplift** of rock formations. Known also as **diastrophism,** tectonism is responsible for the formation of many of our great mountain ranges and for most of the structural deformation that has occurred in the earth's crust. However, these tectonic features (such as folds and faults) are not usually seen until they have been exposed by the process of degradation, or erosion.

In addition, widespread tectonic movements are responsible for certain types of metamorphism. The intrusion of **magma,** more closely associated with volcanism, may also bring about rock deformation by folding.

Volcanism. This term, known also as vulcanism, refers to the movement of molten rock materials within the earth or upon the surface of the earth. Volcanic processes produce the lavas, ashes, and cinders which are ejected from volcanoes. Volcanism is also responsible for the rocks, once molten, which solidified at great depth within the earth.

Minerals

We now know that the geologist is primarily interested in the earth's rocky crust, but before he can study rocks it is necessary to know something about minerals, for these are the building blocks of the earth's crust. Although geologists differ when defining the term mineral, the following definition is generally accepted: **Minerals are chemical elements or compounds which occur naturally within the crust of the earth.** They are **inorganic** (not derived from living things), have a definite chemical composition or range of composition, an orderly internal arrangement of atoms (crystalline structure), and certain other distinct physical properties. It should be noted, however, that the chemical and physical properties of some minerals may vary within definite limits.

Rocks are aggregates or mixtures of minerals, the composition of which may vary greatly. Limestone, for example, is composed primarily of one mineral—calcite. Granite, on the other hand, typically contains three minerals—feldspar, mica, and quartz.

Certain minerals, such as calcite, quartz, and feldspar, are so commonly found in rocks that they are called the **rock-forming** minerals. Other minerals, like gold, diamond, uranium minerals, and silver are found in relatively few rocks.

Minerals vary greatly in their chemical composition and physical properties. Let us now become acquainted with the more important physical and chemical characteristics that enable us to distinguish one mineral from the other.

CHEMICAL COMPOSITION OF MINERALS

Although a detailed discussion of chemistry is not within the scope of this book, an introduction to chemical terminology is necessary if we are to understand the chemical composition of minerals.

All matter, including minerals, is composed of one or more **elements.** An element is a substance that cannot be broken down into simpler substances by ordinary chemical means. Theoretically, if you were to take a quantity of any element and cut it into smaller and smaller pieces, eventually you would obtain the smallest pieces that still retained the characteristics of the element. These minute particles are **atoms.** Although atoms are so small that they cannot be seen with the most powerful microscope (it would take 100 million of them to make a line one inch long) we know a great deal about them. We know, for instance, that the nucleus of an atom is composed of **protons,** positively charged particles, and **neutrons,** or uncharged particles. Outside the nucleus and revolving rapidly around it are negatively charged particles called **electrons.** It is now known, of course, that certain elements have been broken down by atomic fission or "atom-smashing," but these are not considered to be "ordinary chemical means." Although there are only ninety-two elements occurring in nature, several more have been created artificially.

Some minerals, such as gold or silver, are composed of only one element. More often, however, minerals consist of two or more elements united to form a **compound.** For example, calcite is a chemical compound known as calcium carbonate. The chemical composition of a compound may be expressed by means of a chemical formula ($CaCO_3$ in the case of calcite) in which each element is represented by a symbol. The symbol is derived from an abbreviation of the Latin or English name of the element it represents. For many elements, the first letter of the element's name is used as its symbol—thus H for an atom of hydrogen, and C for an atom of carbon. If the names of two elements start with the same letter, two letters may be used for one of them to distinguish between their symbols. For example, an atom of helium may be represented as He, an atom of calcium as Ca. Some symbols have been derived from an abbreviation of the Latin name of the elements: Cu (from *cuprum*) represents an atom of copper, and Fe (from *ferrum*) an atom of iron. The small numerals used in a chemical formula represent the proportion in which each element is present. Hence, the formula for water, H_2O, indicates that there are two atoms of hydrogen for each atom of oxygen present in water.

As mentioned above, ninety-two elements have been found to be present in minerals; however, eight of these elements are so abundant that they constitute more than 98 per cent, by weight, of the earth's crust. These elements, their symbols, and the per cent by weight present in the earth's solid crust are as follows:

Oxygen (O)	46.60
Silicon (Si)	27.72
Aluminum (Al)	8.13
Iron (Fe)	5.00
Calcium (Ca)	3.63
Sodium (Na)	2.83
Potassium (K)	2.59
Magnesium (Mg)	2.09
Total	98.59

As indicated in the above table, two elements, oxygen and silicon, make up approximately three-fourths of the weight of the rocks. Both these elements are **nonmetals,** but the remaining six are **metals.** Metals are characterized by their capacity for conducting heat and electricity, their ability to be hammered into thin sheets (malleability) or to be drawn into wire (ductility), and their luster (the way light is reflected from the mineral's surface). Such minerals as gold, silver, copper, and iron are included in the metals. The nonmetallic, or industrial minerals do not have the properties mentioned above. Some typical nonmetallic minerals are sulfur, diamond, and calcite.

CRYSTALS

When crystalline minerals solidify and grow without interference, they will normally adopt smooth angular shapes known as crystals. The planes that form the outside of the crystals are known as **faces.** These are related directly to the internal atomic structure of the mineral, and the size of the faces is dependent upon the frequency of the atoms in the different planes. The shape of the crystals and the angles between related sets of crystal faces are important in mineral identification.

PHYSICAL PROPERTIES OF MINERALS

Each mineral possesses certain physical properties or characteristics by which it may be recognized or identified. Although some may be identified by visual examination, others must be subjected to certain simple tests.

Physical properties especially useful in mineral identification are (1) hardness, (2) color, (3) streak, (4) luster, (5) specific gravity, (6) cleavage, (7) fracture, (8) shape or form, (9) tenacity or elasticity, and (10) certain other miscellaneous properties. The geologist must know how to test a mineral specimen for the above properties if he is to identify it correctly. Many of these tests do not require expensive laboratory equipment and may be done in the field. Some of them may be made by using such commonplace articles as a knife or a hardened steel file, a copper penny, a small magnet, an inexpensive pocket lens with a magnification of six to ten times, a piece of glass, a piece of unglazed porcelain tile, and a fingernail.

Hardness. One of the easiest ways to distinguish one mineral from another is by testing for hardness. The hardness of a mineral is determined by what materials it will scratch, and what materials will scratch it. The hardness or scratch test may be done with simple testing materials carried in the field. For greater accuracy, one may use the scale of hardness called **Mohs' scale.** This scale, named for the German mineralogist Friedrich Mohs, was devised more than one hundred years ago. In studying his mineral collection, Mohs noticed that certain minerals were much harder than others. He believed that this variation could be of some value in mineral identification, so he selected ten common minerals to be used as standards in testing other minerals for hardness. In establishing this scale, Mohs assigned each of the reference minerals a number. He designated talc, the softest in the series, as having a hardness of 1. The hardest mineral, diamond, was assigned a hardness of 10.

Mohs' scale, composed of the ten reference minerals arranged in order of increasing hardness, is as follows:

No. 1—Talc (softest)
No. 2—Gypsum
No. 3—Calcite
No. 4—Fluorite
No. 5—Apatite
No. 6—Feldspar
No. 7—Quartz
No. 8—Topaz
No. 9—Corundum
No. 10—Diamond (hardest)

Most of the minerals in Mohs' scale are common ones, which can be obtained in inexpensive collections. Diamond chips are more expensive, but not beyond reason. Note that Mohs' scale is so arranged that each mineral will be scratched by those having higher numbers, and will scratch those having lower numbers.

It is also possible to test for hardness by using the following common objects:

ITEM	HARDNESS
Fingernail	About 2½
Copper penny	About 3
Glass	5–5½
Knife blade	5½–6
Steel file	6½–7

Each of the above items will scratch a mineral of the indicated hardness. For example: the fingernail will scratch talc (hardness of 1) and gypsum (hardness of 2), but would not scratch calcite which has a hardness of 3.

In testing for hardness, first use the more common materials. Start with the fingernail; if that will not scratch the specimen, use the knife blade. If the knife blade produces a scratch, this indicates that the specimen has a hardness of between 2½ and 6 (see scale above). Referring to Mohs' scale, it is found that there are three minerals of known hardness within this range. These are: apatite (5); fluorite (4); and calcite (3). If the calcite will not scratch the specimen but the fluorite will, its hardness is further limited as between 3 and 4. Next, try to scratch the fluorite with the specimen. If this can be done, even with difficulty, the hardness is established as 4; if not, then it is between 3 and 4.

Color. Probably one of the first things that is noticed about a mineral is its color. However, the same mineral may vary greatly in color from one specimen to another, and with certain exceptions, color is of limited use in mineral identification. Certain minerals, for example, azurite, which is always blue, malachite, which is green, and pyrite, which is yellow, have relatively constant colors. Others, such as quartz or tourmaline, occur in a wide variety of colors; hence, color may be of little use in identifying these two minerals. Color variations of this sort are primarily due to minor chemical impurities within the mineral.

When using color in mineral identification, it is necessary to take into consideration such factors as (1) whether the specimen is being examined in natural or artificial light, (2) whether the surface being examined is fresh or weathered, and (3) whether the mineral is wet or dry. Each of these may cause color variations in a mineral. In addition, certain of the metallic minerals will tarnish and the true color will not be revealed except on a fresh surface.

Streak. When a mineral is rubbed across a piece of unglazed tile, it may leave a line similar to a pencil or crayon mark. This line is composed of the powdered minerals. The color of this powdered material is known as the streak of the mineral, and the unglazed tile used in such a test is called a **streak plate** (Fig. 3).

The streak in some minerals will not be the same as the color of the specimen. For example, a piece of black hematite will leave a reddish brown streak, and an extremely hard mineral such as topaz or corundum will leave no streak. This is because the streak plate has a hardness of about 7,

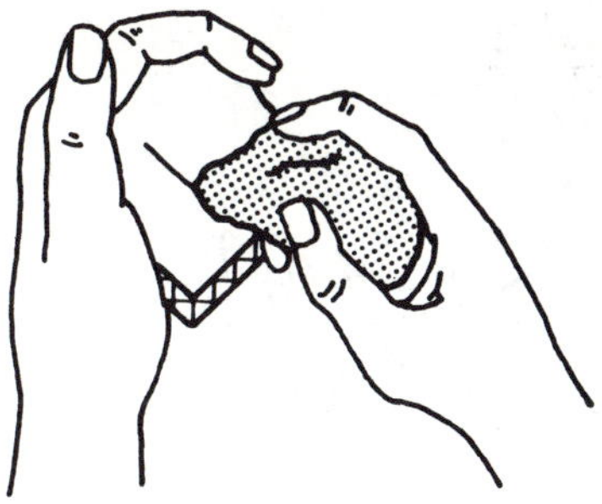

FIGURE 3. Testing for streak by means of streak plate.

and both topaz (8) and corundum (9) are harder than the streak plate, hence the mineral will not be powdered.

Luster. The appearance of the surface of a mineral as seen in reflected light is called luster. Some minerals shine like metals, for example, silver or gold. These are said to have metallic luster. Other lusters are called nonmetallic. The more important nonmetallic lusters and some common examples are shown below:

Admantine—brilliant glossy luster: typical of diamond
Vitreous—glassy, looks like glass: quartz or topaz
Resinous—the luster of resin: sphalerite
Greasy—like an oily surface: nepheline
Pearly—like mother-of-pearl: talc
Silky—the luster of silk or rayon: asbestos or satin-spar gypsum
Dull—as the name implies: chalk or clay

Submetallic luster is intermediate between metallic and nonmetallic luster. The mineral wolframite displays typical submetallic luster.

Terms such as **shining** (bright by reflected light), **glistening** (a sparkling brightness), **splendent** (glossy brilliance), and **dull** (lacking brilliance or luster) are commonly used to indicate the degree of luster present. Here too, one must take into consideration such factors as tarnish, type of lighting, and general condition of the mineral specimen being examined.

Specific Gravity. The relative weights of minerals are also useful in identification, for some minerals, such as galena (an ore of lead), are much heavier than others. The relative weight of a mineral is called its specific gravity. Specific gravity is determined by comparing the weight of the mineral specimen with the weight of an equal volume of fresh water. Thus, a specimen of galena (specific gravity about 7.5) would be about 7½ times as heavy as the same volume of water.

In order to determine the specific gravity of a given specimen, the specimen is weighed in air on a spring scale (sometimes called a Jolly-Kraus balance); then lowered into a container of fresh water and weighed in the water. The specific gravity (Sp. Gr.) equals the weight in air divided by the loss of weight in water. When the specific gravity has been determined, it may then be compared with the known weight of other minerals in order to identify the specimen.

Cleavage and Fracture. Mineral crystals will break if they are strained beyond their plastic and elastic limits. If the crystal breaks irregularly it is said to exhibit **fracture,** but if it should break along surfaces related to the crystal structure it is said to show **cleavage.** Each break or **cleavage plane** is closely related to the atomic structure of the mineral and designates planes of weakness within the crystal. Because the number of cleavage planes

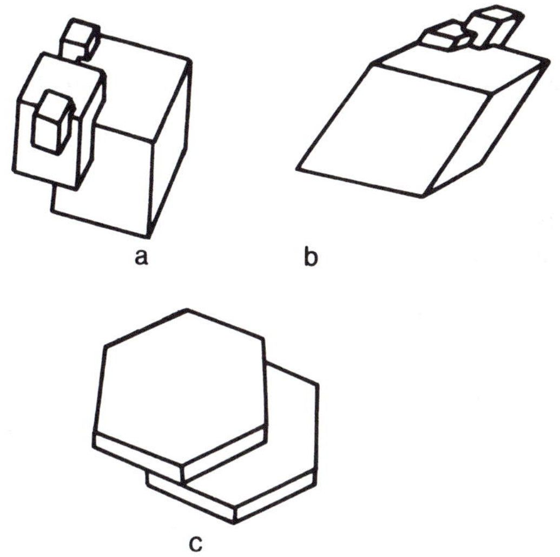

FIGURE 4. Three types of cleavage.
a—Cubic. *b*—Rhombic. *c*—Perfect basal.

present and the angles between them are constant for any given mineral, cleavage is a very useful aid in mineral identification.

Minerals may have one, two, three, four, or six directions of cleavage. The mineral galena, for example, cleaves in three planes (directions) at right angles to one another. Thus, if galena is struck a quick, sharp blow with a hammer, the specimen will break up into a number of small cubes. Calcite, on the other hand, has three cleavage planes that are not at right angles to one another. Therefore it will always produce a number of rhombohedral cleavage fragments. Hence, galena is said to have **cubic** cleavage, calcite **rhombohedral** cleavage.

Many minerals break or fracture in a distinctive way, and for this reason their broken surfaces (Fig. 5) may be of value in identifying minerals.

There are several types of fractures; some of the more common types (with example) are:

Conchoidal—the broken surface of the specimen shows a fracture resembling the smooth curved surface of a shell. This type of fracture is typical of chipped glass: quartz and obsidian.

Splintery or Fibrous—fibers or splinters are revealed along the fracture surface: pectolite.

Hackly—fracture surface marked by rough jagged edges: copper, silver, and certain other metals.

Uneven—rough irregular fracture of surface. This type of fracture is common in many minerals and is, therefore, of limited use in identification: jasper, a variety of quartz.

Even—as the name implies: magnesite.

Earthy—as the name implies: kaolinite.

Tenacity. The tenacity of a mineral may be defined as the resistance that it offers to tearing, crushing, bending, or breaking. Some terms used to describe the different kinds of tenacity are:

Brittle—the mineral can be broken or powdered easily. The degree of brittleness may be qualified by such terms as tough, fragile, etc.: galena or sulfur.

Elastic—the mineral, after being bent, will return to its original form or position: mica.

Flexible—the mineral will bend but will not return to its original shape upon release of pressure: talc.

Other Physical Properties. In addition to those properties discussed above, the mineral characteristics below may also aid greatly in identification. Examples of minerals exhibiting these properties are given.

Play of Colors. Some minerals show variations in color when viewed from different angles: labradorite.

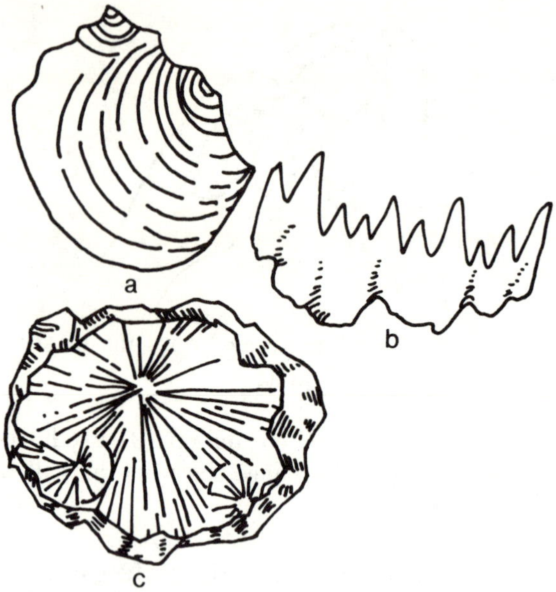

FIGURE 5. Some types of fracture. *a*—Conchoidal. *b*—Hackly. *c*—Splintery.

Sectile—the mineral can be cut with a knife to produce shavings: selenite gypsum and talc.

Malleable—the mineral can be hammered into thin sheets: gold and copper.

Ductile—the mineral can be drawn out into wire: gold, silver, and copper.

Asterism. This may be observed if the mineral exhibits a starlike effect when viewed either by reflected or transmitted light: certain specimens of phlogopite or the star-sapphire.

Diaphaneity or Transparency. This property refers to the ability of a mineral to transmit light. The varying degrees of diaphaneity are:

Opaque—no light passes through the mineral: galena, pyrite, and magnetite.

Translucent—light passes through the mineral but an object cannot be seen through it: chalcedony and certain other varieties of quartz.

Transparent—light passes through the mineral and the outline of objects can be clearly seen through it: halite, calcite, clear crystalline quartz.

Magnetism. A mineral is said to be magnetic if, in its natural state, it will be attracted to an iron magnet: magnetite, or lodestone, and pyrrhotite.

Luminescence. When a mineral glows or emits light that is not the direct result of incandescence, it is said to be luminescent. This phenomena is usually produced by exposure to ultraviolet rays. Exposure to X rays, cathode rays, or radiation from radioactive substances can also cause luminescence. If the mineral is luminous only during the period of exposure to the ultraviolet rays or other stimulus, the material is said to be **fluorescent** (scheelite and willemite are fluorescent). A mineral exhibiting **phosphorescence** will continue to glow after the cause of excitation has been removed.

MINERALOIDS

Although most substances accepted as minerals are crystalline, some lack the ability to crystalize and occur instead as a hardened gel. Substances of this type are commonly referred to as mineraloids. They are also said to be amorphous—that is, without form, for example, opals.

ROCK FORMING MINERALS

Of some two thousand different minerals that are known to be present in the earth's crust, relatively few are major constituents of the more common rocks. Those minerals that do make up a large part of the more common types of rocks are called the rock-forming minerals. Most of the rock-forming minerals are silicates, that is, they consist of a metal combined with silicon and oxygen. Rock-forming minerals are such as feldspars, mica, and quartz.

RADIOACTIVE MINERALS

In this so called "atomic age," radioactive minerals have come to play an ever increasing part in modern technology. A radioactive mineral is distinguished because it emits radioactive isotopes which are detected usually with a geiger counter. Although there are a number of radioactive minerals, the two most widely known are uraninite and carnotite.

METALLIC OR ORE MINERALS

Metals are among the most valuable products known to man, and for this reason the metallic or ore minerals are of great interest to the geologist. These minerals are found in ore deposits —rock masses from which metals may be obtained commercially. Usually occurring with the valuable ore minerals are certain worthless minerals called gangue minerals. These, of course, must be separated from the more valuable ore minerals. Included here are aluminum, gold, copper, lead, and silver.

NONMETALLIC OR INDUSTRIAL MINERALS

Minerals that do not contain metals or that are not used as metals make up this group. It is in this vast category that such varied materials as coal, petroleum, sulfur, fertilizer, building stones, and gem stones are placed.

Metamorphism and Crustal Deformation

Metamorphic rocks are rocks (originally either igneous or sedimentary) that have been buried deep within the earth and subjected to high temperatures and pressures. These new physical conditions usually produce great changes in the solid rock and these changes are included under the term metamorphism (Greek *meta,* "change," and *morphe,* "form" or "shape").

During the process of metamorphism the original rock undergoes physical and chemical alterations which may greatly modify its texture, mineral composition, and chemical composition.

Thus, limestone may be metamorphosed into marble, and sandstone into quartzite. Let us now consider the types of forces that might bring about metamorphic changes.

TYPES OF METAMORPHISM

Although more technical classifications recognize several different kinds of metamorphism, only contact metamorphism, and dynamic, or kinetic, metamorphism will be considered here.

Contact Metamorphism. When country rock (the rock intruded by or surrounding an igneous intrusion) is invaded by an igneous body it generally undergoes profound change. Hence, limestone intruded by a hot magma may be altered for a distance of a few inches to as much as several miles from the igneous sedimentary contact. Some of the more simple metamorphic rocks have been formed in this so-called **baked zone** of the altered country rock (Fig. 6).

Physical change may be produced by contact metamorphism when the original minerals in the country rock are permeated by magmatic fluids which often bring about recrystallization. This process, which typically produces either new or larger mineral crystals, may greatly alter the texture of the rock. In addition, the magmatic fluids commonly introduce new elements and compounds which will modify the chemical composition of the original rock and result in the formation of new minerals.

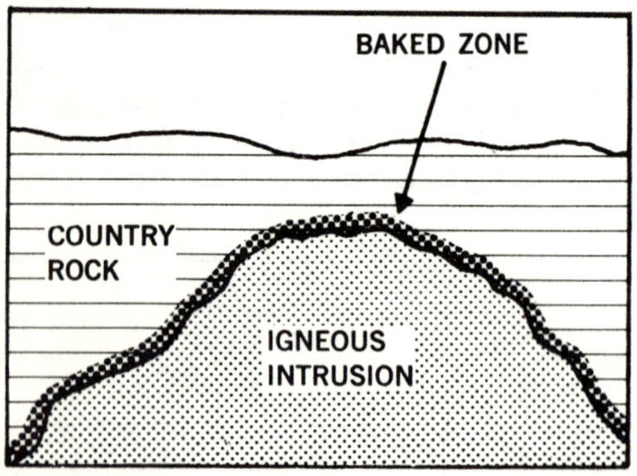

FIGURE 6. Baked zone in country rock surrounding an igneous intrusion.

Dynamic, or Kinetic, Metamorphism. Dynamic metamorphism occurs when rock layers undergo strong structural deformation during the formation of mountain ranges. The great pressures exerted as the rock layers are folded, fractured, and crumpled generally produce widespread and complex metamorphic change. Such pressures may result in tearing or crushing of the minerals, obliteration of any indication of fossils or stratification, realignment of mineral grains, and increased hardness. Because this type of metamorphism takes place on a relatively large scale it is also called **regional metamorphism.**

EFFECTS AND PRODUCTS OF METAMORPHISM

The effects of metamorphism are controlled to a large extent by the chemical and physical characteristics of the original rock and by the agent and degree of metamorphism involved. The more basic changes are in the texture and chemical composition of the rock.

TEXTURE

The rearrangement of mineral crystals during metamorphism results in two basic types of rock texture: foliated and nonfoliated.

Foliated Metamorphic Rocks. Foliated rocks are metamorphic rocks in which the minerals have been flattened, drawn out, and arranged in parallel layers or bands (Fig. 7). There are three basic types of foliation: slaty, schistose, and gneissic. Each of these, and some common rocks which exhibit them, is discussed below.

Slate. A metamorphosed shale, slate is characterized by a very fine texture in which mineral crystals cannot be detected with the naked eye. It does not show banding (see Fig. 7) and splits readily into thin even slabs. Slate occurs in a variety of colors, but is usually gray, black, green, and red. Its characteristic slaty cleavage (not to be confused with mineral cleavage) makes it especially useful for roofing, blackboards, and sidewalks.

Schist. Schist is a medium- to coarse-grained foliated metamorphic rock formed under greater pressures than those which form slate. It consists principally of micaceous minerals in a nearly parallel arrangement called **schistosity.** Schists usually split readily along these schistose laminations or folia, which are usually bent and crumpled. Commonly derived from slate, schists may also be formed from fine-grained igneous rocks. They are named according to the predominant mineral, such as mica schists, chlorite schists, etc.

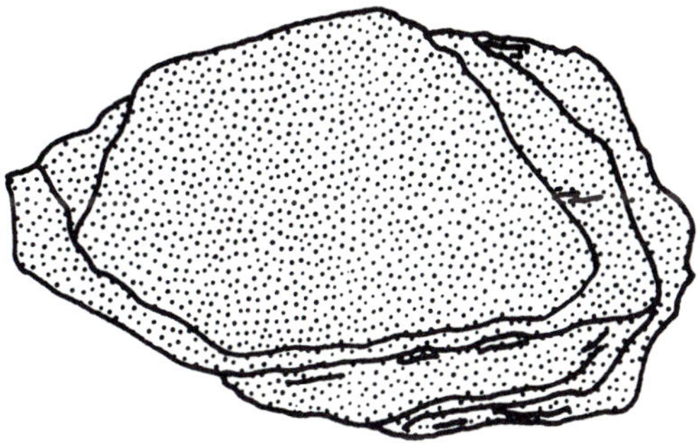

FIGURE 7. Schist, a foliated metamorphic rock.

Phyllite. Derived from the Greek word *phyllon* (a leaf), phyllites are more fine-grained than schists but coarser than slate. On freshly broken surfaces they have a characteristic silky luster or sheen due to the presence of fine grains of mica. Most have been formed from shales which have been subjected to pressures greater than those required to produce slate, but not of sufficient intensity to produce schists.

Gneiss. Gneiss (pronounced "nice") is a very highly metamorphosed coarse-grained banded rock. This rock is characterized by alternating bands of darker minerals such as chlorite, biotite mica, or graphite (Fig. 8). The bands are typically folded and contorted, and although some gneisses resemble schists, they do not split nearly as easily. Banding may be an indication of stratification in

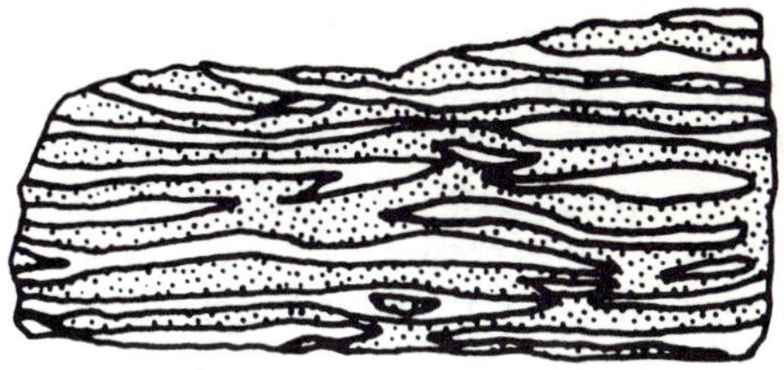

FIGURE 8. Gneiss, a banded metamorphic rock.

the original bedded sedimentary rock, or caused by the alteration of coarse-grained igneous rocks containing light- and dark-colored minerals.

In general, gneisses have undergone a greater degree of metamorphism than have schistose rocks and are commonly formed as a result of intense regional metamorphism.

Nonfoliated Metamorphic Rocks. These are metamorphic rocks which are typically massive or granular in texture and do not exhibit foliation. Although some nonfoliated rocks resemble certain igneous rocks, they can be differentiated from them on the basis of mineral composition.

Quartzite. Quartzite is formed from metamorphosed quartz sandstone. One of the most resistant of all rocks, quartzite is composed of a crystalline mass of tightly cemented sand grains. When formed from pure quartz sand, quartzite is white; however, the presence of impurities may stain the rock red, yellow, or brown.

Marble. A relatively coarse-grained, crystalline, calcareous rock, marble is a metamorphosed limestone or dolomite. It is formed by recrystallization, and any evidence of fossils or stratification is usually destroyed during the process of alteration.

ORIGINAL ROCK	METAMORPHIC ROCK
Sedimentary	
Sandstone	Quartzite
Shale	Slate, phyllite, schist
Limestone	Marble
Bituminous coal	Anthracite coal, graphite
Igneous	
Granitic textured igneous rocks	Gneiss
Compact textured igneous rocks	Schist

TABLE 2. Some common igneous and sedimentary rocks and their metamorphic equivalents.

White when pure, the presence of impurities may impart a wide range of colors to marble.

Anthracite. When bituminous, or soft, coal is strongly compacted, folded, and heated, it is transformed into anthracite, or hard, coal. Because it has undergone an extreme degree of carbonization, anthracite coal has a high fixed carbon content and almost all of the volatile materials have been driven off.

CRUSTAL MOVEMENTS

The crust of the earth has undergone great structural change during past periods of earth history. Even today the earth's crust is continually being altered by three major forces—gradation, volcanism, and tectonism. Gradation and volcanism have been discussed in earlier sections of this book; let us now see how tectonic forces have affected our earth.

TECTONISM

As usually considered, tectonism includes those processes which have resulted in deformation of the earth's crust. Tectonic movements normally occur slowly and imperceptibly over long periods of time. But some—for example, an earthquake—may take place suddenly and violently. In some instances the rocks will move vertically, resulting in uplift or subsidence of the land. They may also move horizontally, or laterally (sidewise), as a result of compression or tension. The two major types of tectonic movements, **epeirogeny** (vertical movements) and **orogeny** (essentially lateral movements) are discussed below.

Epeirogenic Movements. Relatively slow movements accompanied by broad uplift or submergence of the continents are termed epeirogenic movements. Such movements affect relatively large areas, and typically result in tilting or warping of the land. An uplift of this type may raise wave-cut benches and sea cliffs well above sea level; features of this sort are common along certain parts of the Pacific Coast. In a like manner, parts of the Scandinavian coast are rising as much as three feet per century. Subsidence of the continents may also take place. Thus, continental areas sink slowly beneath the ocean and become submerged by shallow seas. Similar movements have caused the British Isles to become isolated from continental Europe and bays to be formed in drowned valleys along the New England coast. (Submergence may, of course, also be caused by a rise in sea level.)

Rock strata involved in epeirogenic movements are not usually greatly folded or faulted (fractured). As noted above, however, such strata may undergo large-scale tilting or warping.

Orogenic Movements. These are more intense than epeirogenic movements, and the rocks involved are subjected to great stress. These movements, known also as orogenies or mountain-making movements, normally affect long narrow areas and are accompanied by much folding and faulting. Igneous activity and earthquakes also commonly occur with this type of crustal disturbance. Although orogenic movements are slow, they do occur somewhat more rapidly than epeirogenic movements.

ROCK STRUCTURES PRODUCED BY TECTONISM

Tectonic movements, whether epeirogenic or orogenic, will result in rock deformation. Under surface conditions, ordinary rocks are relatively brittle and will fracture or break when placed under great stress. Deeply buried rocks, however, are subject to such high temperatures and pressures that they become somewhat plastic. When subjected to prolonged stress these rocks are likely to warp or fold.

Warping. As noted above, warping is usually caused by raising or lowering broad areas of the earth's crust. The rock strata in such areas appear to be essentially horizontal; close study, however, indicates that the strata are gently **dipping** (inclined). Warping movements are typically epeirogenic and are accompanied by little or no local folding and faulting.

Folding. Not only may rocks be tilted and warped, they may also be folded (Fig. 9). Folds, which vary greatly in complexity and size, are formed when rock strata are crumpled and buckled up into a series of wavelike structures. This type of structural development is usually produced by great horizontal compressive forces and may result in a variety of different structures.

Anticlines (Fig. 9a) are upfolds of rock formed when strata are folded upward. **Synclines** (Fig. 9b) may be created when rock layers are folded downward. Broad uparched folds covering large areas are called **geanticlines;** large down-warped troughs are known as **geosynclines.** Great thicknesses of sediments have accumulated in certain geosynclines of the geologic past, and some of these have been elevated to form folded mountain ranges. For example, the Appalachian Geosyncline received sediments throughout much of early Paleozoic time. Then about 225 million years ago these sediments (which had since become sedimentary rocks) were uplifted to form the Appalachian Highlands, of which the Appalachian Mountains are a part.

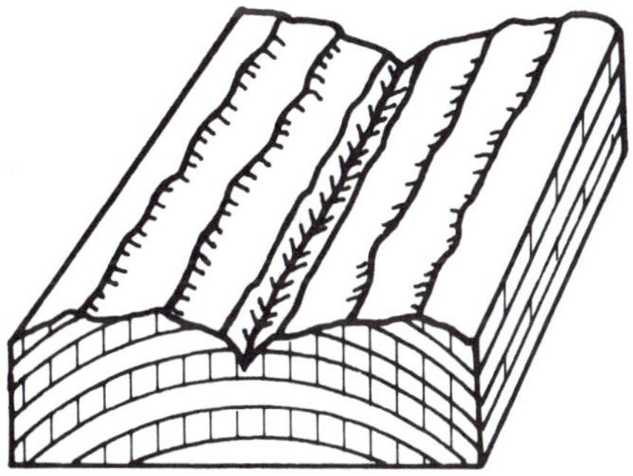
A

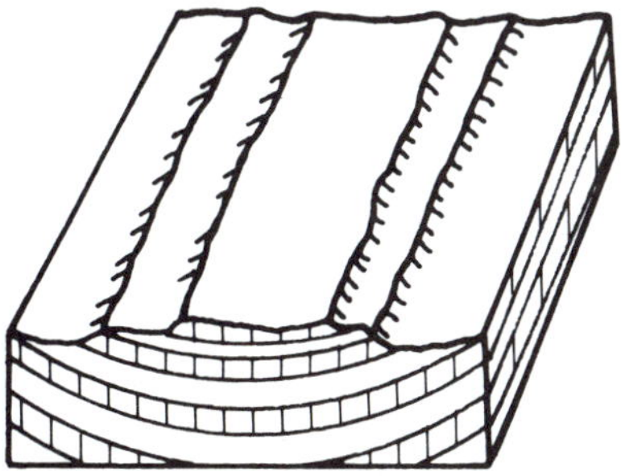
B

FIGURE 9. Types of folds. *a*—Anticline. *b*—Syncline.

In studying folds we must be able to determine the **attitude** of the rock strata. Attitude—a term used to denote the position of a rock with respect to compass direction and a horizontal plane—is defined by **strike** and **dip** (Fig. 10). The strike of a formation is the compass direction of the line formed by the intersection of a bedding plane with a horizontal plane. Dip is the angle of inclination between the bedding plane and a horizontal plane. The direction of dip is always at right angles to the strike; thus, a rock stratum which dips due north would strike east-west.

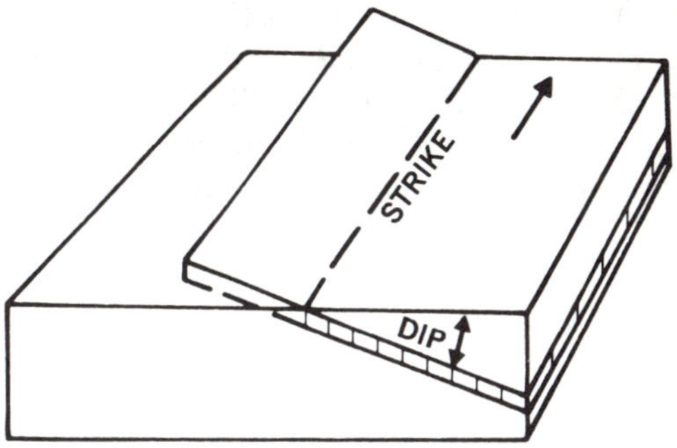

FIGURE 10. Strike and dip. The beds strike north-south and dip to the east.

Other types of folds include **monoclines,** simple steplike folds which dip in only one direction (Fig. 11); **domes,** a fold in which strata dip away from a common center; and **basins,** a fold in which the strata dip toward a common center.

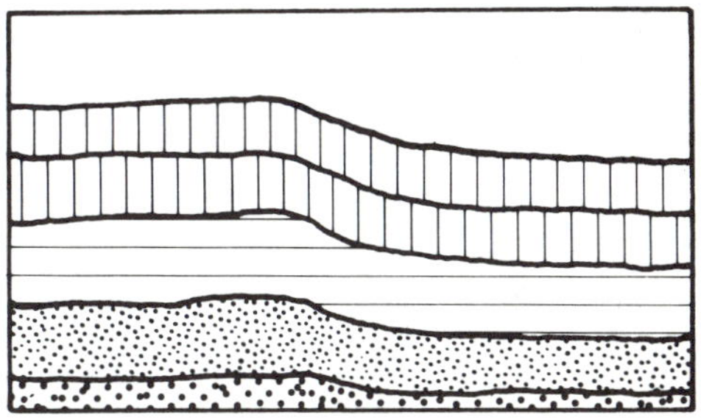

FIGURE 11. A monocline.

Fracturing. Rocks subjected to great stress near the surface are apt to fracture, thus producing joints and faults. A fracture along which there has been little or no movement is called a **joint** (Fig. 12). Joints occur in sets and are usually parallel to one another. Fractures of this sort have formed in igneous rocks as a result of contraction due to cooling and are common in certain dikes and sills. Joints are also created by tension and compression when rocks undergo stress due to warping, folding, and faulting.

Joint systems are developed when two or more sets of joints intersect. These intersecting joint patterns may be helpful in certain quarrying operations and in developing porosity in otherwise impervious rocks. Jointing will also hasten weathering and erosion, for they render the rocks more susceptible to attack from rain, frost, and streams.

Faults are fractures in the earth's crust along which movements have taken place (Fig. 13). The rocks affected by faulting are displaced along the **fault plane.** If the crust is displaced vertically, the rocks on one side of the fault may stand higher than those on the other. This may result in a cliff called a **fault scarp.** Large-scale faulting of this type may produce **fault block mountains,** such as the Sierra Nevada in California and the Lewis Range in Montana.

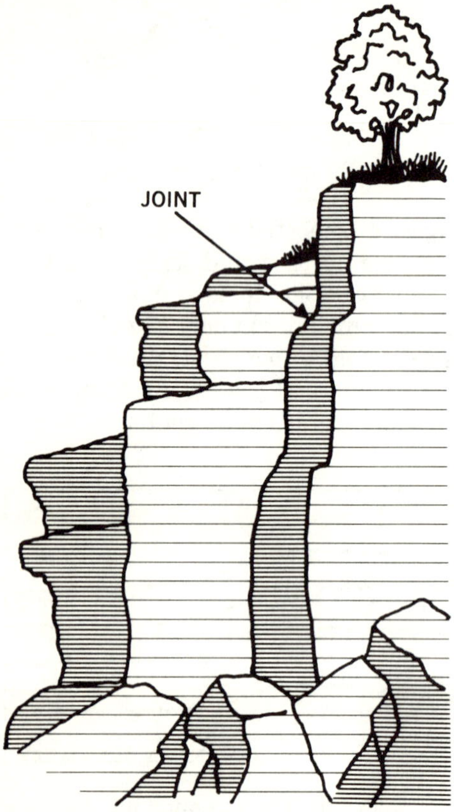

FIGURE 12. Vertical joints in limestone cliff.

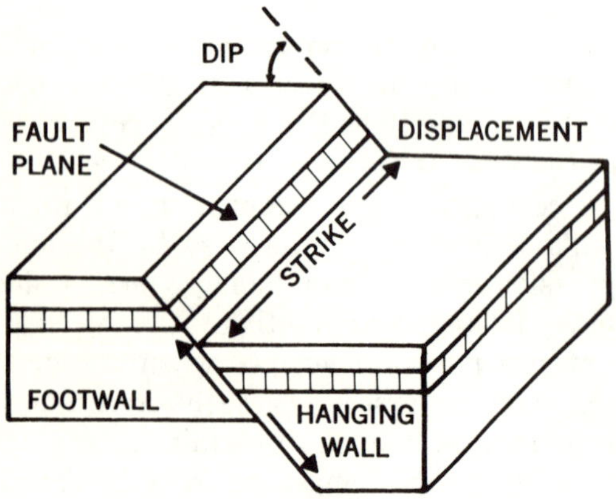

FIGURE 13. A normal fault, showing principal parts and terms used in describing faults.

Some knowledge of fault terminology is prerequisite to an understanding of the different types of faults. (The parts of faults are illustrated in Fig. 13.) The rock surface bounding the lower side of an inclined fault plane is known as the **footwall** and that above as the **hanging wall.** The **strike** of a fault is the horizontal direction of the fault plane; **dip** is determined by measuring the inclination of the fault plane at right angles to the strike. **Displacement** refers to the amount of movement that has taken place along the fault plane.

The various types of faults are classified largely by the direction and relative movement of the rocks along the fault plane. A **normal or gravity fault** is one in which the hanging wall has moved downward with respect to the footwall (Fig. 14).

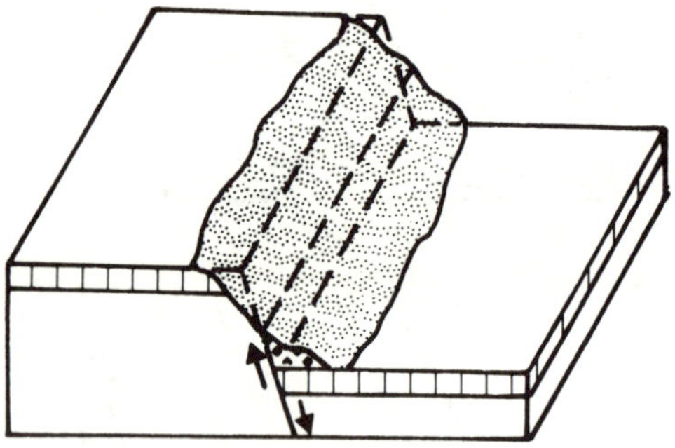

FIGURE 14. Normal or gravity fault.

If the hanging wall has moved upward with respect to the footwall, a **reverse fault** or **thrust fault** is produced (Fig. 15). A **strike-slip fault** will be produced if the movement is predominantly horizontal parallel to the fault plane (Fig. 16).

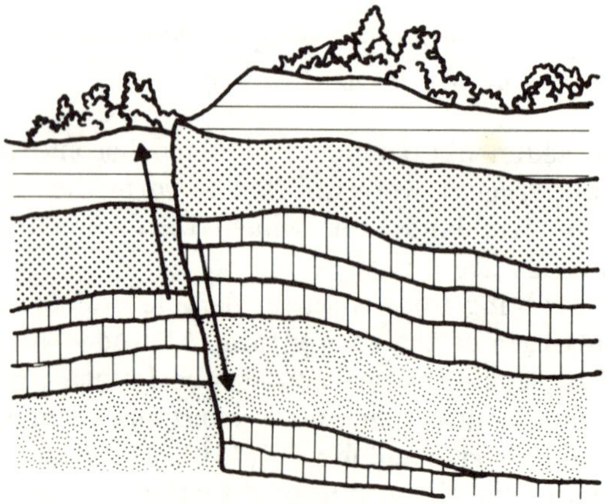

FIGURE 15. Reverse fault.

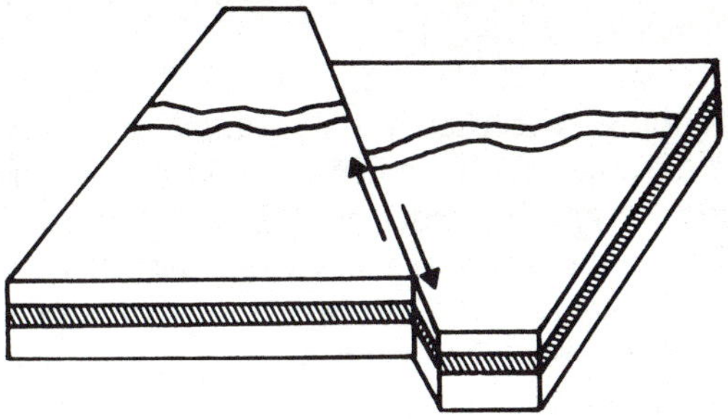

FIGURE 16. Strike-slip fault. (Note the road offset in center of block.)

In some areas a long narrow block has dropped down between normal faults, thereby producing a **graben** (Fig. 17). Large-scale grabens are called **rift valleys.** Two examples of grabens are the upper Rhine Valley and the depression containing the Dead Sea. Sometimes blocks will be raised between normal faults; these elevated blocks are called **horsts** (Fig. 18).

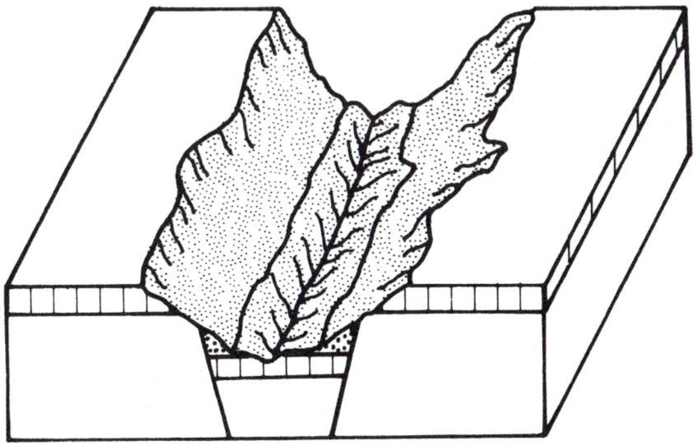

FIGURE 17. A graben.

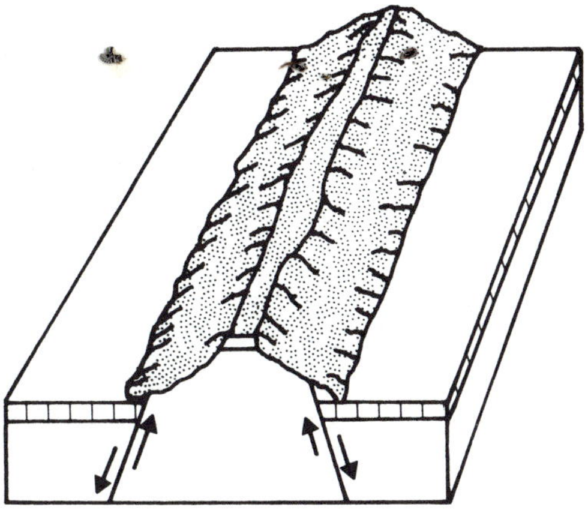

FIGURE 18. A horst.

EVIDENCE OF CRUSTAL MOVEMENTS

The rocks of the earth's crust present much evidence to show that many tectonic movements have taken place in the geologic past. We have already learned, for example, that the fossilized remains of sea plants and animals may be found thousands of feet above sea level. Common also are elevated beaches, coastal plains, and wave-cut cliffs and sea caves. Such features strongly suggest a drop in sea level or an uplift of the continent (possibly both). Similarly, drowned river valleys indicate a rising sea and/or a subsiding land mass.

The occurrence of earthquakes is evidence that similar movements are taking place today. A good example of this can be seen in the Yakutat Bay area of Alaska. Here, in 1899, faulting caused some parts of the coast to be raised as much as 47 feet. Likewise, during the San Francisco earthquake of 1906 the horizontal movement along the fault plane caused certain fences and roads to be offset as much as 20 feet.

CAUSES OF CRUSTAL MOVEMENTS

Although scientists do not agree upon the exact cause of tectonic movements, they have proposed several theories to explain them. A few of these theories are briefly outlined below.

Contraction Theory. According to this theory, the rocks of the outer crust have become crumpled and wrinkled as the interior of the earth cooled and contracted. Shrinkage may also come about as great pressures squeeze the earth into a smaller volume, or when molten rock is extruded upon the surface.

Convection Theory. It has been suggested that convection currents beneath the earth's crust may cause the rocks to expand and push upward. It is thought that the heat to produce such currents may be derived from radioactive elements such as uranium. According to this theory, circulating convection currents would exert frictional drag beneath the crust, thereby causing crustal displacement (Fig. 19).

Continental Drift Theory. This theory suggests that there was originally only one huge continent. At some time in the geologic past this continent

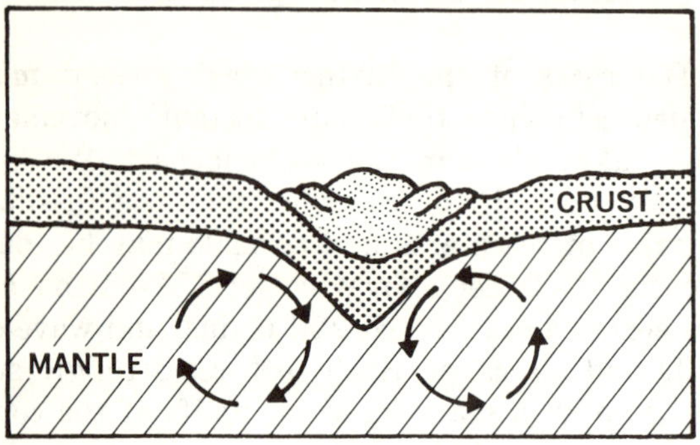

FIGURE 19. Convection currents in the mantle (circling arrows) and their relation to the overlying crust.

broke into several segments and drifted apart. This "drifting" or "floating" was possible because the continents, composed largely of granite, are lighter than the more plastic basaltic material beneath the crust. As the front of the drifting land mass moved forward, frictional drag with subcrustal material caused the continental margins to crumple up, thus forming the folded coastal mountain ranges of Europe and North and South America. Look at a globe and you will see how this idea originated. You will notice that the shorelines along both sides of the Atlantic Ocean match surprisingly well. Moreover, some of the older mountain belts in America appear to be continuations of similar mountain belts in the eastern continents.

Isostasy. The theory of isostasy states that at considerable depth within the earth, different segments of the crust will be in balance with other segments of unequal thickness. The differences in height of these crustal segments is explained as the result of variations in density. Consequently, the continents and mountainous areas are higher because they are composed of lighter rocks; the ocean basins are lower because they are composed of denser (heavier) rocks (Fig. 20). As the continents are eroded and sediments deposited in the ocean, the ocean basin is depressed because of the added weight of the accumulating sediments. This causes displacement of the plastic subcrustal rocks which push the continents up. The upward displacement of the continent is aided by erosion which removes rock materials, thus making the continents lighter and more susceptible to uplift.

Because the movements of isostatic adjustment are essentially vertical in nature, this theory cannot account for forces of horizontal compression. Isostasy does, however, offer some explanation as to why the erosion of the continents and subsequent deposition in the ocean basins have not resulted in a continuous level surface on the face of the earth.

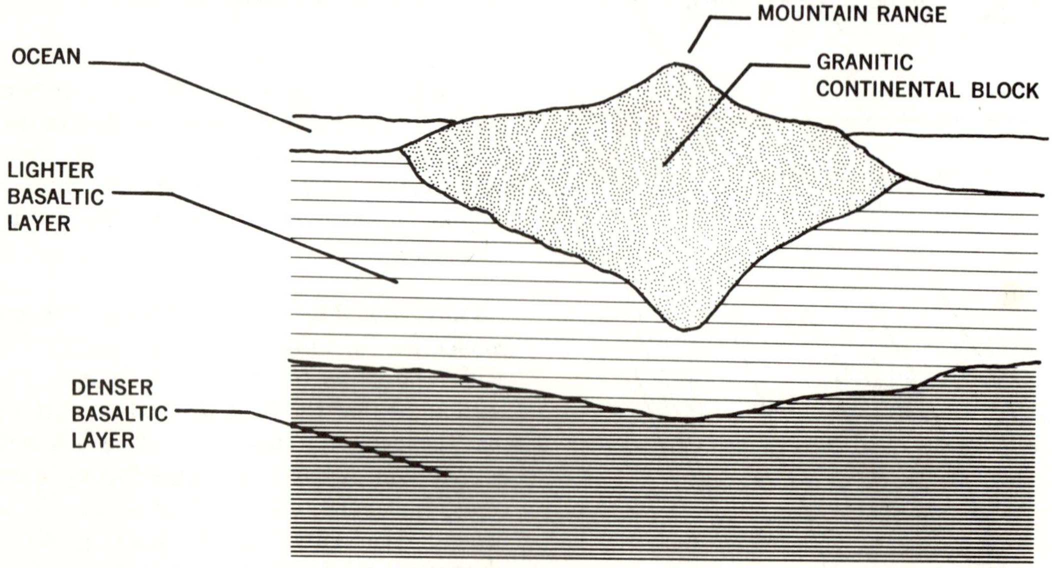

FIGURE 20. Relatively light granitic rocks of continent resting on denser basaltic substratum.

CHAPTER TWELVE

BIOLOGY

Scope and Method

Biology is the study of all living forms, plants and animals, including man, as individuals and as interdependent entities.

To the biologist—who is in the first place and above all a **natural scientist—**the human being is an object of scientific investigation; a very highly specialized protoplasmic structure, reflecting in his life processes the activity of all living animal structures. Biology demonstrates the total and absolute dependence of man—the human animal—on all other forms of life.

Biology covers so vast a field that, to make for greater accuracy and greater ease of study, it has been divided into logical subdivisions or branches. Each subdivision is so vast in itself that a lifetime of study may be devoted to each.

Depending upon his interests, the biologic scientist specializes in a single phase—if in animals, **Zoology**; if in plant life, **Botany**; if in the development of the individual from the "fertilized egg" stage through early stages of life, **Embryology**; if in the structure of the human body, **Anatomy**; if in the functions of the body, **Physiology.**

Another vital biological science is **Genetics,** which explains the phenomena of heredity. For microscope work, there is **Cytology,** the science of cell structure and function, or **Histology,** the science of living tissues. **Protozoology** is a branch of Biology which deals with one-celled animal life; **Bacteriology** is a science of one-celled plant life.

Another important and fascinating branch of Biology is **Ecology,** the study of the relationship of living things to their environment.

Frequently a person who studies Biology from intellectual curiosity becomes intensely interested in a particular division and makes it his hobby or even his lifework, his profession. Biology is the basis of such professions as Medicine, Nursing, Agriculture, Plant and Animal Breeding and even Pharmacy.

How shall we acquaint ourselves with the living world around us? Constant awareness coupled with the curiosity and desire to "dig deeper" will make our immediate surroundings a field and a laboratory for studying life.

A small patch of back yard, a vacant lot, even a window box will provide field for "exploration"; as will the public park, a local wooded area, or the seashore, crowded with plant and animal life for us to observe.

The city streets, for all their concrete pavements and huge structures, have some trees and foliage to watch as they bud in the spring, blossom in the summer, change color in the fall and become bare in the winter.

Even in the heart of the city, one hears the birds which nest nearby or pass through on their migrations. Or one sees an earthworm crawling on the pavement after a heavy rain has driven it out of the soil beneath the pavement. Where there are human beings there must be other forms of plant and animal life!

One of the most famous **Entomologists** (a biologist who specializes in the study of insects), JEAN HENRI FABRE, did most of his field work in his own back yard or in some close-by field. He spent hours watching insects in their daily activities and making notes of his observation.

While some biologists explore the lands, the waters and the skies, others prefer to work in a laboratory, the "workshop" of the scientist. If well equipped, this will have running water in a sink, connections for gas, non-corrosive table tops (usually stone) with air pressure, vacuum, and electricity outlets. In addition there will be glass beakers, jars, flasks, test tubes, bottles, porcelain crucibles, and shelves for various basic chemicals. There will probably be an oven or an incubator, a pressure cooker, and even a refrigerator in some handy place. A well-stocked library of reference books in every branch of Biology is essential.

The individual who has no access to such a laboratory can build one of his own, using materials bought in department stores or even found on the kitchen shelf or in the medicine cabinet. Actual kitchen appliances such as a stove, the pressure cooker, and the refrigerator can be very useful. One can always use cardboard boxes or wooden cheese boxes to house small animals (hamsters, white mice, guinea pigs, insects) for study. One can always plant a window box garden or even a "pocket garden" in a drinking glass to study the growth of a seedling or a sweet potato vine or an avocado pit. It is simple to leave a moist piece of bread or fruit in a warm spot in the house so that mold can grow and flourish.

With this simple equipment you can *think* scientifically and experiment. There are certain steps which a scientist follows, without bias or preconception and in logical order, when thinking scientifically. **This is known as the Scientific Method.**

1. First recognize and state clearly the problem to be solved or the question to be answered.
2. Concentrate on one part of the problem at a time.
3. Collect accurate and complete information from reliable sources.
4. Test this information with new ideas of your own.
5. Answer the question or draw conclusions.

The scientist forms an **hypothesis—a proposition which, although it remains to be tested under controlled, experimental conditions, seems to him the probable explanation of the phenomenon in question.** If subsequent experiments support the hypothesis, it will become the basis of a scientific **theory,** which may in turn be accepted as **natural law,** if it is observed to occur—without failure or variation—in nature.

In every experiment there are usually different factors involved which determine the results. Some examples of these factors are: material used, temperature, air or water pressure, amount of moisture, sunlight and season of the year.

The scientist cannot draw any conclusions unless he has a **control** to his experiment. **This control is an omission or a change of one of the factors.** If there is any difference in the results, the difference must then be due to that one factor which has been omitted or changed. When you perform any experiment at home, you must employ the logical order of the scientific method, and make use of the control.

Let us return to the well-equipped laboratory. Here, in addition to all the equipment that has been mentioned, there must be a **microscope.** It can open to you a marvelous world of living plants and animals that normally cannot be seen at all or only barely seen with the unaided eye.

The microscope, in its simplest form, dates back to the seventeenth century when a Dutch lensmaker, ANTON VAN LEEUWENHOEK, ground and polished a tiny bead of glass until it magnified whatever he looked at. To his great astonishment and awe he found that a drop of stagnant water was teeming with life never before visible to the human eye. For greater convenience, he fashioned a crude microscope of metal in which he inserted and secured this bead of glass.

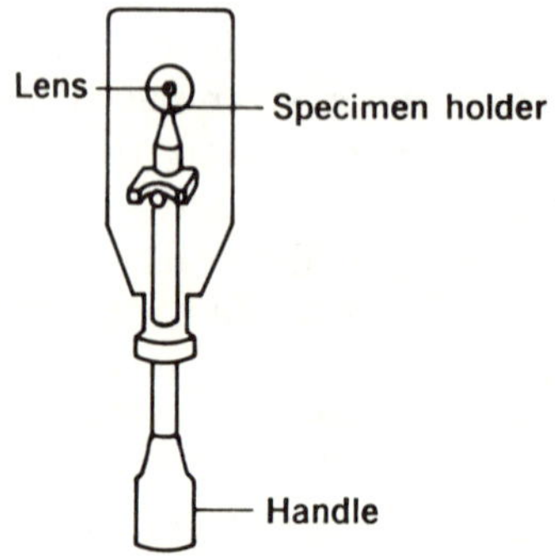

FIGURE 1. Leeuwenhoek microscope

Since that pioneering discovery of a revolutionary new use of optical lenses, there have been vast improvements and advances in magnifying lenses and microscopes. An Englishman, ROBERT HOOKE, made the first **compound microscope.** This type is used today—it can magnify objects clearly as much as 1,800 times. Such a microscope contains many lenses which, combined, *increase* magnification tremendously.

Early in this century, it was discovered that **ultraviolet** light could be used instead of light visible to the human eye, to obtain even higher magnification, as much as 4,000 times the life size of the object. This light cannot be seen by the human eye but can be photographed by the **ultraviolet microscope.**

In very recent years, engineers have developed an **electron microscope** which does not at all look like the compound microscope we are familiar with and which can produce a magnification of 20,000 times.

There is no doubt that microscopes of even greater magnification and accuracy can be de-

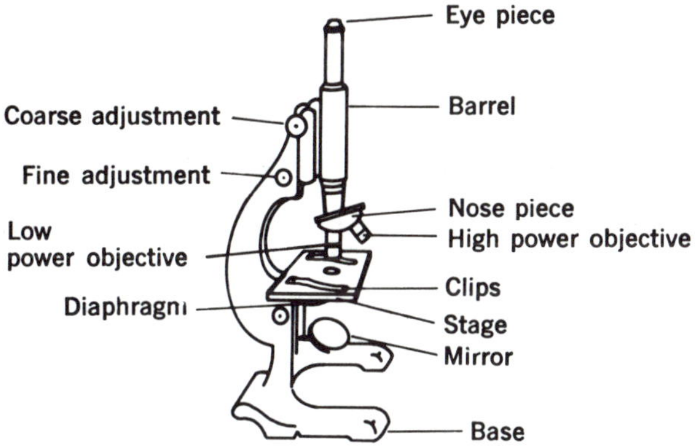

FIGURE 2. Compound microscope

veloped by the large optical companies—and will be in due course.

Because of increasing interest in the use of the microscope by individuals "at home," there are companies in this country and elsewhere which make inexpensive but adequate instruments. They do not, of course, have the magnifying power of a scientist's compound microscope but they are adequate for a home laboratory.

In this "atomic age," we are all becoming very science-conscious. Our curiosity and interests are constantly stimulated. Many newspapers have a science column, frequently biological in nature. Current science news, science facts and advice are presented so that they can be understood and appreciated by the average reader.

There are science digests, science magazines, radio and television broadcasts for the express purpose of informing the average individual. They attempt to whet his desire to seek further information.

The federal government will send literature, on written request, which will provide the most current material on many phases of biology. Write to the Department of Interior and to the Department of Agriculture for a list of their pamphlets on the branch of biology in which you are interested. These booklets may be sent to you free of charge or at a nominal cost.

Among the greatest storehouses of biologic wealth are our museums, our botanical and zoological gardens. In New York City, the Museum of Natural History houses the "story of life" from times historic to modern, with predictions of the future. There are life-size models, lifelike and accurate in every minute detail, set in carefully studied, simulated natural habitats. There are miniatures and fossilized remains. In this museum one can learn just by observing the exhibits, reading the "cards" and listening to the lecturing guides, the entire field of biology with its related subjects. There are such museums in most large cities and universities throughout the country. So, too, with "zoos," zoological gardens.

Spend a day in the springtime at a Botanical Garden. Take your camera with you—make mental pictures as well—of early spring green, of delicate new leaves fresh out of their buds, of pastel-colored blossoms—especially on the fruit trees, on vines and growing from the moist ground. Walk through the hot houses and see the vast variety of plant life which exists in climates other than yours. Smell the heavily fragrant, moist air. See the mist that halos the foliage and the damp rich soil from which it grows. Learn about plant life from growing plants.

"The Cloisters," an adjunct to the Metropolitan Museum of Art in Fort Tryon Park, New York City, has a series of tapestries, the "Unicorn Tapestries," that are world-known not only for the magnificence of their craftsmanship, design and color but for their woven pictures of every plant known in the Middle Ages. In this "imported" monastery are the Gardens of the Monks in which may be found odd flowering plants, every known herb, oddly cultured trees and many other forms of botanic life.

In cities other than New York, in many other states in the country, there are museums and collections of both living and preserved forms of plants and animals—for example, Marineland, Silver Springs, and the Everglades in lower Florida. The National Parks of the West and the Grand Canyon offer exciting and stimulating fields for biologic exploration. There are numerous places in which to study flora and fauna in their natural environments—and few experiences are more rewarding.

The Nature of Life

What is biology? The word comes from the Greek *bios,* meaning "life" and *logos,* meaning "study of" or "science of." Biology is defined as the study of all living things, both plant and animal, including man. If we specify *living* things then we must differentiate between that which is *living* and that which is *non-living.* We may refer to substances in nature that are composed of inorganic chemicals, such as rock, air, water and parts of sand and soil as non-living. We may refer to objects fashioned by man as also being non-living. Through the years of attempting to survive and build stable communities, scientists have studied living plants and animals to determine how they have adapted or adjusted themselves. From these studies and observations, men in many fields of the arts and manufacturing have been able to fashion non-living things that in many ways imitate living things which are well-adapted to their surroundings.

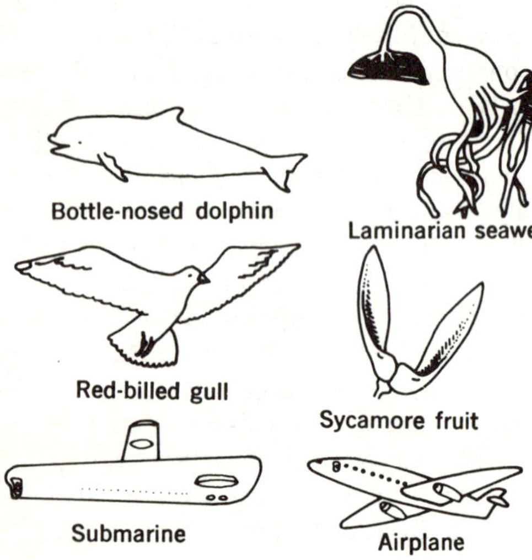

FIGURE 3.

Are you able to recognize man's successful imitation of living things in his building of submarines and planes? Consider the streamline shape of the dolphin, the location of the fins, the dorsally placed nostril, all **natural adaptations** for its life and activities in the water. The seaweed, though not actually propelled through the water, is continually subjected to the tidal currents. Its elongated shape and slimy covering allow the minimum of friction over its surface.

Can you see how man copied the features of a bird when he designed airplanes, and the sycamore fruit when he designed the helicopter? The streamline shape of the bird, its wing shape and spread, its retractable legs, the feather covering for warmth and weatherproofing, the directions its feathers grow are all natural adaptations for its life and activity in the air, on land and on water. The helicopter-bladelike wings of the sycamore fruit are admirably adapted to catch wind currents which will carry it far from the parent plant to colonize new areas.

RECOGNITION OF LIVING FORMS

Yes, non-living, man-made objects resemble the living forms after which they are patterned but there are major differences which set them apart from *living forms.* These differences are:

The *self*-power of *motion* that comes from within the living plant and animal. (Boats and planes move only with the will of man and the energy of fuel he provides for them.)

The *self*-power to *grow,* to add to itself in size. (The house must be added to by the will of man and the materials he provides.)

The *self*-power to *reproduce* plants and animals each of its own kind. This is nature's lease on life. (Only the will of man and the materials he provides can produce more boats, houses, etc.)

The *self*-ability to *respond to stimuli* in the environment, or what is known as sensitivity. The plant seeks sunlight and grows in that direction. (The house must be built that way.) The roots of a tree grow downward in response to the pull of gravity and in the soil in the direction of a water supply. (The foundation of a house is placed in the ground to benefit from the pull of gravity.) Animals seek food and water when their bodies require it—so that they can carry out their daily activities of living. (A machine must be "fed" fuel by man to carry out its activity.)

In plants and simple animals, the responses to various stimuli in the environment are called tropisms.

Animals high in the animal group have specialized *systems* which enable them to respond to stimuli in their environment.

Living things are grouped according to "natural" and logical divisions. The largest and most inclusive of these divisions have been **the Plant Kingdom and the Animal Kingdom.** Yet in view of contemporary evolutionary thought, a new classification has been suggested.

The old system had no place for "in between" organisms. These are primitive life forms that are more closely related to each other than to plants or animals. For example, some systems now place the bacteria and blue-green algae in a kingdom called the Monera. These organisms lack an organized nucleus. Another kingdom, the Protista, is now included in almost every system. It includes the more advanced life forms.

In studying each of these major divisions, biologists have been able to recognize a pattern of further divisions based on the simplicity or complexity of the plant or animal form. For convenience, a *classification* has been made beginning with the simplest form and carrying through to

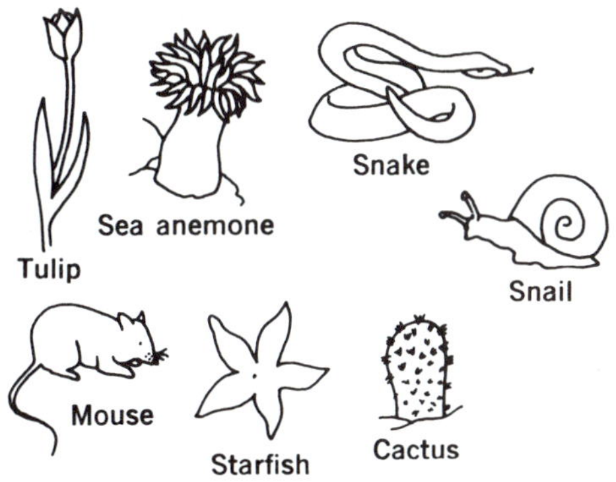

FIGURE 4. Living things

the most complex species of plants and animal life known, up to and including man.

There are forms of life, however, which exist in water, many microscopic forms, which can be grouped only after careful and detailed study, as either plants or animals. Perhaps you have seen coral growing in the warm southern waters, or highly colored sea anemones, sea urchins, or hydra, or even sponges. Have you remarked about the beauty of these underwater "flowers"? Actually they are forms of *animal* life much lower in the animal kingdom than fish or birds.

LIFE FORMS: DIFFERENCES

Perhaps you have examined a drop of water under the microscope and have seen single-celled animated forms of life and wondered—are these plants or animals?

The outstanding characteristics which distinguish plants from animals are:

Plants generally are *stationary*, fixed to a spot. Movement of the plant is usually in response to a stimulus in the immediate environment. Plants do not have the power of *locomotion*. Animals on the other hand, can usually move about—have the power of *locomotion* to seek food and shelter.

Plant growth is *indeterminate*. That is, it is without a definite time or size limit. A plant does not die from old age, but rather from disease or some other external factor. Animal growth, however, is usually determinate.

The most outstanding difference is the ability of the *green* plant to *manufacture* food within itself using the substances in the environment in this process. **This activity or process is known as photosynthesis. All animals, including man, get their food either directly or indirectly from plants.**

In external appearance, plants are usually green, some having varied and colorful flowers and others having no apparent blossoms. Among animals there is a vast variety of sizes, shapes and colors.

The basic difference between plants and animals lies in the unit of structure and function of each, namely, the cell. Plant cells have a **cell wall** which is actually non-living in chemical nature. Animal cells do not have this.

LIFE FORMS: SIMILARITIES

In all other respects, plants and animals are alike. All other activities that keep them alive are common to both. Every plant and animal is equipped to exist in its particular environment or *natural habitat*. Some are better equipped than others, are "hardier," and therefore more likely to survive. All plants and animals are *sensitive* to the need for food, water, certain temperatures and sunlight. In addition, animals are *sensitive* to the need for shelter and protection from their natural enemies.

In plants, chemical changes within the cells occur in response to the stimuli in the environment. Very simple forms of animals respond the same way. Some animals are equipped with nervous systems to respond to these stimuli. In the simpler animals the nervous systems are relatively simple, as are the responses. In the more complex type of animal, including man, this system is highly developed and provides the power of **discrimination.**

All plants and animals require food with which to *grow* and to provide the *energy* to carry on their life activities. Plants manufacture their own food. Animals *secure* their food from external sources and change the food within themselves into materials for growth and energy.

All plants and animals, no matter how simple or complex, are made up of a basic substance called **protoplasm.** This *living material* is identical in chemical nature in all forms of life, therefore its activities are identical.

BRIEF HISTORY OF CELLS

With the advent of the microscope, biologists were able to study the physical characteristics of protoplasm. Just about the time LEEUWENHOEK made his early microscope, the English scientist, ROBERT HOOKE, studied the structure of *cork* (from the bark of an oak tree) with a strong magnifying lens. He found it to be made up of tiny "empty boxes" with thick walls. He named these boxes *cells.*

After the microscope was made available to all scientists, further investigations were made of the structure of tiny water forms, of pieces of human skin, of blood, of parts of leaves, roots and stems of plants and even of parts of insects. They were all found to contain a substance that FELIX DUJARDIN, a French scientist, described as "living stuff," jellylike, grayish matter with "granules" scattered in it.

At the same time (1835–40) in other countries, scientists began to study the basic structure of all living things. In Czechoslovakia, a scientist named EVANGELISTA PURKINJE saw the "living stuff" and gave it the name **protoplasm,** (proto—first; plasm —form). He based his conclusions on the study of embryos of certain animals.

Some fifteen years later, two German biologists, SCHLEIDEN and SCHWANN, working independently, published books on the cellular nature of all plants and animals.

ROBERT BROWN, a botanist and surgeon's mate in the British Army, made an intensive study of orchids. He recognized the cellular structure of each flower part. With the use of stains, he was able to find a slightly thicker "particle" which appeared in every cell. This "particle" seemed to control certain activities of the cells, especially that of *reproduction.* He named this the **nucleus** of the cell.

Scientists in many countries, with the aid of microscopes, working independently and in groups, established what is known as the **Cell Theory:**

Cells are the units of structure of all living things. (All plants and animals are made up of cells.)

Cells are, therefore, the units of function of all living things. (It is within the cells that our life activities occur.)

All living cells come only from other living cells.

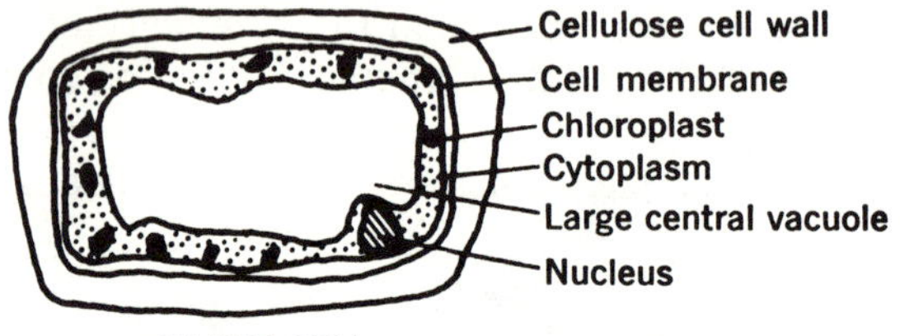

PLANT CELL

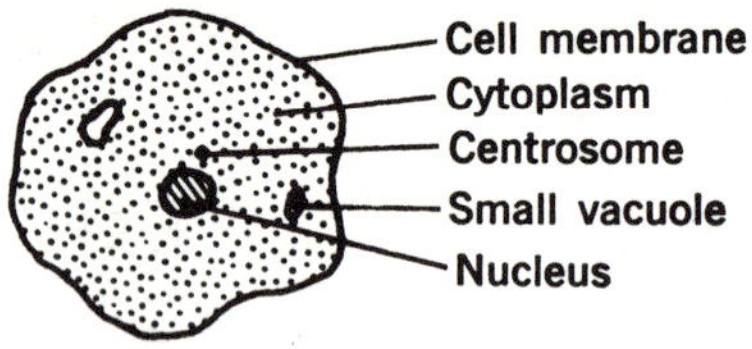

ANIMAL CELL

FIGURE 5.

CELL STRUCTURE

There are certain basic structures which appear in every cell. There are certain structures which differentiate a plant and animal cell, which make the basic differences between the plant and the animal. For convenience of study, let us look at typical plant and animal cells.

Structures present in all cells:

1. Cell membrane or **plasma membrane**—a double membrane surrounding the cell protoplasm or cytoplasm. Its function is to regulate the passage of liquids and gases into and out of the cell. It also provides a surface on which reactions may take place.

2. **Cytoplasm**—the protoplasm of living cells is in a colloid state; that is, it is made up of medium-sized particles hung in suspension. Its particles are too small to settle out and too large to go into solution. Because the particles are small, they provide a great surface area for cellular reactions to take place. They also permit the reaction to take place rapidly. Also, because protoplasm is not in a molecular state it cannot react chemically itself. Yet within the cytoplasm all cellular metabolic activities take place.

3. **Nuclear membrane**—a double membrane which controls the movement of materials into and out of the nucleus.

4. **Nucleus**—a definite structure within every cell. Its function is to control the activities of the cell. The nucleus contains the genetic material responsible for heredity, the *chromosomes.* It also contains the *nucleolus,* a smaller body which aids in the synthesis of protein.

5. **Endoplasmic reticulum**—a cell "skeletal" system. It provides a transport system between cell parts and a surface on which reactions may take place.

6. **Ribosomes**—small bodies which may occur on the surface of the endoplasmic reticulum or free in the cytoplasm. The ribosomes are the sites of protein synthesis.

7. **Mitochondria**—are often called the "powerhouse" of the cell. Here food is oxidized and energy is produced for use in various cellular activities.

8. **Vacuoles**—are storage bodies for water, minerals, etc. In unicellular organisms, vacuoles function in digestion and elimination.

Structures present only in animal cells:

1. **Golgi bodies**—function in the production of secretions of the cell.

2. **Lysosomes**—contain digestive enzymes which are released into the cytoplasm when the lysosomes burst open.

3. **Centrosome** or **centriole**—is located near the nucleus and functions in cell division.

Structures present only in plant cells:

1. **Chloroplasts**—bodies containing green chlorophyll pigments. Chloroplasts may be various shapes. The chloroplast is the site of photosynthesis or food production in a plant cell.

2. **Cell wall**—is composed of two layers. These layers provide support and protection for the cell. Both layers are somewhat waterproof, but they do not prevent the passage of water and substances dissolved in water from passing through. The wall is composed of a substance called cellulose.

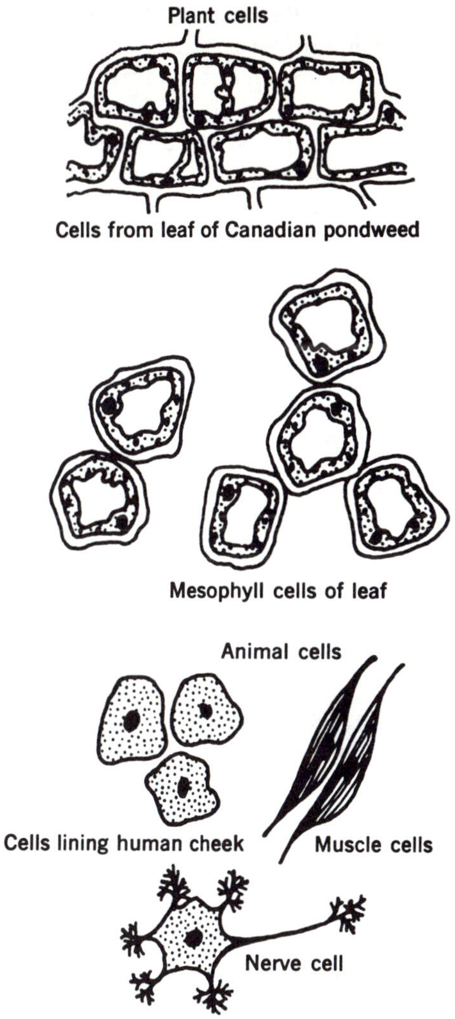

FIGURE 6.

INGESTION

In order to provide the necessary energy for growth and to carry on life's activities, we must take in food or eat. **This process is known as ingestion.**

In the discussion of the adaptations of plant cells it was noted that the cells are provided with structures called chloroplasts which help in the manufacture of food within the green plant. It is only in the green parts of the plant, the leaves and stems, that this food-making takes place.

Green plants in presence of light are able to take in the gas, **carbon dioxide,** from the air and combine it chemically with water to produce their carbohydrates. **This food-manufacturing process is known as photosynthesis.** By combining the sugars and starches made in this way with dissolved mineral salts from the soil, green plants are also able to manufacture their own proteins.

Animals are unable to do this. They secure their food either directly or indirectly from outside sources. Animals are adapted by nature to ingest food either directly into the cell, as in the case of very simple forms, or into parts of the body which prepare the food for all the cells to use.

For example, one of the simplest, one-celled animals, the **ameba,** (alternate spelling *amoeba*) actually surrounds its food with its flowing, ever-changing protoplasmic structure.

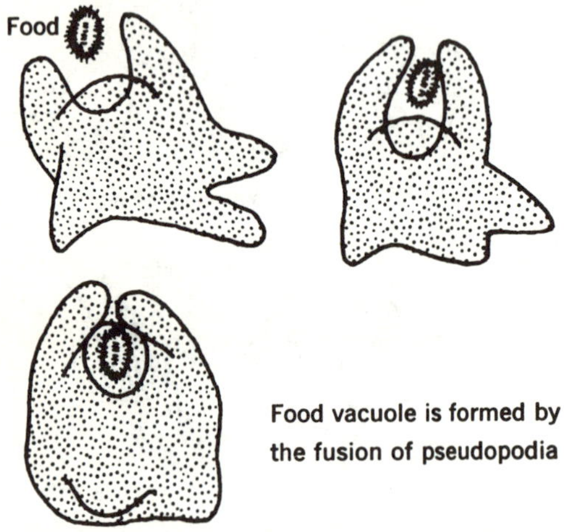

FIGURE 7. Ameba ingesting food

The starfish has an unusual manner of ingesting food. It clamps down with its five arms on an oyster until the muscles of the **bivalve (sea animal with 2 shells)** tire from the force. The oyster, unable to keep itself tense, relaxes. As soon as the starfish feels this, it allows the oyster shells to open, projects its own stomach into the soft tissues of the oyster and proceeds to devour it chemically.

The butterfly takes in food by uncoiling a **long tubelike structure (proboscis),** inserting it into the nectar container of a flower and sipping gently as through a straw.

The frog is an example of another type of feed-getting. He sits quietly on a leaf or log and waits for a flying insect to approach. When the unwary insect is within reach, the frog's long, cleft tongue darts out, catches the prey and directs it into his mouth. See Fig. 9.

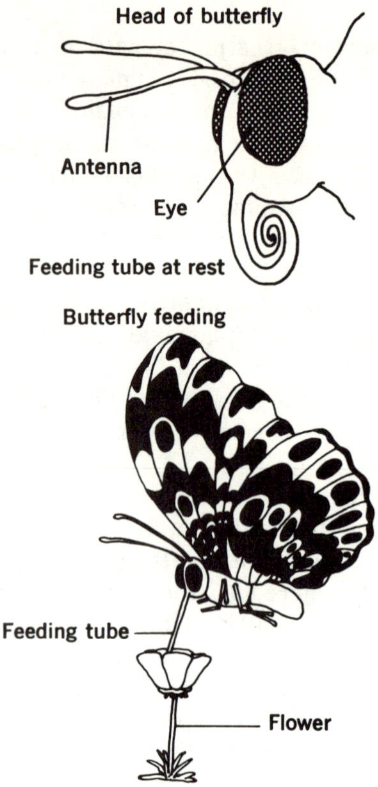

FIGURE 8.

Animals higher in the scale of life are well adapted to move around to choose, secure and to bring food to the "mouth" or part of the body which first takes in food.

DIGESTION

In both plants and animals food must be broken down into its simplest forms and made *soluble.* Only in soluble form are cells able to use food to provide energy for all life processes and to build new protoplasm and repair old. **The process of simplifying food and making it soluble is called digestion. Water is an essential substance in this process.**

The change from insoluble starch, protein and fats to soluble forms is brought about by the action of chemicals called **enzymes** which exist in both plants and animals. These enzymes bring about changes in the composition of foods without being in any way changed themselves or used up in the process. The chemist calls them **activating agents or catalysts.**

In plant cells, during the process of digestion, the starch that is manufactured in the green

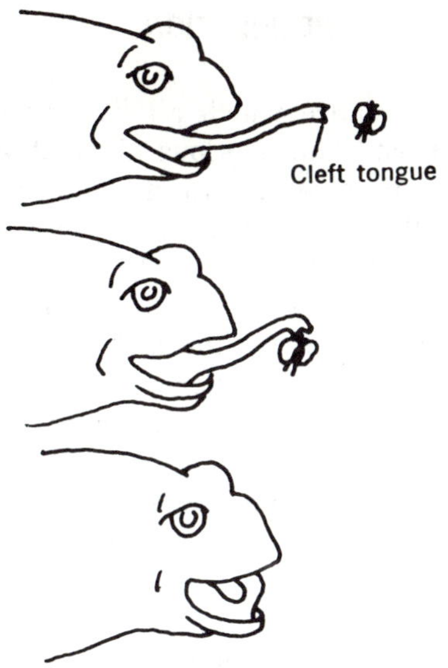

FIGURE 9. Bullfrog ingesting food.

leaves is changed into simple sugars which can be dissolved in water and carried to all other parts of the plant.

In animal cells, much the same is true. Foods containing insoluble starch, proteins, minerals and fats must be digested before they can be made available to all cells. Simple animal forms digest foods within each individual cell. Enzymes provide the necessary stimulus for this process.

More complex animals are especially fitted or adapted for digestion. In the earthworm the digestive system (series of body parts adapted solely for digestion) is extremely simple, merely a single tube extending the length of the body.

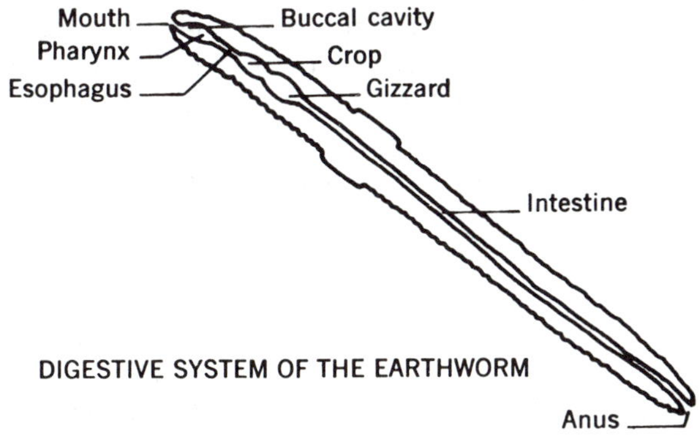

FIGURE 10. Digestive system of the earthworm

Higher in the animal kingdom this tube becomes divided into specialized parts each with a specific function in the process of digestion. In man and other highly developed **vertebrates (animals with backbones)** the digestive system is most specialized. Enzymes produced by glands serve as catalysts in animals as well as in plants.

ABSORPTION

Digested food must reach every cell in the living plant and animal. The cell walls of plants are porous so as to allow soluble food to pass through. The cell membranes are **selective** or **semipermeable:** that is, constructed so that only soluble substances can pass directly through into the cell protoplasm. **This process whereby digested or soluble food passes through the cell membrane is called absorption.**

In plant cells it is a simple process since all cell membranes are suitably adapted.

One-celled and other extremely simple animals contain food vacuoles in which digestion takes place. Digested food is diffused directly into the rest of the cell protoplasm.

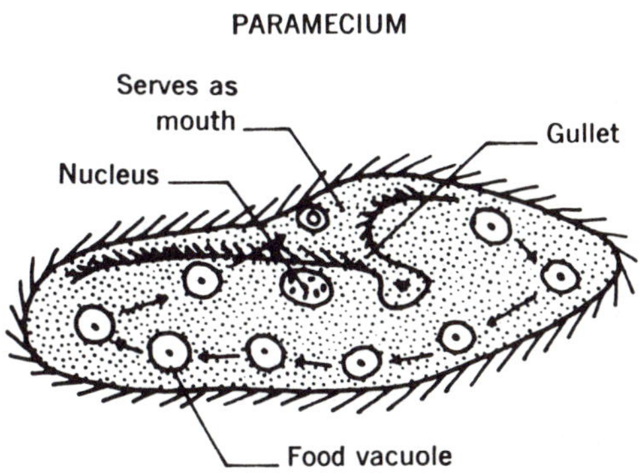

FIGURE 11. Food digestion of paramecium.

In higher animal forms, including man, absorption takes place in specialized parts of the body. For example: in man, the small intestine is adapted to absorb digested food into the blood stream which carries it to all parts of the body.

CIRCULATION

Circulation is the life process in which soluble food and oxygen are distributed to all parts of plant and animal bodies, heat is distributed and waste removed.

The ever-moving protoplasm distributes digested food to all parts of the single-celled plant and animal.

In more highly developed plants there are tubes in the leaves and stems through which food and oxygen are circulated. **Liquid food in plants is known as sap.** Water containing dissolved minerals is transported from the roots up to other plant parts through similar tubes.

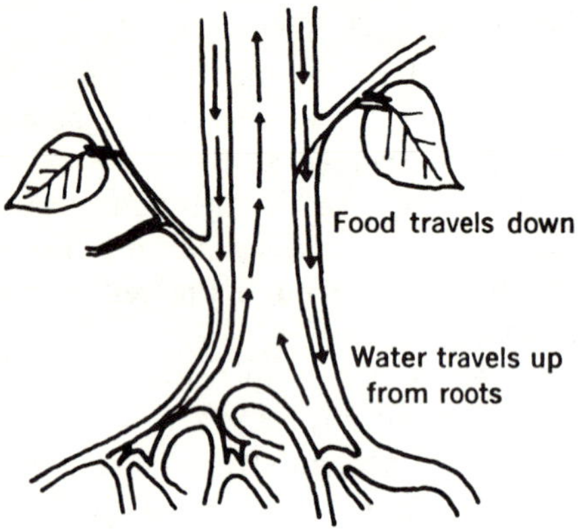

FIGURE 12.

Cut a stem of a growing plant, especially during the active food-making summer season—the stem will "bleed." This is the sap escaping from the severed tubes. Tapping maple trees for their syrup (sap) requires cutting into the tubes through which the maple sap circulates.

In higher types of animals, there is also a specialized series of tubes through which digested food and oxygen are distributed to all parts of the body and waste removed. **In man, circulation is performed by a blood stream which courses in blood vessels (arteries, capillaries and veins) to every cell.**

ASSIMILATION

When digested food reaches the cells in all plants and animals, part of it is chemically combined with oxygen, actually burned (in the process of **oxidation**) to produce heat energy. The rest of it is changed into more protoplasm for growth and repair of cells. This process of changing digested food into protoplasm is called **assimilation.**

RESPIRATION

Another substance which all living things require is **oxygen.** This gaseous element exists in air and also dissolves in water. The mechanical process by which oxygen is taken into the body and later, carbon dioxide (CO_2) released from the body, is called *breathing.* **Respiration** is the utilization of oxygen within each cell which results in the liberation of energy.

Land-living plants and animals naturally secure the necessary oxygen from the air. Plants are provided with small openings on the under surface of leaves, stomata, through which air enters. Within the leaf, oxygen is selected from the air, dissolved in plant sap and circulated to all cells. Oxygen enters the cell membranes and is used by the cytoplasm to combine with digested food (oxidation) to produce the energy with which to carry on all life processes.

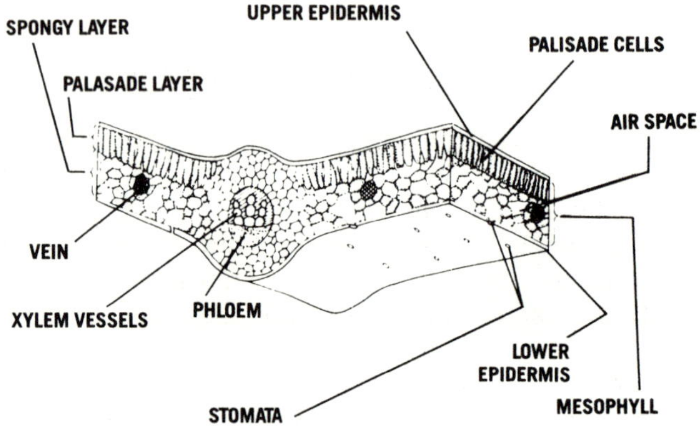

FIGURE 13. Leaf structure.

Characteristic of green plants is their ability to return to the atmosphere oxygen which is a by-product of photosynthesis. This replenishes the supply of oxygen in the air.

Plants that live in water select oxygen from the water via cell membranes. This is true of one-celled water-living animals as well.

Other animals are variously adapted for respiration. Fish are equipped with delicate, well-protected structures, **gills,** on each side of the head for this process. Water enters the mouth of the fish, passes back over the gills and comes out from under the scaly gill coverings. As water passes over the gills, oxygen is absorbed from the air dissolved in the water. It is carried by the blood stream to all parts of the body.

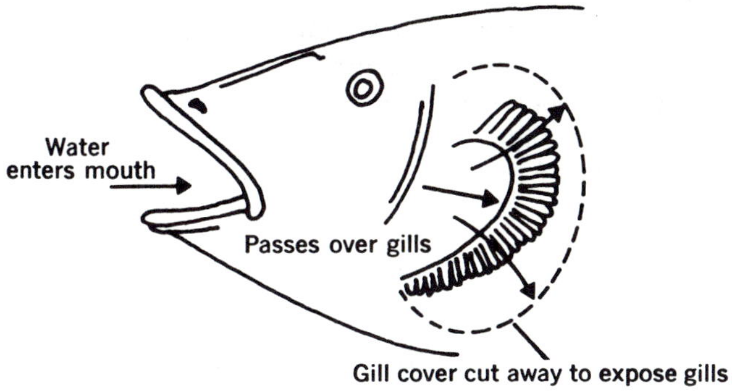

FIGURE 14.

The earthworm, a land-living animal, breathes through its skin—which must be kept moist. Thus the earthworm always seeks damp earth into which to burrow. If the soil around it should become dry and the skin of the animal should dry up, the animal will die from its inability to carry on respiration.

After a heavy rain you will probably see many earthworms on top of the soil in the country or park and on the cement sidewalk in the city. These creatures are not adapted by nature to live under water—they will drown if unable to reach the air.

Land-living animals breathe in air containing oxygen. **Invertebrates (animals without backbones)** have varied adaptations for breathing.

Insects take in air through **spiracles** which are holes on each side of the abdomen. Air is distributed through the tubes **(trachea)** which branch throughout the body. See Fig. 15.

Most land-living vertebrates (including man)

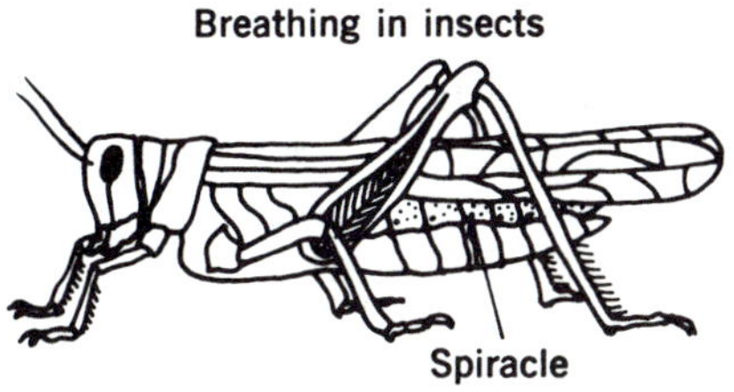

FIGURE 15. Grasshopper

take in air through nose and mouth from which it passes into *lungs*. The blood of these animals selects oxygen from air in the lungs and carries it to all cells where oxidation of food takes place. The blood carries a waste gas (carbon dioxide) and excess water back to the lungs from which they are passed out of the body through the nose and mouth of the animal.

EXCRETION

After plants and animals have oxidized digested food and carried on their life activities, waste products result. Some are common to both plants and animals because of the nature of all protoplasm. These wastes are given off in the process of **excretion.**

Inability of the organism to rid itself of waste materials produces a toxic or poisonous condition within the cells. Such a condition leads to inadequate and abnormal performance of all life processes and may eventually be fatal.

The waste gas, carbon dioxide, and excess water vapor are excreted from plant cells through the stomata in the leaves of green plants. It is believed that other organic wastes accumulated in the leaves during the summer are eliminated when leaves fall in autumn.

Animals are adapted for the process of excretion. In one-celled animals (as well as plants), carbon dioxide and liquid wastes collect in vacuoles and are excreted directly through the cell membranes.

Many-celled animals, of greater specialization, produce solid wastes in addition to carbon dioxide and liquid organic wastes.

Lung-breathers eliminate carbon dioxide and some excess water through mouth and nose after these wastes have been brought by the blood to the lungs. The kidneys and the skin are specialized organs in man which collect and expel liquid wastes. The large intestine excretes solid wastes from the body.

REPRODUCTION

There are two major types of reproduction—asexual and sexual. Asexual reproduction is the more primitive type and results in "daughter" individuals identical to the "mother." Sexual reproduction is more advanced. In its evolution, male and female structures for reproduction have arisen. Sexual reproduction results in daughter individuals which are similar, but not identical, to the parents.

Simple forms of plants and animals reproduce themselves in the most primitive manner, without any special adaptation for the process. Single-celled plants and animals grow to capacity and then split into equal parts, each part becoming an individual. This method of reproduction is called **binary fission.**

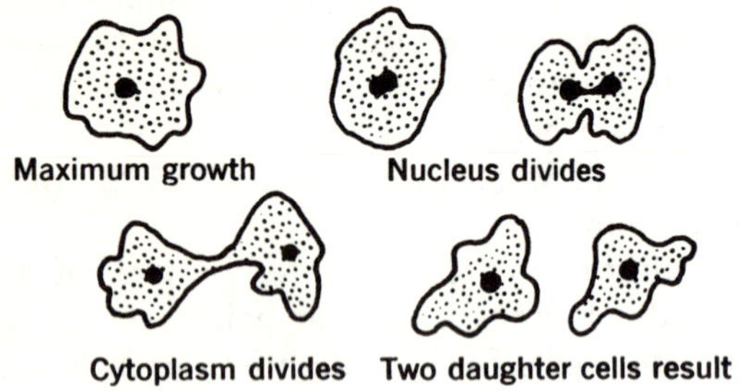

FIGURE 16. Binary fission in Ameba

Multicellular (many-celled) plants are adapted in several ways for the vital function of reproduction. Mosses and ferns produce numerous spores which, when growing conditions are favorable, develop into new moss and fern plants.

Flowering plants are adapted to produce seeds. In this highly specialized form of reproduction the flower is the important part of the plant. Within separate parts of the same flower or within two separate flowers, male and female elements are developed. The combination of male and female cells results in the formation of seeds. A seed contains the **embryo** (the infant plant) which, when conditions are favorable, will develop into the new plant.

In order for most animals to reproduce their kind, male and female cells are necessary. The female reproductive cell is referred to as the **ovum** or **egg cell.** The male reproductive cell is referred to as the **sperm cell.** The union of a sperm cell with an ovum results in a **fertilized egg** which develops into the new infant animal. Since the new animal is a combination of both parent cells it inherits the characteristics of both parents.

Insects, fish, frogs, reptiles and birds produce eggs from which their young develop. Where there is little or no parental care—in the case of most fish, frogs and reptiles—large quantities of eggs are produced to insure the survival of a species.

Where there is some parental care (as in the case of birds) in providing food, shelter and protection against natural enemies, fewer eggs are produced.

Animals classified as **mammals (vertebrates that possess hair or fur and suckle their young)** produce their young alive from eggs fertilized within the body of the female or mother. Man is a member of this group of animals.

MOTION AND LOCOMOTION

Another function of all living things is the power of **motion** and, in some cases, **locomotion.** Since all protoplasm is in constant streaming motion, under normal conditions, then it follows that all living things move in some fashion.

One-celled animals move from place to place independently (locomotion) in their water surroundings.

Plants which are "rooted" in the ground do not have powers of locomotion but they do exhibit types of motion. Leaves, stems and flowers turn in the direction of the sun; tendrils of climbing plants wind about convenient supports; roots turn in the direction of water; some "sensitive" plants respond when touched.

Animals appear to be more "alive," as we commonly know the term, because, with few exceptions they have powers of locomotion. Sponges and corals grow attached at one stage of their lives—and in this way, they resemble plants.

SENSITIVITY AND BEHAVIOR

Sensitivity or **irritability** is another life function common to all protoplasm. **This refers to the response of protoplasm to stimuli or changing conditions in the environment.**

All plants and animals react or respond in some way to light, heat, need for food, physical contact and other external and internal stimuli.

Man bases his claim to superiority over the entire animal kingdom upon his ability to recognize and cope with stimuli in his environment.

The Role of Environment

Living things which exist all over the earth are numerous and extremely varied. Where conditions are favorable, plants and animals are most abundant and successful. Scientists have explored the deepest oceans and the most rarefied heights above the earth's surface and have found evidence of some life. There are relatively few places where no forms of life can exist.

ENVIRONMENT

The nature and success of living things depend upon environmental conditions. **By environment, we mean the immediate surroundings of an individual plant or animal.** The environment furnishes the basic needs for all living things to carry on their life functions.

These essentials are food, air, water and sunlight. Food is necessary to provide the energy to grow and perform life's processes. Air is necessary because it contains oxygen with which food must be oxidized to be changed to heat energy. Water is essential and waste may be removed so that substances can be made soluble for entrance into all cells through the cell membranes.

Since plants need sunlight to aid in the manufacture of food (photosynthesis) and animal food consists directly and indirectly of plants, sunlight is necessary for animals. The heat as well as the light is essential for life to exist.

In addition, the environment includes such factors as other living organisms, gravity, wind, electricity and air or water pressure.

Throughout the years of man's residence on earth, he has learned to improve his environment. To some extent, he has learned to conquer the forces that change his environment and threaten his ability to survive.

HABITAT

The same kinds of plants and animals do not live everywhere on earth. For example, polar bears normally live in frigid, polar regions. Lobsters are found among the rocks in salt water, whereas brook trout live in fresh mountain streams and lakes. The eagle builds its nest and rears its young on a craggy mountain ledge, whereas the sparrow and robin nest in an apple tree on a local farm or a maple tree in the city.

Plants, too, can be found growing in specific areas. Palm trees grow naturally in moist hot regions, whereas pines and other evergreens are more successful in drier and more northern areas. Orchids are flowers characteristic of tropical climate, whereas dandelions grow rampant on lawns in the temperate zones.

The specific environment in which a particular plant or animal or group of plants and animals is found is called its **natural habitat.** All living things are adapted to live in their natural habitats. If they are inadequately adapted, they either die or move to another area for which they are better fitted. If change in habitat occurs gradually, some plants and animals can gradually adapt themselves to the changes and live successfully.

Natural habitats vary greatly, thus the flora and fauna characteristics vary. **Flora refers to the sum of plant life** in a zone or habitat within a given length of time. **Fauna refers to the sum of animal life** of a given region and time period.

Natural habitats are distinguished from one another as follows:

Aquatic—referring to water-dwelling plants and animals. Not all types of aquatic forms live in the same kind of water. The type of indigenous (native to) life depends upon whether the water is fresh or salt, still or flowing, shallow or deep, hot, cold or moderate temperature, smooth or rocky bottom —or a combination of these factors.

Examples of fresh-water life, that is those animals whose natural habitat is ponds, lakes, streams and rivers are: algae, water cress, pondweeds and water lilies; some fish, snakes, snails, crayfish and leeches are among the animals.

Salt-water plants and animals may be divided into three groups:

Those which live on the beach or in shallow shore regions only—such as, sand eels, oysters, crabs and starfish, barnacles and seaweed.

Those which live near the surface of the ocean —such as, most sea fish, jellyfish, sea turtles, sharks, seals, porpoises; diatom plants.

Those which live in the ocean's depths where it is dark and very cold and where food is limited —such as colorless plants (diatoms and some bacteria), a few fish, some barnacles.

Terrestrial—this refers to land-living plants and animals. Although these flora and fauna live either on the surface of the ground or burrow underground, they all need some water to carry on their life processes. Terrestrial plants with few exceptions live on the surface of the ground, most of them anchored to the ground by roots or some sort of processes (stemlike growths). Trees and ferns are examples. Most terrestrial animals live on the surface of the ground. There are a few species that live part of their lives beneath the ground—for example moles, prairie dogs, gophers, earthworms and some insects.

Arboreal—this refers to animals whose existence is confined mostly to trees. Examples are some monkeys, sloths, opossums, lizards and some insects.

Aerial—refers to animals who spend a good part of their lives in the air. Examples are birds, some bats and most insects.

In **mountainous** climates, because of characteristic high altitudes where the oxygen content of the air is less concentrated and there are strong, cold winds, both flora and fauna are relatively limited. Up to a certain line of demarcation, called the timber line, we find hardy oaks and evergreen trees, some poppies, gentians, onion-type grasses, mosses and lichens. This vegetation is low growing and extremely tenacious. Among the animals native to this region are huge spiders, eagles, bears, mountain goats and sheep.

Desert climates provide few factors favorable for most types of plants and animals. Because of the scarcity of water, the sand, and the steady intense light and heat of the sun only hardy plants like cactus, yuccas, sagebrush and tough grasses can exist. These are able to store water for long periods, have extensive roots and are tough enough to withstand the sun's burning intensity and the sharp drops in temperature at night. Such animals as rattlesnakes, horned toads, some lizards, a few more hardy rabbits, in addition to some unattractive birds, buzzards and vultures (scavengers) and a few species of insects, can exist on the desert where food is scarce and water is scarcer.

CLIMATE CONDITIONS

Climate conditions determine in great part the distribution of plants and animals over the world.

In Arctic regions where there is flat, frozen iceland, the flora are limited to low-growing plants such as some mosses and lichens, tough grasses, a few hardy species of dwarf poppies and even forget-me-nots. The fauna are usually confined to penguins, polar bears, seals, walruses and whales.

Plants and animals are greatly varied in **temperate** regions where there is variety in temperatures, and there are four annual seasons.

In **tropical** climates, where there is abundant rain and concentrated sunlight, plant life is luxuriant, always green and varied. Among the plant life are such trees as ebony, mahogany, rubber, date palms, bamboo, banana and thick-stemmed hardy vines; such flowers as orchids, gardenias and other heavily scented, superbly colored ones. Animals such as monkeys, apes, lemurs, sloths, elephants, parrots, birds of paradise, huge beautifully colored butterflies and innumerable insects are indigenous to this region.

NATURAL BARRIERS

There are natural *barriers* (insurmountable obstacles) which prevent the indefinite distribution of successful growing plants and animals. These are large mountain ranges, widespread oceans, and large rivers, far-reaching deserts, soils lacking or overabundant in a certain chemical and the indestructible presence of natural enemies.

Earthquakes, the disappearance of small islands as a result of tumultuous internal earth upheavals, volcanic eruptions and large-scale glacial movements are also factors which produce natural barriers.

COMMUNITY LIVING

Within a given area or community, groups of plants and animals live together in natural coexistence. These living things are adapted or adapt themselves to all the factors in the immediate environment. In a community there always appears to be one or several dominant forms of plant and animal life which are more successful than the other plants and animals which share the community.

An example of community living can be found in a local park. There are trees which grow successfully in that particular climate and type of soil. There are birds which inhabit the trees, build nests and rear their young, feeding on the trees and other plants, and insects that grow in the area. There are insects adapted to live in the air, in the trees, on flowering plants and even in the ground.

Some insects serve as food for other animals, some help to propagate new generations of the local flora. Other animals live on the seeds, roots, stems and other parts of plants in the community. These animals contribute their share in community living by destroying harmful animal pests.

If the environmental factors remain relatively stable, then a balance of living may be achieved and all forms of flora and fauna in the area will live successfully.

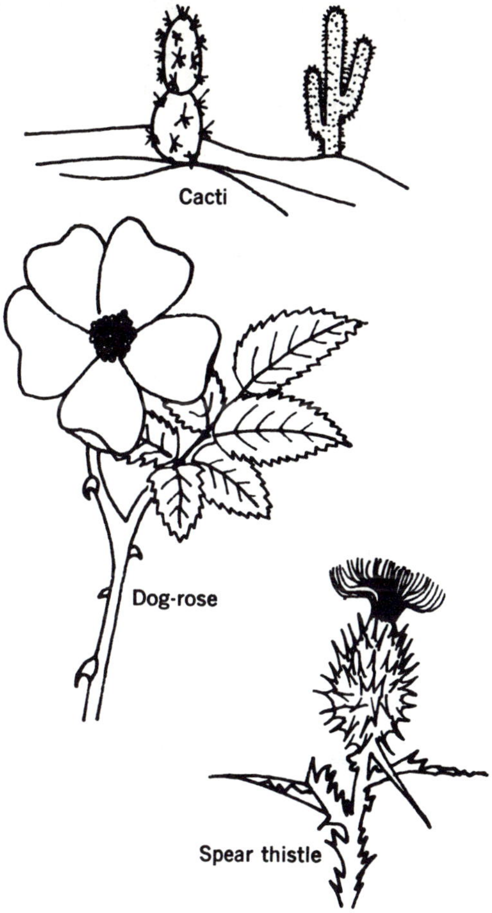

FIGURE 17.

PROTECTIVE ADAPTATIONS

All living things are adapted to secure the necessities of life from their immediate environment.

There appears to be a constant struggle among plants and animals to secure food and living space. Those plants and animals which are best adapted for these activities will be most successful. Those which are weakly adapted will be forced either to "fight" constantly for survival, withdraw to another community, or eventually perish.

Since every form of life has a natural enemy which will seek to destroy it, either to use it as food or in self-protection, all forms of life are adapted to protect themselves. These adaptations are called **protective adaptations.**

Among plants, the rose is a fine example of protective adaptation. Thorns on the stems discourage animals bent on destruction. Another example is the thistle with its needlelike flower cup, stems and leaves. The cactus has horny spines which are most painful to the touch.

The necessity for protective adaptation is great among animals because of their ability to move about (locomotion).

Most animals have some natural color protection from their enemies: that is, they resemble in color their natural surroundings. Most animals have other special adaptations for protection.

Insects, which are so numerous and varied, show interesting and successful adaptations. For example, the green-brown *praying mantis* with its formidable front "claws" and its wary stance, appears most menacing to a potential attacker.

FIGURE 18. Praying mantis

The *walking stick* insect, a gentle animal, is protected by its resemblance to the twig on which it crawls.

The tiny *leaf insect* looks like a spring green leaf on which it alights in its relatively short life on earth.

Beetles have claws and fierce-looking (to another insect) **mandibles (chewing mouth parts)** for protection as well as food-getting.

Bees and *wasps* have painful stinging apparatus for protection against their enemies.

The famous *chameleon* takes on the coloration of whatever it happens to crawl on when it senses the approach of a natural enemy.

Among animals such as rabbits, squirrels and chipmunks, the ability to remain breathlessly motionless as well as their keenness of hearing and sight, their alertness and speed protect them against natural marauders.

FIGURE 19. Walking stick insect

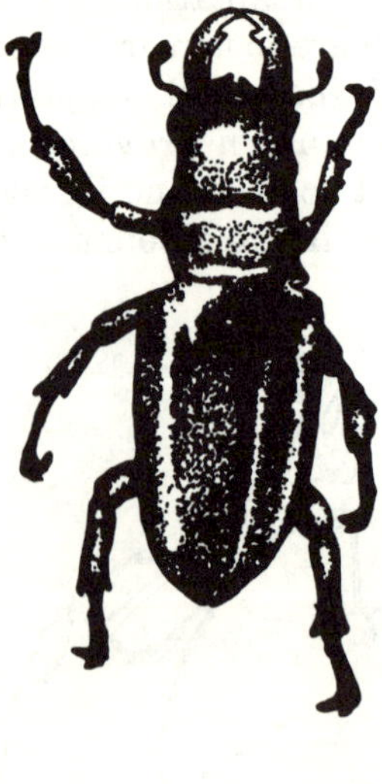

FIGURE 20. Male stag beetle

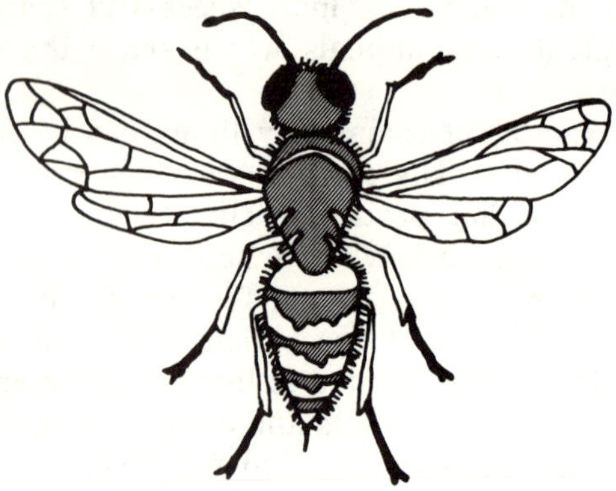

FIGURE 21. Common wasp

The *turtle* is fitted with a thick, horny "shell" which encases its soft body and into which it can withdraw completely for shelter and protection.

FIGURE 22. Turtle

PLANT AND ANIMAL INTERDEPENDENCE

It is obvious that in any environment one plant or one animal cannot survive by itself. All animals depend upon plants and other animals and plants depend upon other living things. Man depends upon other animals and plants for his success on earth. This mutual interdependence is what provides the balance in nature.

Most plants and animals live in groups. Some trees, for example, are adapted to a specific climate and type of soil. Hardy oak and hickory trees grow together in a temporate region where there are dry ridges. Basswood, red maple, elm, willow and birch will be found growing together in more moist areas. Evergreens (firs and pines) are usually found in more northerly climates but can grow elsewhere.

Ferns and mosses flourish together in moist shady places.

Seaweeds and algae grow together in harmony in the salty oceans.

Most animals live gregariously in "communities" or herds. Man is such an animal.

Some insects—bees and ants especially—live in communities and actually share in the many activities of food-getting, shelter-building, care of the young and protection against natural enemies.

In a warm sea-water community certain fish, coral, sponges, lobsters, crabs and jellyfish live together.

Local ponds provide community living for water bugs, frogs, snails, eels and fish.

Such animals as buffalo, elephants, cows and other cattle live in herds for mutual benefits. Wolves and coyotes travel in packs for maximum mutual strength and protection.

Relatively few animals prefer to live alone. Examples of those that do are lions, tigers, some deer and small animals like rabbits. The advantages of solitary living are few. Escape from natural enemies is perhaps easier for a swift, lonely animal; less disturbance and interference in rearing the young; less competition for mating and securing food are sometimes possible advantages.

Generally speaking there is "safety in numbers"; therefore group living is usually the most successful type of living.

SYMBIOSIS

The living together of organisms for mutual benefits is called symbiosis, the plants and animals involved are known as symbionts. An example of symbiosis among animals is the relationship between common ants and plant lice or *aphids*. The aphids suck the sap from rose or other plants. With this plant fluid they produce a sweet substance within their bodies. Ants "milk" the aphids and feed their queen and also the young. (The plant lice are known as "ant cows.") In return for this service, the ant cows are protected by their mutual benefactors against natural enemies and are also given shelter in anthills during the winter.

Another example of mutual "give and take" is found in the *termite*. This wood-eating insect provides food and shelter for a protozoan animal that lives in its intestines. The protozoa rewards its host by producing chemicals which digest the wood fibers for the termite.

Another interesting form of symbiosis between animals exists in the partnership relationship of the hermit crab and the sea anemone (a member of the jellyfish family). The hermit crab lives in a discarded snail shell which covers the soft part of the crab. The anemone lives on top of the snail-shell house and has stinging apparatus which protects it and the crab from natural enemies and captures food. It also gives protective coloration for the crab which, in turn, provides the anemone with transportation and food bits that escape its own mouth.

A classic example of plant symbiotic relationship is the *lichen* which is found growing on rocks

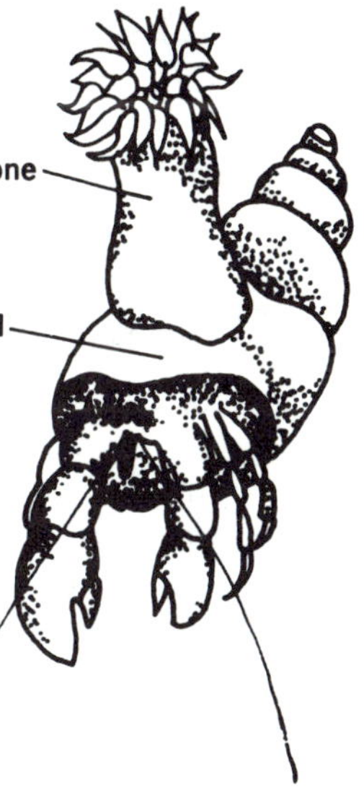

FIGURE 23. Hermit crab

and tree trunks. This is not a single plant but a mutually beneficial combination of a nongreen fungus and a group of one-celled green plants of the algae group. The fungus cannot make its own food. It provides shelter, anchorage, protection, water and carbon dioxide for its algae companions. These simple green plants use the water and carbon dioxide to manufacture food and supply oxygen for the fungus.

PARASITISM

Some plants and animals feed on other living organisms without giving anything in return. **This relationship is known as parasitism; the offender is called a parasite, and the "meal ticket," the host.** In most cases the parasite is structurally degenerate and entirely dependent upon the host. The host may either gradually lose its vitality, be-

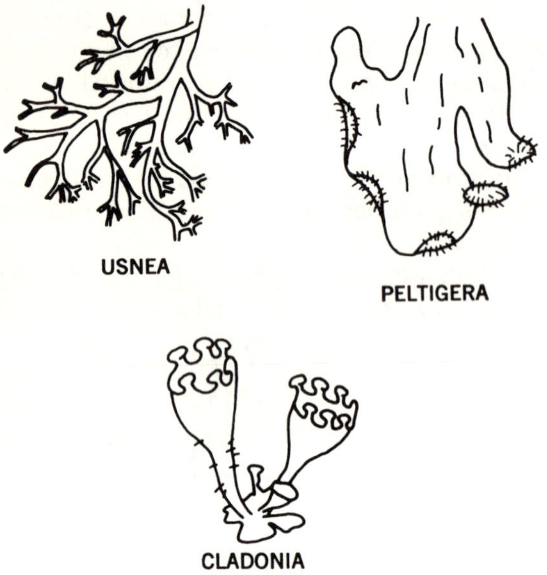

FIGURE 24. Lichen forms

come abnormal and diseased and then die or it may develop a natural protection against the parasite. It may adapt itself to live with and in spite of its burden. In some cases, the host produces a substance which either renders harmless or kills the parasite.

The *mistletoe* plant, which conjures up romantic notions, is actually a parasite incapable of manufacturing its own food, reliant on another plant for its food. Its host, usually an apple, poplar or maple tree, eventually perishes from malnutrition.

Other plant parasites which depend on and slowly devitalize their hosts, causing great economic loss to man, are wheat rust, Dutch elm disease, corn smut and chestnut blight. In each case the tree or plant mentioned in the name is the losing host to the destructive parasite plant.

There are some parasitic plants which do damage directly to man's person. These offenders are members of the **fungus group of plants, that is, a group having no chlorophyll.** The unpleasant "ringworm" and "athlete's foot" ailments are examples.

The most numerous and destructive of all plant parasites are among the **bacteria (a type of single-celled plant).** Some species cause blights on apples, pears, cabbage, cucumbers and other plants. Other species cause diseases in man and are referred to as **pathogenic** bacteria. Among the dreaded pathogenic bacteria are those which produce diphtheria, typhoid fever, Asiatic cholera, bubonic plague and other illnesses, most of which man has been able to control and prevent.

There are some animal parasites which single man out as their unfortunate hosts. Among them are protozoa which cause malaria and sleeping sickness. Hookworm and pork worm—parasitic in man—produce devastating results in their often unsuspecting hosts. Scientists have learned to prevent and control the harmful activities of these animal parasites.

SAPROPHYTES AND SCAVENGERS

Some plants and animals depend for their existence on other, *dead* organisms. Many plants lacking chlorophyll are known as **saprophytes,** examples of which are yeasts, molds and mushrooms.

Animals that live on dead or decaying flesh of other animals are called **scavengers.** Among them are the vultures, buzzards and sea gulls. In the blood stream of man, there are **white blood cells** that resemble ameba which act as tiny scavengers by engulfing and eating unwanted particles including some disease-producing bacteria.

Man, in his position as the superior animal of our universe, has learned to change his environment, sometimes to his misfortune but generally to his advantage, and to improve the welfare of other living things. Because of his powers of observation and reasoning, he has been able, to a great extent, to control many factors of his environment.

Organization and Classification

All living things are made of **protoplasm.** The smallest unit of structure and function of protoplasm is the **cell.** All plants and animals are made up of either a single cell or many cells.

Evolutionists believe that all plants and animals originally arose from a unicellular ancestor. As can be seen by the study of lower plants and animals, particularly those of a single cell, there are many characteristics common to both those called "animals" and those called "plants." It has taken many years of evolution for organisms to acquire their distinct plant or animal-like character. In order to take into account the similarity of the lower plants and animals, recent methods of classification place them together in a group called the Protista. Traditionally, they have been classified separately.

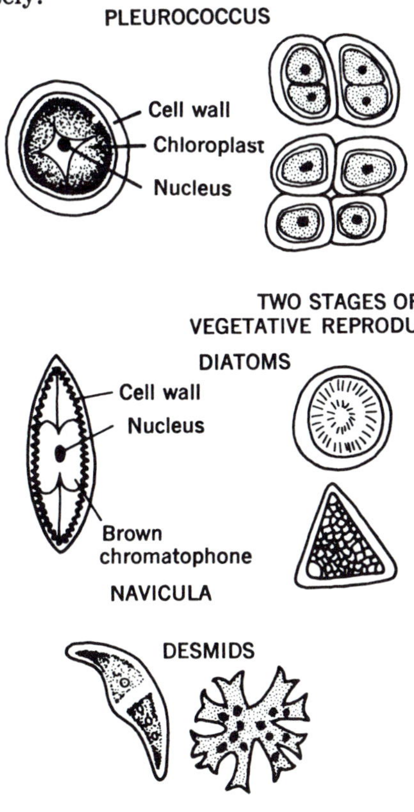

FIGURE 25. Single-celled plants

SINGLE-CELLED LIFE: PLANTS

The simplest form of plant life exists as a single cell which is able to carry on all the necessary life processes. Most one-celled plants belong to the **algae** group which live in water. There are some which live in symbiotic relationship with other plants (lichens) and with animals in a moist environment but out of the water.

A common example of a single-celled plant is the **pleurococcus** which is usually found growing on the north side of moist tree trunks and rocks in the woods. These tiny green plants are legendary

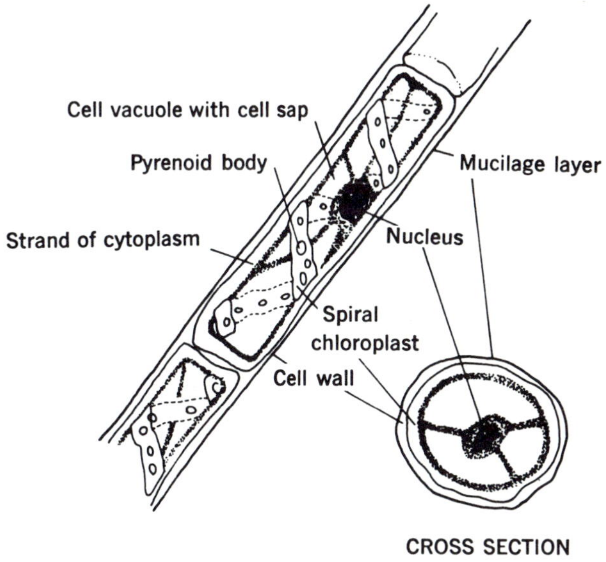

FIGURE 26. Spirogyra (common pond scum)

"Indian's Friend" and "Woodsman's Compasses" because they indicate the direction North.

They contain chlorophyll with which to combine carbon dioxide from the air and water to manufacture food. Under the microscope they appear singly or in colonies, each cell living independently within its colony. See Fig. 25.

A drop of pond water will reveal a variety of single-celled plants. What is commonly known as pond scum is a group of green threadlike colonies called **spirogyra.** They reproduce prolifically and form the greenish scum that appears on the surface of sluggish streams, small ponds and pools. See Fig. 26.

Among the independent single-celled forms which can be viewed under a microscope are the **diatoms** and **desmids.** These plants are curiously symmetrical, each kind having a specific design on its shell-like outer covering which encloses and protects the soft protoplasmic cells.

Diatoms seem to have existed in abundance centuries ago. Large deposits of their empty shells have been discovered in salt as well as fresh water and on land that shows evidence of once having been under water. These deposits, called **diatomaceous earth,** are used commercially as the basis of polishing materials and also for filtering purposes in sugar refineries.

Another common group of single-celled plant life, is found in ocean water, as part of the substance **plankton.** These are tiny green plants that provide much of the food for fish and other sea-living animals.

Many other algae of varied colors inhabit the oceans and shore lines. When they occur in concentration they actually give color to their surroundings—for example, the Red Sea.

Perhaps the most abundant and varied single-celled plants are the **bacteria.** Among this group are many most helpful to man and others, most harmful.

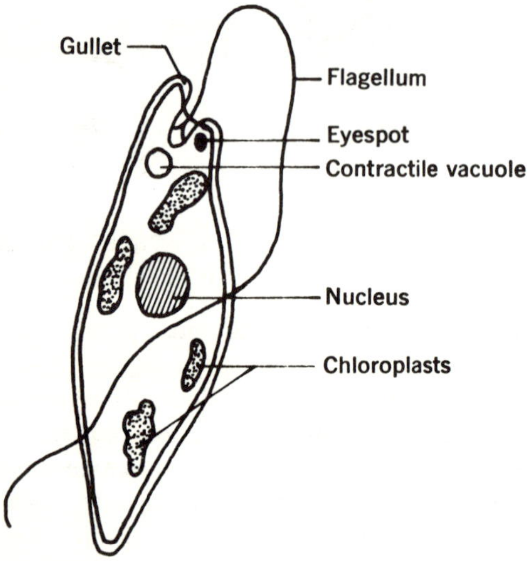

FIGURE 27. Euglena (plant or animal?)

One single-celled form of life, the **euglena,** has created dissension among biologists. Botanists consider it a simple plant because it contains chlorophyll bodies with which it manufactures its own food.

Zoologists, on the other hand, claim that it rightfully belongs to the animal kingdom for several reasons. It contains a contractile vacuole for collecting and eliminating liquid wastes. At one end of the cell there is a form of mouth and gullet into which it takes some food particles from the water. At the mouth region, there is a **whiplike projection (flagellum)** which lashes back and forth, aiding in locomotion and food-getting.

Perhaps this controversial bit of life is proof that one-celled plants and animals have a common ancestor.

SINGLE-CELLED LIFE: ANIMALS

This leads us to the fascinating group of true one-celled animals called **protozoa** (proto—first; zoa—animals). A drop of pond water reveals a variety of tiny animals, some darting about and others moving lazily.

Among the most numerous are paramecia and amebas. Each of these animals is well-equipped within its protoplasm to carry on all the life functions.

The simplest of all animals is the ameba. It has no definite or constant form. The protoplasm within the cell membrane flows into projections known as **pseudopods** or false feet. The presence

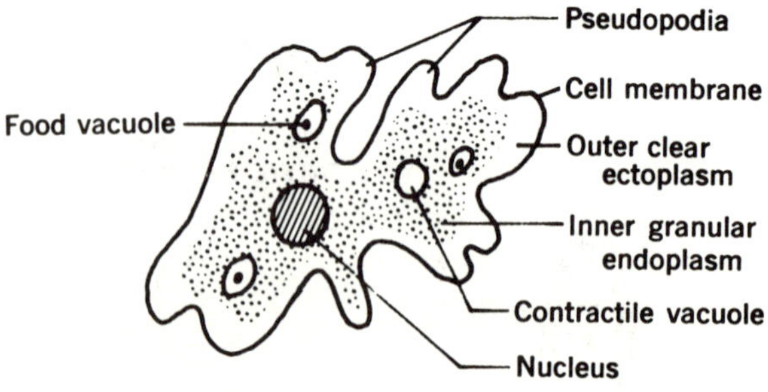

FIGURE 28. Ameba

of food particles in the water seems to stimulate the formation of these false feet which carry the rest of the cell in the direction of the food; thus the animal moves from place to place.

Food is digested within vacuoles and is absorbed directly into the surrounding cell protoplasm. Oxygen dissolved in the water is absorbed directly through any part of the cell membrane. Solid wastes are "left behind" as the ameba flows sluggishly on. A contractile vacuole regulates the water content of the animal and also collects liquid wastes which are expelled through a temporarily thin spot in the cell membrane.

The centrally located nucleus of the ameba controls all cell activities. It splits in half to produce two ameba in the process of reproduction. This simple type of reproduction is known as **binary fission.**

The paramecium, a more advanced type of one-

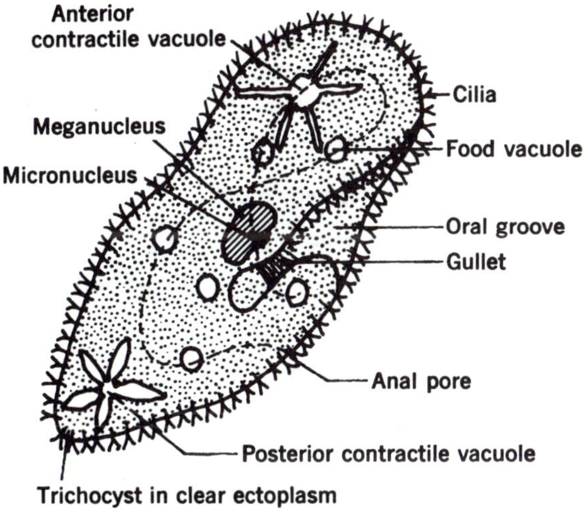

FIGURE 29. Paramecium

celled protozoa, is slipper-shaped and constant in form.

Its cell body is covered with tiny projections of protoplasm called **cilia** which wave back and forth providing means of rapid locomotion in water. Other cilia around the mouth region wave food particles into the "gullet" which is also lined with cilia to push the food into food vacuoles.

Constant flowing motion of the protoplasm within the paramecium cell body distributes each food vacuole to all parts of the cell. Digestion of food takes place in the vacuole. Digested food is absorbed directly into the surrounding protoplasm.

Oxygen dissolved in the water is absorbed directly through the cell membrane into the cell protoplasm.

Solid food wastes are expelled through a weakened area in the cell membrane called an **anal spot.** Liquid wastes are forced through the cell membrane by the contracting action of the contractile vacuoles located one at each end of the tiny animal.

Minute threads of poisonous protoplasm called **trichocysts** are imbedded just inside the cell membrane. These provide means of protection and are expelled with force when the paramecium comes in contact with a hostile form of life.

A well-developed nucleus and a "helper-nucleus" control all life activities and provide the means

CONJUGATION IN PARAMECIUM

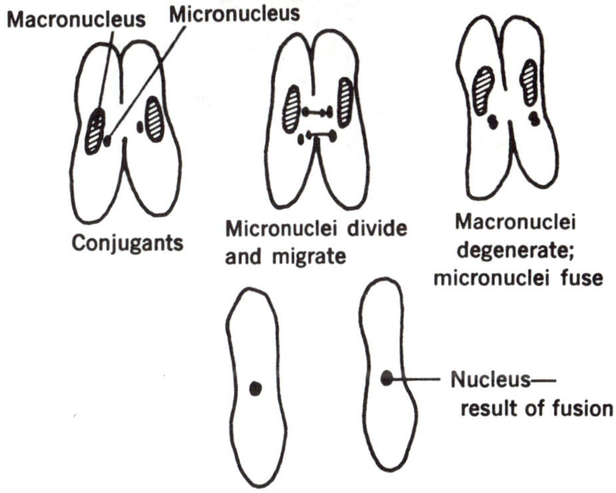

Conjugants separate and divide again by binary fission
This is a simplified version of a more complex process

FIGURE 30.

for reproduction. The paramecium divides by binary fission, similarly to the ameba, and also by a simple type of sexual reproduction called **conjugation.** In this type of reproduction two paramecia fuse temporarily, exchange nuclear material, separate and then each proceeds to divide by binary fission. This process seems to strengthen the species.

There are other types of protozoa which exist individually and still others which live in colonies.

The **vorticella** attaches itself by a long stalk at one end to a stationary object.

Colonial protozoa live in groups, each animal in the colony, functioning independently. Some colonies have a thick, gelatinous substance encasing them while others have glasslike coverings. The famous white cliffs of Dover (Southern England) are composed of countless chalklike shells which have accumulated through the years after the soft protoplasm of each protozoan animal has ceased to exist.

Most one-celled animals live independently but there are some which are parasites. Examples of these are the protozoa that cause malaria and African sleeping sickness in man. Each of these has an alternate host. The malarial plasmodium (protozoan that causes malaria) spends part of its life in the anopheles mosquito. The protozoan which causes sleeping sickness spends much of its life cycle in its alternate host, the tsetse fly, native to the African continent.

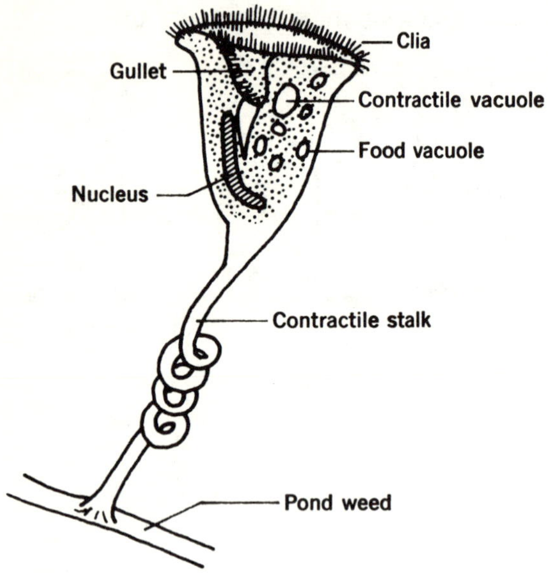

FIGURE 31. Vorticella

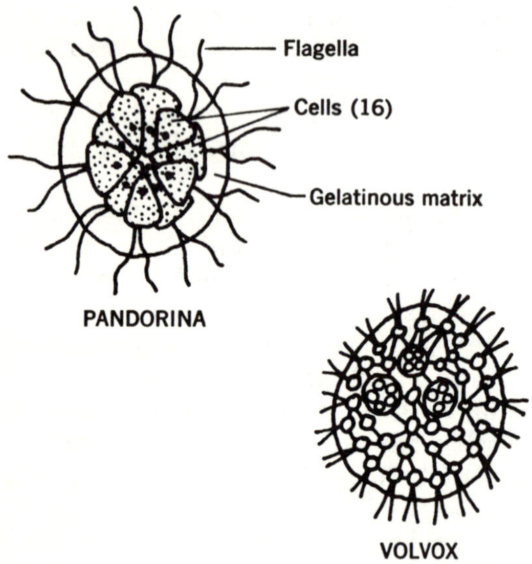

FIGURE 32. Colonial protozoa

CELLULAR ORGANIZATION

Living things that we can readily see and touch are usually made up of many cells, and many groups of cells. Each of these cells or groups of cells is adapted to perform a particular function. All of the groups of cells normally work in harmony for the common welfare of the plant or animal.

One can easily see the gross structure of a geranium plant. To examine the cellular composition of any part of the plant requires a microscope.

Under the microscope the thin lower section of a geranium leaf (surface view) appears to be made up of many cells similar in size and shape, fitted together like a series of bricks in a brick wall. At intervals there are openings "guarded" by two kidney-shaped cells. The same view of the lower epidermis of the leaf appears to be a pattern of well-fitted flagstones among which are guarded openings. See Fig. 33.

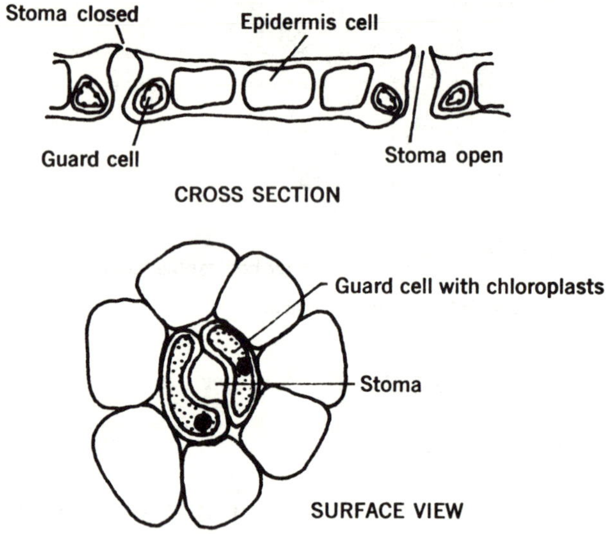

FIGURE 33. Under surface of leaf

The continuous layer of cells is adapted to protect the under surface of the leaf. The openings or **stomata** with their **guard cells** control inward or outward passage of gases. Oxygen is taken into the leaf and carbon dioxide is released during the process of respiration. During the process of photosynthesis carbon dioxide is taken in through these stomata and oxygen is released. Other cells (containing chloroplasts) in the leaf are adapted to combine carbon dioxide and water to produce food for the plant.

In a later discussion of the flowering plants, plant cells and their specialized functions in groups or tissues will be considered in detail. Note a few more examples in Figure 34.

Among many-celled animals, there are also groups of cells similar in structure with a similar common function.

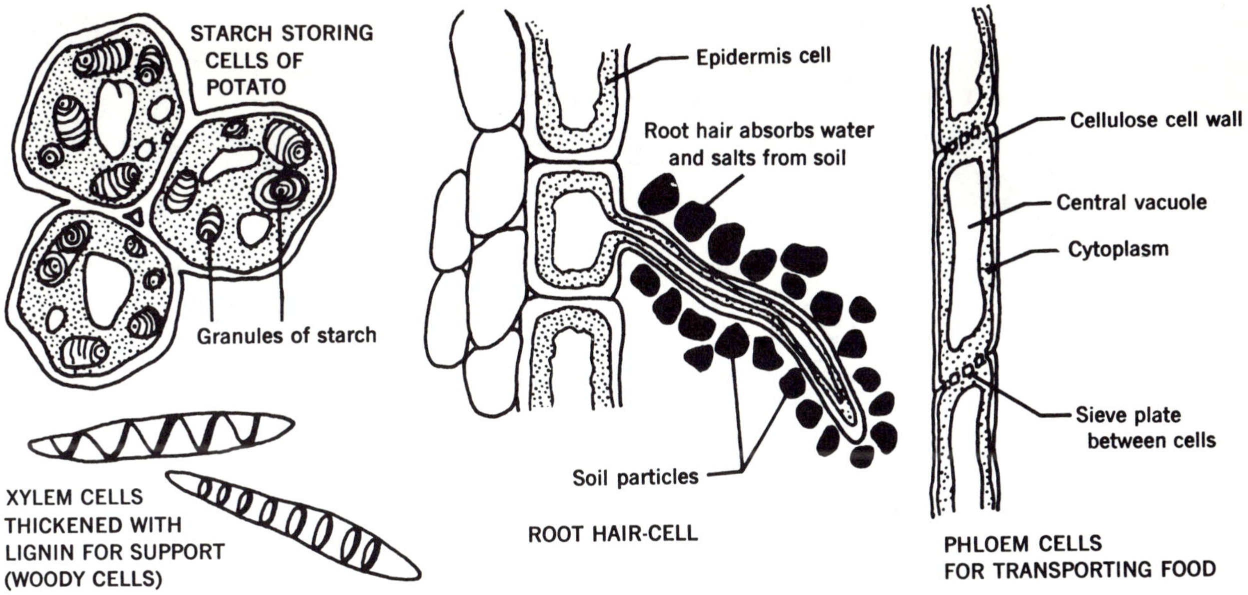

FIGURE 34. Plant tissue cells

For example, examine Figure 35 showing cells from the cheek lining of man. If a microscope is available to you, prepare a slide of cheek lining cells. (Scrape the inner surface of your cheek with the dull edge of a butter knife and mount this in a drop of water on a glass slide.)

These cells are adapted for their job of protecting the softer, inner cells of the mouth.

In Figures 36 and 37 there are surface views of several types of cells found in the human body. Note how they vary in size and shape, also in function.

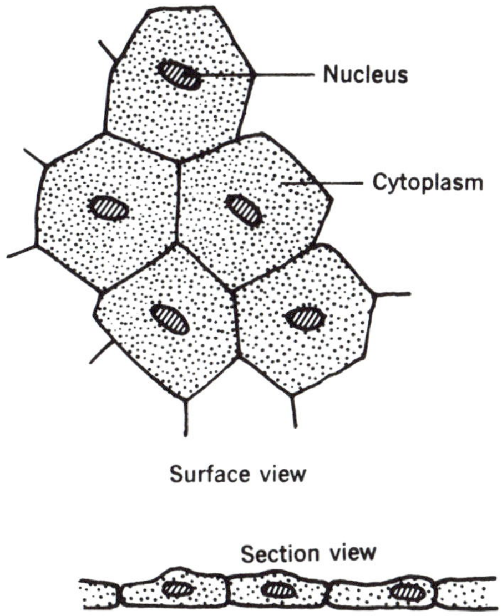

FIGURE 35. Human cheek cells

Groups of cells similar in size, shape and function make up tissues: thus nerve cells working together form nerve tissue; muscle cells grouped together form muscle tissue; and cartilage cells form cartilage tissue.

There are other types of cells in the human body (as well as in all other animals and in plants) that, because of structural and functional similarities, form tissues.

Groups of different kinds of tissues working together to perform a particular function for the plant or animal are called organs.

Examples of plant organs are leaf, stem, roots, flowers, fruits and seeds.

Examples of a few organs found in the human body are larynx, trachea or windpipe and lungs.

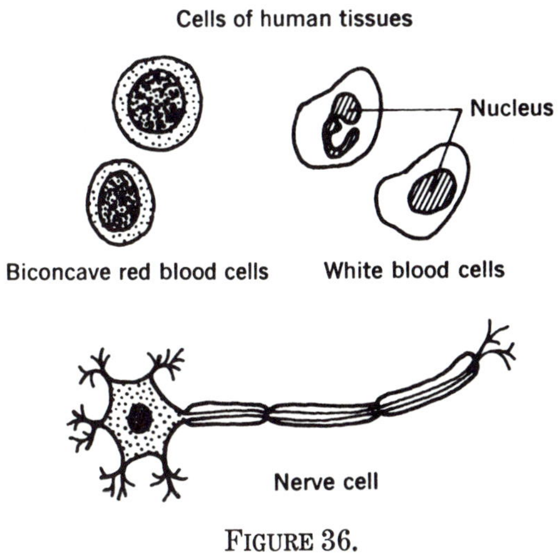

FIGURE 36.

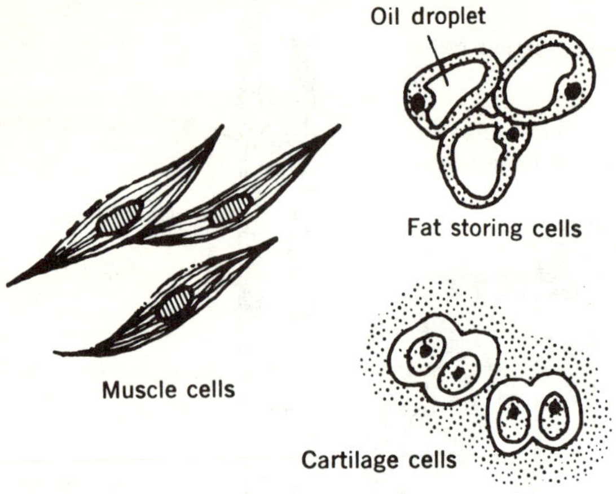

FIGURE 37. More cells of human tissue

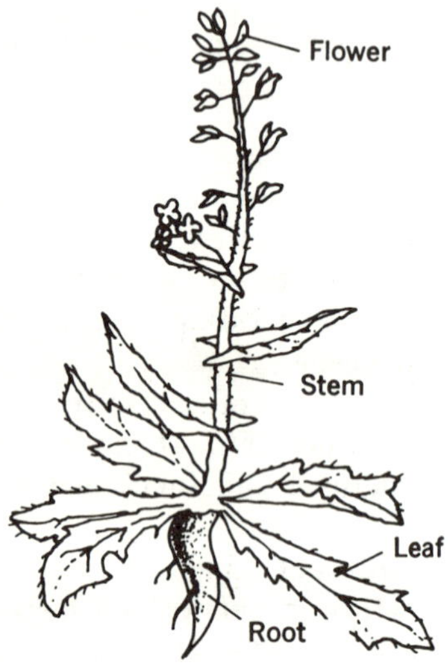

FIGURE 38. Plant organs

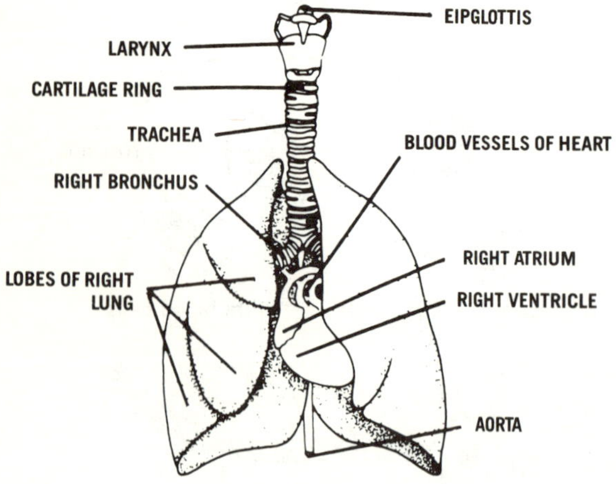

FIGURE 39. Diagram of lungs showing position of heart.

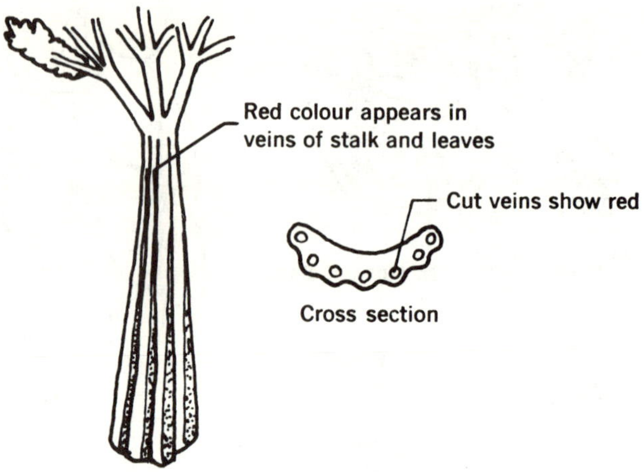

FIGURE 40. Conductive system in celery

A group of organs working together to perform a specific life function is called a system.

A simple experiment which can be performed at home will illustrate the conductive system in plants. Place a stalk of celery (leaves included) in a solution of red ink and water for several hours. Observe the red color which apears in *tubes* or *veins* in the stalk (stem) and leaves. Cut across a piece of the stalk and observe the row of red dots in Figure 40.

This experiment indicates the conductive system through which water containing dissolved minerals from the soil rises up through the stem to all other parts of the plant.

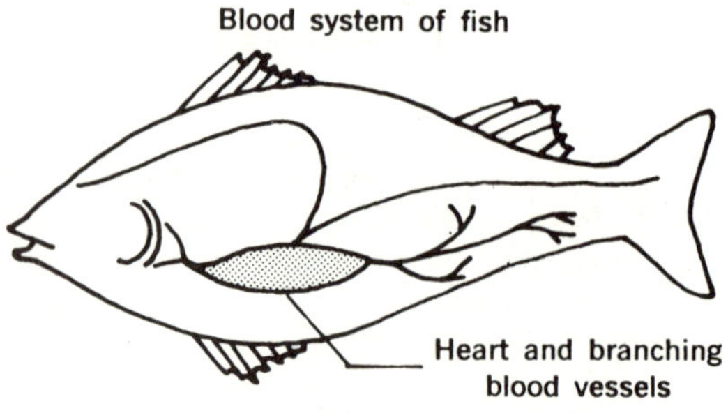

FIGURE 41.

In multicellular animals there are systems which have specialized functions.

The blood or **circulatory system** in fish is one example. A primitive heart and blood vessels (tubes) branching to all parts of the body are the organs which make up this system. Its function is to distribute blood to all cells in the fish. The blood carries digested food and oxygen to the cells and carries waste products away from the cells (to be eliminated).

In a more complex animal there are many different systems, each with a specialized job. We shall mention them briefly at this point:

Digestive system—to digest food.

Absorption system—to absorb digested food and necessary oxygen.

Circulatory system—to circulate or **deliver** digested food and oxygen to all cells **in the body** and to carry away gas and liquid waste products and distribute heat.

Respiratory system—to take in oxygen and release carbon dioxide and excess water vapor from the body.

Excretory system—to rid the body of wastes.

Reproductive system—to produce another generation of human beings.

Nervous system—to control activities of the body.

Skeletal system—to provide for support, protection, and locomotion.

Let us analyze the digestive system to show the organs of which it is composed: the mouth, gullet or esophagus, stomach and intestines. There are glands that produce chemicals (catalysts) which aid the digestive organs in their function.

The sum total of a group of systems working together results in a complete organism, otherwise called a plant or animal.

Over a million varieties of living things have been discovered on our earth. In order that they be studied and recognized they must be grouped in some orderly fashion, or in other words, classified.

For example, books in a library are not just placed on shelves in any haphazard fashion. They are divided first into large general groups, that is, fiction and non-fiction. Each of these groups is divided further into subdivisions. For example, non-fiction are grouped according to their main topics: biography, history, science, art, etc. **Each** of these divisions is further subdivided; for example, science books are classified according to their specialties: astronomy, biology, chemistry, physiology, etc. Subdivisions finally narrow down to individual books.

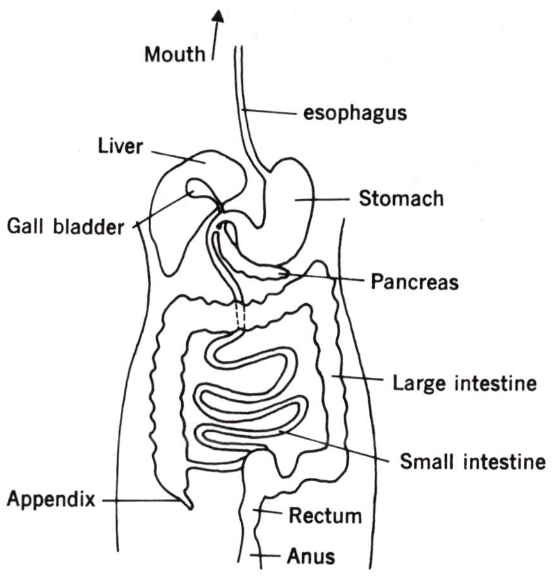

FIGURE 42. Human digestive system

Our modern **system of classification or taxonomy** of all living things was devised by LINNAEUS (Carl von Linné) in the latter part of the eighteenth century. He used Latin names because Latin was the universal language of scholars. He gave names to plants and animals that are short and often descriptive in nature.

The largest groups of living things are the Plant and Animal kingdoms. Each of the kingdoms is divided and subdivided depending first on general and then more detailed structural and functional similarities. The smallest subdivision is the individual plant or animal. For example: The classification of Man.

Kingdom—Animal
Phylum—Chordate (with a skeletal axis)
Subphylum—Vertebrate (having backbone)
Class— Mammal (mammary glands, young born alive, four-chambered heart, have hair)
Order—Primate ("first"; opposable thumb)
Family—Hominidae (mankind)
Genus—Homo (human being)
Species—Sapiens (wise, discerning)
Man—Homo sapiens

See Appendix: Biology Helps Digestive System of the Bullfrog, Fig. A; Human Skeleton, Fig. B.

CHAPTER THIRTEEN

THE NEW MATH

For many years the major emphasis in elementary school mathematics has been on the mechanical aspects of computation. This has created the erroneous and misleading idea that this is all there is to mathematics.

You can become very skillful in computation (learning to add, subtract, multiply, and divide) without really understanding why these mathematical processes work. With the advent of high-speed computers and desk calculators, the ability to compute is fast becoming an unsalable skill.

The tremendous advances taking place in mathematics and science demand that today's children must be taught the *why* as well as the *how* of mathematics. Today's society and, even more so, future societies will face problems that cannot even be predicted today. These problems will not be solved by rote-learned facts alone, but by the ability to think mathematically and to use mathematical methods of attacking the problems. In fact, these new problems will undoubtedly involve and require more new and as yet unknown mathematics.

This chapter is designed to help you go beyond the routine computational skills—to understand the basic structure of and organization of elementary mathematical systems. In most cases, simple illustrations from the physical world are used to help you easily understand the mathematical ideas and concepts.

Your study will be interesting and rewarding if you accept the attitude "Why does it work?" rather than "How does it work?"

Sets, Numbers, Numeration

SETS

In mathematics we are often concerned not with a single object, but with a collection of objects. For example, we hear about and speak of a collection of paintings, a row of chairs, or a set of dishes. Each of these collections is an example of a *set.*

A **set** is simply a collection of things considered as a single entity.

Definition 1:

The things contained in a given set are called **members** or **elements** of the set.

The members of a collection of paintings are the individual paintings in that set. The members of a row of chairs are the individual chairs in that row. The members of a set of dishes are the individual cups, saucers, plates, etc., in that set.

One method of naming sets is shown below.

$$A = \{\text{Bob, Bill, Tom}\}$$

This is read, "A is the set whose members are Bob, Bill, and Tom." Capital letters are usually used to denote sets. The braces, { }, merely denote a set. The names of the members of the set are listed, separated by commas, and then enclosed within braces.

An alternate use of the brace notation is illustrated below.

W = {Monday, Tuesday, Wednesday, Thursday, Friday, Saturday, Sunday}
W = {the days of the week}

The first of these examples lists or tabulates the members of the set W. In the second example a descriptive phrase is enclosed within braces. The latter example is read, "W is the set of days of the week."

Using the set W above, we can say:

Monday *is a member of* W.
Saturday *is a member of* W.

We can abbreviate the phrase "is a member of" by using the Greek letter epsilon, ε, to stand for this phrase. Then we can say:

Monday ε W
Saturday ε W

The slash line or slant bar, /, is often used to negate the meaning of a mathematical symbol. The mathematical symbol ∉ is read, "is not a member of." For set W we can then say:

John ∉ W (John is not a member of W.)
April ∉ W (April is not a member of W.)

The symbols denoting the individual members of a set are generally lower-case letters of our alphabet, such as *a, b, c, d,* and so on.

Exercises 1:

Name the members of each of the following sets.

1. The set of the Great Lakes
2. The set of the last 3 months of the year
3. The set of states in the U.S. bordering the Gulf of Mexico.
4. The set of men over 15 feet tall
5. The set of months in a year
6. The set of states in the U.S. whose names begin with the letter A

Write a description of each of the following sets.

7. $A = \{a,b,c,d\}$
8. $B = \{a,e,i,o,u\}$
9. $C = \{x,y,z\}$

Use the sets given in questions 7–9 above and insert the symbol ε or ∉ in each blank to make the following sentences true.

10. a__A 13. y__A
11. a__B 14. y__B
12. a__C 15. y__C

THE EMPTY SET

Perhaps the preceding Exercise 4 (the set of men over 15 feet tall) caused you to wonder whether a set had been described. Although it seems natural to think of a set as having at least 2 numbers, it is mathematically convenient to consider a single object as a set (*a unit set*). It is also convenient to consider a collection containing no members as a set, called the *empty* set, or the null set, or the void set.

Definition 2:
The empty set is the set that contains no members.

The empty set is usually denoted by Ø (a letter from the Scandinavian alphabet). Ø is read, "the empty set." We can also indicate the absence of members by denoting the empty set by { }.

Other examples of the empty set are: the set of cookies in an empty cookie jar; the set of all living men over 200 years old; or the set of months in our year which contain more than 50 years.

SUBSETS

It is often necessary to think of sets that are "part of" another set or are "sets within a set." The set of chairs (C) in a room is a set within the set of all pieces of furniture (F) in that room. Obviously, every chair in the room is a member of set C and also a member of set F. This leads to the idea of a subset.

Definition 3:
"Set A is a **subset** of set B" means that every member of set A is also a member of set B.

An equivalent definition of a subset might be:

Definition 4:
"Set A is a **subset** of set B" if set A contains no member that is not also in set B.

We can abbreviate the phrase "is a subset of" by using the conventional symbol $\subset$. $A \subset B$ means "set A is a subset of set B," or simply "A is a subset of B."

By using the symbolism already established, we can concisely state Definition 1–3 as follows:

$A \subset B$ if for every $x \in A$ then $x \in B$.

Consider the following sets.

$R = \{a,b,c,d,e\}$

$S = \{a,c,e\}$

Every member of set S is also a member of set R. Hence, $S \subset R$. R is not a subset of S ($R \not\subset S$) because R contains members (b and d) which are not members of S.

All of the possible subsets of set S are given below.

$\{a\} \subset S$	$\{a,c\} \subset S$
$\{c\} \subset S$	$\{a,e\} \subset S$
$\{e\} \subset S$	$\{c,e\} \subset S$
$\{\ \} \subset S$	$\{a,c,e\} \subset S$

The last two subsets of S, as listed above, can lead us to some general conclusions about the subset relation.

Is the empty set a subset of every set? By Definition 1–4, the empty set contains no member which is not also a member of any given set. Hence, we say that *the empty set is a subset of every set.*

Since $S = \{a,c,e\}$ and $\{a,c,e\} \subset S$, we are tempted to ask: "Is every set a subset of itself?" Regardless of the set we choose, every member of the set is obviously a member of the set. Hence, we say that *every set is a subset of itself.*

Exercises 2:

Consider the following sets. Then write the symbol $\subset$ or $\not\subset$ in each blank so that the following become true sentences.

$A = \{a,b,c,d,e\}$ $B = \{b,d,e,g\}$ $C = \{b,d\}$

1. B__A	4. C__B
2. B__C	5. C__A
3. B__B	6. $\emptyset$__C

List all of the possible subsets of each of the following sets.

7. $D = \{x,y\}$
8. $E = \{a,b,c,d\}$

Compare the number of subsets and the number of members of set D, E, and the previously used set $S = \{a,c,e\}$.

9. Can you discover a formula for finding the number of subsets of any set?

SET EQUALITY

Consider the following sets.

$A = \{r,s,t,u\}$

$B = \{t,r,u,s\}$

Since each set contains identically the same members, we say that set A *is equal to set* B or simply $A = B$.

Definition 5:

If A and B are names for sets, $A = B$ means that set A has identically the same members as set B, or that A and B are two names for the same set.

Note that the order in which the members are named does not matter. For example, $\{a,b,c\} = \{c,a,b\} = \{b,a,c\}$.

Whenever the equal sign ($=$) is used, as in $A = B$ or $1 + 2 = 3$, it means that the symbols on either side of it name precisely the same thing.

Consider the following sets.

$K = \{p,q,r,s\}$

$M = \{r,v,x,z\}$

Since K and M do not contain identically the same members, we say K *is not equal to* M, or simply $K \neq M$.

Exercises 3:

Use the sets named below and write $=$ or $\neq$ in each blank so that true sentences result.

$A = \{1,2,3,4\}$

$B = \{a,e,i,o,u\}$

$C = \{\text{the first four counting numbers}\}$

$D = \{\text{the vowels in our alphabet}\}$

$E = \{3,2,1,4\}$

$F = \{o,i,a,w\}$

1. A__B	6. B__C
2. A__C	7. B__D
3. A__D	8. B__E
4. A__E	9. B__F
5. A__F	10. E__F

EQUIVALENT SETS

Suppose you had a set of cups and a set of saucers. Someone asks, "Are there more cups or more saucers?" Would you have to count the objects in each set to answer the question?

All you need do is place one cup on each saucer until all of the members of one of the sets have been used. If there are some cups left over, then there are more cups than saucers. If there are some saucers left over, then there are more saucers. In case each cup is paired with one and only one saucer and each saucer is paired with one and only one cup, we say the sets are matched one-to-one or that there is a one-to-one correspondence between the sets.

Definition 6:

There is a **one-to-one correspondence** between sets A and B if every member of A is paired with one member of B and every member of B is paired with one member of A.

The following illustration shows the six ways of establishing a one-to-one correspondence between the two sets.

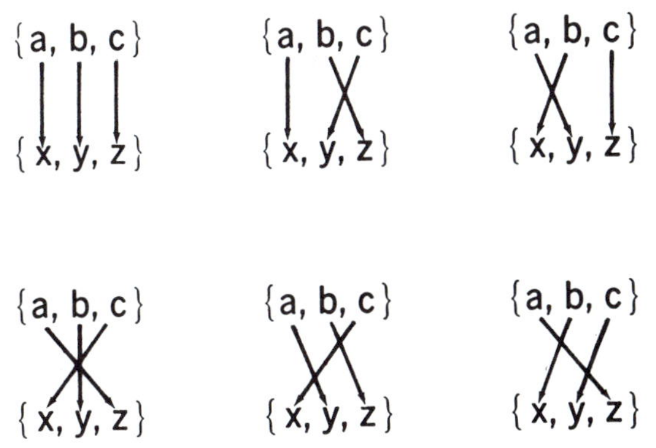

The existence of a one-to-one correspondence between two sets has nothing to do with the way in which the pairing is done.

Definition 7:

Two sets are **equivalent** if there is a one-to-one correspondence between the two sets.

Note that the idea of equivalent sets is not the same as that of equal sets. That is, two sets are equal if they have identically the same members. Two equivalent sets may have different members just so there exists a one-to-one correspondence between them. For example:

$\{a,b,c,d\}$ is equivalent to $\{r,s,t,u\}$.
$\{a,b,c,d\}$ is not equal to $\{r,s,t,u\}$.
$\{a,b,c,d\}$ is equal to $\{c,a,d,b\}$.
$\{a,b,c,d\}$ is equivalent to $\{c,a,d,b\}$.

Exercises 4:

Draw matching lines to show a one-to-one correspondence between the sets in each pair.

1. $\{a,b,c,d\}$

   $\{w,x,y,z\}$
2. $\{1,2,3,4,5,6\}$

   $\{2,4,6,8,10,12\}$

NUMBERS

Let us consider the collection of all sets that are equivalent to $\{a,b,c\}$. For convenience, let us denote a set by drawing a ring around the collection of objects.

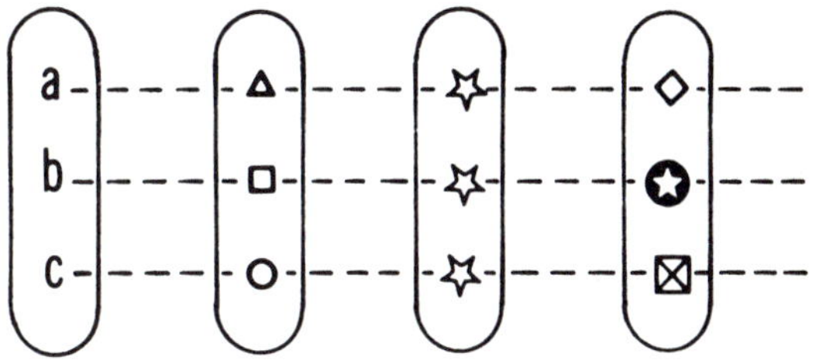

The only thing alike about all of these sets is that their members can be matched one-to-one. That is, they are equivalent sets. The thing that is alike about these sets is called the *number three.*

Of course, other sets belong to this collection also—the set of wheels on a tricycle, the set of people in a trio, and the set of sides of a triangle.

The number three has many names—III, $2 + 1$, 3, and many more. Each of these names is called a **numeral.** A *numeral* is a name for a number. The simplest numeral for the number three is 3.

With every collection of equivalent sets is associated a number, and with each number is associated a simplest numeral.

Set	*Number*	*Simplest Numeral*
$\{\ \}$	zero	0
$\{a\}$	one	1
$\{c,d\}$	two	2
$\{x,y,z\}$	three	3
•	•	•
•	•	•
•	•	•

The dots indicate that we can extend each of the above columns. The set of numbers so derived is called the set of cardinal numbers or the set of *whole numbers*.

Since we usually begin counting "one, two, three, . . ." we call {1,2,3,4,5, . . .} the set of counting numbers or the set of *natural numbers*.

Set of whole numbers: {0,1,2,3,4, . . .}
Set of natural numbers: {1,2,3,4, . . .}

Exercises 5:

Write the simplest numeral for the number associated with each of the following sets.

1. {*q,r,s,t,w,x,y,z*}
2. {the days of the week}
3. {1,2,3,4,5,6,7,8,9}
4. {the months of the year}
5. {all three-dollar bills}
6. {John, James, Jean, Joe}
7. {Presidents of the U.S.}
8. {states in the U.S.}

BASE-TEN NUMERATION

Because of the random arrangement of the members of the set shown below, you may have a hard time determining quickly the number of members in the set.

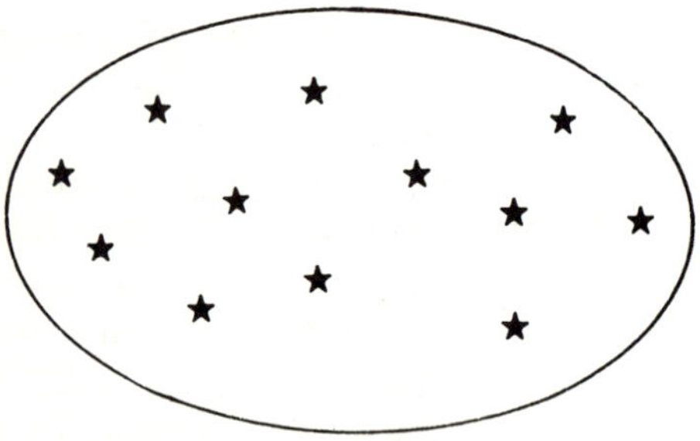

It is easier to determine the number of members if they are arranged as follows.

Since man has ten fingers, he probably matched members of a set one-to-one with his fingers and thereby grouped the objects as follows.

This led to his writing the symbol 12 to mean 1 set of ten and 2 more.

Finally it dawned on man that he could make any kind of grouping in his mind. Then he might group the members and name the number of members in any of the following ways.

10_{twelve}
1 twelve, no more

11_{eleven}
1 eleven, 1 more

12_{ten}
1 ten, 2 more

13_{nine}
1 nine, 3 more

14_{eight}
1 eight, 4 more

15_{seven}
1 seven, 5 more

20_{six}
2 sixes, no more

22_{five}
2 fives, 2 more

30_{four}
3 fours, no more

110_{three}
1 three-three,
1 three, no more

1100_{two}
1 two-two-two,
1 two-two, no
twos, no more

Through the years man has found use for several of these methods of naming the number of the set. But his early ten-finger matching was deep-seated in his memory, and he most frequently grouped by tens. It is this grouping that leads to the *decimal* or *base-ten numeration* system.

Definition 8:

A *numeration system* is a planned scheme or way of naming numbers.

Let us agree that when a numeral is written without a number word to the lower right, such as 23, we shall mean base ten or grouping by tens. Then the numeral 23 means:

2 tens and 3 more
or
2 tens and 3 ones

Since 2 tens can be thought of as 2×10, and 3 ones can be thought of as 3×1, let us name 23 as follows:

$23 = (2 \times 10) + (3 \times 1)$

This is called the *expanded numeral* or *the expanded notation* for 23.

How can we name 427 in expanded notation? The numeral 427 means 4 ten-tens, 2 tens, and 7 ones. Since a ten-ten means 10×10 or 100, we can show the expanded notation for 427 as follows.

$427 = (4 \times 100) + (2 \times 10) + (7 \times 1)$

In a similar way we can write the expanded numeral for 3256 as follows.

3 ten-ten-tens, 2 ten-tens, 5 tens, and 6 ones
$(3 \times 10 \times 10 \times 10) + (2\times 10 \times 10) + (5 \times 10) + (6 \times 1)$
or
$(3 \times 1000) + (2 \times 100) + (5 \times 10) + (6 \times 1)$

Exercises 6:

Write the simplest numeral for each of the following.

1. $(8 \times 10) + (5 \times 1)$
2. $(5 \times 100) + (3 \times 10) + (9 \times 1)$
3. $(7 \times 100) + (3 \times 10) + (0 \times 1)$
4. $(7 \times 100) + (7 \times 10) + (7 \times 1)$
5. $(3 \times 1000 + (4 \times 100) + (3 \times 10) + (2 \times 1)$
6. $(6 \times 1000) + (0 \times 100) + (5 \times 10) + (1 \times 1)$

Write the expanded numeral for each of the following.

7. 46	10. 82
8. 124	11. 3426
9. 629	12. 2041

EXPONENTS

It is inconvenient to write such things as $10 \times 10 \times 10$ and $5\times 5 \times 5 \times 5$ whenever we express a number in expanded notation. Let us invent a short way of saying such things.

In $10 \times 10 \times 10$ we see that 10 is used 3 times in the multiplication. So let us write 10^3 to mean $10 \times 10 \times 10$.

Then $5 \times 5 \times 5 \times 5 = 5^4$ since 5 is used 4 times in the multiplication.

In 10^3, the number 10 is called the *base,* the number 3 is called the *exponent,* and the number named by 10^3 is called the *power.*

Base	*Exponent*
The number used in the multiplication	How many times the base is used

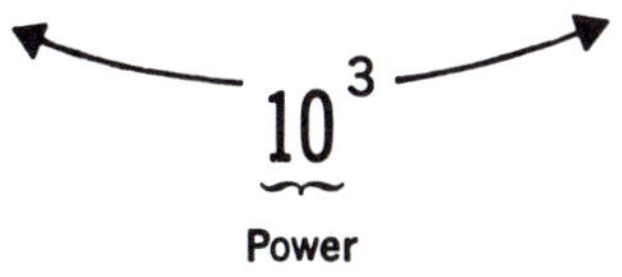

Exercises 7:

Name each of the following as a power.

1. $10 \times 10 \times 10 \times 10 \times 10$
2. 10×10
3. $10 \times 10 \times 10 \times 10$
4. $7 \times 7 \times 7 \times 7$
5. $4 \times 4 \times 4 \times 4 \times 4 \times 4$

Write the meaning of each of the following.

6. 10^3	8. 10^7
7. 10^5	9. 6^4

PLACE VALUE

We have already seen that the place a symbol occupies in the simplest numeral for a number indicates a specific value. For example:

$$328 = (3 \times 10 \times 10) + (2 \times 10) + (8 \times 1)$$
or
$$= (3 \times 10^2) + (2 \times 10^1) + (8 \times 1)$$

Then we can show the meaning of greater numbers by following this pattern of grouping by tens.

$3256 = (3 \times 10^3) + (2 \times 10^2) + (5 \times 10^1) + (6 \times 1)$

$41865 = (4 \times 10^4) + (1 \times 10^3) + (8 \times 10^2) + (6 \times 10^1) + (5 \times 1)$

From this we develop place value in base-ten numeration as indicated in the following illustration.

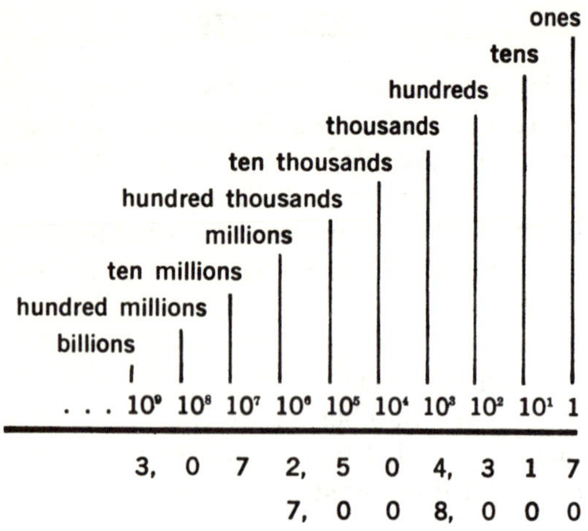

The commas are inserted merely to make it easy to read a numeral. They give no meaning whatsoever to the numeral.

The first numeral above is read: *three billion, seventy-two million, five hundred four thousand, three hundred seventeen.*

The second numeral above is read: *seven million, eight thousand.*

Exercises 8:

Write the simplest numeral for each of the following.

1. one billion, one hundred million, two thousand, eight hundred twenty-six

2. five million, one

3. seven hundred twelve thousand, three hundred nine

4. fifty-two million, eighteen

Addition and Subtraction of Whole Numbers

UNION OF SETS

We are accustomed to joining sets in our daily activities. For example, when you put some coins in your purse, you are joining two sets of coins—the set of coins already in your purse and the set of coins about to be put in your purse. This, and many more examples, form the basis for the idea of the *union* of two sets.

Definition 9:

The **union** of set A and set B, denoted by $A \cup B$, is the set of all objects that are members of set A, of set B, or of both set A and set B.

Consider the following sets.

$R = \{a,b,c,d\}$
$S = \{r,s,t\}$
$T = \{c,d,e,f\}$

According to the definition of union, we can form the following sets.

$R \cup S = \{a,b,c,d,r,s,t\}$
$R \cup T = \{a,b,c,d,e,f\}$
$S \cup T = \{r,s,t,c,d,e,f\}$

For $R \cup T$ there is no need of repeating the names of members c and d. For example, suppose you are referring to a set of 3 girls—named Jane, Mary, and Pam. Then {Jane, Mary, Pam, Mary} is correct but not preferred since Mary is named twice and there are only 3 girls in the set.

Another way of illustrating sets and set operations is to use Venn diagrams. A Venn diagram is merely a closed figure used to denote the set of all points within the figure.

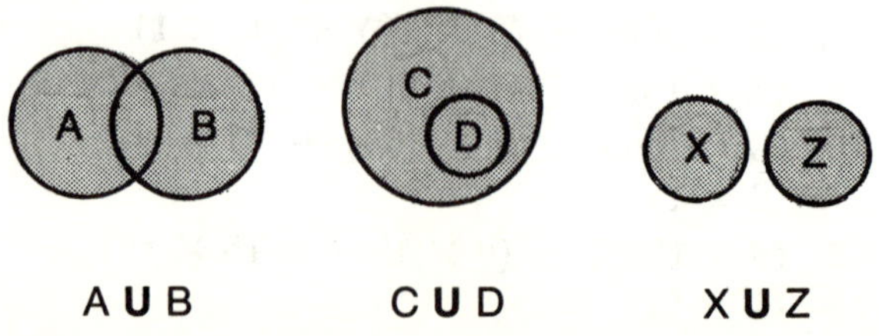

The shaded region in each of these illustrations indicates A ∪ B, C ∪ D and X ∪ Z. Note that the union of two sets includes all of the members in both of the sets.

Exercises 9:

Use the following sets to form the union of each pair of sets given below.

$K = \{3,5,7,9\}$ $M = \{2,4,6,8\}$
$J = \{1,2,3\}$ $N = \{0,5,9\}$

1. $J \cup K$
2. $K \cup M$
3. $K \cup N$
4. $J \cup M$
5. $J \cup N$
6. $M \cup N$
7. $N \cup M$
8. $K \cup K$

INTERSECTION OF SETS

Suppose a teacher asked a class, "How many of you went to the game last night?" Then several children raised their hands. Those who raised their hands are members of the set of children in the class *and* they are also members of the set of all children who went to the game last night.

By using a Venn diagram we can illustrate this situation. Let A = {all children in the class} and let B = {all children who went to the game last night}.

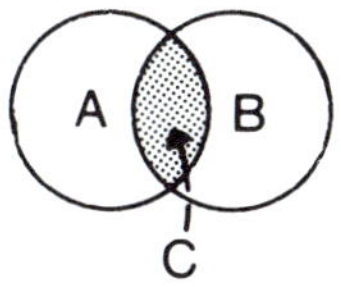

Then C = {all children in A and also in B}, and C is called the intersection of A and B.

Definition 10:

The **intersection** of set A and set B, denoted by $A \cap B$, is the set of all objects that are members of both set A *and set* B.

For example, the shaded region in each of the following illustrations represents $A \cap B$.

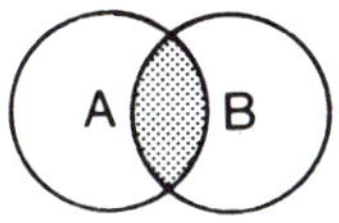

A∩B

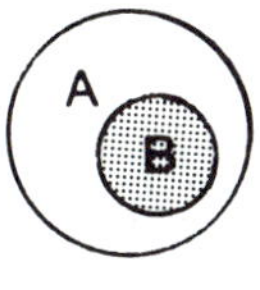

A∩B

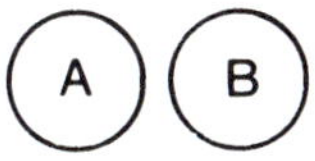

A∩B=∅

Consider the following sets.

$X = \{g,h,i,j\}$
$Y = \{e,f,g,h\}$
$Z = \{a,b,c,d,e\}$

Then: $X \cap Y = \{g,h\}$
$X \cap Z = \emptyset$
$Y \cap Z = \{e\}$
$X \cap X = \{g,h,i,j\}$

Exercises 10:

Use the following sets to form the intersection of each pair of sets given below.

$C = \{2,3,4,5,6\}$
$D = \{1,2,3,7,8\}$
$E = \{3,4,5,6\}$
$F = \{7,8,9,10\}$

1. $C \cap D$
2. $D \cap C$
3. $C \cap E$
4. $C \cap F$
5. $D \cap E$
6. $D \cap F$
7. $E \cap F$
8. $E \cap E$

DISJOINT SETS

It is obvious that some sets have no members in common—such as $\{a,b,c\}$ and $\{r,s,t\}$.

Definition 11:

Set A and set B are called disjoint sets if they have no members in common. Or, set A and set B are *disjoint sets* if $A \cap B = \emptyset$.

In the following diagram, set A and set B do not intersect. Therefore, A and B are disjoint sets.

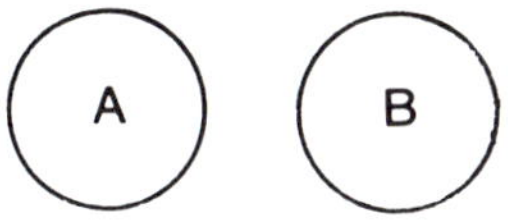

A∩B=∅

Consider the following sets.

$R = \{f,g,h,j\}$
$S = \{a,b,c\}$
$T = \{a,h,j\}$

Sets R and S have no members in common. Hence, R and S are disjoint sets.

Sets R and T are not disjoint sets since they both have h and j as members. Sets S and T are not disjoint sets since they both have a as a member.

Exercises 11:

Tell whether each statement below is *true* or *false*.

1. $\{q,r,s,t\}$ and $\{x,y,z\}$ are disjoint sets.
2. If $Q \cap R = \emptyset$, then Q and R are disjoint sets.
3. If $Q \subset R$, then Q and R are disjoint sets.

4. If $Q \subset R$ and $R \subset Q$, then $R = Q$.
5. If $R \cup Q = R$, then $Q \subset R$.
6. If $R \cap Q = R$, then $R \subset Q$.
7. If $R \cap Q = R \cup Q$, then $R = Q$.
8. If $C \cap D = \{5\}$, then $5 \varepsilon C$ and $5 \varepsilon D$.
9. If $C \cup D = \{3,4,5,6,7\}$, and $5 \varepsilon C$ and $5 \varepsilon D$.
10. If $x \varepsilon H$, then $x \varepsilon H \cup G$.

ADDITION

We already know that with each set there is associated a number. Let us use the symbol n(A) to mean "the number of set A." It is important to note that n(A) is a name for a number.

For $A = \{a,b,c\}$, we have n$(A) = 3$.
For $B = \{g,h\}$, we have n$(B) = 2$.

Let us begin with two disjoint sets, C and D, and find $C \cup D$. That is, we will join set D to set C.

C={□, △, ☆} D={○, ✪}

CUD={□, △, ☆, ○, ✪}

n$(C) = 3$ n$(D) = 2$
n$(C \cup D) = 5$

From this illustration we can say what is meant by addition of whole numbers.

Definition 12:

For *disjoint sets A and B*, the **sum** of n(A) and n(B), denoted by n(A) + n(B), is n$(A \cup B)$ or the number of the union set.

For the above illustration, we have n$(C) = 3$, n$(D) = 2$, and n$(C \cup D) = 5$.

$$n(C) + n(D) = n(C \cup D)$$
$$3 + 2 = 5$$

In an addition statement, the numbers being added are called **addends** and the resulting number is called the **sum.**

Caution! We *add numbers,* not sets. We write 3 + 2, but we do not write $A + B$ for sets. We find the *union of sets,* not numbers. We write $A \cup B$, but we do not write $5 \cup 4$.

To find the sum of 6 and 4, we could think of disjoint sets A and B such that n$(A) = 6$ and n$(B) = 4$. Suitable sets might be:

$A = \{a,b,c,d,e,f\}$
$B = \{r,s,t,u\}$
$A \cup B = \{a,b,c,d,e,f,r,s,t,u\}$

$$n(A) + n(B) = n(A \cup B)$$
$$6 + 4 = 10$$

The numbers six and four are addends. The number ten is the sum. The numerals 6 + 4 and 10 are two names for the sum. The numeral 10 is the simplest name for the number ten.

Exercises 12:

Find each sum.

1.	6 +5	7 +3	8 +4	9 +5	7 +6
2.	4 +3	5 +7	8 +6	2 +8	9 +9
3.	7 +9	5 +5	8 +8	4 +5	7 +8
4.	6 +9	4 +9	9 +3	7 +4	5 +8
5.	3 +8	1 +9	6 +4	7 +7	6 +6

ADDITION IS COMMUTATIVE

If you are to join two sets, you may wonder which set to join to which. Does the order of joining the sets change the union set? Let us examine such a situation.

A={□, ○, △} ← join B to A — B={a, b, c, d}

AUB={□, ○, △, a, b, c, d}

$$n(A) + n(B) = n(A \cup B)$$
$$3 + 4 = 7$$

Now let us reverse the order of joining the two sets.

A={□, ○, △} — join A to B → B={a, b, c, d}

BUA={□, ○, △, a, b, c, d}

$$n(B) + n(A) = n(B \cup A)$$
$$4 + 3 = 7$$

We notice that the union set is unchanged when the order of joining is reversed. We also note the following.

$$3 + 4 = 7 \text{ and } 4 + 3 = 7$$
or
$$3 + 4 = 4 + 3$$

The order of the addends can be changed but the sum remains the same. That is,

For all whole numbers a and b.

$$a + b = b + a.$$

We call this idea the *commutative property of addition.* Or we say that *addition is commutative.*

The phrase "for all whole numbers a and b" means that a and b can be replaced by numerals for any numbers in the set of whole numbers. They may be replaced by the same numeral or by different numerals. When a, b, or any other symbol is used in this manner, it is called a **placeholder** or a **variable** over a specified set of numbers.

Even though we may not know the sum of 557 and 3892, we know the following is true because addition is commutative.

$$557 + 3892 = 3892 + 557$$

Exercises 13:

Think of doing one activity of each pair given below and then doing the other. Do the following pairs illustrate a commutative property?

1. Put on your sock; put on your shoe
2. Take two steps forward; take two steps backward
3. Swim; eat
4. Write the letter "O"; then write the letter "N"
5. Go outside; close the door
6. Eat; brush your teeth

Complete each of the following sentences by using the commutative property of addition.

7. 3 + 7 = 7 + __
8. __ + 15 = 15 + 8
9. 36 + __ = 17 + 36
10. 156 + 13 = __ + 156
11. 129 + 47 = __ + __
12. __ + __ = 218 + 326
13. 327 + __ = 56 + __
14. 651 + 87 = __ + __

IDENTITY NUMBER OF ADDITION

Study the following unions of sets.

$$\{\ \} \cup \{a,b,c\} = \{a,b,c\}$$
$$\{a,b,c\} \cup \{\ \} = \{a,b,c\}$$

Notice that joining the empty set to a given set, or joining a given set to the empty set, does not change the given set.

The addition statements that correspond to the set operations above are:

$$0 + 3 = 3$$
$$3 + 0 = 3$$

Are the following sentences true?

$7 + 0 = 7 \qquad 115 + 0 = 115 \qquad 721 = 0 + 721$

Adding zero to any whole number b, or adding any whole number b to zero, leaves the number b unchanged.

Since zero is the only number with this special property, the number zero is called the **identity element of addition.**

For any whole number b,

$$0 + b = b = b + 0.$$

ADDITION IS ASSOCIATIVE

There are occasions when we join three sets. For example, we might combine a set of forks, a set of spoons, and a set of knives to form a set of silverware.

We might join the spoons to the forks, and then join the knives. Or we might join the knives to the spoons, and then join this set to the forks. Does the method of joining the sets change the resulting set?

Consider joining these sets.

$A = \{a,b,c\} \qquad B = \{g,h,j,k\} \qquad C = \{t,v\}$

$A \cup B = \{a,b,c,g,h,j,k\} \qquad B \cup C = \{g,h,j,k,t,v\}$

$$(A \cup B) \cup C = \{a,b,c,g,h,j,k,t,v\}$$
$$A \cup (B \cup C) = \{a,b,c,g,h,j,k,t,v\}$$

The ( ) in the last two statements indicate which two sets are joined first.

$(A \cup B) \cup C$ means to find $A \cup B$ first.

$A \cup (B \cup C)$ means to find $B \cup C$ first.

Joining sets makes us think of addition. We can add only two numbers at a time. How can we find the sum of three numbers, such as 3, 4, and 2?

Let us use the pattern established for joining three sets.

$$\begin{aligned} 3 + 4 + 2 &= (3 + 4) + 2 \\ &= \quad 7 \quad + 2 \\ &= 9 \\ 3 + 4 + 2 &= 3 + (4 + 2) \\ &= 3 + \quad 6 \\ &= 9 \end{aligned}$$

The ( ) in $(3 + 4) + 2$ means that 4 was added to 3 first. The ( ) in $3 + (4 + 2)$ mean that 2 was added to 4 first.

When finding the sum of three numbers we can group the first two addends or the last two addends and always get the same sum.

This idea is called the **associative property of addition.** Or we say that *addition is associative.*

For all whole numbers a, b, and c,

$$(a + b) + c = a + (b + c).$$

We can add these first,

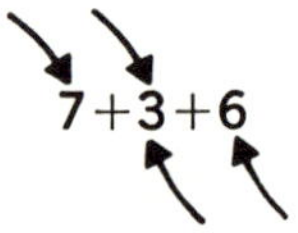

or we can add these first.

We can add these first,

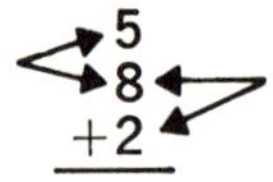

or add these first.

Notice that when we use the associative property of addition the order of the addends is *not* changed as it is when we use the commutative property of addition.

Exercises 14:

Three things are to be combined in each exercise below. Do not change their order, only the grouping. Do the combinations show an associative property?

1. Water, lemon juice, sugar
2. Sand, cement, water
3. Blue paint, red paint, green paint

Complete each of the following sentences by using the associative property of addition.

4. $5 + (7 + 6) = (5 + \_\_) + \_\_$
5. $17 + (15 + 32) = (\_\_ + \_\_) + 32$
6. $(9 + 8) + 7 = \_\_ + (\_\_ + \_\_)$
7. $\_\_ + (\_\_ + \_\_) = (13 + 12) + 6$
8. $(\_\_ + \_\_) + \_\_ = 72 + (31 + 46)$

Find each sum below by using whichever grouping of addends makes the addition easier.

9. $7 + 3 + 6$
10. $12 + 8 + 7$
11. $5 + 5 + 3$
12. $9 + 13 + 7$

USING THE PROPERTIES OF ADDITION

We can show that $5 + (9 + 7) = 7 + (9 + 5)$ without using any addition facts.

$$\begin{aligned} 5 + (9 + 7) &= (5 + 9) + 7 && \text{Assoc. prop.} \\ &= (9 + 5) + 7 && \text{Comm. prop.} \\ &= 7 + (9 + 5) && \text{Comm. prop.} \end{aligned}$$

Exercises 15:

Each of the following sentences is true because of the commutative property of addition, the associative property of addition, or both. Write the letter C, A, or both C and A to tell which property or properties are used.

1. $(9 + 8) + 3 = 9 + (8 + 3)$
2. $(9 + 8) + 3 = 3 + (9 + 8)$
3. $6 + (7 + 12) = 6 + (12 + 7)$
4. $6 + (7 + 12) = (6 + 12) + 7$
5. $(13 + 5) + 14 = 14 + (5 + 13)$
6. $(32 + 9) + 8 = 9 + (32 + 8)$
7. $13 + (9 + 7) = (13 + 9) + 7$
8. $13 + (9 + 7) = (9 + 7) + 13$
9. $13 + (9 + 7) = (13 + 7) + 9$
10. $a + (b + c) = (a + b) + c$

ORDER OF WHOLE NUMBERS

If two sets are not equivalent, then one set contains more members than the other set. For example:

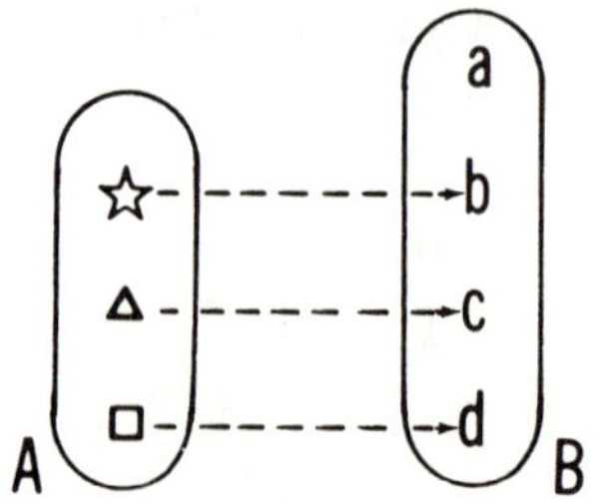

Set B has some members left unmatched after all of the members of set A have been matched. Set B has more members than set A, or set A

has fewer members than set B. We use the symbol $<$ (read: *is less than*) and the symbol $>$ (read: *is greater than*) when comparing the numbers of two sets that are not equivalent.

$$n(A) < n(B) \text{ or } n(B) > n(A)$$
$$3 < 4 \text{ or } 4 > 3$$

THE SUM OF MORE THAN TWO ADDENDS

We can save time and effort by looking for sums of ten, sums of one hundred, and so on, when finding the sum of more than two addends. Think of finding the simplest numeral for the following sum.

$$3 + 6 + 5 + 4 + 7$$

We know that addition is associative, so we can use any grouping we please. We also know that addition is commutative, so we can change the order of addends as we please. By using these two properties of addition, we can think of the addition as follows:

$$\begin{aligned} 3 + 6 + 5 + 4 + 7 &= (3 + 6) + (5 + 4) + 7 \\ &= (5 + 4) + (3 + 6) + 7 \\ &= (5 + 4) + (6 + 3) + 7 \\ &= 5 + (4 + 6) + (3 + 7) \\ &= 5 + 10 + 10 \\ &= 25 \end{aligned}$$

This type of thinking is used when we think about 3 + 6 + 5 + 4 + 7 as follows:

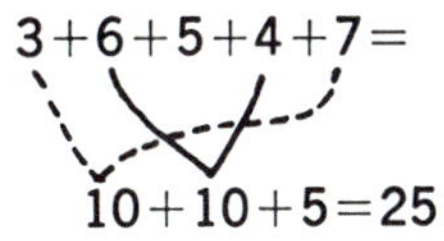

Exercises 16:
Find each sum. Look for sums of ten or one hundred.

1.	5 6 +5	8 2 +7	13 4 +7	25 32 +75	97 9 +3
2.	7 6 4 +3	4 5 5 +6	24 8 2 +6	19 7 1 +2	37 60 13 +40

THE ADDITION ALGORITHM

Everyday problems make us aware of the need to have an easy method for operating with greater numbers. For example, we may want to find the sum of 725 and 273. Both of these numbers have many names. We strive to name the numbers so that it is easy to find their sum.

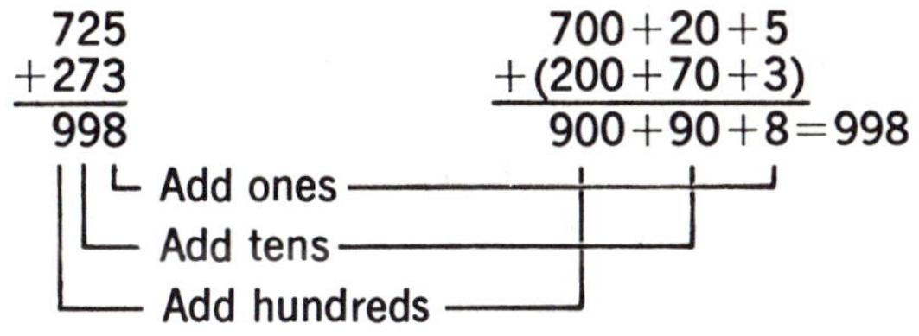

Another situation might require us to find the sum of 3528 and 4361.

$$\begin{array}{r} 3528 \\ +4361 \\ \hline 7889 \end{array} \qquad \begin{array}{r} 3000 + 500 + 20 + 8 \\ +(4000 + 300 + 60 + 1) \\ \hline 7000 + 800 + 80 + 9 = 7889 \end{array}$$

This procedure, or algorithm, of writing numerals and renaming numbers can be extended to finding the sum of greater numbers.

Exercises 17:
Find each sum.

1.	342 +536	3751 +4248	35285 +24713
2.	235 +542	5041 +3806	60027 +28951
3.	624 +65	1826 +153	1423 +36504
4.	43 +325	320 +6468	10726 +8070

RENAMING SUMS IN ADDITION

It may well be the case that the sum of the ones is greater than nine, or the sum of tens is greater than ninety, and so on. All we need do is rename such sums as shown in the following examples.

Rename the sum of the ones:

$$\begin{array}{r} 427 \\ +256 \\ \hline \end{array} \qquad \begin{array}{r} 400 + 20 + 7 \\ +(200 + 50 + 6) \\ \hline 600 + 70 + 13 = \end{array}$$

$$600 + 70 + (10 + 3) = \quad \text{Assoc. prop.}$$

$$600 + (70 + 10) + 3 =$$

$$600 + 80 + 3 = 683$$

Rename the sum of the tens:

$$\begin{array}{r} 3258 \\ +471 \\ \hline \end{array} \qquad \begin{array}{r} 3000 + 200 + 50 + 8 \\ +(400 + 70 + 1) \\ \hline 3000 + 600 + 120 + 9 = \end{array}$$

$$3000 + 600 + (100 + 20) + 9 = \quad \text{Assoc. prop.}$$

$$3000 + (600 + 100) + 20 + 9 =$$

$$3000 + 700 + 20 + 9 = 3729$$

Rename sums of tens and ones:

$$\begin{array}{r} 3456 \\ +2378 \\ \hline \end{array} \qquad \begin{array}{r} 3000 + 400 + 50 + 6 \\ +(2000 + 300 + 70 + 8) \\ \hline 5000 + 700 + 120 + 14 = \end{array}$$

$$5000 + 700 + (100 + 20) + (10 + 4) = \quad \text{Assoc. prop.}$$

$$5000 + (700 + 100) + (20 + 10) + 4 =$$

$$5000 + 800 + 30 + 4 = 5834$$

This procedure can be abbreviated by thinking about the addition as follows.

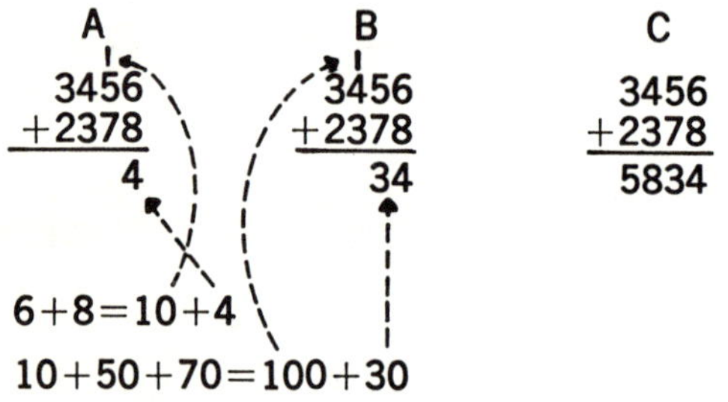

In *A*, 6 + 8 = 14 and 14 = 10 + 4. Write the 4 in ones place of the sum numeral and name the ten by writing a small reminder numeral 1 above the 5 in tens place of the first addend.

In *B*, 10 + 50 + 70 = 130 and 130 = 100 + 30. Write 3 in tens place of the sum numeral to name thirty; then write a reminder numeral 1 above the 4 in hundreds place in the first addend to name the hundred.

In *C*, the sum of hundreds is less than 1000 and the sum of the thousands is less than 10,000, so renaming is not needed.

The above procedure can be extended for addition of more than two numbers and for numbers whose numerals have a greater number of digits.

Exercises 18:

Find each sum.

1.	3426 +2595	61897 +17973	567428 +340754
2.	3058 +4963	47569 +10753	640596 +365437
3.	3246 503 +1174	97654 7965 +89348	297254 34135 +343048
4.	756 82 +1429	507 4296 +39204	30729 1075 +298264

INVERSE OPERATIONS

Many things we do can be "undone." If you take 2 steps backward, you can return to your original position by taking 2 steps forward. If you add 6 to a number, you can obtain the original number by subtracting 6 from the sum.

Any process or operation that "undoes" another process or operation is called an *inverse operation.*

Of course, there are some activities that cannot be undone. Talking cannot be undone by being silent.

Exercises 19:

For each activity given below, tell how to undo it.

1. Close your eyes
2. Stand up
3. Go to school
4. Close your book
5. Take 5 steps forward
6. Untie your shoe
7. Add seven
8. Subtract thirteen

SUBTRACTION

Three ways of thinking about the meaning of subtraction are explained below. The first two ways are helpful for interpreting a physical situation in terms of mathematics. However, their disadvantages will be pointed out. The last way defines subtraction for any mathematical situation.

1. Removing a subset:

John had 7 pennies and spent 4 of them. How many pennies did he have left?

We might illustrate the problem with Venn diagrams. Let $H = \{\text{pennies he had}\}$ and let $S = \{\text{pennies he spent}\}$. Each circular region in the following drawing represents a distinct penny.

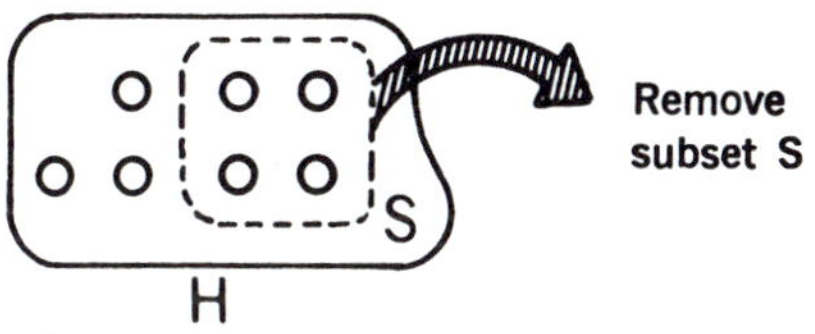

Definition 13:

The difference between $n(H)$ and $n(S)$, denoted by $n(H) - n(S)$, is the number of members in H but not in S.

When subset S is removed from set H, only 3 pennies remain.

$$n(H) - n(S) = 3$$
$$7 - 4 = 3$$

This idea is suitable only for whole numbers and the particular type of problem illustrated.

2. Comparing sets:

Bob has 5 stamps and Jane has 9 stamps. How many more stamps does Jane have than Bob?

Let each □ in the following diagram represent a distinct stamp. Let $B = \{\text{Bob's stamps}\}$ and let $J = \{\text{Jane's stamps}\}$.

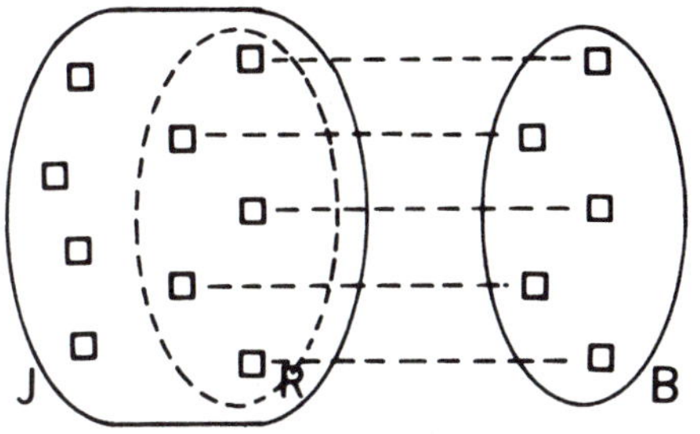

Select a subset R of J by establishing a one-to-one correspondence between set B and subset R. Since $n(R) = n(B)$, we can treat sets J and R as in the previous method.

$$n(J) = 9 \qquad n(B) = n(R) = 5$$
$$n(J) - n(B) = 4$$
$$9 - 5 = 4$$

We now have a method of treating two types of subtraction problems, but as yet subtraction is not defined for all numbers. That is, neither of the above methods is practical for fractional numbers, only for whole numbers.

3. Inverse of Addition:

By using either of the previous methods, we see that addition and subtraction are related—addition and subtraction undo each other. Addition and subtraction are inverse operations.

$$7 - 4 = 3 \text{ and } 3 + 4 = 7$$
$$9 - 5 = 4 \text{ and } 4 + 5 = 9$$

Definition 14:

For any numbers a, b, and c, if $c + b = a$, then c is the **difference** between a and b, denoted by $a - b$.

Note that $a - b$ names a number such that $(a - b) + b = a$. That is, we begin with the number a, subtract b, then add b, and the result is the number a with which we started. This shows the *do-undo* relationship between addition and subtraction.

Also note that $(a + b)$ names a number such that $(a + b) - b = a$. In this case subtraction undoes addition.

Exercises 20:

Write the simplest numeral for each of the following.

1. $(15 - 7) + 7$	5. $57 + (756 - 57)$
2. $621 + (754 - 621)$	6. $(39 - 17) + 17$
3. $(69 + 83) - 83$	7. $(312 + 179) - 179$
4. $(26 - 15) + 15$	8. $(r + s) - s$

Find the simplest numeral for each difference. Think of the corresponding addition if necessary.

9. $15 - 7$	13. $18 - 9$
10. $11 - 8$	14. $13 - 6$
11. $14 - 6$	15. $12 - 5$
12. $9 - 3$	16. $17 - 8$

FINDING UNNAMED ADDENDS

Think about solving the following problem. Randy bought 12 pieces of candy. He ate some of them and has 5 pieces left. How many pieces of candy did he eat?

We might think: If we add the number of pieces of candy he has left (5) to the number of pieces of candy he ate (□), the sum should be the number of pieces of candy he bought (12).

$$5 + \square = 12$$

Now how can we determine the simplest numeral to replace □ so that $5 + \square = 12$ becomes a true sentence?

Using the inverse idea between addition and subtraction, we have

$$5 + \square = 12 \text{ so } 12 - \square = 5.$$

We see that this approach is not too helpful. We might start over again by using the commutative property of addition.

$$5 + \square = 12 \text{ so } \square + 5 = 12$$

Now use the inverse idea.

$$\square + 5 = 12 \text{ so } 12 - 5 = \square$$
$$7 = \square$$

Randy ate 7 pieces of candy.

Note that we could have used any other symbol to represent the number of pieces of candy he ate. That is, we could have used △, ⬡, *a*, *b*, *c*, or any other symbol to hold a place for the numeral. Then, instead of $5 + \square = 12$, we could have written $5 + \triangle = 12$, $5 + ⬡ = 12$, $5 + a = 12$, $5 + b = 12$, $5 + c = 12$, and so on.

Exercises 21:

Find the unnamed addend in each of the following.

1. $9 + \square = 15$
2. $7 + x = 11$
3. $6 + n = 14$
4. $8 + \square = 16$
5. $5 + k = 14$
6. $3 + y = 12$

Write a number sentence for each problem. Solve the number sentence and write an answer for the problem.

7. A boy had 9 scout awards. He earned some more awards, and now he has 12 awards. How many more awards did he earn?
8. Jane made 15 cupcakes. Her brothers ate some of them and there are 7 left. How many of the cupcakes did her brothers eat?
9. Diane invited 12 children to her birthday party. If only 8 of the children came, how many were invited but did not attend?
10. Randy picked 7 apples from one tree and some from another tree. He picked 13 apples in all. How many did he pick from the second tree?

PROPERTIES OF SUBTRACTION

Is subtraction commutative? That is, can we change the order of the numbers without changing the difference?

$$7 - 3 = 4 \text{ but } 3 - 7$$

does not name a whole number, let alone being equal to 4. Hence, subtraction is *not* commutative.

Is subtraction associative? That is, can we change the grouping of the numbers without changing the difference?

$$(12 - 6) - 2 = 6 - 2 = 4$$
$$12 - (6 - 2) = 12 - 4 = 8$$

Since $4 \neq 8$, we see that subtraction is *not* associative.

ZERO IN SUBTRACTION

If the empty set (set of no members) is removed from $A = \{a,b,c,d\}$, the result is set A.

$$n(A) - n(\varnothing) = n(A)$$
$$4 - 0 = 4$$

Since this is true for all sets, it is also true for all whole numbers.

If set A is removed from itself, the result is the empty set.

$$n(A) - n(A) = n(\varnothing)$$
$$4 - 4 = 0$$

Since this is true for all sets, it is also true for all whole numbers.

We can summarize these two special properties of zero as follows:

For any whole number a,

$$a - 0 = a, \text{ and}$$
$$a - a = 0.$$

SUBTRACTION ALGORITHM

As with addition, we should like to devise a scheme of writing the numerals for greater numbers so that subtraction can be done quickly and easily. For example, we may want to find the difference between 758 and 326.

$$\begin{array}{r} 758 \\ -326 \\ \hline 432 \end{array} \qquad \begin{array}{r} 700+50+8 \\ -(300+20+6) \\ \hline 400+30+2=432 \end{array}$$

Subtract ones
Subtract tens
Subtract hundreds

Follow the same procedure for still greater numbers.

$$\begin{array}{r} 6975 \\ -3864 \\ \hline 3111 \end{array} \qquad \begin{array}{r} 6000 + 900 + 70 + 5 \\ -(3000 + 800 + 60 + 4) \\ \hline 3000 + 100 + 10 + 1 = 3111 \end{array}$$

Exercises 22:
Find each difference.

1.	756 −531	9384 −4150	67859 −21536
2.	526 −413	7925 −4912	82756 −62412
3.	837 −216	5987 −2852	49758 −15047

RENAMING NUMBERS IN SUBTRACTION

Think about subtracting 592 from 857.

$$\begin{array}{r} 857 \\ -592 \\ \hline \end{array} \qquad \begin{array}{r} 800 + 50 + 7 \\ -(500 + 90 + 2) \\ \hline ? + 5 \end{array}$$

We notice that 90 is greater than 50, and 50−90 does not name a whole number. But we can name any number in many different ways. Let us rename 857 so that we can subtract the tens.

$$\begin{array}{r} 857 \\ -592 \\ \hline \end{array} \qquad \begin{array}{r} 700 + 150 + 7 \\ -(500 + 90 + 2) \\ \hline 200 + 60 + 5 = 265 \end{array}$$

Another example might be the following, where we must rename 3548 so that we can subtract the ones.

$$\begin{array}{r} 3548 \\ -2419 \\ \hline \end{array} \qquad \begin{array}{r} 3000 + 500 + 30 + 18 \\ -(2000 + 400 + 10 + 9) \\ \hline 1000 + 100 + 20 + 9 = 1129 \end{array}$$

In still other cases we find it impossible to subtract ones or tens or hundreds, and so on, or any combination of these. We merely rename the number subtracted from until subtraction becomes possible in every place-value position.

$$\begin{array}{r} 3426 \\ -1358 \\ \hline \end{array} \qquad \begin{array}{r} 3000 + 400 + 10 + 16 \\ -(1000 + 300 + 50 + 8) \\ \hline ? + 8 \end{array}$$

Rename 3426 in another way so that subtraction of the tens is possible.

$$\begin{array}{r} 3426 \\ -1358 \\ \hline \end{array} \qquad \begin{array}{r} 3000 + 300 + 110 + 16 \\ -(1000 + 300 + 50 + 8) \\ \hline 2000 + 0 + 60 + 8 = 2068 \end{array}$$

This procedure may be abbreviated as shown in the following examples.

$$\begin{array}{r} 315 \\ -172 \\ \hline \end{array} \qquad \begin{array}{r} 200 + 110 + 5 \\ -(100 + 70 + 2) \\ \hline 100 - 40 - 3 \end{array} \qquad \begin{array}{r} \overset{2}{\cancel{3}}\overset{11}{\cancel{1}}5 \\ -172 \\ \hline 143 \end{array}$$

$$\begin{array}{r} 752 \\ -328 \\ \hline \end{array} \qquad \begin{array}{r} 700 + 40 + 12 \\ -(300 + 20 + 8) \\ \hline 400 + 20 + 8 \end{array} \qquad \begin{array}{r} 7\overset{4}{\cancel{5}}\overset{12}{\cancel{2}} \\ -328 \\ \hline 424 \end{array}$$

Exercises 23:
Find each difference.

1.	315 −163	3427 −2109	56349 −21467
2.	408 −226	5382 −3475	47009 −20858
3.	725 −537	6243 −3856	70000 −43197

CHECKING SUBTRACTION

Since addition and subtraction are inverse operations, we can use addition to check subtraction.

$$\begin{array}{r} \textit{Subtraction} \\ 715 \\ -432 \\ \hline 283 \end{array} \qquad \begin{array}{r} \textit{Check} \\ 432 \\ +283 \\ \hline 715 \end{array}$$

Exercises 24:
Check the subtraction in Exercises 23.

Multiplication and Division of Whole Numbers

USING SETS IN MULTIPLICATION

We have described addition of whole numbers in terms of joining disjoint sets. It is also possible to describe multiplication in this way.

A sandwich menu lists three kinds of meat—beef, ham, pork. You can have either white bread or rye bread. What are all the possible kinds of sandwiches if you choose one kind of meat and one kind of bread? The answer might be shown as follows.

(beef, white)	(ham, white)	(pork, white)
(beef, rye)	(ham, rye)	(pork, rye)

We notice that there are 3 choices of meat, 2 choices of bread, and 6 possible kinds of sandwiches. Somehow we have performed an operation on 2 and 3 to obtain 6.

Another example might involve finding the number of street intersections formed by the following situation.

{1st Ave., 2nd Ave., 3rd Ave., 4th Ave.}
{A St., B St., C St.}

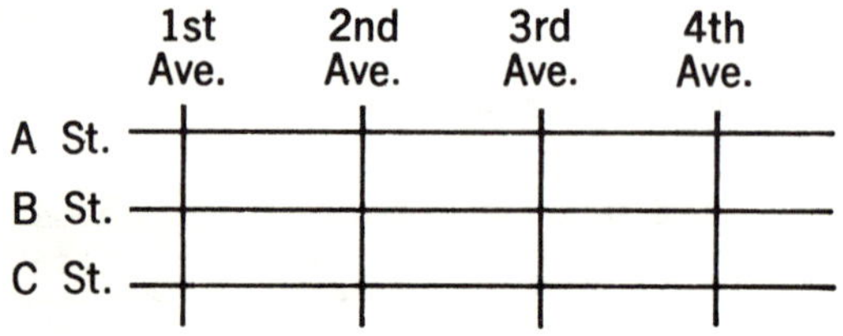

Notice that there are 4 avenues, 3 streets, and 12 intersections. Somehow we have performed an operation on 3 and 4 to obtain 12.

In a game you are to pick one letter from set A below and then pick one number from set B.

$A = \{a,b,c,d,e\}$
$B = \{1,2,3\}$

To show all the possible pairs we could construct the following array.

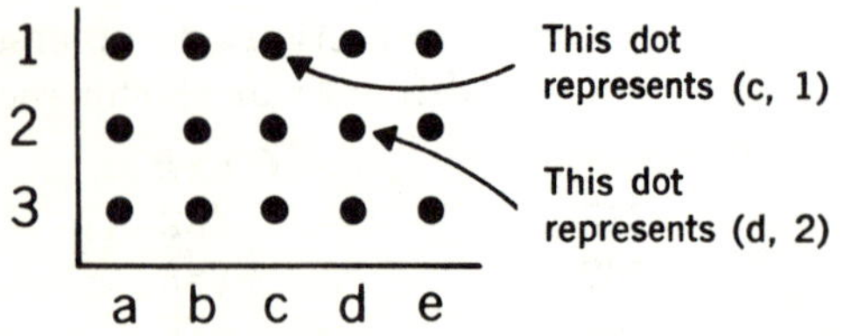

We are to choose first from set A, so let us agree to list the members of this set horizontally when making the array. We are to choose second from set B, so let us agree to list the members of this set vertically.

In other words, the number of columns in the array is the number of the first set and the number of rows is the number of the second set. In this case, the number of columns is $n(A)$ or 5 and the number of rows is $n(B)$ or 3.

Note that the 15 dots indicate that there are 15 possible combinations for picking one letter and one number.

Exercises 25:

Tell how many dots there are in the array for picking one member from the first set below and one member from the second set.

1. {Ed, Bill, Al} and {Jo, Mary, Susan}
2. {?, *} and $\{a,b,c,d\}$
3. {cake, cookies} and {coffee, tea, milk}
4. $\{a,b,c,d,e,f\}$ and {7,8,9,10}

DEFINITION OF MULTIPLICATION

Thinking of arrays for two sets enables us to define the operation of multiplication. Suppose we are given sets A and B such that $n(A) = a$ and $n(B) = b$. We could make an array for these sets so that it has a columns and b rows.

Definition 15:

The **product** of any two whole numbers a and b, denoted by $a \times b$, is the number of dots in the array having a columns and b rows. The numbers a and b are called **factors.**

The symbol $a \times b$ is read "a times b" or "the product of a and b." Hence, 4×5 is read "4 times 5" or "the product of 4 and 5." For a pictorial representation of 4×5 we can set up an array having 4 columns with 5 dots in each column, and then count the number of dots in the array.

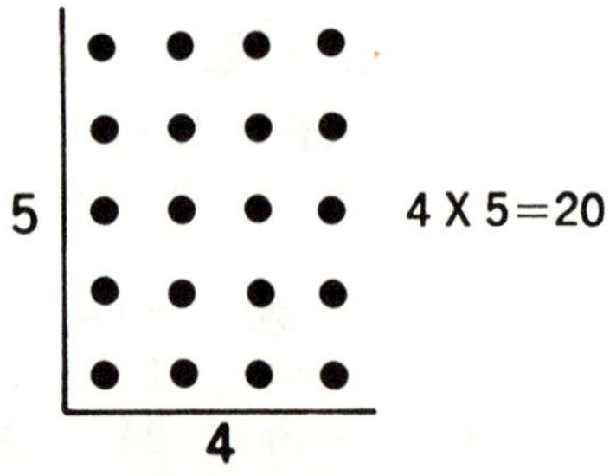

Exercises 26:

Draw an array if necessary and find the simplest numeral for each product below.

1. 3×5	5. 2×8	9. 9×3
2. 4×6	6. 4×4	10. 4×7
3. 2×5	7. 8×3	11. 6×3
4. 7×2	8. 5×6	12. 3×3

MULTIPLICATION AS REPEATED ADDITION

Any array can be thought of as the union of equivalent sets.

5 X 3

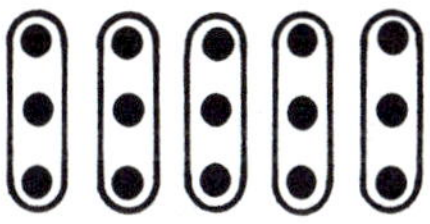

5 sets, 3 members in each set

$\underbrace{3 + 3 + 3 + 3 + 3}_{\text{5 addends}}$

4 X 6

4 sets, 6 members in each set

$\underbrace{6 + 6 + 6 + 6}_{\text{4 addends}}$

These drawings illustrate another way to think about multiplication of whole numbers.

$5 \times 3 = 3 + 3 + 3 + 3 + 3 = 15$
$4 \times 6 = 6 + 6 + 6 + 6 = 24$

This is sometimes referred to as the repeated addition description of multiplication.

Exercises 27:

Write the meaning of each product as repeated addition and give the simplest numeral for the product.

1. 6×2	4. 4×5	7. 6×7
2. 6×1	5. 5×4	8. 4×9
3. 1×6	6. 3×7	9. 5×7

Write each of the following as a product of two factors. Then give the simplest numeral for each product.

10. $8 + 8 + 8 + 8$
11. $5 + 5 + 5 + 5 + 5 + 5$
12. $1 + 1 + 1 + 1 + 1$
13. $9 + 9 + 9 + 9 + 9$
14. $9 + 9$
15. $2 + 2 + 2 + 2 + 2 + 2 + 2 + 2 + 2$

MULTIPLICATION IS COMMUTATIVE

An array having 4 columns and 3 rows can be changed into an array having 3 columns and 4 rows as shown below.

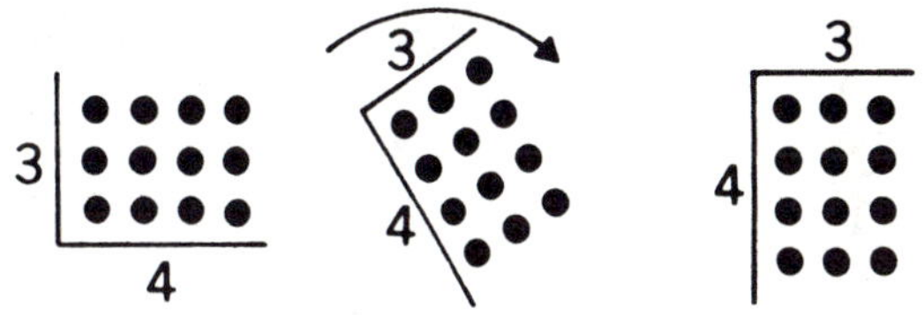

4 X 3 3 X 4

Since $4 \times 3 = 12$ and $3 \times 4 = 12$, we notice that the order of the factors can be changed but the product remains the same.

That is, for all whole numbers a and b,

$$a \times b = b \times a.$$

We call this idea the **commutative property of multiplication.** Or we say that *multiplication is commutative.*

This property of multiplication can also be shown by repeated addition.

$5 \times 4 = 4 + 4 + 4 + 4 + 4 = 20$
$4 \times 5 = 5 + 5 + 5 + 5 = 20$

Therefore, $5 \times 4 = 4 \times 5$.

Exercises 28:

Complete each of the following sentences by using the commutative property of multiplication. Do not find any of the products.

1. $5 \times 9 = 9 \times$ __
2. __ $\times 8 = 8 \times 7$
3. $31 \times 7 =$ __ $\times 31$
4. $12 \times$ __ $= 6 \times 12$
5. $9 \times 17 =$ __ $\times$ __
6. $23 \times$ __ $= 5 \times$ __
7. __ $\times$ __ $= 18 \times 9$
8. __ $\times 13 =$ __ $\times 27$
9. $357 \times 6 =$ __ $\times$ __
10. __ $\times$ __ $= 127 \times 43$

IDENTITY NUMBER OF MULTIPLICATION

Recall that zero is the identity number of addition because for any whole number a, $a + 0 = a = 0 + a$.

We would expect the identity number of multiplication to be some number such that for any whole number a, $a \times$ __ $= a =$ __ $\times a$.

Each array below has but *one* column, and hence the number of dots in the array is the same as the number of dots in the single column.

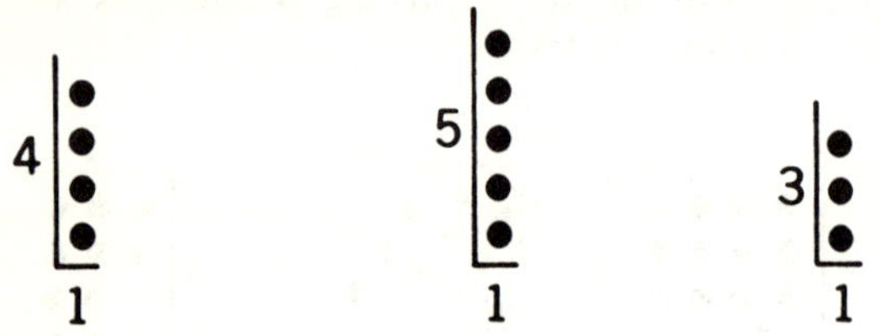

$1 \times 4 = 4$ $\quad 1 \times 5 = 5$ $\quad 1 \times 3 = 3$

Or we can interpret 1×4 as using 4 as an addend only once.

$$1 \times 4 = 4$$

Since multiplication is commutative, we know that $1 \times 4 = 4 \times 1$, and we conclude that $1 \times 4 = 4 = 4 \times 1$.

Multiplying any given whole number by one, or multiplying one by any given whole number, leaves the given number unchanged. Since one is the only number with this special property, we call the number one the **identity number of multiplication.**

For any whole number a, $a \times 1 = a = 1 \times a$.

MULTIPLICATION IS ASSOCIATIVE

Recall that the pattern of the associative property of addition is

$$(a + b) + c = a + (b + c)$$

for all whole numbers a, b, and c.

Is there such a property for multiplication? Let us look at a few examples.

$$(2 \times 3) \times 4 = 6 \times 4 = 24$$
$$2 \times (3 \times 4) = 2 \times 12 = 24$$

Therefore, $(2 \times 3) \times 4 = 2 \times (3 \times 4)$.

$$(3 \times 5) \times 2 = 15 \times 2 = 30$$
$$3 \times (5 \times 2) = 3 \times 10 = 30$$

Therefore, $(3 \times 5) \times 2 = 3 \times (5 \times 2)$.

When finding the product of three numbers, we can group the first two factors or the last two factors and always get the same product.

This idea is called the **associative property of multiplication.** Or we say that *multiplication is associative.*

For all whole numbers a, b, and c,

$$(a \times b) \times c = a \times (b \times c).$$

We can multiply these first

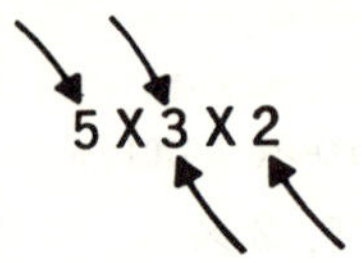

or multiply these first.

Notice that when we use the associative property of multiplication, the order of the factors is *not* changed as it is when we use the commutative property of multiplication.

Exercises 29:

Complete each of the following sentences by using the associative property of multiplication.

1. $(3 \times 7) \times 5 = 3 \times (\_ \times \_)$
2. $4 \times (2 \times 3) = (\_ \times \_) \times 3$
3. $(6 \times 3) \times 2 = \_ \times (\_ \times \_)$
4. $\_ \times (\_ \times \_) = (17 \times 8) \times 5$
5. $(\_ \times \_) \times \_ = 13 \times (9 \times 3)$

Each of the following is true because of the commutative property of multiplication, the associative property of multiplication, or both of these properties. Write the letter C, A, or both C and A to tell which property or properties are used.

6. $(9 \times 8) \times 3 = 9 \times (8 \times 3)$
7. $(9 \times 8) \times 3 = 3 \times (9 \times 8)$
8. $6 \times (7 \times 12) = 6 \times (12 \times 7)$
9. $6 \times (7 \times 12) = (6 \times 12) \times 7$
10. $(13 \times 5) \times 14 = 14 \times (5 \times 13)$
11. $(32 \times 9) \times 8 = 9 \times (32 \times 8)$
12. $r \times (s \times t) = (r \times s) \times t$

ZERO IN MULTIPLICATION

What number is named by 3×0? By thinking of repeated addition,

$$3 \times 0 = 0 + 0 + 0 = 0.$$

Since multiplication is commutative, we know that $3 \times 0 = 0 \times 3$ and that 0×3 must be equal to 0.

It appears that when zero is one of the factors, then the product is zero. That is, for any whole number a,

$$a \times 0 = 0, \text{ and}$$
$$0 \times a = 0.$$

What can we say about the factors if the product is zero? That is, what do we know about the factors a and b if $a \times b = 0$? The only way we can get a product of zero is to use zero as one of the factors. That is:

If $a \times b = 0$, then $a = 0$, $b = 0$, or both factors are zero.

THE DISTRIBUTIVE PROPERTY

Four boys and three girls are planning a party. Each child is to bring 2 gifts. How many gifts did they bring in all?

Two ways of thinking about solving this problem are given below.

1. There are $4 + 3$ or 7 children. Each child will bring 2 gifts. Then, all together they will bring

$(4 + 3) \times 2$ or 7×2 or 14 gifts.

2. Each of the 4 boys will bring 2 gifts. Then the boys will bring 4×2 gifts. Each of the 3 girls will bring 2 gifts. Then the girls will bring 3×2 gifts. All together the children will bring

$(4 \times 2) + (3 \times 2)$ or $8 + 6$ or 14 gifts.

From these ways of thinking about the problem we see that

$$(4 + 3) \times 2 = (4 \times 2) + (3 \times 2).$$

Since multiplication is commutative, we know that we can change the order of the factors. Hence,

$(4 + 3) \times 2 = 2 \times (4 + 3)$,
$4 \times 2 = 2 \times 4$, and
$3 \times 2 = 2 \times 3$.

Then the sentence

$$(4 + 3) \times 2 = (4 \times 2) + (3 \times 2)$$

can be written

$$2 \times (4 + 3) = (2 \times 4) + (2 \times 3).$$

Let us investigate such a pattern with different numbers.

$2 \times (5 + 3) = 2 \times 8 = 16$
$(2 \times 5) + (2 \times 3) = 10 + 6 = 16$
Hence $2 \times (5 + 3) = (2 \times 5) + (2 \times 3)$.

$(4 + 6) \times 3 = 10 \times 3 = 30$
$(4 \times 3) + (6 \times 3) = 12 + 18 = 30$
Hence, $(4 + 6) \times 3 = (4 \times 3) + (6 \times 3)$.

This pattern is also visible in an array.

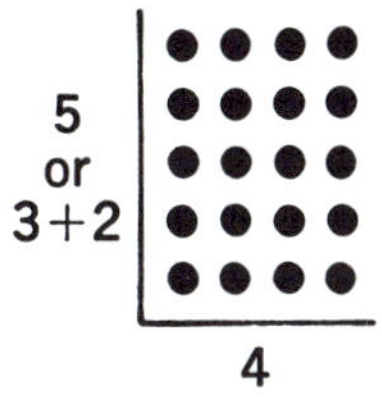

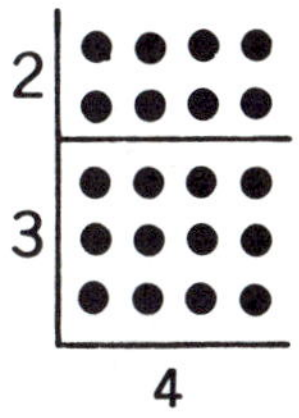

$4 \times (3 + 2)$ $(4 \times 3) + (4 \times 2)$

$$4 \times (3 + 2) = (4 \times 3) + (4 \times 2)$$

By drawing a horizontal line in the array we can separate it into two arrays, one having 2 rows and 4 columns and the other having 3 rows and 4 columns. We have not discarded any of the dots, so the number of dots remains the same.

This property is called the **distributive property of multiplication over addition.**

For all whole numbers a, b, and c,

$$a \times (b + c) = (a \times b) + (a \times c)$$
and
$$(b + c) \times a = (b \times a) + (c \times a).$$

It is important that we realize that the distributive property involves both addition and multiplication. Furthermore, it is important that we are able to "undistribute" as follows.

$(5 \times 3) + (5 \times 6) = 5 \times (3 + 6)$
$(4 \times 6) + (7 \times 6) = (4 + 7) \times 6$

Exercises 30:

Use the distributive property to complete each of the following sentences.

1. $7 \times (2 + 5) = (7 \times \_) + (7 \times \_)$
2. $4 \times (3 + 6) = (\_ \times \_) + (\_ \times \_)$
3. $(4 + 5) \times 3 = (\_ \times 3) + (\_ \times 3)$
4. $(8 + 9) \times 6 = (\_ \times \_) + (\_ \times \_)$
5. $(5 \times 2) + (7 \times 2) = (\_ + \_) \times 2$
6. $(6 \times 3) + (8 \times 3) = (\_ + \_) \times \_$

BASIC MULTIPLICATION FACTS

We can use addition or an array to determine and memorize the basic multiplication facts as shown in the following multiplication table. The first factor is named in the left column and the second factor is named in the top row.

X	0	1	2	3	4	5	6	7	8	9
0	0									
1	0	1								
2	0	2	4							
3	0	3	6	9						
4	0	4	8	12	16					
5	0	5	10	15	20	25				
6	0	6	12	18	24	30	36			
7	0	7	14	21	28	35	42	49		
8	0	8	16	24	32	40	48	56	64	
9	0	9	18	27	36	45	54	63	72	81

Since multiplication is commutative, we need not compute products for the shaded portion of the table. If we need to compute 3×7, we merely commute, $3 \times 7 = 7 \times 3$, and use the table to find that $7 \times 3 = 21$.

Even some of the basic facts can be found in other ways. For example:

$7 \times 8 = 7 \times (3 + 5)$	Rename 8 as 3 + 5
$= (7 \times 3) + (7 \times 5)$	Dist. prop.
$= 21 + 35$	Multiplication
$= 56$	Addition
$9 \times 5 = (5 + 4) \times 5$	Rename 9 as 5 + 4
$= (5 \times 5) + (4 \times 5)$	Dist. prop.
$= 25 + 20$	Multiplication
$= 45$	Addition

FACTORS OF 10, 100, OR 1000

When finding the product of two factors we might draw the array and count the dots. Or we might restate the multiplication as repeated addition and find the sum. Either of these methods become time-consuming and tedious when the factors are greater numbers, such as 615×352. Hence, we should like to discover some "streamlined" way of finding a product.

Let us begin by investigating products where one of the factors is 1, 10, 100, or 1000.

$5 \times 1 = 1 + 1 + 1 + 1 + 1 = 5$

$5 \times 10 = 10 + 10 + 10 + 10 + 10 = 50$

$5 \times 100 = 100 + 100 + 100 + 100 + 100 = 500$

$5 \times 1000 = 1000 + 1000 + 1000 + 1000 + 1000 = 5000$

$7 \times 1 = 1 + 1 + 1 + 1 + 1 + 1 + 1 = 7$

$7 \times 10 = 10 + 10 + 10 + 10 + 10 + 10 + 10 = 70$

$7 \times 100 = 100 + 100 + 100 + 100 + 100 + 100 + 100 = 700$

$7 \times 1000 = 1000 + 1000 + 1000 + 1000 + 1000 + 1000 + 1000 = 7000$

From these examples it is evident that to multiply by 10, annex one zero; to multiply by 100, annex two zeros; to multiply by 1000, annex three zeros.

Exercises 31:

Write the simplest numeral for each product.

1. 6×10
2. 9×100
3. 3×10
4. 8×100
5. 2×100
6. 4×10
7. 4×100
8. 4×1000
9. 100×4
10. 1000×4

Now let us investigate the case where one or both factors are multiples of a power of ten, such as 30, 400, 70, or 900.

$8 \times 20 = 8 \times (2 \times 10)$	Rename 20
$= (8 \times 2) \times 10$	Assoc. prop.
$= 16 \times 10$	Multiplication
$= 160$	Mult. by 10
$50 \times 70 = (5 \times 10) \times (7 \times 10)$	Rename factors
$= [(5 \times 10) \times 7] \times 10$	Assoc. prop.
$= [7 \times (5 \times 10)] \times 10$	Comm. prop.
$= [(7 \times 5) \times 10] \times 10$	Assoc. prop.
$= (7 \times 5) \times (10 \times 10)$	Assoc. prop.
$= 35 \times 100$	Multiplication
$= 3500$	Mult. by 100

Exercises 32:

Write the simplest numeral for each product.

1. 7×30
2. 8×400
3. 50×90
4. 70×20
5. 40×600
6. 700×200

TECHNIQUES OF MULTIPLICATION

To find products of greater numbers, we simply use the properties in such a way that calculation is easy. Notice how the renaming of numbers and the properties of the operations are used in the following examples.

$8 \times 24 = 8 \times (20 + 4)$	Rename 24
$= (8 \times 20) + (8 \times 4)$	Dist. prop.
$= 160 + 32$	Multiplication
$= 192$	Addition
$37 \times 6 = (30 + 7) \times 6$	Rename 37
$= (30 \times 6) + (7 \times 6)$	Dist. prop.
$= 180 + 42$	Multiplication
$= 222$	Addition

To make the addition easier, we can write the above example as follows.

$$\begin{array}{rl} 37 & \\ \times 6 & \\ \hline 42 & = (7 \times 6) \\ 180 & = (30 \times 6) \\ \hline 222 & = (30 \times 6) + (7 \times 6) \end{array}$$

The distributive property of multiplication over addition is used as the factors become greater.

$372 \times 4 = (300 + 70 + 2) \times 4$ Rename 372
Dist. prop.
$= (300 \times 4) + (70 \times 4) + (2 \times 4)$
Multiplication
$= 1200 + 280 + 8$
Addition
$= 1488$

This same product can be computed as follows.

$$\begin{array}{rl} 372 & \\ \times 4 & \\ \hline 8 & = (2 \times 4) \\ 280 & = (70 \times 4) \\ 1200 & = (300 \times 4) \\ \hline 1488 & \end{array}$$

Exercises 33:

Find the simplest numeral for each product.

1. 56×3
2. 78×5
3. 124×6
4. 354×6
5. 37×8
6. 426×9

7. $\begin{array}{r} 47 \\ \times 4 \\ \hline \end{array}$ 8. $\begin{array}{r} 29 \\ \times 5 \\ \hline \end{array}$ 9. $\begin{array}{r} 173 \\ \times 6 \\ \hline \end{array}$ 10. $\begin{array}{r} 321 \\ \times 8 \\ \hline \end{array}$ 11. $\begin{array}{r} 457 \\ \times 3 \\ \hline \end{array}$ 12. $\begin{array}{r} 634 \\ \times 9 \\ \hline \end{array}$

Now let us see what happens when both factors are named by two-digit numerals.

$24 \times 63 = 24 \times (60 + 3)$ Rename 63
Dist. prop.
$= (24 \times 60) + (24 \times 3)$
Rename 60
$= [24 \times (6 \times 10)] + (24 \times 3)$
Assoc. prop.
$= [(24 \times 6) \times 10] + (24 \times 3)$
Multiplication
$= (144 \times 10) + (24 \times 3)$
Mult. by 10
$= 1440 + 72$
Addition
$= 1512$

Another way to think about 24×63 is shown below.

Rename factors
$24 \times 63 = (20 + 4) \times (60 + 3)$
Dist. prop.
$= [(20 + 4) \times 60] + [(20 + 4) \times 3]$
Dist. prop.
$= [(20 \times 60) + (4 \times 60)] + (20 \times 3) + (4 \times 3)$
Assoc. prop.
$= (20 \times 60) + (4 \times 60) + (20 \times 3) + (4 \times 3)$
Multiplication
$= 1200 + 240 + 60 + 12$
Addition
$= 1512$

This, too, can be shown in vertical arrangement.

$$\begin{array}{rl} 24 & \\ \times 63 & \\ \hline 12 & = (4 \times 3) \\ 60 & = (20 \times 3) \\ 240 & = (4 \times 60) \\ 1200 & = (20 \times 60) \\ \hline 1512 & \end{array}$$

Exercises 34:

Find the simplest numeral for each product.

1. $\begin{array}{r} 38 \\ \times 13 \\ \hline \end{array}$ 2. $\begin{array}{r} 27 \\ \times 24 \\ \hline \end{array}$ 3. $\begin{array}{r} 47 \\ \times 35 \\ \hline \end{array}$ 4. $\begin{array}{r} 24 \\ \times 54 \\ \hline \end{array}$ 5. $\begin{array}{r} 78 \\ \times 52 \\ \hline \end{array}$ 6. $\begin{array}{r} 17 \\ \times 58 \\ \hline \end{array}$ 7. $\begin{array}{r} 83 \\ \times 49 \\ \hline \end{array}$ 8. $\begin{array}{r} 57 \\ \times 68 \\ \hline \end{array}$ 9. $\begin{array}{r} 25 \\ \times 93 \\ \hline \end{array}$

THE MULTIPLICATION ALGORITHM

The previous exercises enable us to find the product of still greater factors. You should have noticed by now that the distributive property of multiplication over addition is a powerful tool in making multiplication easy.

$$\begin{array}{rl} 523 & \\ \times 7 & \\ \hline 21 & = (3 \times 7) \\ 140 & = (20 \times 7) \\ 3500 & = (500 \times 7) \\ \hline 3661 & \end{array}$$

```
  346
 ×24
   24 = (6 × 4)
  160 = (40 × 4)
 1200 = (300 × 4)
  120 = (6 × 20)
  800 = (40 × 20)
 6000 = (300 × 20)
 8304
```

```
 346
 ×24
1384
6920
8304
```

By doing 346 × 4 mentally, we can write 1384 in the arrangement at the right. Then write 6920 by doing 346 × 20 mentally.

```
   243
  ×312
   486 = (243 × 2)
  2430 = (243 × 10)
 72900 = (243 × 30)
 75816
```

We can erase the indicated products at the right, and omit writing the final 0's of 2430 and 72,900, and write the short form as follows:

```
  243
 ×312
  486
 243
729
75816
```

Exercises 35:

Find each product.

```
1.  624      4.   432      7. 3426
     ×3          ×312           ×4

2.  532      5    675      8. 4521
    ×24          ×123          ×32

3.  324      6.   843      9. 3421
    ×31          ×324         ×322
```

ESTIMATING A PRODUCT

Often we are interested in estimates rather than the exact answers. Knowing how to multiply by multiples of powers of ten helps us find an estimate of a product very quickly and easily. Suppose you are to find the value of n in $n = 28 \times 53$.

$$20 < 28 \text{ and } 50 < 53,$$
$$\text{so } 20 \times 50 < n \text{ or } 1000 < n.$$
$$30 > 28 \text{ and } 60 > 53,$$
$$\text{so } 30 \times 60 > n \text{ or } 1800 > n.$$

Hence, we know that $1000 < n < 1800$, which is read: 1000 is less than n and n is less than 1800. Another way of saying this is "n is between 1000 and 1800."

Another example might be to find the value of x and $x = 72 \times 587$.

$$70 < 72 \text{ and } 500 < 587,$$
$$\text{so } 70 \times 500 \text{ or } 35000 < x.$$
$$80 > 72 \text{ and } 600 > 587,$$
$$\text{so } 80 \times 600 \text{ or } 48000 > x.$$

Hence, $35000 < x < 48000$, or the value of x is between 35000 and 48000.

Exercises 36:

Find a rough estimate for n in each sentence. Then find the exact answer.

1. $n = 27 \times 65$
2. $n = 82 \times 75$
3. $n = 39 \times 58$
4. $n = 43 \times 94$
5. $n = 47 \times 367$
6. $n = 77 \times 492$
7. $n = 826 \times 52$
8. $n = 572 \times 67$

DIVISION

Division is related to multiplication in much the same way that subtraction is related to addition. When two numbers are added, the addition can be undone by subtraction. Similarly, when two numbers are multiplied, the multiplication can be undone by division. Hence, multiplication and division are inverse operations.

Addition	*Subtraction*
$5 + 7 = 12$	$12 - 7 = 5$
$29 + 5 = 34$	$34 - 5 = 29$
Multiplication	*Division*
$7 \times 6 = 42$	$42 \div 6 = 7$
$24 \times 3 = 72$	$72 \div 3 = 24$

Knowing that multiplication and division are inverse operations, we can interpret $8 \div 2$ as that factor which, when multiplied by 2, yields a product of 8. That is,

$$(8 \div 2) \times 2 = 8.$$

If we should think of an array as we did for multiplication, $8 \div 2$ would be the number of columns in an array of 8 dots having 2 dots in each column.

8÷2 or 4

Or we can think of $8 \div 2$ as the number of disjoint subsets formed when a set of 8 objects is separated into disjoint subsets having 2 objects each.

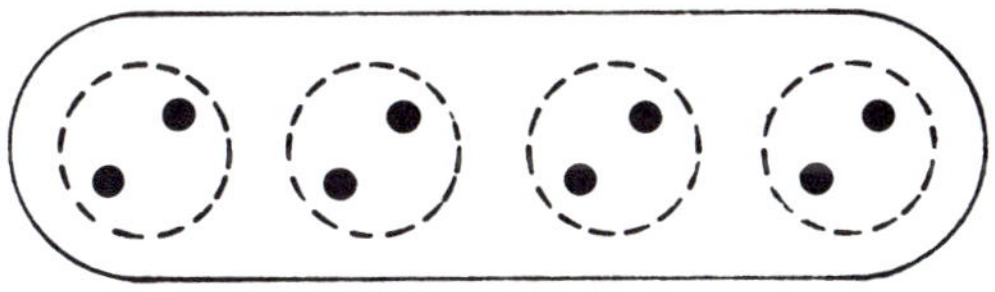

$8 \div 2 = 4$
Set of 8 objects separated into 4 disjoint subsets having 2 objects each.

Exercises 37:

Think of an array or separating a set into disjoint equivalent subsets to tell the number named by each of the following.

1. $12 \div 3$	5. $20 \div 4$	9. $24 \div 8$
2. $6 \div 2$	6. $18 \div 2$	10. $24 \div 12$
3. $15 \div 5$	7. $14 \div 7$	11. $24 \div 3$
4. $16 \div 4$	8. $24 \div 6$	12. $24 \div 4$

ZERO IN DIVISION

First let us investigate a division such as $7 \div 0 = n$. Since multiplication and division are inverse operations, the above division can be restated as a multiplication.

$7 \div 0 = n$ so $n \times 0 = 7$

But we already know that when one of the factors is zero, the product is zero. Hence, there is *no* number n such that $n \times 0 = 7$. That is, $7 \div 0$ does not name a number.

Now let us investigate the special case $0 \div 0 = n$. Restate this as a multiplication.

$0 \div 0 = n$ so $n \times 0 = 0$

In this case, any number we choose for n yields a product of 0. That is, $5 \times 0 = 0$, $721 \times 0 = 0$, $9075 \times 0 = 0$, and so on. If we accept $0 \div 0$ as a name for a number, then we are forced to accept that it names *every* number. This is certainly not very helpful.

The fact that in the first case *no* number is named and in the second case *every* number is named is a source of difficulty in division. Let us rule out both of these cases by agreeing to the following.

Division by zero is meaningless. This means that we shall not define division by zero.

Now let us investigate a case such as $0 \div 8 = n$. Restate this as a multiplication.

$0 \div 8 = n$ so $n \times 8 = 0$

We already know that if the product is zero, at least one of the factors must be zero. Since $8 \neq 0$, then n must be equal to zero. Hence, $0 \times 8 = 0$ and $0 \div 8 = 0$.

This is true regardless of what number we choose for a, except $a = 0$, in the following.

$0 \div a = 0$ if $a \neq 0$.

We can state our finding as follows. When zero is divided by any nonzero number the result is zero.

DEFINITION OF DIVISION

Now let us state a definition of division.

Definition 16:

If $a \times b = c$ and $b \neq 0$, then $c \div b = a$.

We read $c \div b$ as "c divided by b."

The number named by $c \div b$ is called the **quotient**, the number named by b is called the **divisor**, and the number named by c is called the **dividend.**

We can show the relationship between these numbers and the numbers in a multiplication as follows.

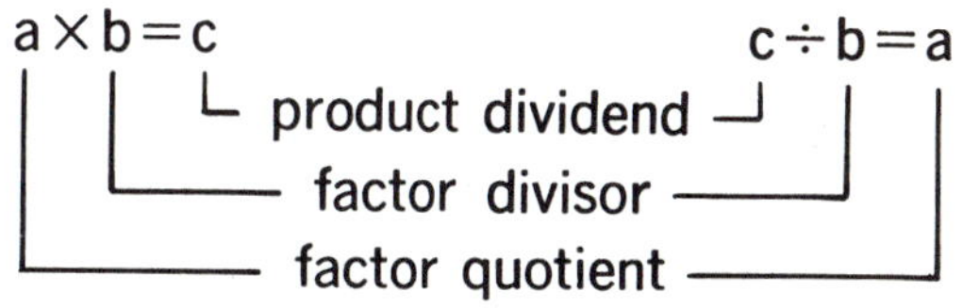

Hence, we see that in a division we are given the product and one of the factors, and we are to find the other factor.

From this definition, and knowing the basic multiplication facts, we can determine the basic definition facts.

Exercises 38:
Find each quotient.

1. $42 \div 7$	5. $36 \div 4$	9. $25 \div 5$
2. $35 \div 5$	6. $21 \div 3$	10. $49 \div 7$
3. $48 \div 8$	7. $45 \div 9$	11. $27 \div 3$
4. $81 \div 9$	8. $32 \div 8$	12. $28 \div 7$

PROPERTIES OF DIVISION

Is division commutative? That is, do $12 \div 4$ and $4 \div 12$ name the same number? $12 \div 4 = 3$, but $4 \div 12$ does not name a whole number, let alone three. Hence, $12 \div 4 \neq 4 \div 12$. Division is *not* commutative.

Is division associative? That is, do $(12 \div 6) \div 2$ and $12 \div (6 \div 2)$ name the same number?

$(12 \div 6) \div 2 = 2 \div 2 = 1$
$12 \div (6 \div 2) = 12 \div 3 = 4$

Hence, $(12 \div 6) \div 2 \neq 12 \div (6 \div 2)$. Division is *not* associative.

Since division is not commutative, we know that $8 \div 1 \neq 1 \div 8$. But let us see what happens when the divisor is 1.

$8 \div 1 = n$ so $n \times 1 = 8$

Since 1 is the identity number of multiplication, we see that $n = 8$ and $8 \div 1 = 8$. That is, when the divisor is 1, the dividend and the quotient are the same.

For all whole numbers a,

$a \div 1 = a.$

If we are to find the value of n in $12 \div 3 = n$, we might rename 12 as $(9 + 3)$. Could it be that division distributes over addition? Let us try it.

$(9 + 3) \div 3 = 12 \div 3 = 4$
$(9 \div 3) + (3 \div 3) = 3 + 1 = 4$

Hence, $(9 + 3) \div 3 = (9 \div 3) + (3 \div 3)$.

We might be tempted to try the other pattern of the distributive property. That is, rename 3 as $2 + 1$ and write $12 \div 3$ as $12 \div (2 + 1)$.

$12 \div (2 + 1) = 12 \div 3 = 4$
$(12 \div 2) + (12 \div 1) = 6 + 12 = 18$

Hence, $12 \div (2 + 1) \neq (12 \div 2) + (12 \div 1)$.

However, it is important to remember that for all whole numbers a, b, and c, where $c \neq 0$,

$(a + b) \div c = (a \div c) + (b \div c).$

We say that *division distributes over addition, but only when the divisor is distributed.*

Study the following examples which show the use of this property.

Example 1:
$$\begin{aligned} 32 \div 4 &= (20 + 12) \div 4 \\ &= (20 \div 4) + (12 \div 4) \\ &= 5 + 3 \\ &= 8 \end{aligned}$$

Example 2:
$$\begin{aligned} 75 \div 5 &= (40 + 35) \div 5 \\ &= (40 \div 5) + (35 \div 5) \\ &= 8 + 7 \\ &= 15 \end{aligned}$$

Example 3:
$$\begin{aligned} 75 \div 5 &= (50 + 25) \div 5 \\ &= (50 \div 5) + (25 \div 5) \\ &= 10 + 5 \\ &= 15 \end{aligned}$$

Exercises 39:
Rename the dividend in each of the following and use the distributive property of division over addition to find each quotient.

1. $16 \div 2$	4. $44 \div 4$	7. $52 \div 4$
2. $65 \div 5$	5. $84 \div 7$	8. $72 \div 6$
3. $39 \div 3$	6. $24 \div 4$	9. $95 \div 5$

REMAINDERS IN DIVISION

If we think of separating a set into disjoint equivalent subsets, we find that some divisions do not yield a whole number as a quotient.

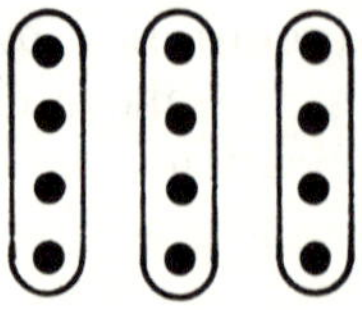

12 objects, 3 disjoint sets,
4 objects in each subset
$12 \div 4 = 3$

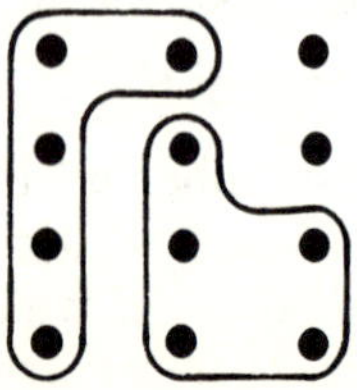

12 objects, 2 disjoint subsets
of 5 objects each, *and* 2 objects
left over

$$12 = (2 \times 5) + 2$$

$$\begin{array}{cc} \uparrow & \uparrow \\ \text{quotient} & \text{remainder} \end{array}$$

As long as we are operating only with whole numbers, we shall give the remainder as such. Later in this chapter we will extend the number system so that we can carry out division without having to use remainders.

A final comment regarding the remainder is the following.

$$20 = (4 \times 5) + 0,$$
so $20 \div 5 = 4$ with remainder 0.

Let us agree that every division of whole numbers has a remainder. That is, for whole numbers a and b, $b \neq 0$, the division $a \div b$ can be stated as

$$a = (q \times b) + r$$

where q is the quotient and r is the remainder. Furthermore, $r = 0$ or $r > 0$ and $r < b$. This means that the remainder is either zero or some whole number between 0 and b.

Exercises 40:

Find each quotient and remainder.

1. $17 \div 5$	4. $31 \div 5$	7. $55 \div 4$
2. $21 \div 6$	5. $40 \div 9$	8. $73 \div 8$
3. $15 \div 7$	6. $33 \div 6$	9. $67 \div 6$

ONE-DIGIT DIVISORS

The definition of division does not tell us how to carry out a division. We should like to discover some method of writing the numerals so that division becomes easy, especially where greater numbers are involved.

Suppose we want to find the simplest numeral for $43 \div 5$. In terms of multiplication we can estimate the result by thinking of $n \times 5 = 43$. Knowing the multiples of 5 helps us in making this estimate.

$$8 \times 5 = 40 \text{ and } 40 < 43$$
$$9 \times 5 = 45 \text{ and } 45 > 43$$

Obviously, $43 \div 5$ does not name a whole number. Perhaps we can state the result in the form $a = (q \times b) + r$. So let us rename 43 as a sum of two addends, the first of which is 40 since we already know it can be named as 8×5.

$$\begin{aligned} 43 &= 40 + 3 \\ &= (8 \times 5) + 3 \end{aligned}$$

$$\begin{array}{cc} \uparrow & \uparrow \\ \text{quotient} & \text{remainder} \end{array}$$

Another way of writing this is:

$$\begin{array}{r} 8 \\ 5\overline{)43} \\ 40 \\ \hline 3 \end{array} \quad 40 = (8 \times 5) \qquad \text{or} \qquad \begin{array}{r} 8 \\ 5\overline{)43} \\ 40 \\ \hline 3 \end{array}$$

Now let us find the simplest numeral for $256 \div 8$.

Think of $n \times 8 = 256$ to estimate the result.

$$\begin{aligned} 10 \times 8 &= 80 \text{ and } 80 < 256 \\ 20 \times 8 &= 160 \text{ and } 160 < 256 \\ 30 \times 8 &= 240 \text{ and } 240 < 256 \\ 40 \times 8 &= 320 \text{ and } 320 > 256 \end{aligned}$$

Hence, the result is between 30 and 40. So let us rename 256 as the sum of two addends, the first addend being 240.

$$256 = 240 + 16$$

We notice that the second addend cannot be the remainder since $16 > 8$. Further, we notice that 16 is a multiple of 8. Then we can use the distributive property of division over addition.

$$\begin{aligned} 256 \div 8 &= (240 + 16) \div 8 \\ &= (240 \div 8) + (16 \div 8) \\ &= \quad 30 \qquad + \quad 2 \\ &= 32 \end{aligned}$$

Another way to write this is:

$$\begin{array}{ccc} & 30 + & 2 = 32 \\ 8\overline{)256} & 8\overline{)240} & + 16 \end{array}$$

Or a more concise method is to think of place value.

$$\begin{array}{r} 3 \\ 8\overline{)256} \\ 240 \\ \hline 16 \end{array} \quad 240 = (30 \times 8) \qquad \begin{array}{r} 32 \\ 8\overline{)256} \\ 240 \\ \hline 16 \\ 16 \\ \hline 0 \end{array} \quad 16 = (2 \times 8)$$

Exercises 41:

Find each quotient.

1. $105 \div 7$	4. $315 \div 5$	7. $3320 \div 8$
2. $156 \div 6$	5. $288 \div 4$	8. $2526 \div 6$
3. $272 \div 8$	6. $201 \div 3$	9. $2464 \div 7$

TWO-DIGIT DIVISORS

Let us extend division to the case where the divisor is expressed by a two-digit numeral. For example, let us carry out the division $624 \div 32$.

We are not as familiar with the multiples of 32 as we are with the multiples of the numbers 1 through 10, so let us think of renaming 624 as the sum of more than two addends. Let us do this by thinking of multiples of powers of 10 as shown below.

$$10 \times 32 = 320 \text{ and } 320 < 624$$
$$20 \times 32 = 640 \text{ and } 640 > 624$$

Now we can rename 624 as follows.

$$\begin{aligned} 624 &= 320 + 304 \\ &= (10 \times 32) + 304 \end{aligned}$$

Certainly 304 cannot be the remainder since $304 > 32$. Now rename 304 as a sum of two addends where the first addend is a multiple of 32. Since 304 is nearly 320 we can expect the value of n in $n \times 32 = 304$ to be nearly 10.

$$8 \times 32 = 256 \text{ and } 256 < 304$$
$$9 \times 32 = 288 \text{ and } 288 < 304$$
$$10 \times 32 = 320 \text{ and } 320 > 304$$

Now we can rename 624 so that the division can be completed easily.

$$\begin{aligned} 624 &= 320 + 288 + 16 \\ &= (10 \times 32) + (9 \times 32) + 16 \\ &= (19 \times 32) + 16 \end{aligned}$$

$$\underset{\text{quotient}}{\uparrow} \qquad \underset{\text{remainder}}{\uparrow}$$

Again, to make the subtraction (necessary in the renaming) easy, let us proceed as follows.

Think

$$\begin{array}{rl} \left.\begin{array}{r} 9 \\ 10 \end{array}\right\} & 10 + 9 = 19 \\ 32\overline{)624} & \\ \underline{320} & = (10 \times 32) \\ 304 & \\ \underline{288} & = (9 \times 32) \\ 16 & \end{array}$$

Write

$$\begin{array}{r} 19 \\ 32\overline{)624} \\ \underline{320} \\ 304 \\ \underline{288} \\ 16 \end{array}$$

Exercises 42:

Carry out each division.

1. $415 \div 25$	4. $328 \div 45$	7. $2091 \div 17$
2. $534 \div 31$	5. $408 \div 24$	8. $2115 \div 17$
3. $715 \div 64$	6. $638 \div 53$	9. $3400 \div 17$

THE DIVISION ALGORITHM

The vertical method makes the division easier to complete since it makes subtraction easy. However, we are faced with subtracting the greatest multiple of the divisor. Suppose we illustrate this with $329 \div 14$.

$$\begin{array}{rl} 1 & \\ 14\overline{)329} & \\ \underline{140} & = (10 \times 14) \\ 189 & \end{array}$$

We see that $189 > (10 \times 14)$, so 10×14 is not the greatest multiple of 14 that we could have subtracted in this process. So let us start over again.

$$\begin{array}{rl} 2 & \\ 14\overline{)329} & \\ \underline{280} & = (20 \times 14) \\ 49 & \end{array}$$

Now estimate the value of n in $n \times 14 = 49$ to obtain the next digit in the answer.

$$3 \times 14 = 42 \text{ and } 42 < 49$$
$$4 \times 14 = 56 \text{ and } 56 > 49$$

Hence, the next digit in the answer must be 3.

Think

$$\begin{array}{rl} 23 & \\ 14\overline{)329} & \\ \underline{280} & = (20 \times 14) \\ 49 & \\ \underline{42} & = (3 \times 14) \\ 7 & \end{array}$$

Write

$$\begin{array}{r} 23 \\ 14\overline{)329} \\ \underline{280} \\ 49 \\ \underline{42} \\ 7 \end{array}$$

Study the following examples and notice how this process is used.

$$\begin{array}{rl} 167 & \\ 21\overline{)3526} & \\ \underline{2100} & = (100 \times 21) \\ 1426 & \\ \underline{1260} & = (60 \times 21) \\ 166 & \\ \underline{147} & = (7 \times 21) \\ 19 & \end{array} \qquad \begin{array}{rl} 81 & \\ 58\overline{)4708} & \\ \underline{4640} & = (80 \times 58) \\ 68 & \\ \underline{58} & = (1 \times 58) \\ 10 & \end{array}$$

Exercises 43:

Carry out each division.

1. $217 \div 34$	5. $5806 \div 47$	9. $8059 \div 25$
2. $836 \div 22$	6. $7052 \div 35$	10. $6072 \div 253$
3. $759 \div 18$	7. $3431 \div 25$	11. $2448 \div 24$
4. $342 \div 32$	8. $5284 \div 25$	12. $6794 \div 79$

Solving Equations and Problems

RELATION SYMBOLS

By using mathematical symbols, we are constantly building a language. In many respects it is more concise than the English language. Because of its brevity we must have a thorough understanding of the meaning of the symbols used in writing a number sentence. Study the meaning of each symbol given below.

$=$ *is equal to*
$\neq$ *is not equal to*
$<$ *is less than*
$>$ *is greater than*

These symbols serve as verbs in number sentences. Since they show how two numbers are related, they are called *relation symbols.*

The sentence $5 + 3 = 8$ is true since $5 + 3$ and 8 are two names for the same number. But the sentence $7 - 3 = 8$ is false since $7 - 3$ and 8 do not name the same number.

What relation symbol can we write between $7 - 3$ and 8 so that a true sentence is formed? Since $7 - 3$ is not equal to 8, we see that $7 - 3 \neq 8$ is a true sentence.

The sentence $5 - 2 < 4 + 3$ is true since $5 - 2$ or 3 is less than $4 + 3$ or 7. But the sentence $8 + 5 < 9 - 6$ is false since $8 + 5$ or 13 is greater than $9 - 6$ or 3. Hence, $8 + 5 > 9 - 6$ is a true sentence.

The sentence $17 - 5 < 12$ is false since $17 - 5$ or 12 is equal to 12. Hence, we can change the relation symbol $<$ to the relation symbol $=$ and form the true sentence $17 - 5 = 12$.

Exercises 44:

Write T before each true sentence below, and write F before each false sentence.

1. $7 + 6 = 15$
2. $14 < 17 + 3$
3. $8 + 2 = 10$
4. $15 - 5 > 6$
5. $23 > 29 + 1$
6. $7 + 6 < 11 - 3$
7. $6 + 9 = 23 - 8$
8. $9 + (-1) = 3 - (-5)$
9. $32 - 2 = 2 \times 15$
10. $3 \times 4 < 5 \times 2$

GROUPING SYMBOLS

Punctuation marks are used in any language to make clear what we want to say. Study how punctuation marks change the meaning of the following unpunctuated sentence.

Bob said Betty is cute.
Bob said, "Betty is cute."
"Bob," said Betty, "is cute."

Punctuation marks are just as important in number sentences as they are in English sentences.

Study the following expression. What number does it name?

$$7 \times 2 + 5$$

Without being told by a symbol or some other means, we do not know whether to do the multiplication or the addition first.

If we multiply first:

$$7 \times 2 + 5 = 14 + 5 = 19$$

If we add first:

$$7 \times 2 + 5 = 7 \times 7 = 49$$

To avoid the confusion of such an expression naming two different numbers, let us use parentheses ( ) to indicate which operation is to be done first.

$$(7 \times 2) + 5 = 14 + 5 = 19$$
$$7 \times (2 + 5) = 7 \times 7 = 49$$

When part of a number sentence is enclosed within parentheses, think of that part as naming but one number. Think of (7×2) as naming 14 and think of $(2 + 5)$ as naming 7.

It is commonly agreed that when more than one operation, or all of the operations, are indicated in the same expression, we multiply and divide first, then add and subtract.

$$5 + 3 \times 4 \text{ means } 5 + (3 \times 4)$$
$$7 - 6 \div 2 \text{ means } 7 - (6 \div 2)$$
$$7 + 3 \times 8 - 5 \text{ means } 7 \times (3 \times 8) - 5$$

In case only addition and subtraction are indicated in an expression (or only multiplication and division), we will perform the operations in the order indicated from left to right.

$$8 + 6 - 9 \text{ means } (8 + 6) - 9$$
$$6 \times 4 \div 3 \text{ means } (6 \times 4) \div 3$$

It is not always necessary to write the multiplication sign. Multiplication is indicated in each of the following.

$6\ (5 + 4)$ means $6 \times (5 + 4)$
$9(15)$ means 9×15
$12n$ means $12 \times n$
$(n + 2)\ (7 - 5)$ means $(n + 2) \times (7 - 5)$

Study how the parentheses are handled in the following sentences.

$$(16 \div 2)\ (7 + 6) = 8 \times 13 = 104$$
$$(13 - 4) + (12 \div 3) = 9 + 4 = 13$$

Sometimes the sentence becomes so complicated that we need more than one set of parentheses. Instead of two sets of parentheses, let us use brackets [ ] for the second set. In such cases, we handle the innermost groupings first.

$$[4 \times (3 + 2)] - 8 = [4 \times 5] - 8 = 20 - 8 = 12$$

$$60 + [(8 \div 2) \times (4 + 3)] = 60 + [4 \times 7] = 60 + 28 = 88$$

Exercises 45:

What number is named by each of the following?

1. $(12 - 8) \times 7$
2. $9 \times (32 \div 8)$
3. $(11 - 6) + 12$
4. $(4 \times 2)\ (20 \div 5)$
5. $28 \div (10 - 3)$
6. $[6 + (7 - 2)] + 8$
7. $40 \div [(18 \div 3) + 2]$
8. $[4 + (7 - 2)]\ (9 - 3)$
9. $[14 \div (6 + 1)] \div 2$
10. $8 - [7(5 - 3) - 6]$

Write parentheses, brackets, or both parentheses and brackets in each of the following expressions so that it will name the number indicated after it.

11. $30 - 12 \div 3 \times 2$ Number: 3
12. $30 - 12 \div 3 \times 2$ Number: 52
13. $30 - 12 \div 3 \times 2$ Number: 12
14. $30 - 12 \div 3 \times 2$ Number: 28
15. $30 - 12 \div 3 \times 2$ Number: 22

NUMBER SENTENCES

The symbols used in writing a number sentence are members of one of the following sets.

Number symbols or numerals:
0, ⅔, 4.7, 5, 72, 119, . . .

Operation symbols:
$+, -, \times, \div, \ldots$

Relation symbols:
$=, \neq, <, >, \ldots$

Grouping symbols:
( ), [ ], . . .

Placeholder symbols or variables:
$\square, n, x, y, t, \ldots$

To write a number sentence we write a relation symbol between two different combinations of the other symbols.

A very important property of a number sentence which does not contain a placeholder symbol is that it is either true or false, but not both. For example, the following number sentences are classified as true or false.

True	*False*
$4 + 7 = 19 - 8$	$6 + 9 = 17 - 8$
$5 \times 3 < 14 + 6$	$27 - 5 < 2 \times 9$
$48 \div 16 \neq 5$	$5 + 4 > 5 \times 4$

Exercises 46:

Write T before each true sentence below and write F before each false sentence.

1. $5\ (3 + 4) = 21 + 14$
2. $(8 \div 4) + 7 < 4 \times 6$
3. $3 \times 4 > 20 - 8$
4. $6 + 8 \neq 15 \div 3$
5. $3(4 + 2) = (3 \times 4) + 2$
6. $(3 + 4)\ (5 - 5) < 5$

OPEN SENTENCES

In previous lessons we determined whether certain sentences were true or false. Now let us examine the following sentences to learn more about when a number sentence is true, when it is false, and when we are unable to determine which it is.

1. Harry Truman was elected President of the United States.
2. Julius Zulk was elected President of the United States.
3. He was elected President of the United States.

You know that sentence 1 is true, and a little checking of history will show that sentence 2 is false. But what about sentence 3?

Until the word *he* is replaced by the name of a person, we are unable to tell whether sentence 3 is true or false.

Now consider the following number sentences.

$$7 + 6 = 13$$
$$9 - 5 = 27$$
$$8 + n = 15$$

Certainly, $7 + 6 = 13$ is true and $9 - 5 = 27$ is false, but we cannot tell whether $8 + n = 15$ is true or false until n is replaced by a numeral.

Definition 17:

Mathematical sentences that contain letters (or some other symbols) to be replaced by numerals, and are neither true nor false, are called *open sentences.*

Examples of open sentences are given below.

$n - 15 = 7$	$3x + 2 < 12$
$(-14)\,t = 64$	$26(y - 3) > 47$

Exercises 47:

Before each sentence below write T if it is true, F if it is false, and O if it is open.

1. $(5 + 3) \div k = 2$
2. $4 - (-6) = 10$
3. $4y + (18 \div 6) < 4$
4. $3 + (-8) = 17 - (2 \times 10)$
5. $72 > (24 \div x) + 56$
6. $(16 \div 4) + 13 < (3 \times 4) + 5$

REPLACEMENT SET

Consider the replacements for the pronoun *she* in the following sentence.

She was a great musician.

Certainly it would be sensible to replace *she* with the name of a person. It would not be sensible to replace *she* with the name of a state, a building, a ship, and so on. If we want the resulting sentence to be meaningful, we must know the set from which we can select the replacements for the pronoun *she.*

This idea also underlies an open sentence. We must know which set of numbers we are allowed to use when replacing a placeholder symbol or variable with a numeral.

Definition 18:

The set of numbers whose names are to be used as replacements for a variable is called the *replacement set.*

Solution Set

Use {1,2,3,4,5,6} as the replacement set for x in the following open sentence.

$$3 + x < 7$$

We can replace x by each of the numerals 1, 2, 3, 4, 5, and 6 to determine which of them make the resulting sentence true.

True	*False*
$3 + 1 < 7$	$3 + 4 < 7$
$3 + 2 < 7$	$3 + 5 < 7$
$3 + 3 < 7$	$3 + 6 < 7$

We see that only the numerals 1, 2, and 3 can replace x to make the resulting sentence true. Hence, {1,2,3} is called the *solution set* for $3 + x < 7$.

Definition 19:

The set of replacements for the variable in an open sentence that make the resulting sentence true is called the *solution set.* Each member of the solution set is called a *solution* or a *root* of the open sentence.

In the previous example, {1,2,3} is the solution set, and the roots of the open sentence are 1, 2, and 3.

Study the following examples of finding a solution set.

Example 1: Find the solution set of $n + 8 = 17$ if the replacement set is the set of whole numbers. We know that $9 + 8 = 17$, so 9 is a solution and belongs in the solution set. If n represents any whole number other than 9, the sentence is false. Hence, the only root is 9 and the solution set is {9}.

Example 2: Find the solution set of $7 - y = 10$ if the replacement set is the set of whole numbers. Since 0 is the least of the whole numbers and $7 - 0 = 7$, we know that y must represent a number less than zero. There is no such whole number, so the solution set is $\emptyset$. This does not mean that there is no solution set. It merely means that there is no solution in the set of whole numbers.

Example 3: Find the solution set of $7 - y = 10$ if the replacement set is the set of integers. Since $7 - (-3) = 10$, we know that -3 is a root. We could try other integer replacements for y to convince ourselves that this is the only root. Hence, the solution set is $\{-3\}$.

Exercises 48:

Using $\{-5,-4,-3,-2,-1,0,1,2,3,4,5,\}$ as the replacement set, find the solution set of each of these open sentences.

1. $n + 7 = 9$	4. $7 - r < 0$
2. $3x + 2 = -7$	5. $(n \div 2) + 3 = 5$
3. $3 + k < 1$	6. $4t - 7 < 10$

7. $21 - n = 21$
8. $13 \times k = -13$
9. $3(2 + n) = 0$
10. $4(15 \div n) = -12$

EQUATIONS

Those number sentences that state that two expressions are names for the same number are called *equations.* The following are examples of an equation.

$$7 + 6 = 13 \quad n = 9$$
$$5 + 2 = 76 \quad 4(5 + r) = 28$$

We see that an equation might be true, such as $7 + 6 = 13$, or it might be false, such as $5 + 2 = 76$, or it might be an open sentence.

If an equation is not an open sentence, all we need do is determine whether it is true or false. Hence, we are primarily concerned with those equations that are open sentences. When no confusion is possible, let us refer to such open sentences as equations.

Definition 20:

To *solve an equation* means to find its solution set.

Throughout this chapter consider the replacement set to be the set of integers for all equations, unless directed otherwise.

In an equation such as $n = 5$ or $k = -56$, the solution set is obvious. We can guess to find the solution set of an equation such as $n + 3 = 5$ or $5t = 15$.

Study how the following equations might be solved mentally.

Solve $3n + 5 = 11$.

By previous agreement, the replacement set for n is the set of integers. Ask yourself: What number plus 5 gives a sum of 11? Since $6 + 5 = 11$, then $3n = 6$. Then ask yourself: 3 times what number gives a product of 6? Since $3 \times 2 = 6$, then $n = 2$. The solution set is $\{2\}$. Check your answer by replacing n by 2 in the original equation ($3n + 5 = 11$) and compute to see if this replacement makes the resulting sentence true.

Exercises 49:

Solve these equations.

1. $n + 5 = 12$
2. $5k = 35$
3. $36 \div y = 4$
4. $16 + x = 10$
5. $7 + 3t = 19$
6. $4r + 20 = 0$
7. $x(12 - 8) = 28$
8. $8k \div 2 = -16$

ADDITION PROPERTY OF EQUATIONS

As we attempt to solve more complicated equations, we become aware that a more systematic or logical procedure is needed. That is, we should like to develop a sequence of reasoning for restating an equation until it becomes simple enough for us to solve mentally. However, each step in the reasoning process should be based on the properties of numbers, the properties of the operations, or on the properties of equations that we shall assume.

Suppose we are to solve $r + 5 = 17$. We already know that $r = 12$ since $12 + 5 = 17$, but let us examine more closely how to arrive at such a root. Can we somehow restate the equation so that only r remains on one side of the equal sign?

Let us begin by thinking of $r + 5$. We can undo the adding of 5 by adding its additive inverse, which is -5.

$$\begin{aligned} (r + 5) + (-5) &= r + [5 + (-5)] && \text{Assoc. prop. } + \\ &= r + 0 && \text{Additive inverses} \\ &= r && \text{Identify number } + \end{aligned}$$

Since $r + 5 = 17$ means that $r + 5$ and 17 are two names for the same number, we must also add -5 to 17 in order that the two new expressions still name the same number. Hence, we could solve the equation as illustrated below.

$$\begin{aligned} r + 5 &= 17 \\ (r + 5) + (-5) &= 17 + (-5) \\ & && \text{Assoc. prop. } + \\ r + [5 + (-5)] &= 12 \\ & && \text{Additive inverses} \\ r + 0 &= 12 \\ & && \text{Identity number } + \\ r &= 12 \end{aligned}$$

The first step in the above solution uses what we call the **addition property of equations.**

For all integers a, b, and c.
if $a = b$, then $a + c = b + c$.

In other words, we can add the same number to both sides of an equation. Of course, we know that adding a negative integer is equivalent to subtracting its opposite. Hence, we do not need such a property for subtraction.

Study the following examples.

Example 1: Solve $17 = n - 8$.

	Add. prop. of equations
$17 + 8 = (n - 8) + 8$	
	Addition
$25 = [n + (-8)] + 8$	
	Assoc. prop. +
$25 = n + [(-8) +]$	
	Additive inverses
$25 = n + 0$	
	Identity number +
$25 = n$	

Example 2: Solve $12 + x = 31$.

Since addition is commutative, we can add -12 on the right or on the left of $12 + x$ and 31.

$12 + x = 31$	
	Add. prop. of equations
$(-12) + (12 + x) = (-12) + 31$	
	Assoc. prop. +
$[(-12) + 12] + x = 19$	
	Additive inverses
$0 + x = 19$	
	Identity number +
$x = 19$	

Exercises 50:

Find the solution set for each equation.

1. $k + 7 = 21$
2. $29 + x = 36$
3. $y - 12 = 43$
4. $8 + r = -9$
5. $-5 + n = 72$
6. $t + 6 = -18$
7. $17 = r + 6$
8. $n - (-3) = 11$
9. $-7 = r + 15$
10. $76 + n = 76$

MULTIPLICATION PROPERTY OF EQUATIONS

We can denote division by several symbols. In an equation such as $n \div 3 = 17$ it is convenient to state $n \div 3$ as $\frac{n}{3}$.

Again, to restate the equation so that it can be solved mentally, we should like to restate the equation so that only n remains on one side of the equal sign.

We can think of undoing the dividing by 3 by multiplying by 3, since multiplication and division are inverse operations.

$$n \div 3 = 17$$
$$(n \div 3) \times 3 = 17 \times 3$$
$$n = 51$$

Another way of writing this is:

$$\frac{n}{3} = 17$$
$$\frac{n}{3} \times 3 = 17 \times 3$$
$$\frac{n \times 3}{3} = 51$$
$$n \times \frac{3}{3} = 51$$
$$n \times 1 = 51$$
$$n = 51$$

In the first step of this solution we used the **multiplication property of equations.**

For all integers a, b, and c, if $a = b$, then $a \times c = b \times c$.

Study how this property is used in solving the following equation.

$$-14 = \frac{a}{4}$$
$$(-14)(4) = \frac{a}{4} \times 4$$
$$-56 = \frac{a \times 4}{4}$$
$$-56 = a \times \frac{4}{4}$$
$$-56 = a \times 1$$
$$-56 = a$$

Fractions occurred in both of the preceding examples. You are probably familiar with the operations on these fractional numbers. These operations will be fully explained in the chapter dealing with rational numbers.

Exercises 51:

Solve the following equations.

1. $\frac{c}{5} = 8$
2. $\frac{x}{-3} = 9$
3. $21 = \frac{n}{10}$
4. $0 = \frac{t}{3}$
5. $\frac{n}{-4} = -7$
6. $\frac{x}{12} = -6$
7. $25 = \frac{c}{3 - 4}$
8. $\frac{a}{-9} = 1$
9. $\frac{a}{2 + 5} = 8$
10. $\frac{t}{4(-5)} = -8$
11. $3(-6) = \frac{n}{5}$
12. $\frac{r}{-1} = 1$

DIVISION PROPERTY OF EQUATIONS

Consider solving the equation $4n = 32$. In this case n is multiplied by 4. Since multiplication and division are inverse operations, we can undo multiplying by 4 by dividing by 4. So we might divide both $4n$ and 32 by 4, as shown in the following example.

$$4n = 32$$
$$\frac{4n}{4} = \frac{32}{4}$$
$$\frac{4}{4} \times n = 8$$
$$1 \times n = 8$$
$$n = 8$$

In this case we have used the **division property of equations.**

For all integers a, b, and c, where $c \neq 0$, if $a = b$, then $\frac{a}{c} = \frac{b}{c}$

We might ask why we have a division property and no subtraction property. Once we have invented the set rational (fractional) numbers, we can show that the division property is no longer needed. Until that time we will use this property of equations.

Study how this property is used in the following examples.

Example 1: Solve $5n = 35$.

$$5n = 35$$
$$\frac{5n}{5} = \frac{35}{5} \quad \text{Div. prop. of equations}$$
$$\frac{5}{5} \times n = 7$$
$$1 \times n = 7$$
$$n = 7$$

Example 2: Solve $-8c = 56$.

$$-8c = 56$$
$$\frac{-8c}{-8} = \frac{56}{-8} \quad \text{Div. prop. of equations}$$
$$\frac{-8}{-8} \times c = -7$$
$$1 \times c = -7$$
$$c = -7$$

Exercises 52:

Solve these equations.

1. $4n = 36$
2. $42 = -6r$
3. $-7k = 63$
4. $-5x = -75$
5. $-k = 47$
6. $72 = 8x$
7. $-52 = -a$
8. $t(5 + 2) = 91$
9. $n(5 - 9) = -24$
10. $x(21 \times 3) = 0$

SOLVING EQUATIONS

As we attempt to solve more and more complicated equations, we may need to use more than one of the properties of equations or use the same property more than once.

In solving an equation such as $5t + 6 = 21$ it is generally advisable to use the property that is most convenient for changing the expression $5t + 6$ to $5t$ first. Then use the property for changing $5t$ to t. Study the following example.

$$5t + 6 = 21$$

Addition property of equations

$$(5t + 6) + (-6) = 21 + (-6)$$

Assoc. prop. +

$$5t + [6 + (-6)] = 21 + (-6)$$

Addition

$$5t + 0 = 15$$

Identity number +

$$5t = 15$$

Division property of equations

$$\frac{5t}{5} = \frac{15}{5}$$

Division

$$t = 3$$

Then we can check our work by replacing t by 3 in the original equation.

$$5t + 6 = 21$$
$$5(3) + 6 = 21$$
$$15 + 6 = 21$$
$$21 = 21$$

Since we have shown that $5(3) + 6$ and 21 name the same number, we know that 3 is a root of the equation.

Since we know that adding a number and its additive inverse is equivalent to adding zero, we can combine some of the steps when writing the previous solution. Also, we may make some of the calculations mentally in the process. However, the example shows the thinking steps necessary in solving the equation.

As you study the following examples, think of the reason or reasons for each step.

Example 1: Solve
$$\frac{n}{4} - 13 = 3.$$

$$\frac{n}{4} - 13 = 3$$
$$\left[\frac{n}{4} + (-13)\right] + 13 = 3 + 13$$
$$\frac{n}{4} = 16$$
$$\frac{n}{4} \times 4 = 16 \times 4$$
$$n = 64$$

Example 2: Solve $\dfrac{x-5}{4} = 6.$

$$\frac{x-5}{4} = 6$$
$$\frac{x-5}{4} \times 4 = 6 \times 4$$
$$x - 5 = 24$$
$$(x - 5) + 5 = 24 + 5$$
$$x = 29$$

Example 3: Solve $\dfrac{3t+7}{2} = 26.$

$$\frac{3t+7}{2} = 26$$
$$\frac{3t+7}{2} \times 2 = 26 \times 2$$
$$3t + 7 = 52$$
$$(3t + 7) + (-7) = 52 + (-7)$$
$$3t = 45$$
$$\frac{3t}{3} = \frac{45}{3}$$
$$t = 15$$

Example 4: Solve $5(2t - 14) = 60.$

Solution 1:
$$5(2t - 14) = 60$$
$$\frac{5(2t-14)}{5} = \frac{60}{5}$$
$$2t - 14 = 12$$
$$(2t - 14) + 14 = 12 + 14$$
$$2t = 26$$
$$\frac{2t}{2} = \frac{26}{2}$$
$$t = 13$$

Solution 2:
$$5(2t - 14) = 60$$
$$10t - 70 = 60$$
$$(10t - 70) + 70 = 60 + 70$$
$$10t = 130$$
$$\frac{10t}{10} = \frac{130}{10}$$
$$t = 13$$

Exercises 53:

Solve these equations. Check your answers by replacing the variable in the original equation with the root you have found.

1. $3n + 4 = 19$
2. $14 = \dfrac{a}{2} - 6$
3. $-26 = 1 - 3x$
4. $15 + 3t = 0$
5. $3t + 5 = 29$
6. $\dfrac{r}{4} + 8 = 7$
7. $4(k + 4) = 0$
8. $\dfrac{3n}{4} = 9$
9. $\dfrac{2c}{5} + 6 = 10$
10. $\dfrac{n+7}{5} = 16$
11. $\dfrac{5n}{3} - 13 = 2$
12. $12 = 11t - 10$
13. $4 = \dfrac{3n-4}{8}$
14. $7t - 18 = 73$
15. $3(4n - 1) = 21$
16. $\dfrac{n+14}{3} = 20$

MORE ABOUT SOLVING EQUATIONS

If a variable occurs more than once in the same equation, it must be replaced by the same numeral in both instances. For example, if either of the letters k in $5k + 2 = 7 + k$ is replaced by the numeral 3, then the other must also be replaced by 3.

Before solving equations where the same variable occurs more than once, let us investigate some expressions of this type.

What is a simpler name for $2y + 5y$? Our first guess would probably be $7y$. We could test our guess for a few replacements of y to see if $2y + 5y = 7y$. For example:

If we replace y by 3, then
$2y + 5y = 2(3) + 5(3) - 6 + 15 = 21$
$7y = 7(3) = 21$

If we place y by -5, then

$$2y + 5y = 2(-5) + 5(-5) = -10 + (-25) = -35$$

$$7y = 7(-5) = -35$$

At least for these two replacements of y the sentence $2y + 5y = 7y$ is true. Since it is impossible to test this equation for all values of y, let us use the properties of numbers and their operations to verify that $2y + 5y = 7y$.

$$\begin{aligned} 2y + 5y &= (2 \times y) + (5 \times y) \\ &= (2 + 5) \times y && \text{Dist. prop.} \\ &= 7 \times y && \text{Addition} \\ &= 7y \end{aligned}$$

We can also use the distributive property to show that $9x - 5x = 4x$.

$$\begin{aligned} 9x - 5x &= 9x + (-5x) \\ &= [9 + (-5)]x \\ &= 4x \end{aligned}$$

Since a placeholder or variable names a number, we can treat it just as we do a numeral when solving an equation, as shown in the following.

Example 1: Solve $9t = 40 + t$.

$$\begin{aligned} 9t &= 40 + t \\ 9t + (-t) &= (40 + t) + (-t) \\ 8t &= 40 \\ \frac{8t}{8} &= \frac{40}{8} \\ t &= 5 \end{aligned}$$

Example 2: Solve $5(2n - 3) = 21 + n$.

$$\begin{aligned} 5(2n - 3) &= 21 + n \\ 10n - 15 &= 21 + n \\ (10n - 15) + (-n) &= (21 + n) + (-n) \\ (-n) + [10n + (-15)] &= 21 + 0 \\ [(-n) + 10n] + (-15) &= 21 \\ 9n + (-15) &= 21 \\ [9n + (-15)] + 15 &= 21 + 15 \\ 9n &= 36 \\ \frac{9n}{9} &= \frac{36}{9} \\ n &= 4 \end{aligned}$$

Exercises 54:

Solve these questions.

1. $7k + 8 = 11k$
2. $8n = 14 + n$
3. $4t - 5 = t + 1$
4. $7r + 3r = 130$
5. $17x - 11x = 42$
6. $c + 3(5 + c) = 23$
7. $a + 14 = 5(a - 2)$
8. $2t + 18 = t + 6$
9. $3(2t - 18) = 11 + t$
10. $15 - t = 2(6 + t)$

TRANSLATING ENGLISH PHRASES

One of the most important skills in problem-solving is the ability to translate a problem stated in the English language into the language of mathematics. That is, we want to write an open sentence that says essentially the same thing as a "story problem."

We know from our study of the English language that sentences may contain phrases. Before translating sentences, let us investigate what we shall call *open phrases,* such as $k + 5$.

Suppose we want to express John's age 6 years ago and we do not know what John's age is now. We might think as follows.

Number of years in John's age now ________ n

Number of years in John's age 6 years ago ________ $n - 6$

Suppose Bob's age is 5 years more than 3 times his sister's age. How can we express Bob's age?

Number of years in his sister's age ________ s

3 times the number of years in his sister's age ________ $3s$

5 years more than 3 times the number of years in his sister's age ________ $3s + 5$.

In making the translation from English to mathematics, we first choose some letter to use as the variable. Then decide which operation or operations say essentially the same thing as the English words.

Exercises 55:

Translate the following English phrases into open phrases. Use the letter n for the variable in each open phrase.

1. Seven more than some number
2. Three less than 2 times some number
3. The sum of a number and twice the number
4. Mary's age 8 years from now
5. The number of cents in n nickels and $(7 - n)$ dimes
6. A man's age is 9 years greater than 2 times his son's age
7. The sum of 3 times some number and 4 times the number
8. Five more than twice the number of dollars Jim has
9. The number of feet in the distance around a square
10. Bob's score on a test if he answered 3 problems incorrectly

TRANSLATING ENGLISH SENTENCES

We usually describe a problem situation in the English language. Some of the English sentences can be translated into mathematical sentences and others cannot be so translated. For example, the sentence "The rose is red" does not lend itself to a mathematical translation.

Consider the following sentence.

John is 14 years old.

This sentence is just as meaningful if stated as follows. Then we can easily translate it into the language of mathematics.

The number of years in John's age	*is*	*14.*
↓	↓	↓
n	$=$	14

Now consider the following sentence.

Six years ago John was 8 years old.

This sentence is just as meaningful if stated as follows.

The number of years in John's age 6 years ago	*was*	8.
↓	↓	↓
n	$=$	8

Notice that both of these sentences were rewritten in order to emphasize that the variable, in this case n, represents a *number*.

Exercises 56:

Translate each of these English sentences into open sentences. Use the letter t for the variable in each open sentence.

1. If Mark spends 3 dollars he will have 4 dollars left.
2. The product of some number and 12 is 32.
3. The difference between 3 times some number and 8 is 7.
4. Alice received 51 votes, which is 7 more votes than George received.
5. When a certain number is divided by 5 the quotient is -9.

SOLVING PROBLEMS

There is no one set of rules for solving problems, nor is there one way to apply mathematics to the physical world. However, some suggestions can be made for solving problems.

a. Study the problem carefully and think about the situation in terms of which operation or operations to use and what open sentence you might write for the problem.

b. Translate the problem into an open sentence.

c. Solve the open sentence.

d. Use the root or roots of the open sentence to answer the problem.

Study how each of the following problems are translated into an open sentence and how the root of the open sentence is used to answer the problem.

Example 1:

The George Washington Bridge has two end spans of the same length and a center span that is 3600 feet long. The overall length of the bridge is 4800 feet. How long is each end span?

Let f = the number of feet in the length of each end span

$$2f + 3600 = 4800$$
$$(2f + 3600) + (-3600) = 4800 + (-3600)$$
$$2f = 1200$$
$$\frac{2f}{2} = \frac{1200}{2}$$
$$f = 600$$

Each end span is 600 feet long.

Example 2:

Jim and Ed were the only candidates for president. Jim received 52 more votes than Ed. If 264 votes were cast, how many votes did each boy receive?

Let e = the number of votes for Ed

$e + 52$ = the number of votes for Jim

$$e + (e + 52) = 264$$
$$(e + e) + 52 = 264$$
$$2e + 52 = 264$$
$$(2e + 52) + (-52) = 264 + (-52)$$
$$2e = 212$$
$$\frac{2e}{2} = \frac{212}{2}$$
$$e = 106$$

Ed received 106 votes.
Jim received $e + 52$ or 158 votes.

Example 3:

Jean's age is 7 years more than twice her sister's age. If Jean is 19 years old, how old is her sister?

Let s = the number of years in her sister's age

$$2s + 7 = 19$$
$$(2s + 7) + (-7) = 19 + (-7)$$
$$2s = 12$$
$$s = 6$$

Her sister is 6 years old.

Exercises 57:

Solve these problems.

1. The sum of two times a certain number and 6 is 22. What is the number?
2. One number is 3 more than a second number. Their sum is 67. What are the two numbers?
3. Ted weighs 9 pounds less than Roger. Their combined weight is 239 pounds. How much does each boy weigh?
4. A rope 26 feet long is cut into 2 pieces so that one piece is 8 feet longer than the other. How long is the shorter piece of rope?
5. A rectangle is 12 inches long. Its perimeter is 44 inches. How wide is the rectangle?
6. The sum of a number and 4 times the number is 75. What is the number?
7. Rita said, "If I had 40 cents more than twice what I have, I would have $3.30." How much money does Rita have?
8. Robert pays 5 cents each for papers and sells them for 8 cents each. Last week he earned $2.70 by selling papers. How many papers did he sell last week?
9. The difference between a number and 5 times the number is 32. What is the number? (Hint: There are two possible answers—one positive and one negative.)

Answers to Exercises

Ex. 1:

1. {Huron, Superior, Erie, Michigan, Ontario}
2. {October, November, December}
3. {Texas, Louisiana, Mississippi, Alabama, Florida}
4. $\emptyset$ or the empty set
5. {January, February, March, April, May, June, July, August, September, October, November, December}
6. {Alaska, Alabama, Arizona, Arkansas}
7. The set of the first 4 letters of the English alphabet
8. The set of vowels in the English alphabet
9. The set of the last 3 letters of the English alphabet

10. $\in$	12. $\notin$	14. $\notin$
11. $\in$	13. $\notin$	15. $\in$

Ex. 2:

1. $\not\subset$	3. $\subset$	5. $\subset$
2. $\not\subset$	4. $\subset$	6. $\subset$

7. $\{x,y\}$, $\{x\}$, $\{y\}$, $\emptyset$
8. $\{a,b,c,d\}$, $\{a,b,c\}$, $\{a,b,d\}$, $\{a,c,d\}$, $\{b,c,d\}$, $\{a,b\}$, $\{a,c\}$, $\{a,d\}$, $\{b,c\}$, $\{b,d\}$, $\{c,d\}$, $\{a\}$, $\{b\}$, $\{c\}$, $\{d\}$, $\emptyset$
9. If a set contains n members, then it contains 2^n subsets.

Ex. 3:

1. $\neq$	3. $\neq$	5. $\neq$	7. $=$	9. $\neq$
2. $=$	4. $=$	6. $\neq$	8. $\neq$	10. $\neq$

Ex. 4:

Answers may vary.

1. $\{a, b, c, d\}$

   $\{w, x, y, z\}$
2. $\{1, 2, 3, 4, 5, 6\}$

   $\{2, 4, 6, 8, 10, 12\}$

Ex. 5:

1. 8	3. 9	5. 0	7. 36
2. 7	4. 12	6. 4	8. 50

Ex. 6:

1. 85 2. 539 3. 730

4. 777 5. 3432 6. 6051

7. (4 × 10) + (6 × 1)
8. (1 × 100) + (2 × 10 + (4 × 1)
9. (6 × 100) + (2 × 10) + (9 × 1)
10. (8 × 10) + (2 × 1)
11. (3 × 1000) + (4 × 100) + (2 × 10) + (6 × 1)
12. (2 × 1000) + (0 × 100) + (4 × 10) + (1 × 1)

Ex. 7:

1. 10^5 3. 10^4 5. 4^6
2. 10^2 4. 7^4

6. 10 × 10 × 10
7. 10 × 10 × 10 × 10 × 10
8. 10 × 10 × 10 × 10 × 10 × 10 × 10
9. 6 × 6 × 6 × 6

Ex. 8:

1. 1,100,002,826 3. 712,309
2. 5,000,001 4. 52,000,018

Ex. 9:

1. $J \cup K = \{1,2,3,5,7,9\}$
2. $K \cup M = \{2,3,4,5,6,7,8,9\}$
3. $K \cup N = \{0,3,5,7,9\}$
4. $J \cup M = \{1,2,3,4,6,8\}$
5. $J \cup N = \{0,1,2,3,5,9\}$
6. $M \cup N = \{0,2,4,5,6,8,9\}$
7. $N \cup M = \{0,2,4,5,6,8,9\}$
8. $K \cup K = \mathrm{K}$

Ex. 10:

1. $C \cap D = \{2,3\}$ 5. $D \cap E = \{3\}$
2. $D \cap C = \{2,3\}$ 6. $D \cap F = \{7,8\}$
3. $C \cap E = \mathrm{E}$ 7. $E \cap F = \emptyset$
4. $C \cap F = \emptyset$ 8. $E \cap E = \mathrm{E}$

Ex. 11:

1. T 4. T 7. T 10. T
2. T 5. T 8. T
3. F 6. T 9. T or F

Ex. 12:

1. 11, 10, 12, 14, 13
2. 7, 12, 14, 10, 18
3. 16, 10, 16, 9, 15
4. 15, 13, 12, 11, 13
5. 11, 10, 10, 14, 12

Ex. 13:

1. No 2. Yes 3. No
4. No 5. No 6. No

7. 3 + 7 = 7 + 3
8. 8 + 15 = 15 + 8
9. 36 + 17 = 17 + 36
10. 156 + 13 = 13 + 156
11. 129 + 47 = 47 + 129
12. 326 + 218 = 218 + 326
13. 327 + 56 = 56 + 327
14. 651 + 87 = 87 + 651

Ex. 14:

1. Yes 2. Yes 3. Yes

4. 5 + (7 + 6) = (5 + 7) + 6
5. 17 + (15 + 32) = (17 + 15) + 32
6. (9 + 8) + 7 = 9 + (8 + 7)
7. 13 + (12 + 6) = (13 + 12) + 6
8. (72 + 31) + 46 = 72 + (31 + 46)

9. 16 10. 27 11. 13 12. 29

Ex. 15:

1. A 4. C, A 7. A 10. A
2. C 5. C 8. C
3. C 6. C, A 9. C, A

Ex. 16:

1. 16, 17, 24, 132, 109
2. 20, 20, 40, 29, 150

Ex. 17:

1. 878, 7999, 59998
2. 777, 8847, 88978
3. 689, 1979, 37927
4. 368, 6788, 18796

Ex. 18

1. 6021, 79870, 908182
2. 8021, 58322, 1006033
3. 4923, 194967, 674437
4. 2267, 44007, 330068

Ex. 19:

1. Open your eyes
2. Sit down (or lie down)
3. Return from school
4. Open your book
5. Take 5 steps backward
6. Tie your shoe
7. Subtract seven
8. Add thirteen

Ex. 20:

1. 15 2. 754 3. 69 4. 26

5. 756 6. 39 7. 312 8. r

9. 8 12. 6 15. 7
10. 3 13. 9 16. 9
11. 8 14. 7

Ex. 21:

1. 6 3. 8 5. 9
2. 4 4. 8 6. 9

7. $9 + n = 12$, 3 awards, answers may vary
8. $15 - n = 7$, 8 cupcakes, answers may vary
9. $12 - 8 = n$, 4 children, answers may vary
10. $7 + n = 13$, 6 apples, answers may vary

Ex. 22:

1. 225, 5234, 46323
2. 113, 3013, 20344
3. 621, 3135, 34711

Ex. 23:

1. 152, 1318, 34882
2. 182, 1907, 26151
3. 188, 2387, 26803

Ex. 24:

1. $\begin{array}{r} 163 \\ +152 \\ \hline 315 \end{array}$ $\begin{array}{r} 2109 \\ +1318 \\ \hline 3427 \end{array}$ $\begin{array}{r} 21467 \\ +34882 \\ \hline 56349 \end{array}$

2. $\begin{array}{r} 226 \\ +182 \\ \hline 408 \end{array}$ $\begin{array}{r} 3475 \\ +1907 \\ \hline 5382 \end{array}$ $\begin{array}{r} 20858 \\ +26151 \\ \hline 47009 \end{array}$

3. $\begin{array}{r} 537 \\ +188 \\ \hline 725 \end{array}$ $\begin{array}{r} 3856 \\ +2387 \\ \hline 6243 \end{array}$ $\begin{array}{r} 43197 \\ +26803 \\ \hline 70000 \end{array}$

Ex. 25:

1. 9 2. 8 3. 6 4. 24

Ex. 26:

1. 15 4. 14 7. 24 10. 28
2. 24 5. 16 8. 30 11. 18
3. 10 6. 16 9. 27 12. 9

Ex. 27:

1. $2 + 2 + 2 + 2 + 2 + 2; 12$
2. $1 + 1 + 1 + 1 + 1 + 1; 6$
3. $6; 6$
4. $5 + 5 + 5 + 5; 20$
5. $4 + 4 + 4 + 4 + 4; 20$
6. $7 + 7 + 7; 21$
7. $7 + 7 + 7 + 7 + 7 + 7; 42$
8. $9 + 9 + 9 + 9; 36$
9. $7 + 7 + 7 + 7 + 7; 35$

10. $4 \times 8 = 32$ 13. $5 \times 9 = 45$
11. $6 \times 5 = 30$ 14. $2 \times 9 = 18$
12. $5 \times 1 = 5$ 15. $9 \times 2 = 18$

Ex. 28:

1. $5 \times 9 = 9 \times 5$ 6. $23 \times 5 = 5 \times 23$
2. $7 \times 8 = 8 \times 7$ 7. $9 \times 18 = 18 \times 9$
3. $31 \times 7 = 7 \times 31$ 8. $27 \times 13 = 13 \times 27$
4. $12 \times 6 = 6 \times 12$ 9. $357 \times 6 = 6 \times 357$
5. $9 \times 17 = 17 \times 9$ 10. $43 \times 127 = 127 \times 43$

Ex. 29:

1. $(3 \times 7) \times 5 = 3 \times (7 \times 5)$
2. $4 \times (2 \times 3) = (4 \times 2) \times 3$
3. $(6 \times 3) \times 2 = 6 \times (3 \times 2)$
4. $17 \times (8 \times 5) = (17 \times 8) \times 5$
5. $(13 \times 9) \times 3 = 13 \times (9 \times 3)$

6. A 8. C 10. C 12. A
7. C 9. C, A 11. C, A

Ex. 30:

1. $7 \times (2 + 5) = (7 \times 2) + (7 \times 5)$
2. $4 \times (3 + 6) = (4 \times 3) + (4 \times 6)$
3. $(4 + 5) \times 3 = (4 \times 3) + (5 \times 3)$
4. $(8 + 9) \times 6 = (8 \times 6) + (9 \times 6)$
5. $(5 \times 2) + (7 \times 2) = (5 + 7) \times 2$
6. $(6 \times 3) + (8 \times 3) = (6 + 8) \times 3$

Ex. 31:

1. 60 4. 800 7. 400 10. 4000
2. 900 5. 200 8. 4000
3. 30 6. 40 9. 400

Ex. 32:

1. 210 3. 4500 5. 24000
2. 3200 4. 1400 6. 140000

Ex. 33:

1. 168 4. 2124 7. 188 10. 2568
2. 390 5. 296 8. 145 11. 1371
3. 744 6. 3834 9. 1038 12. 5706

Ex. 34:

1. 494 4. 1296 7. 4067
2. 648 5. 4056 8. 3876
3. 1645 6. 986 9. 2325

Ex. 35:

1. 1872 3. 10044 5. 83025
2. 12768 4. 134784 6. 273132

7. 13704 8. 144672 9. 1101562

Ex. 36:
1. $1200 < n < 2100$, 1755
2. $5600 < n < 7200$, 6150
3. $1500 < n < 2400$, 2262
4. $3600 < n < 5000$, 4042
5. $12000 < n < 20000$, 17249
6. $28000 < n < 40000$, 37884
7. $40000 < n < 54000$, 42952
8. $30000 < n < 42000$, 38324

Ex. 37:

1. 4	4. 4	7. 2	10. 2
2. 3	5. 5	8. 4	11. 8
3. 3	6. 9	9. 3	12. 6

Ex. 38:

1. 6	5. 9	9. 5
2. 7	6. 7	10. 7
3. 6	7. 5	11. 9
4. 9	8. 4	12. 4

Ex. 39:

1. 8	4. 11	7. 13
2. 13	5. 12	8. 12
3. 13	6. 6	9. 19

Ex. 40:

1. 3 *r*2	4. 6 *r*1	7. 13 *r*3
2. 3 *r*3	5. 4 *r*4	8. 9 *r*1
3. 2 *r*1	6. 5 *r*3	9. 11 *r*1

Ex. 41:

1. 15	4. 63	7. 415
2. 26	5. 72	8. 421
3. 34	6. 67	9. 352

Ex. 42:

1. 16 *r*15	4. 7 *r*13	7. 123 *r*0
2. 17 *r*7	5. 17 *r*0	8. 124 *r*7
3. 11 *r*11	6. 12 *r*2	9. 200 *r*0

Ex. 43:

1. 6 *r*13	5. 123 *r*25	9. 322 *r*9
2. 38 *r*0	6. 201 *r*17	10. 24 *r*0
3. 42 *r*3	7. 137 *r*6	11. 102 *r*0
4. 10 *r*22	8. 211 *r*9	12. 86 *r*0

Ex. 44:

1. F	4. T	7. T	10. F
2. T	5. F	8. T	
3. T	6. F	9. T	

Ex. 45:

1. 28	4. 32	7. 5	10. 0
2. 36	5. 4	8. 54	
3. 17	6. 19	9. 1	

11. $(30 - 12) \div (3 \times 2)$
12. $[30 - (12 \div 3)] \times 2$
13. $[(30 - 12) \div 3] \times 2$
14. $30 - [12 \div (3 \times 2)]$
15. $30 - [(12 \div 3) \times 2]$

Ex. 46:

1. T	3. F	5. F
2. T	4. T	6. F

Ex. 47:

1. O	3. O	5. O
2. T	4. F	6. F

Ex. 48:
1. $\{2\}$
2. $\{-3\}$
3. $\{-3, -4, -5\}$
4. $\emptyset$
5. $\{4\}$
6. $\{-5, -4, -3, -2, -1, 0, 1, 2, 3, 4\}$
7. $\{0\}$
8. $\{-1\}$
9. $\{-2\}$
10. $\{-5\}$

Ex. 49:

1. 7	3. 9	5. 4	7. 7
2. 7	4. −6	6. −5	8. −4

Ex. 50:

1. 14	3. 55	5. 77	7. 11	9. −22
2. 7	4. −17	6. −24	8. 8	10. 0

Ex. 51:

1. 40	4. 0	7. −25	10. 160
2. −27	5. 28	8. −9	11. −90
3. 210	6. −72	9. 56	12. −1

Ex. 52:

1. 9	4. 15	7. 52	10. 0
2. −7	5. −47	8. 13	
3. −9	6. 9	9. 6	

Ex. 53:

1. 5	5. 8	9. 10	13. 12
2. 40	6. −4	10. 73	14. 13
3. 9	7. −3	11. 9	15. 2
4. −5	8. 12	12. 2	16. 46

Ex. 54:

1. 2	4. 13	7. 6	10. 1
2. 2	5. 7	8. −12	
3. 2	6. 2	9. 13	

Ex. 55:

1. $n + 7$	6. $2n + 9$
2. $2n - 3$	7. $3n + 4n$
3. $n + 2n$	8. $2n + 5$
4. $n + 8$	9. $4n$
5. $5n + 10(7 - n)$	10. $n - 3$

Ex. 56:

1. $t - 3 = 4$
2. $12t = 32$
3. $3t - 8 = 7$
4. $t + 7 = 51$
5. $t \div 5 = -9$

Ex. 57:

Typical solutions.

1. $2n + 6 = 22$; 8
2. $n + (n + 3) = 67$; 32 and 35
3. $r + (r - 9) = 239$; Roger 124 pounds and Ted 115 pounds
4. $p + (p + 8) = 26$; 9 feet
5. $2(w + 12) = 44$; 10 inches
6. $n + 4n = 75$; 15
7. $2a + 40 = 330$; \$1.45
8. $p(8 - 5) = 270$; 90 papers
9. $5n - n = 32$ or $n - 5n = 32$; 8 or −8

CHAPTER FOURTEEN

ALGEBRA

Ratio and Proportion

RATIO

A *ratio* is the relation between two like numbers or two like values. The ratio may be written as a fraction, $\frac{3}{4}$; as a division, $3 \div 4$; or with the colon or *ratio sign* (:), 3 : 4. When the last of these forms is used, it is read, 3 *to* 4; or 3 *is to* 4. Ratios may be expressed by the word *per* as in miles per hour, or revolutions per second. In arithmetic these are written miles/hour, revolutions/minute, volts/ampere. Whatever the manner of writing the ratio, its value in arithmetical computations is always the same.

Since a ratio may be regarded as a fraction, you will recognize the following principle as being true:

Rule 1: *Multiplying or dividing both terms of a ratio by the same number does not change the value of the ratio.*

Thus, 2 : 4 = 4 : 8 (multiplying both terms by 2)
or 2 : 4 = 1 : 2 (dividing both terms by 2)

To reduce a ratio to its lowest terms, *treat the ratio as a fraction and reduce the fraction to its lowest terms.*

EXAMPLE 1: Express $\frac{2}{3}$ to $\frac{4}{9}$ in its lowest terms.

SOLUTION: $\frac{2}{3}$ to $\frac{4}{9} = \frac{2}{3} \div \frac{4}{9} = \frac{2}{3} \times \frac{9}{4} = \frac{3}{2}$.

Hence $\frac{2}{3}$ to $\frac{4}{9}$ is the same as 3 to 2.

To separate a quantity according to a given ratio, *add the terms of the ratio to find the total number of parts. Find what fractional part each term is of the whole. Divide the total quantity into parts corresponding to the fractional parts.*

EXAMPLE 2: Three hundred tents have to be divided between two army divisions in the ratio of 1 : 2. How many does each division get?

1 + 2 = 3 (adding the terms)

$$\left.\begin{array}{l}\frac{1}{3} \times 300 = 100 \\ \frac{2}{3} \times 300 = 200\end{array}\right\} \text{ANS.}$$
(Taking corresponding fractional parts of total quantity)

Check: 100 : 200 or $\frac{100}{200} = \frac{1}{2}$ or 1 : 2.

EXAMPLE 3: 1,600 lbs. of coffee have to be distributed to 3 wholesale dealers in the ratio of 8 : 11 : 13. How many lbs. should each dealer receive?

SOLUTION:

8 + 11 + 13 = 32

$\frac{8}{32}, \frac{11}{32}, \frac{13}{32}$ are the fractional parts

$$\left.\begin{array}{l}\frac{8}{32} \times 1{,}600 = 400 \\ \frac{11}{32} \times 1{,}600 = 550 \\ \frac{13}{32} \times 1{,}600 = 650\end{array}\right\} \text{ANS.}$$

Practice Exercise No. 1

PROBLEMS

1 Reduced to its lowest terms, 24 : 32 equals what?

(A) $\frac{1}{3}$ ____ (C) $\frac{6}{8}$ ____
(B) $\frac{1}{2}$ ____ (D) $\frac{3}{4}$ ✓

2 What is the value of the ratio $7 \times 9 : 8 \times 7$?

(A) $\frac{8}{9}$ ____ (C) 8 :9 ____

(B) $1\frac{1}{8}$ ____ (D) $1\frac{23}{49}$ ____

3 If 5 lbs. of vegetables lose 10 oz. in drying, what part of the original weight was water?

(A) $\frac{1}{6}$ ____ (C) 12% ____

(B) $\frac{1}{8}$ ____ (D) $\frac{1}{2}$ ____

4 A mixture requires 2 parts of water to 3 parts of alcohol. What percentage of the mixture is water?

(A) 40% ____ (C) 60% ____

(B) 50% ____ (D) $66\frac{2}{3}$% ____

5 Bronze consists of 6 parts tin to 19 parts copper. How many pounds of tin are there in a 500-lb. bronze statue?

(A) 100 ____ (C) 140 ____

(B) 120 ____ (D) 200 ____

6 $2,000 is to be distributed among 3 members of a family in the ratio of 5 : 14 : 21. How much greater is the largest share than the smallest share?

(A) $900 ____ (C) $500 ____

(B) $800 ____ (D) $750 ____

PROPORTION

A proportion is a statement of equality between two ratios. It may be written with the double colon or **proportion sign** (: :), or with the sign of equality (=).

Thus, 2 : 6 : : 3 : 9 is a proportion that is read, 2 *is to* 6 *as* 3 *is to* 9; *or* $\frac{2}{6}$ *equals* $\frac{3}{9}$.

In any proportion the first and last terms are called the extremes and the second and third terms are called the **means.** In 2 : 6 : : 3 : 9 the *extremes* are 2 and 9; and the *means* are 6 and 3.

Multiply the two extremes and the two means of the proportion 2 : 6 : : 3 : 9 and compare the products.

Extremes: $2 \times 9 = 18$,
Means: $6 \times 3 = 18$.

This result illustrates **Rule 2:** *The product of the* means *is equal to the product of the* extremes.

If you write the proportion in the form of $\frac{2}{6} = \frac{3}{9}$, note that the means and extremes are diagonally opposite each other. This affords another way to pick out your equation.

No proportion is a true proportion unless the two ratios are equal. This is another way of saying that Rule 2 must be satisfied.

By means of this rule you can find the missing term of any proportion if the other 3 terms are given.

EXAMPLE 1: 2 : 6 = 8 : ? Find the value of the missing term. The letter x is traditionally used to denote a missing term or an unknown quantity. Rewriting the proportion we get

$2 : 6 = 8 : x$.

(a) 2 times x = 6 times 8
$2x = 48$

(b) $\dfrac{2x}{2} = \dfrac{48}{2}$
$x = 24$, ANS.

a. Product of the extremes equals product of the means.
b. Both sides of any equation may be divided by the same number without changing the equation.

The above process is the equation method of solving problems containing an unknown.

If you wish to use a strict arithmetic method of finding the missing term in a proportion, you may employ the following two rules.

Rule 3: *The product of the means divided by either extreme gives the other extreme as the quotient.*

2 : 6 : : 8 : 24;
$6 \times 8 = 48$, $48 \div 2 = 24$, $48 \div 24 = 2$.
Thus if given ? : 6 = 8 : 24,
multiply the two means, $6 \times 8 = 48$,
and divide this product by the known extreme; $48 \div 24 = 2$. The quotient here is the unknown term.

Rule 4: *The product of the extremes divided by either mean gives the other mean as a quotient.*

2 : 6 = 8 : 24;
$2 \times 24 = 48$, $48 \div 6 = 8$, $48 \div 8 = 6$.
Thus if given 2 : ? : : 8 : 24,
multiply the two extremes, $2 \times 24 = 48$, and divide this product by the known means; $48 \div 8 = 6$. The quotient again is the unknown term.

Practice Exercise No. 2

Find the missing term.

1 2 : 3 = 4 : ?	6 5 : ? = 25 : 20
2 20 : 10 = ? : 6	7 ? : 5 = 12 : 20
3 2 : ? = 8 : 24	8 ? : 25 = 10 : 2
4 18 : ? = 36 : 4	9 9 : ? = 24 : 8
5 12 : 4 = ? : 7	10 24 : 4 = ? : 3

PROBLEMS IN PROPORTION

In solving problems by the ratio and proportion method it is first necessary to recognize whether a proportion exists and if so what kind it is.

A direct proportion is indicated when two quantities are so related that an increase in one causes a corresponding increase in the other or when a decrease in one causes a corresponding decrease in the other.

The following is a list of typical quantitative expressions in which the variables are directly related when other quantities remain unchanged.

a. The faster the speed, the greater the distance covered.
b. The more men working, the greater the amount of work done.
c. The faster the speed, the greater the number of revolutions.
d. The higher the temperature of gas, the greater the volume.
e. The taller the object, the longer the shadow.
f. The larger the quantity, the greater the cost.
g. The smaller the quantity, the lower the cost.
h. The greater the length, the greater the area.
j. The greater the base, the larger the discount, commission, interest and profit.

EXAMPLE 2: If 20 men assemble 8 machines in a day, how many men are needed to assemble 12 machines in a day?

SOLUTION:

8 machines need 20 men
12 machines need ? men
$8 : 12 = 20 : x$
$8x = 240$
$x = 30$, ANS.

EXPLANATION: Place corresponding values on the same line. Put *like numbers* together. The more machines, the more men needed. ∴ The values are a direct proportion. Solve for x.

EXAMPLE 3: If 12 drills cost $8.00, how much will 9 drills cost?

SOLUTION:

12 drills cost $8.00
9 drills cost ?
$12 : 9 = 8 : x$
$12x = 72,\ x = \$6.$

EXPLANATION: The fewer the drills the lower the cost. ∴ The values are in direct proportion. Solve for x.

Examples 2 and 3 are easily recognized as direct proportions since more men can assemble more machines, and fewer drills cost less money.

CUES IN SOLVING PROPORTION PROBLEMS

In every proportion both ratios must be written in the same order, for instance in Example 2:

$$\frac{\text{Smaller no. mach's}}{\text{Larger no. of mach's}} = \frac{\text{Smaller no. of men}}{\text{Larger no. of men}}$$

In Example 3:

$$\frac{\text{Larger no. of drills}}{\text{Smaller no. of drills}} = \frac{\text{Larger cost}}{\text{Smaller cost}}$$

An inverse proportion is indicated when two quantities are so related that an increase in one causes a corresponding decrease in the other, or vice versa.

The following are quantitative expressions in which the variables are inversely related.

a. The greater the speed, the less the time.
b. The slower the speed, the longer the time.
c. The greater the volume, the less the density.
d. The more men working, the shorter the time.
e. The fewer men working, the longer the time.

EXAMPLE 4: When two pulleys are belted together the revolutions per minute (rpm) vary inversely as the size of the pulleys. A 20-in. pulley running at 180 rpm drives an 8-in. pulley. Find the revolutions per minute of the 8-in. pulley.

SOLUTION:

20 in. makes 180 rpm
8 in. makes ? rpm

$$\frac{8}{20} = \frac{180}{x}$$

$8x = 3{,}600$
$x = 450$ rpm, ANS.

EXPLANATION: First make a table of corresponding values. Put *like numbers* together. The smaller the pulley, the greater the number of revolutions; ∴ the quantities are in inverse ratio. Inverting the first ratio, write the proportion. Solve for x.

CUE: If you write your proportion in this form, $\frac{8}{20} = \frac{180}{x}$, you may note that in the inverse proportion the corresponding numbers are arranged diagonally, *i.e.*, 20 in. and 180 rpm, and 8 in. and x rpm are diagonally opposite each other.

In the direct proportion as in Example 3, $\frac{12}{9} = \frac{8}{x}$, the corresponding numbers are arranged directly on a line with each other, *i.e.*, 12 drills and \$8, 9 drills and \$$x$.

Practice Exercise No. 3

PROBLEMS

1 If a pole 18 ft. high casts a shadow 20 ft. long, how long a shadow would a pole 27 ft. high cast?

(A) 10 ____ (C) 30 ____
(B) 25 ____ (D) 36 ____

2 If a soldier walks 9 miles in 2 hrs. how long will it take him to walk 30 miles?

(A) 6 ____ (C) $8\frac{1}{2}$ ____
(B) $6\frac{2}{3}$ ____ (D) 9 ____

3 If an automobile runs 90 miles on 5 gal. of gas, how far will it run on a full 20-gal. tank?

(A) 300 ____ (C) 450 ____
(B) 360 ____ (D) 280 ____

4 An army camp has provisions for 240 men for 28 days; but only 112 men are sent to the camp. How long will the provisions last?

(A) 60 ____ (C) $13\frac{2}{3}$ ____
(B) 56 ____ (D) 76 ____

5 A train takes 26 hrs. at a speed of 35 miles per hr. to go from Chicago to New York. How fast must the train travel to make the trip in 20 hours?

(A) $39\frac{1}{2}$ ____ (C) $26\frac{12}{13}$ ____
(B) 40 ____ (D) $45\frac{1}{2}$ ____

6 The flywheel on an engine makes 220 revolutions in 2 seconds. How many revolutions does it make in 8 seconds?

(A) 1,7600 ____ (C) 880 ____
(B) 55 ____ (D) 800 ____

Signed Numbers and Algebraic Expressions

Up to the present, all the numbers used here have been positive numbers. That is, none was less than zero (0). In solving some problems in arithmetic it is necessary to assign a *negative* value to some numbers. This is used principally for numbers with which we wish to represent opposite quantities or qualities, and can best be illustrated by use of a diagram. For example consider a thermometer, as in Fig. 1.

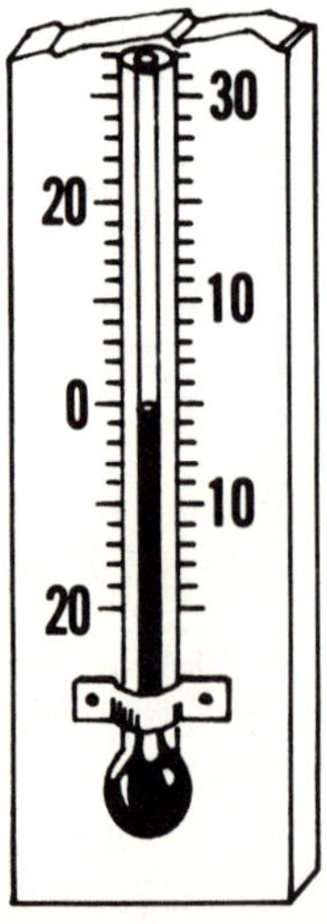

FIGURE 1

If temperatures *above* zero are taken as *positive,* then temperatures *below* zero are considered *negative.*

In measuring distances east and west, as in Fig. 2, if distance *east* of a certain point is taken as *positive,* then distance *west* of that point is considered *negative.*

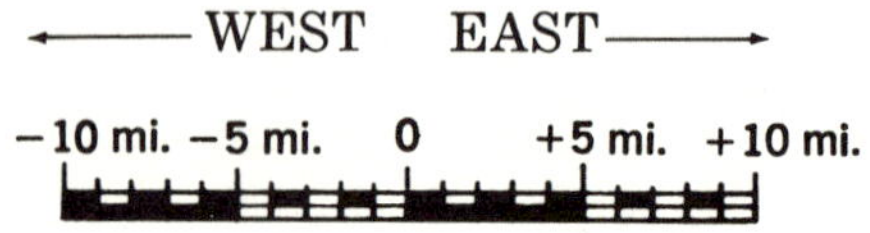

FIGURE 2

Another good example may be taken from commercial bookkeeping, where money in the bank and other *assets* may be considered as *positive* amounts, while money *owed* represents *negative* amounts.

Thus, in general, positive and negative numbers are used to distinguish between opposite qualities. Values above zero are considered positive and take the + sign, while values below zero are considered negative and are written with the − sign. These then become signed numbers, as they are called.

The + and − also continue to be used as signs of addition and subtraction. When no sign is indicated the + sign is understood.

Learning to use signed numbers is an introduction to some of the special rules for algebraic operations and also a preparation for the equation method of solving some difficult arithmetic problems in easier ways.

ADDING SIGNED NUMBERS

To add numbers of like signs, *add the numbers as in arithmetic and give to the result the common sign.*

EXAMPLE 1: -14 added to $-8 = -22$.

EXAMPLE 2: Add $+4$, $+12$, and $+16$. ANS. $+32$.

To add numbers of unlike signs, *combine all positive and negative quantities, subtract the smaller from the larger and give the result the sign of the larger combination.*

EXAMPLE 1: Add $-4\ -8\ +2\ +6\ +10$.

SOLUTION: $(-4) + (-8) = -12$;
$2 + 6 + 10 = 18$
$18 - 12 = 6$, ANS.

EXAMPLE 2: Add $3 + 19 + 4 + (-45)$

SOLUTION: $26 - 45 = -19$, ANS.

What has been done above is called finding the **algebraic sum.** Similarly we can combine numbers that are represented by similar symbols.

EXAMPLE 3: Add $5b + (-11b) + 14b$.

SOLUTION: $19b - 11b = 8b$, ANS.

We cannot arithmetically add terms containing unlike symbols. For instance, if we let b stand for books and p for plates we know from arithmetic that we couldn't combine books and plates as a single quantity of either. Therefore, **to add quantities containing unlike symbols,** *collect like terms and express them separately in the answer.*

EXAMPLE 4: Add $5b + 2p + 7p + 3b$.

SOLUTION: Collecting like terms,

$5b + 3b = 8b$
$2p + 7p = 9p$

Expressing unlike terms separately we get $8b + 9p$, which is an algebraic expression containing two terms, as the answer.

Practice Exercise No. 4

ADDITION OF SIGNED NUMBERS

1 $+5 + 18 =$
2 $-5 + (-17) + (-14) =$
3 $+7 + (-12) + (-6) + 4 =$
4 $-14d + (-6d) =$
5 $7b + (-3b) =$
6 $+22 + (-14) + (-17) + (-12) + 18 =$
7 $5x + (-7x) + 14x =$
8 $3a + 4b + 2a + (-2b) =$
9 $6a + 3b + 9a + (-5b) =$
10 $6a + 3b + 9a + (-5) =$

SUBTRACTING SIGNED NUMBERS

Subtraction means finding the difference between two numbers, or the difference between two values on a scale.

If you were asked what is the difference between $-4°$ centigrade and $+5°$, your answer would be $9°$. You would do this mentally. Now how did you arrive at the answer? First you counted from $-4°$ to zero, then add 5 to that. The rule for subtraction of signed numbers is therefore:

To subtract signed numbers, *change the sign of the subtrahend (the number being subtracted) and apply the rules for addition.*

EXAMPLE 1: Subtract $+20$ from $+32$.

SOLUTION:

$+20$ is the subtrahend or number to be subtracted. Changing its sign and adding, we get $32 - 20 = 12$, ANS.

EXAMPLE 2: From -18 subtract -12.

SOLUTION:

-12 is the subtrahend. Changing its sign and adding, we get $-18 + 12 = -6$, ANS.

Practice Exercise No. 5

SUBTRACTION OF SIGNED NUMBERS

1 $\begin{array}{r} +47 \\ +19 \\ \hline \end{array}$	4 $\begin{array}{r} +54 \\ -12 \\ \hline \end{array}$	7 $(-5) - (-8)$
2 $\begin{array}{r} -26 \\ -17 \\ \hline \end{array}$	5 $\begin{array}{r} 80 \\ -50 \\ \hline \end{array}$	8 $(-7) - (-4)$
3 $\begin{array}{r} -42 \\ -18 \\ \hline \end{array}$	6 $\begin{array}{r} -22ab \\ +18ab \\ \hline \end{array}$	9 $(-9) - (+16)$

MULTIPLICATION AND DIVISION OF SIGNED NUMBERS

Law of signs for multiplication of signed numbers—Rule: *The product of any two numbers that have like signs is positive* (+), *and the product of any two numbers that have unlike signs is negative* (−).

EXAMPLE 1: Multiply −8 by −6.

SOLUTION: The signs are the same.
$\therefore -8 \times -6 = +48$, ANS.

EXAMPLE 2: Multiply +3 by −4.

SOLUTION: The signs are unlike.
$\therefore 3 \times -4 = -12$, ANS.

EXAMPLE 3: Multiply −2 by +5 by −3 by +4.

SOLUTION: $(-2) \times (+5) = -10$,
$(-10) \times (-3) = +30$,
$+ (+30) \times (+4) = +120$, ANS.

Division of signed numbers is carried out by the same process as division in arithmetic, but *the sign of the quotient is positive if the divisor and dividend have the same sign, and negative if the divisor and dividend have opposite signs.*

EXAMPLE 4: Divide −16 by −2.

SOLUTION: $\frac{-16}{-2} = +8$, ANS.

Same signs, ∴ answer is plus (+).

EXAMPLE 5: Divide −35 by +5.

SOLUTION: $\frac{-35}{5} = -7$, ANS.

Opposite signs, ∴ answer is minus (−).

Practice Exercise No. 6

Do the following examples:

1 $2 \times -16 =$	5 $72 \div -24 =$
2 $-18 \times -12 =$	6 $-68 \div -17 =$
3 $-4 \times -6 \times 3 =$	7 $-14 \div -5 =$
4 $4 \times 3 \times -2 \times 6 =$	8 $-24 \times 4 \div 8 =$

ALGEBRAIC EXPRESSIONS

Working with signed numbers is an introduction to using algebraic expressions. An **algebraic expression** is one in which letter symbols are used to represent numbers.

A letter symbol or other type of symbol that represents a number is called a **literal number,** or constant.

If you know the numerical values of the symbols and understand the arithmetic signs of an algebraic expression, then you can find the numerical value of any algebraic expression. *Thus:*

$a + b$ means that b is added to a.
If $a = 2$ and $b = 3$, then $a + b = 5$.

$b - a$ means that a is subtracted from b.
If $b = 6$ and $a = 4$, $b - a = 2$.

$a \times b$ means that b is multiplied by a.
If $a = 7$ and $b = 3$, $a \times b = 21$.

Multiplication can be indicated in four ways in algebra. a multiplied by b can be written $a \times b$, $a \cdot b$, $(a)(b)$, or ab. That is, multiplication can be expressed by a cross ×, by a dot •, by adjacent parentheses, and by directly joining a letter and its multiplier with no sign between them. *Thus* $2a$ means 2 times a, and ab means a times b.

a^2 means $a \cdot a$. You read it: *a squared.*
If $a = 3$, then $a^2 = 3 \cdot 3$ or 9.

a^3 means $a \cdot a \cdot a$. You read it: *a cubed.*
If $a = 3$, then $a^3 = 3 \cdot 3 \cdot 3$ or 27.

$a^2 + b^3$ means that b^3 is to be added to a^2.
If $a = 3$ and $b = 2$, then $a^2 + b^3 = 9 + 8$, or 17.

The small 2 and 3 placed to the right and slightly above the a and the b in writing a^2 and b^3 are called **exponents.**

The number a is called the **base.** a^2 and a^3 are called **powers** of the *base a.*

$3a^2 - 2b^2$ means that $2b^2$ is subtracted from $3a^2$.

The $3a^2$ and $2b^2$ are known as **terms** in the algebraic expression.

The numbers placed before the letters are called **coefficients.** *Thus,* in $3a^2 - 2b^2$, 3 is called the *coefficient* of a^2, 2 is the *coefficient* of b^2. The coefficient so placed indicates multiplication, *i.e.,* $3a^2$ means $3 \times a^2$.

Practice Exercise No. 7

In each of the following write the algebraic expression and find its numerical value if $x = 2$, $y = 3$ and $z = 4$.

1 x added to y =
2 x, y and z added together =
3 Twice x added to twice y =
4 z subtracted from the sum of x and y =
5 The square of x added to the square of y =
6 3 less than y =
7 Twice the product of x and z =

Algebraic Formulas and Equations

In the preceding sections rules in words were used to describe methods to be followed in solving various types of problems. For example, to find the amount of a discount the rule is to multiply the base or price by the rate of discount. By the use of symbols this rule can be expressed in a brief form known as a **formula.**

Thus a short way to express the rule in question is:

a. Discount = Base × Rate

A still shorter way is:

b. $D = B \times R$,

in which *D, B* and *R* means discount, base and rate respectively.

The shortest and algebraic way to express this is:

c. $D = BR$.

DEFINITIONS

A **formula** is a shorthand method of expressing a rule by the use of symbols or letter designations (literal numbers).

At the same time it must be remembered that a formula is an equation. And what is an equation?

An **equation** is a statement that two expressions are equal.

For example, $D = BR$ states that *D*, the discount, is equal to *B*, the base, multiplied by *R*, the rate of discount. Before we can start working with formulas and equations there are a few things that have to be learned about them.

An equation has two equal sides or members. In the equation $D = BR$, *D* is the left side and *BR* is the right side.

Terms are made up of numbers or symbols combined by multiplication or division.

For example, $6DR$ is a term in which the factors 6, *D* and *R* are combined by *multiplication;* $\frac{M}{4}$ is a term in which the quantities *M* and 4 are combined by *division* or in which the factors *M* and $\frac{1}{4}$ are combined by multiplication.

An expression is a collection of terms combined by addition, subtraction, or both, and frequently grouped by parentheses, as in: $(3a + 2b)$, $(2c - 4c + 3b)$, $2x - 3y$.

USING PARENTHESES

Parentheses ( ) or **brackets** [ ] mean that quantities are to be grouped together, and that quantities enclosed by them are to be considered as one quantity. The line of a fraction has the same significance in this respect as a pair of parentheses.

Thus, $18 + (9 - 6)$ is read 18 *plus the quantity* $9 - 6$.

Rule: To solve examples containing parentheses, *do the work within the parentheses first; then remove the parentheses and proceed in the usual way. Within parentheses and in examples without parentheses do multiplications from left to right before doing additions and subtractions.*

It is extremely important to observe this method of procedure, since it is otherwise impossible to solve algebraic problems.

EXAMPLE 1: $94 - (12 + 18 + 20) = ?$
$94 - 50 = 44$, ANS.

EXAMPLE 2: $12(3 + 2) = ?$
$12 \times 5 = 60$, ANS.

EXAMPLE 3: $\frac{18}{2(4 - 1)} = ?$
$\frac{18}{2 \times 3} = \frac{18}{6} = 3$, ANS.

EXAMPLE 4: $3 \times 6 - 4$
$18 - 4 = 14$, ANS.

Note: If in this example the 4 had been subtracted from the 6 before multiplying, the answer would have been 6, but this would be wrong according to the laws of algebra. This example illustrates the absolute necessity of *doing multiplication first* in any cases similar to this.

Practice Exercise No. 8

Clear parentheses and solve.

1 $18 + (19 - 14) =$
2 $22(3 + 2) =$

3 $42 - 9 - (18 + 2) =$
4 $(6 - 4)(8 + 2) =$
5 $(18 \div 3)(9 - 7) =$
6 $(7 \times 8) - (6 \times 4) + (18 - 6) =$
7 $(6 \times 8) \div (8 \times 2) =$
8 $19 + (18 - 14 + 32) =$
9 $(7 \times 6)(6 \times 5) =$
10 $69 \div [35 - (15 - 3)] =$

TRANSLATING WORD STATEMENTS INTO FORMULAS AND ALGEBRAIC EXPRESSIONS

To express word statements as formulas or as brief algebraic expressions, letters and symbols are substituted for words.

EXAMPLE 1: Express briefly, *What number increased by* 6 *gives* 18 *as a result?*

Substituting the letter N for the unknown *what number,* we get

$$N + 6 = 18,$$
$$N = ? \quad \text{ANS.}$$

EXAMPLE 2: Express briefly, *The product of two numbers is* 85. *One is* 5, *find the other.*

$$5N = 85, N = ? \quad \text{ANS.}$$

EXAMPLE 3: Express briefly, *Fifteen exceeds a certain number by* 6. *What is the number?*

$15 - 6 = N$, or $N + 6 = 15$, or $15 - N = 6$, $N = ?$ ANS.

EXAMPLE 4: Express briefly, *Two thirds of a number is* 20. *Find the number.*

$$\tfrac{2}{3}N = 20, N = ? \quad \text{ANS.}$$

In algebra, however, the regular method of writing fractions is to place all factors, as far as may be possible, above or below a single horizontal line. The form $\frac{2}{3}N$, while mathematically correct, is less regular than $\frac{2N}{3}$. Hence to express our problem in approved form we arrive at:

$$\frac{2N}{3} = 20, N = ? \quad \text{ANS.}$$

The foregoing illustrates in simple form the general method of making algebraic statements. In engineering, scientific, industrial and commercial practice, it is common to express certain kinds of facts in algebraic *formulas.* The usual way is to state the formula with symbolic letters and to follow it immediately with an explanation (starting with the words *in which*) to make intelligible to the reader any symbols that may require definition. Examples of this method of formula statement follow.

EXAMPLE 1: The cost equals the selling price minus the margin of profit.

FORMULA: $C = S - M$, in which C stands for cost, S for selling price and M for margin of profit.

EXAMPLE 2: The area of a rectangle equals the base times the height.

FORMULA: $A = bh$, in which A stands for area, b for base and h for height.

EXAMPLE 3: To determine the resistance in ohms of an electrical circuit, divide the number of volts by the number of amperes.

FORMULA: $O = \frac{V}{A}$, in which O stands for ohms, V for volts and A for amperes.

Practice Exercise No. 9

Write the following statements as equations. *Note:* Most of the statements represent formulas commonly used by draftsmen, designers, carpenters, engineers and clerks.

1 The perimeter (p) of a rectangle equals twice its length (l) added to twice its width (w).
2 The distance (d) traveled by an object that moves at a given rate of speed (r) for a given time (t) equals the rate multiplied by the time.
3 To get the horsepower (H) of an electric motor multiply the number of volts (v) by the number of amperes (a) and divide by 746.
4 Interest (I) on money is figured by multiplying the principal (P) by the rate (R) by the time (T).
5 The amperage (A) of an electrical circuit is equal to the wattage (W) divided by the voltage (V).
6 Profit (P) equals the margin (M) minus the overhead (O).
7 The distance (d) that an object will fall in any given time (t) is equal to the square of the time multiplied by 16.
8 The area (A) of a square figure is equal to the square of one of its sides (S).

9 Centigrade temperature (C) is equal to Fahrenheit temperature (F) minus 32°, multiplied by $\frac{5}{9}$.

10 The speed (R) of a revolving wheel is proportional to the number of revolutions (N) it makes in a given time (T).

RULE FOR SOLVING EQUATIONS

When you solve an equation you are finding the value of the unknown or literal number in terms of what has been given about the other numbers in the equation. To do this you must learn the following rules of procedure for treating equations. Primarily, *what you do to one side of an equation you must also do to the other.* This might be called the golden rule of algebra. Its observance is imperative in order to preserve equality.

Rule 1. *The same number may be added to both sides of an equation without changing its equality.*

EXAMPLE 1: If $x - 4 = 6$, what does x equal?

SOLUTION:
$x - 4 + 4 = 6 + 4$. Adding 4 to both sides,
$x = 10$, ANS.

To check the solution of algebraic examples, *substitute the value of the unknown quantity as determined in the answer for the corresponding symbol in the original equation. If both sides produce the same number, the answer is correct.*

EXAMPLE 1: Check the correctness of 10 as the solution of $x - 4 = 6$.

METHOD:
$x - 4 = 6$, original equation,
$10 - 4 = 6$, substituting answer for symbol,
$6 = 6$, proof of correctness.

Rule 2. *The same number may be subtracted from both sides of an equation.*

EXAMPLE 2: If $n + 6 = 18$, what does n equal?

SOLUTION:
$n + 6 - 6 = 18 - 6$. Subtracting 6 from both sides, $n = 12$, ANS.

Check by substituting 12 for n in the original equation. *Thus,* $n + 6 = 18$ becomes $12 + 6 = 18$ or $18 = 18$, which is correct.

Rule 3. *Both sides of an equation may be multiplied by the same number.*

EXAMPLE 3: If $\frac{1}{3}$ of a number is 10, find the number.

SOLUTION:

$$\frac{1}{3}n \text{ or } \frac{n}{3} = 10,$$

$$\frac{n}{3} \times 3 = 10 \times 3, \text{ multiplying both sides by 3,}$$

$$\frac{n}{\not{3}} \times \not{3} = 10 \times 3, \text{ cancelling,}$$

$n = 30$, ANS.
Check the answer.

Rule 4. *Both sides of an equation may be divided by the same number.*

EXAMPLE 4: Two times a number is 30. What is the number?

SOLUTION:
$2n = 30$,

$$\frac{2n}{2} = \frac{30}{2}, \text{ dividing both sides by 2.}$$

$n = 15$, ANS.
Check the answer.

TRANSPOSITION

Transposition is the process of moving a quantity from one side of an equation to the other side by changing its sign of operation. This is exactly what has been done in carrying out the rules in the four examples above.

Division is the operation opposite to multiplication.

Addition is the operation opposite to subtraction.

Transposition is performed in order to obtain an equation in which the unknown quantity is on one side and the known quantity on the other.

Rule: *A term may be transposed from one side of an equation to the other if its sign is changed from + to −, or from − to +.*

Rule: *A factor (multiplier) may be removed from one side of an equation by making it a divisor in the other. A divisor may be removed from one side of an equation by making it a factor (multiplier) in the other.*

Observe again the solution to Example 1.

$x - 4 = 6$,
$x = 6 + 4$,
$x = 10$.

EXPLANATION: To get x by itself on one side of the equation, the -4 was transposed from the left to the right side and made +4.

Observe again the solution to Example 2.

$n + 6 = 18,$
$n = 18 - 6,$
$n = 12.$

EXPLANATION: To get n by itself on one side of the equation, the +6 was transposed from the left to the right side and made −6.

Observe again the solution to Example 3.

$\frac{n}{3} = 10,$
$n = 10 \times 3,$
$n = 30.$

EXPLANATION: To get n by itself on one side of the equation, the divisor 3 on the left was changed to the multiplier $3(\frac{3}{1})$ on the right.

Observe again the solution to Example 4.

$2n = 30,$
$n = \frac{30}{2},$
$n = 15.$

EXPLANATION: To get n by itself on one side of the equation, the multiplier 2 on the left was changed to the divisor 2 on the right.

Note that transposition is essentially nothing more than a shortened method for performing like operations of addition, subtraction, multiplication or division on both sides of the equation.

Changing $x - 4 = 6$ to $x = 6 + 4$ is the same as adding 4 to both sides:

$$\begin{array}{rcr} x - 4 & = & 6 \\ +4 & = & +4 \\ \hline x & = & 10 \end{array}$$

Changing $n + 6 = 18$ to $n = 18 - 6$ is the same as subtracting 6 from both sides:

$$\begin{array}{rcr} n + 6 & = & 18 \\ -6 & = & -6 \\ \hline n & = & 12 \end{array}$$

Changing $\frac{n}{3} = 10$ to $n = 10 \times 3$ is the same as multiplying both sides by 3:

$\frac{n}{3} \times 3 = 10 \times 3$, in which the 3s on the left cancel.

Changing $2n = 30$ to $n = \frac{30}{2}$ is the same as dividing both sides by 2:

$\frac{2n}{2} = \frac{30}{2}$, in which the 2s on the left cancel.

When terms involving the unknown quantity occur on both sides of the equation, *perform such transpositions as may be necessary to collect all the unknown terms on one side (usually the left) andl all the known terms on the other.*

EXAMPLE 5: If $3x - 6 = x + 8$ what does x equal?

SOLUTION:

$3x = x + 8 + 6,$ transposing −6 from left to right.
$3x - x = 14,$ transposing x from right to left.
$2x = 14,$ transposing 2 as a multiplier from left to a divisor at the right.
$x = \frac{14}{2},$
$x = 7,$ ANS.

Check:
$3x - 6 = x + 8,$
$21 - 6 = 7 + 8,$ substituting 7 for x,
$15 = 15.$ proof of correctness.

When using an algebraic formula in actual practice, it may be necessary to change its form from that in which it has been originally expressed. Such changes are effected by transposition.

EXAMPLE 6: If $R = \frac{WC}{L}$, solve for W, C, and L.

SOLUTION:

$R = \frac{WC}{L}$, original formula

$\frac{LR}{C} = W$. To separate W, C and L are transposed.

$\frac{LR}{W} = C$. To separate C, L and W are transposed.

$L = \frac{WC}{R}$. To separate L, L and R are transposed.

Practice Exercise No. 10

Solve:

1	$p + 3 = 8$	$p = ?$
2	$2n = 25$	$n = ?$
3	$\frac{1}{2}x = 14$	$x = ?$
4	$5c - 3 = 27$	$c = ?$
5	$18 = 5y - 2$	$y = ?$
6	$\frac{2}{3}n = 24$	$n = ?$

7 $\frac{a}{2}+\frac{a}{4}=36$ $\quad a = ?$

8 $W=\frac{b}{c}$ $\quad b = ?$

9 $V=\frac{W}{A}$ $\quad A = ?$

10 $H=\frac{P}{AW}$ $\quad W = ?$

FUNDAMENTAL OPERATIONS

Addition is performed thus:

$$\begin{array}{r} 3a - 4b + 2c \\ -8a + 6b - 3c \\ 6a - 4b + 8c \\ \hline a - 2b + 7c \end{array}$$

EXPLANATION: The terms are arranged in columns in such a way that all like terms are in the same column.

Subtraction is performed thus:

$$\begin{array}{r} 8a - 4b + 2c \\ 5a - 6b + 8c \\ \hline 3a + 2b - 6c \end{array}$$

EXPLANATION: To subtract algebraically, whenever you cannot directly subtract a smaller from a larger quantity of like sign, mentally change the sign of the subtrahend and perform an addition.

$8a - 5a = 3a;$ $\quad -4b + 6b = +2b;$
$2c - 8c = -6c.$

Multiplication is performed thus:

$$\begin{array}{l} a^2 - 2ab + b^2 \\ a - b \\ \hline a^3 - 2a^2b + ab^2 \\ \quad - a^2b + 2ab^2 - b^3 \\ \hline a^3 - 3a^2b + 3ab^2 - b^3 \end{array}$$

EXPLANATION: Each term in the multiplicand is multiplied separately by a and then by b. Like terms are set under each other and the whole is added. $+ \times +$ gives $+$; $- \times -$ gives $+$; $+ \times -$ gives $-$.

Division is performed thus:

$$\frac{3a^2b + 3ab^2 + 3a}{3a} = ab + b^2 + 1, \text{ or } b^2 + ab + 1.$$

EXPLANATION: $3a$ is a factor of each term in the dividend. Separate divisions give us $ab + b^2 + 1$. This is changed to $b^2 + ab + 1$ because it is customary to place algebraic terms in the order of their highest powers.

Practice Exercise No. 11

USE OF FORMULAS AND EQUATIONS

1 Diameters of pulleys are inversely proportioned to their rpm. $\frac{D}{d}=\frac{r}{R}$. An 18″ diameter pulley turning at 100 rpm is driving a 6″ diameter pulley. What is the rpm of the smaller pulley?

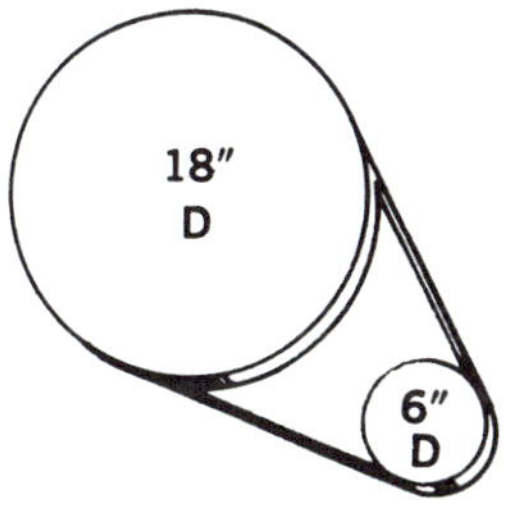

(A) $36\frac{2}{3}$ ____ (C) 300 ____
(B) 600 ____ (D) 900 ____

2 What size pulley at 144 rpm will drive a 9″ pulley at 256 rpm?

(A) 24″ ____ (C) 16″ ____
(B) $5\frac{1}{6}$″ ____ (D) 32″ ____

3 Three times a certain number plus twice the same number is 90. What is the number?

(A) 16 ____ (C) 20 ____
(B) 18 ____ (D) 24 ____

4 The larger of two numbers is seven times the smaller. What is the larger if their sum is 32?

(A) 28 ____ (C) 25 ____
(B) 36 ____ (D) 39 ____

5 Six hundred pairs of shoes are to be divided up among three army units. The second unit is to get twice as many as the first, and the third unit is to get as many as the first and second units together. How many pairs of shoes does the second unit get?

(A) 100 ____ (C) 300 ____
(B) 200 ____ (D) 400 ____

6 Two aviators are 3,000 miles part. They start toward each other, one at a rate of 200 miles per hour and the other at 300 miles per hour. How much distance does the faster one cover up to the time they meet? $R \times T = D$.

(A) 1,200 ____ (C) 1,600 ____
(B) 1,400 ____ (D) 1,800 ____

7 Two soldiers start out from camp in opposite directions. One travels twice as fast as the other. In 10 hours they are 24 miles apart. What is the rate of the faster soldier?

(A) $\frac{4}{5}$ mi. hr. ____ (C) $1\frac{2}{3}$ mi. hr. ____
(B) 1 mi. hr. ____ (D) $1\frac{3}{5}$ mi. hr. ____

8 A man has 3 times as many nickels as quarters. How many nickels has he if the value of both together is \$8.00? Hint: Let n = no. of quarters and $3n$ = no. of nickels and multiply each by their value.

(A) 20 ____ (C) 60 ____
(B) 40 ____ (D) 80 ____

9 When two gears run together the revolutions per minute vary inversely as the number of teeth. A 48-tooth gear is driving a 72-tooth gear. Find the revolutions per minute of the larger gear if the smaller one is running at 160 rpm.

(A) $106\frac{2}{3}$ rpm ____ (C) $66\frac{2}{3}$ rpm ____
(B) 240 rpm ____ (D) 180 rpm ____

10 A teeter board is a form of lever. It is balanced when the weight times the distance on one side equals the weight times the distance on the other side. A weight of 120 lbs. is placed $4\frac{1}{2}$ feet from the fulcrum. What weight is needed to balance this at a distance of 5 feet from the fulcrum on the other end?

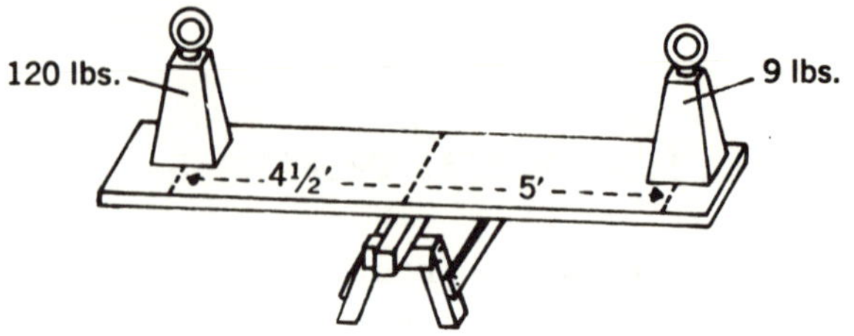

(A) 104 ____ (C) 118 ____
(B) 108 ____ (D) 128 ____

Factors and Roots

A **factor** of a number is an exact divisor of that number. Thus 2 is a factor of 6 because $6 \div 2 = 3$ exactly; 3 is the other factor of 6.

For the number 9, 3 and 3 are equal factors; and for 8, 2, 2 and 2 are equal factors. These equal factors are called roots of the number. Thus:

The number 3 is a *root* of 9.

The number 2 is a *root* of 8.

A root of a number is therefore one of the equal factors which, if multiplied together, produce the number.

The **square root** of a number is one of TWO equal factors which, if multiplied together, produce that number.

$3 \times 3 = 9$, hence 3 is the *square root* of 9.

The **cube root** of a number is one of THREE equal factors which if multiplied together produce that number.

$3 \times 3 \times 3 = 27$, hence 3 is the *cube root* of 27.

A fourth root of a number is one of FOUR equal factors; the fifth root is one of five, and so on.

The square root is the one most frequently used in mathematics.

The sign indicating square root is $\sqrt{\ }$. It is placed over the number whose root is to be found. $\sqrt{25}$ means the square root is 25. It is called the **square root sign** or **radical sign.**

To indicate a root other than square root a small figure called the **index** of the root is placed in the radical sign. Thus: $\sqrt[3]{8}$ means the cube root of 8.

The square root of 4 = 2, of 36 = 6, or 49 = 7.

To check that you have obtained the correct square root of a number, *multiply it by itself. If the product is equal to the original number the answer is correct.*

Practice Exercise No. 12

Find the roots indicated and check.

1 $\sqrt{64}$
2 $\sqrt{100}$
3 $\sqrt{81}$
4 $\sqrt[3]{1000}$
5 $\sqrt{1}$
6 $\sqrt{.04} = \sqrt{.2 \times .2} = .2$

7	$\sqrt[3]{27}$	10	$\sqrt{.09}$
8	$\sqrt[3]{125}$	11	$\sqrt{1.44}$
9	$\sqrt{144}$	12	$\sqrt{.0025}$

Not all numbers have exact square roots. Nor can we always determine square root by *inspection* as you have done above. (Inspection means "trial and error.") There is an arithmetic method of extracting the square roots of numbers whereby an answer may be found that will be correct to any necessary or desired number of decimal places.

METHOD FOR FINDING SQUARE ROOTS

Find the square root of 412,164.

1. Place the square root sign over the number, and then, beginning at the right, divide it into *periods* of two figures each. Connect the digits in each period with tie-marks as shown. In the answer there will be one digit for each period.

```
√41 21 64
```

2. Find the largest number which, when squared, is contained in the first left-hand period. In this case 6 is the number. Write 6 in the answer over the first period. Square it, making 36, and subtract 36 from the first period. Bring down the next period, making the new dividend 5 21.

```
  6
√41 21 64
 36
  5 21
```

3. Multiply the root 6 by 2, getting 12. Place the 12 to the left of 5 21, since 12 is the new trial divisor. Allow, however, for one more digit to follow 12. The place of this missing digit may be indicated by a question mark. To find the number belonging in this place, ignore (cover over) the last number in the dividend 5 21, and see how many times 12 goes into 52. Approximately 4. Place the 4 above its period, 21, and put it in place of the ? in the divisor.

```
       6  4
     √41 21 64
      36
12?4 | 5 21
```

4. Multiply the divisor 124 by the new number in the root, 4. $124 \times 4 = 496$. Place this product under 521 and subtract. Bring down the next period, 64.

```
      6  4
    √41 21 64
     36
124 | 5 21
      4 96
        25 64
```

5. Multiply 64 by 2 to get 128 as the new trial divisor. 128 goes into 256 two times. Place the 2 above the next period in the root and also in the divisor. Then multiply the divisor 1282 by the new root 2, to get 25 64. Subtracting, the remainder is zero. 642 is therefore the exact square root.

```
        6  4  2
      √41 21 64
       36
124   | 5 21
        4 96
128?2 |   25 64
          25 64
              0
```

6. CHECK: $642 \times 642 = 412{,}164$.

FINDING THE SQUARE ROOT OF DECIMALS

A slight variation in method is necessary when it is required to find the square root of a decimal figure.

Mark off periods beginning at the decimal point. Count to the right for the decimal quantities and to the left for the whole numbers. If the last period of the whole numbers contains one figure, leave it by itself, but remember that in such a case the first figure in the root cannot be more than 3 because the square of any number greater than 3 is a two-place number. If the last period of the decimal numbers contains only one figure you may add a zero to it. This is because two digits are necessary to make up a period, while the addition of a zero at the right of a decimal figure does not change its value.

The square root of a decimal will contain as many decimal places as there are periods, or half as many decimal places as the given number.

The operations in obtaining the square root of a decimal number are the same as for whole numbers.

Follow the steps in the example following.

EXAMPLE 1: Find the square root of 339.2964.

```
        1  8. 4  2
      √3 39.29 64
        1
2?8   | 2 39
        2 24
36?4  |  15 29
         14 56
368?2 |     73 64
            73 64
                0
```

1. Beginning at decimal point, mark off periods to left and right.

2. 1 is the largest whole-number square root that is contained in 3, which constitutes the first period.

3. Place decimal point in root after the 8 because the root of the next period has a decimal value.

4. Bring down 29 next to the 15, making 1529 the new dividend. Multiply the root 18 by 2, making 36 the new divisor.

5. Covering the 9 of 1529, 36 seems to be contained about 4 times in this number. Place a 4

in the root above 29, and multiply 364 by 4 to get 1456. Substract this from 1529.

6. Bring down the 64 and repeat the previous process. Since the number is a perfect square, the remainder is zero.

When the given number is not a perfect square, *add zeros after the decimal point, or after the last figure if the original number is already in decimal form, and carry out the answer to the required or desired number of decimal places. Usually two places are sufficient.*

Note: In working a square root example, when a divisor is larger than the corresponding dividend, write zero in the trial divisor and bring down the next period. This is illustrated in the next example.

EXAMPLE 2: Find the square root of 25.63 to three decimal places.

```
          5. 0  6  2+, ANS.
       √25.63 00 00
        25
100?6 | 0 63 00
          60 36
  1012?2 | 2 64 00
           2 02 44
             61 56 remainder
```

To find the square of a fraction, determine separately the square roots of the numerator and of the denominator, and reduce to lowest terms or to a decimal.

EXAMPLE 3: $\sqrt{\frac{33}{67}}$.

$$\sqrt{\frac{33}{67}} = \frac{5.745}{8.185} = .701, \text{ ANS.}$$

USE OF SQUARE ROOTS

Although in many test situations the student may be required to work out square roots as above, in actual practice it is inconvenient to stop work for such calculations. Most mathematics books therefore contain tables giving powers and roots of numbers.

Any formula or problem containing the square of a number or factor, requires a knowledge of square roots for its solution. You will find many such problems and formulas in the material contained in Chapter 15 on geometry.

EXAMPLE 1: Find the length of one side of a square whose area is 225 square feet.

SOLUTION: Let x = length of one side.
Area = base × height. ∴ Area = x^2,
$x^2 = 225$,
$x = 15$, extracting the square root of both sides of the equation.

EXAMPLE 2: $d = 16t^2$ (in which d is distance and t is time) is the formula for measuring the distance an object will fall in t seconds irrespective of its weight. If an object fell 10,000 feet, how long would it take to reach the ground?

SOLUTION:
$10000 = 16t^2$,
$\frac{10000}{16} = t^2$, dividing both sides by 16
$625 = t^2$,
$25 = t$, extracting square root of both sides of the equation.

Practice Exercise No. 13

Work out examples 1–10.

1	$\sqrt{5329}$	6	$\sqrt{676}$
2	$\sqrt{1225}$	7	$\sqrt{1849}$
3	$\sqrt{2937.64}$	8	$\sqrt{3136}$
4	$\sqrt{312.649}$ to 2 places	9	$\sqrt{7225}$
5	$\sqrt{428}$ to 2 places	10	$\sqrt{9409}$

Powers

To square a number is to use that number as a factor twice. Thus $4 \times 4 = 16$, and 16 is said to be the **square** of 4. This is also called raising a number to its **second power.** Using a number as a factor three times (for instance, $4 \times 4 \times 4 = 64$) is called raising it to the **third power.** The given case would be written 4^3, and be *read four cubed.* 4^4 is read *four to the fourth power,* 4^5 is read *four to the fifth power, etc.*

A **power** of a number tells how many times a number has been used as a factor. Raising a number to a given power is the opposite process of finding the corresponding root of a number.

To raise a given number to its indicated power, multiply the number by itself as many times as the power indicated. Thus, $3^5 = 3 \times 3 \times 3 \times 3 \times 3 = 243$. The small five used in writing 3^5 is called an *exponent,* while the number 3 is called the base.

An **exponent** indicates the power to which a number is to be raised. *Thus,* x^3 means that x is to be raised to the third power.

$$\text{If } x^3 = 125,\quad x = ?$$

To raise a fraction to a given power, *raise both the numerator and the denominator to the given power.*

$$(\tfrac{1}{3})^2 = \tfrac{1}{3} \times \tfrac{1}{3} = \tfrac{1}{9},$$
$$(\tfrac{3}{5})^2 = \tfrac{3}{5} \times \tfrac{3}{5} = \tfrac{9}{25}.$$

Any power or root of 1 is 1, because 1 multiplied or divided by 1 any number of times is 1.

Any number **without an exponent** is considered to be the first power or first root of itself. Neither the exponent nor the index 1 is written. *Thus,* x means x^1.

Any number raised to the **zero power,** such as 5^0, is equal to 1. The reason for this will appear when we consider the multiplication of powers of numbers.

When a number has a **negative exponent,** *i.e.,* when the exponent is preceded by the minus sign, as in 3^{-3}, it indicates the reciprocal of the indicated power of the number. Since $3^3 = 27$, $3^{-3} = \frac{1}{27}$, the reciprocal of 27. 12^{-2} means the reciprocal of 12^2, or $\frac{1}{144}$.

When a number has a **fractional exponent** with a numerator of 1, as has $x^{\frac{1}{2}}$, it signifies that the corresponding *root* is to be taken of the number. In other words, $16^{\frac{1}{2}} = \sqrt{16} = 4$.

When a fractional exponent has a numerator greater than one, as has $x^{\frac{2}{3}}$, the numerator indicates the power to which the number is to be raised, while the denominator indicates the root that is to be taken. Accordingly, $4^{\frac{3}{2}} = \sqrt{4^3} = \sqrt{64} = 8$. To reverse this example, $8^{\frac{2}{3}} = \sqrt[3]{8^2} = \sqrt[3]{64} = 4$.

POWERS OF 10

$$10^1 = 10 \qquad 10^{-1} = \frac{1}{10} \text{ or } .1$$
$$10^2 = 100 \qquad 10^{-2} = \frac{1}{100} \text{ or } .01$$
$$10^3 = 1{,}000 \qquad 10^{-3} = \frac{1}{1{,}000} \text{ or } .001$$
$$10^4 = 10{,}000 \qquad 10^{-4} = \frac{1}{10{,}000} \text{ or } .0001$$
$$10^5 = 100{,}000 \qquad 10^{-5} = \frac{1}{100{,}000} \text{ or } .00001$$

From this it is apparent that 10 raised to any positive power is equal to a multiple of 10 bearing as many zeros as are represented by the quantity of the exponent.

Also, 10 raised to any negative power is equal to a multiple of 10 containing as many decimal places as the quantity of the negative exponent.

The above forms are used for writing very large and very small numbers in an abbreviated way. *Thus,*

32,000 may be written as 3.2×10^4,
6,900,000 may be written as 6.9×10^6,
.000008 may be written as 8×10^{-6},
.0000000235 may be written as 2.35×10^{-8}.

A positive exponent moves the decimal point a corresponding number of places to the right. *Thus,* $8.2 \times 10^7 = 82{,}000{,}000$.

A negative exponent moves the decimal point a corresponding number of places to the left. *Thus,* $6.3 \times 10^{-5} = .000063$.

LAWS OF EXPONENTS

To multiply powers of the same base, *add their exponents.*

Thus, 2^2 times $2^3 = 2^5$.
PROOF: $2^2 = 4; 2^3 = 8; 2^5 = 32;$
$4 \times 8 = 32.$

To divide powers of the same base, *subtract the exponent of the divisor from the exponent of the dividend.*

Thus, $3^5 \div 3^3 = 3^2$.
PROOF: $3^5 = 243; 3^3 = 27; 3^2 = 9;$
$243 \div 27 = 9.$

It will now become apparent why *any* number with an exponent of zero is equal to 1. According to the laws just stated—

$$x^3 \times x^0 = x^{3+0} = x^3$$

because if equals are multiplied by equals the products are equal;

$$\text{but } x^3 \times 1 = x^3,$$
$$\therefore x^0 = 1.$$

To generalize this fact, let n denote any positive exponent whatever. Then $x^n \times x^0 = x^n$ and x^0 necessarily equals 1. The same conclusion will be reached if the process is division and the exponents are subtracted. *Thus,*

$$x^n \div x^0 = x^{n-0} = x^n, \therefore x^0 = 1.$$

Practice Exercise No. 14

Perform the indicated operations.

1 $6^2 =$
2 $9^3 =$
3 $25^{\frac{1}{2}} =$
4 $4^{-3} =$
5 $432^2 =$
6 $8^5 =$
7 $\sqrt{81} =$
8 $\sqrt[3]{125} =$
9 $43 \times 10^6 =$
10 $6.2 \times 10^5 =$
11 $(\frac{2}{3})^2 =$
12 $6^{\frac{3}{2}} =$
13 $2.8 \times 10^{-7} =$
14 $25 \times 10^{-4} =$
15 $12.2 \times 10^7 =$

METHOD FOR FINDING CUBE ROOTS

In studying the following example, read step by step the rule that follows it and note how the example illustrates the rule.

EXAMPLE: What is the cube root of 264,609,288?

$$\begin{array}{r} 6 \quad 4 \quad 2 \\ \sqrt[3]{264\ 609\ 288} \end{array}$$

	$6^3 =$	216	
1st Part. Div.	$3 \times 60^2 =$	10800	48 609
	$3 \times 60 \times 4 =$	720	
	$4^2 =$	16	
1st Comp. Div.		11536	46 144
			2 465 288
2nd Part. Div.	$3 \times 640^2 =$	1228800	
	$3 \times 640 \times 2 =$	3840	
	$2^2 =$	4	
2nd Comp. Div.		1232644	2 465 288

The following rule is more readily understood if we bear in mind the formula for the cube of the sum of two numbers:

$$(a + b)^3 = a^3 + 3a^2b + 3ab^2 + b^3$$

Rule: 1. *Separate the given number into periods of three figures each, beginning at the right, and place over it the radical sign with the proper index.*

The extreme left-hand period may contain one, two or three figures.

2. *Determine the greatest cube that is smaller than the first left-hand period, and write its cube root, in the position shown, as the first figure of the required root.*

This root corresponds to a in the formula.

3. *Subtract the cube of this root from the first period and annex the next period to the remainder.*

4. *Multiply this root mentally by ten and write three times the square of this as a partial divisor.*

5. *Make a trial division to determine what the next figure in the root will be and write it in its proper place.*

6. *Add to the partial divisor* (1) *the product of* 3 *times the first part of the root considered as tens multiplied by the second part of the root; and* (2) *the square of the second part of the root. The sum of these numbers is the complete divisor.*

7. *Multiply the complete divisor by the second part of the root and subtract the product from the new dividend.*

Note in the example that at this point $a = 60$ and $b = 4$. When we subtracted 216 we took 216,000 or a^3 out of the given figure. When we multiply the first complete divisor by 4, this is equivalent to multiplying $3a^2$ (10800) by b, producing $3a^2b$; $3ab$ (720) by b, producing $3ab^2$; and b^2 (16) by b, producing b^3. Hence when we write 46144 previous to performing the subtraction we have fulfilled up to this point all the requirements of the formula

$$(a + b)^3 = a^3 + 3a^2b + 3ab^2 + b^3.$$

8. *Bring down the next period and continue the same process until all the figures of the root have been determined.*

When the third figure of the root is found in the example a becomes 640 and b becomes 2. The student should check the manner in which multiplication of the second complete divisor by 2 fulfills the requirements of the formula. The correctness of the complete extraction may of course be checked by multiplying the determined root to its third power.

APPROXIMATE ROOTS OF FRACTIONS

We have seen that the square root of a fraction is the square root of its numerator placed over the square root of the denominator, subject to further reduction or to conversion to a decimal.

When the terms of a fraction are not perfect squares it is often desirable to approximate a square root without going to the trouble of making an exact calculation. This is done by multiplying the terms of the fraction by any number that will make the denominator a perfect square, as in the following example.

EXAMPLE: What is the approximate square root of $\frac{19}{8}$?

$\frac{19}{8} = \frac{38}{16}$, of which the approximate square root, $\frac{6}{4}$, is correct to within $\frac{1}{4}$; or

$\frac{19}{8} \times \frac{32}{32} = \frac{608}{256}$, of which the approximate square root, $\frac{25}{16}$, is correct to within $\frac{1}{16}$.

EXPLANATION: We select a factor that will make the denominator a perfect square. We then extract the square root of the denominator and the square root of the perfect square that is nearest to the numerator. If we write the fraction as $\frac{38}{16}$, the square root of the denominator is 4 and the square root of the nearest perfect square to 38 is 6. The resulting approximate square root, $\frac{6}{4}$, reducible to $\frac{3}{2}$, is correct to within $\frac{1}{4}$.

If we want a closer approximation than this, we multiply by a larger factor. Using 32 as a factor, we get $\frac{608}{256}$. The square root of the denominator is 16. The nearest perfect square to 608 is 625, the square root of which is 25. The resulting approximate square root, $\frac{25}{16}$, is correct to within $\frac{1}{16}$.

It will be noted that the larger the factor the more closely will the result approximate the correct value.

The approximate cube root of a fraction may be found by a similar process.

EXAMPLE: Find the approximate cube root of $\frac{173}{32}$.

$\frac{173}{32} = \frac{346}{64}$, of which the approximate cube root, $\frac{7}{4}$, is correct to within $\frac{1}{4}$; or

$\frac{173}{32} = \frac{2768}{512}$, of which the approximate cube root, $\frac{14}{8}$, is correct to within $\frac{1}{8}$.

EXPLANATION: The denominator has been multiplied by two different factors in order to demonstrate again that the higher factor produces the more nearly accurate answer. It will be noted that the final result in both cases has the same ultimate value since $\frac{14}{8} = \frac{7}{4}$. If, however, we had not worked out the second solution we would not know that $\frac{7}{4}$ is actually correct to within $\frac{1}{8}$.

HIGHER ROOTS

If the index of a higher root contains no other prime factors than 2 and 3, we can find the required root by repeated extraction of square or cube roots, according to the nature of the problem.

EXAMPLE 1: What is the fourth root of 923521?

SOLUTION: $\sqrt{923521} = 961,$

$\sqrt{961} = 31,$ ANS.

EXPLANATION: Since the fourth power of a number is its square multiplied by its square, we find the fourth root of a given number representing such a power by extracting the square root of the square root.

EXAMPLE 2: What is the sixth root of 191102976?

SOLUTION: $\sqrt{191102976} = 13824,$

$\sqrt[3]{13824} = 24,$ ANS.

EXPLANATION: The sixth root is found by taking the cube root of the square root. The order of making the extractions is of course immaterial.

Higher roots with indexes that are prime to 2 and 3 are found by methods based on the same general theory as that underlying the methods for extracting square and cube roots. Thus if it be required to find the fifth root of a number, we consider that $(a + b)^5 = a^5 + 5a^4b + 10a^3b^2 + 10a^2b^3 + 5ab^4 + b^5$. After subtracting a^5 from the first period we must construct a complete divisor which when multiplied by b will satisfy the whole formula. Dividing what follows a^5 in the formula by b we get as the requirement of our complete divisor, $5a^4 + 10a^2b + 10a^2b^2 + 5ab^3 + b^4$. We use the first term of this, $5a^4$, as a trial divisor, but where the complete divisor is so complex several estimates may have to be tried before finding the correct value for b. In actual practice, however, higher roots are more commonly found by the use of logarithms and the slide rule.

HANDY ALGEBRAIC FORMULAS

The following formulas should be memorized.

$(a + b)^2 = a^2 + 2ab + b^2$
$(a - b)^2 = a^2 - 2ab + b^2$
$(a + b)(a - b) = a^2 - b^2$
$(a + b)^3 = a^3 + 3a^2b + 3ab^2 + b^3$

These formulas have many applications, and they are particularly applicable to doing arithmetic by short-cut methods. Compare what is said below with the methods of multiplication starting on page 580.

TRANSLATING NUMBERS INTO ALGEBRA

In the following consider that a represents a number of the tens order, like 10, 20, 30, etc., while b represents a number of the units order.

Squaring a number:

EXAMPLE 1: Multiply 63 by 63.

60 × 60 combined with 3 × 3 = 3609,
6 × 60, or 360, added to 3609 = 3969, ANS.

EXPLANATION: 60 × 60 represents the a^2 of the formula, to which we at once add 9 as the b^2. The $2ab$ is most quickly figured out as 2 × 3 × 60.

EXAMPLE 2: What is the square of 65?

60 × 70 combined with 25 = 4225, ANS.

EXPLANATION: Doing this example by the previous method we would get 3625 + (2 × 5 × 60). But (2 × 5) × 60 = 10 × 60. Hence we at once multiply 60 by 10 more than we otherwise would, or 70.

EXAMPLE 3: What is the square of 89?

8100 combined with 1 = 8101,
8101 − 180 = 7921, ANS.

EXPLANATION: Since the digits are large and 89 is near 90 it is preferable here to use the square of $a - b$, taking a as 90 and b as 1. $a^2 + b^2 = 8101$; $2ab = 2 \times 1 \times 90$ or 180, which in accordance with the formula is subtracted from 8101.

Multiplying a sum by a difference:

EXAMPLE 4: How much is 53 × 47?

2500 − 9 = 2491, ANS.

EXPLANATION: $a = 50$, $b = 3$. $53 = a + b$; $47 = a - b$. $(a + b)(a - b) = a^2 - b^2 = 2500 -$. Note that this method is applicable whenever the units add up to 10 and the tens differ by 10.

Cubing a number:

EXAMPLE: What is the cube of 23?

	8027
(69 × 60)	4140
	12167, ANS.

EXPLANATION: $(a + b)^3 = a^3 + 3a^2b + 3ab^2 + b^3$. $a^3 + b^3$ may be quickly written down as 8027. $3a^2b + 3ab^2 = 3ab(a + b)$. $a + b$ is the given number, in this case 23. We therefore want 3 × 23 or 69 multiplied by ab or 3 × 20 or 60. In other words, to the cubes of the digits properly placed add three times the number multiplied by the product of its digits with an added 0. A little practice makes all this quite simple. For small numbers the method is very much quicker than performing separate multiplications.

In solving examples like the preceding there is of course no reason why a may not represent a number of the hundreds plus the tens order instead of one of the tens order. Consider a few examples:

EXAMPLE 1: Square 116.
12136 + 1320 = 13456, ANS.

EXAMPLE 2: Square 125.
130 × 120 combined with 25 = 15625, ANS.

EXAMPLE 3: Multiply 127 by 113.
14400 − 49 = 14351, ANS. from $(a^2 - b^2)$.

Practice Exercise No. 15

Find the required roots (approximate in the case of fractions).

1	$\sqrt[3]{2460375}$	11	$\sqrt[3]{\frac{2}{3}}\ (\times\frac{72}{72})$
2	$\sqrt[3]{11089567}$	12	$\sqrt[3]{\frac{2}{3}}\ (\times\frac{15552}{15552})$
3	$\sqrt[3]{40353607}$	13	$\sqrt[3]{\frac{2}{3}}\ (\times\frac{124416}{124416})$
4	$\sqrt[3]{403583419}$	14	$\sqrt[3]{5\frac{13}{32}}(\times\frac{2}{2})$
5	$\sqrt[3]{115501303}$	15	$\sqrt[3]{\frac{125}{256}}(\times\frac{2}{2})$
6	$\sqrt{\frac{2}{3}}\ (\times\ \frac{48}{48})$	16	$\sqrt[4]{6561}$
7	$\sqrt{\frac{38}{5}}(\times\frac{5}{5})$	17	$\sqrt[6]{117649}$
8	$\sqrt{\frac{45}{7}}(\times\ \frac{343}{343})$	18	$\sqrt[4]{29\frac{52}{81}}$
9	$\sqrt{10}\frac{1}{2}(\times\frac{200}{200})$	19	$\sqrt[4]{104\frac{536}{625}}$
10	$\sqrt{7\frac{1}{8}}(\times\frac{20000}{20000})$	20	$\sqrt[6]{11\frac{25}{64}}$

Do the following mentally by algebraic methods.

21	21^2		$(a-b)^2$
22	23^2	32	39^2
23	33^2	33	99^2
24	37^2	34	28^2
25	39^2	35	38^2
26	35^2	36	19×21
27	65^2		$(a+b)(a-b)$
28	95^2	37	28×32
29	105^2	38	37×43
30	205^2	39	46×54
31	29^2	40	48×72

Algebraic Processes

DEFINITIONS

A **monomial** is an algebraic expression of one term. *Thus,* $8a$ and $16a^2b$ and $\sqrt{3ax}$ are monomials.

A **polynomial** is an algebraic expression of more than one term. *Thus,* $a + b$, and $a^2 + 2ab + b^2$, and $a^3 + 3a^2b + 3ab^2 + b^3$, are three different *polynomials.*

A **binomial** is a polynomial that contains *two* terms. *Thus,* $a + b$, and $a + 1$, and $\sqrt{2} + \sqrt{3}$, are *binomials.* A **trinomial** contains *three* terms.

FACTORING

Factoring is the process of separating, or resolving, a quantity into factors.

No general rule can be given for factoring. In most cases the operation is performed by inspection and trial. The methods are best explained by examples.

Principle: *If every term of a polynomial contains the same monomial factor, then that monomial is one factor of the polynomial, and the other factor is equal to the quotient of the polynomial divided by the monomial factor.*

EXAMPLE: Factor the binomial $8a^2x^2 + 4a^3x$.

SOLUTION: $8a^2x^2 + 4a^3x = 4a^2x(2x + a)$.

EXPLANATION: We see by inspection that $4a^2x$ is a factor common to both terms. Dividing by $4a^2x$ we arrive at the other factor.

Principle: *If a trinomial contains three terms two of which are squares and if the third term is equal to plus or minus twice the product of the square roots of the other two, the expression may be recognized as the square of a binomial.*

Thus, $a^2x^2 + 2acx + c^2 = (ax + c)^2$, and $9a^2b^2 - 24a^2bc + 16a^2c^2 = (3ab - 4ac)^2$.

Principle: *If an expression represents the difference between two squares, it can be factored as the product of the sum of the roots by the difference between them.*

Thus, $4x^2 - 9y^2 = (2x + 3y)(2x - 3y)$, and $25a^4b^4x^4 - 4z^2 = (5a^2b^2x^2 + 2z)(5a^2b^2x^2 - 2z)$.

Principle: *If the factors of an expression contain like terms, these should be collected so as to present the result in the simplest form.*

EXAMPLE: Factor $(5a + 3b)^2 - (3a - 2b)^2$.

SOLUTION: $(5a + 3b)^2 - (3a - 2b)^2$

$= [(5a + 3b) + (3a - 2b)][(5a + 3b) - (3a - 2b)]$

$= (5a + 3b + 3a - 2b)(5a + 3b - 3a + 2b)$

$= (8a + b)(2a + 5b)$, ANS.

Principle: *A trinomial in the form of* $a^4 + a^2b^2 + b^4$ *can be written in the form of the difference between two squares.*

EXAMPLE: Resolve $9x^4 + 26x^2y^2 + 25y^4$ into factors.

SOLUTION:

$$\begin{array}{l} 9x^4 + 26x^2y^2 + 25y^4 \\ \quad + 4x^2y^2 \qquad\qquad - 4x^2y^2 \\ \hline (9x^4 + 30x^2y^2 + 25y^4) - 4x^2y^2 \\ = (3x^2 + 5y^2)^2 - 4x^2y^2 \\ = (3x^2 + 5y^2 + 2xy)(3x^2 + 5y^2 - 2xy) \\ = (3x^2 + 2xy + 5y^2)(3x^2 - 2xy + 5y^2) \end{array}$$

EXPLANATION: We note that the given expression is nearly a perfect square. We therefore add $4x^2y^2$ to it to make it a square and also subtract from it the same quantity. We then write it in the form of a difference between two squares. We resolve this into factors and rewrite the result so as to make the terms follow in the order of the powers of x.

Principle: *If a trinomial has the form* $x^2 + ax + b$ *and is factorable into two binomial factors, the first term of each factor will be* x*; the second term of the binomials will be two numbers whose product is* b *and whose sum is equal to* a*, which is the coefficient of the middle term of the trinomial.*

EXAMPLE 1: Factor $x^2 + 10x + 24$.

SOLUTION: $x^2 + 10x + 24 = (x + 6)(x + 4)$.

EXPLANATION: We are required to find two numbers whose product is 24 and whose sum is 10. The following pairs of factors will produce 24: 1 and 24, 2 and 12, 3 and 8, 4 and 6. From among these we select the pair whose sum is 10.

EXAMPLE 2: Factor $x^2 - 16x + 28$.

SOLUTION: $x^2 - 16x + 28 = (x - 14)(x - 2)$.

EXPLANATION: We are required to find two numbers whose product is 28 and whose algebraic sum is -16. Since their product is positive they must both have the same sign, and since their sum is negative they must both be negative. The negative factors that will produce 28 are -1 and -28, -2 and -14, -4 and -7. We select the pair whose algebraic sum is -16.

EXAMPLE 3: Factor $x^2 + 5x - 24$.

SOLUTION: $x^2 + 5x - 24 = (x + 8)(x - 3)$.

EXPLANATION: We are required to find two numbers whose product is -24 and whose algebraic sum is 5. Since their product is negative the numbers must have unlike signs, and since their sum is $+5x$, the larger number must be positive. The pairs of numbers that will produce 24, without considering signs, are 1 and 24, 2 and 12, 3 and 8, 4 and 6. From these we select the pair whose difference is 5. This is 3 and 8. We give the plus sign to the 8 and the minus sign to the 3.

EXAMPLE 4: Factor $x^2 - 7x - 18$.

SOLUTION: $x^2 - 7x - 18 = (x - 9)(x + 2)$.

EXPLANATION: We are required to find two numbers whose product is -18 and whose algebraic sum is -7. Since their product is negative the signs of the two numbers are unlike, and since their sum is negative, the larger number must be negative. The pairs of numbers that will produce 18, without considering signs, are 1 and 18, 2 and 9, 3 and 6. We select the pair whose difference is 7, giving the minus sign to the 9 and the plus sign to the 2.

EXAMPLE 5: Factor $x^2 - 7xy + 12y^2$.

SOLUTION: $x^2 - 7xy + 12y^2 = (x - 4y)(x - 3y)$.

EXPLANATION: We are required to find two terms whose product is $12y^2$ and whose algebraic sum is $-7y$. Since their product is positive and their sum negative they must both be negative terms. From the pairs of negative terms that will produce $+12y^2$ we select $-4y$ and $-3y$ as fulfilling the requirements.

When a trinomial factorable into two binomials has the form $ax^2 \pm bx \pm c$, it is resolved into factors by a process of trial and error which is continued until values are found that satisfy the requirements.

EXAMPLE 1: Factor $4x^2 + 26x + 22$

$$\begin{array}{l} 4x + 11 \\ \quad \times \qquad + 11x + 8x = 19x \text{ (reject)}, \\ x + 2 \end{array}$$

$$\begin{array}{l} x + 11 \\ \quad \times \qquad + 44x + 2x = 46x \text{ (reject)}, \\ 4x + 2 \end{array}$$

$$\begin{array}{l} 2x + 11 \\ \quad \times \qquad 22x + 4x = 26x \text{ (correct)}. \\ 2x + 2 \end{array}$$

$\therefore 4x^2 + 26x + 22 = (2x + 11)(2x + 2)$, ANS.

EXPLANATION: We use what is called the *cross multiplication* method to find the required binomials. We consider the pairs of terms that will produce the first and last terms of the trinomials. We write down the various forms of examples that can be worked out with these, and we reject one trial result after another until we find the arrangement that will give us the correct value for the middle term of the given trinomial.

Instead of making a separate example out of each of the possibilities, the process is shortened by simply listing the possible factors involved, in the following manner:

$$\begin{array}{ccc|c} 1 & 4 & 2 & 11 \\ 4 & 1 & 2 & 2 \end{array}$$

Factors to the left of the vertical line represent possible coefficients of x; those to the right of the line represent possible numerical values of second terms. Each pair of x coefficients is written in two positions (1 over 4, 4 over 1, etc.). Accordingly, it is not necessary to write second-term values in more than one position in order to exhaust the possibilities. We proceed with cross multiplication of the numbers on both sides of the vertical line. $(1 \times 2) + (4 \times 11) = 46$ (*too large—reject*); $(4 \times 2) + (1 \times 11) = 19$ (*too small—reject*); $(2 \times 2) + (2 \times 11) = 26$ (*correct.*)

EXAMPLE 2: Factor $24x^2 - 2x - 15$

SOLUTION:

$$\begin{array}{cccccccc|cc} 24 & 1 & 2 & 12 & 3 & 8 & 4 & 6 & 1 & 3 \\ 1 & 24 & 12 & 2 & 8 & 3 & 6 & 4 & 15 & 5 \end{array}$$

We select $\genfrac{}{}{0pt}{}{4}{6}$ and $\genfrac{}{}{0pt}{}{3}{5}$ as the combination of numbers that will give us the required middle term. $\therefore 24x^2 - 2x - 15 = (4x + 3)\ (6x - 5)$, ANS.

EXPLANATION: We write down the possible numerical values in the manner previously described. Inasmuch as the third term of the trinomial is negative the two second terms of its binomial factors must have unlike signs. Considering that the given middle term has a very small value, we conclude that we are more likely to find the answer quickly if we start our cross multiplication at the right of the numerical arrangement rather than at the left. In carrying out this cross multiplication we give the negative sign in each case to the larger of the two products involved. *Thus:* $6(-5) + 4(+3) = -18$ (*reject*); $4(-5) + 6(+3) = -2$ (*correct*). We have been fortunate in finding the correct values so soon. Otherwise we should have had to continue the process of trial and error with the numerical listing—though this is not as lengthy a process as may appear, since many of the wrong results are recognized at a glance without taking the trouble to calculate them. Having selected the correct combination of numbers, we write the factors as $4x + 3$ and $6x - 5$.

Practice Exercise No. 16

Resolve the following into factors

1	$7a^2bc^3 - 28abc$	9	$x^2 + 10x + 21$
2	$15a^2cd + 20ac^2d - 15acd^2$	10	$x^2 - 18x + 45$
3	$4x^2 + 12xy + 9y^2$	11	$x^2 + 5x - 36$
4	$9a^2b^2 - 24a^2bc + 16a^2c^2$	12	$x^2 - 13x + 48$
5	$9a^2x^2 - 16a^2y^2$	13	$x^2 - 14xy + 33y^2$
6	$49x^4 - 16y^2$	14	$6x^2 + 21x + 9$
7	$(2x + y + z)^2 - (x - 2y + z)^2$	15	$15x^2 - 6x - 21$
8	$a^4 + a^2 + 1$ (*Hint: add and subtract* a^2)	16	$12x^2 + 27x - 39$

SIMULTANEOUS EQUATIONS

Simultaneous equations are equations involving the same unknown quantities. *Thus,* $a + 2b = 11$ and $2a + b = 10$ are *simultaneous equations* since they both involve the same unknowns, namely, a and b.

Simultaneous equations involving two unknown quantities are solved as follows:

Rule 1. *Eliminate one of the unknowns.*

Rule 2. *Solve for the other unknown.*

Rule 3. *Find the value of the unknown previously eliminated.*

Elimination may be performed by any one of three different methods:

1. *By addition or subtraction.*
2. *By substitution.*
3. *By comparison.*

ELIMINATION BY ADDITION OR SUBTRACTION:

Rule 1. *Multiply one or both of the equations by such a number or numbers as will give one of the unknowns the same coefficient in both equations.*

Rule 2. *Add or subtract the equal coefficients according to the nature of their signs.*

EXAMPLE: $5x + 2y = 32, 2x - y = 2$. Find x and y.

SOLUTION:

$5x + 2y = 32$

$4x - 2y = 4$, multiplying $2x - y$ by 2,

$9x = 36$

$x = 4$.

$20 + 2y = 32$, substituting 4 for x in first equation,

$2y = 32 - 20$, transposing

$y = 6$.

ELIMINATION BY SUBSTITUTION:

Rule 1. *From one of the equations find the value of one of the unknowns in terms of the other.*

Rule 2. *Substitute the value thus found for the unknown in the other of the given equations.*

EXAMPLE: $2x + 4y = 50, 3x + 5y = 66$. Find x and y.

SOLUTION:

$2x + 4y = 50$,

$2x = 50 - 4y$, transposing,

$x = 25 - 2y$.

$3(25 - 2y) + 5y = 66$, substituting for x in other equation,

$75 - 6y + 5y = 66$,

$-y = 66 - 75 = -9, y = 9$.

$2x + 36 = 50$, substituting 9 for y in first equation,

$2x = 50 - 36 = 14, x = 7$.

ELIMINATION BY COMPARISON:

Rule 1. *From each equation find the value of one of the unknowns in terms of the other.*

Rule 2. *Form an equation from these equal values.*

EXAMPLE: $3x + 2y = 27, 2x - 3y = 5$. Find x and y.

SOLUTION:

$$3x + 2y = 27, 3x = 27 - 2y, x = \frac{27 - 2y}{3}.$$

$$2x - 3y = 5, 2x = 5 + 3y, x = \frac{5 + 3y}{2}.$$

$$\frac{27 - 2y}{3} = \frac{5 + 3y}{2},$$ both being equal to x,

$$27 - 2y = \frac{3(5 + 3y)}{2},$$ multiplying both sides by 3,

$2(27 - 2y) = 3(5 + 3y)$, multiplying both sides by 2,

$54 - 4y = 15 + 9y$, carrying out multiplication,

$-4y - 9y = 15 - 54 = -39, y = 3$.

$3x + 6 = 27, 3x = 21, x = 7$.

Of the foregoing methods, select the one which appears most likely to make the solution simple and direct.

Practice Exercise No. 17

PROBLEMS

1 The hands of a clock are together at 12 o'clock. When do they next meet? (x = minute spaces passed over by minute hand; y = number passed over by hour hand.)

2 A man has $22,000 invested and on it he earns $1,220. Part of the money is out at 5% interest and part at 6%. How much is in each part?

3 Jack is twice as old as Joe. Twenty years ago Jack was four times as old as Joe. What are their ages?

4 There are two numbers: the first added to half the second gives 35; the second added to half the first equals 40. What are the numbers?

5 The inventory of one department of a store increased by one-third of that of a second department amounts to $1,700; the inventory of the second increased by one-fourth of that of the first amounts to $1,800. What are the inventories?

6 Find two numbers such that $\frac{1}{2}$ of the first plus $\frac{1}{3}$ of the second shall equal 45, and $\frac{1}{2}$ of the second plus $\frac{1}{5}$ of the first shall equal 40.

7 A and B invest $918 in a partnership venture and clear $153. A's share of the profit is $45 more than B's. What was the contribution of each one to the capital?

8 Two girls receive $153 for baby sitting. Ann is paid for 14 days and Mary for 15. Ann's pay for 6 days' work is $3 more than Mary gets for 4. How much does each earn per day?

9 In 80 lbs. of an alloy of copper and tin there are 7 lbs. of copper to 3 of tin. How much copper must be added so that there may be 11 lbs. of copper to 4 of tin?

10 Brown owes $1,200 and Jones $2,500, but neither has enough money to pay his debts. Brown says to Jones, "Lend me one-eighth of your bank account and I'll pay my creditors." Jones says to Brown, "Lend me one-ninth of yours and I'll pay mine." How much money has each?

FRACTIONS

To reduce a fraction to its lowest terms, *resolve the numerator and the denominator into their prime factors and cancel all the common factors, or divide the numerator and the denominator by their highest common factor.*

EXAMPLE 1: Reduce $\frac{12a^2b^3c^4}{9a^3bc^2}$.

SOLUTION: $\frac{12a^2b^3c^4}{9a^3bc^2} = \frac{2 \times 2 \times 3a^2bc^2(b^2c^2)}{3 \times 3a^2bc^2(a)}$

$= \frac{4b^2c^2}{3a}$, ANS.

EXPLANATION: The numerical parts of the fraction are separated into their prime factors, and the algebraic parts are divided by their highest common factor. The terms that cancel out are then eliminated. As a guide for determining the highest common factor of monomial terms note that such a factor is made up of the lower (or lowest) of the given powers of each letter involved.

EXAMPLE 2: Reduce $\frac{12x^2 + 15x - 63}{4x^2 - 31x + 42}$.

SOLUTION: $\frac{12x^2 + 15x - 63}{4x^2 - 31x + 42} = \frac{(3x + 9)(4x - 7)}{(x - 6)(4x - 7)}$

$= \frac{3x + 9}{x - 6}$,

$= \frac{3(x + 3),}{x - 6}$ ANS.

EXPLANATION: Numerator and denominator are factored, and the common factor is then cancelled.

A fraction may be reduced to an integral or mixed expression if the degree (power) of its numerator equals or exceeds that of its denominator.

To reduce a fraction to an integral or mixed expression, *divide the numerator by the denominator.*

EXAMPLE 1: Reduce $\frac{x^2 - y^2}{x - y}$ to an integral expression.

SOLUTION: $\frac{x^2 - y^2}{x - y} = \frac{(x - y)(x + y)}{x - y} = x + y.$

EXAMPLE 2: Reduce $\frac{x^2 + y^2}{x + y}$ to a mixed expression.

SOLUTION: $\frac{x^2 + y^2}{x + y} = \frac{(x^2 - y^2) + 2y^2}{x + y}$

$= \frac{(x + y)(x - y) + 2y^2}{x + y}$

$= x - y + \frac{2y^2}{x + y}$, ANS.

EXPLANATION: While $x^2 + y^2$ is not evenly divisible by $x + y$, we recognize that it would be so divisible if it were $x^2 - y^2$. Hence we subtract $2y^2$ to convert it to $x^2 - y^2$ and also add to it the same amount. We divide $x^2 - y^2$ by $x + y$ and write the remainder as a fraction that has $x + y$ for its denominator.

To reduce a mixed expression to a fraction, *multiply the integral expression by the denominator of the fraction; add to this product the numerator of the fraction and write under this result the given denominator.*

EXAMPLE: Reduce $x + 1 + \frac{x + 1}{x - 1}$ to a fraction.

SOLUTION: $\left[\frac{(x + 1)}{1} + \frac{(x + 1)}{(x - 1)}\right]\left(\frac{x - 1}{x - 1}\right) =$

$\left(\frac{x + 1}{1}\right)\left(\frac{x - 1}{x - 1}\right) + \left(\frac{x + 1}{x - 1}\right)\left(\frac{x - 1}{x - 1}\right) =$

$= \frac{x^2 - 1 + x + 1}{x - 1} = \frac{x^2 + x}{x - 1}, \frac{x(x + 1)}{x - 1}$, ANS.

To reduce fractions to their lowest common denominator, *find the lowest common multiple of the denominators and proceed on the same principles that govern arithmetical fractions.*

EXAMPLE: Reduce $\frac{1}{x^2 + 3x + 2}$, $\frac{2}{x^2 + 5x + 6}$ and $\frac{3}{x^2 + 4x + 3}$ to fractions having the lowest common denominator.

SOLUTION: $\frac{1}{x^2 + 3x + 2}, \frac{2}{x^2 + 5x + 6}, \frac{3}{x^2 + 4x + 3}$

$$= \frac{1}{(x+1)(x+2)}, \frac{2}{(x+2)(x+3)}, \frac{3}{(x+1)(x+3)}$$

The LCD is $(x+1)(x+2)(x+3)$.
Dividing this by each of the denominators and multiplying each numerator by the resulting quotient we obtain

$$\frac{x+3}{(x+1)(x+2)(x+3)}, \frac{2x+2}{(x+1)(x+2)(x+3)}, \frac{3x+6}{(x+1)(x+2)(x+3)}, \text{ ANS.}$$

ADDITION AND SUBTRACTION OF FRACTIONS

EXAMPLE 1: Simplify

$$\frac{2a-4b}{4} - \frac{a-b+c}{3} + \frac{a-b-2c}{12}.$$

SOLUTION: $\frac{2a-4b}{4} - \frac{a-b+c}{3} + \frac{a-b-2c}{12}$

$$= \frac{6a-12b-4a+4b-4c+a-b-2c}{12}$$

$$= \frac{3a-9b-6c}{12} = \frac{a-3b-2c}{4}, \text{ ANS.}$$

EXAMPLE 2: Simplify $\frac{a+2x}{a-2x} - \frac{a-2x}{a+2x}$.

SOLUTION: $\frac{a+2x}{a-2x} - \frac{a-2x}{a+2x}$

$$= \frac{(a+2x)^2 - (a-2x)^2}{a^2-4x^2}$$

$$= \frac{a^2+4ax+4x^2-a^2+4ax-4x^2}{a^2-4x^2}$$

$$= \frac{8ax}{a^2-4x^2} \text{ or, } \frac{8ax}{(a-2x)(a+2x)}, \text{ANS.}$$

MULTIPLICATION AND DIVISION OF FRACTIONS

Principle: *The product of two or more fractions is equal to the product of the numerators multiplied together, divided by the product of the denominators multiplied together.*

EXAMPLE 1: Multiply $\frac{7x}{5y}$ by $\frac{3a}{4c}$.

SOLUTION: $\frac{7x}{5y} \cdot \frac{3a}{4c} = \frac{21ax}{20cy}$, ANS.

EXAMPLE 2: Multiply $\frac{2x}{x-y}$ by $\frac{x^2-y^2}{3}$.

SOLUTION: $\left(\frac{2x}{x-y}\right)\left(\frac{x^2-y^2}{3}\right) = \frac{2x(x+y)(x-y)}{3(x-y)}$

$$= \frac{2x(x+y)}{3}, \text{ ANS.}$$

EXAMPLE 3: Multiply $\frac{2(x+y)}{x-y}$ by $\frac{x^2-y^2}{x^2+2xy+y^2}$.

SOLUTION: $\left[\frac{2(x+y)}{x-y}\right]\left[\frac{x^2-y^2}{x^2+2xy+y^2}\right]$

$$= \frac{2(x+y)(x+y)(x-y)}{(x-y)(x+y)^2} = 2, \text{ ANS.}$$

Principle: *Division by a fraction is equivalent to multiplication by the reciprocal of the fraction,* i.e., *the fraction inverted.*

EXAMPLE: Divide $\frac{3a^2}{a^2-b^2}$ by $\frac{a}{a+b}$.

SOLUTION: $\frac{3a^2}{a^2-b^2} \div \frac{a}{a+b} = \frac{3a^2}{a^2-b^2} \cdot \frac{a+b}{a}$

$$= \frac{3a^2(a+b)}{a(a+b)(a-b)} = \frac{3a^2}{a(a-b)} = \frac{3a}{a-b}, \text{ ANS.}$$

Practice Exercise No. 18

1 Reduce $\frac{45x^3y^3z}{36abx^2y^2z}$ to its lowest terms.

2 Reduce $\frac{x^2+2ax+a^2}{3(x^2-a^2)}$ to its lowest terms.

3 Reduce $\frac{x^2+a^2+3-2ax}{x-a}$ to a mixed quantity.

4 Reduce $a + \frac{ax}{a-x}$ to a fraction.

5 Reduce $1 + \frac{c}{x-y}$ to a fraction.

6 Reduce $\frac{x+a}{b}$, $\frac{a}{b}$ and $\frac{a-x}{a}$ to fractions with the LCD.

7 Reduce $\frac{x}{1-x}$, $\frac{x^2}{(1-x)^2}$ and $\frac{x^3}{(1-x)^3}$ to fractions with the LCD.

8 Add $\frac{x+y}{2}$ and $\frac{x-y}{2}$.

9 Add $\frac{2}{(x-1)^3}$, $\frac{3}{(x-1)^2}$ and $\frac{4}{x-1}$.

10 Subtract $2a - \frac{a-3b}{c}$ from $4a + \frac{2a}{c}$.

11 Subtract $\frac{x}{a+x}$ from $\frac{a}{a-x}$.

12 Multiply $\frac{2}{x-y}$ by $\frac{x^2-y^2}{a}$.

13 Multiply $\frac{x^2-4}{3}$ by $\frac{4x}{x+2}$.

14 Divide $\frac{3x}{2x-2}$ by $\frac{2x}{x-1}$.

15 Divide $\frac{(x+y)^2}{x-y}$ by $\frac{x+y}{(x-y)^2}$.

Logarithms

Logarithms are a means of simplifying the manipulation of numbers containing many digits or decimal places. The system of common logarithms, which is the one in most common use, is based on powers of 10.

By this system **the logarithm of a given number** *is the exponent to which* 10 *must be raised to obtain that number. Thus:*

$10^1 = 10$; ∴ the logarithm of 10 is 1.
$10^2 = 100$; ∴ the logarithm of 100 is 2.
$10^3 = 1{,}000$; ∴ the logarithm of 1,000 is 3.
$10^4 = 10{,}000$; ∴ the logarithm of 10,000 is 4.
and so on up.

The logarithm of a number between 10 and 99 is therefore an exponent greater than 1 and less than 2.

The logarithm of a number between 100 and 1000 is an exponent greater than 2 and less than 3. The logarithm of any number other than a multiple of 10 is therefore a whole number plus a decimal.

FINDING THE LOGARITHM OF A NUMBER

The logarithm of 45 should be between 1 and 2. That is, it must be 1 plus something. To find out what this something is, we refer to what is known as a **table of logarithms,** and then we find the logarithm of 45 to be equal to 1.6532. This is written:

$$\text{Log } 45 = 1.6532.$$

The method of finding a logarithm from the table will be explained in detail later.

The **characteristic** is the whole number part of the logarithm. In the above case the *characteristic* is 1.

The **mantissa** is the decimal part of the logarithm, and is the part found in the table of logarithms. In the above case the *mantissa* is .6532.

Finding the Characteristic. *The characteristic is not found in the table but is determined by rule. It is positive for numbers equal to* 1 *or greater, and negative for numbers less than* 1.

By definition,

For numbers between these limits	*the characteristic is*
10,000 and 100,000 *minus*	4
1,000 and 10,000 *minus*	3
100 and 1,000 *minus*	2
10 and 100 *minus*	1
1 and 10 *minus*	0
.1 and 1 *minus*	−1
.01 and .1 *minus*	−2
.001 and .01 *minus*	−3
.0001 and .001 *minus*	−4

Note: The characteristic 4 would apply to numbers from 10,000 to 99,999.999999+ carried to any number of places; characteristic 3, from 1,000 to 9,999.999999 . . . etc. For the sake of simplicity the latter numbers in these groups are expressed as 100,000 minus, 10,000 minus, 1,000 minus, etc.

Rule 1. *For whole numbers the characteristic is one less than the number of figures to the left of the decimal point.*

EXAMPLE 1: What is the characteristic of 82,459.23?

SOLUTION: There are 5 figures to the left of the decimal. $5 - 1 = 4$. ∴ the characteristic is 4.

Rule 2. *The characteristic of decimal numbers is equal to minus the number of places to the right from the decimal point to the first significant figure* (number other than zero).

EXAMPLE 2: What is the characteristic of .001326?

SOLUTION: From the decimal point to 1, the first significant figure, there are 3 places. ∴ the characteristic is −3.

EXAMPLE 3: What is the characteristic of .443?

SOLUTION: There is but one place from the decimal point to the first significant figure. ∴ the characteristic is −1.

Note: If the characteristic of a number (.023) is −2, and the mantissa is 3617, the whole logarithm is written $-2 + .3617$. The mantissa is always considered positive, and therefore negative characteristics are denoted by the placing of the minus sign *above* the characteristic. Another notation used for negative characteristics is $8.3617 - 10$. In this the negative *characteristic* is subtracted from 10, the remainder is made the new characteristic, and the −10 is placed after the mantissa to indicate a negative characteristic.

Practice Exercise No. 19

Write the characteristics of the following.

1	17	6	67.48
2	342	7	7.4
3	78,943	8	.000571
4	4,320	9	.021
5	.42	10	1

Finding the mantissa. The mantissa is found in the table of logarithms on page 843. The mantissa is not related to the position of the decimal point in any number. For example the mantissa of 34,562 is the same as the mantissa of 3,456.2 or 345.62. But the logarithm of these numbers differs with respect to the *characteristic,* which you have learned to find by inspection of the number.

Note: The reason why the mantissa for a given set of digits does not change, no matter how they may be pointed off decimally, will appear from the following. Let us assume that m is any number and the logarithm of this number is $n + p$, in which n is the characteristic and p the mantissa. By definition $m = 10^{n+p}$. If we multiply or divide 10^{n+p} by 10, 100, 1,000, etc. we make corresponding changes in the decimal pointing of m. But by the laws of algebra multiplication or division of 10^{n+p} by 10, 100, 1,000, etc., would be performed by adding or subtracting the exponents of 10^1, 10^2, 10^3, etc. Hence to arrive at any desired decimal pointing of the number m, only the whole-number part of the exponent of 10^{n+p} is modified. This part is n, the characteristic. The mantissa, p, always remains unchanged. Similar considerations will also make it clear why the mantissa still remains positive even when the characteristic is negative.

Let us now use the table of logarithms on page 843 to find the mantissa of the number 345. Find 34 in the left-hand column headed by No. Then move across to the column headed 5. The mantissa is 5378. The characteristic is 2; therefore log $345 = 2.5378$.

By using the same mantissa and simply changing the characteristic we arrive at the following logarithms for various decimal pointings of the digits 345:

$$\log 34.5 = 1.5378$$
$$\log 3.45 = .5378$$
$$\log .345 = -1 + .5378, \text{ or } \bar{1}.5378$$
$$\log .0345 = -2 + .5378, \text{ or } \bar{2}.5378$$

EXAMPLE 1: Find the log of .837.

SOLUTION: Find 83 in the column headed No., move across to column headed 7. The mantissa is .9227; the characteristic is −1.
∴ $\log .837 = \bar{1}.9227$ or $9.9227 - 10$, ANS.

Interpolation is an arithmetic method used to find the value of a mantissa when the original number contains more than three significant (nonzero) figures. (The table printed in the Encyclopedia gives direct answers only for numbers up to 999.)

EXAMPLE 2: Find the log of 6484.

SOLUTION:

log 6480 = 3.8116 } The difference between
log 6490 = 3.8122 } these two logs is .0006.
Difference between 6490 and 6480 is 10.
Difference between 6484 and 6480 is 4.
Difference between mantissas is .0006.
$\frac{4}{10} \times .0006 = .00024$ increment,
$.8116 + .00024 = .81184$.
log 6484 = 3.81184, ANS.

EXAMPLE 3: Find the log of .05368.

SOLUTION:

log .05360 = 2.7292,
log. 05370 = 2.7300.
Difference between logs = .0008.
Difference between numbers is 8.
$.0008 \times .8 = .00064$ increment,
$.7292 + .00064 = .72984$,
log .05368 = 2.72984, ANS.

Practice Exercise No. 20

Find the logarithms of the following:

1	354	6	.234
2	76	7	.00352
3	8	8	6.04
4	6346	9	.0005324
5	3.657	10	672.8

Finding the antilogarithm. The number which corresponds to a given logarithm is called its **antilogarithm.**

The antilogarithm of a logarithm is found by obtaining the number corresponding to the mantissa and determining the position of the decimal point from the characteristic.

EXAMPLE 1: Find the antilogarithm of 1.8531.

SOLUTION: Look for mantissa 8531 in the body of the table on page 843. In the No. column to the left of the row where you have located 8531, you will find the first two figures of the number (71). The third figure (3) is found at the top of the column in which 8531 is located. Since the characteristic is 1, mark off two decimal places in the number, counting from the *left,* to give 71.3.

Usually the mantissa cannot be found exactly in the tables. It is then necessary to interpolate between the two numbers corresponding to the two nearest logarithms.

EXAMPLE 2: Find the antilog of $\bar{3}.5484$

SOLUTION: Given mantissa 5484 is between 5478 and 5490. Hence the first three significant figures of the antilog are 353.

$$\left.\begin{array}{l}\text{Diff. bet. 5490 and 5478} = 0012\\ \text{Diff. bet. 5484 and 5478} = 0006\end{array}\right\} \left.\frac{0006}{0012}\right\} = .5$$

The first four significant figures are therefore 3535. Since the characteristic is $3.535 \times 10^{-3} = .003535$, ANS.

HOW TO USE LOGARITHMS

To multiply by the use of logarithms, *add the logarithms of the numbers to be multiplied and find the antilogarithm corresponding to this sum.*

EXAMPLE: Multiply 25.31 by 42.18.

SOLUTION: log 25.31 = 1.4033,
log 42.18 = 1.6251,
Sum = 3.0284,
Product = antilog of 3.0284 = 1067.5, ANS.

To divide by the use of logarithms, *subtract the logarithm of the divisor from the logarithm of the dividend; the difference is the logarithm of the quotient.*

EXAMPLE 1: Divide 5,280.4 by 67.82.

SOLUTION: log 5,280.4 = 3.7226,
log 67.82 = 1,8313,
difference = 1.8913,
Quotient = antilog 1.8913 = 77.86, ANS.

EXAMPLE 2: Divide 5,280.4 by .06782.

SOLUTION:

log 5,280.4 = 13.7226 − 10
log .06782 = 8.8313 − 10

difference = 4.8913,
antilog = 77860, ANS.

EXPLANATION: log .06782 is negative with a characteristic of −2. In order to perform a subtraction with it we write it as 8.8313 − 10, but before subtraction is possible we must make a corresponding change in the minuend. This we do by both adding to it and subtracting from it the number 10, an operation that does not affect its value. The two −10s are eliminated when we subtract and the resulting logarithm has the correct characteristic.

EXAMPLE 3: Divide 52.804 by 6782.

$$\begin{aligned}\log 52.804 &= 11.7226 - 10\\ \log 6782 &= \ \ 3.8313\\ \hline &\ \ \ \ 7.8913 - 10\\ &= \ \ 3.8913\\ \text{antilog} &= .007786, \quad \text{ANS.}\end{aligned}$$

EXPLANATION: In this case we have to increase and decrease the upper logarithm by 10 in order to perform the subtraction, but the −10 is not eliminated and hence has the effect of giving the remainder a negative characteristic.

To raise to a given power by the use of logarithms, *multiply the logarithm of the number by the given exponent of the number and find the antilogarithm.*

The reason for this may be explained as follows. Let m be a number and n its logarithm. Then—

$$m = 10^n,$$
$$m^2 = 10^n \times 10^n = 10^{n+n} = 10^{2n},$$
$$m^3 = 10^{3n}, \text{ etc.}$$

EXAMPLE 1: Find 46^4.

SOLUTION: $\log 46 = 1.6628$

$$\times 4$$

$$\log 46^4 = 6.6512,$$
$$46^4 = \text{antilog } 6.6512 = 4{,}479{,}000, \quad \text{ANS.}$$

To find a given root by the use of logarithms, *divide the logarithm of the number by the index of the root and find the antilogarithm.*

This may be demonstrated thus:

Let $m = 10^n$.

Then $\sqrt{m} = \sqrt{10^n} = 10^{\frac{n}{2}}$,

$\sqrt[3]{m} = 10^{\frac{n}{3}}$, etc.

EXAMPLE 1: Find $\sqrt[3]{75}$.

SOLUTION: $\log 75 = 1.8751$,

$$\frac{1.8751}{3} = .62503,$$

Root = antilog .62503 = 4.217, ANS.

EXAMPLE 2: Find $\sqrt{.251}$.

SOLUTION: $\log .251 = 1.3997$ or $9.3997 - 10$,

$$\frac{9.3997 - 10}{2} = 4.69985 - 5 = \bar{1}.69985$$

Root = antilog $\bar{1}.69985$ = .5015, ANS.

EXAMPLE 3: Find $\sqrt[3]{.75}$.

SOLUTION:

$$\begin{aligned}\log .75 &= \ \ 9.8751 - 10\\ &+ 20 \qquad\ - 20\\ \hline &\ \ 29.8751 - 30,\end{aligned}$$

$$\frac{29.8751 - 30}{3} = 9.9583 - 10 = \bar{1}.9583$$

antilog = .9084, ANS.

EXPLANATION: Starting in this case with a negative characteristic, we cannot make a direct division by 3 because dividing 10 by 3 would result in a fractional characteristic, which is impossible. We therefore increase and decrease the logarithm by 20 in order to make the division possible and to produce a −10 in the remainder.

Practice Exercise No. 21

Solve by logarithms.

1 3984×5.6	11 $\frac{5}{-7}$
2 25.316×42.18	12 $\frac{-17}{32}$
3 220.2×2209	13 $\frac{6+3}{4}$
4 $5280 \div 33.81$	14 $\frac{8+7}{7}$
5 $7256.2 \div 879.26$	15 $\frac{13-9}{3}$
6 $9783 \div .1234$	16 $\frac{11}{16-7}$
7 77^3	17 $\frac{8}{3 \times 5}$
8 $\sqrt[3]{85}$	18 $\frac{4 \times 6}{11}$
9 $\sqrt[5]{356.07}$	19 $\frac{7 \div 3}{4}$
10 2.43^5	20 $\frac{16}{18 \div 5}$

The principal use of logarithms is in connection with trigonometry, the branch of mathematics that has to do with the measurement of triangles.

ANSWERS TO EXERCISES

Exercise No. 1

1 $\frac{24}{32} = \frac{3}{4}$

2 $63 : 56 = \frac{63}{56} = 1\frac{7}{56} = 1\frac{1}{8}$

3 1 lb. = 16 oz., 5 lb. = 80 oz., $\frac{10}{80} = \frac{1}{8}$.

4 2 parts + 3 parts = 5 parts. Since 2 parts are water, then $\frac{2}{5}$ of (the 100%) total is water, or 40%.

5 6 parts tin + 19 parts copper = 25 parts to

make bronze. The amount of tin in 500 lbs. of bronze is $\frac{6}{25} \times 500$ or 120.

6 $5 + 14 + 21 = 40$ parts = the total of $2,000. $\frac{21}{40} \times 2{,}000 = \$1{,}050$ as the largest share; $\frac{5}{40} \times 2{,}000 = \$250$ as the smallest share; $1,050 − 250 = $800 difference.

Exercise No. 2

1 6	3 6	5 21	7 3	9 3
2 12	4 2	6 4	8 125	10 18

Exercise No. 3

1 $\frac{18}{27} = \frac{20}{x}$ Direct prop. $18x = 540$, $x = \frac{540}{18} = 30$

2 $\frac{9}{30} = \frac{2}{x}$ Direct prop. $9x = 60$, $x = \frac{60}{9} = 6\frac{2}{3}$

3 $\frac{5}{20} - \frac{90}{x}$ Direct prop. $5x = 1{,}800$, $x = \frac{1{,}800}{5} = 360$

4 $\frac{112}{240} = \frac{28}{x}$ Inverse prop. $112x = 6{,}720$, $x = \frac{6{,}720}{112} = 60$

5 $\frac{26}{20} = \frac{x}{35}$ Inverse prop. $20x = 910$, $x = \frac{910}{20} = 45\frac{1}{2}$

6 $\frac{220}{x} = \frac{2}{8}$ Direct prop. $2x = 1{,}760$, $x = \frac{1{,}760}{2} = 880$

Exercise No. 4

1 23	5 $4b$	8 $5a + 2b$
2 −36	6 −3	9 $15a - 2b$
3 −7	7 $12x$	10 $15a + 3b - 5$
4 $-20d$		

Exercise No. 5

1 28	4 66	7 3
2 −9	5 130	8 −3
3 −24	6 $-40ab$	9 −25

Exercise No. 6

1 −32	3 72	5 −3	7 $2\frac{4}{5}$
2 216	4 −144	6 4	8 −12

Exercise No. 7

1 $x + y = 5$	5 $x^2 + y^2 = 13$
2 $x + y + z = 9$	6 $y - 3 = 0$
3 $2x + 2y = 10$	7 $2xz = 16$
4 $x + y - z = 1$	

Exercise No. 8

1 23	4 20	7 3	9 1,260
2 110	5 12	8 55	10 3
3 13	6 44		

Exercise No. 9

1 $p = 2l + 2w$	6 $P = M - O$
2 $d = rt$	7 $d = 16t^2$
3 $H = \frac{av}{746}$	8 $A = S^2$
4 $I = PRT$	9 $C = \frac{5}{9}(F - 32°)$
5 $A = \frac{W}{V}$	10 $R = \frac{N}{T}$

Exercise No. 10

1 $p = 5$	6 $n = 36$
2 $n = 12\frac{1}{2}$	7 $a = 48$
3 $x = 28$	8 $b = Wc$
4 $c = 6$	9 $A = \frac{W}{V}$
5 $y = 4$	10 $W = \frac{P}{AH}$

Exercise No. 11

1 Since $\frac{D}{d} = \frac{r}{R}$ then $rd = DR$, and $r = \frac{DR}{d}$; substituting, $r = \frac{18 \times 100}{6} = \frac{1{,}800}{6} = 300$.

2 Since $DR = dr$, and D is the unknown, then $D = \frac{dr}{R}$; substituting, $D = \frac{9 \times 256}{144} = \frac{2{,}304}{144} = 16$.

3 Let n represent the number. Then $3n + 2n = 90$, $5n = 90$, $n = \frac{90}{5} = 18$

4 Let n represent the smaller number. Then $n + 7n = 32$, $8n = 32$, $n = \frac{32}{8} = 4$, and $7n = 7 \times 4$ or 28.

5 Let x = the amount the first unit gets. Then the second unit receives $2x$, and the third unit receives $x + 2x$ or $3x$. The total $x + 2x + 3x = 6x = 600$, $x = 100$, and $2x = 200$.

6 Rate $\times$ Time = Distance; $R \times t = D$. They both travel the same amount of time. Let t equal the time they travel. Then $300t + 200t = 3{,}000$ mi., $500t = 3{,}000$, $t = \frac{3{,}000}{500} = 6$ hrs. $300 \times 6 = 1{,}800$ mi.

7 $R \times t = D$. Let R = rate of slower soldier. Then $2R$ = rate of faster one. $10R + 20R = 24$ mi., $30R = 24$, $R = \frac{24}{30}$ or $\frac{4}{5}$, and $2R = \frac{8}{5}$ or $1\frac{3}{5}$ mi. per hr.

8 Let n = number of quarters the man has. Then $3n$ = number of nickels, and $.25(n) + .05(3n) = 8.00$ or his total money.

$.25n + .15n = .40n = 8.00$, $n = \frac{8.00}{.40} = 20$

CHECK: $3n = 60$. $20 \times .25 = \$5.00$, and $60 \times .05 = \$3.00$, $\$5.00 + \$3.00 = \$8.00$.

9 Let T and t represent no. of teeth in large and small gears and let R and r represent rpm. Then $\frac{T}{t} = \frac{r}{R}$, and $\frac{72}{48} = \frac{160}{R}$, $72R = 7{,}680$, $R = \frac{7{,}680}{72} = 106\frac{2}{3}$.

10 Weight $\times$ Distance = Weight $\times$ Distance. $\therefore 120 \times \frac{9}{2} = x \times 5$. $5x = 540$, $x = 108$.

Exercise No. 12

1	8	4	10	7	3	10	.3
2	10	5	1	8	5	11	1.2
3	9	6	.2	9	12	12	.05

Exercise No. 13

1	73	4	17.68	7	43	9	85
2	35	5	20.69	8	56	10	97
3	54.2	6	26				

Exercise No. 14

1	36	6	32,768	11	$\frac{4}{9}$
2	729	7	9	12	14.6969
3	5	8	5	13	.00000028
4	$\frac{1}{64}$	9	43,000,000	14	.0025
5	186,624	10	620,000	15	122,000,000

Exercise No. 15

1	135	11	$\frac{5}{6}$	21	441	31	841
2	223	12	$\frac{31}{36}$	22	529	32	1521
3	343	13	$\frac{63}{72}$	23	1089	33	9801
4	739	14	$\frac{7}{4}$	24	1369	34	784
5	487	15	$\frac{6}{8}$	25	1521	35	1444
6	$\frac{10}{12}$	16	9	26	1225	36	399
7	$\frac{14}{5}$	17	7	27	4225	37	896
8	$\frac{124}{49}$	18	$2\frac{1}{3}$	28	9025	38	1591
9	$\frac{65}{20}$	19	$3\frac{1}{5}$	29	11025	39	2484
10	$\frac{1068}{400}$	20	$1\frac{1}{2}$	30	42025	40	3456

Exercise No. 16

1 $7abc\,(ac^2 - 4)$
2 $5acd\,(3a + 4c - 3d)$
3 $(2x + 3y)(2x + 3y)$ or $(2x + 3y)^2$
4 $(3ab - 4ac)(3ab - 4ac)$ or $a^2[(3b - 4c)^2]$
5 $(3ax + 4ay)(3ax - 4ay)$ or $a^2[(3x + 4y)(3x - 4y)]$
6 $(7x^2 + 4y)(7x^2 - 4y)$
7 $(3x - y + 2z)(x + 3y)$
8 $(a^2 + a + 1)(a^2 - a + 1)$
9 $(x + 7)(x + 3)$
10 $(x - 15)(x - 3)$
11 $(x + 9)(x - 4)$
12 $(x - 16)(x + 3)$
13 $(x - 11y)(x - 3y)$
14 $[3(x + 3)](2x + 1)$
15 $(5x - 7)[3(x + 1)]$
16 $(4x + 13)[3(x - 1)]$

Exercise No. 17

1 Let x = no. of min. spaces passed over by min. hand; y = no. passed by hr. hand. $12y = x$; $y = x - 60$. Subtracting, $11y = x - (x - 60) = 60$; $y = 5\frac{5}{11}$. $5\frac{5}{11}$ min. spaces past 12 o'clock gives $1.05\frac{5}{11}$ o'clock.

2 Try elimination by substitution. x = part inv. at 5%; y = part inv. at 6%. $.05x + .06y = \$1{,}220$; $x + y = \$22{,}000$. Multiplying $.05x$ etc. by 20 we get $x + 1.20y = \$24{,}400$, from

which $x = \$24{,}000 - 1.20y$. Substituting this value in other equation, $\$24{,}000 - 1.20y + y = \$22{,}000$; $-.20y = -\$2{,}400$; $y = \$12{,}000$; hence $x = \$10{,}000$.

3 Try elimination by comparison. a = Jack's age; b = Joe's age. $a = 2b$; $a - 20 = 4(b - 20)$; $a = 4(b - 20) + 20$; hence $2b = 4b - 80 + 20$; $2b - 4b = -60$; $b = 30$ years for Joe; $2 \times 30 = 60$ years for Jack.

4 a = first; b = second. $a + \frac{b}{2} = 35$; $\frac{a}{2} + b = 40$. Multiply first equation by 2, $2a + b = 70$. Subtracting second equation from this $1\frac{1}{2}a = 30$; $a = 20$; $a + \frac{b}{2} = 35$; $\frac{b}{2} = 35 - 20$; $\frac{b}{2} = 15$; $b = 30$.

5 $a + \frac{b}{3} = \$1700$; $\frac{a}{4} + b = \$1800$. Multiplying first equation by 3, $3a + b = \$5100$. Subtracting second equation, $2\frac{3}{4}a = \$3300$; $a = \$1200$. Substituting in first equation $\$1200 + \frac{b}{3} = \$1700$; $\frac{b}{3} = \$1700 - \$1200 = \$500$; $b = \$1500$.

6 $\frac{a}{2} + \frac{b}{3} = 45$; $\frac{a}{5} + \frac{b}{2} = 40$. Multiplying both equations, $a + \frac{2b}{3} = 90$; $a + \frac{5b}{2} = 200$. Subtracting the first from the second $\frac{11b}{6} = 110$; $b = 60$. Substituting in first equation, $\frac{a}{2} + 20 = 45$; $\frac{a}{2} = 25$; $a = 50$.

7 a = A's profit; b = B's profit. $a + b = \$153$; $a - b = \$45$. Adding, $2a = \$198$; $a = \$99$; $b = 54$. Dividing \$918 in the proportions of 99 and 54, $\$918 \div 153 = 6$; $\$99 \times 6 = \$594$ for A; $\$54 \times 6 = \$324$ for B.

8 Try substitution. $14A + 15M = \$153$; $6A - 4M = \$3$; $6A = \$3 + 4M$, whence $A = \$.50 + \frac{2M}{3}$. Substituting in other equation $\$7 + \frac{28M}{3} + 15M = \$153$; $9\frac{1}{3}M + 15M = \$153 - \$7$. $\frac{73M}{3} = \$146$; $M = \$6$. Substituting in original equation, $6A - \$24 = \$3$; $6A = \$27$; $A = \$4.50$.

9 There are several ways to solve problems like this. The method by simultaneous equations might be as follows. Select letters to represent values that do not change. a = wt. of copper *to be added;* b = wt. of tin. $b = 80 - \frac{7b}{3} = 24$. $a = \frac{11b}{4} - \frac{7b}{3} = 66 - 56 = 10$ lbs.

10 Eliminate by comparison. $B + \frac{J}{8} = \$1200$; $\frac{B}{9} + J = \$2500$. $B = \$1200 - \frac{J}{8}$; $B = \$22{,}500 - 9J$; $\$1200 - \frac{J}{8} = \$22{,}500 - 9J$; $9J - \frac{J}{8} = \$22{,}500 - \$1200$; $\frac{71J}{8} = \$21{,}300$; $J = \$2400$; $B + \frac{J}{8} = \$1200$; $B + \$300 = \$1200$; $B = \$900$.

Exercise No. 18

1 $\frac{5xy}{4ab}$

2 $\frac{x + a}{3(x - a)}$

3 $x - a + \frac{3}{x - a}$

4 $\frac{a^2}{a - x}$

5 $\frac{x - y + c}{x - y}$

6 $\frac{a(x + a)}{ab}, \frac{a^2}{ab}, \frac{b(a - x)}{ab}$

7 $\frac{x(1 - x)^2}{(1 - x)^3}, \frac{x^2(1 - x)}{(1 - x)^3}, \frac{x^3}{(1 - x)^3}$

8 x

9 $\frac{4x^2 - 5x + 3}{(x - 1)^3}$

12 $\frac{2(x + y)}{a}$

10 $2a + \frac{3(a-b)}{c}$

11 $\frac{a^2 + x^2}{a^2 - x^2}$

13 $\frac{4x(x-2)}{3}$

14 $\frac{3}{4}$

15 $x^2 - y^2$

Exercise No. 19

1	1	4	3	7	0	9	−2
2	2	5	−1	8	−4	10	0
3	4	6	1				

Exercise No. 20

1	2.5490	4	3.8025	7	$\bar{3}.5465$	9	$\bar{4}.7262$
2	1.8808	5	.5631	8	.7810	10	2.8279
3	.9031	6	$\bar{1}.3692$				

Exercise No. 21

1	22310.4	4	156.2	7	456,500	9	3.238
2	1,068	5	8.252	8	4.396	10	84.72
3	486,400	6	79,280				

11 Log 5 = .6990, log 7 = .8451, antilog $\bar{1}.8539$ = .71. Prefix minus sign.

12 Log 17 = 1.2304, log 32 = 1.5051, antilog $\bar{1}.7253$ = .53. Prefix minus sign.

13 First perform addition. Log 9 = .9542, log 4 = .6061, antilog .3521 = 2.25.

14 First perform addition. Log 15 = 1.1761, log 7 = .8451, antilog .3310 = 2.14.

15 First perform subtraction. Log 4 = .6021, log 3 = .4771, antilog .1250 = 1.33.

16 First perform subtraction. Log 11 = 1.0414, log 9 = .9542, antilog .0872 = 1.22.

17 First multiply. Log 8 = .9031, log 15 = 1.1761, antilog $\bar{1}.7270$ = .53.

18 First multiply. Log 24 = 1.3802, log 11 = 1.0414, antilog .3388 = 2.18.

19 $\frac{7 \div 3}{4} = \frac{7}{12}$. Log 7 = .8451, log 12 = 1.0792, log 7 − log 3 − log 4 antilog 1.7659 = .58.

20 $\frac{16}{18 \div 5} = \frac{80}{18} = \frac{40}{9}$. Log 40 = 1.6021, log 9 = .9542, log 16 − (log 18 − log 5) antilog .6479 = 4.44.

CHAPTER FIFTEEN

GEOMETRY

DEFINITIONS AND TERMS

Elementary geometry is the branch of mathematics that deals with space relationships.

Application of the principles of geometry requires an ability to use arithmetic and elementary algebra as taught in the previous sections of this book. A knowledge of geometry in addition to simple algebra and arithmetic is basic to so many occupations (carpentry, stone-masonry, dress design, hat design, display design, sheet metal work, machine-shop work, tool-making, architecture, drafting, engineering, etc.) that no serious student should be without it.

A **geometric figure** is a point, line, surface, solid, or any combination of these.

A **point** is the *position* of the intersection of two lines. It is *not* considered to have length, breadth, or thickness.

A **line** is the intersection of two surfaces. It has *length* but neither breadth nor thickness. It may be *straight, curved,* or *broken.*

Straight
Curved
Broken

A **surface** has *two* dimensions: *length* and *breadth.* A *flat* surface may be called a **plane.**

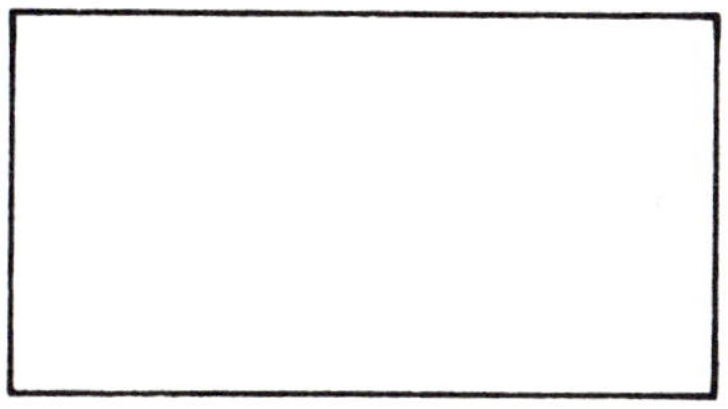

Plane Surface

A **solid** has *three* dimensions: *length, breadth,* and *thickness.*

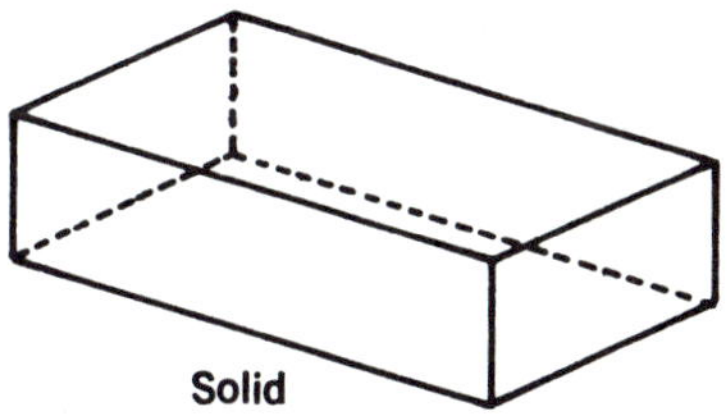

Solid

In solving geometric problems we apply certain general principles called **theorems.** These are systematically demonstrated by means of more basic principles called *axioms* and *postulates.*

Different writers use these last two terms somewhat differently. We may think of the **axioms** used in geometry, however, as *basic mathematical principles* which are so elementary that they cannot be demonstrated by means of still simpler principles. They were once widely called "self-evident truths." Note that the first seven "axioms" listed below are the principles with which you have already become familiar in performing operations upon algebraic equations.

The **postulates** used in geometry are of two different, but closely related, kinds. Some are merely restatements of more general mathematical axioms in specific geometric terms. Others are axiom-like statements which apply only to geometry. For instance, the last three "axioms" below may also be thought of as *geometric postulates.*

AXIOMS

1. Things equal to the same thing are equal to each other.

2. If equals are added to equals, the sums are equal.

3. If equals are subtracted from equals, the remainders are equal.

4. If equals are multiplied by equals, the products are equal.

5. If equals are divided by equals, the quotients are equal.

6. The whole is greater than any of its parts, and is equal to the sum of all its parts.

7. A quantity may be substituted for an equal one in an equation or in an inequality.

8. Only one straight line can be drawn through two points.

9. A straight line is the shortest distance between two points.

10. A straight line may be produced to any required length.

SYMBOLS

The following is a list of symbols used so frequently that they should be memorized.

= equality sign	∠ angle
< is less than	° degree
> is greater than	▭ parallelogram
∴ therefore	⊙ circle
‖ parallel	△ triangle
⊥ perpendicular	≠ unequal

LINES

A **horizontal** line is a straight line that is level with the horizon.

Horizontal

A **vertical** line is a straight line that is perpendicular to the horizon.

Vertical

Two lines are **perpendicular** to each other when the angles at which they intersect are all equal. Such lines are said to be at right angles to each other.

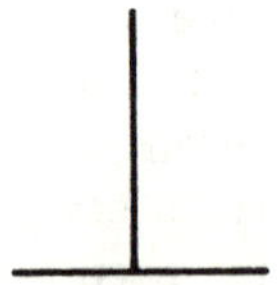

Perpendicular

An **oblique** line is neither horizontal nor vertical.

Oblique

Parallel lines are two or more straight lines which are equally distant from each other at all points and would never meet no matter how far they might be extended.

Parallel

ANGLES

An **angle** is the figure formed by two lines proceeding from a common point called the **vertex.** The lines that form an angle are called its **sides.** If three letters are used to designate an angle, the *vertex* is read between the others. Thus, Fig. 3 is written ∠*ABC*, and is read *angle ABC;* the sides are *AB* and *BC*.

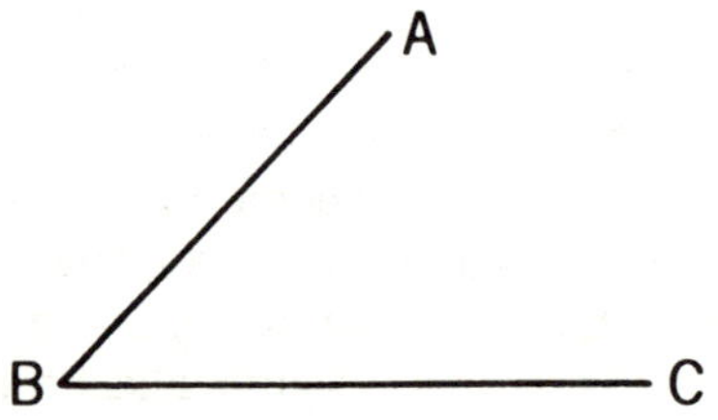

FIG. 3

In measuring an angle remember that you can think of it as composed of the spokes or radii emanating from a point (the vertex) which is at the center of a circle. As shown, there are 360 degrees around a point. The unit of measure for angles is the *degree* (°).

180° in a straight angle

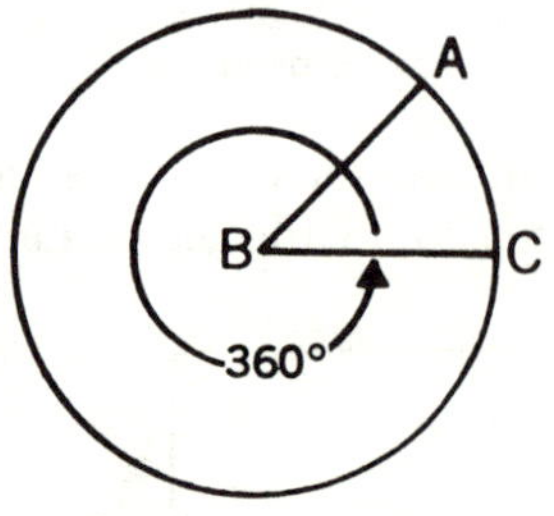

360° in a circle

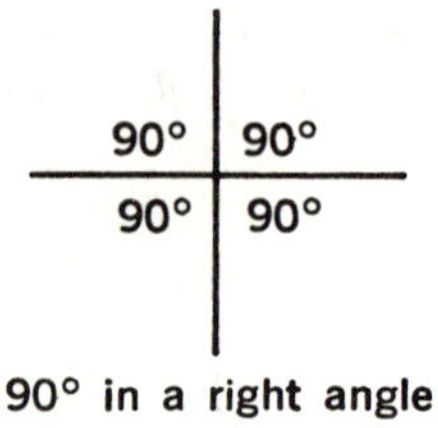

90° in a right angle

One degree is $\frac{1}{360}$th part of the circumference of a circle. It is divided into 60 minutes (′). The minute is divided into 60 seconds ("). An angle of 85 degrees, fifteen minutes, three seconds would be written 85° 15′ 3″.

A **straight angle** is one of 180°. Its two sides lie in the same straight line.

A **right angle** is one of 90°. Hence it is half a straight angle.

An **acute angle** is any angle that is less than (<) a right angle. Thus it must be less than 90°.

An **obtuse angle** is greater than (>) a right angle but less than (<) a straight angle. Hence, it must be *between 90°* and *180°*.

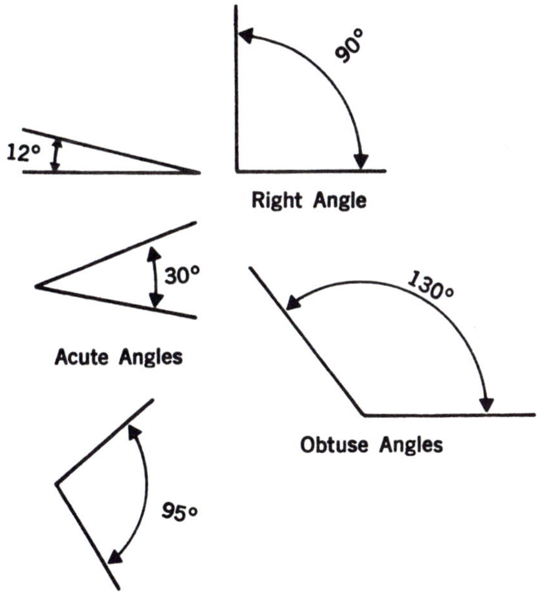

MEASURING ANGLES

Angles are measured by determining the part of a circle that the sides intersect. Therefore one measures the *opening between* the sides of an angle rather than the length of the sides. To measure or lay off angles one uses a protractor as shown in the illustration.

To measure an angle with protractor: *Place the center of the protractor at the vertex of the angle, and the straight side on a line with one side of the angle. Read the degrees where the other side of the angle crosses the scale of the protractor.*

To draw an angle with a protractor: *Draw a straight line for one side of the angle. Place the center of the protractor at the point of the line that is to be the vertex of the angle, and make the*

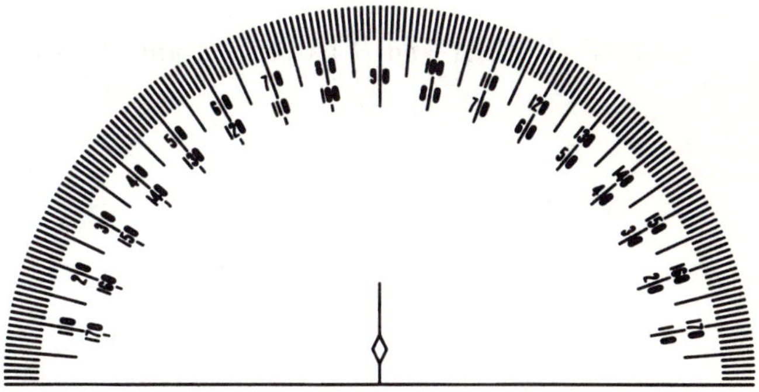

Protractor for Measuring and Laying off Angles

straight side of the protractor coincide with the line. Place a dot on your paper at the point on the scale of the protractor that corresponds to the size of the angle to be drawn. Connect this dot and the vertex to obtain the desired angle.

Practice Exercise No. 1

1 Draw a straight angle.
2 Draw a right angle.
3 Draw an acute angle of 30°.
4 Draw an obtuse angle of 120°.

Use the diagram for the following problems.

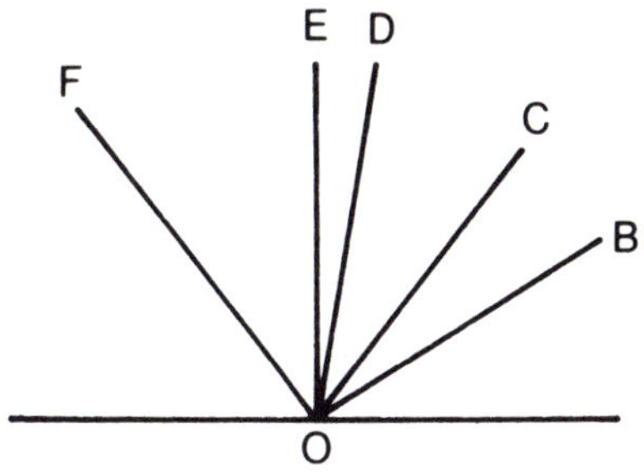

5 Measure angle *AOB*.
6 Measure angle *AOC*.
7 Measure angle *AOD*.
8 Measure ∠*AOE*.
9 Measure ∠*AOF*.
10 Measure ∠*BOF*.
11 Measure ∠*BOD*.

GEOMETRICAL CONSTRUCTIONS

Geometrical constructions, in the strict sense, involve only the use of a straight-edge (un-scaled ruler) and a pair of compasses. These are the only instruments needed to carry out the following constructions. Of course, in actual mechanical drawing the draftsman is not thus limited.

Problem 1: *To bisect a straight line.* (Bisect means to divide in half.)

Method: With *A* and *B* as centers and with a

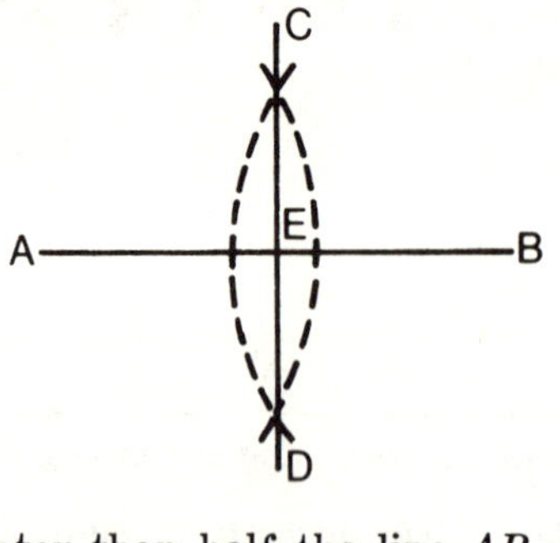

radius greater than half the line *AB*, draw arcs intersecting at points *C* and *D*. Draw *CD*, which bisects *AB* at *E*. (It should be noted that *CD* is perpendicular to *AB*.)

Problem 2: *To bisect any angle.*

Method: With the vertex as center and any radius draw an arc cutting the sides of the angle at *B* and *C*. With *B* and *C* as center and with a

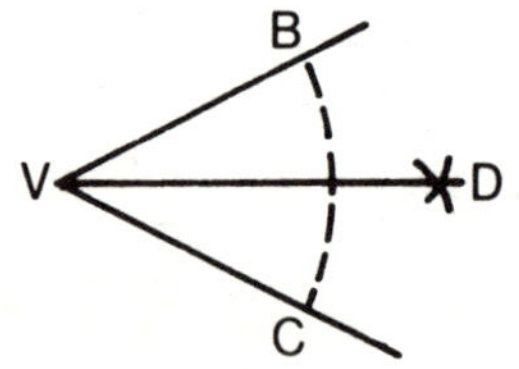

radius greater than half the distance from *B* to *C*, describe two arcs intersecting at *D*. The line *DV* bisects ∠*CVB*.

Problem 3: *At a point on a line to construct a perpendicular to the line.*

Method: From point *P* as center with any radius describe an arc which cuts the line *AB* at *M* and *N*. From *M* and *N* as centers and with a radius

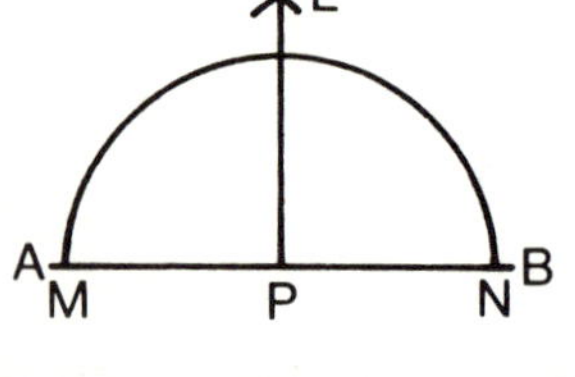

greater than *MP*, describe arcs which intersect at *L*. Draw the line *PL*, which is the required perpendicular.

Problem 4: *From a given point away from a straight line to drop a perpendicular to the line.*

Method: From the given point *P* as center and with a large enough radius describe an arc which cuts line *AB* at *C* and *D*. From *C* and *D* as centers and with a radius greater than half *CD*, describe

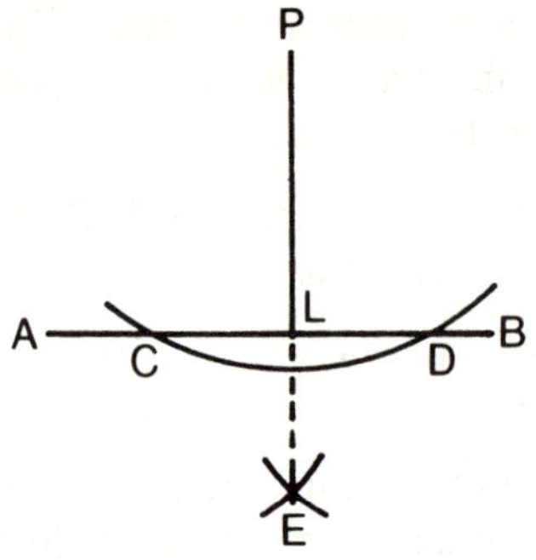

two arcs that intersect at *E*. Connect *PE*. The line *PL* is the required perpendicular to the line *AB*.

Note: For some of the previous constructions and some that are to follow, more than one method is available. To avoid confusion in learning, only one method is here presented.

Problem 5: *To duplicate a given angle.*

Method: Let the given angle be ∠*AVB*. Then from the vertex *V* as center and with a convenient radius, draw an arc that intersects the sides at *C* and *D*. Draw any straight line equal to or greater in length than *VB* and call it *V′B′*. (Read *V prime*

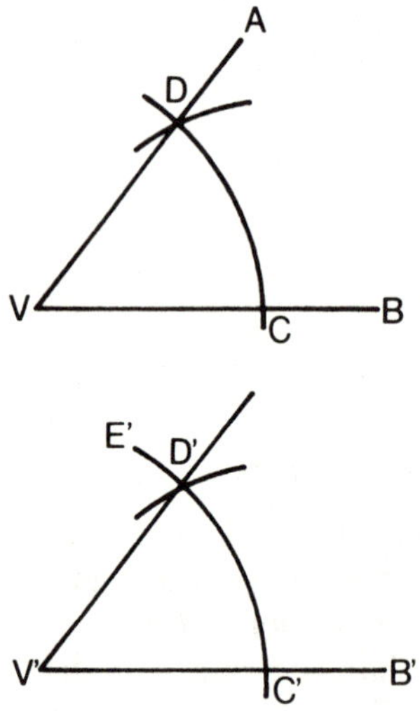

B prime.) With *V′* as center and with the same radius, describe an arc *C′E* that cuts the line at *C′*. From *C′* as center and with a radius equal to *DC*, describe an arc intersecting arc *C′E* at *D′*. Draw *D′V′*. ∠*D′V′C′* is the required angle.

Problem 6: *To duplicate a given triangle.*

Method: Draw any straight line from any point *D* as center, and with a radius equal to *AB* lay off *DE* equal to *AB*. With *E* as center and *BC* as radius, draw an arc. With *D* as center and *AC* as

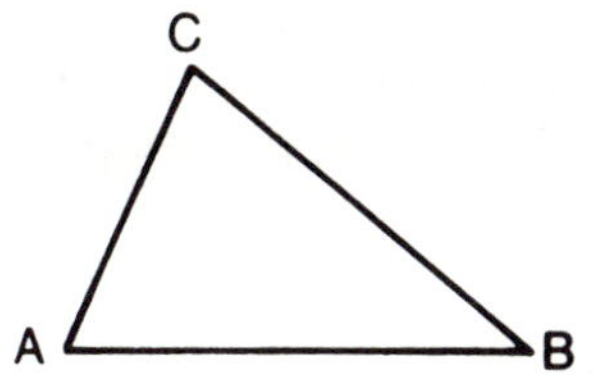

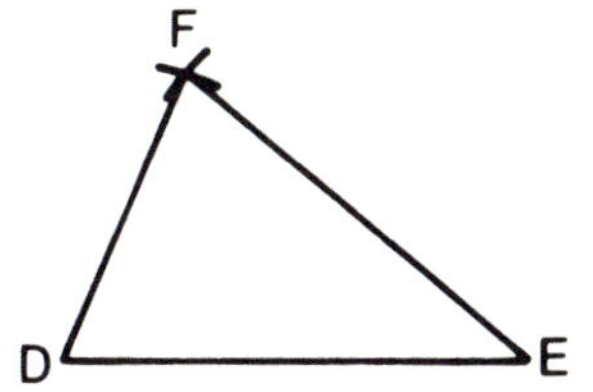

radius, draw an arc which intersects the other arc at *F*. Draw *FE* and *FD*. *DEF* is the required triangle.

Problem 7: *To construct a line parallel to a given line at a given distance.*

Method: If the given line is *AD* and the given distance is one inch, then at any two points *C* and *D* on the given line *AB* erect perpendiculars to *AB*. (See Problem 3.) With *C* and *D* as centers

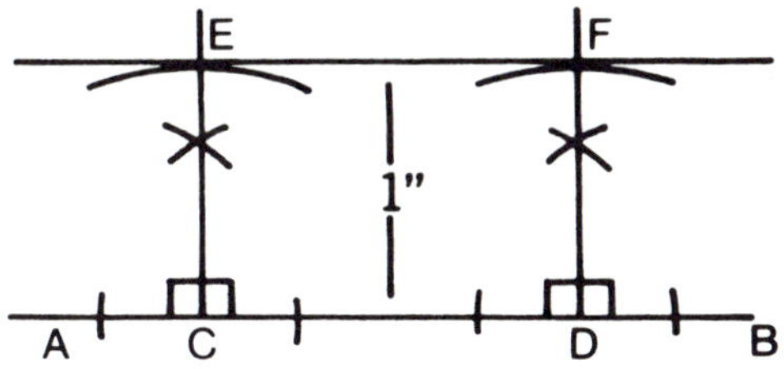

and with a radius equal to one inch, describe arcs cutting the perpendiculars at *E* and *F*. Draw the line *EF*, which is the required parallel line at a distance of one inch from *AB*.

Problem 8: *To divide a line into a given number of equal parts.*

Method: If *AB* is the given line, and if it is to be divided into six parts, then draw line *AC* making an angle (most conveniently an acute angle) with *AB*. Starting at *A* mark off on *AC* with a compass six equal divisions of any convenient length. Connect the last point *I* with *B*. Through points *D, E, F, G* and *H* draw lines parallel to

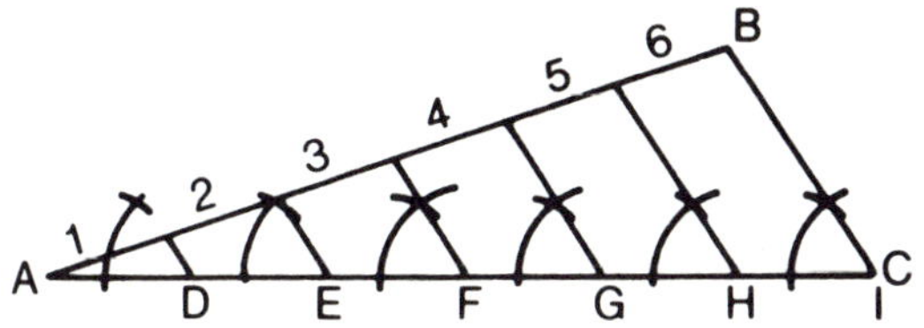

IB by making equal angles. The parallel lines divide *AB* into six equal parts.

Problem 9: *To find the center of a circle or arc of a circle.*

Method: Draw any two chords *AB* and *DE*. Draw the perpendicular bisectors of these chords.

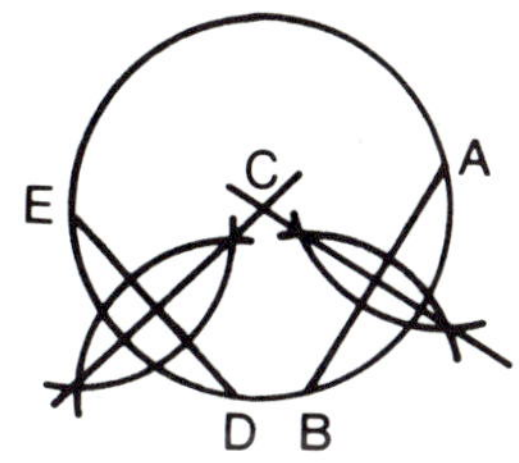

(See Problem 1.) The point *C* where they intersect is the center of the circle or arc.

Problem 10: *To inscribe a regular hexagon in a circle.*

Note: A regular hexagon is a polygon with six equal sides and six equal angles. The length of a side of a hexagon is equal to the radius of a circle circumscribing it.

Method: The radius of the circle is equal to *AG*. Starting at any point on the circle and using the length of the radius as the distance, lay off suc-

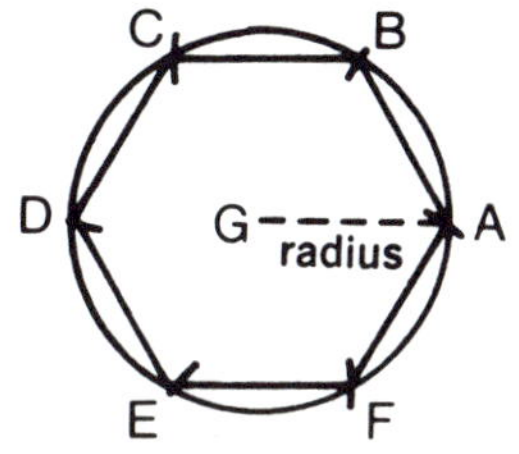

cessive points *B, C, D, E, F* on the circumference of the circle. Connect the points with straight lines to obtain the required hexagon.

LINE AND ANGLE RELATIONSHIPS

Having learned some basic geometric definitions, axioms and constructions, you are now prepared to understand some important relationships between lines and angles.

In demonstrating these relationships it is necessary to introduce additional *definitions, postulates, propositions, theorems* and *corollaries.*

For example, the following are important *postulates.*

Postulate 1. *A geometric figure may be moved from one place to another without changing its size or shape.*

Postulate 2. *Two angles are equal if they can be made to coincide.*

Postulate 3. *A circle can be drawn with any point as center.*

Postulate 4. *Two straight lines can intersect in only one point.*

Postulate 5. *All straight angles are equal.*

A **corollary** is a geometric truth that follows from one previously given and needs little or no proof.

For example, from Postulate 3 above we derive the *corollary:*

Corollary 1. *An arc of a circle can be drawn with any point as center.*

Adjacent angles are angles that have a common vertex and a common side between them.

For example, ∠*CPB* is *adjacent* to ∠*BPA* but not to ∠*DRC.*

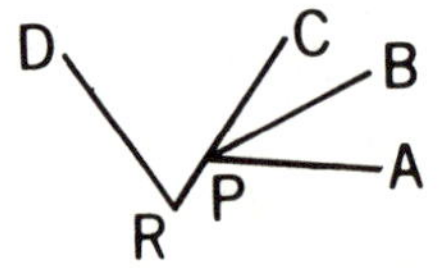

ADDING ANGLES

Postulate 6. *Adjacent angles can be added. Thus:*

∠*AOB* + ∠*BOC* = ∠*AOC.*
∠*DOC* + ∠*COB* + ∠*BOA* = ∠*DOA.*
∠*EOD* + ∠*DOC* + ∠*COB* = ∠*EOB.*

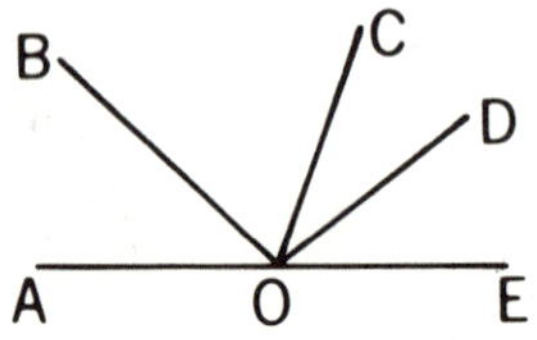

Postulate 7. *The sum of all the adjacent angles about a point on one side of a straight line is equal to one straight angle. Thus:*

If you measure ∠*AOB* + ∠*BOC* + ∠*COD* + ∠*DOE,* it should total 180°. Does it?

COMPLEMENTS AND SUPPLEMENTS

Two angles whose sum is 90°, or one right angle, are called **complementary.** Each of the angles is called the **complement** of the other. *Thus:*

∠*AOB* is the *complement* of ∠*BOC,*
or 35° is *complementary* to 55°,
or 55° is *complementary* to 35°.

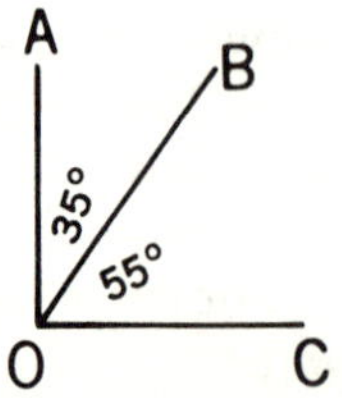

Two angles whose sum is 180° or a straight angle are said to be **supplementary** to each other. *Thus:*

∠*AOC* is the *supplement* of ∠*COB,*
or 150° is *supplementary* to 30°,
or 30° is *supplementary* to 150°.

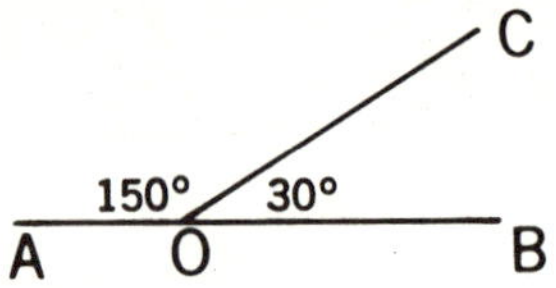

The postulates that follow concerning complementary and supplementary angles are mostly corollaries of axioms and postulates already stated. Hence, the references in parentheses are to axioms and postulates at the beginning of this chapter and this page.

Postulate 8. *All right angles are equal.* Since all straight angles are equal (POST. 5) and halves of equals are equal (AX. 5).

Postulate 9. *When one straight line meets another, two supplementary angles are formed.*

∠1 + ∠2 = ∠*AOB* which is a straight angle. (AX. 6)

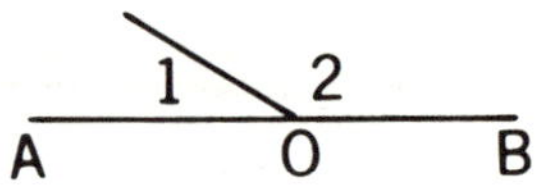

Postulate 10. *Complements of the same angle or of equal angles are equal.* (AX. 3)

Postulate 11. *Supplements of the same angle or of equal angles are equal.* (AX. 3)

Postulate 12. *If two adjacent angles have their exterior sides in a straight line, they are supplementary.*

Postulate 13. *If two adjacent angles are supplementary, their exterior sides are in the same straight line.*

Vertical angles are the pairs of opposite angles formed by the intersection of straight lines. *Thus:*

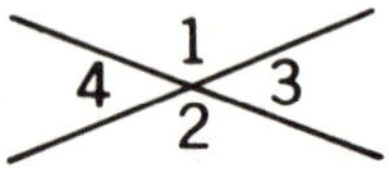

∠1 and ∠2 are *vertical angles.* ∠5 and ∠6 are *vertical angles.* What other pairs are vertical angles?

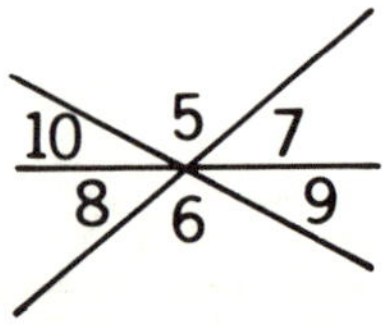

THE METHOD OF DEMONSTRATION IN GEOMETRY

A **proposition** is a statement of either a *theorem* or a *problem.*

A **theorem** is a relationship to be demonstrated.

A **problem** is a construction to be made.

In proving theorems or the correctness of constructions, the procedure is as follows.

If the proposition is a *theorem* requiring proof, you break it up into its two parts: the *hypothesis* and the *conclusion.* In the *hypothesis* certain facts are assumed. You use these given facts in conjunction with other previously accepted geometric propositions to prove the conclusion.

If the proposition is a *problem,* you make the construction and then proceed to prove that it is correct. You do this by listing the given elements and bringing forward previously established geometric facts to build up the necessary proof of correctness.*

For example, let us take the statement, *vertical angles are equal.* This theorem is given as Proposition No. 1 in many geometry textbooks, and is presented as follows.

Given: Vertical angles 1 and 2 as in the diagram next to the definition of vertical angles.

To prove: $\angle 1 = \angle 2$.

Steps	*Reasons*
1. $\angle 2$ is the supplement of $\angle 3$.	1. Two angles are supplementary if their sum is a straight $\angle$.
2. $\angle 1$ is the supplement of $\angle 3$.	2. Same as Reason 1.
3. $\angle 1 = \angle 2$.	3. Supplements of the same $\angle$ are equal. (Post. 4)

* This is the method of procedure followed in most geometry textbooks for demonstrating the truth of established geometric principles. For the purposes of this book, however, it will not be necessary to give formal demonstrations of theorems and problems. It is our purpose to give you a working knowledge of the essential geometric principles, facts and skills that can be put to practical application in office and in shop, in following military pursuits, in indulging a hobby, or in studying higher mathematics as presented in this book and in other more advanced textbooks.

ABBREVIATIONS

The following abbreviations are used:

adj.	adjacent	def.	definition
alt.	alternate	ext.	exterior
	altitude	hyp.	hypotenuse
ax.	axiom	iden.	identity
comp.	complementary	int.	interior
cong.	congruent	rt.	right
const.	construction	st.	straight
cor.	corollary	supp.	supplementary
corr.	corresponding	vert.	vertical

It should also be noted that the plurals of a number of the symbols listed on page 634 are formed by inserting an *s* in the symbol. Thus, ∠s means angles; △s, triangles; |S|, parallels; ⓢ, circles; ▱s, parallelograms, etc.

Practice Exercise No. 2

1 $\angle 1$ coincides with $\angle 2$. $\angle 1 = 30°$. Find $\angle 2$.

2 *BD* is the bisector of $\angle ABC$, which is 45°. Find $\angle ABD$.

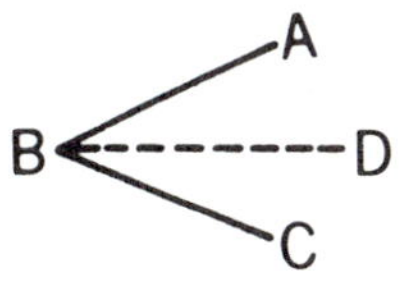

3 $\angle 1 = \angle 5$, $\angle 2 = \angle 1$ and $\angle 3 = \angle 5$. What is the relationship between:

(a) $\angle 1$ and $\angle 3$
(b) $\angle 2$ and $\angle 5$
(c) $\angle 4$ and $\angle 7$

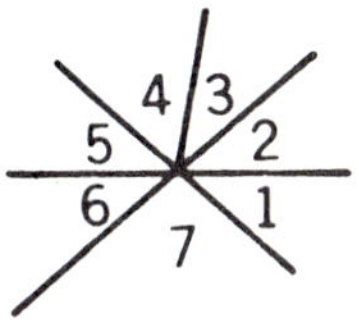

4 In the same figure list the pairs of adj. ∠s.

5 In the same figure list the pairs of vertical angles.

6 In the accompanying figure the opposite ∠s are vertical ∠s; $\angle 1 = 30°$ and $\angle 3 = 100°$. Find the remaining four angles.

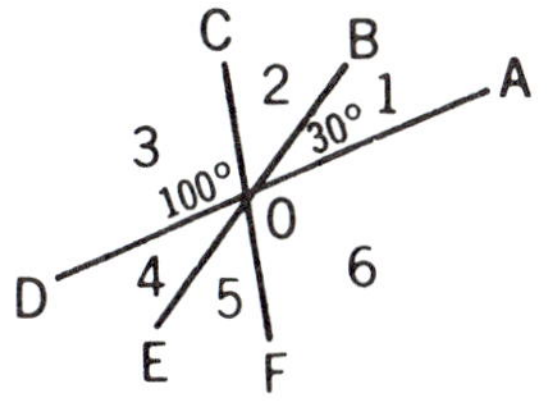

7 In the same figure find the values of $\angle AOC$, $\angle AOD$, $\angle BOE$ and $\angle FOB$.

8 How many degrees are there in (a) $\frac{3}{4}$ of a rt. $\angle$, (b) $\frac{2}{3}$ rt. $\angle$, (c) $\frac{1}{2}$ rt. $\angle$, (d) $\frac{1}{3}$ rt. $\angle$, (e) $\frac{1}{4}$ rt. $\angle$?

9 Find the complement of (a) 68°, (b) 45°, (c) 55°, (d) 32°, (e) 5°, (f) 33° 30′.

10 What is the supplement of (a) 25°, (b) 125°, (c) 44°, (d) 88°, (e) 74° 30′, (f) 78° 30′?

PARALLEL LINES

Postulates Concerning Parallels

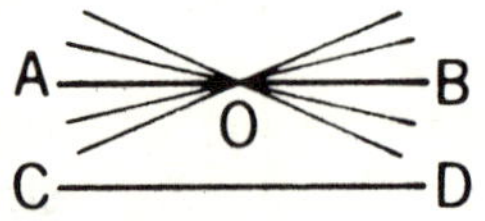

1. Through a given point only one line can be drawn parallel to a given line.

In the diagram, the only line that can be drawn ∥ to *CD* through point *O* is *AB*.

2. Two intersecting lines cannot both be parallel to a third straight line.

3. Two straight lines in the same plane, if produced, either will intersect or else are parallel.

Definitions

A **transversal** is a line that intersects two or more other lines.

When a **transversal** cuts two parallel or intersecting lines, various angles are formed. The names and relative positions of these angles are important. The relationship of angles as shown in the following diagram should be memorized.

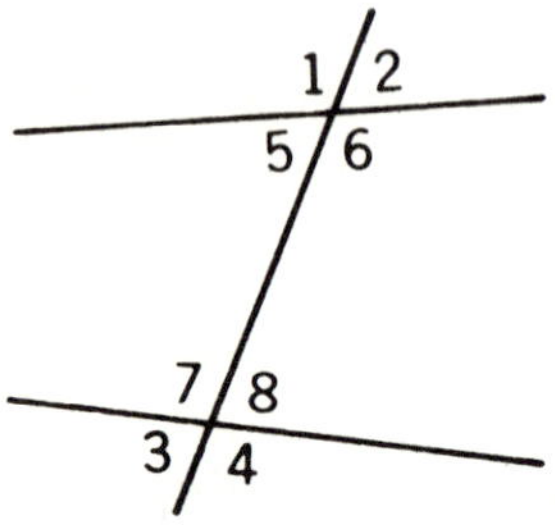

∠1, 2, 3, 4 are termed exterior angles.
∠5, 6, 7, 8 are termed interior angles.

∠1 and 4, ∠2 and 3 } are pairs of **alternate exterior** angles.

∠5 and 8, ∠6 and 7 } are pairs of **alternate interior** angles.

∠1 and 7, ∠2 and 8, ∠5 and 3, ∠6 and 4 } are pairs of **corresponding** angles.

Theorem 1. If two straight lines are parallel to a third straight line, they are parallel to each other.

Given: *AB* and *EF* ∥ to *CD*.
To prove: *AB* ∥ *EF*.

If *AB* is not ∥ to *EF* the two lines would intersect and they would then be two intersecting lines parallel to a third straight line. But this is impossible according to Parallel Postulate 2. Hence *AB* must be parallel to *EF*.

Relationships Formed by Parallels and a Transversal

If two parallel lines are cut by a transversal, certain definite relationships will always be found to exist among the angles that are formed by the parallel lines and the transversal.

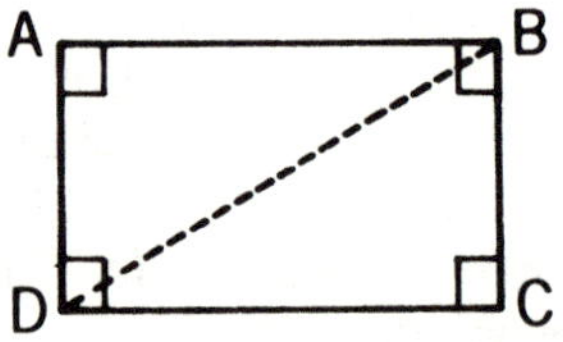

If we take the rectangle *ABCD*, we know that the opposite sides are parallel and equal and that all the angles are right angles. If we then draw the diagonal *DB* we have formed two triangles, △*DAB* and △*DCB*.

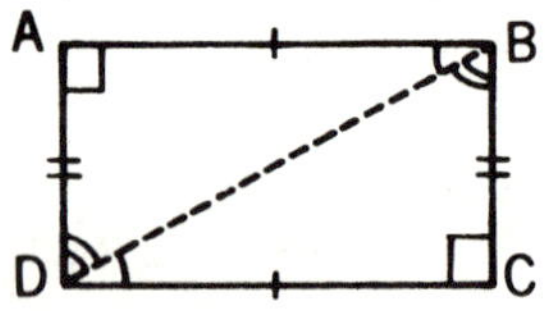

In △s *DAB* and *DCB* we know *AD* = *CB*, *AB* = *DC* and ∠*A* = ∠*C*. As will be shown in the section on triangles, when two sides and the included ∠ of one △ are equal to two sides and the included ∠ of another, the two triangles are said to be congruent. This means that all their corresponding sides and angles are equal. (In the diagram the corresponding sides and angles of each triangle are marked with matched check marks.)

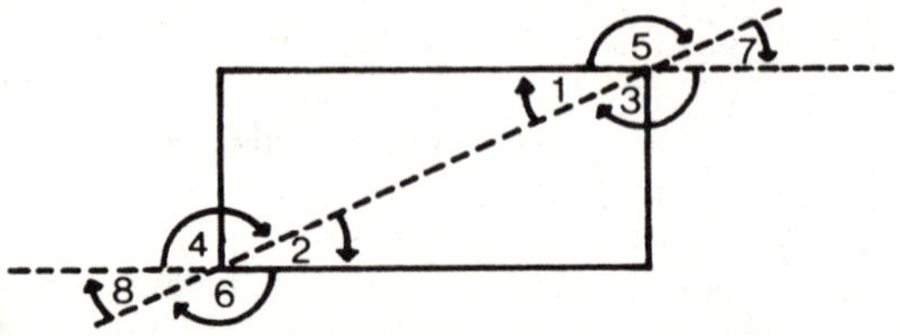

If we extend lines *AB* and *CD*, we have two ∥ lines cut by a transversal. We number the related angles for convenience, and the following relationships become evident.

∠1 = ∠2 (Corr. ∠s of cong. △s.)
∠1 = ∠7 and ∠2 = ∠8 (Vert. ∠s are equal.)

$\therefore \angle 7 = \angle 8 = \angle 1 = \angle 2$ (Things $=$ to the same thing are $=$ to each other.)

$\angle 5$ is supp. $\angle 7$ (Ext. sides form a st. $\angle$s)
$\therefore \angle 6 = \angle 4$ and $\angle 3 = \angle 5$ (Vert. $\angle$ are equal.)
$\therefore \angle 3 = \angle 6, \angle 5 = \angle 6$ and $\angle 3 = \angle 4$ (Things $=$ to the same thing are $=$ to each other. Ax. 1.)

Presenting the above conclusions verbally, the angle relationships that occur when two parallel lines are cut by a transversal may be stated as follows.

1. The alternate interior angles are equal.

$\angle 1 = \angle 2$, and $\angle 3 = \angle 4$

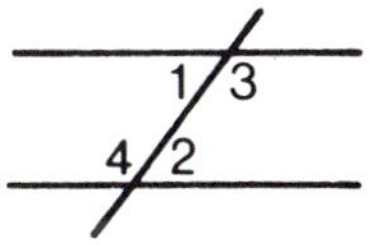

2. The alternate exterior angles are equal.

$\angle 5 = \angle 6$, and $\angle 7 = \angle 8$

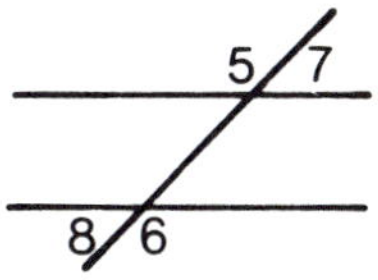

3. The corresponding angles are equal.

$\angle 4 = \angle 5, \angle 3 = \angle 6, \quad \angle 2 = \angle 7, \angle 1 = \angle 8$

4. The two interior angles on the same side of a transversal are supplementary.

$\angle 1$ supp. $\angle 4$, and $\angle 3$ supp. $\angle 2$

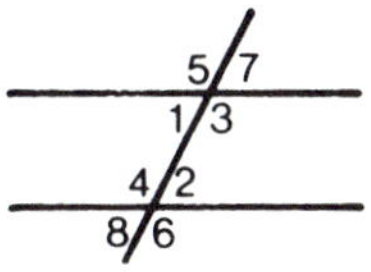

5. The two exterior angles on the same side of a transversal are supplementary.

$\angle 5$ supp. $\angle 8$, and $\angle 7$ supp. $\angle 6$

These angle relationships may now be employed to prove that certain straight lines are parallel. Such proofs are represented by the *converses* of statements 1 to 5, in the form of the following theorems.

Theorems on Parallel Lines

Two lines are parallel if:

Theorem 2. *A transversal to the lines makes a pair of alternate interior angles equal.*

Theorem 3. *A transversal to the lines makes a pair of alternate exterior angles equal.*

Theorem 4. *A transversal to the lines makes a pair of corresponding angles equal.*

Theorem 5. *A transversal to the lines makes a pair of interior angles on the same side of the transversal supplementary.*

Theorem 6. *A transversal to the lines makes a pair of exterior angles of the same side of the transversal supplementary.*

A *corollary* that follows from these theorems is the following.

Corollary 1. *If two lines are perpendicular to a third line they are parallel.*

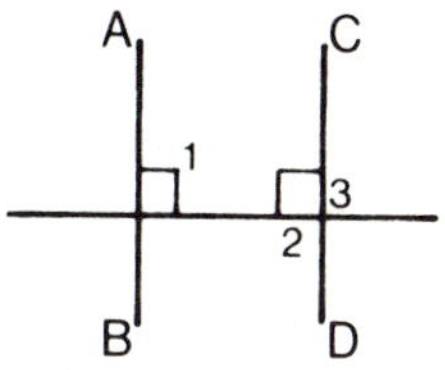

This can be easily proved by showing alt. int. $\angle$s equal as $\angle 1 = \angle 2$, or corr. $\angle$s equal, as $\angle 1 = \angle 2$, etc.

We may summarize the relationships of the angles formed by parallel lines cut by a transversal as follows:

(a) *The four acute angles formed are equal.*

(b) *The four obtuse angles formed are equal.*

(c) *Any one of the acute angles is the supplement of any one of the obtuse angles; that is, their sum equals 180°.*

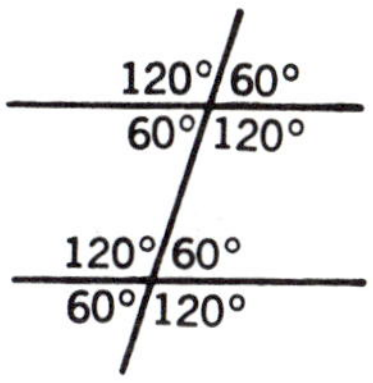

Practice Exercise No. 3

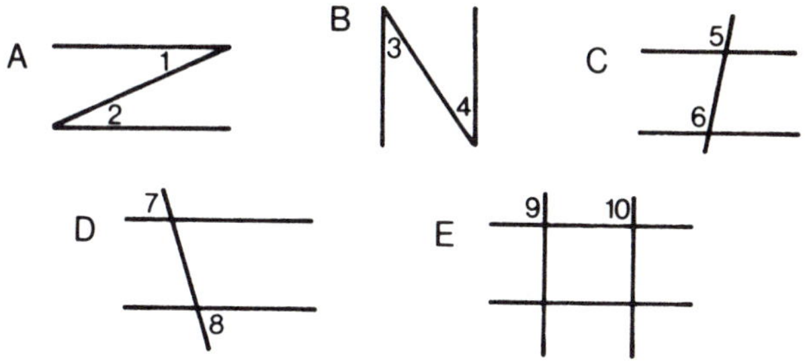

1 In the above diagram identify the kinds of angles indicated.

2 If $\angle 3 = 50°$, what is the value of $\angle 1$, $\angle 2$ and $\angle 4$?

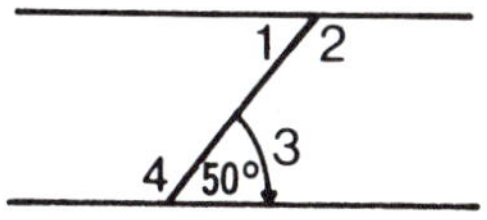

3 If $\angle 5 = 40°$, what is the value of $\angle 6$, $\angle 7$ and $\angle 8$?

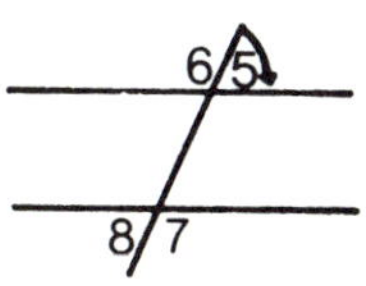

4 *AB* is ⊥ to *CD*. Why would any other line that makes a 90° angle with *CD* be ∥ to *AB*?

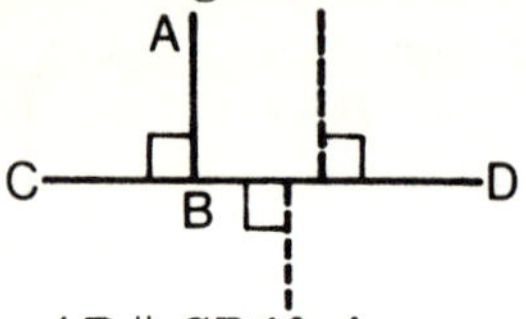

5 Tell why *AB* ∥ *CD* if given:
(a) ∠3 = ∠6
(b) ∠1 = ∠5
(c) ∠2 = ∠7

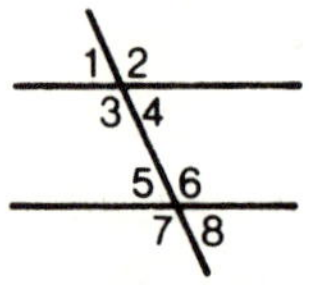

6 If given ∠1 = ∠2, prove that *AB* ∥ *CD*.

7 Given ∠1 = 65° and ∠4 = 115°, prove that the two horizontal lines are ∥.

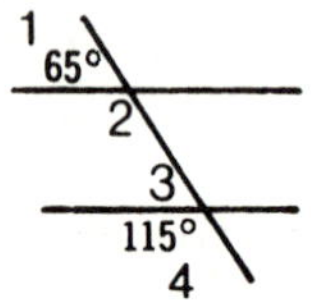

8 If Broadway cuts across Canal Street at an angle of 70°, at what angle does it cut across Broome and Spring Streets, which are ∥ to Canal Street?

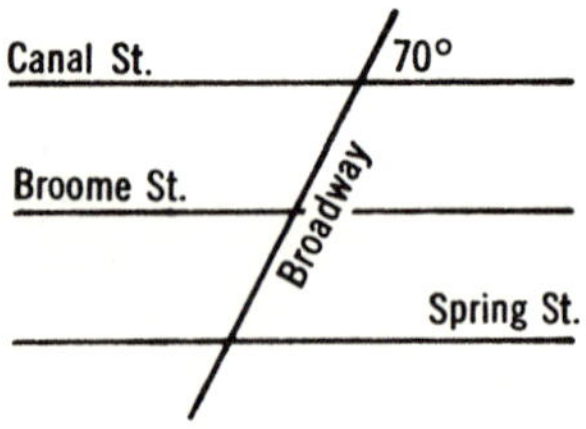

9 Given ∠*ABC* = 60°, construct a line ∥ to *BC* using the principle of corresponding angles being equal.

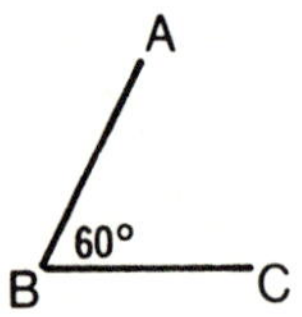

10 Using the drawing-board, T-square and triangle pictured, how would you construct two angles the sides of which are ∥ to each other?

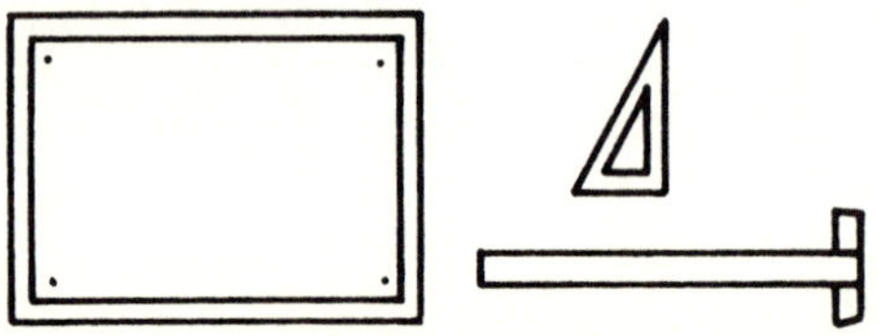

TRIANGLES

A **triangle** is a three-sided figure, the sides of which are straight lines. If you close off any angle a triangle is formed.

Triangles are classified according to their sides as *scalene, isosceles* and *equilateral.*

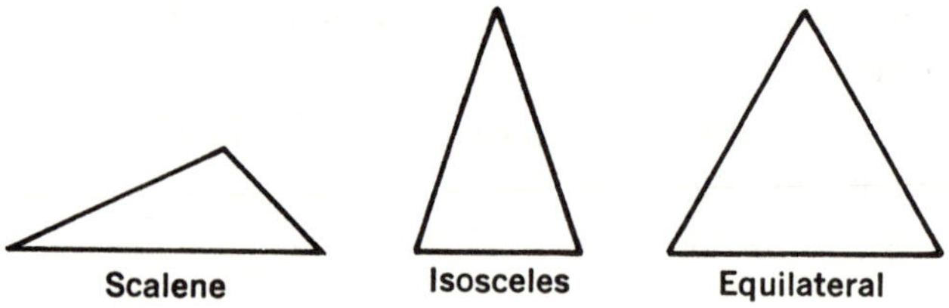

A **scalene triangle** is one in which no two sides are equal. An **isosceles triangle** is one in which two sides are equal. An **equilateral triangle** is one with three sides equal.

Triangles may also be classified with respect to their angles as *equiangular, right, acute* and *obtuse.*

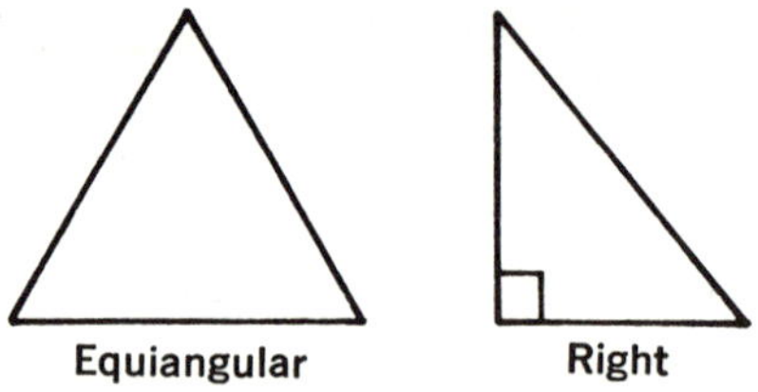

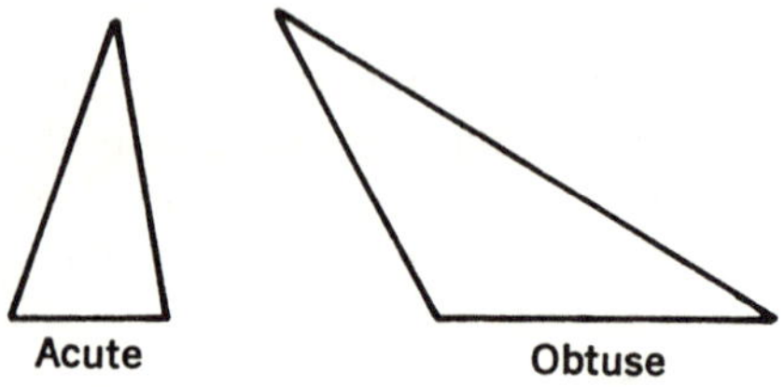

An **equiangular triangle** is one in which all the angles are equal (each measuring 60°).

A **right triangle** (or *right-angled triangle)* contains one right angle (often indicated by placing a small square in the 90° angle).

An **acute triangle** is one in which all angles are less than right angles.

An **obtuse triangle** has one angle greater than a right angle.

Note that an *equiangular triangle* is always *equilateral;* a *right* triangle may be *scalene* or *isosceles,* an *acute* triangle may be *scalene, isosceles,* or *equilateral* (equiangular is merely a special case of acute); an *obtuse* triangle may be *scalene* or *isosceles.*

Note also that either the scalene or the isosceles triangle may be right, acute or obtuse. The scalene cannot be *equiangular,* but the isosceles can, since the equilateral may be considered a special type of the isosceles.

It is a basic theorem that the sum of the angles of any triangle is equal to 180°. (See Theorem 14.)

TRIANGULAR MEASUREMENT

The **height** or **altitude** of a triangle is the perpendicular distance from the base to the vertex of the opposite angle. In Fig. 4, *AC* represents height or altitude of the triangles.

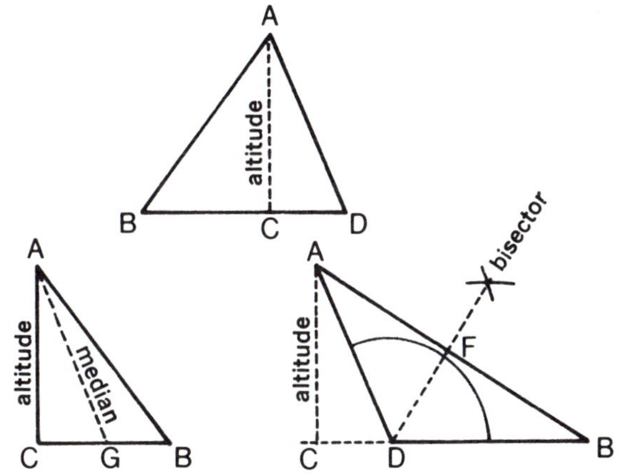

FIG. 4

A **median** is a line drawn from any vertex of a triangle to the middle of the opposite side. *AG* in Fig. 4.

The **bisector** of an angle is the line which divides it into two equal angles. *DF* bisects $\angle BDA$ in Fig. 4.

The **perimeter** of any figure is *the entire distance around the figure.*

Rule: *The area of a triangle equals one half the product of the base and the height.*

Expressed as a **formula:**

$$A = \tfrac{1}{2}bh \text{ or } A = \frac{bh}{2}.$$

EXAMPLE 1: Find the area of the triangle shown.

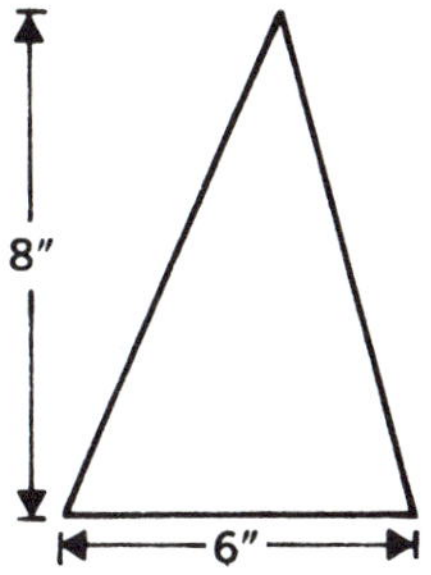

SOLUTION: $A = \dfrac{bh}{2}$

$= \dfrac{6 \times 8}{2}$

$= 24$ sq. in., ANS.

EXAMPLE 2: What is the height of a triangle if its area is 1 sq. ft. and its base 16 in.?

SOLUTION: $A = \dfrac{bh}{2} \therefore h = \dfrac{2A}{b}$

$= \dfrac{2 \times 144}{16} = 18$ in., ANS.

FACTS ABOUT RIGHT TRIANGLES

The **hypotenuse** of a right triangle is the side opposite the right angle.

In the figure below it is shown that the square drawn on the hypotenuse of a right triangle is equal in area to the sum of the areas of the squares drawn on the other two sides.

$(3 \text{ in.})^2 = 9$ sq. in.
$(4 \text{ in.})^2 = 16$ sq. in.
$(5 \text{ in.})^2 = 25$ sq. in.
$9 + 16 = 25$
$3^2 + 4^2 = 5^2$

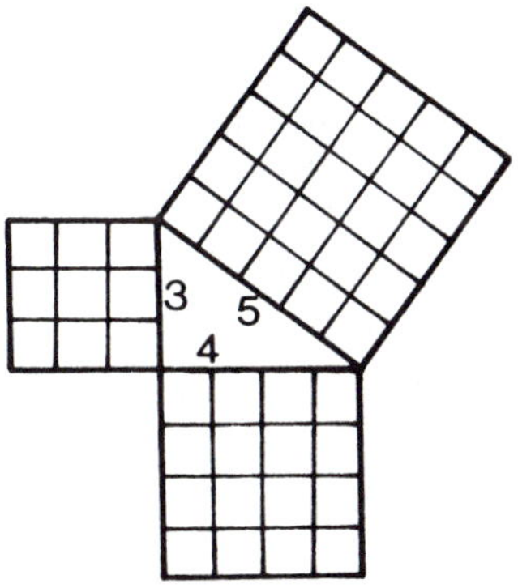

Rule: *The square of the hypotenuse of a right triangle is equal to the sum of the squares of the other two sides.*

From this there arise several self-evident formulas with reference to the right triangle.

Let c = hypotenuse, a = altitude, b = base; then:

Formula 1: $c^2 + a^2 + b^2$

Formula 2: $c = \sqrt{a^2 + b^2}$. (Taking the square root of both sides of the first equation.)

Formula 3: $a^2 = c^2 - b^2$; or, by transposition, $b^2 = c^2 - a^2$.

EXAMPLE 3: Find the hypotenuse of a right triangle whose base is 18 inches and altitude 26 inches.

$c = \sqrt{a^2 + b^2}$ (formula)

$= \sqrt{(18)^2 + (26)^2}$ (substituting)

$= \sqrt{324 + 676}$ (squaring)

$= \sqrt{1000}$ (adding)

$= 31.62$, ANS., extracting the square root.

Practice Exercise No. 4

1 A derrick standing perpendicular to the ground is 45 ft. high, and is tied to a stake in the ground by a cable 51 ft. long. How far is the foot of the derrick from the stake?

(A) 68 ft. ____ (C) 24 ft. ____
(B) 6 ft. ____ (D) 96 ft. ____

2 The base of a triangle is 18 in.; the altitude is $3\frac{1}{2}$ times the base. What is the area?

(A) 1,296 sq. in. ____ (C) 567 sq. in. ____
(B) 600 sq. in. ____ (D) 648 sq. in. ____

3 How much will it cost to fence off an isosceles shaped lot if one side is 75 ft. and the base is 50 ft.? Fencing costs $2.00 a foot.

(A) $40.00 ____ (C) $25.00 ____
(B) $400.00 ____ (D) $50.00 ____

4 In a square baseball field it is 90 ft. from home to first base. How far in a straight line is it from home to second base?

(A) 127 ft. ____ (C) 120 ft. ____
(B) 180 ft. ____ (D) 135 ft. ____

5 The base of a triangle is 20 feet; the altitude is $\frac{1}{2}$ the base. What is the area?

(A) 80 sq. ft. ____ (C) 120 sq. ft. ____
(B) 100 sq. ft. ____ (D) 200 sq. ft. ____

6 To hold a telephone pole in position a 26-ft. wire is stretched from the top of the pole to a stake in the ground 10 ft. from the foot of the pole. How tall is the pole?

(A) 24 ft. ____ (C) 12 ft. ____
(B) 40 ft. ____ (D) 36 ft. ____

7 What must be the length of a ladder to reach to the top of a house 40 ft. high, if the bottom of the ladder is placed 9 ft. from the house?

(A) 36 ft. ____ (C) 41 ft. ____
(B) 45 ft. ____ (D) 54 ft. ____

8 A tree is 100 ft. in a horizontal line from a river and its base is 20 ft. above the river. It is 160 ft. high. A line from its top to the opposite shore of the river measures 500 ft. How wide is the river?

(A) 250.93 ft. ____ (C) 342.89 ft. ____
(B) 366.47 ft. ____ (D) 329.65 ft. ____

DEMONSTRATING THE CONGRUENCE OF TRIANGLES

In demonstrating some fundamental relationships between lines and angles of triangles, a method of proving triangles to be *congruent* is employed.

Congruent figures are those which can be made to coincide or fit on one another. Thus if two triangles can be made to coincide in all their parts, they are said to be congruent.

The symbol for congruence is $\cong$.

In triangles that are congruent the respective equal angles and equal sides that would coincide if one figure were placed on top of the other, are termed **corresponding** angles and *corresponding* sides.

Corresponding parts are also called *homologous* parts. From what has been said it follows that corresponding parts of congruent figures are equal.

In geometry the corresponding or homologous parts of corresponding figures are frequently indicated by using *corresponding check marks* on the respective parts. For example, the corresponding parts in the congruent triangles below are marked with check marks of the same kind.

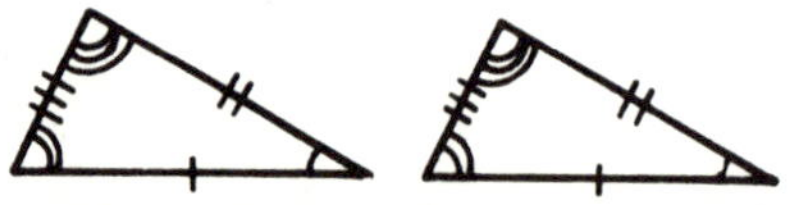

Seven Theorems on Congruence

Theorem 7. *Two triangles are congruent if two sides and the included angle of one are equal respectively to two sides and the included angle of the other.*

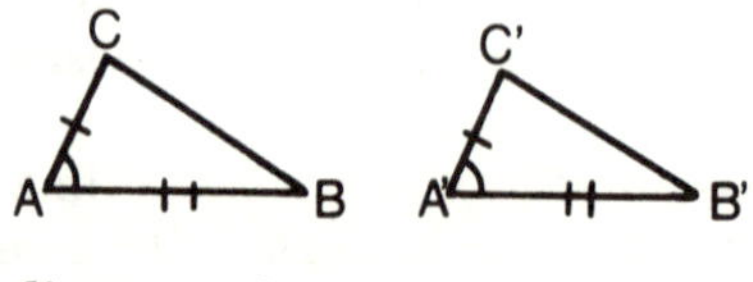

According to this theorem you are given $\angle ABC \cong \triangle A'B'C$, with $AC = A'C'$, $AB = A'B'$ and $\angle A = \angle A'$.

If you construct the figures with the given equal parts and then place $\triangle ABC$ on $\triangle A'B'C'$ so that the given equal parts correspond, it will be seen that the third line, CB, coincides with $C'B'$, making the triangles congruent at all points. Thus all the corresponding parts not given may also be assumed to be respectively equal.

For example, construct AC and $A'C'$ to equal $\frac{3}{8}''$; $\angle A$ and $\angle A' = 60°$; AB and $A'B' = \frac{3}{4}''$. Then measure the distances between CB and $C'B'$, and you will find them to be equal. If you measure $\angle C$ and C' and $\angle B$ and B', you will find these pairs to be equal as well.

Proving congruence by this theorem is known as the *side angle side* method. It is abbreviated *s.a.s.* = *s.a.s.*

By employing a similar approach you can readily verify the following theorems on the correspondence of triangles.*

Theorem 8. *Two triangles are congruent if two angles and the included side of one are equal respectively to two angles and the included side of the other.*

This is known as the *angle side angle* theorem, and is abbreviated *a.s.a.* = *a.s.a.*

Theorem 9. *Two triangles are congruent if the sides of one are respectively equal to the sides of the other.*

This is known as the *side side side* theorem, and is abbreviated *s.s.s.* = *s.s.s.*

Theorem 10. *Two triangles are congruent if a side and any two angles of one are equal to the corresponding side and two angles of the other.*

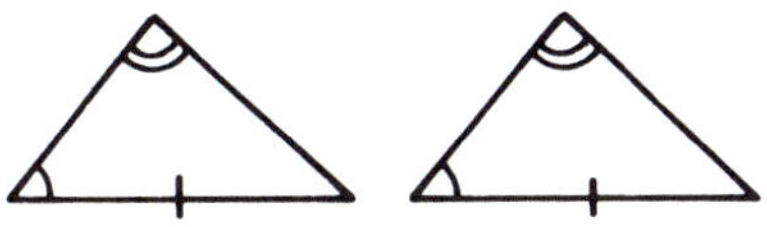

This is known as the *side angle angle* theorem, and is abbreviated *s.a.a.* = *s.a.a.*

Theorem 11. *Two right triangles are equal if the sides of the right angles are equal respectively.*

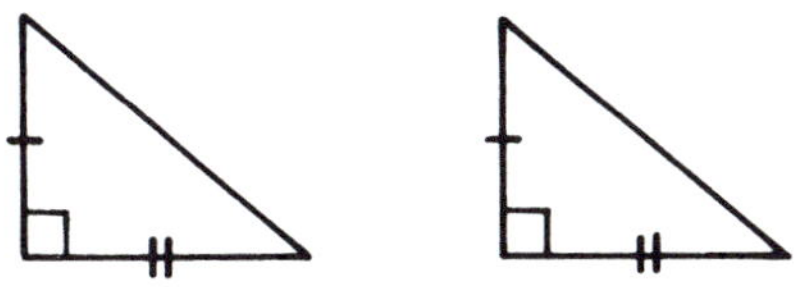

*Formal proofs employing geometric axioms, postulates and theorems to illustrate these cases of congruent triangles are given in regular school textbooks on geometry. The student interested in academic study should refer to such books.

Since the included right angles are equal, this theorem is really a special case of *s.a.s.* = *s.a.s.*

Theorem 12. *Two right triangles are equal if the hypotenuse and an acute angle of one are equal to the hypotenuse and an acute angle of the other.*

Since the right angles are equal, this theorem is a special case of *s.a.a.* = *s.a.a.*

Theorem 13. *Two right triangles are congruent if a side and an acute angle of one are equal to a side and corresponding acute angle of the other.*

Since the right angles are equal, this is again a special case of *s.a.a.* = *s.a.a.*

Practice Exercise No. 5

Note: Mark corresponding parts with corresponding check marks as previously explained. Use the method of demonstration shown under Theorem 14, following lines of reasoning similar to that used in connection with Theorem 7.

1 *Given* $AB = AD$
$\angle 1 = \angle 2$
Prove
$\triangle ABC \cong \triangle ADC$

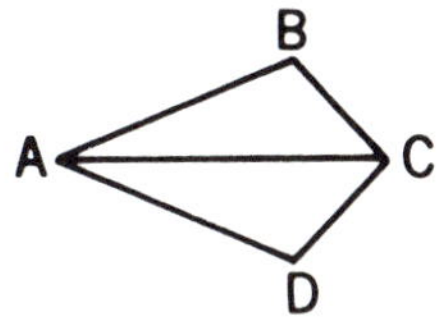

2 *Given* $BD \perp ACD$ is the mid-point of AC
Prove
$\triangle ABD \cong \triangle CBD$

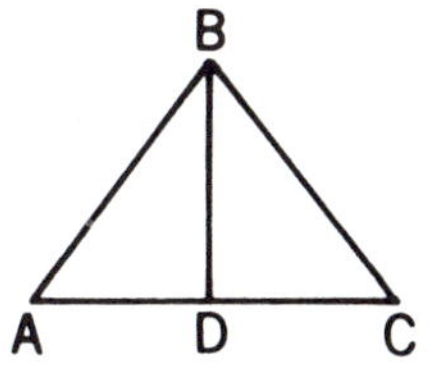

3 *Given* $\angle 3 = \angle 5$ AE is the bisector of BD
Prove
$\triangle ABC \cong \triangle EDC$

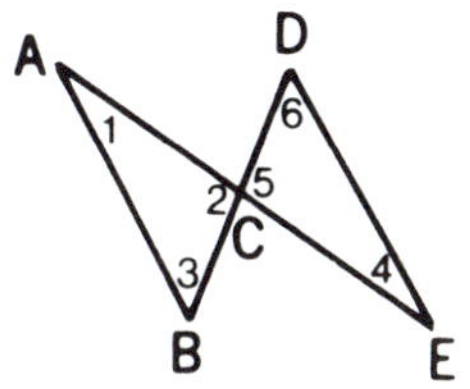

4 *Given* AD and CE bisect each other
Prove $AE \parallel CD$

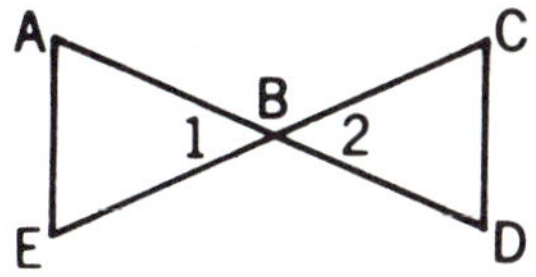

5 *Given* $AD = BC$
$AC = BD$
Prove
$\triangle BAD \cong \triangle ABC$
and $\angle 1 = \angle 2$

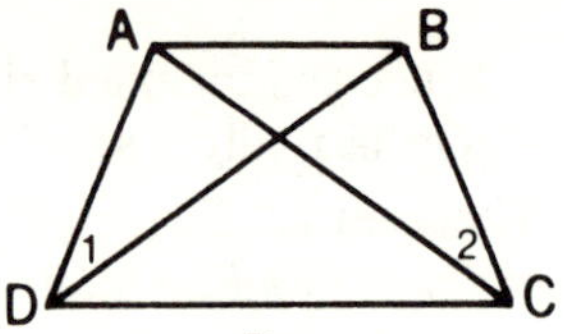

6 *Given* $AB = CB$
$AD = CD$
Prove $\angle 1 = \angle 2$
Hint: Draw BD and then extend it to meet AC at E.

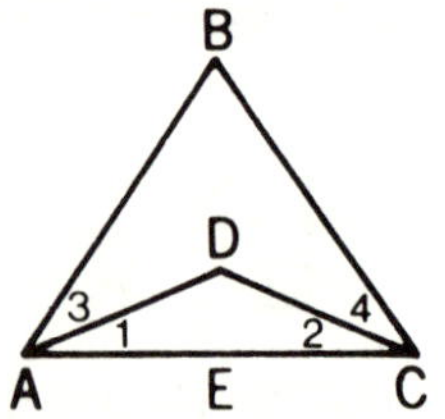

7 *Given* $AB = EF$
$AB \parallel EF$
$BC \parallel DE$
Prove $BC = DE$

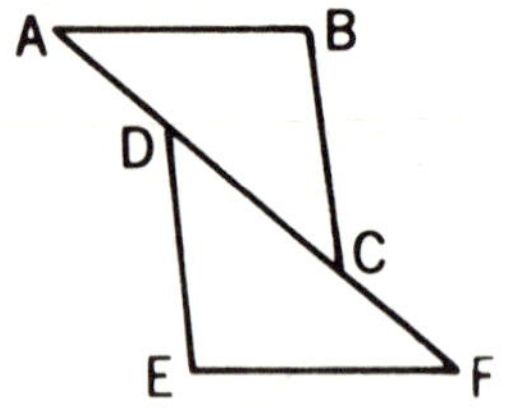

FACTS ABOUT TRIANGLES IN GENERAL

The general properties of the triangle not only form the foundation of trigonometry, but also find a wide application in the analysis and measurement of straight-sided plane figures of every kind.

One of the most important facts about triangles in general is that, regardless of the shape or size of any triangle, *the sum of the three angles of a triangle is equal to a straight angle, or* 180°. Presented as a theorem this proposition is easily proved.

Theorem 14. *The sum of the angles of a triangle is equal to a straight angle.*

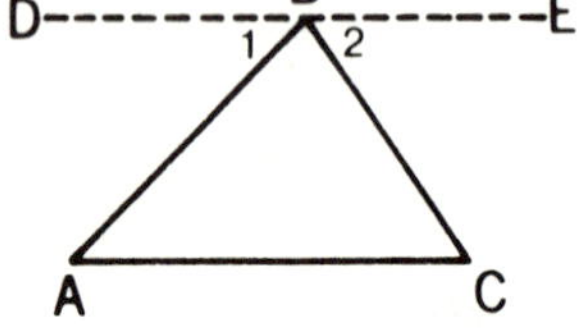

Given: $\triangle ABC$.
To prove: $\angle A + \angle B + \angle C =$ a straight angle.

Steps	*Reasons*
1. Through B draw $DE \parallel AC$.	1. Parallel postulate No. 1.
2. $\angle 1 = \angle A$.	2. Alt. int. ∠s of $\parallel$ lines are =.
3. $\angle 2 = \angle C$.	3. Same reason as 2.
4. $\angle 1 + \angle B + \angle 2 =$ a straight angle.	4. By definition, since the exterior sides lie in a straight line.
5. $\therefore \angle A + \angle B + \angle C =$ a straight angle.	5. Substituting $\angle A$ and $\angle C$ for $\angle 1$ and $\angle 2$ in step 4 by Axiom 7.

From this knowledge of the sum of the angles of a triangle the following corollaries concerning triangles in general become self-evident.

Corollary 1. *Each angle of an equiangular triangle is* 60°.

Since the angles of an equiangular triangle are equal, each angle = 180° ÷ 3, or 60°.

Corollary 2. *No triangle may have more than one obtuse angle or right angle.*

180° minus 90° or more leaves 90° or less, to be split between the two remaining angles, and therefore each of the two remaining angles must be acute, *i.e.*, less than 90°.

Corollary 3. *The acute angles of a right triangle are complementary.*

180° minus 90° leaves two angles whose sum equals 90°.

Corollary 4. *If two angles of one triangle are equal respectively to two angles of another, the third angles are equal.*

This truth is supported by Ax. 3 (page 634), namely, that if equals are subtracted from equals the remainders are equal.

Corollary 5. *Any exterior* angle of a triangle is equal to the sum of the two remote interior angles.*

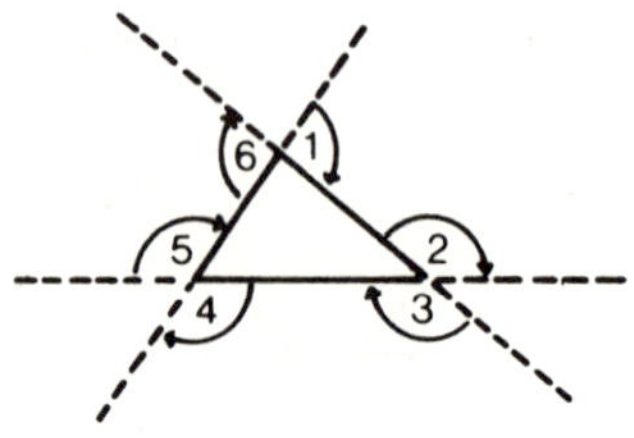

Thus in $\triangle ABC$ if you extend AC to D and draw $CE \parallel AB$, you have the two $\parallel$ lines AB and CE cut by the transversal AD. $\therefore \angle 1 = \angle B$ and $\angle 2 = \angle A$, so that $\angle 1 + \angle 2$, or $\angle BCD = \angle A + \angle B$.

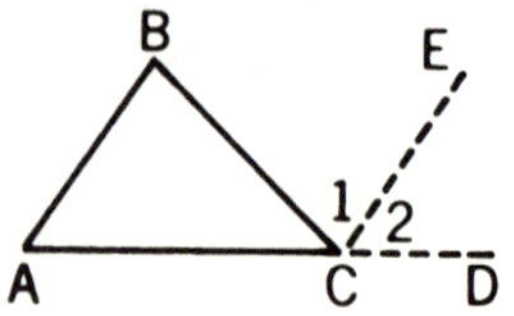

A few characteristic properties of special triangles frequently used are worth noting at this point.

*An exterior angle of a triangle is the angle formed by a side and the extension of its adjacent side. Every triangle has six exterior angles as shown in the diagram.

Theorem 15. *The base angles of an isosceles triangle are equal.*

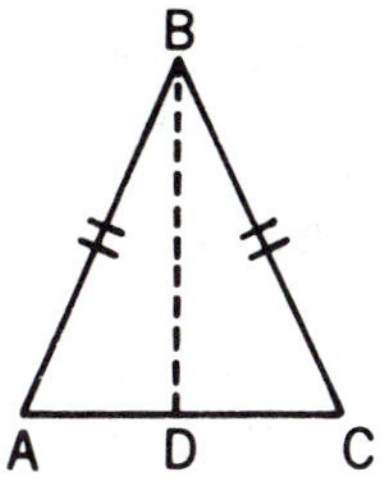

By definition the sides of an isosceles triangle are equal.

∴ if you draw the bisector BD of $\angle B$ it is readily seen that $\triangle ABD \cong \triangle CBD$ by $s.a.s. = s.a.s.$ Hence $\angle A = \angle C$.

This theorem may be stated in another way, namely:

Theorem 16. *If two sides of a triangle are equal, the angles opposite those sides are equal.*

The following corollaries may readily be seen to follow from this theorem.

Corollary 1. *If two sides of a triangle are equal, the angles opposite these sides are equal and the triangle is isosceles.*

Corollary 2. *The bisector of the apex angle of an isosceles triangle is perpendicular to the base, bisects the base and is the altitude of the triangle.*

Corollary 3. *An equilateral triangle is equiangular.*

Theorem 17. *If one acute angle of a right triangle is double the other, the hypotenuse is double the shorter side.* Or

In a 30°–60° right triangle the hypotenuse equals twice the shorter side.

The following properties of bisectors, altitudes and medians of triangles are frequently applied in the practical problems of geometric design and construction that arise in shop and office.

Theorem 18. *Every point in the perpendicular bisector of a line is equidistant from the ends of that line.*

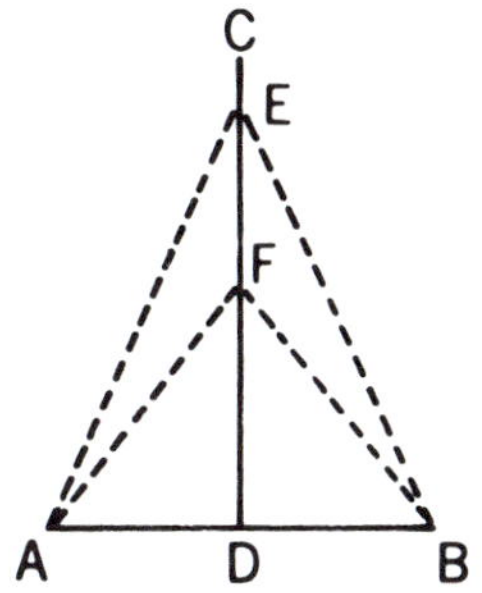

If CD is $\perp$ bisector of AB
Then $DA = DB$
$FA = FB$, etc.

Theorem 19. *Every point in the bisector of an angle is equidistant from the sides of the angle.*

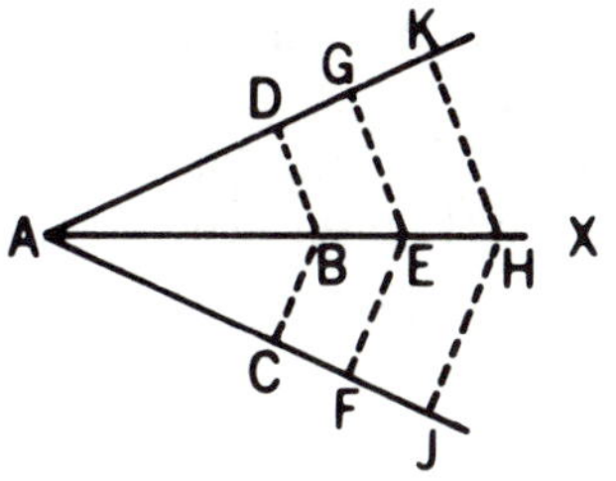

If AX is the bisector of $\angle A$
Then $BC = BD$, $EF = EG$, $HJ = HK$, etc.

Theorem 20. *The perpendicular is the shortest line that can be drawn from a point to a given line.*

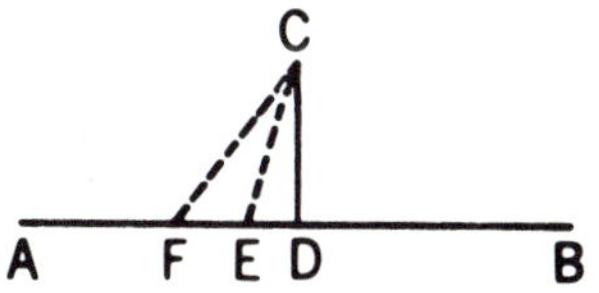

If $CD \perp AB$
Then $CD < CE$,$CD < CF$, etc.

Theorem 21. *The three bisectors of the sides of a triangle meet in one point which is equidistant from the three vertices of the triangle.*

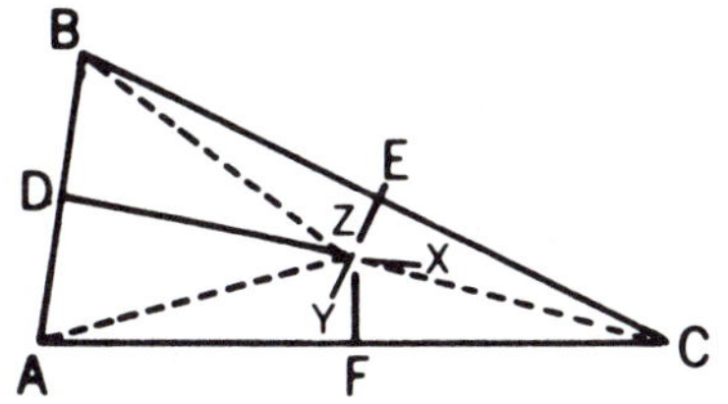

If DX, EY and FZ are bisectors of the sides AB, BC and CA
Then $AO = BO = CO$, and is equal to the radius of the circle circumscribing $\triangle ABC$

Note: This fact is often used as a method for finding the center of a circular object. The procedure consists in inscribing a triangle in the circle and constructing the bisectors of the sides. The point at which they meet is the center of the circle.

Theorem 22. *The three bisectors of the angles of a triangle meet in one point which is equidistant from the three sides of the triangle.*

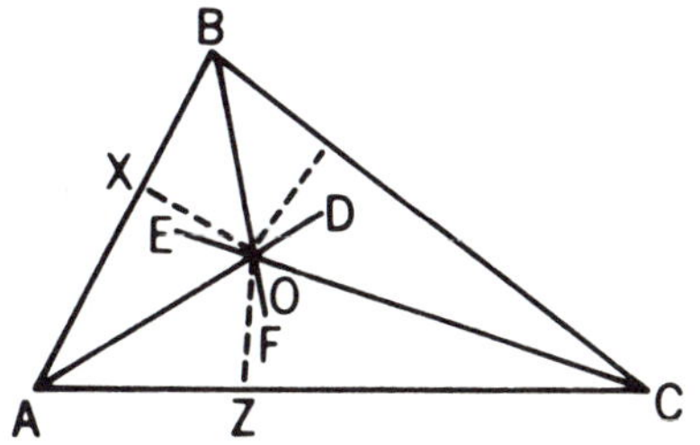

If AD, BF and CE are bisectors respectively of $\angle A$, B and C
Then $OX = OY = OZ$, and is equal to the radius of the circle inscribed in $\triangle ABC$.

Note: This geometric theorem is employed as a method for determining the largest circular pattern that can be cut out of a triangular piece of material.

For practical purposes you should carry out the constructions involved in the theorems of this section. Check the accuracy of your constructions by determining whether the constructed parts fit the hypothesis of the theorem. These very constructions are daily applied in architecture, carpentry, art, machine work, manufacturing, etc.

Practice Exercise No. 6

1 Two angles of a triangle are 62° and 73°. What does the third angle equal?

2 How many degrees are there in the sum of the angles of a quadrilateral?

Hint: Draw the figure and then construct a diagonal.

3 What is the value of an exterior angle of an equilateral triangle?

4 In a certain right triangle the acute angles are $2x$ and $7x$. What is the size of each angle?

5 An exterior angle at the base of an isosceles triangle equals 116°. What is the value of the vertex angle?

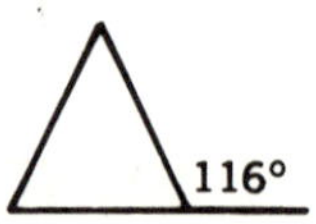

6 In a certain triangle one angle is twice as large as another and three times as large as the third. How many degrees are there in each angle?

7 Draw an equilateral triangle and by it find the ratio between the diameter of the inscribed circle and the radius of the circumscribed circle.

Hint: Refer to Theorems 20 and 22.

8 Given $\angle 1 = \angle 4$, prove that $\triangle ABC$ is isosceles.

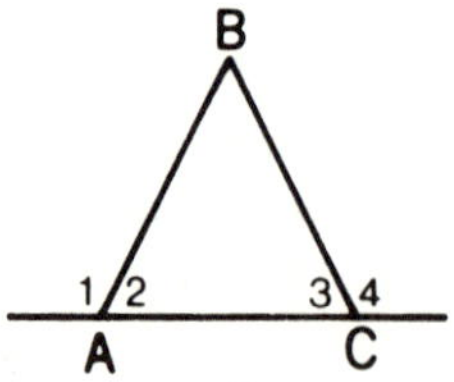

9 Given $BA = BC$ and DE $\parallel$ BC, prove that $DE = DA$.

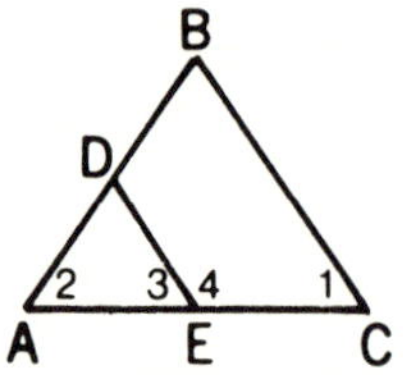

POLYGONS

A **polygon** is a plane geometric figure bounded by three or more sides. Any triangle, for instance, is a polygon.

The **vertices** of a polygon are the angle points where two sides meet.

A **diagonal** of a polygon joins two nonconsecutive vertices. How many diagonals has a triangle? None. How many diagonals can a four-sided figure have? Two.

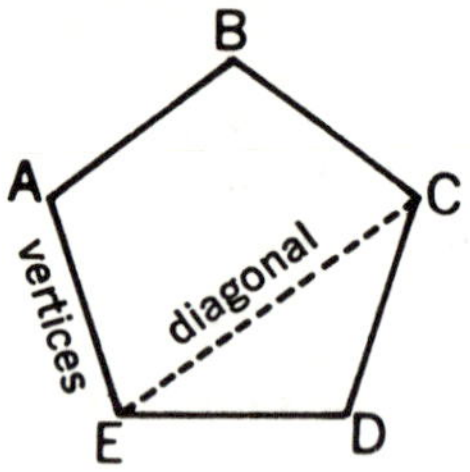

Polygon

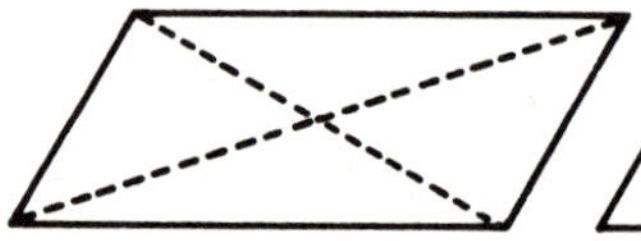
Diagonals

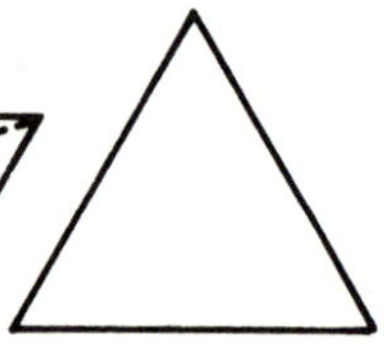
No Diagonals Possible

Polygons derive their names from the number of and nature of the sides and the types of angles included.

Quadrilaterals are polygons with four sides. There are six types of quadrilaterals: the *rectangle*, the *square* (a special form of rectangle), the *rhomboid*, the *rhombus*, the *trapezoid* and the *trapezium*.

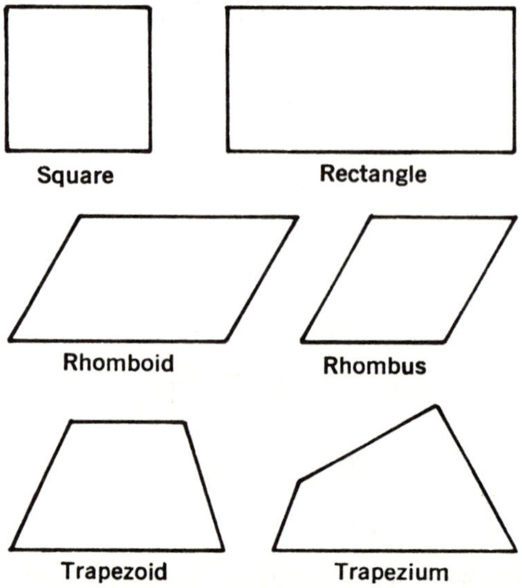

TYPES OF QUADRILATERALS

A **parallelogram** is a quadrilateral in which the opposite sides are parallel and the opposite angles are equal.

A **square** is a parallelogram in which the angles are all right angles and the sides are all equal.

A **rectangle** is a parallelogram that has 4 right angles and in which opposite sides are equal.

A **rhomboid** has opposite sides parallel but no right angles.

A **rhombus** is a parallelogram having four equal sides but no right angles.

A **trapezoid** is a quadrilateral having one pair of parallel sides.

A **trapezium** is a quadrilateral in which no two sides are parallel.

(*Note:* In England these last two definitions are interchanged.)

SURFACE MEASUREMENT OF QUADRILATERALS

The **height** or **altitude** of a **parallelogram** is the distance perpendicular from the base to the opposite side.

Rule: *The area of a rectangle equals the base multiplied by the height.*

Formula: $A = bh$.

EXAMPLE 1: Find the area of a rectangle that is 3 inches high with a 4-inch base.

SOLUTION:
$A = bh$, formula.
$A = 4 \times 3 = 12$.
12 sq. inches, ANS.

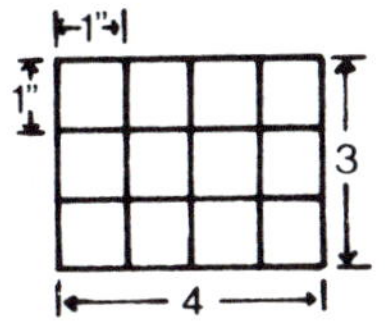

Note: The diagram has been drawn to scale on a $\frac{3}{16}$ basis. There are 4 columns and 3 rows of sq. in. units. The number of sq. in. by count is seen to be 12. The area is thus 12 sq. in.

EXAMPLE 2: Find the height of a rectangle with a 16 ft. base and an area of 80 sq. ft.

SOLUTION: $A = bh. \therefore h = \dfrac{A}{b}$
$= \frac{80}{16} = 5$ ft., ANS.

Rule: *The area of a square is equal to the square of one of its sides.*

Formula: $A = S^2$.

EXAMPLE 3: Find the side of a square whose area is 121 sq. in.

SOLUTION: $A = S^2. \therefore \sqrt{A} = S$
$= \sqrt{121} = 11$ ft., ANS.

Rule: *The perimeter of a square is equal to four times the square root of the area.*

Formula. $P = 4\sqrt{A}$ or $P = 4S$, where P = perimeter, A = area, and S = side of a square.

EXAMPLE 4: Find the perimeter of a square whose area is 144 sq. in.

SOLUTION: $P = 4\sqrt{A}$, $P = 4 \times 12 = 48$ in., ANS.

Rule. *The diagonal of a square equals the square root of twice the area.*

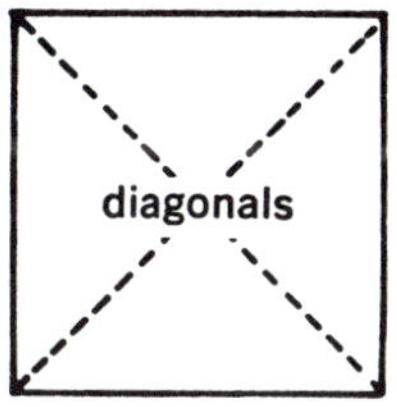

Formula: $D = \sqrt{2A}$

Note: Check back on your right triangle formula.

EXAMPLE 5: Find the diagonal of a square if the area is 49 sq. inches.

SOLUTION: $D = \sqrt{2A}$, $D = \sqrt{98} = 9,899$, ANS.

SOLUTION by rt. triangle formula: $c^2 = a^2 + b^2$, in which c represents the diagonal or hypotenuse while a and b are the sides. Then
$c^2 = 7^2 + 7^2$, $c^2 = 98$
$c = \sqrt{98} = 9.899$, ANS.

Any parallelogram can be converted to a rectangle without changing its area. This is shown in the following diagram.

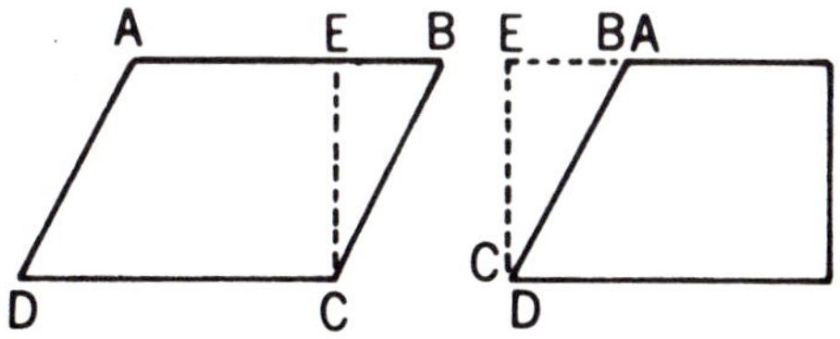

By taking the triangle *EBC* from the figure at the left and changing its position as shown in the figure at the right, we create a rectangle without adding to or deducting from the total area. Hence—

Rule: *The area of a parallelogram is equal to the product of the base times the height.*

EXAMPLE 6: Find the area of a rhomboid whose base is 12 inches and whose height is 8 inches.

SOLUTION: $A = bh. \therefore A = 12 \times 8 = 96$ sq. in.

Rule: *The area of a trapezoid equals half the sum of the parallel sides multiplied by the height.*

PROOF:

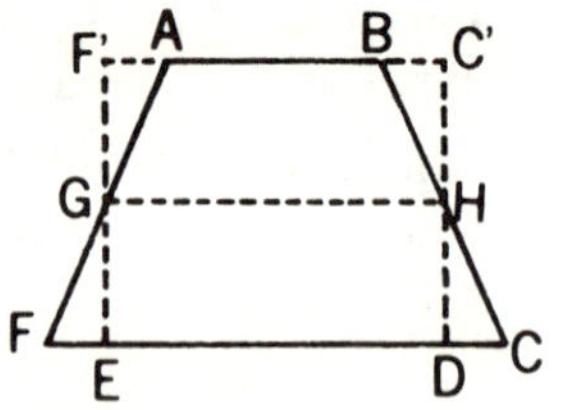

Make a rectangle of the trapezoid *ABCF* by drawing a line *GH* ∥ to the two ∥ sides and midway between them. The length of this line is the average of the two ∥ sides *AB* and *FC*. Perpendiculars from the midline *GH* to the larger base *FC* cut off triangles that are exactly equal to the triangles needed above the midline to form a rectangle of the new figure.

Formula: A of trapezoid $= \frac{B + b}{2} \times h$, in which h is the ⊥ height and B, b are the parallel sides.

EXAMPLE 7: Find the area of a trapezoid whose bases are equal to 20 in. and 30 in. and whose height is 15 inches.

SOLUTION: $A = \frac{B + b}{2} \times h$; $A = \frac{30 + 20}{2} \times 15$
$= 25 \times 15 = 375$ sq. in., ANS.

Practice Exercise No. 7

PROBLEMS

1 An apartment house is rectangular in shape. If its front is 550 ft. and it goes back 390 ft., how far is it all around the house?

(A) 940 ft. ____ (C) 1,880 ft. ____
(B) 1,800 ft. ____ (D) 1,100 ft. ____

2 A rectangular hangar is to house an airplane. What must its area be if you desire a 20-foot allowance on all sides and if the plane is 110 feet wide by 64 feet long?

(A) 23,200 sq. ft. ____
(B) 14,420 sq. ft. ____
(C) 15,600 sq. ft. ____
(D) 14,000 sq. ft. ____

3 How much would it cost to resurface a square plot 75 ft. long at a cost of 20¢ a sq. foot?

(A) $6,000 ____ (C) $1,000 ____
(B) $1,600 ____ (D) $1,125 ____

4 A square field whose area is 1,024 sq. feet is to be completely covered by flagstones 4 ft. square. How many flags will be needed to cover the field?

(A) 32 ____ (C) 64 ____
(B) 56 ____ (D) 84 ____

5 How much barbed wire would be needed to go diagonally across a rectangular piece of land that is 66 ft. wide by 88 ft. long?

(A) 90 ft. ____ (C) 110 ft. ____
(B) 100 ft. ____ (D) 120 ft. ____

6 If you had a square frame for the floor of a tent and if it contained 288 sq. ft., how long a piece of lumber would be needed to brace the frame from one corner to the other?

(A) 12 ft. ____ (C) 21 ft. ____
(B) 17 ft. ____ (D) 24 ft. ____

7 If molding cost 6 cents a ft., how much would it cost to put a border of molding around a square window that had an area of 81 sq. ft.?

(A) $4.86 ____ (C) $1.08 ____
(B) $.54 ____ (D) $2.16 ____

8 What is the area of the figure shown below?

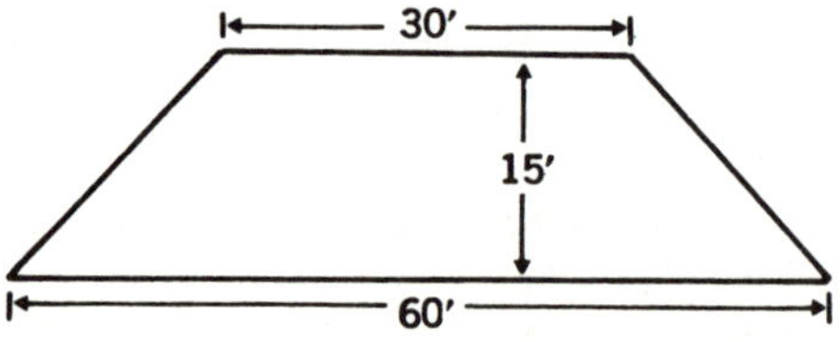

(A) 450 sq. ft. ____ (C) 750 sq. ft. ____
(B) 675 sq. ft. ____ (D) 2,700 sq. ft. ____

9 What is the area of the figure below?

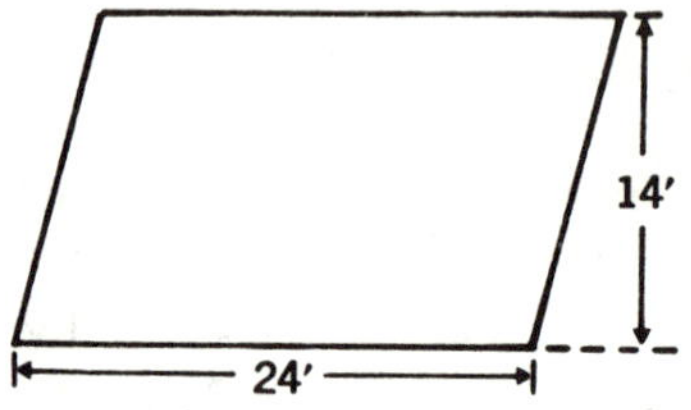

(A) 168 sq. ft. ____ (C) 76 sq. ft. ____
(B) 336 sq. ft. ____ (D) 206 sq. ft. ____

10 What is the area of the figure to the right?

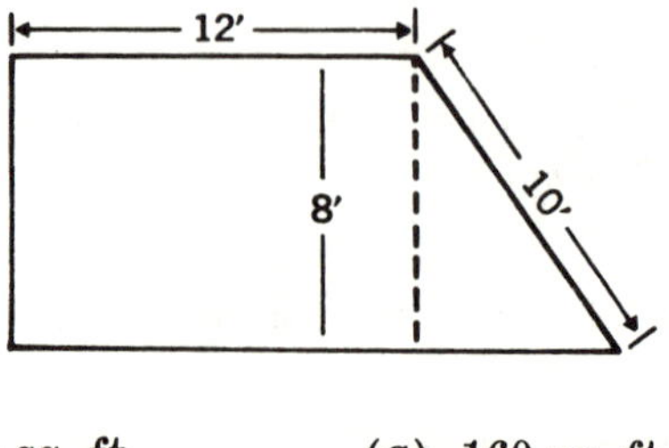

(A) 120 sq. ft. ____ (C) 160 sq. ft. ____
(B) 140 sq. ft. ____ (D) 180 sq. ft. ____

CIRCLES

A **circle** is a curved line on which every point is equally distant from a point within called the **center.**

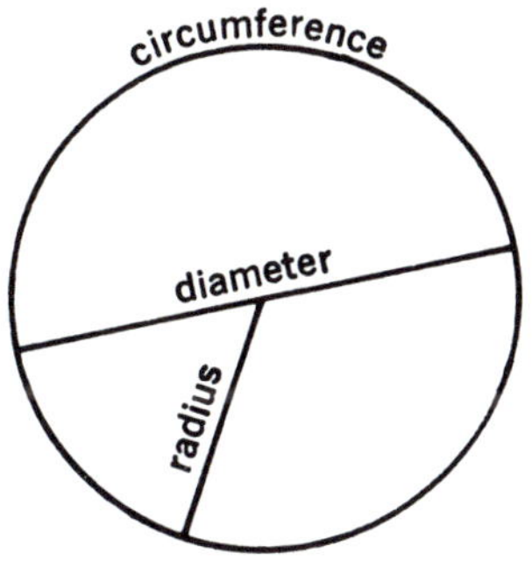

CIRCLE

A **radius** of a circle is a line drawn from the center to the outer edge.

The **diameter** of a circle is a straight line drawn from any point on the outer edge through the center to the outer edge on the opposite side. It is equal to twice any radius.

The **circumference** of a circle is the line representing its outer edge and is equal to the complete distance around the circle. It is analogous to perimeter.

Pi, written π, is the name given to the ratio expressed by dividing the circumference of any circle by its diameter. In quantity it is a constant approximately equal to $3\frac{1}{7}$ or 3.1416. If you measure the distance around any circle, and its diameter, and then divide the distance by the diameter you will always get a result of approximately $3\frac{1}{7}$.

Formula: $\pi = \dfrac{C}{d}$, where C = circumference and d = diameter; or $\pi = \dfrac{C}{2r}$, where r = radius.

Rule: *To find the circumference of a circle multiply the diameter by* π.

Formula: $C = \pi d$; or $C = 2\pi r$.

EXAMPLE 1: The spoke of a wheel is 21 inches. Find its circumference.

SOLUTION: $C = 2\pi r$

$$= 2 \times \frac{22}{\cancel{7}_{1}} \times \cancel{21}^{3} = 132 \text{ in.,} \quad \textit{A}\text{NS.}$$

EXAMPLE 2: The circumference of a pulley is 33 inches. What is its diameter?

SOLUTION: $C = \pi d, \therefore d = \dfrac{C}{\pi}$.

$$d = \frac{33}{\frac{22}{7}} = \cancel{33}^{3} \times \frac{7}{\cancel{22}_{2}} = \frac{21}{2} = 10\tfrac{1}{2} \text{ in.,} \quad \text{ANS.}$$

AREA OF A CIRCLE

Rule: *The area of a circle equals one-half the product of the circumference and the radius.*

This can be reasoned informally as follows. Any circle can be cut to form many narrow triangles as shown in Fig. 5. The altitude of each triangle would be equal to a radius r. The base would be a part of the circumference C. We know the area of each triangle to be equal to $\frac{1}{2}$ the base times the altitude. Since r is the altitude, and the sum of the bases equal the circumference, the area $= \frac{1}{2} r \times C$. Since $C = 2\pi r$, $A = \frac{1}{2} r \times 2\pi r$. $\therefore A = r \times \pi r = \pi r^2$.

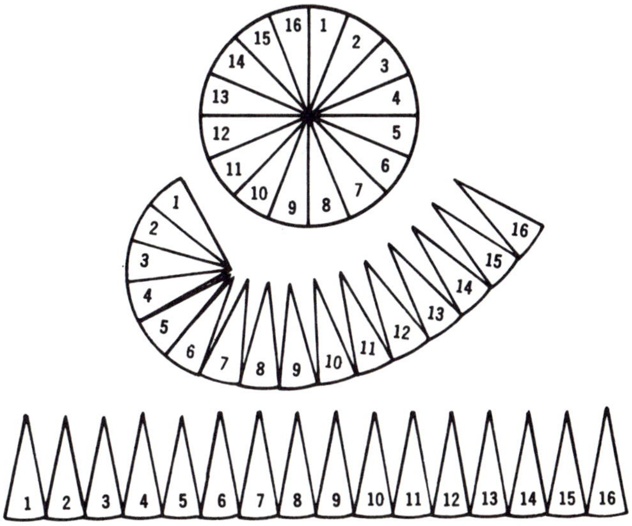

FIGURE 5

Rule: *The area of a circle in terms of the radius is* π *times the radius squared.*

Formula: $A = \pi r^2$.

EXAMPLE 3: Find the area of a circle that has a 6-in. radius.

SOLUTION: $A = \pi r^2 = 3.1416 \times (6)^2$
$= 113.10$ sq. in., ANS.

EXAMPLE 4: The area of a circle is 396 sq. in. Find its radius.

SOLUTION:

$$A = \pi r^2, \quad \frac{A}{\pi} = r^2, \quad \sqrt{\frac{A}{\pi}} = r,$$

$$r = \sqrt{\frac{396}{\frac{22}{7}}} = \sqrt{396 \times \tfrac{7}{22}} = \sqrt{126} = 11.18 \text{ in.}$$

Rule: *The area of a circular ring equals the area of the outside circle minus the area of the inside circle.*

Formula: $A = \pi R^2 - \pi r^2$, where R = radius of larger circle and r = radius of smaller circle.

EXAMPLE: In a circular ring the outside diameter is 8″ and the inside diameter is 6″. What is the area of a cross-section of the ring?

SOLUTION:
$A = \pi R^2 - \pi r^2. \qquad D = 8, \therefore R = 4.$

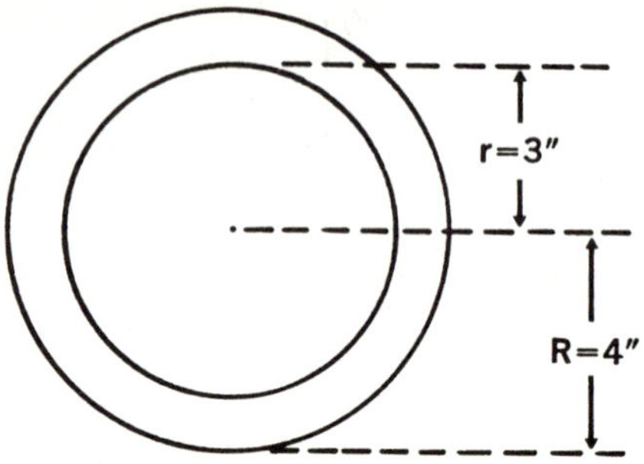

$d = 6, \therefore r = 3. \qquad \therefore A = \pi(4^2 - 3^2).$

$A = \frac{22}{7}(4^2 - 3^2) = \frac{22}{7}(16 - 9)$

$= \frac{22}{\not 7} \times \not 7 = 22$ sq. in., ANS.

SIMILAR PLANE FIGURES

In ordinary language plane figures are similar when they are alike in all respects except size. For instance, all circles are obviously similar.

Two polygons are **similar** when the angles of one are respectively equal to the angles of the other in the same consecutive order.

If the *consecutive* order of the angles is the same, it makes no difference if they follow each other clockwise in one figure and counter-clockwise in the other. Such figures will still be similar because either may be considered as having been reversed like an image in a mirror.

In the case of triangles it is impossible *not* to arrange the angles in the same consecutive order, so that two triangles are similar if only their angles are equal.

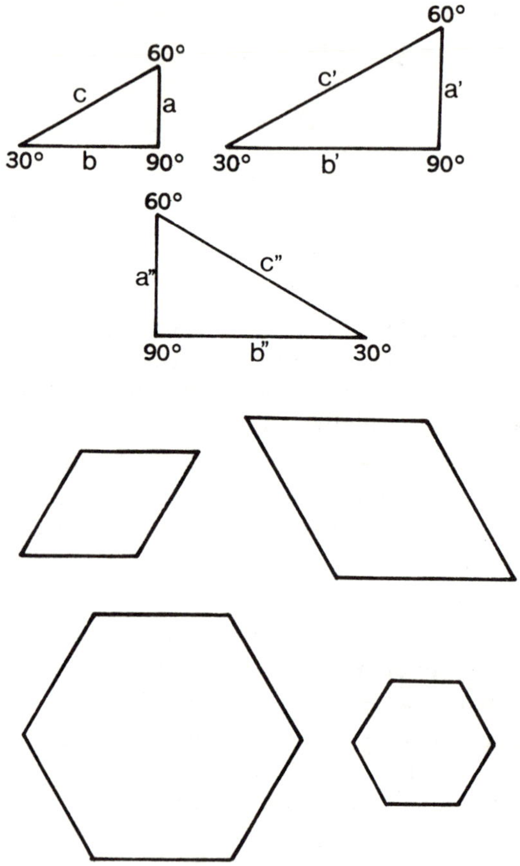

SIMILAR POLYGONS

In the preceding diagram all three triangles are similar because they all have the same angles.

The two rhombuses are similar, though the direction of the lines in one reverses that in the other.

All *regular* polygons with a given number of sides are similar.

Rule 1: *If two figures are similar, the ratio of any line in one to the corresponding line in the other applies to all the lines that correspond in the two figures.*

Rule 2: *If two figures are similar, the ratio of their areas is that of the squares of corresponding lines.*

These rules apply not only to simple geometric figures but to drawings, photographs, engravings, blueprints, etc. presenting the greatest complexity of lines. Because of the broad applicability of the rules governing similar polygons, we have generalized the whole subject.

To find the length of any line in a plane figure that is similar to another plane figure, *apply the ratio that exists between any other two corresponding lines.*

EXAMPLE: In a rhombus measuring 4 inches on a side the longer diagonal is $5\frac{1}{2}$ inches. How long would this diagonal be in a similar rhombus measuring 7 inches on a side?

SOLUTION:

$$D : d :: S : s,$$

$$\frac{D}{5\frac{1}{2}} = \frac{7}{4},$$

$$D = \frac{7 \times 5\frac{1}{2}}{4} = \frac{38\frac{1}{2}}{4} = \frac{77}{2 \times 4} = 9\tfrac{5}{8} \text{ in., } \textsc{Ans.}$$

To find the area of a plane figure that is similar to another plane figure having a known area, *determine the ratio of any two corresponding lines in the two figures and make the required area proportional to the squares of these lines.*

EXAMPLE: A trapezium in which one of the sides measures 6 inches has an area of 54 square inches. What would be the area of a similar trapezium in which a corresponding side measured 15 inches?

SOLUTION:

$$A' : A :: S^2 : s^2,$$

$$\frac{A'}{54} = \frac{15^2}{6^2},$$

$$A' = \frac{225 \times 54}{36} = \frac{225 \times 3}{2} = 337\tfrac{1}{2} \text{ in., } \textsc{Ans.}$$

SOLID GEOMETRY

Plane geometry treats of surfaces or of figures having *two* dimensions, namely *length* and *breadth.* **Solid geometry** treats of **solids** or of **bodies** having *three* dimensions, namely, *length, breadth,* and *thickness.*

RECTANGULAR SOLIDS

A rectangular solid is one in which all the faces are rectangles. The **cube** is a special type of rectangular solid in which all the faces are equal.

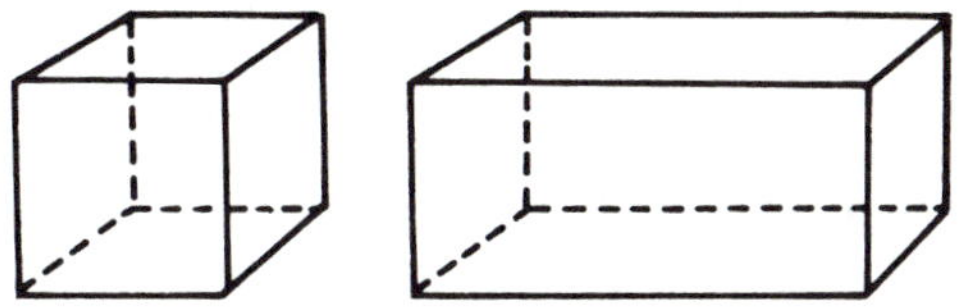

CUBE RECTANGULAR SOLID

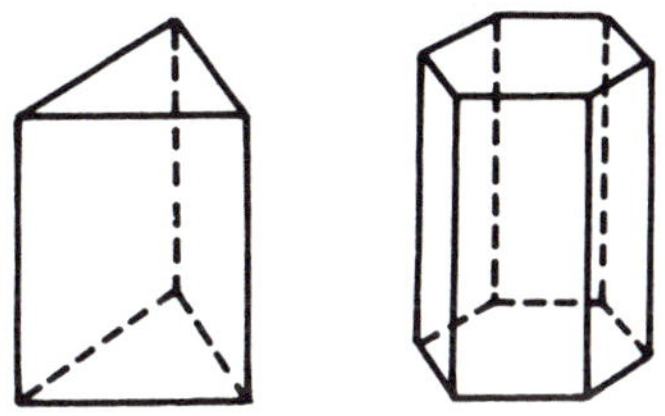

PRISMS

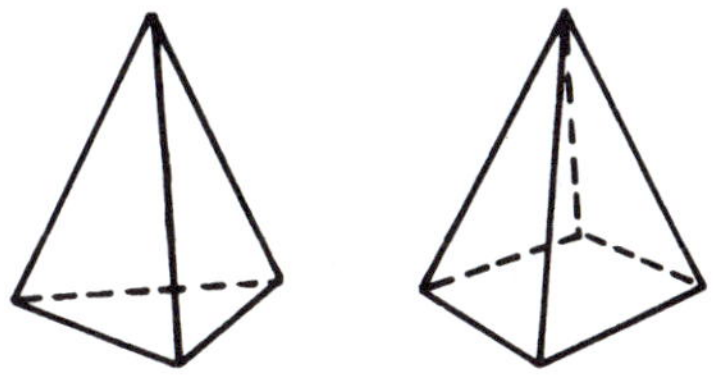

PYRAMIDS

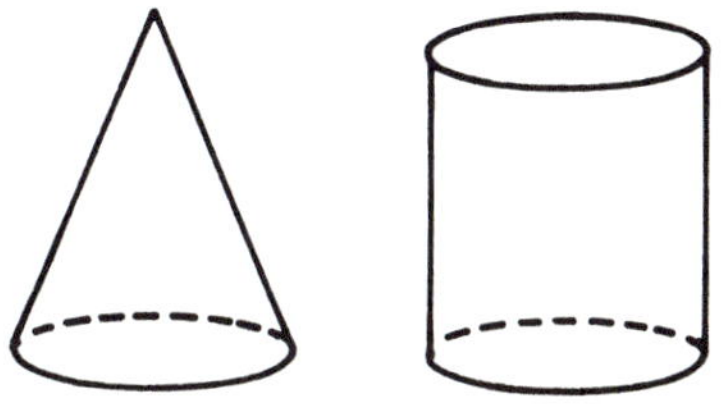

CONE CYLINDER

To find the area of the faces of a rectangular solid, *add the areas of the three different forms of face and multiply by* **2.**

EXAMPLE: A rectangular solid measures $6'' \times 4'' \times 3''$. What is the total area of its faces?

SOLUTION: It has two faces measuring $6'' \times 4''$, two measuring $6'' \times 3''$ and two measuring $4'' \times 3''$.

$(6 \times 4) + (6 \times 3) + (4 \times 3) = 54$ sq. in.

$2 \times 54 = 108$ sq. in., ANS.

To find the area of the faces of a cube, *multiply the area of one face by six.*

To find the cubical contents of a rectangular solid, *multiply together the three dimensions.*

EXAMPLE: What are the cubical contents of a box measuring $11'' \times 6'' \times 4\frac{1}{2}''$?
$11 \times 6 \times 4\frac{1}{2} = 297$ cu. in., ANS.

With solids other than rectangular ones we consider the surfaces and areas of the sides as distinct from those of the bottom and top (if any). We call the area of the sides the **lateral area** and speak of the top as well as the bottom as **bases.**

To find the lateral area of a prism, *multiply the perimeter of one of the bases by the height.*

EXAMPLE: A prism 6″ high has as its base an equilateral triangle measuring $1\frac{1}{2}''$ on a side. What is its lateral area?

SOLUTION:
$(1\frac{1}{2} + 1\frac{1}{2} + 1\frac{1}{2}) \times 6 = 27$ sq. in., ANS.

To find the cubical contents of a prism, *multiply the area of one of the bases by the height.*

EXAMPLE: What are the cubical contents of a prism 8″ high if the area of one of the bases is $3\frac{3}{4}$ square inches?

SOLUTION:
$3\frac{3}{4} \times 8 = 30$ cu. in., ANS.

To find the lateral area of a cylinder, *multiply the circumference of one of the bases by the height.*

EXAMPLE: What is the lateral surface of a cylinder with a base 6″ in diameter if its height is 7″?

SOLUTION:
$6 \times \frac{22}{7} \times 7 = 132$ sq. in., ANS.

To find the cubical contents of a cylinder, *multiply the area of one of the bases by the height.*

EXAMPLE: What are the cubical contents of the cylinder in the preceding example?

SOLUTION:
$3^2 \times \frac{22}{7} \times 7 = 9 \times 22 = 198$ cu. in., ANS.

To find the lateral area of a pyramid, *multiply its slant height by the perimeter and divide by two.*

EXAMPLE: What is the lateral area of a triangular pyramid having a base measuring 2″ on a side and a slant height of 9″?

SOLUTION:
$(2 + 2 + 2) \times 9 \div 2 = 27$ sq. in., ANS.

To find the cubical contents of a pyramid, *multiply the area of the base by the altitude* (not slant height) *and divide by three.*

EXAMPLE: A square pyramid 10 inches high has a base measuring 4 inches on a side. What are its cubical contents?

SOLUTION:

$$\frac{4 \times 4 \times 10}{3} = \frac{160}{3} = 53\tfrac{1}{3} \text{ cu. in., ANS.}$$

To find the lateral area of a cone, *multiply its slant height by the circumference of the base and divide by two.* (Compare this with the rule for finding the lateral area of a pyramid as given above.)

To find the cubical contents of a cone, *multiply the area of the base by the altitude and divide by three.* (Compare this with the rule for finding the cubical contents of a pyramid as given above.)

To find the area of the surface of a sphere, *multiply the square of the radius by 4π.*

EXAMPLE: What is the surface area of a sphere one foot in diameter?

SOLUTION:

$$6^2 \times 4\pi = 36 \times 4 \times \tfrac{22}{7} = \tfrac{3168}{7} = 452\tfrac{4}{7} \text{ sq. in., ANS.}$$

To find the cubical contents of a sphere, *multiply the cube of the radius by $\frac{4\pi}{3}$.*

EXAMPLE: What are the cubical contents of a sphere one foot in diameter?

SOLUTION:

$$6^3 \times \frac{4\pi}{3} = \frac{216 \times 4 \times 22}{3 \times 7} = \frac{6336}{7} = 905\tfrac{1}{7} \text{ cu. in., ANS.}$$

Practice Exercise No. 8

PROBLEMS

1 The diameter of an automobile tire is 28″. What is its circumference?

(A) 66″____ (C) 88″____
(B) 77″____ (D) 99″____

2 The circumference of a wheel is 110 inches. How long is one of its spokes?

(A) 35″____ (C) 15″____
(B) $17\frac{1}{2}''$____ (D) $12\frac{1}{2}''$____

3 To make a circular coil for a magnet you need 49 turns of wire. How much wire will you need if the diameter of the coil is 4″?

(A) $12\frac{4}{7}$ in.____ (C) 324 in.____
(B) $84\frac{2}{7}$ in.____ (D) 616 in.____

4 How many square inches of tin are needed for the top of a can that is 14 inches in diameter?

(A) 616 sq. in. ____ (C) 462 sq. in. ____
(B) 308 sq. in. ____ (D) 154 sq. in. ____

5 You have a circular grazing field 96 ft. in diameter, which is roped around. Concentric with that you have a circular trotting track 128 ft. in diameter. How much will it cost to regravel the trotting track at a price of 10¢ per sq. ft.?

(A) \$426.00 (C) \$826.40
(B) \$563.20 (D) \$968.20

6 The area of canvas needed to just cover the muzzle of a cannon is $50\frac{1}{4}$ sq. in. What is the diameter of the muzzle?

(A) 12 in. ____ (C) 6 in. ____
(B) 8 in. ____ (D) 5 in. ____

7 If the radius of a circle is twice as great as the radius of a smaller circle, how many times as large will the area of the greater circle be than the area of the smaller circle?

(A) 2 ____ (C) 6 ____
(B) 4 ____ (D) 8 ____

8 You have 4 circular garden plots, each having a 14-foot radius. What must the radius be of one large circular plot that will have as much area as the four combined?

(A) 28 ft. ____ (C) 20 ft. ____
(B) 21 ft. ____ (D) 64 ft. ____

9 How much will it cost to re-surface a circular swimming tank that has a diameter of 56 ft. if surfacing costs 25 cents a sq. ft.?

(A) \$154.00 ____ (C) \$462.00 ____
(B) \$308.00 ____ (D) \$616.00 ____

10 If you wish to convert a circular field that has a diameter of 56 feet to a square field with the same area, how long will a side of the square be?

(A) 28 ft. ____ (C) 49.6 ft. ____
(B) 36.8 ft. ____ (D) 46.0 ft. ____

ANSWERS TO EXERCISES

Exercise No. 1

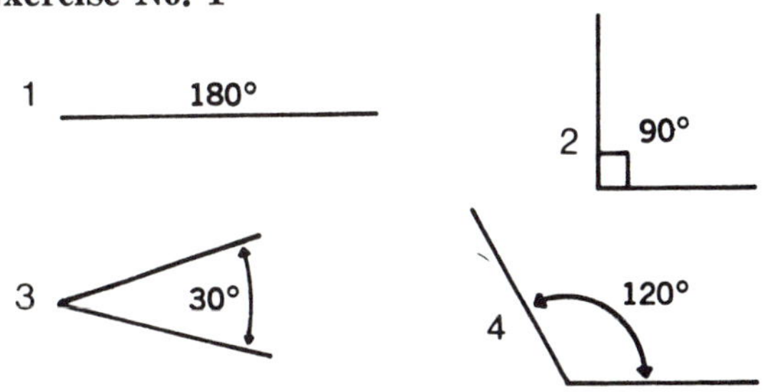

5 30° 7 80° 9 130° 11 50°
6 50° 8 90° 10 100°

Exercise No. 2

1 $\angle 2 = 30°$. $\angle$s that coincide are =.
2 $\angle ABD = 22° 30'$. A bisector divides an $\angle$ in half.
3 (a) $\angle 1 = \angle 3$, (b) $\angle 2 = \angle 5$ } Ax. 1, p. 80
(c) Relationship unknown
4 $\angle 1$ and $\angle 2$, $\angle 2$ and $\angle 3$, $\angle 3$ and $\angle 4$, $\angle 4$ and $\angle 5$, $\angle 5$ and $\angle 6$, $\angle 6$ and $\angle 7$, $\angle 7$ and $\angle 1$
5 $\angle 1$ and $\angle 5$, $\angle 2$ and $\angle 6$
6 $\angle 2 = 50°$, $\angle 4 = 30°$, $\angle 5 = 50°$, $\angle 6 = 100°$
7 $\angle AOC = 80°$, $\angle AOD = 180°$, $\angle BOE = 180°$, $\angle FOB = 130°$
8 (a) 67° 30′, (b) 60°, (c) 45°, (d) 30°, (e) 22° 30′
9 (a) 22°, (b) 45°, (c) 35°, (d) 58°, (e) 85°, (f) 56° 30′
10 (a) 155°, (b) 55°, (c) 136°, (d) 92°, (e) 105° 30′, (f) 101° 30′

Exercise No. 3

1 (a) alt. int., (b) alt. int., (c) corr., (d) alt. ext., (e) corr.
2 $\angle 1 = 50°$, $\angle 2 = 130°$, $\angle 4 = 130°$
3 $\angle 6 = 140°$, $\angle 7 = 140°$, $\angle 8 = 40°$
4 Two lines ⊥ to a third line are ||
5 (a) alt. int. $\angle$s are =
(b) corr. $\angle$s are =
(c) alt. ext. $\angle$s are =
6 If a pair of alt. int. $\angle$s are = the lines are ||.
7 $\angle 3$ is sup. to 115°. ∴ $\angle 3 = 65°$, making corr. $\angle$s =.
8 70°
9 Extend AB to D and construct $\angle BDE$ = to 60°. Then $DE \parallel BC$ because corr. $\angle$s are =.

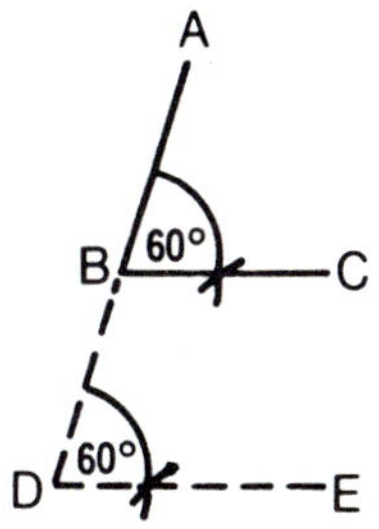

10 If the triangle is moved along the edge of the T-square into any two different positions, then lines drawn along side a will be || to each other, and lines drawn along side b will also be || to each other.

Exercise No. 4

1 $b^2 = c^2 - a^2$, $b = \sqrt{(51)^2 - (45)^2}$
$= \sqrt{2{,}601 - 2{,}025} = \sqrt{576} = 24$

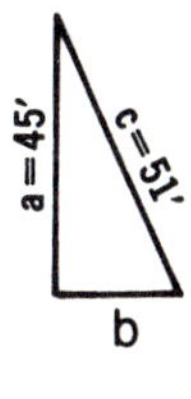

2 $A = \frac{bh}{2}; \frac{18(63)}{2} = 567$ sq. in.

3 Perimeter = sum of 3 sides. In isosceles △ 2 sides are equal.
$75 + 75 + 50 = 200$; $200 \times \$2.00 = \$400.00$

4 $c^2 = a^2 + b^2$
$c = \sqrt{90^2 + 90^2} =$
$\sqrt{8{,}100 + 8{,}100} =$
$\sqrt{16{,}200} = 127.27$

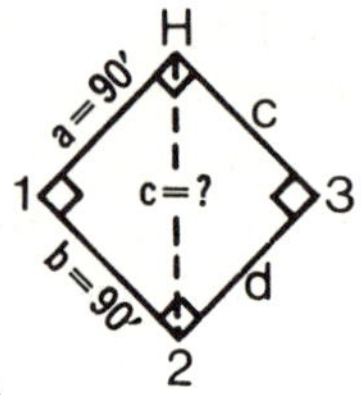

5 Area of $A = \frac{1}{2}bh$; $\frac{20(10)}{2} = 100$ sq. ft.

6 $a^2 = c^2 - b^2$, $a = \sqrt{(c)^2 - (b)^2} =$
$\sqrt{(26)^2 - (10)^2} =$
$\sqrt{676 - 100} = \sqrt{576} = 24$

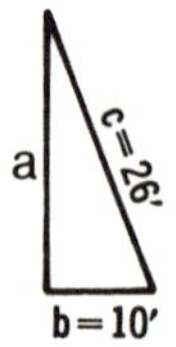

7 Let l = length of ladder, h = height of house, and b = distance from house at base. Then $l = \sqrt{h^2 + b^2} = \sqrt{1600 + 81} = \sqrt{1681} = 41$

8 Form the triangle and make the necessary deduction afterward. Let h = height of tree + elevation = $160 + 20 = 180$; l = line from top of tree to opposite shore; d = horizontal distance from tree to opposite shore. Then $d = \sqrt{l^2 - h^2} = \sqrt{500^2 - 180^2} = \sqrt{250000 - 32400} = \sqrt{217600} = 466.47$. Subtracting 100 ft. leaves 366.47 as the width of the river.

Exercise No. 5

1 $AB = AD$, $\angle 1 = \angle 2$ and $AC = AC$ (by identity) ∴ $\triangle ABC \cong ADC$ by s.a.s. = s.a.s.
2 $AD = DC$, $BD = BD$, and $\angle ADB = \angle CDB$ (all rt. ∠s are =)
∴ $\triangle ABD \cong \triangle CBD$ by s.a.s. = s.a.s.
3 $\angle 3 = \angle 5$, $BC = CD$ (bisected line) and $\angle 2 = \angle 6$ (vert. ∠s are =)
∴ $\triangle ABC \cong \triangle EDC$ by a.s.a. = a.s.a.
4 $AB = BD$, $EB = BC$, $\angle 1 = \angle 2$ (vert. ∠s)
$\triangle ABE \cong \triangle CBD$ by s.a.s. = s.a.s.
$\angle 3 = \angle 4$ (corr. ∠s of cong. △s)
∴ $AE \parallel CD$ (two lines are ∥ if a pair of alt. int. ∠ are =)
5 $AD = BC$, $AC = BD$, $AB = AB$ by identity
∴ $\triangle BAD \cong \triangle CBA$ by s.s.s. = s.s.s.
∴ $\angle 1 = \angle 2$ (corr. ∠ of cong. △ are =)
6 $AB = CB$, $AD = CD$,
$DB = DB$ by identity
∴ $\triangle ABD \cong \triangle CBD$ by s.s.s. = s.s.s.
∴ $\angle 5 = \angle 6$ (corr. ∠s of cong. △s)
∴ $\angle 7 = \angle 8$ (supp. of ∠s are =)
$DE = DE$ by identity
∴ $\triangle ADE \cong \triangle CDE$ by s.a.s. = s.a.s.
∴ $\angle 1 = \angle 2$ (corr. ∠s of cong. △s)

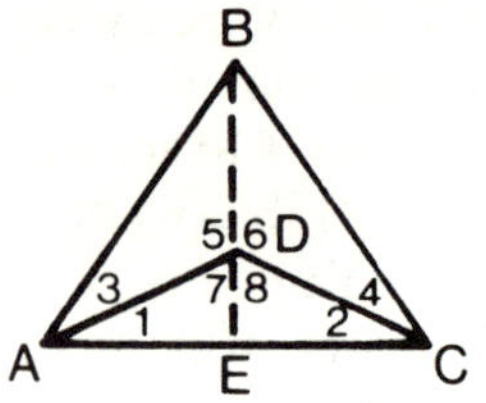

7 $AB = EF$, $\angle A = \angle F$ (alt. int. ∠s) and $\angle C = \angle D$ (alt. int. ∠s)
∴ $\triangle ABC \cong \triangle DEF$ by s.a.a. = s.a.a.
∴ $BC = DE$ (corr. sides of cong. △s)

Exercise No. 6

1 45°
2 360° (any quad. can be divided into 2 △s)
3 120° (∠s of equilateral △ = 60°, and ext. ∠ = sum of 2 int. ∠s)
4 20° and 70° (acute ∠s of a rt. △ are comp. . . $9x = 90°$, $x = 10°$)
5 52° (supp. 116° = 64°; base ∠ of isos. △ are = ∴ $180 - (64° + 64°) = 52°$
6 $32\frac{8}{11}°$, $49\frac{1}{11}°$, $98\frac{2}{11}°$ (Let x = angle; then $x + \frac{1}{2}x + \frac{1}{3}x = 180°$ and $x = 98\frac{2}{11}°$.)
7 Ratio is 1 : 1 or equal.
8 $\angle 2$ supp. $\angle 1$ and $\angle 3$ supp. $\angle 4$
∴ $\angle 2 = \angle 3$ (Ax. 1, page 103)
∴ $AB = BC$ and $\triangle ABC$ is isos. (if 2 ∠s of a △ are = the sides opp. are = and the △ is isos.)
9 In $\triangle ABC$ $\angle 1 = \angle 2$ (base ∠s of an isos. △ are =)
$\angle 1 = \angle 3$ (corr. ∠s of ∥ lines are =)
∴ $\angle 3 = \angle 2$ (Ax. 1)
∴ $DA = DE$ (if two ∠s of a △ are =, the sides opp. are =)

Exercise No. 7

1 Perimeter = sum of 4 sides, and the opposite sides of a rectangle are equal. ∴ $P = 550 + 550 + 390 + 390 = 1{,}880$
2 Area of a rectangle = $l \times w$. $110 + 40 \times 64 + 40 = 150 \times 104 = 15{,}600$
3 Area of a square = S^2. $75 \times 75 = 5{,}625 \times .20 = \$1{,}125$
4 $4^2 = 16$; $1{,}024 \div 16 = 64$

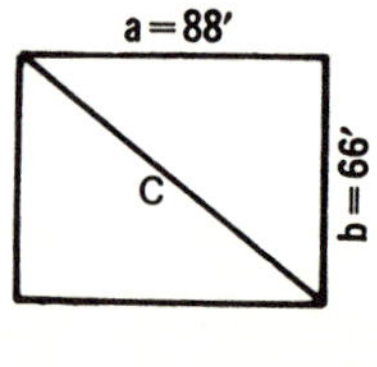

5 Diag. of a rectangle makes 2 rt. angles. $c^2 = a^2 + b^2$.
∴ $c = \sqrt{a^2 + b^2}$,

$c = \sqrt{(88)^2 + (66)^2} = \sqrt{4{,}356 + 7{,}744} = 110$

6 Side of a square is equal to the square root of the area. $S = \sqrt{A} = \sqrt{288}$. Diagonal makes a rt. triangle in which $c^2 = a^2 + b^2$ or $c = \sqrt{288 + 288} = \sqrt{576} = 24$. By formula, diag. of a sq. $= \sqrt{2A}$ or $\sqrt{2 \times 288} = \sqrt{576} = 24$

7 Perimeter = sum of 4 sides. If area = 81, side $= \sqrt{81}$ or 9; $9 \times 4 = 36$; $36 \times .06 =$ \$2.16

8 Area of a trapezoid $= \dfrac{B + b}{2} \times h = \dfrac{60 + 30}{2} \times 15 = 45 \times 15 =$ 675 sq. ft.

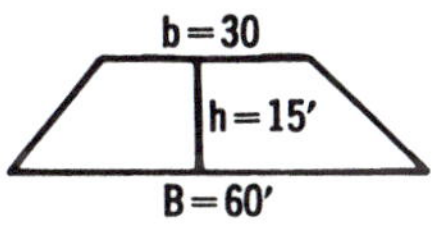

9 Area of a parallelogram equals base times height. $A = bh$. $\therefore =$ $24 \times 14 = 336$ sq. ft.

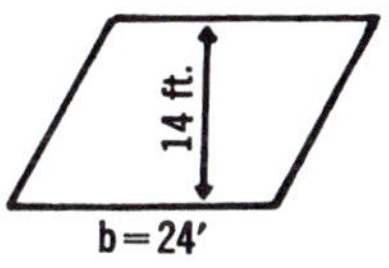

10 To find unknown segment use formula for area of rt. triangle. $c^2 = a^2 + x^2$, or $x = \sqrt{c^2 - a^2} = \sqrt{(10)^2 - (8)^2} = \sqrt{100 - 64} = \sqrt{36} = 6$.

Area of trapezoid $= \dfrac{B + b}{2} \times h$; $\dfrac{18 + 12}{2} \times 8 = 15 \times 8 = 120$

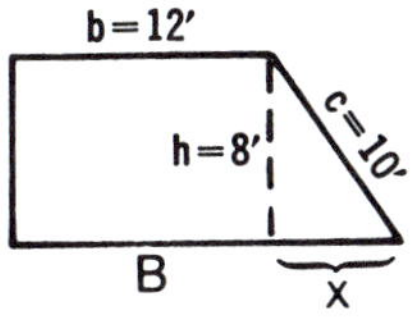

Exercise No. 8

1 $C = \pi d$. $C = \frac{22}{7} \times 28 = 88$ in.

2 $C = 2\pi r$. $r = \dfrac{C}{2\pi}$, $r = \dfrac{110}{\frac{44}{7}} = 110 \times \dfrac{7}{44} = \dfrac{35}{2} = 17\frac{1}{2}$ in.

3 $C = \pi d$. $C = \frac{22}{7} \times 4 = \frac{88}{7}$, $\frac{88}{7} \times 49 = 616$ in.

4 $A = \pi r^2$, $D = 2r$. *If* $D = 14$, then $r = 7$; $A = \frac{22}{7} \times (7)^2 = 154$ sq. in.

5 Area of ring $= \pi R^2 - \pi r^2$. $D = 128$, $d = 96$, $R = 64$, $r = 48$
$A = \pi(64^2 - 48^2) = \frac{22}{7} (4{,}096 - 2{,}304) = \frac{22}{7} \times 1792 = 5{,}632$; $5{,}632 \times .10 =$ \$563.20

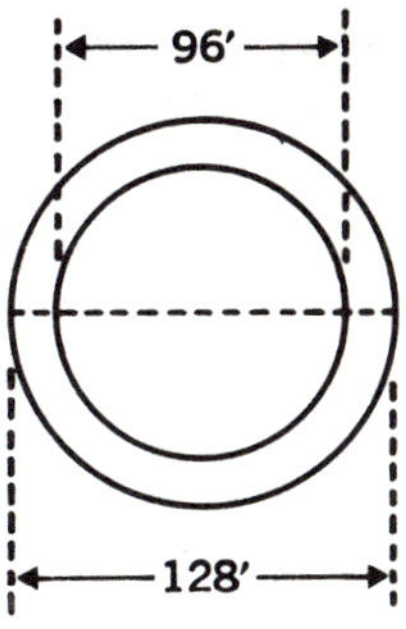

6 $A = \pi r^2$, $r^2 = \dfrac{A}{\pi}$; $r = \sqrt{\dfrac{A}{\pi}} = \sqrt{\dfrac{50\frac{1}{4}}{\frac{22}{7}}} = \sqrt{50\frac{1}{4} \times \frac{7}{22}} = \sqrt{\frac{1407}{88}} = \sqrt{16.1}$. Discarding the decimal, $r = 4$; $D = 2 \times 4$ or 8.

7 Since A = constant times R^2, areas are to each other as the squares of their radii, or $A : a :: R^2 : r^2$. If $R = 2$ and $r = 1$, then $A = \pi \times (2)^2$, and $a = \pi(1)^2$, or 4 to 1. Answer is 4.

8 $R = \sqrt{r^2 + r^2 + r^2 + r^2}$
$= \sqrt{(14)^2 + (14)^2 + (14)^2 + (14)^2}$
$= \sqrt{4(196)} = \sqrt{784} = 28$

9 Area $= \pi R^2 = \frac{22}{7} \times 28^2$. Cost is $\frac{22}{7} \times 28 \times 28 \times \frac{1}{4} = 22 \times 28 =$ \$616.

10 Area of circle $= \pi R^2$. Side of equal square $= \sqrt{\pi R^2} = \sqrt{\frac{22}{7} \times 28 \times 28} = \sqrt{88 \times 28} = \sqrt{2464} = 49.6$ ft.

CHAPTER SIXTEEN

TRIGONOMETRY

Trigonometry is the branch of mathematics that deals with the measurement of triangles. (The word *trigonometry* comes from the Greek and means *to measure a triangle.*) Trigonometry enables us to find the unknown parts of triangles by arithmetical processes. For this reason it is constantly used in surveying, mechanics, navigation, engineering, physics and astronomy.

From geometry you learned that there are many shapes of triangles. For our purpose we can start with the simple case of a right triangle. Starting from this, you will eventually be able to work with all types of triangles because any triangle can be broken down into two right triangles.

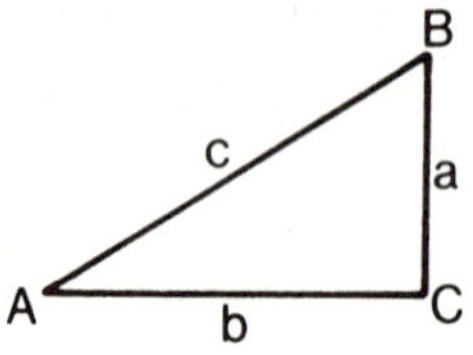

In the right triangle BAC you know from geometry that

(a) $\angle A + \angle B = 90$,

(b) $c^2 = a^2 + b^2$.

From equation (a) you can find one of the acute angles if the other is given, and from equation (b) you can determine the length of any side if the other two are given. But as yet you do not have a method for finding angle A if given the two sides a and b, even though by geometry you could construct the triangle with this information. And this is where trigonometry makes its contribution. It gives you a method for calculating the angles if you know the sides or for calculating the sides if you know the angles.

TRIGONOMETRIC FUNCTIONS OF AN ANGLE

If we take the triangle in the previous figure

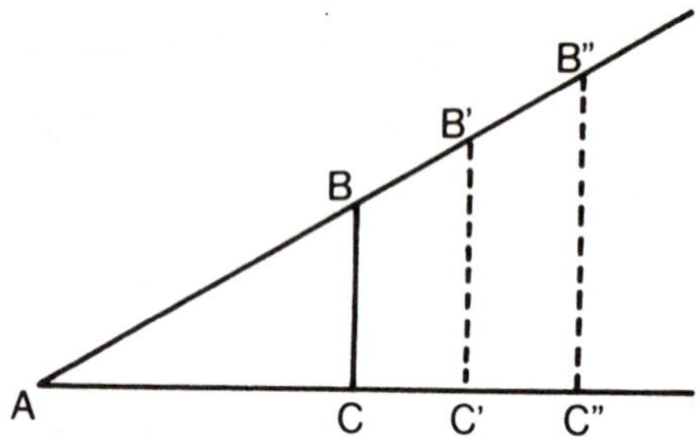

and extend lines AB and AC, and then drop perpendiculars from points B' and B'' to AC, we form three similar triangles:

$$\triangle CAB,\ \triangle C'AB' \text{ and } \triangle C''AB''$$

When two triangles are similar, the ratio of any two sides of one triangle equals the ratio of corresponding sides of the second triangle. Thus in the three triangles of the figure,

$$\frac{BC}{AC} = \frac{B'C'}{AC'} = \frac{B''C''}{AC''}, \text{ or}$$

$$\frac{BC}{AB} = \frac{B'C'}{AB'} = \frac{B''C''}{AB''}.$$

Similar equalities hold for the ratios between the other sides of the triangles.

These equalities between the ratios of the corresponding sides of similar triangles illustrate the fact that *no matter how the size of a right triangle may vary, the values of the ratios of the sides remain the same so long as the acute angles are unchanged.* In other words each of the above ratios is a **function** of angle A.

From algebra and geometry we learn that a variable quantity which depends upon another quantity for its value is called a **function** of the latter value.

Therefore in the above figure the value of the ratio $\frac{BC}{AC}$ is a function of the magnitude of angle A; and as long as the magnitude of angle A remains the same, the value of the ratio $\frac{BC}{AC}$ will be the same.

DESCRIPTION OF THE TANGENT FUNCTION

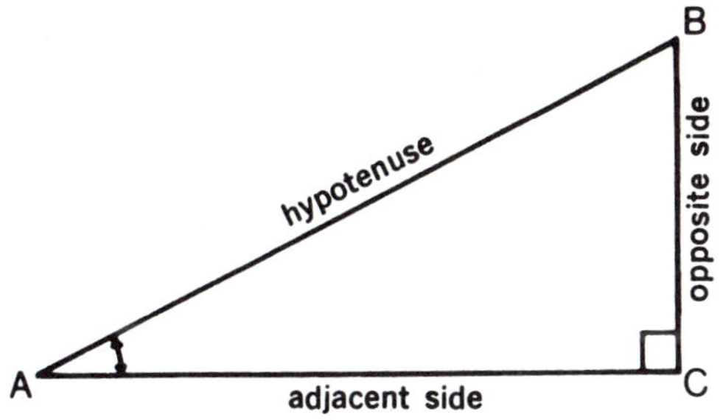

The constant ratio or function, $\frac{BC}{AC}$, is termed the **tangent** of angle A. It will be noted that this function represents the ratio of the side *opposite* angle A divided by the side next to angle A, called the *adjacent* side—that is, the side next to it other than the hypotenuse. Accordingly,

$$\textbf{tangent } \angle A = \frac{\text{opposite side}}{\text{adjacent side}},$$

or

$$\textbf{tan } A = \frac{\text{opp}}{\text{adj}}.$$

MAKING A TABLE OF TRIGONOMETRIC FUNCTIONS

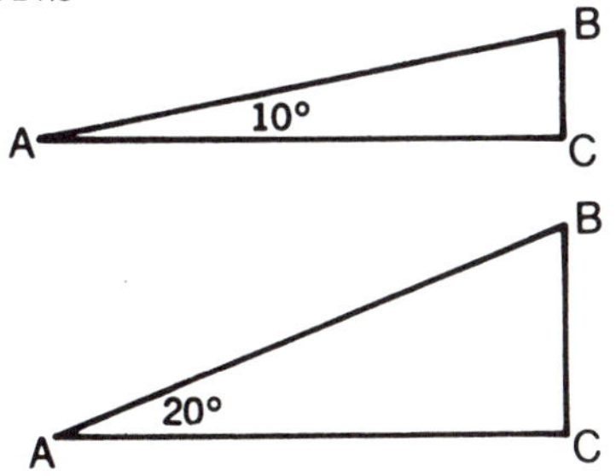

If you construct $\angle A$ equal to 10° and measure BC and AC and then compute the value of $\frac{BC}{AC}$, you will find it to be .176. Then if you construct $\angle A$ to equal 20°, you will find $\frac{BC}{AC}$ equal to .364. For $\angle A$ at 30° you will find $\frac{BC}{AC}$ equal to .577. This means that thereafter you will know that the *tangent* of any angle of 10° in a right triangle is equal to .176, and the tangent of any angle of 20° is equal to .364. Thus by computing the values of the ratios of $\frac{BC}{AC}$ for all angles from 1° to 90° you would obtain a complete table of tangent values. A sample of such a table is shown below.

SAMPLE TABLE OF TRIGONOMETRIC FUNCTIONS

Angle	*Sine*	*Cosine*	*Tangent*
68	.9272	.3746	2.4751
69	.9336	.3584	2.6051
70	.9397	.3420	2.7475
71	.9455	.3256	2.9042
72	.9511	.3090	3.0777

This sample table and the more complete table at the end of this chapter give the tangents of angles to four decimal places. For instance in the table above, to find the value of the tangent of an angle of 69° you first look in the column head *Angle* and find 69°. Then on the same horizontal line in the column headed *Tangent* you find the value 2.6051. This means that tan 69° = 2.6051.

The following example will show how you can solve problems in trigonometry by the use of the table of tangents.

EXAMPLE: An airplane is sighted by two observers. One observer at A indicates it to be directly overhead. The other observer at B, 3,000 feet due west of A, measures its angle of elevation (*see below*) at 70°. What is the altitude of the airplane?

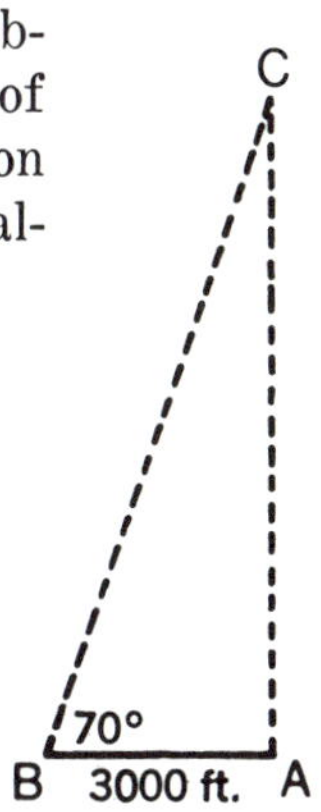

SOLUTION:

$$\tan \angle B = \frac{\text{(opp side)}}{\text{(adj side)}} = \frac{CA}{BA}$$

Since $\angle B = 70°$,
$\tan \angle B = 2.7475.$ (*see table above*)

Substituting, $2.7475 = \frac{CA}{3000}$.

Transposing, $CA = 3000 \times 2.7475$
$= 8242.5$ ft.

Altitude of airplane is 8242.5 ft., ANS.

PRACTICAL OBSERVATION OF ANGLES

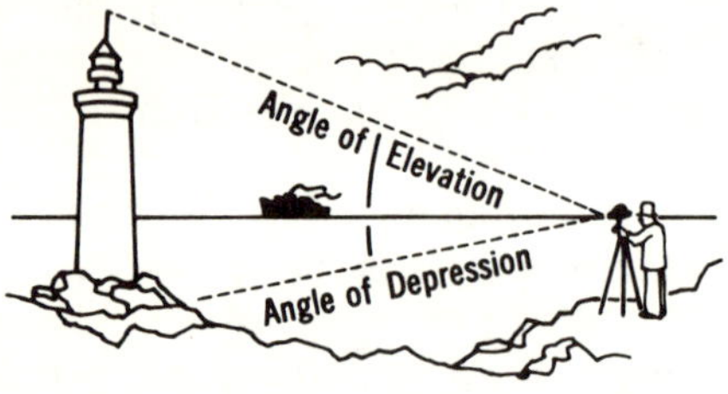

The *angle of elevation or depression* of an object is the angle made between a line from the eye to the object and a horizontal line in the same vertical plane. If the object is above the horizontal line it makes an *angle of elevation;* if below the horizontal line it makes an *angle of depression.*

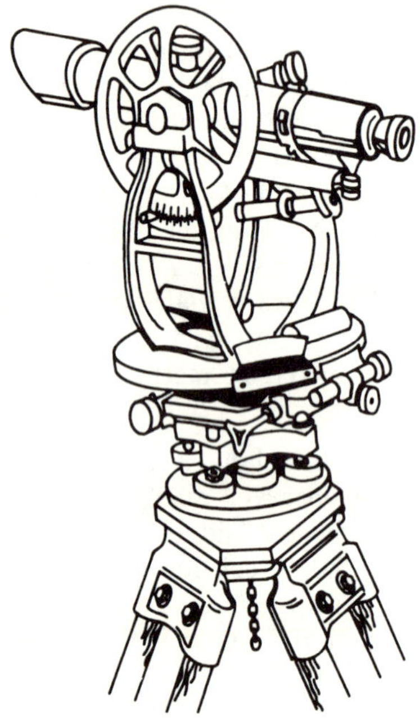

Courtesy of Keuffel & Esser Co., New York

For measuring both vertical and horizontal angles out of doors an engineer's *transit* or *theodolite* is used. As may be seen from the illustration, the instrument combines a telescope with a horizontal and a vertical plate, each of which is graduated by degrees, minutes and seconds. By moving the telescope to right or left, horizontal angles can be measured on the horizontal plate. Vertical angles are measured on the vertical disc by moving the telescope up and down.

THE SIX TRIGONOMETRIC FUNCTIONS

As has been previously pointed out, ratios other than those involved in the *tangent function* exist between the sides of the triangle, and have, like the tangent, an equality of value for a given magnitude of angle, irrespective of the size of the triangle. It is to be expected, therefore, that problems involving the solution of right triangles can be solved by other known trigonometric ratios or functions of the selfsame angle. As a matter of fact, there exist six important ratios or functions for any acute angle of a right triangle. The description and definition of these functions follows.

The sides and angles of triangle *CAB* in the following diagram have been marked in the manner traditionally employed in trigonometry. It is the custom to have the angles represented by capital letters and the sides indicated by the small letter

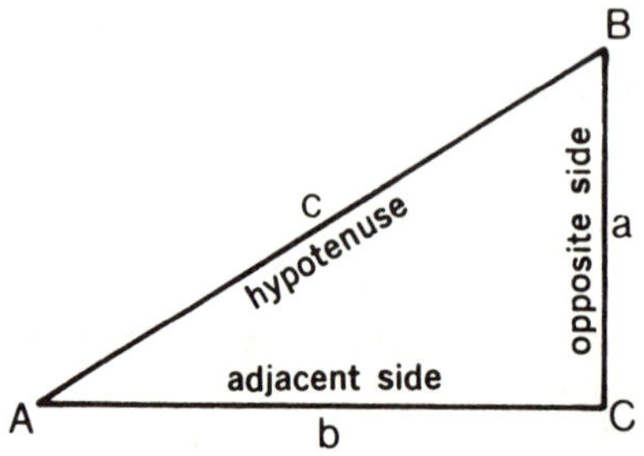

corresponding to the angle opposite the side. Thus the right angle is designated by *C* while the hypotenuse, which is opposite to it, is designated by *c*. Similarly, side *a* is opposite $\angle A$, and side *b* is opposite $\angle B$. Thus we have these six ratios:*

$\frac{a}{c}$ is the **sine** of $\angle A$ (written **sin** *A*).

$\frac{b}{c}$ is the **cosine** of $\angle$A (written **cos** A).

$\frac{a}{b}$ is the **tangent** of $\angle A$ (written **tan** *A*).

$\frac{b}{a}$ is the **cotangent** of $\angle A$ (written **cot** *A*).

$\frac{c}{b}$ is the **secant** of $\angle A$ (written **sec** *A*).

$\frac{c}{a}$ is the **cosecant** of $\angle A$ (written **csc** *A*).

* Two additional functions which are little used are: versed sine $\angle A = 1 - \cos A$ (written vers *A*), and coversed sine $\angle A = 1 - \sin A$ (written covers *A*).

TABLE I

TABLE OF NATURAL TRIGONOMETRIC FUNCTIONS

For explanation of the use of this table see following page.

Angle	Sin	Cos	Tan	Cot	Sec	Csc	
0°	.0000	1.0000	.0000	∞	1.0000	∞	90°
1	.0175	.9998	.0175	57.2900	1.0002	57.2987	89
2	.0349	.9994	.0349	28.6363	1.0006	28.6537	88
3	.0523	.9986	.0524	19.0811	1.0014	19.1073	87
4	.0698	.9976	.0699	14.3007	1.0024	14.3356	86
5°	.0872	.9962	.0875	11.4301	1.0038	11.4737	85°
6	.1045	.9945	.1051	9.5144	1.0055	9.5668	84
7	.1219	.9925	.1228	8.1443	1.0075	8.2055	83
8	.1392	.9903	.1405	7.1154	1.0098	7.1853	82
9	.1564	.9877	.1584	6.3138	1.0125	6.3925	81
10°	.1736	.9848	.1763	5.6713	1.0154	5.7588	80°
11	.1908	.9816	.1944	5.1446	1.0187	5.2408	79
12	.2079	.9781	.2126	4.7046	1.0223	4.8097	78
13	.2250	.9744	.2309	4.3315	1.0263	4.4454	77
14	.2419	.9703	.2493	4.0108	1.0306	4.1336	76
15°	.2588	.9659	.2679	3.7321	1.0353	3.8637	75°
16	.2756	.9613	.2867	3.4874	1.0403	3.6280	74
17	.2924	.9563	.3057	3.2709	1.0457	3.4203	73
18	.3090	.9511	.3249	3.0777	1.0515	3.2361	72
19	.3256	.9455	.3443	2.9042	1.0576	3.0716	71
20°	.3420	.9397	.3640	2.7475	1.0642	2.9238	70°
21	.3584	.9336	.3839	2.6051	1.0711	2.7904	69
22	.3746	.9272	.4040	2.4751	1.0785	2.6695	68
23	.3907	.9205	.4245	2.3559	1.0864	2.5593	67
24	.4067	.9135	.4452	2.2460	1.0946	2.4586	66
25°	.4226	.9063	.4663	2.1445	1.1034	2.3662	65°
26	.4384	.8988	.4877	2.0503	1.1126	2.2812	64
27	.4540	.8910	.5095	1.9626	1.1223	2.2027	63
28	.4695	.8829	.5317	1.8807	1.1326	2.1301	62
29	.4848	.8746	.5543	1.8040	1.1434	2.0627	61
30°	.5000	.8660	.5774	1.7321	1.1547	2.0000	60°
31	.5150	.8572	.6009	1.6643	1.1666	1.9416	59
32	.5299	.8480	.6249	1.6003	1.1792	1.8871	58
33	.5446	.8387	.6494	1.5399	1.1924	1.8361	57
34	.5592	.8290	.6745	1.4826	1.2062	1.7883	56
35°	.5736	.8192	.7002	1.4281	1.2208	1.7434	55°
36	.5878	.8090	.7265	1.3764	1.2361	1.7013	54
37	.6018	.7986	.7536	1.3270	1.2521	1.6616	53
38	.6157	.7880	.7813	1.2799	1.2690	1.6243	52
39	.6293	.7771	.8098	1.2349	1.2868	1.5890	51
40°	.6428	.7660	.8391	1.1918	1.3054	1.5557	50°
41	.6561	.7547	.8693	1.1504	1.3250	1.5243	49
42	.6691	.7431	.9004	1.1106	1.3456	1.4945	48
43	.6820	.7314	.9325	1.0724	1.3673	1.4663	47
44	.6947	.7193	.9657	1.0355	1.3902	1.4396	46
45°	.7071	.7071	1.0000	1.0000	1.4142	1.4142	45°
	Cos	Sin	Cot	Tan	Csc	Sec	Angle

Using self-explanatory abbreviations, we thus have by definition:

$$\sin A = \frac{\text{opp}}{\text{hyp}} = \frac{a}{c}, \qquad \cos A = \frac{\text{adj}}{\text{hyp}} = \frac{b}{c},$$

$$\tan A = \frac{\text{opp}}{\text{adj}} = \frac{a}{b}, \qquad \cot A = \frac{\text{adj}}{\text{opp}} = \frac{b}{a},$$

$$\sec A = \frac{\text{hyp}}{\text{adj}} = \frac{c}{b}, \qquad \csc A = \frac{\text{hyp}}{\text{opp}} = \frac{c}{a}.$$

This table of definitions of the trigonometric functions should be committed to memory.

Practice Exercise No. 1

1 In the preceeding figure, $\tan B = \frac{b}{a}$. Write the other five functions of $\angle B$.

2 Which is greater, $\sin A$ or $\tan A$?

3 Which is greater, $\cos A$ or $\cot A$?

4 Which is greater, $\sec A$ or $\tan A$?

5 Which is greater, $\csc A$ or $\cot A$?

6 $\text{Sin } A = \frac{3}{5}$. What is the value of $\cos A$?
Hint: Use rt. △ formula $c^2 = a^2 + b^2$ to find side b.

7 $\text{Tan } A = \frac{3}{4}$. What is the value of $\sin A$?

8 $\text{Sin } A = \frac{8}{17}$. Find $\cos A$.

9 $\text{Cot } A = \frac{15}{8}$. Find $\sec A$.

10 Find the value of the other five functions of A if $\sin A = \frac{5}{13}$.

RELATIONS BETWEEN FUNCTIONS OF COMPLEMENTARY ANGLES

If you observe the relations between the functions of the two acute angles of the same right triangle, you will note that every function of each of the two acute angles is equal to a different function of the other acute angle. These correspondences of value are demonstrated in the following.

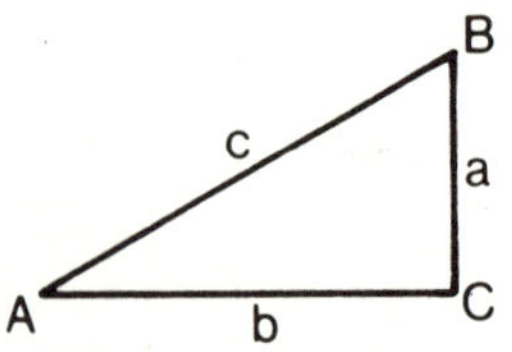

$$\sin A = \frac{a}{c} \text{ and } \cos B = \frac{a}{c},$$

$$\cos A = \frac{b}{c} \text{ and } \sin B = \frac{b}{c},$$

$$\tan A = \frac{a}{b} \text{ and } \cot B = \frac{a}{b}, \text{ etc.}$$

Thus we have:

$$\sin A = \cos B, \qquad \cot A = \tan B$$
$$\cos A = \sin B, \qquad \sec A = \csc B$$
$$\tan A = \cot B, \qquad \csc A = \sec B$$

From these equalities it will be evident that any function of an acute angle of a right triangle equals the co-function of the complement of that angle.*

For example, $\tan 40° = \cot 50°$; $\sin 70° = \cos 20°$; $\csc 41° 20' = \sec 48° 40'$.

Since angles A and B are complementary, another way of writing these equations is as follows:

$$\sin (90° - A) = \cos A, \qquad \cot (90° - A) = \tan A$$
$$\cos (90° - A) = \sin A, \qquad \sec (90° - A) = \csc A$$
$$\tan (90° - A) = \cot A, \qquad \csc (90° - A) = \sec A$$

Practice Exercise No. 2

Fill in the blanks in examples 1–6 with the equivalent co-functions

1 $\sin 26° =$

2 $\tan 43° =$

3 $\cos 24° 28' =$

4 $\cot 88° 50' =$

5 $\sec 6° 10' =$

6 $\csc 77\frac{1}{2}° =$

7 How many degrees must $\angle A$ be if $90° - A = 5A$?

8 What is the value of $\angle A$ if $\tan A = \cot A$?

9 Find A if $90° - A = A$.

10 Find A if $\cos A = \sin 2A$.

HOW TO USE A TABLE OF TRIGONOMETRIC FUNCTIONS

From the foregoing it becomes apparent that you can easily compute the functions of any angle greater than 45° if you know the functions of all angles between 0° and 45°. Therefore in a table of trigonometric functions, such as appears on the preceding page, it is only necessary to have a direct table of functions for angles from 0° to 45°, since the function of any angle above 45° is equal to the co-function of its complement.

* The name *cosine* means *complement's sine.* It is a contraction from the Latin *complementi sinus.* The words *cotangent* and *cosecant* were derived in the same manner.

To find the functions of angles from 0° *to* 45° *read the table from the top down, using the values of angles at the left and the headings at the top of the table. To find the functions of angles from* 45° *to* 90° *read from the bottom up, using the values of angles at the right and the function designations at the bottom of the table.*

If you know the value of the function of an angle and wish to find the angle, look in the body of the table in the proper column and then read the magnitude of the angle in the corresponding row of one or the other of the angle columns.

For example, you are told that the sine of a certain angle is .5000 and wish to find the angle. Look in the *Sin* column, locate .5000 and read the angle value (30°) from the left *Angle* column. If this value had been given to you as a cosine, you would have noted that it does not appear in the column headed *Cos* at the top but does appear in the column that has *Cos* at the bottom. Hence you would then use the *Angle* column at the right and find .5000 to be the cosine of 60°.

You should become thoroughly familiar with the use of the table. To this end you can supplement the following exercise by making up your own examples.

Practice Exercise No. 3

From the table of trigonometric functions find the values required in examples 1–15:

1	sin 8°	6	cos 25°	11	cos 62°
2	sin 42°	7	csc 14°	12	tan 56°
3	tan 40°	8	sin 78°	13	sin 58°
4	cot 63°	9	cot 69°	14	cos 45°
5	sec 22°	10	sec 81°	15	sin 30°

16 Find the angle whose sine is .2588.
17 Find the angle whose tangent is .7002.
18 Find the angle whose cosine is .5000.
19 Find the angle whose secant is 2.9238.
20 Find the angle, whose cotangent is 5.6713.

FUNCTIONS OF 45°, 30°, AND 60° ANGLES

For some rather common angles the exact values of their functions can be easily found by the application of elementary principles of geometry.

Functions of a 45° *Angle*

In the isosceles right triangle *ACB*, if $\angle A = 45°$, then $\angle B = 45°$, and therefore side a = side b. Now if we let side a equal 1 or unity, then from the right triangle formula of

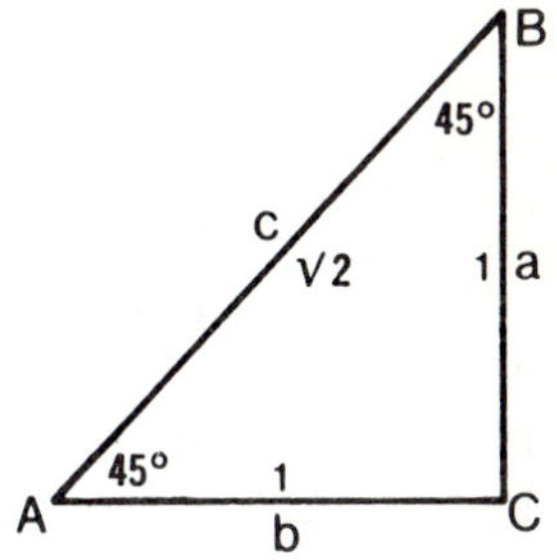

$$a^2 + b^2 = c^2$$

we get

$$c = \sqrt{1+1} \text{ or } \sqrt{2}$$

(taking the square root of both sides of the equation). Now since any trigonometric function of an acute angle is equal to the corresponding co-function of its complement, therefore

$$\sin 45° = \frac{1}{\sqrt{2}} \text{ or } \tfrac{1}{2}\sqrt{2} = \cos 45°,$$

$$\tan 45° = \frac{1}{1} \text{ or } 1 = \cot 45°,$$

$$\sec 45° = \frac{\sqrt{2}}{1} \text{ or } \sqrt{2} = \csc 45°.$$

Functions of 30° *and* 60° *Angles*

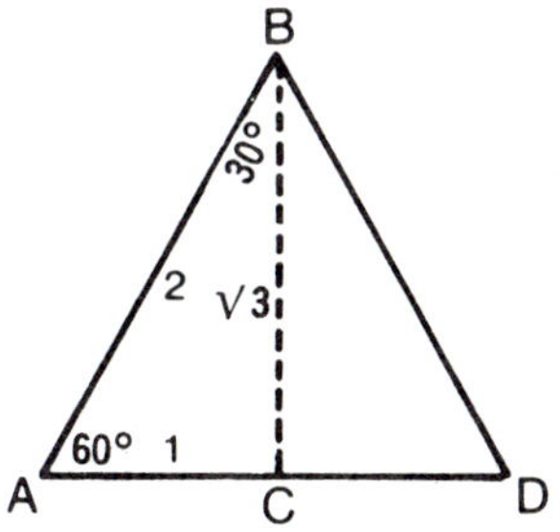

In the equilateral triangle *ABD* the three sides are equal and the three angles each equal 60°. If we drop a perpendicular from *B* to *AD*, it bisects $\angle B$ and the base *AD* at *C*.

If we let the length of each of the sides equal 2 units, then $AC = CD = 1$; and in the right triangle *ACB*.

$$\angle B = 30°, \angle C = 90°, \angle A = 60°$$

$$AC = 1, AB = 2$$

Then, since $(AB)^2 = (AC)^2 + (BC)^2$, it follows that $(BC)^2 = 3$ and $BC = \sqrt{3}$.

Thus in the right triangle *ACB*

$$\sin 30° = \tfrac{1}{2} = \cos 60°,$$

$$\tan 30° = \frac{1}{\sqrt{3}} \text{ or } \tfrac{1}{3}\sqrt{3} = \cot 60°,$$

$$\sec 30° = \frac{2}{\sqrt{3}} \text{ or } \tfrac{2}{3}\sqrt{3} = \csc 60°,$$

$$\cos 30° = \frac{\sqrt{3}}{2} = \sin 60°,$$

$$\cot 30° = \frac{\sqrt{3}}{1} \text{ or } \sqrt{3} = \tan 60°,$$

$$\csc 30^\circ = \frac{2}{1} \text{ or } 2 = \sec 60^\circ.$$

It is an advantage to know the values of the 30°, 45° and 60° angles by heart. To help yourself memorize them, fill in the outline of the table below with the proper values of the functions.

Function	30°	60°	45°
Sine			
Cosine			
Tangent			
Cotangent			
Secant			
Cosecant			

INTERPOLATION

Interpolation is used in trigonometry in connection with the table of functions. For example, if given the function of an angle that is measured in degrees and minutes, such as sin 30° 40′, its exact value could not be found directly from the table but would have to be computed by the method of interpolation. Again, if given the value of a trigonometric function such as tan $A = .7400$, which does not appear in the body of the table, it means that the corresponding angle is expressed in units more exact than the nearest degree and must be found by interpolation. The following examples will illustrate the method of performing interpolations with reference to the table of trigonometric functions.

EXAMPLE 1: Find sin 30° 40′.

SOLUTION: sin 30° 40′ is between sin 30° and sin 31°.

Since there are 60′ in 1°, 40′ = $\frac{2}{3}$ of 1°

From the table sin 30° = .5000
sin 31° = .5150
Difference = .0150

sin 30° = .5000
$\frac{2}{3}$ of .0150 = .0100
sin 30° 40′ = .5100, ANS.

Note: In this case we added the proportional part of the difference (.0100) to the value of sin 30° because the sine of an angle *increases* as the angle increases.

EXAMPLE 2: Find cos 59° 48′.

SOLUTION: cos 59° 48′ is between cos 59° and cos 60°.

48′ is $\frac{4}{5}$ of 1°.

From the table cos 59° = .5150
cos 60° = .5000
Difference = .0150

cos 59° = .5150
$\frac{4}{5}$ of .0150 = .0120
cos 59° 48′ = .5030, ANS.

Note: In this case we subtracted the proportional part of the difference (.0120) from the value of cos 59° because the cosine of an angle *decreases* as the angle increases.

EXAMPLE 3: Find $\angle A$ if tan $A = .7400$.

SOLUTION: From the table, in the tan column, we see that .7400 is between tan 36° and tan 37°.

tan 37° = .7536
tan 36° = .7265
Difference = .0271

tan A = .7400
tan 36° = .7265
Difference = .0135

The proportional difference between tan A and tan 36° is .0135. The difference between tan 36° and tan 37° is .0271.

$\frac{.0135}{.0271}$ of 1° or 60′ equals $\frac{1}{2}$° or 30′

∴ tan A = 36° + 30′ = 36° 30′, ANS.

Further familiarity with the table of functions will indicate the following about variations of the trigonometric functions.

As an angle increases from 0° to 90°, its:

sine *increases* from 0 to 1,
cosine *decreases* from 1 to 0,
tangent *increases* from 0 to ∞,
cotangent *decreases* from ∞ to 0,
secant *increases* from 1 to ∞,
cosecant *decreases* from ∞ to 1.

Also note that:

sines and cosines are never > 1,
secants and cosecants are never < 1,
tangents and cotangents may have any value from 0 to ∞.*

* The symbol ∞ denotes "infinity" and is used in mathematics to represent a number that is indefinitely large, or larger than any preassignable quantity. The sign > means greater than, and < means less than.

Practice Exercise No. 4

Find by interpolation the values of the functions in examples 1–5:

1 sin 15° 30′
2 cos 25° 40′
3 tan 47° 10′
4 cot 52° 30′
5 sec 40° 30′

Find by the interpolation method the value of ∠A to the nearest minute in examples 6–10:

6 $\sin A = .0901$
7 $\tan A = .3411$
8 $\cos A = .4173$
9 $\cot A = .8491$
10 $\csc A = 1.4804$

RECIPROCALS AMONG THE FUNCTIONS

If you inspect the ratios of the six functions of ∠A, you will readily note that they are not independent of each other. In fact, if you line them up as follows:

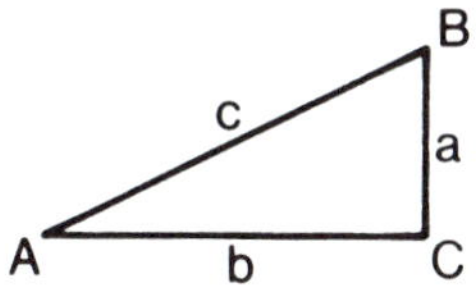

$$\sin A = \frac{a}{c}, \qquad \csc A = \frac{c}{a}$$

$$\cos A = \frac{b}{c}, \qquad \sec A = \frac{c}{b}$$

$$\tan A = \frac{a}{b}, \qquad \cot A = \frac{b}{a}$$

it becomes obvious that *the sine is the reciprocal of the cosecant, the cosine is the reciprocal of the secant, and the tangent is the reciprocal of the cotangent.* Accordingly,

$$\sin A = \frac{1}{\csc A} \qquad \cos A = \frac{1}{\sec A}$$

$$\tan A = \frac{1}{\cot A} \qquad \csc A = \frac{1}{\sin A}$$

$$\sec A = \frac{1}{\cos A} \qquad \cot A = \frac{1}{\tan A}$$

Therefore:

$$\sin A \times \csc A = 1, \quad \cos A \times \sec A = 1$$

$$\tan A \times \cot A = 1$$

In accordance with the usual algebraic method of notation (by which ab is equivalent to $a \times b$) these relationships are usually written:

$$\sin A \csc A = 1, \quad \cos A \sec A = 1$$

$$\tan A \cot A = 1$$

To illustrate such a relation, find, for example, in the table of functions the tangent and the cotangent of 30°.

$$\tan 30° = .5774, \quad \cot 30° = 1.7321$$

$$\tan 30° \cot 30° = .5774 \times 1.7321$$
$$= 1.00011454$$

INTERRELATIONS AMONG THE FUNCTIONS

Since $\tan A = \frac{a}{b}$, $\sin A = \frac{a}{c}$, and $\cos A = \frac{b}{c}$, it follows that

$\tan A = \frac{\sin A}{\cos A}$, and $\sin A = \tan A \cos A$.

The student will the more readily grasp these interrelations if instead of considering only abstract values, he translates these into actual numbers. The 3–4–5 right triangle in the diagram will serve this purpose.

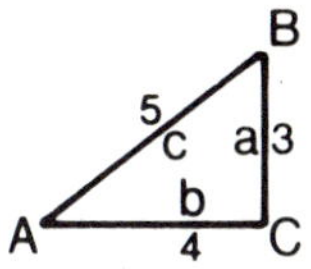

From the interrelations of sine, cosine and tangent it follows that if we know two of these values, we can always find the third.

From the Pythagorean theorem of the right triangle we know that $a^2 + b^2 = c^2$. If we divide both sides of this equation by c^2, we get

$$\frac{a^2}{c^2} + \frac{b^2}{c^2} = 1.$$

Since $\frac{a}{c} = \sin A$ and $\frac{b}{c} = \cos A$, it follows that

(1) $\sin^2 A + \cos^2 A = 1$*

Therefore

(2) $\sin A = \sqrt{1 - \cos^2 A}$ and

(3) $\cos A = \sqrt{1 - \sin^2 A}$

* $(\sin A)^2$ is customarily written as $\sin^2 A$, and likewise for the other functions.

MAKING PRACTICAL USE OF THE FUNCTIONS

With the information on trigonometry outlined in the previous pages you will be able to solve many triangles if you know three parts one of which is a side. And in the case of the right triangle, since the right angle is a part of it, you need only to know two other parts one of which must be a side.

As will be brought out in the practice exercises that follow, these trigonometric methods of solving triangles are used daily in handling problems that arise in military operations, engineering, navigation, shopwork, physics, surveying, etc.

You should adopt a planned method of procedure in solving problems. One such method is as follows.

1. After reading the problem, draw a figure to a convenient scale, and in it show those lines and angles which are given and those which are to be found.

2. Write down all the formulas that apply to the particular problem.

3. Substitute the given data in the proper formulas, and solve for the unknowns.

4. Check your results.

Incidentally we would suggest that you work with a hard lead pencil or a fine-pointed pen. Nothing is of greater help to accuracy in mathematics than neatness of work, and neatness is next to impossible if you use writing instruments that make thick lines and sprawly figures.

Applying the Sine Function,

$$\sin A = \frac{\text{opp}}{\text{hyp}} = \frac{a}{c}$$

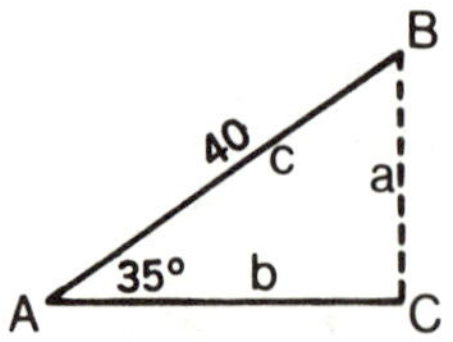

EXAMPLE 1: In the accompanying figure $c = 40$ and $\angle A = 35°$. Find a.

SOLUTION: $\frac{a}{c} = \sin A$, $a = c \sin A$

$\sin 35° = .5736$, $c = 40$
$c \sin A = 40 \times .5736 = 22.944$
$a = 22.944$, ANS.

CHECK: $\frac{a}{c} = \sin A$

$$\frac{22.944}{40} = .5736 \text{ which is } \sin 35°.$$

EXAMPLE 2: Given $c = 48$ and $\angle B = 22°$, find a by means of the sine formula.

SOLUTION: $\frac{a}{c} = \sin A$, $a = c \sin A$,

$\angle A = 90° - \angle B$, $\angle A = 90° - 22° = 68°$,
$\sin 68° = .9272$, $c = 48$,
$c \sin A = 48 \times .9272 = 44.5056$,
$a = 44.50+$, ANS.

CHECK: $\frac{a}{c} = A.$

$$\frac{44.5056}{48} = .9272 \text{ which is } \sin 68°.$$

Practice Exercise No. 5

The problems in this exercise should be solved by using the sine function. Answers need be accurate only to the first decimal place.

1 Given $c = 100$, $\angle A = 33°$, find a.
2 Given $c = 10$, $\angle A = 20°$, find a.
3 Given $a = 71$, $c = 78$, find $\angle A$.
4 Given $a = 14$, $\angle A = 28°$, find c.
5 Given $c = 50$, $a = 36$, find $\angle A$.

6 An airplane is 405 feet above a landing field when the pilot cuts out his motor. He glides to a landing at an angle of 13° with the field. How far will he glide in reaching the field?

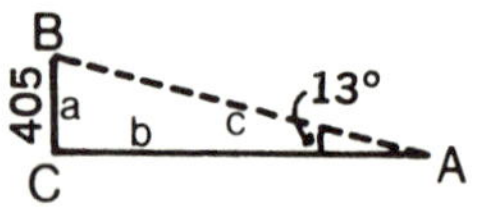

(A) 300 ft. ____ (C) 1,800 ft. ____
(B) 1,248 ft. ____ (D) 1,641 ft. ____

7 An ascension balloon is moored by a rope 150 ft. long. A wind blowing in an easterly direction keeps the rope taut and causes it to make an angle of 50° with the ground. What is the vertical height of the balloon from the ground?

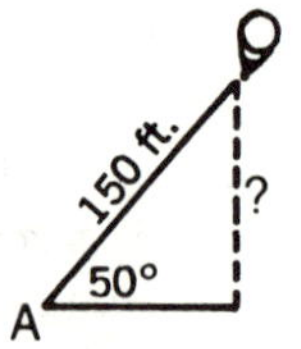

(A) 180 ft. ____ (C) 177.5 ft. ____
(B) 114.9 ft. ____ (D) 189.4 ft. ____

8 A carpenter has to build a ramp to be used as a loading platform for a carrier airplane. The height of the loading door is 12 ft., and the required slope or gradient of the ramp is to be 18°. How long must the ramp be?

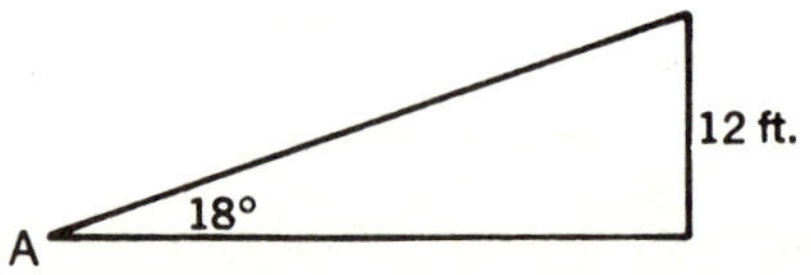

(A) 24 ft. ____ (C) 48.42 ft. ____
(B) 38.83 ft. ____ (D) 10.14 ft. ____

9 The fire department has a new 200-ft. ladder. The greatest angle at which it can be placed against a building with safety is at 71° with the ground. What is the maximum vertical height that the ladder can reach?

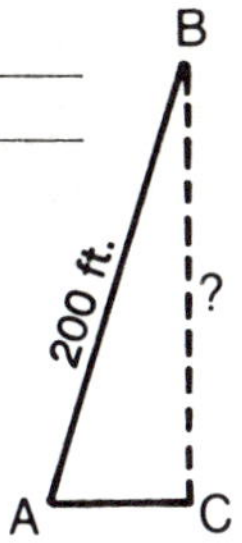

(A) 189.1 ft. ____ (C) 300 ft. ____
(B) 209.4 ft. ____ (D) 162.3 ft. ____

10 A road running from the bottom of a hill to the top is 625 ft. long. If the hill is $54\frac{1}{2}$ ft. high, what is the angle of elevation of the road?

(A) 25° ____ (C) 5° ____
(B) 15° ____ (D) 2° ____

Applying the Cosine Function,

$$\cos A = \frac{\text{adj}}{\text{hyp}} = \frac{b}{c}.$$

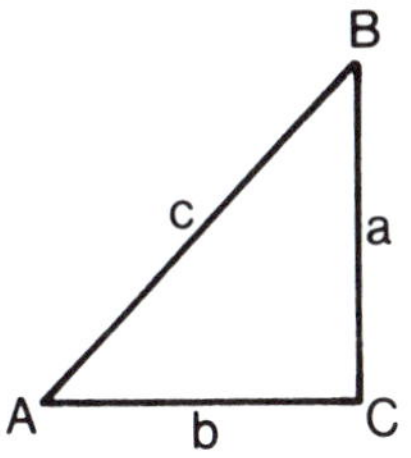

EXAMPLE 1: In the accompanying figure $c = 36$ and $\angle A = 40°$. Find b.

SOLUTION: $\frac{b}{c} = \cos A, \qquad b = c \cos A.$

$\cos 40° = .7660$
$c = 36$
$c \cos A = 36 \times .7660 = 27.576$
$b = 27.58$, ANS.

CHECK: $\frac{b}{c} = \cos A, \frac{27.576}{36} = .7660$ or $\cos 40°$.

EXAMPLE 2: Given $b = 26$ and $\angle A = 22°$; find c.

SOLUTION: $\frac{b}{c} = \cos A, \quad c = \frac{b}{\cos A},$

$b = 26$
$\cos 22° = .9272$

$$\frac{b}{\cos A} = 26 \div .9272 = 28.04$$

$c = 28.04$, ANS.

CHECK: $\frac{b}{c} = \cos A$

$\frac{26}{28.04} = .9272$ which is $\cos 22°$.

Practice Exercise No. 6

Use this cosine function in solving the problems in this exercise.

1 Given $c = 400$, $b = 240$; fiind $\angle A$.
2 Given $c = 41$, $\angle A = 39°$; find b.
3 Given $c = 67.7$, $\angle A = 23° 30'$; find b.
4 Given $c = 187$, $b = 93\frac{1}{2}$; find $\angle A$.
5 Given $b = 40$, $\angle A = 18°$, find c.

6 A carpenter has to build a triangular roof to a house. The roof is to be 30 feet wide. If the rafters are 17 feet long, at what angle will the rafters be laid at the eaves?

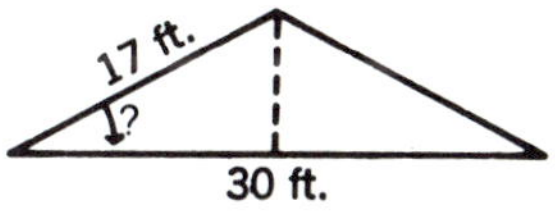

(A) 34° ____ (C) 28° 05′ ____
(B) 19° 30′ ____ (D) 42° 10′ ____

7 Desiring to measure distance across a pond, a surveyor standing at point A sighted on a point B across the pond. From A he ran a line AC, making an angle of 27° with AB. From B he ran a line perpendicular to AC. He measured the line AC to be 681 feet. What is the distance across the pond from A to B?

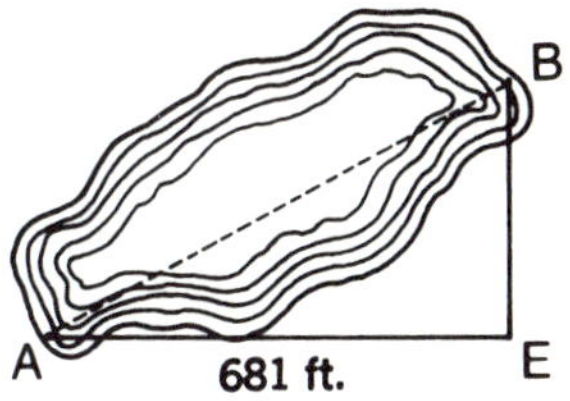

(A) 100 ft. ____ (C) 681 ft. ____
(B) 764.3 ft. ____ (D) 862.8 ft. ____

8 A scout on a hill 125 feet above a lake sights a boat on the water at an angle of depression of 10° as shown. What is the exact distance from the scout to the boat?

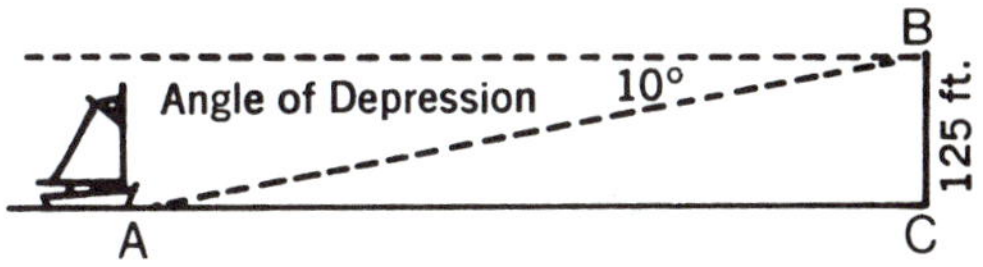

(A) 240.5 ft. ____ (C) 468.4 ft. ____
(B) 720 ft. ____ (D) 1020 ft. ____

9 A mountain climber stretches a cord from the rocky ledge of a sheer cliff to a point on a horizontal plane, making an angle of 50° with the ledge. The cord is 84 feet

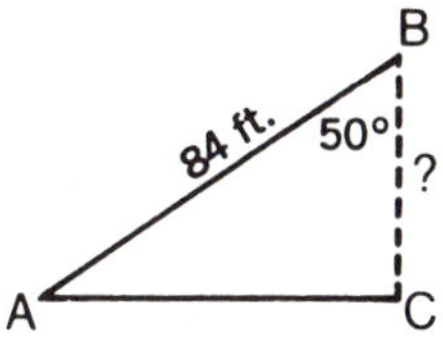

long. What is the vertical height of the rocky ledge from its base?

(A) 45 ft. ____ (C) 76.8 ft. ____
(B) 82 ft. ____ (D) 54 ft. ____

10 A 100-foot ladder is placed against the side of a house with the foot of the ladder $16\frac{1}{2}$ feet away from the building. What angle does the ladder make with the ground?

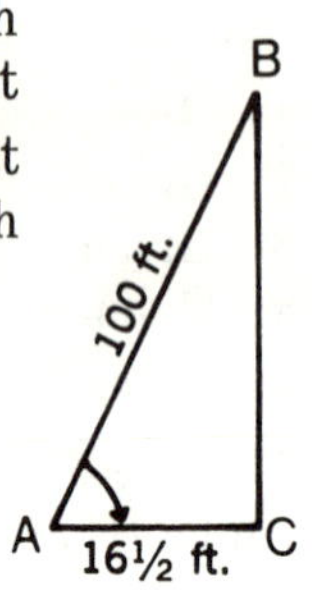

(A) 65° ____
(B) 25° 40′ ____
(C) 80° 30′ ____
(D) 72° 20′ ____

Applying the Tangent Function,

$$\tan A = \frac{\text{opp}}{\text{adj}} = \frac{a}{b}.$$

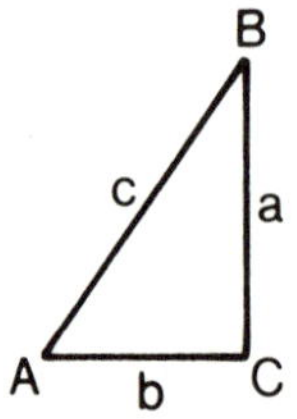

EXAMPLE 1: In the accompanying figure $a = 40$ and $b = 27$. Find $\angle A$.

SOLUTION: $\frac{a}{b} = \tan A, \quad a = 40, \quad b = 27,$

$$\frac{40}{27} = 1.4815,$$

$\tan A = 1.4815, \quad \angle A = 55° \ 59'$, ANS.

CHECK: $a = b \tan A$; $27 \times 1.4815 = 40$ which is a.

EXAMPLE 2: Given angle $A = 28°$ and $a = 29$. Find b.

SOLUTION: $\frac{a}{b} = \tan A, \ b = \frac{a}{\tan A},$

$$a = 29, \quad \tan 28° = .5317, \quad \frac{29}{.5317} = 54.54,$$

$b = 54.54$, ANS.

CHECK: $\frac{a}{b} = \tan A,$

$$\frac{29}{54.54} = .5317 \text{ which is } \tan A.$$

Practice Exercise No. 7

Use the tangent function in solving the problems in this exercise.

1 Given $a = 18$, $b = 24$; find $\angle A$.
2 Given $b = 64$, $\angle A = 45°$; find a.
3 Given $b = 62$, $\angle A = 36°$; find a.
4 Given $\angle A = 70°$, $a = 50$; find b.
5 Given $\angle A = 19° \ 36'$, $b = 42$; find a.

6 An engineer desires to learn the height of a cone-shaped hill. He measures its diameter to be 280 feet. From a point on the circumference of the base he determines that the angle of elevation is 43°. What is the altitude?

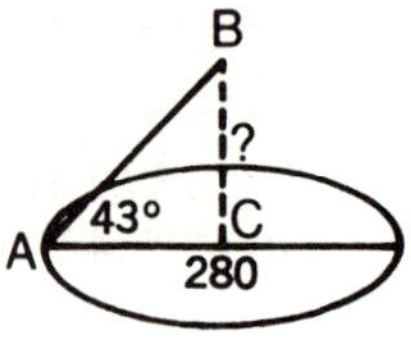

(A) 130.55 ft. ____ (C) 125.45 ft. ____
(B) 260 ft. ____ (D) 560 ft. ____

7 From a lookout tower 240 feet high an enemy tank division is sighted at an angle of depression which is measured to be 10°. How far is the enemy away from the lookout tower if they are both on the same level?

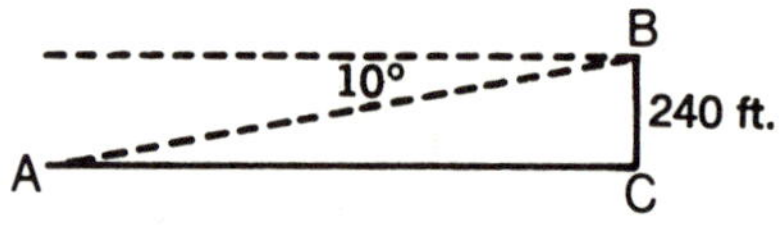

(A) 1,361.11 ft. ____ (C) 866 ft. ____
(B) 642.25 ft. ____ (D) 2,434.16 ft. ____

8 The upper deck of a ship stands 30 feet above the level of its dock. A runway to the deck is to be built having an angle of inclination of 20°. How far from the boat should it start?

(A) 60 ft. ____
(B) 76.25 ft. ____
(C) 82.42 ft. ____
(D) 42.30 ft. ____

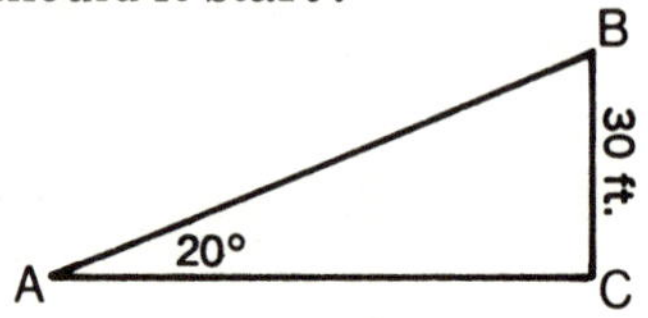

9 From a boathouse 100 feet above the level of a lake two rowing crews were sighted racing in the direction of the boathouse. The boats were directly in a line with each other. The leading boat was sighted at an angle of depression equal to 15°, and the other at 14°. How far apart were the boats?

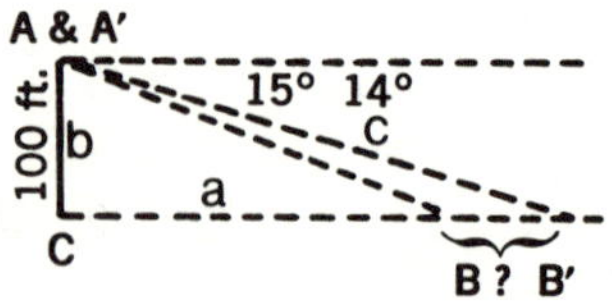

(A) 373.21 ft. ____ (C) 64.14 ft. ____
(B) 27.87 ft. ____ (D) 401.08 ft. ____

10 A clock on the tower of a building is ob-

served from two points which are on the same level and in the same straight line with the foot of the tower. At the nearer point the angle of elevation to the clock is 60°, and at the farther point it is 30°. If the two points are 300 feet apart, what is the height of the clock?

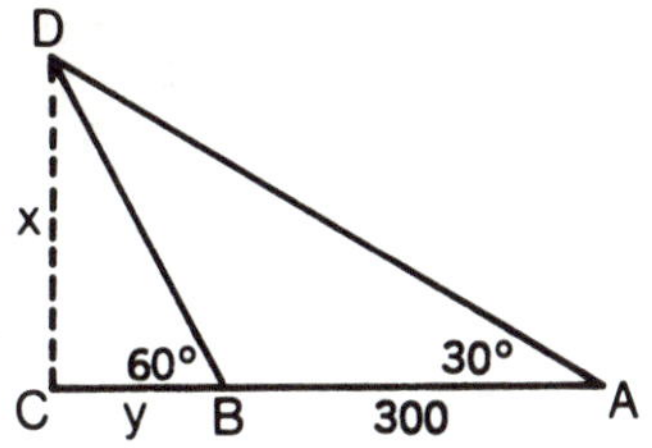

(A) 130.8 ft. ____ (C) 259.8 ft. ____
(B) 400 ft. ____ (D) 360.4 ft. ____

THE OBLIQUE TRIANGLE

As previously stated, you can use right triangle methods to solve most oblique triangles by introducing perpendiculars and resolving the oblique triangle into two right triangles.

For example:

1. Triangle *ABC* can be resolved into right triangles *ADC* and *BDC* by introducing the perpendicular *CD*.

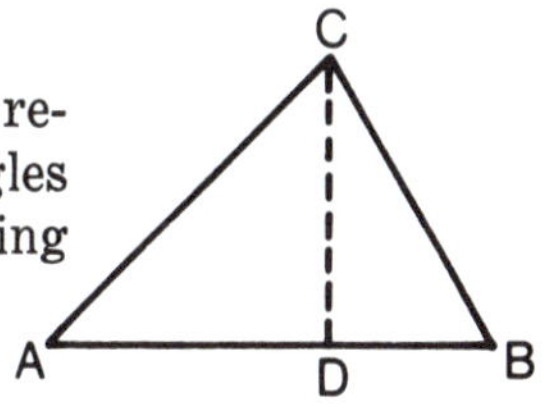

2. Triangle *DEF* can be resolved into right triangles *DGF* and *EGF* by extending *DE* and dropping the perpendicular *FG*.

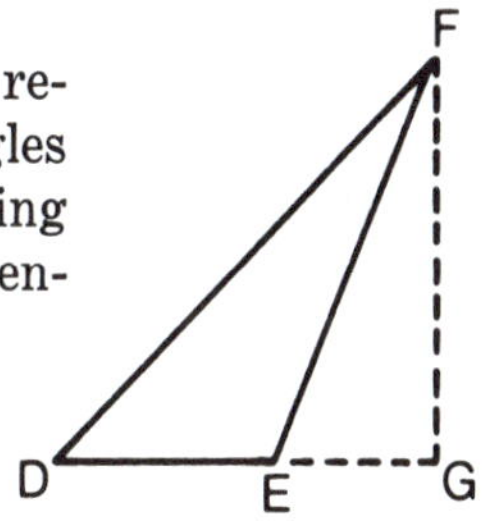

3. Triangle *HJK* can be resolved into right triangles *HLJ* and *KLJ* by introducing the perpendicular *JL*.

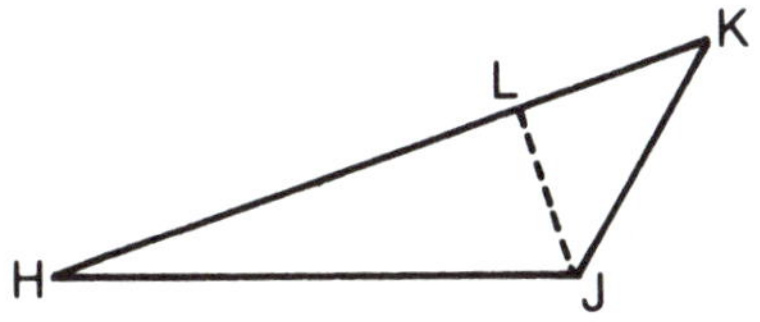

In practical problems, however, it is often impossible or too cumbersome to use a right triangle, and in such cases formulas for oblique angles are needed.*

There are three important formulas that may be used in the solution of triangles of any shape. They are known as the *law of sines*, the *law of cosines* and the *law of tangents*.

For our purposes it will be sufficient to state the law, give the corresponding formulas and show the application of the law to the solution of problems involving oblique triangles.†

The law of sines: *The sides of a triangle are proportional to the sines of their opposite angles:*

$$\frac{a}{\sin A} = \frac{b}{\sin B} = \frac{c}{\sin C}, \text{ or}$$

$$\frac{a}{b} = \frac{\sin A}{\sin B}, \frac{b}{c} = \frac{\sin B}{\sin C}, \frac{a}{c} = \frac{\sin A}{\sin C}.$$

The law of cosines: *The square of any side of a triangle is equal to the sum of the squares of the other two sides minus twice their product times the cosine of the included angle.*

$$a^2 = b^2 + c^2 - 2bc \cos A,$$
$$b^2 = a^2 + c^2 - 2ac \cos B,$$
$$c^2 = a^2 + b^2 - 2ab \cos C, \text{ or}$$
$$a = \sqrt{b^2 + c^2 - 2bc \cos A},$$
$$b = \sqrt{a^2 + c^2 - 2ac \cos B},$$
$$c = \sqrt{a^2 + b^2 - 2ab \cos C}.$$

The law of tangents: *The difference between any two sides of a triangle is to their sum as the tangent of half the difference between their opposite angles is to tangent of half their sum.*

$$\frac{a-b}{a+b} = \frac{\tan \frac{1}{2}(A-B)}{\tan \frac{1}{2}(A+B)},$$
$$\frac{a-c}{a+c} = \frac{\tan \frac{1}{2}(A-C)}{\tan \frac{1}{2}(A+C)},$$
$$\frac{b-c}{b+c} = \frac{\tan \frac{1}{2}(B-C)}{\tan \frac{1}{2}(B+C)},$$

* For work with oblique triangles a more detailed table of functions graduated by tenths of degrees appears at the end of this section. Use of this table will obviate much of the extra arithmetic ordinarily employed in interpolation procedures.

† The interested reader can obtain from any standard textbook on trigonometry a detailed description of the mathematics involved in deriving these formulas.

or if $b > a$, then

$$\frac{b - a}{b + a} = \frac{\tan \frac{1}{2}(B - A)}{\tan \frac{1}{2}(B + A)}.$$

SOLVING OBLIQUE TRIANGLES

Any triangle has six parts, namely, three angles and the sides opposite the angles.

In order to solve a triangle three independent parts must be known in addition to the fact that the sum of the angles of any triangle equals 180°.

In problems involving triangles there occur the following four combinations of parts which if known will determine the size and form of the triangle.

I. *One side and two angles are known*

II. *Two sides and the included angle are known*

III. *Three sides are known*

IV. *Two sides and the angle opposite one of them is known.**

APPLYING THE LAWS OF SINE, TANGENT AND COSINE TO OBLIQUE TRIANGLES

Case I: **One side and two angles are known**

EXAMPLE: Given $\angle A = 56°$, $\angle B = 69°$ and $a = 467$; find b and c.

SOLUTION: We use the law of sines.

Formulas needed:

1. $C = 180° - (\angle A + \angle B)$

2. $\frac{b}{a} = \frac{\sin B}{\sin A}$, $\therefore c = \frac{a \sin B}{\sin A}$,

3. $\frac{c}{a} = \frac{\sin C}{\sin A}$, $\therefore c = \frac{a \sin C}{\sin A}$,

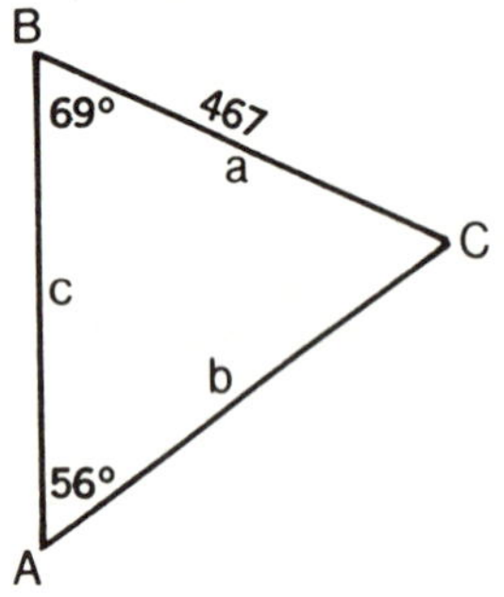

Substituting:

1. $\angle C = 180° - (56° + 69°) = 55°$

2. $b = \frac{467 \times .9336}{.8290} = 525.9$

3. $c = \frac{467 \times .8192}{.8290} = 461.5$

} ANS.

Case II: **Two sides and the included angle are known**

EXAMPLE: Given $a = 17$, $b = 12$ and $\angle C = 58°$; find $\angle A$, $\angle B$ and c.

SOLUTION: We use the law of tangents to obtain $\angle A$ and $\angle B$ and the law of sines to obtain c.

Formulas needed:

1. $A + B = 180° - C$ and $\frac{1}{2}(A + B) = \frac{1}{2}(180° - C)$

When $\frac{1}{2}(A + B)$ has been determined $\frac{1}{2}(A - B)$ is found by the following

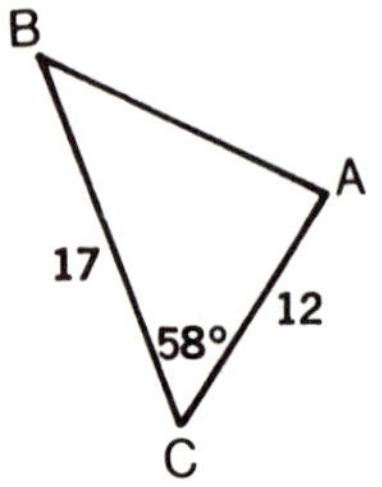

2. $\frac{a - b}{a + b} = \frac{\tan \frac{1}{2}(A - B)}{\tan \frac{1}{2}(A + B)}$

$\therefore \tan \frac{1}{2}(A - B) = \frac{a - b}{a + b} \times \tan \frac{1}{2}(A + B)$

3. $\angle A = \frac{1}{2}(A + B) + \frac{1}{2}(A - B)$ in which the Bs cancel out

4. $\angle B = \frac{1}{2}(A + B) - \frac{1}{2}(A - B)$, in which the As cancel out

5. $\frac{c}{a} = \frac{\sin C}{\sin A}$, $\therefore c = \frac{a \sin C}{\sin A}$.

Substituting:

1. $\frac{1}{2}(A + B) = \frac{1}{2}(180° - 58°) = 61°$

2. $\tan \frac{1}{2}(A - B) = \frac{17 - 12}{17 + 12} \times \tan 61° = .3110$, which is the tan of 17° 16′ and equal to $\frac{1}{2}(A - B)$

3. $\angle A = 61° + 17° 16' = 78° 16'$

4. $\angle B = 60° - 17° 16' = 43° 44'$

5. $c = \frac{17 \times \sin 58°}{\sin 78° 16'} = 14.7$

} ANS.

This example could also be solved by the use of the law of cosines by first finding c ($c = \sqrt{a^2 + b^2 - 2ab \cos C}$). When the three sides and $\angle C$ are known the law of sines can be employed to find $\angle A$ and $\angle B$. For purposes of a check, do this example by the second method.

* This combination is considered an ambiguous case because it is often possible to form more than one triangle to satisfy the given conditions.

Case III: **Three sides are known**

EXAMPLE: Given $a = 5$, $b = 6$ and $c = 7$; find $\angle A$, $\angle B$ and $\angle C$.

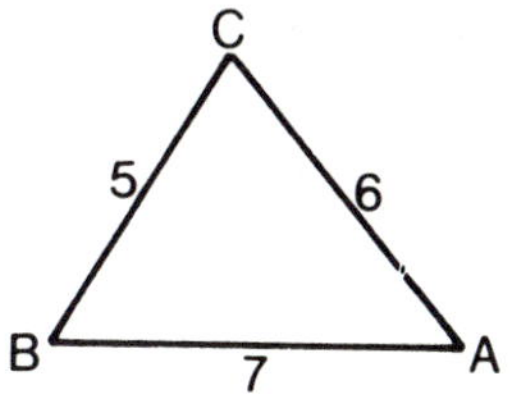

SOLUTION: We use the law of cosines and the law of sines.

Formulas needed:

1. $a^2 = b^2 + c^2 - 2bc \cos A$

$$\therefore \cos A \frac{b^2 + c^2 - a^2}{2bc}$$

2. $\frac{a}{b} = \frac{\sin A}{\sin B}$, $\quad \therefore \sin B = \frac{b \sin A}{a}$

3. $\angle C = 180° - (A + B)$

Substituting:

$$\cos A = \frac{36 + 49 - 25}{2(6 \times 7)} = .7143$$

which is the cos of 44° 25′

$$\sin B = \frac{6 \times .69995}{5} = .8399,$$

which is the sin of 57° 45′

$\angle C = 180° - (44° 25' + 57° 45' = 77° 50'$

$\left.\begin{array}{l} \angle A = 44° 25' \\ \angle B = 57° 45' \\ \angle C = 77° 50' \end{array}\right\}$ ANS.

Case IV (*the ambiguous case*): **Two sides and the angle opposite one of them are known**

When given two sides of a triangle and the angle opposite one of them, there is often a possibility of two solutions unless one of the solutions is excluded by the statement of the problem.

This fact may be clarified by the next figure. It will be seen in the triangle ABC that if $\angle A$ and

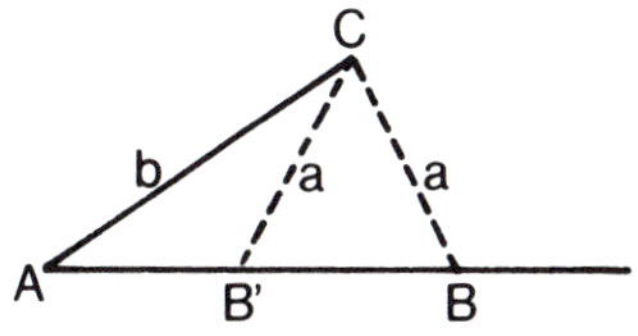

sides a and b are given, either of the triangles ABC or $AB'C$ meet the given conditions.

By varying the relative lengths of a and b and the magnitude of $\angle A$, the following possibilities can be recognized.

If $a > b$, $\angle A > \angle B$, which makes $\angle B$ less than 90°, and allows for only on solution.

If $a = b$, $\angle A = \angle B$; both angles are less than 90° and only an isosceles triangle can be formed.

If $a < b$ and $\angle A$ is acute, two triangles are possible.

If $a = b \sin A$, the figure is a right triangle and only one solution is possible.

If $a < b \sin A$, no triangle is possible.

Before doing a problem of this type you can generally determine the number of possible solutions by making an approximate small-scale drawing of the given parts.

In the cases where there are two possible solutions and the unknown parts are $\angle B$, $\angle C$ and side c, the second set of unknown parts should be designated as $\angle B'$, $\angle C'$ and side c'. They will then be found as follows:

$B' = 180° - B$, because when an angle is determined by its sine, it has two possible values that are supplementary to each other.

$C' = 180° - (A + B')$.

$$c' = \frac{a \sin C'}{\sin A}.$$

EXAMPLE: Given $a = 5$, $b = 8$ and $\angle A = 30°$; find $\angle B$, $\angle C$ and side c.

Here $a < b$ and $\angle A$ is acute. $\therefore$ two triangles are possible.

Formulas needed for $\triangle ABC$:

1. $\frac{b}{a} = \frac{\sin B}{\sin A}$, $\quad \therefore \sin B = \frac{b \sin A}{a}$.

2. $\angle C = 180° - (A + B)$.

3. $\frac{c}{a} = \frac{\sin C}{\sin A}$, $\quad \therefore c = \frac{a \sin C}{\sin A}$.

Substituting:

1. $\sin B = \frac{8 \times .5000}{5} = .8000,$

which is the sin of 53° 8′

2. $\angle C = 180° - (30° + 53° 8') = 96° 52'$

3. $c = \frac{5 \times .9928}{.5000} = 9.928$

$\left.\begin{array}{l} \angle B = 53° 8' \\ \angle C = 96° 52' \\ c = 9.928 \end{array}\right\}$ ANS.

To find $\angle B'$, $\angle C'$ and c':

$\angle B' = 180° - B = 126° 52'$, ANS.

$\angle C' = 180° - (A + B') = 23° 8'$, ANS.

$$c' = \frac{a \sin C'}{\sin A} = \frac{5 \times 3.929}{5} = 3.929, \quad \text{ANS.}$$

Practice Exercise No. 8

In working out the problems in this exercise apply the principles for solving oblique triangles.

1 Given $\angle A = 45°$, $\angle B = 60°$ and $c = 9.562$; find a and b.

2 Given $a = 43$, $\angle A = 43°$ and $\angle B = 68°$; find $\angle C$, b and c.

3 Given $a = 22$, $b = 13$ and $\angle C = 68°$; find $\angle A$, $\angle B$ and c.

4 Given $a = 27$, $b = 26$, $c = 34$; find $\angle A$, $\angle B$ and $\angle C$.

5 Given $a = 8$, $b = 5$ and $\angle A = 21$; find c, $\angle A$ and $\angle B$.

6 Two airplane spotters, A and B, are 1.83 miles apart on the same level of ground. B is due north of A. At the same instant they both spot an airplane to the north, which makes an angle of elevation of 67° 31′ at A and 82° 16′ at B. What is the altitude of the airplane from the ground?

(A) 2.5 mi. ____ (C) 4 mi. ____
(B) 6.6 mi. ____ (D) 3.2 mi. ____

7 An observer on a boat anchored offshore sights on two points, A and B, on the shore. He determines the distance from himself to point A to be 985 feet, and the distance between A and B as 1,460 feet. The angle to the observer subtended by the points on shore is 64° 20′. How far is it from the observer to point B?

(A) 1,585.6 ft. ____ (C) 1,760 ft. ____
(B) 1,242.6 ft. ____ (D) 927.7 ft. ____

8 An observer at a fire tower spots a fire in a forest area extending across a stretch of land from point A to point B. The distance from the tower to A is 5 miles, and to B, $5\frac{1}{2}$ miles. The angle subtended by the stretch of land to the tower is 50°. What is the distance across which the fire extends? (*Note: For practice purposes solve by the tangent law.*)

(A) 6 mi. ____ (C) 3.42 mi. ____
(B) 4.46 mi. ____ (D) 8.5 mi. ____

9 Two scouts start from a point C at the same time and branch out at an angle of 33° to each other. If one scout travels at the rate of 1 mile per hour while the other travels at the rate of 3 miles per hour, how far apart will they be at the end of 2 hours? (*Note: Solve by cosine law.*)

(A) 3 mi. ____ (C) 4.46 mi. ____
(B) 5.42 mi. ____ (D) 8.56 mi. ____

10 A cannon is placed in position at point A to fire upon an enemy fort located on a mountain. The airline distance from the gun to the fort has been determined as 5 miles. The distance on a horizontal plane from the gun to a point C at the base of the mountain is $3\frac{1}{2}$ miles. From this point at the base to the fort itself the distance is 1.8 miles. (a) At what angle of elevation will the cannon have to be set in order to score a direct hit upon the fort? (b) What is the angle of depression from the fort to the cannon?

(a) (A) 27° 21′ ____ (C) 13° 40′ ____
(B) 38° 59′ ____ (D) 16° 8′ ____

(b) (A) 38° 59′ ____ (C) 22° 16′ ____
(B) 27° 21′ ____ (D) 13° 40′ ____

ANSWERS TO EXERCISES

Exercise No. 1

1 $\sin B = \frac{b}{c}$, $\cos B = \frac{a}{c}$, $\cot B = \frac{a}{b}$, $\sec B = \frac{c}{a}$, $\csc B = \frac{c}{b}$

2 tan A 6 $\cos A = \frac{4}{5}$ 10 $\cos A = \frac{12}{13}$, $\tan A = \frac{5}{12}$, $\cot A = \frac{12}{5}$, $\sec A = \frac{13}{12}$, $\csc A = \frac{13}{5}$

3 cot A 7 $\sin A = \frac{3}{5}$

4 sec A 8 $\cos A = \frac{15}{17}$

5 csc A 9 $\sec A = \frac{17}{15}$

Exercise No. 2

1 cos 64° 3 sin 65° 32′ 5 csc 83° 50′

2 cot 47° 4 tan 1° 10′ 6 sec $12\frac{1}{2}°$

7 15° ($90° = 5A + A$; ∴ $90° = 6A$, and $A = 15°$)

8 45° (reciprocals of the cofunctions are =, ∴ $\angle A = 45°$)

9 45° ($90° - A = A$; $90° = 2A$; $A = 45°$)

10 30° ($\cos A = \sin 90° - A$; since $\cos A = \sin 2A$, then $\sin 90° - A = \sin 2A$, $90 - A = 2A$; $3A = 90°$ and $A = 30°$)

Exercise No. 3

1	.1392	6	.9063	11	4695	16	15°
2	.6691	7	4.134	12	1.4826	17	35°
3	.8391	8	.9781	13	.8480	18	60°
4	.5095	9	.3839	14	.7071	19	70°
5	1.079	10	6.3925	15	.5000	20	10°

Exercise No. 4

1	.2672	5	1.315	8	cos 65° 20′
2	.9013	6	sin 5° 10′	9	cot 49° 40′
3	1.079	7	tan 18° 50′	10	csc 42° 30′
4	.7674				

Exercise No. 5

1 $a = 54.46$
2 $a = 3.42$
3 $\angle A = 65° 33'$
4 $c = 29.82$
5 $\angle A = 46° 03'$
6 $\frac{a}{c} = \sin A,\ c = \frac{a}{\sin A} = \frac{405}{.2250} = 1{,}800$ ft.
7 $a = c \sin A = 150 \times .7660 = 114.9$ ft.
8 $c = \frac{a}{\sin A} = \frac{12}{.3090} = 38.83$ ft.
9 $a = c \sin A = 200 \times .9455 = 189.1$ ft.
10 $\frac{a}{c} = \sin A = \frac{54.5}{625} = .0872$ which is the sin of 5°

Exercise No. 6

1 $\angle A = 53° 8'$
2 $b = 31.86$
3 $b = 62.08$
4 $\angle A = 60°$
5 $c = 42$
6 $\frac{b}{c} = \cos A = \frac{15}{17} = .8823$ which is the cos of 28°
7 $\frac{b}{c} = \cos A,\ c = \frac{b}{\cos A} = \frac{681}{.8910} = 764.9$
8 $\angle B = 90° - 10° = 80°,\ \cos B = \frac{a}{c},$

$c = \frac{a}{\cos B} = \frac{125}{.1736} = 720.04$

9 $\cos B = \frac{a}{c},\ a = c \cos B = 84 \times 64828 =$ 53.9952 = 54
10 $\cos A = \frac{b}{c} = \frac{16.5}{100} = .165$ which is the cos of 80° 30′

Exercise No. 7

1 36° 52′
2 64
3 45.04
4 18.19
5 15
6 $\frac{a}{b} = \tan A,\ b = \frac{1}{2}$ of $280 = 140$ ft., $a = b \tan A$ $= 140 \times .9325 = 130.55$ ft.
7 $\tan B = \frac{b}{a},\ \angle B = 90° - 10° = 80°,\ b = a \tan$ $B = 240 \times 5.6713 = 1361.11$ ft.
8 $\tan A = \frac{a}{b},\ b = \frac{a}{\tan A} = \frac{30}{.3640} = 82.42$ ft.
9 $\angle A = 90° - 15° = 75°,\ \angle A' = 90° - 14° = 76°$
$CB = b \tan A = 100 \times 3.7321 = 373.21$ ft.
$CB' = b \tan A' = 100 \times 4.0108 = 401.08$ ft.
$CB' - CB = BB' = 401.08 - 373.21 = 27.87$ ft.
10 Let x = height of tower
y = distance from nearer point to foot of tower

From $\triangle ACD$, $\frac{x}{300 + y} = \tan 30°$; $\tan 30° = \frac{1}{\sqrt{3}}$ $\therefore y = \sqrt{3}x - 300$

From $\triangle BCD$, $\frac{x}{y} = \tan 60°$, $\tan 60° = \sqrt{3}$ $\therefore y = \frac{x}{\sqrt{3}}$

Equating the values of y, $\sqrt{3}x - 300 = \frac{x}{\sqrt{3}}$

$2x = 300 \times 1.732,\ x = 259.8$

Exercise No. 8

1 $a = 7,\ b = 8.57$
2 $\angle C = 69°,\ b = 58.91,\ c = 58.44$
3 $\angle A = 76° 52',\ \angle B = 35° 8',\ c = 20.95$

4 $\angle A = 51° \, 24', \angle B = 48° \, 49', \angle C = 79° \, 47'$

5 $\angle B = 12° \, 56', \angle C = 146° \, 4', c = 12.43$

6 $\angle ABC = 97° \, 44'$

$\angle BCA = 180° - (67° \, 31' + 97° \, 44') = 14° \, 45'$

$\frac{a}{c} = \frac{\sin A}{\sin C}, a = \frac{c \sin A}{\sin BCA}$

$= \frac{1.83 \times .9241}{.2546}$

$= 6.656$

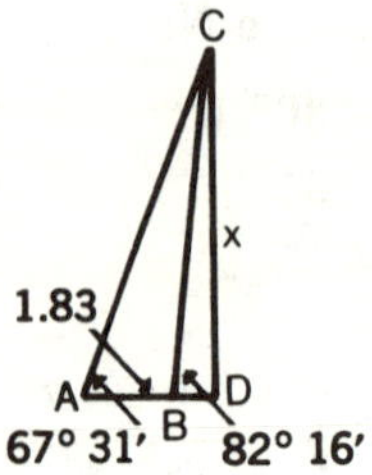

$\sin 82° \, 16' = \frac{x}{6.656},$

$x = .9909 \times 6.656 = 6.595 = 6.6$ mi.

7 $\frac{b}{c} = \frac{\sin B}{\sin C}, \sin B$

$= \frac{b \sin C}{c}$

$= \frac{985 \, (\sin 64° \, 20')}{1460}$

$= .6081$ which is sin $37° \, 27'$

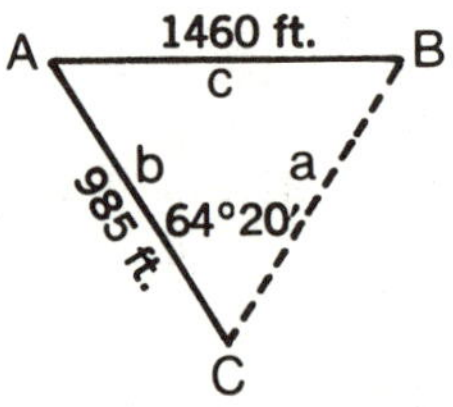

$\angle A = 180° - (64° \, 20' + 37° \, 27') = 78° \, 13'$

$\frac{a}{b} = \frac{\sin A}{\sin B}, a = \frac{b \sin A}{\sin B} = \frac{985 \times .9789}{.6081}$

$= 1585.6$ ft.

8 $A + B = 180° - 50° = 130°, \frac{1}{2} A + B = 65°$

$\tan \frac{1}{2} (A - B) =$

$\frac{a - b}{a + b} \times \tan \frac{1}{2} (A + B)$

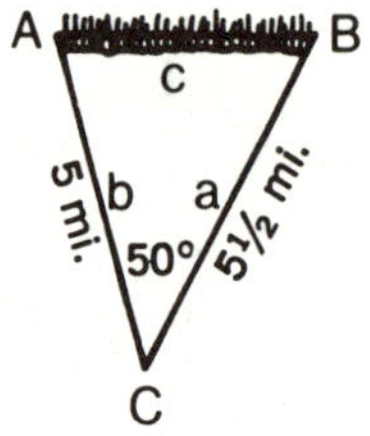

$= \frac{5.5 - 5}{5.5 + 5} \times 2.145 = .102$

which is the tan of $5° \, 50'$

$\angle A = \frac{1}{2}(A + B) + \frac{1}{2}(A - B) = 70° \, 50'$

$\frac{c}{a} = \frac{\sin C}{\sin A}, c = \frac{a \sin C}{\sin A} = \frac{5.5 \times .7660}{.9446} = 4.46$ mi.

9 By cos law, $c = \sqrt{a^2 + b^2 - 2ab \cos C}$

$c = \sqrt{2^2 + 6^2 - 2(2 \times 6) \cos 33°}$

$= \sqrt{19.87}$

$= 4.46$ mi.

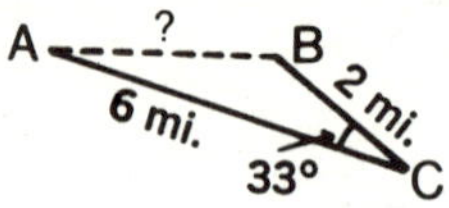

10 By cos law, $a^2 = b^2 + c^2 - 2bc \cos A$

$\therefore \cos A = \frac{b^2 + c^2 - a^2}{2bc}$

(a) $\cos A = \frac{3.5^2 + 5^2 - 1.8^2}{2(3.5 \times 5)} = .9717$

which is the cos of $13° \, 40'$

(b) alt. int. $\angle$s of $\parallel$ lines are $=$;

$\therefore$ angle of depression $= 13° \, 40'$

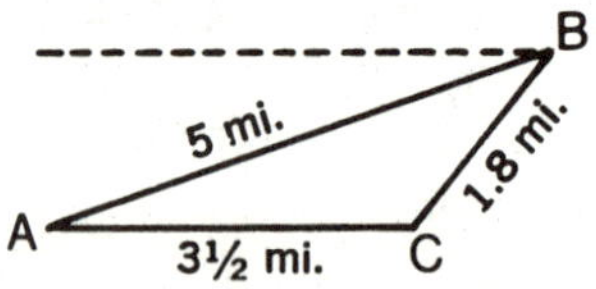

TABLE II

TABLE OF NATURAL TRIGONOMETRIC FUNCTIONS

Degrees	Sin	Cos	Tan	Cot	Sec	Csc	
0° 00′	.0000	1.0000	.0000	——	1.000	——	90° 00′
10	029	000	029	343.8	000	343.8	50
20	058	000	058	171.9	000	171.9	40
30	.0087	1.0000	.0087	114.6	1.000	114.6	30
40	116	9999	116	85.94	000	85.95	20
50	145	999	145	68.75	000	68.76	10
1° 00′	.0175	.9998	.0175	57.29	1.000	57.30	89° 00′
10	204	998	204	49.10	000	49.11	50
20	233	997	233	42.96	000	42.98	40
30	.0262	.9997	.0262	38.19	1.000	38.20	30
40	291	996	291	34.37	000	34.38	20
50	320	995	320	31.24	001	31.26	10
2° 00′	.0349	.9994	.0349	28.64	1.001	28.65	88° 00′
10	378	993	378	26.43	001	26.45	50
20	407	992	407	24.54	001	24.56	40
30	.0436	.9990	.0437	22.90	1.001	22.93	30
40	465	989	466	21.47	001	21.49	20
50	494	988	495	20.21	001	20.23	10
3° 00′	.0523	.9986	.0524	19.08	1.001	19.11	87° 00′
10	552	985	553	18.07	002	18.10	50
20	581	983	582	17.17	002	17.20	40
30	.0610	.9981	.0612	16.35	1.002	16.38	30
40	640	980	641	15.60	002	15.64	20
50	669	978	670	14.92	002	14.96	10
4° 00′	.0698	.9976	.0699	14.30	1.002	14.34	86° 00′
10	727	974	729	13.73	003	13.76	50
20	756	971	758	13.20	003	13.23	40
30	.0785	.9969	.0787	12.71	1.003	12.75	30
40	814	967	816	12.25	003	12.29	20
50	843	964	846	11.83	004	11.87	10
5° 00′	.0872	.9962	.0875	11.43	1.004	11.47	85° 00′
10	901	959	904	11.06	004	11.10	50
20	929	957	934	10.71	004	10.76	40
30	.0958	.9954	.0963	10.39	1.005	10.43	30
40	987	951	992	10.08	005	10.13	20
50	.1016	948	.1022	9.788	005	9.839	10
6° 00′	.1045	.9945	.1051	9.514	1.006	9.567	84° 00′
10	074	942	080	9.255	006	9.309	50
20	103	939	110	9.010	006	9.065	40
30	.1132	.9936	.1139	8.777	1.006	8.834	30
40	161	932	169	8.556	007	8.614	20
50	190	929	198	8.345	007	8.405	10
7° 00′	.1219	.9925	.1228	8.144	1.008	8.206	83° 00′
10	248	922	257	7.953	008	8.016	50
20	276	918	287	7.770	008	7.834	40
30	.1305	.9914	.1317	7.596	1.009	7.661	30
40	334	911	346	7.429	009	7.496	20
50	363	907	376	7.269	009	7.337	10
8° 00′	.1392	.9903	.1405	7.115	1.010	7.185	82° 00′
10	421	899	435	6.968	010	7.040	50
20	449	894	465	6.827	011	6.900	40
30	.1478	.9890	.1495	6.691	1.011	6.765	30
40	507	886	524	6.561	012	6.636	20
50	536	881	554	6.435	012	6.512	10
9° 00′	.1564	.9877	.1584	6.314	1.012	6.392	81° 00′
	Cos	Sin	Cot	Tan	Csc	Sec	Degrees

TABLE OF NATURAL TRIGONOMETRIC FUNCTIONS (*Continued*)

Degrees	Sin	Cos	Tan	Cot	Sec	Csc	
9° 00′	.1564	.9877	.1584	6.314	1.012	6.392	81° 00′
10	593	872	614	197	013	277	50
20	622	868	644	084	013	166	40
30	.1650	.9863	.1673	5.976	1.014	6.059	30
40	679	858	703	871	014	5.955	20
50	708	853	733	769	015	855	10
10° 00′	.1736	.9848	.1763	5.671	1.015	5.759	80° 00′
10	765	843	793	576	016	665	50
20	794	838	823	485	016	575	40
30	.1822	.9833	.1853	5.396	1.017	5.487	30
40	851	827	883	309	018	403	20
50	880	822	914	226	018	320	10
11° 00′	.1908	.9816	.1944	5.145	1.019	5.241	79° 00′
10	937	811	974	066	019	164	50
20	965	805	.2004	4.989	020	089	40
30	.1994	.9799	.2035	4.915	1.020	5.016	30
40	.2022	793	065	843	021	4.945	20
50	051	787	095	773	022	876	10
12° 00′	.2079	.9781	.2126	4.705	1.022	4.810	78° 00′
10	108	775	156	638	023	745	50
20	136	769	186	574	024	682	40
30	.2164	.9763	.2217	4.511	1.024	4.620	30
40	193	757	247	449	025	560	20
50	221	750	278	390	026	502	10
13° 00′	.2250	.9744	.2309	4.331	1.026	4.445	77° 00′
10	278	737	339	275	027	390	50
20	306	730	370	219	028	336	40
30	.2334	.9724	.2401	4.165	1.028	4.284	30
40	363	717	432	113	029	232	20
50	391	710	462	061	030	182	10
14° 00′	.2419	.9703	.2493	4.011	1,031	4.134	76° 00′
10	447	696	524	3.962	031	086	50
20	476	689	555	914	032	039	40
30	.2504	.9681	.2586	3.867	1.033	3,994	30
40	532	674	617	821	034	950	20
50	560	667	648	776	034	906	10
15° 00′	.2588	.9659	.2679	3.732	1.035	3.864	75° 00′
10	616	652	711	689	036	822	50
20	644	644	742	647	037	782	40
30	.2672	.9636	.2773	3.606	1.038	3.742	30
40	700	628	805	566	039	703	20
50	728	621	836	526	039	665	10
16° 00′	.2756	.9613	.2867	3.487	1.040	3.628	74° 00′
10	784	605	899	450	041	592	50
20	812	596	931	412	042	556	40
30	.2840	.9588	.2962	3.376	1.043	3.521	30
40	868	580	994	340	044	487	20
50	896	572	.3026	305	045	453	10
17° 00′	.2924	.9563	.3057	3.271	1.046	3.420	73° 00′
10	952	555	089	237	047	388	50
20	979	546	121	204	048	356	40
30	.3007	.9537	.3153	3.172	1.049	3.326	30
40	035	528	185	140	049	295	20
50	062	520	217	108	050	265	10
18° 00′	.3090	.9511	.3249	3.078	1.051	3.236	72° 00′
	Cos	Sin	Cot	Tan	Csc	Sec	Degrees

TABLE OF NATURAL TRIGONOMETRIC FUNCTIONS (*Continued*)

Degrees	Sin	Cos	Tan	Cot	Sec	Csc	
18° 00′	.3090	.9511	.3249	3.078	1.051	3.236	72° 00′
10	118	502	281	047	052	207	50
20	145	492	314	018	053	179	40
30	.3173	.9483	.3346	2.989	1.054	3.152	30
40	201	474	378	960	056	124	20
50	228	465	411	932	057	098	10
19° 00′	.3256	.9455	.3443	2.904	1.058	3.072	71° 00′
10	283	446	476	877	059	046	50
20	311	436	508	850	060	021	40
30	.3338	.9426	.3541	2.824	1.061	2.996	30
40	365	417	574	798	062	971	20
50	393	407	607	773	063	947	10
20° 00′	.3420	.9397	.3640	2.747	1.064	2.924	70° 00′
10	448	387	673	723	065	901	50
20	475	377	706	699	066	878	40
30	.3502	.9367	.3739	2.675	1.068	2.855	30
40	529	356	772	651	069	833	20
50	557	346	805	628	070	812	10
21° 00′	.3584	.9336	.3839	2.605	1.071	2.790	69° 00′
10	611	325	872	583	072	769	50
20	638	315	906	560	074	749	40
30	.3665	.9304	.3939	2.539	1.075	2.729	30
40	692	293	973	517	076	709	20
50	719	283	.4006	496	077	689	10
22° 00′	.3746	.9272	.4040	2.475	1.079	2.669	68° 00′
10	773	261	074	455	080	650	50
20	800	250	108	434	081	632	40
30	.3827	.9239	.4142	2.414	1.082	2.613	30
40	854	228	176	394	084	595	20
50	881	216	210	375	085	577	10
23° 00′	.3907	.9205	.4245	2.356	1.086	2.559	67° 00′
10	934	194	279	337	088	542	50
20	961	182	314	318	089	525	40
30	.3987	.9171	.4348	2.300	1.090	2.508	30
40	.4014	159	383	282	092	491	20
50	041	147	417	264	093	475	10
24° 00′	.4067	.9135	.4452	2.246	1.095	2.459	66° 00′
10	094	124	487	229	096	443	50
20	120	112	552	211	097	427	40
30	.4147	.9100	.4557	2.194	1.099	2.411	30
40	173	088	592	177	100	396	20
50	200	075	628	161	102	381	10
25° 00′	.4226	.9063	.4663	2.145	1.103	2.366	65° 00′
10	253	051	699	128	105	352	50
20	279	038	734	112	106	337	40
30	.4305	.9026	.4770	2.097	1.108	2.323	30
40	331	013	806	081	109	309	20
50	358	001	841	066	111	295	10
26° 00′	.4384	.8988	.4877	2.050	1.113	2.281	64° 00′
10	410	975	913	035	114	268	50
20	436	962	950	020	116	254	40
30	.4462	.8949	.4986	2.006	1.117	2.241	30
40	488	936	.5022	1.991	119	228	20
50	514	923	059	977	121	215	10
27° 00′	.4540	.8910	.5095	1.963	1.122	2.203	63° 00′
	Cos	Sin	Cot	Tan	Csc	Sec	Degrees

TABLE OF NATURAL TRIGONOMETRIC FUNCTIONS (*Continued*)

Degrees	Sin	Cos	Tan	Cot	Sec	Csc	
27° 00′	.4540	.8910	.5095	1.963	1.122	2.203	63° 00′
10	566	897	132	949	124	190	50
20	592	884	169	935	126	178	40
30	.4617	.8870	.5206	1.921	1.127	2.166	30
40	643	857	243	907	129	154	20
50	669	843	280	894	131	142	10
28° 00′	.4695	.8829	.5317	1.881	1.133	2.130	62° 00′
10	720	816	354	868	134	118	50
20	746	802	392	855	136	107	40
30	.4772	.8788	.5430	1.842	1.138	2.096	30
40	797	774	467	829	140	085	20
50	823	760	505	816	142	074	10
29° 00′	.4848	.8746	.5543	1.804	1.143	2.063	61° 00′
10	874	732	581	792	145	052	50
20	899	718	619	780	147	041	40
30	.4924	.8704	.5658	1.767	1.149	2.031	30
40	950	689	696	756	151	020	20
50	975	675	735	744	153	010	10
30° 00′	.5000	.8660	.5774	1.732	1.155	2.000	60° 00′
10	025	646	812	720	157	1.990	50
20	050	631	851	709	159	980	40
30	.5075	.8616	.5890	1.698	1.161	1.970	30
40	100	601	930	686	163	961	20
50	125	587	969	675	165	951	10
31° 00′	.5150	.8572	.6009	1.664	1.167	1.942	59° 00′
10	175	557	048	653	169	932	50
20	200	542	088	643	171	923	40
30	.5225	.8526	.6128	1.632	1.173	1.914	30
40	250	511	168	621	175	905	20
50	275	496	208	611	177	896	10
32° 00′	.5299	.8480	.6249	1.600	1.179	1.887	58° 00′
10	324	465	289	590	181	878	50
20	348	450	330	580	184	870	40
30	.5373	.8434	.6371	1.570	1.186	1.861	30
40	398	418	412	560	188	853	20
50	422	403	453	550	190	844	10
33° 00′	.5446	.8387	.6494	1.540	1.192	1.836	57° 00′
10	471	371	536	530	195	828	50
20	495	355	577	520	197	820	40
30	.5519	.8339	.6619	1.511	1.199	1.812	30
40	544	323	661	501	202	804	20
50	568	307	703	1.492	204	796	10
34° 00′	.5592	.8290	.6745	1.483	1.206	1.788	56° 00′
10	616	274	787	473	209	781	50
20	640	258	830	464	211	773	40
30	.5664	.8241	.6873	1.455	1.213	1.766	30
40	688	225	916	446	216	758	20
50	712	208	959	437	218	751	10
35° 00′	.5736	.8192	.7002	1.428	1.221	1.743	55° 00′
10	760	175	046	419	223	736	50
20	783	158	089	411	226	729	40
30	.5807	.8141	.7133	1.402	1.228	1.722	30
40	831	124	177	393	231	715	20
50	854	107	221	385	233	708	10
36° 00′	.5878	.8090	.7265	1.376	1.236	1.701	54° 00′
	Cos	Sin	Cot	Tan	Csc	Sec	Degrees

TABLE OF NATURAL TRIGONOMETRIC FUNCTIONS (*Continued*)

Degrees	Sin	Cos	Tan	Cot	Sec	Csc	
36° 00′	.5878	.8090	.7265	1.376	1.236	1.701	54° 00′
10	901	073	310	368	239	695	50
20	925	056	355	360	241	688	40
30	.5948	.8039	.7400	1.351	1.244	1.681	30
40	972	021	445	343	247	675	20
50	995	004	490	335	249	668	10
37° 00′	.6018	.7986	.7536	1.327	1.252	1.662	53° 00′
10	041	969	581	319	255	655	50
20	065	951	627	311	258	649	40
30	.6088	.7934	.7673	1.303	1.260	1.643	30
40	111	916	720	295	263	636	20
50	134	898	766	288	266	630	10
38° 00′	.6157	.7880	.7813	1.280	1.269	1.625	52° 00′
10	180	862	860	272	272	618	50
20	202	844	907	265	275	612	40
30	.6225	.7826	.7954	1.257	1.278	1.606	30
40	248	808	.8002	250	281	601	20
50	271	790	050	242	284	595	10
39° 00′	.6293	.7771	.8098	1.235	1.287	1.589	51° 00′
10	316	753	146	228	290	583	50
20	338	735	195	220	293	578	40
30	.6361	.7716	.8243	1.213	1.296	1.572	30
40	383	698	292	206	299	567	20
50	406	679	342	199	302	561	10
40° 00′	.6428	.7660	.8391	1.192	1.305	1.556	50° 00′
10	450	642	441	185	309	550	50
20	472	623	491	178	312	545	40
30	.6494	.7604	.8541	1.171	1.315	1.540	30
40	517	585	591	164	318	535	20
50	539	566	642	157	322	529	10
41° 00′	.6561	.7547	.8693	1.150	1.325	1.524	49° 00′
10	583	528	744	144	328	519	50
20	604	509	796	137	332	514	40
30	.6626	.7490	.8847	1.130	1.335	1.509	30
40	648	470	899	124	339	504	20
50	670	451	952	117	342	499	10
42° 00′	.6691	.7431	.9004	1.111	1.346	1.494	48° 00′
10	713	412	057	104	349	490	50
20	734	392	110	098	353	485	40
30	.6756	.7373	.9163	1.091	1.356	1.480	30
40	777	353	217	085	360	476	20
50	799	333	271	079	364	471	10
43° 00′	.6820	.7314	.9325	1.072	1.367	1.466	47° 00′
10	841	294	380	066	371	462	50
20	862	274	435	060	375	457	40
30	.6884	.7254	.9490	1.054	1.379	1.453	30
40	905	234	545	048	382	448	20
50	926	214	601	042	386	444	10
44° 00′	.6947	.7193	.9657	1.036	1.390	1.440	46° 00′
10	967	173	713	030	394	435	50
20	988	153	770	024	398	431	40
30	.7009	.7133	.9827	1.018	1.402	1.427	30
40	030	112	884	012	406	423	20
50	050	092	942	006	410	418	10
45° 00′	.7071	.7071	1.0000	1.000	1.414	1.414	45° 00′
	Cos	Sin	Cot	Tan	Csc	Sec	Degrees

CHAPTER SEVENTEEN

COMPUTER SCIENCE

The advancement in this century of the technology, application, and availability of computers has been remarkable. Every year computers become smaller, more efficient, and able to do more complex tasks; and every year computers become more woven into the day-to-day life of Americans. A basic knowledge of computers—how they were developed and how they work—is fast becoming a necessity in today's society.

THE HISTORICAL BACKGROUND

The earliest and most important computing device is the abacus, which has been used for over two thousand years. There are different variations of the abacus, the most common being a series of beads that can be manually positioned along a set of wires. Each wire is given to represent one position in a numerical system of notation, such as ones, tens, hundreds, thousands, etc. By manipulating the beads on the wires, complicated calculations can be performed. The abacus is still used in business and in schools in China and Japan.

Pascal. The French philosopher, physicist, and mathematician, Blaise Pascal (1623–1662), is credited to have designed and built one of the first adding and subtracting machines. This device was built in 1642 and consisted of a complex assortment of gears, rods, and dials. Pascal, who was only nineteen when he constructed his machine, gave a copy of it to Louis XIV, King of France. The use of Pascal's device, however, was not very widespread. Many clerks and accountants refused to accept the machine because they feared that it might someday eliminate their own positions as human calculators.

The first commercially practical adding machines did not appear until about 1820. By the end of the nineteenth century, a variety of manually operated machines were available for business applications. Building calculating machines capable of solving mathematical problems posed by scientists, engineers, and mathematicians developed more slowly.

Charles Babbage. In 1822 the British mathematician Charles Babbage (1792–1871) built a prototype of his "difference engine." This device was an effort to make a machine capable of solving the repetitive computations required to compile mathematical tables. In 1833, Babbage radically changed his theoretical approach to the problem of constructing a computing machine. As a result, he devised plans for a device he termed the "analytical engine." Although Babbage never completed his machine—he had envisioned an enormous array of cogged cylinders powered by a steam engine—his ideas were precursors of what would follow decades after his death.

Babbage had planned that his analytical engine would use punched cards similar to those used on the Jacquard looms of his day. These punched cards would provide the machine with the data and the instructions needed for operation. The machine would also have a primitive memory amounting to the storing of one thousand numbers of up to fifty digits each.

Lord Byron's daughter, the Countess of Lovelace, an accomplished mathematician herself, remarked that Babbage's analytical engine would weave "algebraical patterns just as the Jacquard loom weaves flowers and leaves." She even wrote what could be considered the first computer programming for Babbage's theoretical machine.

Herman Hollerith. The next important development came in 1890 with the work of Herman Hollerith (1860–1929) for the United States Census Bureau. Hollerith developed the first electric machines that could "read" census information which had been punched onto cards. Thus, the statistical work of the Bureau was more easily and quickly prepared. Hollerith's machines were also used for census work in other countries, including Canada and Czarist Russia. In 1896, Hollerith formed the Tabulating Machine Company, which was one of the companies that would join to become International Business Machines (IBM) in 1924.

In the 1920s and 1930s companies marketed computing machines that handled between 50 and 250 punched cards per minute. This is very slow when compared to today's computers and calculators, but it was an important advance over previous technology. In 1928, the astronomers Wallace J. Eckert in America and John Cromie in England devised punched card machines capable of preparing calculations for astronomical and nautical tables.

The desire to build more advanced computers increased with the requirements of World War II. Computers were needed to calculate the trajectories of artillery fire.

ENIAC. In 1943, J. Presper Eckert and John W. Mauchly, with their associates, planned a machine called an "electrical numerical integrator and calculator," which was named "ENIAC." Finally completed in 1946, this all-electric machine was an advancement that incorporated some 18,000 vacuum tubes, expended 180,000 watts of power, and took up the floor area of a two bedroom house. ENIAC would be able to solve ballistics problems in fifteen seconds that formerly would have taken twenty hours if done by a person with a desk-top manual tabulator. ENIAC was also used to perform calculations for the atomic bomb project at Los Alamos, New Mexico.

Mark I. In 1944, the Harvard Mark I was unveiled. This electromechanical machine was developed by Howard Aiken and his associates and could perform the functions Charles Babbage had planned for his analytical engine. The Mark I was eight feet tall and fifty-five feet long and contained some 750,000 parts. It could process 23-decimal place numbers, do all arithmetic operations; and this machine had the capacity to deal with logarithms and trigonometric functions.

An advance in computer design beyond the Mark I occurred in 1945, when John von Neumann proposed the idea of a stored memory capacity. This permitted the computer to store its instructions within itself. Neumann incorporated this concept in his design for the EDVAC machine (Electronic Discrete Variable Automatic Computer), which was completed in 1952.

In 1951, Eckert and Mauchly completed work on UNIVAC (Universal Automatic Computer), which the United States Census Bureau had ordered in 1947. UNIVAC, and other computers similarly designed, had delay-line memories and performed multiplication by repetitious addition.

In the late 1950s the standard for computer memories became ferrite cores, and the transistor, which had been developed in 1948, replaced the cumbersome vacuum tube.

Innovations in the programming of computers were just as important as were the technological advances. The concept of an "assembly language," which translated a computer's binary code into a more easily used set of instructions, came about in the 1950s. Higher-level languages, such as FORTRAN, ALGOL, and COBOL, more closely resembled human language or the logic of mathematics. These computer languages were developed in the late 1950s and early 1960s.

In the 1960s research focused upon building computers with expanded memories and functional capabilities. The two computers that stand out during this period were the "LARC" machine, built by the Sperry-Rand Corporation for the University of California, and "Stretch" built by IBM. Early attempts to photoprint electrical circuitry, thereby making computers smaller and faster, began about 1960.

The use of computers in the business world was also increasing. In 1963, the *Daily Oklahoman-Oklahoma City Times* was the first newspaper to set all classified and editorial text by means of computer. In 1964, American Airlines and IBM created the airlines reservation system called SABRE. The use of computers in science and engineering in the 1960s can best be illustrated by the successful Apollo lunar landing project. Without computers to calculate orbit configurations and rocket specifications, putting men on the moon would probably not have been possible.

The 1970s saw an emphasis placed on scaling down the size and cost of computers. This was especially apparent in the field of hand-held electronic calculators. Yet, the 1970s also witnessed the manufacture of huge, multimillion dollar "supercomputers" used for weather forecasting, oceanographic research, astrophysics, and nuclear engineering.

The 1980s appear to be the decade of the personal computer. Companies such as IBM, Apple, Commodore Business Machines, and the Tandy Corporation are producing microcomputers designed for use in the home or small business. The companies that profited from the home video game craze have also offered hardware that would convert their video games into modest home computers. In education, "computer literacy" is a growing concern for secondary schools; and it has become a 1980s watchword in business, science, and government.

An Alphabet Soup of Early Calculating Machines

ENIAC 1946	Electronic Numerical Integrator and Calculator
EDVAC 1952	Electronic Discrete Variable Automatic Computer
EDSAC 1949	Electronic Delay Storage Automatic Computer
SEAC 1950	Standards Eastern Automatic Computer
UNIVAC 1951	Universal Automatic Computer
MANIAC 1951	Mathematical Analyzer, Numerical Integrator and Computer

THE WAY A COMPUTER WORKS

The modern computer has two basic components: hardware and software. Hardware refers to the physical equipment of a computer system. It may include a keyboard, a video monitor, and a printer. Software refers to the programming instructions that tell the computer how to perform any given task. (The instructions for the operation of computer hardware in an owner's manual may be considered software as well.)

The most important part of a computer is the central processing unit, or CPU. The CPU is composed of an arithmetic and logic section that can perform mathematical functions, such as addition and multiplication, and logical functions, such as comparing two distinct quantities. The CPU also contains a control section that communicates with other parts of the computer system, such as output devices or a data storage disk drive. Although this vital part of the computer is called a *central* processing unit, the actual electrical circuitry that comprises the CPU may not be limited to one location within the computer.

Computers, thanks to semiconducting "chips" of silicon, can be built with two types of memory. RAM, or random-access-memory, is a temporary memory capacity that can be altered by the CPU upon the command of the user. RAM can be thought of as a kind of "scratch pad" upon which the user may write, erase, and write again.

ROM, or read-only-memory, is the computer's permanent memory. The user, through the CPU, can read the ROM, but cannot alter it. Programs that are frequently used can be entered into a computer's ROM during the manufacturing process. Many personal computers are sold with a common language, such as BASIC, already a part of the computer's ROM.

When a computer is turned on, the CPU will automatically read the instructions for it in the "boot ROM," which contains the initial directions a computer needs in order to function. These instructions will direct the CPU to the operating system program, which has been entered onto a section of the RAM so that the CPU can follow it.

But how does a computer process data? The computer must translate all data into a binary code that can be represented as a series of digits of only 0 or 1. Each digit of the binary code is termed a bit. A grouping of eight bits is termed a byte. Within the computer a continuous translation procedure occurs that changes input data into the machine's binary code—and after the data has been processed—back into a form the user can readily understand.

The keyboard is the most common device a user has to input data. When keys are hit, a keyboard processor within the computer interprets the sequence and location of the keys and a translation into machine language occurs. When the translation is completed and the desired task is performed, processed data is sent to an output device, such as a video monitor or a printer. The user may then proceed either to continue data input or to make a transfer of the data to tape or disk for storage.

COMPUTER PROGRAMS

Computers need instructions in order to operate. The central processing unit of a computer understands instructions only if translated into a machine "language" it can read. For this reason different computer languages have been developed to perform the translation process. Still other computer languages have been developed for specific functional tasks.

Languages for computers are divided into two classes: lower and higher. As a computer language more closely resembles a human language, or more closely approximates the way the task at hand is expressed, it is considered a higher-level language. Lower-level languages are more similar in form to the machine's binary code.

Assembly languages are a step more complex than is the machine's binary code. An "assembler," a program to translate assembly language into machine language, was developed in the 1950s, which made programming much easier. Yet more complex is the translator program for higher-level languages, which is called a "compiler."

A query language is a popular user-access language because it closely resembles human language. It is used primarily to make computers more accessible to nonprogrammers. Query languages are very useful in business applications, such as when salesclerks need to query a computer for an inventory or price check.

FORTRAN, a higher-level language developed in the late 1950s, is a language geared for mathematical applications. For example, the algebraic expression $a^3 - 2bc$ can be expressed in FORTRAN as A***3 - 2*B*C*. Scientists and engineers find FORTRAN a very useful computer language.

BASIC, a programming language developed by John G. Kemeny and Thomas E. Kurtz of Dartmouth College, is a simplified rendition of FORTRAN and was designed especially for students. Today, BASIC is a very popular computer language for beginners and one of its variations can be found as an included component of many personal computer systems.

WHAT IS WORD PROCESSING?

Word processing is the term given when a computer and its software are designed specifically for the creation, editing, and production of written text. With a word processor typographical errors, spelling mistakes, and editorial changes can be made before a printed copy is produced. This capability saves time in the preparation of written documents because an error-free final copy can be created the first time.

In the home, word processing might be used to produce personal correspondence, school term papers, and diary entries. In business the word processor could be used to produce "personalized" advertising form letters, memoranda, project proposals, reports, and customer correspondence. The word processor would also have the ability to store on disk or tape anything that it produces. Thus, anything a word processor has created can be filed, retrieved, printed again, or revised more easily than conventional writing methods.

In addition, word processing software gives the writer control of margins, permits word, line, and paragraph deletions or insertions; and some software will check for spelling errors, or automatically construct footnotes or bibliographic citations. With such flexibility it is easy to understand why most major newspapers and book publishers, as well as professional writers, have incorporated the word processor into their business procedures. Some analysts even predict that by the year 2000 more than 60 percent of all Americans will have some form of word processing capability in their homes.

THE PERSONAL COMPUTER

Personal computers, also known as microcomputers, are quickly invading the American home and affecting the American way of life. Sales of home computers in 1983 were about $2.4 billion and this amount is expected to more than double in the next five years. Used for everything from playing video games to tax preparation and word processing, the personal computer has yet to realize its full potential as a household information processor. Many analysts expect that soon the microcomputer will be a major factor in the way the American family banks, shops, communicates long-distance, and gains access to news and reference information.

The person who wishes to buy a personal computer today, however, faces many choices. Which computer system and manufacturer is the best? Why does one system cost so much more than another? And what of all the so-called "peripherals," the devices that can be connected to the computer to expand its applications? Dot matrix versus letter-quality printers, mouses, joysticks, and modems are just a few of the options.

Perhaps the foremost idea to keep in mind, before spending the six hundred to five thousand dollars a microcomputer may cost, is to know exactly what the computer will be used for. A system used primarily for video games and itemizing the family budget need not be as expensive or complete as a system that is expected to serve as a word processor producing letter-quality text.

The prospective computer buyer should also study the software on the market before purchasing the expensive hardware. If needed software requires a large RAM capacity, then this factor will determine one of the specifications of the computer to be purchased.

Of course, it is also worth the time to find a computer retailer who is willing to let customers try out programs and equipment before buying. For example, some keyboards may not be responsive enough for speed-typing, others may be too sensitive. Some software may just be too complicated for the beginner to use. One way to be sure to get the hardware and software you can use is to try it out at the store.

Helpful store personnel will also indicate whether software and hardware are compatible with the customer's current equipment, and whether equipment purchased can be modified later to expand its applications or its memory.

FUTURE POSSIBILITIES

If the next twenty years bring as many innovations in computer science and technology as have the last twenty years, then it is very difficult indeed to foretell the extent to which computers will change our lives. However, some general observations, based on current research into new computer technology and applications, can give us a glimpse of what the future might bring.

As has been the trend for the last fifteen years, computers will become smaller, more efficient, and less costly. Computers will be more economical to use in the home, and in some areas, such as small-scale agriculture, computers will be put to work solving problems that will increase productivity and profits.

In the factory, computers will control robots designed to do the repetitive tasks of assembly line manufacturing. Already there exist automobile assembly lines in Japan, the United States, and Europe that rely almost exclusively upon the work of robots and the computers that control them.

Computers will undoubtedly play an increased role in the advancement of medical science and health care services. Research into "bionics" offers the possibility of replacing diseased or damaged body parts with computer controlled limbs or organs. One application already in operation is a computer accessed data bank of symptoms, which doctors throughout the country can use to help them diagnose disease and illness.

Computers will also change our lifestyle. Some futurists foresee the time when almost all an American family's shopping, banking, communications, and access to information will be by means of a home computer system. Sooner to come will be the wider use of magnetized plastic cards that will automatically debit the customer's bank account when presented at a grocery checkout, gasoline station, or department store. Such a situation would indeed take America closer to becoming a "cashless" society. In a scenario writer Alvin Toffler termed an "electronic cottage," more and more people will have jobs at home working at a computer terminal, rather than in an office.

Technologically, computers will incorporate synthesized voices and be able to add complex speech patterns in a variety of languages to the output capacities now available. Computers will also be able to recognize human language commands; thus, they will be able to "listen" to the user, rather than be limited to a keyboard or keypad for data and command input. The technology for these capabilities exists today. Further research and testing will make them commonplace in the future. Computers may eventually be able to project three-dimensional holograph images. Such a capacity might be used in communications, theater, and art.

Perhaps the most interesting aspect of computer research is in the field of "artificial intelligence." A number of computer scientists, Pulitzer Prize winner Douglas R. Hofstadter among them, are searching for computer programming that would create a "machine consciousness." Hofstadter believes this can be achieved only when a computer has an awareness of itself and of the method of its own problem solving routines.

With whatever the future brings, fear of computers is unjustified; rather, one should fear being ignorant of computers and their potential.

EVERYDAY USES OF COMPUTERS

How do computers affect our lives? Here are just a few of the ways computers have become a part of the American way of life:

At the store: The Universal Product Code is a code of lines and numbers printed on products and packaging. This code is read by a computer controlled sensing device and the price and product name is then printed on the customer's receipt. This system gives the consumer an itemized account of purchases, and it gives the merchant a faster, more efficient means of inventory and sales management.

At the bank: Automatic banking services are a very popular means of doing one's banking quickly and at times when regular banking services are closed. With a personalized magnetically coded plastic card a customer may make withdrawals, deposits, and transfers at any time of the day or night.

In the home: Although sales of video games and video game cartridges dropped substantially in 1983, their popularity is still very high. Video games make use of the same technology as a computer, and most video game manufacturers are offering attachments that can convert the video game into a modest home computer system.

In concert: Beginning with the era of the "moog" synthesizer of the 1970s, computer generated music has expanded to become a permanent part of the contemporary music scene.

In government: Computers are the most effective means of handling the vasts amounts of data used for purposes of Social Security management, tax collection, and military personnel records. In law enforcement, computers are used to help trace stolen property and to transfer information concerning fugitive criminals from one part of the country to another.

In the school: Computers as educational aids are increasing in numbers. Students in elementary schools are learning fundamental language and mathematic skills by interacting with a computer. In secondary schools, students are learning computer languages such as BASIC. In the university, computers are an integral part of the management of school records and the administration of business affairs. In addition, computers are a major factor in the learning experience of science and humanities students.

In the hospital: Computers play an important role in the management of health services. Insurance claims, medical histories, and other information can be stored and accessed by computer. The use of computer controlled diagnostic equipment, such as the "CAT" (Computerized Axial Tomography) scanner, has increased the medical specialist's ability to diagnose illness and disease.

A COMPUTER GLOSSARY

Acoustic Coupler—a device that permits the transmitting of data to or from a computer by way of telephone lines. A modem can be such a device.

Address—a number that reveals the specific location of data within a computer's memory.

ALGOL—Algorithmic Oriented Language, a computer language developed in the 1960s, which is more popular in Europe than in the United States.

Artificial Intelligence—or AI, the capacity of a machine to make choices, solve problems, perceive external stimuli, and learn new tasks.

ASCII—American Standard Code for Information Interchange; this is a seven bit code that symbolizes both letters and numbers.

Assembly Language—a translation of a machine's binary language into a form easier for humans to use.

BASIC—Beginners All-purpose Symbolic Instruction Code; a computer language derivative of and interactive with FORTRAN. It is a very popular computer language, and variations are used in many personal computers.

Baud—the measure of transmission rate expressed in bits per second.

Binary System—the base-2 number system a computer uses. The only digits in base-2 are 0 and 1.

Bit—refers to binary digit, which can be only 0 or 1.

Boot—the initial program that starts the computer into action.

Bubble Memory—a computer memory capacity that uses microscopic cells or "bubbles" to store information that is not lost when the power is shut off.

Bug—a programming error, or an error caused by hardware malfunction.

Byte—a group of eight bits. A byte may represent a single letter, number, or symbol.

COBOL—Common Business Oriented Language, a computer programming language geared for business applications.

Compiler—a program that changes a high-level language into the computer's binary machine language.

CPU—or Central Processing Unit, which is the part within the computer that executes commands, such as process, store, and retrieve.

Chip—electronic circuitry that is "printed" onto a wafer of silicon. A chip may be 3/4-inch square, yet contain thousands of transistors.

Cursor—the movable indicator displayed on a computer's monitor showing the user where inputted information will appear.

Daisywheel—a mechanism in a printer that holds character symbols arrayed on spokes that originate from a common wheel.

Database—a reservoir of data contained in an organized format for easy entry, retrieval, and revision.

Disk—a magnetic plate, usually of plastic, for storage of data. The most common sizes are 5$^1/_2$, 3$^1/_2$, and 8-inch diameters.

Disk Drive—a machine that records data on disks.

Documentation—written instructions to the computer user on the operations of hardware and software.

DOS—Disk Operating System, programs that tell the CPU how to communicate with devices connected to the computer. Common DOS programs include CP/M, MS-DOS, and UNIX.

Dot Matrix—the printing of letters, numbers, or symbols using a matrix of dots. Many computer printers use this concept.

File—a block of data considered by the user as a logical grouping of information and may be handled by the computer as a single unit.

Floppy Disk—a relatively inexpensive disk used for data storage, which must be used with a disk drive.

FORTRAN—Formula Translator, a programming language used primarily for mathematical operations important to engineers and scientists.

Hard Disk—an information storage disk that is most commonly hermetically sealed. A hard disk can store much more data than a floppy disk.

Hardware—includes any of the mechanical or electrical devices of a computer system; excludes software.

Interface—the hardware or software required to couple a computer with another electronic or programming system.

I/O—input/output; refers to the possible ways information may be entered and retrieved from a computer. Common input mechanisms are keyboards, mouse, joystick, and touch-sensitive screens. Output devices include video displays, printers, and voice synthesizers.

K—or kilobyte; the symbol used to represent 1024 bytes.

Keyboard—an input device similar to a set of typewriter keys; some computer keyboards come with a numerical keypad, which is a separate arrangement of numbered keys useful for inputting digital data.

Letter-quality—a designation given to a printer that produces fine quality characters suitable for formal letter or manuscript applications.

LISP—a computer language developed in 1958 that is geared for symbols, characters, and words, rather than for numbers. Computer scientists find it useful in their study of artificial intelligence.

Load—the action of transferring data from a tape or disk into a computer.

Mainframe—the term used to designate a large computer that may be accessed by many terminals.

Menu—a menu permits the user to choose among a list of functions or commands that is displayed on the screen.

Memory—the computer's storage of data; can be "volatile" and lost when power is shut off, or "nonvolatile" and storageable for an indefinite period of time.

Microcomputers—a computer system containing a CPU, memory capacity, I/O devices; any personal computer can be considered a microcomputer.

Modem—Modulating-Demodulating; a device allowing a computer to be connected to a telephone line or a direct line, thereby permitting the transmitting or receiving of data.

Monitor—the video screen on which computer data is displayed.

Mouse—an input device that manipulates a symbol, commonly an arrow, which allows the user to select options displayed on the screen.

PASCAL—a computer language named after French mathematician Blaise Pascal.

Peripheral—a piece of hardware connected to and controlled by a computer, such as a printer, modem, etc.

Pixel—picture element; which is the smallest area of a video screen that can be affected by computer commands.

Printer—an output device that will produce a printed copy of computer generated data.

Program—a list of instructions that tells a computer to perform specified tasks.

RAM—random-access-memory; a temporary data storage capacity that must be transferred to tape, disk, or print-out before power is off, or it is lost.

Real-time processing—handling data quickly enough to influence the environment from which the data came.

ROM—read-only-memory; a memory storage capacity the user can read only and not alter.

Software—the instructions, programs, rules, etc., that make a computer work.

Terminal—a computer without a CPU that is used as an input/output station, by itself or among others, which is connected to an external CPU.

Time-sharing—a concept of handling many computer terminals so that each terminal has a satisfactory response time.

User Friendly—any computer equipment or software that is easy to understand and operate.

Windowing—the capacity of a computer to allow portions of different displays to overlap on the screen at the same time.

Word—a grouping of bits treated as a single unit by the CPU. In microcomputers a word consists of either 8 or 16 bits.

Word Processor—a computer program or system that is geared for the writing, editing, or correcting of written text.

CHAPTER EIGHTEEN

FOUR HUNDRED FAMOUS AMERICANS

It would be impossible to name all of the people who have played an important role in the history of the United States. But in this chapter we list some of the leading Americans from all walks of life, both living and dead, who have left their mark on American society.

You will find leading American authors described under "Authors and Their Works" (pp. 124–151). American Presidents are reviewed on pages 217–256.

AARON, HENRY L. "HANK" (1934–), baseball player. Born in Mobile, Alabama, Aaron began playing for the Indianapolis Clowns of the Negro League in 1952. He joined the Milwaukee Braves as shortstop in 1954 and soon moved to an outfield position. The next year he emerged as top batter of the National League with a .328 average. When the Braves won the World Series in 1957, Aaron was voted the league's Most Valuable Player. He moved with the Braves to Atlanta in 1966, and broke Babe Ruth's home-run record when he hit run number 715 on April 8, 1974 in Atlanta.

ABBOTT, BUD (1896–1974), associated in comedy with Lou Costello. A son of Harry Abbott who served with Ringling Brothers' Circus, he organized a network of burlesque houses in the generation of the Ziegfeld Follies. Abbott starred in several movies, including *One Night in the Tropics, Hold That Ghost,* and *Abbott and Costello Meet Frankenstein.* He promoted the sale of millions of war bonds in World War II and entertained troops during the war. His efforts on behalf of radio, stage, and screen performance made him a well-known entertainer in an age that placed a premium on slapstick.

ABBOTT, LYMAN (1835–1922), an ordained minister of the Congregational Church; prominent journalist and exponent of the "social gospel." Abbott was associated with *Harper's Magazine* and *The Christian Union* (also known as *The Outlook).* He authored *The Life and Literature of the Ancient Hebrews* and other titles that sought to integrate religion and science. After the publication of Charles Darwin's theories of evolution, he became involved with liberal writers and thinkers. Abbott rarely opposed the theological trends of his day. He believed that man was constantly improving, and he affirmed the essential goodness of man. Ira Brown has written an excellent biography titled *Lyman Abbott* (1953).

ABERNATHY, RALPH DAVID (1926–), civil rights leader of the Southern Christian Leadership Conference. Abernathy was closely identified with Dr. Martin Luther King and the human rights revolution of the 1960s. A deliberative preacher committed to nonviolence, he was a member of the Atlantic Ministers Union and Operation Breadbasket. This gave him a unique sensitivity to the religious applications of human needs. During the Montgomery (Alabama) bus boycott he demonstrated strength of purpose and determination that helped to change the social order. He was ordained into the Baptist ministry in 1948.

ACHESON, DEAN (1893–1971), Secretary of State under President Truman; a diplomat in the early stages of the Cold War between the United

States and the Soviet Union. Acheson wrote *Power and Diplomacy,* among other titles. He was largely responsible for the establishment of the North Atlantic Treaty Organization (NATO). During the period of McCarthyism, Acheson refused to testify against his friend Alger Hiss, who had been charged with espionage. He received many honors during his lifetime, including honorary degrees from Yale University and Wesleyan University. He was affiliated with the Democratic Party.

ACUFF, ROY (1903–), born Maynardsville, Tennessee, a noted country-music singer and bandleader. Acuff organized the Smoky Mountain Boys and has been closely associated with Nashville's Grand Ole Opry. He has achieved international fame for his songs, "Wabash Cannon Ball," "That Lonely Mountain of Clay," and "The Great Judgment Morning." He produced a succession of recording classics for Columbia Records and was elected to the Country Music Hall of Fame. An automobile accident in 1965 left him severely injured, but he recovered sufficiently to record "Roy Acuff Sings Famous Opry Favorites" in 1967. He toured college campuses and received considerable recognition for his courage and determination in the face of his injuries.

ADDAMS, JANE (1860–1935), with Ellen Gates Starr organized Hull House in Chicago, Illinois, as a social and humanitarian center. Miss Addams was an early feminist and shared a Nobel Peace Prize. She authored *The Spirit of Youth* and *The City Streets.* Miss Addams was a leader of the Progressive Party and the Women's International Peace and Freedom. She sought legislation to end the corruption of political life in Chicago, and she served as an adviser to several Presidents.

ALI, MUHAMMAD (1942–), a significant figure in American boxing history, known for his colorful and poetic use of language. Born as Cassius M. Clay, he became associated with the Black Muslims and adopted his Muslim name. He refused to be drafted into the military in 1967 and became the center of legal controversies. He won numerous Golden Gloves awards, the Olympic Championship, and the Heavyweight Championship of the world. He has engaged in limited screen roles and frequently appears on television. Leon Spinks won the Heavyweight championship from Ali at Las Vegas, Nevada on February 15, 1978.

ALLEN, ETHAN (1738–1789), author and military figure from the Revolutionary period. During the American Revolution, Allen was captured by the British and was held as a prisoner of war. He organized a militia group in Vermont known as the Green Mountain Boys, and he asked the Continental Congress to raise similar units among the other colonies. He authored a book titled *Reason the Only Grade of Man* (1784), an apology for deism.

ALLPORT, GORDON (1897–1967), outstanding psychologist and teacher. Allport wrote *The Individual and His Religion.* He was associated with Harvard University and produced several new theories of personality and social psychology. Allport was involved in many different organizations, including the British Psychological Society and the National Research Council. He received numerous honors and recognitions, and served as editor of the *Journal for Abnormal and Social Psychology* from 1937 to 1949.

ANDERSON, MARIAN (1902–), black contralto recognized as an outstanding singer within concert and operatic circles. Honored in many countries for her musical excellence, she is a native of South Philadelphia. Miss Anderson authored *My Lord, What a Morning* and has travelled extensively, giving concerts in Great Britain, Scandinavia, Germany, and the Soviet Union. She has worked with Paul Robeson and others to achieve greater freedoms for black Americans. Miss Anderson has received special recognition from the National Association for the Advancement of Colored People (NAACP) and was honored by Howard University and 20 other colleges and universities with honorary doctorates.

Muhammad Ali lands a right to George Foreman during their title bout in Kinshasa, Zaire, on Oct. 29, 1976.

ANTHONY, SUSAN B. (1820–1906), an early proponent of women's rights, identified with the leadership of the American Suffrage Association and several temperance associations. Miss Anthony organized support for the enactment of the fourteenth and fifteenth amendments to the United States Constitution. She was involved in the publication of *The History of Woman's Suffrage* and worked with Ida Harper on *The Life and Work of Susan B. Anthony.*

ARBUCKLE, ROSCOE "FATTY" (1887–1933), American actor and producer born in Smith Center, Kansas. Mr. Arbuckle was identified with numerous motion picture roles in *Moonshine, The Bell Boy,* and *The Sheriff,* among others. He organized the Comique Film Corporation.

ARMSTRONG, LOUIS (1900–1971), jazz trumpeter and vocalist, also known as "Satchmo." Mr. Armstrong appeared in numerous movies, including *Pennies from Heaven, New Orleans, The Glenn Miller Story,* and *Hello Dolly.* Born in New Orleans, he revolutionized American Jazz. After touring the United States with his band, he played at the London Palladium and made numerous appearances before royalty in Sweden, Belgium, Holland, and Denmark. Mr. Armstrong's performance in *High Society* and numerous other recordings have made him an enduring part of the American scene.

ARMSTRONG, NEIL (1930–), veteran astronaut; the first man to set foot on the moon. Born near Wapakoneta, Ohio, he graduated from Purdue University. As a test pilot he was chosen to serve with Edwin Aldrin and Michael Collins on the historic moon flight of July 16, 1969. He also served as the command pilot for the later Gemini 8 program. Mr. Armstrong was an aviator for the United States Naval Reserve from 1949 to 1950. His name will always be associated with the famous words he spoke as he set foot on the moon: "One small step for man; one giant step for mankind."

ARNAZ, DESI (1917–), Latin American musician, comedian, and television producer. Born in Santiago, Cuba, he was associated in comedy with Lucille Ball during the early stages of television. Mr. Arnaz starred in several lesser-known movie musicals until he organized Desilu Productions with his wife, Lucille Ball. He co-starred with Lucille Ball in other movie productions, such as *The Long, Long, Trailer* and *Forever Darling.* He hosted *Desilu Playhouse.* After 1962, he became an independent producer and president of Desi Arnaz Productions. He served during World War II in the United States Army.

ARNOLD, BENEDICT (1741–1801), a patriot and traitor from the Revolutionary period. Arnold organized an army early in the Revolutionary War, but escaped to the British in 1781. His name is synonymous with treachery. In the winter of 1776–1777, he was accused of misconduct and of stealing property from merchants in Montreal during the Canadian campaign. In anger, he resigned his commission in 1777. He conceived the idea of turning over the command of West Point to the English for a ransom; the plot was uncovered and he was forced to seek sanctuary with the English army.

ASBURY, FRANCIS (1745–1816), an early bishop in the Methodist Episcopal Church, associated with John Wesley. Asbury came to America as a missionary and remained to become a leading spokesman for the Independent Methodist Episcopal Church of America. He preached in the Pennsylvania, Maryland, Delaware, and Virginia colonies with a vigor and effectiveness that attracted popular notice. He developed a feud with rival church leader, Thomas Rankin, and during the American Revolution, they were asked to return to England. Rankin left but Asbury remained and became a leading force in the development of religious independence. He authored *Journals and Letters,* edited by Elmer T. Clark (1958).

ASTAIRE, FRED (1899–), American dancer and entertainer. His more famous screen performances include *Easter Parade* (1948), *On the Beach* (1959), and *The Pleasure of His Company* (1961). Mr. Astaire authored *Steps in Time.* His dancing abilities were emphasized in most of his screen performances, such as *The Ziegfeld Follies.* He starred on numerous television specials and occasionally appeared on *The Alcoa Premier.*

ASTOR, JOHN JACOB (1763–1848), American capitalist and entrepreneur. Born in Germany, he immigrated to America and became involved in fur-trading. He organized the American

Fur Company. Mr. Astor's life was characterized by the amassing of incredible wealth. Following the Louisiana Purchase, his trading activities penetrated the Northwest Territories; his traders would collect furs and sell them in the Far East. The town of Astoria was named after the family. After 1800, he became more interested in New York City real estate.

ATTUCKS, CRISPUS (1723–1770), among the group that precipitated the Boston Massacre. Attucks was among the first to die in the struggle that led to the American Revolution. Attucks has been described as a mulatto owned by Deacon William Browne of Framingham, Massachusetts. Although little is known about his life before the Boston Massacre, he has achieved stature as a martyr and patriot. J. B. Fisher, in the *American Historical Record,* Volume I (1872), sought to analyze the deeper meaning of Crispus Attucks' life.

AUDUBON, JOHN J. (1785–1851), a popular naturalist and *ornithologist* (one who studies birds). A man of science, he was responsible for the classification of numerous bird species. Audubon authored *Birds of America,* a classic in the study of birds. His fame extended to Europe. Audubon's earliest research was completed in the wilderness of Kentucky; he travelled to Henderson, Kentucky, to study rare birds. His famous bird drawings evolve from this period. His work is judged as excellent art and science.

AUTRY, GENE (1907–), singer, actor, and entertainer born in Tioga, Texas. Autry made his first record in 1929, singing cowboy songs. He starred in over eighty movies and owns several radio stations in the Southwest and on the West Coast. He has written many songs, including "You're the Only Star in My Blue Heaven" and "Here Comes Santa Claus." He has also produced several television specials.

BAEZ, JOAN (1941–), folk singer and political activist identified with the anti-war protests of the 1960s. Her musical style reflects melancholy and sadness. Miss Baez was a student at Boston University Fine Arts School. Early in her career, she appeared in Ballard Room and Club 47, and she attracted attention at the Newport (R.I.) Folk Festival. She toured college campuses and in 1962 had a successful Carnegie Hall concert. She established the Institute for the Study of Non-violence in Carmel, California.

BAILEY, F. LEE (1933–), defense attorney born in Waltham, Massachusetts. Bailey achieved early fame in the second murder trial of Dr. Sam Sheppard, in which he won Dr. Sheppard's acquittal. He has been described as the most significant criminal lawyer in contemporary America. After Albert DeSalvo's revelations regarding the Boston Strangler Case, he fought for DeSalvo's acquittal but lost. The DeSalvo trial has been regarded as a classic episode in American legal history.

BAILEY, PEARL (1918–), female singer born in Newport News, Virginia. Miss Bailey attended various public schools until she achieved early fame as a popular vocalist with stage bands in New York. She has performed in several Broadway musicals, including *The House of Flowers.* She played significant roles in several screen plays, including *Carmen Jones* and *Variety Girl.*

BALL, LUCILLE (1911–), actress, television personality, producer, and director. Born in Jamestown, New York, she achieved early fame with her first husband, Desi Arnaz, in the successful television comedy series, *I Love Lucy.* She organized the Desilu Production Company and achieved additional successes in several film productions, including *Forever Darling* and *Love From a Stranger.* Miss Ball has been regarded as the most significant personality from the "situation comedy" programs of American television. Her programs have been syndicated around the world.

BALL, THOMAS (1819–1911), sculptor born in Boston, Massachusetts. Ball achieved early fame at the New England Museum. He travelled to Florence, Italy, at the end of the American Civil War, and received several significant commissions. His more famous creations include *Christmas Morning, St. John the Evangelist* and *Love Memories.* He authored an autobiography titled *My Threescore Years and Ten.* He returned to America in 1897. His most famous work done in the United States is the statue of President Washington.

BARNUM, PHINEAS T. (1810–1891), showman and organizer of circus performances. In 1844, Barnum engaged the services of Tom

Thumb, a dwarf, and travelled to Europe for a series of shows. Barnum was responsible for the early and successful appearances of Jenny Lind in America. He ran for Congress and was defeated. He then organized what came to be called "The Greatest Show on Earth," launching the circus firm of Barnum and Bailey in 1881. Barnum authored the *Life of P. T. Barnum Written by Himself* in 1855.

BASIE, WILLIAM "COUNT" (1904-1984), jazz musician, band leader, and composer. Born in Red Bank, New Jersey, Basie has been featured in concerts at Carnegie Hall and Lincoln Center. He has given command performances before the Queen of England and was featured at the Kennedy Inaugural Ball. Basie has also performed on numerous television programs. His new jazz styles and themes have achieved distinction.

BEAN, ROY (1825-1904), rough-and-ready judge of the American frontier. Born in Mason County, Kentucky, Bean worked as teamster and saloonkeeper in the Southwest until he settled in San Antonio, Texas. In 1882, he moved up the Pecos River and established a saloon for workers who were building the Southern Pacific Railroad. Appointed justice of the peace, he made his saloon in Vinegaroon, Texas his courtroom. Bean was noted for his humor. He became known as "the law west of the Pecos."

BEECHER, HENRY WARD (1813–1887), clergyman and public figure born in Litchfield, Connecticut. Beecher attended Amherst College and became a minister. He sought to effect a moral change in the lives of his audience. He edited the *Western Farmer and Gardener,* based in Indianapolis. In 1847, he was called to Park Street Church as minister; he rejected the invitation and launched a public speaking campaign against slavery in the United States.

BEECHER, LYMAN (1775–1863), clergyman and father of Henry Ward Beecher. Born in New Haven, Connecticut, the elder Beecher was instrumental in organizing the American Bible Society. He served as president of Lane Theological Seminary in Cincinnati, and became embroiled in controversies of the General Assembly of the Presbyterian Church in Ohio.

BELL, ALEXANDER GRAHAM (1847–1922), prolific American inventor born in Edinburgh, Scotland. Although the telephone is his most famous invention, Bell developed many early electronic devices for the deaf. His long-time assistant was Thomas Watson. The first words transmitted by telephone on April 3, 1877 were "Mr. Watson, come here; I want you." Bell received many honors, including the Volta Prize awarded by the French Government. He wrote *Duration of Life* and *Condition Associated with Longevity* (1918).

BENNY, JACK (1894–1974), violinist, vaudeville star, radio and motion-picture personality. Born in Waukegan, Illinois, as Benjamin Kubelsky, he took the stage name of Jack Benny. He achieved significant fame through his television program, *The Jack Benny Show.* He entertained the troops during World War II, and was honored by the National Academy of Television Arts and Science in 1957 for his contributions to the world of entertainment.

BERLIN, IRVING (1888–), composer and musician. Born in Russia and migrated to the United States in 1893, Berlin transformed American popular music with his relaxing themes and topical lyrics. Among his famous song titles are: "All Alone," "Remember Reaching for the Moon," and "When I Lost You." His most famous composition was "God Bless America." Berlin composed the stage musicals *Annie Get Your Gun, Call Me Madam,* and *Mr. President.*

BERNSTEIN, LEONARD (1918–), conductor, pianist, and composer. Born in Lawrence, Massachusetts, he became a student of Fritz Reiner and Serge Koussevitsky. He was appointed musical director of the New York Philharmonic, where he achieved worldwide recognition. Among his more famous musical creations have been *West Side Story* (1957) and music for *On the Waterfront* (1954). Bernstein wrote *The Joy of Music* (1959) and *Leonard Bernstein's Young People's Concerts for Reading and Listening* (1962).

BETHUNE, MARY MCLEOD (1875–1955), black educator. Born in Mayesville, South Carolina, she studied at Moody Bible Institute of Chicago and later served as president of Bethune-Cookman College. She was appointed as special adviser for minority affairs to President

Franklin Roosevelt and was associated with the National Association for the Advancement of Colored People (NAACP). For a time, she was president of the Central Life Insurance Company and served with the United Negro College Fund. Mrs. Bethune received many honors and degrees from colleges and universities, including Howard University, Wilberforce University, Atlanta University, and the Tuskegee Institute.

BLACK HAWK (1767–1838), Indian war chief. Born in a Sauk village on the Rock River in Illinois, Black Hawk opposed a treaty negotiated by William Henry Harrison with the Sauk nation in 1804; the treaty gave the United States all Sauk country east of the Mississippi River. Black Hawk assisted the British forces in the War of 1812. During the Black Hawk War, he was taken prisoner and jailed at Fort Armstrong in 1832. In 1833, he dictated the *Autobiography of Black Hawk* to a journalist, J. B. Patterson.

BLACK, HUGO L. (1886–1971), jurist and United States Senator. Born in Harlan County, Alabama, Black attended law school at the University of Alabama. He served as prosecuting attorney for Jefferson County from 1915 to 1917, and was in general law practice from 1919 to 1927. He was elected the United States Senator from Alabama for 1927–1931. He served as an associate justice on the United States Supreme Court from 1937 until his death in 1971. Black favored a liberal interpretation of the United States Constitution. He aided the Earl Warren court rulings in the area of civil rights.

BLOCK, HERBERT "HERBLOCK" (1909–), editorial cartoonist born in Chicago, Illinois. Block has served as a cartoonist with the *Washington Post* and the *Chicago Daily News.* He received the Pulitzer Prize, 1942 and 1954. He has been associated with various civil-liberty causes. Block wrote *The Herblock Book* (1952) and *Straight Herblock* (1964), among others. He was commissioned to design the United States postage stamp to commemorate the 175th anniversary of the Bill of Rights.

BOGART, HUMPHREY (1899–1957), actor and film producer. Born in New York City, Bogart portrayed outstanding screen roles without sentimentality. Among his best-known films were *African Queen, Caine Mutiny,* and *Casablanca.* He was married to Lauren Bacall. Bogart's characterization of Captain Queeg in *Caine Mutiny* received an Academy Award.

BOONE, DANIEL (1734–1820), frontier explorer and Indian fighter. Born near Reading, Pennsylvania, Boone moved to Kentucky in 1767. There he was involved with several expeditions against the Shawnee Indians, and served as captain of the local militia when Kentucky became organized as part of Virginia. Stuart Edward White's *Daniel Boone, Wilderness Scout* (1922) is regarded as the best biography of Boone.

BOOTH, EDWIN T. (1833–1893), actor of international fame. Born in Bel Air, Maryland, Booth played minor roles in *Richard III* (1849) and *The Iron Chest* (1851). Then he travelled west to California, settled in San Francisco, and appeared in leading roles as Richard III, Macbeth, and Hamlet. He went to Australia on tour in 1854 and then to New York, where he obtained a major role in *The Fool's Revenge* in 1864. His younger brother John Wilkes Booth assassinated President Abraham Lincoln.

BOOTH, JOHN WILKES (1838–1865), actor and assassin of President Abraham Lincoln. Born in Bel Air, Maryland, Booth had considerable promise as an actor. He performed with great success at the Boston Museum in 1863. His sympathies were with the South during the Civil War, and he served as a member of the Virginia militia that arrested and executed John Brown. Booth organized the conspiracy that led to the assassination of President Lincoln on April 14, 1865.

BRADY, MATTHEW B. (1823–1896), pioneer photographer. Born in Warren County, New York, Brady began making portraits with the daguerreotype, an early photographic technique developed by S.F.B. Morse and J.W. Draper. Brady published *The Gallery of Illustrious Americans* in 1850. With the approval of President Lincoln, he photographed many historic scenes during the Civil War. His innovations had far-reaching significance in the development of photography.

BRINKLEY, DAVID (1920–), broadcast journalist. Born in Wilmington, North Carolina, Brinkley served as a reporter with Wilmington *Star-News* and then as Washington correspondent for the National Broadcasting Company (NBC). With Chet Huntley, he established a reputation as news analyst and co-anchor for *The NBC News*. Brinkley has received the du Pont and Peabody Awards for outstanding journalism.

BROOKS, PHILLIPS (1835–1893), clergyman, author, and composer. Born in Boston, Massachusetts, Brooks became an outstanding leader in American Protestantism. He came from a family that treasured piety and learning; scholarship and eloquence in preaching were the characteristics of his ministry in Boston. Brooks was a leading voice in the Episcopal Church in America. He delivered several noted lectures on preaching before the Divinity School of Yale College in 1877. Alexander U.G. Allen's *Life and Letters of Phillips Brooks* is the most useful biography.

BROWN, JOHN (1800–1859), abolitionist leader. Brown was born in Tourington, Connecticut. He is remembered for his attack on Harpers Ferry, Virginia before the Civil War. Brown hoped to start a wider revolt among black people by seizing the arsenal and distributing arms among the blacks. But the attack failed; John Brown was indicted on three counts of treason and executed.

BRYAN, WILLIAM JENNINGS (1860–1925), lawyer, editor, orator, and political figure. Born in Salem, Illinois, Bryan ran unsuccessfully for President on three occasions. He was described as "The Great Commoner" because of his policies that favored farmers and common laborers. In 1913, he was named Secretary of State by President Woodrow Wilson. He opposed the United States' entry into World War. Later Bryan defended the anti-evolution educational laws passed by the State of Tennessee. He successfully prosecuted a teacher named Thomas Scopes for violating the anti-evolution statutes.

BUNCHE, RALPH (1904–1971), diplomat and human rights leader. Bunche was born in Detroit, Michigan. He attended the University of California and Harvard University, as well as the London School of Economics. He studied anthropology and colonial policy. Bunche participated in several study projects on race relations and international understanding. He attended the San Francisco Conference of the United Nations as a member of the United States delegation. Later he served as a member of the United Nations' Palestine Commission. He received the Nobel Prize, the Presidential Medal of Freedom, and the Spingarn Medal awarded by the National Association for the Advancement of Colored People (NAACP).

BURBANK, LUTHER (1849–1926), plant breeder and agricultural innovator. Burbank was born in Lancaster, Massachusetts. He was deeply influenced by Charles Darwin's views regarding plants and animal life. With an inheritance of 17 acres, he began a series of experiments that developed the "Burbank potato." He authored a significant publication titled *The Training of the Human Plant*. Burbank received an honorary degree from Tufts University. He was a fellow of the American Association for the Advancement of Science and the Royal Horticultural Society.

BURGER, WARREN (1907–), lawyer and Chief Justice of the United States. Born in St. Paul, Minnesota, Burger was appointed to the Supreme Court by President Nixon. Under his leadership, the Supreme Court has been less activist in legal sentiments than was the Earl Warren court. Burger has been involved with the Mayo Foundation. Prior to his appointment to the Supreme Court, he was a law partner in the firm Fairicy, Burger, Moore, & Costello.

BURR, AARON (1756–1836), lawyer and political figure, Vice-President under Thomas

Aaron Burr

Jefferson. Burr was born in Newark, New Jersey. After his term as Vice-President, he conspired to invade Spanish Territories in the Southwest and organize a separate nation. He killed Alexander Hamilton in a duel, which ended Burr's active involvement in politics until the conspiracy was discovered. He was tried for treason and acquitted on a legal technicality.

BURROWS, ABE (1910–), playwright and director born in New York City. Burrows wrote for the CBS and NBC radio networks. He was writer and star of *The Abe Burrows Show.* He co-authored *Guys and Dolls, Three Wishes for James,* and *How to Succeed in Business without Really Trying,* and he received a Pulitzer Prize for the last. Burrows' music achieved significance in recording with Decca Records.

BUSHNELL, HORACE (1802–1876), Congregational clergyman, author, and educator. Bushnell was born in Bantam, Connecticut. He rejected rigid Puritanism for liberal religious views. He authored *Christian Nurture* (1847), *God in Christ* (1848), and *Nature and the Supernatural* (1858). More conservative Christian thinkers regarded his views as heretical. He denied that religious conversion was necessary.

CAESAR, SID (1922–), actor and comedian born in Yonkers, New York. With the emergence of television, Sid Caesar achieved wide recognition. *Caesar's Hour* and *Sid Caesar Invites You* became popular TV programs. Mr. Caesar often appeared on *The Jackie Gleason Show* and *The Carol Burnett Show.* He starred in the motion picture, *It's a Mad, Mad, Mad, Mad World.* For his work in television, he received the Emmy Award and was named to the United States Hall of Fame.

CALDER, ALEXANDER (1898–1976), sculptor and illustrator. Born in Philadelphia, Pennsylvania, Calder studied at the Stevens Institute of Technology. He built animated wire performers called "the miniature circus" and travelled to Europe with the exhibit. As a result, he developed kinetic sculptures, or mobiles. His designs can be seen at the Lincoln Center, New York, Massachusetts Institute of Technology in Cambridge, and at the UNESCO Gardens in Paris.

CALHOUN, JOHN C. (1782–1850), American statesman and political theorist. Born in South Carolina, he served as a member of both houses of Congress and as Secretary of War in the administration of James Monroe. He served as Vice-President in 1825–1829. Calhoun authored the *South Carolina Exposition* that was a response to the so-called Tariff of Abominations. By 1830, Calhoun was promoting the theory of states' rights embraced in the Nullification Doctrine, which held that states could nullify acts of Congress. Calhoun also wrote *Disquisition on Government* and *Government of the United States,* both published posthumously.

CANTOR, EDDIE (1892–1964), comedian and humanitarian leader. Born in New York City, Mr. Cantor began his career in vaudeville and was later associated with burlesque. He toured as Sam Beverly Moon and starred in the stage productions *Broadway Brevities* (1920), *Make It Snappy* (1922), and *Whoopee* (1929). His first motion picture appearance was in 1926. Mr. Cantor was active in Jewish and Christian charities. He authored *Take My Life: The Way I See It* (1959). He received numerous recognitions for his charity work; Temple University honored him with a Doctor of Humane Letters degree.

CAPONE, ALPHONSE "AL" (1899–1947), gangster; perhaps the most notorious criminal in American history. Born in Naples, Italy, he came

Al Capone is led aboard a train to start his journey to the federal penitentiary in Atlanta, Georgia.

to the United States with his family and settled in Brooklyn, New York. In high school, he took charge of the Five Points gang. In a gang fight, he was slashed across the face with a razor blade, and carried the nickname of "Scarface Al" ever after. In 1920, gang leader Johnny Torrio summoned Capone to Chicago to supervise the sale of bootleg whiskey. Torrio retired in 1925, leaving Capone in charge of Chicago's largest crime racket. "Scarface Al" used murder, bombings, and torture to drive out his competitors. In 1927, he exerted his powers to elect "Big Bill" Thompson as mayor of the city. Capone's henchmen executed seven members of a rival gang in the infamous St. Valentine's Day Massacre of 1929. The United States Treasury Department arrested Capone in 1933 on charges of income-tax evasion. After serving 11 years in Alcatraz Prison, he retired to his Miami Beach estate.

CAPP, AL (1909–1979), newspaper cartoonist. Born in New Haven, Connecticut, Capp attended the Pennsylvania Academy of Fine Arts and the Museum of Fine Arts in Boston. He created the comic strip titled "Li'l Abner," which was widely syndicated throughout the United States. United Feature Syndicate distributed "Li'l Abner." He also served as columnist for the *New York Herald Tribune.* Capp was associated with the People to People program of the United Nations.

CARNEGIE, ANDREW (1835–1919), American industrialist, businessman, and philanthropist. Carnegie was born in Scotland. He became one of the so-called "Captains of Industry" at the turn of the century. In 1848, his family settled in the Allegheny region of Pittsburg. Carnegie was a self-educated lover of books, theater, and classical music. In the 1850s, he took advantage of the rising importance of steel. With his capital, Carnegie constructed the Bessemer Steel Rail Company. Toward the close of the century, he completely dominated the United States steel industry. He authored the article entitled "Wealth," which became the core of what sociologists called the Gospel of Wealth. He believed the rich should spend their fortunes for the welfare of the community. He supported the extensive construction of libraries that bear his name.

CARROLL, JOHN (1735–1815), first bishop of the Roman Catholic Church in America. Born in Upper Marlborough, Maryland, he supported the educational and political integration of the Roman Catholic Church with early America. Carroll sought to unify the several Catholic groups in America, and he obtained religious toleration for Catholics. Regulations developed by his associates became the first canon law in America. Carroll encouraged the establishment of parochial education, secular schools, and colleges at Georgetown (1788) and Baltimore (1799).

CARSON, KIT (1809–1868), soldier, Indian agent, and hunter. Born in Madison County, Kentucky, Carson had no formal education and remained illiterate all his life. He travelled to Arizona and southern California and married an Arapaho woman. He served as John C. Frémont's guide and helped Frémont plan expeditions to Wind River Mountains, the Oregon Trail, the Dalles River, and Klamath Lake. He guided Frémont through the Sierra Nevadas to the Great Salt Lake. Carson served in the Office of Indian Affairs and died in Fort Lyon, Colorado.

CARVER, GEORGE WASHINGTON (1861–1943), black botanist, chemist, and educator. Carver was born in Kansas Territory and attended school in Minneapolis, Kansas, and San Francisco. At Booker T. Washington's invitation, he came to the Tuskegee Institute, where he established an international reputation in horticulture and farming. He became a close friend of Henry A. Wallace, who ran for the United States Presidency. He also developed enduring friendships with Thomas Edison, Luther Burbank, and Harvey Firestone.

CHAMBERLAIN, WILT (1936–   ), professional basketball player. Born in Philadelphia, Pennsylvania, Chamberlain attended Kansas State University. He then served as star center for the Los Angeles Lakers, the Philadelphia 76ers, and the Philadelphia Warriors. In 1967, he led the National Basketball Association in points scored per season. He has achieved stature as an all-time great in the National Basketball Association.

CHANCELLOR, JOHN (1927–   ), broadcast journalist. Born in Chicago, Illinois, he attended DePaul Academy and became a reporter with the *Chicago Sun-Times.* From 1950 to 1965, he was on the staff of NBC News as a newswriter and served as a correspondent in Vienna, London, and Moscow. He served briefly on the NBC *Today* program. Under President Kennedy, Chancellor served as director of the Voice of America. In recent years, he has been anchorman with David Brinkley on the *NBC Nightly News*.

CHANNING, WILLIAM ELLERY (1780–1842), Unitarian theologian and minister. Channing was born in Newport, Rhode Island. He served as minister to the Federal Street Church in Boston most of his life. He held the view that God was merciful and would save all mankind; thus Channing established the basic tenets of Unitarianism and fathered the American Unitarian Association. Through his writings, he sponsored the movement for cultural independence from England. *The Importance and Means of a National Literature* (1830) is the most significant of his writings.

CHAPMAN, JOHN "JOHNNY APPLESEED" (1774-1845), planter of apple orchards on the American frontier. We cannot determine his parentage and place of birth; he was simply known as "Johnny Appleseed." He enjoyed long trips for the study of birds. Chapman's orchards of apple trees became legendary, particularly around Ashland County near Mansfield, Ohio. He said he was a primitive Christian. In 1838, he travelled into Allen County, Indiana. The legend of Johnny Appleseed is closely identified with the Westward expansion.

CHAVEZ, CESAR (1927–), union organizer among migrant farm workers. Chavez was born near Yuma, Arizona. His early activities in the California Community Service Organization established his abilities as an activist and organizer. He became director of the Organized National Farm Workers Association, which then merged with the Agricultural Workers Organizing Committee of the AFL-CIO. Chavez' ability to organize boycotts and strikes made the growers in the Modesto and Sacramento Valleys of California hostile toward his work. Chavez served in the United States Navy Reserve during World War II.

CHISHOLM, SHIRLEY (1924–), black Congresswoman and outspoken political leader born in Brooklyn, New York. She attended Brooklyn College and Columbia University; she has received honorary degrees from Pratt Institute, Hampton Institute, William Patterson College, and Capital University, among others. The Congresswoman has served in numerous organizations that deal with social programs and public policy. In 1972, she made an unsuccessful bid for the United States Presidency. She has written numerous books and pamphlets, including *Unbought and Unbossed* (1970) and *The Good Fight* (1973).

CLARK, WILLIAM (1770–1838), frontier explorer and Indian fighter born in Caroline County, Virginia. Clark served with "Mad" Anthony Wayne in his campaign against the Indians. He joined Meriwether Lewis for expeditions to the Pacific Northwest. Clark was skilled in dealing with Indians and making maps. His diaries of the Lewis and Clark expeditions are essential to our early knowledge of the Northwest Territories. Clark was appointed as superintendent of Indian affairs for the Louisiana Territories. He was a highly regarded soldier and explorer.

CLAY, HENRY (1777–1852), Secretary of State and political leader for a generation (1812–1852). Born in Hanover County, Virginia, Clay fathered the "American System"—a legislative program to unite the industrial East with the farming West. Clay's plan established protective tariffs and provided federal money for public improvements. Clay ran for the Presidency in 1844 as candidate of the Whig Party and lost. He was the

Henry Clay addressing the U.S. Senate

architect of the Compromise of 1850, which delayed the controversies that erupted in Civil War a decade later.

COBB, TY (1886–1961), regarded by many as the greatest offensive player in baseball history; called "the Georgia Peach." He was born in Narros, Georgia. Cobb was a fierce competitor; he appeared in more games (3,033), batted more times (11,429), with more hits (4,191), finished with a higher lifetime average (.367) than any other major league player. Cobb achieved his reputation with the Detroit Tigers, with which he spent 22 seasons. He was elected into the Baseball Hall of Fame in 1936.

CODY, WILLIAM F. "BUFFALO BILL" (1846–1917), Indian fighter whose fame became part of literature and legend; he established a Wild West show that achieved international standing. Cody was born in Scott County, Iowa. After serving in the Civil War, he worked as a civilian scout for the United States Army. He is said to have slaughtered 4,280 buffalo in an eight-month period to provide food for the Army. His reputation in marksmanship was equalled only by his memory of terrain and geography. Cody engaged in over sixteen Indian battles; his popularity as a showman developed later in life.

COFFIN, HENRY SLOANE (1877–1954), clergyman, author and educator. Born in New York City, Coffin became a leader of liberal evangelicalism. He served as president of Union Theological Seminary and was an effective preacher. Coffin sought to apply Christianity to social problems and tried to improve theological education. He served as a fellow of the Corporation of Yale University. He was moderator of the General Assembly of the Presbyterian Church in the U.S.A. Coffin wrote numerous books, including the *Meaning of the Cross* (1931).

COLE, NAT "KING" (1919–1965), singer, entertainer, and jazz pianist. Cole was born in Montgomery, Alabama. He organized the King Cole Trio and later he achieved prominence as a singer. His musical style was relaxed. Cole's most successful recordings included "Nature Boy" and "Walking My Baby Back Home." His name and voice are associated with the song "Unforgettable." He appeared in several motion pictures without distinction.

COPLEY, JOHN SINGLETON (1738–1815), American painter in the realist tradition, born in Boston, Massachusetts. Copley completed several portraits of outstanding Americans, including Paul Revere and Samuel Adams. In 1774, he travelled to Europe to avoid problems of the Revolutionary era. He was elected to the Royal Academy and painted several massive historical scenes, including *Siege of Gibraltar* (1791) and *The Death of the Earl of Chatham* (1781). Copley died in London.

COSTELLO, LOU (1906–1959), film and radio comedian associated with Bud Abbott in comedy. Born in Paterson, New Jersey, Costello worked as a common laborer at Metro-Goldwyn-Mayer Studios and then as a stunt man. After his comic talents emerged, he appeared on the *Kate Smith Hour.* Costello starred in several movies, including *Hold That Ghost, Abbott and Costello in Hollywood,* and *Abbott and Costello Meet the Mummy.* He is best known for his work in the comedy of errors.

CROCKETT, DAVID (1786–1836), political figure, Indian fighter, and celebrity of the American frontier. Born in Hawkins County, Tennessee, Crockett was involved with the so-called Creek War against Creek Indians in Alabama. He was elected to the Tennessee legislature and later won a seat in the United States House of Representatives. After three terms in Congress, he returned to Tennessee to organize an expedition to Texas, looking for new land and challenge. He died in the Battle of the Alamo.

CRONKITE, WALTER (1916–   ), broadcast journalist. Born in St. Joseph, Missouri, Cronkite began his career with the *Houston Post,* where he served as reporter. After a succession of assignments, he became a news correspondent with the American forces in World War II. He began his association with Columbia Broadcasting System (CBS) in 1950 and was assigned to develop the news department. In 1953, he began the narration of a series titled *You Are There;* in 1952, he inaugurated national television coverage of the political conventions; and in 1962, he became anchorman for the *CBS Evening News.* His name is synonymous with television news.

CROSBY, FRANCES J. "FANNY" (1820–1915), Christian composer born in New York City.

She wrote over five thousand hymns, including "Safe in the Arms of Jesus" and "There's Music in the Air." When six weeks old, she lost her eyesight. She entered an institution for the blind at age 15, and taught there from 1847 to 1858. She authored numerous publications that included *The Blind Girl and Other Poems* (1844), *A Wreath of Columbia's Flowers* (1859), and *Autobiography* (1906).

CROSBY, HARRY "BING" (1904–1977), singer, songwriter, and actor. Born in Tacoma, Washington, Crosby's easygoing manner suited the emerging style of popular music. He studied law for a period of time, then entered show business. The songs "Ghost of a Chance" and "When the Blue of the Night" became associated with his voice. He appeared in a series of filmed musical comedies with Bob Hope and Dorothy Lamour. He received an Academy Award for his performance in the film, *Going My Way* (1944). "I'm Dreaming of a White Christmas" is the song commonly associated with Crosby. His autobiography was entitled *Call Me Lucky*.

CURTIS, CYRUS H. K. (1850–1933), magazine publisher. Born in Portland, Maine, Curtis was educated in the public schools. He moved to Philadelphia, where he joined the staff of the *Tribune*. His success in publishing the *Ladies' Home Journal* achieved national recognition, and he became president of the newly organized Curtis Publishing Company. There he pursued other magazine enterprises, including *Country Gentleman* and the *Saturday Evening Post*. Under Curtis' direction, the *Post* achieved a national audience. He acquired the *New York Evening Post* in 1923 in an effort to compete with the Hearst papers and the *New York Times*.

CUSTER, GEORGE (1839–1876), soldier commonly known for his military operations against hostile Sioux and Cheyenne Indians. Custer was born in New Rumley, Ohio. In 1876, he was defeated in an epochal battle at the Little Big Horn in Wyoming. He and his entire army of 655 men were killed by a far superior force of Indians. Custer wrote an interesting commentary titled *My Life on the Plains;* his *War Memoirs* give a useful recollection of the Civil War.

DALEY, RICHARD (1902–1976), leading political figure of the Democratic Party. Born in the Bridgeport district of Chicago, Mr. Daley studied law at De Paul University. He was admitted to the bar in 1933. Through patronage and appointment power, he organized the Illinois Democratic Party with ultimate loyalty to himself. In 1955, he became mayor of Chicago and retained that post until his death, directing one of the most powerful political structures in American history. In 1960, he supported John F. Kennedy's bid for the Presidency and delivered his state for the Democratic presidential contender. In 1968, he was criticized for his treatment of anti-war protesters during the Democratic National Convention in Chicago. In spite of the criticism, political writers considered him the most effective mayor of a large metropolitan city.

DANA, CHARLES A. (1819–1897), newspaper editor and publisher. Dana was born at Hinsdale, New Hampshire. After a series of newspaper jobs, Dana used his friendship with Horace Greeley to secure the position of city editor at the *New York Tribune*. After the Civil War, he acquired the *New York Sun,* which he built into one of New York's greatest daily papers. He was described as a man of wide intellectual interests. Dana wrote *Recollections of the Civil War* (1898), *The Art of Newspaper Making* (1899), and other books.

DANIELS, JOSEPHUS (1862–1948), journalist and statesman, ambassador to Mexico, and Secretary of the Navy under President Woodrow Wilson. Daniels was born in Washington, North Carolina. He became a close friend of William Jennings Bryan and devoted his energies to the Democratic Party. Daniels used considerable restraint in his dealings with the Mexican government; he was a man of great diplomacy and political skill. Daniels authored several books, including *Tar Heel Editor, The Wilson Era: Years of War and After,* and *The Cabinet Diaries of Josephus Daniels.*

DAVIS, JEFFERSON (1808–1889), President of the Confederate States of America. Born in Todd County, Kentucky, Davis attended West Point Military Academy and graduated in 1828. He served with distinction in the Black Hawk Indian War of 1832. He then served as Secretary of War and as a Senator before the outbreak of the Civil War. After the Civil War broke the Confederacy, he lived a sad and helpless existence. Davis wrote *The Rise and Fall of the Confederate Government.*

DE FOREST, LEE (1873-1961), an inventor who pioneered in radio and broadcasting. De Forest was born at Council Bluffs, Iowa. He worked with the Western Electric Company in Chicago, where he invented the audio amplifier. This was the single most significant contribution to the advance of radio, and De Forest is often regarded as the father of radio. He held major responsibilities in the De Forest Wireless Telegraph Company and the Radio Telephone Company. He wrote *Father of Radio* (1950). William R. Maclaurin's *Invention and Innovation in the Radio Industry* explains De Forest's contributions.

DeMILLE, CECIL B. (1881-1959), motion picture producer and director who established a reputation for his spectacular portrayals of biblical themes. DeMille was born in Ashfield, Massachusetts. *The Ten Commandments, The King of Kings, The Sign of the Cross,* and *Samson and Delilah* were some of his best-known films. His screen productions cost millions, yet he was able to produce films that were highly profitable. DeMille rejected criticism that his productions were garish and unartistic by saying that public taste determines the standards of artistry. In later years, he developed movies that reflected historical themes, including *The Greatest Show on Earth, Union Pacific,* and *The Plainsman.*

DEMPSEY, JACK (1895–1983), champion heavyweight boxer. Because Dempsey was born in Manassa, Colorado, he was called the "Manassa Mauler." Initially he won the heavyweight championship from Jess Willard in 1919. The most controversial aspect of his career was the "long count" during the second fight between Dempsey and Gene Tunney. In the seventh round, Dempsey floored Tunney but failed to go to a neutral corner. The count was delayed; Tunney recovered and subsequently won the fight. After retirement, he became a restauranteur in New York City. With Bob Considine and Bill Slocum he co-authored the book, *Dempsey.*

DEWEY, GEORGE (1837–1917), first Admiral of the Navy; hero of the Spanish-American War. Dewey served under Admiral David G. Farragut during the Civil War. In 1897, he requested sea duty in the Pacific as commodore of the new American fleet. He led his six boats into Manila Bay on May 1, 1898, and destroyed the Spanish fleet of 10 ships. In August, he used the American navy to assist General Wesley Merritt's capture of Manila. He returned to a hero's welcome in the United States, where Congress named him Admiral of the Navy. Dewey published his autobiography in 1913.

DEWEY, JOHN (1859–1952), educator and pragmatic philosopher who advocated traditional values of education. Dewey was born in Burlington, Vermont. He believed that science was the highest manifestation of human intelligence. He established his reputation through articles in the *Journal of Speculative Philosophy.* Dewey studied at the University of Vermont, Johns Hopkins, the University of Michigan, and the University of Chicago. At Chicago, he turned to pedagogy and educational philosophy. He authored many books, including *Democracy and Education* (1916) and *Reconstruction in Philosophy* (1920).

DIMAGGIO, JOE (1914–), noted baseball player born in Martinez, California. DiMaggio played as an outfielder with the San Francisco Seals until 1934, when he was purchased by the New York Yankees. In his first year the Yankees recognized him as a potential star; he batted an average of .323, fielded .978, and established the

Admiral Dewey with President McKinley and Cardinal Gibbons, 1899

longest consecutive hitting record by hitting safely in 56 consecutive games. Fans called DiMaggio the "Yankee Clipper." On December 11, 1951, he announced his retirement from baseball. His subsequent marriage to actress Marilyn Monroe drew national attention.

DISNEY, WALTER E. "WALT" (1901–1966), filmmaker, cartoonist, and entertainment entrepreneur. A native of Chicago, Disney developed the cartoon characters Mickey Mouse and Donald Duck in the 1920s. He developed the first feature-length animated cartoons in *Snow White* (1938). Disney's later films *Pinocchio, Bambi, Fantasia,* and *Mary Poppins* achieved spectacular success. The amusement parks named Disneyland and Disney World bear his genius. *The Disney Version: The Life, Times, Art, and Commerce of Walt Disney,* by Richard Schickel (1968) is the most comprehensive study on Disney.

DIX, DOROTHEA L. (1802–1887), humanitarian associated with Dr. William Ellery Channing. Born in Hampden, Maine, Miss Dix became the tutor to Dr. Channing's children. Under Channing's influence, she initiated significant reforms in mental institutions. During the Civil War, she served as a superintendent of nurses; after the war, she continued her efforts on behalf of the mentally ill. Her reforms attracted international attention, particularly in Europe. Francis Tiffany's *The Life of Dorothea Lynde Dix* (1890) is the most definitive biography.

DOOLITTLE, JAMES H. "JIMMY" (1896–), aviator, oil company executive, and war hero. A native of Alameda, California, Doolittle became one of the most famous of American heroes during World War II. He led the first bombing of Japan and commanded thousands of planes in attacks on North Africa, Italy, and Germany. He commanded attacks upon German cities from 1944 to the end of the war in Europe. Doolittle then joined General Douglas MacArthur's command in the Far East until the end of the war in the Pacific. He became an executive of the Shell Oil Company after the war. In the 1950s, he became involved with NACA, which later became the National Aeronautics and Space Administration.

DOUGLAS, STEPHEN A. (1813-1861), United States Senator and candidate for the Presidency, identified with the Democratic Party. Born in Brandon, Vermont, Douglas spearheaded the new Democratic Party in Chicago. He sponsored efforts to make Chicago a significant rail center. The senatorial campaign of 1858 between Douglas and Abraham Lincoln was a rehearsal for the 1860 presidential campaign, even though Lincoln lost. In the famous Lincoln-Douglas debates, Lincoln established his national reputation. Many argue that if Douglas had become President, he could have prevented a Civil War. For a review of this argument, see Gerald M. Capers, *Stephen A. Douglas, Defender of the Union,* edited by Oscar Handlin (1959).

DOUGLAS, WILLIAM O. (1898–1980), liberal justice of the United States Supreme Court. Douglas was born in Yakima, Washington, and attended Columbia Law School. He served briefly as a professor at the Yale Law School, worked on legal matters for the Securities and Exchange Commission. In 1939, he was appointed to the Supreme Court and became the leader of the liberal wing of the court. He challenged tradition in his opinions on obscenity, religion, desegregation, and the rights of criminals. He wrote several books, including *Points of Revolution* (1970). The best study of Douglas' career is *Douglas of the Supreme Court: A Selection of His Opinions,* edited by Vern Countryman (1959).

DOUGLASS, FREDERICK (1817–1895), abolitionist, journalist, and orator. He was born at Tuckahoe, Maryland with the name of Frederick Augustus Washington Bailey. After he escaped from slavery he changed his name to Frederick Douglass. Greatly influenced by William Lloyd Garrison's *The Liberator,* Douglass joined the Massachusetts Anti-Slavery Society. He wrote *The Narrative of the Life of Frederick Douglass, an American Slave* (1845), which some abolitionists thought was too inflammatory. Douglass disagreed with William Lloyd Garrison on proper abolitionist procedures.

DREW, CHARLES RICHARD (1904–1950), a black surgeon who developed the blood bank and new methods for training surgeons. A native of Washington, D.C., Dr. Drew implemented the blood bank in World War II as director of the American Red Cross Bank. He chaired the department of surgery at Howard University and recommended new surgical standards to the National Medical Association. Dr. Drew received the

Spingarn Medal of the National Association for the Advancement of Colored People. He was awarded numerous honorary degrees from colleges and universities.

DU BOIS, WILLIAM E. B. (1868–1963), major black scholar and leader of black protest and panafricanism. Born in Great Barrington, Massachusetts, he received the Master of Arts degree and a doctorate from Harvard University. Dr. Du Bois organized the Niagara group, an all-black protest organization of scholars and professionals. He was one of the founders of the National Association for the Advancement of Colored People (NAACP) in 1909. He edited *Crisis,* a publication of the NAACP, and regarded himself as a Socialist. Dr. Du Bois authored numerous books and pamphlets.

DULLES, JOHN FOSTER (1888–1959), foreign diplomat and Secretary of State under President Dwight D. Eisenhower. Born in the nation's capital, Dulles served at the Paris Peace Conference in 1919. He was legal adviser to the United States delegation at the San Francisco conference on the United Nations. He supported General Eisenhower during the 1952 election. As Secretary of State, Dulles developed the broader aspects of North Atlantic Treaty Organization (NATO). He dealt courageously with the Suez Crisis of 1956 by compelling President Nasser of Egypt to withdraw. Louis L. Gerson's *John Foster Dulles* (1967) is a good biography of Dulles.

DURANTE, JIMMY (1893–1980), entertainer and songwriter born in New York City. Durante began his career in the Bowery district of New York, where he organized a five-piece jazz band for Club Alamo in Harlem. At this time, he was only known as a pianist. In 1923, he opened Club Durante. Other entertainers were attracted to his comedy and musical routines. He wrote many songs after 1923, including "I'm Jimmy, That Well-Dressed Man" and "Did You Ever Have the Feeling That You Wanted to Go?" He appeared in several Broadway musicals, including *Red, Hot and Blue* with Ethel Merman, *Keep off the Grass, Stars in Your Eyes.* He was nicknamed the "Schnozzle" for the generous proportions of his nose. Durante was regarded with great affection as an entertainer.

DUROCHER, LEO (1906–), professional baseball manager. Born in West Springfield, Massachusetts, he played for a time as a second baseman for the New York Yankees. Then he was shortstop for the Cincinnati Reds and St. Louis Cardinals. His fame comes from his management of the Brooklyn Dodgers, who won the National League pennant in 1951 and 1954. He became a television announcer for a short time, then returned as a manager for the Chicago Cubs 1966-1972 and the Houston Astros in 1972-1973. He co-authored a book entitled, *Nice Guys Finish Last* with Ed Linn. That phrase became synonymous with his name.

DWIGHT, TIMOTHY (1752–1817), Congregationalist minister and president of Yale College. Dwight was born in Northhampton, Massachusetts, and received his education at Hopkins Grammar School in New Haven, Connecticut. Dwight served in the Massachusetts Legislature, then taught Latin and Greek. He wrote "The Conquest of Canaan," an epic poem. In 1795, he became the president of Yale College; he administered the affairs of the college, taught moral philosophy, and served in the college pulpit on Sundays. Kenneth Silverman's *Timothy Dwight* is a significant study of his life.

EARHART, AMELIA (1898–1937), aviatrix. A native of Atchison, Kansas, Miss Earhart attended Columbia University and taught extension courses for the Commonwealth of Massachusetts. She was the first woman to cross the Atlantic in an airplane. Miss Earhart became the aviation editor of *Cosmopolitan Magazine* and vice-president of National Airways. She received numerous honors and recognitions, including the Distinguished Flying Cross and the gold medal of the National Geographic Society. She wrote *20 Hours, 40 Minutes* (1928) and *The Fun of It* (1931). Miss Earhart's plane went down in the Pacific Ocean as she was completing a round-the-world flight.

EASTMAN, GEORGE (1854–1932), inventor, industrialist, and mass producer of photographic equipment. Eastman was born in Waterville, New York. He made photography available to the general public. Eastman's discoveries in chemical processing were essential to the United States war effort during World War I. He developed an innovative system of profit-sharing that allowed his employees to enjoy the Eastman Company's profits. Eastman was a lonely man who took his own life. The best single work on Eastman is Carl W. Ackerman's *George Eastman* (1930).

EDDY, MARY BAKER (1821–1910), established the Church of Christ—Scientist in an effort to apply religion to health. She was born at Bow, New Hampshire. Her nervous condition in early life brought several illnesses, which led to her study of science and health. In 1908, she established the *Christian Science Monitor*. Her book, *Science and Health,* became the basis for her religious and scientific theories. Her most significant impact remained in Boston and the East Coast. *The Life of Mary Baker Eddy* by Sibyl Wilbur is the official biography.

EDDY, NELSON (1901–1967), screen star and entertainer, a native of Providence, Rhode Island. Mr. Eddy's baritone voice was matched with the soprano voice of Jeanette MacDonald for several filmed musicals. He starred in popular stage musicals during the 1930s and 1940s, including *Naughty Marietta* (1935), *Rose Marie* (1936), *Girl of the Golden West* (1938), and *Bittersweet* (1940). After his screen career, he entered radio and nightclub entertaining. Eddy made famous the songs, "Ah, Sweet Mystery of Life" and "Indian Love Call." His rich voice singing "Stouthearted Men" was his radio trademark.

EDISON, THOMAS A. (1847-1931), inventor who made outstanding contributions in electric light and electrical devices; his greatest contribution is the incandescent lamp. Born in Milan, Ohio, Edison made significant advances in organized research. Because of deafness, he was exempt from military service. Edison made major contributions to the development of the phonograph, lighting, electric-powered plant, and the movie industry. The Edison Company produced hundreds of movies, and Edison laid the basis for "talking" movies. He also contributed to the development of synthetic rubber. Edison sponsored the early work of Charles Steinmetz and other budding inventors. The best biography of Thomas A. Edison is Matthew Josephson's *Edison: A Biography* (1959).

EDWARDS, JONATHAN (1703–1758), New England minister and missionary, commonly regarded as America's finest preacher and theologian of the eighteenth century. He was born in East Windsor, Connecticut, the son and grandson of clergymen. Edwards' *Personal Narrative* (1740) reflects a close affection for God. He is associated with the Great Awakening, an intense period of revivalism in colonial America. He wrote the influential book entitled, *The Great Christian Doctrine of Original Sin Defended* (1758). His writings and sermons changed the outlook of his entire generation. He became president of the College of New Jersey, now Princeton University.

EINSTEIN, ALBERT (1879–1955), physicist, born in Ulm, Germany, and known for his theory of relativity. Einstein's general and special theories of relativity revolutionized the world of science. He approached President Roosevelt with his theories regarding the development of atomic energy for military purposes. This resulted in the "Manhattan Project" for the development of an atomic bomb. He was expelled from Nazi Germany because of his Jewish heritage, and this had a profound impact on his life. Einstein regarded himself a pacifist and humanitarian. Carl Seelig's biography, *Albert Einstein: A Documentary Biography* (1956), is one of the best portraits of Einstein.

Albert Einstein
This photograph is considered to be the last one made of the physicist. The occasion was Professor Einstein's 76th birthday on Mar. 14, 1955.

Douglas Fairbanks, Sr. (right) and son Douglas, (ca.) 1933

FAIRBANKS, DOUGLAS SR. (1883–1939), distinguished American actor born in Denver, Colorado. His marriages attracted national attention, particularly to Mary Pickford (divorced in 1935) and Lady Ashley. He made his first stage appearance in New York City; among other plays, he appeared in *All For a Girl, The Cub,* and *Show Shop.* He also appeared in motion pictures, such as *His Majesty the American, When the Clouds Roll By, The Mark of Zorro, Robin Hood,* and *The Taming of the Shrew.* He organized his own production company and achieved national attention for his somber portrayals.

FARRAGUT, DAVID G. (1801–1870), naval officer who carried significant assignments during the American Civil War. Born at Campbells Station, Tennessee, he opposed the Southern cause and migrated north to Hastings-on-the-Hudson. His initial assignment was to open the Mississippi to Union battleships. He stationed his gunboats in the Gulf of Mexico, which gave him a more direct striking capability between 1861 to 1864. In 1864, he was assigned to strike at Confederate defenses in Mobile Bay. His success led to the command to strike defenses at Wilmington, North Carolina, which he also accomplished. Farragut was regarded as among the outstanding heroes of the Civil War. A. T. Mahan's *Admiral Farragut* (1892) is still a classic.

FIELD, MARSHALL (1834-1906), merchant and chain-store retailer. Born near Conway, Massachusetts, Field served as a travelling salesman before he was admitted to partnership in the retail firm of Farwell, Field and Company. Unlike A. T. Stewart, John Wanamaker, and other leading retailers of his day, Field was not interested in political activity nor philanthropy; but he did give money to the newly established University of Chicago and fostered the establishment of the Chicago Manual Training School. He was also associated with the establishment of the Field Museum of Natural History in Chicago, and his will provided for the construction of the building in Chicago, and that houses the Field Museum.

FIELDS, W. C. (1879–1946), comedian of the stage, motion pictures, and radio. Fields was born in Philadelphia, Pennsylvania. His first appearances were in vaudeville productions and the Ziegfeld Follies. His fame developed from his movie appearances, in films such as *So's Your Old Man, It's the Old Army Game, One in a Million, David Copperfield, Never Give a Sucker an Even Break,* and his most popular *My Little Chickadee.* He also reached a national audience through his radio broadcast, *The Chase and Sanborn Hour.* Fields was highly regarded for his wry humor.

FINNEY, CHARLES G. (1792–1875), revivalist and educator. Finney was born in Warren, Connecticut. His term as president of Oberlin College gave Presbyterianism a significant voice in educating the ministry. His preaching style contained substance and eloquence. Finney was a strong advocate of temperance; he opposed the use of tobacco, tea, and coffee. Although a Mason, he opposed masonry. Among his more significant book titles: *Sermons on Important Subjects* (1836), *Lectures to Professing Christians* (1837), and *Lectures on Systematic Theology* (1846, 1847). His revivals reached wide audiences and had significant impact on the religious patterns of nineteenth-century America.

FITZGERALD, ELLA (1918–   ), jazz vocalist with an international reputation. Born in Newport News, Virginia, at age fifteen she entered an amateur contest at the Apollo Theatre in New York City. She was hired by Chick Webb for his band. In 1938, she gained worldwide fame with her recording of "A Tisket, a Tasket." Among her more famous recordings are "Love You Madly," "Hard-Hearted Hannah," and "He's My Guy."

Miss Fitzgerald is recognized as an outstanding performer and recording artist. She has received considerable respect in the black community for her civil rights concerns.

FORD, HENRY (1863–1947), automobile manufacturer born in Dearborn Township, Michigan. Ford learned the machinist trade and was the chief engineer for the Edison Illuminating Company. In 1903, he organized the world's largest automobile corporation. In 1914, he announced plans to involve all his workers in a profit-sharing plan, distributing millions of dollars back to his workers. His plan to mass-produce the Model T and Model A made the automobile readily available to the American public at competitive prices. He constructed assembly plants at Highland Park, Michigan, and River Rouge, Michigan; the latter was regarded as the largest single factory in the world. Ford was also active in political and humanitarian efforts. He built the Henry Ford Hospital; in 1918, he ran for the Senate and lost. Ford authored *My Life and Work* (1925) among other titles.

FOSDICK, HARRY EMERSON (1878–1969), clergyman and author who established the Riverside Church in New York, which was distinctive for its interdenominational character. Fosdick was born in Buffalo, New York. His *National Vespers* radio program brought his ideas into the national arena. He was ordained as a Baptist minister, but his theological perspective is associated with a liberal interpretation. Fosdick wrote numerous books, including *The Modern Use of the Bible* (1924) and *A Faith for Tough Times* (1952). His autobiography is contained in *The Living of These Days* (1956). He also wrote numerous hymns.

FOSTER, STEPHEN C. (1826–1864), composer of musical sketches and minstrel songs. At Jefferson College, Foster's musical capacities became evident to his teachers; he continued his education under tutors; his Negro ballads, "O Susanna" and "Away Down South," achieved instant success. In 1851, he began his work with E. P. Christy, who would sing Foster's songs. Each assisted the other. Foster's more famous songs were "The Old Folks at Home," "My Old Kentucky Home," and "Massa's in the Cold, Cold Ground." He remained in Pittsburgh, Pennsylvania most of his life; but his music gave a nostalgic reflection of Negro life in the Old South.

Benjamin Franklin
Signer of the Declaration of Independence

FRANKLIN, BENJAMIN (1706–1790), author, printer, inventor, diplomat, and scientist. Born in Boston, Massachusetts, he began a writing sequence on self-improvement at an early age. These efforts are best reflected in *Poor Richard's Almanack,* which contained slogans on personal improvement, such as: "Necessity never made a good bargain" and "It is hard for an empty sack to stand upright." Franklin became interested in electricity; he initiated projects for community improvement that included the lighting of streets with natural gas. He established police forces and circulating libraries. He also established the American Philosophical Association. Franklin served in the second Continental Congress. He travelled to France in 1776 to negotiate a treaty with the French Government, and negotiated the peace treaty with Great Britain. He served as a member of the Constitutional Convention. The best biography of Franklin is Carl Van Doren's *Benjamin Franklin* (1938).

FREMONT, JOHN C. (1813–1890), soldier and politician born in Savannah, Georgia. His explorations of Minnesota and Dakotas added to his knowledge of science and topography. He travelled the Oregon Trail with Kit Carson and explored the Columbia River. Fremont was regarded as the "Great Pathfinder." He travelled to California and wintered (1845) in Oregon. He then returned to California and served a short term as United

States Senator from California. He ran as a Presidential candidate of the newly formed Republican Party. His autobiographical sketch titled, *My Life* (1887), is a useful overview of the era.

FRIEDMAN, MILTON (1912–), foremost economist in the United States reflecting the conservative perspective. A native of Brooklyn, New York, he served as economic adviser to President Richard Nixon. He wrote *A Monetary History of the United States, 1867–1960* (1963). Friedman advocates the competitive free-market economy, and he originated the negative tax-credit idea. He is a professor at the University of Chicago; his economic theories are commonly associated with the Chicago School. Friedman has received numerous honors and awards, including the Nobel Prize for economics.

FULBRIGHT, J. WILLIAM (1905–), distinguished American political figure. Born in Sumner, Missouri, he attended the University of Arkansas and won a Rhodes scholarship to Oxford University. Fulbright received his law degree from George Washington University. From 1939 to 1941, he served as president of the University of Arkansas. In 1942, he began a political career as Representative to the United States House from the Third District. He called for the creation of the United Nations during World War II. In 1944, he was elected to the United States Senate; he sponsored laws that established an educational exchange program known as the Fulbright-Hays program. Fulbright served on the Senate Banking Committee. He criticized the war in Vietnam from his position as chairman of the Senate Foreign Relations Committee.

FULLER, R. BUCKMINSTER (1895–1983), architect, designer, and inventor. Born in Milton, Massachusetts, his earliest work was the Dymaxion House, a design that blends "dynamism" and "maximum utilization." Dymaxion House, like Fuller's Dymaxion Car, had interest but little direct use in production. He is described as a "catalyst to change." By mid-century some of his more enduring creations were taking form. The United States Pavilion at the Montreal Expo in 1967 was designed by Fuller; he was responsible for the geodesic dome that was built in Dearborn, Michigan for the Ford Motor Company. Fuller's influence is discussed by Roystan Landau, *New Directions in British Architecture* (1968).

FULTON, ROBERT (1765–1815), inventor and engineer born in Lancaster County, Pennsylvania. He built the first successful steamboat. Fulton and Robert R. Livingston designed the steamboat, which came to be called the *Clermont.* In 1807, the *Clermont* made its first trip. H. W. Dickinson's *Robert Fulton: Engineer and Artist: His Life and Works* (1913) is still a classic biography.

GALLUP, GEORGE H. (1901–), public opinion researcher. Born in Jefferson, Iowa, Gallup established his reputation as director of the American Institute of Public Opinion. He graduated from State University of Iowa, then served as a professor of journalism at Drake University and Northwestern University. His work in public opinion surveys evolved from reader-interest surveys that Gallup developed for the Des Moines *Register & Tribune,* the Cleveland *Plain Dealer* and the St. Louis *Post-Dispatch.* He established the American Institute of Public Opinion "impartially to measure and report public opinion." His surveys have become standards for political action or popularity. He has received honorary degrees from many universities, including Northwestern University and Tufts University.

GARFUNKEL, ART (1941–), singer and actor, associated in his early career with Paul Simon. Simon's acoustic guitar and Garfunkel's voice became a national standard of music during the 1960s. In 1964 they cut their first album titled, *Wednesday Morning.* One song that appeared on that album achieved national attention—"The Sound of Silence"; it eventually sold over one million copies. A succession of musical hits brought them international recognition. They composed and performed the music for the film entitled, *The Graduate.* "Bridge Over Troubled Waters" was another significant music success; in 1970, the two parted to pursue their separate careers. Garfunkel was born in Forest Hills, New York.

GARLAND, JUDY (1922–1969), actress and singer. Born in Grand Rapids, Michigan, she achieved instant success in her early portrayal of Dorothy in the film, *The Wizard of Oz.* Her singing of "Somewhere over the Rainbow" in that movie has become an American classic. She was also associated with Mickey Rooney in the Andy Hardy series of films. Her musical successes were highlighted by her performance in the film, *Easter*

Parade (with Fred Astaire); her performance in *A Star Is Born* was also widely acclaimed. In the 1960s, she made a spectacular return by appearances at the London Palladium and Carnegie Hall in New York. She received an Oscar nomination for her dramatic role in *Judgment at Nuremburg*.

GARRISON, WILLIAM L. (1805–1879), editor, reformer, and leader of abolition. In Garrison's day, the anti-slavery movement was split into two camps: those who sought gradual elimination of slavery and those who wanted immediate reform and abolition. Garrison called for the more immediate formula through his newspaper, *The Liberator*. He opposed slaveholders in his book, *Thoughts on Colonization* (1832). He criticized the New England clergy for their reluctance to condemn the broader aspects of slavery. He viewed the Civil War as a means of destroying the institution of slavery, and he wanted to disband the American Anti-Slavery Society after the Civil War. George M. Frederickson's *William Lloyd Garrison* (1969) is an excellent study of his life. Garrison was born in Newburyport, Massachusetts.

GERONIMO (1829–1909), leader of the Apache Indians. He was born with the name *Goyathlay,* and saw his family killed by Mexican troops in 1859. Taking the name *Geronimo* ("Jerome"), he led raids of revenge against white settlements in Arizona and New Mexico until he was confined to a reservation. In 1876, he led his warriors into Mexico, where he plundered white settlers for the next 10 years. He finally agreed to move to a reservation in Florida, but escaped en route. General Nelson A. Miles captured him after 18 months of pursuit. Later, Geronimo was converted to Christianity and lived peaceably with white people. He appeared in President Theodore Roosevelt's inaugural parade in 1905. *Geronimo's Story of His Life* (1906), by S. M. Barrett, gives Geronimo's own account of his experiences.

GERSHWIN, GEORGE (1898–1937), musical composer, distinguished in classical and popular fields. He was born in Brooklyn, New York. With lyricist Irving Caesar, Gershwin composed "Swanee," made famous by Al Jolson in *Sinbad*. In the 1920s he established many successes with his brother Ira: "Oh Kay," "Funny Face," "Rosalie," and "Strike Up the Band." His most distinguished efforts included *Rhapsody in Blue* (1924) for piano and jazz, and *An American in Paris* (1928). He had a fondness for jazz forms and black musical expression, and Gershwin's music reflected the current American scene. The most outstanding biography is David Ewen's *George Gershwin: His Journey to Greatness*. Gershwin's opera, *Porgy and Bess* (1935), was a stinging social commentary on racial prejudice.

Geronimo (center) and his braves shortly before surrendering.

GIBBONS, JAMES (1834–1921), Roman Catholic Cardinal born in Baltimore, Maryland. Gibbons supported the Catholic Church in a generation of change. He wrote *The Faith of Our Fathers* (1875), in which he underscored the practical applications of Catholicism. Known for his religious toleration, Gibbons supported labor organizations such as the Knights of Labor. He had considerable administrative skills, and he blended a profound affection for the church with his deep regard for America. Robert D. Cross gives a masterful summary of his contributions in *The Emergence of Liberal Catholicism in America* (1958).

GLADDEN, WASHINGTON (1836–1918), Congregationalist clergyman who sought to apply Christian principles to social problems. Gladden was born in Norwich, Connecticut. In 1866, he accepted the parish in North Adams, Massachusetts. His writings appeared in the *New York Independent* and *Scribner's Monthly,* usually on ethical themes of everyday living. He served as moderator to the National Council of Congregational Churches, where his scholarship reflected less depth and more of the conventional. He wrote several books on biblical criticism, including *Who Wrote the Bible* (1891), *How Much Is Left of the Old Doctrines* (1899), and *Social Salvation* (1902). Gladden addressed his later writings to municipal reform; he served with some distinction in interchurch associations.

GLENN, JOHN (1921–   ), aviator, astronaut, and United States Senator. Born in Cambridge, Ohio, he attended Muskingum College and trained as a naval air cadet. During World War II he flew 59 fighter bomber missions in the Pacific; he flew 90 missions in the Korean War. Glenn received the Flying Cross on five occasions and was awarded the Air Medal 19 times. He was the oldest of seven astronauts selected in April 1959 for Project Mercury program; but he was selected to make the first orbital flight in 1961. He was the first man to fly at supersonic speeds from Los Angeles to New York. In more recent years, Glenn has distinguished himself in political life as a United States Senator from Ohio.

GODDARD, ROBERT H. (1882–1945), established rocketry and the science of astronautics. Goddard's reputation was established while he was at Clark University, where the focus of his study was rocketry. He was able to perfect a system for liquid-propelled rockets. During World War II he addressed his attention to the potential of rockets in war; he concluded his life as a researcher in the employ of the Curtiss-Wright Corporation. Goddard's importance to the development of aerospace technology and interplanetary travel is great. Milton Lehman's *This High Man: The Life of Robert H. Goddard* is the only definitive biography available. *The Papers of Robert H. Goddard,* edited by Esther C. Goddard and G. Edward Pendray, is a collection of his writings.

GOLDBERG, RUBE (1883–1970), newspaper cartoonist whose funny drawings became world famous. Goldberg's political cartoons reached a wide audience through syndication. He worked for the *San Francisco Chronicle,* the *San Francisco Bulletin,* and the *New York Evening Mail.* He created the characters Lala Palooza, Mike, and Ike before he was offered the position of political cartoonist for the *New York Sun.* His reputation was established from that perspective. His cartoon, "Peace Today," was awarded a Pulitzer Prize in 1948.

GOLDWATER, BARRY M. (1909–   ), United States Senator and candidate for the Presidency in 1964. He suffered a heavy defeat in his quest for the Presidency against President Lyndon Johnson. Born in Phoenix, Arizona, Goldwater attended the University of Arizona but left to manage his family's department stores. During World War II, he served in the Army Air Forces; he helped to organize the Arizona Air National Guard. He was first elected to the Senate in 1952 and was reelected in 1958. After his defeat in 1964, he returned to Arizona for a brief period away from the Senate. The voters sent him back to the Senate in 1966. He has written numerous articles and books on his political philosophy and issues of national importance.

GOODSPEED, EDGAR J. (1871–1962), Greek scholar and Bible translator. Goodspeed studied at Denison, Ohio, Yale, and Chicago universities. In 1898, he came to the University of Chicago as a lecturer, then professor of Patristic Greek. He served as secretary to the president of the university. He devoted considerable work to developing a more readable version of the Bible. He wrote *The Conflict of Severus, The Story of the New Testament, The New Testament—an Ameri-*

can Version, The Complete Bible–an American Version. He was born in Quincy, Illinois.

GOODYEAR, CHARLES (1800–1860), inventor and noted rubber manufacturer. Goodyear was born in New Haven, Connecticut. His father was a hardware manufacturer, and Charles became associated with his father's hardware store in Philadelphia. When the store went bankrupt, he began experiments with rubber products. His fascination with inflated rubber life preservers led to his acquaintance with the American Indian Rubber Company. Goodyear wrote *Gum-Elastic and Its Varieties* and began experiments of treating rubber with sulfur and turpentine. By mid-century, the rubber industry was established in the United States and he migrated to Europe. He was honored by Napoleon III of France for his contributions to the Paris Exposition of 1855.

GOULD, CHESTER (1900–1985), cartoonist famous for his "Dick Tracy" series. Born in Pawnee, Oklahoma, Gould attended Oklahoma A & M and graduated from Northwestern University. He served as cartoonist for the Hearst Newspapers from 1924 to 1929; in 1931, he began working with the *Chicago Tribune* and created the cartoon character Dick Tracy. The character was a serious detective whose primary task was to reckon with criminal elements. "Dick Tracy" reached wide circulation through the Chicago Tribune-New York News Syndicate. The cartoon strip reached hundreds of newspapers throughout the country.

GOULD, JAY (1836–1892), builder of railroads, stock manipulator, and industrial capitalist. Born in Roxbury, New York, Gould began his career as a leather merchant. He established himself as a stock market speculator and helped the Erie Railroad compete against railroad baron Cornelius Vanderbilt. Through unscrupulous practices, he accumulated wealth at the expense of Erie Railroad and many unsuspecting investors. Later he bought an interest in the Wabash and Union Pacific Railroads. His influence extended to Manhattan's rapid transit system and the Western Union Telegraph Company. Louis M. Hacker's *The World of Andrew Carnegie* places Gould and this era into perspective.

GRAHAM, WILLIAM F. "BILLY" (1918–), evangelist and religious thinker. Born in Charlotte, North Carolina, he studied at Wheaton College. After a brief tenure as a pastor in Western Springs, Illinois, Graham became an evangelist. He served with Youth for Christ, then as president of Northwestern College in Minneapolis. He organized the Billy Graham Evangelistic Association for massive evangelism efforts. Through the radio program *Hour of Decision,* he is heard worldwide. He has written *My Answer, World Aflame,* and *Angels,* among many other titles. He has spoken to millions through crusades and television. John C. Pollock's *Billy Graham: The Authorized Biography* is a helpful view of Billy Graham's life.

GREELEY, HORACE (1811–1872), journalist, reformer, and editor. He was an early partner with the *New Yorker,* but the paper lacked profitability. In 1841, he began a more successful experiment known as the *New York Tribune.* Greeley urged social reform and resisted revolutionary approaches. He opposed the pro-slavery Compromise of 1850. Greeley was instrumental in the establishing of the Republican Party; after the Civil War, he became identified with the Radical Republicans. Soon frustrated with that group, he established the Liberal Republican Party. He wrote *Recollections of a Busy Life.* G.G. Van Deusen's *Horace Greeley: Voice of the People* places the man within the context of his generation.

GUGGENHEIM, MEYER (1828-1905), industrialist who established a mining empire. Born in Lengnau, Switzerland, he came to the United States in 1848. He obtained interests in silver-mining in Colorado. Guggenheim later expanded his smelting and mine acquisitions to Mexico. With the establishment of the Guggenheim Exploration Company and the American Smelting Company, his family obtained control of the broader aspects of mining and smelting in the United States. With his seven sons he was able to establish a force that dominated the American industrial scene for generations. The dated but authoritative *The Guggenheims: The Making of an American Dynasty* (1937) by Harvey O'Conner is still an outstanding overview.

HALE, GEORGE ELLERY (1868-1938), noted astronomer and astro-physicist. Born at Chicago, Illinois, Hale attended the Massachusetts Institute of Technology, the Harvard College Observatory, and the University of Berlin. He served as director of the Kenwood Astro-Physical Observatory in Chicago from 1890 to

1896. He invented the spectroheliograph, which was first used in 1892 to discover solar vortices and magnetic fields of sun spots. Hale achieved an international reputation among scientists. He wrote many books, including *The Study of Stellar Evolution, Beyond the Milky Way,* and *The New Heavens.*

HAMILTON, ALEXANDER (1757–1804), political leader and financial advisor. He was born on the island of Nevis in the British West Indies, the illegitimate son of James Hamilton and Rachel Fawcett Lavien. During the early stages of the American Revolution, Hamilton served as a close confidante of General George Washington. He became a member of the Federalist Party after the Revolution and was a co-author of the Federalist Papers. Hamilton served as Secretary of the Treasury under President Washington. He supported the concept of a central banking authority as the United States Bank and authored numerous studies on banking. Hamilton drafted the basic text of Washington's "Farewell Address." He died in a duel with Aaron Burr.

HAMMERSTEIN, OSCAR II (1895–1960), lyricist, theatrical producer, and songwriter. Born in New York City, Hammerstein was a student at Columbia University and received a law degree in 1918. His first musical success was as lyricist with "Wildflower" (1923). He then wrote "Rose Marie" (1924), "Sunny" (1925) and "Desert Song" (1926). With Jerome Kern, he achieved success with *Showboat* (1927). With Richard Rodgers his success became phenomenal. Together they wrote *Oklahoma* (1943), *Carousel* (1945), and *South Pacific* (1949), which received a Pulitzer award. Other successes included *The King and I* (1951), *Flower Drum Song* (1958), and *The Sound of Music* (1959). His more famous musical themes include "The Last Time I Saw Paris," which received an Academy Award, and "Ol' Man River."

HANCOCK, JOHN (1737–1793), first signer of the Declaration of Independence. A Colonial merchant and patriot, Hancock opposed Great Britain's efforts to restrict colonial trade. He resisted the Stamp Act by engaging in smuggling; by 1773, his name was identified with rebellion. Hancock was disappointed when the Continental Congress appointed George Washington to command the armies around Boston as the Revolution mounted. As an accountant for Harvard College, he engaged in erratic bookkeeping that brought embarrassment to him and his family. Hancock later served as president of the States Convention where Massachusetts ratified the United States Constitution. He also served as governor of Massachusetts.

John Hancock
Signer of the Declaration of Independence

HANDY, W. C. (1873–1958), black songwriter regarded as the "Father of the Blues." Born in Florence, Alabama, Handy grew up in a home where both parents were ministers and secular music was regarded with disdain. Yet he organized tours and minstrel performances. His fame grew out of the Mahara Minstrels, a group he led. He travelled to Memphis, Tennessee, where his "Memphis Blues" became famous among musical circles. He also published the classic "St. Louis Blues." Handy was accused of plagiarism on certain musical themes, but he resisted those claims. He organized the W. C. Handy Foundation for the Blind. His book entitled, *Blues: An Anthology* contains some material about his life. He also wrote his autobiography titled *Father of the Blues,* published in 1941.

HARDY, OLIVER (1892–1957), actor and comedian. He was the senior member of a comic team with Stan Laurel. Laurel and Hardy made their first movie in 1926; in their career they were responsible for over two hundred movie features. In the 1950s, they expanded their comedy to the medium of television. The overweight Hardy and the lean Laurel developed a comedy style that reflected the anxieties of life situations. Their slapstick humor was popular in America at the time. Hardy's line, "Another fine mess that you got us into," became associated with the routine.

HATFIELD, MARK O. (1922–), modern political figure. Born in The Dalles, Oregon, Hatfield graduated from Stanford University. He served as instructor and dean of students at Willamette University. From 1950 to 1956, he served as the Secretary of State for Oregon, and as governor from 1959 to 1967. He won election as United States Senator in 1967. Hatfield's involvement in the anti-war movement during the 1960s generated discontent within the Republican Party; he has been identified with the liberal Republicans. Hatfield is a significant leader in evangelical Protestantism. He has written several books, including *Between a Rock and a Hard Place.*

HEARST, WILLIAM RANDOLPH (1863–1951), newspaper publisher and editor. Born in San Francisco, California, Hearst grew up in a wealthy family. He was expelled from Harvard College in 1885, and received permission from his father to work with *The Daily Examiner.* There he sensationalized and fabricated the news in irresponsible fashion. After his father's death, he moved to New York where he used the *New York Morning Journal* to compete against Joseph Pulitzer's *New York World.* In an era of "yellow journalism," Hearst's irresponsible reporting generated a newspaper boom. He established the *Chicago American* in 1900, along with other newspapers in Boston and Los Angeles. Eventually he retired on the Hearst estate at San Simeon in southern California. Ferdinand Lundberg's *Imperial Hearst: A Social Biography* (1936) is an unflattering portrait.

HENRY, CARL F. H. (1913–), minister and educator. Henry was born in New York City. He received the Ph.D. from Boston University and the Th.D. from Northern Baptist Theological Seminary. He established *Christianity Today,* a journal for evangelical Protestantism. Dr. Henry has held faculty positions with Gordon, Fuller, Wheaton Colleges, and numerous other colleges and universities as visiting lecturer. He has authored a number of publications in systematic theology; but his most significant views were shared through his editorials for *Christianity Today,* which he edited from 1956 to 1968.

HENRY, PATRICK (1736–1799), orator and noted political figure born in Hanover County, Virginia. As a member of the Virginia House of Burgesses, Henry spoke against the Stamp Act and opposed the power of Parliament to tax Virginians. He was described as the "Demosthenes of America." His name is synonymous with rebellion, through his impassioned cry, "I know not what course others may take; but as for me, give me liberty or give me death." After the Revolution, he served as governor of Virginia. He opposed the American Constitution because he believed it would concentrate too much power in the central government.

HOFMAN, HANS (1880–1966), cubist and abstract painter. Born in Weissenberg, Germany, Hofman suffered under the political difficulties of postwar Germany. He decided to emigrate to America and accept an appointment at the University of California. During the 1940s, he exhibited his paintings in New York, where his work received wide attention. With exhibitions at the Whitney Museum during the decade of the 1960s, his reputation as a German-American master was assured. His more famous paintings are *Fantasia* (1943), *Liberation* (1947), *The Gate* (1959), and *Agrigento* (1961).

HOGAN, BEN (1912–), an outstanding golfer. Born in Dublin, Texas, Hogan attended Fort Worth public schools. In his professional career as a golfer, he won the United States Open championship on four occasions; the United States Masters twice; won the British Open once. In 1946 and 1948, he won the Professional Golfers Association championship. He has received numerous awards including the Ryder Cup. Hogan was named Golfer of the Year in 1948, 1950, 1951, and 1953. He has written several books on the game of golf, including *Power Golf.*

HOMER, WINSLOW (1836–1910), a well-known American painter in the naturalist tradition. A native of Boston, Massachusetts, Homer began his career by working for *Harper's Weekly* as an illustrator. He proceeded to painting adult subjects in their natural settings; and in 1873, he began his work with watercolors in a graphic style. He moved from New York to the coast of Maine, where he sought a balance in his perspective. Late in life, he moved to the Bahamas, Bermuda, and Florida. At his death, he was regarded as the most significant American painter. *The World of Winslow Homer,* by James Thomas Flexner (1966) gives a good analysis of the man and his generation.

HOOVER, J. EDGAR (1895–1972), first director of the Federal Bureau of Investigation. Upon his initial appointment as acting director in 1924, Hoover established a fingerprint collection and national crime laboratory. The bureau was the center of Prohibition controversies and organized crime. Hoover opposed the emerging menace of Communism, particularly after World War II; he became involved in the McCarthy campaigns, writing books and articles that dealt with the themes of organized crime and Communism. *Masters of Deceit* (1958) is his most famous publication. Hoover was born in Washington, D.C.

HOPE, BOB (1903–), comedian and film star. Born in Eltham, England, Hope developed an instinct for comedy during his early days in vaudeville. He appeared in 1935 in the Ziegfeld Follies with Fanny Brice. He starred in the musical, *Red, Hot, and Blue* with Jimmy Durante and Ethel Merman; he developed a close partnership with Bing Crosby and Dorothy Lamour in a series of films titled *Road to. . . .* During World War II, he entertained troops, particularly during the Christmas holiday season. In 1950, he appeared on the television show, *Star Spangled Revue,* and in October of 1950, he embarked on an entertainment tour for the United States Armed Forces in the Pacific. These tours were continued for over twenty-five years. His television specials draw large audiences. He authored *They've Got Me Covered* (1941), *I Never Left Home* (1944), and *So This Is Peace* (1946).

HOPKINS, JOHNS (1795–1873), merchant and philanthropist. He entered business in partnership with his brothers. In exchange for groceries, the Hopkins Brothers would receive whiskey; then they would sell the whiskey as "Hopkins Best" brand. He developed banking interests by buying up overdue notes. His primary investment was the Baltimore & Ohio Railroad; he became director of it in 1847. He advanced money to the City of Baltimore during periods of financial crisis; he established a hospital and a university that later adopted his name. His biographies have suggested that "he knew how to be generous in large matters."

HOUDINI, HARRY (1874–1926), circus entertainer and escape artist. His real name was Robert Housini. He was born soon after his parents left Budapest, Hungary for Appleton, Wisconsin. In his career as a magician, he took the name Harry Houdini; he learned his magic tricks from a variety of sources—sideshows, circuses, books. His wife Beatrice assisted him in magical routines; they worked the Orpheum circuit. After a sensational escape from Scotland Yard as a publicity stunt, he attracted great attention. Houdini toured the European continent, where he was able to extricate himself from many difficult situations. His return to America was received enthusiastically. He wrote *The Unmasking of Robert Housini* (1908) and starred in three motion pictures after World War I.

HOUSTON, SAMUEL (1793–1863), American statesman and soldier born in Rockbridge County, Virginia. Houston was a Jacksonian Democrat with great oratorical skills and military abilities. He was a lawyer with political ambitions. As a member of Congress and then governor of Tennessee, he became involved with the westward expansion. President Jackson asked Houston to negotiate treaties with various Indian tribes in the Southwest. He moved to Texas, where he advocated statehood for the territory. Houston directed military operations against Mexican president Antonio Lopez dé Santa Anna; from 1845–1859, he served as Senator from Texas. A good biography of Houston was written by Marquis James, *The Raven: A Biography of Sam Houston* (1929).

HOWARD, ROY W. (1883–1964), newspaper publisher who served as director of the Scripps-Howard newspaper chain from 1953 to 1964. Born in Gano, Ohio, his newspaper career began with the *Indianapolis News* in 1902. After he was appointed as general news manager for the United Press, he achieved a broader recognition among publishing circles. While covering World War I, he prematurely reported the signing of the Armistice. Howard negotiated the purchase of the *New York Telegram,* the *New York World,* and the *New York Sun.*

HOWE, ELIAS (1819–1867), inventor who designed the first sewing machine, which revolutionized the garment industry. With ingenuity and persistence, Howe developed a workable sewing machine by 1845 and applied for the appropriate patents. He travelled to England to sell his machine, fell into difficult times, and sold his patents. He returned to America nearly penniless. Through legal proceedings, he was able to get the appropriate license fees on machines that had been produced from 1849 to 1854 in violation of his valid patents. With this newfound wealth, his personal life was stabilized. After the Civil War, sewing machines became major items for mass production.

HUBBLE, EDWIN P. (1889–1953), noted astronomer. Hubble was born in Marshfield, Massachusetts, and pursued a doctorate at the Yerhes Observatory near Pasadena, California. He determined the distances to several galaxies and studied their composition. He led in the development of Mount Palomar's telescope. Hubble wrote an autobiograpical sketch in *The Realm of Nebulae* and *Observational Approach to Cosmology* (both published in 1937). Harlow Shapley's *Through Rugged Ways to the Stars* places Hubble in the context of modern astronomy.

HUGHES, CHARLES EVANS (1862–1948), statesman and chief justice of the United States. After a 20-year period as a lawyer, Hughes became governor of New York State. As governor, he introduced historic reform legislation. President William Taft appointed him to the Supreme Court. In 1916, he was the Presidential candidate for the Republican Party; but he lost to Woodrow Wilson. After World War I, he supported President Wilson's proposal to join the League of Nations. He served as Secretary of State in the scandal-ridden Harding Administration, and gave excellent service. He called the Washington Conference on the limitation of Armaments and dealt with German war reparations. President Herbert Hoover appointed him as Chief Justice of the United States, where his progressive rulings foreshadowed those of the Earl Warren court.

HUGHES, HOWARD R. (1905–1976), business tycoon who achieved great renown through his efforts in aviation technology. After the death of his parents, he took control of the Hughes Tool Company. There he established his reputation and his wealth. Hughes produced motion pictures, and owned hotels, gambling casinos, an airline, television networks, and mines for precious metals. His complex personality contributed to his problems. He required privacy and developed a secretive manner. When Clifford Irving wrote a fraudulent biography on Hughes, the recluse telephoned news reporters to expose the hoax. At his death, many acquaintances of Hughes produced documents that claimed to be his will.

HULL, CORDELL (1871–1955), Congressman, Secretary of State under President Franklin D. Roosevelt. Hull generated the "Good Neighbor" policy toward Latin America. He signed the far-reaching agreement of Montevideo that made it illegal for military powers to intervene in the affairs of nations in the New World. He called for lower tariffs and opposed the expansionism of Japan that preceded World War II. He worked toward the establishment of the United Nations and earned a Nobel Peace Prize in 1945. *The Memoirs of Cordell Hull* (2 vols., 1948) provide a useful overview of the man and his era.

HUMPHREY, HUBERT H. (1911–1978), political figure, United States Senator, and Vice-President of the United States under President Lyndon Johnson. Humphrey was recognized as a spokesman for liberal political views. He was born in Wallace, South Dakota, and attended the University of Minnesota, graduating as a pharmacist from the Denver (Colorado) School of Pharmacy. His father served in the South Dakota state legislature. Hubert studied political science at the University of Minnesota while he served as pharmacist in the family drugstore. He became fascinated by the New Deal of President Franklin Roosevelt. He campaigned for mayor of Minneapolis in 1945 and won. He pursued vigorous reform of urban politics in Minneapolis, and advocated civil rights. Humphrey favored medical insurance through Social Security, the National Defense Education Act, the Peace Corps, and countless other programs of Lyndon Johnson's "Great Society."

HUNTLEY, CHET (1911–1974), television newscaster who achieved national recognition as co-anchorman with David Brinkley on the *Huntley-Brinkley Report,* featured by the National Broadcasting Company. He served as a correspondent on the West Coast for all three television networks. In 1956, he was brought to New York to co-anchor the national political conventions with Brinkley. Their partnership continued until 1970, and their news reporting received every award in broadcasting. Their famous sign-off—"Good night, Chet; Good night, David"—was immediately associated with the report. Huntley returned to Big Sky, Montana, after 1970.

IVES, BURL (1909–   ), singer and actor. Ives worked with the Columbia Broadcasting System as a folk song artist on radio and travelled throughout the states as a troubadour. He has appeared on numerous television programs. Ives' appearances on stage and film reflect a form of character acting. He has been featured in several films, including *East of Eden, Our Man in Havanna,* and *Cat On A Hot Tin Roof.* His television appearances on *The Bold Ones* from 1970 to 1972 developed a new character form—the lawyer.

IVES, CHARLES E. (1874–1954), pioneer in musical expression. Born in Danbury, Connecticut, Ives received initial musical training from his father. He graduated from Yale College in 1898 as a skilled musician and organist. He sold insurance for a time, but continued to compose music. He blended opposite musical forms, using familiar themes within his compositions. He wrote four symphonies, four separate theme works, chamber works, piano sonatas, violin sonatas, hundreds of songs, as well as piano and organ works. Peter Yates' *Twentieth Century Music* (1967) gives particular reference to Ives.

JACKSON, JESSE (1941–), clergyman and civic leader. Born in Greenville, South Carolina, he attended the University of Illinois, received a bachelor's degree from A & T College, Greensboro, North Carolina, and did postgraduate work at the Chicago Theological Seminary. He was ordained to the ministry of the Baptist Church and worked with Dr. Martin Luther King and the Southern Christian Leadership Conference in civil rights efforts. Jackson established Operation Breadbasket and Operation PUSH (People United to Save Humanity). He has been active in the Coalition for United Community Action, and is recognized as a fiery speaker.

JACKSON, MAHALIA (1911–1972), black singer and civil rights activist born in New Orleans, Lousiana. Miss Jackson symbolized black protest by associating with the civil rights movement. She became famous through her singing of "He's Got the Whole World in His Hands" and other popular songs. She achieved recognition in the white community after a widely acclaimed concert at Carnegie Hall in 1950. She was regularly featured in the Newport Jazz Festival after 1958.

JACKSON, THOMAS "STONEWALL" (1824–1863), Civil War general and Confederate hero. Jackson attended the United States Military Academy and served in the Mexican War. In the 1860 election, he supported John C. Breckinridge for the Presidency. After Virginia seceded from the Union he was commissioned to defend Harpers Ferry. At the First Battle of Bull Run, he earned the name "Stonewall" through his determined strategy. He was less successful in the battle to protect Richmond from Union Forces under General McClellan, but he scored a great victory for the South at the Second Battle of Bull Run. At the Battle of Fredericksburg, he was mistaken for a Union soldier and accidentally shot. This proved fatal. In strategy and audacity, Jackson remained unequalled in the Confederate ranks.

JAMES, WILLIAM (1842–1910), philosopher and psychologist.' James was educated at Harvard, and his educational interests reflected a composite of the Renaissance mind. He was a determined advocate of the evolutionary theories of Charles Darwin. He wrote *Principles of Psychology* (1890), in which he underscored the human qualities of habit, emotion, consciousness of self, stream of thought, and will. His concern for individual freedom was reflected in his lectures on "The Will to Believe." His book, *Varieties of Religious Experience,* remains a classic study of the psychology of religion. Bernard P. Brennan's *William James* (1968) is a useful biography.

JAY, JOHN (1745–1829), diplomat, politician, Chief Justice of the United States. Jay served as President of the Continental Congress in 1778; after the American Revolution, he served as the new nation's Secretary for Foreign Affairs. He was a co-author of the *Federalist Papers,* which made him an advocate of the American Constitution. With James Madison and Alexander Hamilton, he called for a more centralized authority. Jay proposed the early outlines of a national judiciary. The treaty that ended the war with Great Britain bears his name; although it was written by Alexander Hamilton, it bore the diplomatic skills of John Jay.

JOLSON, AL (1886–1950), singer and star of motion pictures and radio. Born in St. Petersburg, Russia, his real name was Asa Yoelson and he was the son of a Jewish cantor. In 1909, he joined a minstrel group and entertained in the New York Garden. His role in the motion picture entitled *The Jazz Singer* (1927) is regarded as the first talking

Al Jolson in a scene from the *Jazz Singer* (ca.) 1927

picture. In 1928, he appeared in the film, *The Singing Fool.* His renditions of such songs as "Mammy" and "April Showers" became a permanent part of the American musical scene. He produced George Gershwin's *Rhapsody in Blue,* and the film entitled *The Al Jolson Story* was a phenomenal success.

JONES, E. STANLEY (1884–1973), missionary, author, and spiritual leader. Jones served as a missionary to India. His writings give a balanced, positive expression of Christian experience. He wrote several books, including *A Song of Ascents* (1968), which is his spiritual autobiography. He worked with the Ashram movement in India to communicate a religious message of love and understanding. Jones stressed the need for conversion, transformation, and the abundant life.

JONES, JOHN PAUL (1747–1792), distinguished American Revolutionary officer. His naval operations during the Revolution contributed greatly to the American victory. Historians believe the duel between Jones' ship, the *Bon Homme Richard,* and the British ship *Serapis,* was a significant episode of the war. He managed to seize the copper-bottom ship from the British. Jones received a gold medal and numerous honors for his naval successes. He served a brief period in the Russian navy, and most of his later years were spent in Paris. Alfred Thayer Mahan's book, *The Major Operations of the Navies in the American War of Independence* (1913), remains the classic on John Paul Jones and the Revolution.

JONES, RUFUS M. (1863–1948), college professor and religious leader. Born in South China, Maine, Jones attended Haverford College and the University of Heidelberg. He received his graduate degrees from Harvard and Oxford universities. In 1889, he became instructor at the Oak Grove Seminary in Maine; he taught at Haverford College from 1904 to 1934. Jones served as chairman of the American Friends Service Committee and of the European Relief in 1917–1927 and 1934–1944. He wrote numerous books, including *Autobiography of George Fox: The Story of George Fox* (1919); *The Faith and Practise of the Quakers* (1927); *Re-thinking Religious Liberalism* (1936); and *The Radiant Life* (1944).

JUDSON, ADONIRAM (1788–1850), Baptist missionary to Burma and founder of the American Board of Commissioners for Foreign Missions (1810). Judson was a Congregationalist when he travelled to India under the sponsorship of the board. There he adopted Baptist beliefs and received support from the American Baptist Missionary Union. He then went to Rangoon, Burma, to begin the translation of Scripture into Burmese. His linguistic abilities brought him into contact with broader levels of Burmese royalty. He completed an English-Burmese dictionary.

KEATON, BUSTER (1895–1966), comedian and film star. Born in Piqua, Kansas, Keaton performed in vaudeville before his appearances in Hollywood. He made comic use of pantomime, his portrayals in silent movies established his reputation as a classic performer. Keaton achieved fame in television and as a motion picture actor and director. His performances in *A Funny Thing Happened on the Way to the Forum, Around the World in 80 Days,* and *It's a Mad, Mad, Mad, Mad World* were received with acclaim. He achieved a new standard of excellence in the film, *When Comedy was King.*

KELLER, HELEN (1880–1968), author and humanitarian. Miss Keller was born in Tuscumbia, Alabama. An early illness left her blind and deaf by the age of 18 months. Her tutor Anne Sullivan helped her gain an education; and by age 16, she matriculated at Radcliffe College. She graduated *cum laude.* Her life was dedicated to the broader aspects of education and assistance to the blind and deaf. Miss Keller knew Alexander Graham Bell, whose experiments became essential to her work with the deaf and blind. She authored *Helen Keller's Journal, Out of the Dark,* and *The Story of My Life,* among other works.

KELLY, EMMETT (1898–1979), renowned pantomime clown. Born in Sedan, Kansas, he served as cartoonist for the Advertizing Film Company, where he created the "Wearie Willie" pen-and-ink cartoon. In 1921, he joined the circus as a clown; he worked as a trapeze artist and clown from 1924 to 1931. He appeared in several pictures, including *The Fat Man, The Greatest Show on Earth,* and others. He appeared on television with Ed Sullivan, Garry Moore, Jackie Gleason, Captain Kangaroo, and others.

KELLY, GENE (1912–), dancer, actor, and motion-picture celebrity. Born in Pittsburg, Pennsylvania, he appeared in the New York productions *Leave It To Me* (1938), *Time of Your Life* (1940), *Pal Joey* (1941), and others. Kelly directed the dancers for several movies: *Anchors Aweigh* (1944), *The Pirate* (1948), *An American in Paris* (1950), and *Brigadoon* (1954). Between 1944 and 1946, he served in the United States Naval Reserve. He authored *Take Me Out to the Ballgame* (1948).

KELLY, GRACE (1929-1982), actress, model, and (since 1956) princess of Monaco. Born in Philadelphia, Pennsylvania, she attended the Raven Hall Academy and Stevens School in that city. After early stage productions, she appeared in several motion pictures: *High Noon, Dial M For Murder, Rear Window, The Country Girl, To Catch A Thief,* and *High Society.* She received the Academy award for her role in *Country Girl.* Her marriage to Prince Rainier III of Monaco received considerable attention in America and Europe.

KELLY, WALT (1913–1973), newspaper cartoonist. His fame grew out of the comic strip "Pogo," with the classic line: "We have seen the enemy, and he is us." Kelly's characters reflected an innocent satire on society. Pogo was an opossum who spoke garbled language and had a community of animal friends, such as Howland Owl and the other inhabitants of Okefenokee Swamp. Kelly first worked as an animator for Walt Disney Productions. His comic strip appeared first in the *New York Star;* it reached syndication in over four hundred newspapers. Kelly was named Cartoonist of the Year in 1952.

KENNEDY, EDWARD M. (1932–), United States Senator born in Brookline, Massachusetts. Educated at Harvard and the University of Virginia Law School, he won election to the Senate in 1962 to complete the unexpired term of his brother, John F. Kennedy. In 1964, he was reelected. Mary Jo Kopechne, a campaign worker, died in an automobile accident at Chappaquiddick, Massachusetts that cast shadows on Kennedy's personal integrity. Yet he won reelection in 1970 and 1976. In the Senate, he has established a national health insurance program and favored tax reform. During the 1960s, he loudly opposed the war in Vietnam.

KENNEDY, ROBERT F. (1925–1968), United States Senator assassinated in a Los Angeles hotel after he won the 1968 California Democratic Presidential primary. Kennedy served in the United States Navy during World War II. He graduated from Harvard and received his law degree from the University of Virginia Law School in 1951. He served as assistant counsel to Senator Joseph McCarthy's Permanent Subcommittee on Investigations; and in 1957, he was chief counsel to the Senate Select Committee conducting investigations into labor racketeering. In 1960, he conducted the campaign of his brother, John F. Kennedy, for the Presidency. From 1961 to 1964, he served as Attorney General. From 1965 to his death, he was Senator from New York. Kennedy authored *The Enemy Within* (1960), *Just Friends and Brave Enemies* (1962), and *Pursuit of Justice* (1964).

KETCHAM, HANK (1920–), cartoonist. Born in Seattle, Washington, his real name is Henry King. He worked with Universal Studios and Walt Disney Productions from 1938 to 1942. He created Dennis the Menace and related cartoon characters after 1951. His "Dennis the Menace" cartoon strip was distributed through Field Newspaper Syndicate. He has received numerous awards, including the Billy de Beck Award for Outstanding Cartoonist (1952). He wrote several *Dennis the Menace* cartoon book collections, beginning in 1954, and *I Wanna Go Home* (1965).

KING, MARTIN LUTHER, JR. (1929–1968), civil rights leader who developed and practiced nonviolence as a strategy in dealing with racial prejudice and segregation. King organized a bus boycott to deal with segregation on transportation facilities. He was active in the National Association for the Advancement of Colored Peoples (NAACP); later he organized the Southern Christian Leadership Conference. King participated in the "sit-ins" to integrate lunch counters. The apex of the civil rights movement was achieved in a rally in Washington, D.C., where King delivered his speech, "Let Freedom Ring." In December of 1964, King was nominated for the Nobel Prize. He became involved in the anti-war movement shortly before he was assassinated in Memphis, Tennessee. He authored numerous publications; his most famous was, *I Have a Dream* (1968).

KISSINGER, HENRY (1923-), diplomat and Secretary of State. Born in Furth, Germany, he emigrated to the United States in 1938. Kissinger served during World War II. He received his doctorate from Harvard in 1954. Kissinger received national attention through publication of *Nuclear Weapons and Foreign Policy* (1957). He became a political advisor to Nelson Rockefeller in 1957. In 1968, Richard Nixon named him Presidential Assistant for National Security. Kissinger arranged the visits made by President Nixon to China and the Soviet Union. He was the architect of the treaty that ended the United States involvement in Vietnam. He also began *détente* with the Soviet Union and limited disengagement in the Middle East. Kissinger was recognized as an outstanding Secretary of State.

KOUFAX, SANDY (1935-), baseball pitcher and sportscaster. Born in Brooklyn, New York, he attended the University of Cincinnati. In 1955, he began his professional baseball career with the Brooklyn Dodgers (later the Los Angeles Dodgers). He appeared in World Series championships in 1959, 1963, 1965, and 1966. From 1963 to 1966, he was named to the National League All-Star Team. He was named Major League Player of the Year in 1963 and 1965. In 1963, 1965, and 1966, he received the Cy Young Award. From 1966 to 1972, he was associated with the National Broadcasting Company (NBC) as a sportscaster.

KRESGE, S. S. (1867–1966), merchandiser and businessman who established a network of "five and dime" stores throughout the country to make less expensive merchandise available to a broader market. Kresge was the founder of the S. S. Kresge stores; and from 1907 to 1925, he served as president of the company. From 1913 to 1966, he was chairman of the board; at its peak, over nine hundred thirty general merchandise stores throughout the country bore his name.

KUIPER, GERARD (1905–1973), astronomer. Born in Harencarspel, Netherlands, he analyzed early lunar photos and determined the exact sites where Apollo space craft would land. As chief scientist for the Ranger spacecraft program, he augmented United States efforts in the NASA space projects. The lunar landing of 1969 would not have been possible without his efforts.

LaFARGE, CHRISTOPHER GRANT (1862–1938), modern architect. Born in New York City, LaFarge studied at the Massachusetts Institute of Technology, 1880–1881. He obtained the Master of Fine Arts degree from Princeton University and became a partner in the firm Heins & LaFarge. LaFarge was the architect for the Cathedral of St. John the Divine in New York; St. Matthew's in Washington, D.C.; St. Patrick's in Philadelphia; as well as numerous other churches, hospitals, and governmental structures. He served as general manager of the United States Housing Corporation; also, director of the American Institute of Architects.

LaFOLLETTE, ROBERT M. (1855–1925), political reformer. LaFollette graduated from the University of Wisconsin in 1879 and was admitted to the bar one year later. He served as a member of the United States House of Representatives from

Senator Robert La Follette (left) and Senator Burton K. Wheeler, presidential and vice-presidential candidates of the League for Progressive Political Action

1885 to 1891. He campaigned against political corruption in his own state and was elected governor of Wisconsin in 1900. During his two terms there, he enacted new laws enabling voters to nominate candidates by direct primary elections, regulating government employment, and levying more reasonable taxes on business. LaFollette won election to the United States Senate in 1906 and was reelected twice thereafter. He ran for the Presidency on three occasions—the most successful being in 1924, when he and his running mate Burton K. Wheeler polled five million votes for the League for Progressive Political Action. LaFollette's ideas influenced national policy. He published his *Autobiography: A Personal Narrative of Political Experiences,* in 1913.

LANDON, ALFRED "ALF" (1887–   ), political leader and presidential candidate. Born in West Middlesex, Pennsylvania, Landon graduated from the University of Kansas in 1908. In 1912 and 1914, he worked for the Progressive Party; in 1932, he was elected governor of Kansas. He brought major governmental reform in state finance, water conservation, and utility rate regulation. In 1936 he won the Republican nomination for President, but he carried only Maine and Vermont. He opposed the United States' entry into World War II; after the war, he assumed an independent position and sought recognition of Communist China.

LAUREL, STAN (1890–1965), motion picture comedian. Born in Ulverson, England, he was part of the famous comedy team with Oliver Hardy. The Laurel and Hardy duo made slapstick comedy popular in the 1920s and 1930s. After 1926, he starred with Hardy in a succession of comedies, including *Air Raid Wardens* (1943), *Jitterbugs* (1943), *The Dancing Masters* (1943), *The Big Noise* (1944), *Nothing But Trouble,* and *The Bullfighters* (1945). He also appeared in numerous television roles after 1950; with his partner, he became an enduring part of America.

LAWRENCE, DAVID (1888–1973), editor and columnist. Born in Philadelphia, Pennsylvania, Lawrence began his career as a columnist with the *New York Evening Post* in 1916. His columns were syndicated in over three hundred daily newspapers. In 1947, he became editor of the *U.S. News and World Report.* He wrote numerous books, including *Diary of a Washington Correspondent.* He received the Presidential Medal of Freedom in 1970.

LEE, ROBERT E. (1807–1870), general of the Confederate armies and one of the greatest military strategists of history. Lee was born in

Jefferson Davis and his Cabinet with General Lee in the Council Chamber at Richmond.

Westmoreland County, Virginia, and graduated from the United States Military Academy. He fought in the Mexican War. When the Civil War began, his blood ties in Virginia affirmed his allegiance to the South. He accepted a commission as colonel in the Confederate army. The battles of the war revealed his abilities as a strategist and diplomat—from Manassas where he achieved victory, to Chancellorsville where Stonewall Jackson fell. Gettysburg was a major defeat for Lee. Near the end of the war (Feb. 6, 1985) Lee was appointed to the supreme military office as general-in-chief of the Confederate armies. Historians of war agree that Lee had better strategic than tactical skills. *Gray Fox: Robert E. Lee and the Civil War* by Burke Davis (1956) gives a useful perspective.

LEWIS, JERRY (1926–   ), comedian and television personality. Educated in the public schools of Irvington, New Jersey, Lewis began his career as an entertainer by appearing in the hotels and clubs of the Catskills. He formed a highly successful comedy routine with Dean Martin from 1946–1956. The Martin-Lewis comedy routine appeared on television until an embittered quarrel terminated the association. Lewis appeared in zany roles on screen, including *Sad Sack* (1957), *The Nutty Professor, Big Mouth,* and others. He has appeared on television and has developed a national relationship with the Muscular Dystrophy Association. His yearly telethons have raised millions of dollars for medical research in muscular dystrophy.

LEWIS, JOHN L. (1880–1969), labor leader who organized the Congress of Industrial Organizations (CIO) and was head of the United Mine Workers of America (UMWA). Born in Lucas, Iowa, Lewis worked as a miner in Montana and Utah. After a mine disaster in Wyoming, he dedicated his life to mine safety and defending miner's causes. He used the UMWA as a political base to launch his labor programs in Congress. During the Great Depression and Franklin Roosevelt's New Deal, he differed with the leadership of the American Federation of Labor and organized the CIO. He confronted the steel industry and the automobile industry and gained political leverage. In the 1940 election, he supported the Republican Wendell Willkie in preference to Roosevelt. Saul Alinsky's *John L. Lewis* (1949) is a useful biography.

LEWIS, MERIWETHER (1774–1809), frontier explorer. Born in Albemarle County, Virginia, he explored the territories of the Northwest with William Clark. President Thomas Jefferson, a friend and associate, commissioned their westward expedition. With considerable difficulty, they moved westward into territories inhabited by Indians and wildlife. Lewis' skills in dealing with the Indians proved essential to avoiding war. Upon his return, he was made governor of the Upper Louisiana Territory. However, his journals about the expedition were less persuasive than were those of William Clark, and it is agreed that Clark was an essential component of the expedition. See Bernard DeVoto, *The Journals of Lewis and Clark* (1953).

LINDBERGH, CHARLES A. (1902–1974), aviator who made the first solo non-stop flight across the Atlantic Ocean. Lindbergh was competing for a $25,000 prize posted by Raymond Orteig. He assembled the necessary financial backing to construct the plane he called *Spirit of St. Louis.* On May 20, 1927, he left New York, and in 33½ hours he arrived in Paris. He received numerous awards for the feat. In 1932, he and his wife were horrified at the kidnapping of their infant son; they paid a ranson of $50,000, but the baby was found dead. Lindbergh organized the America First Organization to prevent United States' entry into World War II; after the Japanese attack on Pearl Harbor, he joined the war effort. He wrote *We* (1927) and *The Spirit of St. Louis* (1953); he received a Pulitzer Prize for the latter.

Lindbergh stands under the wing of his plane, the *Spirit of St. Louis,* before taking off on his transatlantic flight.

LINDSAY, JOHN V. (1921–), political leader and news commentator. Born in New York City, Lindsay graduated from Yale in 1944 and served in the Navy during World War II. He represented New York's seventeenth Congressional District in the House of Representatives from 1959 until his election as mayor of New York in 1965. He began his political career as a Republican, but later changed his party affiliation to Democrat. His years as mayor of New York saw a succession of labor difficulties and conflicts. After leaving office, he turned his attention to television and broadcast interests; he has appeared on ABC's *Good Morning, America* program as political and public affairs commentator.

LODGE, HENRY CABOT, JR. (1902–), Senator, government official, author, and lecturer. Lodge graduated from Harvard and Northwestern University, and was elected to the U.S. Senate from Massachusetts in 1936. He resigned the Senate for military service during World War II; he was reelected in 1946. In 1960, he ran with Richard Nixon as the Vice-Presidential candidate for the Republican Party. From 1953 to 1960, he served as the United States representative to the United Nations. He was United States Ambassador to South Vietnam from 1963 to 1964 and 1965 to 1967; there he served a significant diplomatic function. Lodge authored *The Storm Has Many Eyes;* he has received numerous honors and recognitions.

LOUIS, JOE (1914–1981), American boxer and world heavyweight champion. Louis demonstrated his boxing abilities by his successes in the Golden Gloves competition of 1933. Also called the "Brown Bomber," his successes became legendary—particularly over boxers like Billy Conn, Rocky Marciano, and "Jersey Joe" Walcott. During World War II, he boxed on behalf of Army and Navy Relief. He authored *My Life Story* (1947). Jack Olsen's *The Black Athlete: A Shameful Story* (1968) places Louis within the generation of black athletes and racial discrimination.

LUCE, HENRY R. (1898–1967), magazine publisher. Born in Tenchow, China of Presbyterian missionary parents, Luce graduated *summa cum laude* from Yale University. With Briton Hadden, he founded *Time* magazine in 1922; the success of *Time* ushered in a new form of magazine journalism. In 1930, he launched *Fortune,* designed for the business executive. His marriage to playwright Clare Boothe Brokaw was much publicized. In this same period was launched *Life,* a venture into photographic journalism. At the time of his death, the combined circulation of *Life* and *Time* was in the millions. The most definitive study on the man and his ventures is John Kobler's *Luce: His Time, Life, and Fortune* (1968).

MacARTHUR, DOUGLAS (1880–1964), American general with distinguished service in the Far East during the occupation and reconstruction of Japan after World War II. MacArthur graduated from West Point with the highest scholastic average in the history of the academy. His rise within the military was spectacular. In 1936, he was dispatched to the Philippines by President Roosevelt to devise a strategy of defense; MacArthur mistakenly thought that the Japanese

Max Schmeling hangs on the ropes as he is pummeled by Joe Louis in their championship fight on June 22, 1938.

General Douglas MacArthur strides ashore during the landing on Leyte on Oct. 20, 1944.

wouldn't engage in such an attack. During World War II, he reclaimed the Philippines. After the war, he sought to expand American military efforts in the Korean War; because this strategy disagreed with President Truman's, he was dismissed. MacArthur returned to the United States in the midst of sympathy for the military hero. He authored *Reminiscences* (1964), an autobiography.

McCORMICK, CYRUS H. (1809–1884), inventor and manufacturer. He was primarily interested in farm machinery. In 1832, he took out a patent for a horizontal plow. He built a factory in Chicago for manufacturing reapers, and by mid-century he had a national market for reapers. Throughout his life, he competed with Obed Hussey for advantage in the farm machinery market. A contest in London pitted the McCormick reaper against the Hussey, and McCormick won. He expanded his factories in the United States; he developed steam-powered, self-propelled combines. He gave large sums of money to religious causes, and he received numerous honors from governments and organizations. William T. Hutchinson's *Cyrus Hall McCormick* is the standard biography.

MacDONALD, JEANETTE (1907–1965), actress and singer. With Nelson Eddy, she starred in several outstanding musical productions, including *Naughty Marietta* (1935), *Rose Marie* (1936), *Maytime* (1937), *Sweethearts* (1938), and *New Moon* (1940). She appeared in Broadway musicals such as *Love Me Tonight* (1932) and *One Hour With You* (1932). She starred with Clark Gable in *San Francisco* (1936).

McGUFFEY, WILLIAM H. (1800–1873), author of early elementary-school readers. McGuffey served as president of Cincinnati College and sought to promote public education. In 1836, he wrote the *Eclectic Readers;* the last of the now-famous *McGuffey Readers* was completed in 1854. Each of his books contained readings, aphorisms, messages on thrift and initiative. Within the emerging public schools, the readers were popular for several generations. McGuffey became president of Ohio University, and later professor of natural and moral philosophy at the University of Virginia. Richard D. Mosier's *Making the American Mind: Social and Moral Ideas in the McGuffey Readers* (1947) describes the impact of McGuffey's books.

MACHEN, J. GRESHAM (1881–1937), theologian and Bible scholar. Born in Baltimore, Maryland, Machen studied at Johns Hopkins University, Princeton University, and Princeton Theological Seminary. He then became professor and lecturer at Princeton. Machen was ordained as a Presbyterian minister; he became a leading voice of orthodox Protestantism in the early twentieth century. His books include *The Origin of Paul's Religion* (1921), *Christianity and Liberalism* (1923), *New Testament Greek for Beginners* (1923), and *The Virgin Birth of Christ* (1930).

McNAMARA, ROBERT S. (1916–), banker, automobile executive, public servant. McNamara was born in San Francisco, California, and received his undergraduate education at the University of California. He received his graduate degree in business administration from Harvard University. McNamara served for a brief period as a professor at Harvard. He became an executive with the Ford Motor Company in 1946 and president of that firm in 1960. President John Kennedy named him as Secretary of Defense in 1961. His eight years in that office were the most difficult years of the war in Vietnam. In 1968, he became president of the World Bank. McNamara has received numerous honors and recognitions. He authored *The Essense of Security* (1968) and other titles.

MADDOX, LESTER (1915–), segregationist leader and Georgia politician. Born in Atlanta, Georgia, he engaged in various business relationships—real estate, furniture, and a restaurant. As owner of a restaurant, he was told to comply with an integration order. He refused to comply and the restaurant was closed. He subsequently ran for political office and was elected governor of Georgia from 1967 to 1971. He served as lieutenant-governor under Governor Jimmy Carter in 1971–1975.

MALCOLM X (1925–1965), black religious leader. He was born as Malcolm Little in Omaha, Nebraska. Influenced by his father and the "back to Africa" ideas of Marcus Garvey, he resolved to defend the cause of black people. As a child, he saw his father murdered. In Boston, he worked in various menial jobs and was arrested for burglary. While in prison, he was converted to the Black Muslim religion; this provided a new forum for his ideas on race. He became an assistant minister of the Detroit Mosque. After the Kennedy assassination he made certain remarks that caused his suspension from the Black Muslims. He left the Nation of Islam to join the Organization of Afro-American Unity, and was assassinated at a public rally. His experiences were included in *The Autobiography of Malcolm X* by Alexander Haley.

MANCINI, HENRY (1924–   ), popular composer. Born in Cleveland, Ohio, Mancini attended the Juilliard Institute of Music. He served as pianist and arranger for the Tex Beneke Orchestra. As staff composer for Universal Pictures, he wrote scores for *The Glenn Miller Story, The Benny Goodman Story, The Great Waldo Pepper,* and other films. His recordings have achieved national attention. Among them are "Days of Wine and Roses" and "Moon River" (with Johnny Mercer). Mancini has received over twenty Grammy awards; he received Academy Awards for his music in *Breakfast at Tiffany's, Moon River,* and *Days of Wine and Roses.*

MANN, HORACE (1796–1859), educational reformer who promoted education throughout the United States. After graduating as valedictorian from Brown University, he pursued the study of law. His legal studies were interrupted by an interest in tutoring Latin and Greek; but later he returned to his legal studies, graduated from Tapping Reeve, and was admitted to the bar in 1823. He regarded education as "the great equalizer" of society. He abandoned a political career for a position as First Secretary of the State Board of Education. His admiration for Prussian education and non-sectarian study made his views controversial. Mann served as a member of the United States House of Representatives and president of Antioch College. *The Republic and the School: The Education of Free Men* (1957) is the most comprehensive collection of his writings.

MANTLE, MICKEY (1931–   ), baseball player born in Spavinaw, Oklahoma. In 1949, he signed with the New York Yankees. He has appeared with the New York Yankees in numerous World Series and All-Star games. Mantle is regarded as an outstanding baseball player. He was inducted into the Baseball Hall of Fame in 1974.

MARSHALL, GEORGE C. (1880–1959), soldier, statesman, architect of United States foreign policies after World War II. Marshall graduated from Virginia Military Institute and served in World War I under General John Pershing. Appointed Chief of Staff of the Army, he helped to prepare the United States for World War II. He received criticism for his failure to alert our Far East bases of the impending attack by the Japanese; but he directed military operations throughout the war and served as advisor to President Roosevelt. After the war he was named Secretary of State. The Marshall Plan set up a framework for the reconstruction of war-devastated Europe; actually, the plan combined the wisdom of George Kennan and Dean Acheson. Marshall encouraged the formation of the North Atlantic Treaty Organization (NATO). He was Secretary of Defense during the Korean War. The best work on Marshall is Forrest C. Pogue's *George C. Marshall* (2 vols., 1963, 1967).

MARSHALL, JOHN (1755–1835), the fourth Chief Justice of the United States. Marshall consolidated the principle of judicial review and strengthened the powers of the Supreme Court. Marshall was named to the court in 1801; he authored a definitive five-volume biography of George Washington. In 1803, his ruling in the celebrated case of *Marbury* vs. *Madison* established the principle of declaring acts of Congress unconstitutional. In *United States* vs. *Peters* he established the Supreme Court as the final interpreter of Federal law. In *McCulloch* vs. *Maryland* and *Gibbons* vs. *Ogden,* he upheld the principle that allowed the chartering of the Second Bank of the United States and the credit structure for interstate currency. Marshall was one of the truly outstanding Chief Justices in American history. *The Life of John Marshall,* by Albert J. Beveridge (2 vols., rev. ed. 1947) is a significant biography.

MARSHALL, THURGOOD (1908–   ), civil rights lawyer, Associate Justice of the United States Supreme Court. A native of Baltimore, Maryland, Marshall developed techniques for civils rights litigation during his early career as a lawyer. He served as counsel for the Baltimore chapter of the National Association for the Advancement of Colored People (NAACP). In 1938, he was admitted to practice before the United States Supreme Court. He achieved a phenomenal success ratio in his cases before the high court. For example, he argued the successful *Brown* vs.

Board of Education, which overturned segregation in public education. In 1964, President Johnson appointed him Solicitor General; in 1967, he was named to the Supreme Court. He has received numerous honors. An excellent biography is Lewis H. Fenderson's *Thurgood Marshall* (1969).

MARTIN, DEAN (1917–), actor, singer, and comedian. Born in Steubenville, Ohio, Martin became associated with Jerry Lewis in a successful comedy routine. The television series titled *The Martin-Lewis Comedy Hour* achieved considerable attention. His disagreement with Lewis resulted in the break-up of the comedy team. His screen roles have varied from the *Matt Helm* series to *The Bells Are Ringing* (1960), *Oceans II* (1960), *Silences* (1970), and *Airport.* His weekly television program on the National Broadcasting Company was widely received.

MARTIN, MARY (1913–), actress and singer born in Weatherford, Texas. Miss Martin was the singer in *Leave It to Me* (1938). She then starred in numerous musical productions, including *The Great Victor Herbert, Kiss the Boys Goodbye, Birth of the Blues,* and *Night and Day.* She starred in Noel Coward's *Pacific 1860.* Her role as entertainer in tours of United States military forces received acclaim. Her roles in *Annie Get Your Gun* (1948), the stage production of *South Pacific* (1949–1952), *Peter Pan* (1954–1955), and *The Sound of Music* (1959–1961) were widely acclaimed.

MARX, JULIUS "GROUCHO" (1890–1977), comedian and entertainer. In his early days, he joined his brothers Harpo and Chico in comic routines; the vaudeville circuit became the arena for the Marx comedy. With a cigar in hand, Groucho perfected comedy of the lunatic fringe. His scandalous humor was in comedy revues such as *Monkey Business* (1929), *Horsefeathers* (1932), and *Duck Soup* (1933). After the war, he became the host of a radio quiz show, *You Bet Your Life,* which achieved remarkable television success. The last movie effort starring Harpo and Chico was *The Incredible Jewel Robbery* (1959). A useful study of Groucho and his brothers is by Allen Eyles: *The Marx Brothers: Their World of Comedy* (second edition, 1969).

MATHER, COTTON (1663–1728), a leading author from the Puritan era, associated with the Salem witchcraft trials. Mather's youth was as remarkable as his life. At twelve, he was a student at Harvard College. He studied medicine, philosophy, and science in his teens. With his father, Increase Mather, he became a guiding force in the emerging Puritan society. The Salem witchcraft mentality was generated by Cotton Mather; his ill-fated efforts to become president of Harvard College or Yale brought serious disappointments in his later life. He was honored by other means—through election to the Royal Society of London. The best biography on Cotton Mather is Barrett Wendell's *Cotton Mather: The Puritan Priest* (rev. ed., 1963).

MAULDIN, BILL (1921–), editorial cartoonist. Born in Mountain Park, New Mexico, he studied at the Chicago Academy of Fine Arts. Mauldin served as cartoonist for the *St. Louis Post-Dispatch* until 1962, when he joined the staff of the *Chicago Sun-Times.* During World War II, he served with the United States Army; his military service earned him The Purple Heart and Legion of Merit award. Mauldin received the Pulitzer Prize for cartoons in 1944 and 1958. He authored numerous books, including *Bill Mauldin's Army* (1951), *Bill Mauldin in Korea* (1953), and *The Brass Ring* (1972).

MAYS, WILLIE (1931–), professional baseball player born in Westfield, Alabama. In 1950, he joined the New York Giants, which later moved to San Francisco. From 1951 to 1972, he was characterized as a "superstar" of baseball because he held numerous records: National League home run record; National League's Most Valuable Player of 1954 and 1965; and the Sporting News Player of the Year 1954. He wrote *Willie Mays: My Life In and Out of Baseball* (1966).

MEAD, MARGARET (1901–1978), anthropologist and author. Her early studies in Samoa provided new insights into tension, social organization, and adulthood; she authored *Coming of Age in Samoa.* She served as curator of ethnology at the American Museum of National History, then returned to her anthropological studies in New Guinea and wrote *Growing up in New Guinea* (1930). In later writings, she applied her findings to issues of public policy. After World War II, she authored *The Study of Cultures at a Distance* (1953) on cultural integration and analysis. In the 1960s and 1970s, her studies concerned the need for population control.

MEANY, GEORGE (1894–1980), labor leader associated with the American Federation of Labor (AFL). In his early career, Meany was associated with the building trades unions in New York. He promoted the pro-labor legislation of the New Deal; and during World War II, he served on the War Labor Board. In 1952, he was chosen as president of the AFL; later, he became president of the combined AFL and Congress of Industrial Organizations (CIO). Meany committed the organization to social reform and civil rights. Most Presidents since Eisenhower have had to reckon with the labor movement led by George Meany.

MELLON, ANDREW W. (1855-1937), businessman and United States Secretary of the Treasury. While associated with T. Mellon & Sons, he assisted in forming the Aluminum Corporation of America and organized the Gulf Oil Corporation. He then formed the Mellon National Bank of Pittsburgh, which identified him with significant banking and investment leaders. During the 1920s, he assisted the Harding, Coolidge, and Hoover Administrations in planning their monetary policies. His tax policies contributed to the unequal distribution of income that culminated with the Great Depression. Mellon wrote *Taxation: The People's Business* (1924).

MENNINGER, KARL (1893–), psychiatrist and author. Born in Topeka, Kansas, Menninger attended the University of Wisconsin and Harvard, receiving his medical degree *cum laude* from Harvard University. In 1946, he established the Menninger School of Psychiatry; he has been involved in the treatment, education, and rehabilitation of mental disorders. Menninger's books include *The Vital Balance* and *Love Against Hate*.

MILLER, GLENN (1904–1944), band leader of the "swing" era. Born in Chicago, Miller attended schools in Colorado and graduated from the University of Colorado. He began his musical career as a trombone player and as arranger for various orchestras. In 1933, he organized the Glenn Miller Band. The band played on several radio programs, but regularly appeared on the *Chesterfield Radio Program*. He composed many songs that achieved national popularity, including "Moonlight Serenade." Miller died in a plane crash over Holland shortly before the end of World War II.

MONDALE, WALTER (1928–), Vice-President of the United States and former United States Senator. In 1948, he worked in Hubert Humphrey's campaign for the Senate. He left Minnesota to work in Washington, D.C., for the student wing of Americans for Democratic Action; then he returned to Minnesota and graduated from college in 1951. In 1956, he obtained his law degree. In 1964, while serving as attorney general for Minnesota, he was appointed to finish Humphrey's Senate term when Humphrey became Vice-President; he was reelected in 1966 and 1972. On January 20, 1977, he became the forty-second Vice-President of the United States. Mondale has projected the image of a political liberal.

MONROE, MARILYN (1926–1962), motion picture star who built her reputation on a frivolous and sexual image. She was an illegitimate child with the name of Norma Jean Mortenson. Raised by foster parents, she had an unsuccessful marriage to an aircraft worker named James Dougherty. Then she became a photographer's model. In 1954, she married baseball star Joe DiMaggio, but the marriage lasted less than a year. She married playwright Arthur Miller but again was divorced in four years. Her most famous screen roles were in *Gentlemen Prefer Blondes* (1953), *How to Marry a Millionaire* (1953), *The Seven-Year Itch* (1955), *Some Like It Hot* (1959), and *The Misfits* (1961).

MOODY, DWIGHT L. (1837–1899), revivalist and evangelist. While Moody worked as a shoe salesman in Chicago, he became interested in the Young Men's Christian Association (YMCA). He organized "Sunday Schools" for slum families, supported through the YMCA. In 1872, he teamed up with Ira D. Sankey to hold revivals throughout England and Scotland; he then returned to America where he conducted revivals in New York, Philadelphia, Chicago, and Boston. Moody established schools for ministers in Northfield, Massachusetts, and Chicago. Chicago Bible Institute (named after Moody upon his death) achieved a great reputation. James Findlay's *Dwight L. Moody; American Evangelist* (1969) is a good biography.

MORGAN, J. PIERPONT (1837–1913), banker and financier who was instrumental in the financial reorganization of the railroads. During a severe economic crisis in 1893, Morgan managed to sell government bonds for gold. He organized the House of Morgan investment and banking corporation; established United States Steel as the largest corporation of its day; and gained control of major rail routes to the West. He was an avid collector of art; through a personal interest, he provided the funds to make the Metropolitan Museum of Art in New York among the finest museums in the world. Frederick Lewis Allen's *The Great Pierpont Morgan* (1949) is the most readable biography on the man.

MORRIS, GOUVERNEUR (1752–1816), statesman and diplomat. Born in Morisania, New York, he served in the New York provisional congress during the early stages of the American Revolution. He was elected in 1778 as a delegate to the Continental Congress and served as an assistant to Robert Morris, who was Superintendent of Finance. Morris was a significant delegate to the Constitutional Convention in 1787; he helped to draft the American Constitution, which he also signed. Morris served as foreign minister to France from 1792 to 1794. He also served as Senator from New York, and was critical of Jeffersonian Democrats. The diary of Morris is contained in *A Diary of the French Revolution* (2 vols., 1939) edited by B. C. Davenport.

MORSE, SAMUEL F. B. (1791-1872), inventor and designer of the first telegraph system. Morse was born in Charlestown, Massachusetts, the son of a clergyman. He graduated from Yale College. As an artist and painter, his work attracted little attention. Then he developed an interest in electricity. He combined the existing technology of sender, receiver, and code to invent telegraphy. Congress authorized the construction and development of a telegraphic line between Washington, D.C., and Baltimore, Maryland. By 1844, he was able to send the message "What hath God wrought" over this line. Robert L. Thompson's book, *Wiring a Continent* (1947) places Morse within the broader framework of technology.

MOSES, ANNA MARY ROBERTSON "GRANDMA" (1860-1961), painter of the primitive style. Born in Greenwich, New York, she held her first show in New York City in 1940. Subsequently her paintings were exhibited in shows throughout the United States, including the Museum of Modern Art in New York, the Metropolitan Museum in New York, and the Carnegie Institute. From 1950 to 1957, her paintings were exhibited in Europe. She received the Certificate of Merit (1956), the Woman's National Press Club Award (1949), and others. She wrote *My Life's History: Autobiography of Grandma Moses* (1952).

MUHAMMAD, ELIJAH (1897–1975), leader of the black Nation of Islam. Born in Sandersville, Georgia, he became Minister to the Nation of Islam in 1934. He molded the Nation of Islam into an organization of social, economic, and religious importance. Muhammad preached a message of black nationalism and imposed a standard of strict morality. He called for separation from white America and rejected the notion of racial integration. Malcolm X and boxer Muhammad Ali were among the more influential converts to the Nation of Islam.

MURROW, EDWARD R. (1908–1965), broadcast journalist. Born near Greensboro, North Carolina, Murrow spent his early youth in Washington State. He worked in logging camps as he attended Washington State College. In 1935, he joined the Columbia Broadcasting System. He travelled to London in 1937, and there he developed the dramatic "on the spot" style of radio news journalism. He won renown for his broadcasts describing the bombing raids on the city of London. After the war he developed television news journalism through the *See It Now* program; his most famous program was *Person to Person*. In 1961, he was appointed director of the United States Information Agency. Alexander Kendrick's *Prime Time* (1969) is a biography of Murrow.

NADER, RALPH (1934–   ), consumer advocate. Born in Winsted, Connecticut, Nader graduated *magna cum laude* from Princeton University. He later graduated from Harvard Law School. He was appointed as a consultant to the Department of Labor in his initial work on auto safety; served with Senator Abraham A. Ribicoff's Government Operations Subcommittee as a resource expert on safety. Nader wrote *Unsafe at Any Speed: The Designed-In-Dangers of the American Automobile* (1965) and became a bitter foe of the automobile industry. General Motors admitted spying on him, and he sued the company for $26 million in 1966. Nader organized the Center for the Study of Responsive Law in 1969. He has become identified with the consumer protection movement.

The Third-Term Panic, by Thomas Nast.
(The first use of the elephant as the symbol of the Republican Party.)

NAST, THOMAS (1840–1902), caricaturist, painter, and political cartoonist. Nast was born in Ludwig, Bavaria. As a youth he emigrated to the United States. In 1862, he began working for the *Harper's Weekly;* his initial cartoon attacks dealt with the Andrew Johnson Administration. His caricatures of Boss Tweed and the Tammany Hall political machine of New York City achieved national attention. He was offered a $200,000 bribe to stop the series, but he refused the bribe. Nast invented the symbols now associated with the Democratic and Republican parties—the donkey and elephant.

NATION, CARRY (1846–1911), temperance reformer, agitator, and an early leader in the Prohibition movement. Born in Garrard County, Kentucky, she married Dr. Charles Gloyd in 1867. He became an alcoholic and brought considerable hardship to his wife. In 1877, she married David Nation; and in 1890, she began her work with the Women's Christian Temperance Union (WCTU). Mrs. Nation and her associates organized prayer groups outside saloons and bars. In her campaign on behalf the WCTU, she carried a hatchet for breaking up saloon furniture. She displayed an aggressive character in achieving her moral ends.

NEUMANN, JOHN N. (1811–1860), religious leader; first male American saint of the Roman Catholic church. Born in Prachatice (now in Czechoslovakia), Neumann studied at the University of Prague and came to the United States as a Catholic missionary in 1836. After several years of missionary and pastoral work, he was named Bishop of Philadelphia in 1852. Neumann established about one hundred parochial schools and a Catholic seminary; he was well known for his deep personal faith in God. He was declared venerable in 1896, beatified in 1963, and canonized as a saint in 1977.

NICKLAUS, JACK (1940–), professional golfer born in Columbus, Ohio. Nicklaus attended Ohio State University. His career as a professional golfer included winning these major tournaments: United States Open 1962, 1967, 1972; United States Masters 1963, 1965, 1966, 1972, 1975; the British Open 1968, 1970; the Professional Golfer's Association (PGA) 1963, 1971, 1973, 1974. He has won more tournament championships than any other person in the history of professional golf. Nicklaus has authored numerous publications, such as *Ways to Lower Your Golf Score* (1962) and *The Best Way to Better Golf* (1974).

NIEBUHR, H. RICHARD (1894–1962), theologian and sociologist of religion. Born in Wright City, Missouri, Niebuhr graduated from Elmhurst College (1912) and Eden Theological Seminary (1915). He received his Bachelor of Divinity degree and doctorate from Yale University. Niebuhr authored *The Social Sources of Denominationalism* (1929), in which he discusses the relationships of social groups to denominations. His *Kingdom of God in America* (1937) discusses the concept of "Kingdom" in the transformation of Puritan thought to Protestant ideas in American history. He participated in study groups that led to the major assemblies of the World Council of Churches. He was instrumental in the merger between the United Church of Christ, Congregational, and Evangelical and Reformed Churches.

NIEBUHR, REINHOLD (1892–1971), distinguished theologian within the Neo-Orthodox movement. Born in Wright City, Missouri, Niebuhr attended Elmhurst College and Eden Theological Seminary. He received his master's degree from Yale University. Niebuhr pastored a church in Detroit, Michigan, from 1915 to 1928. In 1927, he wrote *Does Civilization Need Religion?* This book criticized the capitalistic values of the American industrial order. In 1928, he joined the faculty of Union Theological Seminary in New York City. There he wrote an attack on liberal Protestantism titled *Moral Man in Immoral Society* (1932). His many books and articles underscored the social and cultural applications of theology. He opposed the expansion of United States military power in Asia during the 1960s.

OAKLEY, ANNIE (1860–1926), an outstanding figure from America's Wild West. Born in Drake County, Ohio, she teamed up with Frank E. Butler in vaudeville and later married him. In spite of her abilities in marksmanship, she was a modest woman. Her exploits inspired the modern musical, *Annie Get Your Gun.* Miss Oakley's religious views were fundamentalist. She was generous with her wealth, and many legends grew out of her reputation after she died. Annie Fern Swarthout's *Missie: An Historical Biography of Annie Oakley* (1947) is a very interesting study.

OCHS, ADOLPH S. (1858–1935), newspaper publisher and philanthropist. Born in Cincinnati, Ohio, Ochs bought and published the *Chattanooga Dispatch* and the *Chattanooga Times.* Then he moved to New York City where, in 1896, he acquired control of the *New York Times.* In an age of "yellow journalism," he sought to establish a newspaper that reflected dignity and trust. He established the *New York Times Index of Current History* (a topical journal) and funded the development of the *Dictionary of American Biography.* Ochs tried to make editorial opinion more objective. Gay Talese's, *The Kingdom and the Power* (1969) is a massive overview of Ochs and the *New York Times.*

President John F. Kennedy, Governor Connally, and Mrs. Jacqueline Kennedy stand under the wing of the presidential plane moments after arriving in Dallas, Texas, on Nov. 22, 1963.

ONASSIS, JACQUELINE KENNEDY (1929–), former wife of John F. Kennedy, the thirty-fifth President of the United States. Born in Southampton, New York, she attended Vassar College and The Sorbonne in Paris, France. After the assassination of President Kennedy, she received national consolation and regard. In 1968, she married Aristotle Onassis, wealthy Greek shipbuilder; the marriage attracted considerable notice. Since Onassis' death she has served as a publishing consultant. In earlier years, she was photographer for the *Washington Times-Herald.* Mrs. Onassis is a trustee of the Whitney Museum of American Art; she has received an Emmy Award for public service.

OPPENHEIMER, J. ROBERT (1904–1967), physicist; director of the atomic energy research project at Los Alamos, New Mexico. Born in New York City, Oppenheimer attended Harvard University and Cambridge University. He joined the staff of the California Institute of Technology in Pasadena, where he established a reputation in quantum mechanics and research in the continuous spectrum. Oppenheimer served as director of the project to develop the atomic bomb. After the development of the bomb, he regretted its devastation. He became the focus of attacks by Senator Joseph McCarthy, who alleged that Oppenheimer had communist sympathies; the allegations were unfounded. In the 1960s, he received the Fermi Award and was appointed director of the Institute for Advanced Study at Princeton University.

OWENS, JESSE (1913-1980), Olympic track star. He was born in Oakville, Alabama, the son of a sharecropper. He soon became an outstanding athlete. In 1935, he competed in the National Intercollegiate Track and Field Championships, where he established new records in broad jump and track. As a member of the United States Olympic team, he won four gold medals and served to refute Adolf Hitler's concept of "Aryan superiority." After several unsuccessful enterprises, Owens was appointed national director of physical education for blacks by the Office of Civilian Defense. He served as director of personnel for Ford Motor Company in Detroit from 1942 to 1946. He has received numerous recognitions and appointments. His autobiography is entitled, *Blackthink: My Life as a Black Man and White Man* (1970).

PALEY, WILLIAM S. (1901–), television network executive. Born in Chicago, Illinois, he attended the University of Chicago and the University of Pennsylvania. In 1928, he joined the staff of the Columbia Broadcasting System, where he rose from president to chairman of the board. He has served on numerous federal commissions, including the White House Conference on Education, Resources for Freedom, and others. He served in the military in World War II and was decorated with the Legion of Honor and Legion of Merit.

PALMER, ARNOLD (1929–), professional golfer born in Youngstown, Pennsylvania. Palmer attended Wake Forest College. As a golfer, he won the Masters Tournament in 1958, 1960, 1962, and 1964; the United States Open in 1960; the British Open in 1961 and 1962; and others. His friendship with President Dwight Eisenhower (and the President's affection for golf) established Palmer as a national celebrity. He is the president of Arnold Palmer Enterprises.

PATTERSON, FLOYD (1935–), boxer and former heavyweight champion, born in Waco, North Carolina. In 1952, Patterson began his boxing career as an Olympic middleweight champion; later in 1952, he fought his first professional fight. In 1956, he won the World Heavyweight Championship by defeating Archie Moore (the title had been vacated by the retirement of Rocky Marciano). After several defenses of the title, he lost it to Ingemar Johansson in 1959. He regained the title from Johansson in 1960, then lost it to Sonny Liston in 1962.

PATTERSON, JOSEPH MEDILL (1879–1946), newspaper publisher. Born in Chicago, Patterson attended the Groton School and Yale University. He began a journalistic career with the *Chicago Tribune* in 1901. In 1919, he founded the *New York Daily News* and remained as editor and publisher of that newspaper from 1919 to 1946. He served during World War I and wrote several books, including *The Fourth Estate* (with J. Keeley and Harriet Ford), *By-Products,* and *Rebellion.* His *New York Daily News* emphasized sensationalism, sex, and crime. After the financial crash of 1929, he addressed the newspaper to social reform and New Deal legislation. Although he supported President Franklin Roosevelt on most items, he felt that the United States should not enter World War II.

PATTON, GEORGE S. (1885–1945), general and military strategist. Born in San Gabriel, California, Patton graduated from the United States Military Academy at West Point. He distinguished himself as a tactician and commander of mobile tank warfare. His strict discipline and colorful language earned him the nickname "Old Blood and Guts." Patton was a student of United States Civil War strategy. Between World Wars, he learned tank warfare. He established his reputation in the North African campaign and the capture of Palermo. His sweep across France with the Third Army was marked by ruthlessness and drive. Patton was strategically involved in the Battle of the Bulge. He authored *War as I Knew It.*

PAULING, LINUS (1901–), atomic chemist. Born in Portland, Oregon, Pauling studied at Oregon State University and California Institute of Technology. He headed the Gates and Crellin Laboratories. His studies involved hemoglobin and protein structures. He is a member of the National Academy of Sciences and numerous other associations. In 1954, he received the Nobel Prize in Chemistry and the Nobel Peace Prize in 1962. Pauling has written numerous articles; his most famous appeared in 1931 and was entitled "The Nature of the Chemical Bond." Pauling advocated military disarmament, as described in *Quest for Peace* (1966) by Mortimer Lipsky.

PEABODY, GEORGE (1795–1869), merchant, financier, and philanthropist. Peabody dealt in securities in London after 1837; he generated capital for American industries. His firm, George Peabody and Company, specialized in foreign exchange. Peabody's international banking earned him a considerable personal fortune. After the Panic of 1837, he purchased several securities that were depressed. His company brought large supplies of capital investment to the United States. His wealth was distributed in various programs of educational reconstruction and poor relief. Franklin Parker's *George Peabody: A Biography* (1971) is highly informative and readable.

PEALE, NORMAN VINCENT (1898–), influential Protestant clergyman. Peale obtained his undergraduate degree from Ohio Wesleyan College in 1920. He was torn between a career in journalism or the ministry; he worked for the *Morning Republican* in Findlay, Ohio, and the *Detroit Journal.* He returned to study at Boston University and was ordained into the Methodist Episcopal Church in 1921. In 1932, he became pastor of the Marble Collegiate Church in New York. He has written numerous books, including *The Art of Living* (1932), *A Guide to Confident Living* (1948), *The Art of Real Happiness* (1950), and his phenomenally successful book, *The Power of Positive Thinking* (1952). Peale also began a radio program titled *The Art of Living,* which began in 1935 on NBC. He has been criticized for his moral pragmatism.

PEALE, REMBRANDT (1778–1860), painter best known for his portraits of Revolutionary heroes. Born in Bucks County, Pennsylvania, Peale was a son of the renowned painter, Charles Willson Peale. He made several trips to France, where he met Jacques Louis David and other leading artists. Peale established the Pennsylvania Academy of Fine Arts. His portrait of George Washington (1822) achieved considerable fame. He was elected president of the American Academy of the Fine Arts in 1825. Peale wrote *Graphics: The Art of Accurate Delineation* (1835). He developed a massive series of paintings on death that reflected several allegorical figures. In an era that emphasized romanticism, Peale's realistic work achieved considerable fame, particularly in Europe.

PEARSON, DREW (1897–1969), controversial newspaper columnist. His syndicated news column "Washington Merry-Go-Round" first appeared in 1932; he shared the writing with Jack Anderson after 1959. Pearson reported President Franklin Roosevelt's plan to pack the Supreme Court; he was generally disliked among Presidents and other public officials. He sponsored humanitarian causes; for example, he organized the Friendship Train to collect food for the people of Europe. He authored several books, including *Washington Merry-Go-Round* (1931) and (with Jack Anderson) *The Case Against Congress* (1968).

PEARY, ROBERT E. (1856–1920), Arctic explorer, famous for his discovery of the North Pole. Peary was born in Cresson, Pennsylvania. After his studies in civil engineering, he served as a county surveyor and draftsman. He was commissioned in the United States Navy in 1881. His early travels to Greenland were a prelude to his subsequent discovery of the North Pole. He reached the North Pole on April 6, 1909; but controversy surrounded Frederick A. Cook's claims that he reached the North Pole in 1908. In later life, Peary became identified with the development and expansion of aviation. John Edward Weems *Race to the Pole* (1960) details the controversy between Cook and Peary.

PENN, WILLIAM (1644–1718), Quaker leader and founder of Pennsylvania. Penn was born in London, where he became associated with the development of Quakerism and the Society of Friends. At Oxford, he was influenced by Puritanism and was expelled from the university. In 1672, he became a Quaker advocate. After the Glorious Revolution of 1688, he came to establish the colony of Pennsylvania. In 1712, he sold the colony to England. His last years were filled with disappointment. Mary M. Dunn's *William Penn: Politics and Conscience* (1967) is a useful analysis of the man.

PENNEY, JAMES C. (1875–1971), business executive and philanthropist born in Hamilton, Ohio. In 1902, he established the J.C. Penney Company, which operated on the principle of the Golden Rule and Christian morality. The department stores that he opened were called Golden Rule Stores; his first store was in Kemmerer, Wyoming. By 1971, his chain of stores numbered 1,660 outlets with gross sales of $4.1 billion. Penney exhibited a deep religious perspective in his personal manner and corporate leadership.

PERRY, OLIVER H. (1785–1819), naval officer and hero of the War of 1812. Born in South Kingston, Rhode Island, Perry held the command of a flotilla at Newport, Virginia, at the outbreak of the War of 1812. Commander Robert H. Barclay challenged Perry on September 10, 1813 in a battle between Perry's *Niagra* and Barclay's *Detroit.* Barclay was defeated, and Perry sent his superiors the famous message: "We have met the enemy and they are ours." This decisive victory strengthened United States claims in the Northwest. Perry retired and received honors from Congress. He later travelled to the Mediterranean, where he died of yellow fever.

PERSHING, JOHN J. (1860–1948), distinguished American commander during World War I. After graduation from West Point in 1886, Pershing was assigned to the campaign against the Apache Indians in the Southwest United States. He was also involved in the Spanish-American War and served as military attache in Tokyo during the Russo-Japanese War (1904–1905). Pershing's most significant service came during World War I, when he called for an independent American army. The Allies questioned his strategy during the last years of the war. Congress awarded him the title General of the Armies, a title given previously to George Washington. He authored *My Experiences in the World War* (1948), which was awarded the Pulitzer Prize.

PICKFORD, MARY (1893-1979), actress and movie star born in Toronto, Canada. Her acting career began at age eight, when she appeared in various melodramas and as a child actress on Broadway. At age 13, she took the name Mary Pickford. She appeared in various roles between 1910 and 1916, when she established the Mary Pickford Film Company. She joined Douglas Fairbanks, Charlie Chaplin, and the United Artists Corporation in 1919. She starred in numerous productions on the silent screen. She aided the work of numerous philanthropic and charity organizations.

PINKERTON, ALLAN (1819–1884), founder of a famous detective agency that bears his name; prototype of the modern crime investigator. Born in Glasgow, Scotland, he migrated to Dundee, Illinois. He supported abolitionists and the Underground Railroad in the years leading up to the Civil War. In 1850, he served as the director of police in Chicago; he then organized his private agency. He worked with the United States Post Office and the Illinois Central Railroad to solve robberies. He prevented an assassination of President Lincoln during the first inaugural. He organized the framework of the most comprehensive detective agency.

POCAHONTAS (ca. 1595–1617), early symbol of the American Indians. The daughter of an Indian chief, her real name was Matoaka; *Pocahontas* means "playful one." According to tradition, she played at the fort at Jamestown. She was taken as a prisoner by Captain Samuel Argall to guarantee the safety of Englishmen who had fallen into Indian hands. She was brought to Jamestown, instructed in Christianity, and baptized. She married colonial leader John Rolfe, and the marriage brought a period of peace between the colonists and the Indians. During a trip to England, she contracted smallpox and died in 1617.

POLLOCK, JACKSON (1912–1956), painter within the abstract, expressionist tradition. Born in Cody, Wyoming, he studied with Thomas Hart Benton between 1929 and 1931. He worked with the Depression-inspired Federal Arts Project from 1938 to 1942. During World War II, his art was influenced by European developments in cubism and surrealism. His paintings attracted the attention of Peggy Guggenheim; and under the Guggenheim influence, his art was shown throughout Europe. Pollock's international reputation became established in this period. During the last years of his life, his work was seen at the Sidney Janis Gallery in New York. In 1956, he was honored by a special exhibition at the New York Museum of Modern Art.

POPE, JOHN RUSSELL (1874–1937), architect; best known for designing the National Gallery of Art in Washington, D.C. Pope was born in New York City and trained at the American Academy at Rome. He was able to duplicate historic architectural styles through his studies. Pope began his architectural career in New York. He designed the Scottish Rite Temple in Washington, D.C., and was chosen to design memorials for Theodore Roosevelt in Washington and Abraham Lincoln in Hodgenville, Kentucky.

POST, ELIZABETH L. "EMILY" (1872–1960), well-known authority on social manners.

Born in Baltimore, Maryland, she began writing short stories and novels in 1904. Her book, *Etiquette,* appeared in 1922 and went through 10 revisions and 89 printings. It served as a guide to proper behavior and manners for ordinary people. Miss Post regarded etiquette as the science of proper living. She also wrote a nationally syndicated newspaper article on etiquette and authored numerous other publications, including *The Personality of a House* (1930), *Children Are People* (1940), and the *Emily Post Cook Book* (1949).

PRESLEY, ELVIS (1935–1977), singer commonly recognized as the father of "rock and roll" music. Presley's performances were filled with emotion and intensity. His gyrating hips and suggestive stage movements became a trademark, and he was idolized by teenagers throughout the world. He signed a recording contract with RCA Victor in 1956; he then recorded success after success. His first 45 records sold over a million copies each. Presley appeared in *Love Me Tender* and a succession of movies. He grossed over $4.3 billion in his 21-year career. His more famous musical titles included "Love Me Tender," "All Shook Up," and "Are You Lonesome Tonight?" His Graceland Mansion in Memphis, Tennessee, was a mecca for his fans.

PULITZER, JOSEPH, SR. (1847–1911), newspaper publisher and editor. Born in Mako, Hungary, he grew up in Budapest and pursued an active interest in military affairs. After being rejected by the French Foreign Legion, he was recruited by the Union forces for the Civil War and obtained passage to Boston. He quickly became identified with journalism through the *Westliche Post* in 1871. He purchased the *St. Louis Post-Dispatch,* which had shaky finances until about 1881. He served as a delegate to the National Democratic Convention and was elected as a member of Congress from New York in 1885. He then purchased the *New York World,* which added strength to his emerging influence. He used the *World* to promote sensational journalism and scandal. Its fiery reports from Cuba drew the United States into the Spanish-American War.

PYLE, ERNEST T. "ERNIE" (1900–1945), outstanding newspaper correspondent of World War II. Born near Dana, Indiana, Pyle studied journalism at Indiana University. After varied assignments, he received permanent appointment with the Scripps-Howard newspaper chain. Pyle developed a column that was syndicated through two hundred daily newspapers. He received a Pulitzer Prize for his coverage of the campaigns in North Africa, Sicily, Italy, and France. Pyle was with United States forces in Iwo Jima, where he died. He authored *Ernie Pyle in England* (1941), *Here Is Your War* (1943), *Brave Men* (1944), and *Last Chapter* (1946).

RAUSCHENBUSCH, WALTER (1861–1918), clergyman associated with the "social gospel." Born in Rochester, New York, Rauschenbusch graduated from Rochester Theological Seminary and assumed a pastorate in the area of New York City known as "Hells Kitchen." His experiences in New York led him to question the capitalistic ethic, and he formulated a theology of Christian socialism. He authored several books, including *Christianity and the Social Crisis, Christianizing the Social Order,* and *A Theology of Social Gospel.*

RAYBURN, SAM (1882–1961), political leader and long-time Speaker of the House of Representatives. Born in Roane County, Texas, Rayburn graduated from Mayo Normal School (now East Texas State University). He taught in rural schools, then ran for the Texas House of Representatives. He attended law school and passed the state bar in 1908. In 1910, he won a seat in the United States House of Representatives; he was subsequently reelected for 23 terms. He served as Speaker of the House for many years. Clearly identified with the Democratic Party and its leadership, he managed the Presidential campaign of Lyndon Baines Johnson in 1960. An interesting analysis of Rayburn's impact on national politics is included in William Leuchtenburg's *Franklin D. Roosevelt and The New Deal, 1932–1940* (1963).

REAGAN, RONALD (1911–), Hollywood actor and political figure. Reagan appeared in over fifty movies. In 1966, he ran for governor of California against incumbent Edmund G. "Pat" Brown and was victorious. He became an important force in the Republican Party. Although he was viewed as a radical conservative because he supported Barry Goldwater for the presidency in 1964, Reagan resisted such labeling. He opposed federally funded welfare programs and the expansion of big government. He was elected President of the United States in 1980.

Presidential candidate Ronald Reagan waves to an enthusiastic crowd on his arrival on Aug. 15, 1976, in Kansas City.

REASONER, HARRY (1923–), broadcast journalist. Born in Dakota City, Iowa, Reasoner began a writing career in 1946 with the *Minneapolis Times.* In 1948, he began an association with radio station WCCO in Minneapolis, a CBS radio affiliate. After a period of time with the United States Information Agency in the Far East, he returned to CBS with a television assignment in New York. He covered the racial crisis in Little Rock, Arkansas, in 1958. During the 1960s, he had numerous assignments with *CBS Reports* and narrated special documentaries on smoking, taxation, and federal aid to schools. He was seen as the weekly anchorman for *CBS Sunday News* until 1970, when he left CBS to join ABC News. He co-anchored news broadcasts at ABC with Howard K. Smith and Barbara Walters, then returned to the staff of CBS News in 1978.

REED, WALTER S. (1851–1902), military surgeon who is credited with having conquered yellow fever. Reed received two medical degrees, one from the University of Virginia and another from Bellevue Hospital Medical College. He served as a professor at the Army Medical School in Washington. He was able to determine the mode of transmission of yellow fever through many controlled experiments. He developed a way to immunize soldiers against the disease. In 1901, he resumed his teaching responsibilities at the Army Medical School. Reed received many honors, including honorary degrees from Harvard University and the University of Michigan. For more information about his life and times, read Albert E. Truby's, *Memorial of Walter Reed: The Yellow Fever Episode* (1943).

REMINGTON, FREDERIC (1861–1909), author and sculptor; painter and illustrator. Remington attended several schools, including Yale School of Fine Arts. His early work reflected his fascination with the West. He often painted horses in action. His work contained a high degree of realism. He represented the cowboy, Indian, and the Western landscape with native color. Remington wrote many significant books, including *Pony Tracks* (1895), *Stories of War and Peace* (1899), and *The Way of an Indian* (1906). A significant collection of his work can be found in the New York Public Library.

RENWICK, JAMES, JR. (1818–1895), architect most famous for St. Patrick's Cathedral in New York City. Born in the Bloomingdale section of New York, Renwick got his abilities in design from his father, James Renwick. He graduated from Columbia College. His designs for several churches brought him to national prominence—Grace Church, Church of the Puritans on Union Square, Church of the Covenant, and St. Patrick's Cathedral. Renwick also designed the New Smithsonian Institution in Washington. He taught a generation of apprentices and draftsmen and was a collector of art objects from his trips abroad.

RESTON, JAMES (1909–), author and journalist born in Clyde-Bank, Scotland. Reston attended the University of Illinois and began his journalistic career with the *Springfield Daily News.* In 1934, he joined the staff of the Associated Press in London. In 1939, he came back to the United States to work with the *New York Times*—first as reporter for the London bureau, then with the Washington bureau, finally as Chief Washington Correspondent (1953–1964). From 1964 to 1968, he was associate editor of the *Times.* He received the Pulitzer Prize in 1945 and 1957. Reston has received numerous other awards, recognitions, and honorary degrees.

RICKENBACKER, EDWARD "EDDIE" (1890–1973), World War I flying ace, racing driver, and executive of a major airline. Rickenbacker worked with the Frayer-Miller company as a race driver and he achieved numerous records. During World War I, he shot down more than twenty-two enemy planes, and became the most decorated pilot of the war. As general manager and later president of Eastern Airlines, he brought innovative promotions to the industry. After World War

II, he supported conservative McCarthyism and the anti-communist crusade. His autobiography is titled, *Rickenbacker—An Autobiography.*

RIDDLE, NELSON (1921-), composer, conductor, and arranger of popular musical themes. He was associated with numerous bands early in his career, including the Tommy Dorsey Band. He served as staff arranger for the National Broadcasting Company in Hollywood, 1947–1950; then he was musical director for Capitol Records, 1951–1962. Riddle has been guest conductor with the Hollywood Bowl and the Atlanta Symphony. He received the Emmy nomination in 1954, 1955, 1956, and 1957, and an Oscar nomination in 1960. Riddle received a Grammy award for *Come Blow Your Horn* and other musical scores. He composed theme music for the television series *Untouchables, Naked City, Route 66,* and others.

ROCKEFELLER, JOHN D., JR. (1874–1960), business entrepreneur and philanthropist. Born in Cleveland, Ohio, Rockefeller was educated at Brown University. After graduation, he became involved in the business affairs of Standard Oil Company, which his father had founded. He disliked the world of business and became involved in philanthrophy. He established the Rockefeller Institute for Medical Research and the Rockefeller Foundation. He supported the education of black people in the South. The last quarter-century of his life was devoted to conservation, the national parks system, and the restoration of Williamsburg. His modesty was in direct contrast to the image that his father projected.

ROCKEFELLER, NELSON A. (1908–1979), former governor of New York and Vice-President of the United States under President Gerald R. Ford. He was a son of John D. Rockefeller, Jr. His government service began as Assistant Secretary of State in 1944–1945. After the war, he chaired the Development Advisory Board. From 1958 to 1973, he was governor of New York, where he inaugurated a major construction program in the state capital of Albany. After President Richard Nixon's resignation, he was named by President Ford to become Vice-President. He was a trustee of the Rockefeller Brothers fund.

ROCKWELL, NORMAN (1894–1978), painter and illustrator of covers for the *Saturday Evening Post* and numerous other magazines, including the *Ladies' Home Journal, Look,* and *McCall's.* Rockwell's *Paintings of Four Freedoms* is represented in the Metropolitan Museum of Art in New York City. During World War I, he served as a first-class painter with the United States Navy. He received numerous recognitions and honorary degrees, and wrote *Norman Rockwell: My Adventures as an Illustrator* (1959), *The Norman Rockwell Album* (1961), *Norman Rockwell: Artist and Illustrator* (1970), and *Norman Rockwell's America* (1975).

RODGERS, RICHARD (1902-1979), noted composer of music. Born near Arverne, New York, Rodgers worked with Lorenze Hart and Jerome Kern in his early years. With Lorenze Hart, he produced a succession of musicals that captured national attention; among their more successful productions were: *On Your Toes* (1936), *Babes in Arms* (1937), and *Pal Joey* (1940). His more popular music with Hart included *My Funny Valentine, With a Song in My Heart, This Can't Be Love,* and *The Lady Is a Tramp.* His association with Oscar Hammerstein resulted in such musical successes as *Carousel* (1945), *South Pacific* (1949), *The King and I* (1951), and *The Sound of Music* (1959). Rodgers' most popular songs include "If I Loved You," "Hello Young Lovers," and "Climb Every Mountain."

ROGERS, WILL (1879–1935), entertainer and newspaper columnist. Rogers was born in Cologah, Oklahoma, of Indian descent; as a young man he was a cowboy—panhandling, twirling rope, and herding steers. In 1902, he joined a Wild West show in Australia. In 1912, he played in his first Broadway musical, *The Wall Street Girl,* and in 1922, he appeared in the Ziegfeld Follies. That same year, he began writing a column that wedded political humor with wit; the column appeared daily in 1926 and was widely syndicated. He authored *Letters of a Self-Made Diplomat to His President* (1926) and *There's Not a Bathing Suit in Russia* (1927). He was an early enthusiast of air travel and was killed in a plane crash en route to Alaska.

ROONEY, MICKEY (1920-), actor and star of films. Born in Brooklyn, New York, he first appeared in vaudeville with his parents. Rooney starred in numerous television and film productions, including *Hold That Kiss, Babes in Arms, National Velvet, Breakfast at Tiffany's, Requiem* *for a Heavyweight,* and the entire *Andy Hardy* series. He starred in the television spectacular *Pinocchio* (1957). Rooney wrote *An Autobiography* (1965).

ROOSEVELT, ELEANOR (1884–1962), author, diplomat, and wife of President Franklin Delano Roosevelt, thirty-second President of the United States. After her husband contracted polio in 1921, she became increasingly involved with his career. She rejected her mother-in-law's notion that Franklin should surrender to his condition. During the Great Depression, she led several New Deal programs for work relief. During World War II, she became involved with several efforts on behalf of the Red Cross and war relief. After the death of her husband in 1945, she assumed international stature in connection with her work on the United Nations. She was a leading voice in the Democratic Party, particularly on behalf of Adlai Stevenson's campaigns for the Presidency. Mrs. Roosevelt authored numerous books, including *On My Own* (1958).

ROOT, ELIHU (1845–1937), Secretary of War and Secretary of State; Senator from New York. Mr. Root attended Hamilton College and graduated from New York University with a law degree. He served as Secretary of War under President William McKinley during the Spanish-American War, and created the Army War College. He was highly regarded by President Theodore Roosevelt; and in 1905, he was named Secretary of State. He was awarded the Nobel Peace Prize in 1912. As Senator from New York (1909–1915), he opposed the progressive program of the Taft Administration, Root authored numerous titles. Richard Jessup's *Elihu Root* (2 vols., 1938) is the official biography.

ROSS, BETSY (1752–1836), legendary maker of the first American flag. Born in Philadelphia, Pennslyvania, she attended the Friends School in Philadelphia and demonstrated a great skill for needlework. In 1773, she eloped with John Ross, whom she married. She was a loyal member of the Society of Free Quakers. The story that George Washington commissioned her to make the first Stars and Stripes is based on tradition; but the flag was adopted as the national flag on June 14, 1777. There is considerable romance and legend associated with her making of the flag.

ROZELLE, PETE (1927–   ), football figure, flamboyant commissioner of the National Football league. Born in South Gate, California, Rozelle, was educated at the University of San Francisco. From 1948 to 1950, he served as the news director of the University of San Francisco; from 1952 to 1955, he was the public relations director for the Los Angeles Rams. Rozelle was general manager of the Los Angeles Rams from 1955 to 1957. In 1960, he was appointed commissioner of the National Football League.

RUBINSTEIN, ARTUR (1887–1982), concert pianist. Born in Lodz, Poland, he made his concert debut in Berlin at the age of twelve. He studied under I. J. Paderewski and began his concert tours with appearances in Paris, London, and the United States in 1905–1906. After World War II, Rubinstein came to live in the United States and continued a hectic pace of concert playing. He is noted for his stirring renditions of classical and patriotic themes.

RUSK, DEAN (1909–   ), Secretary of State during a turbulent era of American-Soviet relations. Appointed by President John Kennedy, he was loyal to the Kennedy-Johnson program of war in Vietnam. He personally confronted the Senate with the Administration's policies in Southeast Asia. Rusk had been president of the Rockefeller Foundation and became identified with foreign policy during the post-World War II period. However, he was unable to chart a course different from the John Foster Dulles policies of the 1950s.

RUTH, GEORGE HERMAN "BABE" (1895–1948), legendary sports figure called the

Babe Ruth hits his 60th home run.

"sultan of swat" for his ability to hit home runs. Ruth began his baseball career as a pitcher for the Boston Red Sox. Because of his reputation as a hitter, he was transferred to the outfield. He became a national celebrity and the perennial home-run king. In 1927, he hit 60 home runs, a record that remained until Roger Maris hit 61 in an extended game. His 714 lifetime home runs remained the record until Hank Aaron surpassed that mark. He is regarded as the game's greatest player. He died of cancer in 1948.

SALK, JONAS (1914–), developed the first vaccine to combat polio. After his study at the College of Medicine of New York, Salk interned at New York's Mount Sinai Hospital. During his stay at the University of Michigan he developed a vaccine for influenza. Working with the National Foundation for Infantile Paralysis, he developed the successful vaccine for polio. Controversies surrounded his achievements; the Sabin oral vaccine competed with his. In 1963, he established the Salk Institute for Biological Studies. For more information, see Richard Carter's *Breakthrough: The Saga of Jonas Salk* (1966).

SALOMON, HAYM (1740–1785), financier, merchant, and banker of the Revolutionary period. Salomon was born in Poland and emigrated to New York in the early 1770s. During the British occupation of New York in 1776, he was arrested as a spy. He induced Hessians to desert the British army, which established his identity among the revolutionaries. Salomon's business and commercial dealings brought him unusual successes in the area of securities. He worked with Robert Morris to maintain a flow of finance and credit during the crucial "last days" of the American Revolution. Following the war, he suffered heavy financial losses.

SARNOFF, DAVID (1891–1971), pioneer radio technician and chairman of the Radio Corporation of America. His early work with John Wanamaker's station in New York allowed him to develop his interests in radio; he was the first to receive the distress call of the S.S. *Titanic* in 1912. Sarnoff became inspector and instructor for the Marconi Institute, which was then merged with the Radio Corporation of America owned by Owen D. Young. Sarnoff supervised the manufacture of radio sets and the expansion of radio programming. RCA became a leader in radio and television broadcast and electronics manufacture. Sarnoff served as communications consultant to President Dwight Eisenhower. He received numerous honors.

SCHECHTER, SOLOMON (1847–1915), a leading voice in Judaism in the United States. Born in Focsani, Romania, his career began as a reader in rabbinics at Cambridge University. During this period, he wrote several books on rabbinic theology. In 1902, he became president of the Jewish Theological Seminary of America in New York and emerged as the leader of conservative Judaism. He became a spokesman for American Zionism. Schechter's numerous writings are contained in his *Seminary Addresses and Other Papers* (1969). He served as co-editor of the *Jewish Quarterly Review.*

SCHLESINGER, ARTHUR, JR. (1917–), distinguished historian and author. His father, Arthur Schlesinger, Sr. was also a historian and professor. The younger Schlesinger graduated from Harvard in 1938, and the following year his thesis was published under the title *Orestes Brownson: A Pilgrim's Progress.* During World War II, he served as a member of the Office of Strategic Services. His book entitled *The Age of Jackson* brought him into national prominence. *The Vital Center* (1949) was his third book. His study of the Roosevelt Presidency resulted in three volumes: *The Crisis of the Old Order, The Coming of the New Deal,* and *The Politics of Upheaval.* He was appointed special adviser to President John Kennedy. His study of the Kennedy Presidency, titled *A Thousand Days,* received national attention.

SCHULLER, ROBERT (1926–), popular clergyman, proponent of "church growth." Born in Alton, Iowa, Schuller attended Hope College and Western Theological Seminary. He established the Garden Grove (California) Community Church in 1955 and began a television and radio ministry. In 1970, he established the Robert H. Schuller Institute for Successful Church Leadership. His leadership has made a national impact. He has authored numerous titles, including *God's Way to the Good Life* (1963), *Your Future Is Your Friend* (1964), *You Can Become the Person You Want to Be* (1973), and others. Dr. Schuller's weekly television broadcast is entitled *The Hour of Power.*

SCHULZ, CHARLES (1922–), newspaper cartoonist, famous for his "Peanuts" series. Born in Minneapolis, Minnesota, he served as cartoonist for the *St. Paul Pioneer Press* and the *Saturday Evening Post* (1948–1949). In 1950, he created the comic strip "Peanuts," with characters Charlie Brown, Lucy, Linus, and Snoopy. Schulz has received the Outstanding Cartoonist Award from the National Cartoonist Association (1956) and an Emmy Award for the television special, *A Charlie Brown Christmas* (1966). His collected cartoons have appeared in books under numerous titles: *Peanuts; More Peanuts; Good Grief, More Peanuts; A Charlie Brown Christmas,* and others.

SCOTT, GEORGE C. (1927–), actor and star of motion pictures. Born in Wise, Virginia, Scott attended Redford High School in Detroit. During World War II, he enlisted in the Marines. Later he entered the School of Journalism of the University of Missouri; there he appeared in several dramatic performances. During the 1950s, he achieved very little. But during his performance in *Comes the Day* on Broadway, Otto Preminger observed Scott's abilities and offered him the lead in the film, *Anatomy of a Murder.* He received an Academy nomination for that role. *The Hustler* (1961) was his next role, followed by *Patton* (1970). Scott has made numerous television appearances in *Playhouse 90, Armstrong Theatre,* and *Hallmark Hall of Fame,* among others.

SEABURY, SAMUEL (1729–1796), the first bishop of the Episcopal Church in America. He was born in Groton, Connecticut as the son of a Congregational minister. He attended Yale College. Seabury worked diligently to maintain union with the British crown; he called for orderly change and petition. His pamphlets were answered by Alexander Hamilton and others who called for revolution. After the Revolution, Anglican officials in Great Britain consecrated him to serve the church in the now-independent colonies. Seabury's sermons and writings were published in *Discourses on Several Subjects* (1793) and *Discourses on Several Important Subjects* (1798).

SELZNICK, DAVID O. (1902–1965), motion picture producer, whose greatest work was the epic *Gone with the Wind* (1939). Selznick's name is associated with other outstanding screen productions, including *A Star is Born* (1937) and *A Farewell to Arms* (1957). He was rated Outstanding Producer for 22 consecutive years. Selznick received Academy Awards for the best production of the year in 1939 and 1940.

SENNETT, MACK (1884–1960), producer of silent movies. In 1912, he organized the Keystone Company; and within the first year, he produced over one hundred forty comedies under the *Keystone* label. Sennett's movies lacked logic or cohesion; they offered a succession of "slapstick" episodes instead. Gloria Swanson added a sexual delight to the Keystone series. In 1928, Sennett was awarded an honor by the Academy of Motion Picture Arts and Sciences for his "contributions to comedy techniques of the screen."

SETON, ELIZABETH B. (1774–1821), first American to be named a saint by the Roman Catholic church. The Seton family travelled to Italy in 1803 to visit the Filicchi family, prominent in banking. There Miss Seton was converted to Catholicism. Upon returning to the United States, she established a boarding school in Baltimore called Sisters of the Charity of St. Joseph. After 1814, she opened orphanages and schools under the same order in New York and Philadelphia. She was declared venerable in 1959, beatified in 1963, and canonized as a saint in 1975.

SEVAREID, ERIC (1912–), broadcaster, news commentator, and author. Born in Velva, North Dakota, Sevareid studied at the University of Minnesota and then travelled to France and enrolled at the Alliance Francaise. After a brief period as a reporter for the *Minneapolis Star,* he joined the staff of the *New York Herald Tribune* in Paris. In 1939, he became a European correspondent for the Columbia Broadcasting System, and broadcast the fall of France to the Nazis. After the war, he became a national correspondent for CBS News. In the 1960s, his editorial commentaries appeared on the *CBS Evening News with Walter Cronkite.* Sevareid received numerous awards, including the George Foster Peabody award in 1949, 1964, and 1968. He authored *Not So Wild a Dream* (1946) and *This Is Eric Sevareid* (1964), among others.

DeSEVERSKY, ALEXANDER P. (1894–1974), aeronautic engineer born in Tiflis (now a part of the U.S.S.R.). DeSeversky served as an aviator for Tzarist Russia and engaged in combat action during World War I. He then served as a lower-level diplomat in America. When Russia closed its Washington embassy in 1918, he decided to remain in the United States. After World War I, he became a strong advocate of strategic air power. He contributed greatly to modern aircraft technology, and developed the first automatic bombsight.

SEWARD, WILLIAM HENRY (1801–1872), Secretary of State under President Abraham Lincoln. Seward graduated from Union College and was admitted to the bar in 1822. He was elected as the Whig candidate for governor of New York; as a two-term governor, he came into conflict with governors from Southern states. Seward wrote *Argument in Defense of William Freeman,* the account of his legal defense of two Negroes. As Secretary of State, Seward was a strong defender of Lincoln. He is considered to be among the greatest Secretaries of State; his most famous action was the purchase of Alaska from Russia.

SHEPARD, ALAN B., JR. (1923–), the first American to travel in space. Born in East Derry, New Hampshire, Shepard graduated from the United States Naval Academy and the Naval War College. He served as a test pilot with the United States Navy Test Pilot School and joined the Project Mercury space program of NASA in 1959. He was the first American in space with a sub-orbital flight on May 5, 1961. He was selected to command the Apollo 14 Lunar Landing Mission in 1971 and became the fifth man to walk on the moon. Shepard has received numerous honors and awards, including a Presidential Citation, the NASA Distinguished Service Award, and the Lungley Award of the Smithsonian Institution.

Apollo 14 astronauts (left to right) Stuart Roosa, Alan Shepard, and Edgar Mitchell

SHRIVER, R. SARGENT (1915–), lawyer and public figure, candidate for the Vice-Presidency with George McGovern in 1972. Shriver graduated from Yale College, *cum laude,* in 1938. He married Eunice Kennedy, sister of the future President John Kennedy. His work as the first director of the Peace Corps in the Kennedy Administration drew international attention. Shriver served as director of the Office of Economic Opportunity under President Johnson and was appointed Ambassador to France. Presently he practices law in Washington, D.C.; he has received numerous honors and awards. His efforts on behalf of the Peace Corps brought him into contact with world leaders in developing countries.

SIKORSKY, IGOR (1889–1972), aeronautical engineer who designed the first multi-motored airplane and the first practical helicopter (in 1939). Sikorsky served as engineering manager and consultant to the Sikorsky Aircraft Division of the United Aircraft Corporation. He designed the S-42 Clipper Ship for Pan American Airlines. United Aircraft developed Sikorsky's helicopter designs, and the V5-300 was the first helicopter to go into mass production. Although helicopters were not used in World War II, they became vital military tools in Korea and Vietnam. Frank J. Delear's *Igor Sikorsky: His Careers in Aviation* is a useful biography.

SIMON, PAUL (1941–), musician and composer who became famous for his compositions with Art Garfunkel. Born in Newark, New Jersey, Simon met Garfunkel in the sixth grade. They began singing together in the mid-1950s as teenagers. Simon entered Queens College to study literature and then went to law school. He and Garfunkel continued singing together, and recorded an album titled, *Wednesday Morning, 3 A.M.* The album achieved success through a song titled "The Sounds of Silence." Simon's success is evident in his musical score for *The Graduate,* for "Bridge Over Troubled Water" and other titles. In 1970, the two singers parted company. On his own, Simon has composed and performed numerous musical selections.

SINATRA, FRANK (1915–   ), singer and actor. Born in Hoboken, New Jersey, Sinatra began his career by touring with the Henry James and Tommy Dorsey Bands. He played leading roles in the movies, *Guys and Dolls, The Tender Trap, Pal Joey, Can Can,* and *Oceans II*. Sinatra received an Academy Award for best supporting role in *From Here to Eternity* (1953). He has received numerous additional awards, including the Peabody and Emmy Awards in 1965, and the Sylvania TV Award.

SIRICA, JOHN (1904–   ), judge who presided over the trials of Watergate scandal, which ousted President Richard Nixon from office. Born in Waterbury, Connecticut, he attended George Washington University Law School. Sirica found the work difficult and had to drop his studies. Later he enrolled at Georgetown University Law School. He graduated and was admitted to the bar in 1926. In 1930, he became Assistant United States Attorney for the District of Columbia; he later built a private law practice and entered Republican politics. In 1957, President Dwight Eisenhower appointed him to the United States District Court for the District of Columbia. By virtue of seniority, he became the chief judge of the District Court. He presided over the case that involved the seven Watergate defendents, including Presidential aides H. R. Haldeman and John Erlichman.

SITTING BULL (1831-1890), a Hunkpapa Sioux medicine man and Indian chief, leader of his tribe at the time of George Custer's massacre. The battle at the Little Bighorn River wiped out Custer and 265 men at the hands of Crazy Horse and his warriors. After 1879, the United States government offered amnesty to Indians who would surrender. Sitting Bull had left for Canada after the episode at Little Bighorn, so he accepted government amnesty. He was placed on a reservation in the Dakota Territory. In 1890, he was arrested on rumors that he would lead the Sioux on the warpath again; he was fatally shot in a struggle that ensued. Robert M. Utley's *The Last Days of The Sioux Nation* (1963) contains a scholarly analysis of Sitting Bull's life.

SLOAN, ALFRED P., JR. (1875–1966), business executive; first president of General Motors. Born in New Haven, Connecticut, Sloan attended public schools and the Polytechnic Institute. He graduated from the Massachusetts Institute of Technology with a bachelor's degree in 1895. His work with the Hyatt Rolling Bearing Company provided steel roller bearings for the automobile industry. Sloane's work came to the attention of William C. Durant, the builder of General Motors. Durant made Sloan the president of United Motors Corporation, which was eventually merged with General Motors. When the control of General Motors passed to the Dupont family, Sloan assumed greater influence. At his retirement, GM controlled 52 percent of the automobile market. He endowed the Alfred P. Sloan Foundation, whose primary contributions have been to the Sloan-Kettering Cancer Research.

SMITH, JOSEPH (1805–1844), religious leader; founder of the Church of Jesus Christ of Latter Day Saints (Mormons). In 1830, he published the *Book of Mormon.* Smith stressed the need for a restored church, and he suggested that he had special revelations from God. He organized a Utopian community of followers and led them westward to Nauvoo, Illinois. Smith admonished his followers against the use of tobacco, alcohol, and hot drinks. Through the theory of the "Hamitic Curse," Smith excluded blacks from the Mormon faith. Smith was murdered on June 27, 1844, while in jail, awaiting trial.

SMITH, HOWARD K. (1914–   ), newscaster and commentator. Born in Louisiana, he attended Tulane University and travelled in Europe after graduation. There Smith accepted a Rhodes scholarship to study at Merton College, Oxford University. During World War II, he served as a reporter with United Press. In 1940, he joined the CBS editorial team. In 1942, Smith wrote *Last Train from Berlin.* After the war, he served as the chief European correspondent for CBS and worked with Edward R. Murrow on the television series, *See It Now.* In 1957, he returned to America, where he became moderator for *The Great Challenge, Face the Nation,* and other programs of public policy. Smith also moderated the first of the Kennedy-Nixon Presidential debates. In October 1961, he resigned his position with CBS over a policy dispute. He moderated ABC's *Issues and Answers* program, and later he was co-anchor with Harry Reasoner on the *ABC Evening News.*

SNEAD, SAM (1912–   ), professional golfer born in Hot Springs, Virginia. Snead became a golfing professional in 1935. He won the Professional Golfer's Association (PGA) Championship in 1942, 1949, and 1951; the British Open in 1946; and the Master's Golf Tournament in 1949, 1952, and 1954. He was inducted into the Professional Golfer's Association Hall of Fame. Snead has written several books, including *How to Hit a Golf Ball* (1940), *How to Play Golf* (1946), and (with Al Stump) *Education of a Golfer* (1962).

SOUSA, JOHN PHILIP (1854–1932), America's foremost composer of music for marching bands. Born in Washington, D.C., he enlisted in the Marine Band. During the Centennial Exposition in Philadelphia, he played in the orchestra conducted by Jacques Offenbach. In 1880, he became the Director of the Marine Band; and in 1892, he organized what he called the New Marine Band. Sousa made several trips to Europe and was widely acclaimed. Some of his compositions achieved an international reputation: "The Stars and Stripes Forever," "The High School Cadets," "The Washington Post," and "The Gladiator." Sousa also wrote comic operas, including *The Bridge Elect.*

SPOCK, BENJAMIN (1903–), physician and educator, noted for his principles of child-rearing. Born in New Haven, Connecticut, Spock received his medical degree from the College of Physicians and Surgeons of Columbia University. As a pediatrician, he authored the *Common Sense Book of Baby and Child Care* (1946), which has gone through numerous printings. Spock's views on child-rearing influenced a generation of parents. In the decade of the 1960s, his opposition to the war in Vietnam brought prestige to the movement of protest and dissent. He authored other books, including *Decent and Indecent* (1970) and *A Teenagers' Guide to Life and Love* (1970). Spock has served on the faculty of the University of Pittsburg and Case Western Reserve, and on the staff of the Mayo Clinic.

STASSEN, HAROLD (1907–), lawyer and controversial candidate for President. A native of West St. Paul, Minnesota, Stassen attended the University of Minnesota and Hamlin University. From 1938 to 1945, he was the governor of Minnesota; and in 1948, he became president of the University of Pennsylvania. In 1953, he left the university to take assignments with the Disarmament Commission and as Special Assistant to the President. During World War II, he served in the South Pacific, where he earned the Legion of Merit and the Bronze Star. He authored *Where I Stand* (1947). Stassen's liberal views made him an unsuccessful contender for the Republican Presidential nomination in 1948, 1964, and 1968. But his ideas affected Republican foreign policy.

Charles Steinmetz

STEINMETZ, CHARLES (1865–1923), mathematician and electrical engineer. Born in Breslau, he came to Yonkers, New York, to work with the electrical inventor Rudolph Eickemeyer in developing alternating-current devices. General Electric hired Steinmetz to do industrial research, and he gave GE a reputation for research and development. Steinmetz perfected the incandescent and arc lights. He also worked on new batteries and other electrical problems. As a consulting engineer with GE, he had freedom to explore projects and problems that were to his liking.

STEVENSON, ADLAI E. (1900–1965), diplomat, governor, and candidate for the United States Presidency. He was the grandson of Adlai E. Stevenson, who served as Vice-President in 1893–1897. He graduated from Princeton University, attended Harvard Law School, and graduated from the Northwestern Law School in 1926. During World War II, he was assistant to the Secretary of the Navy. He served as an adviser to the United States delegation at the San Francisco Conference, which chartered the United Nations. In 1948, he was elected governor of Illinois. He ran for President in 1952 and 1956 and lost. In 1960, President John Kennedy named Stevenson as United States Ambassador to the United Nations.

STOKES, CARL (1927–), the first black mayor of a major American city. Born in Cleveland, Ohio, he passed the bar examination in 1957 and established a law firm with his brother.

Elected to the Ohio House of Representatives in 1962, he became mayor of Cleveland in 1967. *The Cleveland Plain Dealer* lauded his election; he showed a balance in his administration. In 1969, he won reelection; but chose to enter broadcasting instead of attempting another campaign in 1971.

STONE, MELVILLE E. (1848–1929), newspaper executive. Born in Hudson, Illinois, Stone became a newspaper reporter for the *Chicago Republican* in 1867. In 1875, he organized the first penny daily in the United States, the Chicago *Daily News*. He sold out his interests in 1888 and became associated with the Globe National Bank. In 1893, he became the general manager of the Associated Press and moved the AP to New York to compete with the United Press. Stone developed a close relationship between the AP and Reuter Telegram Company of Great Britain for sharing foreign news. His autobiography is titled *Fifty Years a Journalist* (1921).

STRAUS, ISIDOR (1845–1912), merchant and chain-store president born in Otterburg, Bavaria. Educated in public schools, Straus was not able to attend West Point, due to the American Civil War. After the war, he established the enterprise of L. Straus & Son. In 1874, the basement of R. H. Macy and company became the center of Straus merchandising. Throughout Boston, Chicago, and Philadelphia, the Straus family established department stores. Isidor and brother Nathan made R. H. Macy the largest department store in the world. Through underselling, advertising and odd pricing, they controlled the merchandising market. Straus described himself as a Gold Democrat and a friend of President Grover Cleveland. He served as a United States Congressman from 1893 to 1895.

STREISAND, BARBRA (1942–), singer, actress, and film producer. A native of Brooklyn, New York, she began her career playing in summer stock theater. She appeared in numerous clubs, including Bon Soir and The Blue Angel. Miss Streisand starred in the Broadway roles of *I Can Get It For You Wholesale* (1962) and *Funny Girl* (1964–65). As a recording artist for Columbia Records, she became nationally popular. Miss Streisand has appeared in numerous screen roles, including *Funny Girl, Hello Dolly, On a Clear Day You Can See Forever, The Owl and the Pussycat, What's Up Doc? The Way We Were, A Star Is Born* (which she produced), and others. She received the Academy Award as best actress for her role in *Funny Girl* (1968).

STUART, GILBERT (1755–1828), painter and portraitist of the early Republic. During the Revolutionary period, his family moved to London, where he met fellow American exile, Benjamin West. During his London period, Stuart was regarded among the great artists, equal with Joshua Reynolds and Thomas Gainsborough. In 1792, he returned to America and achieved fame through his portraits of Washington. Although Stuart painted President Washington during the later years of his life, little of age is reflected in the portrait of the man. Stuart's portraits of other Revolutionary figures reveal a style that transcends age. He used few colors, but his mixtures reflected shadows and illusions. He set the standard for American portrait painting that prevailed in the nineteenth century.

SUNDAY, WILLIAM A. "BILLY" (1863–1935), preacher and revivalist who introduced America to the "sawdust trail." Born in Ames, Iowa, Sunday began his career as a baseball player with the Chicago White Sox in 1883. He later played with teams in Pittsburgh and Philadelphia. He embraced Christianity and left baseball in 1891 to begin working with the Young Men's Christian Organization. Sunday's preaching reflected the fundamentalist tradition. He opposed Sabbath-breaking and the use of alcohol, and he stirred religious enthusiasm. Sunday wrote several books that coincided with his athletic integration of Christianity, such as *Burning Truths from Billy's Bat* (1914).

SUSSKIND, DAVID (1920–), producer for television, motion pictures, and theatre. Susskind was born in New York City and graduated from Harvard University. He worked with the publicity department of Warner Brothers and Universal Pictures from 1946 to 1948. From 1952, he produced several Broadway plays, including *A Very Special Baby* (1956) and *Brief Lives* (1967). He produced a number of motion pictures: *Raisin in the Sun* (1960), *Requiem for a Heavyweight* (1961), *All Things Bright and Beautiful* (1976), and others. Susskind has been involved in producing several television programs, such as *The du Pont Show of the Month, Kaiser Aluminum Hour, Hallmark Hall of Fame,* and *Kraft Theatre*. He has received the Peabody Award, Academy Awards, and numerous other recognitions and honors.

SWANSON, GLORIA (1899-1983), actress and film celebrity. Born in Chicago, Illinois, she began working with Essanay Studios in Chicago. She later formed her own production company, called Gloria Swanson Productions. From 1971, she organized the Facial Fitness Clinics. Miss Swanson starred in numerous screen productions, including *Airport 1975* and *Sunset Boulevard* (1950). The first picture that recorded her speaking and singing was *The Trespasser* (1929). She appeared in the Broadway production, *Butterflies Are Free* (1970–1972). Miss Swanson is recognized for her acting abilities and business perception.

TAYLOR, ELIZABETH (1932-), actress and movie personality born in London, England. Miss Taylor's first major screen role was in *National Velvet* (1944). She also starred in *A Place in the Sun* (1950), *The Last Time I Saw Paris, Cat on a Hot Tin Roof, Butterfield 8, Cleopatra, The Sand Piper,* and *Who's Afraid of Virginia Wolf?* She received Academy Awards for her roles in *Butterfield 8* and *Who's Afraid of Virginia Wolf?* She has authored *Nibbles and Me* (with Richard Burton) and *World Enough and Time.* She has become notorious for her numerous marriages—to Conrad Nicholas Hilton, Jr.; to Michael Wilding; to Mike Todd; to Eddie Fisher; to Richard Burton (twice); and to John Warner.

TAYLOR, KENNETH (1917-), religious publishing executive. Taylor attended Wheaton (Illinois) College and began his publishing career with Moody Press. In 1963, he became president of his own company, Tyndale Press. He has served as an officer with numerous other organizations, including Living Bibles International and Coverdale Publishers. He has authored numerous titles, including *Is Christianity Credible?* (1946), *Living Letters: The Paraphrased Epistles* (1962), and *The Living Bible* (1971).

TEMPLE, SHIRLEY (1928-), actress, popular child star of movies in the 1930s, and politician. At the age of seven, she was Hollywood's greatest box-office attraction. She is remembered for her singing of "The Good Ship Lollipop." She portrayed a child who was capable of dealing with adult ego and hatred. Her films included *Baby Burlesks, Stand Up and Cheer, Little Miss Marker, Wee Willie Winkie,* and *The Little Princess.* In later life, she married a civic leader in San Francisco and became affiliated with the Republican Party. She ran unsuccessfully for the office of United States Representative to Congress. In 1969, President Nixon appointed her a member of the United States delegation to the United Nations General Assembly.

TESLA, NIKOLA (1856-1943), electrical engineer and inventor born in Smiljan, Croatia (now Yugoslavia). He devised an electrical transformer known as the Tesla coil. He worked briefly with Thomas Edison, designing electrical dynamos; in 1887, he established his own laboratory in New York. Tesla sided with engineers who favored alternating electrical current, rather than direct current (which Edison advocated). The alternating current system was adopted by George Westinghouse and became the basis for power generation from the Niagara Falls to Chicago's Columbian Exposition. Tesla produced motors, transformers, electrical coils, and other devices that contributed greatly to the emerging world of electrical technology.

THOMAS, LOWELL (1892-), radio news commentator, born in Woodington, Ohio. Thomas attended the University of Northern Indiana, University of Denver, Kent College, and Princeton University. In 1915, he made the first of a series of filmed travelogues; he toured extensively and lectured on his travels. President Woodrow Wilson appointed him to the civilian commission on World War I. In 1930, he made his debut on CBS radio; he would regularly conclude his nightly news broadcasts with the words, "So long until tomorrow." He continued producing *Lowell Thomas and the News* until 1976. He was the voice of Movietone News and served in the development of Cinerama movie features. Among his numerous publications are *Beyond the Khyber Pass* (1925), *The Untold Story of Exploration* (1936), and *With Allenby in the Holy Land* (1938).

THURMOND, STROM (1902-), former governor of South Carolina, Presidential candidate, and United States Senator. In 1948, Thurmond launched a Presidential campaign under the "states' rights" banner of the Dixiecrats. He attended Clemson College and was admitted to the bar in 1930. His public career has been identified with the concept of "states' rights" and racial segregation. In 1964, he broke with the Democratic Party and became a Republican. He has served in the United States Senate for over two decades. During World War II, he served in the United States Army during the invasion of Europe. He received the Bronze Star, the Purple Heart, and the Legion of Merit.

TILLICH, PAUL (1886–1965), theologian, religious scholar, and author. Born in Starzeddel, Prussia, Tillich attended the Universities of Berlin, Tübingen, and Halle. He received the Ph.D. from the University of Breslau. Ordained a minister in the Evangelican Lutheran Church, he taught at Marburg, Dresden, and Leipzig before becoming professor at the University of Frankfurt am-Main in 1929. He opposed the Nazis and was dismissed from the university, so he emigrated to the United States. Tillich taught at Union Theological Seminary (1933–1955), Harvard University (1955–1962), and the University of Chicago (1962–1965). He wrote numerous books, including a three-volume *Systematic Theology* (1951–1963).

TRUMBULL, JOHN (1756–1843), painter of historic scenes from the Revolutionary War. Trumbull was born in the Connecticut colony, where his father was governor. He took private painting lessons from John Singleton Copley and graduated from Harvard at age 17. During the Revolution, he served as aide-de-camp to General Washington. In 1780, he sailed to London, where he studied with Benjamin West. A controversy with Thomas Jefferson in 1793 damaged his later career. His art is in the tradition of Peter Paul Rubens; it deals exclusively with the American Revolution. Trumbull's works include the famous *Battle of Bunker Hill* and *Capture of the Hessians at Trenton.* He achieved fame in later life with commissions from Congress for paintings of the *Signing of the Declaration of Independence, Surrender of Cornwallis at Yorktown,* and others that decorate the rotunda of the Capitol in Washington.

TRUTH, SOJOURNER (1797–1883), abolitionist leader whose real name was Isabella Baumfree. Born in Ulster County, New York, she was the daughter of an African couple. After New York had passed an emancipation act, she asked for freedom from her master John J. Dumont. He refused and she ran away with one of her five children. She worked menial jobs and came under the influence of a religious fanatic named Mathias. Eventually she left Mathias and travelled to speak on her own, with the name of Sojourner Truth. She was the first person to test the legality of segregation on Washington, D.C., street cars.

TUBMAN, HARRIET (ca. 1820–1913), black agent for the Underground Railroad. Tubman helped hundreds of slaves flee captivity. She was born a slave herself, in Dorcester County, Maryland. In 1848, she ran away with her two brothers, leaving her husband John Tubman behind. A bounty of $40,000 was placed on her. Before the Civil War, she returned to the South 20 times to help over three hundred slaves to escape. She supported John Brown's insurrection at Harpers Ferry, Virginia. Tubman spoke against slavery and in support of women's rights. During the war, she served as a scout and nurse for the Union forces.

TUNNEY, JAMES J. "GENE" (1898–1978), professional boxer; corporation director. Born in New York City, Tunney won the light heavyweight championship at Paris in 1919. In 1926, he won the heavyweight championship from Jack Dempsey. He retained that title in a return engagement at Chicago in 1927. He retired from boxing in 1928 undefeated. He has served as director to many corporations, including the Bank of Commerce of New York and the Penobscot Building in Detroit. He wrote *A Man Must Fight* (1932) and *Arms for Living* (1941). In later years, Jack Dempsey became Tunney's close personal friend.

TURNER, NAT (1800–1831), black slave leader born in Southampton County, Virginia. He was a restless young man who turned to the Bible for guidance on slavery and freedom. He believed he was appointed of God to deliver his people from slavery, and he understood a solar eclipse to be a sign from God that he was supposed to lead a rebellion. Turner and his friends killed many whites in the rebellion that bears his name. By August of 1831, the tide had turned, and blacks were executed in large numbers. After a brief escape, Turner was caught, tried, and executed. His rebellion galvanized the abolitionist movement. William Styron's *Confessions of Nat Turner* (1968) is an analysis of the man and the movement.

VALENTINO, RUDOLPH (1895–1926), actor and matinee idol of the silent-film era. Born in Castellanetz, Italy, he attended the Dante Alighieri College and the Royal Academy. He came to the United States in 1913 and began his career as a dancer. Valentino joined the Musical Comedy Company and travelled to San Francisco. He entered motion pictures during a stay in Los Angeles, and scored a remarkable triumph as Julio in *The Four Horsemen.* His other performances included *The Conquering Power, Blood and Sand, The Sainted Devil,* and others.

VALLEE, RUDY (1901–), orchestra leader, vocalist, and popular radio personality. In 1929 he starred in the film, *Vagabond Lover;* a succession of screen performances followed: *George White's Scandals* (1934), *Sweet Music* (1935), *Gold Diggers in Paris* (1938), and *Too Many Blondes* (1941). Vallee had a weekly radio program for Standard Brands from 1929 to 1939. He has made frequent nightclub appearances and starred in the musical comedy *How to Succeed in Business Without Really Trying* (1961). During World War I, he served in the United States Navy.

VAN BUREN, ABIGAIL (1918–), writer, lecturer, and newspaper columnist. Born in Sioux City, Iowa, she attended Morningside College. Miss Van Buren has engaged in volunteer activities on behalf of better mental health and the National Foundation for Infantile Paralysis. In 1956, she began writing a column for the *San Francisco Chronicle* titled "Dear Abby." Her column was syndicated through the *Chicago Tribune-New York News Syndicete.* It now appears in foreign press as well, including Brazil, Australia, Japan, Germany, and Holland. In 1963, she established a *Dear Abby* radio program on CBS. She authored *Dear Abby* (1957), *Dear Teen Ager* (1959), and *Dear Abby on Marriage* (1962).

VANDERBILT, CORNELIUS (1794–1877), wealthy builder of railroads and steamship companies. After the success of Robert Fulton and Robert Livingston with steamboats, Vanderbilt became involved with steamboat operations. In a competitive war against Daniel Drew, Vanderbilt was able to establish steamship service between New York and Peekskill. He then opened service between New York, Providence, and Boston. His primary success was achieved in connection with the expansion of railroads after the Civil War. Commodore Vanderbilt again challenged Daniel Drew in pursuit of the Erie Railroad. Illegal maneuvers by Drew, Jay Gould, and James Fisk almost destroyed Vanderbilt in his pursuit of the Erie. He turned his attention to acquiring the Lake Shore, Illinois, and Michigan Central rail companies, which he did.

VAUGHN, SARAH (1924–), jazz vocalist born in Newark, New Jersey. In 1942, she joined the Earl Hines Orchestra; and in 1943, she sang with the Billy Eckstein Band. She has served as vocalist for Mercury Records. In 1942, she won the Apollo Theatre amateur contest. She received the annual Vocalist Award from *Down Beat,* 1946 to 1952; and she has appeared on numerous television programs.

WALLACE, GEORGE (1919–), political leader, governor, and candidate for President. Born at Clio, Alabama, Wallace studied law at the University of Alabama. As governor, he defied a Supreme Court integration order at the University of Alabama. In 1968, his challenge to the Democratic Party resulted in the formation of the American Independent Party. He captured much of the South and nationally obtained 14 percent of the popular vote in that election. In 1972, he became the object of an assassination attempt, which left him paralyzed. He was reelected governor of Alabama, but declining health made him discard plans for another term.

WARHOL, ANDY (1931–), pioneer in pop art and filmmaking. Warhol attended the Carnegie Institute of Technology and received a degree in pictorial design. He began work as a designer with *Glamour* magazine, then *Vogue* and *Harper's Bazaar.* He used the comic-strip characters Dick Tracy, Popeye, and Superman for colorful effects, and he painted Campbell Soup cans in endless rows to show the monotony of American society. After 1965, he concentrated on filmmaking. *The Chelsea Girls* (1966) and *Trash* (1970) received considerable public notice.

WARING, FRED (1900–), musical conductor and entertainer born in Tyrone, Pennsylvania. Waring attended Pennsylvania State College. He composed numerous songs and appeared in several musical shows on Broadway and in motion pictures. He organized an ensemble called "The Pennsylvanians" and began a radio program of the same title in 1933. In 1948, he organized the Fred Waring Music Workshops for Choral Directors. He conducted musical groups for *The Fred Waring Show* on television and produced numerous television programs.

WASHINGTON, BOOKER T. (1856–1915), black educator who was born a slave in Franklin County, Virginia. Booker overheard talk about a school for blacks called the Hampton Institute; the institute had been founded by a Union general and emphasized trades and manual training. In 1881, he was invited to go to Tuskegee to head up the institute, which he discovered had no buildings or program. Under his leadership, the institute became a vital force in education of black youth. In 1895, he delivered the famous "Atlanta Compromise" speech, in which he renounced protest and agitation as a means of achieving educational reform. His views were in contrast to those of Frederick Douglass, who called for racial agitation.

WAYNE, ANTHONY (1745–1796), military hero of early America. Born at Easttown, Pennsylvania, he attended local schools and learned surveying. When the Revolution began, Wayne organized a regiment of infantry and joined General George Washington at Morristown, New Jersey. He gave distinguished service in several battles; he also served with Marquis de Lafayette in Virginia until the British surrender at Yorktown. In 1792, Wayne was asked to serve as Commander-in-Chief of the Army. At Full Timbers, Ohio, he defeated Indians in the first of several battles. Indian tribes recognized his military superiority and signed the treaty of Greenville in 1795.

WAYNE, JOHN (1907–1979), actor and movie personality, noted for his character portrayals from the Old West. Born in Winterset, Iowa, his name was Marian Michael Morrison; but early in life he received the nickname "Duke." On an athletic scholarship, he studied at the University of Southern California. His career as a screen actor began as a stunt man and with bit parts in Westerns. He made two Westerns with Columbia: *Girls Demand Excitement* (1931) and *Three Girls Lost.* Over the next few years he made low-budget Westerns. During and after World War II, he emerged as an actor of some renown; his role in *True Grit* won an Academy Award nomination. During the War in Vietnam, he projected the image of a loyalist to the Administration's expanding of the war. Mike Tomkies' *Duke* (1971) is a useful biography.

WEBSTER, DANIEL (1782–1852), celebrated lawyer and politician. Webster was born in Salisbury, New Hampshire. He graduated from Dartmouth College and then studied law. Identified as a leading spokesman for the Federalists, he was elected to the House of Representatives in 1813. In 1816, his political career temporarily ended, but he achieved prominence in arguing several significant cases before the Supreme Court. For example, Webster defended the Bank of the United States in *McCulloch* vs. *Maryland.* In 1823, he returned to the House of Representatives; and from 1825 to 1829, he supported the Federalist President John Quincy Adams. Webster's Senate record achieved historic importance. He supported President Andrew Jackson on the nullification controversy. His last debate was on behalf of the unpopular Fugitive Slave Law in 1850. He served as Secretary of State in Millard Fillmore's administration.

WEBSTER, NOAH (1758–1843), lexicographer who compiled a dictionary of American usage. Webster was an active literary man; he read widely and was admitted to the bar in 1781. He authored *A Grammatical Institute of the English Language: Part I* in 1783. His grammar book sold over seventy million copies. Webster toured the United States selling his textbooks. As a Federalist, he wrote *Sketches on American Policy* (1785); he authored numerous books and pamphlets, his most famous being *The Effects of Slavery on Morals and Industry* (1793). His dictionaries became his most enduring contribution to American thought and learning.

WEISSMULLER, JOHNNY (1904–1984), Olympic swimmer and movie star as "Tarzan." Born in Windber, Pennsylvania, Weissmuller became a skilled free-style swimmer. In the 1920s, he established world records in over sixty-seven events. Weissmuller was trained as a swimmer at the Illinois Athletic Club in Chicago. In the 1924 and 1928 Olympic games, he won five gold medals; he also won a bronze medal as a member of the United States water polo team. In his acting role as "Tarzan," his abilities as a free-style swimmer made him world famous.

WELCH, RAQUEL (1942–), model, movie actress, and renowned sex symbol. She was born Raquel Tejada in Chicago, Illinois, of Castilian Spanish parents. The family moved to LaJolla, California, where her father worked for General Dynamics. After graduating from high school, she served temporarily as a weather girl for a San Diego television station while attending San Diego State College. After marriage in 1959, she had two children and became a householder. Divorced in 1964, she travelled to Texas where she modeled for Neiman-Marcus department stores. She then returned to Hollywood, where she received minor roles until she appeared in *Life* magazine (October 2, 1964). She soon obtained a contract with Twentieth Century-Fox. She then appeared in *Fantastic Voyage, Bandolero, Lady in Cement, The Magic Christian,* and *Myra Breckinridge,* among others.

WEST, BENJAMIN (1738–1820), noted painter of the Revolutionary era. Born in Springfield Township, Pennsylvania, West was among the most outstanding of America's new artists. He reflected the neo-classical tradition. He lived for a time in Italy, where he attracted numerous patrons. West received encouragement from Joshua Reynolds and won numerous portrait commissions. He became a close friend of King George III; and after the death of Reynolds, he was named president of the Royal Academy. West's more famous paintings include *Death on the Pale Horse* (1802) and *Christ Healing the Sick* (1811). West helped many young artists who visited his studio.

Orson Welles, arms raised, rehearses the *War of the Worlds* broadcast.

WEST, MAE (1892–1980), stage and film actress; her sensuality established her stage presence in early vaudeville days. Miss West made her debut with the Keith vaudeville circuit. When she starred in a sensational Broadway play titled *Sex* (1926), she was jailed for her role and attracted national publicity. She starred in several movies, including *Diamond Lil* (1928); *The Constant Sinner* (1931) and *Night after Night* (1932). During World War II, her name was attached to the inflatable life jackets that were used by Allied soldiers. Her autobiography was titled *Goodness Had Nothing to Do With It* (1959). In 1970, she starred in the screen production of *Myra Breckinridge.*

WELK, LAWRENCE (1903–), famed orchestra leader of the "big band" era. Born in Strasburg, North Dakota, he appeared on radio station WNAX of Yankton, South Dakota in 1920. In 1927, he organized an orchestra that appeared throughout the country. Welk's orchestra appeared on television in Los Angeles from 1950 to 1955, when the American Broadcasting Company syndicated the Lawrence Welk show nationally. The program achieved considerable popularity until it was cancelled in 1971. Welk was a recording artist for Ranwood Records; he has received numerous awards and recognitions, including the Top Dance Band of America award in 1955. His program is now syndicated by the National Broadcasting Company.

WELLES, ORSON (1915–), motion picture actor, director, producer, writer, and photographer. His various theatrical roles have placed him among the outstanding actors of his generation. Born in Kenosha, Wisconsin, he studied at the Art Institute of Chicago. Welles' acting debut was made at Gate Theatre, Dublin, in the fall of 1931. He made his Broadway debut in Shakespeare's *Romeo and Juliet* (1934); he had toured with the Katherine Cornell Company in *Candida* (1933) and *The Barretts of Wimpole Street.* His radio career began with narrating the series, *The March of Time.* His simulation of a Martian invasion in 1938 created a panic among his radio listeners. He has directed numerous Shakespearean plays and has appeared on television.

WESTINGHOUSE, GEORGE (1846–1914), distinguished American inventor and manufacturer; developed the transmission of electrical power. He served with the Union Army in the Civil

War and attended Union College. His fortune came from the patents on his air-brake invention. In 1882, he formed the Union Switch and Signal Company and directed his attention to the orderly transmission of natural gas. In 1886, he formed the Westinghouse Electric Company. In the 1890s, Westinghouse received contracts to develop power from the Niagara Falls. During the 1880s, he received an average of one patent per month for his inventions; his truly significant inventions include the geared turbine and air springs.

WESTMORELAND, WILLIAM C. (1914–), commander of American forces in Vietnam and chief military adviser to President Lyndon Johnson. Westmoreland was born in Spartanburg County, South Carolina, and graduated from West Point in 1936. He commanded the Thirty-Fourth Field Artillery Battalion of the Ninth Infantry Division in Europe during World War II. He served as an instructor at the Command and General Staff College and the Army War College. Between 1960 and 1963, he was superintendent of the U.S. Military Academy, where his effectiveness contributed to his elevation to general. He was assigned to the Military Assistance Program in Vietnam, where he advocated increased bombing and "search and destroy" missions. By 1967, he had over 500,000 men under his command. In 1968, he became Army Chief of Staff. He ran unsuccessfully for governor of South Carolina.

WHISTLER, JAMES A. McNEILL (1834–1903), lithographer and painter; emphasized "art for art's sake." Born in Lowell, Massachusetts, Whistler moved to St. Petersburg, Russia, early in his life when his father worked on a Russian rail project commissioned by Tsar Nicholas I. He returned to America in 1849 and studied at the United States Military Academy. Because he could not conform to the rules, he was dismissed in 1854. He travelled to Europe and studied for a time at the Louvre. In 1859, his first painting appeared; it was titled *At the Piano*. In 1871, he began certain themes titled *Nocturnes* in etchings, including *The Artist's Mother* (1872). His views on aesthetics were summarized in "Ten O'Clock," a lecture delivered at Prince's Hall.

WHITE, WILLIAM ALLEN (1868–1944), prize-winning journalist and author. Born in Emporia, Kansas, he attended Emporia College. He began his journalistic career with work on various newspapers. He purchased the *Emporia Gazette* in 1895 and continued working with that paper until his death. His progressive views ran contrary to conservative political trends. He backed Teddy Roosevelt and the Bull Moose party in 1912; in the 1930s he supported the New Deal of Roosevelt. White worked enthusiastically with "The Committee to Defend America by Aiding the Allies" in generating hostility for Nazism. He received the Pulitzer Prize for *The Autobiography of William Allen White.*

WHITNEY, ELI (1765–1825), inventor who perfected the cotton gin. Whitney was born in Westboro, Massachusetts, and graduated from Yale college. Although a number of cotton gins were in operation in the 1790s, only Whitney's design made practical sense. He manufactured small arms for the federal government, but his delivery of these small arms was hopelessly behind schedule. He substituted machines for hand labor, made uniform parts, and accelerated production. Whitney gave substance to the concept of mass production.

WILKINS, ROY (1901-1981), important civil rights leader. Wilkins was born in St. Louis, Missouri, and attended the University of Minnesota. He served in the local chapters of the National Association for the Advancement of Colored People (NAACP) and edited *Call,* a militant weekly newspaper. In 1931, he joined the executive staff of the NAACP at its national headquarters. He worked on numerous internal studies for the NAACP, and in 1955, became the Executive Director of the organization. He enthusiastically supported the Kennedy Civil Rights program. His organizing abilities, articulate speech, and incisive writing made him a significant leader in the black community. He received the Medal of Freedom from President Nixon in 1969, the Spingarm Award from the NAACP, as well as many other honors and awards.

WILLARD, FRANCES E. (1839–1898), prominent temperance leader. Born in Churchville, New York, she sought independence from her parents at an early age. She attended Northwestern Female College and graduated as class valedictorian. After a brief teaching career, she authored a book titled, *Nineteen Beautiful Years* (1864). Miss Willard toured Europe from 1869 to 1870 and studied at the Sorbonne. She was appointed president of Northwestern Female College in 1871. After 1874, she resigned and accepted the presidency of the Women's Christian Temperance Union (WCTU). She is best known for her work with the WCTU. Miss Willard helped establish the Prohibition Party in 1884; she became president of the World Women's Temperance Union in 1891.

WILLIAMS, ROGER (1603-1683), Puritan clergyman; spokesman for religious toleration and separation of church and state. Williams believed that sinful mankind was hopeless until Christ's return. He refused to serve the Massachusetts Church because it maintained close ties with civil authority. He was banished to Rhode Island in 1635, and there he authored a dictionary titled *A Key into the Language of America* (1643). His quest for perfection made him first a Baptist and then a Seeker. In 1643, he travelled to England and wrote *Queries of Highest Consideration* (1644). Williams opposed the Christian persecution of other Christian groups. He returned to Providence and sought to unify the colony; he disagreed with the local Quakers but granted them toleration nonetheless.

WILLIAMS, TED (1918-), baseball player born in San Diego, California. Williams was professionally associated with the Boston Red Sox of the American League; he compiled a lifetime batting average of .344. Williams' career spanned the years 1939 to 1960. He hit a total of 521 homeruns and won the triple crown of baseball (best average, most home runs, most runs batted in) twice. He was elected to the Baseball Hall of Fame in 1966. He managed the Washington Senators; in his initial year as manager he received the American League Manager of the Year Award.

WINCHELL, WALTER (1897–1972), newspaper columnist and newscaster. Winchell began his radio program with the familiar words, "Good evening, Mr. and Mrs. America and all ships at sea; let's go to press." At first he was a performer in vaudeville. His journalistic career began in 1920 with the *New York Evening Graphic;* later he was associated with the Hearst *New York Mirror*. Winchell introduced a variety of items—political and theatrical—in his column "On Broadway." His column was syndicated in over eight hundred newspapers; his radio career began in 1932. His easily recognized voice narrated the popular television series *The Untouchables*. Later in life, he wrote for the *New York Journal Tribune*.

WINTHROP, JOHN (1588–1649), political leader and historian; a dominant figure in the early development of the Massachusetts Bay Colony. Born in Suffolk County, England, he agreed to go to America in 1629. Winthrop called for a covenant Christian community in his famous sermon, "A Model of Christian Charity." He was the political leader of the colony. New England society in the seventeenth century bore the enduring stamp of John Winthrop.

WOOD, GRANT (1892–1942), regional painter of the 1930s. A native of Anamosa, Iowa, Wood took painting lessons during the family stay at Cedar Rapids, Iowa. During World War I, he took classes in fresco painting at the Chicago Art Institute. He left for Europe in 1923 and spent time at the Academie Julian in Paris. On his return to America, he worked at a factory in Cedar Rapids while painting various subjects. In 1927, he received a commission for a stained-glass window for the Cedar Rapids City Hall. Wood was most famous for his homespun themes. His painting titled *American Gothic* (1930) attracted widespread notice; his satiric sense was evident in *Daughters of the American Revolution*. He opposed conservative political tendencies and directed several projects for the Works Project Administration (WPA).

WOOLWORTH, FRANK (1852–1919), chain-store executive; originator of the "five and dime" store concept. Born in upstate New York, Woolworth opened his first store with a modest three hundred dollars inventory. The growth of his chain stores was spectacular; he derived capital for new stores from profits. He relocated his headquarters in Brooklyn, New York, which brought him into close contact with suppliers and wholesalers. Woolworth emphasized window and counter displays. His enterprises grew rapidly between 1890 and 1910, until his gross business revenue exceeded sixty million dollars annually. In 1913, he began erecting the structure in New York that became the Woolworth Building. At his death, there were over one thousand stores nationwide.

WRIGHT, FRANK LLOYD (1867-1959), the most innovative architect of the twentieth century. Wright's work reflects his fertile imagination. He worked at the firm of Dankmar Adler and Louis Sullivan of Chicago in 1887. He was greatly influenced by Louis Sullivan; and in 1893, he opened his own office. The houses Wright built in Chicago and elsewhere gained particular attention for their innovative spirit. His international fame brought him Japanese and European projects; for example, he designed the Imperial Hotel in Tokyo. Wright blended radical and traditional concepts of architecture. His most famous creations are the Guggenheim Museum in New York, the Administration Building for the Johnson Wax Company, and the Greek Orthodox Church in Milwaukee. Wright was an authentic giant in American architecture and design.

WRIGHT BROTHERS, ORVILLE (1871–1948); WILBUR (1867–1912), aviation pioneers born in Millville, Indiana. In 1892, they opened the Wright Cycle Shop in Dayton, Ohio. The efforts of Otto Lilienthal, glider pilot, attracted the interest of the Wright Brothers. The Wrights were acquainted with the combustion engine, aerodynamics, and basic engineering. Together they developed double-winged gliders and applied motor techniques to the glider. On December 17, 1903, they made the first "heavier-than-air craft" flight (which lasted twelve seconds) at Kitty Hawk, North Carolina. On May 22, 1906, they received a patent for their machine. The federal government demonstrated an interest in the machine, and they received bids for construction and development. The brothers formed the American Wright Company to produce aircraft. The death of Wilbur Wright greatly affected Orville; in 1915, he sold his rights to the company and left manufacturing. He served as a member of the National Advisory Committee for Aeronautics (NACA), the predecessor to NASA. His efforts contributed greatly to the subsequent advances made in aerospace technology.

WYETH, ANDREW (1917–   ), the most significant American painter of his generation. His father was the book illustrator for great American classics such as *Treasure Island.* The most famous of his paintings is *Christina's World.* Wyeth used his neighbors as his subjects; he utilized high and low points of emphasis. He received numerous awards, including the Medal of Freedom. In 1970, Wyeth held a one-man exhibit at the White House. His professional technique and graphic ability have become his legacy to American art.

Flight of the Wright Brothers' first airplane.

YOUNG, BRIGHAM (1801–1877), pioneer leader of the Mormons. In 1832, he read Joseph Smith's *Book of Mormon* and was baptized into the new faith. He formed a Mormon church in Kirkland, Ohio, in 1833. In 1835, he was selected as a member of the Quorum of Twelve Apostles to assist Joseph Smith; he became the fiscal agent for the emerging church in 1841. On December 5, 1847, he was elected president of the Quorum of Twelve Apostles, a position he retained until his death. After Smith was murdered, Young led the Mormons to Utah and established Mormon communities around the Great Salt Lake. He encouraged polygamy and opposed the use of liquor, stimulants, and tobacco. Young established the University of Deseret (now the University of Utah) in 1850.

YOUNG, CHIC (1901–1973), newspaper cartoonist who created the popular feature, "Blondie." Born in Chicago, Illinois, his real name was Murat Bernard. He developed "Blondie," her husband Dagwood, and associated characters. The comic strip was syndicated nationally through King Features. At the time of his death, it was appearing in over sixteen hundred newspapers in 60 countries.

YOUNG, DENTON T. "CY" (1867–1955), baseball player from Gilmore, Ohio. Young began playing for the Cleveland team of the National League in 1890. During his career, he pitched for the St. Louis Cardinals, the Boston Red Sox, the Cleveland Indians, and the Boston Braves. He pitched 751 complete games, winning 511 of them. He also pitched baseball's first "perfect" game (in which no batters reached base) on May 5, 1904. After his death, the major baseball leagues established the Cy Young Award for the best pitcher of the year.

YOUNG, WHITNEY M. (1921–1971), civil rights leader. Born in Lincoln Ridge, Kentucky, he graduated from Kentucky State College and the University of Minnesota. Young was associated with the Urban League in St. Paul, Minnesota, and Omaha, Nebraska. He became dean of the school of Social Work at Atlanta University in 1954. After a period of study at Harvard University, he was named executive director of the Urban League; there he introduced the concept of preferential treatment of blacks in jobs and educational facilities. He tried to mediate between militant civil rights groups and those who advocated more orderly processes. President Richard Nixon awarded him the Medal of Freedom in 1969. Young authored *To Be Equal* (1964) and *Beyond Racism* (1969).

ZAHARIAS, MILDRED DIDRIKSON "BABE" (1914–1956), Olympic athlete; regarded as the greatest woman golfer of all time. She appeared in the Olympic Games at Los Angeles in 1932, where she was the top performer in the 80-meter hurdle and the javelin throw. She excelled in athletic endeavors such as baseball, basketball, swimming, and diving. But her greatest achievements were in golf. From 1935 to 1950, she won every major women's golf championship—the United States National Open in 1948, 1950, and 1954; the national amateur tournament in 1946; and the World Championship four times. In 1947, she became a professional golfer. Stricken with cancer in 1953, she waged a battle to overcome the disease. She continued her athletic successes until her death in 1956. She wrote *This Life I've Led,* her autobiography.

"Babe" Didrikson Zaharias won The AP Award six times, once for starring in track and field and the five others for golfing brilliance. Later, the award was named in her honor.

ZENGER, JOHN PETER (1697–1746), colonial newspaper publisher. Born in the Rhine Country of Germany, he became an apprentice printer to William Bradford. He moved to Chestertown, Pennsylvania, to establish his reputation. Zenger became involved in New York political controversies after he arrived there in 1732. He used his *New York Weekly Journal* to support the political faction of Lewis Morris. Zenger was arrested in 1734 and charged with printing seditious and libelous material. His lawyers were disbarred, so Alexander Hamilton came from Philadelphia to defend Zenger. He was acquitted, and the case became a classic in constitutional law.

ZIEGFELD, FLORENZ (1869–1932), theatrical manager who made burlesque famous. Ziegfeld was born in Chicago, Illinois. In 1906, he developed "The Parisian Model," a revue that attracted popular notice. After viewing the Follies Bergere in Paris, he returned to the United States to assemble the Ziegfeld Follies. He developed several stars; Fanny Brice, Marilyn Miller, W. C. Fields, Eddie Cantor, and Will Rogers were under contract to Ziegfeld. He attempted musical comedy with such productions as *Show Boat, Rio Rita,* and *Bittersweet.* But in 1927, he abandoned the Follies because the Great Depression made it seem inappropriate.

CHAPTER NINETEEN

THE BUSINESS WORLD

Whether or not you work in a business office, you're involved in business dealings every day. When you cash a paycheck, buy groceries, repair your car, or do any number of things, you must handle your money or credit in a business-like way. But how well do you run your own business affairs? This chapter will give you some basic information that should help you handle your money more wisely.

We've included a section on the duties of a secretary to help business executives and secretaries plan their work. At the end of the chapter you'll find an explanation of several common business terms.

How to Make and Use a Family Budget

The most important rule for making a family budget is: *Keep it simple.* If you try to set up a complicated system, you'll waste time with unnecessary bookkeeping. A budget is supposed to help you plan how you will spend your money, and it should help you keep track of how your plan worked. If it's so complex that you can't understand it, why bother?

Design your budget to fit your own needs. Don't try to imitate someone else's budget, because your own income and expenses are unique.

First, notice where you're spending your money now. The easiest way to do that is to study the checks you wrote last month. (The bank sends them back to you after they've been processed.) Make a stack of these, along with any bills or receipts that show how you spent your cash last month.

In another stack, collect the stubs from last month's paychecks and any other checks you received. On a slip of paper, note any cash you received and put it in this stack, too. This can be very important if you get part of your income in cash every month—for example, if you're a waitress and your customers leave you tips.

Now go through each of these stacks, making a list of your income and expenses. Under expenses, you should note how much you spent last month for:

1. Rent or house payments
2. Education
3. Insurance
4. Loan Payments
5. Food
6. Clothing
7. Transportation
8. Medical Expenses
9. Savings
10. Recreation
11. Miscellaneous Expenses

Under the income, list the different sources of your income last month:

1. Fixed Income (your paycheck, Social Security checks, or other regular income)
2. Other Income (income that varies every month, like interest from a savings account or money you get from babysitting)

Now add up the money on each list. If the total of expenses is bigger than the total list of income, it means you're trying to spend more money than you earn. Doing that over a long period of time will drive you into bankruptcy.

How much money *should* you be spending for each item? That depends on your own needs and style of life. The federal government has found that the average family of four in the United States is dividing its money something like this:

HOUSING	33%
FOOD	25%
TAXES	20%
TRANSPORTATION & CLOTHING	10%
MEDICAL EXPENSES	5%
OTHER PERSONAL EXPENSES	7%

This is only an average. Your own budget will probably call for spending more money on certain items and less on others.

Before you make a plan for spending your money, find how much you're able to spend. Work only with your *take-home pay*—your wages or salary *after* your employer has subtracted taxes and Social Security payments.

You must pay a specific amount for some items every month, such as your house rent or mortgage payment, insurance, loan payments, and so on. List these on the budget sheet first. Then look at the expenses that vary each month, such as food, clothing, and transportation. You can control the amount that you spend for these items; so if you need to spend less money, cut the amount you spend for these "variables" first.

If you're planning to make a big purchase (such as a car or a house), decide how much money you can save each month toward this expense and put it in a savings account at your bank. You may also want to put some money in a savings account to build up an emergency fund for unexpected bills.

If you're like most people, you will want to budget some money for recreation, entertainment, and impulse buying. Reduce the money you spend for these things if your budget is pinched.

After you've budgeted a sensible amount of money for every item, you may find that you've exceeded your income. If so, you need to find ways to earn more money or reduce your total spending. You may need to reduce the amount you plan to spend for several items on your budget.

Most people are learning to do some jobs for themselves instead of hiring professionals to do them. You can take care of simple car repairs, home remodeling, and yardwork by yourself. Manufacturers are offering new products to help you do these jobs at a fraction of what you'd pay someone else.

Watch for "sales" on items you know you'll need in upcoming months. Often you can plan your buying to take advantage of seasonal close-outs. For example, you can buy lawn furniture cheaply at the end of the summer and store it to use next summer.

Always try to get the best value for the dollars you spend. When you're buying a new product, compare several brand names to see which one gives you the best quality at the price you can afford to pay.

After you've worked with your budget for a while, you may want to get the advice of a money expert. Ask for help at your local bank or savings-and-loan association. If you belong to a credit union, ask their staff for the advice you need. A stock broker can give you sound advice about investments.

Whatever you do, *stick with the budget you've planned.* You will need to change it from time to time as your personal situation changes. But remember: If you spend more than you planned in one area, you'll need to spend less in other areas. Otherwise, your budget won't balance at the end of the month.

Use good common sense when you plan your budget. Your success or failure depends on you alone. It's your money and you must decide how to spend it.

How to Buy a House

Whether it's large or small, a house is probably the most expensive purchase you'll ever make. It's an important step toward financial security.

But you need to remember several things when you think about buying a house. For one thing, it will require you to spend money on other items besides the house payment. Can you afford the insurance, utilities, property taxes, and maintenance costs that come with a house? You need to know that before you buy.

Take time to compare several houses and find the one that's best for you. You'll probably live there for several years, so get a house you'll enjoy.

Of course, there are all kinds of houses to choose from. So where do you start looking? Naturally, the first big factor is *price*. There's no need to waste time looking at houses you can't afford. Here's a good rule of thumb to use for deciding how much you can spend on a house: *Multiply your annual income by two-and-a-half.* For example, if you earn $20,000, you could probably afford to buy a house that costs $40,000 to $50,000, assuming that the other house money you spend each month doesn't wreck your budget. The basic monthly expenses for your house—the total of mortgage payment, taxes, and insurance—should not be more than one-sixtieth of your annual income. In other words, if you earned $20,000 each year, you'd divide that by 60 and find your basic housing expenses shouldn't be more than $333 each month. Remember, though, that you will be paying for some variable housing expenses, such as utilities and maintenance, on top of that.

The Federal Housing Administration uses another guideline that might help you. The FHA says the total of *all* housing expenses—mortgage payments, taxes, utilities, and maintenance—should be no more than 35 percent of your take-home pay. For example, if your take-home pay is $1,000 per month, you shouldn't spend more than $350 for all of your housing expenses.

Let us say you've decided how much you can afford to pay and you've found the house you want to buy. Now you need to decide how you'll buy it. Most people can't afford to pay cash for the total price of a house, but there are several other ways you might buy it:

1. Contract. The seller may let you pay him a small down payment and sign a contract to pay him the rest in monthly installments. He does not give you the title to the house until you've paid him all of the money that the contract requires.

2. Bank Loan. You can give the seller a down payment of your own and borrow the rest of the money from a bank. The bank will loan you the money only if the house is in good condition and you've made a large enough down payment. The bank requires you to make a smaller down payment for newer houses. Under this plan, the bank holds the title to your house until you pay off the loan. If you fail to make your monthly payments, the bank can sell your house to get the rest of the money you owe. Savings-and-loan associations loan money in the same way, and sometimes they charge less interest than local banks. Mortgage companies and private loan companies can do this, too, but they often charge more interest than the banks.

3. VA Loan. If you've ever served in the United States military, you can borrow money for your house and the Veterans Administration will agree to pay off the loan if you fail to pay. Usually you don't need to put down as much of your own cash, and you pay less interest on the loan. But if you fail to make your monthly payments, the VA can sell your house to get the money you owe.

4. FHA Loan. If at least two banks refuse to loan you the money to buy a house, and if you have a fairly low income, you may get the Farmer's Home Administration to agree to pay off the loan if you fail. If the FHA agrees to do this, you'll need very little money for the down payment and you'll pay less interest than with a regular bank loan. But the FHA will want to make sure that you can afford to make the monthly payments, and the agency will check the house to see that it is a sound investment. The FHA will also require the seller to pay extra fees for setting up this kind of loan. For this reason, some people may not sell their property to you if you plan to buy it with an FHA Loan. You can buy a new house with an FHA Loan; but the house must be modest and economical to maintain. If you have an unusually low income, the FHA may give you *interest credit,* which allows you to pay much less than the normal rate of interest.

When most people buy a house, they seek the

help of a real estate broker. Home sellers usually ask brokers to offer their houses for sale, so a broker can show you several different homes in your price range. The broker will probably ask you to make a small down payment when you offer to buy a house; this is called *earnest money,* because it shows the seller that you're really interested in buying the house. If the seller accepts your offer, the earnest money will go toward buying the house; if he rejects your offer, the broker will usually give your earnest money back to you.

After you've agreed to purchase a house and you've secured the financing, you may be asked to pay certain fees for the transaction. This varies with the different types of loans, and you should ask the broker to explain these *closing costs* before you offer to buy a house.

Be sure that a lawyer examines the title papers on the property. If anything is out of order, the seller should correct it before you close the deal. Otherwise, you may discover later that other debts were standing against the house, and you may have to pay them.

To put it simply, you should know whether you can really afford to buy a house—and if so, how much you can pay—before you begin shopping for one. And you should rely on professional lawyers and real estate brokers to help you make the transaction. If you don't, you could make some costly mistakes.

How to Make a Will

A person writes a *will* to distribute his property after he dies. The will is a legal document that names the persons or institutions who will receive his belongings, and often it tells who will divide this property among the ones who receive it. A husband and wife should each have a will; their wills should work together, so that the property will be handed out properly if *both* of them die at the same time.

You should review your will and update it periodically. As your personal situation changes, you'll probably want to change your will. If you prepare a new will, you should destroy the old ones; two wills would complicate matters after you died.

It is best to consult a lawyer when you're drawing up your will. He will want a list of your property, including any real estate, money, vehicles, insurance policies, or stocks and bonds. Usually you would give all of these things to your spouse, if you are married. But be sure the will explains who will receive these things if you and your spouse die at the same time. Also be sure that the will names someone to care for your children. If you want to give part of your estate to schools, churches, or other organizations, you must name these agencies in your will and tell exactly how much you want each one to receive.

Decide who will distribute your property and carry out the other duties you mentioned in your will; you must name this person in the document. This person is called the *executor* (if male) or an *executrix* (if female).

After you have written your will and gotten a witness to sign it, put it in a secure place. Usually this would be a safety deposit box that you can rent at your local bank. Ask your lawyer to keep another copy in case yours is stolen, lost, or destroyed.

The Business Secretary

Many people dream of being secretary to an important person. The work is varied and full of interest, responsible and challenging. The compensation will match the responsibilities involved. A good secretary is held in high esteem.

Just what must you do to prepare yourself for this valued niche in the world of action?

You should have the background of a good education; your interests should be broad; your reading should be comprehensive. In addition, you should master the tools of your trade. Your stenography and typing must be perfect; you must know how to write good letters and file important papers. A secretarial course at any good business school will see to that. All this, naturally, has to be coupled with your firm determination to emerge as an expert practitioner of the required skills.

But beyond this, there is a *plus* that makes the difference between being just a routine secretary (the kind that comes by the dozen) and that top-notch, "crackerjack" secretary that every busy executive is proud to have. Such a secretary makes life in the office so much smoother for him and the rest of the organization that he is glad to turn over to his secretary much of the work of the office. An executive who has a good secretary is relieved of many of his routine responsibilities and is left free to make the big decisions that can vastly improve the performance of the firm.

PERSONALITY

Understanding, tact, judgment, memory, dependability, initiative, patience, self-control—these might head the list of qualities of the ideal secretary you are aspiring to be.

An employer expects that his secretary will be understanding and well educated, have exemplary manners, know what constitutes good business customs, and be able to practice them. The secretary should also have poise. Who would want a secretary who is shy and afraid to meet people, or one who is brash, forward, obtrusive, and loud? When it comes to personal appearance, the secretary should be neat, but not gaudy. Dress, carriage, grooming, and hair should be attractive without being in any way extreme. The secretary should have a pleasant voice; every caller is exposed to the secretary's voice. It must combine warmth and impersonality, friendliness and restraint. Surely, it is no easy task to be an excellent secretary.

ATTITUDE

Perhaps the word *loyalty* best describes the attitude the secretary should have toward job and employer. It is important to have a sincere interest, not only in the particular work being done, but in the overall welfare of the company. In every task undertaken, the good secretary puts forth the very best effort possible. Loyalty will make the job easy.

Sometimes in large organizations "the boss's secretary" gets into the habit of assuming or taking for granted privileges that others do not have. This is to be avoided. In the last analysis, you are there to do your part—and not an inconsiderable part—to guarantee this smooth functioning of the office.

DUTIES

As secretary, you keep the records; you attend to correspondence, both incoming and outgoing; you see or talk to visitors and telephone callers. In some cases you do the personal filing for your particular employer. You are ready to be called upon for what may be required in the way of business tasks.

Records

When Mr. Jones, president of the ABC Company, arrives at his office in the morning, he naturally wants to know what his day is going to bring, insofar as this is predictable. It is a good idea to let him see at a glance just what appointments and commitments he has for that day. So arrive at the office ahead of him and place on his desk, neatly typed up, a list of the day's activities. To do this, you should keep three calendars: your own, one for your employer, and a follow-up calendar (the so-called tickler file). This third file consists of a file box or drawer with 12 tab cards, one for each month of the year, and 31 tab cards, one for each day of the month. Behind the appropriate month and day (which is moved forward daily to the front of the box or file) you place notations on appointments, meetings, commitments, reminders, and so on. Each morning, you go through the material for the particular day, discarding what may have lost validity and typing up the day's schedule for Mr. Jones' desk.

Mr. Jones may also want to be reminded of significant family dates and anniversaries, holidays, pending trips, dates of payments and taxes due, and the like. If so, you should give him these reminders at the proper time. Thus, if he is planning to send a birthday check or other present to his daughter at college, remind him of this a week in advance, again three days before, and possibly on the very day (since he may want to call her long distance).

If Mr. Jones sets aside a few minutes at the start of the business day for a short conference, during which the two of you can go over the program for the day, it will make the day easier for you both. Of course, that is up to Mr. Jones. But such conferences have worked out splendidly in many offices.

Correspondence

Generally, mail addressed to a particular executive is placed unopened on his secretary's desk as soon as it arrives. It then becomes your duty to open this mail and arrange for its proper distribution. A good idea is to make a preliminary division into four categories:

1. Correspondence
2. Bills and statements
3. Newspapers and periodicals
4. Advertisements and circulars

Each of these initial piles is then further subdivided into: (a) for the employer's attention; (b) for the attention of others in the organization; (c) for the secretary's own attention; (d) possible discards. This last applies only to the fourth category above, and must depend on the very careful discretion of the secretary.

The procedure for mail marked "Personal" varies with the particular organization and the wishes of your employer. Mr. Jones may or may not want you to leave this mail unopened for him to handle himself. Perhaps he prefers to have you open *all* his mail, regardless of the notation on the envelope. He may wish to have such letters placed in a separate folder. You carry out his wishes, of course.

You may prepare letters regarding company business, personal letters, and miscellaneous courtesy letters. When you are expected to write such letters, bear in mind the newspaper reporter's essential five: Who, What, When, Where, and Why. "Short and to the point" is the rule.

For spellings, word divisions, and distinctions among synonyms, *never guess;* consult a standard dictionary. For punctuation, capitalization, and abbreviations, consult the dictionary or a good style book. As for vocabulary and grammar, follow correct usage. Much of what you will need to know will be found in the early sections of this book.

You may need to compose replies to all but the most personal letters. Or it may be Mr. Jones' custom to spend a session with you daily, going over that day's incoming mail. He may dictate all or most of his letters to you, but there are no hard and fast rules. Your employer's wishes are law; carry them out according to the letter and spirit of these wishes.

In general, toward the end of the business day, you bring all outgoing mail to Mr. Jones for his signature. Then you must check every letter to be sure that it is signed, that any enclosures are included, and that the addresses inside the letter and on the envelope conform. Only then is the outgoing mail ready for mailing. You keep copies of any of the letters that your employer wants you to file.

Callers

In seeing your employer's visitors and greeting his telephone callers, you must combine the functions of a receptionist, a diplomat, a welcoming committee, a watchdog, and even a "bouncer." When you greet the caller, you must find out the purpose of his visit and make him comfortable. On some occasions you must be able to get rid of him as quickly and expeditiously as possible. But no matter what your purpose, you must remain polite. You must not convey an air of impatience or hostility. You must not antagonize the visitor or caller; you can be firm, but you must remain friendly. A good secretary soon learns whom an employer wants to see and whom he doesn't, whether to refer the caller to someone else in the organization, or whether to deal with the caller's problem yourself. This aspect of your job calls for excellent judgment and quick decisions. It demands poise, tact, good manners, and adaptability. In making these first contacts with visitors and telephone callers, remember you are serving both your employer and the caller.

Filing

Less than twenty-four hours after the tragic death of President Kennedy, the television screen showed his private files being removed from the Presidential office. In some offices, there is a central filing system that includes all but the most personal correspondence. But in some offices the filing of an executive's private and business correspondence is his secretary's responsibility. It has been said that if you file something correctly, there is only one place where it can be found. But if you file something incorrectly, you may have to look in a thousand places and then not find it. See to it that everything you file is filed in the most logical place it belongs.

Accounting

In today's economy an efficient system of accounting is crucial for the well-being of any organization, whether it be a government, a business or professional concern, a social club, or even an individual family.

Accounting is just what the name implies. It is the art of giving an account, a picture, of an economic state of affairs. By systematically recording, classifying, summarizing, and presenting financial facts, and then by interpreting them, it assesses performance, helps plan and control operations, and provides data for making intelligent decisions regarding the future.

One field of accounting deals with the economic operations of entire nations, but in industry and business accounting subdivides into five specific functions. *Controllership* is in charge of budgeting and expenditures, designing the system of records and seeing that accounting work is done efficiently and effectively. *Auditing* examines and checks financial records to verify correctness. *Financial accounting* prepares and interprets financial statements. *Cost accounting* determines the actual cost of operating including labor, overhead, and materials, to assess the profit/loss situation. *Bookkeeping* is the recording and summarizing of actual business transactions.

Career possibilities are many and varied in the overall field of accounting, ranging from Comptroller General of the United States who oversees the General Accounting Office, possibly the world's largest accounting and auditing organization, down to the combination secretary/bookkeeper in a small shop. Many chief executive officers of large corporations today worked up the career ladder through the financial department ranks. Having computer literacy is almost a necessity for success now.

High schools teach the basics of accounting, bookkeeping, use of business machines, and also courses in economics and business English, math, law and management. Further training is offered in junior colleges and business schools, while a major in accountancy at a four-year college opens more career opportunities in business, governmental, and public accounting. A public accountant is a professional who contracts to perform specific accounting services for business, governmental units, and individuals, such as auditing, preparing income tax returns and special reports, and reviewing and developing bookkeeping and accounting systems. To rise highest in this field people study and pass the qualifying examination to become a CPA (certified public accountant.)

For full information concerning careers in accounting, write:

American Institute
of Certified Public Accountants
1211 Avenue of the Americas
New York, New York 10036

Elemental knowledge of accounting practices is helpful even for those not employed in that occupational field. Individuals and families need to have an accurate picture of their financial situation based on a planned budget and carefully maintained records of savings and expenditures. Treasurers of all clubs, churches, and other such organizations must maintain accurate financial records.

Basic to any company's operations, whatever its size, is a good, accurate system of bookkeeping. There are two bookkeeping systems: single entry and double entry.

Single-entry bookkeeping usually consists of records of cash, amounts receivable from other firms and the amounts that are owed. It is not a complete system and is not used extensively by business firms.

Double-entry bookkeeping is used by most companies because it provides a complete record of all transactions.

It utilizes an equation that states: Assets – Liabilities = Proprietorship. Assets include such items as cash, merchandise, equipment, land, buildings, and accounts receivable from customers.

Liabilities are what the company owes or is obligated to pay: debts to other firms, wages due employees, various taxes and sums due on loans and mortgages, for instance.

Proprietorship or ownership equity is the amount that is left after liabilities are subtracted from assets. For instance, a company with assets totaling $35,000 and liabilities amounting to $3,500 has a proprietorship of $31,500. Thus, proprietorship decreases with funds paid out and increases with each payment received in the form of income. Both sides of the equation, that is, the amount on each side of the = marks, must always balance.

Basic to all double-entry bookkeeping is the account. It usually appears on a page divided down the middle by a double line. The title, or name of what is to be recorded, appears at the top of the page. Increases in the account are recorded on one side and decreases on the other. The difference between the total of each is called the balance and this provides a handy reference for what is in the account at any one time.

There are five basic types of accounts: asset, liability, proprietorship, income, and expense, and a number of accounts may be grouped under each of the types. When a company makes a transaction, at least two of the accounts are affected. It is the job of the bookkeeper to determine which accounts are affected and to make the proper notation.

The terms used for such notations are "debits" and "credits." A cash account, for instance, increases with a cash sale on the left, or debit, side and it decreases when a payment is made on the right, or credit, side.

Certain basic rules have been generally accepted over the years and hence any bookkeeper knows as a matter of course that asset accounts are increased on the left, or debit, side and decreased on the right, or credit, side. But liability and proprietorship accounts are increased on the right, or credit, side and decreased on the left, or debit, side.

Thus the rule is: asset and expense accounts are debited for increases and credited for decreases; liability, proprietorship, and income accounts are credited for increases and debited for decreases.

Regardless of the size of the firm, there are basically two types of books used in the bookkeeping process, journals and ledgers.

The journal contains such daily transactions as sales, purchases, etc., and the ledger contains the record of individual accounts. Daily records from the journal are entered in the ledger.

The debits recorded in the ledger for each entry in the journal are always equal in amount to the credits for that entry. Thus, if no errors are made in posting, the total of all debit amounts in the ledger equals the total of all credit amounts in the ledger. The "trial balance" is a method of testing the accuracy of posting by proving that the debits and credits are the same.

The bookkeeper uses the trial balance information to prepare income statements and balance sheets. The income statement shows the operations of the company by showing all its income, expenses, and net profit. The balance sheet shows the financial condition of the company by listing all its assets and liabilities and its proprietorship. Financial statements are normally prepared each month and summarizing statements every six months and annually.

Business Terms

BUSINESS AND INVESTMENT

ASSETS—those items, property, and services that reflect the total financial value of a person, business, or estate. Assets include the value of all real property and personal property you own.

BALANCE SHEET—a statement of the financial condition of an individual or business at any given time.

BETTER BUSINESS BUREAU—a nonprofit organization that gives information about companies and corporations to the public. In many instances, it provides information you will need when purchasing or using these specific products. The bureau patrols the advertising and marketing methods used by various companies. It may also provide business speakers for different school and civic groups.

BOND—a certificate evidencing a debt of a corporation. In other words, it is the corporation's promise to repay an amount of money that it has borrowed, usually with added interest; the bond holder simply lends his money to the corporation for repayment at a later date. When a corporation issues a bond without any security behind it, the bond is called a *debenture*. When there is security, it is called a *secured bond*.

BOOK VALUE—the assets of a business as shown on its account books. As used in the stock market, the term generally refers to a company's book value for each share of common stock. This value is obtained by dividing the company's total book value by the number of outstanding shares.

BROKER'S COMMISSION—a fee paid to a person for acting as an agent in a contract of sale. This fee is generally decided prior to the transaction and confirmed in writing.

CAPITAL—the total amount of property or assets an individual or business owns.

CAPITAL GAINS/LOSSES—In general, a *capital gain* is the excess of capital assets over the appraised value or cost of an asset. For example, if you've sold a share of stock at a higher price than what you paid for it, the excess is called a capital gain. A *capital loss* exists when an asset costs more than its appraised value, or if the asset is sold at a price less than it originally costs.

Under present tax laws, if an asset is held at least six months and then sold, the gain is considered to be a long-term capital gain and is charged at a lower tax rate.

CHARITABLE CONTRIBUTIONS—An individual or a corporation is allowed to give away a limited amount of money or property and deduct it from taxable income. Many organizations are allowed to receive these contributions. Some of them are churches, tax-exempt organizations, hospital or medical research organizations, or govenment agencies (if the money is used for public purposes).

COMMERCIAL PAPER—a piece of paper used to convey value in a business transaction. This can be exchangeable value, monetary value, or both. A good example of commercial paper would be the checks used in banking; another example would be short-term promissory notes issued by a corporation. Traditionally the charge for using commercial paper as credit is lower than the prime interest rate.

COMMON STOCK—shares of stock that receive equal dividends from a corporation. When a company issues different classes of stock, the shares without special rights are *common*. Most of the stock issued by corporations is common.

COMPOUND INTEREST—interest paid upon interest, as well as upon principal. That is, the interest earned upon the principal is added to the principal, thereby raising the amount of the return to the lender. For example, D promises to repay $100 to C at the end of the year with interest at six percent per annum, compounded quarterly. At the end of the first quarter, the interest earned would be added to the principal. At the end of the second quarter, interest would be computed on the principal plus the preceding quarter's interest. This pattern would continue for the last two quarters as well. Thus, interest would be paid upon interest, as well as upon principal.

CONSUMER PROTECTION AGENCY—an organization created by the federal government to insure a customer's rights in business transactions. This agency offers information about truth in advertising, franchises, business rights, fair debt collection, label information, credit reporting, equal credit opportunity, and truth in lending.

CONVERTIBLE BOND—a bond that may be exchanged for stock in the corporation, under the conditions stated in the bond.

CORPORATION—an association of individuals that has its own distinct legal identity. A corporation has certain legal advantages for carrying on commercial activities. Among these advantages are: (1) continuity of the business. Its work will not be stopped if a member dies or withdraws from the corporation. (2) transferability of its property interest. This is done when the corporation sells stock. In this way, the corporation shares its financial obligations with people outside the corporation. (3) centralization of business control in the hands of its board of directors. (4) little or no individual liability for the debts of the corporation.

A corporation is a separate entity in the eyes of the law. Individuals who own an interest in the corporation (evidenced by their shares or certificates of stock) are called *stockholders*. By owning a share of stock, the stockholder generally enjoys three basic rights: (1) a right to share in the profits, (2) a right to vote upon major business decisions of the corporation, and (3) a right to share in the remaining assets if the corporation is dissolved.

The shares of stock may be given away, traded, or sold. This is generally done at a stock exchange. The exchange simply acts as a place where the various shares of stock can be traded.

DEPRECIATION—the decrease in the value of an asset or property due to wear and tear, obsolescence, and so on.

EX-DIVIDEND—A corporation may declare that it will pay a dividend to everyone who owns shares of its stock at a given date, and pay the dividends at a future date. The shares traded between the given dates will be marked *Ex-Dividend,* meaning they do not entitle the buyer to the new dividend.

FAIR MARKET VALUE—the price arrived at by a buyer and seller who are ready, willing, and able to buy and sell an asset.

FIRST-IN, FIRST-OUT—a method of pricing goods, based on the assumption that a merchant sells or uses goods in the same order in which they are received.

GIFT TAX—a tax upon the transfer of property, rather than on the property itself. This tax is levied during the lifetime of the person making the gift, rather than after his death. The federal gift tax applies only to the transfer of property by individuals, and not to transfers by corporations.

The gift must be made by a taxpayer, and it may be deducted only in the year the gift was made. The Internal Revenue Service has many lengthy rules governing this type of charitable contribution, especially gifts to corporations.

GOOD WILL—an intangible asset of every successful business. A business is said to have "good will" if its customers will probably return to make additional purchases.

INTANGIBLE ASSETS—the powers of a person or business that will allow continuing business success. Intangible assets would include a variety of privileges such as good will, secret processes, patents, and copyrights.

INTEREST—payment that a lender receives for the use of his money. It is usually a fixed percentage of the amount loaned (called *principal*), and it is to be paid at an agreed time.

INVENTORY—a list of the goods or property held by an individual or business.

INVESTMENT TRUST—an organization that accepts money from subscribers and invests it for them. The organization attempts to earn profits that can be distributed to the various subscribers.

LAST-IN, FIRST-OUT—a method of pricing goods, based on the assumption that the goods last received are the goods first sold or used.

LIABILITIES—the debts and obligations of an individual, business, or state.

LISTED STOCK—a stock of a corporation that is listed on the national stock exchange, such as the New York Stock Exchange or the American Stock Exchange. A stock that is not listed on one of the national exchanges is known as *unlisted*. It is sometimes referred to as stock "sold over the counter," or *over-the-counter* stock.

LOAN SHARK—a person who lends money at an exorbitant or illegal rate of interest. This is often called a "shirt-pocket loan." Usually it is for a short time (30 days or less) and its interest rate will be very high—perhaps 40 or 50 percent. Loan sharks often use severe techniques for making loans and collecting them, sometimes resorting to violence.

MONTHLY INVESTMENT PLAN—a plan in which an investor makes monthly payments to his stock broker. With this money, the broker buys as many shares as possible of certain stocks for the investor. If stock prices are low, the investor receives more stocks; if prices are high, he receives less stock. The investor may discontinue his monthly payment at any time.

MUNICIPAL BOND—a city's promise to repay a certain amount of money at a predetermined date and at a stated rate of interest. Federal and state governments levy no income tax on the interest paid by municipal bonds, so this is a very popular source of financing. A city or a county often uses this type of bond to finance large capital improvements.

MUTUAL FUND—an investment company that sells shares to the public, usually at a price determined by supply and demand. The proceeds of the sale are invested to make a profit. As the fund earns higher profits, its shares become more valuable.

NET WORTH—what remains after liabilities or obligations are subtracted from assets. As used in stock-market trading, the term means the net worth of each outstanding share of a company. It is obtained by dividing a company's total net worth by the number of its outstanding shares (i.e., the shares owned by persons outside the corporation).

NO-LOAD MUTUAL FUND—a mutual fund that charges no commission for the shares you buy. It may be hard to purchase shares of a no-load fund; most brokers do not like to sell them because they do not make any money on the sale. Investors usually buy these shares directly from the company that manages the no-load fund.

PREFERRED STOCK—stock that is given priority in the sharing of profits (called *dividends*). The holder of preferred stock is entitled to receive dividends out of the profits of a company at a fixed annual rate, before any profits are distributed to the common stockholders. With some preferred stocks, the fixed dividend is *cumulative.* In that case, if the fixed dividend is not paid within a given year, it must be paid the following year before any profits are distributed to common stockholders. If the preferred stock is *noncumulative,* no such accumulations take place.

PRICE-EARNINGS RATIO—the earnings of a corporation, divided by the number of shares. This ratio is a handy index to the financial condition of the corporation. Generally, as the company becomes more profitable, its price-earnings ratio increases.

PROBATE—official proof that a certain document is valid. For example, a probate court must determine whether a will is valid before the will can take legal effect. Witnesses who have signed the will are usually asked to appear; but it can be probated without their presence. After the court probates a will, it issues a certificate that declares the will legal and official.

PUTS and CALLS—A *put* is an option to sell a fixed amount of a certain stock or commodity at a specified price within a limited amount of time. A *call* is the privilege to buy a stock or commodity at a fixed price within a limited amount of time.

RECEIVABLES—the unpaid claims, bills, and notes of services or merchandise that other merchants have received from a company. These are carried on the company's books as being "due."

RULE OF 78's—the method for computing a refund of interest when a loan contract is paid before maturity. Another name for the Rule of 78's is the *Sum of the Digits.* The number *78* is the sum of the digits 1–12, which stand for the months of the year.

For example, let's say a person borrows $1,000 for 12 months. After two months, he decides to repay the loan. He should be charged only for the amount of time he used the money, so the rule of 78's says this figure would be 24/78 of the interest that would have been charged for the entire year. The borrower can get back 54/78 of the finance charge. *Note:* The rule of 78's applies only to a 12-month contract period.

SAVINGS BOND—a borrowing device that the federal government originated after World War II. The government was heavily in debt and needed a way to raise large amounts of money in a hurry. So it issued savings bonds to attract small loans from private citizens.

Today you can buy a Savings Bond for an amount smaller than its face value and turn it in for the full amount in cash at the end of a seven-year period. The savings bond earns about six percent interest during that time. Savings bonds are not as popular today as they were several years ago, because most banks and savings-and-loan companies pay a higher rate of return.

SECURITY—something given as a promise of repayment. A security may be any note, stock, treasury stock, bond, or debenture. It also includes any document that shows a person's membership or ownership in an organization that has borrowed money from him.

SHORT SALE—a contract to sell shares of stock that the seller does not own, or that are not under his control. The seller hopes that when he has to deliver the stock to the purchaser, its price will be lower than when he made the contract. If it is, he can buy the stock on the open market, deliver it, and make a profit.

SIMPLE INTEREST—interest paid only on the principal balance, and not figured on the accumulated interest. Simple interest is paid simply for the use of the money borrowed.

STOCK SPLIT—A corporation with 100,000 shares outstanding (i.e., owned by private investors) may decide to recall them and issue 200,000 shares, giving each shareholder two shares for one. This is known as a *stock split.* It does not increase or reduce the value of the shareholder's assets; his interest in the corporation remains the same. But if the price of the stock rises after a split, the value of the investor's holdings will increase more rapidly.

STRAIGHT-LINE METHOD—the most common way of figuring depreciation of an asset for tax purposes. Another name for it is *fixed percentage.* It is based on the theory that an asset will loose value at the same rate each year.

To use the straight-line method, estimate the ultimate salvage value of the item and subtract this from its original cost. Divide the result by the number of years you expect to use the item. This will give you the amount of straight-line depreciation for each year.

TREASURY BILL—an obligation of the United States Government to pay the bearer a fixed amount of money after a certain number of days. The Treasury Bill is the most important investment in today's money market. The most common Treasury Bills are the three- and six-month bills; they can be purchased at any Federal Reserve Bank. These bills raise new cash for the federal government. The biggest buyers of Treasury Bills are banks, corporations, and state and local government.

UNIFORM GIFT TO MINORS ACT—a federal law that allows an adult to make a gift to a minor without the minor's having to pay a gift tax. This gift may be in the form of money, security, proceeds from a life insurance policy, or annuities.

The gift can only be made to one minor, and only one person can act as custodian of the gift for the minor. The gift must be final, and the person who gives it must convey its legal title to the minor.

USURY—the act of lending money at an illegally high rate of interest. Usury laws vary from state to state. In some states, a violator of the usury law is required to refund the entire amount of interest paid; in other states, only the amount of excess interest is given back.

WARRANTS AND OPTIONS—A *warrant* confers the right to purchase stock in a corporation at a later date, under stated terms and conditions. A corporation may sell warrants much like it sells common stock. An *option* is similar, except that it is not necessarily sold. The corporation may give an option to a stockholder or friend of the company as a special privilege.

BANKING

BANKER'S ACCEPTANCE—a bank's agreement to accept a bill of exchange or bank draft. Since the bank becomes responsible to pay on the instrument, a person would prefer to exchange a bill or draft for an acceptance.

BILL OF EXCHANGE—a written order to pay a stated amount out of a bank account. A bill of exchange must conform to the following requirements: (1) It must be in writing and signed by the *drawer*—the person issuing the order; (2) It must contain an unconditional order to pay a certain sum in money; (3) It must be payable on demand or at a fixed time; (4) It must state that the amount is payable to a designated person or company, or to the person who holds the bill.

A bank will not honor a bill that does not conform to these requirements. If the bill does conform, it can move about quite freely in business transactions. There is an obvious risk involved in purchasing a bill of exchange that does not conform to any of these requirements, because it may not be honored by the bank that holds the drawer's account. Such a bill would be called a *non-negotiable* instrument.

Many of the common bills of exchange are checks, drafts, trade acceptances, and banker's acceptances. They involve a *drawer* (the person who draws up the bill), a *drawee* (the person who keeps the drawer's account), and a *payee* (a person to whom the bill is paid); so bills of exchange are referred to as *three-party* instruments. Promissory notes are known as *two-party* instruments, since they involve a *maker* (the person who makes the promise to pay) and a *payee* (the person to whom the note is payable).

The drawee is not responsible for the document until he accepts it. He may do this by writing the word *accepted* on the face of the document, followed by his name or initials.

CERTIFICATE OF DEPOSIT—a certificate issued by a bank to acknowledge the deposit of a specific sum of money. The bank promises to pay the depositor the face amount, along with an agreed amount of interest. Most certificates of deposit have an established expiration date; in all cases, the full payment is made only when the depositor gives the certificate back to the bank.

CERTIFIED CHECK—a bank's written promise to pay a specific amount of money on behalf of one of the bank's account holders. In effect, the bank takes funds out of the account and assumes the duty of paying the check when it is negotiated. Thus, it has been said that "a certified check is as good as cash."

CHECK—a bill of exchange drawn on a bank and payable on demand. It is the most common negotiable instrument.

When a depositor opens up a deposit account with a bank, he becomes a lender and a bank becomes his borrower. Under their contract, the bank must surrender the funds of a depositor whenever the depositor gives an order in the form of a check. The check must be presented to the bank within a reasonable time after it is issued.

A bank is not primarily responsible to pay the check; the person who wrote the check is. Therefore, a bank may refuse to honor a check. But if it refuses to pay a valid check, the bank has breached its contract with the depositor, and may be held liable for any losses the depositor incurs because the check was not honored.

COLLATERAL—a pledge of real or personal property to secure the payment of a loan or the extension of credit. Collateral can be in many forms, but it should have enough value to secure the loan. Also, it should be in a form that the lender can convert to cash, if the need arises. Many banks use only the borrower's signature as collateral for small loans. But each lending institution must decide the amount and type of collateral it will accept.

DISCOUNTING—a bank's practice of charging a fee for converting credit instruments into cash. A bank may advance money to the person who holds the instrument and charge him its usual discount rate. Then the bank holds the documents until maturity. If the person or institution that issued the document pays the bank, the transaction is closed. If not, the bank will expect the depositor to return its money.

FEDERAL RESERVE BANK—The Federal Reserve System was established in 1913 by President Woodrow Wilson when he signed the Federal Reserve Act. This act created 12 regional banks across the nation, controlled by the Federal Reserve Board of governors in Washington, D.C. These banks regulate the flow of credit and money. Any bank that wants to use money from the Federal Reserve Bank in its region must become a member of the Federal Reserve System. The Federal Reserve Bank provides many services for its member banks; it handles their reserve accounts, furnishes currency and coins, clears and collects checks, transfers funds by wire, and acts as a depository for the funds handled by government agencies.

INDEPENDENT RETIREMENT ACCOUNT —a bank account for accumulating money that a person will use during retirement. Each year the depositor can put up to fifteen percent of his earned income in the account, up to a maximum of $1,750 each year. This money is not charged Federal income taxes during the current year; it is taxed only when an individual starts withdrawing money. He can do this as early as age 59½, and he must begin withdrawing the money by age 70½. He can take out the deposit in one lump sum or in a certain amount per month.

If both husband and wife are working, each of them can have an Individual Retirement Account. They can set aside a maximum total of $3,000 for these accounts each year. The bank pays interest to these accounts while the money is on deposit; the rate of interest varies from bank to bank.

INTEREST PENALTY—an amount of interest that you forfeit to the bank if you withdraw the money in a time certificate of deposit before it matures. The federal law states that when you cash a certificate of deposit before maturity, you will earn the regular passbook savings rate *minus* 90 days' interest. This means that if you cash a time certificate of deposit early, the bank will not pay interest for 90 days of the time you had the certificate in effect. The bank would pay you the regular passbook rate for the rest of the time you had the money on deposit.

JOINT TENANTS—the partners who jointly own an asset. In banking, this term usually refers to two or more people who jointly own a bank account. If one of the partners dies, his interest or ownership is automatically transferred to the remaining owner(s). Married couples often establish bank accounts as joint tenants.

LINE OF CREDIT—the amount of money that any one person, corporation, or organization can borrow with a certain amount of collateral. Different lending institutions have different ways of arriving at this figure.

For example, let us say that a certain bank has a policy of financing only 75 percent of the value of an automobile. A certain vehicle is valued at $10,000. The bank would loan up to $7,500 for this car; that's the line of credit available.

NONTAXABLE TRUST—an account that an employer uses to provide a stock bonus, pension, or profit-sharing plan for the benefit of his employees. The money deposited in this trust account will not be taxed if it meets all the requirements imposed by federal and state governments.

PRINCIPAL—the original amount of debt, or the initial amount a person owes to another. A bank charges interest only on the principal.

PROMISSORY NOTE—a written promise to pay. A promissory note must conform to the following: (1) It must be in writing and signed by the maker; (2) It must contain an unconditional promise to pay a certain sum of money; (3) It must be payable on demand or at a fixed future time; (4) It must be payable to a designated person or to the bearer.

The payee does not need to hold the note until the maturity date. He may decide to sell it to someone else; in that case, if the instrument is *order paper* (i.e., written to pay a designated person), he endorses the instrument and gives it to the buyer. If it is *bearer paper* (i.e., written to pay the bearer), he simply gives it to the buyer.

PROXY—authorization to allow another person to vote in your absence at a business meeting. In banking, this term usually refers to the proxies that an account holder in a savings-and-loan company may give to the officers of his company.

REDISCOUNTING—If a bank wants to convert some of its holdings into cash, it would submit its bills and notes to its local Federal Reserve Bank for rediscounting. After charging a *rediscount fee,* the Federal Reserve Bank would dispense the cash and hold the instruments until maturity. If all of the debtors pay their notes, the transaction is completed. If not, the Federal Reserve Bank will demand payment from the borrowing bank, which in turn will demand payment from the debtor(s).

SECURED LOAN—a loan that requires the borrower to make a pledge of collateral. Many institutions make only this type of loan. The greater the risk that the loan will not be repaid, the more security the lending institution will require. A good example might be an automobile loan. The bank will hold the title to the car as collateral until the debt has been paid. If the debt isn't paid, the bank may sell the car and recover the money it lended.

SIGNATURE LOAN—a loan that requires only the signature of the borrower as collateral. The lending institution relies on the integrity of the person who borrows the money. In most cases, this type of loan is for a short term and for a low amount.

TENANTS IN COMMON—ownership of an asset by two or more persons, in which each person has an individual interest. In banking, this term usually refers to the common ownership of a bank account. When one of the owners dies, his ownership passes to his heirs or to whomever he has named in his will; the surviving owners do not automatically inherit the account. Tenants in common do not necessarily have equal interests in the account. If one member wishes to dispose of his portion of the account and the others do not, he may force them to convert the account to cash so that he can receive his share.

TRADE ACCEPTANCE—a bill of exchange that arises out of a merchant's purchase of goods. The seller of goods (*drawer*) signs over the debt of the buyer *(drawee),* to a designated agent *(payee).* When the buyer accepts this document, he agrees to pay his debt to the agent.

Let us say that ABC Company has purchased a shipment of goods on credit. The company that sold the goods to ABC issues a trade acceptance. When ABC Company receives the trade acceptance, one of its officers will write the word *accepted* across the face of the document with the date and place of payment, followed by his signature. ABC Company then becomes liable to pay the bill as stated.

TRUST OFFICER—one who manages a trust for someone else. The trust officer may also be called *trustee.*

INSURANCE

ACCIDENT INSURANCE—insurance covering such risks as death, dismemberment, loss of eyesight, or loss of time as a result of accidents. An *accident* is generally defined as an unlooked-for mishap; if someone intentionally cuts off his arm or leg, it would not be an accident. Accident insurance would cover death from accidental means, but no other kind of death.

DOUBLE INDEMNITY—an insurance company's practice of giving twice the amount of insurance benefits when an insured person dies. Double indemnity is most commonly given when the insured person dies in an accident. Many insurance companies do not give double indemnity if the death occurred through suicide, service in time of war, air travel, or disease.

FIRE INSURANCE—insurance that guards against the loss of property by fire. The person who owns a fire insurance policy must have an *insurable interest* in the property involved. In other words, the insured must have a lawful, economic interest in the safety or preservation of the property from loss or destruction. (For example, the average citizen couldn't buy fire insurance on the White House.)

FLOOD INSURANCE—insurance against loss caused by cloudbursts and floods, tidal waves or overflowing streams and rivers. This type of insurance is usually available in low-lying areas and in the vicinity of rivers and dams.

HEALTH INSURANCE—insurance to cover losses caused by illness or sickness.

INCONTESTABILITY—protection against having a life insurance policy cancelled by the insurance company. Most policies state that they are incontestable after two years, unless you fail to pay your premium.

INCREASE OF HAZARD—taking unnecessary or unusual risks. Usually a fire insurance policy will state that the insurance company is not liable for loss or damage if the likelihood of fire is increased by any means within your control. For example, the company may not pay for a fire if you keep fireworks, explosives, gasoline, kerosene, or other highly flammable materials on your property.

INDUSTRIAL LIFE INSURANCE—a fairly small amount of life insurance, for which you pay premiums at weekly or other frequent intervals. Generally, this kind of life insurance policy offers the least amount of protection for the dollars you spend.

INSURABLE INTEREST—Usually a person takes out a life insurance policy on himself. However, you can take out a life insurance policy on someone else and make yourself the beneficiary, if you have an insurable interest in the life of that person. The term *insurable interest* generally means: (1) In the case of persons related by blood or law, an interest that arises from love and affection, or (2) In the case of other persons, a lawful economic interest in protecting the life of the insured person.

LIFE INSURANCE—a form of insurance that pays benefits in the event of death. An insurance company will pay an agreed sum of money to a designated person (called a *beneficiary*) when the insured person dies. The beneficiary may be the estate of the insured, a member of his family, a business associate, or even a stranger. The policy will state whether you can change the name of the beneficiary. If you can't, the beneficiary has what is called a *vested interest*—that is, his interest in the policy may not be stripped from him without his consent. Thus, you may take out a life insurance policy on a member of your family or upon the life of another person who owes you a debt. A business partnership may take out a policy on the lives of its partners. Likewise, a corporation may obtain a life insurance policy for each of its corporate officers. But if you have no insurable interest in the life of the person insured, the law considers it to be a *contract of wager*. Even if an insurance company issues a policy under these circumstances, it is illegal and unenforceable.

MARINE INSURANCE—insurance that covers losses connected with marine activities. This contract may also protect against losses on inland waters or on land, if the losses are connected with a sea voyage. The person or firm obtaining this kind of insurance must have an insurable interest in the subject of the policy (e.g., the boat or the cargo carried by the boat).

MUTUAL INSURANCE—a form of insurance in which the policyholders make up the insurance company. (The *policyholders* are those who buy insurance policies.) Mutual insurance companies only insure the lives and property of their members. When the annual premiums that members pay exceed the amount of losses covered by the company, the company often pays a *dividend* (i.e., a small refund) to the policyholders.

PAID-UP and ENDOWMENT OPTIONS—the opportunity to convert a life insurance policy to another form of insurance, so that you do not have to pay premiums. The original policy may state that when you do this you can keep the same amount of insurance in force *(paid-up option),* or that you will have a declining amount of insurance *(endowment option)*. Usually these options require that: (1) The money you've invested in the policy must be earning interest equal to the amount of your premium. (2) You must ask the company to convert the policy. (3) Your request will be subject to the company's approval. (4) The company will determine how much insurance you can buy under the new plan. (5) If you've borrowed money against your present policy, your new policy will become the collateral for the loan. Not all life insurance policies carry these options.

UNOCCUPANCY—a clause that states that the insurance company will not pay for loss or damage that occurs while an insured building is vacant or unoccupied beyond a certain period of time—usually ten days.

WAIVER OF PREMIUM—a provision that allows you to stop paying premiums on a life insurance policy if you become disabled. Your policy would remain in force, and when your disability ends you resume making the payments.

REAL ESTATE

ABSTRACT OF TITLE—a legal document that shows the history of ownership for a certain piece of property. In most states, the abstract of title passes from the seller to the buyer with each sale of property, and the buyer's name is added to the permanent record. The seller must pay the expense of bringing the abstract up to date. The buyer must have an attorney check the abstract to be sure it is complete.

APPRECIATION—a property's increase in value over a length of time. It is the opposite of *depreciation*. For example, let us say that a tract of land was purchased for $500 per acre five years ago. Today the same land would probably be worth at least $1,000 per acre.

ASSESSMENT—a government's charge against a certain parcel of real estate. This charge is usually made to cover the property owner's share of the cost of a public improvement such as a street or sewer.

BREACH OF CONTRACT—a situation in which one or both parties fail to perform a legal contract. Both parties must accept the breach. If one doesn't accept it for any reason, he may sue the other party to regain what was lost.

EARNEST MONEY—a down payment that a purchaser of real estate makes to show his good faith in the transaction. Earnest money shows the seller that the buyer really means to follow through with the agreement. Sometimes the seller refunds the money if the transaction fails to go through; sometimes he doesn't. This decision is up to the seller.

ESCROW—an account where money is held until a contract has been fulfilled. This type of arrangement is most often used in the sale of real estate. An escrow agent holds the buyer's down payment until the title search is completed and the transaction is closed. The seller receives none of the money until all the legalities are in order. Banks and lawyers are the most common escrow agents.

FEE SIMPLE—the transfer of property to someone and his heirs without limitations. An estate or inheritance that you own completely and without restrictions is called an estate in *fee simple*. You may use it in any way you choose during your life time or after your death (through your will). If you have not made any plans for the distribution of this estate, it must pass to your heirs without any future limitations.

FIRST/SECOND MORTGAGE—a lender's claim to a piece of property that the owner has used as collateral on a loan. If the property owner fails to repay his loan, the lender can force him to sell the property to repay the debt. The only difference between a first and second mortgage is the order in which the lenders file their claim on the property. A second mortgage would only be good after the first mortgage had been satisfied. A lender would prefer to have a first mortgage rather than a second mortgage, since he would be more likely to get his money back.

LIEN—a claim that a person or institution has upon the property of another. The borrower must keep the property as security for the debts. In other words, a lien puts a "hold" on a certain item until its borrower has paid the debt. A lender may hold a lien on real estate, an automobile, or any other item of personal property.

PRORATED TAXES—taxes that are split between the buyer and the seller of a piece of property. When property is sold, the taxes are usually divided according to the time the sale takes place. The buyer should only be expected to pay taxes for the time after he receives title to the property, and not for the entire year.

QUIT-CLAIM DEED—a deed that gives a buyer whatever right, title, or interest that the seller has in a piece of property. It does not indicate whether other persons have an interest in the property, too.

SURVEYOR'S REPORT—a report from a licensed surveyor, which is used to determine limits and boundaries of a piece of property. The surveyor checks legal descriptions of the tract and usually drives stakes at the corners of the property to aid anyone else determining the boundaries at a later time. A surveyor's report should include the measurements of the land in terms of acres, square miles, or square feet. It should also give definite boundaries, the corner locations, and a definite point of beginning the measurement.

The cost of this report varies upon the time required for the research. This fee is customarily paid by a person who is purchasing the property.

TITLE INSURANCE—a contract to protect the owner of real estate against loss arising from defective property titles, hidden liens, or other encumbrances.

Usually title insurance losses are very small, because title insurance companies examine all legal papers very carefully before they will insure them. The premiums paid for title insurance are quite high, because of the amount of time it takes to research the documents. The title company must examine many records of land titles involving many previous owners, deeds, mortgages, and so on. A title insurance policy remains in effect until some further change of ownership takes place, or until a claim is made against a property.

WARRANTY DEED WITH FULL COVENANTS—the most complete form of property title that a seller can give. In this type of deed, a seller guarantees: (1) that he has the right to give the purchaser the title as designated in the contract; (2) that the buyer shall enjoy the premises without having to dispute claims from others; (3) that the premises are free from encumbrances such as tax debts; (4) that the seller will provide any further necessary assurances of the title; and (5) that the seller will forever guarantee the buyer's title to the premises. This is the most valuable form of protection, from the purchaser's viewpoint.

Of course, a buyer can obtain title insurance from a title insurance company for even more protection.

CHAPTER TWENTY

COLLEGES AND UNIVERSITIES

College Entrance Examinations and Questionnaires

At the end of the nineteenth century, a group of colleges, disturbed by the great variety of subjects taught, and by the wide range of marks given, in the secondary schools of the country, set up the College Entrance Examination Board (CEEB). Through the efforts of this organization, greater uniformity of curriculum in secondary schools was obtained. To remedy existing evils, the CEEB began to administer tests of its own construction to those applying to the colleges that originally made up the group. These early tests were of the essay type—usually three-hour tests in which the candidate was asked to discuss several topics rather exhaustively. As the number of college applicants increased greatly after World War I, the CEEB found it necessary to devise simpler testing methods. At this time, the short-answer, multiple-choice question was developed and polished. Studies were conducted to learn the relative values of the various types of tests, and the reliability and validity of short-answer tests were demonstrated to the satisfaction of the colleges involved. They discovered a high degree of correlation between the marks obtained on these short-answer tests and the later success of the students in their college work. Thereupon, the number of colleges making use of these tests grew considerably.

Short-answer tests and the great reliance that some colleges place on them have been attacked, but up to now no better form has been found, and the colleges continue to rely on them.

TYPES OF TESTS

The College Entrance Examination Board of Princeton, New Jersey, through its Educational Testing Service, is today the maker of the most widely used college entrance examinations. Among these are: the Scholastic Aptitude Test (SAT), the Preliminary Scholastic Aptitude Test (PSAT), the Writing Sample Test, achievement tests in various subject-areas, and the Advanced Placement Tests.

The Scholastic Aptitude Test

This test has become a regular part of the college admission procedure for high school seniors throughout the country. The marks achieved in the two fields of verbal aptitude and of mathematical aptitude are a significant factor in most colleges' decisions concerning accepting or rejecting a candidate.

A. The Verbal Section of the SAT

The mark obtained in this section of the test reflects the student's ability to handle language concepts and to reason. Questions of four types are included.

(1) The first type of question tests knowledge of vocabulary.

Example: Each of the questions below consists of a word printed in italics, followed by five words or phrases numbered 1 to 5. Choose the numbered word or phrase which is most nearly opposite in meaning to the word in italics.

1. ***acclaim*—1 discharge 2 denounce 3 applaud 4 divide 5 rationalize**
2. ***zenith*—1 nadir 2 compass 3 summit 4 middle 5 musical instrument**
3. ***superficial*—1 arrogant 2 magnanimous 3 pusillanimous 4 profound 5 young**

Answers (1)2 (2)1 (3)4

(2) The second type of question tests the student's understanding of relationships among words and ideas. The student has to analyze the relationship existing between two words and then match it with another pair that has a similar relationship.

Example: Each of the questions below consists of two words that have a certain relationship to each other, followed by five numbered pairs of words. Select the numbered pair of words that are related to each other in the same way as the original pair of words are related to each other.

1. **carpenter : saw :: 1 magician : wand 2 blacksmith : anvil 3 surgeon : doctor 4 doctor : drugs 5 satirist : words**
2. **facile : pen :: 1 glib : tongue 2 soft : shoe 3 stubborn : mule 4 hasty : pudding 5 easy : pencil**
3. **admiration : love :: 1 parsimony : economy 2 jealousy : envy 3 joy : ecstasy 4 hot : tepid 5 eager : anxious**

Answers (1)5 (2)1 (3)3

(3) The third type of question tests the student's ability to complete a sentence from which one or two words have been removed.

Example: In each of the sentences below there is a blank space indicating that a word has been omitted. Beneath the sentence are five numbered words; from these five words you are to choose the one word which, when inserted in the blank space, *best* fits in with the meaning of the sentence as a whole. In some sentences, two words are omitted; in these sentences, you will be given five pairs of words. Select the pair which best completes the sentence.

1. **You don't win friends by acting ____. 1 professionally 2 nicely 3 generously 4 idealistically 5 superciliously**
2. **My refusal to ____ with your demands was based on the highest intelligence. 1 return 2 abscond 3 recant 4 comply 5 enter**
3. **Only an oaf fails to observe the ____ of life. 1 business 2 proprieties 3 ventures 4 study 5 cessation**

Answers (1)5 (2)4 (3)2

(4) The fourth type of question tests the student's ability to read with understanding.

Example: Read the following passages and answer the questions which follow each passage.

I. While the poll takers are most widely known for their political surveys, the greatest part of their work is on behalf of American business. There are three kinds of commercial surveys. One is public relations research, such as that done for banks, which finds out how the public feels about a company. Another is employee-attitude research, which learns from rank-and-file workers how they really feel about their jobs and their bosses, and which can avert strikes by getting to the bottom of grievances quickly. The third, and probably most spectacular, is marketing research, testing public receptivity to products and designs. The investment a company must make for a new product is enormous—$5,000,000 to $10,000,000, for instance, for just one product. Through the surveys a company can discover in advance what objections the public has to competing products, and whether it really wants a new one. These surveys are actually a new set of signals permitting better communication between business and the general public—letting them talk to each other. Such communication is vital in a complex society like our own. Without it, we would have not only tremendous waste but the industrial anarchy of countless new unwanted products appearing and disappearing.

1. **The title below which best expresses the ideas of this passage is**
   1 The poll taker
   2 Business asks questions
   3 Behind the scenes in business
   4 Our complex business world
   5 Averting industrial anarchy
2. **The passage states that polls can benefit industry by**
   1 reducing waste
   2 establishing fair prices
   3 strengthening people's faith in business

4 saving small businesses
5 serving as a new form of advertising

3. This paragraph is developed by means of
1 cause and effect
2 contrast
3 illustrations
4 anecdotes
5 vivid descriptions

4. Which is *not* mentioned as an area in which polls have been conducted?
1 new products
2 politics
3 public relations
4 labor-management relationships
5 family relationships

5. The passage leads the reader to believe that for business purposes surveys are
1 overrated
2 too widely used
3 often deceptive
4 necessary
5 costly

Answers (1)2 (2)1 (3)3 (4)5 (5)4

B. The Mathematics Section of the SAT

The mathematics section tests a student's ability to handle elementary mathematical concepts in old and new situations. The questions may be answered by those who have had a course in elementary algebra and plane geometry. Those who have had advanced courses in mathematics will, of course, be able to work more rapidly and efficiently. Some typical questions follow:

1. The dial of a meter is divided into equal sections from 0 to 60. When the needle points to 48, the meter registers 80 amperes. What is the maximum number of amperes the meter will register?

(1) 92 (2) 100 (3) 102 (4) 120 (5) 156

2. A box was made in the form of a cube. If a second cubical box has inside dimensions three times those of the first box, how many times as much does it contain?

(1) 3 (2) 9 (3) 12 (4) 27 (5) 36

3. A proper fraction is unchanged in value if both numerator and denominator are
(1) increased by the same number
(2) decreased by the same number
(3) divided by the same number
(4) raised to the second power
(5) replaced by their square roots

4. John's house is 6.3 miles due north of the community center. Dick's home is 5.5 miles due east of it. Find, to the nearest tenth of a mile, the shortest distance between their homes.

(1) 5.9m. (2) 8.3m. (3) 8.4m. (4) 11.8m. (5) 11.9m.

5. An altitude *h* of a triangle is twice the base to which it is drawn. If the area of the triangle is 225 square inches, then altitude *h* is

(1) 15 inches (2) 20 inches (3) 25 inches (4) 30 inches (5) 35 inches

Answers (1)2 (2)4 (3)3 (4)3 (5)4

The SAT is given several times each year during January, March, April, May, July, October, and December. Information about dates, hours, fees, centers, and so on, is contained in the College Board *Student Bulletin* which is available in most high schools or obtainable by writing to the College Entrance Examination Board, Box 592, Princeton, New Jersey, 08540, or Box 1025, Berkeley, California 94701. In general, the April or May examination should be taken by high school juniors who wish to obtain an appraisal of their general aptitude to help them in deciding which college to choose. Juniors who are interested in obtaining an early decision from a college (usually before December 1) should also take these tests. The December or January examinations should be taken by high school seniors.

It is advisable to file the application and fee at least six weeks before the examination date to insure being assigned to the center requested.

Scores obtained on these tests are forwarded to the colleges indicated by the students on the application card and to the student's high school. These scores are usually given to the students six or seven weeks after the examination date. Scores are reported on a scale which ranges from 200 to 800, to be interpreted as follows:

Between 700 and 800
Between 600 and 700-
Between 500 and 600-
500-
Between 400 and 500—
Between 300 and 400—
Between 200 and 300—l

Many colleges will accep scores of 450 or better, bu schools, which have as ma number of applicants that t require scores in the mid schools recognize that any st score of 450 or better is capab tory college work.

The Preliminary Scholastic Apti

Each year in October the Coll test for high school juniors to h how well they can do on aptitu essentialy a shorter form of the and mathematical questions are s and difficulty to the questions des dealing with the Scholastic Aptitud is shorter and costs less to take. T used by a limited number of groups determine winners of various scholarships. The college catalogs and scholarship announcements will indicate whether the test is required.

Arrangements to take this test are usually made by the principal of the high school. Students should inquire of their school advisors in September about the advisability of taking this test.

The Achievement Tests and the Writing Sample Test

Some, but not all, colleges requiring the SAT ask their applicants, in addition, to take one or more Achievement Tests. These are one-hour tests given on the afternoon of the day the SAT is offered. Tests are offered in the following fields:

American History and Social Studies, Biology, Chemistry, English Composition, European History and World Cultures (January and May only), French, German, Hebrew (January only), Latin, Advanced Mathematics, Intermediate Mathematics, Physics, Russian (January only), Spanish.

Most of these tests are of the short-answer type and usually consist of 100 to 150 questions to be answered during the hour. There may be a short essay question or a paragraph to be corrected on the English Composition Test, but this test, too, is basically a short-answer paper.

... are ... school in May if re- ... include Listening Comprehension Tests in French, German, Russian, and Spanish.

The Advanced Placement Tests

For high school seniors who have taken an enriched program of studies—chiefly on the college level—the College Board offers a series of tests for advanced placement in college. Such examinations are now offered in English Composition, Literature, French, German, Latin, Spanish, American History, European History, Mathematics, Biology, Chemistry, and Physics. Unlike the Achievement Tests, these examinations are of the essay type and last for three hours each. Papers are marked and forwarded to the college which has accepted the candidate. Results are reported on a scale of 1 to 5.

(1) fail (2) pass (3) creditable (4) honors
(5) highest honors

The college receiving the grade *may* permit the student to take advanced work in these subject-areas as a freshman.

The teachers of advanced high school courses in these fields will inform students about this test and make the necessary arrangements for the taking of the examination, which is usually given during the spring.

s

n (ACT)
ogram tests
, mathematics,
sciences.
he areas of diction,
ion.
ction covers the first three
mathematics. Stress is laid on
ason.
studies test and the natural science
asize the reading and interpreting of
d passages in the specific field.
udents and colleges receive five scores: one in
ach of the subject-areas, and a composite score.

For information and registration, students should contact their high school counselor. Additional information may be obtained by writing the American College Testing Program, Box 168, Iowa City, Iowa 52240.

This test is used by several colleges in the West and South; most colleges that require this test will accept the CEEB results.

B. The National Merit Scholarship Test

The National Merit Scholarship Corporation annually conducts the country's largest talent search. This nonprofit organization was established in 1955 thanks to grants from the Ford Foundation and the Carnegie Corporation.

Formerly a separate examination, the National Merit Scholarship Qualifying Test (NMSQT) is now the same as the Preliminary Scholastic Aptitude Test, given in October of each year to high school juniors. The students who receive the highest grades (usually in the 99th percentile) are called semifinalists and are asked to take the Scholastic Aptitude Test of the College Board in their senior year. Winners are selected on the basis of their scores on the SAT as well as an evaluation of their high school record.

Most students who take this test do not consider themselves candidates for scholarships, but are interested in learning about their relative strengths and weaknesses as revealed by the test.

C. Many other tests exist, but they have all but disappeared from the examination scene. Tests such as the American Council on Education Psychological Examination, the Ohio State Psycho-

al Test, and the General Education Develop-
ent Test resemble the tests described above. A student who prepares for the SAT or the ACT will be ready for any of these tests if he is asked to take them.

THE "COLLEGE BOARDS"

The College Entrance Examination Board, which prepares the Scholastic Aptitude Test and the various Achievement Tests, is of the opinion that very little can be done to prepare *in the weeks immediately preceding* the taking of the SAT. The College Board discourages students from spending excessive time or money on crash programs to help them prepare for the Scholastic Aptitude Test. Although the Board has slightly modified its stand in the past several years, it still maintains that such programs will do little to improve the student's score on the test. The College Board also points out that time spent on assignments will contribute just as much, if not more, to a high score on the test. The College Board also points out that time spent in this manner is a far better preparation for college than intensive cram courses which have little applicability outside their narrow purpose.

Concerning specific preparation for the tests, the College Board recommends only that the student obtain and thoroughly study the College Board Student Bulletin. This booklet contains directions on how to take the test as well as several pages of sample questions similar to those already given in the *Quick Reference Handbook of Basic Knowledge.* (See page 770 for the address of where to obtain the *Student Bulletin.*)

The idea that "you can't prepare for the College Boards" has been propounded so emphatically by the Board and by teachers and other school personnel who have repeated the statement that many students have gone into the examination without any preparation at all. It has been the experience of many high school teachers, guidance counselors, and college advisors that this statement has often proved deceptive and has actually been harmful to serious students. The disappointingly low marks that frequently resulted became a permanent part of the student's record; occasionally they resulted in a negative decision by the admissions committee of the college of the student's choice.

Intelligent preparation for the "Boards" cannot begin too early in the high school career. A wise student will concentrate on his studies from the time he enters high school. He will read widely. He will explore the world of literature beyond the limits of his work in the English classroom. He will work to develop habits of application which will result in marks that show his real level of ability.

Early in his junior year, the high school student should take the Preliminary Scholastic Aptitude Test. When he gets the results of this test (usually in December), he can evaluate his marks in comparison with his grades in school. The following table may serve as a guide in evaluating performance:

Mark in English or Mathematics	Mark on PSAT Report should be
75%	45–50
80%	50–55
85%	55–60
90%	60–65
95%	65–75

The student who gets a mark that compares favorably with his school grades (as indicated in the table) may feel satisfied with his score; the student who fails to get the indicated mark is definitely in need of help and should begin an intensive program in preparation for the SAT examinations he will take in December or January of his senior year. Preparation should include the following:

1. Obtain a copy of the College Entrance Examination Board's booklet, *The College Board Student Bulletin.* This booklet is distributed, without cost, by school guidance officers to whom you should apply. If you cannot obtain copies in your school, write to the College Entrance Examination Board, Box 592, Princeton, New Jersey, 08540 or to Box 1025, Berkeley, California, 94701.

Read the booklet carefully. Do the illustrative exercises and take the tests in verbal and mathematical ability. Be sure you understand the reasons for the correct answers given in the booklet. This will help you to uncover the areas of mathematics in which you will need to concentrate.

2. Get additional material for study and analysis. Many reference books and study outlines are available, most of them in paperback editions. A good book on building vocabulary skills should prove to be invaluable.

3. Take the College Board Scholastic Aptitude Test in March or May of your junior year, for guidance and practice. A student may reasonably expect an improvement of 40 points over the results on the PSAT. Failure to achieve this improvement indicates the need for additional intensive study before taking the final College Board examinations in December or January of your senior year.

Despite the advice of the College Board indicated above, proper guidance and tutoring have been known to result in impressive improvement in College Board scores. Experience has shown that the best preparation lies in getting an understanding of the nature of the questions asked, and in developing the technique of answering these questions intelligently and quickly. Students who have gotten marks on the College Board examinations that were not commensurate with their scholastic ability, as shown by their school marks, are definitely advised to seek such help. To find a reliable tutoring service, your guidance counselor may be of help. Or you might turn to friends who have had successful experience along these lines.

TAKING THE "BOARDS"

Anyone who has taken the PSAT or who has looked carefully at the questions in the booklets, *A Description of the Scholastic Aptitude Test,* or *How to Prepare for College Entrance Examinations,* will realize that the SAT measures a student's ability to think and to reason. The amassing of factual information or subject matter is relatively unimportant. It is, therefore, advisable for the student to make every effort to be at the peak of mental alertness when he takes the examination. Last-minute "cramming" is valueless. The best way to reach the desired mental acuity is to taper off the studying shortly before the examination. Relaxation and rest will prove more valuable than frantic studying up to the very last moment. A good idea is to stop all studying for the examination at least two days before you take the test. A person who is well rested can analyze questions more quickly and can think more logically than can one who has worked to the point of exhaustion.

When you are taking the examination, it is well to bear in mind three factors: time, "guessing," and experimental questions.

The SAT is usually divided into five or six sections of thirty or forty-five minutes each. Students should not be unduly distressed if they find that they cannot finish the sections in the time allotted. The examination is so designed that even the best students barely have time to finish. In each section, a student can achieve a fair mark by answering correctly approximately fifty percent of the questions. The alert student will answer first those questions that are not too difficult, and then return to those that seem puzzling or confusing. It is a good idea not to spend too much time on any one question.

The College Entrance Board employs a formula to compensate for haphazard guessing, so that "wild guessing" will only result in a lower mark. However, don't be afraid to rely on intelligent analysis of questions that strike you as "tough." If you are able logically to eliminate one or more of the suggested choices, your chance of getting the right answer will be improved. So go ahead and answer such questions. Good students, although they may feel uncertain of their answers to many questions, may possess a fund of background information that will lead them to the correct answer more often than might be expected. Such students should learn to rely on their "hunches." If you feel totally ignorant of the answer to a question, it is wisest to leave that question unanswered.

The knowledge that some questions on the SAT are experimental and do not count toward the mark the student will get, may disturb him. He begins to wonder just which part of the test is the experimental part. Actually, this phase of the examination may well serve as a source of reassurance to the student. Whenever he encounters a difficult section or an unfamiliar type of question that perplexes him, he can console himself with the thought that this may well be the "experimental" part, and that, accordingly, it will not affect his mark adversely. In general, however, students should try to answer all questions to the best of their ability.

The Achievement Tests are tests of mastery of subject matter. Before taking them, the student should review the work of the course as he would in preparing for a final examination in the subject. Most colleges asking for these tests make use of the results for guidance and placement.

U.S. Naval Academy—Michelson Hall, the new science building

Admissions Questionnaires

Each year, many thousands of applications for admission to college are filed by anxious high school juniors and seniors. The questions most frequently asked by students and suggested answers are given below.

Which colleges shall I apply to? The best advice and counsel can be obtained from the high school officials. Late in the junior year or early in the senior year, the student and his parents should confer with the school's college guidance officer or the school's principal. After a careful appraisal of the student's record, his College Board scores, his financial status, and other pertinent data, the school official should be able to offer several colleges for consideration and help the student make a selection.

Having decided on the colleges to apply to, the student should write a brief note to the Director of Admissions of each school asking for a bulletin of information and an application form.

While college application forms vary in the questions asked, they fall into a general pattern. Factual questions can be answered readily. Other questions, however, calling for detailed answers of paragraph or essay length, often give high school students difficulty and cause for worry. In the remainder of this section, we shall analyze and comment on the information requested and the questions you are required to answer.

Name other colleges to which you have applied or intend to apply.

College authorities are realistic. In this day of swollen college enrollments, students are expected to apply to several colleges in order to be certain of acceptance by at least one school. In general, it is wise to apply to different kinds of schools. Thus, your answer should indicate what type of school you are considering, whether it is a large university, a small college, a noncoeducational school, a coeducational institution, or a state-supported school. Not to specify a type will make it difficult to write a convincing answer to questions below.

Who or what has influenced you to consider the college of your choice?

Don't contrive an answer; tell the truth. College advisors, alumni, friends attending the college, representatives of the college who spoke at College Night meetings at your high school may have influenced you in your choice. Mention one or more of these. You may have been influenced by the school's reputation, members of its faculty, its bulletin, the courses offered by the school in the field of your interest, its location (distance from home, etc.), its campus, its facilities (library, laboratories, dormitories), its program of accelerated studies in the field of your interest, etc.

Why do you desire a college education?

This is a more complex question. Do not limit yourself to the vocational or professional preparation aspect. While college is a prerequisite for advanced study, this should not be the sole factor that you discuss. Mention the lasting cultural values that you believe a college education can offer. If you are still undecided about your plans for the future, college may help you to find the field of interest for your life's work.

What challenges do you expect the college to offer you?

Students answering this question have mentioned the confrontation of new ideas, working with gifted teachers and classmates, making of rich and enduring friendships, and the discovery of oneself as an individual and as a member of the community.

What contribution to the life of the college do you hope to make?

The activities you have engaged in while in high school should be continued in college. It is safe to assume that, if you have been active in high school, in publications, dramatics, debating, musical activities, and athletics, you will continue in these activities while in college.

What hobbies or fields of interest do you have?

In discussing your hobby, try to show its educational value to you or to others. What did your hobby give you in addition to pleasure?

What kind of outside reading do you do?

This question appears in many forms:

Name six books you have read during the last two years and tell how the reading of one of them was of value to you.

Write a list of books, not specific course requirements, which you have read in the past year.

Reading is, obviously, an activity that is essential for college work. Your list of books should reveal your interests in many fields. You will, of course, list works of fiction. Try to include works in the fields of biography, your hobby, science, and philosophy as well. This means that during the last year or two of high school you should make ample use of your school and public library.

References

You may be asked to supply the names and addresses of two or more teachers or persons other than teachers to whom the college may refer. Before submitting any name to the college, be sure to ask the individual's permission. It is wise to select a person who can say something specific about your activity. The college knows that all of these letters of reference will be in superlatives; it is wise to have someone write in your behalf who can back up his statement about your character and personality with concrete illustrations.

The autobiographical letter

The instructions for this question range from the very simple "Write an autobiographical sketch of yourself" to the very detailed "Enclose a letter indicating so far as you can (a) your purpose in going to college, (b) the reasons for your interest in the college, (c) how you have spent the past two summers and of what value they have been to you, (d) the nature of any remunerative employment you have had, (e) any experiences—travel, employment, friendship, military service, etc.—which have had an important influence on your development and plans for the future, (f) which of the books you have read during the past two years have been most profitable and enjoyable and why, (g) which of all the things you have accomplished, either in or out of school, has given you the greatest personal satisfaction, (h) any positive or negative factors in your secondary school training which will affect your education at the college."

In writing this statement about yourself and your interests, be frank. College committees can spot the "phony" letter without much trouble. Do not try to impress the readers with long lists of books and activities which your high school record does not substantiate.

Do not begin with data about your early childhood unless the events discussed have had a definite bearing on the kind of person you are. The names and locations of elementary schools are of little importance in determining the kind of person you really are.

Concentrate on your junior and senior high school years. Begin by discussing that which is, in your opinion, the most important influence in making you the kind of person you are today. It may be a subject area which caught your interest, a person who guided your thinking along educational lines, a field of vocational endeavor which gave you an insight into your potential as a student and worker, a hobby which you have decided to follow through your life, or any experience which has colored your thinking about the future.

Describe the kind of work you have been doing in and out of school and discuss your reaction to this work. Mention honors won and positions of responsibility to which you have been appointed or elected.

If illness, or change of school, or any other factor affected your school grades adversely, this letter gives you an opportunity to explain these grades. However, it is advisable to refer to this only if the factor which caused the low marks has been removed or adjusted to.

In general, let the college know why you think you will be a credit to the school you are applying to for admission. You should try to show that you are sufficiently motivated to be eager to carry out college assignments and independent study, that you are resourceful and responsible, and that you are a person of industrious habits. A final word of caution:

Your application for admission to college represents you. Be neat, precise, and accurate. It is advisable to write all answers on another sheet of paper before making any entries on the application blank.

Four-Year Public Colleges and Universities

ALABAMA

Alabama A and M University
Normal, AL 35762
Alabama State University
Montgomery, AL 36195
Athens State College
Athens, AL 35611
Auburn University
Auburn University, AL 36849
Auburn University—Montgomery
Montgomery, AL 36117
Jacksonville State University
Jacksonville, AL 36265
Livingston University
Livingston, AL 35470
Troy State University
Troy, AL 36082
Troy State University—Dothan/Ft. Rucker
Dothan, AL 36301
Troy State University—Montgomery
Montgomery, AL 36104
University of Alabama
University, AL 35486
University of Alabama—Birmingham
Birmingham, AL 35294
University of Alabama—Huntsville
Huntsville, AL 35807
University of Montevallo
Montevallo, AL 35115
University of North Alabama
Florence, AL 35632
University of South Alabama
Mobile, AL 36688

ALASKA

University of Alaska—Anchorage
Anchorage, AK 99504
University of Alaska—Fairbanks
Fairbanks, AK 99701
University of Alaska—Juneau
Juneau, AK 99803

ARIZONA

Arizona State University
Tempe, AZ 85281
Northern Arizona University
Flagstaff, AZ 86011
University of Arizona
Tucson, AZ 85721

ARKANSAS

Arkansas State University
State University, AR 72467
Arkansas Tech University
Russellville, AR 72801
Henderson State University
Arkadelphia, AR 71923
Southern Arkansas University
Magnolia, AR 71753
University of Arkansas
Fayetteville, AR 72701
University of Arkansas—Little Rock
Little Rock, AR 72204
University of Arkansas—Monticello
Monticello, AR 71655
University of Arkansas—Pine Bluff
Pine Bluff, AR 71601
University of Central Arkansas
Conway, AR 72032

CALIFORNIA

California State College—Bakersfield
Bakersfield, CA 93309
California State College—San Bernadino
San Bernadino, CA 92407
California State College—Stanislaus
Turlock, CA 95380
California State Polytechnic University—Pomona
Pomona, CA 91768
California State Polytechnic University—San Luis Obispo
San Luis Obispo, CA 93407
California State University—Chico
Chico, CA 95929
California State University—Dominquez Hills
Carson, CA 90747
California State University—Fresno
Fresno, CA 93740
California State University—Fullerton
Fullerton, CA 92634
California State University—Hayward
Hayward, CA 94542
California State University—Long Beach
Long Beach, CA 90840
California State University—Los Angeles
Los Angeles, CA 90032
California State University—Northridge
Northridge, CA 91330
California State University—Sacramento
Sacramento, CA 95819
Claremont Men's College
Claremont, CA 91711
Humboldt State University
Arcata, CA 95521
National University
San Diego, CA 92108
San Diego State University
Calexico, CA 92231
San Diego State University
San Diego, CA 92182
San Francisco State University
San Francisco, CA 94132
San Jose State University
San Jose, CA 95192
Sonoma State University
Rohnert Park, CA 94928
University of California—Berkeley
Berkeley, CA 94720
University of California—Davis
Davis, CA 95616
University of California—Irvine
Irvine, CA 92717
University of California—Los Angeles
Los Angeles, CA 90024
University of California—Riverside
Riverside, CA 92521
University of California—San Diego
La Jolla, CA 92093
University of California—Santa Barbara
Santa Barbara, CA 93106
University of California—Santa Cruz
Santa Cruz, CA 95064

COLORADO

Adams State College
Alamosa, CO 81102
Colorado School of Mines
Golden, CO 80401
Colorado State University
Fort Collins, CO 80523
Fort Lewis College
Durango, CO 81301
Mesa College
Grand Junction, CO 81501
Metropolitan State College
Denver, CO 80204
United States Air Force Academy
USAF Academy, CO 80840
University of Colorado
Boulder, CO 80309
University of Colorado Springs—Colorado Springs
Colorado Springs, CO 80907
University of Colorado—Denver
Denver, CO 80202
University of Northern Colorado
Greeley, CO 80639
University of Southern Colorado
Pueblo, CO 81001
Western State College of Colorado
Gunnison, CO 81230

CONNECTICUT

Central Connecticut State College
New Britain, CT 06050
East Connecticut State College
Willimantic, CT 06226
Southern Connecticut State College
New Haven, CT 06515
United States Coast Guard Academy
New London, CT 06320
University of Connecticut
Storrs, CT 06268
Western Connecticut State College
Danbury, CT 06810

DELAWARE

Delaware State College
Dover, DE 19901

DISTRICT OF COLUMBIA

University of the District of Columbia
Washington, DC 20004

FLORIDA

Florida A and M University
Tallahassee, FL 32307
Florida Atlantic University
Boca Raton, FL 33431
Florida International University
Miami, FL 33199
Florida State University
Tallahassee, FL 32306

Fort Lauderdale College
Fort Lauderdale, FL 33301
New College of the University of South Florida
Sarasota, FL 33580
Panama Canal College
APO Miami, FL 34002
University of Florida
Gainesville, FL 32611
University of North Florida
Jacksonville, FL 32216
University of South Florida
Tampa, FL 33620
University of West Florida
Pensacola, FL 32504

Georgia

Albany State College
Albany, GA 31705
Armstrong State College
Savannah, GA 31406
Augusta College
Augusta, GA 30910
Columbus College
Columbus, GA 31993
Fort Valley State College
Fort Valley, GA 31030
Georgia College
Milledgeville, GA 31601
Georgia Institute of Technology
Atlanta, GA 30332
Georgia Southern College
Statesboro, GA 30458
Georgia Southwestern College
Americus, GA 31709
Georgia State University
Athens, GA 30303
Kennesaw College
Marietta, GA 30061
Medical College of Georgia
Augusta, GA 30912
North Georgia College
Dahlonega, GA 30533
Savannah State College
Savannah, GA 31404
Southern Technical Institute
Marietta, GA 30060
University of Georgia
Athens, GA 30602
Valdosta State College
Valdosta, GA 31601
West Georgia College
Carrollton, GA 30118

Hawaii

University of Hawaii—College of Arts and Sciences
Hilo, HI 96720
University of Hawaii—Manoa
Honolulu, HI 96822
University of Hawaii—West Oahu College
Aiea, HI 96701

Idaho

Boise State University
Boise, ID 83725
Idaho State University
Pocatello, ID 83209
Lewis-Clark State College
Lewiston, ID 83501
University of Idaho
Moscow, ID 83843

Illinois

Chicago State University
Chicago, IL 60628
Eastern Illinois University
Charleston, IL 61920
Governors State University
Park Forest South, IL 60466
Illinois State University
Normal, IL 61761
National American Educational Service (s)
Chicago, IL 60640
Northeastern Illinois University
Chicago, IL 60625
Northern Illinois University
DeKalb, IL 60115
Sangamon State University
Springfield, IL 62708
Southern Illinois University
Edwardsville, IL 62026
Southern Illinois University—Carbondale
Carbondale, IL 62901
University of Illinois—Chicago Circle
Chicago, IL 60680
University of Illinois—Medical Center
Chicago, IL 60612
University of Illinois—Urbana/Champaign
Urbana, IL 61801
Western Illinois University
Macomb, IL 61455

Indiana

Ball State University
Muncie, IN 47306
Indiana State University—Evansville
Evansville, IN 47712
Indiana State University—Terre Haute
Terre Haute, IN 47809
Indiana University—Bloomington
Bloomington, IN 47405
Indiana University—Kokomo
Kokomo, IN 46901
Indiana University—Purdue University at Fort Wayne
Fort Wayne, IN 46805
Indiana University—Purdue University at Indianapolis
Indianapolis, IN 46202
Indiana University—South Bend
South Bend, IN 46615
Indiana University—Southeast
New Albany, IN 47150
Purdue University
West Lafayette, IN 47907
Purdue University—Calumet
Hammond, IN 46323
Purdue University—North Central
Westville, IN 46391

Iowa

Iowa State University
Ames, IA 50011
University of Iowa
Iowa City, IA 52242
University of Northern Iowa
Cedar Falls, IA 50613

Kansas

Emporia State University
Emporia, KS 66801
Fort Hays State University
Hays, KS 67601
Kansas State University
Manhattan, KS 66506
Pittsburg State University
Pittsburg, KS 66762
United States Army Command and General Staff College
Fort Leavenworth, KS 66027
University of Kansas
Lawrence, KS 66045
University of Kansas—College of Health Sciences and Hospital
Kansas City, KS 66103
Wichita State University
Wichita, KS 67204

Kentucky

Eastern Kentucky University
Richmond, KY 40475
Kentucky State University
Frankfort, KY 40601
Murray State University
Murray, KY 42071
Northern Kentucky University
Highland Heights, KY 41076
University of Kentucky
Lexington, KY 40506
University of Louisville
Louisville, KY 40208
Western Kentucky University
Bowling Green, KY 42101

Louisiana

Grambling State University
Grambling, LA 71245
Louisiana State University—A and M College
Baton Rouge, LA 70803
Louisiana State University—Shreveport
Shreveport, LA 71115
Louisiana Tech University
Ruston, LA 71272
McNeese State University
Lake Charles, LA 70609
Nicholls State University
Thibodaux, LA 70310
Northeast Louisiana University
Monroe, LA 71209
Northwestern State University
Natchitoches, LA 71457
Southeastern Louisiana University
Hammond, LA 70402
Southern University—Baton Rouge
Baton Rouge, LA 70813
Southern University—New Orleans
New Orleans, LA 70126
University of New Orleans
New Orleans, LA 70122
University of Southwestern Louisiana
Lafayette, LA 70504

Maine

Maine Maritime Academy
Castine, ME 04421
University of Maine—Augusta
Augusta, ME 04330
University of Maine—Farmington
Farmington, ME 04938
University of Maine—Fort Kent
Fort Kent, ME 04743
University of Maine—Machias
Machias, ME 04654

University of Maine—Orono
Orono, ME 04473
University of Maine—Presque Isle
Presque Isle, ME 04769
University of Southern Maine
Gorham, ME 04038

MARYLAND

Bowie State College
Bowie, MD 20715
Coppin State College
Baltimore, MD 21216
Frostburg State College
Frostburg, MD 21532
Morgan State University
Baltimore, MD 21239
Salisbury State College
Salisbury, MD 21801
St. Mary's College of Maryland
St. Mary's City, MD 20686
Towson State University
Towson, MD 21204
United States Naval Academy
Annapolis, MD 21402
University of Baltimore
Baltimore, MD 21201
University of Maryland—Baltimore County
Baltimore, MD 21228
University of Maryland—College Park
College Park, MD 20742
University of Maryland—Eastern Shore
Princess Anne, MD 28153
University of Maryland—University College
College Park, MD 20742

MASSACHUSETTS

Boston State College
Boston, MA 02115
Bridgewater State College
Bridgewater, MA 02324
Fitchburg State College
Fitchburg, MA 01420
Framingham State College
Framingham, MA 01701
Massachusetts College of Art
Boston, MA 02215
Massachusetts Maritime Academy
Buzzards Bay, MA 02532
North Adams State College
North Adams, MA 01247
Salem State College
Salem, MA 01970
Southeastern Massachusetts University
North Dartmouth, MA 02747
University of Lowell
Lowell, MA 01854
University of Massachusetts—Amherst
Amherst, MA 01003
University of Massachusetts—Boston
Boston, MA 02125
Westfield State College
Westfield, MA 01085
Worcester State College
Worcester, MA 01602

MICHIGAN

Central Michigan University
Mount Pleasant, MI 48858
Eastern Michigan University
Ypsilanti, MI 48197
Ferris State College
Big Rapids, MI 49307
Grand Valley State Colleges
Allendale, MI 49401
Lake Superior State College
Sault Ste. Marie, MI 49783
Michigan State University
East Lansing, MI 48824
Michigan Technological University
Houghton, MI 49931
Northern Michigan University
Marquette, MI 49855
Oakland University
Rochester, MI 48063
Saginaw Valley State College
University Center, MI 48710
University of Michigan—Ann Arbor
Ann Arbor, MI 48109
University of Michigan—Dearborn
Dearborn, MI 48128
University of Michigan—Flint
Flint, MI 48503
Wayne State University
Detroit, MI 48202
Western Michigan University
Kalamazoo, MI 49008

MINNESOTA

Bemidji State University
Bemidji, MN 56601
Mankato State University
Mankato, MN 56001
Metropolitan State University
St. Paul, MN 55101
Moorhead State University
Moorhead, MN 56560
Southwest State University
Marshall, MN 56258
St. Cloud State University
St. Cloud, MN 56301
University of Minnesota—Duluth
Duluth, MN 55182
University of Minnesota—Morris
Morris, MN 56267
University of Minnesota—Twin Cities
Minneapolis, MN 55455
Winona State University
Winona, MN 55987

MISSISSIPPI

Alcorn State University
Lorman, MS 39096
Delta State University
Cleveland, MS 38733
Jackson State University
Jackson, MS 39217
Mississippi State University
Mississippi State, MS 39762
Mississippi University for Women
Columbus, MS 39701
Mississippi Valley State University
Itta Bena, MS 38941
University of Mississippi
University, MS 38677
University of Mississippi Medical Center
Jackson, MS 39216
University of Southern Mississippi
Hattiesburg, MS 39401

MISSOURI

Central Missouri State University
Warren, MO 64093
Missouri Southern State College
Joplin, MO 64801
Missouri Western State College
St. Joseph, MO 64507
Northeast Missouri State University
Kirksville, MO 63501
Northwest Missouri State University
Maryville, MO 64468
Southeast Missouri State University
Cape Girardeau, MO 63701
Southwest Missouri State University
Springfield, MO 65802
University of Missouri—Columbia
Columbia, MO 65201
University of Missouri—Kansas City
Kansas City, MO 64110
University of Missouri—Rolla
Rolla, MO 65401
University of Missouri—St. Louis
St. Louis, MO 63121

MONTANA

Eastern Montana College
Billings, MT 59101
Montana College of Mineral Science and Technology
Butte, MT 59701
Montana State University
Bozeman, MT 59717
Northern Montana College
Havre, MT 59501
University of Montana
Missoula, MT 59812
Western Montana College
Dillon, MT 59725

NEBRASKA

Chadron State College
Chadron, NE 69357
Kearney State College
Kearney, NE 68847
Peru State College
Peru, NE 68421
University of Nebraska—Lincoln
Lincoln, NE 68508
University of Nebraska—Omaha
Omaha, NE 68182
Wayne State College
Wayne, NE 68787

NEVADA

University of Nevada—Las Vegas
Las Vegas, NV 89150
University of Nevada—Reno
Reno, NV 89557

NEW HAMPSHIRE

Keene State College
Keene, NH 03431
Plymouth State College
Plymouth, NH 03264
University of New Hampshire
Durham, NH 03824

NEW JERSEY

Glassboro State College
Glassboro, NJ 08028
Jersey City State College
Jersey City, NJ 07305
Montclair State College
Upper Montclair, NJ 07043
New Jersey Institute of Technology
Newark, NJ 07102
Rutgers University—Camden College of Arts and Sciences
Camden, NJ 08102

Rutgers University—College of Engineering
New Brunswick, NJ 08903
Rutgers University—College of Nursing—Newark
Newark, NJ 07102
Rutgers University—College of Pharmacy
New Brunswick, NJ 08903
Rutgers University—Cook College
New Brunswick, NJ 08903
Rutgers University—Douglass College
New Brunswick, NJ 08903
Rutgers University—Livingston College
New Brunswick, NJ 08903
Rutgers University—Mason Gross School of the Arts
New Brunswick, NJ 08903
Rutgers University—Newark College of Arts and Sciences
Newark, NJ 07102
Rutgers University—Rutgers College
New Brunswick, NJ 08903
Rutgers University—University College
New Brunswick, NJ 08903
Trenton State College
Trenton, NJ 08625
William Paterson College
Wayne, NJ 07470

New Mexico

Eastern New Mexico University
Portales, NM 88130
New Mexico Highlands University
Las Vegas, NM 87701
New Mexico Institute of Mining and Technology
Socorro, NM 87801
New Mexico State University
Las Cruces, NM 88003
University of New Mexico
Albuquerque, NM 87131
Western New Mexico University
Silver City, NM 88061

New York

CUNY—Bernard Baruch College
New York, NY 10010
CUNY—Brooklyn College
Brooklyn, NY 11210
CUNY—City College
New York, NY 10031
CUNY—College of Staten Island
Staten Island, NY 10301
CUNY—Hunter College
New York, NY 10021
CUNY—John Jay College of Criminal Justice
New York, NY 10019
CUNY—Lehman College
Bronx, NY 10468
CUNY—Medgar Evers College
Brooklyn, NY 11225
CUNY—Queens College
Flushing, NY 11367
CUNY—York College
Jamaica, NY 11432
SUNY—Albany
Albany, NY 12222
SUNY—Binghamton
Binghamton, NY 13901
SUNY—Buffalo
Buffalo, NY 14214
SUNY—College at Brockport
Brockport, NY 14420
SUNY—College at Buffalo
Buffalo, NY 14222
SUNY—College at Cortland
Cortland, NY 13045
SUNY—College at Fredonia
Fredonia, NY 14063
SUNY—College at Genesco
Genesco, NY 14454
SUNY—College at New Paltz
New Paltz, NY 12561
SUNY—College at Old Westbury
Old Westbury, NY 11568
SUNY—College at Oneonta
Oneonta, NY 13820
SUNY—College at Oswego
Oswego, NY 13126
SUNY—College at Plattsburgh
Plattsburgh, NY 12901
SUNY—College at Potsdam
Potsdam, NY 13676
SUNY—College at Purchase
Purchase, NY 10577
SUNY—College of Agriculture and Life Science at Cornell
Ithaca, NY 14853
SUNY—College of Ceramics at Alfred
Alfred, NY 14802
SUNY—College of Environmental Science and Forestry
Syracuse, NY 13210
SUNY—College of Human Ecology at Cornell
Ithaca, NY 14853
SUNY—College of Technology
Utica, NY 13502
SUNY—Empire State College
Saratoga Springs, NY 12866
SUNY—Fashion Institute of Technology
New York, NY 10001
SUNY—Maritime College
Bronx, NY 10465
SUNY—School of Industrial and Labor Relations at Cornell
Ithaca, NY 14853
SUNY—Stony Brook
Stony Brook, NY 11794
SUNY—Upstate Medical Center
Syracuse, NY 13210
United States Merchant Marine Academy
Kings Point, NY 11024
United States Military Academy
West Point, NY 10996

North Carolina

Appalachian State University
Boone, NC 28608
Davidson College
Davidson, NC 28036
East Carolina University
Greenville, NC 27834
Elizabeth City State University
Elizabeth City, NC 27909
Fayetteville State University
Fayetteville, NC 28303
North Carolina Agricultural and Technical State University
Greensboro, NC 27411
North Carolina Central University
Durham, NC 27707
North Carolina School of the Arts
Winston-Salem, NC 27107
North Carolina State University—Raleigh
Raleigh, NC 27650
Pembroke State University
Pembroke, NC 28372
Salem College
Winston-Salem, NC 27108
University of North Carolina
Ashville, NC 28814
University of North Carolina—Chapel Hill
Chapel Hill, NC 27514
University of North Carolina—Charlotte
Charlotte, NC 28223
University of North Carolina—Greensboro
Greensboro, NC 27412
University of North Carolina—Wilmington
Wilmington, NC 28403
Western Carolina University
Cullowhee, NC 28723
Winston-Salem State University
Winston-Salem, NC 27102

North Dakota

Dickinson State College
Dickinson, ND 58601
Mayville State College
Mayville, ND 58257
Minot State College
Minot, ND 58701
North Dakota State University
Fargo, ND 58105
University of North Dakota
Grand Forks, ND 58202
Valley City State College
Valley City, ND 58072

Ohio

Bowling Green State University
Bowling Green, OH 43403
Central State University
Wilberforce, OH 45384
Cleveland State University
Cleveland, OH 44115
Kent State University
Kent, OH 44242
Miami University
Oxford, OH 45056
Ohio State University
Columbus, OH 43210
Ohio State University—Lima
Lima, OH 45804
Ohio State University—Mansfield
Mansfield, OH 44906
Ohio University
Athens, OH 45701
Ohio University—Lancaster
Lancaster, OH 43130
University of Akron
Akron, OH 44325
University of Cincinnati
Cincinnati, OH 45221
Write State University
Dayton, OH 45435
Youngstown State University
Youngstown, OH 44555

Oklahoma

Central State University
Edmond, OK 73034
East Central Oklahoma State University
Ada, OK 74820

Northeastern Oklahoma State University
Tahleguah, OK 74464
Northwestern Oklahoma State University
Alva, OK 73717
Oklahoma State University
Stillwater, OK 74078
Panhandle State University
Goodwell, OK 73939
Southeastern Oklahoma State University
Durant, OK 74701
Southwestern Oklahoma State University
Weatherford, OK 73096
University of Oklahoma—Health
Oklahoma City, OK 73190
University of Oklahoma—Norman
Norman, OK 73019
University of Science and Arts of Oklahoma
Chickasha, OK 73018

OREGON

Eastern Oregon State College
La Grande, OR 97850
Oregon College of Education
Monmouth, OR 97361
Oregon Institute of Technology
Klamath Falls, OR 97601
Oregon State University
Corvallis, OR 97331
Portland State University
Portland, OR 97207
Southern Oregon State College
Ashland, OR 97520
University of Oregon
Eugene, OR 97403
University of Oregon—Health
Portland, OR 97201

PENNSYLVANIA

Bloomsburg State College
Bloomsburg, PA 17815
California State College
California, PA 15419
Cheyney State College
Cheyney, PA 19319
Clarion State College
Clarion, PA 16214
East Stroudsbury State College
East Stroudsbury, PA 18301
Edinboro State College
Edinboro, PA 16412
Grove City College
Grove City, PA 16127
Indiana University of Pennsylvania
Indiana, PA 15705
Kutztown State College
Kutztown, PA 19530
Lock Haven State College
Lock Haven, PA 17745
Mansfield State College
Mansfield, PA 16933
Millersville State College
Millersville, PA 17551
Pennsylvania State University
University Park, PA 16802
Pennsylvania State University—Behrend
Erie, PA 16563
Pennsylvania State University—Capitol
Middletown, PA 17057
Shippensburg State College
Shippensburg, PA 17257
Slippery Rock State College
Slippery Rock, PA 16057
Temple University
Philadelphia, PA 19122
West Chester State College
West Chester, PA 19380

RHODE ISLAND

Rhode Island College
Providence, RI 02908
University of Rhode Island
Kingston, RI 02881

SOUTH CAROLINA

Clemson University
Clemson, SC 29631
College of Charleston
Charleston, SC 29401
Francis Marion College
Florence, SC 29501
South Carolina State College
Orangeburg, SC 29117
The Citadel
Charleston, SC 29409
University of South Carolina
Columbia, SC 29208
University of South Carolina—Aiken
Aiken, SC 29801
University of South Carolina—Coastal Carolina
Conway, SC 29526
University of South Carolina—Spartanburg
Spartanburg, SC 29303
Winthrop College
Rock Hill, SC 29733
Wofford College
Spartanburg, SC 29301

SOUTH DAKOTA

Black Hills State College
Spearfish, SD 57783
Dakota State College
Madison, SD 57042
Northern State College
Aberdeen, SD 57401
South Dakota School of Mines and Technology
Rapid City, SD 57701
South Dakota State University
Brookings, SD 57006
University of South Dakota
Vermillion, SD 57069
University of South Dakota of Springfield
Springfield, SD 57062

TENNESSEE

Austin Peay State University
Clarksville, TN 37040
East Tennessee State University
Johnson City, TN 37614
Memphis State University
Memphis, TN 38152
Middle Tennessee State University
Murfreesboro, TN 37132
Tennessee State University
Nashville, TN 37203
Tennessee Technological University
Cookeville, TN 38501
University of Tennessee—Center for the Health Sciences
Memphis, TN 38163
University of Tennessee—Chattanooga
Chattanooga, TN 37401
University of Tennessee—Knoxville
Knoxville, TN 37916
University of Tennessee—Martin
Martin, TN 38238

TEXAS

Angelo State University
San Angelo, TX 76909
Corpus Christi State University
Corpus Christi, TX 78412
East Texas State University
Commerce, TX 75428
Lamar University
Beaumont, TX 77710
Laredo State University
Laredo, TX 78040
Midwestern State University
Wichita Falls, TX 76308
North Texas State University
Denton, TX 76203
Pan American University
Edinburg, TX 78539
Prairie View A and M University
Prairie View, TX 77445
Sam Houston State University
Huntsville, TX 77340
Southwest Texas State University
San Marcos, TX 78666
Stephen F. Austin State University
Nacogdoches, TX 75962
Sul Ross State University
Alpine, TX 79830
Sul Ross State University—Uvalde Study Center
Uvalde, TX 78801
Tarleton State University
Stephenville, TX 76402
Texas A and I University—Kingsville
Kingsville, TX 78363
Texas A and M University
College Station, TX 77843
Texas A and M University at Galveston
Galveston, TX 77553
Texas Southern University
Houston, TX 77004
Texas Tech University
Lubbock, TX 79409
Texas Woman's University
Denton, TX 76204
University of Houston
Houston, TX 77004
University of Houston—Clear Lake City
Houston, TX 77058
University of Houston—Downtown
Houston, TX 77002
University of Houston—Victoria
Victoria, TX 77901
University of St. Thomas
Houston, TX 77006
University of Texas—Arlington
Arlington, TX 76019
University of Texas—Austin
Austin, TX 78712
University of Texas—Dallas
Richardson, TX 75080
University of Texas—El Paso
El Paso, TX 79968
University of Texas—Health Science Center—San Antonio
San Antonio, TX 78284

University of Texas Medical Branch—Galveston
Galveston, TX 77550
University of Texas—Permian Basin
Odessa, TX 79762
University of Texas—San Antonio
San Antonio, TX 78285
University of Texas—Tyler
Tyler, TX 75701
West Texas State University
Canyon, TX 79016

UTAH

Southern Utah State College
Cedar City, UT 84720
Utah State University
Logan, UT 84322
Weber State College
Ogden, UT 84408

VERMONT

Castleton State College
Castleton, VT 05735
Johnson State College
Johnson, VT 05656
Southern Vermont College
Bennington, VT 05201
University of Vermont
Burlington, VT 05405

VIRGINIA

Christopher Newport College
Newport News, VA 23606
College of William and Mary
Williamsburg, VA 23185
George Mason University
Fairfax, VA 22030
James Madison University
Harrisonburg, VA 22801
Norfolk State University
Norfolk, VA 23504
Old Dominion University
Norfolk, VA 23508
University of Virginia—Clinch
Wise, VA 24293
Virginia Military Institute
Lexington, VA 24450
Virginia Polytechnic Institute and State University
Blacksburg, VA 24061
Virginia State University
Petersburg, VA 23803

WASHINGTON

Central Washington University
Ellensburg, WA 98926
City College
Seattle, WA 98104
Eastern Washington University
Cheney, WA 99004
Evergreen State College
Olympia, WA 98505
University of Washington
Seattle, WA 98105
Washington State University
Pullman, WA 99164
Western Washington University
Bellingham, WA 98225

WEST VIRGINIA

Bluefield State College
Bluefield, WV 24701
Concord College
Athens, WV 24712
Fairmont State College
Fairmont, WV 26554
Glenville State College
Glenville, WV 26531
Marshall University
Huntington, WV 25705
Shepherd College
Shepherdstown, WV 25443
West Liberty State College
West Liberty, WV 26074
West Virginia Institute of Technology
Montgomery, WV 25136
West Virginia State College
Charleston, WV 25312
West Virginia University
Morgantown, WV 26506

WISCONSIN

University of Wisconsin—Eau Claire
Eau Claire, WI 54701
University of Wisconsin—Green Bay
Green Bay, WI 54302
University of Wisconsin—La Crosse
La Crosse, WI 54601
University of Wisconsin—Madison
Madison, WI 53706
University of Wisconsin—Milwaukee
Milwaukee, WI 53201
University of Wisconsin—Oshkosh
Oshkosh, WI 54901
University of Wisconsin—Parkside
Kenosha, WI 53141
University of Wisconsin—Platteville
Platteville, WI 53818
University of Wisconsin—River Falls
River Falls, WI 54022
University of Wisconsin—Stevens Point
Stevens Point, WI 54481
University of Wisconsin—Stout
Menomonie, WI 54751
University of Wisconsin—Superior
Superior, WI 54880
University of Wisconsin—Whitewater
Whitewater, WI 53190

WYOMING

University of Wyoming
Laramie, WY 82071

GUAM

University of Guam
Mangilao, Guam 96913

PUERTO RICO

Bayamon Central University
Bayamon, PR 00619

VIRGIN ISLANDS

College of the Virgin Islands
St. Thomas, VI 00801

Four-Year Private Colleges and Universities

ALABAMA

Birmingham-Southern College
Birmingham, AL 35204
Gately Christian University
Guntersville, AL 35976
Huntingdon College
Montgomery, AL 36106
International Bible College
Florence, AL 35630
Judson College
Marion, AL 36756
Miles College
Birmingham, AL 35208
Mobile College
Mobile, AL 36613
Oakwood College
Huntsville, AL 35806
Samford University
Birmingham, AL 35229
Selma University
Selma, AL 36701
Southeastern Bible College
Birmingham, AL 35256
Spring Hill College
Mobile, AL 36608
Stillman College
Tuscaloosa, AL 35401
Talladega College
Talladega, AL 35160
Tuskegee Institute
Tuskegee, AL 36088

ALASKA

Alaska Bible College
Glennallen, AK 99588
Alaska Pacific University
Anchorage, AK 99504
Sheldon Jackson College
Sitka, AK 99835

ARIZONA

Arizona College of the Bible
Phoenix, AZ 85021
Devry Institute of Technology
Phoenix, AZ 85016
Embry-Riddle Aeronautical University
Prescott, AZ 86301
Grand Canyon College
Phoenix, AZ 85017
Southwestern Baptist College
Phoenix, AZ 85032

University of Phoenix
Phoenix, AZ 85004
Western International University
Phoenix, AZ 85021

Arkansas

Arkansas Baptist College
Little Rock, AR 72202
Arkansas College
Batesville, AR 72501
Central Baptist College
Conway, AR 72032
College of the Ozarks
Clarksville, AR 72830
Harding University
Searcy, AR 72143
Hendrix College
Conway, AR 72023
John Brown University
Siloam Springs, AR 72761
Ouachita Baptist University
Arkadelphia, AR 71923
Philander Smith College
Little Rock, AR 72203

California

Ambassador College
Pasadena, CA 91123
Antioch University—West
San Francisco, CA 94108
Armstrong College
Berkeley, CA 94704
Art Center College of Design
Pasadena, CA 91103
Azusa Pacific College
Azusa, CA 91702
Bethany Bible College
Santa Cruz, CA 95066
Biola College
La Mirada, CA 90639
Brooks Institute
Santa Barbara, CA 93108
California Baptist College
Riverside, CA 92504
California Christian College
Fresno, CA 93703
California College of Arts and Crafts
Oakland, CA 94618
California College of Commerce
Long Beach, CA 90813
California Institute of Technology
Pasadena, CA 91125
California Institute of the Arts
Valencia, CA 91355
California Lutheran College
Thousand Oaks, CA 91360
California Maritime Academy
Vallejo, CA 94590
Center for Early Education
Los Angeles, CA 90048
Chapman College
Orange, CA 92666
Christ College Irvine
Irvine, CA 92715
Christian Heritage College
El Cajon, CA 92021
Cogswell College
San Francisco, CA 94108
Coleman College
La Mesa, CA 92041
College of Notre Dame
Belmont, CA 94002
Columbia College
Los Angeles, CA 90038
Dominican College of San Rafael
San Rafael, CA 94901
Dominican School of Philosophy and Theology
Berkeley, CA 95709
Fresno Pacific College
Fresno, CA 93702
Golden Gate University
San Francisco, CA 94105
Harvey Mudd College
Claremont, CA 91711
Heald Engineering College
San Francisco, CA 94109
Hebrew Union College
Los Angeles, CA 90007
Holy Family College
Fermont, CA 94538
Holy Names College
Oakland, CA 94619
John F. Kennedy University—Evenings
Qrinda, CA 94563
L.I.F.E. Bible College
Los Angeles, CA 90026
Lincoln University
San Francisco, CA 94118
Loma Linda University
Loma, CA 92350
Loma Linda University—La Sierra
Riverside, CA 92515
Los Angeles Baptist College
Newhall, CA 91322
Loyola Marymount University
Los Angeles, CA 90045
Menlo College
Menlo Park, CA 94025
Mills College
Oakland, CA 94613
Monterey Institute of International Studies
Monterey, CA 93940
Mount St. Mary's College
Los Angeles, CA 90049
Music and Arts Institute of San Francisco
San Francisco, CA 94115
New College of California
San Francisco, CA 94110
Northrop University
Inglewood, CA 90306
Occidental College
Los Angeles, CA 90041
Otis Art Institute of Parsons School of Design
Los Angeles, CA 90057
Pacific Christian College
Fullerton, CA 92631
Pacific Oaks College
Pasadena, CA 91103
Pacific States University
Los Angeles, CA 90006
Pacific Union College
Angwin, CA 94508
Patten Bible College
Oakland, CA 94601
Pepperdine University
Los Angeles, CA 90044
Pepperdine University—Seaver College
Malibu, CA 90265
Pitzer College
Claremont, CA 91711
Point Loma College
San Diego, CA 92106
Pomona College
Claremont, CA 91711
San Francisco Art Institute
San Francisco, CA 94133
San Francisco Conservatory of Music
San Francisco, CA 94122
San Jose Bible College
San Jose, CA 95108
Scripps College
Claremont, CA 91711
Simpson College
San Francisco, CA 94134
Southern California College
Costa Mesa, CA 92626
Southern California Institute of Architecture
Santa Monica, CA 90404
Stanford University
Stanford, CA 94305
St. Mary's College of California
Moraga, CA 94575
St. Patrick's College
Mountain View, CA 94042
Thomas Aquinas College
Santa Paula, CA 93060
United States International University
San Diego, CA 92131
University of Judaism
Los Angeles, CA 90024
University of La Verne
La Verne, CA 91750
University of Redlands
Redlands, CA 92373
University of San Diego
San Diego, CA 92110
University of San Francisco
San Francisco, CA 94117
University of Santa Clara
Santa Clara, CA 95053
University of Southern California
Los Angeles, CA 90007
University of the Pacific
Stockton, CA 95211
University of West Los Angeles
Culver City, CA 90230
West Coast Bible College
Fresno, CA 93710
West Coast University—Evenings
Los Angeles, CA 90020
West Coast University—Orange County—Evenings
Orange, CA 92668
Western Apostolic Bible College
Stockton, CA 95205
Western States College of Engineering
Inglewood, CA 90301
Westmont College
Santa Barbara, CA 93108
Whittier College
Whittier, CA 90608
Woodbury University
Los Angeles, CA 90017
World College West
San Anselmo, CA 94960
Yeshiva University of Los Angeles
Los Angeles, CA 90035

Colorado

Baptist Bible College of Denver
Broomfield, CO 80020
Belleview College
Westminster, CO 80030
Colorado College
Colorado Springs, CO 80903
Colorado Technical College
Colorado Springs, CO 80907
Colorado Women's College
Denver, CO 80220

Intermountain Bible College
Grand Junction, CO 81501
Loretto Heights College
Denver, CO 80236
Naropa Institute
Boulder, CO 80302
Regis College
Denver, CO 80221
Rockmont College
Denver, CO 80226
University of Denver
Denver, CO 80210
Western Bible College
Morrison, CO 80465

CONNECTICUT

Albertus Magnus College
New Haven, CT 06511
Bridgeport Engineering Institute
Bridgeport, CT 06606
Connecticut College
New London, CT 06320
Fairfield University
Fairfield, CT 06430
Holy Apostles College
Cromwell, CT 06416
Post College
Waterbury, CT 06708
Quinniplac College
Hamden, CT 06518
Sacred Heart University
Bridgeport, CT 06606
St. Alphonsus College
Suffield, CT 06078
St. Basil's College
Stamford, CT 06902
St. Joseph College
West Hartford, CT 06117
Trinity College
Hartford, CT 06106
University of Bridgeport
Bridgeport, CT 06602
University of Hartford
West Hartford, CT 06117
University of New Haven
West Haven, CT 06516
Wesleyan University
Middletown, CT 06457
Yale University
New Haven, CT 06520

DELAWARE

Goldey Beacom College
Wilmington, DE 19808
University of Delaware
Newark, DE 19711
Wesley College
Dover, DE 19901
Wilmington College
New Castle, DE 19720

DISTRICT OF COLUMBIA

Beacon College
Washington, DC 20009
Benjamin Franklin University
Washington, DC 20036
Catholic University of America
Washington, DC 20064
Corcoran School of Art
Washington, DC 20006
Georgetown University
Washington, DC 20057
George Washington University
Washington, DC 20052
Howard University
Washington, DC 20059
Mount Vernon College
Washington, DC 20007
Oblate College
Washington, DC 20017
Southeastern University
Washington, DC 20024
Strayer College
Washington, DC 20005
The American University
Washington, DC 20016
Trinity College
Washington, DC 20017
Washington International College
Washington, DC 20006

FLORIDA

Barry College
Miami Shores, FL 33161
Bethune-Cookman College
Daytona Beach, FL 32015
Biscayne College
Miami, FL 33054
Clearwater Christian College
Clearwater, FL 33519
College of the Palm Beaches
West Palm Beach, FL 33402
Eckerd College
St. Petersburg, FL 33733
Edward Waters College
Jacksonville, FL 32209
Flagler College
St. Augustine, FL 32084
Florida Beacon College
Largo, FL 33541
Florida Institute of Technology
Melbourne, FL 32901
Florida Institute of Technology—School of Applied Technology
Jensen Beach, FL 33457
Florida Memorial College
Miami, FL 33054
Florida Southern College
Lakeland, FL 33802
Fort Lauderdale College
Fort Lauderdale, FL 33301
Jacksonville University
Jacksonville, FL 32211
Jones College
Orlando, FL 32803
Jones College—Jacksonville
Jacksonville, FL 32211
Miami Christian College
Miami, FL 33167
Nova University
Fort Lauderdale, FL 33314
Palm Beach Atlantic College
West Palm Beach, FL 33401
Ringling School of Art
Sarasota, FL 33580
Rollins College
Winter Park, FL 32789
Southeastern College
Lakeland, FL 33801
Stetson University
Deland, FL 32720
St. John Vianney College Seminary
Miami, FL 33165
St. Leo College
St. Leo, FL 33574
Tampa College Medical Education Center
Tampa, FL 33609
Trinity College
Dunedin, FL 33528
University of Central Florida
Orlando, FL 32816
University of Miami
Coral Gables, FL 33124
University of Sarasota
Sarasota, FL 33577
University of Tampa
Tampa, FL 33606
Warner Southern College
Lake Wales, FL 33853
Webber College
Babson Park, FL 33827

GEORGIA

Agnes Scott College
Decatur, GA 30030
Atlanta Christian College
East Point, GA 30344
Atlanta College of Art
Atlanta, GA 30309
Berry College
Mount Berry, GA 30149
Beulah Heights Bible College
Atlanta, GA 30316
Brenau College
Gainesville, GA 30501
Carver Bible Institute and College
Atlanta, GA 30313
Clark College
Atlanta, GA 30314
Emmanuel College School of Christian Ministries
Franklin Springs, GA 30639
Emory University
Atlanta, GA 30322
Georgia College
Milledgeville, GA 31601
La Grange College
La Grange, GA 30240
Mercer University—Atlanta
Atlanta, GA 30341
Mercer University School of Pharmacy
Atlanta, GA 30312
Morehouse College
Atlanta, GA 30314
Morris Brown College
Atlanta, GA 30314
Oglethorpe University
Atlanta, GA 30319
Paine College
Augusta, GA 30910
Piedmont College
Demorest, GA 30535
Shorter College
Rome, GA 30161
Spelman College
Atlanta, GA 30314
Tift College
Forsyth, GA 31029
Toccoa Falls College
Toccoa Falls, GA 30598
Wesleyan College
Macon, GA 31297

HAWAII

Brigham Young University—Hawaii
Laie Oahu, HI 96762
Chaminade University of Honolulu
Honolulu, HI 96816
Hawaii Loa College
Kaneohe, HI 96744
Hawaii Pacific College
Honolulu, HI 96744
International College
Honolulu, HI 96809

IDAHO

College of Idaho
Caldwell, ID 83605
Northwest Nazarene College
Nampa, ID 83651

ILLINOIS

Aero-Space Institute
Chicago, IL 60610
Antioch—Native American Educational Services
Chicago, IL 60640
Augustana College
Rock Island, IL 61201
Aurora College
Aurora, IL 60507
Barat College
Lake Forest, IL 60045
Blackburn College
Carlinville, IL 62626
Bradley University
Peoria, IL 61625
College of St. Francis
Joliet, IL 60435
Columbia College
Chicago, IL 60605
Concordia College
River Fores, IL 60305
De Lourdes College
Des Plaines, IL 60016
DePaul University
Chicago, IL 60604
DeVry Institute of Technology
Chicago, IL 60618
Elmhurst College
Elmhurst, IL 60126
Eureka College
Eureka, IL 61530
George Williams College
Downers Grove, IL 60515
Greenville College
Greenville, IL 62246
Hebrew Theological College
Skokie, IL 60076
Illinois Benedictine College
Lisle, IL 60532
Illinois College
Jacksonville, IL 62650
Illinois Institute of Technology
Chicago, IL 60616
Illinois Wesleyan University
Bloomington, IL 61701
Judson College
Elgin, IL 60120
Kendall College
Evanston, IL 60201
Knox College
Galesburg, IL 61401
Lake Forest College
Lake Forest, IL 60045
Lewis University
Romeoville, IL 60441
Lincoln Christian College
Lincoln, IL 62656
Loyola University of Chicago
Chicago, IL 60611
MacMurray College
Jacksonville, IL 62650
McKendree College
Lebanon, IL 62258
Midwest College of Engineering
Lombard, IL 60148
Millikin University
Decatur, IL 62522
Monmouth College
Monmouth, IL 61462
Moody Bible Institute
Chicago, IL 60610
Morrison Institute of Technology
Morrison, IL 61270
Mundelein College
Chicago, IL 60660
National American Educational Service(s)
Chicago, IL 60640
National College of Chiropractic
Lombard, IL 60148
National College of Education
Evanston, IL 60201
National College of Education—Urbana
Chicago, IL 60601
North Central College
Naperville, IL 60566
North Park College
Chicago, IL 60625
Northwestern University
Evanston, IL 60201
Olivet Nazarene College
Kankakee, IL 60901
Parks College of Aeronautical Technology of St. Louis University
Cahokia, IL 62206
Principia College
Elsah, IL 62028
Quincy College
Quincy, IL 62301
Rockford College
Rockford, IL 61101
Roosevelt University
Chicago, IL 60605
Rosary College
River Forest, IL 60305
Rush University—Colleges of Nursing and Health Sciences
Chicago, IL 60612
Sangamon State University
Springfield, IL 62708
School of the Art Institute of Chicago
Chicago, IL 60603
Sherwood Music School
Chicago, IL 60605
Shimer College
Waukegan, IL 60085
Spertus College of Judaica
Chicago, IL 60605
St. Xavier College
Chicago, IL 60655
Trinity Christian College
Palos Heights, IL 60463
Trinity College
Deerfield, IL 60015
University of Chicago—The College
Chicago, IL 60637
University of Health Sciences—Chicago Medical School
North Chicago, IL 60062
Vandercook College of Music
Chicago, IL 60616
Wheaton College
Wheaton, IL 60187

INDIANA

Anderson College
Anderson, IN 46011
Bethel College
Mishawaka, IN 46544
Butler University
Indianapolis, IN 46208
Calumet College
Whiting, IN 46394
DePauw University
Greencastle, IN 46135
Earlham College
Richmond, IN 47374
Fort Wayne Bible College
Fort Wayne, IN 46807
Franklin College
Franklin, IN 46131
Goshen College
Goshen, IN 46526
Grace College
Winona Lake, IN 46590
Hanover College
Hanover, IN 47243
Huntington College
Huntington, IN 46750
Indiana Central University
Indianapolis, IN 46227
Indiana Institute of Technology
Fort Wayne, IN 46803
Indiana University—Northwest
Gary, IN 46408
Manchester College
North Manchester, IN 46962
Marian College
Indianapolis, IN 46222
Marion College
Marion, IN 46952
Oakland City College
Oakland City, IN 47660
Rose-Hulman Institute of Technology
Terre Haute, IN 47803
St. Francis College
Fort Wayne, IN 46808
St. Joseph's College
Rensselaer, IN 47978
St. Mary-of-the-Woods College
St. Mary-of-the-Woods, IN 47876
St. Mary's College
Notre Dame, IN 46556
St. Meinrad College
St. Meinrad, IN 47577
Taylor University
Upland, IN 46989
Tri-State University
Angola, IN 46703
University of Evansville
Evansville, IN 47702
University of Notre Dame
Notre Dame, IN 46556
Valparaiso Technical Institute
Valparaiso, IN 46383
Valparaiso University
Valparaiso, IN 46383
Wabash College
Crawfordsville, IN 47933

IOWA

Briar Cliff College
Sioux City, IA 51104
Buena Vista College
Storm Lake, IA 50588
Central College
Pella, IA 50219
Clarke College
Dubuque, IA 52001
Coe College
Cedar Rapids, IA 51402
Cornell College
Mount Vernon, IA 52314
Divine Word College
Epworth, IA 52045
Dordt College
Sioux Center, IA 51250
Drake University
Des Moines, IA 50311

Faith Baptist Bible College
Ankeny, IA 50021
Graceland College
Lamoni, IA 50140
Grand View College
Des Moines, IA 50316
Grinnell College
Grinnell, IA 50112
Iowa Wesleyan College
Mt. Pleasant, IA 52641
Loras College
Dubuque, IA 52001
Luther College
Decorah, IA 52101
Meharishi International University
Fairfield, IA 52556
Marycrest College
Davenport, IA 52804
Morningside College
Sioux City, IA 51106
Mount Mercy College
Cedar Rapids, IA 52402
Mount St. Clare College
Clinton, IA 52732
Northwestern College
Orange City, IA 51041
Open Bible College
Des Moines, IA 50321
Simpson College
Indianola, IA 50125
St. Ambrose College
Davenport, IA 52803
St. Joseph Seminary College
St. Benedict, IA 70457
University of Dubuque
Dubuque, IA 52001
Upper Iowa University
Fayette, IA 52142
Vennard College
University Park, IA 52595
Wartburg College
Waverly, IA 50677
Westmar College
Le Mars, IA 51031
William Penn College
Oskaloosa, IA 52577

Kansas

Baker University
Baldwin City, KS 66006
Benedictine College
Atchison, KS 66002
Bethany College
Lindsborg, KS 67456
Bethel College
North Newton, KS 67114
Friends Bible College
Haviland, KS 67059
Friends University
Wichita, KS 67213
Kansas City College and Bible School
Overland Park, KS 66204
Kansas Newman College
Wichita, KS 67213
Kansas Weselyan
Salina, KS 67401
Manhattan Christian College
Manhattan, KS 66502
Marymount College of Kansas
Salina, KS 67401
McPherson College
McPherson, KS 67460
Mid-America Nazarene College
Olathe, KS 66061
St. Mary College
Leavenworth, KS 66048
Ottawa University
Ottawa, KS 66067
Southwestern College
Winfield, KS 67156
Sterling College
Sterling, KS 67579
St. Mary of the Plains College
Dodge City, KS 67801
Tabor College
Hillsboro, KS 67063
Washburn University of Topeka
Topeka, KS 66621

Kentucky

Ashbury College
Wilmore, KY 40390
Bellarmine College
Louisville, KY 40205
Berea College
Berea, KY 40404
Brescia College
Owensboro, KY 42301
Campbellsville College
Campbellsville, KY 42718
Centre College of Kentucky
Danville, KY 40422
Cumberland College
Williamsburg, KY 40769
Georgetown College
Georgetown, KY 40324
Kentucky Christian College
Grayson, KY 41143
Kentucky Wesleyan College
Owensboro, KY 42301
Lexington Baptist College
Lexington, KY 40502
Louisville School of Art
Louisville, KY 40204
Morehead State University
Morehead, KY 40351
Pikeville College
Pikeville, KY 41501
Seminary of St. Pius X
Erlanger, KY 41018
Simmons University Bible College
Louisville, KY 40210
Spalding College
Louisville, KY 40203
Thomas More College
Fort Mitchell, KY 41017
Transylvania University
Lexington, KY 40508
Union College
Barbourville, KY 40906

Louisiana

Baptist Christian College
Shreveport, LA 71108
Centenary College of Louisiana
Shreveport, LA 71104
Dillard College
New Orleans, LA 70122
Louisiana College
Pineville, LA 71360
Loyola University
New Orleans, LA 70118
Our Lady of Holy Cross College
New Orleans, LA 70114
St. Mary's Dominican College
New Orleans, LA 70114
Tulane University
New Orleans, LA 70118
Xavier University of Louisiana
New Orleans, LA 70125

Maine

Bates College
Lewiston, ME 04240
Bowdoin College
Brunswick, ME 04011
Colby College
Waterville, ME 04901
College of the Atlantic
Bar Harbor, ME 04609
Husson College
Bangor, ME 04401
Nasson College
Springvale, ME 04083
New England Baptist Bible College
Portland, ME 04101
Portland School of Art
Portland, ME 04101
St. Joseph's College
North Windham, ME 04062
Thomas College
Waterville, ME 04901
Unity College
Unity, ME 04988
University of New England— St. Francis College
Biddleford, ME 04005
Westbrook College
Portland, ME 04103

Maryland

Baltimore Hebrew College
Baltimore, MD 21215
Capitol Institute of Technology
Kensington, MD 20795
College of Notre Dame of Maryland
Baltimore, MD 21210
Columbia Union College
Takoma Park, MD 20012
Goucher College
Towson, MD 21204
Hood College
Frederick, MD 21701
Johns Hopkins University
Baltimore, MD 21218
Loyola College
Baltimore, MD 21210
Maryland Institute of College of Art
Baltimore, MD 21217
Mount Saint Mary's College
Emmitsburg, MD 21727
Peabody Conservatory of Music
Baltimore, MD 21202
St. John's College
Annapolis, MD 21404
St. Mary's Seminary and College
Baltimore, MD 21210
Washington Bible College
Lanham, MD 20801
Washington College
Chestertown, MD 21620
Western Maryland College
Westminster, MD 21157

Massachusetts

American International College
Springfield, MA 01109
Amherst College
Amherst, MA 01102
Anna Maria College
Paxton, MA 01612
Assumption College
Worcester, MA 01609
Atlantic Union College
South Lancaster, MA 01561

Babson College
Wellesley, MA 02157
Bentley College
Waltham, MA 02154
Berklee College of Music
Boston, MA 02215
Berkshire Christian College
Lenox, MA 01240
Boston College
Chestnut Hill, MA 02167
Boston Conservatory of Music
Boston, MA 02115
Boston University
Boston, MA 02215
Bradford College
Bradford, MA 01830
Brandeis University
Waltham, MA 02254
Central New England College of Technology
Worcester, MA 01610
Clark University
Worcester, MA 01610
College of Our Lady of the Elms
Chicopee, MA 01013
College of the Holy Cross
Worcester, MA 01610
Curry College
Milton, MA 02186
Eastern Nazarene College
Quincy, MA 02170
Emerson College
Boston, MA 02116
Emmanuel College
Boston, MA 02115
Gordon College
Wenham, MA 01984
Hampshire College
Amherst, MA 01002
Harvard and Radcliffe Colleges
Cambridge, MA 02138
Hebrew College
Brookline, MA 02146
Hellenic College
Brookline, MA 02146
Lesley College
Cambridge, MA 02238
Massachusetts College of Pharmacy and Allied Health Sciences—Hampden
Springfield, MA 01119
Massachusetts Institute of Technology
Cambridge, MA 02139
Merrimack College
North Andover, MA 01845
Mount Holyoke College
South Hadley, MA 01075
New England Conservatory of Music
Boston, MA 02115
Nichols College
Dudley, MA 01570
Northeastern University
Boston, MA 02115
Pine Manor College
Chestnut Hill, MA 02167
Regis College
Weston, MA 02193
School of the Museum of Fine Arts/ Affiliated with Tufts University
Boston, MA 02115
Simmons College
Boston, MA 02115
Simon's Rock Early College of Bard College
Great Barrington, MA 01230
Smith College
Northampton, MA 01063
Springfield College
Springfield, MA 01109
St. Hyacinth College and Seminary
Granby, MA 01033
St. John's Seminary College of Liberal Arts
Brighton, MA 02135
Stonehill College
North Easton, MA 02356
Suffolk University
Boston, MA 02114
Swain School of Design
New Bedford, MA 02740
Tufts University
Medford, MA 02155
Wellesley College
Wellesley, MA 02181
Wentworth Institute of Technology
Boston, MA 02115
Western New England College
Springfield, MA 01119
Wheaton College
Norton, MA 02766
Wheelock College
Boston, MA 02215
Williams College
Williamstown, MA 01267
Worcester Polytechnic Institute
Worcester, MA 01503

MICHIGAN

Adrian College
Adrian, MI 49221
Albion College
Albion, MI 49224
Alma College
Alma, MI 48801
Andrews University
Berrien Springs, MI 49104
Aquinas College
Grand Rapids, MI 49506
Calvin College
Grand Rapids, MI 49506
Center for Creative Studies—College of Art and Design
Detroit, MI 48202
Cleary College
Ypsilanti, MI 48197
Condordia College
Ann Arbor, MI 48105
Detroit College of Business
Dearborn, MI 48126
General Motors Institute
Flint, MI 48502
Grace Bible College
Grand Rapids, MI 49509
Grand Rapids Baptist College
Grand Rapids, MI 49505
Great Lakes Bible College
Lansing, MI 48901
Hillsdale College
Hillsdale, MI 49242
Hope College
Holland, MI 49423
Jordan College
Cedar Springs, MI 49319
Kalamazoo College
Kalamazoo, MI 49007
Kendall School of Design
Grand Rapids, MI 49503
Lawrence Institute of Technology
Southfield, MI 48075
Madonna College
Livonia, MI 48150
Marygrove College
Detroit, MI 48221
Mercy College of Detroit
Detroit, MI 48219
Nazareth College
Nazareth, MI 49074
Northwood Institute
Midland, MI 48640
Olivet College
Olivet, MI 49076
Reformed Bible College
Grand Rapids, MI 49506
Shaw College of Detroit
Detroit, MI 48202
Sacred Heart Seminary
Detroit, MI 48206
Siena Heights College
Adrian, MI 49221
Spring Arbor College
Spring Arbor, MI 49283
St. Mary's College
Orchard Lake, MI 48033
University of Detroit
Detroit, MI 48221
Walsh College of Accountancy and Business Administration
Troy, MI 48084
William Tyndale College
Farmington Hills, MI 48018

MINNESOTA

Augsburg College
Minneapolis, MN 55454
Bethel College
St. Paul, MN 55112
Carleton College
Northfield, MN 55057
College of St. Benedict
St. Joseph, MN 56374
College of St. Catherine
St. Paul, MN 55105
College of St. Scholastica
Duluth, MN 55811
College of St. Teresa
Winona, MN 55897
College of St. Thomas
St. Paul, MN 55105
Condordia College
Moorhead, MN 56560
Concordia College
St. Paul, MN 55104
Dr. Martin Luther College
New Ulm, MN 56073
Gustavus Adolphus College
St. Peter, MN 56082
Hamline University
St. Paul, MN 55104
Macalester College
St. Paul, MN 55105
Minneapolis College of Art and Design
Minneapolis, MN 55404
Minneapolis Bible College
Rochester, MN 55901
North Central Bible College
Minneapolis, MN 55404
Northwestern College
Roseville, MN 55113
Pillsbury Baptist College
Owatonna, MN 55060
St. John's University
Collegeville, MN 56321
St. Mary's College
Winona, MN 55987
St. Olaf College
Northfield, MN 55057

St. Paul Bible College
Bible College, MN 55375

MISSISSIPPI

Belhaven College
Jackson, MS 39202
Blue Mountain College
Blue Mountain, MS 38610
Millsap College
Jackson, MS 39210
Mississippi College
Clinton, MS 39058
Mississippi Industrial College
Holly Springs, MS 38635
Rust College
Holly Springs, MS 38635
Southeastern Baptist College
Laurel, MS 39440
Tougaloo College
Tougaloo, MS 39174
Wesley College
Florence, MS 39073
Whitworth Bible College
Brookhaven, MS 39601
William Carey College
Hattiesburg, MS 39401

MISSOURI

Avila College
Kansas City, MO 64145
Baptist Bible College
Springfield, MO 65803
Calvary Bible College
Kansas City, MO 64147
Cardinal Glennon College
St. Louis, MO 63119
Central Bible College
Springfield, MO 65807
Central Christian College of the Bible
Moberly, MO 65270
Central Methodist College
Fayette, MO 65248
Columbia College
Columbia, MO 65216
Conception Seminary College
Conception, MO 64433
Culver-Stockton College
Canton, MO 63435
Drury College
Springfield, MO 65802
Evangel College
Springfield, MO 65802
Finlay Engineering College
Kansas City, MO 64114
Fontbonne College
St. Louis, MO 63105
Hannibal-Le Grange College
Hannibal, MO 63401
Harris Stowe State College
St. Louis, MO 63103
Kansas City Art Institute
Kansas City, MO 64111
Lincoln University
Jefferson City, MO 65101
Lindenwood Colleges
St. Charles, MO 63301
Maryville College—St. Louis
St. Louis, MO 63141
Missouri Baptist College
St. Louis, MO 63141
Missouri Institute of Technology
Kansas City, MO 64114
Missouri Valley College
Marshall, MO 65340
Ozark Bible College
Joplin, MO 64801
Park College
Kansas City, MO 64152
Rockhurst College
Kansas City, MO 64110
School of the Ozarks
Point Lookout, MO 65726
Southwest Baptist College
Bolivar, MO 65613
Stephens College
Columbia, MO 65215
St. Louis Christian College
Florissant, MO 63033
St. Louis College of Pharmacy
St. Louis, MO 63110
St. Louis Conservatory of Music
St. Louis, MO 63130
St. Louis University
St. Louis, MO 63103
Tarkio College
Tarkio, MO 64491
Washington University
St. Louis, MO 63130
Webster College
St. Louis, MO 63119
Westminster College
Fulton, MO 65251
William Jewell College
Liberty, MO 64068
William Woods College
Fulton, MO 65251

MONTANA

Big Sky Bible College
Lewiston, MT 59457
Carroll College
Helena, MT 59601
College of Great Falls
Great Falls, MT 59405
Rocky Mountain College
Billings, MT 59102

NEBRASKA

Bellevue College
Bellevue, NE 68005
College of St. Mary
Omaha, NE 68124
Concordia Teachers College
Seward, NE 68434
Creighton University
Omaha, NE 68178
Dana College
Blair, NE 68008
Doane College
Crete, NE 68333
Grace College of the Bible
Omaha, NE 68108
Hastings College
Hastings, NE 68901
Midland Lutheran College
Fremont, NE 68025
Nebraska Christian College
Norfolk, NE 68701
Nebraska Wesleyan University
Lincoln, NE 68504
Platte Valley Bible College
Scotts Bluff, NE 69361
Union College
Lincoln, NE 68506

NEVADA

Sierra Nevada College
Incline Valley, NV 89450

NEW HAMPSHIRE

Colby-Sawyer College
New London, NH 03257
Daniel Webster College
Nashua, NH 03063
Dartmouth College
Hanover, NH 03755
Franklin Pierce College
Rindge, NH 03461
Nathaniel Hawthorne College
Antrim, NH 03440
New England College
Henniker, NH 03242
New Hampshire College
Manchester, NH 03104
Notre Dame College
Manchester, NH 03104
River College
Mashua, NH 03060
St. Anselm College
Manchester, NH 03102

NEW JERSEY

Bloomfield College
Bloomfield, NJ 07003
Centenary College
Hackettstown, NJ 07840
College of St. Elizabeth
Convent Station, NJ 07961
Don Bosco College
Newton, NJ 07860
Drew University—College of Liberal Arts
Madison, NJ 07940
Fairleigh Dickinson University—Madison
Madison, NJ 07940
Fairleigh Dickinson University—Rutherford
Rutherford, NJ 07666
Fairleigh Dickinson University—Teaneck
Teaneck, NJ 07666
Felician College
Lodi, NJ 07644
Georgian Court College
Lakewood, NJ 08701
Kean College of New Jersey
Union, NJ 07083
Monmouth College
West Long Branch, NJ 07764
Northeastern Bible College
Essex Fells, NJ 07012
Princeton University
Princeton, NJ 08544
Rabbinical College of America
Morristown, NJ 07960
Ramapo College of New Jersey
Rahway, NJ 07430
Rider College
Lawrenceville, NJ 08648
Seton Hall University
South Orange, NJ 07079
Stevens Institute of Technology
Hoboken, NJ 07030
St. Peter's College
Jersey City, NJ 07306
Thomas A. Edison College
Trenton, NJ 08625
Upsala College
East Orange, NJ 07019
Westminster Choir College
Princeton, NJ 08540

NEW MEXICO

College of Santa Fe
Santa Fe, NM 87501
College of the Southwest
Hobbs, NM 88240

National College of Business—Albuquerque
Albuquerque, NM 87108
St. John's College
Santa Fe, NM 87501
University of Albuquerque
Albuquerque, NM 87140

New York

Adelphi University
Garden City, NY 11530
Albany College of Pharmacy
Albany, NY 12208
Alfred University
Alfred, NY 14802
American University in Cairo
New York, NY 10017
Bard College
Annandale-on-Hudson, NY 12504
Barnard College of Columbia University
New York, NY 10027
Boricus College
New York, NY 10025
Canisius College
Buffalo, NY 14208
Cathedral College of the Immaculate Conception
Douglaston, NY 11362
Clarkson College
Potsdam, NY 13676
Colgate University
Hamilton, NY 13346
College of Human Services
New York, NY 10016
College of Insurance
New York, NY 10038
College of Mount St. Vincent
New York, NY 10471
College of New Rochelle—School of Arts and Sciences
New Rochelle, NY 10801
College of St. Rose
Albany, NY 12203
Columbia University—Columbia College
New York, NY 10027
Concordia College
Bronxville, NY 10708
Cooper Union
New York, NY 10003
Cornell University
Ithaca, NY 14850
Daemen College
Amherst, NY 14226
Dominican College of Blauvelt
Orangeburg, NY 10962
Dowling College
Oakdale, NY 11769
D'Youville College
Buffalo, NY 14201
Eisenhower College of Rochester Institute of Technology
Seneca Falls, NY 13148
Elmira College
Elmira, NY 14901
Fordham University—Lincoln Center
New York, NY 10023
Fordham University—Rose Hill
Bronx, NY 10458
Friends World College
Huntington, NY 11743
Hamilton College
Clinton, NY 13323
Hartwick College
Oneonta, NY 13820
Hebrew Union College
New York, NY 10023
Hobart College
Geneva, NY 14456
Hofstra University
Hempstead, NY 11550
Holy Trinity Orthodox Seminary
Jordanville, NY 13361
Houghton College
Houghton, NY 14744
Iona College
New Rochelle, NY 10801
Ithaca College
Ithaca, NY 14850
Jewish Theological Seminary of America
New York, NY 10027
Julliard School
New York, NY 10023
Keuka College
Keuka Park, NY 14478
Le Moyne College
Syracuse, NY 13224
Long Island University—Brooklyn
Brooklyn, NY 11201
Long Island University—College of Pharmacy/Health Sciences
Brooklyn, NY 11201
Long Island University—C.W. Post College
Greenvale, NY 11548
Long Island University—Southhampton College
Southhampton, NY 11968
Manhattan College
Riverdale, NY 10471
Manhattanville College
Purchase, NY 10577
Mannes College of Music
New York, NY 10021
Marist College
Poughkeepsie, NY 12601
Marymount College
Tarrytown, NY 10591
Marymount Manhattan College
New York, NY 10021
Medaille College
Buffalo, NY 14214
Mercy College
Dobbs Ferry, NY 10522
Molloy College
Rockville Centre, NY 11570
Mount Saint Mary College
Newburgh, NY 12550
Nazareth College of Rochester
Rochester, NY 14610
New School of Social Research
New York, NY 10011
New York Institute of Technology
Old Westbury, NY 11568
New York Institute of Technology—Metropolitan Center
New York, NY 10023
New York School of Interior Design
New York, NY 10022
New York University
New York, NY 10012
Niagara University
Niagara University, NY 14109
Nyack College
Nyack, NY 10960
Pace University
New York, NY 10038
Pace University—College of White Plains
White Plains, NY 10603
Pace University—Pleasant/Briarcliff
Pleasantville, NY 10570
Parsons School of Design
New York, NY 10011
Polytechnic Institute of New York
Brooklyn, NY 11201
Pratt Institute
Brooklyn, NY 11205
Rensselaer Polytechnic Institute
Troy, NY 12181
Roberts Wesleyan College
Rochester, NY 14624
Rochester Institute of Technology
Rochester, NY 14623
Russell Sage College
Troy, NY 12180
Sarah Lawrence College
Bronxville, NY 10708
School of Visual Arts
New York, NY 10010
Siena College
Loudonville, NY 12211
Skidmore College
Saratoga Springs, NY 12866
St. Bonaventure University
St. Bonaventure, NY 14778
St. Francis College
Brooklyn, NY 11201
St. John Fisher College
Rochester, NY 14618
St. John's University Jamaica/Queens/Staten Island
Jamaica, NY 11439
St. Joseph's College
Brooklyn, NY 11205
St. Joseph's College—Suffolk
Patchogue, NY 11772
St. Lawrence University
Canton, NY 13617
St. Thomas Aquinas College
Sparkill, NY 10968
Syracuse University
Syracuse, NY 13210
The King's College
Briarcliff Manor, NY 10510
Touro College
New York, NY 10036
University of Rochester
Rochester, NY 14627
Utica College of Syracuse University
Utica, NY 13421
Vassar College
Poughkeepsie, NY 12601
Wadhams Hall Seminary College
Ogdensburg, NY 13669
Wagner College
Staten Island, NY 10301
Webb Institute of Naval Architecture
Glen Cove, NY 11542
Wells College
Aurora, NY 13026
William Smith College
Geneva, NY 14456
Yeshiva College—Main Center
New York, NY 10033

North Carolina

Atlantic Christian College
Wilson, NC 27893
Barber-Scotia College
Concord, NC 28025
Belmont Abbey College
Belmont, NC 28012
Bennett College
Greensboro, NC 27420

Campbell University
Buies Creek, NC 27506
Catawba College
Salisbury, NC 28144
Duke University
Durham, NC 27706
Elon College
Elon College, NC 27244
Gardner-Webb College
Boiling Springs, NC 28017
Greensboro College
Greensboro, NC 27420
Guilford College
Greensboro, NC 27410
High Point College
High Point, NC 27262
Johnson C. Smith University
Charlotte, NC 28216
Lenoir-Rhyne College
Hickory, NC 28601
Livingstone College
Salisbury, NC 28144
Mars Hill College
Mars Hill, NC 28754
Meredith College
Raleigh, NC 27611
Methodist College
Fayetteville, NC 28301
North Carolina Wesleyan College
Rocky Mount, NC 27801
Pfeiffer College
Misenheimer, NC 28109
Piedmont Bible College
Winston-Salem, NC 27101
Queens College
Charlotte, NC 28274
Roanoke Bible College
Elizabeth City, NC 27909
Sacred Heart College
Belmont, NC 28012
Shaw University
Raleigh, NC 27611
St. Andrew's Presbyterian College
Laurinburg, NC 28352
St. Augustine's College
Raleigh, NC 27611
Wake Forest University
Winston-Salem, NC 27109
Warren Wilson College
Swannanoa, NC 28778
Winston-Salem Bible College
Winston-Salem, NC 27102

North Dakota

Jamestown College
Jamestown, ND 58401
Mary College
Bismark, ND 58501
Northwest Bible College
Minot, ND 58701
Trinity Bible Institute
Ellendale, ND 58436

Ohio

Allegheny Wesleyan College
Salem, OH 44460
Antioch College—Yellow Springs
Yellow Springs, OH 45387
Ashland College
Ashland, OH 44805
Baldwin-Wallace College
Berea, OH 44017
Bluffton College
Bluffton, OH 45817
Borromeo College of Ohio
Wickliffe, OH 44092
Capital University
Columbus, OH 43209
Case Western Reserve University
Cleveland, OH 44106
Cedarville College
Cedarville, OH 45314
Cincinnati Bible College
Cincinnati, OH 45204
Circleville Bible College
Circleville, OH 43113
Cleveland College of Jewish Studies
Beachwood, OH 44122
Cleveland Institute of Art
Cleveland, OH 44106
Cleveland Institute of Music
Cleveland, OH 44106
College of Mount St. Joseph on the Ohio
Mount St. Joseph, OH 45051
College of Wooster
Wooster, OH 44691
Columbus College of Art and Design
Columbus, OH 43215
Defiance College
Defiance, OH 43512
Denison University
Granville, OH 43023
Dyke College
Cleveland, OH 44114
Edgeclift College
Cincinnati, OH 45206
Findlay College
Findlay, OH 45840
Franklin University
Columbus, OH 43215
God's Bible School and College
Cincinnati, OH 45210
Heidelberg College
Tiffin, OH 44883
Hiram College
Hiram, OH 44234
John Carroll University
University Heights, OH 44118
Kenyon College
Gambler, OH 43022
Lake Erie College
Painesville, OH 44077
Malone College
Canton, OH 44709
Marietta College
Marietta, OH 45750
Mount Union College
Alliance, OH 44601
Mount Vernon Bible College
Mount Vernon, OH 43050
Mount Vernon Nazarene College
Mount Vernon, OH 43050
Muskingum College
New Concord, OH 43762
Notre Dame College
Cleveland, OH 44121
Oberlin College
Oberlin, OH 44074
Ohio Dominican College
Columbus, OH 43219
Ohio Institute of Technology
Columbus, OH 43209
Ohio Northern University
Ada, OH 45810
Ohio Wesleyan University
Delaware, OH 43015
Otterbein College
Westerville, OH 43081
Pontifical College Josephinum
Columbus, OH 43085
Rio Grande College/Community College
Rio Grande, OH 45674
Tiffin University
Tiffin, OH 44883
Union for Experimenting Colleges and University
Cincinnati, OH 45202
University of Dayton
Dayton, OH 45469
University of Steubenville
Steubenville, OH 43952
Urbana College
Urbana, OH 43078
Ursuline College
Pepper Pike, OH 44124
Walsh College
Canton, OH 44720
Wilberforce University
Wilberforce, OH 45384
Wilmington College of Ohio
Wilmington, OH 45177
Wittenberg University
Springfield, OH 45501
Xavier University
Cincinnati, OH 45207

Oklahoma

Bartlesville Wesleyan College
Bartlesville, OK 74003
Bethany Nazarene College
Bethany, OK 73008
Cameron University
Lawton, OK 73505
Flaming Rainbow University
Stillwell, OK 74960
Hillsdale Free Will Baptist College
Moore, OK 73153
Langston University
Langston, OK 73050
Midwest Christian College
Oklahoma City, OK 73111
Oklahoma Baptist University
Shawnee, OK 74801
Oklahoma Christian College
Oklahoma City, OK 73111
Oklahoma City University
Oklahoma City, OK 73106
Oklahoma Southwestern College
Oklahoma City, OK 73127
Oral Roberts University
Tulsa, OK 74171
Phillipe University
Enid, OK 73701
University of Tulsa
Tulsa, OK 74104

Oregon

Colegio Cesar Chavez
Mount Angel, OR 97362
Columbia Christian College
Portland, OR 97200
Concordia College
Portland, OR 97211
Eugene Bible College
Eugene, OR 97405
George Fox College
Newberg, OR 97132
Lewis and Clark College
Portland, OR 97219
Linfield College
McMinnville, OR 97128
Marylhurst College for Lifelong Learning
Marylhurst, OR 97036

Mount Angel Seminary
St. Benedict, OR 97373
Multnomah School of the Bible
Portland, OR 97220
Museum Art School
Portland, OR 97205
Northwest Christian College
Eugene, OR 97401
Pacific University
Forest Grove, OR 97116
Reed College
Portland, OR 97202
University of Portland
Portland, OR 97203
Warner Pacific College
Portland, OR 97215
Western Baptist College
Salem, OR 97302
Willamette University
Salem, OR 97301

Pennsylvania

Albright College
Reading, PA 19603
Allegheny College
Meadville, PA 16335
Allentown College of St. Francis De Sales
Center Valley, PA 18034
Alliance College
Cambridge Springs, PA 16403
Alvernia College
Reading, PA 19607
Antioch University—Philadelphia
Philadelphia, PA 19108
Baptist College of Pennsylvania
Clarks Summit, PA 18411
Beaver College
Glenside, PA 19038
Bryn Mawr College
Bryn Mawr, PA 19010
Bucknell University
Lewisburg, PA 17837
Carlow College
Pittsburgh, PA 15213
Carnegie-Mellon University
Pittsburgh, PA 15213
Cedar Crest College
Allentown, PA 18104
Chatham College
Pittsburgh, PA 15232
Chestnut Hill College
Philadelphia, PA 19118
College Misericordia
Dallas, PA 18612
College of the Academy New Church
Bryn Athyn, PA 19009
Combs College of Music
Philadelphia, PA 19119
Curtis Institute of Music
Philadelphia, PA 19103
Delaware Valley College of Science and Agriculture
Doylestown, PA 18901
Dickinson College
Carlisle, PA 17013
Drexel University
Philadelphia, PA 19104
Duquesne University
Pittsburgh, PA 15219
Eastern College
St. Davids, PA 19087
Elizabethtown College
Elizabethtown, PA 17022
Franklin and Marshall College
Lancaster, PA 17604
Gannon University
Erie, PA 16541
Geneva College
Beaver Falls, PA 15010
Gettysburg College
Gettysburg, PA 17325
Gratz College
Philadelphia, PA 19141
Gwynedd-Mercy College
Gwynedd Valley, PA 19437
Hahnemann College of Allied Health Professions
Philadelphia, PA 19102
Haverford College
Haverford, PA 19041
Holy Family College
Philadelphia, PA 19114
Immaculate College
Immaculate, PA 19345
Juniata College
Huntingdon, PA 16652
King's College
Wilkes Barre, PA 18711
Lafayette College
Easton, PA 18042
Lancaster Bible College
Lancaster, PA 17601
La Roche College
Pittsburgh, PA 15237
La Salle College
Philadelphia, PA 19141
Lebanon Valley College
Annville, PA 17003
Lehigh University
Bethlehem, PA 18015
Lincoln University
Lincoln University, PA 19352
Lycoming College
Williamsport, PA 17701
Marywood College
Scranton, PA 18509
Mercyhurst College
Erie, PA 16546
Messiah College
Grantham, PA 17027
Moore College of Art
Philadelphia, PA 19103
Moravian College
Bethlehem, PA 18018
Muhlenberg College
Allentown, PA 18104
Neumann College
Aston, PA 19014
New School of Music
Philadelphia, PA 19103
Philadelphia College of Art
Philadelphia, PA 19102
Philadelphia College of Bible
Langhorne, PA 19047
Philadelphia College of Pharmacy and Science
Philadelphia, PA 19104
Philadelphia College of Textiles and Science
Philadelphia, PA 19144
Point Park College
Pittsburgh, PA 15222
Robert Morris College
Coraopolis, PA 15108
Rosemont College
Rosemont, PA 19010
Seton Hill College
Greensburg, PA 15601
Spring Garden College
Chestnut Hill, PA 19118
St. Francis College
Loretto, PA 15940
St. Joseph's University
Philadelphia, PA 19131
St. Vincent College
Latrobe, PA 15650
Susquehanna University
Selinsgrove, PA 17870
Swarthmore College
Swarthmore, PA 19081
Thiel College
Greenville, PA 16125
Thomas Jefferson University College of Allied Health Sciences
Philadelphia, PA 19107
United Wesleyan College
Allentown, PA 18103
University of Pennsylvania
Philadelphia, PA 19104
University of Pittsburgh
Pittsburgh, PA 15620
University of Pittsburgh—Bradford
Bradford, PA 16701
University of Pittsburgh—Greensburg
Greensburg, PA 15601
University of Pittsburgh—Johnstown
Johnstown, PA 15904
University of Scranton
Scranton, PA 18510
Ursinus College
Collegeville, PA 19426
Valley Forge Christian College
Phoenixville, PA 19460
Villa Maria College
Erie, PA 16505
Villanova University
Villanova, PA 16505
Washington and Jefferson College
Washington, PA 15301
Waynesburg College
Waynesburg, PA 15370
Westminster College
New Wilmington, PA 16142
Widener College
Chester, PA 10913
Wilkes College
Wilkes-Barre, PA 18766
Wilson College
Chambersburg, PA 17201
York College of Pennsylvania
York, PA 17405

Rhode Island

Barrington College
Barrington, RI 02806
Brown University
Providence, RI 02912
Bryant College
Smithfield, RI 02917
Johnson and Wales College
Providence, RI 02903
Newport College—Salve Regina
Newport, RI 02840
Providence College
Providence, RI 02918
Rhode Island School of Design
Providence, RI 02903
Roger Williams College
Bristol, RI 02809
Roger Williams College—Providence
Providence, RI 02809

South Carolina

Allen University
Columbia, SC 29204

Baptist College at Charleston
Charleston, SC 29411
Benedict College
Columbia, SC 29204
Bob Jones University
Greenville, SC 29614
Central Wesleyan College
Central, SC 29630
Claflin College
Orangeburg, SC 29115
Coker College
Hartsville, SC 29550
Columbia Bible College
Columbia, SC 29230
Columbia College
Columbia, SC 29203
Converse College
Spartanburg, SC 29301
Erskine College
Due West, SC 29639
Friendship College
Rock Hill, SC 29730
Furman University
Greenville, SC 29163
Lander College
Greenwood, SC 29646
Limestone College
Gaffney, SC 29340
Morris College
Sumter, SC 29150
Newberry College
Newberry, SC 29108
Presbyterian College
Clinton, SC 29325
Southern Methodist College
Orangeburg, SC 29115
Voorhees College
Denmark, SC 29042
Wofford College
Spartanburg, SC 29301

South Dakota

Augustana College
Sioux Falls, SD 57197
Dakota Wesleyan University
Mitchell, SD 57301
Huron College
Huron, SD 57350
Mount Marty College
Yankton, SD 57078
National College of Business
Rapid City, SD 57709
Sinte Gleska College
Rosebud, SD 57570
Sioux Falls College
Sioux Falls, SD 57101
Yankton College
Yankton, SD 57078

Tennessee

American Baptist College
Nashville, TN 37207
Belmont College
Nashville, TN 37203
Bethel College
McKenzie, TN 38201
Bristol College
Bristol, TN 37620
Bryan College
Dayton, TN 37321
Carson-Newman College
Jefferson City, TN 37760
Christian Brothers College
Memphis, TN 38104
Covenant College
Lookout Mountain, TN 37350
David Lipscomb College
Nashville, TN 37203
Fisk University
Nashville, TN 37203
Freed-Hardeman College
Henderson, TN 38340
Free Will Baptist Bible College
Nashville, TN 37205
Johnson Bible College
Knoxville, TN 37920
Lee College
Cleveland, TN 37311
King College
Bristol, TN 37620
Knoxville College
Knoxville, TN 37921
Lambuth College
Jackson, TN 38301
Lane College
Jackson, TN 38301
Le Moyne-Owen College
Memphis, TN 38126
Lincoln Memorial University
Harrogate, TN 37752
Maryville College
Maryville, TN 37801
Memphis Academy of Arts
Memphis, TN 38112
Mid-South Bible College
Memphis, TN 38112
Milligan College
Milligan College, TN 37682
O'More College of Design
Franklin, TN 37604
Southern Missionary College
Collegedale, TN 37315
Southwestern—Memphis
Memphis, TN 38112
Steed College
Johnson City, TN 37601
Tennessee Temple University
Chattanooga, TN 37404
Tennessee Wesleyan College
Athens, TN 37303
Trevecca Nazarene College
Nashville, TN 37210
Tusculum College
Greeneville, TN 37743
Union University
Jackson, TN 38301
University of the South
Sewanee, TN 37375
Vanderbilt University
Nashville, TN 37212

Texas

Abilene Christian University
Abilene, TX 79601
Abilene Christian University—Dallas
Garland, TX 75041
American Technological University
Killeen, TX 76541
Arlington Baptist College
Arlington, TX 76012
Austin College
Sherman, TX 75090
Baylor College of Medicine
Houston, TX 77025
Baylor University
Waco, TX 76706
Bishop College
Dallas, TX 75241
Dallas Baptist College
Dallas, TX 75211
Dallas Bible College
Dallas, TX 75228
Dallas Christian College
Dallas, TX 75234
East Texas Baptist College
Marshall, TX 75670
Gulf Coast Bible College
Houston, TX 77008
Hardin-Simmons University
Abilene, TX 79601
Houston Baptist University
Houston, TX 77074
Howard Payne University
Brownwood, TX 76801
Huston-Tillotson College
Austin, TX 78702
Incarnate Word College
San Antonio, TX 78209
Jarvis Christian College
Hawkins, TX 75765
LeTourneau College (Le Tourneau Christian College)
Longview, TX 75602
Lubbock Christian College
Lubbock, TX 79407
McMurry College
Abilene, TX 79697
Our Lady of the Lake—University of San Antonio
San Antonio, TX 78285
Paul Quinn College
Waco, TX 76704
Rice University
Houston, TX 77001
Southern Bible College
Houston, TX 77015
Southern Methodist University
Dallas, TX 75275
Southwestern Adventist College
Keene, TX 76059
Southwestern Assemblies of God College
Waxahachie, TX 75165
Southwestern University
Georgetown, TX 78626
St. Edward's University
Austin, TX 78704
St. Mary's University of San Antonio
San Antonio, TX 78284
Texas Christian University
Fort Worth, TX 76129
Texas College
Tyler, TX 78155
Texas Lutheran College
Sequin, TX 78155
Texas Wesleyan College
Fort Worth, TX 76105
Trinity University
San Antonio, TX 78284
University of Dallas
Irving, TX 75061
University of Mary Hardin—Baylor
Belton, TX 76513
University of St. Thomas
Houston, TX 77006
Wayland Baptist College
Plainview, TX 79072
Wiley College
Marshall, TX 75670

Utah

Brigham Young University
Provo, UT 84602
Westminster College
Salt Lake City, UT 84105

Vermont

Bennington College
Bennington, VT 05201
Burlington College
Burlington, VT 05401
College of St. Joseph the Provider
Rutland, VT 05701
Goddard College
Plainfield, VT 05667
Green Mountain College
Poultney, VT 05764
Lyndon State College
Lyndonville, VT 05851
Marlboro College
Marlboro, VT 05344
Middlebury College
Middlebury, VT 05753
Norwick University
Northfield, VT 05663
School for International Training
Battleboro, VT 05301
St. Michael's College
Winooski, VT 05405
Trinity College
Burlington, VT 05401
Vermont College of Norwick University
Montpelier, VT 05602

Virginia

Averett College
Danville, VA 24541
Bluefield College
Bluefield, VA 24605
Bridgewater College
Bridgewater, VA 22812
Eastern Mennonite College
Harrisonburg, VA 22801
Emory and Henry College
Emory, VA 24327
Ferrum College
Ferrum, VA 24088
Hampden-Sydney College
Hampden-Sydney, VA 23943
Hampton Institute
Hampton, VA 23668
Hollins College
Hollins College, VA 24020
Liberty Baptist College
Lynchburg, VA 24506
Longwood College
Farmsville, VA 23901
Lynchburg College
Lynchburg, VA 24501
Mary Baldwin College
Staunton, VA 24401
Marymount College of Virginia
Arlington, VA 22207
Mary Washington College
Fredericksburg, VA 22401
Radford University
Radford, VA 24142
Randolph-Macon College
Ashland, VA 23005
Randolph-Macon Women's College
Lynchburg, VA 24503
Roanoke College
Salem, VA 24153
Shenandoah College and Conservatory of Music
Winchester, VA 22601
St. Paul's College
Lawrenceville, VA 23868
Sweet Briar College
Sweet Briar, VA 24595
University of Richmond
Richmond, VA 23173
Virginia Commonwealth University
Richmond, VA 23284
Virginia Intermont College
Bristol, VA 24201
Virginia Union University
Richmond, VA 23222
Virginia Wesleyan College
Norfolk, VA 23502
Washington and Lee University
Lexington, VA 24450

Washington

Cornish Institute of Allied Arts
Seattle, WA 98102
Fort Wright College
Spokane, WA 99204
Gonzaga University
Spokane, WA 99258
Lutheran Bible Institute
Issaquah, WA 98027
Northwest College
Kirkland, WA 98033
Pacific Lutheran University
Tacoma, WA 98447
Puget Sound College of the Bible
Edmonds, WA 98020
Seattle Pacific University
Seattle, WA 98119
Seattle University
Seattle, WA 98122
St. Martin's College
Lacey, WA 98503
University of Puget Sound
Tacoma, WA 98416
Walla Walla College
College Place, WA 99324
Whitman College
Walla Walla, WA 99362
Whitworth College
Spokane, WA 99251

West Virginia

Alderson Broaddus College
Philippi, WV 26416
Appalachian Bible College
Bradley, WV 25818
Bethany College
Bethany, WV 26032
Davis and Elkins College
Elkins, WV 26241
Salem College
Salem, WV 26426
University of Charleston
Charleston, WV 25304
West Virginia Wesleyan College
Buckhannon, WV 26201
Wheeling College
Wheeling, WV 26003

Wisconsin

Alverno College
Milwaukee, WI 53215
Beloit College
Beloit, WI 53511
Cardinal Stritch College
Milwaukee, WI 53217
Carroll College
Waukesha, WI 53186
Carthage College
Kenosha, WI 53140
Concordia College
Milwaukee, WI 53208
Edgewood College
Madison, WI 53711
Holy Redeemer College
Waterford, WI 53185
Immanuel Lutheran College
Eau Clair, WI 54701
Lakeland College
Sheboygan, WI 53081
Lawrence University
Appleton, WI 54911
Marian College
Fon Du Lac, WI 54935
Marquette University
Milwaukee, WI 53233
Milton College
Milton, WI 53563
Milwaukee Institute of Art and Design
Milwaukee, WI 53211
Milwaukee School of Engineering
Milwaukee, WI 53201
Mount Mary College
Milwaukee, WI 53222
Mount Senario College
Ladysmith, WI 54848
Northland College
Ashland, WI 54806
Ripon College
Ripon, WI 54971
Silver Lake College
Manitowoc, WI 54220
St. Norbert College
De Pere, WI 54115
Viterbo College
La Crosse, WI 54601
Wisconsin Conservatory of Music
Milwaukee, WI 53202

France

American College in Paris 75007
Paris, France

England

New England College
Arundel, Sussex BN18 ODA, England
Richmond College
London W8 5PN, England
University of Warwick
Coventry CVA 7AL, England

West Germany

Schiller International University
6900
Heidelberg, West Germany

Greece

Deree College
Athens, Greece

Hong Kong

Hong Kong Baptist College
Kowloon, Hong Kong

Lebanon

American University of Beirut
Beirut, Lebanon

Mexico

University of the Americas
Puebla, Mexico

Puerto Rico

American College of Puerto Rico
Bayamon, PR 00619
Antillian College
Mayaguez, PR 00708

Catholic University of Puerto Rico
Ponce, PR 00731
Caribbean University College
Bayamon, PR 00618
Conservatory of Music of Puerto Rico
Hato Rey, PR 00918
Inter-American University of Puerto Rico—Arecibo Branch
Arecibo, PR 00612
Inter-American University of Puerto Rico—Metropolitan Campus
Hato Rey, PR 00919
Inter-American University—San German Regional College
San German, PR 00753
International Institute of the Americas of World University
Hato Rey, PR 00917
University of Sacred Heart
Santurce, PR 00924

SWITZERLAND

American College of Switzerland
1854
Leysin, Switzerland

Two-Year Public Colleges and Universities

ALABAMA

Alabama Aviation and Technical College
Ozark, AL 36360
Alabama State University
Montgomery, AL 36101
Alabama Technical College
Gadsden, AL 35903
Alexander City State Junior College
Alexander, AL 35010
Bessemer State Technical College
Bessemer, AL 35021
Brewer State Junior College
Fayette, AL 35555
C. A. Fredd State Technical College
Tuscaloosa, AL 34501
Calhoun State Community College
Decatur, AL 35602
Chattahoochee Valley Community College
Phenix City, AL 36867
Chauncey Sparks State Technical College
Eufaula, AL 36027
Community College of the Air Force
Montgomery, AL 36112
Douglas MacArthur State Technical College
Opp, AL 36467
Enterprise State Junior College
Enterprise, AL 36330
Faulkner State Junior College
Bay Minette, AL 36507
Gadsden State Junior College
Gadsden, AL 35903
George Corley Wallace State Community College
Selma, AL 36701
George C. Wallace State Community College
Dothan, AL 36301
George C. Wallace State Community College
Hanceville, AL 35077
Harper Council Trenholm State Technical College
Montgomery, AL 36108
Harry M. Ayers State Technical College
Anniston, AL 36202
Hobson State Technical College
Thomasville, AL 36784
James H. Faulkner State Junior College
Bay Minette, AL 36507
Jefferson Davis State Junior College
Brewton, AL 36426
Jefferson State Junior College
Birmingham, AL 35215
J.F. Drake State Technical College
Huntsville, AL 35811
John M. Patterson State Technical College
Montgomery, AL 36116
Lawson State Community College
Birmingham, AL 35221
Livingston University
Livingston, AL 35470
Lurleen B. Wallace State Junior College
Andalusia, AL 36420
Northeast Alabama State Junior College
Rainsville, AL 35986
Northwest Alabama State Junior College
Phil Campbell, AL 35581
Patrick Henry State Junior College
Monroeville, AL 36460
S. D. Bishop State Junior College
Mobile, AL 36603
Shelton State Community College
Tuscaloosa, AL 35401
Snead State Junior College
Boaz, AL 35957
Southern Union State Junior College
Wadley, AL 36276
Southern Vocational College
Tuskegee, AL 36083
Southwest State Technical College
Mobile, AL 36690
Tennessee Valley Center—Tuscumbia
Tuscumbia, AL 35674
Walker State Technical College
Sumitron, AL 35148

ALASKA

Anchorage Community College
Anchorage, AK 99504
Ketchikan Community College
Ketchikan, AK 99901
University of Alaska—Juneau
Juneau, AK 99803
University of Alaska—Kenal Peninsula Community College
Soldotna, AK 99669
University of Alaska—Kodiak Community College
Kodiak, AK 99615
University of Alaska—Kuskokwim Community College
Bethel, AK 99559
University of Alaska—Matanuska/Susitna Community College
Palmer, AK 99645
University of Alaska—Northwest Community College
Nome, AK 99762
University of Alaska—Sitka Community College
Sitka, AK 99835

ARIZONA

Arizona Western College
Yuma, AZ 85364
Central Arizona College
Coolidge, AZ 85228
Cochise College
Douglas, AZ 85607
Eastern Arizona College
Thatcher, AZ 85552
Glendale Community College
Glendale, AZ 85302
Maricopa Technical Community College
Phoenix, AZ 85004
Mesa Community College
Mesa, AZ 85202
Mohave Community College—Kingman
Kingman, AZ 86401
Northland Pioneer College
Holbrook, AZ 86025
Phoenix College
Phoenix, AZ 85013
Pima Community College
Tucson, AZ 85709
Scottsdale Community College
Scottsdale, AZ 85253
Yavapai College
Prescott, AZ 86301

ARKANSAS

Arkansas State University—Beebe
Beebe, AR 72012
East Arkansas Community College
Forrest City, AR 72335
Garland County Community College
Hot Springs, AR 71901
Mississippi County Community College
Blytheville, AR 72315
North Arkansas Community College
Harrison, AR 72601

Phillips County Community College
Helena, AR 72342
Southern Arkansas University—El Dorado
El Dorado, AR 71730
Southern Arkansas University—Technical Branch
Camden, AR 71701
University of Arkansas—Little Rock
Little Rock, AR 72204

California

Allan Hancock College
Santa Maria, CA 93454
American River College—Placerville
Placerville, CA 95667
American River College—Sacramento
Sacramento,CA 95841
Antelope Valley College
Lancaster, CA 93534
Bakersfield College
Bakersfield, CA 93305
Barstow College
Barstow, CA 92311
Butte Community College
Oroville, CA 95965
Canada College
Redwood City, CA 94061
Cerritos College
Norwalk, CA 90650
Cerro Coso Community College
Ridgecrest, CA 93555
Chabot College
Hayward, CA 94545
Chaffey College
Alta Loma, CA 91701
Citrus College
Azusa, CA 91702
City College of San Francisco
San Francisco, CA 94112
Coastline Community College
Fountain Valley, CA 92708
College of Alameda
Alameda, CA 94501
College of Marin
Kentfield, CA 94904
College of San Mateo
San Mateo, CA 94402
College of the Canyons
Valencia, CA 91355
College of the Desert
Palm Desert, CA 92260
College of the Redwoods
Eureka, CA 95501
College of the Sequoias
Visalia, CA 93277
College of the Siskiyous
Weed, CA 96094
Compton Community College
Compton, CA 90221
Contra Costa College
San Pablo, CA 94806
Consumnes River College
Sacramento, CA 95823
Crafton Hills College
Yucaipa, CA 92399
Cuesta College
San Luis Obispo, CA 93406
Cypress College
Cypress, CA 90630
De Anza College
Cupertino, CA 95014
Diablo Valley College
Pleasant Hill, CA 94523
East Los Angeles College
Monterey Park, CA 91754
El Camino College
Via Torrance, CA 90506
Evergreen Valley College
San Jose, CA 95135
Foothill College
Los Altos, CA 94022
Fresno City College
Fresno, CA 93741
Fullerton College
Fullerton, CA 92634
Gavilan Community College
Gilroy, CA 95020
Glendale Community College
Glendale, CA 91208
Golden West College
Huntington Beach, CA 92647
Grossmont College
El Cajon, CA 92020
Hartnell College
Salinas, CA 93901
Imperial Valley College
Imperial, CA 92251
Indian Valley Colleges
Novato, CA 94947
Lake Tahoe Community College
South Lake Tahoe, CA 95702
Laney College
Oakland, CA 94607
Lassen College
Susanville, CA 96130
Long Beach City College
Long Beach, CA 90808
Los Angeles City College
Los Angeles, CA 90029
Los Angeles Harbor College
Wilmington, CA 90744
Los Angeles Pierce College
Woodland Hills, CA 91371
Los Angeles Southwest College
Los Angeles, CA 90047
Los Angeles Trade—Technical College
Los Angeles, CA 90015
Los Angeles Valley College
Van Nuys, CA 91401
Mendocino College
Ukiah, CA 95482
Merced College
Merced, CA 95340
Merritt College
Oakland, CA 94619
Mira Costa College
Oceanside, CA 92054
Mission College
Santa Clara, CA 95054
Modesto Junior College
Modesto, CA 95350
Monterey Peninsula College
Monterey, CA 93940
Moorpark College
Moorpark, CA 93021
Mount San Antonio College
Walnut, CA 91789
Mount San Jacinto College
San Jacinto, CA 92383
Napa College
Napa, CA 94558
Orange Coast College
Costa Mesa, CA 92626
Oxnard College
Oxnard, CA 93033
Palomar College
San Marcos, CA 92069
Palo Verde College
Blythe, CA 92225
Pasadena City College
Pasadena, CA 91106
Porterville College
Porterville, CA 93257
Rio Hondo College
Whittier, CA 90608
Riverside City College
Riverside, CA 92506
Sacramento City College
Sacramento, CA 95822
San Bernardino Valley College
San Bernardino, CA 92403
San Diego Evening College
San Diego, CA 92108
San Diego Mesa College
San Diego, CA 92111
San Diego Miramar College
San Diego, CA 92126
San Joaquin Delta College
Stockton, CA 95207
San Jose City College
San Jose, CA 95128
Santa Ana College
Santa Ana, CA 92706
Santa Barbara City College
Santa Barbara, CA 93105
Santa Monica College
Santa Monica, CA 90405
Santa Rosa Junior College
Santa Rosa, CA 95401
Shasta College
Redding, CA 96001
Sierra College
Rocklin, CA 95677
Skyline College
San Bruno, CA 94066
Solano Community College
Suisun City, CA 94585
Southwestern College
Chula Vista, CA 92010
Taft College
Taft, CA 93268
Ventura College
Ventura, CA 93003
West Valley Community College
Saratoga, CA 95070

Colorado

Adams State College
Alamosa, CO 81102
Aims Community College
Greeley, CO 80631
Arapahoe Community College
Littleton, CO 80120
Colorado Mountain College—East
Leadville, CO 80461
Colorado Mountain College—West
Glenwood Springs, CO 81601
Colorado Northwestern Community College
Rangely, CO 81648
Community College of Denver—Auraria
Denver, CO 80204
Community College of Denver—North Campus
Westminster, CO 80030
Community College of Denver—Red Rocks
Golden, CO 80401
Fort Lewis College
Durango, CO 81301
Lamar Community College
Lamar, CO 81052
Mesa College
Grand Junction, CO 81501

Morgan Community College
Fort Morgan, CO 80701
Northeastern Junior College
Sterling, CO 80751
Pikes Peak Community College
Colorado Springs, CO 80916
Pueblo Vocational Community College
Pueblo, CO 81004
Trinidad State Junior College
Trinidad, CO 81081

CONNECTICUT

Asnuntuck Community College
Enfield, CT 06082
Eastern Connecticut State College
Willimantic, CT 06226
Greater Hartford Community College
Hartford, CT 06105
Greater New Haven State Technical College
North Haven, CT 06473
Hartford State Technical College
Hartford, CT 06106
Housatonic Community College
Bridgeport, CT 06608
Manchester Community College
Manchester, CT 06040
Mattatuck Community College
Waterbury, CT 06708
Middlesex Community College
Middletown, CT 06457
Mohegan Community College
Norwich, CT 06360
Northwestern Connecticut Community College
Winsted, CT 06098
Norwalk Community College
Norwalk, CT 06854
Norwalk State Technical College
Norwalk, CT 06611
Quinegaug Valley Community College
Danielson, CT 06329
South Central Community College
New Haven, CT 06511
Thames Valley State Technical College
Norwich, CT 06360
Tunxis Community College
Farmington, CT 06032

DELAWARE

Delaware Technical and Community College—Southern
Georgetown, DE 19947
Delaware Technical and Community College—Stanton
Newark, DE 19702
Delaware Technical and Community College—Terry
Dover, DE 19901
Delaware Technical and Community College—Wilmington
Wilmington, DE 19801

DISTRICT OF COLUMBIA

University of the District of Columbia
Washington, DC 20004

FLORIDA

Brevard Community College
Cocoa, FL 32922
Broward Community College
Fort Lauderdale, FL 33301
Central Florida Community College
Ocala, FL 32670
Chipola Junior College
Marianna, FL 32446
Daytona Beach Community College
Daytona Beach, FL 32015
Edison Community College
Fort Myers, FL 33907
Florida Junior College—Jacksonville
Jacksonville, FL 32202
Florida Keys Community College
Key West, FL 33040
Gulf Coast Community College
Panama City, FL 32401
Hillsborough Community College
Tampa, FL 33622
Indian River Community College
Fort Pierce, FL 33450
Lake City Community College
Lake City, FL 32055
Lake-Sumter Community College
Leesburg, FL 32748
Manatee Junior College
Bradenton, FL 33507
Miami-Dade Community College
Miami, FL 33176
Morris Junior College of Business
Melbourne, FL 32935
North Florida Junior College
Madison, FL 32340
Okaloosa—Walton Junior College
Niceville, FL 32578
Palm Beach Junior College
Lake Worth, FL 33461
Panama Canal College
Dodds, Panama, APO Miami, FL 34002
Pasco—Hernando Community College
Dade City, FL 33525
Pensacola Junior College
Pensacola, FL 32504
Polk Community College
Winter Haven, FL 33880
Sante Fe Community College
Gainesville, FL 32601
Seminole Community College
Sanford, FL 32771
South Florida Junior College
Avon Park, FL 33825
St. John's River Community College
Palatka, FL 32077
St. John's River Community College—Florida School of the Arts
Palatka, FL 32077
St. Petersburg Junior College
St. Petersburg, FL 33733
Tallahassee Community College
Tallahassee, FL 32304

GEORGIA

Abraham Baldwin Agricultural College
Tifton, GA 31794
Armstrong State College
Savannah, GA 31406
Augusta College
Augusta, GA 30910
Brunswick Junior College
Brunswick, GA 31520
Clayton Junior College
Morrow, GA 30260
Columbus College
Columbus, GA 31907
Dekalb Community College
Clarkston, GA 30021
Floyd Junior College
Rome, GA 30161
Georgia Military College
Milledgeville, GA 31061
Georgia State University
Atlanta, GA 30303
Gordon Junior College
Barnsville, GA 30204
Kennesaw College
Marietta, GA 30061
Macon Junior College
Macon, GA 31297
Middle Georgia College
Cochran, GA 31014
Southern Technical Institute
Marietta, GA 30060
South Georgia College
Douglas, GA 31533
Waycross Junior College
Waycross, GA 31501

HAWAII

Hawaii Pacific College
Honolulu, HI 96813
Honolulu Community College
Honolulu, HI 96817
Kapiolani Community College
Honolulu, HI 96814
Kauai Community College
Kauai, HI 96766
Leeward Community College
Pearl City, HI 96782
Maui Community College
Kahului, Maui, HI 96732
University of Hawaii at Hilo—Hawaii Community College
Hilo, HI 96720
University of Hawaii—Windward Community College
Kaneohe, HI 96744

IDAHO

Boise State University
Boise, ID 83725
College of Southern Idaho
Twin Falls, ID 83301
North Idaho College
Coeur D'Alene, ID 83814

ILLINOIS

Belleville Area College
Belleville, IL 62221
Black Hawk College—East
Kewanee, IL 61443
Black Hawk College—Quad—Cities
Moline, IL 61265
Carl Sandburg College
Galesburg, IL 61401
Chicago City College—Daley
Chicago, IL 60652
Chicago City College—Kennedy/King
Chicago, IL 60621
Chicago City College—Loop
Chicago, IL 60601
Chicago City College—Malcolm X
Chicago, IL 60612
Chicago City College—Truman
Chicago, IL 60640
Chicago City College—Wilbur Wright
Chicago, IL 60634
Chicago City-wide College
Chicago, IL 60601
College of Du Page
Glen Ellyn, IL 60137

College of Lake County
Grayslake, IL 60030
Danville Area Community College
Danville, IL 61832
Elgin Community College
Elgin, IL 60120
Highland Community College
Freeport, IL 61032
Illinois Central College
East Peoria, IL 61635
Illinois Eastern Community College—Frontier
Fairfield, IL 62837
Illinois Eastern Community College—Lincoln Trail
Robinson, IL 62454
Illinois Eastern Community College—Olney Central
Olney, IL 62450
Illinois Eastern Community College—Wabash Valley
Mount Carmel, IL 62863
Illinois Valley Community College
Oglesby, IL 61348
John A. Logan College
Carterville, IL 62918
Joliet Junior College
Joliet, IL 60436
Kankakee Community College
Kankakee, IL 60901
Kaskaskia College
Centralia, IL 62801
Kishwaukee College
Malta, IL 60150
Lake Land College
Mattoon, IL 61938
Lewis and Clark Community College
Godfrey, IL 62035
Lincoln Land Community College
Springfield, IL 62708
McHenry County College
Crystal Lake, IL 60014
Moraine Valley Community College
Palos Hills, IL 60465
Morrison Institute of Technology
Morrison, IL 61270
Morton College
Cicero, IL 60650
Oakton Community College
Des Plaines, IL 60016
Olive-Harvey City College of Chicago
Chicago, IL 60628
Parkland College
Champaign, IL 61820
Prairie State College
Chicago Heights, IL 60411
Rend Lake College
Ina, IL 62846
Richland Community College
Decatur, IL 62526
Rock Valley College
Rockford, IL 61101
Sauk Valley College
Dixon, IL 61021
Southeastern Illinois College
Harrisburg, IL 62946
Southern Illinois University—Carbondale School of Technical Careers
Carbondale, IL 62901
Spoon River College
Canton, IL 61520
State Community College of East St. Louis
East St. Louis, IL 62201
Thornton Community College
South Holland, IL 60473
Triton College
River Grove, IL 60171
Waubonsee Community College
Sugar Grove, IL 60554

Indiana

Clark College
Indianapolis, IN 46202
Indiana University—East
Richmond, IN 47374
Indiana University—Kokomo
Kokomo, IN 46901
Indiana University—Purdue University at Fort Wayne
Fort Wayne, IN 46805
Indiana University—Purdue University at Indianapolis
Indianapolis, IN 46202
Indiana University—Southeast
New Albany, IN 47150
Indiana Vocational Technical College—Columbus
Columbus, IN 47201
Indiana Vocational Technical College—Eastcentral
Muncie, IN 47302
Indiana Vocational Technical College—Fort Wayne
Fort Wayne, IN 46805
Indiana Vocational Technical College—Indianapolis
Indianapolis, IN 46202
Indiana Vocational Technical College—Kokomo
Kokomo, IN 46901
Indiana Vocational Technical College—Lafayette
Lafayette, IN 47904
Indiana Vocational Technical College—Northcentral
South Bend, IN 46619
Indiana Vocational Technical College—Northwest
Gary, IN 46409
Indiana Vocational Technical College—Southcentral
Sellersburg, IN 47172
Indiana Vocational Technical College—Southeast
Madison, IN 47250
Indiana Vocational Technical College—Southwest
Evansville, IN 47710
Indiana Vocational Technical College—Terre Haute
Terre Haute, IN 47802
Indiana Vocational Technical College—Whitewater
Richmond, IN 47374
Purdue University
West Lafayette, IN 47907
Purdue University—Calumet
Hammond, IN 46323
Purdue University—North Central
Westville, IN 46391

Iowa

Clinton Community College
Clinton, IA 52732
Des Moines Area Community College—Ankeny
Ankeny, IA 50021
Des Moines Area Community College—Boone
Boone, IA 50036
Ellsworth Community College
Iowa Falls, IA 50126
Hawkeye Institute of Technology
Waterloo, IA 50704
Indian Hills Community Center—Centerville
Centerville, IA 52544
Indian Hills Community College—Airport
Otumwa, IA 52501
Indian Hills Community College—Ottumwa Heights
Ottumwa, IA 52501
Iowa Central Community College
Fort Dodge, IA 50533
Iowa Lakes Community College—Estherville
Estherville, IA 51334
Iowa Lakes Community College—South
Emmetsburg, IA 50536
Iowa Western Community College
Council Bluffs, IA 51501
Iowa Western Community College—Clarinda
Clarinda, IA 51632
Kirkwood Community College
Cedar Rapids, IA 52406
Marshalltown Community College
Marshalltown, IA 50158
Muscatine Community College
Muscatine, IA 52761
Northeast Iowa Technical Institute
Calmar, IA 52132
North Iowa Area Community College
Mason City, IA 50401
Northwest Iowa Technical College
Sheldon, IA 51201
Scott Community College
Bettendorf, IA 52722
Scott Community College—Palmer Campus
Bettendorf, IA 52722
Southeastern Community College—North
West Burlington, IA 52655
Southeastern Community College—South
Keokuk, IA 52632
Southwestern Community College
Creston, IA 50801

Kansas

Allen County Community Junior College
Iola, KS 66749
Barton County Community College
Great Bend, KS 67530
Butler County Community College
El Dorado, KS 67042
Cloud County Community College
Concordia, KS 66901
Coffeyville Community College
Coffeyville, KS 67337
Colby Community College
Colby, KS 67701
Cowley County Community College
Arkansas City, KS 67005
Dodge City Community College
Dodge City, KS 67801
Emporia State University
Emporia, KS 66801

Fort Hays State University
Hays, KS 67601
Fort Scott Community Junior College
Fort Scott, KS 66701
Garden City Community College
Garden City, KS 67846
Haskell Indian Junior College
Lawrence, KS 66044
Highland Community College
Highland, KS 66035
Hutchinson Community College
Hutchinson, KS 67501
Independence Community College
Independence, KS 67301
Johnson County Community College
Overland Park, KS 66210
John Wood Community College
Overland Park, KS 66210
Kansas City Kansas Community College
Kansas City, KS 66112
Kansas State University
Manhattan, KS 66506
Kansas Technical Institute
Salina, KS 67401
LaBette Community Junior College
Parsons, KS 67351
Neosho County Community Junior College
Chanute, KS 66720
Pratt Community College
Pratt, KS 67124
Seward County Community College
Liberal, KS 67901
Washburn University—Topeka
Topeka, KS 66621

Kentucky

Ashland Community College
Ashland, KY 41101
Elizabethtown Community College
Elizabethtown, KY 42701
Hazard Community College
Hazard, KY 41701
Henderson Community College
Henderson, KY 42420
Hopkinsville Community College
Hopkinsville, KY 42240
Jefferson Community College
Louisville, KY 40204
Lexington Technical Institute
Lexington, KY 40506
Madisonville Community College
Madisonville, KY 42431
Maysville Community College
Maysville, KY 41056
Midway College
Midway, KY 40347
Northern Kentucky University
Highland Heights, KY 41076
Owensboro Business College
Owensboro, KY 42301
Paducah Community College
Paducah, KY 42001
Somerset Community College
Somerset, KY 42501
Southeast Community College
Cumberland, KY 40823

Louisiana

Bossier Parish Community College
Bossier City, LA 71111
Delgado College—City Park
New Orleans, LA 70119
Louisiana State University—Alexandria
Alexandria, LA 71301
Louisiana State University—Eunice
Eunice, LA 70535
Northeast Louisiana University
Monroe, LA 71209
Southeastern Louisiana University
Hammond, LA 70401
St. Bernard Parish Community College
Chalmette, LA 70043

Maine

Bangor Community College
Bangor, ME 04401
Central Maine Vocational-Technical Institute
Auburn, ME 04210
Eastern Maine Vocational Technical Institute
Bangor, ME 04401
Southern Maine Vocational Technical Institute
South Portland, ME 04106
University of Maine—Augusta
Augusta, ME 04330
University of Maine—Farmington
Farmington, ME 04938
University of Maine—Fort Kent
Fort Kent, ME 04743
University of Maine—Orono
Orono, ME 04473
University of Southern Maine
Gorham, ME 04038

Maryland

Allegany Community College
Cumberland, MD 21502
Anne Arundel Community College
Arnold, MD 21012
Catonsville Community College
Catonsville, MD 21228
Cecil Community College
North East, MD 21901
Chesapeake College
Wye Mills, MD 21679
Community College of Baltimore
Baltimore, MD 21202
Dundalk Community College
Baltimore, MD 21222
Essex Community College
Baltimore, MD 21237
Frederick Community College
Frederick, MD 21701
Garrett Community College
McHenry, MD 21541
Harford Community College
Bel Air, MD 21014
Howard Community College
Columbia, MD 21044
Montgomery College—Germantown
Germantown, MD 20767
Montgomery College—Rockville
Rockville, MD 20850
Montgomery College—Takoma Park
Takoma Park, MD 20012
Prestonburg Community College
Largo, MD 20870
Wor-Wic Tech Community College
Salisbury, MD 21801

Massachusetts

Berkshire Community College
Pittsfield, MA 01201
Bristol Community College
Fall River, MA 02720
Bunker Hill Community College
Boston, MA 02129
Cape Cod Community College
Barnstable, MA 02668
Essex Agricultural and Technical Institute
Hathorne, MA 01937
Greenfield Community College
Greenfield, MA 01301
Holyoke Community College
Holyoke, MA 01040
Massachusetts Bay Community College
Wellesley Hills, MA 02181
Massasoit Community College
Brockton, MA 02402
Middlesex Community College
Bedford, MA 01730
Mount Wachusett Community College
Gardner, MA 01440
Northern Essex Community College
Haverhill, MA 01830
North Shore Community College
Beverly, MA 01915
Quincy Junior College
Quincy, MA 02169
Qunisigamond Community College
Worcester, MA 01606
Roxbury Community College
Roxbury, MA 02119
Springfield Technical Community College
Springfield, MA 01105
University of Massachusetts—Stockbridge School of Agriculture
Amherst, MA 01003

Michigan

Alpena Community College
Alpena, MI 49707
Bay de Noc Community College
Escanaba, MI 49829
Charles S. Mott Community College
Flint, MI 48503
Cleary College
Ypsilanti, MI 48197
Delta College
University Center, MI 48710
Glen Oaks Community College
Centreville, MI 49032
Gogebic Community College
Ironwood, MI 49938
Grand Rapids Junior College
Grand Rapids, MI 49503
Henry Ford Community College
Dearborn, MI 48128
Highland Park Community College
Highland Park, MI 48203
Jackson Community College
Jackson, MI 49201
Kalamazoo Valley Community College
Kalamazoo, MI 49009
Kellogg Community College
Battle Creek, MI 49016
Kirtland Community College
Roscommon, MI 48653
Lake Michigan College
Benton Harbor, MI 49022
Lake Superior State College
Sault Ste. Marie, MI 49783
Lansing Community College
Lansing, MI 48912

Macomb County Community College—Center
Mt. Clemens, MI 48044
Macomb County Community College—South
Warren, MI 48093
Michigan Technological University
Houghton, MI 49931
Mid Michigan Community College
Harrison, MI 48625
Monroe County Community College
Monroe, MI 48161
Montcalm Community College
Sidney, MI 48885
Muskegon Community College
Muskegon, MI 49442
North Central Michigan College
Petoskey, MI 49770
Northern Michigan University
Marquette, MI 49855
Northwestern Michigan College
Traverse City, MI 49684
Oakland Community College
Bloomfield Hills, MI 48013
Schoolcraft College
Livnoia, MI 48152
Southwestern Michigan College
Dowagiac, MI 49047
St. Clair County Community College
Port Huron, MI 48060
Washtenaw Community College
Ann Arbor, MI 48106
Wayne County Community College
Detroit, MI 48201
West Shore Community College
Scottsville, MI 49454

Minnesota

Anoka-Ramsey Community College
Coon Rapids, MN 55433
Austin Community College
Austin, MN 55912
Bemidji State University
Bemidji, MN 56601
Brainerd Community College
Brainerd, MN 56401
Fergus Falls Community College
Fergus Falls, MN 56537
Hibbing Community College
Hibbing, MN 55746
Inver Hills Community College
Inver Grove Heights, MN 55075
Itasca Community College
Grand Rapids, MN 55744
Lakewood Community College
White Bear Lake, MN 55110
Mankato State University
Mankato, MN 56001
Mesabi Community College
Virginia, MN 55792
Minneapolis Community College
Minneapolis, MN 55403
Normandale Community College
Bloomington, MN 55431
North Hennepin State Community College
Brooklyn Park, MN 55445
Northland Community College
Thief River Falls, MN 56701
Rainy River Community College
International Falls, MN 56649
Rochester Community College
Rochester, MN 55901
University of Minnesota Technical College—Crookston
Crookston, MN 56716
University of Minnesota Technical College—Waseca
Waseca, MN 56093
Vermillion Community College
Ely, MN 55731
Willmar Community College
Willmar, MN 56201
Worthington Community College
Worthington, MN 56187

Mississippi

Coahoma Junior College
Clarksdale, MS 38614
Copiah-Lincoln Junior College
Wesson, MS 39191
East Central Junior College
Decatur, MS 39327
East Mississippi Junior College
Scooba, MS 39358
Hinds Junior College
Raymond, MS 39154
Itawamba Junior College
Fulton, MS 38843
Jones County Junior College
Ellisville, MS 39437
Meridian Junior College
Meridian, MS 39301
Mississippi Delta Junior College
Moorhead, MS 38761
Mississippi Gulf Coast Junior College—Jackson
Gautier, MS 39553
Mississippi Gulf Coast Junior College—Jefferson Davis
Gulfport, MS 39501
Mississippi Gulf Coast Junior College—Perkinston
Perkinston, MS 39573
Northeast Mississippi Junior College
Booneville, MS 38829
Northwest Mississippi Junior College
Senatobia, MS 38668
Pearl River Junior College
Poplarville, MS 39470
Southwest Mississippi Junior College
Summit, MS 39666
Utica Junior College
Utica, MS 39175

Missouri

Crowder College
Neosho, MO 64850
East Central Junior College
Union, MO 63084
Jefferson College
Hillsboro, MO 63050
Longview Community College
Lee's Summit, MO 64063
Maple Woods Community College
Kansas City, MO 64156
Mineral Area College
Flat River, MO 63601
Missouri Institute of Technology
Kansas City, MO 64114
Missouri Southern State College
Joplin, MO 64801
Missouri Western State College
St. Joseph, MO 64507
Moberly Junior College
Moberly, MO 65270
Penn Valley Community College
Kansas City, MO 64111
Pioneer Community College
Kansas City, MO 64111
State Fair Community College
Sedalia, MO 65313
St. Louis Community College—Florissant Valley
St. Louis, MO 63135
St. Louis Community College—Forest Park
St. Louis, MO 63110
St. Louis Community College—Meramec
Kirkwood, MO 63122
Three Rivers Community College
Poplar Bluff, MO 63901
Trenton Junior College
Trenton, MO 64683

Montana

Dawson Community College
Glendive, MT 59330
Flathead Valley Community College
Kalispell, MT 59901
Miles Community College
Miles City, MT 59301
Northern Montana College
Havre, MT 59501
Salish-Kootenai Community College
Pablo, MT 59885
Western Montana College
Dillon, MT 59725

Nebraska

Central Technical Community College
Hastings, NE 68901
Chadron State College
Chadron, NE 69337
McCook Community College
McCook, NE 69001
Metropolitan Technical Community College
Omaha, NE 68103
Mid-Plains Community College
North Platte, NE 69101
Nebraska Western College
Scottsbluff, NE 69361
Northeast Technical Community College
Norfolk, NE 68701
Peru State College
Peru, NE 68421
Platte Technical Community College
Columbus, NE 68601
Southeast Community College—Fairbury
Fairbury, NE 68352
Southeast Community College—Lincoln
Lincoln, NE 68520
Southeast Community College—Milford
Milford, NE 68405
University of Nebraska—Omaha
Omaha, NE 68182

Nevada

Clark County Community College
North Las Vegas, NV 89030
Northern Nevada Community College
Elko, NV 89801
Truckee Meadows Community College—Reno/Sparks Campus
Sparks, NV 89431
Western Nevada Community College
Carson City, NV 89701

New Hampshire

Hesser College
Manchester, NH 03101

New Hampshire Technical Institute
Concord, NH 03301
New Hampshire Vocational Technical College
Berlin, NH 03570
New Hampshire Vocational Technical College
Laconia, NH 03246
New Hampshire Vocational Technical College
Manchester, NH 03102
New Hampshire Vocational Technical College
Nashua, NH 03060
New Hampshire Vocational Technical College
Portsmouth, NH 03801
Plymouth State College
Plymouth, NH 03264
University of New Hampshire—Merrimack Valley
Manchester, NH 03102
University of New Hampshire—Thompson School of Applied Science
Durham, NH 03824

New Jersey

Atlantic Community College
Mays Landing, NJ 08330
Bergen Community College
Paramus, NJ 07652
Berkeley School
Little Falls, NJ 07424
Brookdale Community College
Lincroft, NJ 07738
Burlington County College
Pemberton, NJ 08068
Camden County College
Blackwood, NJ 08012
County College of Morris
Randolph, NJ 07869
Cumberland County College
Vineland, NJ 08360
Essex County College
Newark, NJ 07102
Gloucester County College
Sewell, NJ 08080
Hudson County Community College Commission
Jersey City, NJ 07306
Mercer County Community College
Trenton, NJ 08690
Middlesex County College
Edison, NJ 08817
Passaic County College
Paterson, NJ 07509
Somerset County College
Somerville, NJ 08876
Union County Technical Institute
Scotch Plains, NJ 07076

New Mexico

Eastern New Mexico University—Clovis
Clovis, NM 88101
Eastern New Mexico University—Roswell
Roswell, NM 88201
Institute of American Indian Arts
Santa Fe, NM 87501
New Mexico Junior College
Hobbs, NM 88240
New Mexico Military Institute
Roswell, NM 88201
New Mexico State University—Alamogordo
Almagordo, NM 88310
New Mexico State University—Carlsbad
Carlsbad, NM 88220
New Mexico State University—Grants
Grants, NM 87020
New Mexico State University—Las Cruces
Las Cruces, NM 88003
New Mexico State University—San Juan
Framington, NM 87401
Northern New Mexico Community College
Espanola, NM 87532
University of New Mexico—Gallup
Gallup, NM 87301
Western New Mexico University
Silver City, NM 88061

New York

Adirondack Community College
Glens Falls, NY 12801
Berkeley School—Long Island
Hicksville, NY 11801
Berkeley School—New York
New York, NY 10074
Berkeley School—Westchester
White Plains, NY 10604
Broome Community College
Binghamton, NY 13902
Cayuga County Community College
Auburn, NY 13021
Clinton Community College
Plattsburg, NY 12901
Columbia—Greene Community College
Hudson, NY 12534
Community College of the Finger Lakes
Canandaiga, NY 14424
Corning Community College
Corning, NY 14830
Culinary Institute of America
Hyde Park, NY 12538
CUNY—Borough of Manhattan Community College
New York, NY 10019
CUNY—Bronx Community College
Bronx, NY 10453
CUNY—Hostos Community College
Bronx, NY 10451
CUNY—John Jay College of Criminal Justice
New York, NY 10019
CUNY—Kingborough Community College Manhattan Beach
Brooklyn, NY 11235
CUNY—LaGuardia Community College
Long Island City, NY 11101
CUNY—Medgar Evers College
Brooklyn, NY 11225
CUNY—New York City Technical College
Brooklyn, NY 11201
CUNY—Queensborough Community College
Bayside, NY 11364
Dutchess Community College
Poughkeepsie, NY 12601
Erie Community College—North
Buffalo, NY 14221
Fulton-Montgomery Community College
Johnstown, NY 12095
Genesee Community College
Batavia, NY 14020
Herkimer County Community College
Herkimer, NY 13350
Hudson Valley Community College
Troy, NY 12180
Institute of Design and Construction
Brooklyn, NY 11201
Jamestown Community College
Jamestown, NY 14701
Jefferson Community College
Watertown, NY 13601
Mohawk Valley Community College
Utica, NY 13501
Monroe Community College
Rochester, NY 14623
Nassau Community College
Garden City, NY 11530
Niagara County Community College
Sanborn, NY 14132
North Country Community College
Saranac Lake, NY 12983
Onondaga Community College
Syracuse, NY 13215
Orange County Community College
Middletown, NY 10940
Schenectady County Community College
Schenectady, NY 12305
Suffolk County Community College
Selden, NY 11784
Sullivan County Community College
Loch Sheldrake, NY 12759
SUNY—Agricultural and Technical College—Alfred
Alfred, NY 14802
SUNY—Agricultural and Technical College—Canton
Canton, NY 13617
SUNY—Agricultural and Technical College—Cobleskill
Cobleskill, NY 12043
SUNY—Agricultural and Technical College—Delhi
Delhi, NY 13753
SUNY—Agricultural and Technical College—Farmingdale
Farmingdale, NY 11735
SUNY—Agricultural and Technical College—Morrisville
Morrisville, NY 13408
SUNY—Fashion Institute of Technology
New York, NY 10001
SUNY—Rockland Community College
Suffern, NY 10901
SUNY—Upstate Medical Center
Syracuse, NY 13210
Tompkins Cortland Community College
Dryden, NY 13053
Ulster County Community College
Stone Ridge, NY 12484
Westchester Community College
Valhalla, NY 10595

North Carolina

Anson Technical Institute
Ansonville, NC 28007

Asheville-Buncombe Technical College
Asheville, NC 28801
Bladen Technical College
Dublin, NC 28332
Caldwell Community College and Technical Institute
Lenoir, NC 28645
Cape Fear Technical Institute
Wilmington, NC 28401
Carteret Technical College
Morehead City, NC 28557
Catawba Valley Technical College
Hickory, NC 28601
Central Carolina Technical College
Sanford, NC 27330
Central Piedmont Community College
Charlotte, NC 28204
Cleveland Technical College
Shelby, NC 28150
Coastal Carolina Community College
Jacksonville, NC 28540
College of the Albemarle
Elizabeth City, NC 27909
Craven Community College
New Bern, NC 28560
Davidson County Community College
Lexington, NC 27292
Durham Technical Institute
Durham, NC 27703
Edgecombe Technical Institute
Tarboro, NC 27886
Fayetteville Technical Institute
Fayetteville, NC 28303
Forsyth Technical Institute
Winston-Salem, NC 27103
Guilford Technical Institute
Jamestown, NC 27282
Halifax Community College
Weldon, NC 27890
Hardbarger Junior College of Business
Raleigh, NC 27602
Haywood Technical College
Clyde, NC 28721
Isothermal Community College
Spindale, NC 28139
James Sprunt Technical College
Kenansville, NC 28349
Johnston Technical Institute
Smithfield, NC 27577
Lenoir Community College
Kinston, NC 28501
Martin Community College
Williamston, NC 27892
McDowell Technical College
Marion, NC 28752
Mitchell Community College
Statesville, NC 28677
Nash Technical Institute
Rocky Mount, NC 27801
Pamlico Technical Institute
Grantsboro, NC 28529
Piedmont Technical College
Roxboro, NC 27573
Pitt Community College
Greenville, NC 27834
Randolph Technical College
Asheboro, NC 27203
Richmond Technical Institute
Hamlet, NC 28345
Roanoke-Chowan Technical College
Ahoskie, NC 27910
Robeson Technical College
Lumberton, NC 28358
Rockingham Community College
Wentworth, NC 27375
Rowan Technical Institute
Salisbury, NC 28144
Sampson Technical Institute
Clinton, NC 28328
Sandhills Community College
Carthage, NC 28327
Southeastern Community College
Whiteville, NC 28472
Southwestern Technical Institute
Sylva, NC 28779
Surry Community College
Dobson, NC 27017
Technical College of Alamance
Haw River, NC 27258
Tri-County Community College
Murphy, NC 28906
Vance-Granville Community College
Henderson, NC 27536
Wake Technical College
Raleigh, NC 27603
Wayne Community College
Goldsboro, NC 27530
Western Piedmont Community College
Morganton, NC 28655
Wilkes Community College
Wilkesboro, NC 28659
Wilson County Technical Institute
Wilson, NC 27893

North Dakota

Bismarck Junior College
Bismarck, ND 58501
Lake Region Junior College
Devils Lake, ND 58301
Mayville State College
Mayville, ND 58257
North Dakota State School of Science
Wahpeton, ND 58075
North Dakota State University—Bottineau Branch and Institute of Forestry
Bottineau, ND 58318
Standing Rock Community College
Fort Yates, ND 58538
University of North Dakota—Williston
Williston, ND 58801
Valley City State College
Valley City, ND 58072

Ohio

Bowling Green State University—Firelands
Huron, OH 44839
Central Ohio Technical College
Newark, OH 43055
Cincinnati Technical College
Cincinnati, OH 45223
Clark Technical College
Springfield, OH 45501
Columbus Technical Institute
Columbus, OH 43216
Cuyahoga Community College—Eastern
Warrenville Township, OH 44122
Cuyahoga Community College—Metropolitan
Cleveland, OH 44115
Cuyahoga Community College—Western
Parma, OH 44130
Edison State Community College
Piqua, OH 45356
Hocking Technical College
Nelsonville, OH 45764
Jefferson Technical College
Steubenville, OH 43952
Kent State University—Ashtabula
Ashtabula, OH 44004
Kent State University—East Liverpool
East Liverpool, OH 43920
Kent State University—Geauga
Burton, OH 44021
Kent State University—Salem Regional
Salem, OH 44460
Kent State University—Stark Regional
Canton, OH 44720
Kent State University—Trumbull
Warren, OH 44483
Kent State University—Tuscarawas
New Philadelphia, OH 44663
Lakeland Community College
Mentor, OH 44060
Lima Technical College
Lima, OH 45804
Lorain County Community College
Elyria, OH 44035
Marion Technical College
Marion, OH 43302
Miami University—Hamilton
Hamilton, OH 45011
Miami University—Middletown
Middletown, OH 45042
North Central Technical College
Mansfield, OH 44901
Northwest Technical College
Archbold, OH 43502
Ohio State University Agricultural Technical Institute
Wooster, OH 44691
Ohio State University—Mansfield
Mansfield, OH 44906
Ohio State University—Marion
Marion, OH 43302
Ohio State University—Newark
Newark, OH 43055
Ohio University
Athens, OH 45701
Ohio University—Belmont County
St. Clairsville, OH 43950
Ohio University—Chillicothe
Chillicothe, OH 45601
Ohio University—Ironton
Ironton, OH 45638
Ohio University—Lancaster
Lancaster, OH 43140
Ohio University—Zanesville
Zanesville, OH 43701
Owens Technical College
Toledo, OH 43699
Shawnee State Community College
Portsmouth, OH 45662
Sinclair Community College
Dayton, OH 45402
Southern Ohio College
Cincinnati, OH 45237
Southern State Community College
Hillsboro, OH 45133
Stark Technical College
Canton, OH 44720
Terra Technical College
Fremont, OH 43420
University of Akron—Community and Technical College
Akron, OH 44325

University of Cincinnati
Cincinnati, OH 45221
University of Cincinnati—Raymond Walters College
Cincinnati, OH 45236
University of Toledo
Toledo, OH 43606
Washington Technical College
Marietta, OH 45750
Wayne General and Technical College
Orrville, OH 44667
Wright State University—Western Ohio
Celina, OH 45822
Youngstown State University
Youngstown, OH 44555

Oklahoma

Carl Albert Junior College
Poteau, OK 74953
Claremore Junior College
Claremore, OK 74017
Conners State College
Warner, OK 74469
Eastern Oklahoma State College
Wilburton, OK 74578
El Reno Junior College
El Reno, OK 73036
Murray State College
Tishomingo, OK 73460
Northeastern Oklahoma Agricultural and Mechanical College
Miami, OK 74354
Northern Oklahoma College
Tonkawa, OK 74653
Oklahoma State University Technical Institute
Oklahoma City, OK 73107
Oscar Rose Junior College
Midwest City, OK 73110
Sayre Junior College
Sayre, OK 73662
Seminole Junior College
Seminole, OK 74868
South Oklahoma City Junior College
Oklahoma, OK 73159
Tulsa Junior College
Tulsa, OK 74119
Western Oklahoma State College
Altus, OK 73521

Oregon

Blue Mountain Community College
Pendleton, OR 97801
Central Oregon Community College
Bend, OR 97701
Chemeketa Community College
Salem, OR 97309
Clackamas Community College
Oregon City, OR 97045
Clatsop Community College
Astoria, OR 97103
Lane Community College
Eugene, OR 97405
Linn-Benton Community College
Albany, OR 97321
Mount Hood Community College
Gresham, OR 97030
Oregon Institute of Technology
Klamath Falls, OR 97601
Portland Community College
Portland, OR 97219
Rogue Community College
Grants Pass, OR 97526
Southern Oregon State College
Ashland, OR 97520
Southwestern Oregon Community College
Coos Bay, OR 97420
Treasure Valley Community College
Ontario, OR 97914
Umpqua Community College
Roseburg, OR 97470

Pennsylvania

Bucks County Community College
Newtown, PA 18940
Butler County Community College
Butler, PA 16001
Clarion State College—Venango
Oil City, PA 16301
Community College of Allegheny County—Allegheny
Pittsburgh, PA 15212
Community College of Allegheny County—North
Pittsburgh, PA 15237
Community College of Allegheny County—South
West Mifflin, PA 15122
Community College of Beaver County
Monaca, PA 15021
Community College of Philadelphia
Philadelphia, PA 19107
Delaware County Community College
Media, PA 19063
Edinboro State College
Edinboro, PA 16412
Harrisburg Area Community College
Harrisburg, PA 17110
Indiana University of Pennsylvania—Armstrong County
Kittanning, PA 16201
Indiana University of Pennsylvania—Punxsutawney
Punxsutawney, PA 15767
Lehigh County Community College
Schnecksville, PA 18078
Luzerne County Community College
Nanticoke, PA 18634
Mansfield State College
Mansfield, PA 16933
Montgomery County Community College
Blue Bell, PA 19422
Northampton County Area Community College
Bethlehem, PA 18017
Northeastern Christian Junior College
Villanova, PA 19085
Pennsylvania State University—Allentown
Fogelsville, PA 18051
Pennsylvania State University—Altoona
Altoona, PA 16603
Pennsylvania State University—Beaver
Monaca, PA 15061
Pennsylvania State University—Behrend
Erie, PA 16510
Pennsylvania State University—Berks
Reading, PA 19608
Pennsylvania State University—Delaware County
Media, PA 19063
Pennsylvania State University—DuBois
DuBois, PA 15801
Pennsylvania State University—Fayette
Uniontown, PA 15401
Pennsylvania State University—Hazleton
Hazleton, PA 18201
Pennsylvania State University—McKeesport
McKeesport, PA 15132
Pennsylvania State University—Mont Alto
Mont Alto, PA 17237
Pennsylvania State University—New Kensington
New Kensington, PA 15068
Pennsylvania State University—Ogontz
Abington, PA 19001
Pennsylvania State University—Schuylkill
Schuylkill Haven, PA 17972
Pennsylvania State University—Shenango Valley
Sharon, PA 16146
Pennsylvania State University—Wilkes-Barre
Wilkes-Barre, PA 18708
Pennsylvania State University—Worthington Scranton
Dunmore, PA 18512
Pennsylvania State University—York
York, PA 17403
Reading Area Community College
Reading, PA 19602
Temple University
Philadelphia, PA 19122
Temple University—Ambler
Ambler, PA 19002
Thaddeus Stevens State School of Technology
Lancaster, PA 17602
Westmoreland County Community College
Youngwood, PA 15697
Williamsport Area Community College
Williamsport, PA 17701

Rhode Island

Community College of Rhode Island—Knight
Warwick, RI 02866
Johnson and Wales College
Providence, RI 02903

South Carolina

Aiken Technical College
Aiken, SC 29801
Beaufort County Community College
Beaufort, SC 29902
Beaufort Technical College
Beaufort, SC 29902
Chesterfield-Marlboro Technical College
Cheraw, SC 29520
Clinton Junior College
Rock Hill, SC 29730
Denmark Technical College
Denmark, SC 29042
Florence-Darlington Technical College
Florence, SC 29501
Greenville Technical College
Greenville, SC 29606
Horry-Georgetown Technical College
Conway, SC 29526

Lander College
Greenwood, SC 29646
Midlands Technical College
Columbia, SC 29205
Orangeburg-Calhoun Technical College
Orangeburg, SC 29115
Piedmont Technical College
Greenwood, SC 29646
Rice College
North Charleston, SC 29406
Spartanburg Technical College
Spartanburg, SC 29303
Sumter Area Technical College
Sumter, SC 29150
Tri-County Technical College
Pendleton, SC 29670
Trident Technical College—North
North Charleston, SC 29405
Trident Technical College—Palmer
Charleston, SC 29411
University of South Carolina
Columbia, SC 29208
University of South Carolina—Aiken
Aiken, SC 29801
University of South Carolina—Beaufort
Beaufort, SC 29902
University of South Carolina—Lancaster
Lancaster, SC 29720
University of South Carolina—Salkehatchie
Allendale, SC 29810
University of South Carolina—Sumter
Sumter, SC 29150
University of South Carolina—Union
Union, SC 29379
Williamsburg Technical Education Center
Kingstree, SC 29556

South Dakota

Black Hills State College
Spearfish, SD 57783
Dakota State College
Madison, SD 57042
Northern State College
Aberdeen, SD 57401
Oglala Sioux Community College
Pine Ridge, SD 57770
University of South Dakota—Springfield
Springfield, SD 57062

Tennessee

Belmont College
Nashville, TN 37203
Chattanooga State Technical Community College
Chattanooga, TN 37406
Cleveland State Community College
Cleveland, TN 37311
Columbia State Community College
Columbia, TN 38401
Dyersburg State Community College
Dyersburg, TN 38024
Jackson State Community College
Jackson, TN 38301
Motlow State Community College
Tullahoma, TN 37388
Nashville State Technical Institute
Nashville, TN 37209
Shelby State Community College
Memphis, TN 38104
State Technical Institute—Knoxville
Knoxville, TN 37919
State Technical Institute—Memphis
Memphis, TN 38134
Volunteer State Community College
Gallatin, TN 37066
Walters State Community College
Morristown, TN 37814

Texas

Alvin Community College
Alvin, TX 77511
Amarillo College
Amarillo, TX 79178
Austin Community College
Austin, TX 78768
Bee County College
Beeville, TX 78102
Blinn College
Brenham, TX 77833
Brazosport College
Lake Jackson, TX 77566
Central Texas College
Killeen, TX 76541
Cisco Junior College
Cisco, TX 76437
Clarendon College
Clarendon, TX 79226
College of the Mainland
Texas City, TX 77590
Cooke County College
Gainesville, TX 76240
Del Mar College
Corpus Christi, TX 78404
Eastfield College
Mesquite, TX 75150
El Centro College of the Dallas Community College District
Dallas, TX 75202
El Paso Community College
El Paso, TX 79998
Frank Phillips College
Borger, TX 79007
Galveston College
Galveston, TX 77550
Grayson County College
Denison, TX 75020
Henderson County Junior College
Athens, TX 75751
Hill Junior College
Hillsboro, TX 76645
Houston Community College
Houston, TX 77007
Howard College
Big Spring, TX 79720
Kilgore College
Kilgore, TX 75662
Lamar University—College of Technical Arts
Beaumont, TX 77710
Laredo Junior College
Laredo, TX 78040
Lee College
Baytown, TX 77520
McLennan Community College
Waco, TX 76708
Midland College
Midland, TX 79701
Navarro College
Corsicana, TX 75110
North Harris County College
Houston, TX 77073
Northlake College
Irving, TX 75062
Odessa College
Odessa, TX 79762
Pan American University
Edinburg, TX 78539
Panola Junior College
Carthage, TX 75633
Paris Junior College
Paris, TX 75460
Ranger Junior College
Ranger, TX 76470
Richland College
Dallas, TX 75243
San Antonio College
San Antonio, TX 78284
San Jacinto College—Central
Pasadena, TX 77505
San Jacinto College—North
Houston, TX 77049
South Plains College
Levelland, TX 79336
Southwest Texas Junior College
Uvalde, TX 78801
St. Phillip's College
San Antonio, TX 78203
Tarrant County Junior College District
Fort Worth, TX 76102
Temple Junior College
Temple, TX 76501
Texarkana Community College
Texarkana, TX 75501
Texas Southmost College
Brownsville, TX 78520
Texas State Technical Institute—Amarillo
Amarillo, TX 79111
Texas State Technical Institute—Harlingen
Harlingen, TX 78550
Texas State Technical Institute—Waco
Waco, TX 76705
Tyler Junior College
Tyler, TX 75711
Victoria College
Victoria, TX 77901
Weatherford College
Weatherford, TX 76086
Western Texas College
Snyder, TX 79549
Wharton County Junior College
Wharton, TX 77488

Utah

College of Eastern Utah
Price, UT 84501
Dixie College
Saint George, UT 84770
Snow College
Ephraim, UT 84627
Utah Technical College—Provo
Provo, UT 84601
Utah Technical College—Salt Lake
Salt Lake City, UT 84107
Weber State College
Ogden, UT 84408

Vermont

Castleton State College
Castleton, VT 05735
Community College of Vermont
Montpelier, VT 05062
Johnson State College
Johnson, VT 05656
Vermont Technical College
Randolph Center, VT 05061

Virginia

Blue Ridge Community College
Weyers Cave, VA 24486
Central Virginia Community College
Lynchburg, VA 24502
Dabney S. Lancaster Community College
Clifton Forge, VA 24422
Danville Community College
Danville, VA 24541
Eastern Shore Community College
Melfa, VA 23410
Germanna Community College
Locust Grove, VA 22508
John Tyler Community College
Chester, VA 23831
J. Sargeant Reynolds Community College
Richmond, VA 23241
Lord Fairfax Community College
Middletown, VA 22645
Mountain Empire Community College
Big Stone Gap, VA 24219
New River Community College
Dublin, VA 24084
Northern Virginia Community College
Annandale, VA 22003
Patrick Henry Community College
Martinsville, VA 24112
Paul D. Camp Community College
Franklin, VA 23851
Piedmont Virginia Community College
Charlottesville, VA 22901
Rappahanock Community College
Glenns, VA 23149
Richard Bland College
Petersburg, VA 23803
Southside Virginia Community College
Alberta, VA 23821
Southwest Virginia Community College
Richards, VA 24641
Thomas Nelson Community College
Hampton, VA 23670
Tidewater Community College—Chesapeake
Chesapeake, VA 23320
Tidewater Community College—Frederick
Portsmouth, VA 23703
Tidewater Community College—Virginia Beach
Virginia Beach, VA 23456
Virginia Highlands Community College
Abingdon, VA 24210
Virginia Western Community College
Roanoke, VA 24015
Wytheville Community College
Wytheville, VA 24382

Washington

Bellevue Community College
Bellevue, WA 98007
Big Bend Community College
Moses Lake, WA 98837
Centralia Community College
Centralia, WA 98531
Clark College
Vancouver, WA 98663
Columbia Basin College
Tri-Cities, WA 99302
Edmonds Community College
Lynnwood, WA 98036
Everett Community College
Everett, WA 98201
Fort Steilacoom Community College
Tacoma, WA 98499
Grays Harbor College
Aberdeen, WA 98520
Green River Community College
Auburn, WA 98002
Highline Community College
Midway, WA 98031
Lower Columbia College
Longview, WA 98632
North Seattle Community College
Seattle, WA 98103
Olympia Technical Community College
Olympia, WA 98502
Olympic College
Bremerton, WA 98310
Peninsula College
Port Angeles, WA 98362
Seattle Central Community College
Seattle, WA 98122
Shoreline Community College
Seattle, WA 98133
Skagit Valley College
Mt. Vernon, WA 98273
South Seattle Community College
Seattle, WA 98106
Spokane Community College
Spokane, WA 99207
Spokane Falls Community College
Spokane, WA 99204
Tacoma Community College
Tacoma, WA 98465
Walla Walla Community College
Walla Walla, WA 99362
Wenatchee Valley College
Wenatchee, WA 98801
Whatcom Community College
Bellingham, WA 98225
Yakima Valley Community College
Yakima, WA 98907

West Virginia

Bluefield State College
Bluefield, WV 24701
Fairmont State College
Fairmont, WV 26554
Glenville State College
Glenville, WV 26351
Marshall University
Huntington, WV 25701
Parkersburg Community College
Parkersburg, WV 26101
Potomac State College
Keyser, WV 26726
Shepherd College
Shepherdstown, WV 25443
Southern West Virginia Community College
Williamson, WV 25661
Southern West Virginia Community College—Logan
Logan, WV 25601
West Virginia Institute of Technology
Montgomery, WV 25136
West Virginia Northern Community College
Wheeling, WV 26003
West Virginia State College
Institute, WV 25112

Wisconsin

Blackhawk Technical Institute
James, WI 53545
District One Technical Institute
Eau Claire, WI 54701
Fox Valley Technical Institute
Appleton, WI 54911
Gateway Technical Institute—Elkhorn
Elkhorn, WI 53121
Gateway Technical Institute—Kenosha
Kenosha, WI 53140
Gateway Technical Institute—Racine
Racine, WI 53403
Lakeshore Technical Institute
Cleveland, WI 53015
Madison Area Technical College
Madison, WI 53703
Mid-State Technical Institute—Marshfield
Marshfield, WI 54449
Mid-State Technical Institute—Wisconsin Rapids
Wisconsin Rapids, WI 54494
Milwaukee Area Technical College
Milwaukee, WI 53203
Moraine Park Technical Institute—Fond Du Lac
Fond Du Lac, WI 54935
Moraine Park Technical Institute—West Bend
West Bend, WI 53095
Nicolet College and Technical Institute
Rhinelander, WI 54501
North Central Technical Institute
Wausau, WI 54401
Northeast Wisconsin Technical Institute
Green Bay, WI 54303
Southwest Wisconsin Vocational Technical Institute
Fennimore, WI 53809
University of Wisconsin Center—Baraboo/Sauk
Baraboo, WI 53913
University of Wisconsin Center—Barron County
Rice Lake, WI 54868
University of Wisconsin Center—Fond Du Lac
Fond Du Lac, WI 54935
University of Wisconsin Center—Fox Valley
Menasha, WI 54952
University of Wisconsin—Green Bay
Green Bay, WI 54302
University of Wisconsin Center—Manitowoc County
Manitowoc, WI 54220
University of Wisconsin Center—Marathon County
Wausau, WI 54401
University of Wisconsin—Marinette Center
Marinette, WI 54143
University of Wisconsin—Marshfield/Wood
Marshfield, WI 54449
University of Wisconsin Center—Richland
Richland Center, WI 53581
University of Wisconsin Center—Rock County
Janesville, WI 53545

University of Wisconsin Center—Sheboygan County
Sheboygan, WI 53081
University of Wisconsin Center—Washington County
West Bend, WI 53095
University of Wisconsin Center—Waukesha
Waukesha, WI 53186
University of Wisconsin—Stevens Point
Stevens Point, WI 54481
Waukesha County Technical Institute
Pewaukee, WI 53072
Western Wisconsin Technical Institute
LaCrosse, WI 54601
Wisconsin Indianhead Technical Institute—Ashland
Ashland, WI 54871
Wisconsin Indianhead Technical Institute—New Richmond
New Richmond, WI 54806
Wisconsin Indianhead Technical Institute—Superior
Superior, WI 54880

WYOMING

Casper College
Casper, WY 82601
Central Wyoming College
Riverton, WY 82501
Eastern Wyoming College
Torrington, WY 82240
Laramie County Community College
Cheyenne, WY 82001
Northwest Community College
Powell, WY 82435
Sheridan College
Sheridan, WY 82801
Western Wyoming Community College
Rock Springs, WY 82901

PUERTO RICO

Puerto Rico Junior College
Rio Piedras, PR 00928
University of Puerto Rico—Rio Piedras
Rio Piedras, PR 00931

Two-Year Private Colleges and Universities

ALABAMA

Alabama Christian College
Montgomery, AL 36193
Alabama Lutheran Academy and College
Selma, AL 36701
Booker T. Washington Business College
Birmingham, AL 35203
C.A. Fredd State Technical College
Tuscaloosa, AL 35401
International Bible College
Florence, AL 35630
Lomax-Hannon Junior College
Greenville, AL 36037
Marion Military Institute
Marion, AL 36756
Selma University
Selma, AL 36701
Southern Institute
Birmingham, AL 35255
Southern Junior College of Business
Birmingham, AL 35203

ALASKA

Sheldon Jackson College
Sitka, AK 99835

ARKANSAS

Capital City Business College
Little Rock, AR 72204
Crowley's Ridge College
Paragould, AR 72450
John Brown University
Siloam Springs, AR 72761
Shorter College
North Little Rock, AR 72114
Southern Baptist College
Walnut Ridge, AR 72476

ARIZONA

College of Ganado
Ganado, AZ 86505
DeVry Institute of Technology
Phoenix, AZ 85016
Embry-Riddle Aeronautical University
Prescott, AZ 83602
Navajo Community College
Tsaile, AZ 86556

CALIFORNIA

American Academy of Dramatic Arts—West
Pasadena, CA 91104
Armstrong College
Berkeley, CA 94704
Brooks College
Long Beach, CA 90804
Cabrillo College
Aptos, CA 95003
Center for Early Education
Los Angeles, CA 90048
Christ College—Irvine
Irvine, CA 92715
Coleman College
San Diego, CA 92110
College of Notre Dame
Belmont, CA 94002
Columbia College
Columbia, CA 95310
Columbia College—Hollywood
Hollywood, CA 90038
De Anza College
Cupertino, CA 95014
Don Bosco Technical Institute
Rosemead, CA 91770
D-Q University
Davis, CA 95616
Fashion Institute of Design and Merchandising
Los Angeles, CA 90014
Feather River College
Quincy, CA 95971
Humphreys College
Stockton, CA 95207
Loma Linda University—La Sierra
Riverside, CA 92515
Los Angeles Baptist College
Newhall, CA 91322
Los Angeles Mission College
San Fernando, CA 91343
Los Medanos College
Pittsburg, CA 94565
Marymount Palos Verdes College
Rancho Palos Verdes, CA 90274
Menlo College
Menlo Park, CA 94025
Otis Art Institute of Parsons School of Design
Los Angeles, CA 90057
Pacific Christian College
Fullerton, CA 92631
Saddleback College
Mission Viejo, CA 92691
San Francisco College of Mortuary Science
San Francisco, CA 94109
University of La Verne
La Verne, CA 91750
Vista College
Berkeley, CA 94704

COLORADO

Nazarene Bible College
Colorado Springs, CO 80935
Rockmont College
Denver, CO 80226

CONNECTICUT

Briarwood College
Southington, CT 06489
Hartford College for Women
Hartford, CT 06105
Mitchell College
New London, CT 06320
Mount Sacred Heart College
Hamden, CT 06514
Post College
Waterbury, CT 06708

Quinnipiac College
Hamden, CT 06518
Sacred Heart University
Bridgeport, CT 06606
University of Hartford
West Hartford, CT 06117

Delaware

Brandywine College
Wilmington, DE 19803
Goldey Beacom College
Wilmington, DE 19808
University of Delaware
Newark, DE 19711
Wilmington College
New Castle, DE 19720

Florida

Bauder Fashion College
Miami, FL 33131
College of Boca Raton
Boca Raton, FL 33431
Florida Beacon College
Largo, FL 33541
Florida College
Temple Terrace, FL 33617
Florida Institute of Technology
Melbourne, FL 32901
Florida Institute of Technology School of Applied Technology
Jensen Beach, FL 33457
International Fine Arts College
Miami, FL 33132
Lakeland College of Business and Fashion
Lakeland, FL 33802
Morris Junior College of Business
Melbourne, FL 32935
Palm Beach Atlantic College
West Palm Beach, FL 33401
St. John Vianney College Seminary
Miami, FL 33165

Georgia

Albany Junior College
Albany, GA 31707
Andrew College
Cuthbert, GA 31740
Art Institute of Atlanta
Atlanta, GA 30326
Atlanta Junior College
Atlanta, GA 30310
Bainbridge Junior College
Bainbridge, GA 31717
Brewton-Parker College
Mount Vernon, GA 30445
Crandall College
Macon, GA 31201
Dalton Junior College
Dalton, GA 30720
DeVry Institute of Technology
Atlanta, GA 30341
Draughon's Junior College
Savannah, GA 31406
Emanuel County Junior College
Swainsboro, GA 30401
Emmanuel College
Franklin Springs, GA 30639
Gainesville Junior College
Gainesville, GA 30501
Phillips College
Augusta, GA 30902
Phillips College
Columbus, GA 31901
Reinhardt College
Waleska, GA 30183
Southern Technical Institute
Marietta, GA 30060
Thomas County Community College
Thomasville, GA 31792
Toccoa Falls College
Toccoa Falls, GA 30598
Truett-McConnell College
Cleveland, GA 30528

Hawaii

Chaminade University of Honolulu
Honolulu, HI 96816

Idaho

Northwest Nazarene College
Nampa, ID 83651

Illinois

American Academy of Art
Chicago, IL 60604
Central YMCA Community College
Chicago, IL 60606
DeVry Institute of Technology
Chicago, IL 60618
Felician College
Chicago, IL 60659
Harrington Institute of Interior Design
Chicago, IL 60605
Kendall College
Evanston, IL 60201
Lewis University
Romeoville, IL 60441
Lincoln College (Lincoln Christian College)
Lincoln, IL 62656
MacCormac Junior College
Chicago, IL 60604
Mallinckrodt College
Wilmette, IL 60091
Midstate College
Peoria, IL 61602
Robert Morris College—Carthage
Carthage, IL 62321
Shawnee College
Ullin, IL 62992
Springfield College in Illinois
Springfield, IL 62702

Indiana

Ancilla College
Donaldson, IN 46513
Bethel College
Mishawaka, IN 46544
Butler University
Indianapolis, IN 46208
Calumet College
Whiting, IN 46394
Elkhart Institute of Technology
Elkhart, IN 46514
Fort Wayne Bible College
Fort Wayne, IN 46807
Holy Cross Junior College
Notre Dame, IN 46556
Indiana Business College
Indianapolis, IN 46204
Indiana Central University
Indianapolis, IN 46227
International Business College
Fort Wayne, IN 46804
Lockyear College
Evansville, IN 47706
Marian College
Indianapolis, IN 46222
Northwood Institute
West Baden, IN 47469
Oakland City College
Oakland City, IN 47660
St. Francis College
Fort Wayne, IN 46808
Taylor University
Upland, IN 46989
University of Evansville
Evansville, IN 47702
Valparaiso Technical Institute
Valparaiso, IN 46383

Iowa

American Institute of Private Business
Des Moines, IA 50321
Grand View College
Des Moines, IA 50316
Mount St. Clare College
Clinton, IA 52732
Open Bible College
Des Moines, IA 50321
Sioux Empire College
Hawarden, IA 51023
Vennard College
University Park, IA 52595

Kansas

Central College
McPherson, KS 67460
Donnelly College
Kansas City, KS 66102
Hesston College
Hesston, KS 67062
St. John's College
Winfield, KS 67156

Kentucky

Alice Lloyd College
Pippa Passes, KY 41844
Bellarmine College
Louisville, KY 40205
Brescia College
Owensboro, KY 42301
Kentucky Junior College of Business
Lexington, KY 40508
Kentucky Wesleyan College
Owensboro, KY 42301
Lees Junior College
Jackson, KY 41339
Lindsey Wilson College
Columbia, KY 42728
Pikeville College
Pikeville, KY 41501
St. Catharine College
St. Catharine, KY 40061
Sue Bennett College
London, KY 40741
Sullivan Junior College of Business
Louisville, KY 40205
Thomas More College
Fort Mitchell, KY 41017
Watterson College
Louisville, KY 40218

Louisiana

Loyola University
New Orleans, LA 70118
Our Lady of Holy Cross College
New Orleans, LA 70119
Phillips College of New Orleans
Metairie, LA 70002
Southern University—New Orleans
New Orleans, LA 70126
Southern University—Shreveport—Bossier City
Shreveport, LA 71107

Maine

Andover College
Portland, ME 04101
Beal College
Bangor, ME 04401
Casco Bay College
Portland, ME 04101
Husson College
Bangor, ME 04401
Nasson College
Springvale, ME 04083
Thomas College
Waterville, ME 04901
Unity College
Unity, ME 04988
Westbrook College
Portland, ME 04103

Maryland

Capitol Institute of Technology
Kensington, MD 20795
Charles County Community College
La Plata, MD 20646
Columbia Union College
Takoma Park, MD 20012
Hagerstown Junior College
Hagerstown, MD 21740
Maryland College of Art and Design
Silver Spring, MD 20902
Villa Julie College
Stevenson, MD 21153

Massachusetts

Aquinas Junior College
Milton, MA 02186
Aquinas Junior College
Newton, MA 02158
Bay Path Junior College
Longmeadow, MA 01106
Bay State Junior College of Business
Boston, MA 02116
Becker Junior College—Leicester
Leicester, MA 01524
Becker Junior College—Worcester
Worcester, MA 01609
Blue Hills Technical Institute
Canton, MA 02021
Bradford College
Bradford, MA 01830
Central New England College of Technology
Worcester, MA 01610
Chamberlayne Junior College
Boston, MA 02116
Dean Junior College
Franklin, MA 02038
Emmanuel College
Boston, MA 02115
Endicott College
Beverly, MA 01915
Fisher Junior College
Boston, MA 02116
Forsyth School for Dental Hygienists
Boston, MA 02115
Franklin Institute of Boston
Boston, MA 02116
Laboure Junior College
Boston, MA 02124
Lasell Junior College
Newton, MA 02166
Mount Ida Junior College
Newton Centre, MA 02159
Newbury College—Boston Campus
Boston, MA 02115
Newbury Junior College—Holliston
Holliston, MA 01746
New England Institute of Applied Arts and Sciences for Funeral Service Education
Boston, MA 02215
Pine Manor College
Chestnut Hill, MA 02167
Simon's Rock Early College of Bard College
Great Barrington, MA 01230
Wentworth Institute of Technology
Boston, MA 02115
Worcester Junior College
Worcester, MA 01610

Michigan

Baker Junior College
Flint, MI 48507
Concordia College
Ann Arbor, MI 48105
Davenport College
Grand Rapids, MI 49503
Detroit College of Business
Dearborn, MI 48126
Grand Rapids School of the Bible and Music
Grand Rapids, MI 49506
Kendall School of Design
Grand Rapids, MI 49503
Lawrence Institute of Technology
Southfield, MI 48057
Lewis College of Business
Detroit, MI 48235
Madonna College
Livonia, MI 48150
Marygrove College
Detroit, MI 48221
Mercy College of Detroit
Detroit, MI 48219
Michigan Christian College
Rochester, MI 48063
Muskegon Business College
Muskegon, MI 49442
St. Mary's College
Orchard Lake, MI 48033
Suomi College
Hancock, MI 49930

Minnesota

Bethany Lutheran College
Mankato, MN 56001
Crosier Seminary Junior College
Onamia, MN 56359
Golden Valley Lutheran College
Minneapolis, MN 55422
Minnesota Bible College
Rochester, MN 55901
Pillsbury Baptist Bible College
Owatonna, MN 55060
St. Mary's Junior College
Minneapolis, MN 55454

Mississippi

Clarke College
Newton, MS 39345
Holmes Junior College
Goodman, MS 39079
Mary Holmes College
West Point, MS 39773
Ministerial Institute and College
West Point, MS 39773
Natchez Junior College
Natchez, MS 39120
Phillips College
Gulfport, MS 39501
Prentiss Normal and Industrial Institute
Prentiss, MS 39474

Missouri

Columbia College
Columbia, MO 65216
Cottey College
Nevada, MO 64772
Culver-Stockton College
Canton, MO 63435
Hannibal-LaGrange College
Hannibal, MO 63401
Kemper Military School and College
Boonville, MO 65233
Maryville College—St. Louis
St. Louis, MO 63141
Missouri Valley College
Marshall, MO 65340
Southwest Baptist College
Bolivar, MO 65613
St. Mary's College of O'Fallon
O'Fallon, MO 63366
St. Paul's College
Concordia, MO 64020
Wentworth Military Academy
Lexington, MO 64067

Montana

Carroll College
Helena, MT 59625

Nebraska

College of St. Mary
Omaha, NE 68124
Midland Lutheran College
Fremont, NE 68025
Nebraska Wesleyan University
Lincoln, NE 68504
York College
York, NE 68467

Nevada

Reno Business College
Reno, NV 89502

New Hampshire

Castle Junior College
Windham, NH 03087
Colby-Sawyer College
New London, NH 03257

Daniel Webster College
Nashua, NH 03063
McIntosh College
Dover, NH 03820
Nathaniel Hawthorne College
Antrim, NH 03440
New Hampshire College
Manchester, NH 03104
Notre Dame College
Manchester, NH 03104
Rivier College
Nashua, NH 03060
St. Anselm College
Manchester, NH 03102
White Pines College
Chester, NH 03036

NEW JERSEY

Assumption College for Sisters
Mendham, NJ 07945
Centenary College
Hackettstown, NJ 07840
Edward Williams College
Hackensack, NJ 07601
Felician College
Lodi, NJ 07644
Monmouth College
West Long Beach, NJ 07764
St. Peter's College
Jersey City, NJ 07306
Thomas A. Edison State College
Trenton, NJ 08625
Union College
Cranford, NJ 07016

NEW MEXICO

National College—Albuquerque
Albuquerque, NM 87110
University of Albuquerque
Albuquerque, NM 87140

NEW YORK

Academy of Aeronautics
Flushing, NY 11371
Adelphi University
Garden City, NY 11530
Albany Business College
Albany, NY 12210
American Academy of Dramatic Arts
New York, NY 10016
Boricua College
New York, NY 10025
Branson Art Training Center
New York, NY 10010
Bryant-Stratton Business Institute
Buffalo, NY 14202
Bryant-Stratton Business Institute
Clarence, NY 14031
Bryant-Stratton Business Institute
Rochester, NY 14604
Cazenovia College
Cazenovia, NY 13035
Central City Business Institute
Syracuse, NY 13203
College of Insurance
New York, NY 10038
Concordia College
Bronxville, NY 10708
Culinary Institute of America
Hyde Park, NY 12538
Dominican College
Orangeburg, NY 10962
Elizabeth Seton College
Yonkers, NY 10701
Elmira College
Elmira, NY 14901
Five Towns College
Merrick, NY 11566
Franklin College Switzerland
New York, NY 10021
Harriman College
Harriman, NY 10926
Hilbert College
Hamburg, NY 14075
Houghton College—Buffalo
West Seneca, NY 14224
Interboro Institute
New York, NY 10003
Jamestown Business College
Jamestown, NY 14701
Junior College of Albany
Albany, NY 12208
Katharine Gibbs School
New York, NY 10017
Katharine Gibbs School—Huntington
Melville, NY 11742
Laboratory Institute of Merchandising
New York, NY 10022
Long Island College Hospital School of Nursing
Brooklyn, NY 11201
Maria College
Albany, NY 12208
Maria Regina College
Syracuse, NY 13208
Mater Dei College
Ogdensburg, NY 13669
Mercy College
Dobbs Ferry, NY 10522
Molloy College
Rockville Centre, NY 11570
Monroe Business Institute
Bronx, NY 10468
Nassau Community College
Garden City, NY 11530
New York Institute of Technology—New York
New York, NY 10023
Nyack College
Nyack, NY 10960
Olean Business Institute
Olean, NY 14760
Pace University—Pleasantville/Briarcliff
Pleasantville, NY 10570
Parsons School of Design
New York, NY 10011
Paul Smiths College
Paul Smiths, NY 12970
Powelson Business Institute
Syracuse, NY 13202
Pratt Phoenix School
New York, NY 10016
Rochester Business Institute
Rochester, NY 14604
St. John's University
Jamaica, NY 11439
Taylor Business Institute
New York, NY 10119
Technical Career Institutes
New York, NY 10001
Tobe-Colburn School for Fashion Careers
New York, NY 10021
Trocaire College
Buffalo, NY 14220
Utica School of Commerce
Utica, NY 13501
Villa Maria College of Buffalo
Buffalo, NY 14225
Westchester Business Institute
White Plains, NY 10606
Wood School
New York, NY 10017

NORTH CAROLINA

Asheboro College
Asheboro, NC 27203
Blanton's Junior College
Asheville, NC 28801
Brevard College
Brevard, NC 28712
Cecils Junior College
Asheville, NC 28806
Chowan College
Murfreesboro, NC 27855
Gaston College
Dallas, NC 28034
Lees-McRae College
Banner Elk, NC 28604
Louisburg College
Louisburg, NC 27549
Mayland Technical Institute
Spruce Pine, NC 28777
Montgomery Technical Institute
Troy, NC 27371
Montreat-Anderson College
Montreat, NC 28757
Mount Olive College
Mount Olive, NC 28365
Peace College
Raleigh, NC 27604
Southeastern Baptist Theological Seminary
Wake Forest, NC 27587
Stanly Technical College
Albemarle, NC 28001
St. Mary's College
Raleigh, NC 27611
Wingate College
Wingate, NC 28174
Winsalm College
Winston-Salem, NC 27101
Winston-Salem Bible College
Winston-Salem, NC 27102

NORTH DAKOTA

Northwest Bible College
Minot, ND 58701
Trinity Bible Institute
Ellendale, ND 58436

OHIO

Ashland College
Ashland, OH 44805
Belmont Technical College
St. Clairsville, OH 43950
Bliss College
Columbus, OH 43214
Chatfield College
St. Martin, OH 45118
Cincinnati Bible College
Cincinnati, OH 45204

Davis Junior College
Toledo, OH 43604
Dyke College
Cleveland, OH 44114
Findlay College
Findlay, OH 45840
Franklin University
Columbus, OH 43215
Kettering College of Medical Arts
Kettering, OH 45429
Lourdes College
Sylvania, OH 43560
Malone College
Canton, OH 44709
Miami-Jacobs Junior College of Business
Dayton, OH 45401
Muskingum Area Technical College
Zanesville, OH 43701
Ohio Institute of Technology
Columbus, OH 43209
Rio Grande Community College
Rio Grande, OH 45674
Stark Technical College
Canton, OH 44720
Tiffin University
Tiffin, OH 44883
University of Steubenville
Steubenville, OH 43952
Ursuline College
Pepper Pike, OH 44124
Walsh College
Canton, OH 44720
Wayne General and Technical College
Orrville, OH 44667
Wooster Business College
Wooster, OH 44691

Oklahoma

Bacone College
Muskogee, OK 74401
Bartlesville Wesleyan College
Bartlesville, OK 74003
Hillsdale Free Will Baptist College
Moore, OK 73153
Oklahoma Baptist University
Shawnee, OK 74801
Oklahoma School of Business
Tulsa, OK 74135
Phillips University
Enid, OK 73701
Spartan School of Aeronautics
Tulsa, OK 74151
St. Geogory's College
Shawnee, OK 74801

Oregon

Bassist College
Portland, OR 97205
Columbia Christian College
Portland, OR 97220
Concordia College
Portland, OR 97211
Judson Baptist College
The Dalles, OR 97058
Western Baptist College
Salem, OR 97302

Pennsylvania

Allentown Business School
Allentown, PA 18101
Alliance College
Cambridge Springs, PA 16403
Alvernia College
Reading, PA 19607
Center for Degree Studies
Scranton, PA 18515
Central Pennsylvania Business School
Summerdale, PA 17093
College Misercordia
Dallas, PA 18612
College of the Academy of the New Church
Bryn Athyn, PA 19009
Elizabethtown College
Elizabethtown, PA 17022
Geneva College
Beaver Falls, PA 15010
Gwynedd-Mercy College
Gwynedd Valley, PA 19437
Harcum Junior College
Bryn Mawr, PA 19010
Johnson School of Technology
Scranton, PA 18508
Keystone Junior College
La Plume, PA 18440
Lackawanna Junior College
Scranton, PA 18503
Manor Junior College
Jenkintown, PA 19046
Mount Aloysius Junior College
Cresson, PA 16630
Northeastern Christian Junior College
Villanova, PA 19085
Peirce Junior College
Philadelphia, PA 19102
Pennco Tech
Bristol, PA 19007
Philadelphia College of the Performing Arts
Philadelphia, PA 19102
Pinebrook Junior College
Coopersburg, PA 18036
Point Park College
Pittsburgh, PA 15222
Spring Garden College
Chestnut Hill, PA 19118
United Wesleyan College
Allentown, PA 18103
University of Pittsburgh—Bradford
Bradford, PA 16701
University of Pittsburgh—Titusville
Titusville, PA 16354
Valley Forge Military Junior College
Wayne, PA 19087
Waynesburg College
Waynesburg, PA 15370
Wilson College
Chambersburg, PA 17201

Rhode Island

Bryant College
Smithfield, RI 02917
Johnson and Wales College
Providence, RI 02903
New England Institute of Technology
Providence, RI 20907

South Carolina

Anderson College
Anderson, SC 29621
Columbia Junior College of Business
Columbia, SC 29201
Friendship College
Rock Hill, SC 29730
North Greenville College
Tigerville, SC 29688
Rutledge College
Spartanburg, SC 29303
Spartanburg Methodist College
Spartanburg, SC 29301
York Technical College
Rock Hill, SC 29730

South Dakota

Dakota Wesleyan University
Mitchell, SD 57301
Freeman Junior College
Freeman, SD 57029
Mount Marty College
Yankton, SD 57078
National College of Business
Rapid City, SD 57709
Presentation College
Aberdeen, SD 57401
Sinte Gleska College
Rosebud, SD 57570
Yankton College
Yankton, SD 57078

Tennessee

Aquinas Junior College
Nashville, TN 37205
Belmont College
Nashville, TN 37203
Bristol College
Bristol, TN 37620
Cumberland College of Tennessee
Lebanon, TN 37087
Draughon's Junior College
Memphis, TN 38116
Draughon's Junior College of Business—Knoxville Branch
Knoxville, TN 37919
Draughon's Junior College of Business—Nashville Branch
Nashville, TN 37203
Edmondson Junior College
Chattanooga, TN 37411
Freed-Hardeman College
Henderson, TN 38340
Hiwassee College
Madisonville, TN 37354
John A. Gupton College
Nashville, TN 37203
Martin College
Pulaski, TN 38478
McKenzie College
Chattanooga, TN 37401
Meharry Medical College
Nashville, TN 37208
Morristown College
Morristown, TN 37814
O'More College of Design
Franklin, TN 37604
Steed College
Johnson City, TN 37601
Tomlinson College
Cleveland, TN 37311
Trevecca Nazarene College
Nashville, TN 37210

Texas

Angelina College
Lufkin, TX 75901
Brookhaven College
Farmers Branch, TX 75234
Cedar Valley College
Lancaster, TX 75134
Concordia Lutheran College
Austin, TX 78705
Fashion and Art Institute of Dallas
Dallas, TX 75220
Jacksonville College
Jacksonville, TX 75766
Lon Morris College
Jacksonville, TX 75766
Mountain View College
Dallas, TX 75211
Northwood Institute—Texas
Cedar Hill, TX 75104
Schreiner College
Kerrville, TX 78028
Southwestern Christian College
Terrell, TX 75160
Southwestern Junior College
Waxahachie, TX 75165

Utah

Latter-Day Saints Business College
Salt Lake City, UT 84111
Stevens Henager College
Ogden, UT 84401

Vermont

Burlington College
Burlington, VT 05401
Champlain College
Burlington, VT 05402
College of St. Joseph the Provider
Rutland, VT 05701
Green Mountain College
Poultney, VT 05764
New England Culinary Institute
Montpelier, VT 05602
Southern Vermont College
Bennington, VT 05201
Vermont College of Norwich University—Two Year Division
Montpelier, VT 05602

Virginia

Averett College
Danville, VA 24541
Bluefield College
Bluefield, VA 24605
Eastern Mennonite College
Harrisonburg, VA 22801
Ferrum College
Ferrum, VA 24088
Marymount College of Virginia
Arlington, VA 22207
National Business College
Roanoke, VA 24009
Shenandoah College and Conservatory of Music
Winchester, VA 22601
Southern Seminary Junior College
Buena Vista, VA 24416
Virginia Intermont College
Bristol, VA 24201

Washington D.C.

Mount Vernon College
Washington, DC 20007
Southeastern University
Washington, DC 20024
Strayer College
Washington, DC 20005

West Virginia

Alderson Broaddus College
Philippi, WV 26416
Beckley College
Beckley, WV 25801
Ohio Valley College
Parkersville, WV 26101
Salem College
Salem, WV 26426
Salem College at Clarksburg
Clarksburg, WV 26301
University of Charleston
Charleston, WV 25304
West Virginia Wesleyan College
Buckhannon, WV 26201

Wisconsin

Alverno College
Milwaukee, WI 53215
Cardinal Stritch College
Milwaukee, WI 53217
Concordia College
Milwaukee, WI 53208
Edgewood College
Madison, WI 53711
Fox Valley Technical Institute
Appleton, WI 54911
Immanuel Lutheran College
Eau Claire, WI 54701
Madison Business College
Madison, WI 53703
Milwaukee School of Engineering
Milwaukee, WI 53201
Milwaukee Stratton College
Milwaukee, WI 53202
Mount Senario College
Ladysmith, WI 54848
Silver Lake College
Manitowoc, WI 54220
Wisconsin Lutheran College
Milwaukee, WI 53226

England

Richmond College
London W 8 5PN, England
University of Evansville—British Campus: Harlaxton College
Grantham, Lincolnshire, England

France

American College in Paris
Paris, France 75007

Puerto Rico

American College of Puerto Rico
Bayamon, PR 00619
Caribbean University College
Bayamon, PR 00619
Instituto Tecnico Comercial Junior College
Rio Piedras, PR 00926
Ramirez College of Business and Technology
Santurce, PR 00910
University of the Sacred Heart
Santurce, PR 00924

Spain

Columbus International College
Seville-13, Spain

Switzerland

American College of Switzerland
Les Avants/Montreux, Switzerland 1833

West Germany

Schiller International University
6900 Heidelberg, West Germany

APPENDIX

MUSIC TERMS
SPACE TERMS*
MATHEMATICAL FORMULAS
SQUARES, SQUARE ROOTS, CUBES, CUBE ROOTS
CHEMICAL ELEMENTS
LOGARITHMS
BIOLOGY HELPS
COOKERY AND NUTRITION
METRIC CONVERSIONS

*The material on space exploration was selected from **Space . . . The New Frontier** and **The Challenge of Space Exploration,** prepared by The National Aeronautics and Space Administration, Washington, D.C.

MUSIC TERMS

absolute music—"abstract" or "pure" music; instrumental music requiring for its appreciation neither words nor story nor any association beyond its basic statement.

absolute pitch—the capacity of identifying or singing any tone at proper pitch without the aid of an instrument.

a cappella—choral music sung without accompaniment.

accent—stress or pulse which emphasizes one note over others in a measure.

accidental—a natural, sharp, or flat not indicated by key-signature.

accompaniment—instrumental or choral support for soloists.

adagio—slow tempo; the name often given to a particular section of a musical work so characterized.

allegro—fast tempo; the name often given to a particular section of a musical work so characterized.

alto—a vocal range for a female voice which lies between soprano and contralto; sometimes mistakenly used for contralto; used to describe certain instruments like the viola.

andante—moderately slow tempo; the name often given to a particular section of a musical work so characterized.

antiphonal—the answering or alternation of two groups, choral or instrumental.

aria—a solo song or air in opera, oratorio, or cantata which often lends itself to a display of skill.

arpeggio—a chord, the notes of which are played successively in ascending or descending order.

art song—short song of high dramatic and formal value.

atonality—designating music in which there is no key center; a twentieth-century compositional style sometimes employing a twelve-tone scale.

augmentation—the repetition of a melody with changes provided by the use of proportionately longer notes.

ballet—an elaborate dance usually telling a story, with instrumental or full orchestral accompaniment for theatrical performance.

bar—a measure in musical notation.

baritone—male vocal register between tenor and bass.

baroque—musical style characteristic of composers from 1600 to 1750; includes works of Bach.

bass—deepest male voice.

beat—the rhythmic pulse of music marking time into relatively equal divisions in the measure.

bel canto—operatic singing technique used to produce a lyrical effect.

binary form—notable in music which uses two contrasting themes in a section.

bravura—great skill and expansiveness of style.

buffo—the character-comic in opera.

cadence—chords at the end of a tune, phrase, section, or movement, which have the effect of bringing the statement to a rest.

cadenza—an elaboration of the cadence, displaying the skill of a soloist.

canon—music, such as a round, in which two or more sections repeat the same melody, starting at different times but overlapping.

cantabile—emphasis upon a "singing" quality in the music.

cantata—an elaborate vocal and instrumental form with arias, recitatives, duets, and chorus, but not requiring dramatic or scenic implementation.

castrato—a eunuch with an adult male voice in the female range.

chamber music—music specifically intended for performance in a small hall, each part usually being taken by one instrument as contrasted with groups or sections of instruments in large orchestras.

chord—three or more tones sounded together.

chromatic—music with many half step intervals not in the diatonic scale.

classical music—the musical style of composers between 1750 and 1825, including the works of Mozart and Beethoven.

clef—sign on the left of each staff indicating sound or exact pitch.

coda—passage which rounds out a section or end of a composition.

coloratura—elaborate vocal passage demonstrating skill of both composer and soloist.

concert master—first violinist in orchestra, frequently also an assistant conductor.

concerto—composition for one or more instruments with orchestral accompaniment.

conductor—orchestra leader, chiefly responsible for musical interpretation.

contralto—lowest pitched female voice.

counterpoint—simultaneous use of two or more melodies.

crescendo—becoming gradually louder.

development—compositional exploration and restatement of thematic idea.

diatonic—opposite of chromatic; music confined to the use of notes in a given major or minor key.

discord—*See* dissonance.

dissonance—a combination of clashing tones requiring the addition of other tones for resolution.

divertimento—a light instrumental composition in several short movements.

dominant—fifth tone in the minor or major scale.

downbeat—first strong accent in each measure.

encore—repetition of a piece or performance of an additional one in response to applause.

enharmonic—a tone having several different forms of notation.

ensemble—combination of performers; also, overall quality of musical expression.

equal temperament—division of octave into twelve equal halftones; also characteristic method of tuning instruments.

étude—"study music" composed for practice purposes but often included in concert repertoires.

exposition—in sonata form, among others, a first section containing statement of themes to be developed.

expression—immediate personal and emotional interpretation of music by a performer.

falsetto—adult male voice used in an unnaturally high pitch.

fermata—a long pause.

finale—last section of a composition.

flat—notation indicating the lowering of a tone by a half step.

forte—loud.

fugue—a musical form similar to the canon but one in which various imitations of the melody occur in shorter phrases.

fundamental—primary note of a chord or harmonic series.

glissando—tonal effect produced by sliding finger over the strings or keys of an instrument.

grace note—an embellishing note, printed in smaller type.

Gregorian chant—early church music named for Pope Gregory I; used in Roman Catholic church services.

harmony—the simultaneous combination of tones into chords; also the study of chord functions and structure.

homophony—music composed of a melody supported by harmonic chordal accompaniment.

hymn—originally a religious song in praise of God; also used of songs with a patriotic theme.

imitation—technique of composition

which repeats theme or melody, making use of several instruments or voices as in canon, fugue, or round.

impressionism—the musical style of late nineteenth- and early twentieth-century composers, including Debussy and Ravel.

interval—the difference in pitch between two notes.

intonation—fidelity of pitch.

inversion—reversing or inverting the position of notes in chords or intervals.

-issimo—suffix meaning "very," added to many musical terms.

jazz—music of black American origin, initially called "ragtime," and characterized by syncopated rhythm.

key—scale; relating to a system of tonal relationships developed from a tonic keynote.

keynote—base or principal note from which a scale is derived.

largo—a very slow and deliberate tempo; the name often given to a particular section of a musical work so characterized.

legato—smooth transitions from note to note without breaks.

leitmotiv—thematic melody used recurrently to identify specific characters, events, places, ideas, or emotions; characteristically used by Wagner.

lento—slow tempo between andante and largo.

libretto—the entire literary text of a musical work utilizing singing and speaking.

lyrics—words set to music.

measure—a horizontally lined space between two vertical bar lines which mark off a section of a staff.

medieval music—styles of music developed during the thousand-year period beginning A.D. 500, primarily vocal; greatly influenced by church liturgy, by court and peasant life.

melodrama—scene or play in which a musical background accompanies action and dialogue.

melody—a succession of notes of varying pitch and duration having a distinct pattern.

meter—strong and weak accents in rhythmical pattern.

metronome—a clockwork pendulum invented to insure standard tempi.

mezzo—prefix meaning "half."

mezzo-soprano—female voice between soprano and alto ranges.

M.M.—letters indicating metronomic setting.

mode—general term for system(s) of arranging intervals of a scale.

moderato—moderate tempo.

modern music—styles of music developed from the beginning of the twentieth century, as distinguished from earlier styles still flourishing; among the former, works of Schoenberg and Bartok.

modulation—change of key or tonality through a succession of chords.

molto—very or much more, as in molto adagio (very slowly).

monophony—unaccompanied music composed only of a melodic line.

mordent—a grace note.

motive—a musical phrase which reappears irregularly.

movement—major division of a musical composition.

natural—symbol indicating the return of a tone to its natural pitch from a previous sharping or flatting.

notation—entire system employed for writing Western music.

obbligato—an accompaniment which is an indispensable and intrinsic part of the musical statement; by misuse, in some nineteenth-century music used in the opposite sense to refer to a part which is optional.

octave—the interval covering eight successive notes in the diatonic scale, e.g., middle C to the C above it.

opera—a form of drama set to orchestral music in which most of the dialogue is sung; generally presented in an elaborate production.

opus—a composition or set of compositions; customarily accompanied by a number to indicate its place in the chronological order of a composer's work.

oratorio—a form of drama set to orchestral music and voice; differing from opera in the absence of staging, costumes, and scenery; usually on a religious subject.

overture—introductory instrumental music to an opera or play; also now an independent form.

partita—originally, variations or a set of dances; by extension, used to mean "suite."

phrase—a short distinguishable part of a melody.

piano—softly.

pitch—degree of highness or lowness of a sound.

più—more; as in più lento (more slowly).

poco—a little.

polyphony—music composed of at least two melodies played simultaneously.

polytonality—simultaneous use of two different keys.

prelude—a short composition which can be a piece of a single movement, the beginning of a longer work, or an overture.

presto—very fast tempo; the name often given to a particular section of a musicat work so characterized.

program music—descriptive music which tells a story or describes a place; frequently employs explanatory or supportive program literature; the opposite of "absolute music."

progression—advance from one tone to another or from one chord to another.

quartet—an intimate musical form for four instruments or voices.

quintet—similar to quartet but refers to five instruments or voices.

recapitulation—repetition of a thematic statement after an intervening development and contrast.

reprise—repeat of a segment of music.

rest—musical notation indicating silence.

rhapsody—a very free musical form developed during the nineteenth century.

rhythm—recurrent pattern created by the accent and duration of notes.

rondo—a musical form in which the main theme is consistently repeated throughout.

scale—a series of consecutive tones forming an octave.

scherzo—usually the third movement of a larger composition; humorous and lively.

score—written or printed piece of music in which the different instruments or voices are entered on a separate staff, one above the other.

sharp—notation raising a tone by a half step.

signature—symbol placed at the beginning of a composition specifying key and tempo.

sonata—a composition for one or more instruments.

soprano—the highest female singing voice.

staff—the five horizontal lines and intervening spaces upon which musical notation is made.

symphonic poem—a tone poem; a form of program music.

symphony—major form of orchestral work, divided into movements.

syncopation—kind of rhythm created by altering the natural accent into a weak beat.

tempo (pl: tempi)—the rate of speed at which a piece or passage of music moves.

tenor—highest normal adult male voice; also the range of some instruments.

theme—melody used as the main musical line for development and variation.

tonality—the adherence to the keynote (tonic) as the referent of all chords and harmonies used in a composition or part of a composition.

tone—a note; sound with a fixed pitch.

tone poem—*See* symphonic poem.

transpose—changing key or pitch, leaving all other musical relationships intact.

treble—the highest register of musical sound.

upbeat—weak beat preceding a heavy accent.

variation—alteration of a melody that still retains its essential qualities.

Space Terms*

ablation—the removal of surface material from a body by vaporization, melting, or other process; specifically the intentional removal of material from a nose cone or spacecraft during high-speed movement through a plan etary atmosphere to provide thermal protection to the underlying structure.

absolute zero—the theoretical temperature at which all molecular motion ceases.

acceleration—the rate of change of velocity.

acquisition and tracking radar—a radar set that locks onto a strong signal and tracks the object reflecting the signal.

aerodynamics—the science of the motion of air and other gaseous fluids, and of the forces acting on bodies when the bodies move through such fluids, or of the movement of such fluids against or around the bodies, as "his research in aerodynamics."

aerolite—a meteorite composed principally of stony material.

aerospace—(from aeronautics and space) of or pertaining to both the earth's atmosphere and space, as in "aerospace industries."

aerothermodynamic border—an altitude at about 100 miles, above which the atmosphere is so rarefied that the motion of an object through it at high speeds generates no significant surface heat.

aerothermodynamics—the study of the aerodynamic and thermodynamic problems connected with aerodynamic heating.

airglow—a relatively steady visible emission from the upper atmosphere, as distinguished from the sporadic emission of aurorae.

albedo—the ratio of the amount of electromagnetic radiation reflected by a body to the amount falling upon it, commonly expressed as a percentage.

angel—a radar echo caused by a physical phenomenon not discernible to the eye.

annular eclipse—an eclipse in which a thin ring of the source of light appears around the obscuring body.

aphelion—the point at which a planet or other celestial object in orbit about the sun is farthest from the sun.

apogee—in an orbit about the earth, the point at which the satellite is farthest from the earth; the highest altitude reached by a sounding rocket.

areo—combining form of Ares (Mars) as in "areography."

asteroid—one of the many small celestial bodies revolving around the sun, most of the orbits being between those of Mars and Jupiter. Also called "planetoid," "minor planet."

astroballistics—the study of the phenomena arising out of the motion of a solid through a gas at speeds high enough to cause ablation; for example, the interaction of a meteoroid with the atmosphere.

attitude—the position or orientation of an aircraft, spacecraft, etc., either in motion or at rest, as determined by the relationship between its axes and some reference line or plane such as the horizon.

aurora—the sporadic visible emission from the upper atmosphere over middle and high latitudes. Also called "northern lights."

azimuth—horizontal direction or bearing.

Baker-Nunn camera—a large camera used in tracking satellites.

ballistics—the science that deals with the motion, behavior, and effects of projectiles, especially bullets, aerial bombs, rockets, or the like; the science or art of designing and hurling projectiles so as to achieve a desired performance.

balloon-type rocket—a rocket, such as Atlas, that requires the pressure of its propellants (or other gases) within it to give it structural integrity.

beam-rider—a craft following a beam, particularly one which does so automatically, the beam providing the guidance.

bipropellant—a rocket propellant consisting of two unmixed or uncombined chemicals (fuel and oxidizer) fed to the combustion chamber separately.

blip—*See* **pip.**

boilerplate—as in "boilerplate capsule," a metal copy of the flight model, the structure or components of which are heavier than the flight model.

boiloff—the vaporization of a cold propellant, such as liquid oxygen or liquid hydrogen, as the temperature of the propellant mass rises,as in the tank of a rocket being readied for launch.

booster engine—an engine, especially a booster rocket, that adds its thrust to the thrust of the sustainer engine.

booster rocket—1. a rocket engine, either solid or liquid fuel, that assists the normal propulsive system, or sustainer engine, of a rocket or aeronautical vehicle in some phase of its flight. 2. a rocket used to set a missile vehicle in motion before another engine takes over.

boostglide vehicle—a vehicle (half aircraft, half spacecraft) designed to fly to the limits of the sensible atmosphere, then be boosted by rockets into the space above, returning to earth by gliding under aerodynamic control.

braking ellipses—a series of ellipses, decreasing in size due to aerodynamic drag, followed by a spacecraft in entering a planetary atmosphere.

breakoff phenomenon—the feeling which sometimes occurs during high altitude flight of being totally separated and detached from the earth and human society. Also called the "breakaway phenomenon."

centrifuge—specifically, a large motor-driven apparatus with a long arm at the end of which human and animal subjects or equipment can be revolved and rotated at various speeds to simulate very closely the prolonged accelerations encountered in highperformance aircraft, rockets, and spacecraft.

checkout—a sequence of actions taken to test or examine a launch vehicle or spacecraft as to its readiness to perform its intended function.

chemosphere—the vaguely defined region of the upper atmosphere in which photochemical reactions take place.

cislunar—(Latin *cis,* "on this side") of or

*The material on space exploration was selected from **Space . . . The New Frontier** and **The Challenge of Space Exploration,** prepared by The National Aeronautics and Space Administration, Washington, D.C.

pertaining to phenomena, projects, or activity in the space between the earth and moon, or between the earth and the moon's orbit.

closed ecological system—a system that provides for the maintenance of life in an isolated living chamber such as a spacecraft cabin by means of a cycle wherein exhaled carbon dioxide, urine, and other waste matter are converted chemically or by photosynthesis into oxygen, water, and food.

cold-flow test—a test of a liquid rocket without firing it to check or verify the efficiency of a propulsion subsystem, providing for the conditioning and flow of propellants (including tank pressurization, propellant loading, and propellant feeding).

companion body—a nose cone, last-stage rocket, or other body that orbits along with an earth satellite.

complex—entire area of launch site facilities. This includes blockhouse, launch pad, gantry, etc. Also referred to as a "launch complex."

composite propellant—a solid rocket propellant consisting of a fuel and an oxidizer.

conic section—a curve formed by the intersection of a plane and a right circular cone. Usually called "conic."

console—an array of controls and indicators for the monitoring and control of a particular sequence of actions, as in the checkout of a rocket, a countdown action, or a launch procedure.

control rocket—a vernier engine, retro-rocket, or other such rocket, used to guide or make small changes in the velocity of a rocket, spacecraft, or the like.

corona—the faintly luminous outer envelope of the sun. Also called "solar corona."

cosmic rays—the extremely high energy subatomic particles which bombard the atmosphere from outer space. Cosmic-ray primaries seem to be mostly protons, hydrogen nuclei, but also comprise heavier nuclei. On colliding with atmospheric particles they produce many different kinds of lower-energy secondary cosmic radiation.

cryogenic temperature—in general, a temperature range below about–50° C.; more particularly, temperatures within a few degrees of absolute zero.

deep space probes—spacecraft designed for exploring space to the vicinity of the moon and beyond. Deep space probes with specific missions may be referred to as "lunar probe," "Mars probe," "solar probe," etc.

diplexer—a device permitting an antenna system to be used simultaneously or separately by two transmitters. *Compare with* **duplexer.**

dish—a parabolic type of radio or radar antenna, roughly the shape of a soup bowl.

Doppler shift—the change in frequency with which energy reaches a receiver when the source of radiation or a reflector of the radiation and the receiver are in motion relative to each other. The Doppler shift is used in many tracking and navigation systems.

dosimeter—a device, worn by persons working around radioactive material, which indicates the amount (dose) of radiation to which they have been exposed.

Dovap—from Doppler, velocity and position, a tracking system which uses the Doppler shift caused by a target moving relative to a ground transmitter to obtain velocity and position information.

drogue parachute—a type of parachute attached to a body, used to slow it down; also called "deceleration parachute," or "drag parachute."

duplexer—a device which permits a single antenna system to be used for both transmitting and receiving.

eccentric—not having the same center; varying from a circle, as in "eccentric orbit."

ecological system—a habitable environment, either created artifically, such as in a manned space vehicle, or occurring naturally, such as the environment on the surface of the earth, in which man, animals, or other organisms can live in mutual relationship with each other.

escape velocity—the radial speed which a particle or larger body must attain in order to escape from the gravitational field of a planet or star.

extraterrestrial—from outside the earth.

film cooling—the cooling of a body or surface, such as the inner surface of a rocket combustion chamber, by maintaining a thin fluid layer over the affected area.

flashback—a reversal of flame propagation in a system, counter to the usual flow of the combustible mixture.

flux—the rate of flow of some quantity, often used in reference to the flow of some form of energy.

flying test bed—an aircraft, rocket, or other flying vehicle used to carry objects or devices being flight tested.

g or G—an acceleration equal to the acceleration of gravity, 32.2 feet per second per second at sea level; used as a unit of stress measurement for bodies undergoing acceleration.

gantry—a frame structure that spans over something, as an elevated platform that runs astride a work area, supported by wheels on each side; specifically, short for "gantry crane" or "gantry scaffold."

gas cap—the gas immediately in front of a meteoroid or reentry body as it travels through the atmosphere; the leading portion of a meteor. This gas is compressed and adiabatically heated to incandescence.

geo—a prefix meaning "earth," as in "geology," "geophysics."

geoprobe—a rocket vehicle designed to explore space near the earth at a distance of more than 4,000 miles from the earth's surface. Rocket vehicles operating lower than 4,000 miles are termed "sounding rockets."

gimbal—1. a device with two mutually perpendicular and intersecting axes of rotation, thus giving free angular movement in two directions, on which an engine or other object may be mounted. 2. in a gyro, a support which provides the spin axis with a degree of freedom.

gnotobiotics—the study of germ-free animals.

gravity—the force imparted by the earth to a mass on, or close to the earth. Since the earth is rotating, the force observed as gravity is the resultant of the force of gravitation and the centrifugal force arising from this rotation.

g-suit or G-suit—a suit that exerts pressure on the abdomen and lower parts of the body to prevent or retard the collection of blood below the chest under positive acceleration.

g-tolerance—a tolerance in a person or other animal, or in a piece of equipment, to an acceleration of a particular value.

gyro—a device which utilizes the angular momentum of a spinning rotor to sense angular motion of its base about one or two axes at right angles to the spin axis. Also called "gyroscope."

hardness—of X rays and other radiation of high energy, a measure of penetrating power. Radiation which will penetrate a 10-centimeter thickness of lead is considered "hard radiation."

hot test—a propulsion system test conducted by actually firing the propellants.

hypersonic—1. pertaining to hypersonic flow. 2. pertaining to speeds of Mach 5 or greater.

inertial guidance—guidance by means of acceleration measured and integrated within the craft.

infrared—infrared radiation; electromagnetic radiation in the wavelength interval from the red end of the visible spectrum on the lower limit to microwaves used in radar on the upper limit.

insertion—the process of putting an artificial satellite into orbit. Also the time of such action.

ionosphere—the part of the earth's outer atmosphere where ions and electrons are present in quantities sufficient to affect the propagation of radio waves.

Kepler's laws—the three empirical laws describing the motions of planets in their orbits, discovered by Johannes Kepler (1571–1630). These are: (1) The orbits of the planets are ellipses, with the sun at a common focus. (2) As a planet moves in its orbit, the line joining the planet and sun sweeps over equal areas in equal intervals of time. Also called "law of equal areas." (3) The squares of the periods of revolution of any two planets are proportional to the cubes of their mean distances from the sun.

launch ring—the metal ring on the launch pad on which a missile stands before launch.

launch vehicle—any device which propels and guides a spacecraft into orbit about the earth or into a trajectory to another celestial body. Often called "booster."

launch window—an interval of time during which a rocket can be launched to accomplish a particular purpose, as "liftoff occurred 5 minutes after the beginning of the 82-minute launch window".

lib ration—a real or apparent oscillatory motion, particularly the apparent oscillation of the moon.

Mach number—(after Ernst Mach [1838–1916], Austrian scientist) a number expressing the ratio of the speed of a body or of a point on a body with respect to the surrounding air or other fluid, or the speed of a flow, to the speed of sound in the medium; the speed represented by this number.

manometer—an instrument for measuring pressure of gases and vapors both above and below atmospheric pressure.

mass—the measure of the amount of matter in a body, thus its inertia.

mass-energy equivalence—the equivalence of a quantity of mass m and a quantity of energy E, the two quantities being related by the mass-energy relation $E = mc^2$, *where* c = the speed of light.

meteor—in particular, the light phenomenon which results from the entry into the earth's atmosphere of a solid particle from space; more generally, any physical object or phenomenon associated with such an event.

microwave region—commonly that region of the radio spectrum between approximately one thousand megacycles and three hundred thousand megacycles.

missile—any object thrown, dropped, fired, launched, or otherwise projected with the purpose of striking a target. Short for "ballistic missile," "guided missile."

mockup—a full-sized replica or dummy of something, such as a spacecraft, often made of some substitute material, such as wood, and sometimes incorporating functioning pieces of equipment, such as engines.

module—1. a self-contained unit of a launch vehicle or spacecraft which serves as a building block for the overall structure. The module is usually designated by its primary function as "command module," "lunar landing module," etc. 2. a one-package assembly of functionally associated electronic parts; usually a plug-in unit.

Newton's laws of motion—a set of three fundamental postulates forming the basis of the mechanics of rigid bodies, formulated by Newton in 1687.

The first law is concerned with the principle of inertia and states that if a body in motion is not acted upon by an external force, its momentum remains constant (law of conservation of momentum). The second law asserts that the rate of change of momentum of a body is proportional to the force acting upon the body and is in the direction of the applied force. A familiar statement of this is the equation

$$F = ma,$$

where F is vector sum of the applied forces, m the mass, and a the vector acceleration of the body. The third law is the principle of action and reaction, stating that for every force acting upon a body there exists a corresponding force of the same magnitude exerted by the body in the opposite direction.

normal shock wave—a shock wave perpendicular, or substantially so, to the direction of flow in a supersonic flow field. Sometimes shortened to "normal shock."

nozzle—specifically, the part of a rocket thrust chamber assembly in which the gases produced in the chamber are accelerated to high velocities.

orbital elements—a set of seven parameters defining the orbit of a satellite.

order of magnitude—a factor of 10.

paraglider—a flexible-winged, kite-like vehicle designed for use in a recovery system for launch vehicles or as a reentry vehicle.

passive—reflecting a signal without transmission, as "Echo is a passive satellite." Contrasted with "active."

perigee—that orbital point nearest the earth when the earth is the center of attraction.

photosphere—the intensely bright portion of the sun visible to the unaided eye.

pickoff—a sensing device, used in combination with a gyroscope in an automatic pilot or other automatic or robot apparatus, that responds to angular movement to create a signal or to effect some type of control.

pickup—a device that converts a sound, view, or other form of intelligence into corresponding electric signals (e.g., a microphone, a television camera, or a phonograph pickup).

pip—signal indication on the scope of an electronic instrument, produced by a short, sharply peaked pulse of voltage. Also called "blip."

pitchover—the programmed turn from the vertical that a rocket under power takes as it describes an arc and points in a direction other than vertical.

posigrade rocket—an auxiliary rocket which fires in the direction in which the vehicle is pointed, used for example in separating two stages of a vehicle.

precession—the change in the direction of the axis of rotation of a spinning body or of the plane of the orbit of an orbiting body when acted upon by an outside force.

prestage—a step in the action of igniting a large liquid rocket taken prior to the ignition of the full flow, and consisting of igniting a partial flow of propellants into the thrust chamber.

primary—1. short for "primary body." 2. short for "primary cosmic ray."

primary cosmic rays—high-energy particles originating outside the earth's atmosphere.

probe—any device inserted in an environment for the purpose of obtaining information about the environment, specifically, an instrumented vehicle moving through the upper atmosphere or space, or landing upon another celestial body in order to obtain information about the specific environment.

prominence—a filament-like protuberance from the visible portion of the sun.

proton—a positively charged subatomic particle of a positive charge equal to the negative charge of the electron but of 1,837 times the mass; a constituent of all atomic nuclei.

proving stand—a test stand for reaction engines, especially rocket engines.

purge—to rid a line or tank of residual fluid, especially of fuel or oxygen in the tanks or lines of a rocket after a test firing or simulated test firing.

radar astronomy—the study of celestial bodies within the solar system by means of radiation originating on earth but reflected from the body under observation.

radiosonde—a balloon-borne instrument for the simultaneous measurement and transmission of meteorological data.

reaction control system—a system of controlling the attitude of a craft when outside the atmosphere by using jets of gas in lieu of aerodynamic control surfaces.

readout—the action of a radio transmitter transmitting data either instantaneously with the acquisition of the data or by play of a magnetic tape upon which the data have been recorded.

real time—time in which reporting on events or recording of events is simultaneous with the events.

recombination—the process by which a positive and a negative ion join to form a neutral molecule or other neutral particle.

red shift—in astronomy, the displacement of observed spectral lines toward the longer wavelengths of the red end of the spectrum. *Compare* **space reddening.**

reentry—the event occurring when a spacecraft or other object comes back into the sensible atmosphere after being rocketed to altitudes above the sensible atmosphere; the action involved in this event.

regenerator—a device used in a thermo-dynamic process for capturing and returning to the process heat that would otherwise be lost.

relativity—a principle that postulates the equivalence of the description of the universe, in terms of physical laws, by various observers, or for various frames of reference.

rocket engine—a reaction engine that contains within itself, or carries along with itself, all the substances necessary for its operation or for the consumption or combustion of its fuel, not requiring intake of any outside substance and hence capable of operation in outer space. Also called "rocket motor."

rocketsonde—meteorological rocket.

rockoon—a high-altitude sounding system consisting of a small solid-propellant research rocket launched from a large plastic balloon.

roll—the rotational or oscillatory movement of an aircraft or similar body which takes place about a longitudinal axis through the body—called "roll" for any amount of such rotation.

rotation—turning of a body about an axis within the body, as the daily rotation of the earth.

rumble—a form of combustion instability, especially in a liquid-propellant rocket engine, characterized by a low-pitched, low-frequency rumbling noise; the noise made in this kind of combustion.

scrub—to cancel a scheduled rocket firing, either before or during countdown.

selenocentric—relating to the center of the moon; referring to the moon as a center.

selenographic—1. of or pertaining to the physical geography of the moon. 2. specifically, referring to positions on the moon measured in latitude from the moon's equator and in longitude from a reference meridian.

sensible atmosphere—that part of the atmosphere that offers resistance to a body passing through it.

sensor—the component of an instrument that converts an input signal into a quantity which is measured by another part of the instrument. Also called "sensing element."

service tower—*See* **gantry.**

shock tube—a relatively long tube or pipe in which very brief high-speed gas flows are produced by the sudden release of gas at very high pressure into a low-pressure portion of the tube; the high-speed flow moves into the region of low pressure behind a shock wave.

solar wind—a stream of protons constantly moving outward from the sun.

sounding—1. in geophysics, any penetration of the natural environment for scientific observation. 2. in meteorology, same as upper-air observation. However, a common connotation is that of a single complete radiosonde observation.

space—1. specifically, the part of the universe lying outside the limits of the earth's atmosphere. 2. more generally, the volume in which all spatial bodies, including the earth, move.

space reddening—the observed reddening, or absorption of shorter wavelengths, of the light from distant celestial bodies caused by scattering by small particles in interstellar space. *Compare* **red shift.**

specific impulse—a performance parameter of a rocket propellant, expressed in seconds, and equal to thrust (in pounds) divided by weight flow rate (in pounds per second). *See* **thrust.**

sunspot—a relatively dark area on the surface of the sun, consisting of a dark central umbra and a surrounding penumbra that is intermediate in brightness between the umbra and the surrounding photosphere.

sunspot cycle—a periodic variation in the number and area of sunspots with an average length of 11.1 years, but varying between about 7 and 17 years.

sustainer engine—an engine that maintains the velocity of a missile or rocket vehicle, once it has achieved its programmed velocity through use of a booster engine.

synchronous satellite—an equatorial west-to-east satellite orbiting the earth at an altitude of 22,300 statute miles, at which altitude it makes one revolution in 24 hours, synchronous with the earth's rotation.

synergic curve—a curve plotted for the ascent of a rocket, space-air vehicle, or space vehicle calculated to give the vehicle an optimum economy in fuel with an optimum velocity.

tektite—a small glassy body containing no crystals, probably of meteoritic origin, and bearing no antecedent relation to the geological formation in which it occurs.

telemetry—the science of measuring a quantity or quantities, transmitting the measured value to a distant station, and there interpreting, indicating, or recording the quantities measured.

thermodynamics—the study of the relationships between heat and other forms of energy.

thermonuclear—pertaining to a nuclear reaction that is triggered by particles of high thermal energy.

thrust—1. the pushing force developed by an aircraft engine or a rocket engine. 2. specifically, in rocketry, the product of propellant mass flow rate and exhaust velocity relative to the vehicle.

topside sounder—a satellite designed to measure ion concentration in the ionosphere from above the ionosphere.

transit—1. the passage of a celestial body across a celestial meridian; usually called "meridian transit." 2. the apparent passage of a celestial body across the face of another celestial body or across any point, area, or line.

translunar—of or pertaining to space outside the moon's orbit about the earth.

transponder—a combined receiver and transmitter whose function is to transmit signals automatically when triggered by an interrogating signal.

T-time—any specific time, minus or plus, as referenced to "zero," or "launch" time, during a countdown sequence that is intended to result in the firing of a rocket propulsion unit that launches a rocket vehicle or missile.

ullage—the amount that a container, such as a fuel tank, lacks of being full.

ultraviolet radiation—electromagnetic radiation shorter in wavelength than visible radiation but longer than X-rays; roughly, radiation in the wavelength interval between 10 and 4,000 angstroms.

umbilical cord—any of the servicing electrical or fluid lines between the ground or a tower and an upright rocket missile or vehicle before the launch. Often shortened to "umbilical."

Van Allen Belt, Van Allen Radiation Belt, Van Allen Radiation Region (for James A. Van Allen, 1914–)—the zone of high-intensity radiation surrounding the earth beginning at altitudes of approximately 500 miles.

vernier engine—a rocket engine of small thrust used primarily to obtain a fine adjustment in the velocity and trajectory of a ballistic missile or space vehicle just after the thrust cutoff of the last propulsion engine, and used secondarily to add thrust to a booster or sustainer engine. Also called "vernier rocket."

weightlessness—1. a condition in which no acceleration, whether of gravity or other force, can be detected by an observer within the system in question. 2. a condition in which gravitational and other external forces acting on a body produce no stress, either internal or external, in the body.

yaw—1. the lateral rotational or oscillatory movement of an aircraft, rocket, or the like about a transverse axis. 2. the amount of this movement; i.e., the angle of yaw.

zero g—*See* **weightlessness.**

MATHEMATICAL FORMULAS

CIRCUMFERENCE

Circle .... $C = d\pi$, in which π is 3.1416 and d the diameter.

AREA

Circle .... $A = r^2\pi$, in which π is 3.1416 and r the radius.

Rectangle .... $A = ab$, in which a is the base and b the height.

Sphere .... $A = 4r^2\pi$, in which r is the radius.

Trapezoid .... $A = \frac{h\,(a+b)}{2}$, in which h is the height, a the longer parallel side, and b the shorter.

Triangle .... $A = \frac{ab}{2}$, in which a is the base and b the height.

VOLUME

Cone .... $V = \frac{r^2\pi h}{3}$, in which π is 3.1416, r the radius of the base, and h the height.

Cube .... $V = a^3$, in which a is one of the edges.

Cylinder .... $V = r^2\pi h$, in which π is 3.1614, r the radius of the base, and h the height.

Pyramid .... $V = \frac{Ah}{3}$, in which A is the area of the base and h the height.

Rectangular Prism .... $V = abc$, in which a is the length, b the width, and c the depth.

Sphere .... $V = \frac{4\pi r^3}{3}$, in which π is 3.1416 and r the radius.

FALLING BODIES

Speed per second acquired by falling body: $S = 32t$, in which t is the time in seconds.

Distance in feet traveled by falling body: $D = 16t$, in which t is the time in seconds.

SPEED OF SOUND

Speed of sound in feet per second through any given temperature of air: $S = \frac{1087\sqrt{273+t}}{16.52}$, in which t is the temperature in Centigrade.

ENERGY AND MATTER

Conversion of matter into energy (Einstein's theorem): $E = mc^2$, in which E is the energy in ergs, m the mass of the matter in grams, and c the speed of light in centimeters per second. ($c^2 = 9.10^{20}$).

FORMULAS USED IN SOLID GEOMETRY

LATERAL AREA

Cone of revolution	$L = \pi rs$
Cylinder of revolution	$L = 2\pi rh$
Frustum of cone of revolution	$L = \frac{1}{2}s(c + c')$
Frustum of regular pyramid	$L = \frac{1}{2}s(p + p')$
Prism	$L = ep$
Regular pyramid	$L = \frac{1}{2}sp$

TOTAL AREA

Cone of revolution	$T = \pi r(r + s)$
Cylinder of revolution	$T = 2\pi r(r + h)$
Sphere	$S = 4\pi r^2$
Zone	$S = 2\pi rh$

VOLUME

Circular cone	$V = \frac{1}{3}\pi r^2 h$
Circular cylinder	$V = Bh$
Cube	$V = e^3$
Cylinder of revolution	$V = \pi r^2 h$
Frustum of circular cone	$V = \frac{1}{3}\pi h(r^2 + r'^2 + rr')$
Frustum of pyramid	$V = \frac{1}{3}h(B + B' + \sqrt{BB'})$
Prism	$V = Bh$
Prismatoid	$V = \frac{1}{6}h(B_1 + B_2 + 4M)$
Pyramid	$V = \frac{1}{3}Bh$
Rectangular solid	$V = lwh$
Sphere	$V = \frac{4}{3}\pi r^3$
Spherical sector	$V = \frac{1}{3}rS$

PHYSICAL CONSTANTS

QUANTITY	SYMBOL	VALUE
Gravitational constant	G	$6.67 \times 10^{-11}\ n \cdot m^2/kg^2$
Acceleration of gravity at earth's surface	g	$9.81\ m/sec^2 = 32.2 ft/sec^2$
Atmospheric pressure at sea level	(none)	$14.7\ lb/in^2 = 1.01 \times 10^5\ n/m^2$
Absolute zero	$0^\circ K$	$-273^\circ C$
Boltzmann's constant	k	$1.38 \times 10^{-23}\ j/^\circ K$
Electrostatic constant	C	$9.00 \times 10^9\ n \cdot m^2/coul^2$
Electromagnetic constant	μ	$1.26 \times 10^{-6} \cdot weber/amp \cdot m$
Charge of electron	e	$1.60 \times 10^{-19}\ coul$
Electron rest mass	m_e	$9.11 \times 10^{-31}\ kg$
Proton rest mass	m_p	$1.67 \times 10^{-27}\ kg$
Neutron rest mass	m_n	$1.67 \times 10^{-27}\ kg$
Speed of light	c	$3.00 \times 10^8\ m/sec$
Planck's constant	h	$6.63 \times 10^{-34}\ j \cdot sec$

TABLES OF INTERRELATION OF UNITS OF MEASUREMENT

UNITS OF LENGTH

Units	Inches	Links	Feet
1 inch =	1	0.126 262 6	0.083 333 33
1 link =	7.92	1	0.66
1 foot =	12	1.515 152	1
1 yard =	36	4 545 45	3
1 rod =	198	25	16.5
1 chain =	792	100	66
1 mile =	63 360	8000	5280
1 centimeter =	0.393 700 8	0.049 709 70	0.032 808 40
1 meter =	39.370 08	4.970 970	3.280 840

Units	Yards	Rods	Chains
1 inch =	0.027 777 78	0.005 050 505	0.001 262 626
1 link =	0.22	0.04	0.01
1 foot =	0.333 333 3	0.060 606 06	0.015 151 52
1 yard =	1	0.181 818 2	0.045 454 55
1 rod =	5.5	1	0.25
1 chain =	22	4	1
1 mile =	1760	320	80
1 centimeter =	0.010 936 13	0.001 988 388	0.000 497 097 0
1 meter =	1.093 613	0.198 838 8	0.049 709 70

Units	Miles	Centimeters	Meters
1 inch =	0.000 015 782 83	2.54	0.025 4
1 link =	0.000 125	20.116 8	0.201 168
1 foot =	0.000 189 393 9	30.48	0.304 8
1 yard =	0.000 568 181 8	91.44	0.914 4
1 rod =	0.003 125	502.92	5.029 2
1 chain =	0.012 5	2011.68	20.116 8
1 mile =	1	160 934.4	1609.344
1 centimeter =	0.000 006 213 712	1	0.01
1 meter =	0.000 621 371 2	100	1

UNITS OF VOLUME

Units	Cubic inches	Cubic feet	Cubic yards
1 cubic inch =	1	0.000 578 703 7	0.000 021 433 47
1 cubic foot =	1728	1	0.037 037 04
1 cubic yard =	46 656	27	1
1 cubic centimeter =	0.061 023 74	0.000 035 314 67	0.000 001 307 951
1 cubic decimeter =	61.023 74	0.035 314 67	0.001 307 951
1 cubic meter =	61 023.74	35.314 67	1.307 951

Units	Cubic Centimeters	Cubic decimeters	Cubic meters
1 cubic inch =	16.387 064	0.016 387 064	0.000 016 387 064
1 cubic foot =	28 316.846 592	28.316 846 592	0.028 316 846 592
1 cubic yard =	764 554.857 984	764.554 857 984	0.764 554 857 984
1 cubic centimeter =	1	0.001	0.000 001
1 cubic decimeter =	1 000	1	0.001
1 cubic meter =	1 000 000	1000	1

UNITS OF AREA

Units		Square inches	Square links	Square feet	Square yards
1 square inch	=	1	0.015 942 25	0.006 944 444	0.000 771 604 9
1 square link	=	62.726 4	1	0.435 6	0.048 4
1 square foot	=	144	2.295 684	1	0.111 111 1
1 square yard	=	1296	20.661 16	9	1
1 square rod	=	39 204	625	272.25	30.25
1 square chain	=	627 264	10 000	4356	484
1 acre	=	6 272 640	100 000	43 560	4840
1 square mile	=	4 014 489 600	64 000 000	27 878 400	3 097 600
1 square centimeter	=	0.155 000 3	0.002 471 054	0.001 076 391	0.000 119 599 0
1 square meter	=	1550.003	24.710 54	10.763 91	1.195 990
1 hectare	=	15 500 031	247 105.4	107 639.1	11 959.90

Units		Square rods	Square chains	Acres	Square miles
1 square inch	=	0.000 025 507 60	0.000 001 594 225	0.000 000 159 422 5	0.000 000 000 249 097 7
1 square link	=	0.001 6	0.000 1	0.000 01	0.000 000 015 625
1 square foot	=	0.003 673 095	0.000 229 568 4	0.000 022 956 84	0.000 000 035 870 06
1 square yard	=	0.033 057 85	0.002 066 116	0.000 206 611 6	0.000 000 322 830 6
1 square rod	=	1	0.062 5	0.006 25	0.000 009 765 625
1 square chain	=	16	1	0.1	0.000 156 25
1 acre	=	160	10	1	0.001 562 5
1 square mile	=	102 400	6400	640	1
1 square centimeter	=	0.000 003 953 686	0.000 000 247 105 4	0.000 000 024 710 54	0.000 000 000 038 610 22
1 square meter	=	0.039 536 86	0.002 471 054	0.000 247 105 4	0.000 000 386 102 2
1 hectare	=	395.368 6	24.710 54	2.471 054	0.003 861 022

Units		Square centimeters	Square meters	Hectares
1 square inch	=	6.451 6	0.000 645 16	0.000 000 064 516
1 square link	=	404.685 642 24	0.040 468 564 224	0.000 004 046 856 422 4
1 square foot	=	929.030 4	0.092 903 04	0.000 009 290 304
1 square yard	=	8 361.273 6	0.836 127 36	0.000 083 612 736
1 square rod	=	252 928.526 4	25.292 852 64	0.002 529 285 264
1 square chain	=	4 046 856.422 4	404.685 642 24	0.040 468 564 224
1 acre	=	40 468 564.224	4046.856 422 4	0.404 685 642 24
1 square mile	=	25 899 881 103.36	2 589 988.110 336	258.998 811 033 6
1 square centimeter	=	1	0.000 1	0.000 000 01
1 square meter	=	10 000	1	0.000 1
1 hectare	=	100 000 000	10 000	1

STANDARD CONVERSION FACTORS

1 m/sec = 3.28 ft/sec = 2.24 mi/hr = 3.60 km/hr

1 ft/sec = 0.305 m/sec = 0.682 mi/hr = 1.10 km/hr

1 mi/hr = 1.47 ft/sec = 0.447 m/sec = 1.61 km/hr

1 radian (rad) = 57.30° = 57°18′

1° = 0.01745 rad

1 revolution/minute (rev/min) = 0.1047 rad/sec

1 atomic mass unit (amu) = 1.66 X 10^{-27} kg = 1.49 X 10^{-10} j = 931 Mev

1 newton (n) = 0.225 lb

1 pound (lb) = 4.45 n

1 joule (j) = 0.738 ft.lb = 2.39 X 10^{-4} kcal = 6.24 X 10^{-18} ev

1 kilocalorie (kcal) = 4.186 j

1 foot-pound (ft.lb) = 1.36 j

1 electron volt (ev) = 10^{-6} Mev = 1.60 X 10^{-19} j = 1.18 X 10^{-19} ft.lb = 3.83 X 10^{-23} kcal

1 watt = 1 j/sec = 0.738 ft.lb/sec

UNITS OF CAPACITY LIQUID MEASURE

Units	Minims	Fluid drams	Fluid ounces
1 minim =	1	0.016 666 67	0.002 083 333
1 fluid dram =	60	1	0.125
1 fluid ounce =	480	8	1
1 gill =	1920	32	4
1 liquid pint =	7680	128	16
1 liquid quart =	15 360	256	32
1 gallon =	61 440	1024	128
1 cubic inch =	265.974 0	4.432 900	0.554 112 6
1 cubic foot =	459 603.1	7660.052	957.506 5
1 milliliter =	16.231 19	0.270 519 8	0.033 814 97
1 liter =	16 231.19	270.519 8	33.814 97

Units	Gills	Liquid pints	Liquid quarts
1 minim =	0.000 520 833 3	0.000 130 208 3	0.000 065 104 17
1 fluid dram =	0.031 25	0.007 812 5	0.003 906 25
1 fluid ounce =	0.25	0.062 5	0.031 25
1 gill =	1	0.25	0.125
1 liquid pint =	4	1	0.5
1 liquid quart =	8	2	1
1 gallon =	32	8	4
1 cubic inch =	0.138 528 1	0.034 632 03	0.017 316 02
1 cubic foot =	239.376 6	59.844 16	29.922 08
1 milliliter =	0.008 453 742	0.002 113 436	0.001 056 718
1 liter =	8.453 742	2.113 436	1.056 718

Units	Gallons	Cubic inches	Cubic feet
1 minim =	0.000 016 276 04	0.003 759 766	0.000 002 175 790
1 fluid dram =	0.000 976 562 5	0.225 585 9	0.000 130 547 4
1 fluid ounce =	0.007 812 5	1.804 687 5	0.001 044 379
1 gill =	0.031 25	7.218 75	0.004 177 517
1 liquid pint =	0.125	28.875	0.016 710 07
1 liquid quart =	0.25	57.75	0.033 420 14
1 gallon =	1	231	0.133 680 6
1 cubic inch =	0.004 329 004	1	0.000 578 703 7
1 cubic foot =	7.480 519	1728	1
1 milliliter =	0.000 264 179 4	0.061 025 45	0.000 035 315 66
1 liter =	0.264 179 4	61.025 45	0.035 315 66

Units	Milliliters	Liters
1 minim =	0.061 609 79	0.000 061 609 79
1 fluid dram =	3.696 588	0.003 696 588
1 fluid ounce =	29.572 70	0.029 572 70
1 gill =	118.290 8	0.118 290 8
1 liquid pint =	473.163 2	0.473 163 2
1 liquid quart =	946.326 4	0.946 326 4
1 gallon =	3 785.306	3.785 306
1 cubic inch =	16.386 61	0.016 386 61
1 cubic foot =	28 316.05	28.316 05
1 milliliter =	1	0.001
1 liter =	1000	1

UNITS OF CAPACITY DRY MEASURE

Units	Dry pints	Dry quarts	Pecks
1 dry pint =	1	0.5	0.062 5
1 dry quart =	2	1	0.125
1 peck =	16	8	1
1 bushel =	64	32	4
1 cubic inch =	0.029 761 6	0.014 880 8	0.001 860 10
1 cubic foot =	51.428 09	25.714 05	3.214 256
1 liter =	1.816 217	0.908 108 4	0.113 513 6
1 dekaliter =	18.162 17	9.081 084	1.135 136

Units	Bushels	Cubic inches	Cubic feet
1 dry pint =	0.015 625	33.600 312 5	0.019 444 63
1 dry quart =	0.031 25	67.200 625	0.038 889 25
1 peck =	0.25	537.605	0.311 114
1 bushel =	1	2150.42	1.244 456
1 cubic inch =	0.000 465 025	1	0.000 578 703 7
1 cubic foot =	0.803 563 95	1728	1
1 liter =	0.028 378 39	61.025 45	0.035 315 66
1 dekaliter =	0.283 783 9	610.254 5	0.353 156 6

Units	Liters	Dekaliters
1 dry pint =	0.550 595 1	0.055 059 51
1 dry quart =	1.101 190	0.110 119 0
1 peck =	8.809 521	0.880 952 1
1 bushel =	35.238 08	3.523 808
1 cubic inch =	0.016 386 61	0.001 638 661
1 cubic foot =	28.316 05	2.831 605
1 liter =	1	0.1
1 dekaliter =	10	1

UNITS OF MASS NOT LESS THAN AVOIRDUPOIS OUNCES

Units	Avoirdupois ounces	Avoirdupois pounds	Short hundred weights
1 avoirdupois ounce =	1	0.0625	0.000 625
1 avoirdupois pound =	16	1	0.01
1 short hundredweight =	1 600	100	1
1 short ton =	32 000	2 000	20
1 long ton =	35 840	2 240	22.4
1 kilogram =	35.273 96	2.204 623	0.022 046 23
1 metric ton =	35 273.96	2204.623	22.046 23

Units	Short tons	Long tons	Kilograms	Metric tons
1 avoirdupois ounce =	0.000 031 25	0.000 027 901 79	0.028 349 523 125	0.000 028 349 523 125
1 avoirdupois pound =	0.000 5	0.000 446 428 6	0.453 592 37	0.000 453 592 37
1 short hundredweight =	0.05	0.044 642 86	45.359 237	0.045 359 237
1 short ton =	1	0.892 857 1	907.184 74	0.907 184 74
1 long ton =	1.12	1	1016.046 908 8	1.016 046 908 8
1 kilogram =	0.001 102 311	0.000 984 206 5	1	0.001
1 metric ton =	1.102 311	0.984 206 5	1 000	1

SQUARE, SQUARE ROOTS, CUBES AND CUBE ROOTS OF NOS. 1 TO 100

No.	Sq.	Cube	Sq. Root	Cube Root	No.	Sq.	Cube	Sq. Root	Cube Root
1	1	1	1.000	1.000	51	2601	132651	7.141	3.708
2	4	8	1.414	1.260	52	2704	140608	7.211	3.732
3	9	27	1.732	1.442	53	2809	148877	7.280	3.756
4	16	64	2.000	1.587	54	2916	157464	7.348	3.779
5	25	125	2.236	1.710	55	3025	166375	7.416	3.803
6	36	216	2.449	1.817	56	3136	175616	7.483	3.825
7	49	343	2.646	1.913	57	3249	185193	7.550	3.848
8	64	512	2.828	2.000	58	3364	195112	7.616	3.870
9	81	729	3.000	2.080	59	3481	205379	7.681	3.893
10	100	1000	3.162	2.154	60	3600	216000	7.746	3.915
11	121	1331	3.317	2.224	61	3721	226981	7.810	3.936
12	144	1728	3.464	2.289	62	3844	238328	7.874	3.958
13	169	2197	3.605	2.351	63	3969	250047	7.937	3.979
14	196	2744	3.742	2.410	64	4096	262144	8 000	4.000
15	225	3375	3.873	2.466	65	4225	274625	8.062	4.020
16	256	4096	4.000	2.511	66	4356	287496	8.124	4.041
17	289	4913	4.123	2.571	67	4489	300763	8.185	4.062
18	324	5832	4.243	2.621	68	4624	314432	8.246	4.082
19	361	6859	4.359	2.668	69	4761	328509	8.307	4.102
20	400	8000	4.472	2.714	70	4900	343000	8.367	4.121
21	441	9261	4.583	2.759	71	5041	357911	8.426	4.140
22	484	10648	4.690	2.802	72	5184	373248	8.485	4.160
23	529	12167	4.796	2.844	73	5329	389017	8.544	4.179
24	576	13824	4.899	2.884	74	5476	405224	8.602	4.198
25	625	15625	5.000	2.924	75	5625	421875	8.660	4.217
26	676	17576	5.099	2.962	76	5776	438976	8.718	4.236
27	729	19683	5.196	3 000	77	5929	456533	8.775	4.254
28	784	21952	5.292	3.037	78	6084	474552	8.832	4.273
29	841	24389	5.385	3.072	79	6241	493039	8.888	4.291
30	900	27000	5.477	3.107	80	6400	512000	8.944	4.309
31	961	29791	5.568	3.141	81	6561	531441	9.000	4.327
32	1024	32768	5.657	3.175	82	6724	551368	9.055	4.344
33	1089	35937	5.745	3.208	83	6889	571787	9.110	4.362
34	1156	39304	5.831	3.240	84	7056	592704	9.165	4.371
35	1225	42875	5.916	3.271	85	7225	614125	9.220	4.397
36	1296	46656	6.000	3.302	86	7396	636056	9.274	4.414
37	1369	50653	6.083	3.332	87	7569	658503	9.327	4.431
38	1444	54872	6.164	3.362	88	7744	681472	9.381	4.448
39	1521	59319	6.245	3.391	89	7921	704969	9.434	4.465
40	1600	64000	6.325	3.420	90	8100	729000	9.487	4.481
41	1681	68921	6.403	3.448	91	8281	753571	9 539	4.498
42	1764	74088	6.481	3.476	92	8464	778688	9.592	4.514
43	1849	79507	6.557	3.503	93	8649	804357	9.644	4.531
44	1936	85184	6.633	3.530	94	8836	830584	9.695	4.547
45	2025	91125	6.708	3.557	95	9025	857375	9.747	4.563
46	2116	97336	6.782	3.583	96	9216	884736	9.798	4.579
47	2209	103823	6.856	3.609	97	9409	912673	9.849	4.595
48	2304	110592	6.928	3.634	98	9604	941192	9.899	4.610
49	2401	117649	7.000	3.659	99	9801	970299	9.950	4.626
50	2500	125000	7.071	3.684	100	10000	1000000	10.000	4.641

CHEMICAL ELEMENTS, ATOMIC WEIGHTS

Element	Symbol	Atomic number	Atomic weight	Element	Symbol	Atomic number	Atomic weight
Actinium	Ac	89	(1)	Mercury	Hg	80	200.61
Aluminum	Al	13	26.98	Molybdenum	Mo	42	95.95
Americium	Am	95	(1)	Neodymium	Nd	60	144.27
Antimony	Sb	51	121.76	Neon	Ne	10	20.183
Argon	Ar	18	39.944	Neptunium	Np	93	(1)
Arsenic	As	33	74.91	Nickel	Ni	28	58.71
Astatine	At	85	(1)	Niobium	Nb	41	92.91
Barium	Ba	56	137.36	Nitrogen	N	7	14.008
Berkelium	Bk	97	(1)	Nobelium	No	102	(1)
Beryllium	Be	4	9.013	Osmium	Os	76	190.2
Bismuth	Bi	83	209.00	Oxygen	O	8	[2]16
Boron	B	5	10.82	Palladium	Pd	46	106.4
Bromine	Br	35	79.916	Phosphorus	P	15	30.975
Cadmium	Cd	48	112.41	Platinum	Pt	78	195.09
Calcium	Ca	20	40.08	Plutonium	Pu	94	(1)
Californium	Cf	98	(1)	Polonium	Po	84	(1)
Carbon	C	6	12.010	Potassium	K	19	39.100
Cerium	Ce	58	140.13	Praseodymium	Pr	59	140.92
Cesium	Cs	55	132.91	Promethium	Pm	61	(1)
Chlorine	Cl	17	35.457	Protactinium	Pa	91	(1)
Chromium	Cr	24	52.01	Radium	Ra	88	(1)
Cobalt	Co	27	58.94	Radon	Rn	86	(1)
Copper	Cu	29	63.54	Rhenium	Re	75	186.22
Curium	Cm	96	(1)	Rhodium	Rh	45	102.91
Dysprosium	Dy	66	162.51	Rubidium	Rb	37	85.48
Einsteinium	Es	99	(1)	Ruthenium	Ru	44	101.1
Erbium	Er	68	167.27	Samarium	Sm	62	150.35
Europium	Eu	63	152.0	Scandium	Sc	21	44.96
Fermium	Fm	100	(1)	Selenium	Se	34	78.96
Fluorine	F	9	19.00	Silicon	Si	14	28.09
Francium	Fr	87	(1)	Silver	Ag	47	107.880
Gadolinium	Gd	64	157.26	Sodium	Na	11	22.991
Gallium	Ga	31	69.72	Strontium	Sr	38	87.63
Germanium	Ge	32	72.60	Sulfur	S	16	[3]32.066
Gold	Au	79	197.0	Tantalum	Ta	73	180.95
Hafnium	Hf	72	178.50	Technetium	Tc	43	(1)
Helium	He	2	4.003	Tellurium	Te	52	127.61
Holmium	Ho	67	164.94	Terbium	Tb	65	158.93
Hydrogen	H	1	1.0080	Thallium	Tl	81	204.39
Indium	In	49	114.82	Thorium	Th	90	232.05
Iodine	I	53	126.91	Thulium	Tm	69	168.94
Iridium	Ir	77	192.2	Tin	Sn	50	118.70
Iron	Fe	26	55.85	Titanium	Ti	22	47.90
Krypton	Kr	36	83.80	Tungsten	W	74	183.86
Lanthanum	La	57	138.92	Uranium	U	92	238.07
Lawrencium	Lw	103	(1)	Vanadium	V	23	50.95
Lead	Pb	82	207.21	Xenon	Xe	54	131.30
Lithium	Li	3	6.940	Ytterbium	Yb	70	173.04
Lutetium	Lu	71	174.99	Yttrium	Y	39	88.92
Magnesium	Mg	12	24.32	Zinc	Zn	30	65.38
Manganese	Mn	25	54.94	Zirconium	Zr	40	91.22
Mendelevium	Md	101	(1)				

[1] These values are omitted because the elements do not occur in nature, and their atomic weight depends on which isotope is made.

[2] This is a defined value rather than an indicated one.

[3] Because of natural variations in the abundance ratio of the isotopes of sulfur, the atomic weight of this element has a range of ±0.003.

FOUR-PLACE LOGARITHMS

No.	0	1	2	3	4	5	6	7	8	9
10	0000	0043	0086	0128	0170	0212	0253	0294	0334	0374
11	0414	0453	0492	0531	0569	0607	0645	0682	0719	0755
12	0792	0828	0864	0899	0934	0969	1004	1038	1072	1106
13	1139	1173	1206	1239	1271	1303	1335	1367	1399	1430
14	1461	1492	1523	1553	1584	1614	1644	1673	1703	1732
15	1761	1790	1818	1847	1875	1903	1931	1959	1987	2014
16	2041	2068	2095	2122	2148	2175	2201	2227	2253	2279
17	2304	2330	2355	2380	2405	2430	2455	2480	2504	2529
18	2553	2577	2601	2625	2648	2672	2695	2718	2742	2765
19	2788	2810	2833	2856	2878	2900	2923	2945	2967	2989
20	3010	3032	3054	3075	3096	3118	3139	3160	3181	3201
21	3222	3243	3263	3284	3304	3324	3345	3365	3385	3404
22	3424	3444	3464	3483	3502	3522	3541	3560	3579	3598
23	3617	3636	3655	3674	3692	3711	3729	3747	3766	3784
24	3802	3820	3838	3856	3874	3892	3909	3927	3945	3962
25	3979	3997	4014	4031	4048	4065	4082	4099	4116	4133
26	4150	4166	4183	4200	4216	4232	4249	4265	4281	4298
27	4314	4330	4346	4362	4378	4393	4409	4425	4440	4456
28	4472	4487	4502	4518	4533	4548	4564	4579	4594	4609
29	4624	4639	4654	4669	4683	4698	4713	4728	4742	4757
30	4771	4786	4800	4814	4829	4843	4857	4871	4886	4900
31	4914	4928	4942	4955	4969	4983	4997	5011	5024	5038
32	5051	5065	5079	5092	5105	5119	5132	5145	5159	5172
33	5185	5198	5211	5224	5237	5250	5263	5276	5289	5302
34	5315	5328	5340	5353	5366	5378	5391	5403	5416	5428
35	5441	5453	5465	5478	5490	5502	5514	5527	5539	5551
36	5563	5575	5587	5599	5611	5623	5635	5647	5658	5670
37	5682	5694	5705	5717	5729	5740	5752	5763	5775	5786
38	5798	5809	5821	5832	5843	5855	5866	5877	5888	5899
39	5911	5922	5933	5944	5955	5966	5977	5988	5999	6010
40	6021	6031	6042	6053	6064	6075	6085	6096	6107	6117
41	6128	6138	6149	6160	6170	6180	6191	6201	6212	6222
42	6232	6243	6253	6263	6274	6284	6294	6304	6314	6325
43	6335	6345	6355	6365	6375	6385	6395	6405	6415	6425
44	6435	6444	6454	6464	6474	6484	6493	6503	6513	6522
45	6532	6542	6551	6561	6571	6580	6590	6599	6609	6618
46	6628	6637	6646	6656	6665	6675	6684	6693	6702	6712
47	6721	6730	6739	6749	6758	6767	6776	6785	6794	6803
48	6812	6821	6830	6839	6848	6857	6866	6875	6884	6893
49	6902	6911	6920	6928	6937	6946	6955	6964	6972	6981
50	6990	6998	7007	7016	7024	7033	7042	7050	7059	7067
51	7076	7084	7093	7101	7110	7118	7126	7135	7143	7152
52	7160	7168	7177	7185	7193	7202	7210	7218	7226	7235
53	7243	7251	7259	7267	7275	7284	7292	7300	7308	7316
54	7324	7332	7340	7348	7356	7364	7372	7380	7388	7396
No.	0	1	2	3	4	5	6	7	8	9

No.	0	1	2	3	4	5	6	7	8	9
55	7404	7412	7419	7427	7435	7443	7451	7459	7466	7474
56	7482	7490	7497	7505	7513	7520	7528	7536	7543	7551
57	7559	7566	7574	7582	7589	7597	7604	7612	7619	7627
58	7634	7642	7649	7657	7664	7672	7679	7686	7694	7701
59	7709	7716	7723	7731	7738	7745	7752	7760	7767	7774
60	7782	7789	7796	7803	7810	7818	7825	7832	7839	7846
61	7853	7860	7868	7875	7882	7889	7896	7903	7910	7917
62	7924	7931	7938	7945	7952	7959	7966	7973	7980	7987
63	7993	8000	8007	8014	8021	8028	8035	8041	8048	8055
64	8062	8069	8075	8082	8089	8096	8102	8109	8116	8122
65	8129	8136	8142	8149	8156	8162	8169	8176	8182	8189
66	8195	8202	8209	8215	8222	8228	8235	8241	8248	8254
67	8261	8267	8274	8280	8287	8293	8299	8306	8312	8319
68	8325	8331	8338	8344	8351	8357	8363	8370	8376	8382
69	8388	8395	8401	8407	8414	8420	8426	8432	8439	8445
70	8451	8457	8463	8470	8476	8482	8488	8494	8500	8506
71	8513	8519	8525	8531	8537	8543	8549	8555	8561	8567
72	8573	8579	8585	8591	8597	8603	8609	8615	8621	8627
73	8633	8639	8645	8651	8657	8663	8669	8675	8681	8686
74	8692	8698	8704	8710	8716	8722	8727	8733	8739	8745
75	8751	8756	8762	8768	8774	8779	8785	8791	8797	8802
76	8808	8814	8820	8825	8831	8837	8842	8848	8854	8859
77	8865	8871	8876	8882	8887	8893	8899	8904	8910	8915
78	8921	8927	8932	8938	8943	8949	8954	8960	8965	8971
79	8976	8982	8987	8993	8998	9004	9009	9015	9020	9025
80	9031	9036	9042	9047	9053	9058	9063	9069	9074	9079
81	9085	9090	9096	9101	9106	9112	9117	9122	9128	9133
82	9138	9143	9149	9154	9159	9165	9170	9175	9180	9186
83	9191	9196	9201	9206	9212	9217	9222	9227	9232	9238
84	9243	9248	9253	9258	9263	9269	9274	9279	9284	9289
85	9294	9299	9304	9309	9315	9320	9325	9330	9335	9340
86	9345	9350	9355	9360	9365	9370	9375	9380	9385	9390
87	9395	9400	9405	9410	9415	9420	9425	9430	9435	9440
88	9445	9450	9455	9460	9465	9469	9474	9479	9484	9489
89	9494	9499	9504	9509	9513	9518	9523	9528	9533	9538
90	9542	9547	9552	9557	9562	9566	9571	9576	9581	9586
91	9590	9595	9600	9605	9609	9614	9619	9624	9628	9633
92	9638	9643	9647	9652	9657	9661	9666	9671	9675	9680
93	9685	9689	9694	9699	9703	9708	9713	9717	9722	9727
94	9731	9736	9741	9745	9750	9754	9759	9763	9768	9773
95	9777	9782	9786	9791	9795	9800	9805	9809	9814	9818
96	9823	9827	9832	9836	9841	9845	9850	9854	9859	9863
97	9868	9872	9877	9881	9886	9890	9894	9899	9903	9908
98	9912	9917	9921	9926	9930	9934	9939	9943	9948	9952
99	9956	9961	9965	9969	9974	9978	9983	9987	9991	9996
No.	0	1	2	3	4	5	6	7	8	9

Biology Helps

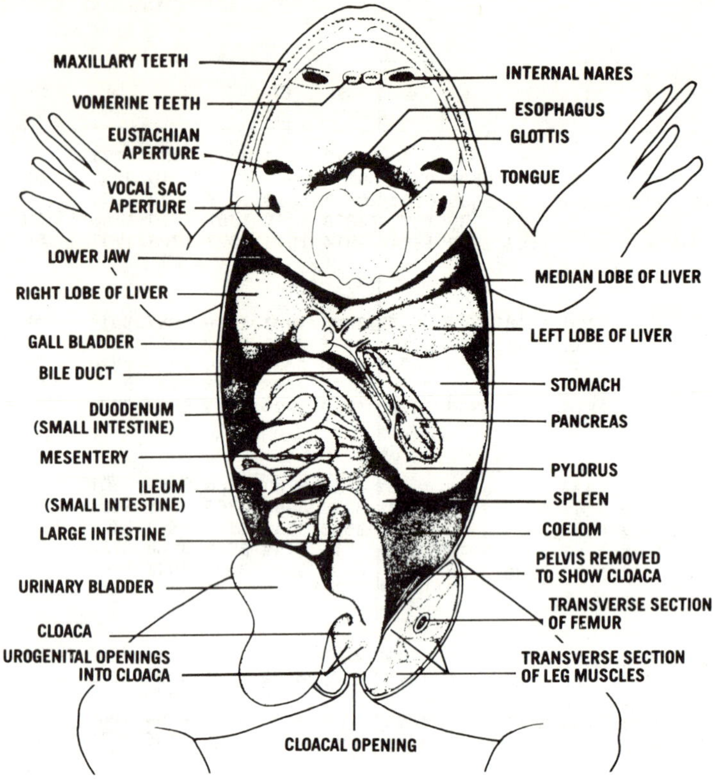

Digestive System of the Bullfrog
FIGURE A.

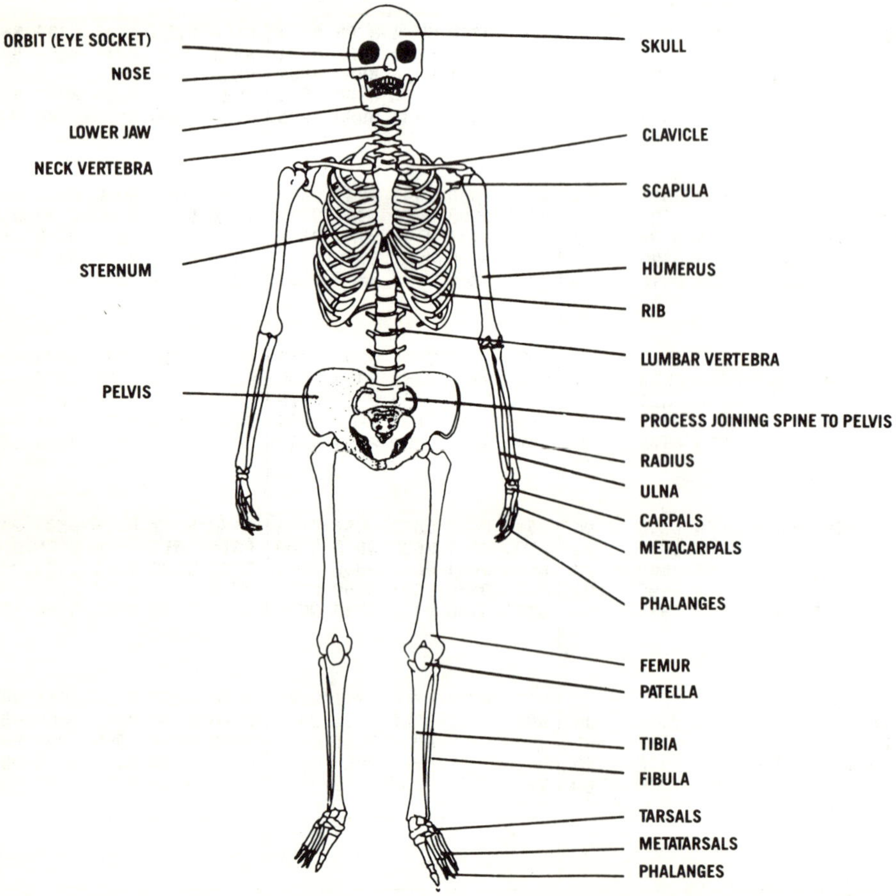

Human Skeleton
FIGURE B.

Cookery and Nutrition

Every penny you spend on food should be an investment in good health. This doesn't mean that you have to devote hours every day to working with charts and slide rules. But to make the most of your food dollars, you do have to understand what kinds of food you need and what and how each contributes to basic nutritional requirements.

Quite simply, good nutrition means meeting the body's needs for growth, maintenance, energy, and tissue repair. Good nutrition also means family meals that are satisfying and enjoyable.

PLANNING YOUR MENUS

Well-balanced meals are easy to plan if you include a variety of foods that meet everyone's daily nutritional needs. While it's possible to provide a proper diet without following a daily plan, it's easier to stay within your budget while meeting your family's nutritional needs if you build your menus around the Basic Four Food Groups. All of us need something from each section every day, and since the foods within each group are similar in value, they can be used interchangeably for variety and interest. (The sample menu chart that follows shows you how to turn basic foods into excitingly different meals.) To review briefly, groups are:

1. Dairy. Included are milk, cheese, ice cream or ice milk—all of which supply calcium, riboflavin, protein, and Vitamin A, along with other essentials. *Daily need:* Three to four cups of milk for children and teenagers; two or more cups for adults; three or more cups for pregnant women; four cups for nursing mothers.

2. Meats. Other sources are poultry, fish, and eggs which we must have for animal protein, thiamine, riboflavin, niacin, and iron. *Daily need:* Two servings.

3. Fruits and vegetables. A daily must for nearly all of our Vitamin C and much of our Vitamin A, they also contribute minerals, calcium, iron, and some riboflavin. *Daily need:* Four or more servings, including one rich in Vitamin C and one of a dark green or yellow variety.

4. Breads and cereals. Alternates are spaghetti, macaroni, noodles, hominy, grits, rice, and crackers or other baked foods which provide essential B vitamins and iron. *Daily need:* Four or more servings.

Fortunately, all of the foods containing these nutrients are readily found in supermarkets. While each nutrient contributes to building, regulating, and repairing the body, it's important to remember that they work together as a team. An extra supply of one can't take the place of another.

Only the amounts of food should vary to meet individual needs based on age and activity—for example, smaller servings for children and dieters, larger servings for very active adults and teenagers. Following these pages you'll find a chart that lists the major nutrients, the reasons why they are needed, and their principal sources. Use it for quick reference; with a little practice, you'll notice that you soon think of each food in terms of what it provides.

Fiber While it is not a nutrient, fiber is essential to health. It consists of the indigestible elements of foods which pass through our bodies primarily unchanged. To keep our digestive systems functioning properly, we all need a certain amount every day. Whole-grain cereals and breads—especially bran—fruits, vegetables, and nuts are top contributors.

NUTRITIONAL LABELING—WHAT'S ITS USE?

Labels that spell out what's inside are now found on any canned, frozen, processed, or packaged foods for which a manufacturer makes a nutritional claim, or on foods to which nutrients have been added (fortified cereals or enriched breads). Read these labels carefully, for they can help you:

1. learn more about nutrition;
2. plan better balanced meals;
3. meet the nutritional needs of every member of your family;
4. count calories;
5. know how much of a specific nutrient a food contains.

At the same time, keep in mind that meats and fresh fruits and vegetables do not yet carry nutritional labels. Therefore, you can't use this information as your *only* guide to selecting foods.

Conveniently, all listings stated on the labels are given in single servings (2 slices, 1 cup, 1 ounce), along with the total servings in the container. This enables you to compare the nutritive values of different products, and as a result, find your best buys.

On the label, you'll also notice the term U.S.

RDA. This means Recommended Daily Allowances, the nutritional standards based on the amounts of nutrients the National Research Council believes are adequate for most healthy people. Since RDA's are given in percentage of the day's total, they can help you keep tabs on how your menus stack up nutritionally.

A GOOD BREAKFAST

For good health and energy, everyone should start the day with at least a quarter of his daily needs for protein, vitamins, minerals, and calories. Children and adults who skip or skimp on the day's first meal slow down in mid- or late morning because of fatigue. With no breakfast, weight control is harder since noontime hunger is greater, and the dieter is more likely to overeat.

A sound, basic breakfast pattern can be as simple as fruit or juice, cereal and milk, toast with butter or margarine, and extra milk as a beverage for youngsters or coffee for adults. Even though a family eats in shifts, this menu is easy enough for most children of school age to fix for themselves.

HOW IMPORTANT ARE SNACKS?

For good health, at any age, it isn't necessary to eliminate them—just plan them so that they carry their weight in food value.

Children's energy needs are great, so most need something to keep them going between meals. Cereal and milk, pudding, ice cream, fruit, crackers, raw vegetables, cheese, and peanut butter are top nutritional choices. It's best not to allow snacking too close to mealtime, however, or appetites won't be up to par for the next meal.

For teenagers, snacks are a part of their social life, and for boys, particularly, a source of the extra calories they need. But whatever they eat should provide more than just calories. Wise choices are hamburgers or cheeseburgers, pizza, milk, milk shakes, and high-protein chocolate-flavored beverages that come in the soft drink section of the supermarket.

Girls benefit from meat and cheese sandwiches, ice cream, fruit and fruit juices, and dry cereals to eat out of hand. All of these supply particular nutrients that are often lacking—or low—in their diets.

Adults and waistline-watchers can also enjoy snacks if they select them wisely and count their calories as part of their day's permitted total. Fruit and vegetable juices, bouillon, skimmed milk or buttermilk, and raw vegetable relishes take the edge off hunger, yet contain few calories.

COOK TO SAVE NUTRIENTS

How you cook is equally as important as what you cook, since sloppy methods or overcooking can destroy food value. This is particularly true of vegetables that lose their bright color and fresh flavor when drowned in water or left on the heat too long.

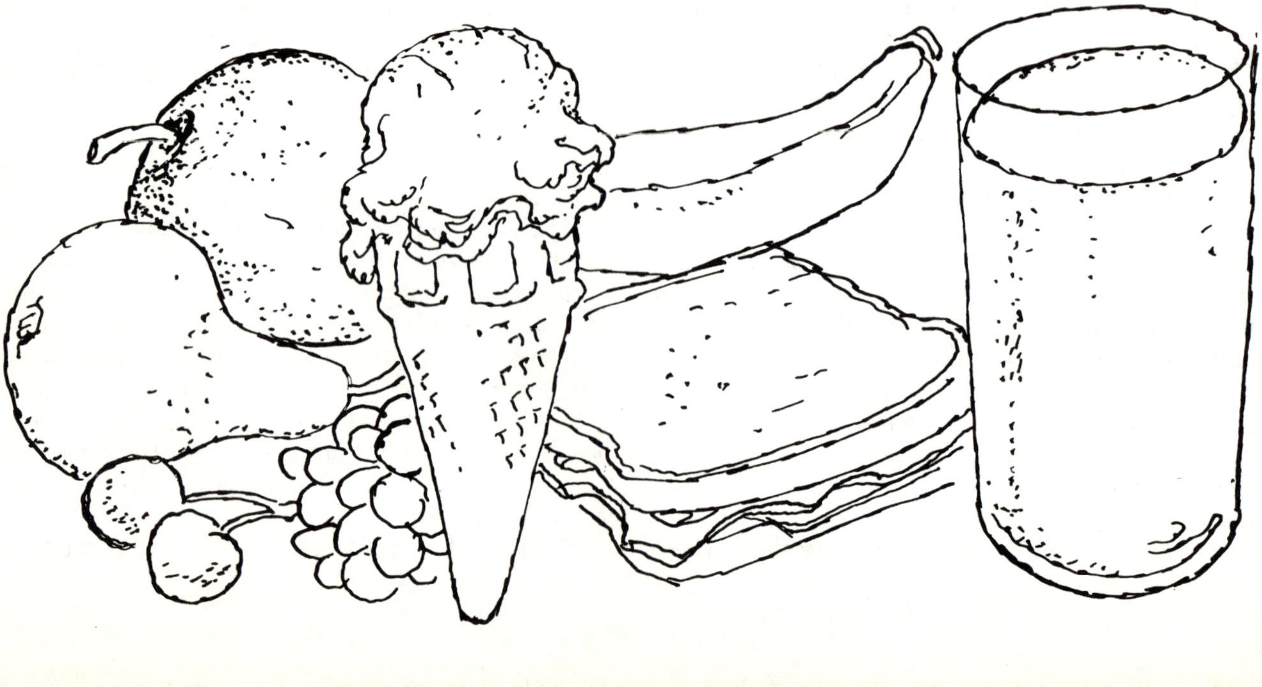

SAMPLE SEVEN-DAY MENU GUIDE TO KEEP YOUR FAMILY FIT

BREAKFAST	LUNCH	DINNER
Chilled Grapefruit Juice 40% Bran Flakes Broiled Corned-beef Hash on Toasted Hamburger Buns Milk, Tea or Coffee	Chicken-vegetable Soup Tuna Casserole Raw Carrot Sticks Fresh Fruit Compote Milk, Tea	Beef Patties Parslied Noodles Green Beans Waldorf Salad Strawberry Sundaes Pineapple Drop Cookies Milk, Tea or Coffee
Sliced Oranges Toasted Frozen Waffles with Hot Blueberry Sauce Milk, Tea or Coffee	Lentil Soup Toasted Italian Bread Shredded Cabbage Salad with Cranberry-mayonnaise Dressing Canned Apricot Halves Milk, Tea	Salmon Soufflé Baked Potatoes Pimiento Peas and Limas Marinated Yellow Squash Sticks on Lettuce Butterscotch Pudding Milk, Tea or Coffee
Sliced Bananas with Granola-type Cereal Raisin French Toast Maple-blended Syrup Milk, Tea or Coffee	Spanish Rice with Shrimp Tossed Green Salad with Oil-and-vinegar Dressing Raspberry Gelatin Cubes with Custard Sauce Milk, Tea	Lamb Stew Pear, Orange, and Avocado Salad with French Dressing Chocolate Layer Cake Milk, Tea or Coffee
Tangerine Sections Scrambled Eggs with Diced Ham Toasted English Muffins Milk, Tea or Coffee	Broiled Hamburger Patties Hamburger Buns with Mustard Butter Mixed Raw Relishes and Pickles Caramel Cup Custards Milk, Tea	Baked Chicken and Rice Green Salad with Shredded Carrot and Sliced Cauliflowerets Corn Sticks Lemon Pie Milk, Tea or Coffee
Chilled Mixed Vegetable Juice Hot Oatmeal Cinnamon Toast Milk, Tea or Coffee	Bologna Sandwiches Lettuce Wedges with Russian Dressing Chocolate Ice Cream Bars Milk, Tea	Consommé Baked Haddock Potatoes au Gratin Steamed Spinach Mixed Green Salad with Cherry Tomatoes Peach Betty with Cream Milk, Tea or Coffee
Grapefruit Halves Open-face Toasted Cheese Sandwich Milk, Tea or Coffee	Spaghetti with Meat Balls Hot Garlic French Bread Celery Spears Fresh Apples and Grapes Milk, Tea	Sautéed Liver and Onions Whipped Potatoes Steamed Broccoli Raw Relish Tray Baking Powder Biscuits Gingerbread with Lemon Sauce Milk, Tea or Coffee
Chilled Orange Juice Small Whole-wheat Pancakes Brown-and-serve Link Sausages Strawberry Preserves Milk, Tea or Coffee	Mushroom Omelets with Cheese Sauce Marinated Mixed Vegetables on Lettuce Italian Bread Sticks Lemon Pudding Milk, Tea	Beef Pot Roast Romaine-radish Salad with Italian Dressing Hot Butterflake Rolls Dill Pickles Apple Pie Milk, Tea or Coffee

MAJOR NUTRIENTS: THEIR ROLES AND SOURCES

NUTRIENT	WHY NEEDED	WHERE FOUND
Protein	Promotes growth and repair of body tissues; supplies energy; helps to fight infections; forms an important part of blood, enzymes, and hormones to regulate body functions.	Lean meats; poultry; fish; shellfish; eggs; milk; cheese. Next best are the vegetable proteins such as dry beans and peas; nuts; peanut butter; bread; cereals; wheat germ. If served with a complementary animal protein food such as cheese, the combined protein value is high.
Carbohydrates (Starches and sugars)	Supply energy; spare protein for body building and repair; also necessary for bulk and proper elimination.	Breads; cereals; grits; corn; rice; potatoes; the macaroni and noodle families; bananas; sugar; honey; syrup; jam; jelly; molasses.
Fats	Supply concentrated energy; improve taste of food; help body use other nutrients; help maintain temperature; lubricate intestinal tract.	Butter; margarine; whole milk; ice cream; cheese; egg yolk; shortening; lard; chocolate; chocolate candy; pies; puddings; salad oils.
Calcium	Builds sturdy bones and teeth; helps blood clot; helps to keep nerves, muscles, and heart healthy; aids in healing wounds; helps fight infections.	Milk; ice cream; cheese; cottage cheese; kale; collards; mustard and turnip greens; salmon; sardines.
Iodine	Helps thyroid gland work properly in regulating energy.	Iodized salt; salt-water fish and shellfish.
Iron	Necessary to form hemoglobin (red substance in blood) which carries oxygen from lungs to body cells.	Liver; heart; kidneys; oysters; lean meats; egg yolk; clams; whole-grain and enriched cereals; dry beans; molasses; raisins and other dried fruits; dark green leafy vegetables.
Sodium	Preserves water balance in body.	Salt; meat; fish; poultry; eggs; olives.
Potassium	Keeps nerves and muscles healthy; helps to maintain fluid balance.	Meat; fish; fruits; cereals.
Phosphorus	Essential (with calcium) for bones and teeth; helps fat do its job in the body; aids enzymes used in energy metabolism.	Milk; ice cream; cheese; meat; poultry; whole-grain cereals; dry beans and peas; fish; nuts.
Magnesium	A must for strong bones and teeth; helps muscle contraction; aids in transmitting nerve impulses.	Cereals; dry beans; meats; milk; nuts.
Vitamin A	Helps maintain eyesight, especially in dim light; aids growth of healthy skin, bones, and teeth; promotes growth; helps resist infection.	Liver; broccoli; turnips; carrots; pumpkin; sweet potatoes; winter squash; apricots; butter; fortified margarine; egg yolk; fish-liver oils; cantaloupe.
Thiamine (Vitamin B_1)	Helps body cells obtain energy from food; aids in keeping nerves healthy; promotes good appetite and digestion.	Pork; lean meats; poultry; fish; liver; dry beans and peas; egg yolk; whole-grain and enriched cereals and breads; soybeans.
Riboflavin (Vitamin B_2)	Helps body use protein, fats, and carbohydrates for energy and for building tissues; aids in maintaining eyesight; promotes radiant skin.	Milk; cheese; liver; kidneys; heart; eggs; green leafy vegetables; enriched cereals and breads; yeast.
Niacin	Required for healthy nervous system, skin, and digestive tract; aids energy production in cells.	Lean meats; poultry; fish; variety meats; dark green leafy vegetables; whole-grain and enriched cereals and breads; peanuts; peanut butter.
Vitamin C (Ascorbic acid)	Aids in building the materials that hold cells together; helps in healing wounds and resisting infection; needed for healthy teeth, gums, and blood vessels.	Citrus fruits; strawberries; cantaloupe; tomatoes; potatoes; Brussels sprouts; raw cabbage; broccoli; green and sweet red peppers.
Vitamin D	Helps body use calcium and phosphorus to build bones and teeth.	Fortified milk; fish-liver oils; egg yolks; liver; salmon; tuna. Direct sunlight also produces Vitamin D.
Vitamin B_6	Aids body to use protein and maintain normal hemoglobin in blood.	Meats; wheat germ; liver; kidneys; whole-grain cereals; soybeans; peanuts.
Vitamin B_{12}	A necessity for producing red blood cells and for building new proteins in the body.	Meats; liver; kidneys; fish; eggs; milk; cheese.
Vitamin E	Function is not clearly understood, although it is thought to help form red blood cells, muscle, and other tissue.	Wheat-germ oil; salad oils; green leafy vegetables; nuts; dry beans and peas; margarine.
Vitamin K	Promotes normal blood clotting.	Green leafy vegetables; cauliflower; egg yolk; liver; soybean oil.
Water	Forms a vital part of all cells; carries nutrients to cells and waste from body; necessary for digestion; regulates body temperature.	Water; beverages; soups; fruit juices; milk; fruits and vegetables.

EVERYDAY HELPS

With all of our modern kitchen appliances, minute minders, and space savers, cooking is a joy, yet push buttons just can't do everything. Recipes still call for a human touch, and here's where it pays to know the techniques and shortcuts that will make the job easier and the results surer.

The following helps will give you quick answers to many of your daily cooking questions. How-to's on measuring ingredients and utensils help guarantee success and become second nature once you learn the right way. If you want to know how many whole onions it takes to make a cupful after they've been chopped, look here for a handy chart listing a number of foods.

For easy at-home reference—perhaps when you're planning meals or making up your shopping list—another table tells you what size cans certain foods come in so you can pick the pack that best fits your needs. Still another will guide you through emergency situations when you've started a recipe and find you've run out of a particular item you thought you had on hand. Sometimes there's an equally good counterpart you can use in its place, and this chart includes a few that have been worked out scientifically to eliminate mistakes and failures.

Finally, for these days when everyone's trying to save energy, there are tips to help you conserve it as well as get the most from what you do use.

BASIC COOKING TERMS AND WHAT THEY MEAN

BAKE: To cook food by dry heat in an oven or oven-type appliance.

BARBECUE: To roast or broil food on a rack or spit over or under a heating unit. Usually a special sauce is brushed over the food as it cooks.

BASTE: To moisten food as it cooks to prevent drying and add flavor. Pan drippings, fruit juices, salad oil, or special sauces are most often used.

BEAT: To make a mixture smooth with a quick even motion, using a spoon, wire whisk, or hand or electric beater.

BLANCH: To dip into boiling water to loosen skin from some foods or to scald as a step in preparing vegetables for freezing.

BLEND: To thoroughly mix two or more ingredients. Or to prepare food in an electric blender.

BOIL: To cook in liquid in which bubbles constantly rise to the surface and break.

BRAISE: To cook food slowly in a small amount of liquid in a tightly covered pan.

BROIL: To cook by direct heat on a rack or spit.

CARAMELIZE: To heat sugar slowly in a skillet until it melts and turns golden-brown.

CHILL: To refrigerate food or let it stand in a pan of ice and water until cold.

CHOP: To cut into small pieces with a knife or electric blender.

COAT: To cover all sides of food with another ingredient such as flour or bread crumbs.

CREAM: To make a mixture soft and smooth by beating with a spoon or electric mixer. Usually refers to blending fat and sugar together. Another meaning is to cook food in, or serve it with, a white or creamy sauce.

CRISP: To make a food firm and brittle by letting it stand in ice water or heating it in the oven.

CUBE: To cut food into cubes.

CUT: To combine shortening or solid fat with flour or other dry ingredients by using a pastry blender to distribute the shortening evenly.

DEEP-FRY: To cook in hot fat that's deep enough so the food floats on top.

DEVIL: To combine foods with one or more spicy-hot seasonings.

DICE: To cut foods into very small cubes, usually about ¼ inch.

DOT: To scatter bits of an ingredient such as butter or margarine over the surface of another food.

DREDGE: To coat or cover food with some dry ingredient such as flour, cornmeal, or sugar.

DUST: To sprinkle food with a dry ingredient such as flour or confectioners' powdered sugar.

FOLD: To combine delicate ingredients with other foods by cutting vertically down through the mixture with a spoon or spatula, sliding it across the bottom of the bowl, and bringing some of the mixture up and over the surface.

FRY: To cook in hot fat.

GRATE: To cut food into fine particles by rubbing it against a grater.

GREASE: To rub the surface of dish or pan

with shortening or other fat to keep food from sticking.

GRILL: To cook by direct heat.

GRIND: To cut food into tiny particles by putting it through a grinder.

JULIENNE: To cut food into long, slender strips.

KNEAD: To work a food mixture with hands by folding it toward you, then pressing down and pushing it away.

LARD: To cover meat with strips of fat or to insert them into meat to add flavor and prevent drying.

MARINATE: To let food stand in liquid for a period of time to enhance flavor or produce tenderness.

MELT: To use heat to turn a solid food into liquid.

MINCE: To cut into very fine pieces.

MIX: To combine ingredients until evenly blended.

PANBROIL: To cook, uncovered, in a skillet without fat.

PANFRY: To cook in a skillet in a small amount of fat.

PARBOIL: To boil food until partly cooked.

PARE: To trim skin, peeling, or outer covering from food with a knife or vegetable parer.

PEEL: To pull outer covering from food with hands.

PIT: To remove seed.

POACH: To cook gently in simmering liquid.

PUREE: To press food through a fine sieve or food mill, or twirl in a blender, until it becomes smooth.

RECONSTITUTE: To add water to concentrated food to return it to its natural form.

ROAST: To cook, uncovered, by hot air.

SAUTÉ: To cook in a small amount of hot fat.

SCALD: To heat a liquid to a point just below boiling.

SCORE: To make shallow cuts or slits in the surface of food to prevent fat from curling, to decorate, or to increase tenderness.

SEAR: To brown the surface of meat quickly by intense heat.

SHRED: To cut food into thin strips or slivers with a knife or shredder.

SIFT: To put through a sieve or sifter.

SIMMER: To cook slowly in liquid with the surface of the liquid barely rippling.

SKEWER: To fasten with wooden or metal pins.

STEAM: To cook directly over boiling water in a tightly covered container.

STEEP: To extract color and flavor by letting food stand in hot liquid.

STEW: To simmer in liquid.

STIR: To mix food with a circular motion for uniform consistency.

TOAST: To brown by dry heat.

TOSS: To mix foods lightly by lifting them with two forks or spoons.

WHIP: To beat rapidly to incorporate air and expand volume.

THE RIGHT WAY TO MEASURE

Start with proper equipment. Every cook should have these basics: a set of four nested measuring cups for dry ingredients, a 1-cup measure for liquids, and a set of four measuring spoons.

Nested—or graduated—cups in metal or plastic include ¼-, ⅓-, ½-, and 1-cup sizes. Liquid measures, available in glass or plastic, are designed with a rim above the cup level to prevent spilling, as well as lines that mark less than 1-cup amounts. For measuring larger quantities or bulky foods such as bread cubes or apple slices, pint and quart sizes are also handy. Standard measuring-spoon sets include a quarter and half teaspoon, one teaspoon, and one tablespoon.

To measure dry ingredients. Lightly spoon flour, granulated sugar, or confectioners' powdered sugar into cup or spoon until it overflows, then level it off with the edge of a spatula. Two other reminders in measuring flour: Be careful not to pack it down and never shake or tap the cup.

On the other hand, pack brown sugar into the cup with the back of a spoon, then level off. If properly measured, the sugar should hold the shape of the cup when it's turned out.

Solid shortening also calls for nested cups. Spoon the shortening directly from can to cup, packing it down lightly; level off; scrape the cup out cleanly with a rubber spatula.

Most stick butter and margarine comes in wrappers that are designed with tablespoon measurements, so it's easy to cut off what you need with a knife. If your particular brand isn't marked, remember that one-quarter pound or one stick makes ½ cup. For smaller amounts, follow the rule for solid shortening.

For all other solid ingredients—fruits, nuts, cereals, grated cheese, coconut, bread crumbs, biscuit mixes, and rice—use your nested cups.

Many times a recipe calls for ⅛ teaspoon of some ingredient such as salt, an herb, or a spice. In this case, measure ¼ teaspoon and level off, then divide the amount in half by drawing a knife lengthwise through the center. Push half back into the bottle or jar and use the other half.

To measure liquids. Place cup on a level surface and fill it to the line marked on the side, then bend down so you can read the amount at eye level. For spoon measurements, pour the liquid right to the rim but don't let it spill over. Never measure, even small amounts, directly over the food to which the liquid is being added. Your hand may tremble or slip and pour out more than you need.

Measure liquid shortening, salad oils, and melted butter or margarine the same as milk, water, fruit juices, wine, or other liquids.

HOW TO MEASURE PANS AND MOLDS

For best results, it pays to use the exact size pan, casserole, or mold called for in your recipe. This ensures attractive foods and even cooking, and avoids spillovers.

Many manufacturers stamp the size or capacity on the bottom of baking pans and dishes, pie plates, custard cups, and molds. But if you should have some that aren't marked, here's how to determine their size:

Casseroles and molds: Pour measured amounts of water into the utensil up to the rim. The total amount tells you how many cups or quarts the utensil holds.

Round cake pans and pie plates: For diameter, use a ruler and measure across the top from inside edge to inside edge. If it's depth you need, stand the ruler straight up along side.

Rectangular or square pans: Use your ruler again to measure length and width.

FAMILIAR CAN SIZES

NET WEIGHT OR FLUID MEASURE	CUPS	SERVINGS	PRODUCT PACKED
8 ounces	1	1 to 2	Fruits and vegetables; *specialties.
10½ to 12 ounces	1¼	2 to 3	Condensed soups; some fruits, vegetables, meats, and fish; *specialties.
12 ounces	1½	3 to 4	Mostly vacuum-pack corn.
14 to 16 ounces	1¾	3 to 4	Pork and beans; baked beans; meat products; cranberry sauce; blueberries; *specialties.
16 to 17 ounces	2	4	Fruits and vegetables; some meat items; ready-to-serve soups; *specialties.
20 ounces or 18 fluid ounces	2½	5	Juices; ready-to-serve soups; pineapple; apple slices; pie fillings; *specialties.
27 to 29 ounces	3½	5 to 7	Fruits; some vegetables such as pumpkin, sauerkraut, spinach, and tomatoes.
51 ounces or 46 fluid ounces	5¾	10 to 12	Fruit and vegetable juices; juice drinks; pork-and-beans.

*Specialties include such items as macaroni-and-cheese, Spanish rice, Mexican foods, and Chinese foods.

Juices now come canned or bottled in several sizes besides 18 or 46 fluid ounces.

Infant and junior foods are available in small cans and jars suitable for small servings. Check labels for content.

Cooking Measures

Dash (liquid) = Few drops
Dash, pinch, or few grains (dry) = Less than 1/8 teaspoon

3 teasp.	1 tablesp.
1/3 of 1 tablesp.	1 teasp.
1/3 of 2 tablesp.	2 teasp.
1/3 of 5 tablesp.	1 tablesp. + 2 teasp.
1/3 of 7 tablesp.	2 tablesp. + 1 teasp.
1/2 of 1 tablesp.	1 1/2 teasp.
1/2 of 3 tablesp.	1 tablesp. + 1 1/2 teasp.
1/2 of 5 tablesp.	2 tablesp. + 1 1/2 teasp.
1/2 of 7 tablesp.	3 tablesp. + 1 1/2 teasp.
2 tablesp.	1/8 cup
4 tablesp.	1/4 cup
5 tablesp. + 1 teasp.	1/3 cup
8 tablesp.	1/2 cup
10 tablesp. + 2 teasp.	2/3 cup
12 tablesp.	3/4 cup
16 tablesp.	1 cup
1/3 of 1/4 cup	1 tablesp. + 1 teasp.
1/3 of 1/3 cup	1 tablesp. + 2 1/3 teasp.
1/3 of 1/2 cup	2 tablesp. + 2 teasp.
1/3 of 2/3 cup	3 tablesp. + 1 2/3 teasp.
1/3 of 3/4 cup	1/4 cup
1/2 of 1/4 cup	2 tablesp.
1/2 of 1/3 cup	2 tablesp. + 2 teasp.
1/2 of 1/2 cup	1/4 cup
1/2 of 2/3 cup	1/3 cup
1/2 of 3/4 cup	6 tablesp.
2 cups	1 pt.
2 pt.	1 qt.
1 qt.	4 cups
4 qt.	1 gal.
8 qt.	1 peck
4 pecks	1 bushel
16 oz. (dry measure)	1 lb.

Oven Temperatures

	Fahrenheit
Very Slow	250°–275°
Slow	300°–325°
Moderate	350°–375°
Hot	400°–425°
Very Hot	450°–475°
Extremely Hot	500°–525°

Cooking Substitutes

■ 1 teaspoon baking powder = 1/3 teaspoon baking soda plus 1/2 teaspoon cream of tartar.

■ 1 cup bread crumbs = 3/4 cup cracker crumbs.

■ 1 cup butter = 1 cup margarine or 7/8 cup vegetable oil.

■ 1-ounce square unsweetened chocolate = 3 tablespoons cocoa plus 1 tablespoon margarine.

■ 1 tablespoon cornstarch, as thickener = 2 tablespoons flour.

■ 1 cup heavy cream = 3/4 cup milk plus 1/3 cup butter.

■ 1 cup light cream = 3/4 cup milk plus 3 tablespoons butter.

■ 2 egg yolks = 1 whole egg.

■ 1 cup all-purpose flour = 1 cup whole wheat flour.

■ 1 cup cake flour = 1 cup less 1 tablespoon all-purpose flour.

■ 1 teaspoon lemon juice = 1/2 teaspoon vinegar.

■ 1 cup whole milk = 1/2 cup evaporated milk plus 1/2 cup water.

■ 1 cup sour milk = 1 cup yogurt or buttermilk.

■ 1 cup sour cream, in baking = 7/8 cup buttermilk or sour milk plus 3 tablespoons margarine.

■ 1 cup sour cream = 1 cup yogurt.

■ 1 cup sugar, in baking bread = 1 cup honey plus a pinch of baking soda.

■ 1 cup sugar, main dishes = 3/4 cup honey.

■ 1 cup sugar, in baking = 7/8 cup honey plus a pinch of baking soda.

■ 1 cup brown sugar = 1 cup white sugar plus 2 tablespoons molasses.

■ 1/2 cup dry red or white wine = 2 tablespoons sherry or port.

■ 1 cup molasses, in baking = 1 cup sugar, omit baking soda, use baking powder.

■ 3/4 cup maple syrup, in baking = 1 cup sugar, increase liquid in recipe by 3 tablespoons.

■ 1 cup grated coconut = 1 1/3 cup flaked coconut.

■ 2 teaspoons tapioca, as thickener = 1 tablespoon flour.

■ 1 cup yogurt = 1 cup buttermilk.

■ 1 cup zucchini = 1 cup summer squash.

■ 1 pound almonds, in shell = approximately 3/4-1 cup shelled.

■ 1 pound apples = approximately 3 cups pared and sliced.

■ 1 pound dried apricots = approximately 3 cups.

Metric Conversions

TEMPERATURE

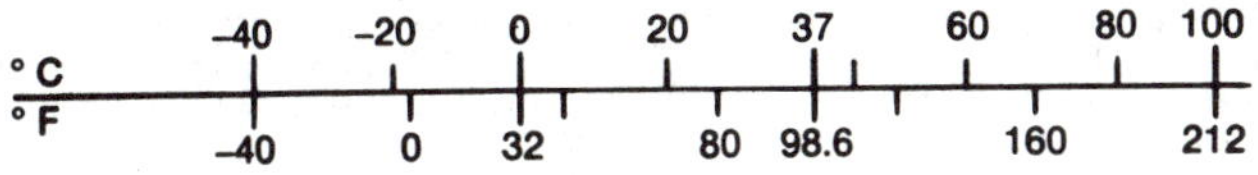

To Convert Celsius to Fahrenheit:
Multiply the Celsius temperature by 2, subtract 10%, and add 32.
Example: 25″ C x 2 = 50 – 5 = 45 + 32 = 77″ F

To Convert Fahrenheit to Celsius, Reverse the Procedure.
Example: 72″ F – 32 = 40 + 4 = 44 ÷ 2 = 22″ C

Temperatures in degrees Celsius, as in the familiar Fahrehheit system, can only be learned through experience. The following may help to orient you with regard to temperatures you normally encounter.

0″ C	Freezing point of water (32″ F)
10″ C	A warm winter day (50″ F)
20″ C	A mild spring day (68″ F)
30″ C	Quite warm — almost hot (86″ F)
37″ C	Normal body temperature (98.6″ F)
40″ C	Heat wave conditions (104″ F)
100″ C	Boiling point of water (212″ F)

30 centimeters = 1 foot

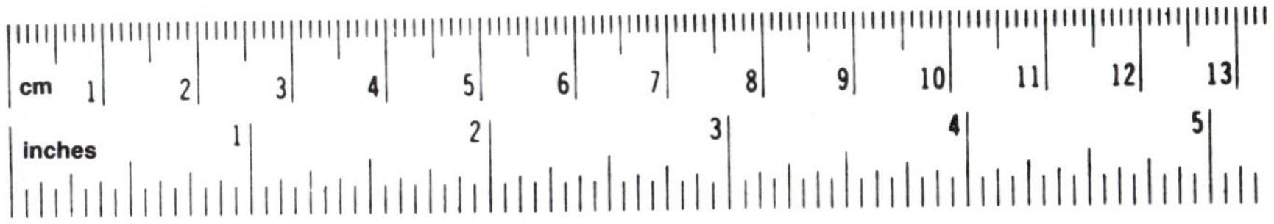

KILOMETERS

MILES PER HOUR

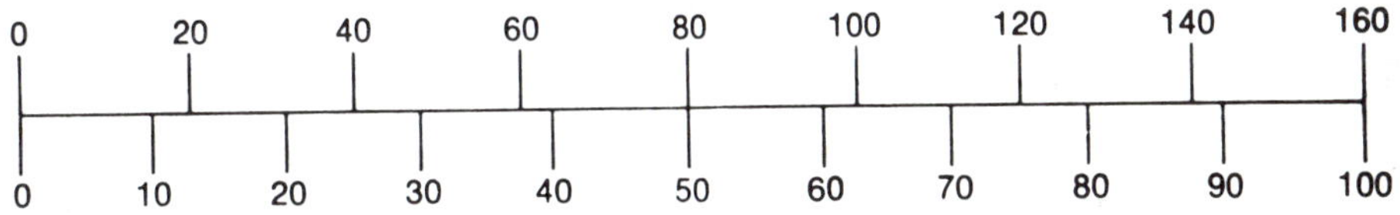

Inches	Millimeters
1/32	.79
1/16	1.59
1/8	3.175
1/4	6.35
3/8	9.53
1/2	12.7
5/8	15.88
3/4	19.05
7/8	22.3
1.0	25.4
1 1/2	38.1
2.0	50.8
2 1/2	63.5
3.0	76.2
3 1/2	88.9
4.0	101.6
4 1/2	114.3
5.0	127.0
5 1/2	139.7
6.0	152.4
6 1/2	165.1
7.0	177.8
7 1/2	190.5
8.0	203.2
8 1/2	215.9
9.0	228.6
9 1/2	241.3
10.0	254.0
10 1/2	266.7
11.0	279.4
11 1/2	292.1
12.0	304.8

Feet	Meters
1	0.3
2	0.6
3	0.9
4	1.2
5	1.5
6	1.8
7	2.1
8	2.4
9	2.7
10	3.0
15	4.6
20	6.1
25	7.6
30	9.1
35	10.7
40	12.2
45	13.7
50	15.2
55	16.8
60	18.3
65	19.8
70	21.3
75	22.9
80	24.4
85	25.9
90	27.4
95	29.0
100	30.5

Pounds	Kilograms
1	0.5
2	0.9
3	1.4
4	1.8
5	2.3
6	2.7
7	3.2
8	3.6
9	4.1
10	4.5
11	5.0
12	5.4
13	5.9
14	6.4
15	6.8
16	7.3
17	7.7
18	8.2
19	8.6
20	9.1
25	11.34
30	13.61
40	18.14
50	22.68
60	27.22
70	31.75
80	36.29
90	40.82
100	45.36

Ounces	Grams
1/4	7.1
1/2	14.2
3/2	21.3
1	28.4
2	56.7
3	85.0
4	113.4
5	141.7
6	170.1
7	198.4
8	226.8
9	255.1
10	283.5
11	311.8
12	340.2
13	368.5
14	396.9
15	425.2
16	453.6

Pints	Liters
1/2	.236
1.0	.473
1 1/2	.709
2.0	.946
2 1/2	1.183
3.0	1.419
3 1/2	1.656
4.0	1.893
4 1/2	2.129
5.0	2.366
5 1/2	2.602
6.0	2.839
6 1/2	3.075
7.0	3.312
7 1/2	3.549
8.0	3.786

Gallons	Liters
1	3.8
2	7.6
3	11.4
4	15.1
5	18.9
6	22.7
7	26.5
8	30.3
9	34.1
10	37.9
11	41.6
12	45.4
13	49.2
14	53.0
15	56.8
16	60.6
17	64.3
18	68.1
19	71.9
20	75.7
30	113.6
40	151.4
50	189.3
60	227.1
70	264.9
80	302.8
90	340.7
100	378.5

INDEX

B

C

D

N

O

P

Q

R

S

T

U

V

W